The Late Victorian Folksong Revival

The Persistence of English Melody, 1878–1903

E. David Gregory

The Scarecrow Press, Inc.
Lanham, Maryland • Toronto • Plymouth, UK
2010

SCARECROW PRESS, INC.

Published in the United States of America
by Scarecrow Press, Inc.
A wholly owned subsidary of The Rowman & Littlefield Publishing Group, Inc.
4501 Forbes Boulevard, Suite 200, Lanham, Maryland 20706
www.scarecrowpress.com

Estover Road
Plymouth PL6 7PY
United Kingdom

British Library Cataloguing in Publication Information Available

Library of Congress Cataloging-in-Publication Data

Gregory, E. David.
  The late Victorian folksong revival : the persistence of English melody, 1878–1903 / E. David Gregory.
      p. cm.
  Includes bibliographical references and index.
  ISBN 978-0-8108-6988-2 (hardcover : alk. paper) — ISBN 978-0-8108-6989-9 (ebook)
  1. Folk songs, English—England—History and criticism. 2. Ballads, English—England—History and
criticism. I. Title.
  ML3652.G73 2010
  782.42162'21009034—dc22   2009025388

Printed in the United States of America

This book is dedicated to my wife, Rosaleen Gregory, whose singing introduced me to English traditional music forty years ago; and to the two American scholars who taught me most about the discipline of history, Dr. Walter Simon and Dr. John Sherwood.

Contents

Figures

Preface

Salvador Dali's painting *The Persistence of Memory* has long fascinated me. Whatever Dali may have intended his languid watches and clocks to symbolize, to me they suggest the idea of a past that remains ineradicably present, yet has become malleable and distorted. Memory keeps alive what the inexorable march of time would have destroyed, but only in a form that we in the present can accept and comprehend. Tradition is memory writ large, and the persistence of melody in oral tradition parallels the persistence of memory in Dali's painting. The melodies we now possess that were noted from oral tradition during the last decades of the nineteenth century are echoes of earlier times. They have been mediated through the memories of tradition bearers, through the act of transcription by song collectors, and by the decisions of editors influenced by the mores of the time. Most of the songs have probably not been transformed as radically as Dali's clocks, but some element of distortion is always likely to be present, if only because the song-catchers of the Late Victorian era sought to capture in written notation living performances that defied exact representation in that form. And in a minority of instances the distortion was much greater, usually the result of a deliberate choice. In the minds of the Late Victorian collectors not everything that they recovered from the field was publishable, and they did their best to create songbooks that would at once preserve in print the best of what they had obtained from their source singers and still be acceptable to publishers and readers alike.

It is my aim in this book to explore, as systematically as possible, both what the Late Victorian folksong collectors discovered in the field and what they published for posterity. In doing so, I have tried to be mindful of the two distorting processes that may have rendered the songs as we have them all too much like Dali's clocks. There is not much we can do about the distortion inherent in transcription by ear to notepad, except to recognize that traditional folksong is often modal and rhythmically flexible, and that the use of standard musical notation (especially key signatures, time signatures, and bar lines) may impose an inappropriate formal structure upon it. However, transcriptions were—and are—intended only as a sort of *aide mémoire* for the basic melody of a song, and provided we keep this in mind we can recognize their value while remaining aware of their limitations.

As for the other kind of distortion—that introduced consciously or unconsciously by collectors seeking to publish their treasures—this is a factor that requires study in detail. It has been assumed by previous scholars, for example by Dave Harker in *Fakesong* and by Georgina Boyes in *The Imagined Village*, that it was systematic and huge.[1] These authors go so far as to claim that the first folksong revival (including the Edwardian phase as well as the Late Victorian phase) was vitiated by its creation (or, perhaps, perpetuation) of a Romantic myth of 'the folk.' I beg to differ. To my mind the 'myth of the folk' is itself a myth, a figment of the academic imagination. But, like most myths, there is a reality behind it. The reality is the *limited* extent to which the collectors distorted what they had found when they sought to publish the results of their research. That tension—between what was collected and what was published—makes a fascinating study. Unfortunately, it is not possible to pursue this question in every case. For many, indeed most, folksong collectors in the Victorian era we have no record of their fieldwork. Only their publications survive. Yet for the three most important figures in the Late Victorian phase of the revival (Sabine Baring-Gould, Frank Kidson, and Lucy Broadwood) we do possess some archival records. So I have attempted in this book to work from these primary sources as far as possible, and in each case to make an overall judgment as to the faithfulness of their publications to their field collecting.

The other principal goal of the book is to provide a reliable overall survey of the birth of a movement: the first folksong revival. Much of the existing secondary literature suggests that this was a phenomenon of the Edwardian era, associated, of course, with such mighty figures as Cecil Sharp, Ralph Vaughan Williams, and Percy Grainger, to name just a few of the best-known folksong collectors in the decade before World War I. That is another myth. As I demonstrated in *Victorian Songhunters*, the roots of the folksong revival are to be found in the early-mid Victorian era, and the revival itself began in the late 1870s.[2] The Late Victorian phase deserves to be accorded equal weight and equal interest to the Edwardian phase, yet it has been largely neglected by scholars. My hope is to begin to remedy this undeserved neglect. Since history is a seamless web, there is always an element of arbitrariness in sub-dividing it chronologically, and the Victorian era is no exception. Yet because England changed substantially between 1837 and 1901 we do for practical purposes need to distinguish the last decades of the Victorian period from that which went before. This book is focused on the twenty-five years from 1878 to 1903, a period which I call the Late Victorian era. The year 1878 is admittedly a somewhat arbitrary and arguable date to choose for the beginning of this era. One could easily make a case for 1875, when the century still had a quarter of its span to run and, although of course no one knew it at the time, so did the Queen's reign. The obvious alternative, 1880, restricts the era to the last two decades of the century. 1878 roughly splits the difference, and, moreover, it works best for the history of song collecting. This book is a sequel to *Victorian Songhunters*, which covered years 1820-1883, and so there is necessarily some overlap between the final chapter of that work and the early chapters of this one. However, the reader will find here a greater breadth and depth of treatment of the half-decade covered in both books. At the other end of the Late Victorian era I have chosen to be a little flexible with dates. The old Queen died in 1901 but, for reasons that will become more evident in chapter 14, I decided to continue the story until the year before Sharp and Vaughan Williams emerged as major folksong collectors. And, for the sake of completeness, I have included a brief epilogue tracing the work of two major figures, Frank Kidson and Lucy Broadwood, through the Edwardian era to their deaths in the late 1920s.

I would like to emphasize that this is an empirical study that aims to place its subject in a context, that of Late Victorian English history. My perspective is that of a cultural historian, not that of a folklorist or ethnomusicologist. The book obviously falls within the broad field of cultural studies, but I would not claim to have followed the methodological prescriptions of any of the rival schools that co-exist somewhat uneasily within that academic territory. Nor have I employed the arcane terminology favored by so many contributors to the field. On the contrary, I have tried to avoid the jargon and theoretical baggage that so often renders academic writing impenetrable to the non-academic reader. Of course my interpretation cannot be entirely value free—by necessity I select and comment on my material—but I hope that it does avoid the anachronism of assessing and criticizing historical figures by the values and theoretical assumptions of a later age. After all, the primary task of a historian is to understand and explain, not to attack and pass adverse judgment.

One other statement of purpose seems to be in order. I confess to finding disappointing and unsatisfactory books about folksong that fail to provide the reader with appropriate musical examples of the subject matter under discussion. I have done my best to avoid that fundamental and unfortunately very widespread mistake. The reader will find as many vernacular song tunes and texts—traditional ballads, broadside ballads, folk lyrics, occupational songs, carols, shanties, etc.—as I could squeeze into the book. I could not avoid quite a few minor discrepancies between the fragments of song lyrics given alongside tune transcriptions and the full sets of words printed after (or sometimes before) the melody. Those small differences usually reflect discrepancies in the original sources, usually between brief sets of words scribbled in tune manuscripts and the full song-texts, whether written down in manuscripts, found on broadsheets, or printed in published collections. Certain words, such as "bonny" or "chase," are frequently found with alternative spellings (e.g. "bonnie" or "chace") that appear to have been used indiscriminately, and articles (especially "the") are sometimes included and sometimes omitted. I have tried to rationalize and minimize such differences, usually giving precedence to the words that best fit the tune, but this has not always been feasible, so some inconsistencies remain, normally when I have retained the spelling or usage employed in the source manuscript. It is a judgment call whether to aim for full linguistic consistency (as proofreaders urge) or complete faithfulness to the primary sources (on which some historians would insist). One cannot do both, and for song titles and texts I have tried to find and follow a middle road that favors consistency without making a fetish of it. No doubt there will be some readers who disagree with my choices in particular instances but that seems inevitable. Moreover, it is quite possible that some inadvertent transcription errors of my own have also crept in, although naturally I have tried to avoid them. However, I am fairly confident that any errors or discrepancies that remain are very minor ones.

I wish there were even more musical illustrations in the book. Had there been space, I would have willingly included many others. If this publication achieves nothing else, I trust that it will have demonstrated the abundance and high quality of the songs recovered by the collector/editors whose endeavors I have traced. To them I believe we owe a very considerable debt of gratitude.

In writing this book I have had help from three scholars: Martin Graebe (on Sabine Baring-Gould), Roy Palmer (on Frank Kidson), and Irene Shettle (on Lucy Broadwood). Of course, they are not responsible for the willful opinions and many minor errors that the book no doubt contains despite their sage advice. Athabasca University generously gave me a President's Award for Research and Scholarship, which provided me with a four month break from teaching and administration, during which time I converted the first draft into something approaching the final version. I would also like to thank the Academic Research Fund and the helpful staff in the Interlibrary Loan office at Athabasca University, at the Surrey History Centre, Woking, Surrey, at the Mitchell Library, Glasgow, and at the Vaughan Williams Memorial Library at Cecil Sharp House, Camden Town, London. I am especially grateful to my wife, Rosaleen Gregory, who commented on my first draft, improved my English in many places, and, above all, encouraged me to keep researching and writing when I felt snowed under with other responsibilities.

Notes

1. Georgina Boyes, *The Imagined Village: Culture, Ideology and the English Folk Revival* (Manchester: Manchester University Press, 1993). Dave Harker, *Fakesong: The Manufacture of British 'Folksong' 1700 to the Present Day* (Milton Keynes, U.K.: Open University Press, 1985).
2. E. David Gregory, *Victorian Songhunters: The Recovery and Editing of English Vernacular Ballads and Folk-Lyrics, 1820-1883* (Lanham, Md. & Oxford, U.K.: The Scarecrow Press, 2006).

Part 1

Concepts and Legacies

1

The Concept of Folksong

Philosophers have long debated whether or not it is possible to have a concept without a term for it, or, to put the issue another way, whether a concept can exist *prior* to there being an agreed-upon word that denotes it. Some think not. Language, they would argue, is a social construct and a concept is a mutually shared representation. To have a notion of something without a word for it—so this argument runs—would be to have a private language, and a private language is, by its very nature, impossible. In other words, an individual may dream up a new idea but that idea cannot become a functional concept without a commonly agreed term for it among a community of users. This philosophical position derives from the theory of language set forth in Ludwig Wittgenstein's *Philosophical Investigations*.[1] The other side in the debate seems to have its roots in a much older philosophical tradition going back to Plato, a tradition often called Idealism. Idealists (or at least some of them) claim that, on the contrary, the mental concept—the Platonic Idea, if you will—necessarily comes first, and that a name for a thing comes into existence only *after* a given linguistic community already has a collective notion of what that thing is.

This introductory essay is not primarily philosophical, but it does seek to examine the parameters and history of the difficult and controversial concept that is used in the very title of this book. My aim is to find a preliminary answer to the question: what concept or concepts of folksong did the Late Victorian collectors inherit from their predecessors? To do so requires finding when and how the term first came into use. But it also necessitates exploring whether earlier Victorian song collectors had a working notion of folksong before then. To sort out these issues one must examine two somewhat different histories: the history of the English word *folksong* and the history of Victorian vernacular song collecting. The way in which these two stories intertwine may then shed some light on both the empirical question and the philosophical issue of whether a concept can exist prior to an agreed term for it.

The Term

From Folklore to Folksong

Let us begin with the simpler of these two stories, that of the term. The word *folk* is almost as old as the English language itself, having been used by both Langland (in his *Vision of Piers Plowman*) and Chaucer (in the *Canterbury Tales*). The term *folklore*, on the other hand, seems to have been an invention of the early nineteenth century, and it was in fairly common use in book titles by mid-century. William J. Thoms, for example, published a book on *The Folk-lore of Shakespeare* in 1847,[2] and four years later one could purchase a copy of Thomas Sternberg's treatise on *The Dialect and Folk-lore of Northamptonshire*.[3] Many other mid-Victorian examples could be cited, but two publications from the 1860s merit particular attention because they were by folklorists who were also song collectors: Llewelyn Jewitt's *Notes on the Folk-lore of Fungi*[4] and John Harland and Thomas Wilkinson's *Lancashire Folk-lore*.[5] Incidentally, the British Folk-Lore Society began publishing its journal in 1878, by which time there was already in existence a regional folklore periodical published in Shrewsbury, namely *Salopian Shreds and Patches, or, Miscellaneous Notes on the History, Antiquities, Folklore, etc. of the County*.[6]

It was not a huge jump from routinely employing the term *folklore* to inventing the term *folksong,* but pinning down the first use of the term is not quite as straightforward as one would like. It appears that American usage preceded British, since in 1865 John Williams Palmer published in New York a book with the title *Folk Song*.[7] This was billed as a collection of literary texts, some of the items were poems rather than songs, and there were no tunes, but the term had been invented and applied, perhaps for the first time. The earliest usage that I have discovered in England is William E. A. Axon's *Folk Song and Folk-Speech of Lancashire*.[8] This was published in Manchester by Tubbs & Brook, but no date is given on the title page. It is usually cited as 1871, and internal evidence does suggest that the text was written around that time. However, the only copy that I have been able to obtain includes advertising matter that proves it was printed commercially some sixteen years later, in 1887, and I suspect that any earlier edition was merely for private circulation. Yet even with a publication date of 1887 Axon's little book still seems to have priority within the British Isles. The next contender appears to be Heywood Sumner's *The Besom-Maker and Other Country Folk Songs*, which came off the press the next year, in 1888.[9] The trickle only gradually turned into a flood. William Alexander Barrett's *English Folk-Songs* followed in 1891,[10] and Sabine Baring-Gould's *A Garland of Country Song: English Folk Songs with their Traditional Melodies* appeared in 1895.[11] The Folk-Song Society was founded in 1898. Not everyone chose to adopt the term immediately, but it seems fair to say that it was in general use by the end of the nineteenth century.

Two Opposing Perspectives

According to the Wittgensteinian theory of language mentioned earlier, a community of users employing the term in the same way is required before a meaningful and functional concept exists. For the term *folksong* such a linguistic community had evidently come into existence by the Edwardian era, and in 1907 Cecil Sharp made his famous—if controversial—attempt to define and explain the meaning of the concept in *English Folk Song: Some Conclusions*.[12] In fact, Sharp was articulating in print and spelling out in detail the implications inherent in the notion of folksong that he had inherited from one of his Victorian precursors, Sabine Baring-Gould. In *A Garland of Country Song* Baring-Gould drew a sharp distinction between the old English songs reprinted by William Chappell in *Popular Music of the Olden Time* and "genuine folk songs" preserved in oral tradition by the peasantry of Devon and Cornwall. The former—such songs as "Greensleeves," "The Lass of Richmond Hill," "Sally in Our Alley," and "The Vicar of Bray"—were "old parlour and concert-hall music" and were "exactly the music which is *not* sung by the peasantry."[13] The true folksongs were those that Baring-Gould had collected in the Devon villages around Lew Trenchard from local agricultural laborers, hedgers, masons, and blacksmiths. In reality, like that of his successor, Baring-Gould's theoretical definition of folksongs as those noted from the mouths of the "peasantry"—(his word and Sharp's too)—did not quite jibe with his own practice, since he collected as readily from local artisans as from farm laborers. Yet it is clear that he considered folksong to be *rural* in nature and to be transmitted by *oral tradition*. Here, then, we have a reasonably clear Victorian concept of folksong, one which Sharp merely refined and made more explicit.

Not everyone wholeheartedly endorsed the Baring-Gould/Sharp theory of folksong. An alternative perspective was shared by Frank Kidson, Lucy Broadwood, and Alec Fuller Maitland, among others. They were not comfortable with Baring-Gould's sharp dichotomy between folksongs and also-rans, and they tended to avoid using the term *folksong* in the titles of their collections because they wanted to indicate that they had included a broader array of vernacular material. Thus Kidson's *Old English Country Dances* included such songs as "Ge[e] Ho, Dobbin" and "The Maid of Honour,"[14] while *Traditional Tunes* reprinted a good number of broadside ballads, including "Spencer the Rover" and "Polly Oliver."[15] Broadwood and Fuller Maitland's *English County Songs* included an industrial song, "The Collier's Rant," several carols, such national songs as "A North-Country Maid" and "The Cheerful Arn," and a number of broadside ballads including "The Undaunted Female" and "The Barkshire Tragedy."[16] It was a more eclectic vision that encompassed a wider territory than that surveyed by Baring-Gould.

With the formation of the Folk-Song Society in the late 1890s, Kidson and Broadwood became reconciled to the term folksong. Rather than explicitly redefining it they simply used it in the looser fashion, employing it to denote the wider pool of vernacular songs that they had previously called country songs, county songs, or simply old English songs. They slipped easily into this broader usage because it was already current in some circles. In fact they unconsciously inherited their less doctrinaire approach—their alternative language game, if you prefer Wittgensteinian terminology—from their mid-Victorian predecessors. So we find that in the Late Victorian era there were in existence two alternative usages of the word folksong: Baring-Gould's strict definition (old songs preserved in oral tradition by the 'peasantry'), and the broader and looser notion employed in practice by Kidson, Broadwood, and others. To understand what they (and their precursors) had in mind we must therefore examine this other, inchoate, *idea* of folksong. To do so requires going back several decades prior to the emergence of the term itself.

History of the Idea

To start with, can we find earlier song collectors who, despite not having the term itself, appear to be working with the same notion of folksong as Baring-Gould and Sharp? Does an earlier *idea* of folksong foreshadow the more restrictive use of the term? The answer seems to be "yes." During the 1820s the Romantic poet John Clare noted approximately fifty song texts, some from his illiterate parents, others from villagers who lived in or near Helpston in Northamptonshire. They included such traditional ballads as "Lord Randall," "The Demon Lover," and "The Cruel Brother," and such lyrics as "Ten Thousand Mile," "Bushes and Briars," and "All Jolly Fellows That Follow the Plough." Clare never used the word *folksong*, but his subject matter and, significantly, the way he limited it, was very similar to Baring-Gould's. Although he never published his manuscript collection, his working title was *National and Provincial Melodies Selected from the Singing and Recitations of the Peasantry* and the songs were collected exclusively from rural oral tradition.[17] During the next half-century other songhunters, including the Reverend John Broadwood, followed in Clare's footsteps, and the quest for "peasant songs" was an ongoing current within the broader stream of Victorian song collecting. John Broadwood's published collection, for example, was titled *Old English Songs, as now sung by the Peasantry of the Weald of Surrey and Sussex.*[18] His small book can also be seen as representative of another phenomenon, the beginning of regional song collecting. This was most common in the northeast of England, the pioneers including Joseph Ritson,[19] John Bell,[20] and Cuthbert Sharp,[21] each of whom noted some items from oral tradition.

Meanwhile, a rival current had emerged. In 1823 William Kitchiner compiled *The Loyal and National Songs of England* and *The Sea Songs of England*,[22] thereby pioneering the revival of what quickly came to be known as 'national songs.' These were composed songs, almost all by known authors, which had lasted in popularity beyond their initial success and had become in some sense identified with the spirit of the nation. Some, such as "The British Grenadiers" and "Fairest Isle," were overtly patriotic, but others, such as "Black-eyed Susan," "Tom Bowling," and "Fill the Flowing Bowl," were not. A few years after Kitchiner's books were published Edward Utterson edited *A Little Book of Ballads*,[23] a small collection of broadside ballads that served as a reminder of the long tradition of ballad editing that went back to the anonymous *A Collection of Old Ballads*,[24] and included the work of Joseph Ritson [25] and Thomas Evans.[26]

So when Victoria's reign began in 1837 there were, quite independent of each other, four parallel phenomena: the collecting of rural ('peasant') songs from oral tradition; a growth in regional collecting which was by no means exclusively rural in character; a deliberate revival of late seventeenth- and eighteenth-century national songs; and a renewed interest in black-letter broadside balladry from the late sixteenth and seventeenth centuries. The early to mid-Victorian era would witness an intermingling but as yet incomplete merger of these four strands.

The Percy Society and Vernacular Song

In contrast to these rival collections of old ballads, local songs, 'peasant' songs, and national songs, certain Victorian song collectors developed a broader and more inclusive notion of lower class vocal music. They did not achieve consensus on what to call it, variously employing such phrases as "ballads and songs," "old songs," "country songs," "traditional songs," and "songs of the people," so for the sake of a single working label, I will call this kind of music *vernacular song*.

The early Victorian era—the 1840s and 1850s—was the critical period. The dominant force in these years was the Percy Society, which was responsible for the publication in 1846 of James Henry Dixon's groundbreaking *Ancient Poems, Ballads and Songs of the Peasantry of England.*[27] Dixon made extensive use of broadsheets and garlands as sources of song-texts in addition to his own and others' collecting from oral tradition.[28] Broadsides, of course, were urban in origin, and he included the work of commercial ballad-mongers as well as more traditional ballads. Both were of interest. "Arthur O'Bradley," "The Blind Beggar of Bethnal Green," and "The Golden Glove" were just three of the vernacular ballads that Dixon reprinted but Francis James Child would reject.[29] Another Percy Society member, Charles Mackay, concentrated more on non-narrative songs. His *The Book of English Songs, from the Sixteenth to the Nineteenth Century*[30] contained, along with such rural items as "Dame Durden" and "John Barleycorn," such national songs as "The Lass of Richmond Hill," "The Miller of Dee," and "The Vicar of Bray."

The Percy Society member who became most widely identified with the resurrection of older national songs was William Chappell. His first important publication was *A Collection of National English Airs*,[31] which was followed in the late 1850s by his *magnum opus, Popular Music of the Olden Time*, which bore the subtitle *A Collection of Ancient Songs, Ballads and Dance Tunes, illustrative of the National Music of England.*[32] Chappell was much more catholic than Kitchiner. Broadly speaking, the songs in *Popular Music of the Olden Time* can be divided into three main groups. There were commercial compositions with known authors, for example Henry Carey, Charles Dibdin, and William Shield, that had survived to become street songs. There were broadside ballads, many of unknown authorship but others linked to such figures as Thomas Deloney, Martin Parker, and Laurence Price. And there were anonymous songs from oral tradition. A section titled "Traditional Songs of Uncertain Date" included, among others, "Cupid's Garden," "Early One Morning," "The Grey Cock," "The Lincolnshire Poacher," and "The Mermaid." Chappell was fascinated by all three kinds of old popular songs, and he did not pick favorites among them.

So if we take the published work of the leading Percy Society members as a whole we find a wide range of song-types. Implicit in the Percy Society perspective was a broad and inclusive notion of vernacular song that recognized, in addition to oral tradition, manuscripts, broadsheets, garlands, and early printed books as legitimate sources of old songs that were worth reviving. It was an eclectic vision and perhaps rather indiscriminate in its scattergun approach, but refreshingly open and flexible.

Regional Collections and "Songs of the People"

Another Percy Society activist, James Orchard Halliwell, resumed the collection and reprinting of English regional song pioneered by Joseph Ritson, John Bell, and Cuthbert Sharp. Halliwell's collections included *The Norfolk Anthology*, *The Palatine Anthology* (covering Lancashire and Cheshire), and *The Yorkshire Anthology*.[33] Other regional collections followed. The most important published during the 1860s included Llewelynn Jewitt's *Ballads and Songs of Derbyshire*,[34] Davison Ingledew's *The Ballads and Songs of Yorkshire*,[35] and two works by John Harland, *Ballads and Songs of Lancashire* and *Lancashire Lyrics*.[36] As we have seen, Jewitt and Harland were both folklorists with publications that used the term folk-lore in their titles.

Harland's books had a significant impact on the Victorian notion of vernacular song. *Ballads and Songs* printed quite a variety of material, including traditional ballads such as "The Two Sisters," border ballads, broadsides, May Day and wassail songs, drinking songs, old comic songs, local verses reflecting Lancashire life and customs, and occupational songs by the county's spinners and weavers. The latter were usually in dialect. The best-known, "Jone o' Grinfilt Junior," was reworked and popularized by Ewan MacColl as "The Four Loom Weaver." In *Lancashire Lyrics* Harland printed some songs that he called "traditional," such as "The Seeds of Love" and "The Sprig of Thyme," but many more that had been composed during the previous fifty years by popular Lancashire poets. They included such industrial songs as "Th' Shurat Weyvur's Song," "The Factory Lass," "Eawt o' Work," and "Hard Times." Harland's collective term for all this material was "songs of the people."

As mentioned earlier, it was Harland's friend and assistant, William Axon, who made the terminological leap from folklore to folksong. His *Folk Song and Folk-Speech of Lancashire*[37] was a commentary on the material in Harland's two collections. By "folk songs" Axon meant the same as had Harland by "songs of the people," that is, any vernacular songs created and sung by local people, whether or not the composers' names were known and whether or not they were in dialect. This early usage of the term *folksong* was therefore broad in conception, extending to contemporary political and occupational song as well as to traditional and broadside balladry and shorter love lyrics. Because the region was industrializing rapidly and its popular culture included the songs of textile mill workers as well as those of handloom weavers and other artisans, Lancashire folksong was urban as well as rural. A century before A. L. Lloyd[38] argued for a broader definition of folksong than Cecil Sharp's, Harland and Axon had effectively done the same.

It has to be admitted that although Harland's books became recognized as the standard collections of Lancashire vernacular song, Axon's essay was soon forgotten. I would therefore not go so far as to maintain that Axon's usage of the term 'folk song' quickly became a standard one. The truth is that most folksong collectors during the 1890s and 1900s were not very interested in industrial or urban songs, and the movement's focus was primarily rural. But the term had come into existence, and it was now available for anyone who had a use for it.

Moreover, the legacy of Dixon, Mackay, Chappell, Harland, and the other Victorian collectors was pervasive and could scarcely be ignored. Some late Victorian and Edwardian figures, such as Baring-Gould and Sharp, reacted against it, and took delight in excoriating Chappell in particular. Others were more appreciative, and tried to build on their predecessors' work. Frank Kidson, for example, was methodologically a disciple of Chappell, and he had inherited Chappell's love of broadside ballads and national songs as well as traditional ballads and folk lyrics. Lucy Broadwood did extensive research among broadside collections and old songbooks in the British Museum, and she was perhaps the first English scholar/collector to absorb thoroughly the work of Francis James Child. Child's antipathy to broadsides is well known but, paradoxically, a considerable number of the English—as opposed to Scottish—variants he had found of his "popular" ballads were broadside texts, which underlined the importance of print as an early medium of song transmission.[39]

As a result of their historical investigations into broadsides, garlands, and old songbooks, Kidson and Broadwood came to recognize that many songs that they first encountered in oral tradition had enjoyed earlier careers as broadside ballads or as songs composed for the London pleasure gardens. Kidson was the most outspoken advocate of an eclectic approach to vernacular song. Throughout his involvement with the folksong movement he championed the sometimes unpopular view that folk lyrics, traditional ballads, broadside ballads, and the most memorable commercial popular songs were all part of a broader tradition of national song. What mattered, he argued, was not the mode of transmission but whether they possessed "vital melodies."[40] If a song did, it would survive from generation to generation and would become part of the wide and deep pool of English vernacular music. Even Sabine Baring-Gould eventually came to much the same conclusion: *English Minstrelsie* contained a much wider range of material than his earlier collections. Nonetheless, his editorial response in *English Minstrelsie* was to narrow further the number and kind of songs that he was prepared to label folksongs, and to create instead a second (very large) category that he called "old English songs."[41] The other option, of course, would have been to assimilate all, or at least most, of these vernacular items under a more liberally interpreted category called folksong.[42]

Some Provisional Conclusions

This brief examination of the pre-history and early history of the concept of "folksong" in Victorian England leads us to several conclusions. The first is that the English term *folksong* was a spin-off from the term *folklore*. That was in use in England by at least as early as the 1840s, but it took several decades before folklorists decided that they needed a new term for what they had previously been content to call "old songs and ballads." The person who most likely coined the word *folksong* in England was William Axon. He probably did so in the early 1870s, under the influence of two folklorists who loved and collected vernacular songs, John Harland and Thomas Wilkinson.

A second conclusion is a negative one: that the German notion of *Volkslied* had no significant influence and there was probably no translation of this term before Carl Engel's *The Literature of National Music*.[43] Engel in any case muddied the water and caused endless confusion by translating *Volkslied* as "national song" rather than folksong. There were undoubtedly Victorian intellectuals who were aware of the work and ideas of Herder and other German Romantics—Thomas Carlyle, Matthew Arnold, and George Eliot come to mind—but they seem not to have been interested in collecting English folksongs, nor, apparently, did they influence those who were.

Third, it appears that the term *folksong* came into fairly general use only in the 1890s, stimulated by Heywood Sumner's use of it in *The Besom Maker and Other Country Folk Songs* and by William Alexander Barrett's larger and better distributed *English Folk-Songs*. Adoption of the term by the enthusiasts behind the formation of the Folk-Song Society in 1898—in conscious imitation of the existing Folk-Lore Society—was critical in consolidating its acceptance by a community of users, some of whom had previously shown reluctance to embrace it.

Fourth, Sabine Baring-Gould's use of the term in the subtitle of *A Garland of Country Song*, and his narrow definition of it in that work and in *English Minstrelsie*, was very influential. From 1895 onwards one high-profile usage restricted folksongs to songs noted from oral tradition in the countryside from unlettered rural inhabitants. This was the definition adopted and further refined by Cecil Sharp, and accepted by Ralph Vaughan Williams and others in the Edwardian era. It continued to be championed by Maud Karpeles within the English Folk Dance and Song Society in the 1930s and in International Folk Music Council circles during the post-war era.

A fifth conclusion is that there was also in existence a rival usage that embraced a wider range of vernacular songs including broadside ballads and the more lyrical and less overtly patriotic kind of national songs, although there was still a presumption that such songs would be found in villages and small towns rather than cities. This perspective derived from the work of such early and mid-Victorian collectors as Dixon, Chappell, and Harland. It was adopted in the late Victorian period by Frank Kidson, Lucy Broadwood, Alec Fuller Maitland, Arthur Somervell, and others. Within Folk-Song Society circles in the years before World War I they had some success in defending it against Sharp's more doctrinaire perspective.

Another, decidedly minority, usage extended the term further, to include industrial and urban vernacular song, in fact any "songs of the people," no matter where those people resided or how they earned their living, but this definition, although suggested by William Axon in the 1870s, failed to find much favor before the 1950s. It would then be championed by A. L. Lloyd, Ewan MacColl, John Hasted, and Eric Winter, among others, and find expression in the pages of *Sing* magazine.

Let us return, finally, to the philosophical issue with which we began. It is evident that each of the first two notions of folksong existed and developed for several decades before actually receiving the label. The narrow version was implicit in the practice of both John Clare and John Broadwood, although the word was first applied in this sense by Heywood Sumner in 1888. A broader version was implicit in the practice of James Henry Dixon and other members of the Percy Society, and, in effect, it was adopted (although not unambiguously) by the Folk-Song Society in 1898. The broadest of the three was implicit in the work of John Harland and was articulated by William Axon, but it would not become a widely used definition until after World War II. In any event, we can say with some assurance that by the death of the old Queen in 1901 there were three rival usages (or definitions) of the term *folksong* extant in England. Moreover, it would appear that the history of the concept lends support to the Idealist theory of language: in each case the *idea* of folksong (whether conceived narrowly or broadly) preceded the invention and widespread use of the term.

Notes

1. Ludwig Wittgenstein, *Philosophical Investigations*, translated by G. E. M. Anscombe (2nd edition. Oxford: Basil Blackwell, 1967).

2. William J. Thoms, *The Folk-lore of Shakespeare* (London: J.R. Smith, 1847).

3. Thomas Sternberg, *The Dialect and Folk-lore of Northamptonshire* (London: J. R. Smith, 1851).

4. Llewelyn Jewitt, *Notes on the Folk-lore of Fungi* (London, n.p., 1860).

5. John Harland and Thomas T. Wilkinson, *Lancashire Folk-lore* (London: F. Warne, 1867).

6. This was published from 1874 to 1892.

7. John Williams Palmer, ed., *Folk Song* (New York: Scribner, 1865).

8. William E. A. Axon, *Folk Song and Folk-Speech of Lancashire* (Manchester: Tubbs & Brook, n.d. [1871?], reissued 1887).

9. Heywood Sumner, ed., *The Besom Maker and Other Country Folk Songs* (London: Longmans, Green & Co, 1888).

10. William Alexander Barrett, ed., *English Folk-Songs* (London & New York: Novello, Ewer & Co., 1891).

11. Sabine Baring-Gould and H. Fleetwood Sheppard, eds., *A Garland of Country Song: English Folk Songs with their Traditional Melodies* (London: Methuen, 1895).

12. Cecil J. Sharp, *English Folk Song: Some Conclusions* (Taunton: Barnicott & Pearce, 1907).

13. Baring-Gould, *Garland of Country Song*, vi.

14. Frank Kidson, ed., *Old English Country Dances* (London: William Reeves, 1890).

15. Frank Kidson, ed., *Traditional Tunes, a Collection of Ballad Airs, chiefly obtained in Yorkshire and the South of Scotland, together with their appropriate words from broadsides and from oral tradition* (Oxford: Charles Taphouse & Son, 1891; reprint: East Ardsley: S.R. Publishers, 1970).

16. Lucy E. Broadwood and J. A. Fuller Maitland, eds., *English County Songs: Words and Music* (London: The Leadenhall Press, 1893; reprinted London: Cramer, 1915).

17. Ms. A41, *John Clare Collection*, Peterborough Museum, Peterborough, Northamptonshire, England, U.K.

18. [John Broadwood] and Geoffrey Dusart, eds., *Old English Songs, as now sung by the Peasantry of the Weald of Surrey and Sussex* (London: Betts & Co., [1847 not 1843, as often given]).

19. Joseph Ritson, ed., *Northern Garlands* (London: Triphook, 1810). This was a reprint, in one volume, of four small collections made by Ritson and published separately between 1784 and 1802: *The Bishopric Garland, or Durham Minstrel* (1784, revised edition 1792), *The Yorkshire Garland* (1788), *The Northumberland Garland* (1793), and *The North-Country Chorister* (1802).

20. John Bell, ed., *Rhymes of Northern Bards* (Newcastle-upon-Tyne, U.K.: Bell & Angus, 1812; reprinted, Newcastle-upon-Tyne, U.K.: Frank Graham, 1971).

21. Sir Cuthbert Sharp, ed., *The Bishoprick Garland, or a collection of Legends, Songs, Ballads, etc., belonging to the county of Durham* (London: Nichols and Baldwin and Cradock, 1834).

22. William Kitchiner, ed., *The Loyal and National Songs of England, for one, two, and three voices, selected from original manuscripts and early printed copies in the Library of W. Kitchiner* (London: Hurst, Robinson & Co., 1823); William Kitchiner, ed., *The Sea Songs of Charles Dibdin, with a Memoir of his Life and Writings* (London: G. & W. B. Whittaker & Clementi and Co., 1823); William Kitchiner, ed., *The Sea Songs of England, selected from original manuscripts and early printed copies in the Library of W. Kitchiner* (London: Hurst, Robinson & Co., 1823).

23. [Edward V. Utterson, ed.,] *A Little Book of Ballads* (Newport, U.K.: Yelf & Co., for the Roxburghe Club, 1836).

24. *A Collection of Old Ballads, Corrected from the best and most Ancient Copies Extant, with Introductions Historical, Critical or Humorous*, 3 vols. (London: J. Roberts, 1723-1725).

25. Joseph Ritson, ed., *Ancient Songs from the Time of King Henry the Third to the Revolution* (London: J. Johnson, 1790); expanded edition as *Ancient Songs and Ballads from the Reign of King Henry the Second to the Revolution*, 2 vols. (London: Payne & Foss, 1829).

26. Thomas Evans, ed., *Old Ballads, Historical and Narrative, with some of Modern Date, Collected from Rare Copies and Mss.*, 2 vols. (London: Evans, 1777; 2nd edition, 4 vols.: London: Evans, 1784).

27. James Henry Dixon, ed., *Ancient Poems, Ballads and Songs of the Peasantry of England* (London: The Percy Society, 1846). Dixon also edited for the Percy Society a selection from the manuscripts of Peter Buchan titled *Scottish Traditional Versions of Ancient Ballads* (London: The Percy Society, 1846).

28. Dixon's own collecting was done mainly in the Yorkshire Dales. His helpers included such other Percy Society members as William Sandys and William Chappell. He apparently also drew on material in the archives of the Newcastle-upon-Tyne antiquarian society.

29. That is to say, exclude from his canon of 305 items in *The English and Scottish Popular Ballads*, 10 parts in 5 vols.(Boston, Mass.: Houghton, Mifflin & Co., 1882-1898; reprinted: New York: Dover, 1965). Child's earlier collection, *English and Scottish Ballads*, 8 vols. (Boston, Mass.: Little Brown & Co., 1857-59. 2nd edition, 1860. 3rd edition, 1866) was more eclectic.

30. Charles Mackay, ed., *The Book of English Songs, from the Sixteenth to the Nineteenth Century* (London: Office of the National Illustrated Library, 1851).

31. William Chappell, ed., *A Collection of National English Airs consisting of Ancient Song, Ballad and Dance Tunes*, 2 vols. (London: Chappell, Simkin, Marshall & Co., 1838).

32. William Chappell, ed., *Popular Music of the Olden Time, a collection of Ancient Songs, Ballads and Dance Tunes, illustrative of the National Music of England*, 2 vols. (London: Cramer, Beale & Chappell, 1858-59; reprinted: New York: Dover, 1965).

33. James Orchard Halliwell, ed., *The Norfolk Anthology: A Collection of Poems, Ballads, and Rare Tracts Relating to the County of Norfolk* (Brixton Hill, U.K.: Halliwell, 1852); *The Palatine Anthology: A Collection of Ancient Poems and Ballads Relating to Lancashire and Cheshire* (London: Halliwell, 1850); *Palatine Garland, being a Selection of Ballads and Fragments Supplementary to the Palatine Anthology* (London: Halliwell, 1850): *The Yorkshire Anthology* (London: Halliwell, 1851).

34. Llewelynn F. W. Jewitt, ed., *Ballads and Songs of Derbyshire* (London: Bemrose & Lothian, 1867).

35. C. J. Davison Ingledew, ed., *The Ballads and Songs of Yorkshire* (London: Bell & Daldy, 1860).

36. John Harland, ed., *Ballads and Songs of Lancashire, chiefly older than the 19th Century* (London: Whittaker, 1865; 2nd edition, 1875); *Lancashire Lyrics: Modern Songs and Ballads of the County Palatine* (London: Whittaker, 1866).

37. See note 8.

38. A. L. Lloyd, *Folk Song in England* (London: Lawrence & Wishart, 1967).

39. On Child, see (among others) David Atkinson, with Tom Cheeseman, "A Child Ballad Study Guide with Select Bibliography and Discography" in *Ballads into Books: The Legacies of Francis James Child,* ed. Tom Cheeseman and Sigrid Rieuwerts. (Bern, Switzerland: Peter Lang, 1997), 259-80; Michael J. Bell, "'No Borders to the Ballad Maker's Art': Francis J. Child and the Politics of the People," *Western Folklore* 47 (1988): 285-307; Rosaleen Gregory and David Gregory, "Jewels Left in the Dunghills: Broadside and other Vernacular Ballads Rejected by Francis Child," *Canadian Journal for Traditional Music* 29 (2002): 69-80; Sigrid Rieuwerts, "The Ballad Society: a forgotten chapter in the history of English ballad studies," in *Folk Song: Tradition, Revival, and Re-Creation,* ed. Ian Russell and David Atkinson (Aberdeen, U.K.: The Elphinstone Institute, University of Aberdeen, 2004), 28-40; Sigrid Rieuwerts, "The Folk-Ballad: The Illegitimate Child of the Popular Ballad," *Journal of Folklore Research* 33 (1996): 221-26; Sigrid Rieuwerts, "From Percy to Child: The 'Popular Ballad' as 'a distinct and very important species of poetry,'" in *Ballads and Boundaries: Narrative Singing in an Intercultural Context,* ed. James Porter (Los Angeles: Department of Ethnomusicology and Systematic Musicology, University of California at Los Angeles, 1995), 13-20; Sigrid Rieuwerts, "'The Genuine Ballads of the People': F. J. Child and the Ballad Cause," *Journal of Folklore Research* 31, nos. 1-3 (1994): 1-34; and Sigrid Rieuwerts, "In Memoriam: Francis James Child (1825-1896)," in *Ballads into Books*, ed. Tom Cheeseman and Sigrid Rieuwerts, 19-25.

40. Frank Kidson, "Notes on Old Tunes," thirty-two articles published in the *Leeds Mercury Weekly Supplement* between 6 November 1886 and 25 June 1887; Frank Kidson, "New Lights upon Old Tunes," *Musical Times*, 1 October 1894, 1 February 1895, 1 May 1895, 1 September 1895, 1 June 1896, 1 September 1896, and 1 August 1897; Frank Kidson, "The Vitality of Melody," *Proceedings of the Musical Association* 34 (1907-1908): 81-95.

41. Sabine Baring-Gould, ed., *English Minstrelsie: A National Monument of English Song*, vols. 1-8 (Edinburgh: Jack & Jack, 1895-1898).

42. Sharp's influence mitigated against this solution in England during the interwar era, but it would be widely adopted in the second folksong revival of the 1950s and 1960s. See, for example, the editorial policy of *Sing* magazine, an influential periodical which printed an eclectic mixture of traditional songs and contemporary political songs. *Sing* was modeled on the American magazine *Sing Out!*, which did the same.

43. Carl Engel, *The Literature of National Music* (London: Novello, Ewer & Co., 1879).

2

Legacies from the Past

The story of English vernacular song fits quite well into the general picture of British history in the nineteenth century. Although earlier surges of activity had alternated with times when the current slowed to a trickle, the Victorian movement to recover and publish (or reprint) old songs had since the late 1850s flowed energetically onwards, gathering momentum like a brook rushing towards a lake. Moreover, in the last twenty-five years of the century we can observe, with the benefit of hindsight, the genesis and early development of something new, the phase that I have chosen to call the first English folksong revival.[1] It began slowly in the mid-1870s, but by 1878 Victorian England was, at least in this respect, entering a new phase of its cultural history and the stream of vernacular song was becoming a powerful river fed by several tributaries. The aim of this chapter is to survey the state of English collecting and research just as that new wave of activity began. To some degree it will cover ground that has been surveyed briefly in the previous chapter, but the emphasis here is not on the concept of folksong but on the actual work of collecting, editing, and publishing old songs. As we shall see, there were in fact various rivulets, gills, brooks, and creeks, but they had not yet merged to form that river of Late Victorian song.

Folksong enthusiasts in the Late Victorian period could draw upon a considerable body of previously collected material. In hunting for songs they had no need to start from scratch. Far from it. They had a choice: they could begin collecting in the field oblivious to what had been done before, or they could first—or at least simultaneously—become familiar with the work of earlier collectors. Not that the Late Victorians were always fully aware—or appreciative—of what had been done before them, but the results of their predecessors' labors could be found on library shelves by anyone who cared to take down and dust off those weighty volumes. So if, in 1878, someone newly captivated by English traditional song—perhaps a young lady named Marianne Harriet Mason, Laura Smith, Charlotte ("Lotty") Burne, or Lucy Broadwood, each of whom we shall meet later in these pages—had set out to find out how many of the 'old songs' had already been published and who had collected them, what would she have come up with? In 1910 one of those four women, Charlotte Burne, the author of *Shropshire Folk-Lore*, would become the first female President of the Folk-Lore Society. Another, Lucy Broadwood, would be by then the editor of the *Journal of the Folk-Song Society* and the co-editor of three major folksong collections, *Sussex Songs*, *English County Songs*, and *English Traditional Songs and Carols*.[2] And both Laura Smith and Marianne Mason would also have played significant roles within the Victorian movement to collect and revive old song, including editing important collections. So evidently each one of them came to know a great deal about folk music, and each must have gone through an interesting learning process to obtain that knowledge.

Unfortunately we do not have enough documentary evidence to follow in sufficient detail the early intellectual development of any of these four women, so it is not possible to reconstruct precisely how even one of them acquired the extensive knowledge of folk music and balladry that she came eventually to possess. Nor do we have a better male candidate. Sabine Baring-Gould, Frank Kidson, Alec Fuller Maitland, and John Stokoe all await their biographers.[3] As more primary sources become available it may turn out to be possible to reconstruct in the kind of detail we are looking for their intellectual development and their early involvement with folksong. Baring-Gould is perhaps the best bet, and the completion of Martin Graebe's forthcoming major work on this key figure is hopefully not too far distant. For now the closest we can come is with Lucy Broadwood, but our best source of information about her early years, her extant diaries, begins only in late 1882, and our knowledge of her (rather limited) involvement with folksong before 1886 is sketchy.[4] Broadwood's formative years will be discussed in chapter 10, and it will then be quite evident that the year 1878 is too early for her to have obtained much of the information outlined in this background chapter.

I suspect, therefore, that no individual who was involved with folksong in the late 1870s attempted systematically to assimilate the legacy of previous generations' attempts to collect and preserve English traditional balladry and vernacular song. A wealth of information and a large body of already collected song existed, but, as a whole, it was not well known. This existing heritage of song became apparent to Baring-Gould, Broadwood, Kidson, and others only gradually during the next two decades. Frank Kidson was fascinated by the history of popular song and he collected books and broadsides avidly, so it is likely that he fairly quickly obtained a good background in printed materials. It was probably Lucy Broadwood, the only one of these three with access to excellent library facilities in London as well as a wide circle of knowledgeable musical friends living in various regions of the country, who eventually achieved the most comprehensive familiarity with all that had gone before. The important point, however, is that the Late Victorian era was when the achievements of earlier collectors, including the many Victorians working before the 1880s, gradually came to be appreciated by their successors in a way that had never previously occurred. It was a time of consolidation as well as advance.

Nonetheless, since the Late Victorian folksong revival did not suddenly spring from nowhere, *sui generis*, but in fact built on the work of earlier collectors, we do need to survey briefly the intellectual and cultural background to this phenomenon. That means doing two things: sketching the pre-history of the revival, and placing it in the context of the times. This chapter is intended to cover the first of these two tasks. The political, cultural, and intellectual context for the 1880s is sketched in chapter 3, and for the 1890s in chapter 9. Readers well versed in the history of Late Victorian England may wish to skip those two chapters, but others may find that they provide a useful framework in which to place the more specialized activity of song collecting. Similarly, readers already familiar with the earlier history of English vernacular song may wish to skip the summary provided in this chapter and go on to the main story. On the other hand, readers who want more information than can be included in a short survey are referred to my book *Victorian Songhunters*, which not only treats in detail the story of vernacular song collecting and editing during the early and mid-Victorian eras but also provides a brief account of the work of the earlier seventeenth- and eighteenth-century collectors.[5]

Varieties of Vernacular Song: Ballads, Folksongs, and National Songs

Victorian songhunting was quite a diverse activity, and the practitioners included antiquarians, ballad scholars, musicians, music historians, and various other amateur song collectors. There was a division of labor between them: they tended to split into either song catchers or ballad editors. Ballad editing was something of a specialized field and divided into two wings: traditional balladry and broadside balladry. There was some disagreement over terminology, but, broadly speaking, ballads—that is, any songs that told stories in narrative form—were seen as dividing into two kinds: 'popular' (or traditional) ballads (putatively the work of medieval minstrels or other anonymous rural songsmiths of centuries past), and broadsides (printed texts, usually the work of professional 'ballad-mongers' who flourished from the mid sixteenth century to the Georgian era). Each of these types of ballad had its Victorian experts who specialized in compiling and editing them.

Let us take so-called 'popular'—(meaning 'of the people')—balladry first. The best-known (and best-selling) collection of traditional ballads in mid-Victorian England was the work of Irish poet/editor William Allingham. Titled *The Ballad Book,* it was first published in 1864.[6] Although not a slim volume, it comprised only a selection from the best available texts of the most striking or beautiful examples of the ballad-maker's art, and occasionally its editor had not scrupled to create his own composite version where he believed no extant variant fully captured the essence of the ballad in question. The student of traditional balladry who wanted more—and more authentic—texts had to look further afield, which meant, in practice, to the work of American literary historian Francis James Child. Between 1857 and 1859 Child had edited for the Little, Brown publishing company of Boston, Massachusetts, an eight-volume compilation titled *English and Scottish Ballads.*[7] He had intended this huge, sprawling, eclectic work to include all the examples of popular early English narrative poetry known to exist, and he had come close to achieving his aim, perhaps in part because he had not been overly concerned to differentiate between different kinds of ballads but had cheerfully included just about everything of which he was aware at the time. Child made minor revisions to his collection several times during the 1860s, but the version of the work that was most readily available to an English audience was the second edition (1860), which was reprinted by a London publisher, Sampson Low.[8] This, then, was the standard reference work and source of ballad texts available to Late Victorian students of narrative song, although, of course, it was always possible to go beyond Child to the earlier printed sources from which he himself had compiled his massive collection. They included

Thomas Percy's *Reliques of Ancient English Poetry*,[9] Joseph Ritson's *Ancient Songs and Ballads from the Reign of King Henry the Second to the Revolution*,[10] Sir Walter Scott's *Minstrelsy of the Scottish Border*,[11] and a host of other publications by Scottish ballad collectors from David Herd to Peter Buchan and William Motherwell. One could also consult an important manuscript source that had been unavailable to Child: *Bishop Percy's Folio Manuscript,* edited by John W. Hales and Frederick J. Furnivall and published in four volumes in 1867-68.[12] And there were other, more minor but still useful, English sources, including Ritson's other publications and the work of various members of the Percy Society in the 1840s.

The other wing of ballad scholarship was the recovery and republication of broadside texts. Many thousands of individual broadsheets and small collections of broadsides called 'garlands' had been printed and reprinted since the Tudor era by a host of small backstreet publishers. Beginning in the seventeenth century, efforts had been made to collect these ephemeral publications, and by the Victorian era several large collections of broadsides existed. They included the Pepys, Madden, Douce, Wood, Halliwell, Huth, Bagford, and Roxburghe collections, but unfortunately most were in university or private libraries and hence inaccessible to the general public. The two major exceptions were the Bagford and Roxburghe collections, which had been purchased by the British Museum. Selections from the Roxburghe collection found their way into print from the 1840s onwards, but it was not until Frederick Furnivall founded the Ballad Society in 1868 that a vehicle existed whereby an entire broadside collection might be reproduced as a whole. The task of editing the Roxburghe ballads for the Ballad Society's comprehensive edition fell to the distinguished Victorian music historian William Chappell. It was a formidable task, and Chappell would not live to see the project anywhere near completed. But he made a good start. Between 1869 and 1873 he saw into print the first two volumes (in five parts) of *The Roxburghe Ballads,* and in 1875 the first part of Volume III saw the light of day.[13]

Yet while the Ballad Society's edition—and Chappell's scholarship—was far superior to any previously published selection from a broadside collection, it was obviously frustrating for a student of balladry in 1878 to have available only a small part of the Roxburghe. That meant supplementing the Ballad Society's work with earlier publications. One could go back to the anonymous three-volume *A Collection of Old Ballads* (1723-25),[14] to Thomas Evans's *Old Ballads, Historical and Narrative* (1784)[15] or to a variety of publications by members of the Percy Society in the 1840s and 1850s. More recently, in 1860, antiquarian W. Walker Wilkins had edited a two-volume edition of *Political Ballads of the Seventeenth and Eighteenth Centuries,*[16] while in 1867 publisher Joseph Lilly had issued a selection from the Huth Collection titled *A Collection of 79 Black Letter Ballads and Broadsides printed in the Reign of Queen Elizabeth.*[17] And then there was *A Pedlar's Pack of Ballads and Songs*, edited by William H. Logan in 1869.[18] Based on James Maidment's broadside collection, this publication conveniently arranged its material by subject matter, grouping the ballads into ten main categories: nautical lyrics, military lyrics, ballads about highwaymen, gypsy and begging songs, songs about madness, ballads about financial speculation ("Bubblemania"), drinking songs ("Bacchanalia"), festive and sporting songs, two sets of ballads about relations between the sexes ("Ante-Matrimonial" and "Matrimonial"), and a final group of miscellaneous items that didn't fit into any of the previous chapters. In practical terms, this one-volume compilation of Logan's was the single most useful reprint of broadsides available in the 1870s.

A Pedlar's Pack included a number of non-narrative items, which explains the inclusion of the word 'songs' in addition to 'ballads' in the title. Ballad terminology—especially that tricky distinction between traditional and broadside—was difficult enough, but when one came to discuss old *songs* one found a lack of consensus on the best way to label different kinds of lyrics. The magisterial work in the field of Victorian songhunting was William Chappell's two-volume *Popular Music of the Olden Time* (1858-59), which reprinted (with scholarly commentary) a wide variety of popular songs, narrative and non-narrative, composed between the thirteenth and eighteenth centuries.[19] Chappell, a formidable musical detective, had made it his goal, wherever possible, to match tunes and texts and to discover the composers of each song, but, notwithstanding years of painstaking research, many of the melodies and/or lyrics he reproduced remained anonymous. Although the term *Volkslied* had been current on the Continent for several decades, and he was familiar with Romantic *lieder* that drew upon German folk music, Chappell, as we saw earlier, did not employ the term 'folksong.' In his first major publication, *A Collection of National English Airs* (1838),[20] he had contented himself with the phrase "ancient songs, ballads and dance tunes," and a later publication of his was titled *Old English Ditties.*[21] In *Popular Music of the Olden Time* he usually referred to his subject matter as 'old songs,' without further distinction. Yet while he was not inclined to overemphasize the differences between types of old song—he championed them all equally —he did in practice distinguish between 'national songs,' (items by known composers that in his view expressed something of the English spirit or character), 'carols' (ceremonial or religious songs), 'ballads,' and 'traditional songs of uncertain date.' Indeed, there appears to be a strong similarity between his 'traditional songs' and what most later collectors would term 'folksongs.'

As I have argued in the previous chapter, the conceptual distinction between 'national songs' and 'folksongs' (narrowly defined) goes back to the earlier part of the nineteenth century. As early as 1823 William Kitchiner had published *The Loyal and National Songs of England* (a pioneering collection which firmly established the notion of a 'national song' that was not explicitly patriotic),[22] while both James Henry Dixon's *Ancient Poems, Ballads and Songs of the Peasantry of England* (1846)[23] and John Broadwood and Geoffrey Dusart's *Old English Songs, as now sung by the Peasantry of the Weald of Surrey and Sussex* (1847)[24] employed the concept, although not the term, of folksong to reference anonymous lyrics and tunes current in oral tradition among lower class inhabitants of rural England. On the other hand, the distinction between composed songs and folksongs had been absent in such earlier, eighteenth-century, song collections as Thomas D'Urfey's six-volume *Pills to Purge Melancholy* (1719-20)[25] or Joseph Ritson's *A Select Collection of English Songs in Three Volumes* (1783).[26] In the Victorian era it was still absent from such eclectic regional collections as C. J. Davison Ingledew's *The Ballads and Songs of Yorkshire* (1860)[27] or Llewelynn F. W. Jewitt's *Ballads and Songs of Derbyshire* (1867),[28] although implicit in the division of labor between John Harland's *Ballads and Songs of Lancashire, chiefly older than the 19th Century* (1865)[29] and its sequel, *Lancashire Lyrics: Modern Songs and Ballads of the County Palatine* (1866).[30]

To summarize: the items found in the major Victorian song collections could be divided into five main, if overlapping categories, although the distinctions between them were frequently ignored in the contemporary literature. Apart from the two main types of narrative song—traditional ballads and broadside ballads—there were three kinds of shorter lyric: the popular songs of earlier centuries that had been preserved in collections such as *Pills to Purge Melancholy* and *Popular Music of the Olden Time;* a subset of these, conventionally called 'national songs,' that were seen as expressing something essentially English; and a group of anonymous 'traditional' or 'folk' songs preserved orally in the countryside. Each of these types of song, of course, comprised both lyric and melody, but the ballad collections rarely provided the tunes, and many of the other song collections were also limited to words only.

Clearly, more work was needed in collecting tunes. And it was readily apparent that there were many regions of the country where little or no song collecting had ever been done. In short, although one could quickly discover that there was a large body of material on 'old songs' to explore and that much of it was the work of earlier Victorian collectors and editors, it was also evident that much remained to be done. Song collecting in Late Victorian England was a field in which there was still plenty of scope for newcomers to make substantial contributions.

Old Songs: Medieval to Georgian

Anyone poring over musty volumes of old music in the British Museum, or in public libraries in Plymouth, Shrewsbury, Leeds, or Newcastle, would have soon realized that there was a significant difference between two kinds of collection. There were retrospective collections of songs created many decades or even centuries before and there were also compilations of the popular songs of the day, such as D'Urfey's *Pills,* Ramondon's *Merry Musician* [31] or Davidson's *Universal Melodist.*[32] A few of the historical collections aimed at comprehensiveness, most notably Child's *English and Scottish Ballads* and Chappell's *Popular Music of the Olden Time,* but most of them were quite specialized, focusing on a circumscribed subject matter (such as sea songs or Robin Hood ballads), a particular type of song (such as carols or historical ballads), or a certain period (such as the Middle Ages or the Restoration era). Samuel Pepys's diaries suggest that song collecting had already become an avocation by the late seventeenth century, but the earliest of these specialized compilations to have been published appears to have been the anonymous *A Collection of Old Ballads* which appeared during 1723-25.[33] Song editing had become a profession later in the eighteenth century, if not with Thomas Percy's *Reliques of Ancient English Poetry* then certainly with the publications of Joseph Ritson, who made collecting and editing old songs and ballads his life's work. But, of course, collecting—in the sense of making compilations of currently popular songs, either for personal use or for commercial publication—went back much farther than the seventeenth century, in fact all the way back to the Middle Ages.

There were no published medieval song collections (printing had yet to be invented, of course), but the British Museum possessed a few relevant manuscripts dating from the Late Middle Ages. Some of these had been reprinted in the early Victorian era by such Percy Society stalwarts as James Orchard Halliwell or Thomas Wright. Examples are Wright's edition of *Songs and Carols now first printed from a Manuscript of the Fifteenth Century*[34] and his impressive compilation of *Political Poems and Songs relating to English History from Edward III to Richard III.*[35] There were few ballads in these collections, but if one delved into the mass of material that Francis J. Child had assembled in his *English and Scottish Ballads* one would have found a number of items that appeared—on the basis of subject matter and the moral codes embodied in the texts—to have their roots in the medieval era. Unfortunately Child was not of great help in sorting out which ballads were genuinely medieval and which reflected Tudor or seventeenth-century ballad-mongers' imaginative recreations of the Middle Ages.

The question of when and how the oldest ballads had been composed had been raised by Thomas Percy in the *Reliques,* and his answer—that they had been created by medieval minstrels and their Tudor successors—had become the conventional wisdom among ballad *aficionados,* although it had been questioned by both Joseph Ritson and Frederick Furnivall. The *Reliques*—an early Romantic bestseller—was easily available, and so too (at a price) was Furnivall and Hales's scholarly edition of *Bishop Percy's Folio Manuscript,* which demonstrated that Percy's sources were in fact mainly seventeenth-century rather than 'ancient' or medieval ones.[36] Percy was thus not of much use in the search for *genuine* medieval ballads and songs, and Thomas Wright's researches remained the best guide. As for tunes, the most fruitful source was Chappell's *Popular Music of the Olden Time,* although his chapter on the Middle Ages was thin compared to those on later periods; still, he had found both text and melody for (among other things) "Summer Is Icumen In" and an early Christmas carol, "Nowell, Nowell," and he had texts for the old wassail "Bring Us In Good Ale" and for the ballad "Chevy Chace." The earliest Robin Hood ballads, "Robin Hood and the Monk" and "Robin Hood and the Potter," also dated from the fourteenth century, although the original tunes had been lost.

The invention of printing had made the broadside ballad possible, and although only a small proportion of the black-letter broadsides that had been published in the Tudor era had survived, there were nonetheless hundreds to be found in those major collections of broadsides in libraries at Oxford, Cambridge, and London. Some, too, had been reprinted by the Percy Society, the Ballad Society, or by independent antiquarians. The first volume of *The Roxburghe Ballads* included most of the sixteenth-century texts in that collection, and, as we have seen, Lilly had recently reprinted a considerable portion of the Huth collection. Earlier in the Victorian era the Percy Society had made reprinting Tudor literature —including balladry—one of its priorities, and its many publications had included, for example, John Payne Collier's *Old Ballads from Early Printed Copies*[37] and reprints of two collections by Elizabethan ballad-monger Thomas Deloney, *Strange Histories*[38] and *The Garland of Goodwill.*[39] And if the chapter on medieval song in *Popular Music of the Olden Time* seemed rather slim, Chappell had no lack of Tudor material: ballads, dance tunes, lute tunes, and many popular songs, some by known composers and others anonymous. To the early Tudor period (the reigns of Henry VII and Henry VIII) he had dated, for example, the traditional ballad "The Three Ravens," the broadside ballad "John Dory," the drinking song "I Cannot Eat But Little Meat," such pretty lyrics as "Westron Wynde" and "The Hawthorn Tree," and a number of popular dance tunes, including "Dargason" and "Sellinger's Round." Moreover, to the second half of the sixteenth century Chappell had ascribed several of the better-known traditional ballads, including "The Knight and the Shepherd's Daughter," "Little Musgrave and Lady Barnard" and "Lord Thomas and Fair Ellinor," as well as such popular broadsides as "The Blind Beggar's Daughter of Bethnal Green," "The Bailiff's Daughter of Islington," and "The Spanish Lady's Love." The Elizabethan era was also noteworthy for such beautiful lyrics as "Greensleeves," "Walsingham," and "Lady, Lie Near Me," for such drinking songs as "Watkin's Ale" and "When Joan's Ale Was New," for instrumentals like "Packington's Pound" and "Staines Morris," and for many love songs from the plays of Marlowe, Shakespeare, and other dramatists, including "Come Live With Me and Be My Love" and "O Mistress Mine."

Yet if primary sources of English song were becoming plentiful by the time Chappell reached the Elizabethan era, this profusion was nothing compared to that surviving from the seventeenth century. Apart from a brief period during the Civil War and Commonwealth when religion and politics combined to make broadside publishing rather hazardous, the seventeenth century had been the golden era of the broadside ballad. Not surprisingly, then, the great broadside collections held in Oxford and Cambridge contained thousands of items dating from this century, and the same was true of the two British Museum collections reprinted by the Ballad Society, the *Bagford Ballads* (edited by Joseph Ebsworth)[40] and *The Roxburghe Ballads* (edited initially by William Chappell).[41] But Victorian reprints were not limited to broadside collections. Chappell, for example, also edited for the Percy Society a reprint of the 1612 edition of Richard Johnson's *Crown Garland of Golden Roses.*[42] Indeed, songs that proved popular on the streets had often been anthologized in garlands or other booklets, and a few composers (such as Deloney and Johnson) had even collected together their best items for republication in book or booklet form. Other older printed collections of songs and ballads included *Deuteromelia,*[43] *Melismata*[44] and *Wit Restor'd,*[45] and in 1651 John Playford had issued the first of many editions of his celebrated tunebook *The English Dancing Master.*[46] The theatre, too, was an important source, with dramatists continuing to incorporate songs and instrumental music in their plays throughout the Jacobean era, and resuming the practice with vitality in the Restoration era.

Chappell's *Popular Music of the Olden Time* provided the best guide to the popular music of the Early Stuart era and the period of the Civil War and Commonwealth. Its author could date with confidence only a few traditional ballads, such as "Fair Margaret and Sweet William," to the early decades of the seventeenth century, but he ascribed to the same period a host of shorter lyrics, including "Come Ye from Newcastle?" "Love Will Find Out the Way," and "The Jovial

Beggar." A new crop of Robin Hood ballads, no doubt reflecting popular discontent with the Crown, was another feature of the Early Stuart period. The interregnum produced such political songs as "When the King Enjoys His Own Again" and other plaintive lyrics that reflected either the dislocation caused by military conflict or the need to move to an urban center to make a living, such as "The North Country Lass," "The Broom of Cowdon Knowes," and "I Live Not Where I Love." If one wanted to see more examples of the broadside literature from these years one could dip into Thomas Wright's *Political Ballads Published in England during the Commonwealth*,[47] while many of the non-political Cavalier songs of the time could be found in Joseph Ebsworth's editions of the *Choyce Drollery*,[48] the *Merry Drollery*,[49] and the *Westminster Drolleries*.[50] But perhaps the best window on the popular music of the mid-seventeenth century was provided by that invaluable manuscript collection compiled during the 1640s, the so-called *Bishop Percy's Folio Manuscript*.

The famous folio manuscript was such an important primary source that an interested reader could spend many an hour poring over the pages of Hales and Furnivall's printed edition. Publishing the manuscript in its entirety—a project that had been frustrated for the best part of a century—had been one of the major victories of mid-Victorian scholarship. Internal evidence suggests that it probably dated from between 1643 and 1649 (although slightly later is possible), and it was likely compiled by or for a lawyer named Thomas Blount. The orthography suggests that many of the texts were written down hurriedly as if from singing or recitation, although others may have been copied from broadsides. Anyway, the manuscript provides an intriguing snapshot of mid-seventeenth century popular song, although, of course, it is difficult to tell how representative that snapshot may have been. Certainly the material in the manuscript is quite eclectic. Broadly speaking the contents divide into four categories: poetry, ballads, shorter lyrics, and bawdy ditties. Narrative items predominate, and they are of three kinds: verse romances (usually lengthy in nature), traditional ballads, and broadside ballads. Eight of the ballads are about Robin Hood, and another dozen derive from Arthurian romances or other romances set vaguely in the early Middle Ages, including "King Arthur and the King of Cornwall," "Sir Lancelott of Dulake," and "Merline." Others, although hardly specific as regards time and place, appear to be set later in the medieval period, including, for example, "The Child of Ell" (a variant of "Earl Brand"), "The Heir of Lin," "Old Robin of Portingale," and "Sir Aldingar." Certain ballads, such as "Agincourte," "King John and Bishoppe," "Flodden Field," and "Captaine Carre," are ostensibly historical in character, dealing with actual events and/or people. By no means all of these historical ballads are medieval in setting; for example, "Thomas Lord Cromwell" is about the chancellor of Henry VIII who masterminded his sovereign's break with Rome, the events related in "King James and Browne" took place in Scotland between 1572 and 1580, and "Marye Aubree" deals with the putative exploits of a female soldier in the Netherlands in 1584.

The quality of the ballad texts in the folio manuscript naturally varies, and some are fragmentary, but there are interesting versions of some of the finest traditional ballads, including "Glasgerion," "Child Waters," "Lord Barnard and Little Musgrave," and "Childe Maurice," and some striking broadsides too, most notably "Bessie off Bednall" (a version of "The Blind Beggar's Daughter of Bethnal Green"), "The King Enjoyes His Rights Againe" (a variant of Martin Parker's composition with a similar title), and two of Thomas Deloney's best creations, "The Spanish Lady's Love" and the beautiful "Walsingham." Only a few of the shorter lyrics, such as "Came You Not from Newcastle?" and "Balowe," would usually be classified as folksongs, but there are also love songs by Cavalier poets, including Richard Lovelace's "When Love with Unconfined Wings." Other songs are political in subject matter, or touch on social issues of the time, such as "Darksome Cell" (a "Tom of Bedlam" song about madness), or "Come My Dainty Doxeys" (a defense of gypsy life). As for the more than forty so-called "loose and humorous songs," which were hived off to a separate volume and edited by Furnivall alone (Hales had wished to omit them entirely, as Percy had a century earlier), not all of them are bawdy and others merely mention sexual relations in a straightforward and non-erotic manner. The most interesting are "Lillumwham," a rather doggerel version of the religious ballad "The Maid and the Palmer," and "The Sea-Crab" (about the danger of keeping a live crab in a chamber pot). Others include "A Mayden Head" (an attack on virginity), "A Maid and a Younge Man (about a midsummer encounter in the woods), "Walking in Meadow Gren" (on the theme of impotence), "Off a Puritane" (a satire on licentious Puritan ministers and holy sisters), "Lye Alone" (on the want of a man) and "Come Wanton Wenches" (advice from an old courtesan). Such items are presumably representative of a type of popular song common in the Elizabethan and early Stuart eras.

Chappell had assembled a wealth of material from the late seventeenth century—which he believed witnessed a renaissance of English popular music rivaling only the Elizabethan era—and the second volume of *Popular Music of the Olden Time* included a lengthy chapter of over one hundred pages devoted to the reigns of Charles II, James II, and William and Mary. The Restoration era was a time when drinking songs, harvest homes, comic ditties satirizing rural life, and "Scotch" songs were particularly prevalent, but perhaps the most popular of all was the political satire "Lilliburlero." A substantial sampling of the popular music of the period could be found in a celebrated contemporary compilation,

Henry Playford's *Wit and Mirth, or Pills to Purge Melancholy* (1698-1706).[51] Chappell naturally drew on this invaluable source, but he also dated to this period such folksongs as "The Seeds of Love," such broadsides as "The Jovial Companions," "Turn Again, Whittington," and "Tobacco Is an Indian Weed" and several traditional ballads, including "Barbara Allen," "The Three Sisters," "The Baffled Knight," and "A Noble Riddle Wisely Expounded."

For anyone investigating the eighteenth-century sources of folksong and balladry Chappell's *magnum opus* again provided the most convenient and systematic introduction. The next chapter covered the reigns of Queen Anne and the first two Georges. The early Hanoverian period had seen the publication of several collections of contemporary popular songs, including Thomas D'Urfey's expanded, six-volume, edition of *Pills to Purge Melancholy* (1719-20).[52] Chappell excluded D'Urfey's more salacious or suggestive material, but he still had plenty of love songs (such as Henry Carey's hugely popular "Sally in Our Alley" and Richard Leveridge's "Black-eyed Susan") and rollicking tavern songs (including "Old King Cole" and "Down among the Dead Men") to reprint. The early eighteenth century had produced a considerable number of 'national' songs, both patriotic compositions such as "Rule Britannia" and "God Save the Queen" and a variety of other lyrics that captured less blatantly the resilient spirit of the nation, including "Heart of Oak," "The Vicar of Bray," and "The Miller of Dee." Sailors' songs were now much in evidence, including "Jack's the Lad," "The Mermaid," and "Spanish Ladies." Other folksongs that Chappell identified as definitely originating during the early Georgian era included "The Keel Row," "Gossip Joan," and "Cupid's Garden," but he noted that many of them were difficult to date and, in recognition of this, followed his chronological coverage with an extra section devoted to "Traditional Songs of Uncertain Date." These were vernacular songs that he believed probably antedated the reign of George III but which might—or might not—also antedate that of George I. They included many that would subsequently be collected from oral tradition, including "Early One Morning," "The Lincolnshire Poacher," "The Grey Cock," and "The Barley Mow." Broadside ballads continued to be written and printed in the early Georgian era, and a few of them caught the popular imagination and entered oral tradition, for example "Admiral Benbow," "Polly Oliver's Ramble," and "O Rare Turpin Hero." For other, usually more prosaic, broadsides one could go to that first anonymous compilation, *A Collection of Old Ballads* (1723-25). Of course Chappell's selection from the commercial popular music of the time was hardly exhaustive, and one could go beyond him to several contemporary printed collections. If D'Urfey's *Pills* were insufficient one could also dip into Lewis Ramondon's *Merry Musician, or, A Cure for the Spleen* (1728-1730)[53] or the ballad operas that proliferated after the successful debut of *The Beggar's Opera* in 1728.

The late eighteenth century—the long reign of George III—had witnessed the ballad revival sparked by Thomas Percy's notorious but much-loved *Reliques of Ancient English Poetry* (1765).[54] Percy had presented his collection as an edition of an old folio manuscript containing minstrel songs and ballads. In fact it was no such thing, as Furnivall and Hales's accurate printing of the folio manuscript clearly demonstrated, but Percy had kept his deception effectively hidden and the *Reliques* had won the hearts of a generation of ballad *aficionados*, among whom were to be numbered such Scottish collectors as David Herd, Robert Burns, Sir Walter Scott, and their many disciples. Between them these Scottish ballad editors had produced an extensive body of literature, of variable quality, to be sure, but far surpassing the extant English sources of traditional balladry. One could never be sure to what extent a ballad printed in Scott's *Minstrelsy of the Scottish Border* or in any other of these late eighteenth-century Scottish collections had been touched up by its collector/editor, and Scott, for one, had followed a deliberate policy of combining fragments into composite versions that he believed recreated the original (partially lost) ballad. The work of the pioneers had been complemented by a second wave of Scottish collectors, of whom William Motherwell and Peter Buchan were the most important. Although in his own case it was largely a matter of "do what I say" rather than "do what I do," Motherwell had, in the preface to his *Minstrelsy Ancient and Modern*,[55] set out the principle of printing exactly what the informant had sung (or recited), while Buchan had followed the same approach in his two published collections.[56] Anyone who had trouble obtaining the latter could turn instead to James Henry Dixon's selection from Buchan's manuscripts, *Scottish Traditional Versions of Ancient Ballads*, published by the Percy Society in 1846.[57] Similarly, the readily available collection of *Legendary and Romantic Ballads of Scotland* edited by Charles Mackay had drawn heavily upon Motherwell's field work.[58] Moreover, there were English versions of many, although not all, of the traditional ballads collected from oral tradition north of the border. Percy's critic and rival, Joseph Ritson, had also played an important role in the ballad revival, publishing the first edition of his *Ancient Songs* in 1790[59] and his collection of Robin Hood ballads in 1795,[60] while an omnibus edition of his field collection had appeared in 1810 as *Northern Garlands*.[61] His pioneering song collecting in the north of England had been continued by John Bell, resulting in the publication of the latter's *Rhymes of Northern Bards* in 1812.[62]

Victorians who enjoyed Romantic poetry were likely familiar with John Clare's *Poems Descriptive of Rural Life and Scenery* (1820), *The Village Minstrel* (1821), and *The Shepherd's Calendar* (1827),[63] but they probably did not know that his lyrics had their roots in the ballads and songs he had collected from oral tradition in and around his native village of Helpston in Northamptonshire.[64] A handful of other song collectors—Davies Gilbert, William Sandys, and

Cuthbert Sharp—had similarly obtained items from oral tradition in other corners of rural England during the early decades of the nineteenth century. The 1820s had also witnessed, in the work of William Kitchiner, a forceful championing of 'national songs' by means of two publications, *The Loyal and National Songs of England* and *The Sea Songs of England* (both 1823).[65] Most important of all, William Chappell, the man who had dedicated himself with tenacity to carrying on the work of Joseph Ritson, had in 1838 printed *A Collection of National Airs*, his first attempt to compile the best of English vernacular music, the 'national songs,' folksongs, and tunes that had become part of the national heritage.[66]

The Victorian Vernacular Song Revival

Chappell, an active member of both the Percy Society in the 1840s and the Ballad Society in the 1860s, may be said to have personified the Victorian vernacular song revival. There were several sides to his work, but at the heart of his lifelong project was a desire to discover, document, and publicize the entire tradition of English song and ballad writing. He cared little whether a given item was anonymous and traditional or the commercial product of a known songsmith or ballad-monger, but he always (or almost always) saw them as treasures in which melody and lyrics were fused together to create more than the sum of the parts. For Chappell, rescuing old songs from oblivion meant not only locating and reprinting them but, above all, restoring texts to tunes and tunes to texts, a difficult task which required a great deal of detective work, ingenuity, and sheer hard labor in libraries, archives, and private collections. In articulating this visionary program and then attempting to carry it out, first in *A Collection of National English Airs* and later in *Popular Music of the Olden Time*, Chappell was an intellectual pioneer of the first order. Yet, of course, although he took a leading role, he was only one figure among many collectors and editors who played a part in the cultural movement we call the Victorian vernacular song revival. He and his fellow enthusiasts had accomplished a great deal since 1840 and quite a variety of publications had to be consulted to obtain the full picture of their activity, but it would not have taken long for an avid researcher to realize that the key institution in the early phase of the Victorian vernacular song revival was the Percy Society.

The Society's active members, who, of course, included Chappell, were primarily antiquarians, amateur scholars for whom songhunting and editing was more than a hobby but less than a profession. Such freelance academics as John Payne Collier, Frederick Fairholt, Thomas Wright, and James Orchard Halliwell (among others) made use of their expertise in English literary history to locate and publicize the existence of early (late medieval and Tudor) manuscript song collections, and they put almost as much time and effort into the work of excavating and reprinting black-letter broadsides. The core of the Percy Society's work was the publication of a thirty volume series of edited reprints of both manuscripts and early printed texts. It was scholarly work that should, perhaps, have been undertaken by professors at Oxford and Cambridge universities, but the unpaid Percy Society stalwarts took on the job that the professional academics failed to do. Not only did they republish garlands and other primary sources, they also edited selections of ballads from particular historical periods or dealing with specific themes. There were too many Percy Society publications to list more than a sampling here, but a few examples of what could be found on Victorian library shelves will give the flavor of the Society's work. Collier's most important contributions were his sampler of Elizabethan broadsides, *Old Ballads from Early Printed Copies*, and his edition of Deloney's *Strange Histories*. Fairholt was similarly responsible for three specialized collections of (mainly) broadsides: *The Civic Garland: A Collection of Songs from London Pageants*, *Satirical Songs and Poems on Costume*, and *Poems and Songs relating to George Villiers, Duke of Buckingham*.[67] Wright and Halliwell, two of the mainstays of the Society, did even more.

Wright, an extraordinarily industrious and prolific archaeologist, historian, and literary critic, was one of the Society's most energetic and reliable activists. His first important collection, *The Political Songs of England, from the Reign of John to that of Edward II*,[68] antedated the formation of the Percy Society, but the latter published his similar work on a later period, *Political Ballads Published in England during the Commonwealth*.[69] Wright saw it as his mission to print the best manuscripts of late medieval songs that he had found in archival collections, and the Percy Society obliged in 1847 by printing *Songs and Carols now first printed from a Manuscript of the Fifteenth Century*, a collection that dated from the time of the Wars of the Roses.[70] Another document, the British Museum's Sloane MS. 2593, arguably the best of Wright's archival 'finds,' was published a decade later under the confusingly similar title *Songs and Carols from a Manuscript in the British Museum of the Fifteenth Century*.[71] Wright continued his research into medieval song after the demise of the Percy Society, and although he had difficulty in finding a publisher, he eventually saw into print a sequel to his earlier work titled *Political Poems and Songs relating to English History from Edward III to Richard III*.[72] He then moved on to the Tudor period, and in 1860 edited a manuscript collection that he titled *Songs and Ballads, chiefly from the Reign of Philip and Mary*.[73]

Halliwell, the youngest member of the Percy Society, was a friend and protégé of Wright's, and together they edited a large, two-volume collection of primary sources titled *Reliquiae Antiquae*,[74] one highlight of which was a thirteenth century religious ballad, "Judas," possibly the oldest extant ballad in the English language. Between 1840 and 1850 Halliwell edited seventeen publications for the Percy Society. Several of these were reprints of early literary works, but others were collections of ballads and/or songs. They included *The Early Naval Ballads of England*,[75] *The Nursery Rhymes of England* (an innovative compilation),[76] and an edition of *The Loyal Garland*.[77] Halliwell, a book dealer by profession, had his own small printing press, and several of his own limited edition publications were of significance also, for example his *Ballads and Poems respecting Hugh of Lincoln*[78] and such pioneering regional collections as *The Palatine Anthology*,[79] *The Yorkshire Anthology*,[80] and *The Norfolk Anthology*.[81]

All this was the antiquarian side of the Percy Society's activities, but it was also a forum for less academic song collectors who were interested in recovering vernacular carols, ballads, and folk lyrics from oral tradition as well as from manuscript and printed sources. This group of men, who were mainly lawyers and journalists by profession, were often amateur musicians. In addition to Chappell, they included Charles Mackay, William Sandys, James Henry Dixon, and Edward Rimbault. Mackay, a friend and disciple of Chappell, first edited for the Percy Society a collection of (mainly) broadside ballads titled *Songs and Ballads relative to the London Prentices and Trades*,[82] but he was really more interested in popular songs, as was evident in two of his other publications, *The Book of English Songs, from the Sixteenth to the Nineteenth Century*[83] and its companion, *The Illustrated Book of Scottish Songs, from the Sixteenth to the Nineteenth Century*.[84] Although he lived in London, Mackay was a Scot by birth and he retained a keen interest in Scottish balladry, which he believed was insufficiently known and appreciated south of the border. To remedy this he published a collection titled *The Legendary and Romantic Ballads of Scotland*,[85] which, as we have seen, drew heavily on the fieldwork of William Motherwell and reprinted the latter's ground-breaking manifesto "Preliminary Essay on Scottish Ballad Literature," in which Motherwell argued that ballad editors should refrain from making composite versions and should treat all variants collected from oral tradition as possessing equal textual authority. Mackay's many other publications included a collection of Scottish Jacobite texts[86] and a book of songs from the time of the English Civil War and the Restoration, *The Cavalier Songs and Ballads of England from 1642 to 1684*.[87]

Folklorist William Sandys's published output was less voluminous than Mackay's but more original. In 1833 he had made the most comprehensive collection of folk carols yet assembled, *Christmas Carols, Ancient and Modern*, many of which he had noted in the counties of Devon and Cornwall.[88] This he followed with another specialized work on vernacular songs, *Festive Songs, principally of the Sixteenth and Seventeenth Centuries*, which was in fact a history and collection of drinking songs from the twelfth century to the eighteenth.[89] Sandys subsequently made Cornwall the focus of his collecting, publishing an important regional collection of stories, poems, ballads, and songs titled *Specimens of Cornish Provincial Dialect*, which included (among other things) a version of "Hal-an-Tow" that he had noted during the Furry Day ceremonies at Helston.[90] As a collector who viewed local song and dance not in isolation but as part of a broader spectrum of rural folklore, Sandys offered a model that fitted well with other folklorists' interest in the customs and tales as well as the music of their own county or region.

Perhaps the single most important of the Percy Society's many publications was the work of lawyer James Henry Dixon. Before moving to London, Dixon had been a member of the Newcastle-upon-Tyne Society of Antiquaries, and he had done some collecting of his own in Yorkshire and Northumberland. Like Mackay, Dixon was an admirer of the Scottish ballad collectors and did his best to publicize south of the border the collecting of Peter Buchan, editing a selection from Buchan's manuscripts as *Scottish Traditional Versions of Ancient Ballads*.[91] His major work, though, was titled *Ancient Poems, Ballads and Songs of the Peasantry of England*.[92] Published in 1846, it was effectively the first sizeable general collection of English folksongs, although Dixon did not employ the term. In assembling its contents he drew both on songs and ballads collected orally from informants in the countryside and items that he and his collaborators had found in manuscript and early printed sources. Much of the material in the poetry section was taken from broadsides and some of the items were clearly intended to be sung. The ballad section mixed traditional ballads and broadsides, and a handful of them had been noted from oral tradition, mainly in Yorkshire and Northumberland; they included variants of "Lord Bateman," "Lord Delaware," "The Death of Parcy Reed," "The Baffled Knight," and "The Highwayman Outwitted." Dixon possessed his own small collection of broadside ballads, but he also drew upon the Bagford and Roxburghe collections, reproducing such traditional ballads as "Lord Lovel," "The Merry Broomfield," and "The Outlandish Knight," and such broadsides as "The Golden Glove," "The Sailor from Dover," and "John Barleycorn." The quality of his texts varied considerably, some blessed with poetic simplicity while others were longwinded doggerel. Much the same was true of the shorter folk lyrics in the third section of the book. Several of these related to agriculture, such as "The Painful Plough," "The Mow," "The Farmer's Son," "The Haymaker's Song," and three harvest homes. There were items associated with rural ceremonies and rituals: the "Helston Furry-day Song" (aka "Hal-an-Tow"), the

"Cornish Midsummer Bonfire Song," a Gloucestershire wassailers' song, a "Sword Dancers' Song," and "The Maskers' Song." Others were linked with particular counties, such as "Richard of Taunton Dean" (from Somerset), "Trelawny" (Cornwall), "Jone o' Greenfield's Ramble" (Lancashire), and "The Yorkshire Horse Dealer." Drinking songs were fairly numerous and included "The Barley Mow," "The Leathern Bottel," and "Joan's Ale Was New." Other eminently singable folksongs included "The New-Mown Hay," the sea song "Spanish Ladies," the poaching ballad "Thornehagh-Moor Woods" and a beautiful version of "The Seeds of Love." Dixon's collection had its faults—there was insufficient information about the sources of the songs, the quality of the texts was inconsistent, and tunes were lacking—but it was nonetheless the best general collection of English vernacular songs to be assembled in the early Victorian era. In the form of a second, expanded, edition published under Robert Bell's name as editor, it remained so for nearly half a century.[93]

While Dixon focused primarily on texts, other Victorian collectors recognized the need to retrieve the tunes to which ballads and lyrics were sung. Edward Rimbault was another innovative song catcher whose varied work can be seen in retrospect as particularly valuable. Although he also served as its secretary, Rimbault's primary role in the Percy Society was to provide a service few other members except Chappell could offer, that of locating missing tunes to partner song and ballad texts recovered by other collectors. Some of his publications were quite modest in size and scope: they included *Old Ballads Illustrating the Great Frost of 1683-84*,[94] *A Little Book of Christmas Carols*,[95] *Nursery Rhymes*,[96] and *A Little Book of Songs and Ballads*.[97] Not all of these included melodies, but Rimbault provided an invaluable tune appendix to John Gutch's comprehensive compilation of Robin Hood texts, *The Robin Hood Garlands and Ballads, with the Tale of 'The Lytell Geste.'*[98] Even better, he set out to find the appropriate melodies for many of the items in Percy's *Reliques,* a project that eventually gave rise to his most important publication, *Musical Illustrations of Bishop Percy's Reliques of Ancient English Poetry.*[99] This included tunes for more than twenty traditional ballads and a variety of shorter lyrics. The ballads included "Barbara Allen's Cruelty," "Little Musgrave and Lady Barnard," "King John and the Abbott of Canterbury," "Chevy Chace," "The Jew's Daughter," "Queen Eleanor's Confession," and "Lord Thomas and Fair Ellinor," while the shorter lyrics included "Waly, Waly," "John Anderson My Jo," "Love Will Find Out the Way," "Come Live With Me and Be My Love," and "Lilliburlero." All in all, it was an impressive collection, one of the very few works by Victorian collectors that rivaled as well as complemented Chappell's *Popular Music of the Olden Time.*

Of course not all the early Victorian collectors were members of the Percy Society. There are always outsiders, and Frederick Sheldon, who in 1847 had published *The Minstrelsy of the English Border,*[100] a book evidently intended to be an English equivalent of Sir Walter Scott's famous collection, was certainly a maverick. Sheldon claimed to have done extensive field collecting in the villages of Cumberland and Northumberland, but he rarely provided detailed information about his sources and the reader was left wondering to what extent the texts were really authentic. Some, such as "The Outlandish Knight" and "The Fair Flower of Northumberland" apparently derived from broadsides, while a few, notably "The Laird of Roslin's Daughter" (a variant of "Captain Wedderburn's Courtship") appeared to be genuinely the product of oral tradition. But others looked suspiciously like Sheldon's own compositions or, at the very least, the result of substantial reworking. Sheldon, like his mentors Percy and Scott, apparently took considerable liberties in repackaging his raw material in a way that he thought would show it off to its best advantage.

Much more confidence could be placed in the work of another independent collector, John Broadwood, whose *Old English Songs* was published the same year.[101] This was a small collection of folksongs gathered mainly on the border of Surrey and Sussex, and its importance lies in the fact that Broadwood insisted that the tunes be printed exactly as he had noted them rather than modified to accommodate the piano arrangements provided by his music editor, Geoffrey Dusart. Broadwood's texts were sometimes fragmentary or even non-existent, but the sixteen items in the collection were authentic examples of vernacular music preserved by oral tradition in the countryside of southern England. The ballads for which Broadwood had noted traditional melodies included "Lord Bateman," "The Bailiff's Daughter of Islington," "The Lost Lady Found" (aka "Gipsy Song"), and two maritime broadsides, "The Privateer" and "The Fourteenth of July." Songs of rural life included "The Woodcutter," "The Ploughboy," "The Servingman and the Husbandman," and a ballad that celebrated poaching, "In Thorny Woods." So, although small in size, and published only in a limited edition, *Old English Songs* was a pioneering work. Broadwood was not the first English collector from oral tradition, but his little book *was* the first to consist exclusively of tunes noted in the field.

Another Victorian publication of some value was Robert Bell's *Songs from the Dramatist,* a compilation that aimed at bringing together the best song texts from all the plays staged in England between the early Tudor period and the late eighteenth century.[102] Bell was also the editor of two other useful collections, *Early Ballads Illustrative of History, Traditions and Customs* (1856)[103] and the revised edition of Dixon's *Ancient Poems, Ballads and Songs of the Peasantry of England* mentioned earlier, which appeared the next year.[104] Some items were unfortunately deleted by Bell because he had 'borrowed' them for *Early Ballads,* but he compensated by adding several new ballads and various political songs,

songs of rural life, and songs of custom and ceremony. The additions included the traditional ballads "Earl Brand" and "The Death of Queen Jane," the broadsides "The Bowes Tragedy" and "The Crafty Lover, or the Lawyer Outwitted," and such shorter lyrics as "The Lincolnshire Poacher," "A-Begging We Will Go," "Jockey to the Fair" and "The Sweet Nightingale." But, as with Dixon's original collection, there were no tunes to go with this valuable compilation of folksong texts. So where, apart from Chappell and Rimbault's publications, could a folksong enthusiast go to find tunes for these old songs?

There was no good answer to that question, but one partial solution was provided by *Davidson's Universal Melodist.*[105] This huge two-volume work, published and presumably compiled by G. H. Davidson, was a compendium of over 1600 old songs. Melodies were provided, but usually only a token verse or two of text for each item. There was no editorial matter of any significance, no notes to the songs, and no obvious method of arrangement of the material. Each volume had an alphabetical list of contents, but the songs themselves were arranged neither alphabetically nor in accordance with any other plan. In essence the *Universal Melodist* was a raw database, its contents were assembled randomly and there was no listing of songs by composer/lyricist or by first line, which made the lack of any index particularly problematic. As a reference work the book was singularly inept. Nonetheless a very large number and wide variety of songs were to be found within its pages. Topical songs and folksongs were not plentiful although they did exist, but the *Universal Melodist's* real strength was its comprehensive cataloguing of the commercial popular music of the Georgian era, with song after song by Robert Burns, Thomas Arne, Charles and Thomas Dibdin, Henry Carey, Henry Russell, William Shield, Stephen Storace and a host of other songwriters. The compendium likely made a significant contribution to the re-diffusion of elderly pop songs and, among other things, played a role in promoting Burns's songs in England. As such it helped broaden English vernacular tradition, since few community songbooks in the future would be without "Annie Laurie," "Charlie Is My Darling," and a handful of songs by Burns. It also reinforced the vogue for 'national songs' by including not only large numbers of overtly patriotic songs ("The Blood Red Flag of England" or "Rule Britannia" may serve as examples) but also such popular lyrics as "Sally in Our Alley," "The Lass of Richmond Hill," and "Black-eyed Susan" and a host of sea songs, from "Tom Bowling" and "Poor Jack" to "The *Arethusa*" and "The Heart of a True British Sailor." And this huge compendium was also important in a negative way: by resurrecting such a large number of forgotten and unmemorable 'pop' songs of former decades, *Davidson's Universal Melodist* implicitly underlined the difference between truly vernacular songs—those with 'vital melodies' that allowed them to survive in oral tradition, whatever their origin—and the vast mass of other compositions that had, at best, enjoyed a short time in the sun.

Whatever its faults, the *Universal Melodist* was premised on the important—and at the time quite radical—contention that songs without tunes were incomplete. That underscored the basic problem with much mid-Victorian song collecting and ballad editing: there was frequently a dissociation between texts and tunes. This was particularly the case with regard to ballads. The mid-Victorian era had been a time of considerable progress in ballad editing. As noted earlier, the two most important ballad collections of the period were William Allingham's *Ballad Book* and Francis James Child's *English and Scottish Popular Ballads.* While they hardly supplanted completely such classics as Scott's *Minstrelsy of the Scottish Border* or *Bishop Percy's Folio Manuscript,* these were the secondary sources to which one could most readily turn to find a standard version of any particular traditional ballad for which one was looking. But the tunes were not so easy to find. And that was often also true for non-narrative songs, especially folk lyrics of the kind that might be collected in the villages and small towns of rural England.

Regional Song Collections

Any Late Victorian folksong enthusiast contemplating song collecting in the countryside near his or her home would likely have been interested in examining all the existing English regional song collections in print. Several had appeared since the middle of the century, but if one lived in London or the home counties there was nothing from very close to home, apart, that is, from John Broadwood's small collection from the Surrey/Sussex border. The nearest county to London to attract a mid-Victorian songhunter was Derbyshire: Llewelynn Jewitt's *Ballads and Songs of Derbyshire* was published in 1867.[106] Compiled, according to its editor, from manuscripts and oral tradition as well as broadsides and garlands, the book did include a number of items collected from local vernacular culture. They included dialect songs, hunting songs, and poems about local scenery, of which the best ("Derbyshire Hills") was by a wandering minstrel named James Bannard, while "The Beggar's Ramble," which consisted mainly of rhyming lists of Derbyshire place-names, was ascribed to a legendary local ballad singer, Singing Sam. Other local songs were more recent compositions, such as "The Ashborne Foot-Ball Song" and "The Flax-Dresser's Wife of Spondon and the Pound of Tea." More than half the collection consisted of broadside ballads with links with Derbyshire. These included "The Derbyshire Miller,"

"The Blink-Ey'd Cobbler," "The Taylor's Ramble," and four Robin Hood ballads. One of the best broadsides, for which Jewitt even provided a tune from oral tradition, was "King Henry V, His Conquest of France," while other historical ballads included "The Most Pleasant Song of Lady Bessie," "The Complainte of Anthonie Babington," and "Sir Richard Whittington's Advancement." Non-narrative songs included "The Gipsies Song" (another of the handful of items for which Jewitt had a tune) and the humorous "The Derby Ram." Although more than half the book's contents were texts composed by educated members of the county's middle class, *Ballads and Songs of Derbyshire* did nonetheless demonstrate that local singing traditions existed in the English midlands, and that there were still songwriters, poets, and balladmongers at work adding to the heritage of regional song. Traditional songs and ballads represented only a small proportion of the book's total number of items, but there were enough to suggest that a more concerted effort to collect Derbyshire folksongs would likely prove worth the trouble.

Further north in Yorkshire James Orchard Halliwell's pioneering work[107] had been supplanted at the beginning of the 1860s by a new collection of vernacular material made by C. J. Davison Ingledew. *The Ballads and Songs of Yorkshire*[108] was an attempt to bring together in one volume all previously published items relating to the county. Ingledew had found seventy-six texts, ranging from Robin Hood ballads to fox-hunting, horse-racing, and poaching songs, as well as comic songs in dialect. There were six of the former, including "Robin Hood and Guy of Gisborne," "The Jolly Pindar of Wakefield," "The Noble Fisherman," "Robin Hood and the Curtall Fryer," and "The Bishop of Hereford's Entertainment." Other historical or pseudo-historical ballads included "The Deposing and Murder of Richard II" (set in 1399), "The Rising in the North" (dealing with the events of 1569), and William Elderton's celebrated "Yorke, Yorke, for My Monie." Broadsides reflecting local events or personalities included ballads about local politics ("The Mayor of Doncaster"), horse trading ("The Yorkshire Horse-Dealers"), highwaymen ("Bold Nevison"), and murder ("The Romanby Tragedy"). Among the more popular broadsides were "The Soldier in Yorkshire" (in which a local lass discovers that her soldier lover is already a husband and father), "The Crafty Plough Boy" (a classic tale of a highwayman outwitted by his intended victim), and two pro-poaching ballads, "Bill Brown" and "The Sledmere Poachers." Comic ballads were also common, such as "Dolly's Gaon; or the Effects of Pride," "The Yorkshire Lad in London" and "Mother Shipton," and there was a selection of dialect verse, some items derived from broadsides, others the work of local poets, such as Benjamin Preston of Bradford whose contributions included "Natterin' Nan" and "Aw Niver Can Call Hur My Wife." Ingledew's collection was thus quite varied in nature and, despite a fair amount of dross, contained some interesting material. But it lacked industrial songs, even mining songs, and there were no tunes.

The parallel collection dealing with the vernacular music of the north of England on the other side of the Pennines was John Harland's *Ballads and Songs of Lancashire, chiefly older than the 19th Century,* a second edition of which appeared in 1875.[109] It was of particular interest. First published ten years earlier, the book contained an even wider range of song types and, as such, had marked something of a breakthrough in regional collecting. There were several border ballads, other narrative ballads, May Day and wassail songs, drinking songs, old comic songs, occupational songs by spinners and weavers, and a great deal of regional material reflecting the county's daily life and customs. Harland's sources were also varied, including regional publications, old manuscripts, broadsides, compositions by local poets, and items noted from oral tradition. He arranged the collection in roughly chronological order; the older narrative songs included two accounts of the battle of Flodden Field and several broadsides depicting events of local history, such as "The Liverpool Tragedy." Other old songs reflecting Lancashire life included "Warrington Ale," "Warrikin Fair," "Long Preston Peggy," "The Burnley Haymakers," and "The Lancashire Witches." Most of these items had come from printed sources, but Harland had also recovered a few songs and ballads that he believed to be remnants of minstrelsy handed down orally. They included Richard Sheale's "A Love Song" and three versions of the traditional murder ballad "The Two Sisters." There were also several wassails and wakes, for example the "Droylesden Wakes Song" and a "Wassail Cup Song," plus a group of seven May Day songs, two of which Harland had collected himself from local merrymakers in Swinton. The book also included a number of occupational songs reflecting the lives of workers in the Lancashire textile industry, some humorous but others overtly critical of mechanized production and factory owners. They included a cycle of songs about Jone o' Grinfelt and such titles as "Grimshaw's Factory Fire," "Hand-Loom versus Power-loom," and "The Hand-loom Weavers' Lament." The best of these industrial songs were compelling in their matter-of-fact realism, a good example being "Jone o' Grinfilt Junior" (latterly better known as "The Four Loom Weaver"), which was noted by Harland's collaborator John Higson from a weaver at Droylsden. Harland was more punctilious than Ingledew about documenting his printed and manuscript sources, but, apart from revealing that several of the industrial songs had been collected by Higson at Gorton from a weaver named John Grimshaw, he was unfortunately not very forthcoming about his local informants. Nor did the book contain any tunes.

In 1866 Harland published a sequel to *Ballads and Songs of Lancashire* titled *Lancashire Lyrics: Modern Songs and Ballads of the County Palatine,* which aimed to carry the story of Lancashire vernacular song up to the mid-nineteenth century.[110] The book began with a small group of ballads that included "Black Bess" (a highwayman ballad about Dick Turpin) and "Derwentwater's Fate" (about the execution of a Jacobite nobleman in 1716). The second section consisted of shorter lyrics, mainly love songs. The folk lyrics among them included "The Seeds of Love" and "The Sprig of Thyme." There was also a rather miscellaneous group of patriotic songs, drinking songs, religious songs, and songs about exile and death, plus a separate small group of sea songs. The remainder of the collection featured the work of a considerable number of popular Lancashire poets (Thomas Brierley, James Ramsbottom, Richard Bealey, Edwin Waugh, Samuel Laycock, and John Critchley Prince, among others) writing, usually in regional dialect, about their county and its people. Examples included the anonymous "Moi Owd Mon," Waugh's "Come Whoam to thi Childer an' Me," Laycock's "Mi Gronfeyther," Brierley's "Heaw Quare Is this Loife," Bealey's "My Piece Is O bu' Woven Eawt," and Prince's "The Songs of the People." Several of these authors had also composed songs about a recent period of severe recession in the textile industry during 1862-64. These contemporary industrial songs included Laycock's "Th' Shurat Weyvur's Song," Ramsbottom's "The Factory Lass" and "Eawt o' Wark," and James Bowker's "Hard Times." Collectively they provided a powerful expression of the hardships undergone by working class families reduced to poverty by the "cotton famine" resulting from the American Civil War.

Harland's books were greatly admired by William Axon and stimulated Axon to write *circa* 1871 his own *Folk Song and Folk-Speech of Lancashire*.[111] As we have seen, this modest offering appears to have been the first English publication to employ 'folk song' in its title, an indication that the term was coming into use in the mid-Victorian era, although it was not yet common. Axon's principal interest lay in dialect poetry but he recognized that in Lancashire there was no sharp dividing line between vernacular poetry and vernacular song, especially among the lower classes. Indeed Axon suggested that the local poets' most successful verses had been written with popular airs in mind, and, as a result, were sung in all manner of working class homes, from the smallest villages to the industrial cities. His extended essay was not intended as a song collection but it did include a considerable number of songs to illustrate its author's historical survey of the development of Lancastrian dialect in verse and prose. His oldest example of a rural dialect song was "Warriken Fair," which he dated to the mid-sixteenth century. Early ballads included "Fair Ellen of Radcliffe" and "The Liverpool Tragedy"; "The Tyrannical Husband" was a typical example of a seventeenth-century comic ditty, and "Preston Prisoners to the Ladies about Court and Town" was the best of a small group of Jacobite songs. Axon argued that the beginnings of modern Lancastrian dialect song could be found in the eighteenth century, especially in such anonymous lyrics as "Owd Ned's a Rare Strung Chap" and "A Mon o' Measter Grundy's," but the genre really came into its own in the first decades of the nineteenth century with such classics as the "Droylsden Wakes Song," Alexander Wilson's "Johnny Gren's Wedding," and Sam Bamford's "Tim Bobbin's Grave." Axon's list of the best contemporary dialect songwriters was similar to Harland's, and he singled out Sam Laycock as the most popular of them all. Fiercely proud of this regional song tradition, which he regarded as a direct expression of Lancashire working class character, Axon admired it as much for the values it expressed (stoicism, independence, good humor, neighborliness, and a sense of community) as for the creativity of its artisan-poets.

Another northern region that found a local editor/publisher interested in its heritage of popular song and poetry was Northumberland. Beginning in 1862, a set of several small booklets of song texts was published in Newcastle-upon-Tyne by Thomas Allan, and a decade later he reprinted them, with additions, as a book titled *Allan's Illustrated Edition of Tyneside Songs*.[112] The geographical compass of the book was wider than its title suggested, covering the counties of Northumberland and Durham rather than focusing exclusively on the Newcastle area. If anything, Geordie dialect was even more difficult for non-locals to understand than Lancashire dialect, and in both cases the use of dialect restricted a song's audience while making it more attractive to local listeners. Allan's collection was thus aimed primarily at a regional rather than national market, and—like those edited by Jewitt, Ingledew, and Harland—its use and usefulness was also limited by the lack of tunes.

In addition to this proliferation of regional song collections, two other developments occurred in the 1860s and 1870s that deserved notice. While one form of specialization was to focus on a single county, another was to concentrate on a subgenre of vernacular song. William Henry Husk's *Songs of the Nativity* (1864, revised 1868) was a good example of this.[113] It was at once a synthesis of the earlier work done by Gilbert, Sandys, Wright, and Rimbault, and an attempt to carry it further to create the most comprehensive collection of folk carols yet assembled. Divided between forty-three "religious carols" and thirty-nine "festive carols and songs," the book included many interesting and unusual texts in each section, and, moreover, Husk added an appendix of a dozen melodies. His oldest material was late medieval in origin, consisting of five fifteenth-century carols ("Welcome Yule," "A Yule-tide Carol," "The Virgin and Child," "A Carol for St. Stephen's Day," and "A Babe Is Born"). Tudor carols were slightly more numerous and included "A Carol of the Innocents" and "Be We Merry in This Feast" from Richard Kele's *Christmas carolles newely Imprinted*, which probably dated from the reign of Henry VIII. Other items from the Tudor period were culled from manuscripts in the

British Museum or from the compositions of Elizabethan musicians such as William Byrd. The early seventeenth century was also a period during which a considerable number of carols had been created, including "Remember, O Thou Man," the earliest composition for which Husk could provide a melody, which he took from Ravenscroft's *Melismata*. Apart from those reprinted from earlier collections, most of Husk's other religious carols were derived from broadsides sold in the West Country (for example "A Virgin Most Pure" and "The Moon Shone Bright") or the West Midlands ("The Carnal and the Crane," "The Holly and the Ivy," "The Seven Virgins," "A Worcestershire Carol," and "Dives and Lazarus"). Such items were difficult to date with precision, especially when found as reprints on eighteenth-century broadsheets, but Husk suspected that most of them were at least two hundred years old. Other carols that derived from old broadsides included several of the most popular, such as "I Saw Three Ships Come Sailing In," "God Rest You Merry Gentlemen," "The Cherry Tree Carol," "The Twelve Good Joys of Mary," and "The Holy Well."

The second half of *Songs of the Nativity* was devoted to festive carols and other songs associated with Christmas that had little or no explicit religious content. Many reflected traditional customs such as wassailing or the processional entry of the boar's head at a feast. Husk was as much interested in the folklore of Christmas as in its songs, arguing (for example) that the custom of "wenches" (as they were called) going from house to house with a decorated bowl of mulled and spiced ale was initially associated with Twelfth Night and dated back at least to the reign of Henry VII. He emphasized that such traditions as the boar's head ceremony, decking the halls with holly and ivy, and wassailing were still living customs in parts of rural England, and local carol-making was itself an art that had not yet died out, especially in such counties as Gloucestershire and Yorkshire. The best known among the festive songs collected by Husk was undoubtedly "The Twelve Days of Christmas," but he had also found a goodly number of wassails (including "A Jolly Wassail-Bowl," "All You That in this House Be Here," and a Yorkshire "Wassailers' Carol") and a group of songs about the supposed rivalry between holly and ivy: "Holly and Ivy," "Here Comes Holly," "Ivy, Chief of Trees," and "The Contest of the Ivy and the Holly." Interesting broadsides from the Commonwealth and Restoration eras included "Christmas's Lamentation" (an expression of popular discontent with Puritans' attempts during Cromwell's rule to make Christmas less festive and more religious) and "The Return of Old Christmas" (which celebrated the return to unbridled merrymaking after the accession of Charles II).

But while Husk had assembled plenty of song texts he had experienced difficulty collecting tunes for them. Indeed he had obtained melodies for only four items in the second half of the book: "The Boar's Head Carol" (for which he had found eight variant texts), "A Merry Christmas Carol," "All You That Are Good Fellows," and a "Gloucestershire Wassailers' Song." The latter he had noted himself on New Year's Eve, 1864, in the hamlet of Over, performed by a troop of wassailers from the neighboring village of Minsterworth. It was presumptive evidence that the venerable—if rather pagan—tradition of wassailing was alive and well in Victorian England. Like such regional collectors as Jewitt, Ingledew, Harland, Axon, and Allan, Husk was fiercely proud of English local traditions and the songs associated with them, and he saw his work as a contribution to both the preservation and the wider dissemination of the carols and wassails he loved. There was much to be learned from Husk's book. One could appreciate his catholic use of a variety of different kinds of primary and secondary sources, his folklorist's way of embedding the songs in traditional custom, his insistence that tradition was a living force in rural society, and his attempt (albeit only partially successful) to preserve the musical as well as the textual aspects of the songs. When one placed *Songs of the Nativity* alongside *Ballads and Songs of Lancashire* one might well wonder if it might be possible to create a regional collection that combined the best of Harland's and Husk's approaches to vernacular song. This would be attempted, with varying degrees of success, in the Late Victorian era.

Another significant development, which suggested that the musical climate with regard to folksong was changing, occurred right at the end of the 1870s. In 1866 Carl Engel, a German music historian living in London, had published a book titled *An Introduction to the Study of National Music*.[114] It was a pioneering essay in comparative musicology that analyzed the similarities and differences between a wide range of musical cultures around the world. Its learned author discussed different kinds of musical scales, varying approaches to melody and harmony, different ways of combining music and poetry, the social uses of music in various cultures, national dances, and the characteristics of typical national airs. He even examined the sources of "God Save the King" and included a few pages on Welsh and Scottish musical traditions. Yet the book lacked any discussion of the traditional music of England. The implication was that England lacked a distinctive national form of art music because it also lacked a body of folk music upon which 'serious' composers could draw for inspiration. England, in short, was (allegedly) a country without an indigenous musical culture. This was nonsense, of course, but it seemed to bolster the belief, apparently widely held in Europe, that England was a "Land ohne Musik." A decade later Engel published a series of articles in *The Musical Times*. They appeared monthly between July 1878 and March 1879, and were immediately reprinted in book form as *The Literature of National Music*.[115] Intended as a guide to the available song and tune collections and to the secondary literature on the music of a variety of different countries, the format of the publication forced Engel to discuss England along with Scotland, Ireland, Wales, and the Isle of Man. He now knew more about English music, and had changed his mind about it. He acknowledged the existence of several substantial collections of popular songs, mentioning Playford's *The Dancing Master*, D'Urfey's *Pills*, Ritson's *Select Collection of English Songs*, Rimbault's *Musical Illustrations to Bishop Percy's Reliques*, and Chappell's *Popular Music of the Olden Time*. Yet he still claimed that very few of the airs contained in these books could be regarded as "national airs in the strict sense of the term." In contrast to what Kitchiner and Chappell had meant by the term, Engel used 'national song' as an equivalent of *Volkslied*, a word usually translated nowadays as 'folksong.' All these compendia of old English songs, he explained, contained the popular songs of previous eras, what in German would be called *Volksthumliches Lied*. In his view they were not *Volkslied*, songs created by the ordinary people of a nation.[116]

Arguing that almost every other European nation possessed several comprehensive collections of *Volkslieder*, Engel now saw it as surprising that England had no such "printed collection of its national songs with the airs as they are sung at the present day."[117] He identified two small publications that included the right kind of English *Volkslied*, namely Edward Jones's *Popular Cheshire Melodies*[118] and Robert Topliffe's *Selection of the Most Popular Melodies of the Tyne and Wear*.[119] But these, he argued, were "too insignificant to supply the desideratum," and in any case they were too old to illustrate *Volkslied* melodies as currently sung in the English countryside. This apparent absence of genuine *Volkslieder* raised for Engel an interesting question: had there merely been a failure to collect them, or was there no such thing in England? It had been claimed, he noted, that, unlike their counterparts on the continent, rural workers in England rarely sing while at work in the fields or on their way home in the evenings, and that the kind of evening social gathering at which Germans routinely sing *Volkslieder* has no parallel in England. Engel now doubted that this was true. His (revised) opinion was that English folksongs probably did exist, but not in urban England. Because England was the most industrialized and urbanized of all countries, one would have to make a special effort to seek out folksong in the more remote and isolated rural regions of the land.[120]

Engel's library research (and knowledge of British geography) left much to be desired. He seems to have been unaware of the work of Jewitt, Ingledew, Axon, and Allan, but he cited two examples of regional collections that suggested that English *Volkslieder* might, after all, exist: John Harland's *Ballads and Songs of Lancashire* and George Henderson's *The Popular Rhymes, Sayings and Proverbs of the County of Berwick*.[121] The song-texts printed in such books were clues, he argued, "that there must be, belonging to the ditties, airs which have never been written down, and are only orally preserved by the people."[122] In one very brief visit to Llangollen he himself had noted from an old blind harper a previously uncollected tune called "Dixon's Hornpipe," a further indication that there was still much folk music waiting to be collected in the unindustrialized parts of the United Kingdom.[123] Moreover, Jane Williams's *Ancient National Airs of Gwent and Morganwg*[124] had demonstrated what "remarkably beautiful" melodies could be found in the Vale of Neath, and even if the folk airs of central and eastern England were less beautiful than those of Wales they should nonetheless prove to be "in every other respect equally interesting."[125]

Having done his best to demonstrate that a concerted attempt to collect folksongs in rural England would undoubtedly bear fruit, Engel issued an appeal to English piano teachers, organists, and music professors to get out of their drawing rooms and start "collecting airs from the lips of the peasantry." All that was required, he suggested, was that they look upon collecting tunes as a labor of love, something to be enjoyed while visiting the remoter counties, such as Cornwall or Northumberland, on vacation. The rewards could be great, since so little had been done so far and the field was wide open for discoveries similar to those already made in the Scottish lowlands.[126]

This was clearly a call to arms. Engel underestimated the extent to which folksong tunes as well as texts had already been collected by Victorian antiquarians and musicians, but he was right to proclaim the need for a more systematic effort to obtain popular melodies from oral tradition. Although there were some very important exceptions (Broadwood, Rimbault, and Chappell being the most obvious ones), early and mid-Victorian editors of ballad and folksong collections had tended to concentrate on words rather than tunes, and they all too frequently left out the music entirely. Yet unknown to Engel, change was already in the air. Tunes would soon gain parity with texts.

Notes

1. The first English folksong revival dates from the late 1870s to the end of the 1920s, and was divided into two main phases, the Late Victorian phase (the subject of this book) and a subsequent Edwardian phase (associated with such figures as Cecil Sharp, Percy Grainger, and Ralph Vaughan-Williams, among others). The second English folksong revival is usually thought of as occurring after

World War II, although its roots may be traced back to the 1930s. It is associated with such figures as Pat Shuldham-Shaw, Peter Kennedy, A. L. Lloyd, Ewan MacColl, John Hasted, and Eric Winter.

2. Lucy E. Broadwood and Herbert Birch Reynardson, eds., *Sussex Songs (Popular Songs of Sussex)* (London: Lucas & Weber, 1889) [actually 1890]. Lucy E. Broadwood and J. A. Fuller Maitland, eds., *English County Songs: Words and Music* (London: The Leadenhall Press, 1893; reprinted London: Cramer, 1915). Lucy E. Broadwood, ed., *English Traditional Songs and Carols* (London: Boosey, 1908).

3. It is my hope that sooner rather than later we will see biographies of Sabine Baring-Gould by Martin Graebe and of Frank Kidson by John Francmanis. See the bibliography for their existing publications on these collectors.

4. I understand that Dorothy De Val is working on a biography of Lucy Broadwood. I am also hoping to explore more fully Broadwood's song collecting and editorial work for the Folk-Song Society in collaboration with Irene Shettle, who has already done much by means of talks and concerts to publicize Broadwood's legacy.

5. E. David Gregory. *Victorian Songhunters: The Recovery and Editing of English Vernacular Ballads and Folk Lyrics, 1820-1883* (Lanham, Md.: Scarecrow Press, 2006).

6. William Allingham, ed., *The Ballad Book: A Selection of the Choicest British Ballads* (London: Macmillan, 1864).

7. Francis James Child, ed., *English and Scottish Ballads,* 8 vols. (Boston: Little, Brown & Co., 1857-59).

8. Child, *English and Scottish Ballads,* 8 vols. (2nd edition, London: Sampson Low, 1860).

9. Thomas Percy, ed., *Reliques of Ancient English Poetry, consisting of old heroic ballads, songs, and other pieces of our earlier poets (chiefly of the lyric kind),* 3 vols. (London: Dodsley, 1765. 5th edition, London: Rivington & Longman, 1812).

10. Joseph Ritson, ed., *Ancient Songs and Ballads from the Reign of King Henry the Second to the Revolution,* 2 vols. (London: Payne & Foss, 1829).

11. Sir Walter Scott, ed., *Minstrelsy of the Scottish Border, consisting of historical and romantic ballads, collected in the southern counties of Scotland, with a few of modern date, founded on local tradition,* 2 vols. (Kelson, U.K.: J. Ballantyne, 1802. 2nd edition, three volumes: Edinburgh: Ballantyne, 1803. 5th edition, 1812. New edition, ed. T. F. Henderson, 3 vols.: Edinburgh: William Blackwood & Sons, 1902).

12. John W. Hales and Frederick J. Furnivall, eds., *Bishop Percy's Folio Manuscript.* 3 vols. & Supplement of "Loose and Humorous Songs" (London: Trubner, 1867-68).

13. William Chappell and J. W. Ebsworth, eds., *The Roxburghe Ballads,* 8 vols. (Hertford, U.K.: The Ballad Society, 1869-99).

14. *A Collection of Old Ballads, Corrected from the best and most Ancient Copies Extant, with Introductions Historical, Critical or Humorous,* 3 vols. (London: J. Roberts, 1723-25) [attributed to Ambrose Philips, ed., but this attribution has been questioned].

15. Thomas Evans, ed., *Old Ballads, Historical and Narrative, with some of Modern Date, Collected from Rare Copies and Mss.,* 2 vols. (London: Evans, 1777. 2nd edition, 4 vols., London: Evans, 1784).

16. W. Walker Wilkins, ed., *Political Ballads of the Seventeenth and Eighteenth Centuries,* 2 vols. (London: Longman, Green, Longman & Roberts, 1860).

17. Joseph Lilly, et al., eds., *A Collection of 79 Black Letter Ballads and Broadsides printed in the Reign of Queen Elizabeth* (London: Lilly, 1867).

18. W. H. Logan, ed., *A Pedlar's Pack of Ballads and Songs, with Illustrative Notes* (Edinburgh: William Paterson, 1869; reprinted: Detroit, Mich.: Singing Tree Press, 1968).

19. William Chappell, ed., *Popular Music of the Olden Time, a collection of Ancient Songs, Ballads and Dance Tunes, illustrative of the National Music of England,* 2 vols. (London: Cramer, Beale & Chappell, 1858-9; reprinted: New York: Dover, 1965).

20. William Chappell, ed., *A Collection of National English Airs consisting of Ancient Song, Ballad and Dance Tunes,* 2 vols. (London: Chappell, Simkin, Marshall & Co., 1838).

21. William Chappell, G. A. Macfarren, Natalia Macfarren and J. Oxenford, eds., *Old English Ditties, selected from W. Chappell's "Popular Music of the Olden Time," with a New Introduction,* 2 vols. (London: Chappell & Co., n.d.).

22. William Kitchiner, ed., *The Loyal and National Songs of England, for one, two, and three voices, selected from original manuscripts and early printed copies in the Library of W. Kitchiner.* (London: Hurst, Robinson & Co., 1823).

23. James Henry Dixon, ed., *Ancient Poems, Ballads and Songs of the Peasantry of England.* (London: Percy Society, 1846).

24. Geoffrey Dusart [and John Broadwood], eds., *Old English Songs, as now sung by the Peasantry of the Weald of Surrey and Sussex.* (London: Betts & Co., [1847]). The publication date of this book is often erroneously given as 1843, the year in which Dusart harmonized the tunes.

25. Thomas D'Urfey, ed., *Wit and Mirth: or Pills to Purge Melancholy,* 6 vols. (London: D'Urfey, 1719-20. Reprint: New York: Folklore Library Publishers, 1959).

26. Joseph Ritson, ed., *A Select Collection of English Songs in Three Volumes,* 3 vols. (London: J. Johnson, 1783).

27. C. J. Davison Ingledew, ed., *The Ballads and Songs of Yorkshire* (London: Bell & Daldy, 1860).

28. Llewelynn F. W. Jewitt, ed., *Ballads and Songs of Derbyshire* (London: Bemrose & Lothian, 1867).

29. John Harland, ed., *Ballads and Songs of Lancashire, chiefly older than the 19th Century* (London: Whittaker, 1865; 2nd edition, 1875).

30. John Harland, ed., *Lancashire Lyrics: Modern Songs and Ballads of the County Palatine* (London: Whittaker, 1866).

31. Lewis Ramondon, ed., *The Merry Musician, or, A Cure for the Spleen,* 3 vols. (2nd edition, London: J. Walsh, 1730).

32. G. H. Davidson, ed., *Davidson's Universal Melodist,* 2 vols. (London: Davidson, 1848).

33. *A Collection of Old Ballads,* 3 vols. (London: J. Roberts, 1723-25).

34. Thomas Wright, ed., *Songs and Carols now first printed from a Manuscript of the Fifteenth Century* (London: Percy Society, 1847).

35. Thomas Wright, ed., *Political Poems and Songs relating to English History from Edward III to Richard III,* 2 vols. (London: Longman, Green, Longman & Robert, 1859-61).

36. John W. Hales and Frederick J. Furnivall, eds. *Bishop Percy's Folio Manuscript,* 3 vols. & Supplement of "Loose and Humorous Songs" (London: Trubner, 1867-68).

37. John Payne Collier, ed., *Old Ballads from Early Printed Copies* (London: Percy Society, 1840).

38. Thomas Deloney, *Strange Histories, or, Songes and Sonets, of Kings, Princes, Dukes, Lordes, Ladyes, Knights, and Gentlemen* (London: W. Barley, 1607); reprinted as *Strange Histories, consisting of Ballads and other Poems* (London: Percy Society, 1841).

39. Thomas Deloney, *The Garland of Good Will* (London: publisher unknown, c. 1595). Republished, edited by J. H. Dixon, as part of volume 30 of *Early English Poetry, Ballads, and Popular Literature of the Middle Ages* (London: C. Richards for the Percy Society, 1851).

40. Joseph W. Ebsworth, ed., *The Bagford Ballads,* 2 vols. (Hertford, U.K: The Ballad Society, 1876-78).

41. William Chappell and J. W. Ebsworth, eds., *The Roxburghe Ballads,* 8 vols. (Hertford, U.K.: The Ballad Society, 1869-1899).

42. William Chappell, ed., *The Crown Garland of Golden Roses, Part II, from the Edition of 1659* (London: Percy Society, 1845).

43. Thomas Ravenscroft, ed., *Deuteromelia* (London: n.p., 1609).

44. [Thomas Ravenscroft, attrib. ed.,] *Melismata: Musicall Phansies, Fitting the Court, Cittie, and Countrey Humours* (London: n.p., 1611).

45. [Thomas Deloney, attrib. ed.,] *Wit Restor'd* (London: n.p., 1658); reprinted in *Facetiae: Musarum Deliciae, Wit Restor'd & Wits Recreations,* 2 vols. (London: n.p., 1817).

46. John Playford, ed., *The English Dancing Master* (London: Playford, 1651).

47. Thomas Wright, ed., *Political Ballads Published in England during the Commonwealth* (London: Percy Society, 1841).

48. Joseph Ebsworth, ed., *Choyce Drollery: Songs & Sonnets, being a Collection of Divers Excellent Pieces of Poetry. Of Several Eminent Authors, to which are added the extra songs of Merry Drollery, 1661, and an Antidote Against Melancholy, 1661* (Boston, U.K: Robert Roberts, 1876).

49. Joseph Ebsworth, ed., *Merry Drollery Compleat, being Jovial Poems, Merry Songs, both parts, 1661, 1670, 1691.* (Boston, U.K.: Robert Roberts, 1875).

50. Joseph Ebsworth, ed., *Westminster Drolleries, both parts, of 1671, 1672, being a Choice Collection of Songs and Poems sung at Court and Theatres* (Boston, U.K.: Robert Roberts, 1875).

51. Henry Playford, ed., *Wit and Mirth: or Pills to Purge Melancholy,* 4 vols. (London: Playford, 1698-1706. A fifth volume was issued in 1714).

52. Thomas D'Urfey, ed., *Wit and Mirth: or Pills to Purge Melancholy,* 6 vols. (London: D'Urfey, 1719-1720; Reprinted, New York: Folklore Library Publishers, 1959).

53. Lewis Ramondon, ed., *The Merry Musician, or, A Cure for the Spleen,* 3 vols. (2nd edition, London: J. Walsh, 1730).

54. Thomas Percy, ed., *Reliques of Ancient English Poetry, consisting of old heroic ballads, songs, and other pieces of our earlier poets (chiefly of the lyric kind),* 3 vols. (London: Dodsley, 1765. 5th edition, London: Rivington & Longman, 1812).

55. William Motherwell, ed., *Minstrelsy Ancient and Modern* (Glasgow: John Wylie, 1827).

56. Peter Buchan, ed., *Gleanings of Scarce Old Ballads* (Peterhead, U.K.: Buchan, 1825). *Ancient Ballads and Songs of the North of Scotland,* 2 vols. (Edinburgh: Laing & Stevenson, 1828).

57. James Henry Dixon, ed., *Scottish Traditional Versions of Ancient Ballads* (London: Percy Society, 1846).

58. Charles Mackay, ed., *The Legendary and Romantic Ballads of Scotland* (London: Griffin, Bohn, 1861).

59. Joseph Ritson, ed., *Ancient Songs from the Time of King Henry the Third to the Revolution* (London: J. Johnson, 1790; expanded, two volume edition: London: Payne & Foss, 1829).

60. Joseph Ritson, ed., *Robin Hood: A Collection of All the Ancient Poems, Songs and Ballads now extant relative to that celebrated English Outlaw,* 2 vols. (London: J. Johnson, 1795. 2nd edition: London: William Pickering, 1832).

61. Joseph Ritson, ed., *Northern Garlands* (London: Triphook, 1810). A reprint, in one volume, of four small collections made by Ritson and published separately between 1784 and 1802: *The Bishopric Garland, or Durham Minstrel* (1784, revised edition 1792), *The Yorkshire Garland* (1788), *The Northumberland Garland* (1793), and *The North-Country Chorister* (1802).

62. John Bell, ed., *Rhymes of Northern Bards* (Newcastle-upon-Tyne, U.K.: Bell & Angus, 1812; reprinted, Newcastle-upon-Tyne, U.K.: Frank Graham, 1971).

63. John Clare, *Poems Descriptive of Rural Life and Scenery* (London: Taylor, Hessey & Drury, 1820). *The Village Minstrel and Other Poems,* 2 vols. (London: Taylor, Hessey & Drury, 1821). *The Shepherd's Calendar, with Village Stories and Other Poems* (London: Taylor, 1827).

64. George Deacon, *John Clare and the Folk Tradition* (London: Sinclair Browne, 1983).

65. William Kitchiner, ed., *The Loyal and National Songs of England, for one, two, and three voices, selected from original manuscripts and early printed copies in the Library of W. Kitchiner* (London: Hurst, Robinson & Co., 1823). *The Sea Songs of England, selected from original manuscripts and early printed copies in the Library of W. Kitchiner* (London: Hurst, Robinson & Co., 1823).

66. William Chappell, ed., *A Collection of National English Airs consisting of Ancient Song, Ballad and Dance Tunes*, 2 vols. (London: Chappell, Simkin, Marshall & Co., 1838).

67. Frederick W. Fairholt, ed., *The Civic Garland: A Collection of Songs from London Pageants* (London: Percy Society, 1845). *Satirical Songs and Poems on Costume: From the 13th to the 19th Century* (London: Percy Society, 1849). *Poems and Songs relating to George Villiers, Duke of Buckingham, and his assassination by John Felton, August 23, 1628* (London: Percy Society, 1850).

68. Thomas Wright, ed., *The Political Songs of England, from the Reign of John to that of Edward II* (London: Camden Society, 1839).

69. Thomas Wright, ed., *Political Ballads Published in England during the Commonwealth* (London: Percy Society, 1841).

70. Thomas Wright, ed., *Songs and Carols now first printed from a Manuscript of the Fifteenth Century* (London: Percy Society, 1847).

71. Thomas Wright, ed., *Songs and Carols from a Manuscript in the British Museum of the Fifteenth Century* (London: T. Richards for the Warton Club, 1856).

72. Thomas Wright, ed., *Political Poems and Songs relating to English History from Edward III to Richard III*, 2 vols. (London: Longman, Green, Longman & Robert, 1859-61).

73. Thomas Wright, ed., *Songs and Ballads, chiefly from the Reign of Philip and Mary* (London: J. B. Nichols & Sons, 1860).

74. Thomas Wright and James Orchard Halliwell, eds., *Reliquiae Antiquae: Scraps from Ancient Manuscripts*, 2 vols. (London: n.p., 1845).

75. James Orchard Halliwell, ed., *The Early Naval Ballads of England* (London: Percy Society, 1841).

76. James Orchard Halliwell, ed., *The Nursery Rhymes of England, collected principally from oral tradition* (London: Percy Society, 1842).

77. James Orchard Halliwell, ed., *The Loyal Garland: A Collection of Songs of the Seventeenth Century* (London: Percy Society, 1850).

78. James Orchard Halliwell, ed., *Ballads and Poems respecting Hugh of Lincoln* (Brixton Hill, U.K.: [Halliwell,] 1849).

79. James Orchard Halliwell, ed., *The Palatine Anthology: A Collection of Ancient Poems and Ballads Relating to Lancashire and Cheshire* (London: Halliwell, 1850).

80. James Orchard Halliwell, ed., *The Yorkshire Anthology* (London: Halliwell, 1851).

81. James Orchard Halliwell, ed., *The Norfolk Anthology: A Collection of Poems, Ballads, and Rare Tracts Relating to the County of Norfolk* (Brixton Hill, U.K.: Halliwell, 1852).

82. Charles Mackay, ed., *A Collection of Songs and Ballads relative to the London Prentices and Trades, and to the Affairs of London Generally* (London: Percy Society, 1841).

83. Charles Mackay, ed., *The Book of English Songs, from the Sixteenth to the Nineteenth Century* (London: Office of the National Illustrated Library, 1851).

84. Charles Mackay, ed., *The Illustrated Book of Scottish Songs, from the Sixteenth to the Nineteenth Century* (London: Illustrated London Library, 1852).

85. Charles Mackay, ed., *The Legendary and Romantic Ballads of Scotland* (London: Griffin, Bohn, 1861).

86. Charles Mackay, ed., *The Jacobite Songs and Ballads of Scotland from 1688 to 1747, with an appendix of modern Jacobite songs* (London: R. Griffin, 1861).

87. Charles Mackay, ed., *The Cavalier Songs and Ballads of England from 1642 to 1684* (London: G. Bohn & Co., 1863); reprinted as *The Songs and Ballads of the Cavaliers* (London: C. Griffin & Co., 1864).

88. William Sandys, ed., *Christmas Carols, Ancient and Modern, including the most popular in the West of England, and the airs to which they are sung. Also specimens of French Provincial Carols* (London: Richard Beckley, 1833).

89. William Sandys, ed., *Festive Songs, principally of the Sixteenth and Seventeenth Centuries* (London: Percy Society & T. Richards, 1848).

90. William Sandys, ed., *Specimens of Cornish Provincial Dialect...[and] a Selection of Songs and other pieces connected with Cornwall* (London: J. R. Smith, 1846).

91. James Henry Dixon, ed., *Scottish Traditional Versions of Ancient Ballads* (London: Percy Society, 1846).

92. James Henry Dixon, ed., *Ancient Poems, Ballads and Songs of the Peasantry of England* (London: Percy Society, 1846).

93. Robert Bell, ed., *Ancient Poems, Ballads and Songs of the Peasantry of England* (London: John Parker & Sons, 1857).

94. Edward Rimbault, ed., *Old Ballads illustrating the Great Frost of 1683-84 and the Fair on the River Thames* (London: Percy Society, 1844).

95. Edward Rimbault, ed., *A Little Book of Christmas Carols, with the Ancient Melodies to which they are Sung* (London: Cramer, Beale & Co., 1847).

96. Edward Rimbault, ed., *Nursery Rhymes* (London: Cramer, Beale & Co., 1849).

97. Edward Rimbault, ed., *A Little Book of Songs and Ballads* (London: Smith, 1851).

98. John Gutch, ed., *The Robin Hood Garlands and Ballads, with the Tale of 'The Lytell Geste': A Collection of Poems, Songs and Ballads relating to this Celebrated Yeoman*, 2 vols. (London: J. R. Smith, 1850).

99. Edward Rimbault, ed., *Musical Illustrations of Bishop Percy's Reliques of Ancient English Poetry* (London: Cramer, Beale & Co., 1850).

100. Frederick Sheldon, ed., *The Minstrelsy of the English Border, being a collection of Ballads, ancient, remodelled, and original, founded on well known Border legends* (London: Longman, Brown, Green & Longmans, 1847).

101. [John Broadwood and] Geoffrey Dusart, eds., *Old English Songs, as now sung by the Peasantry of the Weald of Surrey and Sussex.* (London: Betts & Co., 1847).

102. Robert Bell, ed., *Songs from the Dramatists* (London: John Parker & Sons, 1854).

103. Robert Bell, ed., *Early Ballads Illustrative of History, Traditions and Customs* (London: John Parker & Sons, 1856).

104. Robert Bell, ed., *Ancient Poems, Ballads and Songs of the Peasantry of England* (London: John Parker & Sons, 1857).

105. G. H. Davidson, ed., *Davidson's Universal Melodist*, 2 vols. (London: Davidson, 1848).

106. Llewelynn F. W. Jewitt, ed., *Ballads and Songs of Derbyshire* (London: Bemrose & Lothian, 1867).

107. James Orchard Halliwell, ed., *The Yorkshire Anthology* (London: Halliwell, 1851).

108. C. J. Davison Ingledew, ed., *The Ballads and Songs of Yorkshire* (London: Bell & Daldy, 1860).

109. John Harland, ed., *Ballads and Songs of Lancashire, chiefly older than the 19th Century* (London: Whittaker, 1865. 2nd edition, 1875).

110. John Harland, ed., *Lancashire Lyrics: Modern Songs and Ballads of the County Palatine* (London: Whittaker, 1866).

111. William E. A. Axon, *Folk Song and Folk-Speech of Lancashire* (Manchester, U.K.: Tubbs & Brook, [1871], reissued 1887).

112. Thomas Allan, ed., *Allan's Illustrated Edition of Tyneside Songs and Readings* (Newcastle-upon-Tyne, U.K.: Thomas & George Allan, 1872; revised edition, 1891). The 1872 edition appears to be very rare and I was unable to find a copy of it, so this brief account is based upon the 1891 edition.

113. William Henry Husk, ed., *Songs of the Nativity; Being Christmas Carols, Ancient and Modern* (London: John Camden Hotten, 1864; revised edition, 1868).

114. Carl Engel, *An Introduction to the Study of National Music* (London: Longmans, Green, Reader & Dyer, 1866).

115. Carl Engel, *The Literature of National Music* (London: Novello, Ewer & Co., 1879).

116. Engel, *Literature*, 34.

117. Engel, *Literature*, 32.

118. Edward Jones, ed., *Popular Cheshire Melodies* (London: Jones, 1798).

119. Robert Topliffe, ed., *Selection of the Most Popular Melodies of the Tyne and Wear, consisting of 24 original airs peculiar to the counties of Durham and Northumberland* (London: R. Topliffe, 1820).

120. Engel, *Literature*, 32-33.

121. George Henderson, ed., *The Popular Rhymes, Sayings and Proverbs of the County of Berwick* (Newcastle-upon-Tyne: W. S. Crow, 1856). The county of Berwick, incidentally, is in Scotland, just across the border from Northumberland.

122. Engel, *Literature*, 33.

123. Engel, *Literature*, 99.

124. Maria Jane Williams and Daniel Huws, eds., *Ancient National Airs of Gwent and Morganwg* (Llandovery, Wales: W. Rees, 1844).

125. Engel, *Literature*, 31 and 33.

126. Engel, *Literature*, 99-100.

Part 2

The Rediscovery of Melody, 1878-1889

3

Prelude: England in the 1880s

Before exploring the genesis of the Late Victorian folksong revival in the north of England, let us pause briefly to examine the society within which this new cultural movement was born. At the beginning of the 1880s the United Kingdom had a population of about 35 million, some 26 million of whom lived in England and Wales, the remainder divided roughly evenly between Scotland and Ireland. Although only a little more than half the size of the United Kingdom's population today, this figure is approximately the same as the current population of Canada. By the end of the decade it would grow to 37.7 million, with the population of England and Wales rising to nearly 29 million.[1]

Economy and Society

One could make the case that the island of Britain was already overpopulated in 1880; certainly it had lost its ability to feed itself from its own agricultural production and was dependent for survival on imports of cattle, grain, sugar, tea, and other staples from the Americas and Asia. The United Kingdom could pay for those imports, and at the same time make huge capital investments at home and overseas, because it was still the industrial workshop of the world. Exports, worth £223 million per annum in 1880, were still growing slowly (they would reach £233 million by the end of the century). While in certain traditional markets (the USA, Germany, and France in particular) competition was becoming fiercer, trade with the rest of Europe, Canada, South America, Africa, India, and the Far East was still very profitable. One of the most important areas in which British industry was still dominant was in steel production. Steel was rapidly replacing iron as the strongest and most durable construction material, and the United Kingdom's output of steel rose from 1.3 million tons in 1880 to 3.6 million tons in 1890. Yet if the 1880s were an age of steel, they were also the beginning of the age of electricity. Towns and houses were still lit by gaslight, but Joseph Swan, (beating Edison by a year), had invented the electric light bulb in 1878 and the first electric trams appeared in cities during the next decade. Another key breakthrough was the application of refrigeration on an industrial scale, which made possible the wholesale import of meat (rather than live cattle and sheep) from South America, Australia, and New Zealand.

In broad terms the 1880s were a time of continued economic expansion for this industrial economy, although growth was slower (around 2% per annum on average) and more spasmodic than in the heady days of the mid-Victorian era. The 1870s had witnessed a shallow but fairly prolonged depression that had reached bottom in the bad years of 1878-79 with an unemployment rate of nearly 11%. Growth returned at the beginning of the new decade, but that classic characteristic of an unregulated, *laissez-faire*, economy, a cycle of boom and bust, was severely evident. Thus a four-year period of expansion reaching a crest in 1883 with unemployment down to 2.5% was followed by a sharp recession that bottomed out in 1886 with unemployment back at 9.5%. The next boom lasted three years, cresting in 1889 with unemployment at a near record low of 2.0%, but the new decade opened with the beginnings of another downturn again evident.[2]

Victorian England was a harsh, class-ridden society with extremes of wealth and poverty. No solutions had been found, or even seriously sought, for the problems of cyclical unemployment, the permanently unemployed, and the aged poor. Pauperism was endemic in both town and country, but the condition of this underclass living in extreme poverty was exacerbated during each recession when large numbers of unemployed workers and their families joined the ranks of the very poor. At such times the palliative of voluntary charity was totally inadequate, nor could the Poor Law system, which was often inhumane and was widely hated by its victims, cope with the volume of cases. For the average urban worker times were good in the boom years with real wages tending to rise, but this gain was offset by the real possibility of losing one's job during each recession and by the complete lack of unemployment insurance or other form of social security net except the dreaded workhouse. During the worst slumps starvation stalked industrial slums and rural cottages alike. It did not help that bread was cheap if one had nothing with which to buy it and the rent was still to pay.[3]

Cheap grain from the prairies of North America and cheaper meat from Australasia meant that the 1880s were a time when the prices of basic commodities were, on the whole, either stable or falling. The decline was most marked in the case of wheat and consequently of bread: wheat sold for approximately 44 shillings per quarter in 1880 but was down to 32 shillings by 1890, while four pounds of bread cost 8 pence in 1880 and only 6 pence in 1890. This did mean rising living standards for most working families, at least in boom times when unemployment was low, but it was obviously bad news for farmers and everyone else dependent on the rural economy. The dividing line between town and country is difficult to draw other than arbitrarily, and England had for long been a land with many large villages that might be called small towns (and vice versa), but even if one counted small market towns as rural, this was now predominantly an urban society: between three-fifths and two-thirds of the population lived in cities or in the larger towns. Moreover a substantial part of urban England, especially in the Midlands and the North, was industrial, and the factories were now predominantly powered by steam and dependent on a fossil fuel, coal. There were industrial villages as well as towns: textile mills and coalmines were often located in the countryside, especially in South Wales, in the counties of Lancashire and Yorkshire, and in the Northeast.

On the other hand, the topography of most of England, and by far the majority of Wales, Scotland, and Ireland, was still rural. Proportionately less people lived in the countryside than before, but farmland and moorland was still extensive, and farming was still an important sector in the economy. It was also the weakest sector, threatened by free trade and by those growing imports of meat and already huge imports of grain. Low prices meant that British agriculture had to become more efficient to survive, and that meant increased mechanization and the non-cultivation of marginal land. The total acreage under arable production fell by about 10% during the decade of the 1880s, although this was compensated for in some degree by an increase in cattle rearing of about 7%. These changes meant that employment opportunities in rural areas were declining, and farmers were tempted to reduce further the already meager wages of agricultural laborers. Attempts at unionization, led by Joseph Arch in the 1870s, had failed with the onset of the depression, with the result that wages had fallen from the already low figure of about 2 shillings a week to around 1 shilling and 6 pence. This was at a time when London dockers successfully struck for a wage of 6 pence per hour. Not surprisingly, there was in this decade a marked drift of the unemployed and underemployed away from the English (and Scottish and Irish) countryside, resulting in the continued population growth of the larger cities and industrial areas such as the coalfields.[4]

By the Late Victorian era England—and to a lesser extent the less populated parts of the United Kingdom—already possessed a quite extensive railway network, so increased travel opportunities, including the possibility of seaside vacations, was a feature of everyday life for the middle class and for the better-off members of the working class. But once one got off the train, it was normally back to some form of horse-drawn conveyance if one had luggage that required transportation. In the cities most public transportation, except for the first electric trams, was still horse-drawn and the streets were often cobbled; in the countryside the roads still left much to be desired, especially in wet weather. The advent of the bicycle had considerably increased mobility for those who did not keep their own horse, and was having the side-effect of making clothing, especially women's clothing, more practical. Cycling was a new means of transportation, but it was also for some a leisure activity that permitted a more extensive exploration of the countryside than had previously been possible. Hiking, especially in mountainous or moorland areas, was also on the increase. The 1880s, too, were a time when participation in such sports as cricket and tennis was growing, and, like soccer and rugby, they were also becoming spectator sports. Association football (soccer) officially became a professional sport in 1885, although professionalism was still rejected by the English Rugby Union. Cricket, played on Saturdays by amateur teams on village greens all across England, also had its professionals, the most famous being Dr. W. G. Grace, whose remarkable exploits as a batsman stimulated its growth as a spectator sport, as did the beginning of international contests with the Australians. Lawn tennis had been invented only in the mid-1870s but by the beginning of the next decade the Wimbledon All England Croquet and Lawn Tennis Club had finalized the rules, its popularity was spreading like wildfire, and courts were springing up in suburban gardens as well as country houses. Golf, too, made rapid progress in the 1880s, facilitated by the decision to allow women to play on the main links rather than special nursery ones.[5]

Political Life

The greatest spectator sport in Late Victorian England was still parliamentary politics. One could follow it daily in the pages of one's chosen newspaper, which cost one penny. For Conservatives it was a choice between the *Daily Telegraph*, the *Standard*, or the *Morning Post*. Liberals would opt for the *Daily News* or the *Daily Chronicle*, or, if they lived in the North, the *Manchester Guardian*. Avid politics-watchers might also purchase *The Times*, but that cost three pence and could no doubt be found at one's club or in the local library. To be properly informed it was also necessary to canvass the intellectual debates in the best periodicals, such as the Conservative *Saturday Review* and the Liberal *Spectator* and *Fortnightly Review*.

The politicians who ruled the United Kingdom had already taken (in the early Victorian era) the one basic economic policy decision with which they had been confronted: whether to opt for free trade or to protect British agriculture from lower-cost imports. The choice had been to sacrifice the rural economy in the interests of manufacturers and exporters who thereby benefitted from cheaper labor costs than their French or German competitors. Other than this, the government had very little control over the economy, nor did it believe that intervention would be prudent or effective. It was content to do nothing to alleviate the huge disparities that existed in wealth and income: approximately two-thirds of the national income went to the wealthiest twelve percent of the population. That economic elite was also, by and large, the political elite, that is to say those who participated in one way or another in the political process. Britain did have a form of representative, parliamentary government, but it was far from a democracy. The Second Reform Act of 1867 had doubled the electorate and redistributed seats but in most places voting was still mainly restricted to adult males with property. The result was that approximately one tenth of the population—around 3 million people—actually had the vote at the beginning of the 1880s. This would increase to about 5.7 million after the Franchise Act of 1884 again reduced voter qualifications and further rationalized the distribution of seats, but genuine democracy was still far away: neither women nor the poorer segments of society were enfranchised.[6]

The end of the 1870s saw Benjamin Disraeli in power at the head of a Tory government that had ruled since 1874.[7] An occasional and moderate reformer, Disraeli had initiated a brief burst of legislation after taking over the reins of government. His reform legacy had included a Trade Union Act (making collective bargaining and strikes legal but maintaining other restrictions imposed on trade unions by a hostile judiciary), an Artisans' Dwelling Act (aimed at improving working-class living conditions), a Sale of Food and Drugs Act (attempting to reduce the widespread adulteration of food and medicine), and a Public Health Act. Combined with William Gladstone's earlier reforms, this package, although limited in scope and often ineffective in practice, seemed almost enough to warrant the claim that Victorian society was one in which abuses and social problems would be identified and solved. Progress might be slow and erratic, but it did seem to be gradually coming about.[8]

The latter years of Disraeli's last term in office were marred by a series of crises. The misery caused by the severe recession of these years provoked widespread discontent with a government that seemed preoccupied with foreign affairs. A crisis in the Balkans, during which Disraeli pursued an anti-Russian policy, provoked outrage at the government's support of a corrupt and repressive Turkish government, a sentiment stirred up by Gladstone's eloquent pamphlet, *The Bulgarian Horrors and the Question of the East*. Disraeli's diplomacy failed to prevent a Russian military victory in 1878, and although he emerged from the subsequent Congress of Berlin proclaiming "peace with honour" his critics could plausibly argue that a morally wrong policy had ended with a political defeat. This might not have mattered had not Disraeli's government not found itself dealing at the same time with two fairly major colonial conflicts: the inglorious and costly Zulu War of 1879 and the embarrassing Afghan War of the same year. During the latter conflict the British legation in Kabul was massacred and a major military expedition was needed to regain control of Kabul and to prevent a similar fate befalling a garrison in Kandahar. Nor was Disraeli's decision to purchase shares in the Suez Canal a popular measure among those liberal critics who foresaw, quite correctly, that it would sooner than later result in Egypt becoming in effect a British protectorate with all the ensuing headaches that that would involve. Even his proclamation of Queen Victoria as "Empress of India" drew fire, although it seems to have been surprisingly popular in India as well as among English voters.

The most difficult problem of all facing Disraeli, and one that neither he nor his successors managed to solve, was that of Ireland. A predominantly agricultural and Catholic country, Ireland was controlled by mainly Protestant and frequently absentee landlords, and it had been hit very hard by the depression and falling prices for farm produce. Rents were too high for most peasant cultivators to afford and eviction rates were high, resulting in widespread misery, discontent, and protest, sometimes violent. Since the Ballot Act of 1872 it was much easier for Irish voters to elect candidates who were not beholden to the landed elite, and in the late 1870s Charles Stewart Parnell took over from Isaac Butt as the leader of a parliamentary group of Irish liberals demanding Home Rule for Ireland.[9] Home Rule was the political dimension of Parnell's program, while its economic dimension was land reform, a cause championed by the Irish National Land League, formed in 1879 as an alliance between Parnell and the more radical Fenian movement. To Parnell and the Fenians Disraeli had no answer but to try to enforce law and order, a policy doomed merely to exacerbate a situation that required rapid and decisive action before the problem became an insurmountable crisis.

With the support of the Irish independents, Gladstone won the election of April 1880. The new Liberal government had a modest reform agenda and brought in such legislation as the Married Women's Property Act of 1882, the Settled Land Act of the same year, the Bankruptcy Act of 1883, and the Corrupt Practices Act (also 1883). As we have seen, the Liberals also nearly doubled the electorate and redistributed seats to urban areas by means of the Franchise Act of 1884. This was the philosophy of cautious progress seen at work once again, and one of Gladstone's most successful periods in office, but he was plagued by similar foreign policy problems to those that had afflicted the elderly Disraeli (who died in 1881). A renewed Afghan War resulted in a defeat for British forces at the battle of Maiwand and a heroic forced march by other troops to prevent the loss of the vulnerable Kandahar garrison. Gladstone wisely extracted himself from this mess by effectively ceding Afghan independence. His approach to dealing with another colonial crisis in South Africa was similar. Disraeli had annexed the Transvaal but a revolt against British rule by the Transvaal Boers resulted in successive defeats of British forces at the battles of Laing's Nek and Majuba Hill. By the Pretoria Convention of 1881 the Liberal government effectively acknowledged the independence of the Transvaal. Yet even Gladstone was not prepared to relinquish British control of the Suez Canal, so vital a part of the fastest sea-route to India, and he was gradually drawn into a full-fledged occupation of Egypt in order to protect it. The question then became: how far south should British control extend? General Gordon favored a forward policy and occupied the Sudan, but he was unable to hold it and the relief expedition tardily sent to save him failed to reach Khartoum in time. The massacre of Gordon and his garrison by the Mahdi in 1885 was a major foreign policy setback for Gladstone and certainly contributed to his defeat in the next general election.

So too did his unpopular Irish policy, although it reflected a genuine attempt to cooperate with Parnell and to bring about the land reform that the country desperately needed. The previous government's policy of coercion without reform had provoked a crisis situation in which 'Captain Moonlight' took anonymous but violent action against oppressive landlords, while Parnell and the Land League launched a highly effective campaign of ostracism directed against evicting landlords and replacement tenants, a campaign which introduced the word 'boycott' into the English language. Gladstone's approach was to combine a new Crimes Bill (aimed at appeasing the 'law and order' lobby) with an Irish Land Reform bill along the lines suggested by Parnell, but before he could implement it his government was defeated on a budget matter, and he resigned in favor of a minority Conservative government led by Lord Salisbury. Salisbury was a conservative imperialist whose enthusiasm for Britain's colonial 'mission' rivaled, although perhaps not in eloquence, that of historian and propagandist Sir John Seeley, whose *The Expansion of England* had been published in 1883.[10] He used the opportunity of his first brief spell as Prime Minister to annex Burma. He was unwilling to bring in the kind of radical land reform that Ireland required but he did introduce the first state-assisted scheme aimed at facilitating land purchase by the Irish peasantry (it was too little, too late). He also tricked Parnell into believing that a form of Home Rule might be obtained more easily from the Tories (who at least controlled the House of Lords) than from the Liberals. Parnell then advised Irish voters in English constituencies to vote Conservative, with the result that the Liberals lost seats at the General Election of 1885 although they still won a majority. Back in power once again, Gladstone determined to grasp the Irish nettle and brought a Home Rule Bill to the House of Commons, only to see it defeated by the Tories and by rebels within his own party. He then dissolved parliament and fought an election on the issue, only to discover that Home Rule was even more unpopular in the country at large than in the House.

Apart from the elderly Gladstone, there was no intellectual spokesman for Victorian liberalism in the 1880s with the eloquence and vision to rival that of John Stuart Mill, but two figures of some importance should nonetheless be noted: James Bryce, whose *The American Commonwealth* (1888) championed the development of democracy in the USA, and John Morley, who, along with Bryce, was a member of Gladstone's brief third ministry in 1886. Morley, Gladstone's future biographer, was an influential essayist as well as historian; he had edited the *Fortnightly Review* from 1867 to 1882, and he continued to write articles and books (his biographies of Cobden, Rousseau, and Walpole were published in the 1880s). The defeat of the Liberal government in 1886 brought to the end a fairly lengthy period in which Liberal ideas and policies, although not always Liberal administrations, had dominated Victorian intellectual and political life. Except for a brief spell between 1892 and 1894, politician-intellectuals such as Morley and Bryce would henceforth be consigned for the rest of the Victorian era to the opposition benches. Of course they continued to try to influence voters through their speeches and published writings but, in the main, it seemed that they were swimming against the current.[11]

So, if the first half of the 1880s was a time when Victorian liberalism was in the ascendant, the latter half of the decade belonged to the Conservatives. Lord Salisbury returned to office in 1886, although his Conservative government was dependent for its majority on support from seventy-eight Liberal Unionists opposed to Home Rule. On Ireland Salisbury was committed to the old Tory policy of repression and coercion, orchestrated from now on by his nephew, A. J. Balfour. The failure of Parnell's attempts to obtain a Tenants' Relief Bill had been followed by another spate of evictions, and the Irish Land League responded with a new 'Plan of Campaign' that attempted to organize tenant farmers for collective bargaining with their landlords. The government responded to increased unrest in Ireland with a more draconian Crimes Act, which it used to jail, among others, the Lord Mayor of Dublin, the English poet William Scawen Blunt, and an Irish M.P., William O'Brien. There was also an attempt to discredit Parnell by publishing in *The Times* letters that supposedly showed him condoning murder. Parnell was eventually able to prove that they were forgeries, but the combination of repressive legislation and the attacks on their leaders drove the Irish to more extreme acts of lawlessness. Ireland was in a virtual state of civil war, and it was evident that Salisbury's and Balfour's policy of coercion without meaningful reform was not working. They were saved by the revelation of Parnell's affair with Mrs. O'Shea, which resulted in Gladstone's refusal to work with him and his loss of support among the Irish clergy. Parnell attempted to retain his leadership of the Irish cause, with the result that his parliamentary group split, and so did the Land League. Despite his death in 1891 the antagonistic divisions that had surfaced within the Irish nationalist movement continued to impair its effectiveness for several decades and ensured that the Irish Question would be left unsolved for another generation.

The Salisbury government was equally repressive in its dealings with dissent at home. Peaceful protest meetings were legal in England and opposition groups traditionally held open air assemblies in Hyde Park and in Trafalgar Square. In February 1886, at the height of the recession, an angry protest meeting of unemployed workers in Trafalgar Square that got out of hand resulted in the prosecution of four of its organizers, the socialist H. M Hyndman and three labor leaders (John Burns, H. H. Champion, and Jack Williams). They were subsequently acquitted by a sympathetic jury. An even larger demonstration, (50,000 strong), in Hyde Park later that month was attacked and broken up by police. The next year witnessed an even more flagrant abuse of power by the authorities: the 'Bloody Sunday' incident. A demonstration planned for Trafalgar Square on 13 November 1887 to call for the release of O'Brien was arbitrarily banned by the Commissioner of Police, Sir Charles Warren, but went ahead anyway. Police and troops attacked the demonstrators, killing two people and wounding over a hundred more, and the meeting's organizers, who included Burns and an M.P., R. Cunninghame Graham, were given heavy jail sentences. Needless to say, public assemblies to celebrate Queen Victoria's first Jubilee that same year were permitted without question. Burns would get his revenge by leading the successful London Dock Strike in 1889.

The Salisbury government, albeit mainly tacitly and by diplomacy rather than military action, encouraged and supported renewed colonial expansion, which was usually initiated by such ambitious entrepreneurs as Cecil Rhodes, William Mackinnon, and George Taubman Goldie. This was the time of the so-called 'scramble for Africa,' and in support of the commercial interests of the Royal Niger Company (1886), the British East Africa Company (1888), and the British South Africa Company (1889), Salisbury laid claim to substantial portions of both West and East Africa (including the regions that would become the colonies of Nigeria, Kenya, Uganda, and Rhodesia). These claims were subsequently approved by an international conference of imperialist powers held in Berlin in 1890.[12] In domestic matters Salisbury's legacy was much less weighty, his government's most important piece of legislation being the Local Government Act of 1888, which created county councils and borough councils, thus facilitating municipal reform projects (such as clean water supplies and sewage systems) where the local municipalities were willing to take on the financing of such schemes. On this matter, unlike many others, the Conservative government did not block reform, but by and large the second half of the 1880s were a time when the Victorian ideology of progress was but poorly implemented in practice.

Christianity and Its Critics

If ameliorism and imperialism were two prevalent Late Victorian ideologies, Christian evangelicalism was a third. On the surface Christianity in Victorian England was fragmented among a variety of institutions, ranging from the Catholic Church through Anglicanism to a variety of dissenting sects, including Methodists, Baptists, Presbyterians, and Quakers. In practice the divide between church and chapel was not so great, since most Victorian Christians believed—or at least practiced without question—a similar form of the religion. This involved a more or less literal reading of the Bible, belief in an afterlife and in salvation through prayer, good works, and keeping the Ten Commandments, and a commitment to family prayers and to Sunday worship, in which hymn-singing and the sermon played key roles. There were sections of the industrial cities where this ideology and conventional behavior had hardly penetrated, but in the main it had taken root, in one form or another, among the urban middle classes and among the better-off sections of the working classes, and it was dominant in rural England, Wales, Scotland, and Ulster. Yet just as the Conservatives were but lukewarm adherents of the liberal creed of progress through gradual reform, and many liberals shared Gladstone's wariness about imperialist expansionism, so too evangelicalism had its critics, both within and outside institutional Christianity. Within the Anglican Church it was challenged by a strong minority movement, Anglo-Catholicism, which demanded a return to a sacramental theology and to worship expressed through music and ceremony. At the other end of the theological spectrum, more liberal Christian thinkers recognized that the King James edition of the New Testament, a magnificent but faulty translation of a Latin translation of the original *koine* Greek, could not be relied on as the literal word of God, and that there were significant theological differences among the Gospels and between them and the Old Testament. Noticeable too was a renewed interest in theosophy, which asserted that all the world's religions shared a common core and aimed to research in a more empirical manner humankind's latent faculties and connections with the spiritual world. The Theosophical Society had been founded by Helena Blavatsky and others in New York in 1875 and although its headquarters moved (with Blavatsky) to India four years later, an English wing was active in London by the early 1880s, and the man who was to become its most eloquent English spokesman, G. R. S. Mead, joined the movement at that time. Blavatsky launched her journal *Lucifer* and settled in London in 1887, and before long Mead and Annie Besant had both joined her inner circle. Their influence was as yet small but they symbolized the Late Victorian search for a more rational and ecumenical form of spirituality than that offered by conventional Christianity.[13]

Evangelicalism was also under covert attack by those who disliked its anti-hedonistic streak, which it had inherited from seventeenth-century Puritanism but which had been reinforced by Methodism and the temperance movement. It is perhaps going too far to identify a hedonist movement in Late Victorian England, but there was something of a reaction against asceticism as an ideal and against Sunday observance as a rigid practice. The Prince of Wales was not only the leader of fashionable London society but also very popular with the masses, and his lifestyle (which included Sunday evening dinner parties, gambling, and a certain laxity in the matter of sexual liaisons) hardly accorded with conventional mores. On a more intellectual and artistic level there was the cult of aestheticism. Walter Pater was the acknowledged spokesman of the aesthetic movement, and he published his greatest work, *Marius the Epicurean*, in 1885, followed later in the decade by *Imaginary Portraits* and *Appreciations: with an Essay on Style*. The world of Victorian art and literature lost Dante Gabriel Rossetti in 1882 (he published his last literary collection, *Ballads and Sonnets*, in 1881), but Algernon Charles Swinburne recovered from a severe bout of alcoholism and poor health to embark on an extraordinarily productive decade in which he created much poetry (including *Tristram of Lyonesse and Other Poems* and *Poems and Ballads: Third Series*), historical dramas (*Mary Stuart*), tragedies (*Marino Faliero*), and literary criticism (studies of Shakespeare, Christopher Marlowe, Thomas Middleton, Ben Jonson, and Cyril Tourneur). Although his greatest works were yet to come, the young Oscar Wilde began his literary career in the late 1880s with *The Happy Prince and Other Tales*. The aesthetic movement was not anti-Christian *per se* but its ethos suggested an indifference to conventional Victorian morality that paralleled the Prince of Wales' lifestyle and, in a similar fashion, helped undermine its pervasive dominance.[14]

More radical and overtly confrontational were the critiques of biblical orthodoxy made by such prestigious humanists as Matthew Arnold and Thomas Huxley, whose skepticism reinforced doubts created by the unresolved clash between science and religion. Arnold was one of the few mid-Victorian sages who was still active in the 1880s: Charles Dickens had died in 1870, John Stuart Mill in 1873, Thomas Carlyle in 1881, and John Ruskin, although still a controversial professor of art history, was past his prime. Arnold's last attempt to explain his views on Christianity (*God and the Bible*) had been published in 1875, but his swansong, *Essays in Criticism, Second Series* appeared as late as 1888. There was no shortage of other thinkers ready and willing to debate the controversial intellectual issues of the day. Because of the many technological advances made possible by discoveries in physics and chemistry, the natural sciences had great prestige in Late Victorian England, and a positivist climate was evident in the new social sciences, including political economy, the still youthful discipline of sociology, and the emergent study of folklore (the Folklore Society was founded in 1878). The continued influence of John Stuart Mill's books, especially *Utilitarianism* and *Principles of Political Economy*, and of the writings of Comteans such as Frederic Harrison, president of the English Positivist Committee from 1880 to 1905, demonstrated that the Enlightenment ideal of a comprehensive science of society was far from dead in Victorian England.

Neither was the controversy over evolution and its implications for religion. Far from it. Although it was now over twenty years since Darwin had published *On the Origin of Species* (1859) only a decade had passed since the appearance of *The Descent of Man*, which spelled out more clearly the implications of discoveries in the fields of paleontology and biology. Thomas Huxley, who had been labeled "Darwin's bulldog" after the publication of his forthright *Man's Place in Nature* (1863), continued to engage his clerical opponents in the pages of such periodicals as the *Fortnightly Review* and *The Nineteenth Century*. It was becoming more and more difficult to square the circle of scientific skepticism and biblical fundamentalism, although it was as yet unfashionable to admit outright to atheism or even agnosticism. Huxley had already coined the latter term, however, and a handful of other leading intellectuals, including Harrison, Matthew

Arnold, and the young dramatist and literary critic George Bernard Shaw, could obviously be counted as secular humanists rather than Christians. Hardly surprisingly, the issue of religious doubt was one taken up by Victorian novelists, of whom one of the most popular was Mary (Mrs. Humphrey) Ward, the niece of Matthew Arnold. Her most successful book, *Robert Elsmere* (1888), evoked the crisis of Victorian faith and portrayed the various alternatives, ranging from the Oxford movement to Christian socialism, open to her hero, an earnest clergyman assailed by qualms about the truth and efficacy of mainstream Anglicanism. Gladstone himself reviewed it most enthusiastically.

In the late 1870s Christian socialism was temporarily in decline due to the death of its most influential mid-Victorian theorist, F. D. Maurice, but Frederick Furnivall, Stewart Headlam, and John Clifford each took up the cause and it was soon making headway again. However, neither Headlam nor Clifford would pen their most influential writings until the next decade and the movement, condemned by the Anglican hierarchy, was still mainly confined to Nonconformists.[15] It also had a formidable rival in the Salvation Army, formed by William Booth in 1878 but named only in 1880. Christians were not the only ones to concentrate their efforts on helping (and trying to convert) the working classes. Another important development in the 1880s, with which William Morris and George Bernard Shaw (among others) were involved, was the resurgence of secular socialism. The Marxist wing of this took an organizational form in 1881 with the foundation of the Democratic Federation by H. M. Hyndman, a leading English disciple of Karl Marx. It was later renamed the Social Democratic Federation, and Morris joined it in 1883, although he soon left to create his own Socialist League the next year. 1884 also saw the beginnings of the Fabian Society, in which Shaw would coexist uneasily with Annie Besant and Sidney and Beatrice Webb; the Fabians' first influential collection, *Fabian Essays*, was published in 1889. During these years, too, Edward Carpenter developed his own eccentric but imaginative version of communal socialism, an attempt to fuse some of the best elements from the thought of Walt Whitman, John Ruskin, Henry David Thoreau, and even the *Bhagavadgita*. Although dismissed by most as an eccentric, Carpenter was simply ahead of his time. Most of the progressive causes with which he was associated, including women's rights, sexual liberation, vegetarianism, anti-vivisection, and environmentalism, would come to the fore only in the next century.[16] Morris was another of the influences on Carpenter's eclectic vision. At his most militant in the late 1880s, Morris took time from the Arts and Crafts movement to write *The Dream of John Ball*, which was first published in serial form in *Commonweal* (1886-1887), and then his even more popular *News from Nowhere*, which would appear in the same periodical in 1890.[17]

Literature

The Late Victorian novelist whose works, in the tradition of Charles Dickens but strongly influenced by the realism of Honoré de Balzac and the naturalism of Emile Zola, most painstakingly set out to illustrate the plight of the urban lower classes was George Gissing. His first novel, *Workers in the Dawn*, was published in 1880, followed by (among others) *Demos* in 1886 and *The Nether World* in 1889, although his two most famous works (*New Grub Street* and *Born in Exile*) appeared early in the next decade.[18] In contrast to the urban focus of Gissing's novels, that of Thomas Hardy was rural, his fictional Wessex being primarily based on his native county of Dorset. Hardy had emerged as a major literary figure—he was a prolific poet and an occasional dramatist as well as a novelist and short story writer—in the 1870s, and one of his finest novels of "character and environment" (his own descriptor), *The Return of the Native*, had been published in 1878. During the next decade his output included two more works of this type, *The Mayor of Casterbridge* (1886) and *The Woodlanders* (1886), as well as a collection of short stories in the same vein, *Wessex Tales* (1888). He also wrote two novels that he characterized as "romances," *The Trumpet Major* (1880), one of his most popular works, and *Two on a Tower* (1882), which conventional opinion regarded as too daring. Hardy's strong sense of suffering and injustice and his ironic vision of humanity's struggle against an indifferent and implacable force of nature were often denounced as immoral and excessively pessimistic, and his work certainly undercut any naïve faith in progress.[19]

The Anglo-Irish novelist George Moore also had trouble with critics' prudery and faced censorship by circulating libraries, his first novel, *A Modern Lover* (1883), evoking the same disapproval as *Two on a Tower*. Moore retaliated with an outspoken defense of artistic freedom and of the literary technique of realism/naturalism. The influence of Balzac and Zola is evident in his novels in the 1880s: *A Mummer's Wife* (1884), *A Drama in Muslin* (1886), and *A Mere Accident* (1887) were each explorations of human character in different social environments, while *Confessions of a Young Man* (1888) was autobiographical in nature.[20] Also preoccupied with the study of character were George Meredith and Henry James. Meredith was a well-established figure on the Victorian literary scene by the 1880s since the novel for which he is chiefly remembered, *The Egoist*, had appeared in 1879. It was followed the next year by *The Tragic Comedians*, although it was only with *Diana of the Crossways* in 1885 that Meredith achieved widespread popularity among the reading public.[21] Henry James, an American who had taken up residency in London, had written his first important novel, *Roderick Hudson*, in the mid-1870s, but the next decade saw him creating two of his most celebrated works, *A Portrait of a Lady* (1881) and *Princess Casamassima* (1886), as well as *The Bostonians* (1886) and *The Aspern Papers* (1888).[22]

All the novelists mentioned so far wrote works that employed fiction to explore questions of significance, either on the micro level of how human beings respond to personal crises or in an attempt to raise and comment on major social issues. Less weighty in their approach were a group of best-selling writers whose books were intended primarily as entertainment, although this did not always rule out an underlying serious purpose. A good example of an author who deliberately wrote on two levels is Robert Louis Stevenson. His very popular trio of *Treasure Island*, *Kidnapped*, and *Dr. Jekyll and Mr. Hyde* appeared between 1883 and 1886, with *The Master of Ballantrae* following in 1889.[23] Another master of the adventure novel—he wrote thirty-four of them in total—was Henry Rider Haggard, whose exciting tales of *King Solomon's Mines*, *She*, and *Allan Quartermain* were among the most read books of the years 1886-1887.[24] Haggard conjured the landscape, wildlife, tribal society, and mystery of Africa, while Rudyard Kipling was the Late Victorian writer who most sensitively portrayed the sights and sounds of British India. He was only beginning his long literary career at this time, but two of his early works, *Departmental Ditties* (1886) and *Plain Tales from the Hills* (1888) were already available.[25] One other popular Late Victorian writer must be noticed, although his work is largely forgotten now. Sabine Baring-Gould's *Mehalah* was one of the best-selling novels of 1880, and he followed it with nearly thirty more, including, during the 1880s, *John Herring* (1883), *Red Spider* (1887), and *Richard Cable, the Lighterman* (1888). A polymath of incredible energy, he also wrote many works on religion, travel, local history, folklore, and, as we shall see, played a major role in the Late Victorian folksong revival.[26]

The Fine Arts

If borrowing books, particularly novels, from public libraries or such circulating libraries as Mudie's, Smith's, or Boots, was the prevalent intellectual pastime of middle-class Victorians, particularly women, another favorite activity—albeit more of a minority interest—was viewing works of art at local galleries.The fine arts played a much more important role in Victorian culture than they do nowadays. The mainstream of Victorian painting in the 1880s, as exhibited at the Royal Academy, was conservative, with portraiture and landscape painting its mainstays. Ruskin's *Modern Painters* had successfully championed the works of John Constable and Joseph Turner and they were now widely accepted as masters, but no major successors emerged to dominate the field in the way they had in the early Victorian era.[27] There were some very competent minor figures, however, an example being John Singer Sargent, a popular portraitist and painter of flowers and gardens. His best works included *Carnation, Lily, Lily, Rose* (1886) and the striking *Ellen Terry as Lady Macbeth* (1889). Some of his paintings reflect an interesting minority current that is evident in the visual arts of the Late Victorian period: a fascination with the techniques and 'look' of Chinese and Japanese calligraphy and landscape painting.[28]

Perhaps the most noteworthy mainstream painter to develop her art in the 1880s was Helen Allingham, although her style was conventional and her paintings mainly depicted landscapes or groups of figures.[29] She is important because she was fascinated by the old buildings of rural England, especially cottages dating from the Middle Ages or the sixteenth century. Her family scenes included *In the Hayloft* (1880) and *The Children's Tea* (1882) but she is chiefly remembered for her visual records of country lanes and domestic houses, including *In Whitley Village* (1884), *In Wormley Wood* (1886), and *Cottage at Chiddingford* (1889). Allingham's work was not grand enough for the Royal Academy, and the variant on traditional representational painting that found most institutional favor in this decade was the neo-classical style of Frederic Leighton and Lawrence Alma-Tadema, who also favored subjects drawn from antiquity. Examples of Leighton's work from this period include *Memories* (1883), *Antigone* (1884) and *Desdemona* (1888),[30] while Alma-Tadema, whose grasp of perspective and technique were outstanding, created *The Triumph of Titus* in 1885, although it would be another decade before his masterpiece, *A Coign of Vantage*, would appear.[31]

Leighton and Alma-Tadema were both influenced by the Pre-Raphaelites, and by the 1880s the work of this group of artistic rebels had become more widely accepted, with their shows usually held in the Grosvenor Gallery. Stylistically their art laid emphasis on the meticulous depiction of detail combined with a pictorial use of color that emulated medieval art. Their subjects were often religious or drawn from medieval Romance. [32]As mentioned earlier, one of the school's most celebrated members, Dante Gabriel Rossetti, died in 1882, his last important painting being *The Day-Dream* (1880).[33] Other artists associated with the movement continued to paint. For example, George Frederick Watt's contributions in these years included *Hope* (1885) and *Sir Galahad* (1888), while William Holman Hunt painted *The Lady of Shalott* in 1886-87. The prolific John William Waterhouse also chose *The Lady of Shalott* as a subject in 1888, the same year he created *Cleopatra*; *Ophelia* followed in 1889, while his earlier paintings included *Diogenes* (1882) and *Magic Circle* (1886). The leader of the school and its most distinctive artist, however, remained Edward Burne-Jones. His works included *The Mill* (1882), *The Wheel of Fortune* (1883), *King Cophetua and the Beggar Maid* (1884), and *The Baleful Head* (1887).

If the Pre-Raphaelite school was on the verge of assimilation into the mainstream of Victorian art, the same could not be said for the French Impressionists (who had staged their first exhibition in Paris in 1874), or James Whistler, the American artist working in London who most closely shared their ideas and techniques. Whistler's series of *Nocturnes* (including *Nocturne in Black and Gold: The Fallen Rocket*) had been shown at the Grosvenor Gallery in 1877 and had elicited a storm of condemnation by art critics, including, perhaps surprisingly, John Ruskin, who had notoriously accused the artist of flinging a paint-pot at the canvas. The indignant Whistler sued for defamation and won his case, only to be awarded the derisory damages of one farthing. He retired, bankrupt, to the continent to lick his wounds, but returned to London in 1880 to exhibit his *Venice* etchings, while later in the decade he produced one of his finest paintings, *Sarasate* (1886), a portrait of virtuoso violinist Martin Sarasate.

The other most innovative artistic trend in the 1880s was the growth of Art Nouveau. Inheriting its ideals from both Pre-Raphaelitism and the Arts and Crafts movement of the mid-Victorian era, Art Nouveau sought to re-beautify domestic and public objects: book covers, wall-paper, curtain material, lampshades, lamp-stands, and statuary, among other things. It was also noticeably influenced by the vogue for *Chinoiserie* and the renewed interest in all things Japanese that produced, in a different art form, *The Mikado*. Art Nouveau's early proponents included Walter Crane, Arthur Mackmurdo, Charles Vosey, and Alfred Gilbert. Notable examples of their work included Crane's *Baby's Bouquet* (1878), Mackmurdo's *Peacock* wallpaper (1882) and the title page of his book *Wren's City Churches* (1883), Vosey's *Design for a Printed Textile* (1888), and, most celebrated of all, Gilbert's *Eros*, begun in 1887 and erected in Piccadilly Circus in 1893. During the next decade the movement would find in Aubrey Beardsley its most talented and famous exponent, but that was still largely in the future. In the 1880s it was still rather difficult to distinguish the products of this new school from those of the more venerable Arts and Crafts movement from which it had sprung.[34]

The leading spokesman for Arts and Crafts, William Morris, while also turning his attention to literature and socialist thought, continued to work as an artist/craftsman, moving his factory to Merton Abbey in 1881 and opening a shop in Manchester two years later.[35] A good example of his work in textile design during this period is *The Honeysuckle* (1883). He continued to collaborate with the Pre-Raphaelites, executing, for example, Burne-Jones' designs for stained-glass windows, including *David's Charge to Solomon* and *The Worship of the Magi* for a church in Boston, Massachusetts. He also worked with the leading potter of the age, William De Morgan, providing him with designs for ceramic tiles. De Morgan was well aware of Art Nouveau, as his own designs, such as *Plate with Gazelle* (made sometime between 1882 and 1888), demonstrate.[36]

The Arts and Crafts movement also continued to provide a more comfortable and less grandiose stylistic alternative to the dominant force in Victorian architecture, the Gothic revival. Philip Webb, who had collaborated with Morris on the famous Red House in Bexleyheath, designed various beautiful town houses in Kensington and Chelsea, and one of his best country houses, Clouds (in Wiltshire), was built during the early 1880s, while at the end of the decade he designed Standen in East Sussex (built in 1891-94). Webb influenced Richard Norman Shaw, the architect who emerged in the latter decades of the century as the designer most associated with the 'Old English' style of country house, with its mullioned windows and tall brick chimneys. His buildings in the 1880s included Craigside in Northumberland and Adcote in Shropshire. A more modest version of the style, intended for smaller buildings such as town houses, came to be known as 'Queen Anne'; domestic examples are to be found in Hampstead, Chelsea, and Queen's Gate (London) and Newnham College, Cambridge. Most of the leading proponents of Victorian Gothic, such as George Gilbert Scott, William Butterfield, and Alfred Waterhouse, were past their prime by the 1880s, but the Gothic Revival showed no signs of abating and it was carried on by Scott's son, George Gilbert Scott Jr., G. F. Bodley, and John Loughborough Pearson (among others). The style worked best for grand buildings such as churches, colleges, town halls, and, above all, cathedrals. Examples built (mainly) in the 1880s include the beautiful Cattistock church in Dorset, Keble College, Oxford (both by the Scotts), and one of the most impressive Victorian recreations of medieval religious architecture, Truro Cathedral (by Pearson).[37]

Music

Neither British painting nor British architecture was strongly influenced in the 1880s by developments on the continent of Europe. British music, on the other hand, although it evolved in its own way, kept in touch with some of the most important developments across the Channel, particularly those in Germany and Austria but to a lesser degree also in France, Norway, and Russia.[38] The influence of foreign composers came in different ways. It was partly the work of European musicians such as Clara Schumann, Josef Joachim, Hans Richter, and Charles Hallé, who either toured England extensively or came to live and work permanently in the country. Younger English composers and instrumentalists studied abroad, and brought back news (and scores) of important works they had encountered. And there were some European composers, such as Richard Wagner, whose revolutionary music caused such a stir that it was impossible to ignore. Wagner had completed the *Ring* cycle with *Götterdämmerung* in 1873, but it was not until 1882 that his last major opera, *Parsifal*, was performed. It stimulated many pilgrimages to Bayreuth to hear it (and *Tristan und Isolde* and the *Ring*) performed. Wagner's disciple Anton Bruckner was not yet as well known in England, but he wrote three of his major symphonies, Nos. 6, 7, and 8, as well as his *Te Deum*, during the 1880s. The young Gustav Mahler composed his first symphony in 1888, preceded by his first three song cycles.

Much better known in England were the compositions of Johannes Brahms. Josef Joachim, a virtuoso violinist, championed his Violin Concerto in D (1878) and his Double Concerto (1887) as well as various chamber works, but Brahms also composed his second Piano Concerto in 1881, and followed this with his third and fourth symphonies in 1883 and 1885 respectively. Hans Richter did much to make not only Wagner's but Richard Strauss's compositions known in England; Strauss began writing his celebrated tone poems in the mid-1880s with *Aus Italien*, but *Macbeth*, *Don Juan*, and *Death and Transfiguration* followed in quick succession during 1887-89. The only other continental composer to rival in popularity Wagner and Brahms was Edvard Grieg. He had composed the incidental music to Ibsen's play *Peer Gynt* in 1875, but it was only when the first *Peer Gynt Suite* (which included "Morning Mood") was issued in 1888 that he became a household name in England. The best-loved Russian composer of the time was Pyotr Tchaikovsky; he composed his Symphony No. 5 in 1888, and the ballet music for *Sleeping Beauty* the next year. Nikolai Rimsky-Korsakov had in the meanwhile completed Modest Mussorgsky's unfinished opera *Khovaschina* in 1881 and written his own successful opera, *The Snow Maiden*, the same year, but it was only later in the decade with such shorter pieces as *Capriccio Espagnol* and *Scheherezade* that he reached a wider audience. In the world of opera the elderly Giuseppe Verdi, whose *Otello* appeared in 1887, continued to rival Wagner and the Russians, while a revival of French opera at the hands of Georges Bizet (*Carmen*, 1875) and Léo Delibes (*Lakmé*, 1883) showed the diversity of approach possible within the genre.

These events on the continent influenced and formed the background to parallel developments in the United Kingdom. The 1880s witnessed the growing impetus to reform and renewal that was already evident, albeit in an embryonic way, in the English art music of the previous decade. Six British composers were collectively responsible for this resurgence, three in a preliminary way and three more directly. The oldest of the group was George Macfarren, professor of music at Cambridge University, Principal of the Royal Academy of Music since 1875, and knighted for his services to English music in 1883. Much of his best work was already done by this time, but he composed his oratorio *King David* (1883), two cantatas, and the opera *Kenilworth* during the 1880s. Macfarren's own music owed little to English folksong, but as a friend and collaborator of William Chappell's he had contributed piano arrangements to *Popular Music of the Olden Time*, and subsequently joined with Chappell and others to edit a selection of material from that two-volume opus as *Old English Ditties*.[39]

Frederic H. Cowen, a proficient pianist and conductor as well as a composer, was German-trained, and influenced by Mendelssohn, Liszt, and Brahms (he met the latter two while studying in Germany in the 1860s). He had burst onto the English music scene in 1869 with performances of his Piano Concerto in A minor and his Symphony No. 1, but it was his third symphony, the "Scandinavian," written in 1880 but first performed in Vienna in 1882, which would become his most popular work. Others of his symphonies included No. 4 "Welsh" (1884) and No. 5 "Cambridge" (1887), and an earlier Sinfonietta (1881). During this decade Cowen also composed several cantatas (including *The Deluge, St. Ursula*, and *St. John's Eve*) as well as two oratorios (*Ruth* and *Song of Thanksgiving*) and an opera (*Thorgrim*), but apart from his symphonies his most attractive works were shorter orchestral pieces such as the suites *The Language of Flowers* (1880) and *In the Olden Time* (1883), which showed off his flair for melody and colorful orchestration.[40]

Arthur Sullivan, the best known of all Late Victorian composers, was the most prolific supplier of musical works for the London stage in the 1880s. His partnership with W. S. Gilbert had first found commercial success with *Trial By Jury* in 1875 and had been consolidated by the enthusiastic reception for *HMS Pinafore* in 1878. The decade of the 1880s witnessed a succession of such comic operas at the newly built Savoy Theatre, the first to be lit by electricity: *Patience* (1881), *Iolanthe* (1882), *Princess Ida* (1884), *The Mikado* (1885), *Ruddigore* (1887), *The Yeomen of the Guard* (1888), and *The Gondoliers* (1889). These works were good for Sullivan's pocket-book, as were his many songs and drawing-room ballads, but they interfered with his ambitions as a serious art-music composer. By this time he had almost abandoned extended orchestral composition, although he did write some incidental music for *Macbeth* in 1888. However, he composed two odes (one a setting of Tennyson for the Colonial and Indian Exhibition in 1886), a sacred music drama, *The Mayor of Antioch* (1880), and a cantata, *The Golden Legend*, in 1886, while his *Te Deum* was performed at the Crystal Palace in 1887.[41]

Alexander Mackenzie took over from Macfarren as Principal of the Royal Academy of Music in 1888 and retained the position for thirty-six years. His teaching and administrative work curtailed his activity as a composer in later life, but in the 1880s he was highly prolific, writing cantatas (including *The Bride*, *Jason*, and *The Cottar's Saturday Night*), oratorios (*The Rose of Sharon*, 1884), odes (*A Jubilee Ode*, 1887), and two operas (*Colomba* and *The Troubadour*) as well as orchestral and instrumental works; the latter included *Rhapsodie écossaise* (1880), a Violin Concerto (1885), *Overture to Twelfth Night* (1888), and *Pibroch Suite* (1889). If Berlioz, Lizst, and Wagner were his biggest musical influences, Mackenzie, a Scotsman, also valued Scottish traditional music and loved the poetry of Robert Burns, and several of his best works, most notably *Scenes in the Scottish Highlands* for solo piano, *The Cottar's Saturday Night*, *Pibroch Suite*, and the opera *Colomba*, sought to create a distinctly Scottish form of art music. This nationalist ideal was not lost on his contemporaries Hubert Parry and Charles V. Stanford.[42]

A particularly significant event in the history of English music occurred in 1883—the opening of the Royal College of Music. This would provide a valuable alternative to the more conservative RAM for those seeking the best musical education available in the United Kingdom. It was no longer necessary to study abroad to become a proficient instrumentalist, singer, or composer. Two of the best professors at the Royal College were Parry and Stanford. Charles Villiers Stanford, the College's professor of composition and the conductor of its orchestra, was Anglo-Irish by origin, German-trained, and an admirer of Brahms, but he played an important role in the genesis of the English musical renaissance through his insistence on high standards and his influence on such students as Frank Bridge, George Butterworth, George Dyson, Ivor Gurney, Herbert Howells, John Ireland, Jack Moeran, and Ralph Vaughan Williams (among others). Although he also served as professor of music at Cambridge University, conducted the orchestra of the Cambridge University Music Society and for a while ran the Bach Choir, he still found time to write much of his best music during the 1880s. This included his 'Irish' symphony (No. 3, 1887), but it would not be until the 1900s that he composed the five Irish rhapsodies that best illustrated his vision of how art music might draw upon the traditional melodies of his homeland. The other symphonies he composed in the 1880s were his second, the Elegiac (1882), and No. 4 (1888), while other orchestral compositions included the incidental music to two ancient Greek plays, Euripides's *The Eumenides* (1885) and Sophocles's *Oedipus Tyrannus* (1887), and a festival overture *Queen of the Seas* (1888). Other significant works were a Cello Concerto (1880), a Piano Quintet (1886), and a Piano Trio (1889). A regular composer of large-scale choral works for festivals, Stanford's odes, oratorios and other works for chorus and orchestra included a Walt Whitman setting (*Elegiac Ode*), the biblical oratorio *The Three Holy Children*, and three Tennyson settings (*The Revenge: A Ballad of the Fleet*, *Carmen saeculare*, and *The Voyage of Maeldune*). He also hoped to re-establish British opera, composing three such works in this decade: *The Veiled Prophet of Khorassan* (first performed in Hanover in 1881), *Savonarola*, and *The Canterbury Pilgrims* (both of which were staged in London in 1884).[43]

Even more instrumental in the genesis of the English musical renaissance was Hubert Parry. Also German-trained, Parry began his musical career as an enthusiastic Wagnerian, attending a performance of the *Ring* cycle at Bayreuth in 1876 and seeing *Parsifal* three times in 1882. Employed as a sub-editor by George Grove for the first edition of the great *Dictionary of Music and Musicians*, he wrote over one hundred articles for the work, and this experience, combined with the quality of his early compositions, landed him the post of professor of music history at the Royal College of Music in 1883. He eventually became its director in 1895, and was knighted three years later. His career as a composer began in the mid-1870s but his first important orchestral work was the concert overture *Guillem de Cabestanh* (1878), which revealed his debt to Wagner, as did his early cantata, *Scenes from Prometheus Unbound* (1880). Parry soon developed into perhaps the greatest English symphonist before Elgar, composing his first symphony in 1882 and one of his most popular, the Cambridge (No. 2), the next year. Two more followed at the end of the decade, the English (No. 3) and the untitled fourth symphony, both composed in 1889. Other orchestral pieces included his incidental music to Aristophanes's *The Birds* (1883) and *Suite Moderne* (1886), while his most notable chamber work in these years was the Quintet in E flat (1884). Even more than Mackenzie and Stanford, Parry was an avid composer of choral music, much of it commissioned by leading choral festivals such as those at Gloucester, Leeds and Norwich. His choral odes included *The Glories of Our Blood and State* (1883), the hugely popular *Blest Pair of Sirens* (1887), and *Ode on St. Cecilia's Day* (1889), while he also wrote music for an Anglican evening service (*The Great*, 1881), an oratorio (*Judith*, 1888), and the cantata *L'Allegro ed Il Pensiero* (1890). His one attempt at opera, *Guenever* (1886), was regrettably rejected by the London opera houses. Like Stanford, Parry exerted a huge influence on a considerable number of young composers, and it was significant that he would be the individual invited to give the "Inaugural Address" to the first Annual General Meeting of the Folk-Song Society in February 1899. By then he was the grand old man of English music and had come to symbolize not only the resurgence of English music in the Late Victorian era but also the desire to see it rooted both in folksong and in older English art-music traditions.[44]

Ballad Editing

Before concluding this brief overview of Victorian social, political, intellectual, artistic, and musical life in the 1880s, there is one additional subject that needs to be addressed in order to provide background information that the reader will require later in the book. Ballad editing was a specialist topic in which only relatively few late Victorian intellectuals had any interest but it was of considerable importance to English folksong collectors. It tended to divide into two camps: those scholars who focused on traditional balladry, as found in manuscript collections and oral tradition, and those interested primarily in the print traditions accessible through collections of broadsheets and garlands. As we have seen in the previous chapter, the Victorian era had witnessed several attempts to compile and edit collections of traditional balladry, but by the Late Victorian era a consensus was building that none of these were sufficiently comprehensive or methodologically adequate. Paradoxically, the most important new development in the field of British traditional ballad studies occurred not in England, or even in another part of the British empire, but in the United States of America. It was the work of a Harvard philologist and professor of literature turned comparative folklorist, Francis James Child (1825-1896).

Francis James Child and *The English and Scottish Popular Ballads*

In 1857-59 Child had published the most comprehensive collection of narrative song texts compiled to that date. *English and Scottish Ballads* was a sprawling, eclectic work that ran to eight volumes, and the second edition, which appeared in 1860, was published in England as well as America.[45] During the next two decades, despite several attempts, no English ballad editor came close to rivaling Child's achievement. Yet Child himself soon became dissatisfied with the work. The lack of tunes eventually came to bother him, but that was a problem which he recognized only belatedly and was never able to address fully. The authenticity of certain texts that he had reprinted was the worrying question that came more rapidly to dominate his thinking. Before long, he decided that his great compendium was fatally flawed, and that the only thing to be done was to start over, right from the very beginning. It was a courageous judgment, and one that entailed adopting a quite different approach to editing English-language ballad texts than anyone (including Child himself) had ever employed before. Essentially Child had to retrain and retool himself as a folklorist rather than a literary historian. Since he was aware of recent publications by European folklorists, he was not working entirely without precedents, and he solicited (and received) advice from the Danish ballad scholar Svend Grundtvig. Nonetheless, it was Child himself who had the imagination to conceive and plan the new project, and it was he who had the fortitude to carry it out. Doing so involved decades of hunting down authentic and variant texts, and a huge amount of research into the sources of the ballads and their parallels in other (mainly European) languages.

So for the decade of the 1860s Child worked hard to find the manuscript sources that he needed. He investigated the primary documents that previous generations of ballad editors had utilized, and he systematically attempted to purchase them or to have them copied. By the mid-1870s his perspective on traditional balladry and his approach to ballad editing had changed significantly. Influenced by William Motherwell's introductory essay in *Minstrelsy: Ancient and Modern* and by Grundtvig's *Danmarks gamle Folkviser*,[46] he had now become a folklorist. He was in the process of developing a theory about the nature of a "true popular ballad," a concept that undoubtedly owed a lot to Grundtvig, and he had come to differentiate sharply between 'popular' (i.e., traditional) and broadside ballads. Although he recognized that a ballad editor had perforce to rely sometimes on broadside texts (or had to include them as variants if he was aiming at completeness of coverage), he was more hostile to broadsides than he had been in the late 1850s. Unaware of the wealth of material that could still be recovered from oral tradition, he looked primarily to unpublished, hand-written documents, in particular to the Percy folio manuscript and to the manuscripts on which the published Scottish ballad collections had been based. The task was a daunting one and more than two decades elapsed before he was ready to begin publishing the fruits of his research.

Child's new collection was called *The English and Scottish Popular Ballads,* and it was issued in ten parts (subsequently bound in five volumes) between 1882 and 1898.[47] He had not wanted to begin publication until he had "at command every valuable copy of every known ballad" and although he had not quite achieved this goal by the early 1880s, he believed that he was very close, remarking in the preface that "what is still lacking is believed to bear no great proportion to what is in hand, and may soon come in, besides."[48] In the event, more did come in, resulting in the need for a section titled "Additions and Corrections" at the end of each newly published volume. Although the new compilation turned out not to be quite as exhaustive as Child had hoped, it was nonetheless seen as definitive, and it has dominated the field of ballad scholarship ever since.

The change of title was significant. Child's new goal was to make a comprehensive collection of *authentic* old folk-ballads. He called such ballads 'popular' to distinguish them from literary productions by the educated classes. He could not define precisely what was and what was not a ballad, nor exactly what he meant by popular, but he did have an intuitive sense of what he meant: traditional narrative songs that had been part of rural folklore. One might have expected to find at the beginning of the first volume of *The English and Scottish Popular Ballads* a preface in which Child explained his concept of 'popular' balladry and his notion of a ballad era that antedated the emergence of printed literature as an art form. But the looked-for introduction was conspicuous only by its absence. To get some sense of the theoretical underpinning of Child's new project one had to consult an entry titled "Ballad Poetry" that he had written for Rossiter Johnson's *Universal Cyclopedia* in 1874.[49] In this article, which Johnson (presumably with Child's acquiescence) reprinted in 1884 in a new edition of his encyclopedia, Child claimed that 'popular' balladry was a "distinct and very important species of poetry," that it was historically "anterior to the poetry of art," and that it reflected a time-period (the ballad era) *before* the emergence of significant differences between upper- and lower-class culture. He explained the genesis and special characteristics of the 'popular' ballad as follows:

> Whenever a people in the course of its development reaches a certain intellectual and moral stage, it will feel an impulse to express itself in literature, and the form of expression to which it is first impelled is...not prose but verse, and in fact narrative verse. The condition of society in which a truly national or popular poetry appears, explains the character of such poetry. It is a condition in which the people are not divided by political organization and book-culture into markedly distinct classes, in which consequently there is such community of ideas and feelings that the whole people form an individual...The fundamental characteristic of popular ballads is therefore the absence of subjectivity and self-consciousness. Though...a man and not a people has composed them, still the author counts for nothing, and it is not by mere accident, but with the best reasons, that they have come down to us anonymous...The primitive ballad then is popular, not in the sense of something arising from and suited to the lower orders of a people. As yet, no sharp distinction of high and low exists, in respect to knowledge, desires, and tastes.[50]

In the Balkans, Child suggested, this kind of relatively classless society still existed and the ballad era was still going strong in Serbia, Bosnia, and Montenegro. In Western Europe it was a different story: the ballad era was long over, although Child believed that there was compelling evidence that it had once existed. He postulated that there had been two periods in which popular balladry had flourished: the first in the early Middle Ages, and a second at the end of the medieval era. Traces of the 'primitive' balladry of the early Middle Ages had been preserved in the epic literature of various European countries, with Denmark, Norway, and Spain possessing the best collections. In England the first phase was poorly represented, although Child claimed that several extant narrative poems in Anglo-Saxon "might be called ballads" and he speculated that there had once been outlaw ballads celebrating the deeds of Hereward the Wake and Fulk Fitz-Warin. The earliest Robin Hood ballads, although they dated from the fourteenth century, were late exemplars of the same phenomenon.[51]

Child dated the second phase of the ballad era to the late Middle Ages and the early Renaissance. "During the fifteenth and the early part of the sixteenth centuries," he wrote, "a second growth of the genuine popular song appears, some of it springing, doubtless, out of shoots from the old stock which had lived through this long interval, some of it a fresh product of the age." He was quick to emphasize that the balladry of this period still complied with his idiosyncratic definition of the term 'popular.' "These [late medieval and Renaissance era] ballads," he claimed, "were popular in the large and strict sense; that is, they were the creation and the manifestation of the whole people, great and humble, who were still one in all essentials, having the same belief, the same ignorance, and the same tastes, and living in much closer relations than now." It was only after the invention of printing and the Reformation that the educated classes developed a more sophisticated literature of their own and left what had been a common treasure, the corpus of popular balladry, to the lower classes, "the ignorant or unschooled mass."[52]

What Child's perspective meant, when applied to England, was that although there were evidently a few ballads that could be ascribed to the late Middle Ages, most traditional balladry must have been created during the early Tudor era. By the reign of Elizabeth I (1558-1603) class divisions were clearly evident in English society and poetry had already become an art form, so by then even the second phase of the ballad era was over. And certainly by the seventeenth century—the golden era of the broadside—the split into 'high' and 'low' literature was well established, and popular balladry (in Child's sense) was long gone, except as a derivative remnant of an earlier age.

Child was at pains to emphasize that broadside balladry was *not* an expression of the ballad era and that it must not be confused with popular balladry. On this point he was quite categorical, insisting that "the popular ballad is not originally the product or the property of the lower orders of the people." Indeed, his repudiation of the broadside was unequivocal:

> The vulgar ballads of our day, the "broadsides" which were printed in such large numbers in England and elsewhere in the sixteenth century or later, belong to a different genus; they are products of a low kind of *art*, and most of them are, from a literary point of view, thoroughly despicable and worthless.[53]

For Child, then, broadside balladry and popular balladry were distinct species. He wanted to have as little to do with the former as possible. He was determined to rule out ballads *composed* (as opposed to transmitted or reworked) by broadside ballad-mongers, just as he ruled out those created by poets, intellectuals, and other professional writers. That meant excluding items he suspected to be fraudulent (i.e., imitation ballads passed off as 'ancient' and texts rewritten extensively by poet-editors such as Thomas Percy), and also all original compositions by commercial ballad-writers.

However, theory was one thing, practice was another. In reality, Child could not entirely avoid either literary ballads or broadsides. He did include certain literary versions of ballads, such as Sir Walter Scott's, when he believed them to be closely based on authentic originals, but only under sufferance and when he had no access to the primary sources on which they were based. As we have seen, his intention was to work as far as possible from original manuscripts, and he was obviously very proud of his use of a large number of manuscript collections, especially those created or owned by Percy, White, Herd, Scott, Jamieson, Kinloch, Motherwell, and Buchan. Child was also dependent on the holdings of various libraries, especially the British Museum, Cambridge University Library, and the Bodleian Library in Oxford, not only for manuscript collections but also for collections of broadsides. He was discriminating in his use of the latter, including them only when he believed them to derive from 'popular' tradition, yet he included over two hundred and fifty texts taken from broadsides or garlands. He also included hundreds of texts from printed sources, which he listed chronologically in the final Part of the work. Finally, his sources included a certain amount of "gathering [direct] from [oral] tradition," but he acknowledged this latter component to be "meagre, and generally of indifferent quality."[54]

In *The English and Scottish Popular Ballads,* Child identified three hundred and five old narrative ballads that he believed derived from popular (i.e., rural lower class) tradition, and he also found manuscript sources of tunes for forty-six of them. The tunes were not integrated with the texts, but were relegated to Part X, which was not published until 1898, after Child's death. Perhaps the biggest problem facing its editor was how to organize the collection. Dissatisfied with his earlier attempt at grouping ballads by subject matter, Child searched for an alternative method of organization. Attracted by Chappell's historical approach in *Popular Music of the Olden Time,* he decided to attempt a chronological structure in which the oldest of the ancient ballads would come first and the most recent additions to the genre would be placed at the end. The problem with this idea was that it was extremely difficult to carry out. Dating individual ballads, even approximately, was often well-nigh impossible. Child's friend and mentor, the Danish ballad scholar Svend Grundtvig, argued that the metrical structure of ballads had evolved over the centuries, and so the verse-forms of the texts provided clues to the approximate age of the ballads. Attracted by the convenience of this (albeit dubious) theory, Child apparently tried to adopt it, although it conflicted with another one of his principles, which was that all variants of a ballad should be printed together, notwithstanding their different verse forms and putative ages. He acknowledged in his preface that *The English and Scottish Popular Ballads* "closely followed the plan of Grundtvig's *Old Popular Ballads of Denmark,*" and fulsomely praised Grundtvig's work as a ballad scholar, thanking him for his "criticism and advice...and aid in many ways."[55]

One very useful idea that Child did borrow from Grundtvig was the simple but clever device of identifying clusters of similar texts with a single ballad number but then labeling each version with an upper case letter and each variant occurrence of that version with a lower case letter. This is best explained by means of a simple example. The oldest extant version of the cluster of ballad texts titled "The Fair Flower of Northumberland" dated from the late sixteenth century, having been printed in Deloney's *Pleasant History of John Winchcomb, in his younger years called Jacke of Newberie,* so this became 9Aa, whereas a very similar (and derivative) variant printed in Ritson's *Ancient Songs* was labeled 9Ab. The next oldest version of the same ballad, Kinloch's manuscript version, became 9Ba, whereas the variant text printed by Kinloch in *Ancient Scottish Ballads* (which had been taken down from Miss E. Beattie's recitation) became 9Bb. Child similarly labeled a third version of the ballad (from Buchan's manuscript notebooks) 9Ca, and the virtually identical variant printed in Buchan's *Ballads of the North of Scotland* became 9Cb. A fragment in Motherwell's manuscript collection received the label 9D, and a fifth version found in Robert White's papers was labeled 9E. In short, Child's numbering system was systematic but flexible, although, of course, it was premised in each instance on an editorial judgment about which ballad texts belonged to a given ballad cluster. It also required in many instances a difficult judgment as to whether a particular text was a new version of a ballad or merely a variant of a version already given a capital letter.

Child was nothing if not thorough, and he aimed to make *The English and Scottish Popular Ballads* exhaustive and definitive. Although he was not a lover of broadsides—he called the Pepys and Roxburghe collections "veritable dung-hills, in which, only after a great deal of sickening grubbing, one finds a very moderate jewel"[56]—yet, as we have seen, he included for the sake of completeness over two hundred and fifty texts taken from broadsides or garlands. He also accepted hundreds of texts from printed sources, which he listed chronologically in the final part of the work, beginning with an item dating from the early sixteenth century, the anonymous *A Gest of Robyn Hode*. This meant that, in the case of some ballads, he ended up with a very large number of variants: "The Twa Sisters," for example, runs to the letter U, which gives a singer twenty-one alternative texts to choose between, although admittedly some are mere fragments. A logical corollary of the decision to print all versions plus significant variants of those versions was that Child was freed from the invidious task of deciding which single text of a ballad was the best one, and from the temptation to collate texts in order to provide a complete version. But it meant that for each ballad one ended up with a cluster of (often imperfect) texts rather than a single definitive version. This approach to ballad editing thus sacrificed 'singability' to historical accuracy, with the result that *The English and Scottish Popular Ballads* would never be much use as a songbook. It was a case of losing on the roundabout what one gained on the swings.

Given the size of *The English and Scottish Popular Ballads*, it is impossible here even to list fully its contents, but one needs some sense of what it contained in order to appreciate the sweep and depth of Child's scholarship. Child, of course, was interested in Scottish balladry as well as English, and a higher proportion of his texts derived from Scottish sources. As mentioned, Part I of Volume 1 was issued in 1882 and comprised twenty-eight ballads, presumably the ones that Child considered the oldest that had been preserved through oral tradition, in early manuscripts, or in broadsides. His notes reveal that he considered all these texts to have early medieval roots—in part because of their numerous parallels to similar medieval ballads and tales found in other European countries—but that he was unable to date them to specific centuries. He assigned pride of place to "Riddles Wisely Expounded," followed by "The Elfin Knight," "The Fause Knight upon the Road," and "Lady Isabel and the Elf-Knight." Other traditional ballads with some connection to the medieval era (or at least to the transitional period between the late Middle Ages and the Renaissance) in Part I included "Earl Brand," "The Fair Flower of Northumberland," "The Cruel Brother," "Hind Horn," "The Three Ravens," and the incest ballad "Sheath and Knife." Other well-known narrative song texts in this first selection of ballad clusters included "The Twa Sisters," "Lord Randal," "Edward," and "The Cruel Mother," while there were three religious ballads: "The Maid and the Palmer," "St. Stephen and Herod," and "Judas."

Part II (the second half of the first volume) of *The English and Scottish Popular Ballads* followed in 1884, comprising ballad clusters numbers 29-53. It began with a body of material that was set in the Middle Ages and possibly derived from texts originally written during the late medieval or early Tudor era. This included quite a varied mix of ballads based on Arthurian legends and tales involving historical personages (for example, "King Henry" and "King John and the Bishop"). The relevant broadside literature available to Child included quite a large number of 'legendary' ballads on Arthurian subjects, yet he chose to include only three of these: "The Boy and the Mantle," "King Arthur and King Cornwall," and "The Marriage of Sir Gawain." Clearly the dividing line between what to include and what to exclude was proving difficult to draw with clarity, and at this point Child, who had no love for broadsides, was inclined to stringency in applying his selection criteria. Unfortunately, he failed to make those criteria explicit. He was also having difficulty with the tension between two conflicting principles of organization. He wanted, whenever possible, to place ballads of a similar type or theme together. Yet he also wanted to maintain his approximately chronological mode of organization. He had begun Part I with several ballads of the supernatural, and he might well have included more in the same group. But he had less confidence that such ballads as "Thomas Rymer," "Tam Lin," and "The Twa Magicians" could really be traced back to the fifteenth century or earlier, and his only sources for them were late Scottish ones.

Part II therefore comprised texts that Child was less confident had genuinely medieval roots but which nonetheless seemed to have some connection with the Middle Ages. He began with three ballads of Arthurian romance: "The Boy and the Mantle," "King Arthur and King Cornwall," and "The Marriage of Sir Gawain." He followed these with a small group that involved witchcraft and the rescue of women from their enchanted forms as loathsome beasts, ghosts, or old hags. These magical ballads, "King Henry," "Kempy Kay," "Kemp Owyne," "Allison Gross," and "The Laily Worm and the Machrel of the Sea," were, with one exception, of exclusively Scottish provenance. Four fine ballads about encounters between human beings and elfin folk, "Thomas Rymer," "The Wee Wee Man," "Tam Lin," and "Hind Etin," were similarly available to Child only in Scottish versions. Even "Clerk Colvill," about a deadly encounter between a man and a mermaid, lacked English variants, as did "The Twa Magicians." "The Broomfield Hill," on the other hand, was to be found on an English broadside as well as in Scottish oral tradition. It was one of several ballads in Part II that explored relationships (often unusual or tragic) between the sexes. Others included "Captain Wedderburn's Courtship," "Proud Lady Margaret," "The King's Dochter Lady Jean," "Young Andrew," and "Young Beichan." "Lizzie Wan" was another incest ballad, while "The Twa Brothers" was another tragic tale of fratricide. Yet for most of these fine ballads Child had no English versions, the two exceptions being "Captain Wedderburn's Courtship" and "Young Beichan" (aka "Lord Bateman").

Child's great project was now well underway, and he made good progress with it during the middle years of the decade. Parts III and IV of the new collection appeared in 1885 and 1886 respectively, and were subsequently bound together as Volume 2. He began Part III (which comprised ballad clusters numbers 54-82) with several religious ballads, for which he was indebted to earlier Victorian collecting and scholarship: "The Cherry Tree Carol," "The Carnal and the Crane," and "Dives and Lazarus." These provided a transition to the main focus of Part III, which was on tragic ballads set in the Middle Ages. In most cases Child had no direct evidence to suggest that these narratives had been first created during the medieval era, but he apparently believed that they probably did have their origins in the second phase of his putative ballad era. He was certainly correct to identify a medieval ambiance in this group of ballads, but it was possible that this was a matter of subject rather than source. The ballads may well reflect a seventeenth-century or even eighteenth-century perspective on an earlier historical period, but one could say with justification that there was a thematic connection to the Middle Ages in each case. For example, one such narrative, "Sir Patrick Spens," was apparently based on an actual historical event, and others were set in medieval courts or featured medieval kings or knights.

More than half of the items dealt with loving or loveless relationships between men and women. In "Fair Annie" and "Childe Waters" the women, although treated harshly, survived, but in "Glasgerion," "Lord Thomas and Fair Annet," "The Lass of Roch Royal," and "Little Musgrave and Lady Barnard" the outcomes were all tragic. Tragic ballads in which men were the victims included "Young Hunting" and "Clerk Saunders," while ballads involving supernatural appearances of the dead included "Sweet William's Ghost," "The Unquiet Grave," and "The Wife of Usher's Well." For nearly half of the items in Part III Child had only Scottish, or sometimes Scottish and Irish, sources. This did not mean that English versions would never be found for any of these, but rather it was a reflection of the fact that Child had many more Scottish than English manuscript sources available to him. It was often the case that even when he knew that a ballad's geographical provenance included England, he had only one or two English variants and many more Scottish texts. Moreover, his most complete English text was frequently that found in the Percy folio manuscript. That was the case, for example, with "Sir Aldingar," which Child called "one of the most important of all that the Percy manuscript has saved from oblivion."[57]

If the ballads in Part III were related in one way or another to the Middle Ages, Part IV, the second half of Volume 2, comprised ballad clusters numbers 83-113 and took the collection into the early Renaissance and perhaps beyond. It opened with "Childe Maurice" and included some very well-known ballads, such as "Bonny Barbara Allen," "The Young Maid Freed from the Gallows," and "Willie o' Winsbury," as well as one of the most horrible, "Lamkin." Others of note included "The Great Silkie of Sule Skerry," "Lady Alice," "The Bailiff's Daughter of Islington," "The Knight and Shepherd's Daughter," and the frequently-found comic ballad about a failed seduction, "The Baffled Knight."

The English and Scottish Popular Ballads now seemed well on its way to becoming *the* definitive collection of narrative song texts, but a delay then ensued and several years went by with nothing further published. Yet just when it seemed that the ambitious project had perhaps ground to a premature halt, Part V appeared in 1888, followed by the remainder of Volume 3 the next year. Child continued to follow an approximately chronological mode of organization, and the setting of most of the ballads he reproduced in this volume was still vaguely medieval in ambiance. He did not make explicit claims about their medieval origins, except in a few instances where the texts could be dated back to the fourteenth century, but his underlying assumption seems to have been that they all derived, directly or indirectly, from the second phase of the putative ballad era, or perhaps even, in just a few cases, from the first, early medieval, phase.

Part V, which covered ballad clusters 114-155, was devoted mainly to ballads about Robin Hood and other outlaws. Several previous ballad collectors and scholars had devoted themselves to this corpus of material, most notably Joseph Ritson, whose pioneering *Robin Hood: A Collection of All the Ancient Poems, Songs and Ballads now extant relative to that celebrated English Outlaw* had first appeared in 1795, and John Mathew Gutch, whose large and eclectic two volume compendium *The Robin Hood Garlands and Ballads, with the Tale of 'The Lytell Geste': A Collection of Poems, Songs and Ballads relating to this Celebrated Yeoman* was published in 1850. Child's task was largely confined to deciding which ballads from Gutch's collection he should omit as inauthentic. He also had to make up his mind concerning his predecessors' rival theories about the historical figure underlying the Robin Hood of the ballads. To put Child's work into context one therefore needs to understand what he saw himself combating: a body of existing scholarship that he regarded as fanciful and undiscriminating. It was time, he believed, to wield Occam's razor. Putting Robin Hood balladry on a scientific footing meant omitting all imitation ballads and rejecting speculative theories. In the event, he followed such other outlaw ballads as "Johnie Cock" and "Adam Bell, Clim of the Clough, and William of Cloudesly" with a clutch of thirty-eight Robin Hood ballads, ranging from late medieval provenance to the products of seventeenth-century ballad-mongers.

Part VI (issued in 1889), which covered ballad clusters 156-188, seemed at first glance a rather chaotic mixture of material, much of it very Scottish in character but some of it obviously the work of late Tudor or early Stuart ballad-mongers. However, if one examined the contents more carefully, it became evident that there was method in Child's madness. In fact there was a logic to his mode of organization. Starting with "Queen Eleanor's Confession," which dealt with an event supposed to have occurred in the late twelfth century, during the reign of Henry II, the ballads were arranged in ascending chronological order, not according to when they had been written (that was often very difficult to determine) but by the date or approximate date of the incidents they described. The earliest incident with a precise date about which a ballad had been composed was the battle of Durham in 1346, but other landmark dates celebrated in ballads included the battle of Harlaw in 1411, the end of the Wars of the Roses in 1485, the birth of the future Edward VI in 1537, and the Northern Rebellion of 1569. This entire corpus of 'historical' balladry (thirty-two texts in total) dealt with three main kinds of subject matter. One theme was conflict in the lands north and south of the English/Scottish border. A second was other historical events of some significance: uprisings, battles, murders, and the like. The third theme might be characterized as pseudo-historical: ballads about people and deeds that it is difficult to verify actually existed. While figures such as Hugh Spencer and Mary Hamilton may have had some basis in historical reality, they seem, like Robin Hood, to be at least partially creations of the ballad muse. Some of this historical material was quite well known to Child's Victorian readers, and a third of it was exclusively Scottish, but there were nonetheless many interesting English variants that the volume made more readily accessible. One reason was that Child drew extensively on texts extant in the Percy folio manuscript but, whenever he could, provided their broadside equivalents. Just as in Part V he could draw upon the prior labors of Ritson and Gutch, in Part VI he could build on the scholarship of Hales and Furnivall.

A dozen of the texts in Part VI might reasonably be classified, on the basis of their subject matter, as 'border ballads.' This convenient label, however, actually subsumes three rather different kinds of material. There were, for example, ballads that depicted major battles between the Scots and English that took place in either the north of England or the Scottish lowlands. The earliest of these was "Durham Field," about a conflict that took place during the reign of Edward III, the military-minded monarch known as the 'hammer of the Scots.' The battle of Otterburn in 1388, during the reign of Richard II, was similarly described by a minstrel or poet, while "Flodden Field" (recounting a conflict which took place in 1513) was the work of Elizabethan ballad-monger Thomas Deloney. Finally "Musselburgh Field" recorded a successful military operation against the Scots by Edward VI's uncle, the Protector Somerset. A second group of ballads were about the activities of the warlords who controlled the lands on either side of the border, and who periodically engaged in armed conflict with each other during the fifteenth and sixteenth centuries. The most famous ballad about these clashes between the Northumbrian Percy family and the Scottish Douglas clan was "The Hunting of the Cheviot" (aka "Chevy Chace"), but a later example is "Northumberland Betrayed by Douglas." The third kind of 'border ballad' dealt with more minor incidents, acts of violence resulting from cattle rustling across the border. Examples included "Johnie Armstrong," "Dick o the Cow," "Kinmont Willie," "Jock o the Side," and "Archie o Cawfield." Essentially they were Scottish equivalents to the Robin Hood cycle, but their historical setting was the sixteenth century rather than the medieval era. Part VI also included a few other quasi-historical ballads that would become better known than the majority of the border ballads, such as the pirate ballad "Sir Andrew Barton," the murder ballad "The Bonny Earl of Murray," "The Death of Queen Jane" (about Henry VIII's wife, Jane Seymour, and the birth of her son, the future Edward VI), and the tragic Scottish ballad "Mary Hamilton."

Child's second published collection was thus incomplete and still far from finished when the decade of the 1880s drew to a close. He was over halfway, but he still had more than one third of his chosen 305 ballad clusters to cover. In fact he had only six more years to live, and sadly would never see the complete work in print. The last part would have to be published posthumously by his disciples. On the other hand, by the end of the 1880s he had done enough to suggest that *The English and Scottish Popular Ballads,* when eventually completed, would become widely recognized as *the* definitive printed ballad collection. Child had also demonstrated the systematic and comparative methodology that he believed was essential to any 'scientific' ballad editing project. And he had advanced an attractive, if flawed, theory of ballad origins and communal transmission that would strongly influence later ballad editors, folklorists, and folksong collectors. However, it would take time before Child's work became widely known and assimilated in the United Kingdom. During the 1880s the work of collecting old songs—including, of course, ballads—would go on in the field, but it would be essentially parallel to and independent of his project. Only in the 1890s would the two endeavors begin to interact to some limited degree, as English folksong collectors gradually became aware of Child's later work and of the ongoing release of installments of *The English and Scottish Popular Ballads.*

Joseph Ebsworth and *The Roxburghe Ballads*

Although Child's huge project was the single most important phenomenon in the world of ballad editing during the 1880s, it was not the only one. There was also the work of the Ballad Society, an organization that was predominantly the creation of Frederick Furnivall and which had committed its resources to a major project: publishing the entire collection of broadside ballads in the Roxburghe collection held by the British Museum. This was a huge undertaking that would take several decades to bring to completion, and its first editor, William Chappell, would not live to see the project finished. But he did make a substantial start on it, beginning work in the late 1860s on the task of indexing and copying the 1,466 ballads that were gathered into four large folio volumes of broadsides in the Museum. His first two printed volumes of *The Roxburghe Ballads* reproduced, albeit with some variation, most of the first folio in the British Museum, in which the broadsides were bound in an approximately alphabetical order. He saw these two volumes into print in 1869-71 and 1872-74, respectively,[58] and in 1875 he issued a supplement (eventually included in the third volume) which reprinted the remaining 66 ballads from the first folio.[59]

The beginning of the 1880s saw Chappell complete the publication of the third volume of the Ballad Society's edition of *The Roxburghe Ballads*. The remainder of this volume comprised two more segments (Parts 2 and 3, also referred to as Parts VIII and IX) that were published serially, in 1879 and 1880 respectively.[60] Together they reprinted ninety-three items taken mainly from the second folio. Chappell continued his policy of reprinting the ballads in essentially the same order in which they had been bound together. This second folio was organized alphabetically, and consisted mainly of ballads printed between the mid-1650s, when Cromwell sanctioned the resumption of broadside publishing, and the end of the seventeenth century. The texts thus came from the Commonwealth years, from the late Stuart era, and from the reign of William and Mary, but the majority dated from the reign of Charles II. In the appendix to Volume 3 Chappell announced that he was handing over editorship of the remaining Roxburghe ballads to Joseph W. Ebsworth. The loss of Chappell was a major blow to the Ballad Society, which already had enough problems without a change in editorship of its flagship project. Yet even without him it would still prove to be functional, albeit sometimes only barely so, for another two decades.

The new editor got to work at once, and throughout the 1880s progress with publishing additional volumes would be fairly steady, if slow. Joseph Ebsworth successfully issued Volume 4 in two parts in 1882-83, and Volume 5 appeared in three parts during 1884-85.[61] He devoted almost the entire fifth volume (comprising close to 800 pages in total) to political ballads from the 1680s, a topic which interested him greatly as a historian of the period but which evidently did not thrill most of the Ballad Society's subscribers. Ebsworth had at his disposal several hundred more political ballads illustrating the course of events from the Glorious Revolution of 1688 through the reigns of William and Mary and Anne to the early Georgian era, but the response of Ballad Society members to his tenure as editor had been far from encouraging. The majority of subscribers wanted to see him reprinting broadside versions of traditional ballads rather than historical documents about late seventeenth-century politics. Some had already voted with their feet by refusing to purchase Volume 5, and from this point on, if not before, the Ballad Society and its flagship project faced financial disaster. The solution was to give them what they wanted. Volume 6, Ebsworth announced, would be devoted to ballads of true love, naval ballads, ballads of good fellowship, and legendary and romantic ballads. The latter, he predicted, would be greeted with an especially ecstatic "chorus of jubilation" by lovers of "Old Ballads."[62]

The massive sixth volume of *The Roxburghe Ballads* duly appeared, in four parts, between 1886 and 1889.[63] What Ebsworth called, rather misleadingly, his "Group of True-Love Ballads" took up the entire first part and half of the second. They were ballads about male/female relationships, mostly amorous, but by no means all of them depicted true love. Some were more about casual sex than about love, and a good number of them were laments by maidens wooed, won, and deserted. Many of them employed the pastoral convention, so there were many mournful shepherds and languishing swains appealing to shepherdesses who were sometimes cruel and sometimes kind. Naturally, these love ballads varied in quality, with some of the better ones the work of such well-known ballad-mongers as Laurence Price, Tobias Bowne, and Thomas D'Urfey. Ebsworth followed them with a fairly large group of naval ballads, which included several vernacular ballads that would later be counted as folksongs. The same was true when he eventually reached the long anticipated group of "Legendary and Romantic Ballads" in the Roxburghe collection. It was 1889 before Ballad Society members received the remaining two parts (parts III and IV) of Volume 6 that contained these songs, but they were well worth waiting for.[64] They included, among others, "Little Musgrove and the Lady Barnet," "Lord Thomas and Fair Eleanor," "Fair Margaret and Sweet William," "The Lass of Occram," "Sir Hugh the Graeme," and "Johnny Armstrong's Last Good-night." There were also numerous historical—or pseudo-historical—ballads of note, including "Queen Eleanor's Confession," "The Spanish Lady's Love," "King John and the Abbot of Canterbury," "King Henry V, his Conquest of France," and "Chevy Chace." William Chappell, the first editor and Ebsworth's friend and mentor, had unfortunately not lived to see the completed Volume 6, having died in 1888. Ebsworth had promised Chappell that he would see the entire project through to the end, but he was worried that the Ballad Society's funds would be insufficient. As the 1880s drew to a close, the fate of the complete edition of *The Roxburghe Ballads* was hanging in the balance.

John Ashton and Broadside Balladry

When reproducing old broadsides for a modern audience, one had a simple choice: publishing either a comprehensive edition of a single collection or a thematic selection from one or more collections. The Ballad Society had opted for the first route, but it meant reprinting a large amount of dross along with the "moderate jewels."[65] The other option was an easier one, and—in the short term—apparently more productive. Ballad enthusiasts could be involved in the publication of smaller but more attractive and less costly collections of a more limited nature. The most important of these initiatives was the work of John Ashton, a social historian but also a ballad *aficionado* from a young age. Quite a number of individuals made personal collections of broadsides during the Victorian era, one of the most notable collectors being Sir Frederick Madden, who worked as a curator at the British Museum. Such personal collections were not—or not yet—available for public access *in situ* let alone in published form. Historian John Ashton, however, realized the importance of making key texts accessible to anyone who was interested. It was he who took the lead in making what he considered the best of broadside balladry available to the general public in the late Victorian era.

Ashton's approach to vernacular song was quite different from that of the other editors whose work we have so far examined. He was well aware that, given enough time and money, the Ballad Society would eventually make available to the public at least one of the huge collections of broadsides in the British Museum. Yet he also recognized that such a vast compilation would be mind-boggling to any reader except a devoted antiquarian or broadside ballad specialist. A collection such as the Roxburghe was huge and inchoate; one felt dizzy in the face of such a massive amount of unsorted primary source material. Help was needed if folksong enthusiasts were to come to terms with such potentially invaluable sources of song-texts, which could be used to expand fragments collected from oral tradition. And amateur historians needed to be shown the kind of valuable and intriguing source material that could be unearthed in the archival collections. By selecting important (and singable) ballad texts, and by organizing them into a variety of useful categories, W. H. Logan had begun providing the public with that discriminating expertise some two decades before in *A Pedlar's Pack of Ballads and Songs*.[66] That, essentially, was the work which Ashton took up again and carried forward in the late 1880s and early 1890s. A diligent collector of broadsheets who was fascinated by historical ballads and sea songs, he was also interested in and fond of vernacular song. He located, extracted, and made accessible in a coherent manner hundreds of broadsides that had captured in print the words of folksongs and other vernacular songs. In doing so, he, like Logan, performed a valuable and needed service of which the Late Victorian, and especially the Edwardian, collectors would make good use.

In terms of size and organization Ashton's first book, *A Century of Ballads,* published in 1887, was a substantial work.[67] There were eighty seventeenth-century broadsides, complete with original wood-cuts, apparently reprinted from broadsides in Ashton's own collection. Not all of the items were new to Ballad Society members and other ballad enthusiasts, since some had appeared in previously published collections. However, Ashton had a good working knowledge of the available material, his selection was sensible, and his book was well organized. He divided the ballads into nine categories: social ballads, supernatural ballads, historical ballads, love ballads, drinking ballads, sea ballads, naval and military ballads, sporting ballads, and "local and miscellaneous" ballads. Like several of his Victorian predecessors, Ashton made a plea that it was unfair to condemn the balladry of the past as "coarse and brutal" because sixteenth and seventeenth-century people "wrote and printed as they talked, and, on delicate subjects, so openly as to suggest primal innocence." Yet he recognized that the language of many broadsides was too forthright and down-to-earth for "the fastidious taste" of his own era, and that "many could not now be published at all."[68] He concluded that since most seventeenth-century broadsides provided some illustration of "social manners, customs, tastes, dress, etc.," his task was to select, from among those ballads that dwelt particularly on social subjects, the ones that were most appropriate for "family reading." Censorship had thus once again reared its head, and it appears that Ashton's own sense of what was and was not indelicate played a not inconsiderable role in his selection of texts.

Although Ashton's primary aim was to illustrate seventeenth-century social history, he was clearly also interested in the history of broadside balladry, and he discussed its origins in his introduction. The seventeenth century, he argued, was the heyday of the broadside, a time when political ballads had an enormous influence, with invective and scurrility routinely employed by both government and its opponents. At a time when there were no cheap newspapers, ballads had an "immense power...in forming public opinion among an uneducated nation." They were an excellent source of information about not only the politics but also the "social life and manners of the times."[69] *A Century of Ballads* was thus intended to provide the raw materials for a history of seventeenth-century popular culture and society.

Ashton's first category of "social ballads" was especially suited to illustrating seventeenth-century social life. The twenty ballads in this group included Martin Parker's "Time's Alteration," a classic conservative complaint about the degeneracy of the age, bewailing the expensiveness of necessities, the decline in hospitality, and the prevalence of dissipation.[70] Many of the others were in one way or another about marriage: advice that country girls made better wives than city girls, instructions from a mother to her betrothed daughter, descriptions of customs and ceremonies, and advice on how to handle a scold. Two of this group stand out: "A Penny-worth of Good Counsell" (a lament on the inadequacies of a husband who has "no fore-cast in him," a rather transparent euphemism), and "A Woman's Work Is Never Done." Ashton's second group, of so-called "supernatural ballads," included two kinds of material.[71] There were credulous religious ballads, such as "The Kentish Miracle," "A Warning for Swearers," "A Poore Man in Essex and the Devil," "Strange and True News from Westmorland," and "Witchcraft Discovered and Punished." There were also three tragic ballads in which the ghosts of dead lovers played key roles in the outcome: "The Two Faithful Lovers' Tragedy," "The Suffolk Miracle," and a broadside which is also known as "The Cruel Ship's Carpenter" but in Ashton's copy was titled "The Gosport Tragedy, or The Perjured Ship Carpenter." Of the six historical ballads in the third section of the book, five were accounts of royal coronations and deaths featuring every monarch from Charles I to Mary II. By far superior to these in content and execution was Martin Parker's "The King Enjoys His Own Again."[72] Most notable among the six love ballads in the next section were "True-Love Requited" (better known as "The Bailiff's Daughter of Islington") and a rather pedestrian version of the traditional ballad "Barbara Allen," titled "Barbara Allen's Cruelty, or, the Young-Man's Tragedy."[73]

The second half of the book saw a return to ballads depicting social activities of various kinds. It opened with a section titled "Drinking Ballads."[74] Two of the items in this small group of convivial songs were well known, "The Leather Bottel" and "Sack for my Money." The others were ballads in praise of ale, the hostesses who served it, and the good companions with whom it was drunk. Ashton's sixth section, devoted to sea ballads, was one of his most interesting.[75] It included several popular favorites, such as "The Sailors Only Delight" (aka "The *George Aloe* and the *Sweepstake*") and "Neptune's Raging Fury" (better known as "When the Stormy Winds Do Blow"). Others of interest were ballads against the press-gang ("The Distressed Damsels") and against slavery ("The Algerian Slaves Releasement"), while the pick of the group was "Sir Walter Raleigh Sailing in the Low-lands" (aka "The *Sweet Trinity*" or "The *Golden Vanity*"). The four naval and military ballads that came next were inferior in quality to the best of these sea ballads, while the four sporting ballads were on the subjects of fox hunting and horse racing.[76] Ashton's last, miscellaneous, category included material that he might easily have apportioned to one or another of his earlier groupings.[77] There were two ballads about highwaymen, and murder ballads were much in evidence, but the gem in this last section was undoubtedly a tragic ballad, "Fair Margaret and Sweet William" (Child no. 74), here titled "Fair Margaret's Misfortunes."[78]

In 1888 Ashton followed *A Century of Ballads* with *Modern Street Ballads,* a similar compilation of broadsides, but drawing on late eighteenth-century and early nineteenth-century sources rather than seventeenth-century publications.[79] He seems to have taken most of the ballads that he selected for reprinting from the catalogue of a leading London broadside publisher, Catnach of Seven Dials or his successor, Fortey, but some of them at least came from his own collection, built up since he began collecting them in his youth. He described these more recent broadsides as "rough" but rarely "coarse," although he admitted to screening out some that he had collected to make sure that his book contained "nothing which can offend anybody except an absolute prude."[80] He claimed that his selections represented the modern street ballad at its stylistic best, and that he had chosen those ballads that best illustrated the manners and customs of the first half of the nineteenth century.

For this book Ashton had sorted his material into eight categories: social, humorous, country, sea, the Queen, historical, political, and miscellaneous. As with his previous collection, the first section, his "social" category, was large, and contained quite a variety of songs ranging from satirical attacks on women's fashions, policemen and the income tax to street cries ("The Cries of London"), drinking songs ("I Likes a Drop of Good Beer"), celebratory accounts of a prize fight ("Bendigo, Champion of England"), and the sights of London ("Crystal Palace" and "The Treats of London").[81] Some of the ballads, such as "Women's Sayings" (a catalogue of superstitions and old wives' saws) and "Sale of a Wife," clearly reflected the social conditions and practices of an earlier, pre-industrial society, but others were serious commentaries on the social ills of the Victorian era. They included several advocating teetotalism, laments about poverty and unemployment ("The Mechanic's Appeal to the Public"), and a pro-labor ballad supporting weavers', postmen's, and cabmen's strikes in the 1850s. Ashton's second section, "Humorous," was the largest in the book, comprising thirty-four items.[82] The influence of the music hall was evident here. Much of this humorous material was urban in character, making fun of city dwellers or describing comic incidents that were clearly set in the streets of London. Ashton's next category, in contrast, was called "Country," and ploughmen, poachers, and farmers were the subjects of many of the songs.[83] Gentrified farmers and country bumpkins were satirized in "The New Fashioned Farmer" and "Hodge in London," while there were ballads about horse races ("The Humours of the Races"), cock fighting ("The Bonny Grey"), and fishing ("The Jolly Angler"). Many of these songs were light-hearted, but there were also serious ballads, such as "The Honest Ploughman, or 90 Years Ago," that lamented the changes that had taken place in the English countryside, especially the introduction of Poor Law bastilles. Sympathy with the countryman struggling to make ends meet in difficult times was evident in this and other ballads, including those about poaching. "Death of Poor Bill Brown," for example, was a lament for a fellow poacher murdered by a gamekeeper and an account of the justified revenge taken for that death. "The Bold Poacher" (aka "The Lincolnshire Poacher") was a similarly defiant celebration of poaching in which the gamekeeper was again the villain, unless he turned a blind eye to what was clearly regarded as a legitimate way of obtaining food or making an income.

Ashton's next category, "Sea," consisted in part of broadsides relating naval battles: "Victory," for example, related the fate of a lover forced by a press-gang to sail and die with Nelson at Trafalgar. "The New York Trader" provided an account of a dreadful voyage that ended only when the captain, a confessed murderer, was thrown overboard to appease the angry elements. Several ballads in this group were about smuggling, while whaling was the subject of "The Greenland Whale Fishery." Some broadsides presented romanticized stories of encounters between ordinary sailors and royalty, some related equally unlikely stories of women trans-dressing and happily accompanying their lovers at sea, and others more realistically rejoiced in the safe return of sailors to port, sometimes to their waiting fiancées, or, more often, to sample the joys of tavern and bawdy-house. The latter were graphically pictured in "Ratcliffe Highway in 1842," but perhaps the most popular of the ballads in this section, one that certainly entered oral tradition, was "Bold William Taylor," a story of infidelity and revenge in which the sea played only an incidental role.[84] The next two sections of *Modern Street Ballads* contained mainly ephemeral broadsides about political and military events. Nine items about Queen Victoria were followed by six about prominent figures in the military and political history of earlier decades of the century, such as King George IV, Robert Peel, the Duke of Wellington, and Lord Nelson.[85] These patriotic items were, in the main, rather pedestrian, the best of the bunch being those celebrating victories at the battles of Trafalgar and Waterloo. More interesting were some of the political broadsides in the next section, although, again, few of them are likely to have been sung once the controversies in question had passed into history. There were, for example, three ballads in support of the Anti-Corn Law League and one in favor of parliamentary reform. The advent of the Chartist movement had also stimulated compositions, both pro and con. Ashton strongly disapproved of Chartism and characterized a song by Chartist leader Ernest Jones as "inflammatory rubbish," but to his credit he did reprint it, albeit only as a good example of "the sort of stuff that was disseminated among the people at the time of agitation for 'the Charter.'"[86]

The last section, "Miscellaneous," was indeed a mish-mash of broadsides on disparate subjects.[87] One of the best, "The Three Butchers," told the story of a woman used as a decoy in the robbery and murder of a man deceived into trying to rescue her. There were several confessional ballads supposedly written by convicted murderers about to be hanged. Others, including "Botany Bay" and "Van Dieman's Land," related the deeds and coming fate of convicts about to be transported. Other broadsides were more defiant. "My Bonny Black Bess," for example, celebrated the career of highwayman Dick Turpin, "The Collier Swell" depicted the rough manners of a working-class couple, and "The Wild Rover" was an early broadside version of what would become a popular folksong. The curious absence of a section in the book devoted to male/female relationships—a very common subject of broadside ballads—was underscored by the belated inclusion of such texts as "The London Merchant," "Riley's Farewell," "Young William," and "The Broken Hearted Gardener," all ballads about true love thwarted by fickleness or unsympathetic parents.

Modern Street Ballads served to underscore the vibrancy of the broadside tradition well into the nineteenth century. It demonstrated the way in which oral tradition and the printing press had gone hand in hand in preserving an older vernacular culture and, indeed, in keeping that culture up-to-date and flourishing. There was a lesson to be learned here, both by other ballad editors and by folksong collectors preoccupied exclusively with oral tradition. A few prominent figures in the late Victorian folksong movement, such as Frank Kidson, were listening, but most initially turned deaf ears to Ashton's enthusiasm for the corpus of late broadside balladry. They were more interested in remedying the most obvious element lacking in the published work of Child, the Ballad Society, and Ashton: the absence of tunes.

Notes

1. Historical census data is available online at www.visionofbritain.org.uk/census/index.jsp.

2. On the economic history of Late Victorian England, in addition to the standard works on the British Industrial Revolution, see especially the following: N. F. R. Crafts, S. J. Leybourne, and T. C. Mills, *The Climacteric in Late Victorian Britain: A Reappraisal of the Evidence* (Leeds: University of Leeds School of Economic Studies, 1987); François Crouzet, *The Victorian Economy* (New York: Routledge, 1982); Maurice Flamant and Jeanne Singer-Kérel, *Modern Economic Crises and Recessions* (New York: Harper & Row, 1970); James Foreman-Peck, *New Perspectives on the Late Victorian Economy: Essays in Quantitative Economic History, 1860-1914* (New York: Cambridge University Press, 2003); Eric J. Hobsbawm, *Industry and Empire,* vol. 3 of *The Pelican Economic History of Britain* (Harmondsworth: Penguin, 1969); Eric J. Hobsbawm, *The Age of Empire, 1875-1914* (London: Weidenfeld & Nicolson, 1987); Deirdre N. McCloskey, *Enterprise and Trade in Victorian Britain* (London: Routledge, 1981); R. S. Sayers, *A History of Economic Change in England, 1880-1939* (London: Oxford University Press, 1967).

3. Standard works on the general history of Late Victorian England include R. C. K. Ensor, *England, 1870-1914* (Oxford: Clarendon Press, 1960) and J. F. C. Harrison, *Late Victorian Britain, 1875-1901* (London: Routledge, 1991). There appears to be no modern social history of Britain that covers this period systematically and in detail, but aspects of the subject are treated in the following: Eugene C. Black, *Victorian Culture and Society* (New York: Harper & Row, 1973); Simon Gunn and Rachel Bell, *Middle Classes: Their Rise and Sprawl* (London: Cassell, 2002); Elizabeth T. Hurren, *Protesting About Pauperism: Poverty, Politics and Poor Relief in Late Victorian England, 1870-1900* (Woodbridge, England: Boydell Press, 2007); Gareth Stedman Jones, *Outcast London: A Study in the Relationship Between Classes in Victorian Society* (Oxford: Clarendon Press, 1971); Helen M. Lynd, *England in the Eighteen-Eighties: Toward a Social Basis for Freedom* (New Brunswick, N.J.: Transaction Books, 1984); John M. Mackenzie, ed., *The Victorian Vision: Inventing New Britain* (London: V&A Publications, 2001); Hugh McLeod, *Class and Religion in the Late Victorian City* (London: Croom Helm, 1974); Henry Pelling, *Popular Politics and Society in Late Victorian Britain: Essays* (London: Macmillan, 1968); Clarence Swisher, ed., *Victorian England* (San Diego, Calif.: Greenhaven Press, 2000); Donna Thomas, *The Problem of the Aged Poor: Social Reform in Late Victorian England* (Edmonton, Canada: University of Alberta Press, 1969).

4. On rural England, see David J. Eveleigh, *The Victorian Farmer* (Princes Risborough, U.K.: Shire, 1991); David Souden, *The Victorian Village* (London: Collins and Brown, 1991); Sadie B. Ward, *Seasons of Change: Rural Life in Victorian and Edwardian England* (London: Allen & Unwin, 1982); for a snapshot of one county, John Lowerson, *Victorian Sussex* (London: BBC, 1972).

5. Richard Holt, *Sport and the British: A Modern History* (New York: Oxford University Press, 1989); Mike Huggins, *The Victorians and Sport* (London: Hambledon and London, 2004); Mike Huggins, *Disreputable Pleasures: Less Virtuous Victorians at Play* (London: Frank Cass, 2004).

6. Eric J. Evans, *Parliamentary Reform, c. 1770-1918* (Harlow, England: Longman, 2000).

7. The standard biography of Disraeli is Robert Blake, *Disraeli* (New York: St. Martin's Press, 1962). Other more recent accounts include Richard Aldous, *The Lion and the Unicorn: Gladstone vs. Disraeli* (New York: Norton, 2006); Sarah Bradford, *Disraeli* (New York: Stein & Day, 1983); E. J. Feuchtwanger, *Disraeli* (London: Arnold, 2000); Ian St. John, *Disraeli and the Art of Victorian Politics* (London: Anthem Press, 2005); Stanley Weintraub, *Disraeli: A Biography* (New York: Dutton, 1993).

8. All biographers of Gladstone are indebted to John Morley, *The Life of William Ewart Gladstone* (London: Macmillan, 1903). The standard modern work was Philip Magnus, *Gladstone: A Biography* (New York: Dutton, 1954), until Richard Shannon, *Gladstone*, 2 vols. (Chapell Hill, N.C.: University of North Carolina Press, 1984 & 1999). See also Peter Stansky, *Gladstone: A Progress in Politics* (Boston: Little, Brown, 1979); Roy Jenkins, *Gladstone: A Biography* (New York: Random House, 1997).

9. Parnell remains a fairly controversial figure. See, among other works, David G. Boyce, *Parnell in Perspective* (London: Routledge, 1991); Michael Hurst, *Parnell and Irish Nationalism* (London: Routledge & Kegan Paul, 1968); Robert Kee, *The Laurel and the Ivy: The Story of Charles Stewart Parnell and Irish Nationalism* (New York: Penguin, 1993); Noel Kissane, *Parnell: A Documentary History* (Dublin: National Library of Ireland, 1991); F. S. L. Lyons, *Charles Stewart Parnell* (New York: Oxford University Press, 1972); and R. Barry O'Brien, *The Life of Charles Stewart Parnell, 1846-1891* (New York: Haskell House, 1968).

10. Michael Blake, *Lord Salisbury's World: Conservative Environments in Later Victorian Britain* (Cambridge, England: Cambridge University Press, 2001); Robert Blake and Hugh Cecil, *Salisbury: The Man and His Policies* (New York: St. Martin's Press, 1987); Peter Marsh, *The Discipline of Popular Government: Lord Salisbury's Domestic Statecraft, 1881-1902* (Hassocks, England: Harvester Press, 1978); E. D. Steele, *Lord Salisbury: A Political Biography* (London: UCL Press, 1999); Robert G. Taylor, *Lord Salisbury* (New York: St. Martin's Press, 1975).

11. Arthur Anthony Baumann, *The Last Victorians* (London: Benn, 1927); Murney Gerlach, *British Liberalism and the United States: Political and Social Thought in the Late Victorian Age* (London: Palgrave Macmillan, 2001); H. S. Jones, *Victorian Political Thought* (New York: St. Martin's Press, 2000); Gary Kelly and Ed Applegate, *British Reform Writers, 1832-1914* (Detroit: Gale Research, 1998).

12. There is a huge secondary literature on British Imperialism. One of the most useful books is a documentary collection edited by George Bennett, *The Concept of Empire: Burke to Attlee, 1714-1947* (London: Black, 1962). A systematic overview of the subject is provided in Woodruff D. Smith, *European Imperialism in the Nineteenth and Twentieth Centuries* (Chicago: Nelson Hall, 1982), while an extensive sampling of different perspectives can be found in Harrison M. Wright, ed., *The "New Imperialism": Analysis of*

Late Nineteenth-Century Expansion (Lexington, MA: Heath, 1976). James Morris, *Pax Britannica*, 3 vols. (London: Faber and Faber, 1973-78) provides a systematic and colorful narrative account of the British experience. Eric J. Hobsbawm, *The Age of Empire, 1875-1914* (London: Weidenfeld & Nicolson, 1987) is concise and analytical. More recent treatments include Andrew S. Thompson, *Imperial Britain: The Empire in British Politics, c. 1880-1932* (Harlow, England: Pearson Longman, 2000), Anthony Webster, *The Debate on the Rise of the British Empire* (Manchester, England: Manchester University Press, 2006); E. Spencer Wellhofer, *Democracy, Capitalism and Empire in Late Victorian Britain, 1885-1900* (London: Palgrave Macmillan, 1996).

13. Clare Goodrick-Clarke and Nicholas Goodrick-Clarke, eds., *G.R.S. Mead and the Gnostic Quest* (Berkeley, Calif.: North Atlantic Books, 2005).

14. William E. Buckler, *Walter Pater: The Critic As Artist of Ideas* (New York: Cambridge University Press, 1982); Hilary Fraser, *Beauty and Belief: Aesthetics and Religion in Victorian Literature* (New York: Cambridge University Press, 1986); Wolfgang Iser, *Walter Pater: The Aesthetic Moment* (New York: Cambridge University Press, 1987); Elizabeth Prettejohn, *Art for Art's Sake: Aestheticism in Victorian Painting* (New Haven, Conn.: Yale University Press, 2007); Margaret D. Stetz and Mark Samuels Lasner, *England in the 1880s: Old Guard and Avant-garde* (Charlottesville,Va.: University Press of Virginia, 1989).

15. Peter d'Alroy Jones, *The Christian Socialist Revival, 1877-1914: Religion, Class, and Social Conscience in Late Victorian England* (Princeton, N.J.: Princeton University Press, 1968).

16. Tony Brown, *Edward Carpenter and Late Victorian Radicalism* (London: Routledge, 1990).

17. The classic study of William Morris's political and social thought is E. P. Thompson, *William Morris: Romantic to Revolutionary* (London: Lawrence and Wishart, 1955). See also Florence S. Boos and Carole G. Silver, eds., *Socialism and the Literary Artistry of William Morris* (Columbia, Ms.: University of Missouri Press, 1990); Paul Meier, *William Morris, the Marxist Dreamer* (Sussex, England: Harvester Press, 1978); Paul Richard Thompson, *The Work of William Morris* (New York: Oxford University Press, 1991).

18. Jacob Korg, *George Gissing: A Critical Biography* (London: Methuen, 1965).

19. Secondary works on Hardy are legion. They include: James Gibson, *Thomas Hardy: A Literary Life* (New York: St. Martin's Press, 1996); Molly Lefebvre, *Thomas Hardy's World: The Life, Times and Works of the Great Novelist and Poet* (London: Carlton Books, 1997); Norman Page, *The Oxford Reader's Companion to Hardy* (New York: Oxford University Press, 2000); Norman Page, *Thomas Hardy* (London: Routledge & Kegan Paul, 1981); F. B. Pinion, *Thomas Hardy: His Life and Friends* (New York: St. Martin's Press, 1992); Ralph Pite, *Thomas Hardy: The Guarded Life* (New Haven, Conn.: Yale University Press, 2006); Claire Tomain, *Thomas Hardy* (New York: Penguin, 2007); Paul Turner, *The Life of Thomas Hardy: A Critical Biography* (Oxford: Blackwell, 1998); Carl T. Weber, *Hardy of Wessex: His Life and Literary Career* (New York: Columbia University Press, 1965); and Sarah B. Wright, ed., *Thomas Hardy A to Z: The Essential Reference to His Life and Work* (New York: Facts on File, 2002).

20. Adrian W. Frazier, *George Moore, 1852-1932* (New Haven, CN: Yale University Press, 2000); Tony Gray, *A Peculiar Man: A Life of George Moore* (London: Sinclair-Stevenson, 1996); and Elizabeth Grubgeld, *George Moore and the Autogenous Self: The Autobiography and Fiction* (Syracuse, N.Y.: Syracuse University Press, 1994).

21. Mervyn Jones, *The Amazing Victorian: A Life of George Meredith* (London: Constable, 1999).

22. There is a extensive body of secondary literature on Henry James. It includes George Bishop, *Henry James: Life, Work and Criticism* (Fredericton, NB: York Press, 1991); Leon Edel, *Henry James: A Life* (London: Flamingo, 1996); Kenneth Graham, *Henry James: A Literary Life* (New York: St. Martin's Press, 1995); Philip Horne, ed., *Henry James: A Life in Letters* (New York: Penguin, 1999); Fred Kaplan, *Henry James: The Imagination of a Genius: A Biography* (Baltimore, Md.: Johns Hopkins University Press, 1999); Harry T. Moore, *Henry James* (London: Thames & Hudson, 1974); and Miranda Seymour, *A Ring of Conspirators: Henry James and his Literary Circle* (London: Scribner, 1988).

23. Ian Bell, *Dreams of Exile: Robert Louis Stevenson, A Biography* (New York: H. Holt, 1993); Bryan Bevan, *Robert Louis Stevenson: Poet and Teller of Tales* (New York: St. Martin's Press, 1993); Philip Callow, *Louis: A Life of Robert Louis Stevenson* (Chicago: Ivan R. Dee, 2001); Hunter Davies, *The Teller of Tales: In Search of Robert Louis Stevenson* (London: Sinclair-Stevenson, 1994); William Gray, *Robert Louis Stevenson: A Literary Life* (New York: Palgrave Macmillan, 2004); Claire Harman, *Myself and the Other Fellow: A Life of Robert Louis Stevenson* (New York: Harper Collins, 2005); and Frank J. McLynn, *Robert Louis Stevenson: A Biography* (New York: Random House, 1993).

24. Victoria Manthorpe, *Children of the Empire: The Victorian Haggards* (London: Gollancz, 1996); and Tom Pocock, *Rider Haggard and the Lost Empire* (London: Weidenfeld & Nicolson, 1993).

25. John Adams, *Kipling* (London: Haus Books, 2005); Charles Allen, *Kipling Sahib: India and the Making of Rudyard Kipling* (London: Little, Brown, 2007); Andrew Lyall, *Rudyard Kipling* (London: Weidenfeld & Nicolson, 1999); Phillip Mallett, *Rudyard Kipling: A Literary Life* (New York: Palgrave Macmillan, 2003); Harry Ricketts, *Rudyard Kipling: A Life* (New York: Carroll & Graf, 2006); Martin Seymour-Smith, *Rudyard Kipling* (London: Papermac, 1990).

26. Bickford Dickinson, *Sabine Baring-Gould: Squarson, Writer and Folklorist, 1834-1924* (Newton Abbott: David & Charles, 1970); Harold Kirk-Smith, *'Now the Day Is Over': The Life and Times of Sabine Baring-Gould, 1834-1924* (Boston, England: Richard Kay, 1997); William E. Purcell, *Onward Christian Soldier: A Life of Sabine Baring-Gould* (London: Longman, Green, 1957).

27. Russell Ash, *Victorian Masters and their Art* (London: Pavillion, 1989); Hugh Brigstocke, ed., *The Oxford Companion to Western Art* (New York: Oxford University Press, 2001); Françoise Cachin, ed., *Arts of the Nineteenth Century: Volume Two, 1850 to 1905* (New York: Abrams, 1999); Peter Corbett and Lara Perry, *English Art, 1860-1914: Modern Artists and Identity* (New Brunswick, N.J.: Rutgers University Press, 2001); Paula Gillett, *The Victorian Painter's World* (Gloucester, England: Sutton, 1990); Luke

Hermann, *Nineteenth Century British Painting* (London: Giles de la Mare, 2000); Lionel Lambourne, *Victorian Painting* (London: Phaidon, 1999).

28. Elizabeth Prettejohn, *Interpreting Sargent* (New York: Stewart, Tabon & Chang, 1998).

29. J. Marsden, ed., *The Victorian World of Helen Allingham* (London: Brockhampton Press, 1999).

30. T. J. Barringer, ed., *Frederic Leighton: Antiquity, Renaissance, Modernity* (New Haven, Conn.: Yale University Press, 1999); Wyke Bayliss, *Five Great Painters of the Victorian Era: Leighton, Millais, Burne-Jones, Watts, Holman Hunt* (London: Low, Marston, 1904).

31. Russell Ash, *Sir Lawrence Alma-Tadema* (New York: Abrams, 1990); R. J. Barrow, *Lawrence Alma-Tadema* (New York: Phaidon, 2001); Edwin Becker and Elizabeth Prettejohn, *Sir Lawrence Alma-Tadema* (New York: Rizzoli, 1972); Jennifer G. Lovett, *Empire Restored, Elysium Revisited: The Art of Sir Lawrence Alma-Tadema* (Williamstown, Mass.: Sterling and Francine Clark Art Institute, 1991).

32. Timothy Hilton, *The Pre-Raphaelites* (New York: Abrams, 1971); Elizabeth Prettejohn, *The Art of the Pre-Raphaelites* (Princeton, N.J.: Princeton University Press, 2000); Edmund Swinglehurst, *The Art of the Pre-Raphaelites* (New York: Shooting Star Press, 1994); Tate Gallery, *The Pre-Raphaelites* (London: Penguin, 1984); Jon Whiteley, *Oxford and the Pre-Raphaelites* (Oxford: Ashmolean Museum, 1989); Christopher Wood, *The Pre-Raphaelites* (New York: Viking, 1981).

33. Alicia G. Faxon, *Dante Gabriel Rossetti* (New York: Abbeville Press, 1989).

34. S. Tschudi Madsen, *Art Nouveau* (London: Weidenfeld and Nicolson, 1967).

35. Linda Parry, *William Morris* (New York: Abrams, 1996); Diane Waggoner, *"The Beauty of Life": William Morris and the Art of Design* (New York: Thames and Hudson, 2003); Elizabeth Wilhide, *William Morris: Décor and Design* (New York: Abrams, 1991).

36. Rosalind P. Blakesley, *The Arts and Crafts Movement* (London: Phaidon, 2006); Nikolaus Pevsner, *Pioneers of Modern Design* (Harmondsworth: Penguin, 1960); Peter Stansky, *Redesigning the World: William Morris, the 1880s, and the Arts and Crafts Movement* (Princeton, N.J.: Princeton University Press, 1985).

37. Hugh Braun, *A Short History of English Architecture* (London: Faber, 1978); David Watkin, *English Architecture: A Concise History* (London: Thames and Hudson, 1979).

38. Standard histories of European classical music include Donald Jay Grout, *A History of Western Music* (3rd edition, New York: Norton, 1980), and K. Marie Stolba, *The Development of Western Music* (2nd edition, Dubuque, Iowa: Brown & Benchmark, 1994); see also articles in *Grove Music Online*.

39. At present there appears to be no full-length modern study of Macfarren and his music. For further information on him see the article in *Grove Music Online* and two older works: Charles Willeby, *Masters of English Music* (London: Osgood, McIvaine & Co., 1893), and Donald F. Tovey, *Some English Symphonists* (New York: Oxford University Press, 1941).

40. Like Macfarren, Cowen has been neglected by music historians and musicologists. Willeby's *Masters of English Music* [see previous note] still appears to provide the most extensive treatment of his career and compositions. See also the article in *Grove Music Online*.

41. Arthur Jones, *Arthur Sullivan: A Victorian Musician* (New York: Oxford University Press, 1984). There is a fairly extensive literature on Gilbert and Sullivan, including: Michael Ainger, *Gilbert and Sullivan: A Dual Biography* (New York: Oxford University Press, 2002); Leslie Baily, *Gilbert and Sullivan: Their Lives and Times* (Harmondsworth: Penguin, 1974); David Eden, *Gilbert and Sullivan: A Creative Conflict* (Rutherford, NJ: Fairleigh Dickinson University Press, 1986); Alan James, *Gilbert and Sullivan* (New York: Omnibus Press, 1989).

42. As with Macfarren and Cowen, insufficient scholarly attention has been paid to the life and work of Sir Alexander Mackenzie. See Willeby's *Masters of English Music* [note 39] and, more recently, Nicholas Temperley, ed., *The Athlone History of Music in Britain, Volume 5: The Romantic Age, 1800-1914* (London: Athlone Press, 1981). Also the article in *Grove Music Online*.

43. J. A. Fuller Maitland, *The Music of Parry and Stanford: An Essay in Comparative Criticism* (Cambridge: Heffer, 1934); John F. Porte, *Sir Charles V. Stanford* (New York: Da Capo, 1976); Paul Rodmell, *Charles Villiers Stanford* (Burlington, Vt.: Ashgate, 2002); Nicholas Temperley, ed., *The Athlone History of Music in Britain, Volume 5: The Romantic Age, 1800-1914* (London: Athlone Press, 1981); Nicholas Temperley, ed., *Music in Victorian Society and Culture: A Special Issue of Victorian Studies* (Bloomington, Ind.: Indiana University Press, 1986).

44. Michael Allis, *Parry's Creative Process* (Burlington, Vt.: Ashgate, 2003); Jeremy Dibble, *C. Hubert Parry: His Life and Music* (New York: Oxford University Press, 1992); J. A. Fuller Maitland, *The Music of Parry and Stanford: An Essay in Comparative Criticism* (Cambridge: Heffer, 1934); Nicholas Temperley, ed., *The Athlone History of Music in Britain, Volume 5: The Romantic Age, 1800-1914* (London: Athlone Press, 1981); Nicholas Temperley, ed., *Music in Victorian Society and Culture: A Special Issue of Victorian Studies* (Bloomington: Indiana University Press, 1986); Donald F. Tovey, *Some English Symphonists* (New York: Oxford University Press, 1941).

45. Francis James Child, ed., *English and Scottish Ballads,* 8 vols. (Boston, Mass.: Little, Brown & Co., 1857-59. 2nd edition, 1860. 3rd edition, 1866. The English edition, which was a reprint of the second American edition, was published in London by Sampson Low in 1861).

46. Svend Grundtvig, Axel Olrik, et al., eds., *Danmarks gamle Folkviser,* 12 vols. (Kjöberhavn: Samfundet til den danske literaturs fremme, 1853-1976).

47. Francis James Child, ed., *The English and Scottish Popular Ballads,* 10 parts in 5 vols. (Boston, Mass.: Houghton, Mifflin & Co., 1882-1898; reprinted: New York: Dover, 1965). Subsequent references are to the Dover edition, vols. 1-5.

48. Child, *Popular Ballads,* 1: vii

49. F[rancis]. J[ames]. Child, "Ballad Poetry," in *Johnson's Universal Cyclopedia,* ed. Rossiter Johnson (New York: Johnson, 1874), 464-468; reprinted in *Universal Cyclopedia and Atlas,* ed. Rossiter Johnson (New York: Johnson, 1884), 365-367. Quotations are from the 1884 edition.

50. Child, "Ballad Poetry," 365.

51. Child, "Ballad Poetry," 366.

52. Child, "Ballad Poetry," 366.

53. Child, "Ballad Poetry," 367.

54. Child, *Popular Ballads,* 1: vii.

55. Child, *Popular Ballads,* 1: ix. Given Child's full and straightforward public recognition of his debt to Grundtvig, it seems churlish to complain, as Dave Harker does, that "Child acknowledges Grundtvig's help sparingly" (Harker, *Fakesong,* 120).

56. Francis James Child, Letter to Professor Svend Grundtvig, 25 August 1872; reprinted in Appendix A of Sigurd B. Hustvedt, *Ballad Books and Ballad Men: Raids and Rescues in Britain, America, and the Scandinavian North since 1800* (Cambridge, Mass.: Harvard University Press, 1930), 254.

57. Child, *Popular Ballads,* 2: 33.

58. William Chappell, ed., *The Roxburghe Ballads,* vols. 1 & 2 (Hertford, U.K.: The Ballad Society, 1869-1874).

59. For an analysis of the contents of the first two volumes of *The Roxburghe Ballads,* see Gregory, *Victorian Songhunters,* 330-343.

60. William Chappell, ed., *The Roxburghe Ballads,* vol. 3 (Hertford, U.K.: The Ballad Society, 1875-1880).

61. Joseph W. Ebsworth, ed., *The Roxburghe Ballads,* vols. 4 & 5 (Hertford, U.K.: The Ballad Society, 1882-85).

62. *Roxburghe Ballads,* 6, pt. 1: xx.

63. Joseph W. Ebsworth, ed., *The Roxburghe Ballads,* vol. 6 (Hertford, U.K.: The Ballad Society, 1886-89).

64. Part 3 was dated 1888, but a note from Ebsworth at the head of the table of contents suggests that it was actually issued simultaneously with Part 4, which was dated 1889 and published that year.

65. Francis James Child's phrase, in a letter to Professor Svend Grundtvig, 25 August 1872; reprinted in Hustvedt, *Ballad Books and Ballad Men,* 254.

66. W. H. Logan, ed., *A Pedlar's Pack of Ballads and Songs, with Illustrative Notes* (Edinburgh: William Paterson, 1869; reprinted: Detroit: Singing Tree Press, 1968).

67. John Ashton, ed., *A Century of Ballads* (London: Elliot Stock, 1887).

68. Ashton, *Century of Ballads,* xx.

69. Ashton, *Century of Ballads,* xx.

70. Ashton, *Century of Ballads,* 5-73.

71. Ashton, *Century of Ballads,* 79-122.

72. Ashton, *Century of Ballads,* 129-48.

73. Ashton, *Century of Ballads,* 153-75.

74. Ashton, *Century of Ballads,* 181-96.

75. Ashton, *Century of Ballads,* 201-24.

76. Ashton, *Century of Ballads,* 229-63.

77. Ashton, *Century of Ballads,* 271-352.

78. Ashton, *Century of Ballads,* 345-47.

79. John Ashton, ed., *Modern Street Ballads* (London: Chatto & Windus, 1888).

80. Ashton, *Modern Street Ballads,* vi-vii.

81. Ashton, *Modern Street Ballads,* 1-84.

82. Ashton, *Modern Street Ballads,* 85-183.

83. Ashton, *Modern Street Ballads,* 184-216.

84. Ashton, *Modern Street Ballads,* 218-70.

85. Ashton, *Modern Street Ballads,* 271-312.

86. Ashton, *Modern Street Ballads,* 338.

87. Ashton, *Modern Street Ballads,* 343-405.

4

Stirrings in the North

Having traced the emergence of the concept of folksong in Victorian England, examined briefly the history of English vernacular song-collecting up to and including the 1870s, and sketched the political and cultural background within which the Late Victorian folksong revival took place, it is time to begin to explore in detail the new impetus to collect and disseminate traditional song that was evident in England in the late 1870s and the 1880s. Although this was not universally the case, it was, on the whole, characterized by a more systematic effort to note folksong tunes in addition to (or even instead of) texts. This chapter will discuss the work of five collectors and editors: Marianne Harriet Mason, T. T. Wilkinson, Collingwood Bruce, John Stokoe, and Joseph Crawhall. We will notice considerable continuity with the early-mid Victorian past. Mason's initiative was stimulated and influenced by that of an early Victorian collector whom we met in chapter 2, John Broadwood. Wilkinson was concerned to make sure that the wealth of regional song-texts collected earlier by his friend and colleague John Harland would remain accessible to a national audience. Bruce and Stokoe were working with materials that had, in the main, been noted by earlier collectors associated with the Newcastle-upon-Tyne Society of Antiquaries. Crawhall was the most recent example of a regional collector attempting to assemble together in publishable form the best items from a local—and still vibrant—musical tradition.

We have seen how, in a series of articles published in *Musical Times* during 1878-79, musicologist Carl Engel called upon musicians and teachers to get out of their drawing rooms and organ lofts and start noting down the vernacular tunes still extant in oral tradition in the English countryside. He did not know it, but even before his plea appeared in print a handful of individuals in different parts of England had begun to do just that. One pioneer of the new approach—which emphasized the importance of collecting both tunes and texts from oral tradition—was Marianne Harriet Mason (1845-1932), whose *Nursery Rhymes and Country Songs* was published in 1878.[1]

Nursery Rhymes and Country Songs

Biographical information on Harriet Mason is scarce, but she was born in Marylebone (West London) in 1845, and seems to have spent some of her childhood at the country estate of the Mitford family, close to the village of Mitford, near Morpeth, in Northumberland. By her mid-twenties she was living with her parents at Morton Hall, East Retford, Nottinghamshire, where her father was a Justice of the Peace. She did not marry, but devoted herself during the 1870s and early 1880s to working with children who had come under the care of the local Poor Law guardians. She acted as volunteer supervisor of all Poor Law boarding-out committees in Nottinghamshire, and served on the executive of both the Girls' Friendly Society and the Young Men's Friendly Society. This record of devoted charity work led to her employment from 1885 onwards as a Local Government Board inspector of the conditions of children placed in foster care, a task that took her all over England and Wales. She worked in this capacity until her retirement in 1910, having been promoted to senior inspector in 1899.[2]

Mason was living in Nottinghamshire when she published *Nursery Rhymes and Country Songs*, but it was during her childhood stay in the northeast of England that she learned more than two dozen nursery rhymes and other children's songs from her grandmother, Mrs. Mitford, to whom she dedicated her slim publication. In her youth she evidently also lived for shorter periods in a variety of other locations in England including Derbyshire, Nottinghamshire, Lancashire, and Devon, as well as Carmarthenshire in Wales. In each of these counties she noted a few songs from oral tradition, to add to her fairly small Northumbrian collection. Her family was also related to the Broadwoods of Lynne in Surrey, and Henry Broadwood gave her a copy of the privately printed draft version of the book that the Reverend John Broadwood published with Geoffrey Dusart in 1847 as *Old English Songs, as now sung by the Peasantry of the Weald of Surrey and Sussex.*[3] As a result, *Nursery Rhymes and Country Songs,* although less than sixty pages in length, comprised fifty-seven items, of which six derived from the Broadwood family and thirty-three from the Mitford family. Most of the latter were Northumbrian in origin, although a few were Scottish, reflecting the proximity of the region to the Scottish border.

More than half the book's contents consisted of either nursery rhymes or children's songs of one kind or another, and most, but not quite all, of these had been learned from Grandmother Mitford. Among the exceptions were a Derbyshire game-song, "Rosy Apple," the Lancastrian ditty "There Was a Pig Went Out to Dig," and two children's songs from Nottinghamshire, "The Jacket and Petticoat" and "Whose Little Pigs Are These?" In Devon Mason had picked up a well-known cumulative song, "The Tree in the Valley," and she had learned another, "I Love a Sixpence" from some American visitors, although the song was clearly English in origin. And, although she did not reveal where and from whom she had obtained them, she had two versions of a riddle song, titled "A Paradox," which posed such questions as "How can there be a chicken without any bone?" and "How can there be a cherry without any stone?" More than two dozen of Mason's children's songs came from Northumbrian sources.

The bulk of the Northumbrian items were thus juvenile in nature, as were a handful of those from unidentified locations. Along with such well-known nursery rhymes as "Pat-a-cake," "See-Saw, Margery Daw," "Goosey, Goosey, Gander," "Little Bo-Beep," and "Dickory, Dickory Dock" were less familiar ones with a 'folk' flavour, such as "Wing Wang Waddle, O!" "Robertin Tush," "I Had a Little Moppet," "The Little Market Woman," and "There Was an Old Woman Tossed in a Basket." As an illustration of this type of juvenile English folk ditty, here is one of Grandmother Mitford's nursery songs, "King Arthur's Servants":

King Arthur's Servants

Anon

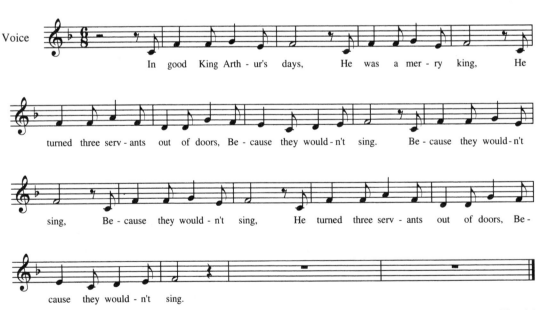

Fig. 4.1

In good King Arthur's days,	Because they wouldn't sing,
He was a merry king,	Because they wouldn't sing,
He turned three servants out of doors	He turned three servants out of doors
Because they wouldn't sing.	Because they wouldn't sing.

The first he was a miller,
The second he was a weaver,
The third he was a little tailor,
Three thieving rogues together.
Three thieving rogues, etc.

The miller he stole corn,
The weaver he stole yarn,

The little tailor he stole broadcloth,
To keep these three rogues warm.
To keep these three, etc.

The miller was drowned in his dam,
The weaver was hanged in his yarn,
The devil ran off with the little tailor,
With his broadcloth under his arm,
With his broadcloth, etc.[4]

Other well-known children's songs from Grandmother Mitford's repertoire included "Old King Cole," the game-song "Looby Light" and "The Frog's Wooing." Harriet had learned from her grandmother two quite different versions of the latter song, each complete with its own tune. This was one of them:

The Frog's Wooing

Anon

Fig. 4.2

There was a frog lived in a well, farding link-a-laddie,
And a merry mouse lived in a mill, faddy,
Oh! faddy, Oh! faddy, Oh! faddy, Oh! farding lay.

This frog he would a-wooing ride, farding link-a-laddie,
Sword and buckler by his side, faddy, Oh!, &c.

He rode till he came to the mouse's hall, farding link-a-
                                               laddie,
And there did knock and there did call, faddy, Oh! &c.

"O Mistress Mouse, are you within?" farding link-a-
                                               laddie,
"Yes, kind sir, I sit and spin," faddy, Oh! &c.

"O Mistress Mouse, will you marriage make," farding
                                 link-a-laddie,
"With the frog that is so blake?" faddy, Oh! &c.

"Uncle Rat is not at home," farding link-a-laddie,

"I can't consent till his return," faddy, Oh! &c.

When Uncle Rat came home at night, farding link-a-laddie,
"Has any one been here since I went out?," faddy, Oh! &c.

"Yes, there's been a gentleman," farding link-a-laddie,
"Who says he'll marry me if he can," faddy, Oh! &c.

"We'll have the marriage in the mill," farding link-a-laddie,
"The drums shall beat and the bells shall ring," faddy, Oh!
                                               &c.

The drums did beat and the bells did ring, farding link-a-
                                               laddie,
When in came the cat, and her kitling, faddy, Oh! &c.

The cat, she seized the rat by the crown, farding link-a-laddie,
The kitling knocked the mousey down, faddy, Oh! &c.

The frog he jumped into a brook, farding link-a-laddie,
Where he was gobbled up by a duck, faddy, Oh! &c.[5]

Some of the children's songs were more regional in nature. For example, "Nancy Dawson," sung to the tune of "Here We Go Round the Mulberry Bush," was an interesting blend of lyrics from two folksongs associated with northeast England, "Elsie Marley" and "Bobby Shaftoe."

Nancy Dawson

Anon

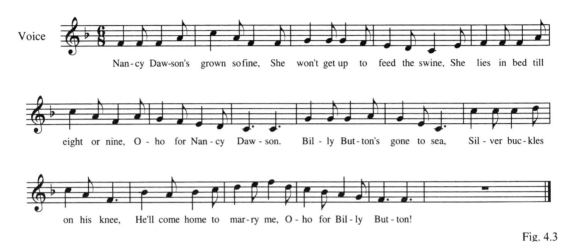

Nan-cy Daw-son's grown so fine, She won't get up to feed the swine, She lies in bed till eight or nine, O - ho for Nan-cy Daw-son. Bil - ly But-ton's gone to sea, Sil - ver buc-kles on his knee, He'll come home to mar-ry me, O - ho for Bil - ly But-ton!

Fig. 4.3

Nancy Dawson's grown so fine, she won't get up to feed the swine,
She lies in bed till eight or nine; O - ho! for Nancy Dawson!

Billy Button's gone to sea, silver buckles on his knee,
He'll come home to marry me; O – ho! for Billy Button![6]

However, by no means all the songs in the book were intended primarily for children. Although fairly small, *Nursery Rhymes and Country Songs* was in fact an important collection of folksongs derived from oral tradition, and it foreshadowed the major field-collection efforts of coming decades. In particular, the book included a number of narrative ballads, some learned from Grandmother Mitford, others noted elsewhere in England.

Perhaps the most interesting Northumbrian version of a traditional ballad noted by Mason was "There Was a Lady in the West." This was not the first time the ballad had been found in oral tradition. William Motherwell had collected two versions of "Riddles Wisely Expounded" in southern Scotland during the early years of the nineteenth century and Davies Gilbert had published a version that he had heard in the south-west of England.[7] An earlier printed source was Thomas D'Urfey's 1719 edition of *Wit and Mirth: or Pills to Purge Melancholy*, while the ballad was also common as a broadside, with copies in the Douce, Pepys, Rawlinson, and Wood collections (among others).[8] In most versions of the ballad the stranger is an eligible bachelor come to seek a wife, but in Mason's variant he is the devil in disguise, which makes it a cross between "Riddles Wisely Expounded" and "The False Knight on the Road," although it should probably be counted as a variant of the former rather than the latter. One of Motherwell's versions also portrays the wooer as the devil.

There was a lady in the West,
Lay the bank with the bonnie broom,
She had three daughters of the best,
Fa lang the dillo,
Fa lang the dillo, dillo, dee.

There came a stranger to the gate,
Lay the bank, &c.
And he three days and nights did wait,
Fa lang the dillo, &c.

The eldest daughter did ope the door,
The second set him on the floor.
The third daughter she brought a chair,
And placed it that he might sit there.

"Now answer me these questions three,
Or you shall surely go with me."

"Now answer me these questions six,
Or you shall surely be Old Nick's."

"Now answer me these questions nine,
Or you shall surely be all mine."

"What is greener than the grass?"
"What is smoother than crystal glass?"
"What is louder than a horn?'
"What is sharper than a thorn?"

"What is brighter than a light?"	"Hunger is sharper than a thorn."
"What is darker than the night?"	
	"Truth is brighter than a light,"
"What is keener than an axe?"	"Falsehood is darker than the night."
"What is softer than melting wax?"	
	"Revenge is keener than an axe,
"What is rounder than a ring?"	Love is softer than melting wax."
"To you we thus our answers bring."	
	"The world is rounder than a ring,
"Envy is greener than the grass,	To you we thus our answers bring."
"Flattery, smoother than crystal glass."	
	"Thus you have our answers nine,
"Rumour is louder than a horn,"	And we never shall be thine."[9]

There Was a Lady in the West

Anon

There was a lad - y — in the West, Lay the bank with the bon - ny broom, She

had three daught-ers of — the best, Fa lang the dil - lo, Fa lang the dil lo dil lo

dee.

Fig. 4.4

Other traditional ballads in the collection included "Giles Collin" (aka "Lady Alice"), a truncated version of "Clerk Colvill," a tragic ballad that warned against the dangers of sexual infidelity and of meddling with the supernatural. Mason's version provided an interesting example of how a fine ballad could degenerate while yet retaining some elements of the original story. It was probably derived from a broadside version titled "Giles Collins and Proud Lady Alice," in which the tale had been stripped of its magic and turned into a mildly comic parody; Robert Bell had picked up a stall copy of this and included it in his 1857 edition of James Henry Dixon's *Ancient Poems, Ballads and Songs of the Peasantry of England*,[10] while a slightly different broadside version had earlier appeared in the 1810 edition of *Gammer Gurton's Garland*.[11] However, if one counted it as a separate ballad (as Francis James Child would, allotting it number 85 in *The English and Scottish Popular Ballads*[12]), this was the first time the song had been noted from oral tradition.

Giles Collin he said to his mother one day,	And died before it was noon.
"Oh! mother, come bind up my head;	
For tomorrow morning, before it is day,	Lady Alice was sitting in her window,
I'm sure I shall be dead."	All dressed in her night-coif;
	She saw as pretty a corpse go by,
"Oh! mother, oh! mother, if I should die,	As ever she'd seen in her life.
And I am sure I shall,	
I will not be buried in our churchyard,	"What bear ye there, ye six tall men?
But under Lady Alice's wall."	What bear ye on your shourn?"
	"We bear the body of Giles Collin,
His mother she made him some water gruel,	Who was a true lover of yourn."
And stirred it up with a spoon;	
Giles Collin he ate but one spoonful,	

"Down with him, down with him, upon the
                                                grass,
The grass that grows so green;
For tomorrow morning before it is day,
My body shall lie by him."

Her mother made her some plum-gruel,
With spices all of the best;
Lady Alice she ate but one spoonful,
And the doctor he ate up the rest.

Giles Collin was laid in the lower chancel,
Lady Alice all in the higher;
There grew up a rose from Lady Alice's breast,
And from Giles Collin's, a briar.

And they grew and they grew to the very church top,
Until they could grow no higher,
And twisted and twined in a true-lover's knot,
Which made all the parish admire.[13]

Giles Collin

Anon

Fig. 4.5

Mason's version of the anti-Semitic traditional ballad "The Jew's Daughter" (aka "Hugh of Lincoln") was titled "Little Sir William." It was noticeably different from the better known version, derived from Scottish tradition, that Thomas Percy had included in the *Reliques of Ancient English Poetry* and Victorian antiquarian James Orchard Halliwell collated in his publication, *Ballads and Poems respecting Hugh of Lincoln.*[14] Although the storyline had been compressed and the melody was less poignant, this was an effective variant with a vigorous and attractive tune:

Little Sir William

Anon

Fig. 4.6

Easter Day was a holiday, of all days in the year;
And all the little school fellows went out to play, but Sir William was not there.

Mamma went to the Jew's wife's house and knocked at the ring,
Saying "Little Sir William, if you are there, Oh! let your mother in!"

The Jew's wife opened the door and said, "He is not here to-day;
He is with the little schoolfellows out on the green, playing some pretty play."

Mamma went to the Boyne water that is so wide and deep,
Saying "Little Sir William, if you are there, Oh! pity your mother's weep!"

"How can I pity your weep, mother, and I so long in pain?
For the little penknife sticks close in my heart, and the Jew's wife has me slain."

"Go home, go home, my mother dear, and prepare my winding sheet;
For tomorrow morning, before eight o'clock, you with my body shall meet."

"And lay my prayer-book at my head, and my grammar at my feet,
That all the little schoolfellows, as they pass by, may read them for my sake."[15]

In addition to these traditional ballads, Mason's collection included some broadsides that had entered oral tradition. The more notable were "The Silly Old Man" (a variant of "The Highwayman Outwitted"), the sentimental but very popular "Babes in the Wood," and a compact version of "Spencer the Rover." It had been noted in Derbyshire from the singing of a local agricultural laborer—Mason called him a "Derbyshire peasant"—who had also provided a similarly moralistic lyric called "The Spider," which lamented the extremes of wealth and poverty present in the English countryside.

Spencer the Rover

Anon

When Spencer the rover, who'd wander'd all over,
And gone through most parts of Great Britain and Wales,
Near Rotherham in Yorkshire arrived on his rambles,
And, weary of trav'ling, had sat down to rest.

At the foot of yon mountain, where runs a clear fountain,
With bread and cold water he did him content;
He found it was sweeter than the gold he had wasted,
And sweeter than honey, the pleasure it lent.

As night was approaching, to the woods he resorted,
With woodbine and ivery his bed he did make;
He dreamt about crying, lamenting, and sighing,
"Go home to thy family, and rambling forsake!"

Fig. 4.7

> "Last fifth of November, I've cause to remember,
> My children were round me, care driving away;
> United together, like birds of one feather,
> Like bees in one hive, we contented will stay!"[16]

Other broadside ballads in *Nursery Rhymes and Country Songs* derived from John Broadwood's previously mentioned collection of tunes and lyrics noted mainly in northern Sussex, near the border with Surrey.[17] Examples are "'Tis of a Noble Lord," "'Tis of a Young Damsel" (a version of "The Lost Lady Found"), "The Privateer" (a patriotic sea ballad), and the poaching ballad, "In Thorny Woods." The other items that Mason had decided to include from Broadwood's book were two songs that fulsomely extolled the pleasures of living and working in the countryside, "The Rosebuds in June" and "A Sweet Country Life."

There were also various other folksongs in *Nursery Rhymes and Country Songs*, such as "There Was an A'd Man Cam' Over the Lea" (aka "An Old Man Came A-Courting"), "When I Was a Maiden," and a fragment from a Christmas mumming play, "The Old Horse," which was sung by Nottinghamshire wassailers as the hobby horse entered each house. Another example of the valuable (and highly singable) material in the collection was one of the oldest songs, "The Cutty Wren," one of two items that Mason had learned in her childhood from a nurse while staying in the Welsh county of Carmarthenshire. Although it has been suggested (by A. L. Lloyd) that this song has late medieval origins and refers to the Peasants' Revolt of 1381, it seems more likely that it reflects the social and political conflict of the 1640s, and that the *persona* of John the Red Nose in the song may depict Oliver Cromwell (Cromwell's family were brewers and he was often portrayed with a red nose in the broadside literature of the Civil War period).

The Cutty Wren

Anon

Fig. 4.8

"O, where are you going?" says Milder to Malder;
"O, I cannot tell," says Festel to Fose;
"We're going to the woods," says John the Red Nose,
"We're going to the woods," says John the Red Nose.

"O, what will you do there?" says Milder to Malder,
"O, I cannot tell," says Festel to Fose;
"We'll shoot the Cutty Wren," says John the Red Nose,
"We'll shoot the Cutty Wren," says John the Red Nose.

"O, how will you shoot her?" says Milder to Malder,
"O, I cannot tell," says Festel to Fose;

"With arrows and bows," says John the Red Nose,
"With arrows and bows," says John the Red Nose.

"O, that will not do," says Milder to Malder,
"O, what will do then?" says Festel to Fose;
"With cannons and guns," says John the Red Nose,
"With cannons and guns," says John the Red Nose.

"O, how will you bring her home?" says Milder to Malder,
"O, I cannot tell," says Festel to Fose;

"On four strong men's shoulders," says John the Red Nose,
"On four strong men's shoulders," says John the Red Nose.

"O, that will not do," says Milder to Malder,
"O, what will do then?" says Festel to Fose;
"In waggons and carts," says John the Red Nose,
"In waggons and carts," says John the Red Nose.

"O, what will you cut her up with?" says Milder to Malder,
"O, I cannot tell," says Festel to Fose;
"With knives and with forks," says John the Red Nose,
"With knives and with forks," says John the Red Nose.

"O, that will not do," says Milder to Malder,
"O, what will do then?" says Festel to Fose;

"With hatchets and cleavers," says John the Red Nose,
"With hatchets and cleavers," says John the Red Nose.

"O, how will you boil her?" says Milder to Malder,
"O, I cannot tell," says Festel to Fose;
"In kettles and pots," says John the Red Nose,
"In kettles and pots," says John the Red Nose.

"O, that will not do," says Milder to Malder,
"O, what will do then?" says Festel to Fose;
"In cauldrons and pans," says John the Red Nose,
"In cauldrons and pans," says John the Red Nose.

"O, who'll have the spare-ribs?" says Milder to Malder,
"O, I cannot tell," says Festel to Fose;
"We'll give them to the poor," says John the Red Nose,
"We'll give them to the poor," says John the Red Nose.[18]

Nursery Rhymes and Country Songs thus included quite a variety of interesting material, from traditional ballads and broadsides to songs of agricultural life and political history, as well as the children's game songs and nursery rhymes alluded to in the title. Yet the most significant thing of all about this pioneering publication was that *all* fifty-eight items came complete with tunes. So, although it was not a very bulky collection, Mason's slim songbook was significant in two very important ways: it drew exclusively upon oral tradition, and it respected folksongs as holistic fusions of text and melody. The collecting and editorial approach adopted by Marianne Harriet Mason thus represented a significant methodological step forward, and it foreshadowed the new folksong revival that would begin to emerge in the 1880s.

Ballads and Songs of Lancashire

It appears that by the early 1880s compilations of regional songs and poetry were beginning to find a market. As indicated in chapter 2, John Harland's *Ballads and Songs of Lancashire*, which had been published in 1865, was one of the pioneering mid-Victorian regional collections. It included not only texts of such ballads as "The Cruel Sister" and folk lyrics such as "The Seeds of Love" and "The Sprig of Thyme," but also many vernacular songs reflecting the daily life of both rural and industrial Lancashire. It was particularly notable for its inclusion of traditional May Day songs, wassails and wakes, and for printing the texts of a number of songs created by communities of textile workers.[19] In 1882 Harland's friend T. T. Wilkinson edited a new (third) edition of this important work, and expanded its contents significantly by drawing on another of Harland's song collections, *Lancashire Lyrics*.[20] Unfortunately, the one major drawback of this otherwise very valuable collection, the absence of any music, was not remedied in the new edition.

The 1882 version of *Ballads and Songs of Lancashire* was divided into two main parts, the first (comprising over two hundred pages) titled "Ancient Songs and Ballads" and the second (another three hundred and fifty pages) called "Modern Songs and Ballads."[21] The first part included several border ballads, other narrative ballads, May Day and wassail songs, drinking songs, old comic songs, and such regional material as "The Liverpool Tragedy," "The Lancashire Miller," "The Burnley Haymakers," "The Praise of Lancashire Men," and "The Lancashire Witches," as well as the industrial songs of the county's spinners and weavers (for example, "Jone o' Grinfelt's Ramble," "Hand-loom versus Power-loom" and "The Hand-loom Weaver's Lament"). The second part contained only a few traditional songs and consisted mainly of imitation ballads by local poets and more recently composed songs (whose authors were usually named). Its mode of organization was interesting, however: it was subdivided into seven categories: "Romantic and Legendary Ballads" (including "Derwentwater's Fate"), "Love Songs and Praises of the Fair" (this section included a few folk lyrics taken from broadsides), "Songs of Home and Its Affections," "Songs of Life and Brotherhood" (this section included an odd mixture of patriotic songs, drinking songs, religious songs, and songs about exile and death), "Lays of the Cotton Famine" (including "The Mill-Hand's Petition," "The Factory Lass," "Eawt o' Wark," "The Smokeless Chimney," "Hard Times," and "Th' Shurat Weyvur's Song"), "Sea Songs" and a final miscellaneous section.

Most of Wilkinson's additions were modern compositions, but he had found a few extra items for Part 1 as well. As an example, here is a humorous anti-military song, written partly in dialect, "The Owdham Recruit":

When I're a young lad, sixteen years ago,
I lov'd a pretty lass, and followed the plough;
But somehow or other I was ne'er content,
Till I like a noddy for a sodger went.
There were such shouts of miorth and glee,
For I thowt I should a Captain be.
Bud ah! by gum! I wur varra much mista'en,
And monny a time I wished mysel' at t' plough-tail again.

So we march'd and march'd abeawt Owdham streets,
Where they tried to persaude me 'twas my turn to treat;
I treated them all till we geet drunk as foos,'
Between serjeant, me, and corporal, there wur nod mich to chuse,
I thowt that my brass wod never ha been done,
Thinks I but we shall live a life of rare fun.
Bud ah! by gum! I wur varra much mista'en,
And monny a time I wished mysel' at t' plough-tail again.

Bud when my brass wur o spent and dun,
They pushed me about for a bit of roaring fun;
By gum, they'd like to throttled me; eh what a sin;
With a collar stiff as steel just stuck under my chin,
They cut my hair so close, sure, and gathered such a crop,
They made me soon i' th' regiment a real dandy fop.
Bud ah! by gum! &c.

I'st never forget what a fuss of me they made,
When we went to a pleck ut they coed their parade;
If I could look to pleeos um theer, may I indeed be brunt,
For they wanted all at once my een, left, reet, and front;
Then o in a row like fire potters we wur stood,
And my toes wouldn't turn in let me do wot I could;
I listed for a Captain; but, by gum, I wur mista'en,
And monny a time, &c.

I wondered wot the dickens could ever be the matter,
For they shut me in the guard-house to live on bread and watter;
And when I offered then to quit that ugly place,
A soldier with his bagnet stood staring in my face:
I began then a thinkin' that my case was varra bad,
For I're wur off by far than when I' th' awkward squad.
I listed for a Captain; but, by gum, &c.[22]

Despite its presentation of much interesting regional material (in particular, the industrial songs reflecting the hardships of workers in the Lancashire textile industry), there were two main drawbacks with *Ballads and Songs of Lancashire*: a good half of the contents were literary rather than vernacular in character, and, as we have seen, there were no tunes. Even the revised edition, therefore, was essentially a work of mid-Victorian scholarship rather than a contribution to the new wave of folksong collecting with its emphasis on the recovery of melodies in addition to texts. It was nonetheless a useful publication that underlined the existence and value of industrial songs as well as country ones, and which implicitly argued that broadside ballads and recently composed vernacular songs were as interesting and important as traditional ballads and older songs noted from oral tradition. And, of course, it demonstrated that the north was likely to be a fruitful hunting ground for anyone interested in tapping into the living tradition of English regional and national song.

Northumbrian Minstrelsy

As it so happened, it was the northeast rather than the northwest of England that provided the second foundational document of the Late Victorian folksong revival. The same year (1882) in which Wilkinson's edition of *Ballads and Songs of Lancashire* appeared also witnessed the publication of a major folksong collection that has since become a classic,

John Collingwood Bruce & John Stokoe's *Northumbrian Minstrelsy*.[23] At first glance it appeared to represent a significant advance on all previous publications: here, at last, was a substantial collection of folk music that apparently included many authentic texts, with tunes, plus substantive information about the songs and their sources, who were often local carriers of oral tradition. Although only a regional collection, the book was wide in scope. It comprised one hundred and forty-four items, divided into two main sections: ballads and songs, complete with melody lines, and small-pipe tunes. The volume also seemed to have been carefully edited, with informative notes by John Stokoe that usually included the source of the ballad, song, or tune. In the main, Collingwood Bruce (1805-1892) was responsible for the texts and Stokoe for the tunes. Bruce, incidentally, was a retired Presbyterian divine and school-teacher. An enthusiastic amateur archaeologist, whose main hobby was studying the chronology of Hadrian's Wall, he lived in Newcastle-upon-Tyne.[24] John Stokoe, also a member of the local Society of Antiquaries, was a journalist and an amateur musician who played the Northumbrian pipes.[25]

Appearances can be a little deceptive, however, and the *Northumbrian Minstrelsy* has proven a controversial work. Scholarly assessments of the book differ markedly, reflecting the critics' own ideological biases. Some have been favorable. A. L. Lloyd wrote a "Foreword" to a 1965 facsimile reprint of the book, and while he pointed out some of the work's deficiencies (particularly the editors' occasional modifications to tunes and texts) his overall assessment of *Northumbrian Minstrelsy* was positive. "Beside the weight of the *Minstrelsy's* virtues," he concluded, "its defects are as a feather. The songs and tunes of this quite modest nineteenth century volume do what no other distinguished collection of English folk song does: they look back on the rural feudal past but also they look forward to the urban industrial present."[26] In contrast, the book has drawn heavy criticism from proponents of the 'cultural studies' approach to folk music. In Dave Harker's opinion, for example, Bruce and Stokoe imposed their "class-bound values and assumptions" onto their source material by borrowing from earlier publications without proper acknowledgement, by avoiding or censoring erotic material, and by privileging the northern, more rural, part of the region. He argues that they "excised any piece which smacked of working-class struggle, downgraded worker-musicians at every opportunity and generally reconstructed a musical culture...from a very obviously ideological perspective, for the benefit of the Duke, members of the Society of Antiquaries, musical antiquarians elsewhere in the country, and all these people's connections in polite society."[27] It is, of course, true that the publication was aimed at a middle-class market and therefore represented, to some degree, a cultural transfer across class lines. But Harker's detailed criticisms are not entirely fair: there seems nothing wrong with concentrating on material from north of Durham in a book titled *Northumbrian Minstrelsy*; the editors did acknowledge their debt to John Bell's *Rhymes of Northern Bards*; and they included a variety of dialect and other vernacular songs, not to mention dozens of pipe tunes. On the other hand, a few of their texts were unreliable. Retired clergyman Bruce insisted on excluding or modifying lyrics that he judged indecent. Moreover, since the publication of Hales & Furnivall's edition of Blount's folio manuscript, he had no excuse for relying on Percy's *Reliques of Ancient English Poetry* for ballad texts, nor was Scott's *Minstrelsy of the Scottish Border* an unimpeachable source. Judged by modern editorial standards *Northumbrian Minstrelsy* was far from perfect, and the progress made was only relative.

Moreover, it is important to recognize that Bruce and Stokoe's publication was not, in the main, the product of *recent* collecting from oral tradition in the counties of Northumberland and Durham (the region of northeastern England that the term Northumbria in the title was intended to designate). It was, in fact, a selection of materials from the archives of the Newcastle-upon-Tyne Society of Antiquaries, and its contents had been gathered over a lengthy period, effectively between 1813 (when the Society was formed) and 1877, when local musician Joseph Crawhall published a small collection of *Tunes for the Northumbrian small pipes, violin or flute*. The book could—and should—have been published in the early 1860s, and it probably would have been but for a series of events that delayed its completion. In 1855 a subcommittee of the Society of Antiquaries had been formed to undertake the task of pulling together a collection of the region's traditional songs and tunes played by local pipers. Collingwood Bruce was a member, along with lawyer John C. Fenwick, but two other men were also keenly involved in the original project. One of these, William Kell, died in 1862, after a painful illness that had for some time incapacitated him. Another driving force, antiquarian and song collector Robert White, died in 1870. After Fenwick moved to London, Bruce was left with sole responsibility for the project, and he lacked the musical expertise required. He therefore eventually recruited local journalist and musician John Stokoe to work on the musical aspect of the planned publication. As mentioned, Stokoe played the Northumbrian pipes, and it may have been his idea to divide the book into two parts, the first focusing on traditional songs and the second on pipe tunes. Bruce appears to have retained control over the ballad and song texts.

Given Bruce's age and history of procrastination, it was probably Stokoe who did the lion's share of preparing *Northumbrian Minstrelsy* for publication. He wisely decided not to attempt to provide piano arrangements for the songs, providing instead simple melody lines, as he also did for the pipe tunes. The sources he had to work with were quite varied: some printed, some in manuscript, and some items noted from oral tradition. The oldest seem to have been two of

Joseph Ritson's songbooks, *The Bishopric Garland, or Durham Minstrel* (1784, revised edition 1792) and *The Northumberland Garland* (1793). Next came a tunebook by John Peacock, a celebrated piper employed by the city of Newcastle around the turn of the century: his *Favourite Collection of Tunes with Variations Adapted for the Northumbrian Small Pipes* was published locally *circa* 1804. Another major printed source, John Bell's *Rhymes of the Northern Bards*, dated from 1812. This contained no tunes, but while compiling it Bell had collected about one hundred melodies and made fair copies of them in a manuscript book subsequently preserved in Newcastle's Black Gate Museum. Stokoe had access to this manuscript, and he made extensive use of it. He also had a copy of Sunderland musician Robert Topliffe's *A Selection of the Most Popular Melodies of the Tyne and the Wear,* published locally *circa* 1815, which he used as the foundation for the second half of the *Minstrelsy.* He supplemented this with a few items from Crawhall's more recent, but apparently less reliable, *Tunes for the Northumbrian small pipes, violin or flute.* Another printed source was Sir Cuthbert Sharp's *The Bishoprick Garland, or a collection of Legends, Songs, Ballads, etc., belonging to the county of Durham* (1832).

Stokoe also had other material at his disposal, and some of this had been noted in the field. Thomas Doubleday had collected songs in the streets of Newcastle, and he had made both texts and tunes available to the Society in the 1820s. Robert White had done some collecting of his own, including noting some ballads and songs from the singing of his sister, Mrs. Andrews, who had learned them from their mother. A friend of White's, the shepherd and writer James Telfer, had during the 1840s noted forty-nine song texts in Liddesdale, Redesdale and elsewhere near the Scottish border, and a decade later he had returned with a musician friend to obtain the tunes. James Henry Dixon, while a member of the Newcastle Society of Antiquaries in the 1830s (i.e., before he moved to London and joined the Percy Society), had contributed several items to its archives. His book, *Ancient Poems, Ballads and Songs of the Peasantry of England,* was also used as a source for the words of songs when the local variants were corrupt or incomplete. A local singer, Thomas Hepple of Kirkwhelpington, had submitted the texts and tunes of various old ballads and traditional songs that he had known since childhood. His cousin, piper John Baty of Wark, had lent the committee a large manuscript tunebook that had been compiled in 1770 by another local piper, William Vickers. Another Northumbrian piper, Robert Bewick, had similarly shared the sixty melodies from his manuscript tunebook. It is evident, therefore, that Stokoe had no shortage of material to choose from. The selections in the second half of the *Minstrelsy* were probably largely his own, but the Reverend Bruce clearly had a strong voice in deciding what went into the first part.

Notwithstanding its blemishes, *Northumbrian Minstrelsy* was a major collection, with a wide range of different kinds of material, including narrative ballads, broadsides, folk lyrics, regional songs, and local instrumental pieces. Above all, it systematically printed tunes as well as texts. One significant aspect of the book was the inclusion (with tunes) of northern English versions of a number of fine narrative ballads. To begin with there were several lengthy ballads about military operations, skirmishes, cattle raids and other conflicts in the countryside along the Scottish border. These included "Chevy Chace" (for which several alternative tunes were provided), "The Bewick and the Graeme," "Jock o' the Syde," and "The Death of Parcy Reed." To illustrate this component of the collection, here is a Northumbrian version of "Earl Brand." The ballad, which is possibly of late medieval origin, was collected fairly extensively from Scottish oral tradition by Sharpe, Kinloch, and Motherwell, and Sir Walter Scott printed a version in his *Minstrelsy of the Scottish Border.* It was also extant south of the border. A fragment of an earlier English version (dating from no later than the mid-seventeenth century) may be found in the Percy folio manuscript, there was apparently a rather rare broadside edition, and Robert Bell had included a variant in his edition of *Ancient Poems, Ballads and Songs of the Peasantry of England.*[28] Bruce's source for the text, which was slightly incomplete, was a manuscript by Newcastle antiquarian Robert White, who had apparently taken down the ballad from the recitation of a local fiddler. Stokoe's source for the tune was the singing of White's sister, Mrs. Andrews, who had learned it from her mother.

O did you ever hear of the brave Earl Brand?
Hey lillie, ho lillie, lallie;
He's courted the King's daughter o' fair England,
I' the brave nights so early!

She was scarcely fifteen years that tide,
Hey lillie, etc.;
When sae boldly she came to his bedside,
I' the brave nights, etc.

"O, Earl Brand, how fain wad I see,
A pack of hounds let loose on the lea."

"O lady fair, I have no steed but one,
But you shalt ride, and I will run."

"O, Earl Brand, but my father has two,
And thou shalt have the best o' tho'."

Brave Earl Brand and the King of England's Daughter

Anon

O did you ev-er hear of the brave Earl Brand? Hey lil-ie, ho lil-lie,

lal - lie. He's court-ed the King's daugh-ter o' fair Eng - land, I' the brave nights so ear - ly.

Fig. 4.9

Now they have ridden o'er moss and moor,
And they have met neither rich nor poor.

Till at last they met with old Carl Hood,
He's aye for ill and never for good.

"Now, Earl Brand, an' ye love me,
Slay this old Carl and gar him dee."

"O lady fair, but that would be sair,
To slay an auld Carl that wears grey hair.

My own lady fair, I'll not do that,
I'll pay him his fee....."

"O, where have you ridden this lee lang day,
And where have you stown this fair lady away?"

"I have not ridden this lee lang day,
Nor yet have I stown this lady away.

For she is, I trow, my sick sister,
Whom I have been bringing fra' Winchester."

"If she's been sick and nigh to dead,
What makes her wear the ribbon sae red?

If she's been sick and like to die,
What makes her wear the gold sae high?"

When came the Carl to the lady's yett,
He rudely, rudely rapped thereat.

"Now where is the lady of this hall?"
"She's out with her maids a-playing at the ball."

"Ha, ha, ha! Ye are all mista'en,
Ye may count your maidens owre again.

I met her far beyond the lea,
With the young Earl Brand his leman to be."

Her father of his best men armed fifteen—
And they're ridden after them bidene.

The lady looked owre her left shoulder then,
Says, "O Earl Brand, we are both of us ta'en."

"If they come on me one by one,
You may stand by me till the fights be done.

But if they come on me one and all,
You may stand by and see me fall."

They came upon him one by one,
Till fourteen battles he has won.

And fourteen men he has them slain,
Each after each upon the plain.

But the fifteenth man behind stole round,
And dealt him a deep and a deadly wound.

Though he was wounded to the deid,
He set his lady on her steed.

They rode till they came to the river Doune,
And there they lighted to wash his wound.

"O, Earl Brand, I see you heart's blood."
"It's nothing but the glent and my scarlet hood."

They rode till they came to his mother's yett,
So faintly and feebly he rapped thereat.

"O my son's slain, he is falling to swoon,
And it's all for the sake of an English loon."

"O say not so, my dearest mother,
But marry her to my youngest brother."

"To a maiden true he'll give his hand,

To the king's daughter o' fair England,   To a prize that was won by a slain brother's brand,
                                                           I' the brave nights so early."[29]

Another ballad about the abduction of an English girl across the border into Scotland was "The Fair Flower of Northum-berland." This dated from the late Tudor era, and the source of the oldest known version was silk weaver Thomas Delo-ney, who had included it in his *Pleasant History of John Winchcomb*.[30] A leading ballad-monger during the last years of the reign of Elizabeth I, Deloney was probably the author of the text reprinted in *Northumbrian Minstrelsy*, although Bruce may have actually copied it from Joseph Ritson's *Ancient Songs from the Time of King Henry the Third to the Revolution*.[31] Stokoe had in any case previously contributed a version of the ballad to a local newspaper, the *Newcastle Courant*, and, since neither Deloney nor Ritson provided a melody, it seems very likely that he had, as he indicated there, noted the tune (and perhaps also the entire text or just part of it) on collecting expeditions in the Tynedale, Reed-water, and Liddesdale districts of Northumberland and the Scottish borderlands. Both melody and text are significantly different from the Scottish versions of the ballad collected by Kinloch, Motherwell, and Buchan. Robert White's papers, which were apparently available to Bruce and Stokoe, contained another version of the ballad with an equally if not more attractive tune, but Stokoe chose to go with the oldest set of words and the tune that he had found to match them.

The Fair Flower of Northumberland

Anon

Fig. 4.10

It was a knight, in Scotland born,
Follow, my love, come over the strand,
Was taken pris'ner and left forlorn,
Even by the good Earl of Northumberland.

Then was he cast in prison strong,
Follow, my love, etc.,
Where he could not walk nor lay along,
Even by the good Earl, etc.

And as in sorrow thus he lay,
Follow, my love, etc.
The Earl's sweet daughter passed that way,
And she the fair flower of Northumberland.

And passing by, like an angel bright,
Follow, my love, etc.,
The prisoner had of her a sight,

And she the fair flower, etc.

And aloud to her this knight did cry,
Follow, my love, etc.
The salt tears standing in her eye,
And she the fair flower, etc.

"Fair lady," he said, "take pity on me,"
Follow, my love, etc.
"And let me not in prison dee,
And you the fair flower," etc.

"Fair sir, how should I take pity on thee,"
Follow, my love, etc.
"Thou being a foe to our countree,
And I the fair flower," etc.

"Fair lady, I am no foe," he said,
Follow, my love, etc.
"Through thy sweet love here was I stayed,
And thou the fair flower," etc.

"Why should'st thou come here for love of me,
Having wife and bairns in thy own countree?"

"I swear by the blessed Trinity,
That neither wife nor bairns have I."

"If courteously thou wilt set me free,
I vow that I will marry thee."

"Thou shalt be lady of castles and towers,
And sit like a queen in princely bowers."

Then parted hence this lady gay,
And got her father's ring away.

Likewise much gold got she by sleight,
And all to help this forlorn knight.

Two gallant steeds, both good and able,
She likewise took out of the stable.

And to the gaoler she sent the ring,
Who the knight from prison forth did bring.

This token set the prisoner free,
Who straight went to this fair lady.

A gallant steed he did bestride,
And with the lady away did ride.

They rode till they came to a water clear,
"Good sir, how shall I follow you here?"

"The water is rough and wonderful deep,
And on my saddle I shall not keep."

"Fear not the ford, fair lady!" quoth he,
For long I cannot stay for thee."

The lady prickt her gallant steed,
And over the water swam with speed.

From top to toe all wet was she,
"This have I done for love of thee."

Thus rode she all one winter's night,
Follow, my love, come over the strand,

Till Edinborough they saw in sight—
The fairest town in all Scotland.

"Now choose," quoth he, "thou wanton flower:
If thou wilt be my paramour.

For I have a wife and children five,
In Edinborough they be alive.

And if thou wilt not give thy hand,
Then get thee home to fair England.

This favour thou shalt have to boot –
I'll have thy horse; go thou on foot."

"O false and faithless knight," quoth she;
"And canst thou deal so bad with me?

Dishonour not a lady's name,
But draw thy sword and end my shame."

He took her from her stately steed,
And left her there in extreme need.

Then she sat down full heavily,
At length two knights came riding by.

Two gallant knights of fair England,
And there they found her on the strand.

She fell down humbly on her knee,
Crying, "Courteous knights, take pity on me.

I have offended my father dear,
For a false knight that brought me here."

They took her up beside them then,
And brought her to her father again.

And now you fair maids be warned by me,
Follow no Scotchman over the strand;

Scots never were true, nor ever will be,
To lord nor lady nor fair England.[32]

If Deloney was indeed the composer, "The Fair Flower of Northumberland" could (and perhaps should) be counted as a broadside rather than a traditional ballad, and the same might be said of "The Outlandish Knight," which also related the abduction of a naïve maiden by a stranger from the "North lands" (read Scotland). Bruce and Stokoe claimed they had found it on a "stall copy of considerable antiquity," although they obtained the tune from Mrs. Andrews.[33] In fact their text was identical to that provided by James Henry Dixon in *Ancient Poems, Ballads and Songs of the Peasantry of England*,[34] whereas the broadside text in the Roxburghe Collection (in the British Museum) differed. At any rate, it was the addition of Mrs. Andrews's melody that made this reprint a significant contribution to the corpus of English balladry.

The Outlandish Knight

Anon

Fig. 4.11

An outlandish knight came from the North lands, and he came a wooin' to me;
He told me he'd take me unto the North lands, and there he would marry me.

"Come fetch me some of your father's gold, and some of your mother's fee,
And two of the best nags out of the stable, where they stand thirty and three."

She fetched him some of her father's gold, and some of her mother's fee;
And two of the best nags out of the stable, where they stood thirty and three.

She mounted her on her milk-white steed, he on a dapple grey,
They rode till they came unto the sea-side, three hours before it was day.

"Light off, light off, thy milk-white steed, and deliver it unto me!
Six pretty maids have I drowned here, and thou the seventh shall be.

Pull off, pull off, thy silken gown, and deliver it unto me!
Methinks it looks too rich and too gay to rot in the salt sea.

Pull off, pull off, thy silken stays, and deliver them unto me;
Methinks they are too fine and gay to rot in the salt sea.

Pull off, pull off, thy Holland smock, and deliver it unto me;
Methinks it looks too rich and gay to rot in the salt sea."

"If I must pull off my Holland smock, pray turn thy back to me,
For it is not fitting that such a ruffian a naked woman should see."

He turned his back towards her, and viewed the leaves so green;
She catched him around the middle so small and tumbled him into the stream.

He dropped high, he dropped low, until he came to the side—
"Catch hold of my hand, my pretty maiden, and I will make you my bride."

"Lie there, lie there, you false-hearted man, lie there instead of me!
Six pretty maids have you drowned here, and the seventh has drownèd thee."

She mounted on her milk-white steed, and led the dapple grey;
She rode till she came to her own father's hall, three hours before it was day.

The parrot being in the window so high, hearing the lady, did say,
"I'm afraid that some ruffian has led you astray, that you've tarried so long away."

"Don't prittle or prattle, my pretty parrot, nor tell no tales of me;
Thy cage shall be made of the glittering gold, although it is made of a tree."

The king being in the chamber so high, and hearing the parrot, did say,
"What ails you, what ails you, my pretty parrot, that you prattle so long before day?"

"It's no laughing matter," the parrot did say, "but so loudly I call unto thee;
For the cats have got into the window so high, and I'm afraid they will have me."

"Well turned, well turned, my pretty parrot, well turned, well turned for me;
Thy cage shall be made of the glittering gold, and the door of the best ivory."[35]

    Northumbrian Minstrelsy contained, in addition to the border ballads already mentioned, several other traditional ballads, although Bruce and Stokoe may have again resorted to printed sources for their texts. Of note, for example, was their version of "Binnorie, or, The Cruel Sister," about which Stokoe remarked that "the popularity of this ballad in England extends over more than a couple of centuries. Mr. Rimbault printed a version from a broadside, dated 1656. It also appeared in *Wit Restored,* 1658...The tune is a true Northumbrian melody, never before published."[36]

Binnorie; or, The Cruel Sister

Anon

There   were   twa   sis-ters   sat   in   a   bow'r,   Bin-nor-ie,   O   Bin-no-rie;   There

came   a___knight   to   be___   their   woo'r,   By   the   bon-nie   mill   dams   o'   Bin-no-rie.

Fig. 4.12

There were twa sisters sat in a bow'r,
Binnorie, O Binnorie,
There came a knight to be their woo'r,
By the bonnie mill-dams of Binnorie.

He courted the eldest wi' glove and ring,
Binnorie, etc.,
But he lo'ed the youngest aboon a' thing.
By the bonnie, etc.

He courted the eldest wi' broach and knife,
But he lo'ed the youngest aboon his life.

The eldest she was vexed sair,
And sore envied her sister fair.

The eldest said to the youngest ane:
"Will you go and see our father's ships come in."

She's ta'en her by the lily hand,
And led her down to the river strand.

The youngest stude upon a stane,

The eldest cam' and pushed her in.

She took her by the middle sma,'
And dashed her bonnie back to the jaw.

"O sister, sister, reach out your hand,
And ye shall be heir of half my land."

"O sister, I'll not reach my hand,
And I'll be heir of all your land.

Shame fa' the hand that I should take,
It's twined me, and my world's make."

"O sister, reach but me your glove,
And sweet William shall be your love."

"Sink on, nor hope for hand or glove,
And sweet William shall better be my love.

Your cherry cheeks and your yellow hair
Garr'd me gang maiden ever mair."

Sometimes she sunk, sometimes she swam,
Until she came to the miller's dam.

The miller's daughter was baking bread,
And gaed for water as she had need.

"O father, father, draw your dam!
There's either a mermaid or a milk-white swan."

The miller hasted and drew his dam,
And there he found a drown'd woman.

You couldna see her yellow hair
For gowd and pearls that were sae rare.

You couldna see her middle sma,'
Her gowden girdle was sae braw.

You couldna see her lily feet,
Her gowden fringes were sae deep.

A famous harper passing by,
The sweet pale face he chanced to spy;

And when he looked that lady on,

He sighed and made a heavy moan.

"Sair will they be, whate'er they be,
The hearts that live to weep for thee."

He made a harp o' her breast bone,
Whose sounds would melt a heart of stone;

The strings he framed of her yellow hair,
Their notes made sad the listening ear.

He brought it to her father's ha,'
There was the court assembled a.'

He laid the harp upon a stane,
And straight it began to play alane—

"O yonder sits my father, the king,
And yonder sits my mother, the queen;

And yonder stands my brother Hugh,
And by him my William, sweet and true."

But the last tune that the harp played then
Was—"Woe to my sister, false Helen!"[37]

Another traditional ballad of note was "Lay the Bent to the Bonny Broom" (aka "Riddles Wisely Expounded"). We have seen that Harriet Mason learned a version of this from her grandmother and included it in *Nursery Rhymes and Country Songs*. Bruce and Stokoe's text came courtesy of James Henry Dixon who had found it on a Restoration era broadside in the Bodleian Library, Oxford, and their tune derived from Thomas D'Urfey's *Wit and Mirth, or Pills to Purge Melancholy*.[38] In this variant the riddling stranger is a knight seeking a bride who possesses wit as well as beauty, and in the original broadside text it is evident that the youngest sister spends the night with him before undergoing her intelligence test.

Lay the Bent to the Bonny Broom

Anon

Voice: There was a la-dy in the North coun-trie, Lay the bent to the bon-nie broom, And she had love-ly daught ers three, Fa la la la la la la la la re.

Fig. 4.13

Bruce omitted the following segment of the broadside text for propriety's sake:

The youngest sister that same night,
She went to bed to this young knight.

And in the morning, when it was day,
These words unto him she did say:

"Now you have had your will," quoth she,
"I pray, sir knight, will you marry me?"[39]

This is the text printed in *Northumbrian Minstrelsy*. Bruce's substitutions will be obvious.

There was a lady in the North countrie,
Lay the bent to the bonnie broom,
And she had lovely daughters three,
Fa, la la la, fa, la la la ra re.

There was a knight of noble worth,
Lay the bent, &c.,
Who also lived in the north,
Fa, la la la, &c.

This knight was of courage stout and brave,
Nothing but love could his heart enslave.

This knight he knocked at the lady's gate,
One evening when it was full late.

The eldest sister let him in,
And pinned the door with a silver pin.

The second sister she made his bed,
And laid soft pillows under his head.

The youngest sister fair and bright,
Was resolved to wed this valiant knight.

And in the morning when it was day,
These words unto him she did say:

"Now (as I love you well)" quoth she,
"I pray, sir knight, will you marry me?"

The young brave knight to her replied—
"Thy suit, fair maid, shall not be denied;

If thou canst answer me questions three,
This very day I will marry thee."

"Kind sir, in love, O then," quoth she,
"Tell me what your questions be?"

"O what is longer than the way?
Or what is deeper than the sea?

Or what is louder than the horn?
Or what is sharper than the thorn?

Or what is greener than the grass?
Or what is worse than woman e'er was?"

"O true love is longer than the way,
And hell is deeper than the sea.

And thunder is louder than the horn,
And hunger is sharper than the thorn.

And poison is greener than the grass,
And the Devil is worse than woman e'er was."

When she these questions answered had,
The knight became exceeding glad.

And having tried so hard her wit,
He much commended her for it.

And after it was verified,
He made of her his lovely bride.

Now, fair maidens, all adieu,
This song I dedicate to you.

I wish that you may constant prove,
Unto the men that you do love.[40]

Bruce and Stokoe also included a singable, although very lengthy, broadside version of "Lord Beichan," which had been acquired by James Henry Dixon while a member of the Newcastle-upon-Tyne Society of Antiquaries. There was also a northern English variant of the comic ballad, "The Keach i' the Creel." Some of the other ballads reprinted in *Northumbrian Minstrelsy* were probably the work of educated authors rather than anonymous products of oral tradition. "The Laidley Worm o' Spindleston Heugh," for example, appears to have been the work of the Reverend Robert Lambe of Norham, "Derwentwater's Farewell" was likely written by Robert Surtees, and "Derwentwater" may have been crafted (or, more likely, just reworked) by Allan Cunningham.

A second category of material in the *Northumbrian Minstrelsy* consisted of folk lyrics. It is not always easy to draw the dividing line between ballads (story songs of one kind or another) and shorter lyrics, since the latter may derive from ballads or may contain an element of narrative. "Whittingham Fair," for example, is conventionally reckoned a part of a longer ballad that is usually titled "The Elfin Knight." Bruce and Stokoe's version of "Whittingham Fair" was, they stated, "popular in the north and west of the county of Northumberland," a plausible claim, since the village of Whittingham is located about ten kilometers west of Alnwick. Both tune and words were similar to the better-known version of the same song called "Scarborough Fair," although "Whittingham Fair" seems to pre-date its Yorkshire cousin.

Whittingham Fair

Anon

Fig. 4.14

Are you going to Whittingham fair,
Parsley, sage, rosemary, and thyme;
Remember me to one who lives there,
For once she was a true love of mine.

Tell her to make me a cambric shirt,
Parsley, sage, etc.
Without any seam or needlework,
For once she was, etc.

Tell her to wash it in yonder dry well,
Where never spring water nor rain ever fell.

Tell her to dry it on yonder thorn,
Which never bore blossom since Adam
was born.

Now he has asked me questions three,
Parsley, sage, etc.
I hope he will answer as many for me,
For once he was, etc.

Tell him to find me an acre of land,
Betwixt the salt water and the sea sand.

Tell him to plough it with a ram's horn,
And sow it all over with one pepper corn.

Tell him to reap it with a sickle of leather,
And bind it up with a peacock's feather.

When he has done and finished his work,
O tell him to come and he'll have his shirt.[41]

"Whittingham Fair" was an example of a song that was not specific to the north of England but could be found elsewhere in the British Isles, and *Northumbrian Minstrelsy* contained several other vernacular songs that fell into this same category. There was, for instance, a version of "The Twelve Days of Christmas," a cumulative carol that was national rather than regional in provenance, as was another festive song, "Christmas Day in the Morning." "Let No Man Steal Your Thyme," which Bruce and Stokoe unnecessarily re-titled "The Willow Tree, or Rue and Thyme," was a Northumbrian variant of a beautiful folk lyric found in several English counties:

Beware, young maids, beware, beware and read my rhyme,
And see that you keep your garden well, and let no one steal your thyme.

O, when my thyme was new, it flourished both night and day,
Till bye there came a false young man, and he stole my thyme away.

And now my thyme's all gone, and I can plan no new,
And the very place where my thyme was set is all o'ergrown with rue.

And rue runs over all, and nothing can it stop,
But there grows a flower in my father's garden, they call it the fair maid's hope.

"Now spring up hope," said I, and be not afraid of rue,
And if ever that young man should come again, he'll surely find me true.

The gardener standing by, I bade him choose for me;
He chose me the lily, the violet, and the pink, but I refused all three.

The lily I refused, because it fades so soon,
The violet and the pink I did them overlook, and vowed I would wait till June.

In June the red rose buds, and that is the flower for me,
But on laying my hands on the red rose bush I thought of the willow tree.

The willows they grow long, the willows they grow strong,
And the whole world over may very well know that false love has done me wrong.

It's good to be drinking the beer, it's good to be drinking the wine,
But it's better far to be on the bonny laddie's knee that's stolen this heart of mine.

Farewell to all fading flowers, farewell to young lovely June,
For the grass that once was trodden under foot, perhaps it may rise again.[42]

The Willow Tree; or, Rue and Thyme

Anon

Fig. 4.15

There were also versions of such traditional songs as "Broom, Green Broom," "Blow the Winds, I-Ho!" "Bobby Shaftoe" and "I Drew My Ship into Harbour." "The Oak and the Ash and the Bonny Ivy Tree" had a northern provenance, but not necessarily a Northumbrian one, although Bruce and Stokoe cited the authority of Sir Walter Scott in claiming it for Northumberland. Their text appears to have been a broadside in the British Museum's Roxburghe collection, and the tune probably came (via William Chappell) from the 1650 edition of John Playford's *Dancing Master.*

A north-countrie lass up to London did pass,
Although with her nature it did not agree,
Which made her repent, and so often lament,
Still wishing again in the north for to be.
"O, the oak and the ash, and the bonny ivy tree
 Do flourish at home in the north countrie."

"Fain would I be in the north countrie,
Where the lads and lasses are making the hay,
There should I see what is pleasant to me,
A mischief light on them enticed me away.
O, the oak and the ash, etc.

At wakes and at fairs, being void of all cares,
We there with our lovers did use for to dance,
Then hard hap had I my ill fortune to try,
And so up to London my steps to advance.
O, the oak and the ash, etc.

But still I perceive I a husband might have,
If I to the City my mind could but frame,
But I'll have a lad that is north-countrie bred,
Or else I'll not marry in the mind that I am.
O, the oak and the ash, etc.

Then, farewell my daddy, and farewell my minny,
Until I do see you I nothing but mourn,
Rememb'ring my brothers, my sisters, and others,
In less than a year I hope to return.
Then the oak and the ash, and the bonny ivy tree,
I shall see them at home in my ain countrie."[43]

The Oak and the Ash and the Bonny Ivy Tree

Anon

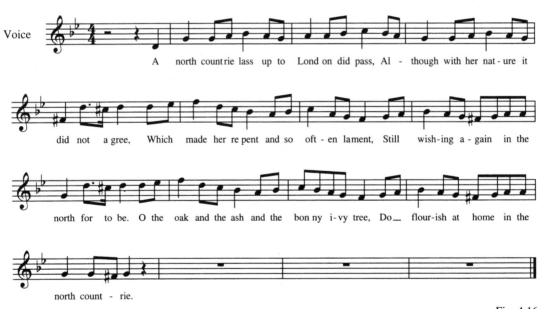

Fig. 4.16

A third kind of material in the *Minstrelsy* was even more regional in nature. It consisted of vernacular songs about Northumbrian people or places, songs by local composers whose names were known, and songs in local dialect, usually Geordie (i.e., from the Newcastle area). One well-known Tyneside personality in the late Georgian era was Blind Willie Purvis (1752-1832), a street minstrel who sang and played the fiddle but also made a living selling brooms and broadsheets.[44] His best-loved composition was "Buy Broom Buzzems," a song that served to advertise his wares as well as entertain his audience.

If you want a buzzem,   Ye may hae your choose.
For to sweep your hoose,
Come to me, maw hinnies,   CHORUS: Buy broom buzzems,

Buy them when they're new,
Fine heather bred 'uns,
Better never grew.

Buzzems for a penny,
Rangers for a plack;
If you winnot buy,
Aw'll tie them on my back.

If aw had a horse,
Aw wad hey a cairt;
If aw had a wife,

She wad tyek me pairt.

Had aw but a wife,
Aw care not what she be—
If she's but a woman,
That's enuf for me.

If she liked a droppie,
Her and I'd agree;
If she didn't like it,
There's the mair for me.[45]

Buy Broom Buzzems

Blind Willie Purvis

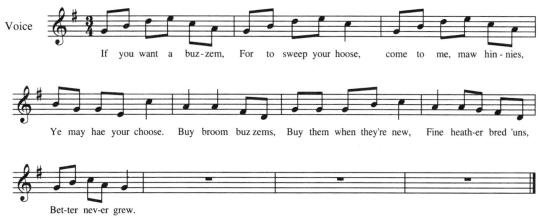

If you want a buz-zem, For to sweep your hoose, come to me, maw hin - nies,

Ye may hae your choose. Buy broom buz zems, Buy them when they're new, Fine heath-er bred 'uns,

Bet-ter nev-er grew.

Fig. 4.17

Elsie Marley (d. 1768), the proprietress of a public house called *The Barley Mow* in the mining community of Picktree, a village halfway between Durham and Newcastle, had been another colorful and well-known local personality. The popularity of her tavern, her penchant for extravagant clothes, the perception that financial success led her to put on airs, and an incident when she lost the week's takings were the subject of a comic song that entered local oral tradition and was still being sung more than a century after it was composed. This is the version of "Elsie Marley" included in the *Minstrelsy*:

Di' ye ken Elsie Marley, honey,
The wife that sells the barley, honey?
She lost her pocket and all her money,
Aback o' the bush i' the garden, honey.

CHORUS: Elsie Marley's grown so fine,
She won't get up to serve the swine,
But lies in bed till eight or nine,
And surely she does take her time.

Elsie Marley is so neat,
It's hard for one to walk the street,
But every lad and lass you meet
Cries – Di' ye ken Elsie Marley, honey?

Elsie Marley wore a straw hat,

But now she's gotten a velvet cap;
The Lambton lads mun pay for that,
Di' ye ken Elsie Marley, honey?

Elsie keeps rum, gin and ale,
In her house below the dale,
Where every tradesman, up and down,
Does call and spend his half-a-crown.

The farmers, as they come that way,
They drink with Elsie every day,
And call the fiddler for to play
The tune of "Elsie Marley," honey.

The pitmen and the keelmen trim,
They drink bumbo made of gin,

And for the dance they do begin
To the tune of "Elsie Marley," honey.

The sailors they do call for flip
As soon as they come from the ship,
And then begin to dance and skip
To the tune of "Elsie Marley," honey.

Those gentlemen that go so fine,

They'll treat her with a bottle of wine,
And freely they'll sit down and dine
Along with Elsie Marley, honey.

So to conclude, these lines I've penned,
Hoping there's none I do offend,
And thus my merry joke doth end,
Concerning Elsie Marley, honey.[46]

Elsie Marley

Anon

Voice

Di' ye ken El - sie Mar - ley, hon-ey, The wife that sells the bar - ley, hon-ey, She
lost her pock et and all her mon ey, A - back o' the bush i' the gard - en, hon - ey, El - sie Mar ley's
grown so fine,— She won't get up to serve the swine, But lies in bed till
eight or nine, And sure - ly she— does take her time...—

Fig. 4.18

The *Northumbrian Minstrelsy* also contained other examples of local songs from the northeast of England, such as "The Hexhamshire Lass," "The Keel Row," "The Water of Tyne," "The Bonny Fisher Lad," and "The Mode o' Wooing." While much of the regional material in the book avoided (or was translated from) Geordie dialect, the texts of some items did contain words unfamiliar to southerners. The dialect songs included "Up the Raw," "Dol-Li-A," "Maw Canny Hinny," "A U Hinny Burd," and a simple but poetic lyric, "Bonny at Morn," which had the virtue of a particularly beautiful tune. In this instance the meaning of the dialect words could be easily guessed:

The sheep's in the meadow, the kye's in the corn,
Thou's ower lang in thy bed, Bonny at morn.
Canny at night, Bonny at morn,
Thou's ower lang in thy bed, Bonny at morn.

The bird's in the nest, the trout's in the burn,
Thou hindes they mother in many a turn,
Canny at night, Bonny at morn,
Thou's ower lang in thy bed, Bonny at morn.

We're all laid idle wi' keeping the bairn,
The lad winnot work, and the lass winnot lairn,
Canny at night, Bonny at morn,

Thou's ower lang in thy bed, Bonny at morn.[47]

Bonny at Morn

Anon

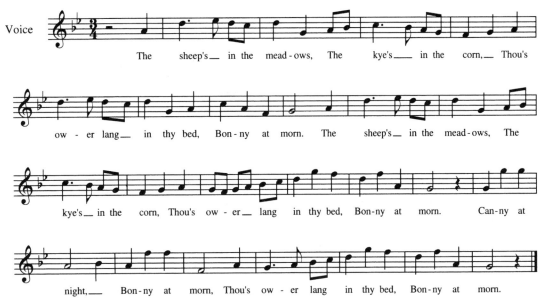

Fig. 4.19

Since he played the Northumbrian small-pipes it is not surprising that John Stokoe had sole responsibility for choosing the seventy-three tunes that made up the second half of *Northumbrian Minstrelsy*. These melodies were played at local dances and on ceremonial occasions, and they included a few slow airs (including a tune for the ballad of "Chevy Chace") as well as such favorites as "The Lads of Alnwick," Noble Squire Dacre," "Shew's the Way to Wallington," "Morpeth Lasses," and "Peacock's Fancy." Most of these pipe tunes were given as melodies only, but a few of them had lyrics associated with them. Examples of the latter included "Felton Lonnin,'" "The Miller's Wife o' Blaydon," "My Dearie Sits Woer Late Up," "Andrew Carr," and "Blaw the Wind Southerly." When used for a song, the tune was often slightly different from the instrumental version for the pipes. In this section of the *Minstrelsy* Stokoe was primarily interested in pipe tunes rather than songs, so although he occasionally printed lyrics associated with particular tunes, the words did not always fit the melody exactly. As just one example of a well-known pipe tune that also became a vernacular song, here is "The Bonnie [or Bonny] Pit Laddie." As a song it existed in two forms ("Bonny Pit Laddie" and "Bonny Keel Laddie"), reflecting two of the most common working class occupations in the region: coal mining and bargeing.

The bonny pit laddie, the canny pit laddie,
The bonny pit laddie for me, O!
He sits in his hole as black as a coal,
And brings the white siller to me, O!

The bonny pit laddie, the canny pit laddie,
The bonny pit laddie for me, O!
He sits on his cracket and hews in his jacket,
And brings the white siller to me, O!

THE BONNY KEEL LADDIE

My bonny keel laddie, my canny keel laddie,
My bonny keel laddie for me, O!
He sits in his keel as black as the deil,
And he brings the white money to me, O!

Hae ye seen owt o' my canny man,
And are ye sure he's weel, O!

He's gaen o'er land wiv a stick in his hand,
To help to moor the keel, O!

The canny keel laddie, the bonny keel laddie,
The canny keel laddie for me, O!
He sits in his hudduck and claws his bare buttock,
And brings the white money to me, O![48]

The Bonnie Pit Laddie

Anon

Fig. 4.20

As will be evident from the items mentioned, this regional collection, whatever its faults, included a wealth of fine tunes and dozens of beautiful, interesting or amusing folk lyrics and ballads. The *Northumbrian Minstrelsy* was, however, only one of several collections of vernacular songs to come out of the north of England in the late Victorian era. For example, Newcastle publisher Thomas Allan had in 1872 published an anthology of poems and songs by local poets under the title *Tyneside Songs*, and in 1891 he would bring out a much expanded version of the compilation as *Allan's Illustrated Edition of Tyneside Songs*.[49] Although interesting, especially to local readers, few of the items gathered by Allan rivaled in quality most of the material in the *Minstrelsy* or even that in *Nursery Rhymes and Country Songs*, but they reinforced the sense that a movement to collect, preserve and publish northern English vernacular song was emerging in some force during the decades of the 1880s and early 1890s. We will return to this subject in a later chapter, but to recognize fully the importance of John Stokoe's contribution to the birth of the northern folksong revival in the 1880s we must briefly examine another regional collection with which he was involved as music editor.

A Beuk o' Newcassel Sangs

A Beuk o' Newcassel Sangs was published in 1888, six years after *Northumbrian Minstrelsy*, as a collection of local songs made by Newcastle businessman, sportsman, and artist, Joseph Crawhall (1821-1896). Although only Crawhall's name appeared as editor, the *Beuk* actually marked the second of Stokoe's three attempts to demonstrate the richness of vernacular song in Northumberland. The volume's contents were ostensibly entirely urban in character, the songs having been apparently composed or noted in and around the city of Newcastle-upon-Tyne. The title also proclaimed the dialect character of much of Crawhall's and Stokoe's material, and indeed the book, which was plentifully illustrated with woodcuts similar to those found on the more sophisticated broadsides of an earlier period, included such local favorites as "A U Hinny Burd," "Buy Broom Buzzems," "The Keel Row," "Aboot the Bush, Willy," "The Collier's Rant," "The Sailors are a' at the Bar," and "The Sandgate Lass's Lament."[50] Most of these were anonymous vernacular songs, as heard on the streets and in the pubs of Newcastle. Other songs, although mostly still in dialect, were more formal compositions by local poets whose names were well-known in the Tyneside region.

Even among the dialect songs there was considerable overlap with the contents of *Northumbrian Minstrelsy*, a publication with which Crawhall was very familiar, although he had begun putting together his own collection years before its publication. Indeed, in 1877 he had published a small collection of Northumbrian pipe-tunes upon which Stokoe had drawn when compiling the second half of the *Minstrelsy*. As an example of the overlap between the two collections, here is one of the dialect songs that appeared identically in both works. "Up the Raw," for which John Bell had earlier given a dialect text (but no tune) in *Rhymes of Northern Bards*, now came with a distinctive melody:

Up the raw, maw bonny hinny, up the raw, lass, ivvery day;
For shape an' colour, maw bonny hinny, thou bangs thy mother, maw canny bairn.
Black as a craw, maw bonny hinny, thou bangs them a', lass, ivvery day;
Thou's a' clag-candied, maw bonny hinny, thou's double japanded, maw canny bairn.

Up the Raw, doon the Raw, up the Raw, lass, ivvery day;
For shape an' colour, maw bonny hinny, thou bangs thy mother, maw canny bairn.
For hide an' hue, maw bonny hinny, thou bangs the crew, maw canny bairn;
Up the Raw, maw bonny hinny, thou bangs them a', lass, ivvery day.[51]

Up the Raw

Anon

Fig. 4.21

As a second example of a song in Geordie dialect that appeared in both books, here is "Sair Fyel'd, Hinny," a simple but poignant lyric about aging, with a distinctive tune:

Sair Fyel'd, Hinny

Anon

Fig. 4.22

Sair fyel'd hinny,   Sin' I kenn'd thou.
Sair fyel'd noo,   I was young an' lusty,
Sair fyel'd hinny,   I was fair an' clear,

I was young an' lusty,   Sair fyel'd hinny, etc.
Mony a lang year.
Sair fyel'd hinny, etc.   Then said the auld man
                                           To the oak tree,
When I was young and lusty,   "Sair fyel'd is 'e,
I could loup a dyke,   Sin' I kenn'd thee!"
But now, at five-and-sixty,   Sair fyel'd hinny, etc.[52]
Canna do the like.

"The Collier's Rant" may stand as an illustration of a dialect song that had not been included in *Northumbrian Minstrelsy*. This sardonically humorous piece came from the Northumberland and Durham coalfield, situated south of Newcastle, and reflected the occupational language of mining as much as the local dialect. It too had a memorable and distinctive tune, although Stokoe's version slightly minimized its modal character:

The Collier's Rant

Anon

As me and my mar-ra was gan-nin' to wark, We met wi' the dee-vil, It was i' th' dark; Aw up wi' my pick, it being i' the neet, I knock't off his horns, like-wise his club-feet. Foll-ow the hors-es, John-ny my lad-die! Fol-low them through, my can-ny lad, oh! Fol-low the hors-es, John ny my lad-die! Oh laddie lye a way can-ny lad, oh!

Fig. 4.23

As me an' my marra was gannin' to wark,   O marra, oh, marra! Oh what does t'u think?
We met wi' the devil, it was i' th' dark;   Aw've broken my bottle, an' spilt a' my drink;
Aw up wi' my pick, it being in the neet,   Aw've lost a' my shin-splints among the big stanes,
I knock't off his horns, likewise his club-feet. Draw me to the shaft, it's time to gan hyem.
Follow the horses, Johnny my laddie!   Follow the horses, &c.
Follow them through, my canny lad, oh!
Follow the horses, Johnny my laddie!   O marra! oh, marra! where hes t'u been?
Oh laddie lye away, canny lad, oh!   Drivin' the drift frae the law seam,
                                                  Drivin' the drift frae the law seam:
As me an' my marra was puttin' the tram,   Had up the lowe, lad! De'il stop oot thy e'en!
The lowe it went oot, an' my marra gat wrang;   Follow the horses, &c.
You wad ha'e laughed had ye seen the gam,
The De'il gat my marra an' aw gat the tram.   O marra! oh, marra! this is wor pay week,
Follow the horses, &c.   We'll get penny loaves an' drink to wor beek;
                                                  We'll fill up a bumper, and round it shall go;
                                                  Follow the horses, Johnny lad oh!

Follow the horses, &c.

Theer's my horse, an' theer's my tram;
Twee horns full o' grease will myek her to gan,

Theer's my pit hoggars, likewise my half-shoon,
An' smash my heart, marra, my putting's a' deun!.
Follow the horses, &c.[53]

Anonymous dialect songs were not the only type of material in the collection. About half of the thirty-eight items were the work of local poets who had turned their hands to writing new lyrics for old tunes. These creations included "Canny Newcassel" by Thomas Thompson, "The Fiery Clock-fyece" by Robert Nunn, "The Floatin' Grunstane" by William Armstrong, "Use and Abuse, or The Pitman and the Preachers" by J. P. Robson, and "My Lord Size" by John Shield. "Gee-ho! Dobbin" was a favorite tune: Robert Gilchrist used it for "The Amphitrite" and William Mitford did the same for "Cappy's the Dog." Another Mitford lyric, "The Pitman's Courtship," could be sung to either "The Night before Larry was Stretch'd" or "The Irish Drops o' Brandy." John Cunningham also contributed two lyrics: "The Holiday Gown" and "Newcastle Beer," while dialect poet Thomas Wilson provided "The Weshin'-day." The words of some of these pieces had been printed previously by Thomas Allan in one of the early editions of *Tyneside Songs,* but the all-important difference was that they now came equipped with tunes. As an example of the self-deprecating humor that often characterized these dialect poems and songs, here is Joseph Wilson's "Aw Wish Thy Muther Wad Cum."

Aw Wish thy Muther Wad Cum

Joseph Wilson

Fig. 4.24

Come, Geordie ha'd the bairn,
Aw's sure aw'll not stop lang:
Aw'd tyek the jewel me sel,
But really aw's not strang.
Thor's floor an' coals to get,
The hoose-wark's not half deun,
Sae—haud the bairn for fairs,
Thou's often deun't for fun.

Then Geordie held the bairn,
But sair agyen his will:
The poor bit thing wes good,

But Geordie had nee skill:
He haddent its Muther's ways,
He sat byeth stiff an' numb;
Afore five minutes was gyen,
He wish'd its Muther wad cum.

His wife had hardlys gyen,
The bairn began to squall,
With hikin't up an' doon
He varry nigh let it fall.
It nivver wad ha'd its tung,
Tho' some aud teun he'd hum—

"Jack and Jill went up the hill"—
"Aw wish thy Muther wad cum."

What weary toil said he
This nursin' bairns mun be:
A bit on't's weel eneuf,
Aye, quite eneuf for me.
To ha'd a blubberin' bairn,
It may be grand to some:
A day's wark's not as bad—
"Aw wish thy Muther wad cum."

Men seldom give a thowt
To what their wives endure;
Aw thowt she'd nowt to dee
But clean the hoose, aw's sure,
Or myek my dinner an' tea—
(It's startin' to sook its thumb:
The poor thing wants its tit)—

"Aw wish thy Muther wad cum."

What a selfish world this is!
There's nowt mair sae than Man;
He laffs at Wimmins' toil,
An' nivver'll norse hiw awn—
(It's startin' to cry agyen –
Aw see tuts throo it's gum:)
Maw canny bit pet, O dinna thoo fret—
"Aw wish thy Muther wad cum."

But kindness dis a vast—
It's nee use gettin vext—
It'll niver please the bairn,
Or ease a mind perplext.
At last it's gyen to sleep,
The Wife'll not say aw's numb—
She'll think aw's a real good nurse—
But—"Aw wish thy Muther wad cum."[54]

There were also a few vernacular songs that were (mainly) not in Geordie dialect, although they apparently had been taken from oral tradition. Examples are "Andrew Carr," "Bobby Shaftoe," "The Sandgate Lass's Lament," and "Aboot the Bush, Willie." The collection was rounded out with a handful of pipe tunes without words, such as "Fenwich o' By-well," "Blackett o' Wylam," "My Love Is Newly Listed," and "Sandhill Corner." But our final example demonstrating the high quality of much of the material in *A Beuk o' Newcassel Sangs* is this simple but beautiful regional lyric, "Water o' Tyne":

The Water of Tyne

Anon

Fig. 4.25

I cannot get to my love if I would dee,
The water of Tyne runs between him and me;
And here I must stand, with the tear in my e'e,
Both sighing and sickly my sweetheart to see.

O where is the boatman? My bonny hinny!
O where is the boatman? Bring him to me—

To ferry me over the Tyne to my honcy,
And I will remember the boatman and thee.

O bring me a boatman—I'll give any money,
And you for your trouble rewarded shall be,
To ferry me over the Tyne to my honey,
Or scull him cross that rough river to me.[55]

The importance of *A Beuk o' Newcassel Sangs* was three-fold. The book provided tunes as well as texts, and although many of the songs had been published earlier, there was additional local material that had not previously been available in print. Moreover, Stokoe's tunes were verified by a co-editor who had lived all his life on Tyneside and had collected the songs independently of the small group of collaborators who had worked on *Northumbrian Minstrelsy*. Furthermore, Crawhall's texts appear to have escaped the kind of puritanical editing imposed by Bruce. Taken together, these features meant that *A Beuk o' Newcassel Sangs* marked a slight step beyond the *Minstrelsy* in terms of authenticity.

Just as T. T. Wilkinson's third edition of John Harland's *Ballads and Songs of Lancashire* suggested that there was a living tradition of vernacular song in that county and that future collecting initiatives there would bear plentiful fruit, so the work of Harriet Mason, John Stokoe, and Joseph Crawhall made it abundantly evident that the counties of Northumberland and Durham possessed a wealth of local song and instrumental music that would repay more concerted exploration. As we saw in chapter 2, there was no reason to believe that this would not also be true of Yorkshire, the very large county that lay to the east of Lancashire and to the south of Durham, especially since in 1860 C. J. Davison Ingledew, building on prior work by James Orchard Halliwell, had already compiled *The Ballads and Songs of Yorkshire*.[56] And what about the Midlands and the south of England? Were parallel beginnings of a movement to collect folksong tunes as well as texts to be found elsewhere in the England of the 1880s? The answer is yes, but as yet only by a few isolated individuals. To see who they were, we now turn our attention southwards.

Notes

1. M[arianne] H[arriet] Mason, ed., *Nursery Rhymes and Country Songs: Both Tunes and Words from Tradition* (London: Metzler, 1878).

2. Katherine Field, "Mason, (Marianne) Harriet," *Oxford Dictionary of National Biography*, www.oxforddnb.com/articles/48/48847-article.html.

3. [John Broadwood] and Geoffrey Dusart, eds., *Old English Songs, as now sung by the Peasantry of the Weald of Surrey and Sussex* (London: Betts & Co., [1847]; the publication date is often erroneously given as 1843).

4. Mason, *Nursery Rhymes and Country Songs*, 7.

5. Mason, *Nursery Rhymes and Country Songs*, 8.

6. Mason, *Nursery Rhymes and Country Songs*, 13.

7. Davies Gilbert, ed., *Some Ancient Christmas Carols with the Tunes to which they were formerly sung in the West of England, together with Two Ancient Ballads* (2nd edition: London: John Nichols, 1823), 65.

8. Thomas D'Urfey, ed., *Wit and Mirth: or Pills to Purge Melancholy*, 6 vols. (London: D'Urfey, 1719-1720. Reprint: New York: Folklore Publishers, 1959), vol. 4, 130.

9. Mason, *Nursery Rhymes and Country Songs*, 31.

10. Robert Bell, ed., *Ancient Poems, Ballads and Songs of the Peasantry of England* (London: John Parker & Sons, 1857), 127.

11. *Gammer Gurton's Garland, or, The Nursery Parnassus* (London: n.p., 1810).

12. Francis James Child, ed., *The English and Scottish Popular Ballads*, 10 Parts in 5 vols. (Boston, Mass.: Houghton, Mifflin & Co., 1882-1898; reprinted: New York: Dover, 1965), vol. 2, 279-80

13. Mason, *Nursery Rhymes and Country Songs*, 46.

14. James Orchard Halliwell, *Ballads and Poems respecting Hugh of Lincoln* (Brixton Hill, U.K.: [Halliwell,] 1849).

15. Mason, *Nursery Rhymes and Country Songs*, 46.

16. Mason, *Nursery Rhymes and Country Songs*, 44.

17. [Broadwood] and Dusart, *Old English Songs*. See note 3.

18. Mason, *Nursery Rhymes and Country Songs*, 47.

19. John Harland, ed., *Ballads and Songs of Lancashire* (London: Whittaker, 1865).

20. John Harland, ed., *Lancashire Lyrics: Modern Songs and Ballads of the County Palatine* (London: Whittaker, 1866).

21. John Harland and T. T. Wilkinson, eds., *Ballads and Songs of Lancashire* (3rd edition: London: Heywood, 1882).

22. Harland and Wilkinson, *Ballads and Songs of Lancashire*, 155-57.

23. J. Collingwood Bruce and John Stokoe, eds., *Northumbrian Minstrelsy: A Collection of the Ballads, Melodies, and Small-Pipe Tunes of Northumbria* (Newcastle-upon-Tyne: Society of Antiquaries of Newcastle-upon-Tyne, 1882; reprinted, with a foreword by A. L. Lloyd: Hatboro, Pennsylvania: Folklore Associates, 1965).

24. *Oxford Dictionary of National Biography*, http://www.oxforddnb.com/articles/3/3741-article.html.

25. Biographical information on John Stokoe seems hard to find; there is, for example, no entry for him in the *Oxford Dictionary of National Biography*.

26. A. L. Lloyd, "Foreword," in 1965 reprint edition of *Northumbrian Minstrelsy,* ed. Bruce and Stokoe, xxii.

27. Dave Harker, *Fakesong: The Manufacture of British 'folksong', 1700 to the present day* (Milton Keynes: Open University Press, 1985), 165-166.

28. Bell, *Ancient Poems, Ballads and Songs*, 122.

29. Bruce and Stokoe, *Northumbrian Minstrelsy,* 31-33.

30. Thomas Deloney, *The Pleasant History of John Winchcomb, In his younger years called Jacke of Newberie, the famous and worthy Clothier of England* (London: Young & Wright, 1633 [originally published 1597]), 61.

31. Joseph Ritson, ed., *Ancient Songs from the Time of King Henry the Third to the Revolution* (London: J. Johnson, 1790), 169.

32. Bruce and Stokoe, *Northumbrian Minstrelsy,* 51-55.

33. Bruce and Stokoe, *Northumbrian Minstrelsy,* 50.

34. James Henry Dixon, ed., *Ancient Poems, Ballads and Songs of the Peasantry of England* (London: Percy Society, 1846), 74.

35. Bruce and Stokoe, *Northumbrian Minstrelsy,* 48-50.

36. Bruce and Stokoe, *Northumbrian Minstrelsy,* 63.

37. Bruce and Stokoe, *Northumbrian Minstrelsy,* 61-63.

38. D'Urfey, *Pills,* vol. 4, 130. The broadside is in the Pepys, Douce, and Rawlinson collections.

39. D'Urfey, *Pills,* vol. 4, 130.

40. Bruce and Stokoe, *Northumbrian Minstrelsy,* 76-77.

41. Bruce and Stokoe, *Northumbrian Minstrelsy,* 79-80.

42. Bruce and Stokoe, *Northumbrian Minstrelsy,* 90-91.

43. Bruce and Stokoe, *Northumbrian Minstrelsy,* 86-87.

44. On Blind Willie Purvis see Dave Harker, "The Making of the Tyneside Concert Hall," *Popular Music* 1 (1981): 27-56.

45. Bruce and Stokoe, *Northumbrian Minstrelsy,* 118-19.

46. Bruce and Stokoe, *Northumbrian Minstrelsy,* 112-13.

47. Bruce and Stokoe, *Northumbrian Minstrelsy,* 88.

48. Bruce and Stokoe, *Northumbrian Minstrelsy,* 150.

49. Thomas Allan, ed., *Allan's Illustrated Edition of Tyneside Songs and Readings* (Revised edition, Newcastle-upon-Tyne, U.K.: Thomas & George Allan, 1891).

50. Joseph Crawhall, ed., *A Beuk o' Newcassel Sangs* (Newcastle-upon-Tyne: Mawson, Swan, & Morgan, 1888. Reprinted, Newcastle-upon-Tyne: Harold Hill, 1965).

51. Crawhall, *Beuk,* 45-46.

52. Crawhall, *Beuk,* 41-43.

53. Crawhall, *Beuk,* 29-32.

54. Crawhall, *Beuk,* 97-101.

55. Crawhall, *Beuk,* 15.

56. C. J. Davison Ingledew, ed., *The Ballads and Songs of Yorkshire* (London: Bell & Daldy, 1860).

5

Village Singers and Gypsies

It is now time to leave the northeast of England for a while and to make our geographical focus broader in scope. First we will travel to the county of Shropshire in the West Midlands, but in this and the subsequent chapter we will also discover that the pioneer Late Victorian collectors found folksongs not only in the villages but also in the caravans of traveling people and the many seaports of coastal England. This chapter surveys some of the varied achievements during the 1880s of four more vernacular song collectors: Charlotte Burne, Heywood Sumner, Francis Groome, and Laura Smith. We begin in the West Midlands with the work that I regard, along with *Nursery Rhymes and Country Songs* and *Northumbrian Minstrelsy*, as the third foundational document of the English folksong revival, *Shropshire Folk-Lore*, by Charlotte Burne.

Shropshire Folk-Lore

Separated from it by Cheshire, the county of Shropshire lies south of Lancashire, in the borderlands between the English Midlands and North Wales. Pioneer Salopian local historian and folklorist Georgina Jackson had spent several decades gathering data on the customs and beliefs of the inhabitants of her native county. She planned to set out her findings in a large work that would be illustrated with copious examples of the stories, sayings, and songs of Shropshire's rural inhabitants. Jackson had amassed plenty of suitable material and had organized it into categories that were to form the chapters of her book, but she did not live to write the text of the work. In 1872 she had made friends with a young woman whose manuscript notes on the folklore of the Severn Valley had impressed her, and by 1875 she had enlisted the help of that young woman, Charlotte ("Lotty") Burne, with her own project. A severe illness in the summer of 1877 resulted in Jackson's being forced to give up fieldwork, and by the end of the decade she was apprehensive that she would be unable to finish her book. It seems very likely that by the spring of 1880 she had decided to hand over all her materials to Burne, who by then was actively collecting Salopian lore (including folksongs) on her own account. The transfer was complete by December 1881 at the latest.[1]

Charlotte Sophia Burne (1850-1923) was the eldest daughter of Charlotte and Sambrooke Burne, members of the Shropshire gentry. Her father, a country squire, who died of a hunting accident while she was young, was the owner of Loynton Hall, located near Newport, Shropshire. The family seat was inherited by Lotty's brother, and she spent her childhood partly at Loynton, partly in the nearby village of Edgmond, and partly in the Staffordshire village of Pyebirch, near Eccleshall. It is therefore hardly surprising that she was very familiar with the countryside of the Shropshire/Staffordshire border, and she did most of her collecting of folklore (including folksongs) in that area.[2] To Jackson's material Burne added a considerable amount of her own. The result of the two women's labors appeared in three installments in 1883, 1885, and 1886, and was titled *Shropshire Folk-Lore: A Sheaf of Gleanings from the Collections of Georgina F. Jackson*.[3] The sub-title was a little misleading, in that the book also made extensive use of Burne's own field research.

Shropshire Folk-Lore is a huge and fascinating compendium of legends about local heroes, giants, devils, bogies, fairies, ghosts, witches, superstitions, charms, and medicinal lore. At 663 pages in length, the book covers all the main sub-genres of folklore studies, including some subjects that were rarely treated at the time, such as riddles, jingles and mottoes, proverbs, local sayings and rhymes, and other aspects of verbal folklore. There are sections on Salopian customs and superstitions associated with different seasons and special times of the year, such as Shrovetide, Whitsuntide, May Day, Midsummer, Harvest and All Saints' Day as well as Christmas, New Year, and Easter. Chapters in the second half of the work describe the county's traditional church-wakes, fairs, agricultural shows, sports (including bull-baiting and bear-baiting), feasts, games (including children's games), and music. While there is much else of interest in the book, it is on the songs collected by Jackson and Burne that we must focus here. They are to be found mainly in Chapter XXXIV titled "Ballads, Songs, and Carols," and in an Appendix containing twenty-three tunes.[4] There are twelve items identified as ballads by Burne, eight of which have tunes, and about twenty other items described as "local songs." These include broadsides, carols, comic songs, instrumental pieces, and various fragments sung by children.

In late nineteenth-century Shropshire traditional music came in several different forms. It was a component of most local dramatic performances, which included rustic stage plays and masques performed by morris dancers. It was an essential part of country dancing, which thrived in the county. And there were singing traditions among village women, farm hands, artisans, and travelers. Georgina Jackson had been more interested in stories and customs than in music, and the number of her informants who sang was not large. Nonetheless, although Jackson was not a musician and she seems to have collected only a handful of songs, she had planned a chapter on the region's ballads and songs. During the early and mid-1870s, with the help of associates who wrote down the tunes, she obtained some suitable material. For example, in 1872 she noted texts of "Cold Blows the Wind," a variant of "The Unquiet Grave" (Child no. 78), and "Lord Thomas and Fair Eleanor" (Child no. 73), while in 1874, with the aid of local musician E. Roessel, she took down a version of "The Outlandish Knight" (Child no. 4).

Charlotte Burne was more interested than Jackson in the local singers and their repertoire, and she quickly recognized the need to supplement Jackson's materials. Although she played the piano and harmonium she was not an accomplished musician and found it difficult to note melodies by ear. She therefore recruited a friend called James Smart to note the tunes, and he transcribed about a dozen for her. A few other individuals, whom we know only by their initials, also helped out in this regard.

When Burne and Smart began collecting together in 1879 they naturally first returned to the village of Edgmond, where Lotty had once lived and Georgina Jackson had found some traditional ballads. They rediscovered a small group of women who had been singing together for at least a decade. The principal singers were Jane Butler, Harriet Dowley, and Sally Withington. Their repertoire was particularly interesting because it included a number of traditional ballads. For example, Jane Butler sang "The Outlandish Knight," which we have seen (in chapter 4) reproduced in Bruce and Stokoe's *Northumbrian Minstrelsy*. This is Jane's version of the melody:

The Outlandish Knight

Anon

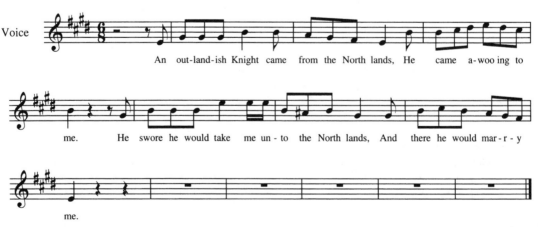

An out-land-ish Knight came from the North lands, He came a-woo-ing to me. He swore he would take me un-to the North lands, And there he would mar-r-y me.

Fig. 5.1

None of the Edgmond singers could quite remember all the words of this ballad, but Burne had also heard it recited by an old nurse at Ross in nearby Herefordshire and was able to supply a few missing lines; the text turned out to be almost the same (except for a few minor details) as the broadside reprinted by Bruce and Stokoe, so there is no need to set it out again here. The tune had been transcribed for Georgina Jackson in 1874 by her musical assistant at the time, E. Roessel, and, as can be seen, was similar, although not identical, to Stokoe's. It is interesting that the Northumbrian and Salopian versions proved to be so close in both text and tune. This suggests not only a common broadside source for the text but a common source for the melody too, an instance where words and tune did not become dissociated in oral transmission but were passed from generation to generation in distinct geographical locations in a remarkably faithful way.

Jane Butler also sang "Cold Blows the Wind" (aka "The Unquiet Grave"). This song had previously been collected in Scotland by Peter Buchan, and would also be found in various parts of England, including the counties of Suffolk and Sussex. The Edgmond version contained a reference to the nearby Staffordshire village of Clifton Camville as the place where the dead lover had met his fate—it had been the site of a minor battle during the Wars of the Roses, which suggests that the ballad may date from the fifteenth century. One can debate whether "Cold Blows the Wind" is really a ballad or merely a lament, but it has a beautiful melody and is a good example of the kind of traditional song still prevalent in rural Shropshire in the 1870s.

Cold Blows the Wind (The Unquiet Grave)

Anon

Fig. 5.2

Cold blows the wind o'er my true love, cold blow the drops of rain,
I never had but one true love, and in Camville he was slain.
I'll do as much for my true love as any young girl may,
I'll sit and weep down by his grave for twelve months and one day.

But when twelve months were come and gone this young man he arose,
"What makes you weep down by my grave? I can't take my repose."
"One kiss, one kiss, of your lily-white lips, one kiss is all I crave,
One kiss, one kiss, of your lily-white lips, and return back to your grave!"

"My lips they are as cold as my clay, my breath is heavy and strong,
If thou wast to kiss my lily-white lips, thy days would not be long!"
"O, don't you remember the garden-grove where we was used to walk?

Pluck the finest flower of them all, 'twill wither to a stalk!"

"Go fetch me a nut from a dungeon deep, and water from a stone,
And white milk from a maiden's breast [that babe bare never none]."
"Go dig me a grave both long, wide, and deep, as quickly as you may,
I will lie down in it and take one sleep, for twelvemonth and one day.
I will lie down in it and take one sleep, for twelvemonth and one day!"[5]

Harriet Dowley's repertoire was a mix of traditional ballads and more recent compositions learned from broadsides. The most striking was the tragic ballad of "Lord Thomas and Fair Eleanor." This had been collected in the field in Scotland on a variety of occasions during the early nineteenth century by (among others) Robert Jamieson, George Kinloch, William Motherwell, and Peter Buchan, but an earlier broadside version had been published in England during the Restoration era, and a copy of this was extant in the Pepys Collection in Cambridge. The broadside had been reprinted in the anonymous compilation *A Collection of Old Ballads* (1723), and included by Joseph Ritson in the second volume of his *A Select Collection of English Songs* (1783), while Thomas Percy had also printed a reworked variant in his *Reliques of Old English Poetry* (1765). However, the ballad had not previously been noted from oral tradition in England, so this was a significant discovery by Burne and by James Smart, who transcribed the tune for her in 1879. Dowley's rendition was clearly indebted to the English broadside but omitted some verses and modified others.

Lord Thomas and Fair Eleanor

Anon

Lord Thom as he was   a   bold for-est-er,   Chas - ing   of the king's

deer.___ Fair   El - ean or was___ a   fine___ wo-man, And Lord Thom as he lov-ed ___ her dear.

Fig. 5.3

Lord Thomas he was a bold forester,
Chasing of the king's deer,
Fair Eleanor she was a fine woman,
And Lord Thomas he lovéd her dear.

It happenéd on a high holiday,
As many another beside,
Lord Thomas he went unto fair Eleanor
That should have been his sweet bride.

"What news, what news, Lord Thomas?" she said,
"What news have you brought unto me?"
"I come to bid thee to my wedding
And that is bad news unto thee."

"O God forbid," fair Eleanor cried,
"That ever such thing should be done!
I thought to ha' bin the bride my own sel,
And thee to ha' bin the bridegroom!"

She dresséd herself in rich attire,
Her merry men all in green,

In every town that she rode through
They took her to be some queen.

And when that she raught to Lord Thomas's door,
So boldly she tirled at the pin,
O who was so ready as Lord Thomas
For to let Fair Eleanor in?

He took her by the lily-white hand,
He led her through the hall,
He took her into the drawing-room,
And fixed her above them all.

The brown girl had a knife in her hand,
It was both keen and sharp,
And 'twixt the long ribs and the short
She prickéd fair Eleanor's heart.

"O what is the matter?" Lord Thomas he says,
"Methinks you look wondrous wan,
Which you used to have as fair a colour

As ever the sun shone on."

"O are you blind, Lord Thomas?" she says,
"Or cannot you very well see?
O cannot you see my own heart's blood
Run trickling down to my knee?"

Lord Thomas having a sword in his hand,
It was both keen and small,
He took off the brown girl's head
And threw it against the wall.

He stick'd the haft against the floor,

The point against his own heart,
O never so soon did three lovers meet,
And never so soon did part!

Lord Thomas was buried in the lower chancél,
Fair Eleanor in the higher;
Out of Lord Thomas there grew a wild rose,
And out of her a briar.

They grew so high, they grew so wide,
They raught to the chancel-top,
And when that they could grow no higher
They knit of a true-lover's knot.[6]

Sally Withington provided two traditional ballads, "Barbara Allen" and "Lord Bateman." The tune of the latter was noted by Smart, also in 1879. It was another example of a narrative song that had been collected extensively from oral tradition in Scotland and published as "Young Beichan" by Robert Jamieson in *Popular Ballads and Songs* (1806) and by George Kinloch in *Ancient Scottish Ballads* (1827), but which had also been printed on an English broadside as "The Loving Ballad of Lord Bateman." The text sung by Withington followed this broadside quite closely, although she omitted several verses, including the last one. This is her version:

Lord Bateman

Anon

Fig. 5.4

Lord Bateman was a noble lord,
A noble lord of high degree,
He shipped himself upon a ship,
Some foreign country for to see.

He sealéd [sailed] east, he sealéd west,
Until he came to [proud] Turkey,
Where he was taken and put i' prison,
Until his life it was weary.

This Turk he had one only daughter,
The fairest creature I ever did see,
She stole the keys of her father's prison,
Saying, "Lord Bateman I will set free."

She took him to her father's arbour,
And gave to him the best of wine,
And every health she drank unto him,
"I wish, Lord Bateman, you were mine.

Now seven years I'll make a vow,
And seven years I'll keep it strong,
If you will wed with no other woman,
I will wed with no other man."

The seven years were over and past,
And forty days were over and gone,
When she packed up her gay gold clothing,
And said, "Lord Bateman I will go see."

When she got to Lord Bateman's castle
So boldly she rung the bell,
O who was so ready as the young proud porter
For to let this fair creature in?

"Is this Lord Bateman's castle?" she says,
Or is his lordship now within?"
"O yes, O yes," cried the young proud porter,
He's just now taken his young bride in."

"Tell him to send me a slice of bread,
And a bottle of the best of wine,
And not to forget the fair young lady
That did release him when close confined."

Away, away, went the young proud porter,
Away, away, away went he,
Until he came to Lord Bateman's chamber,
He fell down on his bended knee.

"O there is one of the fairest creatures,
That ever my two eyes did see,
She has got rings on every finger,
On one of them she has got three,
And as much gay gold about her middle
As would buy all Northumberland.

"She bids you give her a slice of bread,

And a bottle of the best of wine,
And not to forget the fair young lady
That did release you when close confined."

Then Lord Bateman flew in a passion,
And broke his sword in splinters three,
Saying, "I'll give all my father's riches
If Sophia has crossed the sea!"

Then up and spake the young bride's mother,
(She never was heard to speak so free),
"You'll not forget my only daughter,
If Sophia has crossed the sea!"

"Take back, take back your daughter, Madam,
She's neither better nor worse for me,
She came to me with a horse and saddle,
She shall go back with a coach and three!"[7]

Burne recognized the tune of "Cruel Barbara Allen," which she stated was sung by Sally Withington and others at Edgmond on several occasions between 1870 and 1880, as the same as that given by William Chappell in his first collection, *National English Airs* (1840). She commented that the Shropshire variant was probably older than that in Thomas Percy's *Reliques of Ancient English Poetry* and, in her opinion, "decidedly superior to it." She particularly relished the detail of the blood and tears mingled in a basin, and noted that the young men carrying the coffin were in accord with traditional Salopian funeral custom. Withington's version had some lines in common with an English broadside preserved in the Roxburghe Collection in the British Museum, but it did differ significantly from this and from the variant printed by Percy. It also had different verses than either of the Scottish versions collected by Allan Ramsay and William Motherwell. Again, this seems to have been the first time that the song, which would become one of the best known and most performed of all traditional ballads, was noted from oral transmission in England.

Cruel Barbara Allen

Anon

Twas in the morn - ing month of may,   When   flowers they are   a

spring ing,   A   young man on   his   death bed lay,   For   love of Bar - b'ra   All en.

Fig. 5.5

Twas in the morning month of May,
When flowers they are a springing,
A young man on his death-bed lay
For love of Barb'ra Allen.

He sent one of his servant-men
To the place where she was dwelling,
Saying, "You must come down to my master's
        house,
If your name's Barb'ra Allen!"

Then she arose, and put on her clothes,
And slowly she crept nigh him,
And said, when she entered his bed-room,
"Young man, I see you're dying!"

"One kiss from you would cure me yet,
[Were I on my death-bed lying."]
"A kiss from me you shall not have,
Although I think you're dying!"

"Look up, look up, to my bed's head!

You'll see a napkin hanging;
'Tis my gold watch and silver brooch,
Give them to Barb'ra Allen!"

"Look down, look down, to my bed's foot!
You'll see a basin standing;
'Tis my heart's blood and tears I've shed,
For love of Barb'ra Allen!"

As she was walking through the fields
She heard the death-bell tolling,
In every stroke she heard it say,
"Hard-hearted Barb'ra Allen!"

And as she walked along the road
She met his corpse a-coming;
"O put him down, O put him down,

That I may gaze upon him!"

The more she gazed, the more she smiled,
The further she kept from him;
The young men cried, "O fie for shame!
Hard-hearted Barb'ra Allen!"

"O mother, mother, make my bed,
And make it soft and easy;
For my young man has died to-day,
And I'll die for him to-morrow!"

"O father, father, dig my grave,
And dig it long and narrow;
For my young man has died for love,
And I'll die for him for sorrow!"[8]

The Edgmond women were not the only local sources of traditional and broadside balladry, although some Shropshire informants recited rather than sang their material, and in a few cases Burne received texts in written form. In total she obtained over a dozen ballads, although in some instances forgotten lines had to be supplied from broadsides. Some of these ballads were well known, for example the very popular "Gipsy Laddie," and "The Outlandish Knight," which, as we have seen, was recited to her by an old nurse at Ross, in the nearby county of Herefordshire, as well as sung by Jane Butler. Also quite common—in England, Scotland, and even New England—was "Hugh of Lincoln" (aka "Sir Hugh" or "The Jew's Daughter"). This was already familiar to Victorian antiquarians and folklorists, having been the subject of James Orchard Halliwell's 1849 publication *Ballads and Poems respecting Hugh of Lincoln*.[9] Percy had included a Scottish version in the *Reliques of Ancient English Poetry* and variants had subsequently been collected in Scotland by David Herd, Robert Jamieson, and William Motherwell. It would later turn up in a variety of English counties, including Lincolnshire, Northamptonshire, Buckinghamshire, Surrey, Kent, as well as in different parts of London. Burne's version, which resembled a fragment noted from oral tradition by Halliwell, was obtained from an antiquarian periodical titled *Salopian Shreds and Patches*, which had in 1875 printed a text gleaned from the recitation of a local nursemaid sometime between 1810 and 1820. Burne consequently had no tune for the song, while her text for "Hugh of Lincoln," although recognizably the same ballad, was quite different from that printed by Harriet Mason in *Nursery Rhymes and Country Songs*.

It hails, it rains, in Merrycock land,
It hails, it rains, both great and small,
And all the little children in Merrycock land
They have need to play at ball.

They tossed the ball so high,
They tossed the ball so low,
Amongst all the Jews' cattle
And amongst the Jews below.

Out came one of the Jew's daughters
Dressed all in green,
"Come, my sweet Saluter,
And fetch the ball again."

"I durst not come, I must not come,
Unless my little playfellows come along,

For if my mother sees me at the gate
She'll cause my blood to fall."

She showed me an apple green as grass,
She showed me a gay gold ring,
She showed me a cherry red as blood,
And so she enticed me in.

She took me in the parlour,
She took me in the kitchen,
And there I saw my own dear nurse,
A-picking of a chicken.

She laid me down to sleep
With a Bible at my head and a Testament at my feet,
And if my playfellows come to *quere* for me,
Tell them I am asleep.[10]

On the other hand, certain other ballads that Burne found in Shropshire oral tradition were less common. "Lord Derwentwater's Death," a historical ballad about the execution of one of the ringleaders of the Jacobite rebellion defeated at the battle of Preston in 1715, was recited to her in 1881 by Mrs. Dudley of Much Wenlock. Again Burne had no tune, but she gave it pride of place in her set of song texts, commenting that "the ballad is singularly early in style for the period at which it must have been 'made,'" which was presumably soon after the protagonist's execution in 1716. Mrs. Dudley had apparently learned the ballad from her grandfather, evidently himself a Jacobite sympathizer, who had informed her that "the sun was the colour of blood the day it [the beheading] happened."[11] Burne was aware that John Harland had published a modernized version of the ballad in the second (1875) edition of *Ballads and Songs of Lancashire*, but she did not mention the fragment that John Bell had printed in *Rhymes of Northern Bards* or any of the Scottish variants noted by Kinloch, Motherwell, and Buchan.[12] This is Mrs. Dudley's text, which reads as though it was derived from a broadside, and the first part of which closely resembles Bell's fragment:

The King he wrote a letter
And sealed it with gold,
And sent it to Lord Derwentwater
To read it if he could.

The first three lines he looked upon,
They made him to smile;
And the next three lines he looked upon
Made tears fall from his eyes.

O then bespoke his gay lady
As she on a sick-bed lay,
"Make your will, my lord,
Before you go away."

"O there is for my eldest son
My houses and my land,
And there is for my youngest son
Ten thousand pounds in hand.

"There is for you, my gay lady,
My true and lawful wife,
The third part of my whole estate
To maintain you a lady's life."

Then he called to his stable-groom
To bring him his grey steed;
For he must to London go,
The king had sent indeed.

When he put his foot in the stirrup
To mount his grey steed,

His gold ring from his finger burst,
And his nose began to bleed.

He had not gone but half a mile
When it began to rain,
"Now this is a token," his lordship said,
"That I shall not return again."

When he unto London came
A mob did at him rise,
And they called him a traitor,
Made the tears fall from his eyes.

"A traitor, a traitor! His lordship said,
["Tell me how that can be?]
Is it for keeping eight score men
To fight for pretty Jimmee?"

O then bespoke a grave man
With broad axe in his hand:
"Hold your tongue, Lord Derwentwater,
Your life lies at my command."

"My life, my life," his lordship said,
"My life I will give to thee,
And the black velvet coat upon my back,
Take it for thy fee."

Then he laid his head upon the block,
He did such courage show,
And asked the executioner
To cut it off at one blow.[13]

Other ballads obtained by Burne included "An English Lady," a local variant of "The Pretty Ploughboy," which evoked the geographical location of Shropshire on the border with Wales and the lower social status of the Welsh peasantry. "The Widow Woman," noted in March 1883 by one of Burne's helpers, Hubert Smith, as recited by an elderly fisherman at Bridgnorth who had learnt it in his youth from his grandmother, was a variant of "The Wife of Usher's Well." It was a pity that Burne and Smith were unable to obtain a tune because no other English version of this ballad was extant, although Sir Walter Scott had published in *Minstrelsy of the Scottish Border* a text noted in West Lothian and George Kinloch had acquired a variant sung in Peeblesshire. This is the English version, as collected by Smith and printed by Burne:

There was a widow-woman lived in far Scotland,
And in far Scotland she did live,
And all her cry was upon sweet Jesus,
Sweet Jesus so meek and mild.

Then Jesus arose one morning quite soon,
And arose one morning betime,
And away He went to far Scotland,
And to see what the good woman want.
And when he came to far Scotland

Crying, "What, O what, does the good woman want,
That is calling so much on Me?"

"It's you go rise up my three sons,
Their names, Joe, Peter, and John,
And put breath in their breast,
And clothing on their backs,
And immediately send them to far Scotland,
That their mother may take some rest."

Then He went and rose up her three sons,
Their names, Joe, Peter, and John,
And did immediately send them to far Scotland
That their mother may take some rest.

Then she made up a supper so neat,
As small, as small, as a yew-tree leaf,
But never one bit they could eat.

Then she made up a bed so soft,
The softest that ever was seen;
And the widow-woman and her three sons
They went to bed to sleep.

There they lay about the middle of the night,
Bespeaks the youngest son,
"The white cock he has crowed once,
The second has, so has the red."

And then bespeaks the eldest son,
"I think, I think, it is high time
For the wicked to part from their dead."

They laid [= led] her along a green road,
The greenest that ever was seen,
Until they came to some far Chaperine
Which was builded of lime and sand;
Until they came to some far Chaperine
Which was builded with lime and stone.

And then He opened the door so big
And the door so very wide,
Said He to her three sons, "Walk in!"
But told her to stay outside.

"Go back, go back!" sweet Jesus replied,
"Go back, go back!" says He,
"For thou hast nine days to repent
For the wickedness that thou hast done."

Nine days then was past and gone,
And nine days then was spent,
Sweet Jesus called her once again
And took her to Heaven with Him.[14]

While most of the ballads collected by Burne and her helpers would usually be classed as traditional, a few (including "An English Lady," "The Golden Glove" and "The Disdainful Lady") were clearly derived from broadsides printed in the county town of Shrewsbury, although they had passed into local singing tradition. The Edgmond singers' repertoires contained several of these broadside ballads. Harriet Dowley, for example, sang the courtship ballad titled "The Disdainful Lady," a variant on "The Keys of Canterbury."

The Disdainful Lady

Anon

Fig. 5.6

Yonder stands a comely creature,
With her breast as white as snow,
I'll go court her for her feature,
Though her answer'll perhaps be no!

"Madam, I am com'n a-courting,
If your favour I can gain,
And if you will entertain me,
Perhaps that I may come again."

"Sit you down, young man, you're welcome,
If your face I see no more,

For I will have a handsome young man,
Whether he be rich or poor."

"Madam, I've got gold and silver,
Madam, I've got house and land,
Madam, I've got great stores of riches,
They all shall be at your command."

"What care I for gold and silver,
What care I for your house and land,
Or what care I for all your treasures
If I can have but a handsome man?"

"Madam, you talk much of beauty,
It's a flower that soon decays,
The finest flower in the summer,
It doth soonest fade away.

The ripest apple's soonest rotten,
The hottest love is soonest cold,

A young man's word is soon forgotten,
So, pretty maid, don't be so bold.

But fare you well, my dearest creature,
Since I have no more to say." –
"O turn again, young man! I'll have you!"
But his answer was, "Nay, Nay!"[15]

Sally Withington provided "The Golden Glove," a broadside ballad frequently found in oral tradition, which she had learned during the 1820s from the singing of her mistress when she had been working as a maid on a local farm:

The Golden Glove

Anon

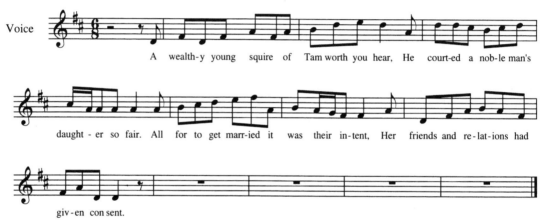

Voice

A wealth-y young squire of Tam-worth you hear, He court-ed a nob-le man's

daught-er so fair. All for to get marr-ied it was their in-tent, Her friends and re-lat-ions had

giv-en con-sent.

Fig. 5.7

A wealthy young squire of Tamworth you hear,
He courted a nobleman's daughter so fair,
All for to be married it was their intent,
Her friends and relations had given consent.

The time was appointed for the wedding-day,
A farmer was chosen to give her away;
As soon as this lady the farmer did spy,
Love inflamed her heart: "O my heart!" she did cry.

She turned from the squire but nothing she said,
Instead of being married she went to her bed,
The thoughts of the farmer still run in her mind,
A way for to gain him she soon then did find.

Coat, waistcoat, and breeches, this lady put on,
And a-hunting she went with her dog and her gun;
She hunted all around where the farmer did dwell,
Because in her heart she lovéd him well.

She oftimes fired, but nothing she killed,
At length this young farmer came into the field,
[And to discourse with him it was her intent,
With her dog and her gun to meet him she went.]

"I thought you had been at the wedding," she cried,
"To wait on the squire and give him his bride."
"O no," said the farmer, "if truth I must tell:
I'll not give her away for I love her too well."

The lady was pleased for to hear him so bold,
She gave him a glove that was flowered with gold,
And told him she'd found it as she came along,
As she was a-hunting with her dog and her gun.

The lady went home with her heart full of love,
And gave out a speech that she had lost her glove:
"The man that will find it and bring it to me,
That man that will find it, his bride I will be."

The farmer was pleased for to hear such news,
With his heart full of love to the lady he goes,
Saying, "Dear honoured lady, I've picked up a glove,
If you will be pleased for to grant me your love."

"It's granted already," the lady replied;
"I love the sweet breath of a farmer," she cried;
"I'll be mistress of his dairy and the milking of his cows,
While my jovial brisk young farmer goes a-whistling to
        plough.[16]

Shropshire singers evidently made no distinction between traditional and broadside ballads, embracing both, but it is significant that about three-quarters of the ballads that Burne chose to print would be incorporated into the Child canon. This may mean, although we cannot be sure, that she did not bother to take down from her singers broadside ballads for which she already possessed printed texts. On her own testimony she had accumulated a "great number" of broadsides but she considered most of them "very inferior pedlar's pack sort of productions," and unfortunately she omitted these from her book.[17] So *Shropshire Folk-Lore* reprinted only a select few broadsides that Burne considered significantly superior to the general run of the genre.

In seeking to supplement the relatively small number of songs collected in the field by (or with) Georgina Jackson, Burne and Smart looked to local "gypsies" (Burne's term) as a suitable source of oral tradition. On four occasions between May and November 1885 they visited travelers camping near the North Shropshire/Staffordshire border. The adults were too busy or too suspicious to sing, but their children were ready to oblige, and Burne obtained several songs and ballads from them. The best singers were Eliza Wharton and her brothers. Apart from children's game songs, they offered three fairly distinct types of material: fragments of love lyrics, carols, and traditional ballads.

As regards the ballads, Burne noted traveler versions of "The Gipsy Laddie" and "The Cruel Mother." The latter was another example of a narrative song that had been collected extensively in Scotland but rarely in England, although there was a broadside version in the Pepys Collection in Cambridge. The rollicking chorus and some of the language in the verses of Eliza's version of "The Cruel Mother" suggested that, notwithstanding its painful subject, the ballad had become a vehicle for a children's game:

The Cruel Mother

Anon

Fig. 5.8

There was a lady lived in York,
Ri fol i diddle i gee wo!
She fell a-courting in her own father's park,
Down by the greenwood side, O!

She leaned her back against the stile,
Ri fol i diddle &c.
There she had two pretty babes born,
Down by the greenwood &c.

And she had nothing to lap 'em in,
But she had a penknife sharp and keen.

She did not care if they felt the smart,
There she stabbed them right through the heart.

She wiped the penknife in the sludge,
The more she wiped, the more the blood showed.

As she was walking in her own father's park,
She saw two pretty babes playing with a ball.

"Pretty babes, pretty babes, if you were mine,"
"I'd dress you up in silks so fine."

"Dear mother, dear mother, when we were thine,"
"You dressed us not in silks so fine!"

"Here we go to the heavens so high,"
"You'll go to bad when you do die!"[18]

Given its subject matter, it is hardly surprising that "The Gipsy Laddie" was one of the traditional ballads that most appealed to the traveler community, and the Wharton children had picked it up from their parents' singing. Whether or not the ballad had its roots in an actual incident that took place in early seventeenth-century Ayrshire, Scottish versions of it were common, the earliest published being that included by Allan Ramsay in the 1740 edition of his *Tea-Table Miscel-*

lany.[19] An English broadside, *circa* 1720, a copy of which is in the Roxburghe Collection, antedated Ramsay's version, and it remained in London broadside publishers' catalogues until at least the mid-nineteenth century. The gypsy version noted by Burne and Smart from the Wharton children on 23 May 1885 was incomplete, but it differed textually from the English broadside and from all the Scottish variants. These are the words and tune sung by Eliza and her brothers:

The Gipsy Laddie

Anon

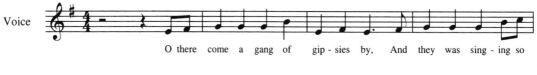

O there come a gang of gip-sies by, And they was sing-ing so

mer-ry gay, And they was sing-ing so mer-ry__gay, Till they gain'd a the heart of my la-dy, O.

Fig. 5.9

There come a gang of gipsies by,
And they was singing so merry gay,
And they was singing so merry gay,
Till they gain'd a the heart o' my lady, O.

As soon as the lawyer [*read,* lord he] did come in,
Enquirèd for his lady, O!
And some o' the servants did-a reply,
"Her's away wi' the gipsy laddie, O!"

"O saddle me the bay, and saddle me the grey,
Till I go and sarch for my lady, O!"
And some o' the sarvants did a-reply,
"Her's away wi' the gipsy laddie, O!"

And he rode on, and he rode off,
Till he come to the gipsies' tent-ie, O!

And there he saw his lady gay
By the side o' the gipsy laddie, O!"

"Didn't I leave you houses and land?
And didn't I leave you money, O?
Didn't I leave you three pretty babes
As ever was in yonder green island, O?"

"What care I for houses and land?
And what care I for money, O?
What do I care for three pretty babes
[Compared to my gipsy laddie, O?]

"The tether night you was on a feather bed,
Now you're on a straw one, O!"
[*imperfect stanza*] [20]

The traveler children also sang snatches of love songs that they had heard from adults, and Burne commented that these were "evidently genuine wild-flowers, though probably of but recent growth."[21] Perhaps because she did not have James Smart with her on that occasion, she did not note the tune, but this, "My True Love Came Whistling By," is one of the love lyrics that Burne collected on 29 August 1885:

My mother sent me for some water,
[Over the stepping-stones high and dry,]
My foot slipped and in I tumbled,
My true love came whistling by.

My mother said as I shouldna have him,
'Cos that he would break my heart;

I don't care what my mother tells me,
I shall take my true love's part.

He will buy me silks and satins,
He will buy me a guinea-gold ring,
He will buy me a silver cradle,
For to lap my baby in.[22]

As a folklorist, Burne had a particular interest in children's games, which she divided into six types: choral games, dramatic and dialogue games, obscure and archaic games, games of strife and skill, Christmas games, and nursery and other trifling games. Although more than one type of game sometimes had associated music, the choral games had the most elaborate texts and tunes and were the only ones for which Burne and Smart saw fit to record the melodies. They included, among others, "Oats and Beans and Barley Grow!" "Oliver, Oliver, Last in the Ring," "Sally, Sally Water,"

"Ring o' Roses" and "The Wind, Wind Blows." Of the game songs noted from the traveler children, "Green Gravel" was one that Burne and Smart heard Eliza Wharton perform:

Green Gravel

Anon

Fig. 5.10

Green gravel, green gravel, the grass is so green,
The fairest young lady that ever was seen;
I'll clothe you in silk,
And I'll wash you in milk,
And I'll write down your name with a gold pen and ink.

O Sally, O Sally, your true love is dead,
He's sent you a letter to turn round your head.[23]

The carols that the Wharton children knew were also very interesting, although the texts were somewhat fragmentary. They included a Christmas carol that Eliza associated with Easter and sang in May, and "The Moon Shines Bright." Another was "Christ Made a Trance." Burne classified this as a variant of "The Moon Shines Bright," but her informant, Eliza, apparently regarded it as a different carol:

Christ made a trance one Sunday view, all with his own dear hands,
He made the sun clear, and the moon, like the water on dry land.

[All for the saving of our souls] Christ died upon the cross,
What shall we do for our Saviour like He has done for us?

He's the rose, the rose, and the gen-teel rose, the fyarn that grows so green,
And God give us grace in ever-i place [to pray for our youthful Queen].

Go you down, go you down, to yonder little town, as far as the hol-i well,
And there you'll see sweet Jesus Christ with his body nailed to a tree.

"O my dear son, what hast thou done, [that thou'rt nailed to a tree?]"
"Dear mother, dear mother, take young John [and love him instead of me.]"

"For it's O my dear son, that never can be done, that I should lather John
So well as my own dear son Jesus that I bore from my own bodie."[24]

Christ Made a Trance

Anon

Christ made a trance one Sun-day view, All with his own dear hands, He made the sun clear and the moon, like the wat - er on the dry — land.

Fig. 5.11

Other folk-carols in *Shropshire Folk-Lore* included "As I Sat on a Sunny Bank" (aka "I Saw Three Ships"), "The Seven Virgins," and various imperfectly remembered fragments.

Although Burne clearly regarded the ballads as the most important musical material that she and Jackson had collected, she thought it worthwhile to reproduce a selection of other local folksongs. This was how she introduced them to her readers:

> The six remaining songs comprise a humorous song on that favourite topic, clownish courtship, a hunting song, a war song, and three thoroughly local ditties, dealing with cock-fighting, bear-baiting, and rustic jokes, of which the village cobbler seems to have been the favourite butt...Here we come to the purely Shropshire compositions, which are chiefly *topical*...It is still quite a usual practice in Shropshire to "make a ballet" on any passing event of interest, such as an unusually good run with the hounds, a singularly melancholy death, and so forth...One such songmaker, commonly called "the Muxton Carter," lived in the parish of Lilleshall within my memory. He "used to think the verses over in his mind when he was going with the horses, and when he got home at night he would put them down." It was doubtless such unlettered poets as these who supplied the matter for the 'broadsides' which emanated in great numbers from Waidson's press at Shrewsbury during the earlier years of the present century. I have had a great number of these placed at my disposal, but only two—the *Shropshire Militia Boys* and the *English Lady in Love*—appear in the present collection.[25]

Three of the songs referred to here by Burne were "Country Courtship" (obtained from an eighty-year-old inhabitant of the village of Pulverbatch, West Shropshire), "The Three Jolly Huntsmen" (a song traditional in Burne's own family for fifty years or more) and "The Shropshire Militia Boys" (reprinted from a Waidson broadsheet). Another, "The Lee Bridge Cocking," depicted a cock-fight held in 1799 near the village of Wem. One of the humorous songs, "The Loppington Bear," recorded an incident that happened in 1822. This, together with "The Cobbler and the Jackass," a comic song making fun of an avaricious artisan—Joseph Harper, a shoemaker from the neighboring village of Wolverley—who was not content to buy his raw materials locally, was collected in Loppington. Both songs seem to have been examples of group composition, perhaps in the local pub, by blacksmith William Williams and cobbler Richard Davies (presumably a competitor of Harper's). As an illustration of Shropshire humor, here is "The Loppington Bear," in which Harper, likely the worse for drink, sees what he takes to be a bear and rouses the entire village:

> In Loppington town there now doth dwell a cobbler who is known full well;
> In Loppington town there now doth dwell a cobbler who is known full well;
> He went to milk one morning fa'r, in Elkes's fallow he spied a bar.
> Tal-jal-la, ra-li, gee wo! Tal-lal-la, ra-li, gee wo!
>
> Then down he throws his milking can, and off he runs to his wife Ann;
> Then down he throws his milking can, and off he runs to his wife Ann;
> He says, "My dear, I do declar,' in Elkes's fallow I've see'd a bar!"
> Tal-jal-la, ra-li, gee wo! Tal-lal-la, ra-li, gee wo!
>
> "My dear, what do you tell me now? For sure the bar he'll bite our cow!
> Sure they are the most dreadful things for they can bite as well as grin."

Then off to Freeman's he did run to fetch the big dog and the gun,
Cart-ropes and pikels, likewise stakes to bait the bar at Loppi'ton Wakes.

The village it did quickly rise to hear the cobbler's mournful cries;
They surely thought he had been bitten, but they were very much mistaken.

Bold Alexander run with speed, he vow'd he kill the monstrous jeed;
Likewise the blacksmith with his shovel, and vowed he'd kill the monstrous devil.

The Milner gazing in his room, "You fools, it's only the full o' the moon!
But if it really should be so, the whole o' the town will have to go."

Says Todd, "This is a curious thing, for bars are apt to bite and grin;
But if she proves their overthrow, the Milner and I shall be forced to go."

Now munna this cobbler ha' bin bould to ha' walked twice round him while he growled?
And munna-d his hearing ha' bin good to ha' heard the growls of a chump o' wood?[26]

The Loppington Bear

Richard Davies and William Williams

Fig. 5.12

Burne was also particularly interested in songs that were associated with traditional Shropshire customs such as mumming plays and Morris dancing. At Christmas, local Morris dancers, called "guisers," performed a traditional play, loosely based on the legend of St. George and the Dragon. Burne was familiar with three different versions of the play, one staged at Newport, one at Eccleshall, and one at Edgmond. One of the characters was a Fool called Bellzebub, and the "Tinker's Song" was incorporated into one of his speeches:

> I am a jovial tinker, I've traveled both far and near,
> And I never did meet with a singer, without he could drink some beer.
> O it's then with a friend we'll a merry life spend,
> Which I never did yet, I vow.
> With my rink-a-tink tink, and a sup more drink,

I'll make yer old kettles cry sound, sound, sound!
I'll make yer old kettles cry sound!

I am a jovial tinker, and have been all my life,
So now I think it's time to seek a fresh young wife,
And then with a friend, we'll a merry life spend,
Which I never did yet, I vow.
With my rink-a-tink tink, etc.

They drawed me to the barracks, they drawed me up and down,
They draw me to the barracks and put my poor legs in pound,
But now with a friend, we'll a merry life spend,
Which I never did yet, I vow.
With my rink-a-tink tink, etc.

My jacket's all pitches and patches and on it I give a sly look,
My trousers all stitches and starches wouldn't quite suit a lord or a duke,
But it's pitches and patches I wear till I can get better or new,
I take the world as I find it,
[With my rink-a-tink tink, and a sup more drink,]
Brave boys, if I'm ragged I'm true, true, true!
Brave boys, if I'm ragged I'm true.[27]

Tinker's Song

Anon

Fig. 5.13

In Shropshire, Hallowe'en or All Saints' Night was usually called All Souls' Night, and the custom associated with it was souling. Souling involved a party of merrymakers visiting local farms and cottages and singing a traditional request for apples, ale, and soul cakes. Burne collected souling ditties in fifteen different villages, including this one at Market Drayton, the version that she considered the "purest and oldest":

> Soul! Soul! For a soul-cake!
> I pray, good missis, a soul-cake!
> An apple or pear, a plum or a cherry,
> Any good thing to make us merry,
> One for Peter, two for Paul,
> Three for Him who made us all,
> Up with the kettle and down with the pan,
> Give us good alms, and we'll be gone.[28]

Of the many souling songs that Burne collected, only two had melodies that she deemed worthy of including in her tune appendix. She had encountered the following ditty in six different villages, and although the verses varied from village to village the tune was the same and it was clearly the same song. She therefore made a composite version by collating the fragments, indicating in brackets after each verse the villages in which she had heard it sung.

Souling Song No. 1

Anon

God bless the mas-ter of this house, And the good mis-sis too, And

all the lit-le child-ren that a-bout the tab-le go.

Fig. 5.14

God bless the master of this house
And the good missis too,
And all the little children
That about the table go.
(Whittington, Westfelton, Oswestry,
Ellesmere, Wellington)

God bless your man and maiden,
Your cattle and your store,
And all that is within your gates
I wish you ten times more.
(Whittington)

Your pockets lined with silver,
Your barrels full of beer,
Your pantry full of pork-pies,
I wish I had some here!
(Oswestry)

Your streets is very dirty,
The night is very cold,
And this night to come a-souling

We do make bold.
(Whittington)

The roads are very dirty,
My shoes are very thin,
I've got a little pocket
To put a penny in.
(Oswestry, Ellesmere, Newport)

Go down into your cellar,
And see what you can find,
The barrel is not empty,
I hope you will prove kind.
(Whittington, Westfelton, Ellesmere, Newport)

I hope you will prove kind
With your apples and strong beer,
And we'll come no more a-souling
Till this time next year!
(Whittington, Westfelton, [and part] Oswestry)[29]

The second souling song with a melody was sung in three locations: Wellington, Newport, and Market Drayton. Again Burne created a composite, indicating after each verse the source or sources of that couplet.

We are three jolly boys all in a mind:
We are come a-souling, I hope you'll prove kind.
(Market Drayton)

Souling time's coming, and we're souling here,
And all that we're souling for is apples and good
                                              beer. *(Wellington)*

Put your hand in your pocket and pull out your keys,
Go down in your cellar and draw what you please. *(Market Drayton, Newport)*

I hope you'll prove kind with your ale and strong beer,
And we'll come no more a-souling till this time next year.
(Market Drayton) [30]

Souling Song No. 2

Anon

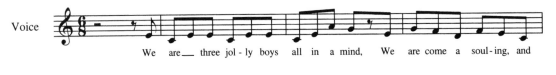

Fig. 5.15

Other songs reflecting traditional local activities included a hunting song ("Three Jolly Huntsmen") that Burne collected in two versions, a dance tune called "Shrewsbury Quarry," and a broadside in praise of the "Shropshire Militia." She closed her chapter on local ballads and songs with a wassail sung annually at Christmas on the streets of Shrewsbury. The "Wassail Cup Carol," also known locally as "The Wessel Cup Hymn," seems to have been a regional variant of "Here We Come A-Wassailing." Some overlap between the words of the wassail and the words of local souling songs was evident.

Oh, here we come a-wassailing
Among the leaves so green,
Oh, here we come a-wassailing
So far to be seen.
God send you happy! God send you happy!
God send you all a Happy New Year.

We are not daily beggars
That beg from door to door,
But we are neighbours' children
That you have seen before.
God send you happy, etc.

Call up the butler of this house,
Put on his golden ring,
And let him bring a pint of beer,

And the better we shall sing.
God send you happy, etc.

The streets are very dirty,
Our shoes are very thin,
We've got a little pocket
To put a penny in.
God send you happy, etc.

God bless the master of this house,
Likewise the missis too,
And all the little children
That about the table go.
God send you happy, etc. [31]

Wassail Cup Carol

Anon

Oh here we come a-wass-ail-ing, A - mong the leaves so green. Oh here we come a-wass ail-ing, so far— to be seen. God send you hap-py! God send you hap-py! God send you all— a— Hap py New Year!

Fig. 5.16

Burne's presentation of her material unfortunately dissociated words from music, with the latter consigned to an appendix. In some instances she provided tunes but only abbreviated texts (for example, the two Souling songs), and at other times she had been unable to collect melodies—as when her informants recited rather than sang ballads, or when her broadside or chap-book sources failed to give tunes. Yet even when she could provide both texts and tunes, she hived the melodies off to the back of the book. Why she did this we do not know for sure, but the most likely reason is a very practical one—it saved on printing costs. If so, it was an understandable, if still regrettable, decision. Luckily it is not too difficult to put the words and music back together again, as I have done for the examples given above.

Although Charlotte Burne's focus was hardly narrow, we nonetheless know that she had in her possession many ballads and folksongs that she decided to omit from her book. The material that she presented in *Shropshire Folk-Lore* was thus very selective. One cannot help wishing that she had expanded the scope of her single chapter on Shropshire folksong. What she did publish provides a good glimpse, but still only a glimpse, into a world of rural singing traditions that had not yet been corrupted by the music hall or by other more modern forms of popular culture. If nothing else, the book demonstrated that the county of Shropshire (and its neighboring counties) would be a very promising area in which to supplement the relatively small amount of songhunting undertaken there by Jackson, Burne, and Smart. Indeed, it provided a tantalizing taste of the riches likely to be found in the lands along the Welsh border. Surprisingly, although Ralph Vaughan Williams would go collecting with Ella Leather in nearby Herefordshire during the Edwardian revival, it would not be until the 1950s, when Peter Kennedy arrived with a BBC tape recorder, that the traditional music of Shropshire would again attract serious attention.

Burne herself apparently never collected any more folksongs from local singers on the Shropshire/Staffordshire border. She did, however, continue to collect English folklore, and went on to play a significant role in the Folk-Lore Society. *Shropshire Folk-Lore* was well received by anonymous reviewers in the *Folk-Lore Journal* in 1884 and again in 1886; indeed the latter declared that it was "the best collection of English folklore that has yet appeared."[32]

The Besom Maker and Other Country Folk Songs

Heywood Sumner (1853-1940) was a Hampshire artist and artisan. Although trained as a lawyer, he made his career as an etcher, painter, and interior decorator. A close friend of metalwork designer W. A. S. Benson, who introduced him to William Morris, Sumner became associated with the Arts and Crafts movement in the early 1880s, and with the Century Guild from 1884. He worked in a variety of media, including textiles, wallpaper, tapestries, and stained glass. He also specialized in the technique of sgraffito, a way of decorating walls by incising designs on colored plaster. In the early 1880s Sumner published two books of landscape etchings, *The Itchen Valley* (1881) and *The Avon from Naseby to Tewkesbury* (1882), and in 1883 he contributed twelve etchings to a new edition of J. R. Wise's guide to *The New Forest.*

Other works that he illustrated included two by F. H. K. De La Motte, *Sintram and his Companions* (1883) and *Undine* (1888).[33] His sole contribution to the burgeoning folksong revival was *The Besom Maker and Other Country Folk Songs,* which appeared in 1888.[34]

Sumner's *Besom Maker,* although visually a work of art, seemed at first glance a slight offering. It was twenty-six pages in length, many of which were taken up with illustrations, and there were only nine songs. Yet, small though it was, the collection had the virtue of including music as well as texts. Since Sumner's collecting was done in the counties of Sussex, Hampshire, and Somerset, there was no doubt that these were songs from rural southern England. Although no specific sources were given for the items, Sumner indicated that they had been noted from elderly rural dwellers. In his preface he affirmed that (with one unspecified exception) the songs had been collected from countrymen at labor in the fields or while merrymaking at harvest suppers:

> This little book contains a few old fashioned country songs. Songs which still may be heard where ploughmen strike their furrows, and still sung at harvest suppers by the old folk who do not change their tune to the times. Indeed when thus heard Song & Singer seem to be inseparable, for singers such as these have a quaint personal style & an unexpected manner of prolonging their best notes which cannot be imparted & which almost baffles notification [*sic*]. Nevertheless, apart from their local rendering and though these simple tunes are caged in bars, I hope that there still remains a true echo of the country in these "terrible old fashioned" songs as here presented. Respecting their authenticity and antiquity I will hazard no opinion... [but] I would express my belief that the tunes & versions here given are not included in any current British song & ballad book.[35]

This was Sumner's way of emphasizing that the collection, small though it was, consisted entirely of authentic old folksongs noted from oral tradition in the countryside of southern England. Agriculture and other aspects of rural life provided the subjects of more than half of them. He affirmed that he had printed each song "like hi't wer' gun' 'ter me," as regards both words and melody.[36] In this respect, the songbook therefore followed closely in the footsteps of Broadwood's *Old English Songs* and Mason's *Nursery Rhymes and Country Songs.* However, the book's most original aspect, apart from its decorative illustrations, may have been the use of the word "folk song," which although not a first, was one of the earliest occasions on which the term appeared in the title of a collection of vernacular songs.

The title song of *The Besom Maker* was a variant of the ditty that Blind Willie Purvis had made his own on Tyneside as "Buy Broom Buzzems." The diction was much more formal than the version in *Northumbrian Minstrelsy* and one wonders whether Sumner, notwithstanding his claim that all the songs in the book were exactly as collected, had tidied it up for publication. The text of his version, with its sexual imagery, suggested that the singer was a woman, and it would be interesting to know the gender of his informant (which he did not reveal). His illustrations portrayed the besom maker as an elderly male but this may have been a deliberate attempt to distract the reader from the song's subtext. On the other hand, it is just possible, although unlikely, that Sumner simply missed the metaphor:

> I am a besom maker, come listen to my tale,
> I am a besom maker that lives in yonder vale,
> Sweet pleasure that I do enjoy both morning night and noon,
> Going o'er the hills so high O, in gathering of green broom.
> So it's O come buy my besoms, my besoms fine and new,
> Bonny green broom besoms, better never grew.
>
> One morning as I was roving all over the hills so high
> I met the jolly squire all with his rolling eye,
> He tips to me the wink and I sing to him my tune,
> So I ease him of his drink O, in gathering of green broom,
> So it's O come buy my besoms, etc.
>
> One morning as I was roving until my native vale
> I met Jack Sprat the miller and he asked me to turn tail,
> His mill I rattle round and I grind his grits so clean,
> So I lease him of his drink O, in gathering broom so green.
> So it's O come buy my besoms, etc.
>
> One morning as I was a roving until my native cot
> I met a jolly farmer so happy was his lot.
> He ploughed his furrows deep and he laid his corn so low,
> And there it would bide asleep till spring and the broom she'd grow.

So it's O come buy my besoms, etc.

And when the corn grew up upon its native soil
All like a little baby bright with its waving smile,
Then I bundles up my broom cuts and I binds 'em tight and spare,
And my besoms folks they please 'ems for I'm the darling of the fair.
So it's O come buy my besoms, etc.[37]

The Besom Maker

Anon

Fig. 5.17

Apart from the title song, the songbook's overtly agricultural items included "God Speed the Plough," "The Jolly Ploughboy," and "The Reaphook and the Sickle." As a second illustration of *The Besom Maker's* contents, here is another of these songs of country life, a harvest health:

Come all you lads and lasses, together let us go,
Into some pleasant cornfield our courage for to show,
With the reaphook and the sickle so well we clear the land,
The farmer says, "Well done, my lads, here's liquor at your command."

By daylight in the morning, when birds so sweetly sing,
They are such charming creatures they make the valley ring,
We will reap and scrape together till Phoebus do go down,
With the good old leathern bottle and beer that is so brown.

Then in comes lovely Nancy, the corn all for to lay,
She is my charming creature, I must begin to pray:
See how she gathers it, binds it, she folds it in her arms,
Then gives it to some waggoner to fill a farmer's barns.

Now harvest's done and ended, the corn secure from harm,
All for to go to market, boys, we must thresh in the barn.
Here's a health to all your farmers, likewise to all you men,
I wish you health and happiness till harvest comes again.[38]

The Reaphook & the Sickle

Anon

Come all you lads and las - ses, to - geth - er let us go, In to some pleas - ant corn - field, our cour age for to show. With reap - hook and the sick - le, so well we clear the land, The farm - er says "Well done, my lads, here's liqu - or at your com - mand."

Fig. 5.18

Sumner was also interested in local customs, and he had collected the tune of a local wassail song, although he may have supplemented the text from a printed source. The wassail was employed primarily as a means of obtaining free ale on New Year's Eve, although the text suggests that it may also have been sung when caroling on Christmas Eve. We have seen that wassailing was still an active custom in Shropshire, where Charlotte Burne noted a "Wassail Cup Carol" as well as several souling songs. The practice seems to have survived also in the south and southwest of England. Sumner had apparently noted his "Wassail Song" in Hampshire, but commented that a close variant of the chorus was employed on Epiphany Eve in western Somerset as part of a fertility ceremony intended to bring about a bumper apple crop, from which cider would be made.

Pray master and mistress if you are within,
Please open the door and let us come in.
For we are come with our Christmas carol,
We are come if you please to help empty your barrel.
Wassail, wassail, all around the town,
Our cup is white and our ale is brown.

Our bowl is made of a good ashen tree,
And here my kind fellow we drink to thee.
We are in the old Time: the new Time comes fast,
The new Time comes fast—the old Time is past.
So I wish you all a happy New Year,
Your pockets full of money, your barrels full of beer.
Wassail, wassail, etc.

We'll drink master's health and our mistress' beside,
And all the pretty family around the fireside,
And all that he has got, I know he does not mind,
We'll drink master's health in water or in wine.
Wassail, wassail, etc.

We'll drink master's health with the star all on his breast,
And when that he is dead we hope his soul will rest—
So I wish you all a happy New Year,
So I wish you all a happy New Year.
Wassail, wassail, etc.[39]

The Wassail Song

Anon

Fig. 5.19

The Besom Maker also included three children's game songs ("Hobblety Bobblety," "The Two Young Men of Kenilworth," and "Forty Dukes a Riding"), and one love song, "My Johnny Was a Shoemaker," which Sumner may have also collected from local children. Although the underlying subject of the song appears to have been the press gang, and the lyric suggests a residual distaste for the life of an ordinary sailor, this was no anti-war song. It optimistically predicted that the cobbler-turned-mariner would succeed in his new trade, rise in the ranks, and eventually return unscathed to his lover, whom he would find waiting patiently in his native village. Just as "The Reaphook and the Sickle" glossed over the hardships of life as an agricultural laborer in Late Victorian England, so "My Johnny Was a Shoemaker" glossed over the perils of making a living in either the merchant marine or the Royal Navy. It seems likely that the singers of these ditties, whose names have unfortunately gone unrecorded, knew full well the darker side of life at sea and in the countryside but used the songs as a way of looking on the brighter side. Celebrating the good things that interspersed their daily routine perhaps made that incessant cycle of toil easier to bear. This is Sumner's version of "My Johnny Was a Shoemaker":

> My Johnny was a shoemaker and dearly he loved me,
> My Johnny was a shoemaker but now he's gone to sea,
> With nasty pitch to soil his hands
> And sail across the stormy sea..ea..ea,
> My Johnny was a shoemaker.
>
> His jacket was a deep sky blue and curly was his hair,
> His jacket was a deep sky blue, it was I do declare,
> To reef the topsail now he's gone
> And sail across the stormy sea..ea..ea,
> My Johnny was a shoemaker.
>
> And he will be a captain by and by, with a brave and gallant crew,
> And he will be a captain by and by, with a sword and a spy glass too,
> And when he is a captain bold
> He'll come back to marry me..ee..ee,

My Johnny was a shoemaker.[40]

My Johnny Was a Shoemaker

Anon

Fig. 5.20

Although not a major work, Sumner's little book was a useful addition to the relatively small stock of English folksongs for which integrated tunes and texts now existed in published form. It was not, however, a balanced collection, since it over-emphasized the 'country life' component of this heritage of rural vernacular song. Sumner himself would continue to participate, albeit in a modest way, in the folksong revival as it developed during the early 1890s, becoming one of Lucy Broadwood's collaborators on the project that resulted in *English County Songs*. But he never again published a folksong collection of his own.

In Gipsy Tents

In Gipsy Tents, first published in 1880, before either *Shropshire Folk-Lore* or *The Besom Maker*, was Francis Hindes Groome's memoir of his encounters with Romany gypsies in the byways of England and Wales. Groome (1851-1902), already the author of the article on "Gipsies" in the ninth edition of *Encylopaedia Britannica* (1879), was one of the leading Victorian apologists for the traveling families that he admired. He had first become fascinated with gypsy life and lore while a student at Ipswich Grammar School in the late 1860s. While studying at Corpus Christi College, Oxford, he came to know intimately the local gypsy communities, and from 1873 to 1876 he lived as a Romany, traveling extensively with gypsy bands in Germany, Hungary, and Romania as well as throughout the United Kingdom. Groome settled in Edinburgh in 1876 and from then on made a living as a writer and encyclopedia editor, but he renewed his ties with Suffolk, where his parents lived, and edited "Suffolk Notes and Queries" for the *Ipswich Journal*. He also resumed his contacts with British gypsies and continued his study of Romany life, lore, and history. His early romanticism was gradually superseded by a more scientific spirit, but he never lost his love of gypsy ways and Romany culture. A founder-member of the Gipsy-Lore Society and a frequent contributor to its *Journal*, Groome quickly became recognized as one of the two or three leading scholars on the subject of Romany migrations and their influence on European culture. He summarized his views in an influential paper, "The Influence of the Gypsies on the Superstitions of the English Folk," which was published in 1891 in the *Transactions of the International Folk-Lore Congress*[41]. He would later publish a novel of gypsy life, *Kriegspiel* (1896),[42] and an important collection of *Gypsy Folk-Tales* (1899),[43] which is usually seen as his most important contribution as a scholarly folklorist.[44]

Nostalgia for a way of life and for a body of folklore that was in danger of being swept away by a tide of urbanization and industrialization permeates *In Gipsy Tents*, but it was nonetheless intended as a faithful record of Groome's encounters with the Romany and as an accurate picture of their lives and customs. He appears to have tracked them down mainly in central Wales or along the Scottish border, although he also knew one family living in or near London. Groome was not searching for folksongs when he conducted interviews with his Romany informants and by no means all his traveler acquaintances were singers, but on more than one occasion he found himself in a gypsy camp when singing was the order of the day. Luckily he recognized the value of noting some of the ballads current in oral tradition. A few were in the Romany language, but most were in English. For example, from a traveler named Starlina Lovell he obtained the following lyric, sometimes known as "Died for Love":

A brisk young sailor came courting me,
He stole away my sweet liberty;
My heart he stole with a free good will,
He's got it now, and he'll keep it still.

There is an alehouse in yonders town,
Where my first lover is sitting down,
And he takes another lass on his knee;
Oh! Don't you think it's a grief to me?

A grief to me, and I'll tell you why,
Because she has more gold than I;
But her gold will flash, and her beauty pass,
And she'll become like me at last.

Her father came home, it was late one night,
Inquiring for his heart's delight;
Upstairs he went, and the door he broke,
And found her hanging by a rope.

He took his knife, and he cut her down,
And in her bosom this note he found,
And on the note these few lines was wrote—
"O Johnny, O Johnny, my heart you have broke.

Come dig me a grave both wide and deep,
And marble stone from head to feet,
And on the top then a turtle-dove,
To show the world that I died for love."[45]

The text of this song may have been learned from a broadside but it was sung to a "buzzing, quavering tune" that for Groome evoked a vision of an alehouse with "smock-frocked drinkers, oak settle and mugs of cider," a scene that he declared much preferable to "the glare and din of music halls." Another ballad that he heard that day, "Cold Blows the Wind," sung by Grandmother Lementina Lovell, had a "lovely old air" that Groome carried for a while in his head but found impossible to set down on paper. "Myself," he commented ruefully, "I know the tunes but not the notes, so am just as serviceable as an inkless pen; but let the first musician that lights on Boswell, Stanley, Lovell, or Herne [the surnames of some of his singing informants] secure this air and those that followed it."[46] Another member of the Lovell family, Lucretia, contributed "Hugh of Lincoln," a variant of the traditional anti-Semitic ballad, "The Jew's Daughter." Groome had previously heard this sung by a London traveler called Amy North, who had performed it with much emotion and a plethora of runs, trills, and grace notes. Although recognizably the same song as the "Little Sir William" collected by Harriet Mason, the words (and, no doubt, the tune) were somewhat different. It was much closer to the Shropshire version printed by Charlotte Burne, and it is possible that the same broadside may have been the ultimate source of both variants.

Down in merry merry Scotland,
It rained both hard and small,
Two little boys went out one day,
All for to play with a ball.

They tossed it up so very very high,
They tossed it down so low,
They tossed it into the Jew's garden,
Where all the flowers do blow.

Out came one of the Jew's daughters,
Dresséd in green all—
"If you come here, my fair pretty lad,
You shall have your ball."

She showed him an apple as green as grass,
The next thing was a fig,
The next thing a cherry as red as blood,
And that would 'tice him in.

She set him on a golden chair,
And gave him sugar sweet;
Laid him on some golden chest of drawers,
Stabbed him like a sheep.

"Seven foot Bible
At my head and my feet:
If my mother pass by me,
Pray tell her I'm asleep."[47]

Not all the songs with which this traveler family regaled Groome were traditional ballads—Anselo performed a plough-boy's song ("Here's a health to every labouring lad that ploughs and sows the land") and Pyramus a drinking song ("The Leather Bottel")—but another of the female gypsies, Sinfi by name, sang "to a kind of monotonous chant, sad and suggestive as a river's flow" a version of "Babylon" that she knew as "The Bonny Banks of Airdrie." She had learned it from the wife of a Scottish traveler named Jocky Neilson:

There were three sisters going from home,
All in a lea and alony, oh!
They met a man, and he made them stand,
Down by the bonny banks of Airdrie, oh.

He took the first one by the hand,
All in a lea, etc.
He turned her round, and he made her stand,
Down by the bonny banks, etc.

Saying, "Will you be a robber's wife?
Or will you die by my penknife?"

"Oh! I won't be a robber's wife,
But I will die by your penknife."

Then he took the second by the hand,
He turned her round, and he made her stand.

Saying, "Will you be a robber's wife?
Or will you die by my penknife?"

"Oh! I won't be a robber's wife,
But I will die by your penknife."

He took the third one by the hand,
He turned her round, and he made her stand.

Saying, "Will you be a robber's wife?
Or will you die by my penknife?"

"Oh! I won't be a robber's wife,
And I won't die by your penknife.

If my two brothers had been here,
You would not have killed my sisters two."

"What was your two brothers' names?"
"One was John, and the other was James."

"Oh, what did your two brothers do?"
"One was a minister, the other such as you."

"Oh, what is this that I have done?
I have killed my sisters all but one,

And now I'll take out my penknife,
And here I'll end my own sweet life."[48]

Unlike some of the other ballads, which were sung unaccompanied, this was performed to a "masterly" fiddle accompaniment that to Groome's ears "pled for the murdered, raved at the murderer, and moaned for his remorseful suicide."[49] Groome evidently appreciated the artistry with which his favorite traveler family performed its repertoire of traditional and broadside ballads, but, regrettably, he noted down—or saw fit to print—only a handful of the songs that he heard. But his book at the very least had the merit of alerting collectors of vernacular song to the potential value of travelers as a repository of oral tradition. Charlotte Burne was not the only other folklorist to take notice during the 1880s. There was also Laura Smith.

Through Romany Songland

Laura Alexandrine Smith, about whose life little information seems to be available,[50] will be remembered primarily for her two song collections, both published towards the end of the 1880s. She was apparently domiciled in Newcastle-upon-Tyne in the late 1880s, but she appears to have lived in South Wales and in the London area earlier in the decade, while she was collecting material for her books. Smith sometimes worked as a freelance journalist, traveling extensively in the United Kingdom and probably also on the continent of Europe. An amateur musician, she corresponded with professional musicians (including Sir George Macfarren) who she thought might be able to guide her investigations, and she had great admiration for, and probably some contact with, the small group of men (including George Henry Borrow, Charles Godfrey Leland, and George Smith of Coalville) whom she recognized as sympathetic students of and advocates for gypsy culture. A disciple of Francis Hindes Groome in her fascination with and admiration for traveler life and lore, Smith's approach to gypsy song was one of open-minded eclecticism. Her largest and most important work, which dealt with shanties and other sea songs, was published in 1888. It was titled *The Music of the Waters* and will be discussed in the next chapter. The other, *Through Romany Songland,* was published one year later.[51]

The scope of this book was Europe-wide. It had chapters devoted to French gypsies, Gitanos (Spanish gypsies), Zigeuner (German and Scandinavian gypsies), Magyar (Hungarian) gypsies, Russian Romany songs, and Indian gypsy songs and dance tunes. There were also chapters on Scottish tinkers and on Anglo-Romany songs. In her brief Scottish section Smith printed versions of such ballads as "The Gypsie Laddie," "Hughie the Graeme," and "The Tinker and the

Lass o' Gallowa." Although she argued that these narrative songs were beloved of Scottish travelers, the texts she provided were usually taken from printed sources, such as Scott's *Minstrelsy of the Scottish Border*[52] and John Finlay's *Scottish Historical and Romantic Ballads*.[53] The latter, for example, was her source for "The Gypsie Laddie," although she was also familiar with the version printed by Charlotte Burne in *Shropshire Folk-Lore*. Smith did have a few previously unpublished items that she ascribed to Scottish "tinklers" but she was often reticent about her sources. One, which she titled "Tinkler's Song" and attributed to Yetholm (a village close to the border with Northumberland), was identical to that printed by Burne as "Tinker's Song." It was an interesting example of exactly the same song (including the melody) being noted from oral tradition in widely separated parts of the United Kingdom, a fact presumably explained by the itinerant lifestyle of the tradition bearers. Another gypsy song that Smith claimed had been noted in Scotland was credited to collector George Smith (a resident of Coalville, a town in Leicestershire, England), whom she characterized as "the gypsy's best friend."[54] It was untitled, and lacking a tune, but probably an authentic Romany jingle:

Shela, Shela,
Shela gang a' rue,
Shela gang a',
Ricki, dicki,
Shela gaggie o;
Shela gang a',
Lagghi dagghi.
Sweet malori
Sweet Jamie's the lad

That I'll gang wi'.
I'll due my petticoatie,
I'll dye it red,
And wi' my bonnie laddie
I'll beg my bread;
And wi' my bonnie laddie
I'll beg my bread.
Sweet Jamie's the lad
That I'm gaen wi'.[55]

Smith's chapter on Romany songs from England was more extensive, and included several gypsy dance tunes as well as songs in both Romany and English. Although some of her material was culled from printed sources, she had done some collecting of her own from travelers camped in the Plaistow marshes (near London). From an unnamed female informant she noted the words (but no tune) of this ballad, "The Squire and the Gypsy Maid":

One spring morning early a squire was straying
Over the beauteous lands that nature gave birth;
The primrose bloomed forth and the young lambs
                        were straying;
He sings, "I am lonely on this beauteous earth."

"But what are those notes that echo the valley?
Yon smoke that's ascending, it shall be my guide,
Let her be what she may, both wealthy or lowly,
I'll swear by my powers I'll make her my bride!"

He had not strayed far when struck with such beauty,
He'd scarcely trot far in the deep woody dell,
By the side of the tent two eyes shone like diamonds,
And there he beheld the dark gypsy girl.

"Shall I tell you your fortune?" "Oh, dearest, I know
                        it—
The fortune I crave for, is you for my bride;
You shall live in a castle surrounded by servants,
Silks and fine satins shall be your attire;
My sweet gypsy bride shall be looked on with envy
As she rides in her carriage the wife of a squire."

"You promise to me a grand proposal,
You promise to make me as rich as a queen;
Throw them all to the dirt, while I so light-hearted
Can ride on my neddy that stands on the green."

"So fly with me now, in a few months we'll marry,
As man and as wife together can dwell.
I am not of age, that's the reason I tarry,
But I am sure for to marry the dark gypsy girl!"

"O you are a squire, and I'm a poor gypsy:
Both wealth and great beauty are at your command.
There's more honour and virtue in the poor and the lowly,
Than in half your proud ladies that walk through the land.

O you are a squire, and I'm a poor gypsy:
Both wealth and great beauty are at your command.
Some other fair beauty is won by false flattery,
And the poor gypsy wanderer is turned on the street.

But I'll tell you a secret, my virtuous young squire,
The gypsy will not to such misery be led.
The bright golden circle must be on my finger;
Then through the churchyard is the way to my bed."

How this matter ended I did not stop to listen:
Some months passed away and winter drew near;
I passed by a mansion, all was joy and splendour,
And the valleys they echoed with cheer after cheer.

These words met my ear, and filled my heart with pleasure:
"May they well prosper, and God be their guide.
Hail! Hail! to the squire with these little treasures—
Long life to Selina, the dark gypsy bride."[56]

Smith's informants at Upton Park and Canning Town told her that the sentimental lyric "Banks of the Beautiful Severn" was very popular in these gypsy encampments. She failed to obtain the tune of this song, but she did write down the words:

On the banks of the beautiful Severn,
One ev'ning that long since has gone by,
We strayed till the clock struck eleven,
My own little Annie and I.
Her cheeks wore a blush like the roses,
Her breath like the hay newly mown,
Her eyes sparkled like the dew that reposes
In crystal-like drops on the foliag'd-clad thorn.

CHORUS: On the banks of the beautiful Severn,
One evening that long since has gone by,
We strayed till the clock struck eleven,
My own little Annie and I.

We strayed hand in hand together,
Our hearts beating high with true love;
We gazed on the stars as they twinkled,

And peep'd from the blue vault above.
She talked of the days of her childhood,
When gathering flowers on the lea;
And clasped her sweet hands as she nestled close to me,
And cried, "Dearest, now do you love me?"
CHORUS: On the banks of the beautiful Severn, etc.

We soon reached the door of her cottage,
Where Granny was waiting to see
The face of her own little darling
That was dearer than life unto me.
We stood at the gate for a moment,
Till Granny cried fiddle-de-dee,
She teased me, and squeezed me, and pressed me so tight,
She kissed me, and wished me a very good-night.
CHORUS: On the banks of the beautiful Severn, etc.[57]

One of Smith's informants was called Jim Lee, and he and other London travelers contributed a number of items in the Romany language. Lee and his companions were bilingual, and in some cases their songs were also sung in English versions. That was the case for the children's song "Little Bingo," which Smith nonetheless believed to be "of gypsy parentage," and on this occasion she did note the unusual tune as well as the words. She printed lyric and melody separately, however, and her representation of the latter is rather difficult to decipher. The following is a tentative attempt to combine them:

Little Bingo

Anon

Fig. 5.21

A farmer's dog leap'd over the stile,
His name was little Bingo.
There was B with an I, I with an N;
N with a G, G with an O—
There was B I N G O,
And his name was little Bingo.

The farmer lov'd a cup of good ale,
And called it very good stingo;
There was S with a T, T with an I,
I with an N, N with a G, G with an O,
There was S T I N G O,
And called it very good stingo.

The farmer lov'd a pretty young lass,	Now is not this a nice little song?
And gave her a wedding-ring, O;	I think is is, by Jingo!
There was R with an I, I with an N,	There was J with an I, I with an N,
N with a G, G with an O,	N with a G, G with an O,
There was R I N G O,	There was J I N G O,
And gave her a wedding ring, O.	I think it is, by Jingo![58]

According to her own testimony, Smith could speak only a few words or phrases of the Romany tongue, but she claimed that she did understand quite a lot of it. This made it possible for her to jot down some simple items sung in Romany. As an example of a humorous ditty that she heard in both languages, here is the Romany version of "Mullo Balor" followed by the English translation ("Dead Pig"):

Oh! I jassed to the ker,	I went to the farmhouse,
An' I tried to mang the balor,	Where I knew a pig had died,
Tried to mang the mullo balor,	And to get it I implored 'em,
When I jassed to the ker.	Till I pretty nearly cried.
But the rani wouldn't del it,	But the lady wouldn't give it,
For she pennas les os drabbered,	And she 'inted rather free,
For she pennas les os drabbered,	As 'twas poisoned by some gypsy,
Penn's the Romany chal had drabbed the balor.	And that gypsy man was *me*.[59]

Smith had no tune for this item, but from other London gypsies located in Wandsworth, Hampstead, and Hampton she had picked up a Romany whittling song and a melody with which she was already familiar under the title "Money Makes the Mare to Go." She printed the tune and text separately, so this attempt to put them back together is also a trifle speculative:

Can You Rokra Romany?

Anon

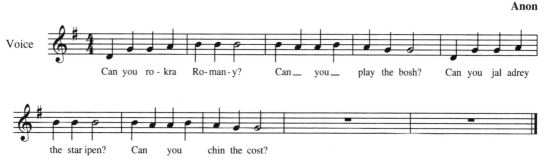

Fig. 5.22

Can you rokra Romany?	Can you speak the Romany tongue?
Can you play the bosh?	Can you play the fiddle?
Can you jal adrey the staripen?	Can you eat the prison loaf?
Can you chin the cost?	Can you cut and whittle?[60]

The traveler from whom Smith noted that song, Job Lee, was a crippled fiddle-player. She described him as wearing "a ragged blue Guernsey and blue Tam-o'-Shanter cap, which served to add a touch of wildness to his already *farouche* appearance."[61] He not only regaled her with fiddle tunes but also sang her a verse of an Irish Romany ballad with which Smith was already familiar from Charles Godfrey Leland's book, *The Gypsies*.[62] This is the text, with a translation:

Cosson kailyard corrum me morro sari,	Coming from Galway tired and weary
Me gul ogalyach mir;	I met a woman;
Rahet manent trasha moroch	I'll go bail by this time to-morrow
Me tu sosti mo diele.	You'll have enough of me.[63]

Smith did not rely entirely on her own collecting for her chapter on "Anglo-Romany Songs." Much of her account was derived from secondary sources. As we've seen, she was familiar with *In Gipsy Tents* and with *Shropshire Folk-Lore* and she reprinted several of the songs obtained by Charlotte Burne from the Wharton family of local travelers. These included such ballads as "Cold Blows the Wind" and "The Cruel Mother" and several carols, including "The Moon Shines Bright."[64] She also drew on another published work by Charles Leland, *English-Gipsy Songs,*[65] and she obtained some manuscript material from George Smith. Some of her other sources, such as Lord Lytton's novel *The Disowned*[66] and George Borrow's *The Romany Rye*[67] and *Romano Lavo Lil,*[68] were primarily literary publications. However, the most valuable items in her book were the handful that she collected herself from Jim and Job Lee and from other un-named Romany travelers that she met in London and its environs. Smith's work was rhapsodic and often disorganized, but her enthusiasm for her material was not to be denied and she deserves credit as a pioneer collector of gypsy songs and ballads in the field.

This chapter has spanned a fairly wide range of vernacular material, from the traditional and broadside ballads of the villagers of Edgmond in Shropshire through the varied repertoires of gypsy singers (including children) in various parts of England. In the main, its geographical focus has been the West Midlands, Hampshire, and the London area. Each of the collectors whose work we have examined was operating independently of the others, although we have seen that Charlotte Burne worked initially with folklorist Georgina Jackson and later with James Smart. Heywood Sumner appears to have done his collecting entirely independently and on his own initiative, although he would later compare notes with such other collectors as Lucy Broadwood and Alec Fuller Maitland. Laura Smith, whose collecting was done towards the end of the decade, was familiar with both Burne's *Shropshire Folk-Lore* and Francis Hindes Groome's *In Gipsy Tents*, and she made use of both those books when compiling *Through Romany Songland*. Her approach to vernacular song was particularly eclectic, although the subjects of her books were specialized. None of these collectors was a professional musican, although several were amateur singers or pianists. Groome recognized the importance of noting tunes as well as texts, and lamented that he lacked the ear-training that would have allowed him to do so. Burne had difficulty noting melodies by ear, although she did have some musical training and proficiency, so she usually took a better musician along with her on her collecting expeditions. Smith claimed to have noted most of her Romany material herself, but she apparently often found the tunes too much of a challenge, especially when the songs were in the Romany tongue.

As regards authenticity, there appears to be little reason to doubt the accuracy of Burne's texts and tunes, nor those of Sumner. Groome and Smith no doubt romanticized the travelers they so evidently admired, but they had no motive to distort the texts they obtained, and Smith did her honest best with the tunes, although she may have made some mistakes here and there. These were all pioneering efforts, and they each had their faults: Burne dissociated texts and tunes, and excluded most broadside ballads that she encountered in her researches; Sumner provided very little information about his source singers and their locations; Groome was unable to note tunes and was often vague about specifics; Smith's book on gypsy songs was mainly (although not entirely) based on second-hand information.

Yet if we cannot in all cases be sure that these publications reflected with complete accuracy what the various source singers actually sang, we can nonetheless be grateful for the glimpses that they provided into previously unex-plored aspects of popular culture. Notwithstanding their inadequacies, these were significant collections. During the 1880s Groome, Burne, Sumner, and Smith (in that chronological order) collectively began the process of opening up musical worlds that had previously been closed to all but the village singers and gypsies who had made the songs part of their daily lives. Their work complemented that achieved in the north of England during the same decade by Harriet Ma-son, T. T. Wilkinson, Collingwood Bruce, John Stokoe, and Joseph Crawhall. Moreover, it should be recognized that these nine individuals were not the only people involved in noting songs from vernacular culture in England. They some-times drew on the work of earlier collectors and occasionally they had collaborators, some identified and some anonym-ous, who helped them note tunes or provided additional items. The pages of the eclectic periodical *Notes & Queries* also demonstrate that during this (and the next) decade other rural correspondents occasionally collected individual items (usually fragments of ballad texts, or folk lyrics) from elderly informants.[69]

Laura Smith's collecting was not limited to gypsy lore and songs. In fact her major published work was devoted to the shanties and other sea songs of sailors in England's many seaports. Her endeavors in this regard were undertaken independently of a parallel initiative by Frederick Davis and Ferris Tozer. In the next chapter we examine the pioneering efforts made at the end of the 1880s and the beginning of the 1890s to discover and record for posterity the heritage of occupational (and other) sea songs to be found in the coastal regions of southern England, south Wales, and the seaports of Bristol, Plymouth, Liverpool, and Newcastle-upon Tyne.

Notes

1. Gillian Bennett, "Charlotte Sophia Burne: Shropshire Folklorist, First Woman President of the Folklore Society, and First Woman Editor of *Folklore.* Part 2: Update and Preliminary Bibliography," *Folklore* 112, no. 1 (2001): 98.

2. Gordon Ashman and Gillian Bennett, "Charlotte Sophia Burne: Shropshire Folklorist, First Woman President of the Folklore Society, and First Woman Editor of *Folklore.* Part 1: A Life and Appreciation," *Folklore* 111, no. 1 (2000): 3-4.

3. Charlotte Sophia Burne, ed., *Shropshire Folk-Lore: A Sheaf of Gleanings from the Collections of Georgina F. Jackson* (London: Trubner & Co., 1883-86).

4. Burne, *Shropshire Folk-Lore,* 532-68 and 650-56.

5. Burne, *Shropshire Folk-Lore,* 542-43 and 651.

6. Burne, *Shropshire Folk-Lore,* 545-46 and 651.

7. Burne, *Shropshire Folk-Lore,* 547-48 and 651.

8. Burne, *Shropshire Folk-Lore,* 544-45.

9. James Orchard Halliwell, ed., *Ballads and Poems respecting Hugh of Lincoln* (Brixton Hill, U.K.: [Halliwell], 1849).

10. Burne, *Shropshire Folk-Lore,* 539-540; reprinted from *Salopian Shreds and Patches*, 21 July 1875.

11. Burne, *Shropshire Folk-Lore,* 537.

12. Burne, *Shropshire Folk-Lore,* 537.

13. Burne, *Shropshire Folk-Lore,* 537-39.

14. Burne, *Shropshire Folk-Lore,* 541-42.

15. Burne, *Shropshire Folk-Lore,* 551-52 and 652.

16. Burne, *Shropshire Folk-Lore,* 553 and 652.

17. Burne, *Shropshire Folk-Lore,* 535.

18. Burne, *Shropshire Folk-Lore,* 540 and 651.

19. Allan Ramsay, ed., *The Tea-Table Miscellany, or A Collection of Choice Songs, Scots & English,* 4 vols. (Edinburgh: Ramsay, 1724-1732; revised edition, 1740).

20. Burne, *Shropshire Folk-Lore,* 551 and 652.

21. Burne, *Shropshire Folk-Lore,* 533.

22. Burne, *Shropshire Folk-Lore,* 554-55.

23. Burne, *Shropshire Folk-Lore,* 510 and 656.

24. Burne, *Shropshire Folk-Lore,* 565, 567 and 655.

25. Burne, *Shropshire Folk-Lore,* 533-35.

26. Burne, *Shropshire Folk-Lore,* 560-61 and 653.

27. Burne, *Shropshire Folk-Lore,* 487-88 and 650.

28. Burne, *Shropshire Folk-Lore,* 383.

29. Burne, *Shropshire Folk-Lore,* 384-85 and 655.

30. Burne, *Shropshire Folk-Lore,* 385 and 656.

31. Burne, *Shropshire Folk-Lore,* 568.

32. Anon. "Review of *Shropshire Folk-Lore*," *Folk-Lore Journal* 4 (1886): 365.

33. Jane Barbour, "Sumner, (George) Heywood Maunoir (1853-1940), Artist and Archaeologist," *Oxford Dictionary of National Biography*, http://www.oxforddnb.com/view/article/38033.

34. Heywood Sumner, ed. *The Besom Maker and Other Country Folk Songs* (London: Longmans, Green & Co., 1888).

35. Sumner, *Besom Maker,* "Preface" (unpaginated).

36. Sumner, *Besom Maker,* "Preface" (unpaginated).

37. Sumner, *Besom Maker,* 1-3.

38. Sumner, *Besom Maker,* 13-14.

39. Sumner, *Besom Maker,* 9-10.

40. Sumner, *Besom Maker,* 11-12.

41. Francis Hindes Groome, "The Influence of the Gypsies on the Superstitions of the English Folk," in *International Folk-Lore Congress: Papers and Transactions, 1891* (London: n.p., 1892), 292-308.

42. Francis Hindes Groome, *Kriegspiel* (New York: Ward, Lock & Bowden, 1896).

43. Francis Hindes Groome, ed. *Gypsy Folk-Tales* (London: Hurst & Blackett, 1899).

44. David Patrick, "Groome, Francis Hindes (1851-1902): Scholar of Gypsy Life and Writer," *Oxford Dictionary of National Biography*, http:www.oxforddnb.com/view/article/33588. Michael Owen Jones, "Francis Hindes Groome: 'Scholar Gypsy and Gypsy Scholar'," *Journal of American Folklore* 80 (1967): 71-80.

45. Francis Hindes Groome, *In Gipsy Tents* (Edinburgh: Nimmo, 1881), 142-43.

46. Groome, *Gipsy Tents,* 142.

47. Groome, *Gipsy Tents,* 145-46.

48. Groome, *Gipsy Tents,* 143-45.

49. Groome, *Gipsy Tents*, 145.

50. Neither the *Oxford Dictionary of National Biography* nor *The Oxford Companion to English Literature* nor any of the standard biographical dictionaries such as the *Cambridge Biographical Encyclopedia* or *Chambers Biographical Dictionary* accord her an entry. My searches in a number of online databanks, including *Jstor, Ebsco,* and *Google Scholar,* have also all proved fruitless.

51. Laura Alexandrine Smith, *Through Romany Songland* (London: David Stott, 1889).

52. Sir Walter Scott, ed., *Minstrelsy of the Scottish Border, consisting of historical and romantic ballads, collected in the southern counties of Scotland, with a few of modern date, founded on local tradition,* 2 vols. (Kelson, U.K.: J. Ballantyne, 1802; 2nd edition, 3 vols., Edinburgh: Ballantyne, 1803).

53. John Finlay, ed., *Scottish Historical and Romantic Ballads, Chiefly Ancient* (Edinburgh: J. Ballantyne for J. Smith & Son, 1808).

54. Smith, *Romany Songland,* 169.

55. Smith, *Romany Songland,* 169-70.

56. Smith, *Romany Songland,* 146-48.

57. Smith, *Romany Songland,* 153-54.

58. Smith, *Romany Songland,* 116-17.

59. Smith, *Romany Songland,* 122.

60. Smith, *Romany Songland,* 120.

61. Smith, *Romany Songland,* 150.

62. Charles Godfrey Leland, *The Gypsies* (Boston: Houghton Mifflin, 1882).

63. Smith, *Romany Songland,* 151-52.

64. Smith, *Romany Songland,* 109-56.

65. Charles Godfrey Leland, ed., *English-Gipsy Songs, In Romany, with metrical English translations* (Philadelphia, Penn.: Lippincott, 1875).

66. Bulwer Lytton, *The Disowned* (London: H. Colburn, 1829).

67. George Borrow, *The Romany Rye* (London: John Murray, 1857).

68. George Borrow, ed., *Romano Lavo Lil: World Book of the Romany; or, English Gypsy Language* (London: John Murray, 1874).

69. This is a topic that was in practice beyond the scope of this study but would almost certainly repay further research.

6

Songs of the Sea

The Late Victorian folksong revival would have a mixed record in the area of occupational song. Agriculture was well represented among the songs noted in the field, as were such related rural subjects as hunting, poaching, and even black-smithing and bell-ringing, but other kinds of work song were collected only occasionally. One notable exception to this generalization, however, was that of sailors' songs. Shanties appear to have been noted in England for the first time during the 1880s, and other songs about seafaring were also quite common among the collections made during this and the subsequent decade. The pioneer collectors who focused their efforts on shanties and other sailors' songs were Laura Smith and Frederick Davis, and they were soon to be joined in the early 1890s by John Ashton. Laura Smith's first book, a bigger and better one than *Through Romany Songland*, was titled *The Music of the Waters*. It was published a year earlier in 1888. The lengthy subtitle gave a good indication of its contents; it was *A Collection of the Sailors' Chanties, or Working Songs of the Sea, of All Maritime Nations. Boatman's, Fishermen's, and Rowing Songs, and Water Legends.*[1] This was not a songbook *per se*, although it included a considerable number of songs, but rather a discursive examination of various different kinds of sea songs, profusely illustrated with examples noted from British sailors and also, to a lesser extent, from seafarers of other nationalities from the Baltic, the Mediterranean, the Indian Ocean, and the China Sea.

The Music of the Waters

Only the first quarter of the *The Music of the Waters* was devoted to shanties, but Smith provided a fairly comprehensive, if at times rather chaotic, survey of the subject, distinguishing between different types of shanty and providing examples of each. Using Newcastle-upon-Tyne, Cardiff, Portsmouth, and London as her main bases, Smith had collected most of her material herself, in these and other ports all around the British Isles. She was at pains to emphasize that she had "taken down myself the greater part from the sailors; sometimes at my own house, sometimes at one of theirs, occasionally in a hospital, or on board ship."[2] It appears she also visited homes for retired sailors, and she certainly obtained quite a lot of her material in the Newcastle sailors' home. Just as she saw the travelers whose culture she promoted in *Through Romany Songland* as a maligned and misunderstood community, so she responded warmly to the elderly sailors she encountered and leapt to their defense in her "Introduction" to *Music of the Waters*. The British seaman, she contended, should not be judged harshly by the same moral standards as a landsman, because his daily life was so different and so much more demanding:

> So much rougher discipline, so much more severe, that no wonder during their sometimes short holidays our tars squander their substance in the riotous manner that has become proverbial of them. Think how many months they spend in exile, enduring many serious hardships, beside which the trials of shore-men seem insignificant; scanty rations, often of the most revolting description, always of the coarsest; hard, rough work in the most terrible degrees of heat and cold, wretched accommodation, and at all times the presence of imminent peril…and yet, for all that, taking them as a class, they are healthy, hearty fellows, and well deserving of the epithet of "Jolly Tars."[3]

In her encounters with these retired "Jolly Tars," Smith was looking to collect a variety of sea songs, both work songs and the other ballads and ditties preferred by sailors when gathered together to make their own entertainment in forecastle or tavern. Despite the fact that she was happy to take the items that she sought for what they were—unpolished, functional work songs or sometimes bawdy evocations of girls waiting in the ports—and even warned her readers against looking for "drawing-room rose-water sentiment in the ideas that originate and find favour amongst the hardy toilers of the briny ocean,"[4] she did not find it easy to persuade her informants to sing everything in their repertoires. As she put it, "there have been difficulties often in my way, in spite of the great kindness I have everywhere had shown me."[5] Reading between the lines, we can guess the major obstacle that she encountered in her fieldwork: the self-censorship imposed by her informants when singing to a young lady. This meant that Smith's texts were bowdlerized, but such would also be the case with many later shanty collections edited by men who were familiar with, but declined to print, bawdier versions of the same songs.

Notwithstanding her difficulties, Smith succeeded in noting a large number of English (and American) sea songs, the majority of them shanties, and she supplemented her own collecting with items taken from earlier publications, especially William Chappell's *Popular Music of the Olden Time*.[6] The long chapter on English sea songs with which *Music of the Waters* opened contained about thirty shanties, plus over a dozen other sea-related songs that were not used as work songs. Smith made a sharp distinction between the shanties, which she regarded as the true creations of seamen themselves while plying their trade on the oceans of the world, and the other sea songs, which she characterized, somewhat dismissively, as the work of landsmen, some of whom were quite ignorant of life at sea. But she recognized that some of the landsmen's songs had resonated—and still did—with sailors, anything from such Elizabethan ballads as "John Dory" and "The *Golden Vanity*" to Charles Dibdin's "Poor Jack" and "'Twas in the Good Ship." Indeed she reported that one of the most popular of all forecastle songs was "I'm the Pirate of the Isles," while Dibdin's "Tom Bowling," which she regarded as his masterpiece, never failed "to elicit hearty cheers and rapturous applause whenever and wherever it [was] heard."[7]

Smith was evidently fascinated by the shanties she had collected, and the logical layout of *Music of the Waters* suffered because she was repeatedly drawn back to them, even when she had moved on to discussing a different kind of sea song. She defined "the chanty" (her spelling) as "an essential part of the work on ship-board, it mastheads the topsail yards when making sail, it starts and weights the anchor, it brings down the main-tack with a will, it loads and unloads cargo, it keeps the pumps a-going; in fact it does all the work where unison and strength are required."[8] She distinguished between several different kinds of shanty. There were, she thought, four main types: those sung at the capstan while lifting the anchor, those suitable for hauling on ropes, those employed for pumping bilge water, and those used when doing such tasks as "holy-stoning" the decks and stowing cargo.[9]

Capstan shanties were also known as "windlass shanties" (from the name of the winding machinery) and "outward-bound" shanties because they were associated with leaving port. Smith observed that their tunes were often mournful, the meter was in general long, and subject matter often about parting and the voyage ahead. One of her favorites, which she characterized as "the wildest and most mournful of the sailor songs" was "Lowlands." She commented that the chorus was "even more than usually meaningless" but the song was "the sighing of the wind and the throbbing of the restless ocean translated into melody."[10] She had recorded only one stanza, but had noted the melody as follows:

Lowlands

Anon

Fig. 6.1

I dreamt a dream the other night,
Lowlands, Lowlands, Hurrah, my John!

I dreamt I saw my own true love,
My lowlands a-ray![11]

The majority of the work songs noted by Smith were, according to her classification, capstan shanties. Another of the many she collected was "Old Stormy." This shanty illustrates a problem that she encountered frequently: that a given song would be sung with different words, and sometimes a different tune, by different informants or even, on occasion, by the same informant. It was also known as "Storm Along" or "Stormalong." The widespread existence of multiple variants seems to have bothered, or at least perplexed, Smith, to the point where she almost abandoned her project. As she remarked, "I have found these same discrepancies over and over again, and many times have almost given up the idea of the collection, in consequence. It is the same amongst all nations of sailors."[12] Later shanty collectors would often criticize Smith's versions as inaccurate because they differed from what they themselves had noted from sailors, but it seems probable that her versions were just as authentic as any others: shanties, like ballads, come as clusters of variants, and it is difficult, and perhaps fruitless, to try to determine which variant came first. Smith obtained three different versions of "Old Stormy," the first of which she considered the best, and perhaps oldest, variant:

Old Stormy

Anon

Fig. 6.2

Old Stormy, he is dead and gone,
To me way, hay, storm along, John!

Old Stormy, he is dead and gone,
Ah, ha! Come along, get along, storm along, John. [13]

Smith's second version was American and had a tune that she thought was "of decidedly negro origin." This, she suggested, indicated that the legend of Stormy might have African rather than nautical roots.

Old Stormy, he was a bully old man,
To me way, you storm along;

Old Stormy, he was a bully old man,
Fi – i – i, massa, storm along.[14]

Old Stormy

Anon

Fig. 6.3

A third variant, "Old Storm Along," had the following words:

Old Storm Along is dead and gone,	I hove him up with an iron crane,
Ay! Ay! Ay! Mr. Storm Along!	And lowered him down with a golden chain.
When Stormy died I dug his grave,	Old Storm Along is dead and gone,
I dug his grave with a silver spade,	Ay! Ay! Ay! Mr. Storm Along.[15]

Other examples of the many capstan shanties mentioned by Smith include "Outward Bound," "Valparaiso," "Round the Horn," "Santa Anna," "Oceanida," "Johnny's Gone," "The Black Ball Line," "Sally Brown," and "Shenandore." As mentioned, they were employed primarily, although not exclusively, when leaving port and getting the ship set for a long voyage. She collected too many work songs of this type to list in full, let alone reproduce, but here is one more example of a popular capstan shanty for which she noted both text and tune, "Rio Grande":

The ship went out sailing over the bar,
O Rio! O Rio!
They pointed her nose for the Southern Star.
And we're bound for the Rio Grande,
Then away, love, away, away down Rio,
Then fare you well, my pretty young girl,
We're bound for the Rio Grande.

Were you ever in Rio Grande?
Away you Rio!
O were you ever in Rio Grande?
I am bound to the Rio Grande.
Then away, love, away, away you Rio,
Fare you well, my pretty young girl,
I am bound for the Rio Grande.

As I was going down Broadway Street,
Away you Rio!
A pretty young girl I chanced to meet,
And I'm bound for the Rio Grande.
Then away, &c.

O where are you going, my pretty maid,
Away you Rio!
O where are you going, my pretty maid,
I am bound to the Rio Grande.
Then away, &c.

I am going a milking, sir, she said,

Away you Rio!
I am going a milking, sir, she said,
And I'm bound for the Rio Grande,
Then away, &c.

What is your fortune, my pretty maid,
Away you Rio!
What is your fortune, &c.

My face is my fortune, sir, she said,
Away you Rio!
My face is my fortune, &c.

What is your father, my pretty maid,
Away you Rio!
What is your father, &c.

My father's a farmer, sir, she said,
Away you Rio!
My father's a farmer, &c.

What is your mother, my pretty maid,
Away you Rio!
What is your mother, &c.

Wife to my father, sir, she said,
Away you Rio!
Wife to my father, &c.

Then I can't marry you, my pretty maid,
Away you Rio!
Then I can't marry you, &c.

Nobody asked you, sir, she said,
Away you Rio!

Nobody asked you, sir, she said,
And I'm bound for the Rio Grande.
Then away, love, away, away down Rio,
So fare you well, my pretty young girl,
We're bound for the Rio Grande.[16]

Rio Grande

Anon

Voice

The ship went sail-ing out ov-er the bar, O Ri - o! O Ri - o! They

point-ed her nose for the Sou - th ern Star, and we're bound for the Ri - o Grande.___ Then a -

way, love, a - way,___ a - way,___ down Ri - O!___ Then fare you well___ my

pret - ty young girl,___ we're bound for the Ri - o Grande.

Fig. 6.4

According to Smith, certain capstan shanties were also used when the ship was tacking, to trim the sails. "Haulin' the Bowlin,'" "Johnny Polka," "Lowlands Away," "Across the Western Ocean," and "Old Storm Along" were all examples of such dual purpose shanties. Since trimming the sails involved pulling the sheets tight, the shanties used for this task might have been classified as "hauling shanties," but Smith's informants apparently insisted that they were all primarily capstan shanties.[17]

Many shanties evidently had multiple uses, and in fact a fairly large number of those noted by Smith were called "hauling shanties" by the sailors from whom she obtained them. This was her second main category. She divided the "hauling shanties" into two main types: "the hand-over-hand song, in very quick time" and "the long-pull song, when there are, perhaps, twenty or thirty men pulling on a rope." As a well-known example of a quick-time shanty employed to hoist the topsail-yards, Smith cited "Blow the Man Down," noting that "Sally Racket" was another used for the same purpose. About "Blow the Man Down" she commented that "it is very tuneful, and though, perhaps, the words are scarcely to be admired, still it is a genuine chanty, and has a *verve* and vigour about it that speak of its value as an incentive to the labor of hoisting the topsail-yards or any other hauling work."[18] This is her version:

I'm a true English sailor, just come from Hong-Kong,
Tibby, Heigh, ho, blow the man down!
My stay on the old English shore won't be long,
Then give me some time to blow the man down.

CHORUS:
Then we'll blow the man up, and we'll blow the man
                                        down, Tibby!

Heigh, ho, blow the man down,
So we'll blow the man up, and we'll blow the man down,
Oh, give me some time to blow the man down.

As I was a-walking down Winchester Street,
Heigh, ho, blow the man down;
A pretty young girl I happened to meet,
Then give me some time to blow the man down.[19]

Blow the Man Down

Anon

Voice

I'm a true Eng-lish sail-or, Just come from Hong-Kong, Tib-by, Heigh, ho,

blow the man down! My stay on the old Eng-lish shore won't be long, Then give me some time to

chorus

blow the man down. Then we'll blow the man up, and we'll blow the man down, Tib-by! Heigh, ho,

blow the man down! So we'll blow the man up, and we'll blwo the man down! Then give me some time to

blow the man down.

Fig. 6.5

For heavier work, or when hands were few, hauling shanties with a longer meter were used. These employed a regular pattern of solo voice followed by a chorus, with the pull always made on the same word in the collective response. "Reuben Ranzo" was, according to Smith, the greatest favorite among such long-haul shanties, perhaps because of its mournful, haunting tune. This was the version included in *The Music of the Waters:*

[solo] Pity Reuben Ranzo,
[chorus] Ranzo, boys, a Ranzo,
[solo] Pity Reuben Ranzo,
[chorus] Belay there, boys, belay.
[solo] Reuben was no sailor,
[chorus] Ranzo, boys, a Ranzo,
[solo] By trade he was a tailor,
[chorus] Belay there, boys, belay.

He went to school on Monday,
Ranzo, boys, a Ranzo,
He went to school on Monday,
Belay there, boys, belay.
Learnt to read on Tuesday,
Ranzo, boys, a Ranzo,
Learnt to read on Tuesday,
Belay there, boys, belay.

He learnt to write on Wednesday,

He learnt to fight on Thursday.

On Friday he beat the master,
On Saturday we lost Reuben.

And where do you think we found him?
Why, down in yonder valley.

Conversing with a sailor,
He shipped on board of a whaler.

He shipped as able seamen do,
The captain was a bad man.

He took him to the gangway,
And gave him five-and-forty.

The mate he was a good man,
He taught him navigation.

Now he's captain of a whaler,   And now they both are happy,
Married the captain's daughter.   This ends my little ditty.[20]

Reuben Ranzo

Anon

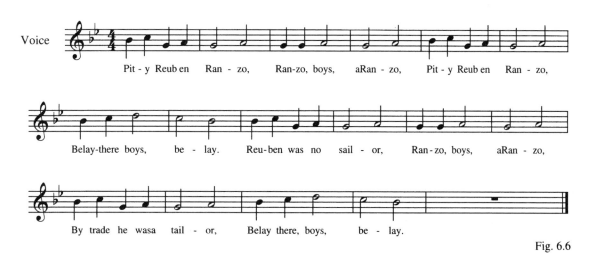

Pit - y Reub en   Ran - zo,   Ran-zo, boys,   aRan - zo,   Pit - y Reub en   Ran - zo,

Belay-there boys,   be - lay.   Reu-ben was no   sail - or,   Ran-zo, boys,   aRan - zo,

By trade he wasa   tail - or,   Belay there, boys,   be - lay.

Fig. 6.6

Other hauling shanties with this chorus/response pattern included "Whisky Johnny," "Tommy's Gone to Hilo," "A Yankee Ship," and "Bonny Was a Warrior." Of these Smith determined, from the number of times it was offered to her and the several different variants that she encountered, that "Whisky Johnny" was not only well known among sailors but also appeared to be a "great favourite." In her view it did not betray much "delicacy or refinement of expression" but it evidently served the purpose for which it was intended, namely regulating and lightening work at sea.[21] This is one of the versions that she noted:

Whisky Johnny

Anon

Oh,   whis-ky   is   the   life of — man, Oh,   whis-ky!   Oh,   John ny!   Oh,

whis - ky   is   the   life   of man! Oh,   whis - ky   for   my   John - ny!

Fig. 6.7

Oh, whisky is the life of man, [solo]   Oh, whisky! Oh, Johnny!
Oh, whisky! Oh, Johnny! [chorus]   Oh, whisky makes me pawn my clothes,
Oh, whisky is the life of man! [solo]   Oh, whisky for my Johnny!
Oh, whisky for my Johnny! [chorus]

                                                 Oh, whisky gave me a broken nose,
Oh, whisky makes me pawn my clothes,   Oh, whisky, etc.

I thought I heard the old man say,
Oh, whisky, etc.

I thought I heard the old woman say.
Oh, whisky up and whisky down.

I thought I heard the steward shout, [solo]
Here's whisky for my Johnny, [chorus]
If I can't get whisky, I'll have rum, [solo]
Oh, whisky for my Johnny!

Oh, that's the stuff to make good fun.
Oh, whisky for my Johnny,

For whisky men and women will run,
Oh whisky, Oh Johnny.

I'll drink whisky when I can
Oh, whisky, etc.

That's the stuff to make you frisky
Oh, whisky, etc.

Give me whisky and I'll give you tin.
If you have no whisky, give me gin.
Belay there![22]

Smith's third category was that of pumping shanties. According to her information, any quick, lively tune could serve as suitable music for a pumping shanty, but certain songs seemed to be particularly associated with the chore of bilge pumping. She provided far fewer examples of these than of capstan and hauling shanties, although she did cite "Pay Me the Money Down," "Highland Day and Off She Goes" and "Run, Let the Bull Chimes Run."[23] For the latter she supplied both tune and a fragment of text, but gave no indication of how the two fitted together.

Run, Let The Bull Chimes Run

Anon

Voice

Fig. 6.8

CHORUS: Run, let the bull chimes run
            We'll run,—

SOLO: Away to America.

CHORUS: Way aha, way aha!
            Way aha, way aha!

SOLO: We'll pump her dry and get our grog

CHORUS: Run, let the bull chimes run.

SOLO: We'll pump her dry and away we'll go,

CHORUS: Away to America![24]

A rather distant variant on the same shanty was "Let the Bulgine Run" or, as Smith titled it, "The Black Cross Line." She had only one verse and chorus, and found the words largely unintelligible, but commented that the song had a "true melody" and was "deservedly popular."[25]

The Black Cross Line

Anon

Fig. 6.9

Smith's organization of her material was sometimes rather erratic, and she did not make it completely clear whether her next group of shanties was intended to illustrate her fourth category of songs sung while performing such tasks as scrubbing decks and stowing cargo. Presumably they were, since such songs as "The *Lion* Man-o'-War," "Home, Dearie, Home," "The Spanish Canoe," and "Homeward Bound," as Smith presented them, were seemingly neither capstan nor hauling nor pumping shanties.[26] Smith had gathered from the merchant seamen that she interviewed that they had little respect for the sailors of the Royal Navy whose daily chores were regulated not by shanty singing but by blasts on a whistle. Certain sea songs celebrating the exploits of military vessels were nonetheless popular among merchant seamen, one example being "The *Lion* Man o' War" which recorded an encounter between the French navy and a British fighting ship out of Portsmouth, the port where Smith noted the ballad. "The Spanish Canoe" was apparently more popular in northern ports; it was a variant of the Tudor ballad "The *Golden Vanity*." "Homeward Bound" was a specimen of the kind of song that Smith found hard to get sailors to sing to her, one that celebrated Poll, Bet, lovely Sue, and the other girls who were always happy to help Jack spend his pay at the Dog and Bell near St. Catherine's Dock. The text she printed, however, would not have offended a Victorian clergyman.

Some of Smith's items in this group were not traditional shanties but more recent compositions imitating the genre. They had, however, entered into oral tradition and become vernacular songs. "Home, Dearie, Home," for example, was an interesting composite, in part an adaptation of the song that we saw Bruce and Stokoe print in *Northumbrian Minstrelsy* as "The Oak and the Ash and the Bonny Ivy Tree." It also included a stanza reminiscent of "Rosemary Lane." Smith did not collect a full text for the song, and the verse that she gave with the music lacked continuity with the others she printed, so it seems likely that her informant had forgotten some intervening stanzas.[27] This, however, is what she had available:

> Oh, Amble is a fine town, with ships in the bay,
> And I wish with my heart I was only there to-day;
> I wish with my heart I was far away from here,
> A-sitting in my parlour, and talking to my dear.

Home, Dearie, Home

Anon

And if it be a lass, she shall wear a gold-en ring; And if it be a lad, he shall

live to serve his king; With his buckles and his boots and his lit-tle jack-et blue, He shall

Chorus

walk the quar-ter deck, as his dad-dy used to do.... And it's home, dear-ie, home! Oh, it's

home I want to be! My top-sails are hoist-ed, and I must out to sea; For the oak and the ash and the

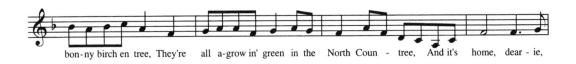

bon-ny birch en tree, They're all a-grow in' green in the North Coun-tree, And it's home, dear-ie,

home!

Fig. 6.10

CHORUS:
And it's home, dearie, home! Oh it's home I want to be,
My top-sails are hoisted, and I must out to sea,
For the oak, and the ash, and the bonny birchen tree,
They're all a-growin' green in the North Countree;
And it's home, dearie, home!

And if it be a lass, she shall wear a golden ring;

And if it be a lad, he shall live to serve his king;
With his buckles and his boots, and his little jacket blue,
He shall walk the quarter deck, as his daddy used to do.[28]

Although her fourth category of shanties seemed to blur the distinction, Smith had on several occasions drawn a sharp line between shanties (seamen's work songs) and "forecastle favorites," songs of the sea heard on board when off-duty sailors were entertaining themselves and on shore wherever seamen were congregated together.[29] She pointed out that many of these "rattling old sea-songs" were centuries old, some having remained current since the last decades of Queen Elizabeth's reign. Examples of such old favorites were "John Dory," "The Spanish Lady," "We Be Three Poor Mariners," and "Farewell to You, Ye Fine Spanish Ladies," while more recent additions to the stock were "The Mermaid," "Cawsand Bay," "Bay of Biscay," "Hearts of Oak," and even "The Eton Boat-Song."[30] Most of these songs, however, Smith had not noted herself from her informants in the sailors' homes but had been sent by correspondents, or, in many instances, had copied from William Chappell's *Popular Music of the Olden Time*.[31]

The second chapter of *The Music of the Waters* was titled "Gaelic Boat Songs and Scotch Sea Songs," and it included several Gaelic songs (with English translations) taken from Donald Campbell's *Language, Poetry and Music of the Highland Clans*.[32] There were also a few English-language songs such as "A Crab Song" and "The Skye Boat Song."[33] This chapter was followed by one titled "Keelmen's and Fishermen's Songs, and Songs of the Press Gang on Tyneside." While based in Newcastle, Smith had the chance to collect not only shanties but other vernacular songs common among Northumbrian fishermen and sailors. She made good use of the opportunity and obtained from local oral tradition tunes and texts for many of the songs found in northern regional collections, from John Bell's *Rhymes of the Northern Bards*[34] to Bruce and Stokoe's *Northumbrian Minstrelsy* and Joseph Crawhall's *Beuk o' Newcassel Sangs*. The songs in this section included, as might be expected, such regional favorites as "Well May the Keel Row," "Captain Bover," "Here's the Tender Coming," "The Bonny Keel Laddie," "The Bonny Fisher Lad," "Blaw the Wind Southerly" and "The Water of Tyne." John Bell had collected "The Sandgate Lass's Lament," but *Rhymes of the Northern Bards* provided no tune for the song. Smith's text was inferior to Bell's, but she had noted a good melody:

The Sandgate Lass's Lament

Anon

Fig. 6.11

I was a young maiden truly, and lived in Sandgate Street,
I thought to marry a good man, to keep me warm and neat,

Some good-like body, some bonny body, to be with me at noon;
But last I married a keelman, and my good days are done.

I thought to marry a parson, to hear me say my prayers,
But I have married a keelman, and he kicks me down the stairs;
Some good-like body, &c.

I thought to marry a dyer, to dye my apron blue,
But I have married a keelman, and he makes me sairly rue.
Some good-like body, &c.

I thought to marry a joiner, to make me chair and stool,
But I have married a keelman, and he's a perfect fool.
Some good-like body, &c.

I thought to marry a sailor, to bring me sugar and tea,
But I have married a keelman, and that he lets me see.
Some good-like body, &c.[35]

In geographical terms, the second half of *The Music of the Waters* ranged much more widely. It comprised songs that Smith had collected from sailors who had disembarked in Newcastle from the ships of many different nations. These were mainly foreign-language songs, or often just the tunes of such songs. Where she was able (as with French, Italian, German, Scandinavian, and even Indian songs), Smith supplied English translations of the lyrics, but her chapters on Russian, Greek, Egyptian, and Japanese boating songs provided mainly tunes without words. Scantier still, but quite fascinating, were the examples Smith provided of river songs from China, Maori canoeing songs, and the water-music of the Tonga Islands. However, interesting though it was, this second part of *The Music of the Waters* represented a synthesis of secondary sources, whereas in the first half of the book Smith had been a pioneer collector of English sea shanties from sailors who had sung them at sea during the last years of the sailing ship era.

The originality and value of Laura Smith's work was not always appreciated at the time. In *The Musical Times* an anonymous, and rather haughty, reviewer took delight in pointing out a number of minor transcription errors. His condescending conclusion was that "Miss Smith has a superabundance of enthusiasm, but she is conspicuously bereft of critical instinct...Only a scholar and a musician could do justice to such a subject, and she unfortunately is neither."[36] One can understand his point—the book was somewhat chaotic and breathless—but his uncharitable critique ignored the originality of *Music of the Waters*. It also failed to recognize the considerable volume of field collecting done by Smith. In any case, most suitably qualified scholar-musicians had neglected to respond to Carl Engel's call, and it would be quite some time before any of them bothered to devote themselves to collecting the occupational songs of the lower classes. Smith's books were far from perfect, but her achievements deserve better recognition than they have so far been accorded.

Sailors' Songs or "Chanties"

Although she was well versed in the published work of William Chappell, Bruce and Stokoe, and Charlotte Burne, and she had made a fairly thorough search of the older Victorian literature for the kind of items in which she was interested, Laura Smith was seemingly unaware of a small book titled *Sailors' Songs or "Chanties."* This lacked a publication date, but it seems to have been first issued in 1886 or perhaps the next year, thereby antedating *The Music of the Waters* by a year or so. Its editors were Frederick Davis and Ferris Tozer, and their publication seems to have been the first of its kind in England.[37] It was a songbook rather than a study of the occupational and other songs sung by working seamen, and there was virtually nothing in the way of commentary about the songs. In this respect it differed quite markedly from Laura Smith's discursive work in which musical examples were integrated into a text that discussed, albeit in a rather haphazard way, the nature and provenance of different types of sea song. Moreover, the focus of *Sailors' Songs or "Chanties"* was exclusively on shanties. Davis and Tozer claimed to be filling "a want long felt" by providing the first "complete collection" of sailors' work songs.[38]

The first edition of the songbook comprised twenty-four items. They were all contributed from memory by one of the editors, Frederick Davis, a seaman who had served in both the Royal Navy and the P. & O. Royal Mail Service. His home port was apparently Devonport, near Plymouth, and he presumably learned his shanties on mail boats rather than in the Royal Navy. However, it was by no means certain that Davis had personally sung all the items as a lead shantyman, although the lyrics were derived from versions he had heard at sea. He appears to have cleaned them up for public consumption, omitting verses that he considered too bawdy for print. As for the shanty tunes, the authors claimed that their melodies had "been handed down from one sailor to another for many years" and were therefore "to a certain extent traditional."[39] Ferris Tozer provided piano arrangements, a marketing necessity since the little book was issued by music publisher Boosey and Company, most of whose list was aimed at amateur performers singing with piano accompaniment in middle-class drawing rooms. That same market dictated the degree of self-censorship that Davis evidently practiced.

Davis and Tozer defined "chanties" as "the songs sung by sailors to lighten their labour when weighing anchor, setting or taking in sail, pumping the ship out, or at other duties where heaving or pulling is required."[40] This definition accorded well with Laura Smith's, so there was substantial agreement on the purpose and use of the songs. And, as befitted a collection of work songs, Davis divided his shanties into groups according to the tasks being performed when they were routinely sung. He called the largest group "anchor songs" (that is, hauling songs used by sailors to lighten their labor when weighing anchor). These were the equivalent of Laura Smith's "capstan" or "windlass" shanties. Davis recalled nine of them: "Sally Brown," "Away for Rio," "We're All Bound to Go," "The Wide Missouri" (a variant of "Shenandoah"), "Leave Her Johnnie," "Can't You Dance a Polka?" "The Black Ball Line," "Hoodah Day," and "Homeward Bound." The surprise inclusion here was "Homeward Bound," which Smith had concluded was more often a general purpose shanty used for deck scrubbing and stowing cargo, but, in the main, Davis's list of capstan shanties accorded well with Smith's. As an example of this category, here is the "chanty" with which Davis opened the volume, "Sally Brown":

Sally Brown

Anon

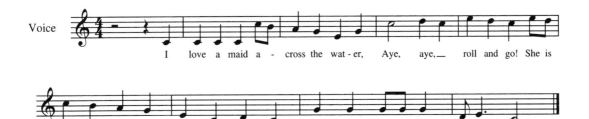

Fig. 6.12

I love a maid across the water,
Aye, aye, roll and go!
She is Sal herself, yet Sally's daughter,
Spend my money on Sally Brown.

Seven long years I courted Sally,
Aye, aye, etc.,
She called me "boy and Dilly Dally,"
Spend my money, etc.

Seven long years and she wouldn't marry,
And I no longer cared to tarry.

So I courted Sal, her only daughter,

For her I sail upon the water.

Sally's teeth are white and pearly,
Her eyes are blue, her hair is curly.

The sweetest flower of the valley,
Is my dear girl, my pretty Sally.

Oh! Sally Brown, I had to leave you,
But trust me that I'll not deceive you.

Sally Brown, I love your daughter,
For her I sail upon the water.[41]

Davis's second category was that of songs used for setting sails, and he offered eight shanties of this type: "Whisky for my Johnnie," "Reuben Ranzo," "Blow, Boys, Blow," "Blow the Man Down," "Tom's Gone to Ilo," "Hanging Johnnie," "Haul Way, Jo," and "Haul the Bowlin." This group corresponded to Smith's set of hauling shanties, and the two authors were in agreement on most of the items they included in the category. One exception was "Haul the Bowlin," which

Smith had counted as a capstan shanty, but Davis's claim that it was primarily used for hauling ropes when hoisting sails seems more plausible, given its title.

Despite their general agreement on capstan and hauling shanties, Smith's and Davis's texts often differed markedly. Whereas Smith's versions had been obtained from a variety of maritime sources and her singers had been employed on many different types of sailing ships, Davis's shanties reflected the singing tradition of the P. & O. line. His versions were usually longer, and presumably more complete than hers, although no doubt similarly bowdlerized. Here, as an example, is his version of "Blow the Man Down," which contrasts the predatory nature of man with the neighborliness of the creatures of the deep:

Blow the Man Down

Anon

Fig. 6.13

I'll sing you a song, a good song of the sea,
[chorus] To my aye, aye, blow the man down!
And trust that you'll join in the chorus with me,
[chorus] Give me some time to blow the man down.

There was an old skipper, I don't know his name.
To my aye, aye, &c.
Although he once played a remarkable game,
Give me some time, &c.

For his ship lay becalmed in the tropical sea,
And he whistled all day, but in vain, for a breeze.

But a seal heard his whistle and loudly did call,
"Roll up your white canvas, jib, spanker and all."

"I'll bring some good fish to consult, if you please,
The best way to get you a nice little breeze."

The first fish to come was a hoary old shark,
Saying, "I'll eat you up if you play any lark."

The next was a whale, aye, the biggest of all,

He climbed up aloft and he let each sail fall.

The mack'rel came next, with his pretty striped back,
He hauled aft each sheet and he boarded each tack.

The herring came, saying, "I'm King of the Seas,
If you want any wind I'll blow you a breeze."

But the skipper the mackerel ate for his tea,
The herring he salted, the seal harpooned he.

He baited a hook, and he thought it a lark,
To catch as he did, that hoary old shark.

Then he killed the old whale, which was no easy task,
And soon with the sperm oil he had filled up each cask.

Then the breeze it blew gaily, and gaily went he,
But what an old rascal that skipper must be.

Blow the man down, Johnny, blow the man down,
If he be white man, or black man, or brown.[42]

Smith had divided her broad category of "hauling chanties" into two different types: those used for quick, short hauls "hand over hand," and those employed in coordinating long hauls when dozens of men pulled at regular intervals on the same rope. Davis made a different distinction: between shanties used for hoisting the sails and those employed for furling them. His next category was therefore devoted to songs used for furling sails. Surprisingly, he could offer only one example of a song designed specifically for this task, namely "Paddy Doyle's Boots."

Paddy Doyle's Boots

Anon

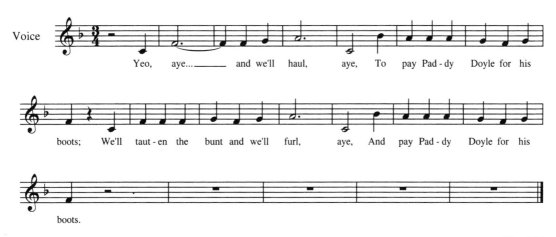

Fig. 6.14

Yeo, aye, and we'll haul, aye,
To pay Paddy Doyle for his boots;
We'll tauten the bunt and we'll furl, aye,
And pay Paddy Doyle for his boots.

Yeo, aye, and we'll sing, aye,
To pay Paddy Doyle for his boots;
We'll bunt up the sail with a fling, aye,
And pay Paddy Doyle for his boots.[43]

Davis's fourth type of shanty was that employed when pumping out bilge water. Smith had also identified this as a separate category of shanty, but she had had difficulty in finding good examples, and had been unable to provide the full text and tune of a single one, although she had offered several fragments, including her incomplete version of "Let the Bull Chimes Run." Davis argued that "Storm Along," which Smith had counted as a capstan shanty, was in fact a pumping shanty. His version was more complete than any of her three fragments and it provides an interesting comparison with what she had obtained from several different oral traditions. This is Davis's variant, apparently sung when pumping bilge water from the clipper ships that used to take mail to and from the far-flung corners of the British empire:

Storm Along

Anon

Fig. 6.15

Oh, Stormie's gone, the good old man,
To my aye, storm along!
Oh, Stormie's gone, that good old man,
Aye, aye, aye, Mister Storm along.

They dug his grave with a silver spade,
To my aye, etc.
His shroud of the finest silk was made,
Aye, aye, aye, etc.

He was a sailor bold and true,
A good old skipper to his crew.

Of captains brave, he was the best,
But now he's gone and is at rest.

He lies low kin an earthen bed,
Our hearts are sore, our eyes are red.

He's moored at last and furled his sail,
No danger now from wreck or gale.

Old Storm has heard the angel call,
So sing his dirge now, one and all.[44]

Davis provided two other examples of pumping shanties: "Mobile Bay" and this somewhat sanitized version of "A-Roving," in which the woman in question is not a prostitute but a lover left behind in Holland.

A-Roving

Anon

Fig. 6.16

In Amsterdam there lives a maid,
Mark you well what I say!
In Amsterdam there lives a maid,
And she is mistress of her trade,
I'll go no more a-roving from you, fair maid.
A-roving, a-roving, since roving's been my ruin,
I'll go no more a roving from you, fair maid.

Her eyes are like two stars so bright,
Mark you well what I say!
Her eyes are like two stars so bright,
Her face is fair, her step is light,
I'll go no more a-roving from you fair maid.
A-roving, a-roving, etc.

Her cheeks are like the rosebuds red,
There's wealth of hair upon her head.

I often take her for a walk,
And love to hear her merry talk.

I love this fair maid as my life,
And soon she'll be my little wife.

And if you'd know this maiden's name,
Why soon like mine, 'twill be the same.[45]

Davis rounded out his collection with three items that he simply called "general songs." These were "Salt Horse," "Eight Bells," and a multi-purpose shanty which is often known as "Poor Old Man." Its simple and repetitive structure—solo voice followed immediately by a short choral response—suggested that it was probably another song used mainly for hauling ropes. Davis titled it "The Dead Horse," an allusion to a common seafaring term for the first month of a long voyage, during which the sailors were working off the cash advance they had received (and spent) before leaving port.

The Dead Horse

Anon

Fig. 6.17

They say "my horse is dead and gone,"
[chorus] And they say so, and they hope so!
They say "my horse is dead and gone."
[chorus] Oh! Poor old man!

For one long month I rode him hard,
And they say so, &c.
For one long month I rode him hard,
Oh! Poor old, &c.

If he's not dead, I'll ride him again,

If he's not dead, I'll ride him again.

But if he's dead, I'll bury him low.
But if he's dead, I'll bury him low.

I'll hoist him to the mainyard-arm.
I'll hoist him to the mainyard-arm.

Then drop him to the depths of the sea.
Then drop him to the depths of the sea.[46]

Sales of Davis and Tozer's collection seem to have been brisk. A second edition added sixteen more shanties, and a third edition would eventually bring the total to fifty.[47] The publication of *The Music of the Waters* soon after *Sailors' Songs or "Chanties"* likely helped create an interest in shanties and so boosted the songbook's sales, which were obviously good enough to warrant the second and third editions. Davis had almost exhausted his personal repertoire, but he was not averse to borrowing from Smith's book for extra items to expand his later editions. The two works in fact complemented each other. Smith provided more background information and a more extended discussion of the shanties' functions and their provenance, whereas Davis's versions were usually more complete and had the virtue of being based on first-hand experience. One should not be too surprised at the discrepancies between the versions of those shanties included in both books, since it had become evident to Smith during her research that the lyrics of all the best-known shanties existed in multiple versions and that their tunes, while often related, also varied considerably from singer to singer. The Edwardian revival would see something of a boom in shanty collecting and publishing, with even Cecil Sharp participating in the hunt.[48]

Real Sailor Songs

We have seen that in the late 1880s, with *A Century of Ballads* and *Modern Street Ballads*, John Ashton had pioneered a renewal of interest in broadside balladry and underlined the substantial textual overlap with parallel material recovered from oral tradition. This lesson was not thoroughly embraced by the English folk music community—such as it was—in the 1880s, with the notable exception of Frank Kidson, but it would gradually sink in during the next decade. Meanwhile

Ashton continued to plough his own furrow. His third compilation, which appeared in bookstores in 1891, was more specialized than either of his previous publications, and strictly speaking, because of its date of publication, the work belongs to the ongoing history of ballad editing in the decade of the 1890s. However, because of its subject matter, it is more useful to discuss the book at this point in our story.

Titled *Real Sailor Songs,* Ashton's new collection comprised over one hundred and twenty-five broadsides that related to seafaring in one way or another.[49] As with his previous books, no tunes were provided, but the selection of texts was sensible and he had plenty of interesting material to offer. The ballads that he had identified as worthy of reprinting included many accounts of battles and songs that reflected the realities of the press-gang, the loss of ships and the crews in storms, and sailors' varied relationships with the women who waited on shore. What Ashton omitted from this collection, in addition to the missing tunes, was work songs used by merchant sailors on the clipper ships. Shanties were thus conspicuous by their absence. However, there was a wealth of broadside texts, which Ashton divided into six categories: sea fights, press-gang, disaster, ashore, love, and miscellaneous.

The largest section of the book was the first, which featured ballads celebrating the exploits of such admirals as Nelson, Benbow, Duncan, Keppel, Killigrew, Napier, and Russel.[50] Only a few of these historical texts had caught the popular imagination sufficiently to become vernacular songs, but those that did included "Admiral Benbow," "Captain Ward and the *Rainbow*," "The *Arethusa*" (actually a popular song from William Shield's 1796 opera *Lock and Key*), "The Sailor's Only Delight" (aka "The *George Aloe* and the *Sweepstake*"), and "The *Shannon* and the *Chesapeake*" (about a hard-fought encounter near Boston in 1813 between a British ship and an American frigate). A large number of these patriotic songs purported to describe and praise the bravery of English sailors in sea battles, usually against the French. They reflected the way in which broadside ballads and drinking songs had functioned as jingoistic propaganda during the Napoleonic wars. One of the shorter examples, which was probably intended for use in recruitment, was "The Game Cocks of Old England." The last line was almost certainly repeated, but Ashton's text did not indicate this:

Well Met, brother Tar,
What news do you hear
Concerning the present Campaign?
Why I never will rest
'Till we attack Brest,
Where ev'ry Tar will die game, my brave boys.

The Shipwright, ne'er doubt,
Will build ships strong and stout,
And able to scour the main;
When we give the French chase,
They ne'er will us face,
But steer to their harbours again, my brave boys.

There's the jolly Montrose,
Never at a loss,
In bombing their forts and their towns;
They are lusty and stout,
And they'll never give out,
Until their high buildings come down, my brave boys.

There's Tinkers and Taylors
For Soldiers and Sailors,
Translators and Weavers the same;

The draw boys you know,
For five pounders will go,
For every one will die game, my brave boys.

There's the Blacksmith, you know,
Is ready to go,
He'll scour them with his iron rods;
If this man blows the bellows,
It makes the French jealous,
For he'll burn all their wooden Gods, my brave boys.

There's the Butcher we know,
Is stout, at one blow
He is able to knock down an ox:
His man is the same,
They both will die game,
And cut the French all in the chops, my brave boys.

So here's a good health
To George our King,
And he that refuses the same,
I wish him in France,
On a Gallows to dance,
Whilst Soldiers and Sailors die game, my brave boys.[51]

Ashton's second section, "Press-Gang," contained just nine broadside texts, all of which contained at least passing references to the feared and hated institution of the press-gang and reflected the human costs of warfare.[52] They included "The Press'd Man's Lamentation," "The Ship Carpenter's Love to the Merchant's Daughter" (aka "The Merchant's Daughter of Bristol"), a tragic ballad about a drowned lover, "Young William," and the most singable item in the group, "The Sailor Laddie":

My love has been in London City,
So has he been in Port Mahon,
My love is away at Greenland,

I hope he will come back again.
Oh! My bonny sailor laddie,
Oh! My bonnie sailor, he,

Well I love my sailor laddie,
Blyth and merry may he be.

Greenland altho' it is no City,
Yet it is a bonny place,
Soon will he come back to England,
Then to court his bonny lass.
Oh! My bonny sailor laddie, etc.

Fisher lads go to the fishing,
Bonny lasses to the braes,
Fisher lads come home at even,
Tell how their fishing goes.
Oh! My bonny sailor laddie, etc.

Sailor lads come home at even,
Casting off their tarry cloaths,
Calling for their own true lovers,
And telling how the trading goes.
Oh! My bonny sailor laddie, etc.

Sailor lads has gold and silver,
Fisher lads has nought but brass,
Well I love my sailor laddie,
Because I am a sailor's lass.
Oh! My bonny sailor laddie, etc.

Our noble Captain's gone to London,
Oh! Preserve them from the press,
Send him safely back to Terry,
There to court his bonny lass.
Oh! My bonny sailor laddie, etc.

How can I be blyth and merry,
And my true love so far from me,
When so many pretty Sailors
Are prest, and taken to the Sea?
Oh! My bonny sailor laddie, etc.

When my love he was in Terry,
He came and saw me once a night;
But now he's prest to the St. Ann's
And is kept quite out of my sight.
Oh! My bonny sailor laddie, etc.

Oh! I wish the press was over,
And all the wars was at an end;
Then every bonny sailor laddie
Would be merry with his friend.
Oh! My bonny sailor laddie, etc.

Here has been so much disturbance,
Our sailor lads dare not look out,
For to drink with their own lasses,
Or to have a single rout.
Oh! My bonny sailor laddie, etc.

My love he's a bonny laddie,
Blyth and merry may he be,
If the wars were at an end,
He would come and marry me.
Oh! My bonny sailor laddie, etc.

Some delight in jolly farmers,
Some delight in soldiers free;
But my delight's in a sailor laddie,
Blyth and merry may he be.
Oh! My bonny sailor laddie, etc.

Oh, I wish the war was over,
And peace and plenty come again,
Then every bonny sailor laddie
Would come sailing o'er the main.
Oh! My bonny sailor laddie, etc.

If the wars they were all over,
And all our sailors were come home,
Then every lass would get her laddie,
And every mother get her son.
Oh! My bonny sailor laddie, etc.

Come you by the Buoy and Nore,
Or come you by the Roperie,
Saw you of my love sailing,
Oh, saw you coming home to me.
Oh! My bonnie sailor laddie,
Oh! My bonnie sailor, he,
Well I love my sailor laddie,
And my sailor he loves me.[53]

This fairly brief section was followed by another short one on the subject of disasters at sea. It comprised eleven broadsides, most of which involved the loss of ships and/or members of their crews. A few of these ballads related incidents with happy endings, while others were straightforward accounts of ships sinking in storms or running aground on jagged rocks. The most popular item in this group was undoubtedly "The Mermaid." The next category, "Ashore," consisted of eleven texts.[54] A recurring theme was the rueful recognition that returning sailors were welcomed by publicans, prostitutes, and even their sweethearts only when and while they had plenty of money in their pockets. Many of these songs were humorous accounts of carefree sailors on leave spending their accumulated pay fast and free on wine, women, and song. Representative of the genre, but a cut above the rest because of its use of allegory and its colorful language, was "The Sailor's Frolic, or, Life in the East" (meaning the East End of London):

Come, all you jolly Seamen,
And listen unto me;
Avast a while, I'll make you smile,
And tell you of a Spree.

There's a funny craft in Wappin,
In streaming colours gay,
And Pirates too, and Fire Ships,
In Ratcliffe Highway.

So, mind those buxom lasses
In their flying colours gay,
Or soon they'll clear your lockers,
In Ratcliffe Highway.

The Old Three Crowns I anchor'd in,
O such a jolly crew;
There's rough and smooth from ev'ry clime,
And copper colour too.
Such lasses there, so neat and fair,
With hair both grey and red,
Some with no nose, and some no teeth,
And damag'd figure head.
So, mind those buxom lasses, etc.

The Blue Anchor next I enter'd in,
A Frigate took in tow,
I was run aground, my cargo lost,
I found that I must go.
I sail'd into another Port,
And so by the next day,
My hulk well rigg'd and water tight,
Was in Ratcliffe Highway.
So, mind those buxom lasses, etc.

Then there's the Three Jolly Sailors,
Such grog is there galore,
And lasses, too, there's twenty,
I think as many more.
There's foot it there so neatly,
But mind, without a doubt,
You'll find they'll cut your Cable,
So keep a good look out.
So, mind those buxom lasses, etc.

The Old Rose, and Britannia,
Such Frigates there's at hand,

There's crooked Loo, and squinting Sue,
And bandy Mary Anne.
There's skinny Nell the yellow girl,
And flash Maria neat,
There's bouncing Het, and brazen Bet,
That's been all through the Fleet.
So, mind those buxom lasses, etc.

Then, in the fam'd King William,
That's in New Gravel Lane:
There's Jenny Jones, all skin and bones,
And ugly Molly Payne.
Thick lipp'd Kate as black as jet,
With bustle such a size,
And snuffing Liz, with such a phiz,
And Sukey gravy eyes.
So, mind those buxom lasses, etc.

At the fam'd Old Barley Mow,
Hail'd a Frigate tight,
Steer'd away, without delay,
And boarded her that night.
She took my watch and money too,
And clothes, without delay,
Two bullies soon they turn'd me out
Into Ratcliffe Highway.
So, mind those buxom lasses, etc.

So all you jolly sailors,
I'd have you bear in mind,
There's Pirate Craft in every port,
And Fire Ships you'll find.
If you wish to have a Spree
When out upon a Cruise,
Get moor'd all right, so snug and tight,
In the port of the Paddy's Goose.
So, mind those buxom lasses, etc.[55]

Ashton's fifth category was a much larger one, containing thirty-one items, all of which dealt with male/female relationships under the general heading of "Love."[56] A number of them were popular broadside ballads, such as "The Bold Lieutenant" (aka "The Fan in the Lion's Den"), "Beautiful Nancy," "Susan's Adventures in a Man of War" (aka "On Board a Man of War"), and "The Merchant's Daughter of Bristol." One of the best examples of the genre, which would frequently be found in oral tradition, was "Fair Phoeby and her Dark Eyed Sailor." Another of the broadsides assigned to this category was "The Distressed Ship's Carpenter," a version of the traditional ballad usually called "The Daemon Lover" (Child no. 243, "James Harris"). Interestingly, this text, which was probably an eighteenth-century one, contained no hint of the supernatural element often found in traditional versions of the ballad, yet it had been rewritten substantially from the oldest known text, Laurence Price's seventeenth-century broadside, "A Warning to Married Women":

Well met, well met, my own true Love,
Long time I have been seeking thee,
I am lately come from the salt salt Sea,
And all for the Sake, Love, of thee.

I might have had a King's Daughter,
And fain she would have married me,
But I've forsaken all her Crowns of Gold,
And all for the Sake, Love, of thee.

If you might have had a King's Daughter,

I think you much to blame,
I would not for Five Hundred Pounds,
That my Husband should hear the same.

For my Husband is a Carpenter,
And a young Ship Carpenter is he,
And by him I have a little Son,
Or else, Love, I'd go along with thee.

But, if I should leave my Husband dear,
Likewise my little Son also,

What have you to maintain me withal,
If I along with you should go?

I have seven Ships upon the Seas,
And one of them brought me to Land,
And Seventeen Mariners to wait on thee,
For to be, Love, at your Command.

A pair of Slippers thou shalt have,
They shall be made of beaten Gold,
Nay, and be lin'd with Velvet Soft,
For to keep thy Feet from Cold.

A gilded Boat then thou shalt have,
Thy Oars shall be gilded also,
And Mariners to row thee along,
For to keep thee from thy overthrow.

They had not been long upon the Sea,
Before that she began to weep;
What weep you for my Gold? He said,
Or do you weep for my Fee?

Or do you weep for some other young Man,
That you love much better than me?
No, I do weep for my little Son,
That should have come along with me.

She had not been upon the Seas,
Passing Days three or four,
But the Mariner and she were drown'd,
And never were heard of more.

When Tidings to Old England came,
The Ship's Carpenter's wife was drown'd,
He wrung his Hands, and tore his Hair,
And grievously fell in a Swoon.

Oh! Cursed be those Mariners,
For they do lead a wicked life,
They ruin'd me a Ship Carpenter,
By deluding away my Wife.[57]

Another interesting item in this category was the very popular eighteenth-century song, "Cupid's Garden." Despite its rather confusing lyric, it had entered oral tradition as well as becoming a best-selling broadsheet. A good example of a non-traditional ballad that had rapidly become a vernacular song, it was nonetheless debatable whether it should be counted as a folksong. Ashton clearly thought it should.

Ashton's final group of ballads was something of a rag-bag, as might be expected in a category named "Miscellaneous."[58] In fact, several of the twenty-nine items might reasonably have been allocated to an earlier group, but it is difficult to see where else he could have fitted in "Britain's Glory," "Hearts of Oak," "Doll of Wapping," "The Female Smuggler," "Davey Jones's Locker," or "The Great Sea Snake." He again included "Sir Walter Raleigh Sailing in the Low-lands," which, as we have seen, was an early broadside version of "The *Golden Vanity*" (Child no. 286, "The *Sweet Trinity*").[59] This section also included several murder ballads replete with ghosts: "Captain Glen," "Bill Jones" and "The Gosport Tragedy, or the Perjured Ship Carpenter." The latter, although rather long, is worth reproducing as a splendid example of the broadside genre. The ballad's story comprises courtship, a reluctant lover, extra-marital intercourse, an unwanted pregnancy, deceit, murder, haunting, confession, madness, vengeance, and, to cap it all, a moralistic ending:

In Gosport, of late, there a damsel did dwell,
For Wit and for beauty, did many excel;
A young man did court her to be his dear,
And he by his trade was a ship-carpenter.

He said, Oh! Dear Molly, if you will agree,
And will consent to marry me;
My love, you will ease me of sorrow and care,
If you will but wed a ship-carpenter.

With blushes more charming than Roses in June,
She answer'd, Sweet William, To wed, I'm too young;
Young men are so fickle, I see very plain,
If a maid is not coy, they will her disdain.

They flatter and swear their charms they adore,
When gain'd their consent, they care for no more;
The handsomest creature that ever was born,
When a man has enjoy'd, he will hold in scorn.

My charming Molly, what makes you say so?

Thy beauty's the haven to which I would go:
So unto that country I chance for to steer,
There will cast anchor and stay with my dear.

I ne'er shall be cloy'd with the charms of my love,
My love is as true as the turtle dove;
And all I crave is to wed with my dear,
And when thou art mine, no danger I fear.

The life of a virgin, Sweet William, I prize,
For marriage brings sorrows and troubles likewise;
I am loth to venture, and therefore forbear,
For I will not wed with a ship-carpenter.

For in time of war, to the sea you must go,
And leave wife and children in sorrow and woe;
The seas they are perilous, therefore forbear,
For I will not wed with a ship-carpenter.

But yet all in vain, she his suit did deny,
Though he still did press her to make her comply;

At length, with his cunning he did her betray,
And to lewd desire, he led her away.

But when with child, this young woman were,
The tidings she instantly sent to her dear;
And by the good Heaven he swore to be true,
Saying I will wed no other but you.

Time passed on, till at length we hear,
The King wants sailors, to sea he repairs;
Which grieved the damsel unto the heart,
To think she so soon with a lover must part.

She said, My dear William, 'ere thou go'st to sea,
Remember the vow that thou madest to me;
But, if you forsake me, I never shall rest,
Oh! Why doest thou leave me with sorrow opprest?

Then, with kind embraces, to her he did say,
I'll wed thee, dear Molly, 'ere I go away;
And, if, tomorrow, to me thou doest come,
A licence I'll buy, and it shall be done.

So with kind embraces he parted that night,
She went to meet him, in the morning light:
He said, dear Charmer, thou must go with me,
Before we are wedded, a friend for to see.

He led her through valleys and groves so deep,
At length this Maiden began to weep;
Saying, William, I fancy thou lead'st me astray,
On purpose my innocent life to betray.

He said, that is true, and none you can save,
For I this night have been digging a grave:
Poor innocent soul, when she heard him say so,
Her eyes like a fountain began for to flow.

O perjured creature, the worst of men,
Heavens reward thee when I am dead and gone;
O pity the infant, and spare my life,
Let me go distrest, if I am not your wife.

Her hands, white as lilies, in sorrow she wrung,
Beseeching for mercy, saying, what have I done
To you, my dear William, what makes you severe,
For to murder one that loves you so dear?

He said here's no time disputing to stand,
And instantly taking the knife in his hand;
He pierced her body till the blood it did flow,
Then into the grave her body did throw.

He cover'd her body, then home he did run,
Leaving none but the birds her death for to mourn;
On board the *Bedford* he entered straightway,
Which lay at Portsmouth out bound for the sea.

For Carpenter's mate he was enter'd, we hear,
Fitted for his voyage, away he did steer;

But, as in his Cabbin one night he did lie,
The Voice of his sweetheart he heard for to cry.

O perjured Villain, awake now and hear,
The Voice of your love, that lov'd you so dear:
This ship out of Portsmouth never shall go,
Till I am revenged for this overthrow.

She afterwards vanish'd with shrieks and sighs,
Flashes of lightning did dart from her eyes;
Which put the ship's crew into great fear,
None saw the ghost, but the voice they did hear.

Charles Stuart, a man of courage so bold,
One night was going into the Hold;
A beautiful creature to him did appear,
And she, in her arms had a daughter most fair.

The charms of this so glorious a face,
Being merry in drink, he goes to embrace;
But to his surprise, it vanished away,
So he went to the Captain without more delay.

And told him the story, which when he did hear,
The Captain said, some of my men, I do fear,
Have done some murder, and if it be so,
Our ship in great danger to the sea must go.

One at a time then his merry men all,
Into his cabbin he straightway did call;
And said, my lads, the news I do hear,
Doth much surprise me with sorrow and fear.

The ghost which appear'd in the dead of the night,
Which all my Seamen so sadly did fright;
I fear has been wrong'd by some of my crew,
And, therefore, the person I fain would know.

Then William affrighted, did tremble with fear,
And began, by the powers above, for to swear;
He nothing at all of the matter did know,
But, as from the Captain he went to go

Unto his surprise his true love did see;
With that he immediately fell on his knee,
And said, here's my true love, where shall I run,
O save me, or else I am surely undone.

Now he the murder confessed out of hand,
And said, before me my Molly doth stand:
Sweet injured ghost, thy pardon I crave,
And soon will I seek thee in the silent grave.

No one but this wretch did see this sad sight,
Then, raving distracted, he dy'ed in the night;
As soon as her parents these tidings did hear,
They sought for the body of their daughter dear.

Near a place call'd Southampton, in a valley deep,
The body was found, while many did weep;

At the fall of the damsel, and her daughter dear,
In Gosport Church, they buried her there.
I hope this may be a warning to *All*,

Young men how innocent maids they enthrall;
Young men, be constant, and true to your love,
Then a blessing indeed will attend you above.[60]

Despite some imperfect texts, there was thus a great deal of very interesting material in *Real Sailor Songs,* including not only some of the finest broadside ballads about the sea and sailors but several traditional ballads and folk lyrics as well. Essentially Ashton's book replaced James Orchard Halliwell's earlier attempt to cover much of the same ground in the Percy Society publication, *The Early Naval Ballads of England* (1841).[61] His research into broadside texts complemented the pioneering work of Laura Smith in *Music of the Waters,* and, because of his lack of shanty material, implicitly reinforced the importance of Davis and Tozer's equally pioneering *Sailors Songs or "Chanties."* The book was therefore a useful contribution, but it was nonetheless a pity that Ashton had not concerned himself with tunes as well as texts. His achievement in editing *A Century of Ballads*, *Modern Street Ballads*, and *Real Sailor Songs* was essentially to popularize a large but still limited number of items selected from the huge number of broadsides that lay unsorted and largely unread in public and private archives. While it pales by comparison with the parallel work of Francis James Child and Joseph Ebsworth, it was nonetheless of considerable value in selecting and popularizing some of the best examples of broadside literature.

Sea songs of various kinds were indeed an important branch of the tree of English vernacular music, and these three publications served as a reminder of this fact. Together they made a substantial first step in the recovery and publicizing of maritime folksong. Admittedly they had their faults. Ashton's book had no tunes and the texts were sometimes bowdlerized. Smith's was somewhat chaotic in organization, lacked sufficient documentation, was fraught with minor errors, and her texts clearly suffered from her singers' self-censorship: they were simply too polite to offend a lady's ears. Davis and Tozer provided virtually nothing in the way of context and documentation, and their texts also appear to have been sanitized. All Late Victorian publications (except under the counter pornography) were effectively subject to censorship with regard to matters of sexuality, and it would have been surprising if the shanty texts offered by Smith and Davis had not been cleaned up. They, like Ashton, knew what was not permissible in a songbook intended for use in Victorian drawing rooms. It is, however, a pity that no manuscript versions of Davis's shanties have survived since it would have been very interesting to compare what he sang (or heard) on board ship with what he and Tozer actually printed.

Ashton's work, like that of Child and Ebsworth, raised the question of how many tunes could be found, either in old songbooks or in oral tradition, for this particular branch of broadside balladry. Tune-hunting would be the main focus of Sabine Baring-Gould, Frank Kidson, Lucy Broadwood, and others during the last two decades of the Victorian era. To complete our survey of vernacular songhunting in the 1880s we will devote a chapter to each of these three important figures. First we move to the county of Devon to find the Reverend Sabine Baring-Gould.

Notes

1. Laura Alexandrine Smith, ed., *The Music of the Waters: A Collection of the Sailors' Chanties, or Working Songs of the Sea, of All Maritime Nations. Boatman's, Fishermen's, and Rowing Songs, and Water Legends* (London: Kegan Paul, Trench & Co, 1888).

2. Smith, *Music of the Waters*, 30.

3. Smith, *Music of the Waters*, xxiii.

4. Smith, *Music of the Waters*, 28.

5. Smith, *Music of the Waters*, 30.

6. William Chappell, ed., *Popular Music of the Olden Time, a Collection of Ancient Songs, Ballads and Dance Tunes, illustrative of the National Music of England*, 2 vols. (London: Cramer, Beale & Chappell, 1858-1859).

7. Smith, *Music of the Waters*, xxx.

8. Smith, *Music of the Waters*, xxiii-xxiv.

9. Smith, *Music of the Waters*, 7.

10. Smith, *Music of the Waters*, 14-15.

11. Smith, *Music of the Waters*, 15.

12. Smith, *Music of the Waters*, 30-31.

13. Smith, *Music of the Waters*, 16.

14. Smith, *Music of the Waters*, 16.

15. Smith, *Music of the Waters*, 16-17.

16. Smith, *Music of the Waters*, 10-12.

17. Smith, *Music of the Waters*, 12-17.

18. Smith, *Music of the Waters*, 18.

19. Smith, *Music of the Waters*, 18-19.

20. Smith, *Music of the Waters*, 19-20.

21. Smith, *Music of the Waters*, 28.

22. Smith, *Music of the Waters*, 28-29.

23. Smith, *Music of the Waters*, 23-24.

24. Smith, *Music of the Waters*, 24-25.

25. Smith, *Music of the Waters*, 46-47.

26. Smith, *Music of the Waters*, 25-28.

27. The song was of recent vintage, and may well have been a composition, in deliberately archaic style, by W. E. Henley. It nonetheless borrowed lines from a much older folk lyric or ballad.

28. Smith, *Music of the Waters*, 25-27.

29. Smith, *Music of the Waters*, xix, xxv-xxvii, 7, and 58-61.

30. Smith, *Music of the Waters*, 60-76.

31. Smith, *Music of the Waters*, 61-70.

32. Donald Campbell, *A Treatise on the Language, Poetry and Music of the Highland Clans* (Edinburgh: Collie, 1862).

33. Smith, *Music of the Waters*, 91 and 101.

34. John Bell, ed., *Rhymes of the Northern Bards* (Newcastle-upon-Tyne, U.K.: Bell & Angus, 1812).

35. Smith, *Music of the Waters*, 110-11.

36. *Musical Times and Singing Class Circular* 30, no. 557 (1 July, 1889): 393-94.

37. Frederick Davis and Ferris Tozer, eds., *Sailors' Songs or "Chanties"* (London: Boosey & Co., n.d. [1886 or 1887]).

38. Davis and Tozer, *Sailors' Songs*, preface [unpaginated].

39. Davis and Tozer, *Sailors' Songs*, preface [unpaginated].

40. Davis and Tozer, *Sailors' Songs*, preface [unpaginated].

41. Davis and Tozer, *Sailors' Songs*, 5.

42. Davis and Tozer, *Sailors' Songs*, 26-27.

43. Davis and Tozer, *Sailors' Songs*, 35.

44. Davis and Tozer, *Sailors' Songs*, 38-39.

45. Davis and Tozer, *Sailors' Songs*, 36-37.

46. Davis and Tozer, *Sailors' Songs*, 44-45.

47. Frederick Davis and Ferris Tozer, eds., *Sailors' Songs or "Chanties"* (3rd edition, London: Boosey & Co., [1907]).

48. Cecil J. Sharp, ed., *English Folk-Chanteys* (London: Schott, 1914).

49. John Ashton, ed., *Real Sailor Songs* (London: Leadenhall Press, 1891; reissued, New York: Benjamin Blom, 1972).

50. Ashton, *Real Sailor Songs*, 21-87.

51. Ashton, *Real Sailor Songs*, 76-77.

52. Ashton, *Real Sailor Songs*, 91-127.

53. Ashton, *Real Sailor Songs*, 101-2.

54. Ashton, *Real Sailor Songs*, 131-49.

55. Ashton, *Real Sailor Songs*, 145-46.

56. Ashton, *Real Sailor Songs*, 153-217.

57. Ashton, *Real Sailor Songs*, 216-217; Francis James Child, ed., *The English and Scottish Popular Ballads*, 5 vols. (Boston: Houghton, Mifflin & Co., 1882-1898; reprinted: New York: Dover, 1965), 4: 360-69.

58. Ashton, *Real Sailor Songs*, 221-71.

59. Ashton, *Real Sailor Songs*, 221-22. Child, *Popular Ballads*, 5: 135-142.

60. Ashton, *Real Sailor Songs*, 250-52.

61. James Orchard Halliwell, ed., *The Early Naval Ballads of England* (London: Percy Society, 1841).

7

Western Pioneer: Sabine Baring-Gould

The Reverend Sabine Baring-Gould (1834-1924) was a figure of some stature in Late Victorian intellectual and cultural life. The son of a retired officer of the East India Company, as a youth he traveled extensively in Europe with his parents, picking up several languages and becoming interested in archeology and the classics. Always religious, in the 1850s, while a student at Clare College, Cambridge, he was attracted to the Tractarian movement and declared his intention of becoming a clergyman, but this aspiration was initially thwarted by parental opposition. For nearly a decade he turned instead to teaching, mainly at Hurstpierpoint College, expressing his faith in part by composing hymns and by running a choir. In 1863 his parents relented, and two years later Baring-Gould, now an ordained Anglican priest, took up his ministry as a curate in the mill town of Horbury Brig in Yorkshire, where he met his future wife, a mill-girl, Grace Taylor. Married in 1868, the couple would have five sons and ten daughters, most of whom survived infancy. During his spell as a curate in Horbury and later at Dalton (also in Yorkshire), Baring-Gould continued to compose hymns, but he also wrote books about folklore: *The Book of Were-Wolves*[1] and *Curious Myths of the Middle Ages*.[2] In 1868 he published his first novel, *Through Flood and Flame*, which was mainly autobiographical.[3] Interested in church history and theology, and influenced by the debate over Darwin's theory of evolution, Baring-Gould worked out his own perspective on Christianity in *The Origin and Development of Religious Belief*.[4] This attracted hostile reviews from both Catholics and fundamentalist Protestants but William Gladstone liked the book, and in 1871, as Prime Minister, he appointed the author to the crown living of East Mersea in Essex. While vicar of East Mersea, Baring-Gould took the opportunity to travel in Europe and to write more books, including *The Vicar of Morwenstowe: A Life of Robert Stephen Hawker*[5] and fifteen volumes of *Lives of the Saints*,[6] which the Roman Catholic Church saw fit to place on the Index. He also created his best-selling novel, *Mehalah*,[7] which Swinburne compared to *Wuthering Heights*. In 1872 he had inherited his father's estate at Lew Trenchard[8] in the county of Devon, but the local church still had an elderly minister, so it was only in 1881 that Baring-Gould was able to take over the family living and move his family to Lew House.[9]

For the rest of his life Sabine Baring-Gould was the local squire and vicar of the parish of Lew Trenchard on the edge of Dartmoor, in South West England. Known to the general public as a best-selling novelist and as the composer of the texts of a number of popular hymns, including "Onward Christian Soldiers" and "Now the Day Is Over," he was something of a polymath, although his interests were mainly antiquarian. As an amateur archeologist at a time when the profession was in its infancy he led the way in identifying and excavating paleolithic barrows and stone circles on Dartmoor. As a geographer he explored and documented the physical landforms of Iceland. And as a folklorist, he wrote about the history of European customs and beliefs, and pioneered the collection of the traditional music of Devon and Cornwall. Indeed he was one of the very first folksong collectors to spend days and sometimes weeks at a time hunting for songs in the isolated cottages and hamlets, villages and small towns of rural England. He was also a pioneer in publishing a large collection of regional folksongs equipped with scholarly critical notes. His best known work, *Songs of the West*,[10] a revised and expanded edition of the earlier *Songs and Ballads of the West*,[11] was the biggest, and, for a while, the best collection of folksongs noted in the field during the first folksong revival.

Baring-Gould wrote in the second volume of his autobiography, *Further Reminiscences,* that his work as a song-collector was his greatest accomplishment, commenting that he considered "the recovery of our West-country melodies...the principal achievement of my life."[12] This suggests that, looking back, he saw his work with Devon and Cornish folksong as even more important than his pastoral work as a churchman, his secondary career as a successful novelist and travel writer, or his discoveries in the fields of archeology, geography, history, and folklore (other than folksongs).[13] If so, he was probably correct. He was a conscientious and caring Anglican minister, but his contributions to theology were not exceptional and his parishioners' lives would not have been greatly different had another man preached the weekly sermons in the local church. His novels, with the exception of *Mehalah*, have largely been forgotten. Most of his work as an archeologist, historian, geographer, and folklorist, although at the time useful contributions to the development of these disciplines, has been superseded. His collection of folksongs alone remains unique and irreplaceable.

There is no doubt that Baring-Gould was an energetic and prolific, if idiosyncratic, contributor to the late Victorian folksong revival. Despite their flaws, his published song collections were pioneering works of major importance. Moreover, as a collector and editor Baring-Gould had virtues that not all other first revival collectors exhibited, and his work raised in acute form issues that they would all have to confront. Unfortunately his exceptionally valuable field work was somewhat vitiated by his propensity as an editor to 'doctor' his texts. It is therefore important to examine how and from whom he collected folksongs, how he preserved and processed the fruits of his labors, what songs he selected for publication, and the editorial approach in his three published collections. This chapter focuses on his early work during the 1880s.

The Problem

We are dealing with the legacy of a major Victorian folklorist. Yet Baring-Gould is a controversial figure. His work raises tricky questions of censorship and authenticity, and he has received a bad press. Criticisms of his published collections have centered on two issues: the undeniable fact that Baring-Gould, as he openly admitted, was unable to print certain bawdy or sexually explicit songs in the form that he collected them, and the claim that many of his other song-texts are composites of his own creation or even outright forgeries. Let us clear the decks by examining these criticisms in turn.

Over fifty years ago A. L. Lloyd and John Hasted began to examine attitudes to sex in traditional folk lyrics, and in 1958 literary critic James Reeves published *The Idiom of the People*, a very influential book that compared the published versions of folksong lyrics collected by Cecil Sharp with the originals in his manuscripts in the Vaughan Williams Memorial Library.[14] This revealed that a significant degree of censorship had been imposed on Sharp's Edwardian era publications, by either Sharp himself, his collaborator the Reverend Charles Marson, or their publisher, Novello. The revelation stimulated inquiries to determine if the same was the case with other earlier songhunters, and Reeves published a sequel, *The Everlasting Circle*, in which he printed the original versions of selected folksongs from the Baring-Gould, H. E. D. Hammond, and George Gardiner manuscript collections.[15] It was evident that in many instances a similar process of sanitization had been imposed, and Baring-Gould was perceived to have been the worst offender, perhaps because he was the most candid about what he had done and why. In folk-revival circles in England during the 1960s he was sometimes referred to as the "Reverend Dr. Bowdler."[16]

Did Baring-Gould really deserve this kind of criticism? On the face of it, yes. The best way to illustrate why is with an example. One of the songs most closely associated with him is "Strawberry Fair." This is the published version in his first major published song collection, *Songs and Ballads of the West*:

As I was going to Strawberry Fair,
Singing, singing, buttercups and daisies,
I met a maiden taking her ware,
Fol-de-dee!
Her eyes were blue and golden her hair,
As she went on to Strawberry Fair,
Ri-fol, Ri-fol, Tol-de-riddle-li-do,
Ri-fol, Ri-fol, Tol-de-riddle-dee.

"Kind Sir, pray pick of my basket!" she said,
Singing, etc.
"My cherries ripe, or my roses red,
Fol-de-dee!
My strawberries sweet, I can of them spare,
As I go on to Strawberry Fair."
Ri-fol, etc.

"Your cherries soon will be wasted away,
Singing, etc.
Your roses wither and never stay,
Fol-de-dee!
'Tis not to seek such perishing ware,
That I am tramping to Strawberry Fair."
Ri-fol, etc.

"I want to purchase a generous heart,
Singing, etc.
A tongue that neither is nimble nor tart,
Fol-de-dee!
An honest mind, but such trifles are rare,
I doubt if they're found at Strawberry Fair."
Ri-fol, etc.

'The price I offer, my sweet pretty maid,
Singing, etc.
A ring of gold on your finger displayed,
Fol-de-dee!

So come make over to me your ware,
In church today at Strawberry Fair.'
Ri-fol, etc.[17]

When we compare this with the original "Strawberry Fair" taken down by Baring-Gould and his friend, musician H. Fleetwood Sheppard, from John Masters at Bradstone (Devon) in 1891, we find some significant differences. The tune and chorus are much the same, but the buttercups and daisies are nowhere to be seen.

Strawberry Fair

Anon

Fig 7.1

These are the verses as sung by Masters:

As I was going to Strawberry Fair,
Ri-tol-ri-tol, riddle tol-de-lido,
I saw a fair maid of beauty rare,
Tol-de-dee.
I saw a fair maid go selling her ware,
As she went on to Strawberry Fair,
Ri-tol-ri-tol, riddle-tol-de-lido,
Ri-tol, ri-tol, riddle tol-de lee.

"O pretty fair maiden, I prithee tell,
Ri-tol-ri-tol, etc.
My pretty fair maid, what do you sell?
Tol-de-dee.
O come tell me truly, my sweet damsel,
As you go on to Strawberry Fair."
Ri-tol-ri-tol, etc.

"O I have a lock that doth lack a key,
Ri-tol, etc.
O I have a lock sir," she did say.
Tol-de-dee.

"If you have a key then come this way,
As we go on to Strawberry Fair."
Ri-tol, etc.

Between us I reckon that when we met,
Ri-tol, etc.
The key to the lock it was well set,
Tol-de-dee.
The key to the lock it well did fit,
As we went on to Strawberry Fair.
Ri-tol, etc.

"O would that my lock had been a gun,
Ri-tol, etc.
I'd shoot the blacksmith, for I'm undone.
Tol-de-dee.
And wares to carry I now have none,
That I should go to Strawberry Fair."
Ri-tol, etc.[18]

Instead of a chaste pastoral idyll, with fruit and flowers, moral virtues, and wedding bells, we find overt sexual symbolism, a suggestion that the woman may be a prostitute, an unwanted pregnancy, and a desire for violent revenge. Clearly the lyric has been cleansed and the meaning of the song has been transformed. The case for the prosecution seems irrefutable, and the "Reverend Doctor Bowdler" tag appears eminently justified.

Yet the situation is not as simple as it first appears. To start with, we are not dealing with literary fraud on the part of Baring-Gould. He did not pretend that he had collected the words as printed in *Songs of the West* and in its predecessor, *Songs and Ballads of the West*. On the contrary, he explicitly acknowledged that he had altered them in the interests of propriety. In a note on the song, he commented that it could be traced back to the fifteenth century but that the original words were "very indelicate" and he had been "forced to re-write" them.[19]. Such, indeed, was his normal practice. In the alphabetical index at the back of *Songs and Ballads of the West* he divided the songs into three categories: those with traditional lyrics, those with lyrics that he had modified or supplemented, and those he had completely rewritten. He also indicated the few occasions when he had set a lyric to a different melody than that sung by his informant. So there was no deception involved, only heavy-handed editing done for an evident, and acknowledged, purpose.

Baring-Gould in fact regretted not being able to publish songs such as "Strawberry Fair" exactly as he found them, and he was eager to make publicly available, as best he could, the songs *as collected*. He promised to deposit copies of the originals in the Plymouth Public Library, and, in a sense, he was as good as his word. The Plymouth Central Library contains a manuscript titled "Songs and Ballads of the West (Devon and Cornwall)" that contains some two hundred songs, with tunes and variants. For more than a century it has been possible to compare the versions in this manuscript with printed versions. However, the manuscript is not a field notebook, and the entries are fair copies made years after the songs were collected. They are usually close to the originals, but they are not always precise replicas of the corresponding items in Baring-Gould's and his collaborators' field notebooks. So even when we consult this fair copy manuscript we cannot be sure that we are seeing tunes and texts exactly as Baring-Gould's informants sang to him. The same is true even when we consult the comprehensive set of fair copy manuscripts that he kept for his own use. One suspects that censorship has sometimes occurred between the field notebooks and the fair copies, as well as between the fair copies and the published versions.

Since the 1960s Baring-Gould has continued to be a fashionable subject for attack in English folk music circles. For example, in *Folk: A Portrait of English Traditional Music, Musicians and Customs,* published in 1976, Dave Pegg likened him to a butterfly collector, the implication being that he killed his specimens in the process of collecting them.[20] This was actually quite unfair to Baring-Gould, who showed considerable concern for the wellbeing of his informant-parishioners and was eager to see the songs he had rescued from oblivion performed at concerts, both by his source singers themselves and by trained-voice singers appropriately sensitive to and appreciative of the material. He was scathing in his criticisms of middle-class performers who had no empathy with the songs.

Yet although some of the arrows shot at Baring-Gould have missed their mark, the question of the reliability of his published material, and even that of the fair copies he made for his own use and to share with other collectors, has been cast in doubt by evidence that suggests that, at least on occasion, he was prone to make his own composite versions of song-texts, without always acknowledging what he had done. Such composites were compiled from fragments he had noted in the field from several different singers and sometimes also from related broadside ballad texts. The creation of composite versions of ballad texts had been a standard editorial procedure during the nineteenth century, so Baring-Gould was by no means unique in this regard. Singers, of course, routinely do it to this day. However, the approach was challenged by Francis James Child in *The English and Scottish Popular Ballads* and is now widely regarded by folklorists and other academics as something akin to an intellectual crime. Steve Gardham, for example, has argued that Baring-Gould was a "literary hoaxer" who probably invented at least two ballads ("The Gypsy Countess" and "The Brown Girl") that he sent to Francis James Child for inclusion in *The English and Scottish Popular Ballads*.[21] While it may seem unfair to generalize from just two examples, Gardham's article has certainly reinforced a fairly widespread perception that Baring-Gould is simply not to be trusted as a collector/editor. Indeed he is sometimes seen as a notorious example of the bourgeois expropriator of the people's music denounced so vigorously and comprehensively by Dave Harker in *Fakesong*.[22]

Let us examine the case of "The Brown Girl" to make clear the kind of *faux pas* of which Baring-Gould is accused. This is the ballad as found in Baring-Gould's own fair copy manuscript book, ascribed to source-singer John Woodrich:

I am as brown as brown can be,   Did scorn and passed me by.
And my eyes as black as sloe,
I am as brisk as a nightingale,   Me did he send a love letter,
As wild as forest doe.   And he sent it from the town,
My love he was so high and proud,   Saying no more he loved me,
His fortune too so high,   For that I was so brown.
He for another fair pretty maid   I sent his letter back again,

For his love I valued not,
Whether that he would fancy me,
Whether that he would not.

When that six months were overpassed,
Were overpassed and gone,
Then did my lover, once so bold,
Lie on his bed and groan.
When that six months were overpassed,
Were gone and overpassed,
My lover once so bold and proud,
With love was sick at last.

First sent he for the doctor's man,
"You, doctor, must me cure!
The pains that now do torture me
I cannot long endure."
Next did he send from out the town,
O next did send for me,
He sent for me, the brown, brown girl
Who once his wife should be.

O never a bit the doctor's man
His sufferings could relieve.
O never a one but the brown, brown girl
Who could his life reprieve.
O now you shall hear what love she had
For this poor love-sick man,
All of this day, a summer's day,

She walked but never ran.

When that she came to his bedside,
Where he lay sick and weak,
O then for laughing she could not stand
Upright upon her feet.
"You flouted me, you scouted me,
And marry another one;
And now the reward has come at last
For all that you have done."

She took the rings from off her hands,
The rings by two and three.
"O take, O take these golden rings,
By them remember me."
She had a white wand in her hand,
She strake him on the breast:
"My faith and troth I give back to thee,
So may thy soul have rest."

"Prithee,' said he, "forget, forget,
Prithee forget, forgive:
O grant me yet a little space,
That I may be well and live."
"O never will I forget, forgive,
So long as I have breath:
I'll dance above your green, green grave
Where you do lie beneath."[23]

The Brown Girl

Anon

Fig. 7.2

The melody was noted by F. W. Bussell, apparently in 1888 or 1889. In the fair copy manuscript the duration of some notes is not clear, nor do they always fit properly Bussell's barring, so I have had to interpret the original a little in order to reproduce the tune here. Nonetheless, it is probably very close to what Woodrich sang. It is not so certain, however, that he remembered, or even knew, the words of the ballad. Gardham claims that this version of "The Brown Girl" is in fact a "concoction" created by the Devon cleric himself. He further suggests that Baring-Gould forged the ballad in order to play a hoax on Child.[24] The materials from which Baring-Gould allegedly compiled "The Brown Girl" were, in Gardham's opinion, actually a broadside version of the ballad from an eighteenth-century garland in the British Museum titled *The Brown Girl's Garland*, and another, somewhat similar, song (also found on broadsheets as well as in oral tradition) titled "Sally and her True Love Billy." Gardham's claim that Baring-Gould forged "The Brown Girl" is based on a textual analysis that purports to demonstrate that his text is rather clumsily stitched together from these two disparate sources.

Here is the broadside version of "The Brown Girl," which was actually titled "The Bonny Brown Girl":

"I am as brown as brown can be,
My eyes as black as sloe;
I am as brisk as a nightingale,
And as wilde as any doe.

"My love has sent me a love-letter,
Not far from yonder town,
That he could not fancy me,
Because I was so brown.

"I sent him his letter back again,
For his love I valu'd not,
Whether that he could fancy me
Or whether he could not.

"He sent me his letter back again,
That he lay dangerous sick,
That I might then go speedily
To give him up his faith."

Now you shall hear what love she had
Then for this love-sick man;
She was a whole long summer's day
In a mile a going on.

When she came to her love's bed-side,
Where he lay dangerous sick,
She could not for laughing stand
Upright upon her feet.

She had a white wand all in her hand,
And smoothd it all on his breast;
"In faith and troth come pardon me,
I hope your soul's at rest.

"I'll do as much for my true-love
As other maidens may;
I'll dance and sing on my love's grave
A whole twelvemonth and a day."

There is actually no evidence that Baring-Gould was familiar with either this broadside or the broadside of "Sally and Her True Love Billy." Neither of them appear to be in his own broadside collection (now mainly deposited in the British Library). However, copies of both broadsides did exist in the (then) British Museum and so he *may* have seen one or both of them there. If he did "concoct" his version he must, at the very least, have copied part of it from "The Bonny Brown Girl." If so, where did he find the other elements of his composite? There is in fact another source that appears more likely than the broadside of "Sally and Her True Love Billy." It is a (related) song titled "Pretty Dorothy." John Woodrich knew this song and Baring-Gould did collect it from him. Here is the text of "Pretty Dorothy":

I once was a bachellor
From London Town I came
I courted pretty Dorothy
And Dorothy her name
But she was proud and lofty
Her fortune was so high
And for another bachellor
She scorn'd and passed me by

When six long months were over (gone)
Were overgone and past
This damsel she was taken sick
With love was sick at last
She sended for the doctor-man
For him she fain would see
She sended for the bachellor
Whose wife she wished to be.

O Dolly I'm the doctor's-man
That you were fain to see
O Dolly I'm the bachellor
Whose wife you wish to be
If that you be a doctor-man
You me must kill or cure
The pains that now do torture me
I can not long endure

O Dorothy, proud Dorothy
Thou haughty Dorothy
Remember how in time that's past
You scorned and slighted me
You flouted me, you scouted me
And many another one
And now reward has come at last
For all that you have done

She took her rings from off her fingers	O William yet forgive, forget
Her rings by two and three	O pray forget, forgive
Then take of me these golden rings	And grant me yet a little space
By them remember me	That I may love or live
Remember me so proud and cold	O no, thou haughty Dorothy
When I am dead and gone	So long as I have breath
And then perchance you'll grieve for me	I'll dance upon your green, green grave
For what to me you've done	Whilst that you lie beneath.[25]

So it is quite *possible* that by drawing on both "The Bonny Brown Girl" and "Pretty Dorothy" Baring-Gould could have made up his own composite version of "The Brown Girl." While the main structure of his ballad follows the broadside, his fourth stanza looks as though it might have been borrowed in part from "Pretty Dorothy," as does stanza six (about the rings). Yet it is not clear why he would have then passed off the result as an item noted entirely from Woodrich. It seems equally possible that Woodrich had heard or seen "The Bonny Brown Girl" but could not remember it exactly and, when attempting to sing it to Baring-Gould, included appropriate verses, suitably adapted, from "Pretty Dorothy." This kind of blending of elements from different songs is quite common in oral tradition. In short, the composite version of "The Brown Girl" *may* have been collected from oral tradition, as Baring-Gould claimed, notwithstanding that it apparently incorporates lines from "Pretty Dorothy" (or, for that matter, from "Sally and Her True Love Billy").

Personally, I do not find Gardham's forgery thesis very convincing. Baring-Gould, in my estimate, was neither a congenital liar and hoaxer nor was he a faker of traditional songs. On the other hand, he was often careless, and he *was* sometimes willing to create a composite from several imperfectly remembered versions of the same ballad. He did so, usually for publication purposes, in order to obtain a complete version of the song or ballad. It is therefore possible that Woodrich sang only "Pretty Dorothy" and that Baring-Gould elaborated this into a version of "The Brown Girl," drawing up stanzas from the broadside to fill in missing verses. On the other hand, it is also possible that Woodrich sang "The Brown Girl" very much as it is in Baring-Gould's fair copy. The problem is, we do not know for sure which was the case. Suspicion is not proof, and in this particular case I think we must give Baring-Gould the benefit of the doubt. It is by no means certain that his version of "The Brown Girl" is a reconstruction, but even if it is, he was no doubt honestly attempting to re-create the original ballad. As we have seen, when he wrote, or re-wrote, lyrics, he usually did so because he knew he could not print the originals, and he routinely informed his readers when he had done so. However, it has to be admitted that the question of "The Brown Girl," when added to that of "Strawberry Fair," does make one wary about accepting Baring-Gould's song-texts as completely authentic. More "tidying up" may have taken place than we would nowadays find acceptable. Nonetheless, in my view he was not a forger.

The Layers of the Onion

To explore further the issue of the discrepancies between what Baring-Gould collected and what he published we must try to pare away the accumulated detritus that separates his publications from the original field notes upon which they were loosely based. There are four layers of this onion. We can quickly dispose of the outer, twentieth-century, layer. Baring-Gould was an elder statesman of the Edwardian phase of the folksong revival during the decade between 1904 and 1914. He had by then ceased to collect actively on his own behalf, but he remained a friend and correspondent of Lucy Broadwood and a friend and collaborator of Cecil Sharp. In 1906 he worked with Sharp on the very influential *English Folk Songs for Schools*,[26] employed by successive generations of elementary school teachers. It was a successful rival to *The National Song Book: A Complete Collection of the Folk-Songs, Carols, and Rounds suggested by the Board of Education,* edited by Sir Charles Villiers Stanford,[27] and to earlier collections of national songs published in the 1890s.[28] *English Folk Songs for Schools* was still in use in the 1950s, and, over the decades, millions of young school children must have sung songs from its pages. Baring-Gould's more than two dozen contributions to *English Folk Songs for Schools* were taken mainly from *Songs of the West*, published the previous year (1905), an omnibus compilation of folksongs that he had collected, for which Cecil Sharp had served as music editor.[29] This reprinted, in modified form, a large selection from the first two of the three major vernacular song collections Baring-Gould had made during the Late Victorian era. The outer (fourth) layer of the onion thus comprises these two Edwardian era publications: *Songs of the West* (1905) and *English Folk Songs For Schools* (1906). They need not detain us further.

Moving backwards in time and a step closer to Baring-Gould's collecting in the field we come to his three major publications in the Late Victorian era. They were *Songs and Ballads of the West: A Collection made from the Mouths of the People,*[30] *A Garland of Country Song: English Folk Songs with their Traditional Melodies,*[31] and the eight volume *English Minstrelsie: A National Monument of English Song* (1895-98).[32] These books comprise the third layer of the onion. While not as well known as his two later, better selling, publications that were co-edited with Cecil Sharp, they represent his most important public contribution to the Late Victorian revival. The versions of West Country folksongs in these collections are the ones that were known to most folk music enthusiasts, concert goers, and listeners to BBC radio throughout the first half of the twentieth century and during much of the post-war folksong revival in the United Kingdom. As we have seen, their texts were fairly frequently bowdlerized or otherwise rewritten although their tunes, when stripped of their overly elaborate piano arrangements, were accurate and authentic.

Peeling away this third layer we come to the manuscript sources on which the books were based. I call this the second or 'fair copy' layer. It comprises two manuscripts: one in Plymouth Library titled "Songs and Ballads of the West (Devon and Cornwall)" (also known as the "Plymouth Fair Copy Manuscript") and the so-called "Personal Copy" (aka "The Killerton Manuscript"), which is very large.[33] The first part of "The Personal Copy" is similar to the Plymouth manuscript, but more songs were added as Baring-Gould collected them or received them in the mail from other collectors, with the result that this document expanded over the years to three large exercise books. It became his master file of all the folksongs that he had collected or obtained from other people. His numbering system identifies 568 discrete song-clusters, but it is faulty and there are in fact over 650 different items in the entire collection. It is not entirely clear which of these fair copy manuscripts came first. While it is probable that the Plymouth Fair Copy Manuscript was compiled from "The Personal Copy," it is also possible that it was the first fair copy manuscript that Baring-Gould created, perhaps as he edited the successive parts and editions of *Songs and Ballads of the West*; the preface is dated 1892 but it was submitted to the Plymouth Library in October 1900. "The Personal Copy," on the other hand, although started earlier, perhaps in 1888, was compiled more gradually and episodically over an even longer period of time. It documents Baring-Gould's later collecting as well as the initial burst reflected in *Songs and Ballads of the West*.

The inner core of the onion—the first or 'field-collecting' layer—consists of Baring-Gould's field notebooks, and those of his collaborators H. Fleetwood Sheppard and F. W. Bussell. They date from 1888 onwards. Baring-Gould typed up fourteen separate alphabetical indexes to these notebooks, but at least nineteen short manuscripts appear to be extant, and others may be missing. What remains is divided into two sets of papers. One set, usually called the "Rough Copy Notebook(s)," contains mainly tunes. The second, usually called the "Plymouth Notebook(s)," comprises mainly song lyrics. There are far more tunes than texts. Most of Baring-Gould's scribbled field notes were replaced by fair copies written out when he got home, and the "Plymouth Notebook(s)" are a remnant that somehow survived against the odds. The "Rough Copy Notebook(s)" apparently includes some tunes (perhaps all the tunes) that Baring-Gould collected on his own, but most were noted by Sheppard or Bussell. Differences in handwriting provide clues to who noted each melody. There is some doubt as to the accuracy of the minority of tunes written down by Baring-Gould himself. He was apparently a competent pianist, but, by his own admission, he had trouble noting melodies by ear in the field; his preferred method was therefore to bring the singer to a place where there was a piano. As a last resort, if he heard something valuable in a pub or a parishioner's residence, he would keep singing the tune over and over to himself until he got home to his own piano. It must also be recognized that some of the notebooks appear to consist of initial fair copies made at home after collecting expeditions rather than being actual field-work manuscripts. On the whole, however, it seems reasonable to place reliance on both the tunes and texts found in the "Rough Copy Notebook(s)" and the "Plymouth Notebook(s)." Indeed we have no choice: they are the closest we can get to what Baring-Gould's informants actually sang to him and his collaborators.

Hence in studying Baring-Gould's work we are fortunate to possess three kinds of sources: his field notebooks, his manuscript fair copies, and his published collections. Moreover, most of this is now available on microfiche, courtesy of the Baring-Gould Heritage Project.[34] The microfiche collection comprises four main parts. The first set of items (section 1) consists of Baring-Gould's notebooks and those of his collaborators. There are thirteen volumes of rough copy notebooks presented to Plymouth Library by Baring-Gould, two other notebooks subsequently acquired by the Plymouth Library, a notebook from Baring-Gould's personal library (the "Killerton Notebook"), and a small collection of material that Baring-Gould sent by mail to Francis James Child (the "Harvard Manuscript"). As mentioned earlier, the thirteen Plymouth rough copy notebooks contain mainly tunes, and appear to be in several hands, so they preserve some of the melodies collected by H. Fleetwood Sheppard and/or F. W. Bussell, as well as a few noted by Baring-Gould himself. The other two Plymouth notebooks are mainly in Baring-Gould's handwriting and contain the words of songs as he noted them in the field. The "Killerton Notebook" and "Harvard Manuscript" contain fair copies (and some rough drafts) of song lyrics, but no accompanying music. Two additional notebooks were discovered after the microfiche collection was filmed, and these are preserved in the Devon County Record Office (Exeter): they contain some early attempts at fair copies and were also used for rough notes.

A second category of material available on microfiche (section 2) comprises the two large and important fair copy manuscripts. As mentioned earlier, the "Plymouth Fair Copy Manuscript" contains two hundred songs, with melodies, including, in some instances, several variants of tune and/or text. It was begun in 1892 (the short preface carries that date), but includes variants collected as late as 1900. It was donated to the Plymouth Library shortly thereafter. Baring-Gould titled the manuscript "Songs and Ballads of the West (Devon and Cornwall)" and added a subtitle, "as taken down, words and melodies, from the mouths of the People." His frontispiece contains the following comment:

> I give these as near as possible, but singers sometimes vary the words and the airs slightly, when singing at intervals of time. Also where there have been four or five versions of the same, slightly varying, I have not always noted all the differences. This, in my opinion, when I first started collecting, in 1888, was not necessary; as I was under the impression that they were all taken from Broadsides. Later, I came to a different opinion; and I now hold that in a good many cases the traditional forms are earlier and sometimes more correct than the broadsides, which were taken down in many cases from oral recitation in London or Manchester, or other large towns, where correct forms were less likely to be preserved than in country villages.[35]

These, then, were fair copies of the material that Baring-Gould and his collaborators had collected in the field, mainly during the late 1880s, and from which the songs in Baring-Gould's first published collection, *Songs and Ballads of the West,* were selected. They are the transcriptions that represent his best effort to record accurately for posterity what he had found in the field.

The second fair copy manuscript is the one conventionally known as "The Personal Copy," although it is sometimes referred to as the "Killerton Fair Copy Manuscript," to distinguish it from the "Plymouth Fair Copy Manuscript." This manuscript was discovered only after Baring-Gould's personal library was moved from Lew Trenchard to Killerton House in the 1970s. As mentioned earlier, it contains over 650 items (tunes and words, with variants) in three volumes and provides the single most comprehensive source for Baring-Gould's *oeuvre* as a folksong collector. It was evidently compiled over several decades, with the earliest entries dating from the 1880s and the last ones from as late as 1917. The first volume, in particular, appears to have been used as the model upon which the "Plymouth Fair Copy Manuscript" was based. It may be fairly safe to assume that the two hundred items in the Plymouth manuscript were copied from the Killerton manuscript, and that the versions of those songs in "The Personal Copy" represent Baring-Gould's initial fair copies. There are some differences between texts in these two documents, but the variations are not major, and, *prima facie*, these two fair copy manuscripts possess roughly the same degree of authority. In most cases of conflict, however, "The Personal Copy" should perhaps be accorded priority because it contains Baring-Gould's own working copies of all his folksong materials, whether he obtained them from his own field work, from that of other collectors, or from printed sources such as broadsides and songbooks. However, there are rare instances when the "Plymouth Fair Copy Manuscript" appears more definitive.

The microfiche collection also includes two other types of material. Section three comprises Baring-Gould's interleaved and annotated copies of two of his own publications, *Songs and Ballads of the West* (four parts in the two-volume edition of 1891), and *A Garland of Country Song* (1895). Section four contains eleven volumes of printed popular literature collected by Baring-Gould, including seven volumes of broadside ballad texts, one volume of other broadside song texts, and three volumes of chapbooks.

Ideally one would like to trace the evolution of a song—text and tune—through all four layers of the onion, starting with the field notes and ending with the product as republished for school use in 1906. In practice, this is rarely possible since relatively few of the songs are to be found in every layer. *English Folk Songs for Schools* and the field notebooks unfortunately do not match up very well. The problem is most severe at the first layer since only fragments of the field notebooks have survived. However it is usually possible to compare the more legible and complete items in the field notebooks with versions in "The Personal Copy," and items in the latter can frequently be juxtaposed with the printed versions in *Songs and Ballads of the West* or *A Garland of Country Song.* That way we can get some sense of the reliability of the second and third layers of the onion. And sometimes we can also reach the outer layer. *English Folk Songs for Schools* includes only a small sampling from the many hundreds of songs that Baring-Gould noted, but much more of his collecting (over 120 items) was included in *Songs of the West.* Occasionally, if a song was also included in *English Folk Songs for Schools,* we can follow it through the complete set of metamorphoses. There are many difficulties in practice, however, and to illustrate them I will examine two examples.

"Sweet Nightingale" is an example of a song that one can seemingly trace through all four layers of the onion. This is how the tune appears in *Songs and Ballads of the West* and in *English Folk Songs for Schools,* accompanied on each occasion by five verses.[36] The item was actually a composite, so from where had Baring-Gould obtained the melody and the words?

Sweet Nightingale

Anon

Fig. 7.3

Initially obtained from a Cornish correspondent, E. F. Stevens of St. Ives, essentially the same tune as that in Fig. 7.3 is written down in what was probably Stevens's own hand in the "Rough Copy Notebook" [microfiche 1.1]. One verse of text is scribbled underneath the music, in a different hand, likely Baring-Gould's. Probably in response to a newspaper request, Baring-Gould also received a very similar, although not quite identical, melody from another correspondent, Plymouth brushmaker Henry Whitfield. This, along with Stevens's tune, is included in "The Personal Copy" [microfiche 2.2] and in the "Plymouth Fair Copy Manuscript" [microfiche 2.1]. In the latter manuscript, underneath Stevens's tune, Baring-Gould wrote "same air sung by H. Westaway, Belstone; by J. Parsons, Lew Down."[37] Another slightly different tune, but still very similar to Stevens's and Whitfield's, is to be found in the "Plymouth Notebook" [microfiche 1.2]. Baring-Gould apparently collected the song twice, from James Parsons, who lived nearby,[38] and from one of his Dartmoor singers, Harry Westaway.[39] The "Plymouth Notebook" tune is a little different from either of the variants attributed to Stevens and Whitfield, which increases the probability that it was indeed noted in the field from either Parsons or Westaway, although we do not know which. This version from oral tradition may be found below, as Fig. 7.4.[40] A comparison of this version with the melody printed in *English Folk Songs for Schools* shows that, although they are very similar, Baring-Gould and Sharp made adjustments to the tune, the most significant being a decision to end the long melisma on A rather than G. Musically this is arguably an improvement, and in this respect the result accords with the Stevens version. However, it means that the published version does not replicate exactly what Baring-Gould thought he heard from Parsons or Westaway.

Baring-Gould believed the lyric of "Sweet Nightingale" to have been derived from an eighteenth-century ballad opera, *Thomas and Sally,* the libretto for which had been written by Isaac Bickerstaff and the music composed by Thomas Arne, but Arne's melody was not the same as that sung by Parsons and Westaway or those obtained from either Stevens or Whitfield. Baring-Gould also discovered that there was a version of the song in Robert Bell's 1857 publication, *Ancient Poems, Ballads and Songs of the Peasantry of England*, which differed somewhat from that in Bickerstaff's libretto, and he initially assumed, without providing any evidence, that Bell had likely modified or even rewritten Bickerstaff's words. It is possible that this was in fact not the case: Bell's text may have been taken from a broadside in his, or in James Henry Dixon's possession, since many of the songs in *Ancient Poems, Ballads and Songs* derived from broadsides, although others were the product of Dixon's field collecting. It is just possible, although less likely, that Bell collected it himself from oral tradition. The five verses given in the "Plymouth Notebook" [microfiche 1.2] seem to have been taken from Bell, but there is only one verse in the "Plymouth Fair Copy Manuscript" [microfiche 2.1] and only three in "The Personal Copy" [microfiche 2.2], although the latter also includes an extract from Bickerstaff's libretto. *Songs and Ballads of the West* makes use of Bell's five verses, and these are retained in *Songs of the West* and *Folk Songs for Schools.*

Baring-Gould's two Devon singers must have known some words for the "Sweet Nightingale" tune even if they could not remember them all. It appears that he obtained only one verse (at most) from Stevens and/or Whitfield, so the three verses in "The Personal Copy" are probably those that he obtained from Parsons and Westaway. The most authentic version that we can reconstruct of "Sweet Nightingale" is therefore this short text, together with the version of the tune in the "Plymouth Notebook." It suggests that the original song was about a failed attempt at seduction.

The Sweet Nightingale

Anon

Fig. 7.4

Sweet heart, come along, don't you hear the fond song,
The sweet notes of the nightingale flow?
Don't you hear the fond tale of the sweet nightingale,
As she sings in the valleys below?

Pretty Betty, don't fail, for I'll carry your pail,
Safe home to your cot as we go;
You shall hear the fond tale of the sweet nightingale,
As she sings in the valleys below.

Pray let me alone, I have hands of my own,
Along with you, sir, I'll not go,
To hear the fond tale of the sweet nightingale,
As she sings in the valleys below.[41]

Yet once Bell's longer text is taken into account we can see that it was not unreasonable for Baring-Gould to conclude that the verses he had obtained from oral tradition were incomplete. Arguably they comprised a large fragment (three fifths) of a longer song that paralleled closely (and was derived from) the first part of a broadside ballad that had been taken from Bickerstaff's libretto or, alternatively, upon which Bickerstaff's text was based. Most likely "The Sweet

Nightingale" is really a longer narrative song in which the *dénouement* reverses the initial situation and the seduction is successful. These are the additional two verses found in the "Plymouth Notebook," *Songs and Ballads of the West* and *English Folk Songs for Schools*:

> Pray sit yourself down with me on the ground,
> On this bank where sweet primroses grow,
> You shall hear the fond tale of the sweet nightingale,
> As she sings in the valleys below.
>
> The couple agreed; they were married with speed,
> And soon to the church they did go.
> She was no more afraid for to walk in the shade,
> Nor yet in those valleys below:
> Nor to hear the fond tale of the sweet nightingale,
> As she sang in the valleys below,
> As she sang in the valleys below.[42]

This, then, was what Baring-Gould had to work with when he prepared "The Sweet Nightingale" for publication in (initially) *Songs and Ballads of the West.* For a tune he could choose between Arne's melody employed in *Thomas and Sally,* or one of three very similar tunes obtained from Stevens, Whitfield, and his own collecting. However, we find that the tune provided in *Songs and Ballads* is actually said to have been noted by H. Fleetwood Sheppard. It therefore seems probable that Baring-Gould had Sheppard check one of his local singers' (probably Parsons's) rendition of the melody. As we have seen, the differences between Sheppard's published transcription and the one given in the "Plymouth Notebook" are minor. The singer may have sung it slightly differently, or possibly Sheppard made the changes on his own initiative. Essentially all versions (except Arne's) are the same tune, with only slight variations. There thus seems no good reason to doubt the essential authenticity or accuracy of the melody published by Baring-Gould. It most likely closely reproduces what Sheppard heard in the field, although it only approximates what Baring-Gould himself heard (assuming he made the first transcription and got it down accurately).[43]

As for the lyrics, Baring-Gould apparently concluded that three of Bell's five verses were essentially the same as those also to be found in Devon oral tradition, and that perhaps, after all, Bell had not reworked them extensively. If the source singers' lyrics and Bell's text both derived from a broadside, it was legitimate to suppose that the two missing verses would have been much the same as Bell's. He therefore reproduced them verbatim, but with one exception: he omitted the additional three lines of the last verse. In this instance, then, Baring-Gould's editorial decisions seem reasonable, and there is a high probability that "The Sweet Nightingale," as printed in *Songs and Ballads of the West* and later publications, does closely resemble the vernacular ballad of that name as it was sung in Devon during the last half of the nineteenth century, although it is not exactly the same. Yet it is also possible that the texts, or text fragments, that Parsons and Westaway sang were different (and perhaps bawdy), and that Baring-Gould simply discarded them in favor of Bell's, leaving no record of them anywhere in his papers. However, I have found no evidence to prove, or even suggest, this. On the whole, I think the scenario that I have outlined is the most plausible, because the "Plymouth Fair Copy Manuscript" was intended by Baring-Gould to be an accurate record of his own collecting and because only three verses were set down in "The Personal Copy," which was also primarily (although not exclusively) a compilation of all his collecting.[44] However, we have to admit that while we have drilled down satisfactorily to the bottom layer of the onion in the case of the tune, we cannot get beyond the second layer with regard to the lyric, which means that we cannot be certain that the published words match those noted in the field. They may well do so (three verses, that is), but firm proof is lacking. This test case does therefore underline the difficulties involved in reconstructing exactly what occurred in any given instance.

Of all James Parsons's songs, the one that seems to have delighted Baring-Gould the most was "The Trees They Do Grow High." This ballad was an important discovery, and it may serve as another example of the transformative process that Baring-Gould's material sometimes underwent between source singer and published version. In this instance we can examine what happened to both tune and text. In the "Plymouth Notebook" we find an eight-verse text ascribed to James Parsons, and in the "Rough Copy Notebooks" two versions of the tune, one of which is ascribed to Parsons. In the "Plymouth Fair Copy Manuscript" we find six different texts, three collected in Devon, one in Ireland, one in Scotland, and one a Catnach broadside. In "The Personal Copy" we find eight texts and eleven variants of the tune, including one collected by Lucy Broadwood in Surrey. In both fair copy manuscripts, the 'A' text comprises twelve verses, is ascribed to Parsons *and* Matthew Baker, and is evidently a composite, while the 'A' tune (Parsons's) is the same as that in the "Rough Copy Notebooks." The published version in *Songs and Ballads of the West* gives Parsons's tune and six verses from Parsons's text, plus two additional verses that appear to have been composed by Baring-Gould. In *Songs of the West* Sharp replaced Sheppard's rather complex piano arrangement with his own simpler one, but left tune and text the same. The ballad was omitted from *Folk Songs for Schools*.

The two attempts to capture the melody of "The Trees They Are So High" in the "Rough Copy Notebooks" are apparently by different hands. The first (Fig. 7.5) is rather tentative, the second is more confident. According to a note in the "Plymouth Fair Copy Manuscript" the first transcription was made by Baring-Gould himself in September 1888. He seems to have had some difficulty deciding the exact pitch and rhythm of Parsons's melody, his barring is imperfect, and his score is unclear in places. One is given the impression that although he made a determined effort (and did in fact catch the main outline of the tune) he was dissatisfied with the result. He made several rather messy corrections to his notation, and this is therefore no more than a best guess at interpreting the manuscript score. I have had to adjust the barring in order to make the transcription.

The Trees They Are So High

Anon

Fig. 7.5

Dissatisfied with his own transcription of the tune, Baring-Gould revisited Parsons the next year, accompanied by Fleetwood Sheppard. The latter's transcription was more confident, although he apparently changed his mind about the time signature, initially choosing 4/4 and then finding that the tune better fitted waltz time. Fig. 7.6 reproduces Fleetwood Sheppard's version of the melody, as sung by Parsons.

The words of "The Trees They Are So High," as Baring-Gould first noted them from Parsons, are found in both the "Plymouth Notebook" [microfiche 1.2] and the "Killerton Notebook" [microfiche 1.3], the latter apparently a slightly modified fair copy of the former. This is apparently what Baring-Gould scribbled down as Parsons sang:

The trees they are so high,
The leaves in summer green,
The day is gone, my pretty love,
That you and I have seen.
It is cold this winter's night
And I must lie alone,
Once my pretty lad was young
And was growing.

In a garden as I walked
I heard them laugh and call,
It was four and twenty playing there,
They played with bat and ball.
O the rain is on the roof

And here I make my moan,
Then my pretty lad was young
And was growing.

I listened in the garden,
I looked over the wall,
Amidst five and twenty gallants, love,
My lad exceeded all.
Oh the wind is in the thatch
And here alone I weep,
Then my pretty lad was young
And was growing.

O father, father dear,

Great harm to me is done,   And I am bitter cold,
Why should I married be this day   Still my pretty lad is young
   Before the set of sun?   And is growing.
   At the buffle of the gale
   I turn and can not sleep,   At fourteen he wedded was,
   Then my pretty lad was young   A father at fifteen,
   And was growing.   And then his face was white as milk
       And then his grave was green,
   O daughter, daughter dear,   And the daisies there was spread
   A lady thou shalt be,   And buttercups of gold,
   In court and stall, in stately hall Ah! My lad who was so young
   And bower of tapestry.   Hath ceased growing.[45]
   But the snow the snow flakes fall

The Trees They Are So High

Anon

Fig. 7.6

On the second occasion he visited (this time with Sheppard), Baring-Gould obtained two more verses that Parsons had apparently forgotten first time around. Moreover, he discovered that another of his informants, Matthew Baker of Lew Down, knew the ballad and could contribute additional verses that fitted the same tune. Drawing on both singers' texts, Baring-Gould put together a composite in which the stanzas were arranged in what he considered the most logical order. This long version is in the "Plymouth Fair Copy Manuscript" [microfiche 2.1]:

All the trees they are so high   You've done to me great wrong,
And the leaves they are so green,   That I should married be this day
The day is past and gone, sweetheart,   Unto a lad so young.
That you and I have seen.   [O the rain on the roof]
'Tis a cold winter's night,   Here and I must make my moan,
You and I must be alone,   Whilst my pretty lad is young,
Whilst my pretty lad is young,   And is growing.
Yet is growing.
        O daughter, daughter dear,
O father, father dear,   No wrong to thee is done,

For I have married thee this day
Unto a rich man's son.
    [O the wind on the thatch]
    Here and I alone must weep,
    Whilst my pretty lad is young,
    And is growing.

    O father, father dear,
    If that you think it fit,
    Then send him to the school awhile,
    To be a year there yet.
    At the huffle of the gale
    Here I toss and cannot sleep,
    Whilst my pretty lad is young,
    And is growing.

    To let the lovely ladies know
    They may not touch and taste,
    I'll bind a bunch of ribbons red
    About his little waist.
    And I'll wait another year,
    [O the roaring of the sea,]
    Whilst my pretty lad is young,
    And is growing.

    In a garden as I walked
    I heard them laugh and call,
    There were four and twenty playing there,
    They played with bat and ball.
    I must wait, awhile must wait,
    And then his bride will be,
    O my pretty lad so young,
    Still is growing.

    I listened in the garden,
    I looked o'er the wall,
    Of four and twenty scholars there
    My love exceeded all.
    O the snow, the snow flakes fall,
    O and I am chill and freeze,
    But my pretty lad so young,
    Still is growing.

    I'll cut my yellow hair,

    I'll cut it cross my brow,
I'll go unto the college–re– [sic]
And none shall know me so,
O the clouds are driving by,
And they shake the leafy trees,
But my pretty lad so young,
Still is growing.

To the college I did go,
I cut my yellow hair,
To be with him in sun and shower
His sports and studies share.
O the taller that he grew,
The sweeter still grew he,
O my pretty lad so young,
Still a-growing.

As it fell upon a day,
A bright and summer's day,
We went into the greenwood,
To frolic and to play.
O what did there befall
I tell not unto thee,
But my pretty lad so young,
Was still growing.

At thirteen he married was,
A father at fourteen,
And then his face was white as milk,
And then his grave was green,
And the daisies were outspread
And the buttercups of gold,
O'er my pretty lad so young,
Now ceased growing.

I'll make my pretty love
A shroud of Holland fine,
And all the time I'm making it,
My tears run down the twine.
And as the bell doth knell
I shiver as one cold
And weep o'er my pretty lad,
Now done growing.[46]

However, the ultimate version for publication involved more than a mere collation of verses from different sources. There was some interventionist editing too. As sung by Baring-Gould's informants, the young man in the ballad is married at the age of thirteen and a father at the age of fourteen, although the woman is in her early twenties. In another version, a broadside, the lovers are aged twelve and thirteen. Baring-Gould considered sexual activity at such a young age improper (especially for women, no doubt) and concluded that the ballad would have to be made a little more decent for public consumption. In his notes to the ballad in *Songs and Ballads of the West* he admitted that "in most versions, the age of the boy when married is 13, and he is a father at 14. I advanced his age a little, in deference to the opinion of those who like to sing the song in a drawing-room or at a public concert."[47] For publication in *Songs and Ballads of the West* he also reduced the number of verses, which he regarded as too many for performance purposes. The result of these editorial decisions was a text abridged and embellished by an imaginative editor confident of his literary flair, while the printed tune was a slightly modified version of Fleetwood Sheppard's transcription. This is the published version of the ballad in both *Songs and Ballads of the West* and *Songs of the West*. In both cases it was presented with piano accompaniment, in the former by Sheppard, in the latter by Sharp. It was omitted from *English Folk Songs for Schools*, no doubt because the lyric, even in its slightly bowdlerized form, was considered unsuitable for young ears.

The Trees They Are So High

Anon

Fig. 7.7

All the trees they are so high, and the leaves they are so green,
The day is past and gone, sweetheart, that you and I have seen.
It is cold winter's night, you and I must bide alone:
Whilst my pretty lad is young and is growing.

In a garden as I walked, I heard them laugh and call;
There were four and twenty playing there, they played with bat and ball.
O the rain on the roof, here and I must make my moan:
Whilst my pretty lad is young and is growing.

I listened in the garden, I looked o'er the wall;
Amidst five and twenty gallants there my love exceeded all.
O the wind on the thatch, here and I alone must weep:
Whilst my pretty lad is young and is growing.

O father, father dear, great wrong to me is done,
That I should married be this day, before the set of sun.
At the huffle of the gale, here I toss and cannot sleep:
Whilst my pretty lad is young and is growing.

My daughter, daughter dear, if better be, more fit,
I'll send him to the court awhile, to point his pretty wit.
But the snow, snowflakes fall, O and I am chill as dead:
Whilst my pretty lad is young and is growing.

To let the lovely ladies know they may not touch and taste,
I'll bind a bunch of ribbons red about his little waist.
But the raven hoarsely croaks, and I shiver in my bed;
Whilst my pretty lad is young and is growing.

I married was, alas, a lady high to be,

In court and stall and stately hall, and bower of tapestry,
But the bell did only knell, and I shuddered as one cold:
When I wed the pretty lad not done growing.

At seventeen he wedded was, a father at eighteen,
At nineteen his face was white as milk, and then his grave was green;
And the daisies were outspread, and the buttercups of gold,
O'er my pretty lad so young now ceased growing.[48]

To summarize, we find some minor differences between the version of the tune initially collected by Baring-Gould and the version published in *Songs and Ballads of the West* and *Songs of the West*, but these changes mainly reflect Sheppard's more confident noting of the melody as sung by Parsons second time around. The published version of the text is a composite, and although all but two of the verses appear to have been derived from source singers some additional touching up of the text seems to have taken place. However, apart from a significant adjustment to the age of the lad—a clear case of bowdlerization, but for a stated (and quite understandable) reason—all the changes appear to be fairly minor apart from the addition of two verses composed by Baring-Gould. In short, the published "The Trees They Are So High" is essentially the same ballad, but it differs in many details, most but not all of them minor, from that collected in the field by Baring-Gould.

My overall conclusion is that we must beware of rash generalizations about Baring-Gould's editorial practices: while in some instances we may find that the difference between the inner and outer layer of the onion is considerable, in other cases we may find that it is minimal. Ultimately, however, one is forced to make a judgment concerning Baring-Gould's honesty as an editor. Mine is that one can normally expect him to censor ribald texts for publication but one can usually trust him in *Songs and Ballads of the West* to indicate when he has done so. One can also usually, but not always, rely on the fair copy texts in the "Plymouth Fair Copy Manuscript" and "The Personal Copy," although some do appear to be composites. One also strongly suspects that the editorial process (including some censorship) may occasionally have begun *before* Baring-Gould made his fair copies or, alternatively, occurred during the actual creation of "The Personal Copy."

Baring-Gould's Informants

Although it was, of course, through his publications that Baring-Gould played his most major role in the Late Victorian folksong revival, *Songs and Ballads of the West* and *A Garland of Country Song* are best understood in relation to the large body of material collected from informants in Devon and Cornwall during the late 1880s and early 1890s. In reassessing Baring-Gould's legacy, the best place to start is therefore with his field notebooks and his fair copy manuscripts rather than with his printed collections. Baring-Gould's attitude to his source singers was in fact quite different from the way Dave Pegg presented it in *Folk*.[49] As a song collector, as in other spheres of his life, he was extraordinarily energetic and industrious, while his pastoral work and life-experience as a clergyman who cared about his parishioners usually helped him establish an effective working relationship with his singers. He was not blind to their character faults, but he admired their good qualities and he respected their musicianship. In return they sensed his sympathy for their hardships and his genuine interest in their songs, and some of them were unusually willing to share their entire repertoires with him, often over a period of several years. In short, Baring-Gould clearly had a flair for song collecting. The exceptional size and quality of his work, however, ultimately depended not only on his skill as a collector but also on the remarkable store of words and music preserved in the memories of his informants. They therefore deserve center stage in any account of his work.

The date when Baring-Gould began researching and collecting folksongs is not easy to determine with certainty. In *Further Reminiscences, 1864-1894* he titled chapter fifteen "Folk Songs, 1887-88," which suggests that he began collecting seriously in 1887. However in the opening sentence of that same chapter he remembered the critical year as 1888. He portrayed his conversion to the cause as a sudden revelation, claiming that his road to Damascus ran between the villages of Mount Tavy and Lew Trenchard. This is how he recalled the incident:

> I was dining at Mount Tavy, at the hospitable table of Mr. Daniel Radford...when the conversation turned upon Devonshire songs. Some of those present knew "Arscott of Tetcott" and some knew "Widdecombe Fair," but none could recall others such as "The Oxen Ploughing" and "Green Broom" in their entirety, though some remembered snatches of them. I remembered how, when I was a boy, I had ridden round Dartmoor, and had put up at little taverns. In them I had seen men sitting and smoking, and had heard them sing ballads. I mentioned this. My host said

to me: "Come, you are the man to undertake the job of collecting these songs and airs. It must be done at once, or it cannot be done at all, for in a few years they will be lost." I shall not forget my walk back next day from Mount Tavy to Lew. My mind was in a ferment. I considered that I was on the outstart of a great and important work; and to this day I consider that the recovery of our West-country melodies has been the principal achievement of my life.[50]

Despite its matter-of-fact appearance, there may be an element of romanticism in this autobiographical account. The incident may have actually occurred a year earlier, in 1887, and, in any case, it may suggest a too specific date for the beginning of what may have been a more gradual process.[51] Baring-Gould had in fact encountered, and shown some interest in, local vernacular songs well before the late 1880s. In *Old Country Life* he mentioned that as a youth he had traveled around his native county, staying at local village inns where he witnessed "gatherings where the local song-man entertained the company."[52] He subsequently described one evening he spent in the bar at the Oxenham Arms in the village of South Zeal during the early 1850s, when he used to ride his pony on Dartmoor. It was a day when local miners had received their pay and had gathered together for an evening of conviviality:

> At the table and in the high-backed settle sat the men, smoking, talking, drinking. Conspicuous among them was one man with a high forehead, partly bald, who with upturned eyes sang ballads. I learned that he was given free entertainment at the inn, on condition that he sang as long as the tavern was open, for the amusement of the guests. He seemed to be inexhaustible in his store of songs and ballads; with the utmost readiness, whenever called on, he sang, and skillfully varied the character of his pieces – to grave succeeded gay, to a ballad a lyric. At the time I listened, amused, till I was tired, and then went to bed, leaving him singing.[53]

Although the young horseman made no attempt to collect any songs at that time, he did not forget his experiences: "snatches of the songs and wafts of the strains lingered in my head."[54] Baring-Gould also remembered vividly that on his travels he discovered that "Somerset had its own type of songs with peculiar cadences, and Devon and Cornwall were rich to overflow in melodies."[55] Moreover, in a manuscript dated 1892 (that is, more than three decades before the publication of *Further Reminiscences*) he seemingly referred to 1880 as the time when he began collecting folksongs, although, given the difficulties posed by Baring-Gould's handwriting, it is also possible to construe the date as 1888.[56]

It is therefore almost certain that Baring-Gould was familiar with some West Country folksongs well before 1888, and that he may have even noted one or two songs in the early to mid-1880s. It also seems quite possible that his revelation about his mission came a year earlier than he dated it in *Further Reminiscences*. However, it was only in 1887 or 1888 that he decided to devote his considerable energy to collecting songs in a systematic way. Although he read music and played the piano, he was not adept at translating the tunes he heard sung in fields, pubs and cottages into notes on paper, at least when there was no piano available. For this reason he obtained the help of two musicians on many of his collecting trips among the villages of Devon and Cornwall. They were the Reverend H. Fleetwood Sheppard, rector of Thurnscoe and choir-master in Doncaster (in south Yorkshire), and F. W. Bussell, an Oxford undergraduate whose mother rented a cottage on the Lew Trenchard estate and who subsequently became a clergyman and professor (he taught Classics, philosophy, and divinity). On a given field trip one or the other would note tunes by ear while Baring-Gould wrote down the words of the songs. Other local musicians were occasionally pressed into service too: William Huggins of Lydford, and fiddler Peter Isaacs of South Fleming, both of whom Baring-Gould commissioned to collect songs for him. He described his initial encounter with Isaacs in a letter to Lucy Broadwood:

> I made the acquaintance of a poor old ragged fiddler with white hair, a beautiful intelligent face, a man whose occupation is gone; he is somewhat of a dreamer, and not a little given I fear to liquor, but a genuine musical enthusiast, and desperately poor. I have promised him 6d for every genuine old ballad air he can pick up for me, and he is going round this county for that purpose.[57]

Isaacs took his commission seriously, but in the process of songhunting he slept rough in a barn and made the mistake of smoking his pipe there, an offense for which he landed in Exeter jail. This episode prompted Baring-Gould to comment to Broadwood: "The singing birds are not, I am sorry to say, a very reputable lot—but I love them and I am sure they love me."[58]

Baring-Gould did some of his initial collecting in his own parish of Lew Trenchard and in neighboring villages, but he soon ventured further afield. Several of his collecting trips took him across Dartmoor, and on one of the earliest he found two of his best singers. The occasion stuck in his memory, and he describes it as follows in *Further Reminiscences:*

A Plymouth dentist, Mr. Spence Bate, who had retired from business, had a house at South Brent. He wrote to inform me that there were living in the place a miller, John Helmore, ruined by the setting up of a steam-mill, and a crippled stone-breaker, named Robert Hard; both notable song-men. He invited Mr. Sheppard and me to pay him a visit and gather up the fragments of folk music that remained to be discovered at South Brent. Accordingly we went. It was the depth of winter, and the weather was bitter. Mr. Bate's house was built over a stream from the moor, a so-called "leet," and it was like an ice-house. After dinner we adjourned to the kitchen, where there was a roaring fire, and the old men were set up with jugs and tankards of ale. But some neighbouring gentlemen and ladies, notably the latter, had been invited to be present at the performance. This I saw at once would never do. Tunes have to be repeated several times to be noted with accuracy, as peasant singers are disposed to embroider them with twirls and flourishes of their own device; and further, I was not at all sure that the words of the ballads would in all cases be fit for ladies' ears. And so it proved. For after the singing of "The Mole-Catcher" by John Helmore, the aged miller, there ensued a rapid dissolution of the company. I inserted the song in the last edition of *Songs of the West*, but to much chastened words.

On the following day Mr. Sheppard and I had the two old men to ourselves, and between us we recovered the words and airs of some very interesting pieces. In the summer I went to Mr. Bate's house along with Mr. Bussell, and gleaned more songs. Finally I went alone in the winter of 1890, and the Vicar of South Brent very kindly surrendered to me his drawing-room and piano, and gave me a good fire. I had in old Hard. Then and there I obtained from him a further crop of old ballads. That was the last reaping, for in the ensuing bitter frost the aged man was found dead, frozen on a heap of stones by the roadside. John Helmore, the miller, after his wife's death, ended his days in the Workhouse. [59]

Baring-Gould probably misremembered the date of this last collecting session with Robert Hard, who actually died in 1892. He may also have been misinformed about the details of Hard's death.[60] Yet the social chasm between the well-to-do parson and these poverty-stricken old men, for whom there were no pensions or any other form of social security net except the hated workhouse, is only too evident in this account. Baring-Gould's language, as in his metaphor of harvesting a crop, may make it appear as though he regarded singers such as Robert Hard and John Helmore as merely sources of what he wanted, to be cultivated briefly and then thrown aside and left to their fate. However, when one reads *Further Reminiscences* in conjunction with another of Baring-Gould's books, *Old Country Life,* and the notes to *Songs and Ballads of the West* and *A Garland of Country Song,* one realizes that this is a false impression. Not only was this clergyman/author a compassionate and observant human being who noticed and recorded much that others would have missed or disregarded, he also had a genuine interest in—even love and admiration for—his informants as people, not just as singers. When he could, he tried to help them financially by putting on concerts of Devonshire songs and distributing the proceeds among his poorest informants.[61]

Baring-Gould obtained some of his material from correspondents such as H. Whitfield, a brushmaker from Plymouth, but almost all the source singers from whom he noted texts and tunes in person were from the lower classes, either farm laborers or village artisans by occupation, and they all lived in rural locations. He discovered more than a dozen singers with sizeable repertoires who became his principal sources. This core group included not only Hard (the crippled stone-breaker from the village of South Brent on the edge of Dartmoor) and Helmore (the miller, also from South Brent) but also Matthew Baker (a cripple from Lew Down), Jonas Coaker (a blind man from Post Bridge, Dartmoor), Sam Fone (a miner from Black Down, near Lydford), Edmund Fry (a thatcher from Lydford), Roger Hannaford (from Lower Widecombe, Dartmoor), Roger and William Huggins (masons from Lydford), Roger Luxton (a retired farm laborer from Halwell), John Masters (a bedridden old man at Bridestone, near Lifton), James Olver (a tanner from Launceston, Cornwall), James Parsons (a hedger from Lew Down), Sally Satterley (a housewife from Huccaby (or Huckaby) Bridge, Dartmoor), Harry Westaway (a yeoman farmer from Belstone), and John Woodrich (a blacksmith from Wollacott Moor, Thrushelton). All except James Olver were Devonians, and all except Sally Satterley were male, and most were elderly.[62]

Each of Baring-Gould's core group contributed at least one song to *Songs and Ballads of the West,* and several of them provided many more. Sam Fone would eventually prove the most prolific of all, but Baring-Gould discovered him later than most of the other members of his core group and so Fone does not figure as largely in the early collecting as he would do in the 1890s. However, Hard, Masters, Olver, Parsons, and Woodrich also had large repertoires upon which Baring-Gould drew gratefully, and Parsons's songs in particular showed up frequently in *Songs and Ballads of the West.* There were, of course, many other informants who contributed just a song or two to Baring-Gould's collection. A few of the other informants mentioned in *Further Reminiscences* or in other publications by Baring-Gould include Moses Cleve (a youth at Huccaby, Devon, who later committed suicide), William Friend (a laborer at Lydford, Devon), William Rice (a laborer at Lamerton, Devon), John Richards (also from Lamerton), and John Woolrich (a laborer at Broadwoodwidger, not to be confused with blacksmith John Woodrich of Thrushelton).

In all, over fifty singers provided items for *Songs and Ballads of the West,* although, as might be expected, there was some duplication of titles. Insufficient space precludes quoting more than a handful of Baring-Gould's pen-portraits of these men and women, but a selection will give a sense of who these informants were and what they were like. There are thumb-nail sketches of eight of them in *Old Country Life,* and photographs or drawings of three of the men (Robert Hard, John Helmore, and James Olver) are to be found in other books. This is Baring-Gould's description of the two South Brent singers whom he had first met at Mr. Bate's house:

> On the south of Dartmoor live two men also remarkable in their way—Richard [*sic*] Hard and John Helmore. The latter is an old miller, with a fine intelligent face and a retentive memory. He can read, and his songs have to be accepted with caution. Some are very old, others have been picked up from song-books. Hard is a poor cripple, walking only with the aid of two sticks, with sharply-chiselled features—he must have been a handsome man in his youth—bright eyes, a gentle, courteous manner, and a marvellous store of old words and tunes in his head. He is now past stone-breaking on the roadside, and lives on 4 pounds per annum. He has a charming old wife; and he and the old woman sing together in parts their quaint ancient ballads. That man has yielded up something like eighty distinct melodies. His memory, however, is failing; for when the first lines of a ballad in some published collection is read to him, he will sometimes say, "I did know that some forty years ago, but I can't sing it through now." However, he can very generally "put the tune to it." [63]

Songs collected from John Helmore included "The Mole-Catcher," "The Miller and His Sons," "The Chimney Sweep," and "The Sailor's Farewell." The original text of "The Mole-Catcher" does not seem to have been preserved by Baring-Gould, although there is an expurgated version in "The Personal Copy." "The Spotted Cow," on the other hand, is in the "Killerton Notebook" [microfiche 1.3], although a note by Baring-Gould indicates that he failed to obtain all the verses. These are the four that he did note from Helmore:

As early in the month of May	"No longer weep, no more complain,
I from my cottage strayed,	She is not lost, my dear,
Just as the sun proclaimed the day	I saw her now in yonder grove,
I met a lovely maid.	Come, I will show you where."
"Good morning, sir." "Good morn," said I	They traversed many a pleasant field,
"O whither wander now?"	And many a flowery dale,
This pretty maid she answered,	And she forgot the spotted cow,
"I seek my spotted cow."	And harkened to his tale.[64]

Among the two dozen songs Baring-Gould noted from Robert Hard were "The Scolding Wife," "'Twas On a Sunday Morning," "Fathom the Bowl," "The Hearty Good Fellow," "The Tythe Pig," "Nancy," and "A Nutting We Will Go." One of the most unusual was "Blow Away Ye Morning Breezes." This was a dialogue song which Hard likely performed with Helmore. Baring-Gould considered it "very old" and "odd" (both attributes were recommendations in his eyes), and it had a catchy tune that Fleetwood Sheppard appreciated and duly noted:

Refrain: Blow away ye morning breezes,	For thou shalt drink the puddle foul,
Blow ye winds, hey ho!	And I the crystal clear."
Blow away the morning kisses,	
Blow, blow, blow.	"I shall not sorrow," etc.
"O thou shalt rue the very hour	"O thou shalt rue that e'er thou wo'ld
That e'er thou knewest the man,	Behold a love of mine,
For I will bake the wheaten flour	For thou shalt sup the water cold,
And thou shalt bake the bran."	But I will sup red wine."
"I shall not rue the very hour	"I shall not rue," etc.
That e'er I knew the man	
But I will bake the wheaten flour	"Thou shalt lament in grief and doubt,
And thou shalt bake the bran."	Thou spake'st with him at all,
Refrain: Blow away ye morning breezes,	For thou shalt wear the sorry clout,
etc.	And I the purple pall."
"O thou shalt sorrow thro' thy soul	"I shall not lament," etc.
Thou stood'st to him so near,	

"O thou shalt curse the day of birth,
And curse thy dam and sire,
For I shall warm me at the hearth,

And thou shalt feed the fire,"

"I shall not curse, etc."[65]

Blow Away Ye Morning Breezes

Anon

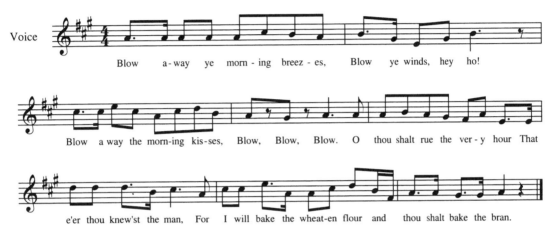

Fig. 7.8

Although they lived in the same village, these two men's repertoires seem to have been, in the main, quite different. Occasionally, however, they overlapped: Helmore's "The Dark Eyed Sailor," for example, was essentially the same ballad as Hard's "The Broken Token." Here are the words of Helmore's version, as recorded by Baring-Gould in the "Killerton Notebook." The square brackets around the fifth verse suggest that Baring-Gould interpolated it:

"'Twas of a comely lady fair,
Abroad she went to take the air.
She met a sailor on her way,
So she listened, so she listened,
So she listened to hear what he would say.

Said he "Why lady, roam alone?
The night is come, the day is gone."
She said as tears from eyes did flow,
"A dark eyed sailor,
A dark eyed sailor proved my woe."

"'Tis three years since he left this land,
He took his gold ring from my hand,
He broke the token, half gave me,
And his lies deep,
And his lies deep beneath the sea."

Said he "Now cast him from your mind,
Some other lover, thou wilt find,
Love changes fast and cold doth grow,
As a winter morning,
As winter's morning white the land like snow.

[She answered, "Nay, that cannot be,
Though my love lies beneath the sea,
As holly standeth ever green,
So true love bides,
So true love bideth what it e'er has been.]

Then half the ring, did William show,
Away was fled her doubt and woe,
"O welcome to my heart and fold,
Your faithful maiden,
Your (faithful maiden) to your heart of gold."[66]

And here is the touched-up version, with the tune, that Baring-Gould attributed to Robert Hard in *Songs and Ballads of the West*:

One summer evening, a maiden fair,
Was walking forth in the balmy air,
She met a sailor upon the way;
"Maiden stay," he whisper'd,
"Maiden stay," he whisper'd,

"O pretty maiden, stay!"

"Why art thou walking abroad alone?
The stars are shining, the day is done."
O then her tears they began to flow,

For a dark eyed sailor,
For a dark eyed sailor
Had filled her heart with woe.

"Three years are pass'd since he left this land,
A ring of gold he took off my hand,
He broke the token, a half to keep,
Half he bade me treasure,
Half he bade me treasure,
Then crossed the briny deep."

"O drive him damsel from out your mind,
For men are changeful as is the wind,
And love inconstant will quickly grow,
Cold as winter morning,
Cold as winter morning

When lands are white with snow."

"Above the snow is the holly seen,
In bitter blast it abideth green,
And blood-red drops it as berries bears,
So my aching bosom,
So my aching bosom,
Its truth and sorrow wears!"

Then half the ring did the sailor show,
Away with weeping and sorrow now!
In bands of marriage united we,
Like the broken Token,
Like the broken Token
In one shall welded be.[67]

The Broken Token

Anon

Fig. 7.9

James Parsons, who lived in the nearby village of Lewdown,[68] provided about twenty-five ballads and songs, including some that appeared to be "of a very early and archaic character, certainly not later than the reign of Henry VII."[69] As he lived so close to Lew Trenchard, he would occasionally walk over to spend an evening with Baring-Gould, who naturally encouraged him to sing and to talk about his repertoire. This brief account of Parsons is to be found in *Old Country Life:*

> James Parsons, a very infirm man, over seventy, asthmatic and failing, has been a labourer all his life, and for the greater part of it on one farm. His father was famed through the whole country side as "The Singing Machine," he was considered to be inexhaustible. Alas! he is no more, and his old son shakes his head and professes to have but half the ability, memory, and musical faculty that were possessed by his father. He can neither read nor write. From him I have obtained some of the earliest melodies and most archaic forms of ballads. Indeed the majority of his airs are in the old church modes, and generally end on the dominant.[70]

Another pen-portrait written a couple of years later reveals more about the two men's relationship: how they sang together, and the way in which Parsons regarded himself as the vicar's tutor in matters of song:

> He sits by a settle by my hall fire, turns up his eyes, crosses his hands on his breast, and sings. Then I sing after him, and he is most particular that I should have all the turns right. "You mun give thickey (that) a bit stronger," he says—and by stronger he means take a tone or semitone higher. He will not allow the smallest deviation from

what he has to impart. "It's just no use at all," says he, "my singing to you if you won't follow correct. Thickey turn came out of your head, not mine!" Then I must go back again till I have got the tune exact. "I be maister, and you be scholar," he says, "and a scholar mun learn what he be taught; and larn it right."[71]

Baring-Gould made good use of Parsons's large repertoire in *Songs and Ballads of the West*. More than twenty songs are attributed to him, including "Roving Jack," "As Johnny Walked Out," "The Saucy Sailor," "The Squire and the Fair Maid," "My Ladye's Coach," "A Sweet Pretty Maiden," "The Forsaken Maiden," "The Warson Hunt," "The Green Bushes," "Nancy," "Fair Girl, Mind This!" "The Blackbird," "The Drowned Lover," and "The Wreck Off Scilly." One of the first items the clergyman heard from this singer was two verses of a song that is usually called "Let No Man Steal Your Thyme" but which Baring-Gould renamed "Flowers and Weeds." It had a poetic lyric and an attractive melody, and Baring-Gould would subsequently collect another, more complete, text and a variant of the tune from one of his most prolific Cornish informants, Joseph Dyer. This is the original version from Parsons:

In my garden grew plenty of thyme,
It would flourish by night and by day;
O'er the wall came a lad, he took all that I had,
And stole my thyme away,
[And he stole my thyme all away].

My garden with heart's ease was bright,
And pansy so pied and so gay,
One slipped through the gate, and alas! cruel fate,
My heart's ease stole away,
[My heart's ease he stole all away].[72]

Flowers and Weeds

Anon

Fig. 7.10

One of the most interesting, if puzzling, of James Parsons's ballads is "The Bonny Bunch of Roses." The standard version of this song is at once a love lament and a quasi-allegorical commentary on the rise and fall of Napoleon Bonaparte, in which the bunch of roses stands for the British Isles. Baring-Gould noted that he and Sheppard had "taken down a great number of versions" of this very popular ballad, and remarked that "the melody is everywhere the same, with insignificant variations, and a very fresh and charming air it is."[73] Fleetwood Sheppard noted the tune in the field in October 1888 from an anonymous singer at South Brent who may have been Robert Hard rather than Parsons. In *Songs and Ballads of the West* Baring-Gould and Sheppard changed the key from B-flat to C, made some minor adjustments to the rhythm, and evened out the tempo. In "The Personal Copy," on the other hand, the tune is written in the key of B-flat and the singer gives the impression of speeding up at the end. Yet if the changes made to the tune for publication were minor, the same was not true for the lyric. The ballad is best known from an early nineteenth-century broadside version, in which the protagonist is clearly Napoleon, and Baring-Gould possessed a copy. But the song was also extant in oral tradition in Devon, and he noted several different versions. One, taken down from William Friend of Lydford, was similar to the broadside, while Robert Hard's variant also had Napoleon as the protagonist. However, we find a different variant in one of Baring-Gould's field notebooks. It has only three verses:

Beside the rolling ocean, all in the month of June,
When feathered, warbling songsters were changing note and tune,
I overheard a damsel complain in words of woe,
With tears on cheek, she thus did speak, O for the bunch of Roses, O.

Then up and spake Charles Edward, "That rosy bunch I'll gain,
But flowers such I doubt not are hardly plucked at whim,
The roses are with prickles set and dyed with blood I trow,
No sharper thorn of bush is born, than is the bunch of Roses, O.

Then sadly spake his mother, the tear was in her eye,
"Adventure not, my gallant son, or surely thou wilt die.
Thy father he adventured and now his head lies low,
Be then afraid, his mother said, of the bunch of Roses O"[74]

The Bunch of Roses

Anon

Fig. 7.11

Evidently this fragment is not about the Napoleonic wars but is an anti-Jacobite song from a century earlier. The text of James Parsons's version in "The Personal Copy" has no explicit "Charles Edward" reference but in other respects three of its five verses are similar to this fragment. In *Songs and Ballads of the West* Baring-Gould commented that "the song is unmistakably an anti-Jacobite production, adapted at the beginning of the century to Napoleon, when an additional verse was added relative to Moscow. In this later form it issued from Catnach's press."[75] He omitted that extra verse and other Napoleonic references in order to restore the Jacobite provenance of the original song. For his text he used a composite of Parsons's version and the fragment in the "Plymouth Notebook." This was the result, a composite in which neither text nor tune was exactly as noted in the field, although both were close. Baring-Gould's practice would not be acceptable by modern editorial standards, but he would have likely argued that the end justified the means in this case:

Beside the rolling ocean, one morning in the month of June,
The feathered warbling songsters were sweetly changing note and tune.
I overheard a damsel fair complain in bitter woe,
With tear on cheek, she thus did speak, "O for the bonny bunch of roses, O!"

Then up and spake her lover and grasped the maiden by the hand,
"Have patience, fairest, patience! A legion I will soon command.
I'll raise ten thousand soldiers brave, thro' pain and peril I will go,
A branch will break, for thy sweet sake, a branch of the bonny Bunch of Roses, O!"

Then sadly said his mother, "As tough as truest heart of oak,
That stem that bears the roses, and is not easy bent or broke.
Thy father he essayed it first and now in France his head lies low,
For sharpest thorn is ever borne, O by the bonny Bunch of Roses, O!

He raised a mighty army and many nobles joined his throng,
With pipe and banner flying to pluck the rose he march'd along:
The stem he found was far too tough, and piercing sharp the thorn, I trow;
No blossom he rent from the tree, all of the bonny Bunch of Roses, O!"

"O mother, dearest mother! I lie upon my dying bed,
And like my gallant father must hide an uncrowned, humbled head.
Let none henceforth essay to touch that rose so red, or full of woe,
With bleeding hand he'll fly the Land, the land of the bonny Bunch of Roses, O!"[76]

The Bonny Bunch of Roses

Anon

"O, for the bon-ny bunch of ros-es, O!"

Fig. 7.12

Roger Luxton was another elderly Devonian countryman who still knew the old songs. Luxton was a farm laborer whose outlook on life typified that of an older generation for whom Baring-Gould had a great deal of affection and respect. His sketch of Luxton attempted to reproduce the old man's character and mode of speech as well as his opinions on music and the modern world:

At Halwell, in North Devon, lives a fine old man named Roger Luxton, aged seventy-six, a great-grandfather, with bright eyes and an intelligent face. He stays about among his grandchildren, but is usually found at the picturesque farm-house of a daughter at Halwell, called Croft. This old man was once very famous as a song-man, but his memory fails him as to a good number of the ballads he was wont to sing. "Ah, your honour," said he, "in old times us used to be welcome in every farm-house, at all shearing and haysel and harvest feasts; but, bless'y! now the farmers' da'ters all learn the pianny, and zing nort but twittery sorts of pieces that have nother music nor sense in them; and they don't care to hear us, and any decent sort of music. And there be now no more shearing and haysel and harvest feasts. All them things be given up. 'Taint the same world as used to be - 'tain't so cheerful. Folks don't zing over their work, and laugh after it. There be no dances for the youngsters as there used to was. The farmers be too grand to care to talk to us old chaps, and for certain don't care to hear us zing. Why for nigh on forty years us old zinging-fellows have been drove to the public-houses to zing, and to a different quality of hearers too. And now I reckon the labouring folk be so tree-mendous edicated that they don't care to hear our old songs nother. 'Tis all *Pop goes the Weasel* and *Ehren on the Rhine* now. I reckon folks now have got different ears from what they used to have, and different hearts too. More's the pity." [77]

Luxton's repertoire was smaller than that of some of Baring-Gould's other informants, but to *Songs and Ballads of the West* he contributed "Henry Martyn," "Plymouth Sound," "Furze Bloom," and "Constant Johnny." He also sang "Rosemary Lane," but the clerical songhunter considered it unsuitable for polite ears, commenting that "the words are objectionable." However, a short text is extant in the "Killerton Notebook":

I served my apprentice in Rosemary Lane,
To keep the good will of my master and dame.
A sailor came by, and he wanted to lie,
And there it began all my misery.

The sailor was drowsy and laid down his head,
He asked for a candle to light him to bed,
I lit him to bed, as another might do,
Said he, "Pretty maid, come my bed now unto."

A silly young maiden I thought it no harm,
To lie in his bed and keep his back warm,

But what happened then I will never declare,
I would that short night was extended seven year.

Next morning so early the sailor arose,
And into my apron three guineas he throws,
Saying, "Take these, my dearest, a fare on my score,
Ten thousand times [indistinct] that t'is all [indistinct] o'er.

And if 'tis a girl she shall sit at her ease,
And if it's a boy he shall cross the salt seas,
With his slight little shoes and his ribbons to fly,
And climb the high rigging, ten thousand feet high."[78]

One of Baring-Gould's more prolific informants was John Woodrich, an ex-blacksmith from Wollacott Moor, near Thrushelton, Devon. Woodrich, whom Baring-Gould described as "a small, dwarfish man, living in a lonely spot," had been the youngest of fourteen children and had spent much of his childhood living with his grandmother, from whom he learned many songs and ballads. His father was a pub singer, and after returning to his parent's house at the age of ten, the boy learned a different kind of repertoire. In his mid-teens he ran away from home, and rambled about the country, finding work, wages and more songs wherever he could. This itinerant life eventually got him into serious trouble. He had obtained a job as a blacksmith's assistant (operating the bellows), married a pretty young woman, and started a family, but domesticity was more than he could endure. He got bored and his wanderlust returned. Refusing to let his family chain him down, he deserted them, and ended up as a vagrant in Wales. Because his sick wife and his children then became a burden on the parish ratepayers, he was tracked down and thrown in jail. His wife died of cancer, and when Baring-Gould found him he was earning a meagre living as a stone-breaker. Yet he had a good voice and was always welcome in the local pubs, where, as Baring-Gould put it, "he got his drink for nothing out of his own pocket."[79] His travels had given him a large stock of tavern songs, and, as he readily explained, he had inherited from his father an ability to quickly and easily learn new ones. This was apparently no idle boast. Baring-Gould noted that Ginger Jack, as he was known, could "generally pick up a melody and retain it, if he has heard it sung once; that of a song twice sung, he knows words and music, and rarely, if ever, requires to have it sung a third time to perfect him."[80] Woodrich was a character with a dubious reputation and a checkered career, but this does not seem to have bothered Baring-Gould, who counted him as a "valuable man."[81]

Among the many songs in Ginger Jack's repertoire were "Go Way from My Window," "Green Broom," "Haymaking Song," "The Blue Kerchief," "The Rout Is Out," "The Gipsy Countess," "The Everlasting Circle," and two songs that Baring-Gould considered required completely new lyrics for drawing-room consumption, "The Mallard" and "The Oxford Tragedy." "Blue Muslin," a variant of "The Keys of Canterbury," was a cumulative song and the singer had to be sure to get the verses of the second half in exactly reverse order, a challenge when drunk. Woodrich told Baring-Gould that he would often sing it in a pub to show that he was still sober and could be offered another pint or two.

"O will you accept of the mus-e-lin so blue,
To wear all in the morning, and to dabble in the dew?"
"No, I will not accept of the mus-e-lin so blue,
To wear all in the morning, and to dabble in the dew,

Nor to walk, nor to talk with you!"

"O will you accept of the pretty silver pin,
To pin your golden hair with the fine mus-e-lin?"

"No, I will not accept of the pretty silver pin,
To pin my golden hair with the fine mus-e-lin,

Nor I'll walk, nor I'll talk with you!"

Blue Muslin

Anon

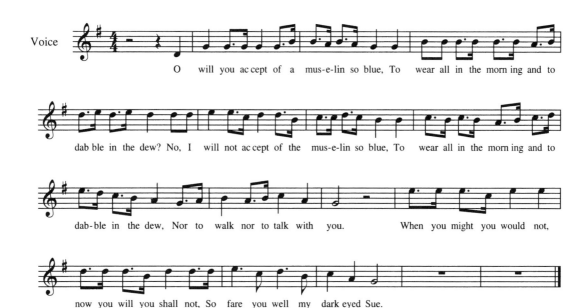

Fig. 7.13

"O will you accept of a pair of shoes of cork,
The one is made in London, the other's made in York?"
"No, I will not accept of a pair of shoes of cork,
The one that's made in London, the other's made in York,
Nor I'll walk, nor I'll talk with you!"

"O will you accept of the keys of Canterbury,
That all the bells of England may ring and make us merry?"
"No, I will not accept of the keys of Canterbury,
That all the bells of England may ring and make us merry,
Nor I'll walk, nor I'll talk with you!"

"O will you accept of a kiss from a loving heart,
That we may join together and never more may part?"
"Yes, I will accept of a kiss from a loving heart,
That we may join together and never more may part,
And I'll walk and I'll talk with you!"
"When you might you would not,
Now you will you shall not,
So fare you well, my dark-eyed Sue."

"O will you accept of the keys of Canterbury,
That all the bells of England may ring and make us merry?"
"Yes, I'll accept of the keys of Canterbury,
That all the bells of England may ring and make us merry,
And I'll walk and I'll talk with you!"

"When you might you would not,

Now you will you shall not,
So fare you well, my dark-eyed Sue."

"O will you accept of a pair of shoes of cork,
The one is made in London, the other's made in York?"
"Yes, I'll accept of a pair of shoes of cork,
The one that's made in London, the other's made in York,
And I'll walk and I'll talk with you!"

"When you might you would not,
Now you will you shall not,
So fare you well, my dark-eyed Sue."

"O will you accept of the pretty silver pin,
To pin your golden hair with the fine mus-e-lin?"
"Yes, I'll accept of the pretty silver pin,
To pin my golden hair with the fine mus-e-lin,
And I'll walk and I'll talk with you!"

"When you might you would not,
Now you will you shall not,
So fare you well, my dark-eyed Sue."

"O will you accept of the mus-e-lin so blue,
To wear all in the morning, and to dabble in the dew?"
"Yes, I'll accept of the mus-e-lin so blue,
To wear all in the morning, and to dabble in the dew,

And I'll walk and I'll talk with you!"   Now you will you shall not,
                                                                    So fare you well, my dark-eyed Sue."[82]
"When you might you would not,

As one further illustration of the type of amateur singer who supplied Baring-Gould with material, here is his depiction of Cornish artisan James Olver:

> Another of my singers is James Olver, a fine, hale old man, with a face fresh as a rose, and silver hair, a grand old patriarchal man, who has been all his life a tanner. He is a Cornishman, a native of St. Kewe. His father was musical, but a Methodist, and so strict that he would never allow his children to sing a ballad or any profane song in his hearing, and fondly fancied that they grew up in ignorance of such things. But the very fact that they were tabooed gave young Olver and his sister a great thirst to learn, digest, and sing them. He acquired them from itinerant ballad-singers, from miners, and from the village song-men. Olver was apprenticed to a tanner at Liskeard.[83]

Among Olver's many songs Baring-Gould singled out "Ormond the Brave" as one of the rarest and oldest political ballads that he had found anywhere, but other songs in the Cornishman's repertoire included "Why Should We Be Dullards Sad?" "Come My Lads, Let Us Be Jolly," "The Grey Mare," "The Wrestling Match," "The Duke's Hunt," and "The *Golden Vanity*." Olver was just one of three informants from whom he noted "The Streams of Nancy." This was a song which particularly intrigued the clergyman. It is a beautiful love lyric, set in a place not clearly identified but which was probably on the mainland opposite St. Michael's Mount in Cornwall. The "Plymouth Fair Copy Manuscript" and "The Personal Copy" each give four variants of the tune and five versions of the lyric, the latter taken mainly from broadsides. The broadside texts were more elaborate than those collected from oral tradition, and it appears likely that James Olver's version of the song derived from the Davenport broadside, of which Baring-Gould already had a copy when they first met in May 1889. The only set of words that Baring-Gould obtained aurally from an informant were three verses that he noted from Matthew Baker in July 1889. The melody was obtained from Olver; this is how F. W. Bussell transcribed it:[84]

The Streams of Nancy

Anon

Fig. 7.14

O the sweet streams of Nancy,   They do meet their sweethearts.
They divide in two parts,   There in drinking strong liquor
Where the young men in dancing   It makes my heart sing,

And the sound of the viol	And it shines in the night.
It does make my heart ring.	
	On yonder high moorland
On yonder tall mountain	The wild fowl do fly;
A castle doth stand.	There is one fair among them
It is built of white ivory	Soars than others more high.
All above the black sand.	My heart is an eagle
All of ivory builded,	With wings wide outspread,
And of diamonds bright,	It soareth and flyeth
And with gold it is gilded	In pursuit of my maid.[85]

About the song Baring-Gould commented:

Taken down from Matthew Baker, a cripple, aged 72, who can neither read nor write, Lew Trenchard. Music noted down by Mr. Sheppard. Again from James Olver, Launceston, and from Matthew Ford, shoemaker, Menheniot, practically the same melody. This song is "The Streams of lovely Nancy," of the broadsides. It was printed in 1830 by Keys of Davenport...The Nancy of the broadsides is Nant-(something or other). Nant or Nan is firstly a falling stream, and then secondly a valley or glen. Nankivell is the Horse-vale, Nanteglos the church-dale, Nanvean is the small vale; there are hundreds of dales and streams with names beginning Nan or Nant, in Cornwall.[86]

When he came to print the song in *Songs and Ballads of the West,* Baring-Gould modified the title, and rewrote some of the words, borrowing a few phrases from a broadside, although he used Matthew Baker's text as the basis for his reconstruction. He preferred Baker's tune to Olver's. This was the result:

The Streams of Nantsian

Anon

Fig. 7.15

O the streams of Nantsian in two parts divide,
Where the young men in dancing meet sweethearts and bride,
They will take no denial, we must frolic and sing,
And the sound of the viol, O it makes my heart ring.

On the rocky cliff yonder a castle up-stands;

To the seamen a wonder above the black sands.
'Tis of ivory builded with diamonds glazed bright,
And with gold it is gilded, to shine in the night.

Over yonder high mountain the wild fowl do fly,
And in ocean's deep fountain the fairest pearls lie.
On eagle's wings soaring, I'll speed as the wind;
Ocean's fountain exploring, my true love I'll find.

O the streams of Nantsian divide in two parts,
And rejoin as in dancing do lads their sweethearts.
So the streams, bright and shining, tho' parted in twain,
Re-unite, intertwining, once henceforth remain.[87]

It would be easy to cull from *Old Country Life* and *Further Reminiscences* additional pen-portraits of singers, or to quote several picturesque stories about how Baring-Gould collected such ballads as "The Trees They Are So High" (from Matthew Baker), "The Death of Queen Jane," "The Duke's Hunt" (both from miner Sam Fone), "King John and the Abbot of Canterbury" (from an old woman at Kingswear), or "The Bold Dragoon" (from a youth named Moses Cleve at Huccaby on Dartmoor). One more must suffice. Where he had no contacts in a community, Baring-Gould's method of collecting was to go to the local public house in the hope that it would prove to be the gathering place for local singers. He and Bussell did this on one occasion (the year is unspecified) at the village of Two Bridges, in the heart of Dartmoor:

> One New Year's Eve, Mr. Bussell and I were at the "Saracen's Head," an inn at Two Bridges, on Dartmoor. It has since become an important hotel. Then it was but a modest tavern. We sat in the kitchen in the evening, where a number of moor-men were gathered to drink and welcome the New Year. One of the singers gave us "Barbara," or, as he called her, Barbaroo-Allen, with some additional verses to those in print. This was capped by another, who sang "The Brown Girl," of a somewhat similar character...But the most delightful melody we then obtained was "The Bell-ringers." We learned something from the singers; not to press these men to give more, at a time, than a limited number of songs, for they are inclined to mix the tunes.[88]

The title of the last song mentioned here by Baring-Gould was actually "The Bell Ringing." It was noted from William George Kerswell, an elderly moorland farmer, and Baring-Gould commented that when he sang it beside a roaring fire in the pub's kitchen, "his clear, robust voice imitating the bells," the effect produced had "an indescribable charm."[89]

One day in October,
Neither drunken nor sober,
O'er Broadbury Down I was wending my way,
When I heard of some ringing,
Some dancing and singing,
I ought to remember that Jubilee Day.

Refrain: 'Twas in Ashwater town,
The bells they did sound,
They rang for a belt and a hat laced with gold.
But the men of North Lew
Rang so steady and true,
That never were better in Devon, I hold.

'Twas misunderstood,
For the men of Broadwood,
Gave a blow on the tenor should never have been.
But the men of North Lew,
Rang so faultlessly true,
A difficult matter to beat them I ween.
Refrain: 'Twas in Ashwater town, etc.

They of Broadwood being naughty
Then said to our party,

We'll ring you a challenge again in a round;
We'll give you the chance,
At St. Stephen's or Launceston,
The prize to the winner's a note of five pound.
Refrain: 'Twas in Callington town
The bells next did sound, etc.

When the match it came on,
At good Callington,
The bells they rang out o'er the valleys below.
Then old and young people,
The hale and the feeble,
They came out to hear the sweet bell music flow.
Refrain: 'Twas at Callington town
The bells then did sound, etc.

Those of Broadwood once more
Were obliged to give o'er,
They were beaten completely and done in a round.
For the men of North Lew
Pull so steady and true,
That no better than they in the West can be found.
Refrain: 'Twas in Ashwater town,
Then at Callington town, etc.[90]

The Bell Ringing

Anon

One day in Oct-o-ber, neither drunk en nor sob-er, O'er Broad bur-y Down I was

wend ing my way, When I heard of some ring ing, some danc ing and sing ing, I ought to re mem ber that

Jub-il-ee day. 'Twas in Ash-wat-er town, the bells they did sound, They rang for a belt and a

hat laced with gold, But the men of North Lew rang so stead-y and true.., that nev-er were bet-ter in

Dev-on I hold.

Fig. 7.16

It was indeed the tunes that Baring-Gould was primarily seeking. As we have seen, he gave the impression that in the main he obtained them not from well-to-do farmers but from agricultural workers and artisans of the lowest social class. These informants were usually uneducated, and were prone to alter or even make nonsense of the words of ballads, but the best of them had an ear for traditional melody that enchanted the song-hunting cleric. These are Baring-Gould's reflections in *Further Reminiscences* on the class and gender of his singers:

> It was necessary to drop to a lower level [than that of farmers and yeomen] if we were to tap the spring of tradi-
> tional music. I speedily discovered that what I wanted was to be obtained mainly from such men as could neither
> read nor write. At the outset we did not attempt to extort songs from the old women; in fact, we worked that field
> very little, and very inadequately.[91]

However, it seems that this generalization should have been heavily qualified because there were many exceptions to the rule. In the main, it appears that Baring-Gould exaggerated the age, rusticity, and low social class of his informants. According to Chris Bearman's research, nearly half those traceable in census returns were either much the same age as Baring-Gould or younger, while about a third were either farmers or tradesmen.[92] As regards his source singers' reliability as informants, Baring-Gould made the following interesting comments:

> I soon learned to mistrust the words of the songs, which were often, but not always, corruptions of Broadside Bal-
> lads, transmitted orally. Thus "the Northern Knight" was changed to "the Northern Cat," and the expression "And
> she the laurel wore" had become "And she was lorriowere." In the ballad of "Death and the Lady," the former was
> described as "he was of the Branchy Tree," in place of "he was an Anatomy." The printed ballads of Such, Fortey,
> Ryle, Catnach and others are not trustworthy. The Broadside Ballad publishers received the songs and ballads that
> they printed from itinerant singers, extremely illiterate, who had themselves received them orally, and had cor-
> rupted them unintentionally...There were, however, a certain number of ballads that we received from our "song-

men," that were obviously more correct in diction than those produced by the publishers who furnished the sheets that were hawked about at fairs. That which became daily more evident was that the melodies were incomparably more valuable than the words. The latter might be borrowed, and be in common circulation over England, but the tunes were for the most part local. And, what was more, the melodies had a character of their own distinct from those of Somerset and Dorset.[93]

The melodies, then, were in Baring-Gould's eyes the most important thing, and he eventually concluded that they derived from one or other of two sources: the village bards themselves, or "the ancient wandering minstrels, whose tunes live still, orally transmitted through many generations."[94] In his view such folk melodies were "the expression of the minds, artistic sense, and feelings of the people, just as truly as are the songs of the thrush, blackbird and nightingale."[95] In *Old Country Life* Baring-Gould developed a quite elaborate account of the decline and transformation of English minstrelsy in the late Tudor and Jacobean eras. He argued that the Elizabethan government had hounded itinerant musicians as "sturdy rogues and vagabonds," and that the Puritan governments of the Commonwealth had driven secular music underground. This killed the musical life of urban England that had flourished under the early Tudors, but it made remote villages the refuge of thousands of unemployed professional musicians and their instruments, and thus stimulated rural music making in an unprecedented manner. The village bard or "song-man" was therefore the successor to the medieval minstrel, and in Baring-Gould's view the oral tradition carried by such bards had preserved the old ballads and songs of the early Tudor era. He acknowledged that the broadside had also played its part in the process of transmission, but he regarded the communal memory of the song-man as more important:

> The village bard or song-man is the descendant of the minstrel. Now the minstrels were put down by Act of Parliament in 1597, and were to be dealt with by the magistrates with severity as rogues and vagabonds. That sealed the doom of the old ballad. All such as were produced later are tame and flat in comparison with the genuine songs of the old times, and can at best be regarded only as modern imitations. The press has preserved in Broadsides a good number of ballads, and *The Complete Dancing Master* and other collections have saved a good number of the old tunes from being irrevocably lost. But by no means all were thus preserved; a great many more continued to be sung by our peasantry, and I quite believe the old men when they say, that at one time they knew some one hundred and fifty to two hundred distinct songs and melodies; their memories were really extraordinary. But then they could neither read nor write, and the faculty of remembering was developed in them to a remarkable extent.[96]

As examples of early songs that survived in this way, Baring-Gould cited not only the Robin Hood songs and such Child ballads as "Chevy Chace," "King Henry V's Conquest of France," "Barbara Allen," and "The *Golden Vanity*," but also such ballads and songs as "The Golden Glove," "The Maid and the Box," "Early One Morning," "Cupid's Garden," and "Spanish Ladies." He was uncomfortable with the convenient, but in his view misleading, division of ballads into two categories: traditional and broadside. He was convinced that there were genuinely traditional ballads that Child had missed or had deliberately omitted, and he even tried sending Child a few that he had collected.[97] The fundamental problem, however, was that "the old fellows who had these songs were fast dying off, and their sons and grandsons despised the ballads and the tunes in the Gregorian mode, and sang only the last vulgar music-hall ditties." There was therefore no time to be lost in saving these precious melodies for posterity.[98]

All this said, it is by no means clear that Baring-Gould had already come to these views in the late 1880s when he was collecting the songs that would appear, sometimes in rather transformed guise, in *Songs and Ballads of the West*. That statement that he "soon learned" to distrust broadside texts and the impression that he quickly recognized that orally transmitted versions of ballads were often "obviously more correct in diction" may be deceptive. It is possible that the learning process was much slower, and was even influenced by the views promulgated by Cecil Sharp in *English Folk-Song: Some Conclusions* (1907), views that he certainly expressed to Baring-Gould during the period of collaboration that culminated in Sharp's role as music editor for *Songs of the West*. Initially, as he acknowledged, Baring-Gould had the impression that much of his singers' material, in particular their narrative songs, were derived ultimately from broadside ballads, even if they themselves had received them through oral transmission from their parents or other older singers. In time he amassed a considerable library of broadsides, so he certainly knew whereof he spoke, but it is one thing to make the aesthetic judgment, as Cecil Sharp and many other collectors and literary critics have done, that the best versions of ballads noted from oral tradition surpass in quality the broadside versions, and quite another to assume, without evidence, that the broadsides were inferior copies of older traditional folk ballads. In reality the print and oral traditions intermingled in a complex way from the sixteenth century onwards, and, on the whole, it is rare for ballads to have been noted from oral tradition at an earlier date than the oldest broadside printing. This fact may give a false impression that the broadsides were usually the origin of both print and oral traditions but, *prima facie*, that *is* what much of the evidence would seem to suggest. Baring-Gould may therefore have been correct first time around, and his later thesis of a continuous line of oral transmission between medieval minstrel and nineteenth-century village bard may have been a reasonable hypothesis that now seems less likely to be true.

One would like to know even more about Baring-Gould's informants than he told us, but this eccentric clergyman must be credited as the first song hunter to be genuinely interested in the singers as well as the songs. He was the first folksong editor to tell his readers about the lives and characters of his informants. He was also one of the first to provide fairly detailed notes about his sources for each item that he printed. Admittedly, he did not do so in a very systematic way, and in a few cases the singers remained anonymous or were given pseudonyms (but only in works such as *Further Reminiscences*, not in the notes to *Songs and Ballads of the West* or "The Personal Copy"), but the fact remains that, by and large, one obtains from Baring-Gould much more information about the sources of the songs he collected and the singers who performed them than from any other Victorian folksong collector.

Songs and Ballads of the West

According to Baring-Gould's own testimony, he was actively engaged in folksong research for well over a decade, and he never ceased to be interested in the subject.[99] Yet it is one thing to make a collection of folksongs 'in the field' and another to make those songs publicly available in published form. Baring-Gould had no intention of sitting on his findings. As a successful novelist, he had the connections with publishers needed to get his work into print in a timely manner. So it was not long before the first fruits of his and Sheppard's initial researches in Devon and Cornwall appeared in print. As we have seen, the first fascicle of *Songs and Ballads of the West, a Collection made from the Mouths of the People* was published in 1889, and three more parts appeared during the next three years.[100] H. Fleetwood Sheppard was credited as co-collector and co-editor. A second (collected) edition in a single volume appeared in 1895, and then a third edition in 1905. There were significant differences between these editions. The first two were very similar, each including one hundred and ten songs, although Baring-Gould did change two of them and he also rewrote many of the notes, usually including additional information about the songs and/or singers but sometimes cutting out material too. The two songs that were omitted, "Thomasine Enys" and "On the Settle," were both original compositions by Baring-Gould himself, set to tunes composed by Sheppard. In response to criticism by Frank Kidson and Lucy Broadwood of their inclusion in a collection of folksongs they were replaced by a ballad, "Ormond the Brave" and by a folk lyric, "The Oxen Ploughing."

The third edition, however, was titled *Songs of the West: Folk Songs of Devon and Cornwall*, and F. W. Bussell was added as one of the collectors, while Cecil Sharp was named as the new musical editor.[101] That new edition omitted twenty-four songs that had been included in one or other of the earlier ones but, in compensation, added thirty-three new songs. As explained earlier, it also drew on material from *A Garland of Country Song*, so it was really a 'best of' compilation. Another change was in the way the songs were arranged: all three editions provided both tunes and text, with the melodies harmonized for piano accompaniment. In the first two editions the accompaniments, which were quite elaborate, were the work of Sheppard, who had collected almost all of the tunes. Most of the additional tunes in the third edition had been collected by Bussell, and the piano arrangements, which were simpler, were by Cecil Sharp. Lucy Broadwood and Frank Kidson, among others, judged Sharp's less florid arrangements to be a significant improvement, but Baring-Gould himself seems to have preferred Sheppard's.

Editorial responsibility for the song-texts in all three editions seems to have been primarily, perhaps exclusively, in the hands of Baring-Gould, although he consulted Sharp when selecting the songs to be added to and omitted from the 1905 edition.[102] The net result was that, taken together, *Songs of the West* and the two editions of *Songs and Ballads of the West* presented in total one hundred and forty-three songs, rather less than half the approximately three hundred "airs" that Baring-Gould stated that he and his collaborators had collected between 1888 and 1895.[103]

The importance of *Songs and Ballads of the West* was three-fold. To start with, this very substantial and original publication presented both tunes and texts for every item that was included. Although it had but rarely been the case in the past, this practice now established a norm that would usually be followed by other collectors in the future. Second, the collection was a major regional survey which contained a large number of songs that would quickly become well known examples of the genre, and variants of which would be discovered in other parts of the United Kingdom. Some of the best-known folksongs included in it were "The Trees They Are So High," "Sweet Nightingale," "Widdecombe Fair," "The Bonny Bunch of Roses," "Green Bushes," "Henry Martyn," "The Painful Plough," "The *Golden Vanity*," "Strawberry Fair," "The Spotted Cow," "John Barleycorn," "Flora, Lily of the West," and "The Keeper." As such, *Songs and Ballads of the West* helped to define what a "folksong" was, and the term was used confidently in the revised title of the third edition. Third, there was the claim made in the subtitle to all three editions that this was a collection made entirely from oral tradition. Baring-Gould backed up this claim by discussing the age, occupation, and/or place of residence of some of his principal informants, and often (although not always) referencing these source singers in the notes to each song. While this claim was by no means always valid for the song texts, it was apparently largely true for the melodies.

Having provided a preliminary indication of the rich fare to be found in *Songs and Ballads of the West,* let us now examine in a little more detail the contents of this chaotic collection. The one hundred and ten songs in *Songs and Ballads of the West* seem not to have been arranged in any particular order. There was no subdivision of the book into sections, nor do the contents appear to have been grouped by theme or subject matter. Baring-Gould did not even trouble to separate ballads from folk lyrics, let alone distinguish between traditional (or Child) ballads and broadside ballads. Perhaps a quarter of the items were ballads (in the sense of narrative songs with events and consequences). Although there were not many West Country versions of Child ballads in the collection there were a lot of other narrative songs. While many of these appear to have been derived from broadsides, others, such as "The Trees They Do Grow High," were traditional ballads that apparently fitted Child's (admittedly imprecise) notion of a "popular" ballad. Certainly they had become vernacular ballads in Devon or neighboring counties. Only a few of them would be accepted by Child into his canon although others perhaps should have been. "Cold Blows the Wind" was a variant of "The Unquiet Grave" (Child no. 78), and Baring-Gould noted it from several of his informants, including John Woodrich, Sally Satterley (aka Mary Satcherley), and Ann Roberts of Scobbetor, Widdecombe-in-the-Moor.[104] Five other items were versions of ballads that Child would include in the final two volumes of *The English and Scottish Popular Ballads,* namely "The Gipsy Countess" (Child no. 200, "The Gypsy Laddie"), "Dead Maid's Land" (Child no. 219, "The Gardener"), "Henry Martyn" (Child no. 250), "The Silly Old Man" (Child no. 283, "The Crafty Farmer"), and "The *Golden Vanity*" (Child no. 286). The most unusual of these was "Dead Maid's Land," and this is the ballad as Baring-Gould printed it in *Songs and Ballads of the West:*

Dead Maid's Land

Anon

Fig. 7.17

There stood a gardener at the gate
And in each hand a flower;
"O pretty maid, come in," he said,
"And view my beauteous bower."

"The lily it shall be thy smock,
The jonquil shoe thy feet;
Thy gown shall be the ten-week stock,
To make thee fair and sweet.

The gilly-flower shall deck thy head,
The way with herbs I'll strew,
Thy stockings shall be marigold,
Thy gloves the vi'let blue."

"I will not have the gilly-flower
Nor herbs my path to strew,

Nor stockings of the marigold,
Nor gloves of vi'let blue.

I will not have the ten-week stock,
Nor jonquils to my shoon;
But I will have the red, red rose,
That flow'reth sweet in June."

"The red, red rose it hath a thorn
That pierceth to the bone."
"I little heed thy idle rede;
I will have that or none."

"The red, red rose it hath a thorn,
That pierceth to the heart."
"The red, red rose, O I will have,
I little heed the smart."

She stooped down unto the ground
To pluck the rose so red,
The thorn it pierced her to the heart,
And this fair maid was dead.

There stood a gardener at the gate,
With cypress in his hand.
And he did say, "Let no fair may
Come into Dead Maid's Land."[105]

It is interesting to compare this version with the one that Baring-Gould collected in 1889 from Joseph Paddon of Holcombe Burnell in North Devon. Paddon's words were much the same, except that he began the song with three verses that are usually associated with "The Seeds of Love." His tune was also very similar to that usually used for "The Seeds of Love" and it was quite different from the one given above. Here is Paddon's tune, with the three extra verses:

A garden was planted around with flowers of every kind,
I chose of the best to wear in my breast the flowers best pleased my mind,
The flowers best pleased my mind.

A gardener standing by I asked to choose for me,
He chose the lily, the violet, the pink, but I liked none of the three,
But I liked none of the three.

A violet I don't like, a lily it fades so soon,
But as for the pink I cared not a flink, I said I would stop till June,
I said I would stop till June.[106]

Dead Maid's Land

Anon

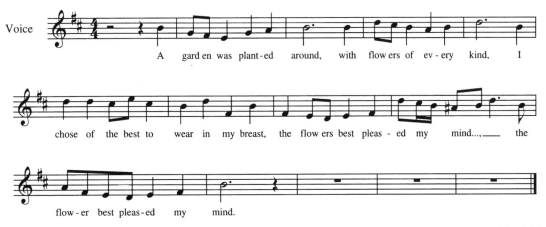

Fig. 7.18

It was understandable that Baring-Gould should decide to omit these extra verses since they belonged to another song and were, in any case, redundant in "Dead Maid's Land." But why had he dispensed with Paddon's tune, and where had his alternative tune come from? The answer was to be found in his notes. With Paddon's tune in mind, he had written a song of his own, "Shower and Sunshine," and this he printed as the next item in the book. Rather than use the same melody twice, he had cast about for an alternative tune for "Dead Maid's Land." Fleetwood Sheppard had noted a distinctive melody from Ann Roberts's singing of "Cold Blows the Wind" that conveniently fitted the meter and mood of "Dead Maid's Land." In the major it was a hymn tune, but in the minor it sounded like a traditional ballad air. So this had become the new tune for "Dead Maid's Land."[107] It was an example of Baring-Gould's creative editing at its most interventionist.

Most of the other narrative songs in *Songs and Ballads of the West* would normally be classified as broadside ballads, although many had a traditional feel to them and Baring-Gould had collected versions of them all from oral tradition in Devon and/or Cornwall. They dealt with a variety of different subjects. "The Hearty Good Fellow" was an example of a male fantasy in which a penniless traveler at an inn bluffs his way through a game of cards, receives free bed, board, and booze, and departs the next day with money in his pocket and a farewell kiss from the landlady. "The Orchestra" was a humorous tale of several local musicians competitively serenading the same girl, while "The Wrestling Match" related a sporting encounter between two local champions. The only political ballad was "Ormond the Brave," about the persecution of a favorite of Queen Anne during the reign of George I.

We saw in the previous chapter that England possessed a wealth of sea songs of various types, many of which were collected for the first time in the 1880s. Baring-Gould made a significant contribution to this body of maritime song. Sailors figured in quite a few of the ballads in *Songs and Ballads of the West*. These included, among others, "Nancy," "The Rambling Sailor," "The Sailor's Farewell," "Farewell to Kingsbridge," "Plymouth Sound," and "The Green Bed." The latter portrayed the fickle responses of an inn-keeper and his daughter to a sailor looking for lodgings. "The Wreck Off Scilly" related the loss of a ship at sea, and the subsequent unhappy fate of the sole survivor, reduced to a life of begging in the streets of Plymouth after he finds that his sweetheart, thinking him dead, has married another.

Although death, the supernatural and religious faith were relatively uncommon subjects, a few ballads dealt with them. Three of the more chilling were "My Ladye's Coach," "Broadbury Gibbet," and "Death and the Lady." Others touching on the subject of death were "The Blue Flame" and the moralistic "Tobacco is an Indian Weed," while overtly Christian ballads included "Brixham Town," "Adam and Eve," "Shower and Sunshine," and a "May Day Carol." But of all the tragic ballads, perhaps the most striking was a local composition about the treacherous nature of Dartmoor in winter time, "Childe the Hunter." Baring-Gould obtained the words from Jonas Coaker, a blind man in his eighties, who lived in Post Bridge, and the melody, which he believed to be a harp tune dating from the reign of Henry VII, from two Miss Phillips and a Mrs. Gibbons.

Childe the Hunter

Anon

Come list-en all both great and small, to__ you a tale I'll__ tell: What on this bleak and bar-ren moor, in__ an-cient__ days__ be-fell.

Fig. 7.19

Come listen all, both great and small,
To you a tale I'll tell:
What on this bleak and barren moor,
In ancient days befell.

It so befell, as I've heard tell,
There came the hunter Childe,
All day he chased on heath and waste,
On Dart-a-moor so wild.

The winds did blow, then fell the snow,
He chased on Fox-tor mire;
He lost his way, and saw the day,
And winter's sun expire.

Cold blew the blast, the snow fell fast,
And darker grew the night;
He wandered high, he wandered low,

And nowhere saw a light.

In darkness blind, he could not find
Where he escape might gain,
Long time he tried, no track espied,
His labours all in vain.

His knife he drew, his horse he slew,
As on the ground it lay;
He cut full deep, therein to creep,
And tarry till the day.

The winds did blow, fast fell the snow,
And darker grew the night,
Then well he wot, he hope might not
Again to see the light.

So with his finger dipp'd in blood,

He scrabbled on the stones—
"This is my will, God it fulfil,
And buried be my bones.

Who'er he be that findeth me
And brings to a grave,
The lands that now to me belong,

In Plymstock he shall have."

There was a cross erected then,
In memory of his name;
And there it stands, in wild waste lands,
To testify the same.[108]

The remainder of the ballads dealt with male/female relationships in one form or another, and in about half of these the course of true love eventually ran smooth. The latter included not only "The Broken Token" but also "Green Broom" (about a marriage across class lines), "As Johnny Walked Out" (a romantic tale of a joint search for a lost lamb), "The Simple Ploughboy" (the story of a press-gang victim rescued by his lover), and "I Rode My Little Horse" (in which the man finally returns to his love despite her lack of a fortune). On the other hand, "The Trees They Are So High," "The Squire and the Fair Maid," "The Bold Dragoon," "The Grey Mare," "The Barley Raking," and "The Green Bushes" all described encounters or relationships that did not work out, usually because of the infidelity, avariciousness, or death of one of the partners.

Indeed, close to half of all the songs in the collection were in one way or another about relations between the sexes. Apart from the ballads already mentioned there were many love lyrics, love laments, and shorter lyrics about male/female encounters or relationships. About a dozen of them were laments: songs about absent or lost lovers, or lyrics regretting that a hoped-for love-match was not to be. Often set to beautiful if mournful minor-key or modal melodies, the former included "The Drowned Lover," "I'll Build Myself a Gallant Ship," "The Rout Is Out," "The Green Cockade," and "Blow Away Ye Morning Breezes," while examples of the latter are "Flowers and Weeds," "The False Lover," "Something Lacking," "On a May Morning So Early," and "Down by a Riverside." It is difficult to choose just one of these songs to illustrate the category, but here is "Deep in Love," which Baring-Gould collected in both Cornwall and Devon. One of his Devonian sources was Sally Satterley (aka Mary Satcherley), who lived near Huckaby (or Huccaby) Bridge on Dartmoor. Although elderly and illiterate, she had a good memory and was his most useful female informant. He also collected the song from William Nichols of Whitchurch, near Tavistock, who had learned it from his grandmother, the hostess of a village inn during the last decade of the Georgian era. This is the (apparently composite) version in *Songs and Ballads of the West*:

Deep In Love

Anon

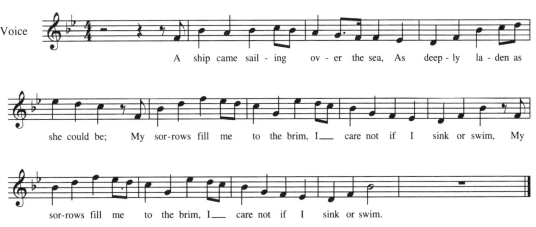

A ship came sail-ing ov-er the sea, As deep-ly la-den as she could be; My sor-rows fill me to the brim, I__ care not if I sink or swim, My sor-rows fill me to the brim, I__ care not if I sink or swim.

Fig. 7.20

A ship came sailing over the sea,
As deeply laden as she could be;
My sorrows fill me to the brim,
I care not if I sink or swim.

Ten thousand ladies in the room,
But my true love's the fairest bloom,
Of stars she is my brightest sun,
I said I would have her or none.

I leaned my back against an oak,
But first it bent and then it broke;
Untrusty as I found that tree,
So did my love prove false to me.

Down in a mead the other day,
As carelessly I went my way,
And plucked flowers red and blue,
I little thought what love could do.

I saw a rose with ruddy blush,
And thrust my hand into the bush,
I pricked my fingers to the bone,
I would I'd left that rose alone!

I wish! I wish! But 'tis in vain,
I wish I had my heart again!
With silver chain and diamond locks,
I'd fasten it in a golden box.[109]

An equal number of ballads and folk lyrics were poetic expressions of love, or songs celebrating mutually satisfactory sexual encounters and/or enduring partnerships. The ballads and longer love songs included "By Chance It Was," "The Roving Journeyman," "The Loyal Lover," "Constant Johnny," "Fair Susan," "Trinity Sunday," "An Evening So Clear," "Cupid the Ploughboy," and a celebration of long years of marriage, "Fair Girl, Mind This!" The shorter songs depicting male/female encounters—like the longer ballads on the same subject—included some with happy outcomes and some with more negative consequences. Joyful relationships were celebrated in "The Blue Kerchief" and "Upon a Sunday Morning." Occasionally, despite Baring-Gould's propensity to wield his red pencil, the encounters were implicitly sexual in nature, as in "The Blackbird," "The Barley Straw," "The Spotted Cow," and "A Nutting We Will Go." In other songs, such as "Strawberry Fair," more overt sexual metaphors were expunged and the lyrics rendered innocuous. Quite a few of these songs described meetings between the sexes that did not flourish; for example in "Cecily Sweet" the male suitor is rejected as a clown, while in "The Saucy Sailor," "The Hostess' Daughter" and "Blue Muslin" (aka "The Keys of Canterbury") the man decides that the girl is not right for him. "Within a Garden" suggests that the maid will be left grieving, and "The Jolly Goss-hawk" is an allegorical account of female infidelity. Love is as often painful as it is joyful.

About one quarter of the material in *Songs and Ballads of the West* was unequivocally regional in nature, reflecting local traditions or places. Examples of songs that explicitly refer to particular places in the West Country include (among others) "Plymouth Sound," "The Wreck Off Scilly," "The Bell Ringing," "Childe the Hunter," "The Warson Hunt," and perhaps the most familiar song collected by Baring-Gould, "Widdecombe Fair." It was, he reported, known almost everywhere and was, in his view, probably the most popular of all Devonshire vernacular ballads. He first obtained the song from W. F. Collier, of Woodtown, near Horrabridge, while from Harry Westaway he noted the same words to a different tune. "Other versions, slightly varying," he commented, "then poured in," and he was able to establish that the original Uncle Tom Cobleigh lived near Yeoford Junction, while all the other people mentioned in the chorus lived in the village of Sticklepath. This is Baring-Gould's composite version, a slimmed-down synthesis of the many variants he came across:

Tom Pearce, Tom Pearce, lend me your grey mare,
All along, down along, out along lee,
For I want to go to Widdecombe Fair,
Wi' Bill Brewer, Jan Stewer, Peter Gurney,
Peter Davy, Dan Whiddon, Harry Whiddon,
Harry Hawk, old Cobley and all,
Old Uncle Tom Cobley and all.

"And when shall I see again my grey mare?"
All along, etc.
"By Friday soon, or Saturday noon,
Wi' Bill Brewer, Jan Stewer," etc.

Then Friday came, and Saturday noon,
All along, etc.
But Tom Pearce's old mare hath not trotted home,
Wi' Bill Brewer, etc.

So Tom Pearce he got up to the top o' the hill,
All along, etc.
And he seed his old mare down a making her will,

Wi' Bill Brewer, etc.

So Tom Pearce's old mare, her took sick and died,
All along, etc.
And Tom he sat down on a stone, and he cried,
Wi' Bill Brewer, etc.

But this isn't the end o' this shocking affair,
All along, etc.
Nor, though they be dead, of the horrid career,
Of Bill Brewer, etc.

When the wind whistles cold on the moor of a night,
All along, etc.
Tom Pearce's old mare doth appear, gashly white,
Wi' Bill Brewer, etc.

And all the long night be heard skirling and groans,
All along, etc.
From Tom Pearce's old mare in her rattling bones,
And from Bill Brewer, etc.[110]

Widdecombe Fair

Anon

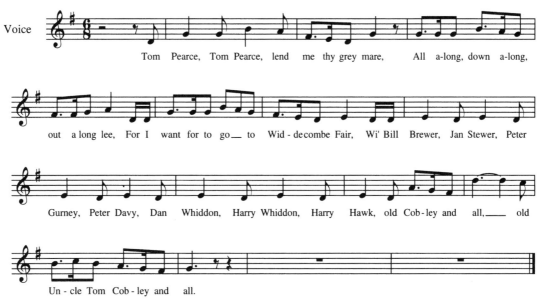

Voice

Tom Pearce, Tom Pearce, lend me thy grey mare, All a-long, down a-long,

out a long lee, For I want for to go— to Wid-decombe Fair, Wi' Bill Brewer, Jan Stewer, Peter

Gurney, Peter Davy, Dan Whiddon, Harry Whiddon, Harry Hawk, old Cob-ley and all,— old

Un - cle Tom Cob - ley and all.

Fig. 7.21

Another category of material found quite extensively in the book reflected the rhythms of country life, either in a general way (as, for example, in "The Seasons" or "Furze Bloom") or by dealing with one specific aspect, such as ploughing, haymaking, milling, hunting, bell-ringing, tithe-collecting, or market-day. Not surprisingly, there were songs that reflected various aspects of agriculture and the lives of those engaged in farming. These included "The Oxen Ploughing," "The Painful Plough," "The Country Farmer's Son," and "Haymaking Song." There were even songs about farm animals, such as "Poor Old Horse" and "The Tythe Pig," the latter a satire on the greediness of the country parson. The role of the church in village life was also reflected in "The Bell Ringing," and that of the village bard in "The Old Singing Man." Millers, also perceived as grasping, were satirized in "The Miller and his Sons," while the adventure of traveling to the county fair was reflected in "Strawberry Fair" and, of course, "Widdecombe Fair." Of all the songs celebrating country life, perhaps the most complacent in tone was "The Cottage Thatched with Straw," which Baring-Gould found to be rivaled in popularity among tavern singers only by "Widdecombe Fair." He and Fleetwood Sheppard noted the words and tune respectively from John Watts, a quarryman, who lived at Alder, near Thrushelton. They subsequently heard it sung elsewhere in Devon, as well as at Looe in Cornwall.

In days of yore there sat at his door
An old farmer and thus sang he,
"With my pipe and my glass, I wish every class
On the earth were as well as me!"
For he en-vi-ed not any man his lot,
The richest, the proudest, he saw;
For he had home brewed, brown bread,
And a cottage well thatch'd with straw.

Chorus: And a cottage well thatch'd with straw,
And cottage well thatch'd with straw,
For he had home brewed, brown bread,
And a cottage well thatch'd with straw.

My dear old dad this snug cottage had,
And he got it, I'll tell you how,
He won it, I wot, with the best coin got,
With the sweat of an honest brow.
Then says my old dad, "Be careful lad
To keep out of the lawyer's claw.
So you'll have home brew'd, brown bread,
And a cottage well thatch'd with straw."

The ragged, the torn, from my door I don't turn,
But I give them a crust of brown,
And a drop of good ale, my lad, without fail,
For to wash the brown crust down.
Tho' rich I may be, it may chance to me,

That misfortune should spoil my store,
So I'd lack home brewed, brown bread,
And a cottage well thatch'd with straw.

Then in frost and snow to the church I go,
No matter the weather how,
And the service and prayer that I put up there

Is to Him who speeds the plough.
Sunday saints, i 'feck, who cheat all the week,
With a ranting and a canting jaw,
Not for them is my home brewed, brown bread,
And my cottage well thatch'd with straw.

The Cottage Thatched With Straw

Anon

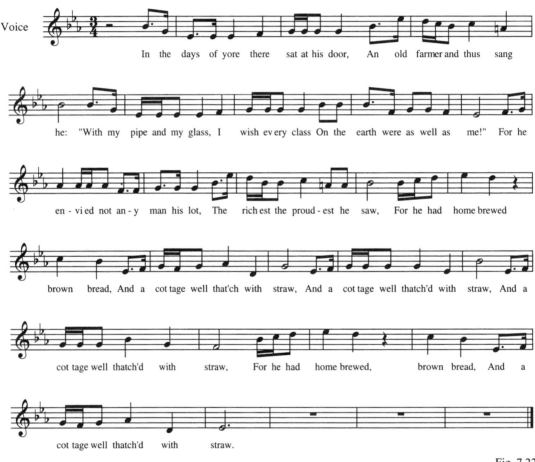

Fig. 7.22

In Baring-Gould's judgment "The Cottage Thatched with Straw" was not a very old song, dating most likely from the early years of the nineteenth century. Nonetheless he preferred it to another, older, song that he found very popular among agricultural laborers in Devon. This was "The Seasons," a lengthy ballad which he described as a crudely written creation set to an old dance tune. He reported that there were numerous variants of this song in existence but his preference was for the following version, which he and Fleetwood Sheppard had noted from J. Potter of Post Bridge:

First comes January
When the sun lies very low;
I see in the farmer's yard
The cattle feed on stro',

The weather being so cold
While the snow lies on the ground.
There will be another change of moon
Before the year comes round.

The Seasons

Anon

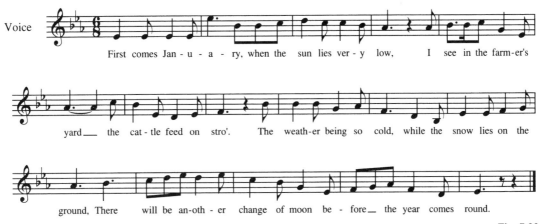

Voice

First comes Jan-u-a-ry, when the sun lies ver-y low, I see in the farm-er's

yard— the cat-tle feed on stro'. The weath-er being so cold, while the snow lies on the

ground, There will be an-oth-er change of moon be-fore— the year comes round.

Fig. 7.23

Next is February,
So early in the spring;
The farmer ploughs the fallows,
The rooks their nests begin.
The little lambs appearing
Now frisk in pretty play.
I think upon the increase,
And thank my God, today.

March it is the next month,
So cold and hard and drear.
Prepare we now for harvest
By brewing of strong beer.
God grant that we who labour
May see the reaping come,
And drink and dance and welcome
The happy harvest home.

Next of months is April,
When early in the morn
The cheery farmer soweth
To right and left the corn.
The gallant team come after,
A-smoothing of the land.
May Heaven the farmer prosper
What e'er he takes in hand.

In May I go a walking
To hear the linnets sing,
The blackbird and the throstle
A-praising God the King.
It cheers the heart to hear them
To see the leaves unfold,
The meadows scattered over
With buttercups of gold.

Full early in the morning

Awakes the summer sun,
The month of June arriving,
The cold and night are done.
The cuckoo is a fine bird,
She whistles as she flies,
And as she whistles, cuckoo,
The bluer grow the skies.

Six months I now have named,
The seventh is July.
Come lads and lasses gather
The scented hay to dry,
All full of mirth and gladness
To turn it in the sun,
And never cease till daylight sets
And all the work is done.

August brings the harvest,
The reapers now advance,
Against their shining sickles
The field stands little chance.
Well done! exclaims the farmer,
This day is all men's friend,
We'll drink and feast in plenty
When we the harvest end.

By middle of September
The rake is laid aside,
The horses wear the breeching
Rich dressing to provide,
All things to do in season,
Me-thinks is just and right.
Now summer season's over,
The frosts begin at night.

October leads in winter,
The leaves begin to fall.

The trees will soon be naked
No flowers left at all.
The frosts will bite them sharply
The elm alone is green.
In orchard piles of apples red
For cyder press are seen.

The eleventh month, November,
The nights are cold and long,
By day we're felling timber,
And spend the night in song.
In cozy chimney corner,

We take our toast and ale,
And kiss and tease the maidens,
Or tell a merry tale.

Then comes dark December,
The last of months in turn.
With holly, box, and laurel,
We house and church adorn.
So now, to end my story,
I wish you all good cheer.
A merry, happy Christmass,
A prosperous New Year.[111]

Hunting was a rural pastime in which the poorest members of the village community did not engage, but Baring-Gould still managed to collect five hunting songs: "The Warson Hunt," "The Duke's Hunt," "The Hunting of Arscott of Tetcott," "The Hunting of the Hare," and "Parson Hogg," a satirical song about a vicar who would much rather hunt than attend to his pastoral duties. Drinking in the local tavern was an activity indulged in by all members of rural society, although the more well-to-do would likely choose the saloon bar rather than the public bar. Also very suitable for whiling away long winter evenings either at home or in the pub were cumulative songs. Baring-Gould included two good examples of these, "The Everlasting Circle" and "The Dilly Song." In his visits to Devon pubs he picked up a handful of drinking songs, of which he chose four to include in *Songs and Ballads of the West:* "Fathom the Bowl," "Why Should We Be Dullards Sad?" "Come My Lads, Let's Be Jolly," and "The Drunken Maidens." The latter, he noted, was an old ballad that had been printed, *circa* 1710, in *Charming Phillis' Garland,* although he had located it in Devonshire oral tradition, his informant being Edmund Fry of Lydford.

The Drunken Maidens

Anon

Fig. 7.24

There were three drunken maidens,
Came from the Isle of Wight,
They drank from Monday morning,
Nor stay'd till Saturday night.
When Saturday did come, sirs!
They would not then go out,
Not the three drunken maidens,
As they pushed the jug about.

Then came in bouncing Sally

With cheeks as red as bloom:
"Make space my jolly sisters,
Now make for Sally room,
For that I will be your equal,
Before that I go out."
So now four drunken maidens,
They pushed the jug about.

It was woodcock and pheasant,
And partridges and hare,

It was all kinds of dainties,
No scarcity was there.
It was four quarts of Malaga,
Each fairly did drink out,
So the four drunken maidens,
They pushed the jug about.

Then down came the landlord
And asked for his pay.
O! a forty-pound bill, sirs!
The damsels drew that day.
It was ten pounds apiece, sirs!

But yet, they would not out.
So the four drunken maidens,
They pushed the jug about.

"O where be your spencers?
Your mantles rich and fine?"
"They all be a-swallowed
In tankards of good wine."
"O where be your characters,
Ye maidens brisk and gay?"
"O they be a-swallowed!
We've drunk them clean away."[112]

Although Baring-Gould did most of his collecting in the county of Devon, he periodically visited Cornwall and seems to have stayed on various occasions at St. Mawgan-in-Pyder, where he collected from Joseph Dyer, at Launceston, where he found James Olver, and at Liskeard, where he noted the words of "Ormond the Brave" from a tanner named J. Peake. He was interested in the annual May Day ceremonies at Padstow and Helston, and from *Songs and Ballads of the West* one might easily conclude that he also went to Helston one May 8 to observe the Flora Day festival celebrating the coming of spring. Apparently he never made it, and his account is at second-hand, based on that by a correspondent named J. Mathews who lived in St. Austell. He also used several printed sources.[113] The ceremonies included the famous Furry Dance, which is described as follows in *Songs and Ballads of the West*:

> Very early in the morning a party of youths and maidens goes into the country, and returns dancing through the streets to a quaint tune, peculiar to the day, called the "Furry Dance." At eight o'clock the "Hal-an-tow" is sung by a party of from twenty to thirty men and boys who come into the town bearing green branches, with flowers in their hats, preceded by a single drum, on which a boy beats the furry Dance. They perambulate the town for many hours, stopping at intervals at some of the principal houses. At one o'clock a large party of ladies and gentlemen, in summer attire,—the ladies decorated with garlands of flowers, the gentlemen with nosegays and flowers in their hats, assemble at the Town Hall, and proceed to dance after the band, playing the traditional air...The "Helston Furry Dance" is a relic of part of the Old English May Games. These originally comprised four entirely distinct parts. 1st. The election and procession of the King and Queen of the May, who were called the Summer King and Queen. 2nd. The Morris Dance, performed by men disguised, with swords in their hands. 3rd. The "Hobby Horse." 4th. The "Robin Hood"...In the Helston performance we have a fragment only of the original series of pageants; the bringing home of the May and the dance, and the song about Robin Hood. At Padstow, the Hobby-horse still figures...The "Helston Furry Dance" tune was first printed in Davies Gilbert's *Christmas Carols,* 2nd Ed., 1823. His form is purer than ours, which is as now sung."[114]

The tune and some of the words of "Hal-an-Tow," as printed in *Songs and Ballads of the West,* were obtained from Mathews, although Baring-Gould also knew three previously published versions of the song. He suggested that "Aunt Mary Moses" in the last verse was a corruption of an original Cornish name, "Modryb Maria," a result of the decline of the Cornish language as the normal vehicle for everyday speech in the area. Although there does not seem to be an exact match between words and tune, this is the version of "Hal-an-Tow" printed by Baring-Gould:

Robin Hood and Little John
They both are gone to the fair, O!
And we will to the merry greenwood,
To see what they do there, O!
And for to chase, O,
To chase the buck and doe!

Refrain:
With Hal-an-tow, jolly rumble O,
To chase the buck and doe,
And we were up as soon as the day, O,
For to fetch the summer home,
The Summer and the May, O!

Now the Winter is a gone, O.

Where are those Spaniards
That make so great a boast, O!
Why, they shall eat the grey goose feathers,
And we will eat the roast, O!
In every land, O,
The land where'er we go.
Refrain: With Hal-an-tow, jolly rumble O, etc.

As for that good Knight, St. George,
St. George he was a Knight, O!
Of all the knights in Christendom,

St. George he is the right, O!
In every land, O,
The land where'er we go.
Refrain: With Hal-an-tow, jolly rumble O, etc.

God bless Aunt Mary Moses
And all her power and might, O!

And send us peace in merry England,
Send peace by day and night, O!
To merry England, O!
Both now and ever mo'.
Refrain: With Hal-an-tow, jolly rumble O, etc.[115]

Hal-an-Tow

Anon

Voice

Rob - in Hood and Lit - tle John, They both are gone to the fair O,

And we will to the mer - ry green wood, To see what they do there O.

And for to chase O, to chase the buck and doe.... With Hal - an-Tow, jol-ly

rum - ble O, to chase the buck and doe....

Fig. 7.25

There are too many interesting songs in *Songs and Ballads of the West* to mention, let alone quote or even describe them all. The book's faults are obvious. Its organization is chaotic, yet when one becomes familiar with the songs it would be difficult to deny their varied nature and often high quality. The main frustration is with the substitutions: it is irritating to find so many lyrics replaced or altered by Baring-Gould or Sheppard, usually accompanied by a tantalizing statement to the effect that "for very sufficient reasons we could not employ the words as sung, which were very vulgar." Which brings us back to the issue that I posed at the beginning of this chapter, the question of Baring-Gould's interventionist editing in the interest of propriety.

Baring-Gould as Editor

I warned earlier about the difficulty of making fair and accurate generalizations about Baring-Gould's methods as an editor, but now I must try to draw some conclusions from the foregoing discussion. At first glance, *Songs and Ballads of the West* appears to be the real McCoy, a genuine and scholarly collection of folk music, taken down from oral tradition in the rural southwest of England. In fact it is not, although it nonetheless contains much that is authentic. By and large, one can rely on the tunes, but one has to be very careful about the printed lyrics. The examples given above demonstrate that Baring-Gould sometimes, although not always, subjected his discoveries to a stringent editing process, although this usually only involved the song texts. He normally attempted to provide what he considered the best version of a song, and in order to do so he more than occasionally made composite versions from fragments and variants. He also edited out lines, stanzas, or even entire song texts that he felt were not suitable for the eyes of polite society. He sometimes seems to have regretted having to do this, and he did not disguise what he had done and why. Indeed he provided a running commentary in the notes in *Songs and Ballads of the West* on the extent to which he had felt compelled to modify each item. When one reads carefully the book's preface and the extensive notes to the songs, and especially when one compares the published song texts to the fair copy manuscript texts that he deposited in Plymouth Public Library, a picture gradually emerges of his systematically interventionist approach to editing.

Baring-Gould was evidently quite clear about what he was doing and what he believed to be the compelling reasons for it. He defended his editorial approach as follows in the "Introduction" to *Songs of the West*:

> In giving these songs to the public, we have been scrupulous to publish the airs precisely as noted down, choosing among the variants those which commended themselves to us as the soundest. But we have not been so careful with regard to the *words*. These are sometimes in a fragmentary condition, or are coarse, contain *double entendres*, or else are mere doggerel. Accordingly, we have re-written the songs whenever it was not possible to present them in their original form. This was done by the Scotch. Many an old ballad is gross, and many a broadside is common-place. Songs that were thought witty in the Caroline and early Georgian epochs are no longer sufferable; and broadside ballads are in many cases vulgarised versions of earlier ballads that have been lost in their original forms. What a change has taken place in public feeling with regard to decency may be judged by the [admiring] way in which Addison speaks of D'Urfey...Why—D'Urfey's *Pills* must now-a-days be kept under lock and key. The fun so commended by the pious and grave Addison is filth of the most revolting description...A good many of the ditties in favour with our rural song-men are, it must be admitted, of the D'Urfey type; and what is more some of the very worse are sung to the daintiest early melodies. Two courses lay open to us. One, that adopted by Dr. Barrett and Mr. Kidson, was to print the words exactly as given on the broadsides, with asterisks for the undesirable stanzas. But this would simply have killed the songs. No one would care to warble what was fragmentary. On the other hand, there is that adopted by the Scotch and Irish collectors, which consists in re-writing or modifying where objectionable or common-place. This has been the course we have pursued. It seemed a pity to consign the lovely old melodies to the antiquary's library, by publishing them with words which were fatal to the success of the songs in the drawing room or the concert hall...As, however, to the antiquary everything is important, exactly as obtained, uncleansed from rust and unpolished, I have deposited a copy of the songs and ballads with their music exactly as taken down, for reference in the Municipal Free Library, Plymouth.[116]

Unfortunately, this latter claim was ambiguous. If Baring-Gould meant that the *tunes* were accurate and authentic he was correct, with a few minor exceptions. If he meant that the *songs* (i.e., both tunes and words) were "exactly as taken down" his statement was not strictly true. While the "Plymouth Fair Copy Manuscript" and "The Personal Copy" are fairly reliable as primary sources, they do not always follow exactly Baring-Gould's field notebooks. As we have seen, some editing has sometimes already taken place during the process of making fair copies. Moreover, Baring-Gould apparently did not always bother to take down the original words of a song when he deemed it too "coarse," so even the notebooks do not always provide an exact record of what he and his collaborators found.

Baring-Gould's attitude to his material was similar to that of the Scottish collector William Christie. Both men regarded the tunes as more important than the words and they were willing to make compromises in order to see the melodies in print. It is hardly surprising that Baring-Gould, a Victorian clergyman, believed that for public consumption it was essential to bowdlerize or to replace lyrics that he deemed offensive. Personally he was no prude, but he had a strong sense for what respectable society would find unacceptable, he had a reputation to maintain, and he wanted his publications to find a market. He was therefore determined not to offend middle-class taste and mores. We have seen in detail how and why he modified or excluded, among other songs and ballads, "Strawberry Fair," "Rosemary Lane," and "The Trees They Are So High." Anyone who troubled to read the notes provided to the items in *Songs and Ballads of the West* would have learned that James Parsons's "A Sweet Pretty Maiden" dealt with "a topic not advisable to be sung about in the drawing room" and so an entire set of new words had been substituted for the source singer's objectionable lyric.[117] The same was true for Roger Luxton's "Plymouth Sound," the original words of which Baring-Gould deemed "not only very poor, but somewhat coarse."[118] As for "The Bold Dragoon," he considered the "original too coarse to be presentable" and so recast the ballad, adding a chimpanzee to the story for good measure.[119] In the case of "The Hostess' Daughter" it was obvious to the cleric that "the frankness and rudeness of the original words demanded modification before the song was fitted for the drawing room."[120] Similarly, it was "not possible" to give "On a May Morning So Early" in its original form, so on this occasion it was Sheppard who rewrote it.[121] "A Nutting We Will Go" also had to be toned down to make it "tolerable for polite ears."[122] Again, the words of "Barley Straw" were "very vulgar," which prompted Sheppard to rewrite them,[123] while "for very sufficient reasons" the editors could not employ the original words of "The Saucy Ploughboy."[124] And so it went on. One could multiply even more examples, but to do so would be tedious. As a result of these sensitivities, Baring-Gould, like Bishop Percy, ended up rewriting a substantial portion of his material, although unlike Percy he did usually indicate when and why he had done so.

Baring-Gould's criteria for what he believed drawing-room society would regard as not "objectionable" were tough: the slightest suggestion of female promiscuity incurred his editorial red pencil, as did metaphorical allusions to sexual intercourse. On the other hand, he was not as hard on males sowing, or attempting to sow, their wild oats, and in rewriting songs he sometimes reversed the sexes to render the situation less improper. So there was a double standard at work here. In addition, he regarded most broadside texts as corrupt and inferior, and consequently had no compunction about rewriting any songs where he suspected the singer had inherited the words from a broadside source. Occasionally he seems to have missed the sexual meaning implicit in certain metaphors, or else he believed them to be too obscure to be decoded by polite society. But the more obvious ones were systematically removed.

It is easy to feel indignant at this kind of bowdlerization and to condemn out of hand Baring-Gould's decision to act as a censor, but it is clear that he (and other folksong editors of the time) felt that they had no choice in the matter. At the very least, we should allow him to restate his defense. This was how he addressed the matter in retrospect in *Further Reminiscences:*

> Of course, it is only some, and they are not very numerous among the popular lyrics, that are objectionable, and the singers have no thought that they are offending ears polite, when they mention in their songs and ballads matters not generally talked about, and when they call a spade "a spade" and not "an agricultural instrument employed by gardeners." The relation of the sexes is the basis of most poetical compositions that circulate among the peasantry...It is therefore necessary for the editor to modify words, expressions, even statements of events recorded, so as to make the ballads and songs tolerable to men and women of culture. Burns, as already said, undertook this task for the Scottish songs. Sir Walter Scott did the same for the Border Ballads. The task had—and has—to be undertaken so as to rescue exquisite melodies from being killed by the words to which they are wedded. To do this, an editor must be imbued with the feeling of the folk-poet, and must divest himself of literary tricks. In a word, he must reverse the process of the early Stuart rhymers, who tricked out the ancient ballads with gew-gaws of their own fancy, and made them trip to unaccustomed measures.[125]

So how extensively was the material in *Songs and Ballads of the West* rewritten? What was the net result of Baring-Gould's somewhat puritanical yet pragmatic and creative approach to folksong editing? According to his own count, twenty-four of the songs in the first edition of the book were either Fleetwood Sheppard's compositions or his own, and he admitted altering another nineteen. The remainder, he averred, were the "old" (i.e., original, as collected) words, and he also claimed to have restored the "old words" to three more songs in the 1895 edition. In effect, then, he was suggesting that about two-thirds of the songs in the second edition were fully authentic, and he was also claiming that all but twenty-one were substantially the same as collected. In reality, this was an overstatement and somewhat economical with the truth. In addition to the twenty-one "new songs" composed by the editors, twenty songs in the 1895 edition were substantially rewritten, while another thirty-one more were modified, either by minor editorial changes or by the omission of verses. At best thirty-eight songs were printed with the original words, and in some cases at least these were composite versions made by taking the best verses from two or more variants.

Nor did Baring-Gould change his approach in 1905, when *Songs and Ballads of the West* was re-edited as *Songs of the West* in collaboration with Cecil Sharp, whose avowed intent was to provide simpler piano arrangements that would reflect more faithfully the spirit of the songs as collected. Authenticity remained low on Baring-Gould's list of editing criteria. He was often ready to sacrifice accurate reporting of what he found in the field to his own aesthetic and moral judgments. Of the thirty-three new songs in *Songs of the West,* at least ten were to some degree the poetic creations of the editor. To give just three of many possible illustrations, we find him commenting in his notes to "Flora, the Lily of the West" that he "thought it well to cut out the murder and the trial," while with "The Keeper" he was "compelled to rewrite most of the song which in the original is very gross"; and for "Old Adam, the Poacher" he remarks bluntly that "I wrote the words." Yet, as usual, he was careful to indicate in his notes when he had felt constrained to modify or rewrite a song. The inauthentic folksongs in *Songs of the West,* as in *Songs and Ballads of the West,* were not fakes, since there was no intention to defraud. They were merely traditional tunes with overtly edited or (sometimes) completely recomposed texts. Like many folksingers before and after him, Baring-Gould was making his own contribution to 'the folk process'. He no doubt saw himself as a sort of 'song-man,' in his own way a musical descendant of the Tudor minstrels and the village bards of later centuries. But it will be for his collecting rather than his song writing that he will be remembered with gratitude.

Notes

1. Sabine Baring-Gould, *The Book of Were-Wolves* (London: Smith, Elder, 1865).

2. Sabine Baring-Gould, *Curious Myths of the Middle Ages* (London: Rivingtons, 1866).

3. Sabine Baring-Gould, *Through Flood and Flame* (London: Smith, Elder, 1868).

4. Sabine Baring-Gould, *The Origin and Development of Religious Belief* (London: Rivingtons, 1870).

5. Sabine Baring-Gould, *The Vicar of Morwenstowe: A Life of Robert Stephen Hawker* (London: King, 1876).

6. Sabine Baring-Gould, *Lives of the Saints*, 15 vols. (London: Hodges, 1872-88).

7. Sabine Baring-Gould, *Mehalah* (London: Smith, Elder, 1880).

8. The village is now called Lewtrenchard but in Baring-Gould's day it was commonly known as Lew Trenchard and that is the way he normally spelled it.

9. Brenda Colloms, "Gould, Sabine Baring- (1834-1924)," *Oxford Dictionary of National Biography*, http://www.oxforddnb.com /articles/30/30587-article.html; Bickford Dickinson, *Sabine Baring-Gould: Squarson, Writer and Folklorist, 1834-1924* (Newton Abbott, U.K.: David & Charles, 1970); Harold Kirk-Smith, *'Now the Day Is Over': The Life and Times of Sabine Baring-Gould, 1834-1924* (Boston, U.K.: Richard Kay, 1997); William E. Purcell, *Onward Christian Soldier: A Life of Sabine Baring-Gould* (London: Longman, Green, 1957); David Roberts, "His 'Magpie Mind' Made Baring-Gould a Rare Bird Indeed," *Smithsonian* 24, no. 4 (1993): 74-83.

10. Sabine Baring-Gould, H. Fleetwood Sheppard, F. W. Bussell, and Cecil J. Sharp, eds., *Songs of the West: Folk Songs of Devon and Cornwall, Collected from the Mouths of the People* (London: Methuen, 1905).

11. Sabine Baring-Gould and H. Fleetwood Sheppard, eds., *Songs and Ballads of the West, a Collection made from the Mouths of the People,* 4 parts, subsequently bound in 2 vols. (London: Patey & Willis, [1889-92]; 2nd edition, London: Methuen and Patey & Willis, [1891-95], reprinted in one volume, 1895).

12. Sabine Baring-Gould, *Further Reminiscences, 1864-1894* (London: John Lane, The Bodley Head, 1925), 184.

13. He may not have meant to include his life-long service as a clergyman in this comparison, but he certainly seems to have regarded his folksong collecting as ultimately more successful and valuable than his work as a geographer, archeologist, folklorist, historian of religion, composer of church music, novelist, or travel writer.

14. James Reeves, ed., *The Idiom of the People* (London: William Heinemann, 1958).

15. James Reeves, ed., *The Everlasting Circle: English Traditional Verse from the Manuscripts of S. Baring-Gould, H.E.D. Hammond, and George B. Gardiner* (London: Heinemann, 1960).

16. For example, I remember that the phrase was used in an article in *Sing* magazine by Hylda Sims (at the time a protégée of John Hasted's). Unfortunately I have so far been unable to locate the bibliographical details of this article.

17. Baring-Gould and Sharp, *Songs of the West,* 140-41.

18. John Masters, "Strawberry Fair," as recorded by Baring-Gould in the "Killerton Notebook," no. CXXXV, unpaginated. Baring-Gould microfiche collection, 1.3.

19. Baring-Gould, et al., eds., *Songs of the West,* 20.

20. Dave Pegg, *Folk: A Portrait of English Traditional Music, Musicians and Customs* (London: Wildwood House, 1976), 12.

21. Steve Gardham, "The Brown Girl" (Child 295B): A Baring-Gould Concoction?" in *Folk Song: Tradition, Revival, and Re-Creation*, edited by Ian Russell and David Atkinson (Aberdeen, U.K.: Elphinstone Institute, University of Aberdeen, 2004), 363-76.

22. Dave Harker, *Fakesong: The Manufacture of British 'Folksong' 1700 to the Present Day* (Milton Keynes, U.K.: Open University Press, 1985). For a critique of the Harker thesis, see my *Victorian Songhunters*, 398-400.

23. "The Personal Copy" [microfiche collection 2.2], no. CXI, 220-221.

24. Gardham, "The Brown Girl," 369-70.

25. "Killerton Notebook 1," unpaginated. Baring-Gould also noted a more fragmentary version of the same song from James Parsons, although Parsons's version was titled "Pretty Barbara." A comment on the manuscript (in Baring-Gould's handwriting) indicates that he thought the song was a variant of "Barbara Allen." For this information I am indebted to Martin Graebe.

26. Sabine Baring-Gould and Cecil J. Sharp, eds. *English Folk Songs for Schools* (London: Curwen, 1906).

27. Sir Charles Villiers Stanford, ed., *The National Song Book: A Complete Collection of the Folk-Songs, Carols, and Rounds suggested by the Board of Education* (London: Boosey, 1905).

28. John L. Hatton and Eaton Faning, eds., *The Songs of England: A Collection of 272 English Melodies, including the most popular Traditional Ditties, and the Principal Songs and Ballads of the Last Three Centuries,* 3 vols. (London: Boosey & Co., [1890]); William Alexander Barrett, ed., *Standard English Songs* (London: Augener, [1890]); Harold Boulton and Arthur Somervell, eds., *Songs of the Four Nations: A Collection of Old Songs of the People of England, Scotland, Ireland and Wales* (London: Cramer, 1892); Frank Kidson and Alfred Moffat, eds., *The Minstrelsy of England: a collection of 200 English songs with their melodies, popular from the 16th century to the middle of the 18th century* (London: Bailey & Ferguson, 1901).

29. Baring-Gould, et al., *Songs of the West.* See note 10.

30. Baring-Gould and Fleetwood Sheppard, *Songs and Ballads of the West.* See note 11.

31. Sabine Baring-Gould, and H. Fleetwood Sheppard, eds., *A Garland of Country Song: English Folk Songs with their Traditional Melodies* (London: Methuen, 1895).

32. Sabine Baring-Gould, ed., *English Minstrelsie: A National Monument of English Song,* 8 vols. (Edinburgh: Jack & Jack, 1895-98).

33. The term "The Personal Copy" was coined by Baring-Gould expert Martin Graebe. It is useful because it suggests, correctly, that the voluminous manuscript represented Baring-Gould's consolidated record, in fair copy, of vernacular songs that he had collected, along with some variants that other collectors had sent him.

34. The Baring-Gould Heritage Project microfiche collection. Copies are held at the Vaughan Williams Memorial Library (Cecil Sharp House, London), Plymouth Public Library, and the Devon County Records Office (Exeter).

35. Baring-Gould, "Songs and Ballads of the West (Devon and Cornwall)," front page. Manuscript in Plymouth Central Public Library [also included in Baring-Gould microfiche collection, 2.1, as "Plymouth Fair Copy Manuscript"].

36. Baring-Gould and Fleetwood Sheppard, *Songs and Ballads of the West,* 3-33; Baring-Gould and Sharp, *English Folk-Songs for Schools,* 62.

37. "Plymouth Fair Copy Manuscript" [microfiche 2.1], item no. 15.

38. Baring-Gould's relationship to Parsons and the latter's repertoire are discussed later in this chapter.

39. "Plymouth Notebook" [microfiche 1.2], unpaginated.

40. "Plymouth Notebook" [microfiche 1.2], unpaginated. The bar-lines are very faint on the microfiche and the last bars of the tune in particular are difficult to read, but I believe that this is accurately transcribed.

41. "The Personal Copy" [microfiche 2.2], no. 15.

42. "Plymouth Notebook" [microfiche 1.2], unpaginated.

43. It is of course also possible that Sheppard made the original tune transcription, although the hand appears to be Baring-Gould's and the song is in the "Plymouth Notebook" (Baring-Gould's own field notebook) rather than in one of the Rough Copy notebooks that mainly preserve his collaborators' tune transcriptions in the field.

44. The fact that "The Personal Copy" has only three verses seems to me to be quite significant; had the text been copied directly from Bell all five verses would likely have been set down there. Martin Graebe demurs. In a personal communication to the author he is skeptical that the partial texts in the "Plymouth Fair Copy Manuscript" and "The Personal Copy" reflect what Parsons or Westaway sang or even a fragment obtained from Whitfield. He suggests that Baring-Gould simply had Bell's text and, as a result of a newspaper request, obtained a tune for it from Stevens, put them together, and published the result. This interpretation, however, apparently ignores the evidence that Baring-Gould did note the song (or part of it) from both Parsons and Westaway, and also that he evidently took the trouble to have Fleetwood Sheppard verify the accuracy of the melody current in Devon oral tradition. Nor does it explain why only three verses were included in "The Personal Copy."

45. "Plymouth Notebook" [microfiche collection 1.2], unpaginated.

46. "Plymouth Fair Copy Manuscript" [microfiche collection 2.1], no. IV, unpaginated.

47. See Reeves, *The Everlasting Circle,* 265-269, for an alternative discussion of variant texts.

48. Baring-Gould and Fleetwood Sheppard, *Songs and Ballads of the West,* 2nd edition (1895), 8-9.

49. Pegg, *Folk,* 12.

50. Baring-Gould, *Further Reminiscences,* 184.

51. In this I concur with Martin Graebe's conclusion in "Sabine Baring-Gould and his old singing-men," in *Folk Song: Tradition, Revival, and Re-Creation,* edited by Ian Russell and David Atkinson (Aberdeen, U.K.: The Elphinstone Institute, University of Aberdeen, 2004), 176.

52. Sabine Baring-Gould, *Old Country Life* (London: Methuen, 1890), 264.

53. Sabine Baring-Gould, "Among the Western Song Men," *English Illustrated Magazine* 102 (1892): 468. I am grateful to Martin Graebe for alerting me to this source.

54. Baring-Gould, "Among Western Song Men," 468.

55. Baring-Gould, *Old Country Life,* 265.

56. "Plymouth Fair Copy Manuscript" [microfiche collection 2.1], front page. The date in the manuscript is ambiguous. It can certainly be read as 1888—Baring-Gould's handwriting is sloping and often difficult to decipher—but on close examination of the manuscript the last digit does look to me more like a zero than an eight. That was how I read it before I realized that there might be an issue here, and I have returned to the Plymouth archive to re-examine it and my conclusion is the same as before. Martin Graebe, who almost certainly has more experience reading Baring-Gould's handwriting than anyone else, interprets that last digit as an eight, but I find that problematic because it appears to be formed differently. The two eights preceding are virtually identical but the third digit does not look like them. 1886 would be another possibility, but the third digit looks more like a zero or an eight than a six. Of course the date 1880 poses a difficulty: it is surprisingly early, since Baring-Gould was still vicar of East Mersea at the time. Nonetheless, he did pay fairly frequent visits to Lew Trenchard at that time and he could well have noted a song or two from a villager. He may also have been vague about the exact year, and merely meant the beginning of the 1880s, which would fit well with his return to Devon.

57. Sabine Baring-Gould to Lucy Broadwood, undated. Vaughan Williams Memorial Library, Lucy Broadwood Manuscript Collection, LEB/4/39.

58. Baring-Gould to Broadwood, 10 March, 1893. VWML, Broadwood Collection, LEB/4/34.

59. Baring-Gould, *Further Reminiscences,* 189-90.

60. Hard's death was reported in the *Totnes Times and Devon News,* 3 December 1892; the report implies that Hard died in his bed after a short illness. For a discussion of this incident, see Graebe, "Sabine Baring-Gould and his old singing-men" in *Folk Song: Tradition, Revival, and Re-Creation,* 178-179. Graebe concludes that the account in *Further Reminiscences* shows Baring-Gould at his "most misleading." However, the newspaper obituary may have deliberately (or unknowingly) concealed the circumstances of Hard's demise, and the slip over the date is understandable in an account written from memory over thirty years after the incident.

61. Baring-Gould and Fleetwood Sheppard, *Songs and Ballads of the West,* 1895 edition, xxiii.

62. Baring-Gould also mentions a Mary Satcherley but Martin Graebe is certain that this was actually the same woman as Sally Satterley (the housewife at Huccaby). Probably Baring-Gould initially misheard the name or misremembered it.

63. Baring-Gould, *Old Country Life,* 278-280. In this book Baring-Gould consistently gives Hard's first name as Richard. In subsequent works, from *Songs and Ballads of the West* to *Further Reminiscences,* it is always given as Robert. It would appear likely that Baring-Gould initially misheard the name and made an error in *Old Country Life,* a mistake that he subsequently corrected. Of course, it is also possible that he was right the first time and consistently wrong thereafter.

64. "Killerton Notebook" [microfiche collection 1.3], no. XXXVI, 48.

65. Baring-Gould and Fleetwood Sheppard, *Songs and Ballads of the West,* 2nd edition (1895), 52-53.

66. "Killerton Notebook" [microfiche collection 1.3], no. XXIII, 32.

67. Baring-Gould and Fleetwood Sheppard, *Songs and Ballads of the West,* 2nd edition (1895), 93.

68. My thanks to Martin Graebe for pointing out that James Parsons was not, as I had supposed, a parishioner of Baring-Gould's since Lewdown, although geographically very close to Lew Trenchard, was in fact in the neighboring parish of Marystow.

69. "Preface," *Songs and Ballads of the West,* 2nd edition, vii.

70. Baring-Gould, *Old Country Life,* 270-271.

71. Baring-Gould, "Among the Western Song Men," *English Illustrated Magazine* 102 (1892): 477.

72. "Plymouth Fair Copy Manuscript" [microfiche collection 2.1], no. VII, unpaginated.

73. Baring-Gould and Fleetwood Sheppard, *Songs and Ballads of the West,* 2nd edition (1895), xxii.

74. "Plymouth Notebook" [microfiche collection 1.2], unpaginated.

75. Baring-Gould and Fleetwood Sheppard, *Songs and Ballads of the West,* 2nd edition (1895), xxii.

76. Baring-Gould and Fleetwood Sheppard, *Songs and Ballads of the West,* 2nd edition (1895), 56-57.

77. Baring-Gould, *Old Country Life,* 275-76.

78. "Killerton Notebook" [microfiche collection 1.3], no. XCVII, pagination unclear but possibly 126.

79. Baring-Gould, *Further Reminiscences,* 199.

80. Baring-Gould, *Further Reminiscences,* 199.

81. Baring-Gould, *Old Country Life,* 277-78.

82. Baring-Gould and Fleetwood Sheppard, *Songs and Ballads of the West,* 2nd edition (1895), 46-47.

83. Baring-Gould, *Old Country Life,* 272.

84. I have had to slightly adjust a few notes in order to retain Bussell's barring.

85. "Plymouth Fair Copy Manuscript" [microfiche 2.1], no. XCIII, 237.

86. Baring-Gould and Fleetwood Sheppard, *Songs and Ballads of the West,* 2nd edition (1895), xl.

87. Baring-Gould and Fleetwood Sheppard, *Songs and Ballads of the West,* 2nd edition (1895), 198-99.

88. Baring-Gould, *Further Reminiscences,* 201.

89. Baring-Gould and Fleetwood Sheppard, *Songs and Ballads of the West,* 2nd edition (1895), xxxvii.

90. Baring-Gould and Fleetwood Sheppard, *Songs and Ballads of the West,* 2nd edition (1895), 175-77.

91. Baring-Gould, *Further Reminiscences,* 185.

92. Martin Graebe has pointed this out in "Sabine Baring-Gould and his old singing-men," in *Folk Song: Tradition, Revival, and Re-Creation,* 178. He credits Chris Bearman for the census and demographic data on the basis of which he makes the observation. Some of Bearman's pioneering work may be found in his excellent doctoral dissertation, Christopher James Bearman, "The English Folk Music Movement 1898-1914," Ph.D. thesis, University of Hull, 2001. Graebe also references "In the Beginning: Methods and Results of the Pioneer Folk Song Collectors," an unpublished paper by Bearman delivered at the Baring-Gould Study Day, Okehampton, 24 October 2001.

93. Baring-Gould, *Further Reminiscences,* 185-86.

94. Baring-Gould, *Further Reminiscences,* 187.

95. Baring-Gould, *Further Reminiscences,* 211.

96. Baring-Gould, *Old Country Life,* 260-61.

97. "Harvard Notebook" [microfiche 1.4].

98. Baring-Gould, *Further Reminiscences,* 212.

99. Baring-Gould, *Further Reminiscences,* 212.

100. See note 11.

101. See note 10.

102. Baring-Gould, et al., *Songs of the West,* xi.

103. Baring-Gould and Fleetwood Sheppard, *Songs and Ballads of the West,* 2nd edition (1895), xii. When I give the title of the work as *Songs (and Ballads) of the West*, it is my shorthand way of referring to all three editions together. There was never an edition which had "and Ballads" in parentheses; the words were included in the first two editions and omitted in the third.

104. Baring-Gould seems to have been uncertain whether to spell her Christian name as Ann or Anne.

105. Baring-Gould and Fleetwood Sheppard, *Songs and Ballads of the West,* 2nd edition (1895), 226-27.

106. "Plymouth Fair Copy Manuscript" [microfiche 2.1], no. CVII, unpaginated.

107. Baring-Gould and Fleetwood Sheppard, *Songs and Ballads of the West,* 2nd edition (1895), xlii.

108. Baring-Gould and Fleetwood Sheppard, *Songs and Ballads of the West,* 2nd edition (1895), 68-69.

109. Baring-Gould and Fleetwood Sheppard, *Songs and Ballads of the West,* 2nd edition (1895), 184-85.

110. Baring-Gould and Fleetwood Sheppard, *Songs and Ballads of the West,* 2nd edition (1895), 34-35.

111. Baring-Gould and Fleetwood Sheppard, *Songs and Ballads of the West,* 2nd edition (1895), 40-41.

112. Baring-Gould and Fleetwood Sheppard, *Songs and Ballads of the West,* 2nd edition (1895), 200-1.

113. For this information I am indebted to Martin Graebe, in a personal communication.

114. Baring-Gould and Fleetwood Sheppard, *Songs and Ballads of the West,* 2nd edition (1895), xx-xxi.

115. Baring-Gould and Fleetwood Sheppard, *Songs and Ballads of the West,* 2nd edition (1895), 50-51.

116. Baring-Gould, et al., *Songs of the West,* x-xi.

117. Baring-Gould and Fleetwood Sheppard, *Songs and Ballads of the West,* 2nd edition (1895), xxiv.

118. Baring-Gould and Fleetwood Sheppard, *Songs and Ballads of the West,* 2nd edition (1895), xxix.

119. Baring-Gould and Fleetwood Sheppard, *Songs and Ballads of the West,* 2nd edition (1895), xxxii.

120. Baring-Gould and Fleetwood Sheppard, *Songs and Ballads of the West,* 2nd edition (1895), xxxiii.

121. Baring-Gould and Fleetwood Sheppard, *Songs and Ballads of the West,* 2nd edition (1895), xxxiv.

122. Baring-Gould and Fleetwood Sheppard, *Songs and Ballads of the West,* 2nd edition (1895), xxxviii.

123. Baring-Gould and Fleetwood Sheppard, *Songs and Ballads of the West,* 2nd edition (1895), xl.

124. Baring-Gould and Fleetwood Sheppard, *Songs and Ballads of the West,* 2nd edition (1895), xli.

125. Baring-Gould, *Further Reminiscences,* 191-92.

8

Northern Pioneer: Frank Kidson

One of the most knowledgeable and independent-minded personalities to play a major role in the Late Victorian folk-song revival, Frank Kidson (1855-1926) was credited by Lucy Broadwood with being "one of the first people in England to discover the beauty and interest of our English traditional songs."[1] The fruits of this discovery appeared in *Traditional Tunes*, a ground-breaking collection that was first printed in 1891.[2] The contents of the book had been collected during the 1880s, and during the second half of that decade its editor had also begun to make a name for himself as a journalist and musicologist whose knowledge of the history of popular song rivaled that of William Chappell. The aim of this chapter is to explore who this pioneer Yorkshire collector was, how and from whom he began folksong collecting, what his early views were on the nature of vernacular song, and the kind of material he amassed for inclusion in *Traditional Tunes* and the smaller publications that preceded that work.

Traditional Tunes was Kidson's most important publication, but it was by no means the first indication of his interest in folk lyrics and other old vernacular songs, which he appears to have inherited from his grandfather, his mother Mary (née Roberts), and possibly also his father, Francis Kidson, who died in 1872, when young Frank was sixteen and a student at Shadwell boarding school, near Leeds.[3] Francis Kidson, although he earned his living first as a butcher and later, in the employ of the Leeds municipal government, as a rate collector, was in his spare time a published poet who specialized mainly in religious verse,[4] while Frank's grandfather, John Roberts, had also been a poet and enthusiastic book collector with sufficient wealth to indulge his hobby. While growing up Frank had access to his grandfather's library, and later in life he told Lucy Broadwood that, from the age of eight, he had read voraciously novels by Charles Dickens, Frederick Marryat, Fenimore Cooper, and Sir Walter Scott, and that, in particular, Marryat's *Jacob Faithful* had stimulated his interest in vernacular song. At that time he was especially fond of singing sea songs, including some of Charles Dibdin's.[5] The youngest of seven sons, Frank was apprenticed in his late teens to his brother Joseph, who had his own business selling jewelry and antique china. Another brother, Henry, who lived in Liverpool, also dealt in china as well as artworks and antiques, so it is hardly surprising that Frank also became an expert on the subject, publishing (with Joseph) in 1892 a book titled *Historical Notices of the Leeds Old Pottery*.[6]

Frank Kidson's spell as his brother's assistant apparently ended in 1876 when he inherited some shares and rental property from his grandfather. From that time on he had a comfortable, if fairly modest, private income, and no longer had to work for a living. He became a landscape painter and, later, a freelance journalist, activities that also left him time for scholarly pursuits. He continued to live in Leeds, looking after his mother until her death in 1890, and, incidentally, noting down some of the songs that she had sung to him in his adolescence. He initially devoted most of his newly found free time to painting. Throughout his life, however, he added to his grandfather's and father's collection of rare books, which included old music manuscripts, broadsides, chapbooks, and other printed songbooks. He never married, but after his mother's death in 1890 he informally adopted as his daughter his niece, Emma Mary (known as Ethel), who became his housekeeper and assistant. Ethel, who was a talented amateur musician as well as a painter, novelist, and dramatist, usually accompanied him on sketching and song collecting expeditions. She proved very helpful in noting tunes. His early collecting, however, was done without her assistance.

Kidson's career as a painter—his specialty was landscapes, in both water-color and oil—lasted from the mid-1870s into the early twentieth century, and he fairly frequently went on sketching expeditions with other local artists, who included his brother Henry, his first teacher, George Alexander, the flamboyant George Cammidge, and an amateur musician, Edwin Henry Holder. They traveled far afield, their destinations including the Thames valley, the English West Country, the English south coast, North Wales, and southern Scotland, although the Yorkshire Moors seem to have been their favorite location. Kidson also vacationed on the continent, visiting Holland, Belgium, France, and Spain. He exhibited his work through the Leeds Society of Artists, which organized occasional art shows, for example the Yorkshire Fine Art Exhibition (1880), the First Autumn Exhibition of Works by Yorkshire Artists in 1885, and the Leeds Winter Exhibition the following year.[7] He also contributed letters and articles to a periodical titled *The Artist*, becoming a regular columnist for a time. Kidson's sketching expeditions were important not only for his work as a painter. They also provided the opportunity to collect songs from the rural inhabitants with whom he found lodgings, especially when Holder, who sang and played the guitar, helped get music making underway beside the fireplace in farm kitchens.[8]

As mentioned, Kidson probably inherited his love of vernacular song and dance from his parents and grandparents. According to his own testimony he became seriously interested in folksong during the mid-1870s, when he was in his early twenties and working for his elder brother Joseph.[9] During his boyhood he had heard both his grandfather and his mother sing vernacular songs, and decades later he could still recall several ballads and folk lyrics from their repertoires. One of his grandfather's favorite songs was "The Spinning Wheel," while his mother sang, among other items, a version of Robert Burns' "Highland Mary," and two broadside ballads, "The Grey Mare" and "The Summer Morning." "Highland Mary" might not be considered a folksong, but the young Kidson was interested in any vernacular songs that had good tunes and poetic lyrics, whether or not they had known authors. He was also aware that Burns had used an older song, "Katherine Ogie," as the basis for "Highland Mary," and furthermore he had come across a broadside text which included verses seemingly not penned by Burns. His mother, along with another "elderly lady" who also knew the song, sang two of these extra verses, which Kidson considered traditional. In any case, their tune was not the one employed by Burns, being instead a local air "sung early in the present century in the streets of Leeds to Burns' verses."[10] This, then, was at least part of Mary Kidson's version of "Highland Mary," which apparently included the first verse of Burns's song (perhaps more) plus the two "traditional" verses found on the broadside:

Highland Mary

Anon/Robert Burns

Fig. 8.1

Ye banks and braes and streams around
The castle o' Montgomery,

Green be your woods and fair your flowers,
Your waters never drumlie;

There, simmer first unfauld her robes,
And there the langest tarry,
For there I took my last farewell
Of my sweet Highland Mary.

All in the silent hour of night,
Through the green churchyard I'll wander,
Right hearty well I know the spot,
Where Mary she lies under;
I'll weep it o'er with silent grief,
I'll sit and ne'er be weary,

For pleasure there is none for me
Without sweet Highland Mary.

And round sweet Highland Mary's grave,
I'll plant the fairest lily,
The primrose sweet, and violet blue,
Likewise the daffodilly;
But since the world is grown so wild,
In the wilderness I'll tarry;
Come welcome death, thou friend true,
I'll sleep with Highland Mary.[11]

During the early or mid-1880s Kidson apparently began collecting folksongs more systematically. In addition to his mother, his sources were friends, local acquaintances, and street singers, as well as the informants he met on his sketching expeditions. By the mid-1880s, too, he had already amassed a small collection of broadsheets, garlands, and tune books that would become more and more comprehensive as time went by. Around this time, he started researching and writing historical articles on old songs for such local newspapers as the *Leeds Mercury* and the *Yorkshire Post,* as well as for the *Musical Times.* In particular, during 1886-1887 he wrote thirty-two short articles under the general title "Notes on Old Tunes" in the *Leeds Mercury Weekly Supplement,* and a few years later, in 1890-91, he contributed to the same newspaper another thirty-two part series, titled "Old Songs and Airs: Melodies Once Popular in Yorkshire." The year 1890 saw the publication of Kidson's first book, a collection of fiddle and pipe tunes titled *Old English Country Dances,*[12] and, as we have seen, his pioneering collection *Traditional Tunes* was printed the next year, albeit only in a limited edition of two hundred copies. He would follow that publication with other work in the field of vernacular song collecting and scholarly analysis, but in this chapter we will concentrate on his work up to and including *Traditional Tunes.*

As with Baring-Gould, we are fortunate in possessing some archival material that allows us to penetrate to some degree beyond Kidson's books and articles to his actual collecting. This is mainly housed in the Mitchell Library in Glasgow, although there are also a few items in Leeds Central Library and a few others in the British Library. The Kidson archive in Glasgow has been described by Roy Palmer in two publications, "Kidson's Collecting"[13] and *Checklist of Manuscript Songs and Tunes collected from Oral Tradition by Frank Kidson.*[14] There are five manuscript volumes in Kidson's handwriting and each was supplied (perhaps by Kidson's niece, Ethel) with a typewritten list of contents. Yet, as Palmer points out, only a handful of the songs contained in these manuscripts reflect Kidson's early collecting. Seven items date from the years 1888-1890, but they do not correspond with songs or tunes included in Kidson's first two books. The items are "I'Anson's Racehorse," noted by Kidson's friend, T. C. Smith, in 1888, plus five songs apparently collected in or near Leeds by Kidson in 1890, and one noted in North Yorkshire, perhaps while Kidson was on vacation in the North York Moors. Of the five, one song, "In Leinster There Dwelt a Young Damsel," was noted from an unnamed Irish street singer in August, while in October 1890 Kidson obtained "The Foggy Dew" from Robert Holliday of Newtondale in the North Riding. That same year a Mr. Clarke of Wortley, near Leeds, sang Kidson "The Pretty Ploughboy" (aka "The Lark in the Morning"), while his most prolific informant was a Mr. Carr of Bradford, who contributed "Drink Old England Dry," "The One Pound Note," and "The Cuckoo's Nest." And, sadly, that is it for the pre-1891 collecting in the Glasgow archive. Those songs in the manuscripts that we can date with certainty to the year 1891—a batch of five items noted from Kate Thompson, mainly in November and December—were evidently collected too late for use in *Traditional Tunes.*

In short, the Mitchell Library's archival materials, while undoubtedly valuable for his later activities, cast virtually no light upon the origins of the tunes and lyrics that he printed in 1890-91. We will therefore leave a more detailed discussion of them until chapter thirteen, when we will examine Kidson's activities during the 1890s. For his earlier work one is left with little more than that which can be deduced from his publications. Although printed at the beginning of the 1890s, his first two books, *Old English Country Dances* and *Traditional Tunes,* were evidently both based on the collecting and research that he did during the previous decade. At approximately the same time he was also writing his first set of articles for the *Leeds Mercury Weekly Supplement.* Published earlier than his books, this remarkably scholarly journalism gives us the first available glimpse into the mind of the leading music historian of the late Victorian folksong revival.

"Notes on Old Tunes"

Kidson's first important publication relating to folksong was "Notes on Old Tunes," a series of thirty-two articles that he wrote for the magazine supplement of his local newspaper, the *Leeds Mercury*, between 6 November 1886 and 25 June 1887.[15] There are too many to examine each one in detail, but even a quick look at some of the highlights reveals much about Kidson's views on vernacular song at the time. The subject matter of the majority of these short pieces indicates that he was as interested in 'national songs' as in folksongs and old ballads. Not that the latter were completely ignored, since the series included discussions of a Gloucestershire wassail, the Tyneside industrial song "The Keel Row," Martin Parker's broadside ballad "When the King Enjoys His Own Again," and the well-known traditional ballad "The Gypsy Laddie." There were also discussions of several songs which Kidson had obtained from oral tradition and which he considered to be generally known around the north of England and lowland Scotland, such as "Peggy Roy," "The Goose and the Gander," "Caller Herring," and "Pretty Peg o' Derby-O." With these exceptions, most of the individual tunes chosen for analysis had known (if sometimes disputed) authors, and many of them dated from the eighteenth century. They included, among others, "Sally in Our Alley," "The Country Lass," "Tobacco," "Marlbrook," "The Gentle Shepherd," "Bonny Dundee," "Bow Wow Wow," "Dulce Domum," "Auld Lang Syne," and even "God Save the King." Kidson had an explanation for why he was concentrating to such an extent on eighteenth-century national songs. His aim, he stated, was to complement the work of William Chappell, who had focused more on the sixteenth and seventeenth centuries in *Popular Music of the Olden Time*. Right from the outset it was clear that he had a tremendous admiration for Chappell's work, and that he saw himself as the disciple who could pick up where the master had left off:

> It is somewhat singular, considering the general liking there is for old songs, that so little has been written on their history. With regard to English songs, Chappell's *Popular Music of the Olden Time*, excluding short essays and notes to ballad collections, is the only work we have on the subject. It is a perfect marvel of research, and will undoubtedly serve, as it has hitherto done, the purpose of a text-book as long as interest in the subject remains. Chappell appears to have...got together such a mass of books and Mss of ballad music as to have enabled him to completely supersede all future labours. His book, containing about four hundred airs, is, however, necessarily limited, and as he has devoted the bulk of his space to the older class of airs, he leaves the easier task of the collection of eighteenth century airs to other hands.[16]

Kidson evidently saw himself as one of the "other hands," and he believed that the printed sources which Chappell had employed predominantly, (although not exclusively, since he also consulted manuscripts and noted some songs from oral tradition), could and should be complemented by "the songs that have come down to us personally from the singing of father, mother, or more distant relatives, who in turn have received them more directly from the time of their popularity."[17] In these statements we can see elements of the fundamental thesis underlying both "Notes on Old Tunes" and *Traditional Tunes*: that good old songs have come down to us in a variety of ways—in print, on manuscripts, and by oral tradition—and that these different modes of transmission complement each other; moreover, there are various kinds of old songs—folk lyrics, traditional ballads, broadside ballads, and national songs—all of which are equally valuable, at least in principle, and the collector should concern himself or herself with all of them rather than discriminate arbitrarily between types. It was a manifesto in favor of eclecticism and an open mind, one that, like Kidson's championing of the achievements of William Chappell, would find a mixed reception among the English folk music community in the 1890s and 1900s.

In addition to his articles on individual songs, Kidson inserted into this series several general pieces devoted to such topics as John Playford, *Pills to Purge Melancholy*, broadside collections, Jacobite songs, and ballad operas. His aim in doing so was to provide a historical overview of song collecting in England, and to stress the value of the early printed collections as sources for the original tunes to which various vernacular songs were—and are—sung. He argued that no significant song collections were published before the seventeenth century, and that the breakthrough was primarily the work of John Playford:

> The common lyrical productions of the people, while they delighted thousands, were deemed to be of too trivial a nature to be passed into print, and although there were several books of airs published at the latter end of the sixteenth century, yet they are of a very scholastic type of composition. John Playford was the first man who brought forward the popular ditties, and he and his sons succeeding him were the principal music printers of the day. His principal work was *The English Dancing Master*...dated 1651 but really published the preceding year. This is a collection of such ballad airs as were suitable for country dances, and is the chief source from which we are able to draw our knowledge of the lyric music of the period. The work was so popular that no less than eighteen editions were issued, but as in each edition certain tunes were withdrawn and others added, as they lost or came into

favour, each may be considered a separate work. The first edition is in quarto and contains 104 tunes...Of this work the British Museum is possessed of a complete and unique set, enriched with Ms. notes by Mr. William Chappell, from whom the principal part was purchased.[18]

Kidson justified his "somewhat lengthy account" of *The Dancing Master* on the grounds that it was "impossible to quote any historical notice of our English songs without constantly referring to it" because the tunes printed in its various editions were the airs employed in singing the ballads of the day. The texts of the songs, on the other hand, were preserved in such broadside collections as the Pepysian and Roxburghe. He explained to his readers what these collections were, and how they could be used by a music historian in conjunction with *The Dancing Master* and later tune collections such as *Pills to Purge Melancholy, The Merry Musician,* and Watts's *Musical Miscellany*:

> "[T]he Roxburghe ballads...are a vast number of black-letter broadsides collected by Robert, Earl of Oxford, and which were carefully mounted in volumes about the year 1773. Some of these ballads date from Elizabeth's reign but they are mainly of seventeenth century date. Subsequent possessors have increased the collections with more modern ones and they now form four large folio volumes, safely enshrined in the large room in the British Museum. Many selections have been made and published but the collection is too large to reprint in entirety. We are able to identify many airs which occur in *The Dancing Master* and other publications by these ballads as the name of the tune to which each is to be sung is always given, and in some few instances given the musical notes. The Pepysian is a smaller collection, formed by Samuel Pepys, of the Diary, and now at Cambridge. It also is most valuable, but much more difficult of access. The musical collections issued after the first edition of *The Dancing Master* were very numerous, and can but be alluded to here. One of the most famous books of catches and glees was John Hilton's, with the appropriate title, *Catch as Catch Can* (1685), *Musick's Handmaiden for the Virginals* (1673), Playford's *Theatre of Musick* (1685?), *Choice Ayres* (1676), etc. Most of these seventeenth-century collections were merely noted down for some instrument, as the violin, etc., and it was not till the appearance of *Wit and Mirth, or, Pills to Purge Melancholy*...that a regular collection of songs with their airs was attempted. *Wit and Mirth*, on reaching its sixth volume in 1720, contained nearly 800 songs. A similar book was *The Merry Musician, or a Cure for the Spleen*. This is in four volumes [1716-c.1725 (?)]. One of the best gatherings of this period was *Watts' Musical Miscellany*, six volumes, ranging in date from 1729-1731.[19]

In two subsequent articles Kidson focused on what he regarded as the other major printed source for traditional tunes, the scores of eighteenth-century ballad operas. "Few people," he argued, "have any idea of the important part [the ballad operas of the last century] have played in the matter of our lyrics. A very great proportion of our popular songs first appeared in opera, and have been left high and dry in public favour long after even the name of the opera has ceased to be remembered."[20] As examples he cited "Rule Britannia" (from Thomas Arne's masque *Alfred*), "Hearts of Oak" (from the pantomime, *Harlequin Invasion*), and "Stingo," "Packington's Pound," "Greensleeves," "Up in the Morning Early," "Lilliburlero," and "Babes in the Wood" (tunes that were all utilized in the first successful English ballad opera, John Gay's *The Beggar's Opera*). Similarly Gay's follow-up creation, *Polly*, employed an eclectic mix of Scottish and English melodies: "'Twas within a furlong of Edinburgh," "O Waly, Waly," "Corn Rigs," "Through the Woods, Laddie," "The Collier Has a Daughter," "Tweedside," "Katharine Ogie," "Hark the Bonny Christ Church Bells," "There Was a Jovial Beggar" (aka "A Hunting We Will Go"), and "To You Fair Ladies Now at Hand." Subsequent ballad operas that drew upon the wealth of English traditional music still readily available for re-use in the eighteenth century included *Momus Turned Fabulist, or Vulcan's Wedding* (1729), *The Devil to Pay, or Wives Metamophosed* (1731), *The Rival Milliners, or the Humours of Covent Garden,* and *The Village Opera*. From *Momus Turned Fabulist* Kidson reproduced the tune of "Woman's Work Is Never Done" plus an appropriate verse from a broadside in the Roxburghe collection:

> Here is a song for maids to sing,
> Both in the winter and the spring;
> It is such a pretty conceited thing,
> Which will much pleasure to them bring.
> Maids may sit still, go, or run,
> But a woman's work is never done.[21]

Woman's Work Is Never Done

Anon/Kidson

Fig. 8.2

Kidson had a more extensive and detailed knowledge of these seventeenth- and eighteenth-century printed sources for folksong and ballad tunes than any other participant in the late Victorian vernacular song revival, but, as we have seen, his interests went well beyond print. He was a folklorist, enthusiastically studying local customs, especially the ceremonial festivities associated with Christmas, Easter, and harvest time. One of his articles in the "Notes on Old Songs" series was about wassailing. He lamented that the custom of wassailing was dying out in Yorkshire, and that even carol singing was degenerating in nature, with the old folk carols being superseded by more recent religious or even commercial creations. To provide his readers with a good example of a wassail song recently noted from oral tradition he was forced to have recourse to one collected on Christmas Eve a few years before by a Gloucestershire friend. He explained that it was "sung by the farm labourers on Christmas Eve, a small band of them going about to the various large farmers carrying a wassail-bowl decorated with ribbons…The verses which were sung are not sparkling with point or wit, but doubtless served the purpose for which they were intended, and my friend told me that the quantity was largely dependent on the beer forthcoming; for if you gave them liquor enough they would sing half the night."[22] He supplemented this item with a Christmas rhyme that he had noted in Yorkshire, commenting that he believed the simple melody was actually derived from "one of our oldest traditional ballad tunes." Its date of composition was no later than the fifteenth century, and, in his opinion, it was in fact an early version of the tune used for "Greensleeves." The children's rhyme was called "Dame Get Up":

Dame Get Up

Anon/Kidson

Fig. 8.3

Dame get up and bake your pies,
Bake your pies, bake your pies,
Dame get up and bake your pies,
On Christmas Day in the morning.

Dame, what makes your maidens lie,
Maidens lie, maidens lie,
Dame, what makes your maidens lie,
On Christmas Day in the morning.

Dame, what makes your ducks to die,
Ducks to die, ducks to die,
Dame, what makes your ducks to die,
On Christmas Day in the morning.

Their wings are cut and they cannot fly,
Cannot fly, cannot fly,
Their wings are cut and they cannot fly,
On Christmas Day in the morning.[23]

Kidson was also interested in traditional balladry, and he argued that the Jacobites had often made use of ballad airs when creating the corpus of older songs associated with the various anti-Orange and anti-Hanoverian rebellions. As an example he gave the Jacobite song "Wae's Me for Prince Charlie," the tune of which derived from that given for "Johnnie Faa, or The Gypsy Laddie" by William McGibbon in his *Collection of Scots Tunes*, a book that Kidson described as one of the most dependable Scottish ballad collections and a fountainhead of later folksong melodies. In this case, moreover, it was possible to trace the tune even further back, to a dance tune titled "Ladie Camille's Lilt" in the Skene manuscript.[24] He also discussed the popular Scottish air "Lochaber No More," commenting that its prototype was the tune of an old ballad that was once well known on both sides of the English-Scottish border, "Lord Randal" or "Lord Ronald, My Son." Robert Burns, he pointed out, picked up the tune from oral tradition in Ayrshire and inserted it in Johnson's *Musical Museum* with a fragment of the ballad, while the same air was also to be found in Bunting's Irish collection, as "Limerick's Lamentation." He concluded that since there was little difference between the traditional music of northern Ireland and that of southern Scotland, the tune, which was probably in common currency among soldiers, could have traveled either way between the two countries.[25]

Kidson also stressed that the political boundary between England and Scotland was in no sense a musical one, and that Northumbrian and lowland Scottish folk music had so much in common that it was often impossible to tell whether a given tune had started its life north or south of the border. Addressing the question of whether "Auld Lang Syne" and "The Keel Row" were examples of the Scottish stealing Northumbrian tunes and passing them off as their own, he argued that no definitive answer was possible in either case, but what evidence there was tended to favor the Scots. While the tune of "Auld Lang Syne" was apparently composed by William Shield, a native of Newcastle, for his opera *Rosina* (1753), Shield's tune, like Burns's variant of it, was actually based on two older airs "I fee'd a lass at Martinmas" and "The Miller's Wedding," at least one of which was Scottish. Similarly, although "The Keel Row" was located by Chappell in several late eighteenth-century manuscripts as well as in Topliffe's *Selection of Melodies of the Tyne and Wear*, it was also printed in an earlier book of Scottish airs, *A Collection of Favourite Scots Tunes*, edited by Charles MacLean and published in Edinburgh during the 1770s. The book includes "Johnnie Cope" and other Jacobite material, and MacLean was associated with the Jacobite faction in Scotland. Kidson therefore suggested that "Well May the Keel Row" might well have originated as a Jacobite air during the 1745 rebellion. The lyric, on the other hand, seemed to link the song with Tyneside, but even that was not conclusive since the word "keel" was used to mean a barge on both sides of the border, and Scottish versions of the song refer to Canongate (in Edinburgh) rather than Sandgate in Newcastle. He ended this article by remarking that "anyone who has made the subject his study will know the difficulty in settling the nationality of traditional airs. Fiddlers were constantly in request and consequently passing from one country to another with batches of tunes; these being picked up by ear or heard imperfectly quickly got the national character of the music being grafted on to them for the future puzzle of musical antiquaries."[26] Pointing out that lowland Scots and Northumbrian dialects also sounded very similar, he concluded that it was impossible to separate the music of the north of England from the south of Scotland.

One more example of Kidson's musical detective work in "Notes to Old Tunes" must suffice. He enjoyed old comic songs, and took the genre as the subject for another one of his articles, focusing on the tune "Bow, Wow, Wow." He claimed that "the comic song writer of the old days differed in many respects from the modern specimen" because to be successful he had to be witty as well as licentious and because he was expected to set his humorous new lyric to a well-known tune. There were, in fact, about a dozen stock airs from which he had to choose:

> The stock airs for humorous songs may be almost counted on the fingers. Nearly all had a refrain or burden and the metre of the song as well as the original refrain, which was generally retained, at once identified the air to which it was intended to be sung. The stock airs, then, were—the two versions of "Derry Down," "Gee Ho, Dobbin," "Bow, Wow, Wow," "The Black Joke," "Alley Croaker," "Langolee," "Balline-Mona-Ora," "Push about the Forum," and one or two others.[27]

Kidson then discussed the history of "Bow, Wow, Wow," finding it first in *Calliope, or the Vocal Enchantress* (1788). He commented that the words had little value, their rather feeble humor consisting of comparing the lawyer, the parson, and the courtier to dogs of various description. The reason that the song had survived and become a vernacular one, he suggested, was primarily because the air was "good, simple and taking." It was even adopted by Charles Dibdin for his jocularly patriotic ditty "The Mammoth and Buonaparte" and by Tom Dibdin for another anti-Napoleon song, "The Negotiation, or, John Bull versus Buonaparte," both of which made use of a variant of the air and the catchy "Bow, wow, wow" refrain.[28]

While Kidson never spelled it out explicitly in "Notes on Old Tunes," one can easily read between the lines the basic thesis that he was already developing on the relationship of English folksong to commercial popular song. He was convinced of three very important, if controversial, truths. One was that the pool of authentic traditional melody was not coterminous with England but rather extended to much of the United Kingdom, including lowland Scotland and northern and eastern Ireland. Second, just as by examining carefully the large collections of broadsides in the British Museum and other libraries one could locate, and often date, the original words to many folksongs and ballads, so too by carefully researching a large array of publications from Playford's *The English Dancing Master* onwards one could locate and date early versions of their tunes. Tunes and texts could then be reunited. Third, because of the numerous and widespread debts owed by seventeenth- and eighteenth-century composers to the rich legacy of traditional song, and because, on the other hand, country singers took up and made the best commercial songs part of oral tradition, it was ultimately pointless to try to draw hard-and-fast distinctions between broadside ballads and traditional ballads and between folksongs and national songs. If a song was good enough to survive beyond its initial airing and became, *de facto*, a vernacular song, it was worth singing and studying, whether or not its author's name was known. And, of course, the same was true for instrumental tunes.

Old English Country Dances

Old English Country Dances, a collection of instrumental tunes that Kidson published in 1890, was a work of antiquarian research rather than field collecting. Some of the melodies printed in it were taken from old manuscript tune books that Kidson had found in second-hand book stalls in Leeds and elsewhere, but most were derived from such seventeenth- and eighteenth-century printed sources as John Playford's *The Dancing Master,* John Walsh's *Compleat Country Dancing Master,* John Johnson's *Choice Collection of 200 Favourite Country Dances*, and Peter Thompson's *Complete Collection of 200 Favourite Country Dances*. Kidson's aim was to rescue from oblivion fine tunes that had once been much loved but had since been neglected; he commented in his "Preface" that his collection consisted "not of the most popular, but of the least known, country dances having merit, and is selected to show the variety of styles in vogue from the middle of the 17th to the beginning of the 19th century."[29]

The small book was innovative: not only was it novel to focus on dance tunes and other instrumentals rather than song tunes, but a depth of scholarship about the subject was evident that was rare for the time. Kidson clearly had an extensive and detailed knowledge of the entire history of English music publishing from its beginnings in the Tudor era, and he included a very useful chronological bibliography of printed collections of country dance music. The earliest publications that he listed were those edited by John Playford in the mid-seventeenth century, and the earliest tunes that he printed derived from Playford's *The Dancing Master*. An example is "Once I Loved a Maiden Fair," taken from the first (1651) edition. Kidson chose this particular tune because it was the mid-seventeenth-century melody to which a broadside ballad in the Roxburghe collection was intended to be sung. It differed from that included by William Chappell in *Popular Music of the Olden Time.* Although Kidson was a disciple of Chappell, he was quite willing to dispute his mentor's findings when he thought necessary, and on this occasion he concluded that Chappell's version reflected an eighteenth-century corruption of Playford's original.[30]

Once I Loved a Maiden Fair

Anon

Fig. 8.4

As a Yorkshireman, Kidson was especially interested in the dance music and songs of northern England, especially the northeast. That included the border balladry of Northumberland and the popular music of Tyneside. We have seen that he included in the series of "Notes on Old Tunes" that he wrote for the *Leeds Mercury Weekly Supplement* an article on "The Keel Row," in which he discussed the tricky issue of whether the tune was Scottish or Northumbrian.

Well May the Keel Row

Anon

Fig. 8.5

The melody was clearly one of his favorites, and he duly included it in *Old English Country Dances*. Although his version was taken from an early Scottish source and he believed that the tune might well have originated north of the border, he pointed out that the best-known version of the song exhibited clear links with the river and coastal shipping of Newcastle-upon-Tyne and the other ports serving the Northumberland and Durham coalfields.[31]

As a conscientious music historian, Kidson was well aware of the published work of earlier Yorkshire collectors, including James Orchard Halliwell and Davison Ingledew. From his perspective the main problem with their work was that while they had diligently located and reprinted texts, including many broadside ballads, their books contained no tunes. Kidson in some respects closely resembled Halliwell: they were both avid purchasers of broadsheets and they shared an antiquarian love of old books, especially those that had anything to do with song or dance. Where Kidson sought to go beyond Halliwell was in putting the tunes and texts of broadsides back together, and he correctly believed that whereas the Ballad Society was making good (if slow) progress in making broadside texts again accessible to the public, virtually no work had been done on broadside tunes. He therefore included in *Old English Country Dances* a considerable number of tunes that were commonly used by seventeenth- and eighteenth-century ballad-mongers.

Many of the fifty-three tunes in *Old English Country Dances* were purely instrumental pieces, but others had lyrics associated with them. Although Kidson did not normally print all the words with the melodies, he usually provided a verse or two for illustrative purposes in his scholarly notes. A good example of a standard tune employed by broadside ballad writers, not to mention the writers of bawdy songs, is "Ge[e] Ho, Dobbin!"[32]

Ge Ho, Dobbin

Anon

Fig. 8.6

As I was a driving my wagon one day,
I met a young damsel tight—buxom and gay;
I kindly accosted her with a low bow,
And I felt my whole body I cannot tell how;
Ge ho, Dobbin! Hi ho, Dobbin!
Ge ho, ge Dobbin! Ge ho, ge ho!, &c.[33]

About this tune Kidson made the following comment:

This has ever been a most popular air, and a countless number of humorous songs have been set to it. It being a good and catching melody, with a refrain which everybody knew, caused it so largely to be employed. The original song is called—"The Waggoner, or Ge ho, Dobbin!" and is in *Apollo's Cabinet, or the Muses Delight*, 1757...The present copy (with the terminal strain added from *Apollo's Cabinet*) is from *Thompson's Country Dances*, vol. 1, *circa* 1759. A song in [the ballad opera] *Love in a Village*, 1762, is set to this air. The modern tune has considerable difference from this original one, and is frequently published.[34]

The original song had eight verses, but Kidson included only one—for illustrative purposes—in his notes to the tune. The lyric was ribald, and this is an example of his heavy hand as an editor. In this instance he was just as guilty of bowdlerization as Baring-Gould, and, worse, he failed to indicate what he had done and why.

Another example is "The Dame of Honour,"[35] a tune found in a late (1728) edition of the *Dancing Master* but also used by Thomas D'Urfey for one of his own compositions in the first volume of his edition of *Pills to Purge Melancholy*, and then subsequently employed in a string of ballad operas in the 1720s and 1730s.

The Dame of Honour

Anon

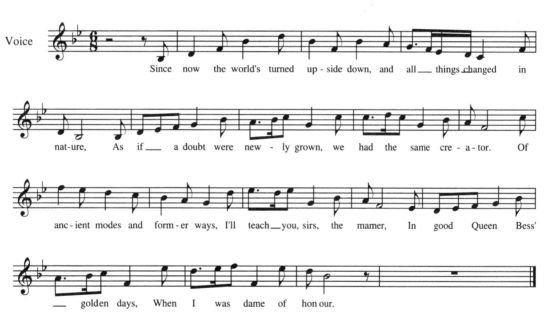

Fig. 8.7

It was the tune with which Kidson was primarily concerned. In *Old English Country Dances* he included only one verse of what had been, in the early eighteenth century, a highly popular vernacular song:

Since now the world's turned upside down and all things changed in nature,
As if a doubt were newly grown we had the same creator,
Of ancient modes and former ways, I'll teach you sirs the manner,
In good Queen Bess's golden days when I was Dame of Honour.[36]

He later printed two more verses in an article in *Musical Times:*

I had an ancient noble seat, tho' now is come to ruin,
Where mutton, beef, and such good meat in hall were daily chewing;
Of humming beer my cellar full, I was the yearly donor,
Where toping knaves had many a pull, when I was Dame of Honour.

> My men of homespun honest grays had coats and comely badges;
> They wore no dirty ragged lace, nor e'er complained for wages;
> For gawdy fringe and silk o' th' town I fear'd no threat'ning dunner,
> But wore a decent grogram gown, when I was Dame of Honour.[37]

A fourth verse eventually turned up in Kidson and Moffat's *The Minstrelsy of England:*

> My neighbours still I treated round and strangers that came near me,
> The poor, too, always welcome found, whose prayers did still endear me,
> Let, therefore, who at court would be no churl nor yet no fawner,
> Match in old hospitality Queen Bess's Dame of Honour.[38]

Old English Country Dances was an early fruit of what became Kidson's passion for the remainder of his life: research into the history of popular melodies and music publishing. While it was not based on field collecting, its extensive bibliography and informative notes demonstrated that Kidson already had a comprehensive knowledge of the history of English popular music. In researching the detailed history of music publishing he had taken up where Chappell left off, and was probably already the leading Victorian scholar in the field. What this meant was that Kidson would have a unique knowledge base to draw upon when assessing the relationship of songs noted from oral tradition to other vernacular songs known from old printed sources. *Old English Country Dances* was followed one year later by the most important of his many publications, *Traditional Tunes* (1891), his first published foray into the realm of folksong collecting from oral tradition. However, it is evident that Kidson had some years earlier begun collecting song melodies (and some song texts) as well as instrumental tunes. So, before we examine *Traditional Tunes*, let us try to reconstruct the pattern and nature of his early song collecting during the 1880s.

Informants and Early Collecting

Kidson's early folksong collecting appears to have been quite eclectic. The songs he noted were varied in nature, and some of the earliest of them appear to have been obtained quite casually, from family and friends or from individuals encountered by chance in the street. Apart from the seven items preserved in manuscript in the Mitchell Library, *Traditional Tunes* provides our only evidence about what he collected during the 1880s, which means that the examples cited and quoted in this section are by necessity taken from that book. However, there is an important qualification to be made at the outset. Not all of his collecting was in fact done by Kidson personally. He mobilized a small network of friends to find songs for him. The two most prolific of these helpers, who were source singers in their own right but who also sought out other singers on Kidson's behalf, were Charles Lolley and Benjamin Holgate. One way or another Lolley would contribute twenty-five items to *Traditional Tunes,* while Holgate was credited with twelve.

Both men were personal friends of Kidson. Benjamin Holgate was a draughtsman, accountant, and company secretary, and he eventually became a director of a local engineering firm; he had a strong interest in science and technology, and was a Fellow of the Geological Society. He came from Headingley (on the outskirts of Leeds) and focused his collecting efforts on the districts to the north and west of the city. Charles Lolley was an artisan turned businessman. He initially made his living as a bricklayer, then worked as a foreman for a firm of Leeds building contractors, William Nicholson and Son. In 1891 he became the firm's manager, a job which took him on frequent trips away from Leeds to other parts of northern England. He collected songs mainly in the East Riding of Yorkshire, especially in the Howden area, where he had grown up. Lolley's role in *Traditional Tunes* was so large that one is almost tempted to regard the work as a joint effort between him and Kidson. Nonetheless, it was Kidson who was the lynchpin of this collaborative effort. He was the spider at the center of a web of informants that stretched from Liverpool on the west coast to Hull on the east coast and north to Flamborough on the North Yorkshire coast and beyond to the Scottish border country.

Kidson's sources can be divided into seven main categories: family, friends in Leeds, residents of the villages surrounding Leeds, inhabitants of towns and villages on the North York Moors and the coast nearby, informants from the East Riding of Yorkshire, a small number of individuals elsewhere in England, and a group of Scottish informants. We will examine each in turn.

As we've seen, Kidson's initial collecting was almost certainly from his mother's singing, and possibly also from other family members, including his grandfather. Of the three items we know that he noted from his mother, her version of "Highland Mary" has been given earlier. "The Grey Mare" was a comic ballad about a suitor who tries to bargain too hard over his intended's dowry and ends up losing both bride and fortune. "The Summer Morning," which laments the results of military recruitment practices that ensnared unsuspecting countrymen, was also known as "[The] White Cockade":

White Cockade (The Summer Morning)

Anon

It was one sum-mer morn-ing, As I went o'er the moss, I had no thought of list-ing, Till the sold-iers did me cross; They kind-ly did in-vite me, To a flow-ing bowl, and down They ad-vanc-ed, they ad-vanc-ed, they ad-vanc-ed, they ad-vanc-ed, They ad-vanc-ed me some mon-ey, Ten guin-eas and a crown.

Fig. 8.8

It was one summer morning as I went o'er the moss,
I had no thought of 'listing, till the soldiers did me cross;
They kindly did invite me to a flowing bowl, and down
They advancèd, they advancèd, they advancèd, they advancèd,
They advancèd me some money, ten guineas and a crown.

'Tis true my love has 'listed, he wears a white cockade,
He is a handsome tall young man, besides a roving blade,
He is a handsome young man, and he's gone to serve the King,
Oh, my very heart is breaking, my very heart is breaking,
Oh, my very heart is breaking, all for love of him.

My love is tall and handsome, and comely for to see,
And by a sad misfortune a soldier now is he,
I hope the man that 'listed him may not prosper night or day,
For I wish that the Hollanders, I wish that the Hollanders,
I wish that the Hollanders may sink him in the sea.

Oh, may he never prosper, oh, may he never thrive,
Nor anything he takes in hand so long as he's alive;
May the very grass he treads upon the ground refuse to grow,
Since he's been the only cause, since he's been the only cause,
Since he's been the only cause of my sorrow, grief, and woe.

Then he pulled out a handkerchief and wiped her flowing eyes,
"Leave off these lamentations, likewise these doleful sighs,
Leave off your grief and sorrow, while I march o'er the plain,

We'll be married, we'll be married, we'll be married, we'll be married,
We'll be married, we'll be marrièd, when I return again."

Oh, now my love has 'listed, and I for him will rove,
I'll write his name on every tree that grows in yonder grove;
Where the huntsman he does hallo, and the hounds do sweetly crie,
To remind me of my ploughboy, to remind me of my ploughboy,
To remind me of my ploughboy until the day I die.[39]

Kidson next turned to his circle of middle-class friends who lived in and around Leeds. They included not only the two singer-collectors mentioned earlier, Benjamin Holgate and Charles Lolley, but also John Briggs, William Cheetham, John Holmes, Thomas Hewson, and Washington Teasdale. These men represented the progressive wing of the local bourgeoisie. They were liberal, even radical, thinkers, who combined a strong commitment to natural science with an interest in ameliorating social problems. William Cheetham, a successful cloth manufacturer and a Fellow of the Geological Society, supplied versions of the ballads "Chevy Chace" and "Henry Martin." John Holmes, a philanthropist and social activist as well as a businessman, provided "The Three Ravens." From John Briggs Kidson obtained just one song that would be included in *Traditional Tunes*, "When Adam Was First Created." It was a substantial fragment of a mildly sexist, quasi-religious ballad of which James Henry Dixon had previously collected a text in the northeast of England and printed it in *Ancient Poems, Ballads and Songs of the Peasantry of England* as "Old Adam." Kidson was thus able to reunite text and tune.[40] Thomas Hewson, a civil engineer in charge of the city's waterworks, was the source for Kidson's version of "Young Bucks A-Hunting Go." Washington Teasdale, also an engineer, was an extraordinarily energetic man with a wide range of scientific interests. Fascinated by photography, astronomy, and archeology, he wrote a book about Stonehenge, pioneered the use of the lantern slide for illustrating lectures, and brought the art of flash photography to Leeds. Kidson noted three songs from Teasdale: "The Brewer Laddie," "The Jolly Shilling," and "The Card Song."

One would like to give several examples to illustrate the kind of material Kidson acquired from these middle-class friends, but one must suffice. It was quite a *coup* to find a good tune for the venerable border ballad "Chevy Chace," so here is the one that William Cheetham heard sung in a "doleful voice" by a ballad singer in the West Riding of Yorkshire. Kidson commented that the melody, noted from oral tradition, was not the same as any of "the many published airs to which Chevy Chace is found united." Claiming that the ballad text was "much too long and too well known" for inclusion in his publication, Kidson would print only two verses in *Traditional Tunes*. The melody was the important thing:

Chevy Chace

Anon

God prosper long our noble king, Our lives and safe-ties all;__ A__
nob-le hunt-ing did there once In__ Chev-y Chace be-fall.__

Fig. 8.9

God prosper long our noble king,   To drive the deer with hound and horn,
Our lives and safeties all;   Earl Percy took his way;
A woeful hunting did there once   The child may rue that is unborn
In Chevy Chace befall.   The hunting of that day.[41]

Charles Lolley was a fiddler and tradition carrier as well as a songhunter. He sang to Kidson five items that he had learned in his youth at Howden, a small town located on the River Ouse about halfway between Leeds and the seaport of

Hull. They were "The *Nightingale*," "The Spotted Cow," two versions (with different tunes) of "My True Love Once He Courted Me," and one ballad that Francis Child would accept into his canon. Lolley could remember the tune but only part of one verse, so Kidson took the text of "Geordie" from a Scottish printed source, Johnson's *Museum*:

Geordie

Anon

There was a bat-tle in the North, And nob - les there were man - y, And

they hae killed Sir Char-lie__ Hay, And laid the wyte on Geor - die.

Fig. 8.10

There was a battle in the North, and nobles there were many;
And they hae killed Sir Charlie Hay, and laid the wyte on Geordie.

O, he has written a lang letter, he sent it to his lady -
"Ye maun come up to Edinbro' town, to see what words o' Geordie."

When first she looked the letter on, she was baith red and rosy;
But she hadna read a word but twa, till she wallow't like a lily.

And she has mounted her gude grey steed, her menzie a' gaed wi' her;
And she did neither eat nor drink, till Edinbro' town did see her.

At first appear'd the fatal block, and syne the axe to head him,
And Geordie coming down the stair, wi' bands of iron on him.

O, she's down on her bended knees—I wat she's pale and weary—
"O! pardon, pardon, noble king, and gie me back my dearie.

I hae borne seven sons to my Geordie, dear, the seventh ne'er saw his daddy;
O! pardon, pardon, noble king, pity a waefu' lady."

"Gar bid the headin' man mak haste," our king replied fu' lordly;
"O! noble king, tak a' that's mine, but gie me back my Geordie."

An aged lord at the king's right hand, says, "Noble king, but hear me,
Gar her tell down five thousand pounds, and gie her back her dearie."

Some gae her marks, some gae her crowns, some gae her dollars many;
And she's tell'd down five thousand pounds, and gotten again her dearie.

He claspit her by the middle sma', and he kissed her lips sae rosy—
"The fairest flower o' woman kind, is my sweet, bonnie lady!"[42]

Charles Lolley's own repertoire as a singer was seemingly not large, and was mainly confined to songs that he had learned as a youth. Although there is some ambiguity over a few items, by and large we can separate what Lolley sang to Kidson and what he collected on Kidson's behalf, almost invariably in the East Riding of Yorkshire. Of all Kidson's informants and helpers Lolley was by far the most important, in terms of both the quality and quantity of the songs that he supplied, as we shall see when we examine the songs that Kidson obtained from the East Riding.

In the case of Kidson's other major informant from Leeds, Benjamin Holgate, it is not so easy to make the distinction between Holgate's own repertoire as a singer and what he collected with Kidson's project in mind. It seems that when Holgate obtained a song that he liked from another singer he would make it his own, before presenting it to Kidson. So, as far as we can tell, Kidson noted down from Holgate's own singing the dozen items he credited to his friend in *Traditional Tunes*. They included two Child ballads, "The Knight and the Shepherd's Daughter" and "Barbara Allen," and several broadside ballads, including "The Farmer's Boy" and "Mary across the Wild Moor." Other titles were "Come All Ye Bold Young Countrymen," "Forty Miles," "Three Maidens A-Milking Did Go," "Execution Song," "The Roving Heckler Lad," "I Am a Rover," and "My True Love Once He Courted Me." It is difficult to choose a single song from this list as most typical of Holgate's collecting and/or singing repertoire, but this was another of his broadside ballads, "The Banks of Sweet Dundee":

The Banks of Sweet Dundee

Anon

Fig. 8.11

It's of a farmer's daughter, so beautiful, I'm told,
Her father died and left her five hundred pound in gold!
She lived with her uncle, the cause of all her woe,
But you soon shall hear, this maiden fair did prove his overthrow.

Her uncle had a ploughboy young Mary loved full well,
And in her uncle's garden their tales of love they'd tell;
But there was a wealthy squire who oft came her to see,
But she still loved her ploughboy on the banks of sweet Dundee.

Her uncle and the squire rode out one summer's day,
"Young William is in favour," her uncle he did say;
"Indeed, 'tis my intention to tie him to a tree,
Or else to bribe the press-gang on the banks of sweet Dundee."

The press-gang came to William when he was all alone,
He boldly fought for liberty, but they were six to one;
The blood did flow in torrents: "Pray, kill me now," said he,
"I would rather die for Mary on the banks of sweet Dundee."

This maid one day was walking, lamenting for her love,
She met the wealthy squire down in her uncle's grove;
He put his arms around her: "Stand off, base man," said she,
"You sent the only lad I love from the banks of sweet Dundee."

He clasped his arms around her and tried to throw her down,
Two pistols and a sword she spied beneath his morning gown;
Young Mary took the pistols and the sword he used so free,
But she did fire and shot the squire on the banks of sweet Dundee.

Her uncle overheard the noise, and hastened to the ground,
"O, since you've killed the squire, I'll give you your death wound!"
"Stand off!" then young Mary said, "Undaunted I will be."
The trigger drew and her uncle slew on the banks of sweet Dundee.

A doctor soon was sent for, a man of noted skill,
Likewise came his lawyer for him to sign his will;
He left his gold to Mary who fought so manfully,
And closed his eyes no more to rise on the banks of sweet Dundee.[43]

When Kidson began to collect from informants whom he had not known previously he seems to have first visited a number of villages that lay on the outskirts of Leeds. He was not always very forthcoming about the details of his collecting in what he sometimes called "the Leeds district." For example, we know that three songs, "Through the Grove," "The Goose and the Gander," and "The Death of Bill Brown" were found near (but outside) Leeds, but we do not know exactly where or the names of the informants who sang them. One version of "The Spotted Cow" came from the village of Calverley, and "The Holbeck Moor Cock-Fight" was collected at both Holbeck and at the neighboring village of Hunslet, another place where cockfighting was a traditional pastime. Horsforth was where Kidson's friend William Cheetham lived, while John Holmes's and Thomas Hewson's residences were in Roundhay. Best of all was Alderhill, near Meanwood, where Kidson found Mrs. Holt. He never tells us her first name, but she proved a valuable informant, providing him with a full version of another Child ballad, "Lord Bateman," several broadside ballads ("Green Bushes," "The Golden Glove," and "The Farmer's Boy"), an eighteenth-century vernacular song from the Vauxhall pleasure gardens, "Colin and Phoebe," and a local song about country courting, "Young Roger of the Valley." Indeed she was the most prolific of his informants in the villages surrounding Leeds. This is her version of "The Farmer's Boy." It has a melody different from, although perhaps related to, the tune to which these words are usually sung:

The sun was sunk behind yon hill,
Across yon dreary moor;
When poor and lame, a boy there came,
Up to a farmer's door:
"Can you tell me if here it be
That I can find employ,
To plough and sow, and reap and mow,
And be a farmer's boy?"

"My father is dead, and mother is left
With five children, great and small;
And what is worse for mother still,
I'm the oldest of them all.
Though little, I'll work as hard as a Turk,
If you'll give me employ,
To plough and sow, to reap and mow
And be a farmer's boy."

"And if that you won't me employ,
One favour I've to ask,—
Will you shelter me, till break of day,
From this cold winter's blast?

At break of day, I'll trudge away
Elsewhere to seek employ,
To plough and sow, and reap and mow,
And be a farmer's boy."

"Come, try the lad," the mistress said,
"Let him no further seek;"
"O, do, dear father!" the daughter cried,
While tears ran down her cheek;
"He'd work if he could, so 'tis hard to want food,
And wander for employ;
Don't turn him away, but let him stay,
And be a farmer's boy."

And when the lad became a man,
The good old farmer died,
And left the lad the farm he had,
And his daughter for his bride.
The lad that was, the farm now has,
Oft smiles, and thinks with joy,
Of the lucky day he came that way,
To be a farmer's boy.[44]

The Farmer's Boy

Anon

Voice

The sun was sunk be - hind yon hill, A cross yon dr-ear-y moor,___ When

poor and lame a boy there came, Up to a fam-er's door:___ "Can you tell me, if here it be, That

I can find em - ploy?___ To plough and sow, to reap and mow, And be a farm-er's boy."

Fig. 8.12

Kidson seems to have visited the North Riding of Yorkshire quite frequently, to paint or to go walking on the North York Moors or along the sea coast in the vicinity of Flamborough, Whitby, and Robin Hood's Bay. He collected at least twenty songs in the region, but, as with his collecting in the villages around Leeds, we find his documentation rather haphazard. Ten of the twenty items that would be printed in *Traditional Tunes* are ascribed to anonymous informants. We know neither the name nor the location of the person in the North Riding from whom Kidson obtained "The Outlandish Knight" and one of his versions of "The Indian Lass." "The Pretty Ploughboy" was apparently sung by a ploughman in North Yorkshire but exactly where and by whom we are not told. One version of "Barbara Allen" was apparently picked up in the Northallerton district, just west of the North York Moors, whereas most of the other anonymous items came from along the coast to the east of the moors. "As We Were A-Sailing" is identified as having been collected on the Yorkshire coast, but precisely where is not revealed. Fishermen at Flamborough contributed one Child ballad, "Henry Martin," and a local song, "The Drowned Sailor," which is set further down the coast near Robin Hood's Bay.

On Stowbrow, on Stowbrow, a fair young maid did dwell,
She loved a handsome sailor and he loved her quite as well,
He promised he would marry her when back he did return,
But, ah! what misfortunes the world it does contain.

As they were a-sailing, a-sailing by night,
The moon it was shaded, and dismal was the night,
The storm it was raging, and the waves the vessel bore,
Till they dashed these poor sailors all on the rocky shore.

Some of them were single, and some of them had wives,
And all of these poor sailor lads had to swim for their lives;
But this unhappy sailor who tried his life to save,
Instead of being married he found a watery grave.

Now as she was walking from Stowbrow to Bay,
She saw a drowned sailor that on the sand did lay,
The nearer she drew to him it brought her to a stand,
She spied it was her true love by the mark upon his hand.

She kissed him, she caressed him, ten thousand times all o'er,
And said, "These awful billows have washed my love ashore."

But soon this pretty damsel she lay down by his side,
And in a few moments she kissed him and died.

Now, this couple was buried in Robin Hood's churchyard,
And for them a memorial stone at their head was raised;
And all you true lovers that do this way pass by,
Pray shed a tear of pity from out your glistening eye.[45]

The Drowned Sailor

Anon

On Stow-brow, on Stow-brow, a fair young maid did dwell, She loved a handsome sail-or, and he loved her quite as well, He prom-ised he would mar-ry her when back he did re-turn, But, ah! what mis-fort-unes the world it does con-tain.

Fig. 8.13

In either Whitby or a village nearby Kidson noted one Child ballad, "Lord Thomas and Fair Eleanor," and a fragment of another, "Scarborough Fair." And at Fylingdale, a village just inland from Whitby, he picked up a local hunting song, the "Fylingdale Foxhunter's Song." At Newtondale Kidson discovered Robert Holliday, who knew the broadside ballad "Polly Oliver" and who also sang the folk lyric "My True Love Once He Courted Me." His most prolific informant in the region was a railwayman who had befriended him during his earlier career as a landscape painter, Allan Wardill of Goathland, a village in the heart of the North York Moors. Seven songs from Wardill's repertoire would be included in *Traditional Tunes*: "Barbara Allen," "Scarborough Fair," "An Auld Man He Courted Me," "The Bonny Scotch Lad," "The Farmer's Boy," "When I Was a Maid," and "Forty Miles." The latter song was also in the repertoire of another singer that Kidson found in Goathland, Newell Pennock. Wardill knew two variants of "Barbara Allen," each differing from the most common version in both text and tune. The first of these had the more attractive melody but the second a more comprehensive set of lyrics, so when brought together they constitute a fine composite version derived from Kidson's collecting on the North York Moors. The verse with the music (on the next page) gives the words that Wardill associated with the first melody, while the full text provided here was that associated with the other variant.

In Reading town, there I was born,
In Scotland was my dwelling;
O, there I courted a pretty, fair maid,
Her name was Barbara Allen,
O, there I courted a pretty, fair maid,
Her name was Barbara Allen.

I courted her for months and years,
Thinking that I should gain her;
And I oft times vowed and did declare
No other man should have her,
And I oft times, etc.

I sent a man to yonder town,
To ask for Barbara Allen,
Saying, "You must come to my master's house,
If your name be Barbara Allen."

So slowly she put on her clothes,
So slowly she came to him;
And when she got to his bedside,
"Young man," she said, "you're dying."

If you look under my pillow,
You'll find a napkin lying,
And it is soaked with my heart's blood,

For the love of Barbara Allen.

He put his hand right out of bed,
Thinking to draw her nigh him;
But she whipped her heels and away she ran,
Straightway from him she flew.

So he turned his face unto the fall,
And death came slowly to him;
"Adieu, adieu to all my friends,
Farewell to Barbara Allen."

As she was walking across yon fields,
She heard his death-bell tolling,

And every toll it seemed to say—
Hard-hearted Barbara Allen.

"O, dear mother, make me my bed,
And make it fit to die on;
There's a young man died for me to-day,
And I'll die for him to-morrow."

And he did die on one good day,
And she died on the morrow,
O, he did die for the love of her,
And she did die for sorrow.[46]

Barbara Allen

Anon

Voice

In Scotland I was born and bred, O, there it was my dwell-ing;___ I

court-ed there a pret-ty maid, O, her name was Bar-b'ra All-en.___

Fig. 8.14

The third region of Yorkshire from which Kidson obtained folksongs was the East Riding. In practice, this meant just two locations: the seaport of Hull and the surrounding coastline, and Howden and Goole, a pair of small towns located inland along the river Ouse. Kidson does not seem to have done much of his own collecting in either of these areas, relying almost entirely on the skill and enthusiasm of his most active collaborator, Charles Lolley, who had grown up in Howden and who retained connections with friends and family there. However, there are a few songs in *Traditional Tunes* which were collected in Howden and Goole and which are not credited to Lolley, so it is possible that Kidson himself noted "Brocklesby Fair" from an anonymous informant at Howden and also collected "Hares in the Old Plantation," "Down by the Derwent Side," and "The Golden Glove" at Goole. As for the North Sea coastline, here is an example of a broadside ballad collected, probably by Kidson himself, from a sailor near Hull. It employs the common theme of a young woman cross-dressing in order to go to sea with her sailor lover.

Young Susan was a blooming maid, so valiant, stout and bold,
And when her sailor went a-board, young Susan, we are told,
Put on a jolly sailor's dress, and daubed her hands with tar,
To cross the raging seas for love, on board of a Man-of-War.

It was in Portsmouth harbour this gallant ship was moored,
And when young Susan shipped there were nine hundred men aboard;
'Twas then she was contented, all bedaubed with pitch and tar,
To be with her sweet William on board of a Man-of-War.

When in the Bay of Biscay, she aloft like lightning flew,
Respected by the officers and all the jovial crew;
In battle she would boldly run, not fearing wound or scar,
And did her duty by her gun, on board of a Man-of-War.

She faced the walls of China, where her life was not insured,
And little did young William think his Susan was on board;
But by a cruel cannon ball she did receive a scar,
And she got slightly wounded, on board of a Man-of-War.

When on the deck young Susan fell, of all the whole ship's crew,
Her William was the very first who to her assistance flew;
She said, "My jolly sailor, I've for you received a scar,
Behold your faithful Susan bold, on board of a Man-of-War."

Then William on his Susan gazed with wonder and surprise,
He stood some moments motionless, while tears stood in his eyes,
He cried, "I wish instead of you I had received that scar,
O, love, why did you venture on board of a Man-of-War?"

At length to England they returned, and quickly married were,
The bells did ring, and they did sing, and banished every care!
They often think upon that day when she received that scar,
When Susan followed her true love on board of a Man-of-War.[47]

On Board of a Man-of-War

Anon

Young Su-san was a bloom-ing maid, so val-liant, stout and bold, And
when her sail-or went a-board, young Su-san we are told, Put on a jol-ly
sail-or's dress, And daubed her hands with tar, To cross the rag-ing seas for love, on
board of a Man-of-War.

Fig. 8.15

All the other songs noted in the East Riding of Yorkshire were collected by Lolley. He had picked up two songs, "The Soldier's Dream" and Burns's "Highland Mary," from his mother, who probably still lived in Howden. Other songs collected there were "My Valentine" and "The White Hare." Nearby Goole supplied "The Death of Bill Brown." Most of the remainder of Lolley's twenty-one items in *Traditional Tunes* were vaguely ascribed to the East Riding. They included a number of broadside ballads, such as "The Golden Glove," "The Bold Privateer," "The Banks of Sweet Dundee," and "Saddle to Rags." Lolley also noted one Child ballad, "The Outlandish Knight," one folk lyric, "The Sprig of Thyme," and several sentimental or religious songs, such as "The Stolen Child" and "Time to Remember the Poor." From sailors, presumably either in Hull itself or in nearby coastal villages, he picked up three items: "Just As the Tide

Was Flowing," "The Indian Lass" and a shanty, "Outward Bound." At least in terms of tunes, these sea-songs were among the highlights of his collecting. "Just As the Tide Was Flowing" is a good example:

Just As the Tide Was Flowing

Anon

Fig. 8.16

One morning in the month of May, down by a rolling river,
A jolly sailor he did stray, and there beheld a lover,
She carelessly along did stray, a viewing of the daisies gay;
She sweetly sang a roundelay, just as the tide was flowing.

Her dress it was as white as milk, and jewels did adorn her skin,
It was as soft as any silk, just like a lady of honour.
Her cheeks were red, her eyes were brown, her hair in ringlets hanging down,
Her lovely brow without a frown, just as the tide was flowing.

I made a bow and said, "Fair maid, how come you here so early?
My heart by you it was betrayed, and I could love you dearly.
I am a sailor come from sea, if you'll accept my company,
To walk and see the fishes play, just as the tide is flowing."

No more was said, but on her way we both did gang together;
The small birds sang, the lambs did play, and pleasant was the weather.
We both being weary sat us down, beneath a tree with branches round;
Then to the church we soon were bound, just as the tide was flowing.[48]

The last category of Kidson's early collecting comprises ballads and other songs noted outside of Yorkshire. His material from elsewhere in the north of England was paltry. It came mainly from Lancashire, and was largely dependent on items sent to him by correspondents. So, for example, James B. Shaw of Cornbrook, Manchester, provided him with a Lancashire Morris Dance tune and a tune (with one verse and chorus) for a political song in support of universal manhood suffrage, "With Henry Hunt We'll Go." But here, as an example of Kidson's personal collecting in the northwest of England, is a short lyric with a distinctive tune called "Johnny Todd," which he obtained from a group of Liverpool schoolchildren:

Johnny Todd

Anon

John ny Todd he took a no tion, for to go a-cross the sea, And he left his love be hind him,

weep - ing by   the Liv-er pool sea.

Fig. 8.17

Johnny Todd he took a notion, for to go across the sea,
And he left his love behind him, weeping by the Liverpool sea.

For a week she wept full sorely, tore her hair and wrung her hands,
Till she met another sailor, walking on the Liverpool sands.

"Why, fair maid, are you a-weeping, for your Johnny gone to sea?
If you'll wed with me to-morrow, I will kind and constant be.

I will buy you sheets and blankets, I'll buy you a wedding ring,
You shall have a gilded cradle for to rock your baby in."

Johnny Todd came back from sailing, sailing o'er the ocean wide,
But he found his fair and false one, was another sailor's bride.

All young men who go a-sailing, for to fight the foreign foe,
Don't you leave your love like Johnny—marry her before you go.[49]

Most of Kidson's remaining material was obtained in Scotland, where he often spent his holidays or went on sketching expeditions. Eleven songs in *Traditional Tunes* were of Scottish origin, more than half of them collected in Dumfriesshire. Only one Scottish informant is named by Kidson, Mrs. Calvert of Gilnockie, Eskdale, Dumfriesshire, who contributed "The Mammy's Pet" and "The Dowie Dens of Yarrow." Another Gilnockie informant, an anonymous man, sang "Coupshawholme Fair," and an unnamed Dumfriesshire girl provided "The Banks of Claudy" and "Braes of Strathblane." Other informants living in the same county contributed "The Plains of Waterloo" and "Rother Glen," while a lady in Dumfermline was responsible for "Maggie's Smile" and "Glowerowerum." Kidson's Scottish collecting was rounded out with two other songs, "Robin Tamson's Smiddy" and "The Bonny Irish Boy," from anonymous Scottish informants whose locations also remained undisclosed.

From this batch of songs Kidson, when later writing to Lucy Broadwood, singled out "The Dowie Dens of Yarrow" as the cream of the crop. He pointed out that Mrs. Calvert was the granddaughter of the Tibbie Shiel who lived at St. Mary's Loch and was employed as a servant by James Hogg's father. James Hogg or Sir Walter Scott had apparently noted the words of the ballad from Shiel, and Mrs. Calvert's version was nearly identical to that on a manuscript copy found among Scott's papers.[50] In his note to the ballad in *Traditional Tunes* Kidson emphasized the differences between Mrs. Calvert's rendition and the ballad as printed in Scott's *Minstrelsy of the Scottish Border*, thereby implying that Scott had done a lot of touching up of his original source. Peter Buchan's variant in *Ancient Ballads of the North*, on the other hand, "more nearly resembled" the Shiel/Calvert version.[51] This is how Kidson would give the ballad in *Traditional Tunes*:

The Dowie Dens of Yarrow

Anon

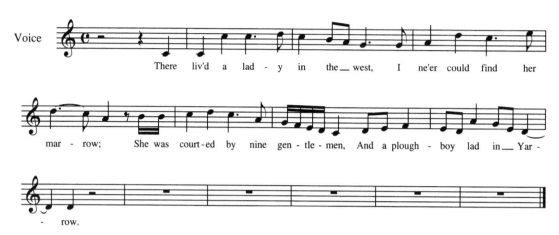

Fig. 8.18

There liv'd a lady in the west,
I ne'er could find her marrow;
She was courted by nine gentlemen,
And a ploughboy lad in Yarrow.

These nine sat drinking at the wine,
Sat drinking wine in Yarrow;
They made a vow among themselves,
To fight for her in Yarrow.

She washed his face, she kaimed his hair,
As oft she'd done before, O!
She made him like a knight sae bright,
To fight for her in Yarrow.

As he walked up yon high, high hill,
And down by the homes of Yarrow;
There he saw nine armed men,
Come fight with him in Yarrow.

"There's nine of you, there's one of me,
It's an unequal marrow;
But I'll fight you all one by one,
On the dowie dens of Yarrow."

There he slew, and there they flew,
And there he wounded sorely;
Till her brother John, he came in beyond,
And pierced his heart most foully.

"Go home, go home, thou false young man,
And tell thy sister, Sarah,

That her true love, John, lies dead and gone
On the dowie dens of Yarrow."

"Oh, father dear, I dreamed a dream,
I'm afraid it will bring sorrow;
I dreamed I was pulling the heather bell,
In the dowie dens of Yarrow."

"Oh, daughter dear, I read your dream,
I doubt it will prove sorrow;
For your true love, John, lies dead and gone
On the dowie dens of Yarrow."

As she walked up yon high, high hill,
And down by the homes of Yarrow,
There she saw her true love, John,
Lying pale and dead on Yarrow.

Her hair it being three quarters long,
The colour it was yellow;
She wrapped it round his middle sma'
And carried him hame to Yarrow.

"Oh father dear, you've seven sons,
You may wed them a' to-morrow;
But a fairer flower I never saw
Than the lad I loved in Yarrow."

This fair maid being great with child,
It filled her heart with sorrow;
She died within her lover's arms,
Between that day and morrow.[52]

As can be seen from the names in the foregoing discussion, Kidson's informants were predominantly, but not exclusively, male. A significant number of them, including Washington Teasdale, William Cheetham, and Benjamin Holgate, were middle-class urban dwellers. It is possible that some of the many informants who remained anonymous were female, but we know there were at least three women: Mrs. Holt of Alderhill, Mrs. Calvert of Gilnockie, and the unnamed girl from Dumfriesshire. By far the majority of the songs that Kidson noted personally (or with the help of his niece Ethel) were from two regions: Leeds and the surrounding villages, and the North Riding of Yorkshire. More than one third of his early material appears to have been collected on his behalf, mainly by Benjamin Holgate and Charles Lolley, although it is not always possible to draw a sharp line between Lolley's collecting and Kidson's.

Traditional Tunes

Discussion of Kidson's informants and collaborators has necessarily involved many references to the major work he published, albeit in a limited edition, in 1891, *Traditional Tunes*. Writing an obituary of Kidson in November 1926, Lucy Broadwood would claim that this publication "marked a turning-point in the history of folk-song" because it was "the first book of English traditional songs in which tunes and texts, given in 'undoctored' form, [were] accompanied by scholarly critical notes."[53] The 'undoctored' claim was not quite correct, but it was true that *Traditional Tunes* was a highly important regional collection, and, moreover, its editorial approach was indeed quite different from any previously published collection of folksongs. So despite the fact that I have already quoted extensively from the publication, it is now necessary to provide an overview of the book's structure and contents.

The subtitle of *Traditional Tunes* said it all: this was *A Collection of Ballad Airs, chiefly obtained in Yorkshire and the South of Scotland, together with their appropriate words from broadsides and from oral tradition.* Note the deliberate emphasis on tunes and on oral tradition. Kidson's introduction revealed his love of vernacular song and his motive for publishing the book. He quoted from an essay by Joseph Addison in the *Spectator*, No. 70: "it is impossible that anything should be universally tasted and approved by the multitude, though they are only the rabble of the nation, which hath not in it some peculiar aptness to please and gratify the mind of man"; and he remarked that his was a collection of just such "homely ditties...as were sung by the humbler classes in England round the fireside of farm kitchens or at the plough tail." One should not expect much "wit or brilliancy," he added, and the songs should not be judged by too high a standard; nonetheless, they were of some interest ("the themes being in most cases familiar subjects"). Moreover, because they would soon be gone for ever, it was high time that someone preserved them for posterity.[54] Kidson insisted that this work of preservation was urgent, and becoming more difficult by the day:

> This class of song is fast disappearing before the modern productions, and any young ploughboy who should sing the songs his father or grandfather sung, would be laughed to scorn. Before easy means of transit existed, the songs of a country side remained unaltered for a great length of time, and people delighted to sing the songs which were venerable with age. Now, however, cheap trips to the larger towns enable the country lad to compete with the town's boy in his knowledge of popular musical favourites. The old traditional songs are fast dying out, never to be recalled. They are now seldom or never sung, but rather *remembered,* by old people. I have found in the course of my search how quickly this class of old airs is disappearing, for I have frequently been told of some old man, then dead, from whom I could have got certain songs had I been a few months earlier in my inquiries. Although from some country singers I have met with the utmost sympathy and aid, yet from others, from shyness or from a difficulty of seeing the utility of collecting these old things, I have not found my task a light one. Another source of trouble has been the notation of tunes from singers who, by reason of great age and quavering voices, sang the melody flat and out of tune. The type of tunes here gathered together, is one which never got into print, for they were sung by a different class of people to those catered for by the music publisher.[55]

Kidson was thus convinced that the tunes, in particular, of these old vernacular songs were unique, and that a wealth of melody was doomed to oblivion unless rescued immediately. He was very interested in the question of how old such traditional melodies actually were, but he was well aware of the difficulties involved in trying to date them with accuracy. He distinguished between three categories of old songs: ballads deriving from an old minstrel tradition; songs from the sixteenth and seventeenth centuries; and more recent (i.e., eighteenth-century) compositions:

> Of course the tunes in the present collection vary very much as to age, but the older class of airs is, I think I may safely say, the remnants of early minstrel melody. Such (and I believe musical antiquaries will bear me out), are—"The Three Ravens," "The Knight and Shepherd's Daughter," "The Dowie Dens of Yarrow," "Lord Thomas and Fair Eleanor," and several more. Of a later period, but still, I feel sure, very early specimens of melody, are—"My True Love Once He Courted Me," "Green Bushes," "The Pretty Ploughboy," "The Nightingale," "The Sprig of Thyme," "Polly Oliver's Ramble," etc. While airs of the last century appear

to find examples in—"Colin and Phoebe," "The Indian Lass," "The Spotted Cow," "Young Bucks A-Hunting Go," [and] "The White Hare," besides many others.[56]

Kidson then put forward a rather speculative account of how these tunes had survived through a process of oral transmission. The earliest airs, he argued, had a "peculiar plaintive strain" and were joined to stories of a "more or less melancholy character; the tune in the minor mode, of one strain, simple in structure, of little compass, and being queer and odd in interval." But as time went on "the airs lost a good deal of their ruggedness, and towards the middle of the last century became more ornamental in character," although they were still different in feel from the published songs of the time. Both types of melody, he was convinced, had survived only in the countryside, having been passed on from generation to generation:

> From the early days these songs have passed down from mouth to mouth, and as printed music and musical instruments became more common, they were abandoned for newer and more fashionable music, till it was left for the cottage to preserve what the hall had cast aside. Many of the airs somewhat later have been evolved by rustic fiddlers or crowders for the amusement of a rustic audience, and, like their predecessors, passed down in a country side for many ages. They would be carried from place to place by pedlars and by journeymen who travelled to ply their trade. The question naturally arises, what changes have the tunes undergone in their passage down to our time? Undoubtedly, in many instances, much corruption has crept in: in some cases by the wilful alterations of singers and performers, and in other instances by reason of imperfect acquirement of the air...This being the case, it is much to be wondered at that some few tunes are found so little altered in different districts, and it satisfactorily accounts for the variations in others. The fact certainly remains that tradition is wonderfully accurate, and this is so in more things than in old tunes.[57]

Kidson provided several examples ("The Banks of Sweet Dundee," "The Summer Morning" and "Forty Miles") of songs with traditional tunes that had been noted in widely separate parts of the United Kingdom. In such cases the distinctive melodies had been preserved almost note for note by the various local tune-carriers. In other cases, however, tunes for the same song-text came to differ widely from region to region, as in the case of "Polly Oliver," "Henry Martin," and "My True Love Once He Courted Me." Local singers would even sometimes invent a new air, or use the tune of a different song. By and large, Kidson concluded, song texts were more stable than tunes, simply because of the prevalence of ballad sheets, which only rarely included melody lines along with the words. Kidson did not, in general, have a high opinion of the literary quality of broadside texts or of the lyrics of folksongs preserved by oral tradition; it must be conceded, he remarked with a touch of sarcasm, that "the rustic muse produced better melody than poetry or even rhyme."[58]

Kidson's way of editing a folksong collection was unique for his time. Most earlier Victorian editors had concentrated exclusively on texts but we have seen that several Late Victorian editors, together with such precursors as Edward Rimbault and William Chappell, viewed folksongs as combinations of tune and text in which both elements were equally significant. Other Late Victorian editors often aimed to go a step further, creating songbooks with fleshed-out lyrics and music harmonized for the piano, so that amateur musicians might easily perform the songs. Kidson, on the other hand, was much more interested in the melodies than the texts, and he believed (correctly) that traditional tunes, whether sung unaccompanied or played on such traditional melody instruments as fiddles or pipes, were rarely if ever harmonized. They should therefore be left in their natural state, and not embellished with inappropriate accompaniments. He stated his editorial policy bluntly in the preface to *Traditional Tunes:*

> The compiler's wish has been to at least temporarily rescue from oblivion some few of the old airs, which, passing from mouth to mouth for generations, are fast disappearing before the modern effusions of the music hall and concert room...He has endeavoured to set down the airs as far as musical notes will permit with the utmost fidelity, scrupulously avoiding an attempt at arrangement or emendation, for, however desirable it might be in some instances to amend the airs from corruptions which have crept in, the Editor has considered that he would be scarcely justified in tampering with them, as such an attempt at revisal would greatly detract from the antiquarian value of the whole...To the above may be added that the traditional airs forming the present volume have perhaps *never* been harmonized. They have either been sung by a single singer (or by parties of singers in unison), or performed on such a simple instrument as the flute or the fiddle. Is it, then, desirable to put such old wine into new bottles?[59]

Kidson's focus in the book was thus on traditional tunes that could still be found in oral tradition in Yorkshire and in the countryside on either side of the Scottish border. He argued that such melodies had been passed down from singer to singer for a century or more, and in many cases oral transmission preserved them with extraordinary accuracy. Proof of this was to be found in the way in which a tune might be found "as near note for note as possible in places so widely apart as the South of Scotland, and the North and West Ridings of Yorkshire, and in Berkshire and Oxfordshire."[60] As we have seen, Kidson cited several examples of this phenomenon, but he also admitted that in other cases a tune might be "found either greatly changed in different districts or a totally fresh air used for the song."[61] There was thus no rule of thumb concerning the effectiveness of oral transmission: sometimes it preserved texts and melodies extraordinarily faithfully, and on other occasions the passage of time brought corruption, change, and occasionally imaginative renewal. Any attempt to generalize about the process, he concluded, was fruitless: one had to research what had actually happened in any given case, and it was no use attempting to prejudge the result of the inquiry.

Traditional Tunes contained eighty-three songs, but for quite a number of them Kidson printed variants: one or more alternative tunes and/or texts in addition to his primary version. That brought the total number of items to one hundred and seven. In collecting these songs Kidson relied quite heavily on a dozen main informants. We have already met most of these, but it will be useful to recap the names of the most important ones and the places where they lived. Although there were numerous occasions when Kidson failed to reveal his sources, on the whole he was fairly good at crediting informants and collectors, especially when he printed several different variants of the same ballad or tune. It is noticeable that the same names keep appearing in the notes to *Traditional Tunes*. Charles Lolley of Leeds was the source of at least twenty-five items, Benjamin Holgate (of Headingley) contributed twelve, Allan Wardill (of Goathland in the North Riding of Yorkshire) seven, Mrs. Holt (of Meanwood, near Leeds) six, Mary Kidson and Washington Teasdale (both from Leeds) three each, and William Cheetham (from Horsforth in the West Riding), Robert Holliday (from Newtondale in the North Riding) and James Shaw (from Manchester in Lancashire) two each. Other named contributors living in England were John Briggs (of Leeds), Mr. C. Butteriss (of Leicestershire), Thomas Hewson (of Roundhay, near Leeds), John Holmes (also of Roundhay), Newell Pennock (of Goathland), and Kidson's grandfather, John Roberts.

The influence of Francis Child's work on Kidson, or at least the prestige of narrative ballads in folksong circles, can be detected in the organization of *Traditional Tunes*. The first eleven items, contributed by Holgate, Lolley, Holmes, Wardill, Cheetham, Mrs. Calvert, and Mrs. Holt, were traditional ballads. They included "The Dowie Dens of Yarrow" (collected from Mrs. Calvert of Gilnockie, Eskdale), "The Outlandish Knight" (the text taken from Dixon but the air collected in the North Riding of Yorkshire), "Lord Bateman" (from Mrs. Holt of Alderhill), "Lord Thomas and Fair Eleanor" (the text from a broadside but the melody collected at Whitby on the Yorkshire coast), and "Scarborough Fair" (a variant of "The Elfin Knight," also collected from a Whitby street singer). Moreover, there were two versions of "Henry Martin" and three versions of "Barbara Allen." This was material of high quality, so where was Kidson getting it from? Some of his texts were from broadsides or from printed sources such as Johnson's *Scots Musical Museum* and Dixon's *Scottish Traditional Versions of Ancient Ballads*, but his tunes and some other texts were taken from oral tradition. As we have seen, William Cheetham was the source for one version of "Henry Martin," while Kidson collected the other from a fisherman at Flamborough. Holgate and Wardill provided two of the melodies for "Barbara Allen," while the third tune was collected (presumably by Kidson himself) at Northallerton in the North Riding. Here is the variant of "Henry Martin" that Kidson noted at Flamborough, along with the text that he ascribed to the same informant (notwithstanding the slight discrepancy between the words given with the music and those of the longer text):

In Scotland there lived three brothers of late,
In Scotland there lived brothers three;
Now, the youngest cast lots with the other two,
Which should go rob on the salt sea.

The lot it did fall to bold Henry Martin—
The youngest of all the three;
And he had to turn robber all on the salt seas,
To maintain his two brothers and he.

He had not been sailing past a long winter's night,
Past a long winter's night before day,
Before he espied a lofty, fine ship,
Come sailing all on the salt sea.

"O! where are you bound for?" cried Henry Martin,
"O! where are you bound for?" cried he;
"I'm a rich loaded ship bound for fair England,
I pray you to let me pass free."

"O, no! O, no!" cried Henry Martin,
"O, no! that never can be;
Since I have turned robber all on the salt sea,
To maintain my two brothers and me."

"Heave down your main tack, likewise your main tie,
And lig yourself under my lee;
For your rich glowing gold I will take it away,
And your fair bodies drown in the salt sea."

Then broadside to broadside they merrily fought,
For fully two hours or three,
When, by chance, Henry Martin gave her a broadside
And right down to the bottom went she.

Bad news! Bad news! Unto old England,
Bad news I tell unto thee;
For your rich glowing gold is all wasted away,
And your mariners are drown'd in the salt sea.[62]

Henry Martin

Anon

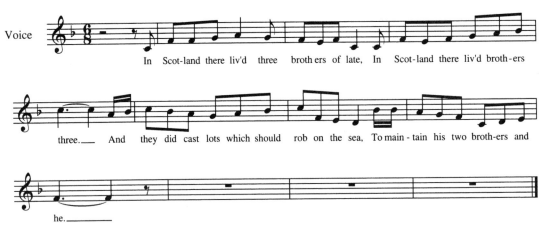

Fig. 8.19

Traditional Tunes also included a considerable number of ballads that are not part of the Child canon. Most were broadsides, but Kidson's primary interest was in the melodies to which the broadside texts were sung, and he often did not bother to print the entire set of words. This was true also when the text was to be found in a fairly well-known printed collection. For example, Kidson had noted a tune for "The Spinning Wheel" from the singing of his grandfather and had discovered a different tune, along with a full set of words, in the second volume of *Pills to Purge Melancholy*. He opted for his grandfather's tune but decided to reproduce only a portion (five verses) of D'Urfey's text.[63] On the other hand, if his informant had been able to remember all the verses and there was nothing indecent about them, Kidson usually did print them all, even when he had a low opinion of their literary worth. An example is this version of "Spencer the Rover," about the source of which all we know is that he collected it somewhere in Yorkshire. It may be compared with the shorter version noted by Harriet Mason and printed in *Nursery Rhymes and Country Songs* (see fig 4.7).

Spencer the Rover

Anon

Fig. 8.20

These words were composed by Spencer the Rover,
Who travelled o'er most parts of Great Britain and Wales;
He being much reduced, which caused great confusion,
And that was the reason that a rambling he went.

In Yorkshire, near Rotherham, he being on his ramble,
Being weary of travelling, he sat down to rest,
At the foot of yon mountain there runs a clear fountain,
With bread and cold water he himself did refresh.

It tasted more sweet than the gold he had wasted,
Sweeter than honey, and gave more content;
Till the thoughts of his babies lamenting their father,
Brought tears in his eyes and caused him to lament.

The night being approaching, to the woods he resorted,
With woodbine and ivy his bed for to make;
He dreamed about sighing, lamenting, and crying,
Come home to your children and rambling forsake.

On the fifth of November, I've reason to remember,
When first I arrived to my family and wife;
She stood so surprised to see my arrival,
To see such a stranger once more in her sight.

My children flocked round me with their prit-prattling story,
With their prit-prattling story to drive away care;
So we'll be united, like ants live together,
Like bees in one hive contented we'll be.

Now I am placed in my cottage contented,
With primroses and woodbine hanging round my door;
As happy as they that have plenty of riches,
Contented I'll stay, and go rambling no more.[64]

Other broadside ballads for which Kidson found tunes included "The Golden Glove" (two versions, one from Charles Lolley, the other from Mrs. Holt), "The Banks of Claudy" (as sung by the anonymous Dumfriesshire girl), "The Banks of Sweet Dundee" (obtained from Benjamin Holgate), "Bold Brennan on the Moor" (the tune noted by Kidson, the words from a broadside), "Saddle to Rags" (about the outwitting of a highwayman by an old man, the tune noted by Charles Lolley in the East Riding of Yorkshire), and "The Plains of Waterloo" (a lengthy description of the battle, for which Kidson found three different airs).

While some of these ballads had happy outcomes, many were tragic. "Mary across the Wild Moor" (which relates the death by exposure of an unwed mother and her child, shut out of her parent's home) is one example. Kidson came across it on several occasions, but he first noted it from the singing of Benjamin Holgate.

It was one winter's night, when the wind
It blew bitter across the bleak moor,
When poor Mary she came with her child,
Wand'ring home to her own father's door.

She cried—"Father, O pray, let me in,
Do come down and open your own door,
Or the child at my bosom will die,
With the wind that blows on the wild moor."

"Why ever did I leave this cot,
Where once I was happy and free,
Doomed to roam without friend or a home,

O! Father have pity on me."

But her father was deaf to her cry,
Not a voice nor a sound reached the door,
But the watch dog's bark and the wind
That blew bitter across the wild moor.

Now, think what her father he felt,
When he came to the door in the morn,
And found Mary dead, and her child
Fondly clasped in its dead mother's arms.

Wild and frantic he tore his grey hairs,

As on Mary he gazed at the door,
Who on the cold night there had died,
By the wind that blew on the wild moor.

Now, her father in grief pined away,
The poor child to its mother went soon,
And no one lived there to this day,

And the cottage to ruin has gone.

The villagers point to the cot
Where a willow droops over the moor,
They cry out there poor Mary died,
With the wind that blew o'er the wild moor.[65]

Mary Across the Wild Moor

Anon

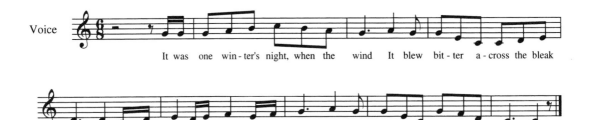

It was one win-ter's night, when the wind It blew bit-ter a-cross the bleak moor,— When poor Mar-y she came with her child, Wand'ring home to her own fath er's door.—

Fig. 8.21

Other tragic ballads included "The Drowned Sailor" (noted by Kidson at Flamborough, Yorkshire), "The Death of Bill Brown" (about a poacher killed by a gamekeeper), "Young Henry the Poacher" (about transportation to Van Dieman's Land), "Spence Broughton" (the ostensible confession of a murderer), and "The Awful Execution of John Bird Bell" (about the hanging of a sixteen-year-old criminal).

Kidson's expansion of the corpus of singable ballads beyond those in the Child canon was one of his greatest contributions to the late Victorian folksong revival. But there were also other kinds of material in *Traditional Tunes*. The remainder of the collection consisted mainly of shorter folk lyrics of various kinds. Here too Kidson was not much interested in variant texts but he was quite prepared to include different tunes for a song if he considered them worthy. For instance, "My True Love Once He Courted Me" appeared in four different versions, and "The Farmer's Boy" and "Forty Miles" had three, although in each case only one full set of words was included. Other examples of songs with variant tunes were "The Spotted Cow," "Colin and Phoebe," "The Gray Mare," "Highland Mary," "The Indian Lass," "The Plains of Waterloo," and "I Am a Rover."

Not surprisingly, a considerable number of the shorter lyrics in *Traditional Tunes* were either love songs, songs about amorous encounters, or laments by deserted lovers. Those in which the course of true love ran smooth included "Forty Miles," "Colin and Phoebe," and "The Foggy Dew." Amorous encounters relayed in song (but often censored by Kidson) included "My Valentine," "The Spotted Cow," "Three Maids a Milking Did Go," and "Brocklesby Fair" (aka "Young Ramble Away"). Love laments were fairly numerous, a few examples being "Through the Grove," "Highland Mary" (a variant of Robert Burns's composition), "I Am a Rover," "The Bonny Irish Boy," and "The Sprig of Thyme." The latter, recalled from childhood by Charles Lolley, was related to "The Seeds of Love" and similar, but not identical, to the song collected by Baring-Gould as "Flowers and Weeds" (aka "Let No Man Steal Your Thyme").

Come, all you pretty fair maids,
That are just in your prime;
I would have you weed your garden clear,
And let no one steal your thyme.

I once had a sprig of thyme,
It prospered both night and day;
By chance there came a false young man,
And he stole my thyme away.

Thyme is the prettiest flower,
That grows under the sun;
It's time that brings all things to an end,
So now my thyme runs on.

But now my old thyme's dead,
I've got no room for any new,
For in that place where my old thyme grew,
I changed to a running rue.

It's very well drinking ale,   But it's far better sitting by a young man's side
And it's very well drinking wine,   That has won this heart of mine.[66]

The Sprig of Thyme

Anon

Come, all you pret - ty fair maids, That are just in your prime, I

would have you weed your gar - den clear, And let no— one steal your thyme.

Fig. 8.22

The theme of such love laments was often the inconstancy of young men contrasted with the faithfulness of women to their lovers, but just as often the man was not responsible for his failure to return. Sailors were lost at sea, and quite frequently the cause of separation was the induction of the young man into the armed forces, usually the army, either because he was press-ganged or because he enlisted while drunk. "The Summer Morning" (aka "[The] White Cockade"), "The Bonny Scotch Lad," and "Polly Oliver" are three examples of songs collected by Kidson about such soldier lovers.

Traditional Tunes included quite a large number of songs that in one way or another depicted or reflected aspects of rural life. Two songs ("The Farmer's Boy" and "The Pretty Ploughboy") praised agricultural occupations, while "Coupshawholme Fair" provided a graphic description of a regional fair. Reading between the lines of the lyrics of these ballads one can sense some of the underlying but omnipresent difficulties and tensions of rural life. "Brocklesby Fair" suggests that fairs could be dangerous places for the innocent, a scene of robbery, exploitation, and seduction, a subject that Kidson declined to dwell upon, printing only one of seven verses. "Down in Our Village" and "Young Roger of the Valley" treat the subject of courtship in a genial manner, the tenderness edged with humor. But it is evident that economic realities stand in the way of marriage. In "Down in Our Village" the lovers are "resolved to tarry…till money we've both sav'd a sum," while in "Young Roger" the entire arrangement turns on a pooling of assets that will allow the married couple to purchase a cow of their own. This is "Young Roger of the Valley":

Young Roger of the valley,
One morning very soon,
Put on his gay apparel,
Likewise his Sunday shoon;
And he would go a-courting,
To bonny, buxom Nell,
"Adzooks!" cried he, "can'st fancy me,
For I like thy person well,
For I like thy person well."

"My horses I have dress'd,
And gi'en them corn and hay,
Put on my best apparel,
And have come this way;
Let's sit and chat a while,
With thee, my bonny Nell;
Dear lass," cries he, "could'st fancy me,
I like thee wondrous well."

"Young Roger, you're mistaken,"
The damsel then reply'd,

"I'm not in such a haste
To be a ploughman's bride;
Know I then live in hopes,
To marry a farmer's son."
"If it be so," says Hodge, "I'll go,
Sweet mistress, I have done."

"Your horses you have dress'd,
Good Hodge, I heard you say,
Put on your best apparel,
And being come this way;
[Let's sit and chat a while."]
"O no, indeed, not I,
I'll neither wait, nor sit, nor prate,
I've other fish to fry."

"Go, take your farmer's son,
With all my honest heart;
What tho' my name be Roger,
That goes with plough and cart?
I need not tarry long,

I soon may gain a wife:
There's buxom Joan, it is well known,
She loves me as her life."

"Pray, what of buxom Joan?
Can't I please you as well?
For she has ne'er a penny,
And I am buxom Nell,
And I have fifty shillings."
(The money made him smile)
"O then, my dear, I'll draw a chair,

And chat with thee a while."

Within the space of half-an-hour,
This couple a bargain struck,
Hoping that with their money,
They both would have good luck;
"To your fifty I've forty,
With which a cow we'll buy;
We'll join our hands in wedlock bands,
Then who but you and I?"[67]

Young Roger of the Valley

Anon

Fig. 8.23

The cruelty and violence of village life was also reflected in some of the songs collected by Kidson and Lolley. "The Holbeck Moor Cock Fight" depicted one popular local amusement that Kidson was happy to report had largely died out during the nineteenth century. Cock-fighting was one of three country sports celebrated in song, the others being hunting and poaching. Hunting songs in *Traditional Tunes* included "The Fylingdale Fox Hunt," "Young Bucks A-Hunting Go" and "The White Hare." Little sympathy for the victim was evidenced in these glorifications of the riding prowess of local squires and other galloping "sportsmen," and Kidson plainly did not like them very much. He excused himself from printing more than two verses of "The Fylingdale Fox Hunt" on the grounds that the other eighteen were "highly interesting to those who know the descendants of the [huntsmen] mentioned, but rather monotonous to the general reader," and about "The White Hare" he commented, "Musicians will, I think, congratulate Mr. Lolley upon obtaining such a fine and sterling old air. I wish I could say as much for the words."[68] Poaching songs included "Hares in the Old Plantation" and a striking ballad titled "The Death of Bill Brown" (the tune noted by Lolley from an informant at Goole, near Leeds). This defiant and militantly pro-poaching statement was quite different from the broadside ("Bill Brown, the Poacher") reprinted by Davison Ingledew in *The Ballads and Songs of Yorkshire* (1860), although its subject was the same: the shooting of a poacher by a gamekeeper near the village of Brightside in 1769. It clearly revealed the economic role played by poaching in village life, and the degree of class hatred between wealthy estate owners (and their servants) and those they excluded from the moors and woodlands that surrounded the villages. Nor was the ballad a rarity. Kidson reported that another of his correspondents (he did not say who) had collected the same tune as Lolley, and that he had found a complete set of words on a different broadside. The following combines tune and (adjusted) text:

The Death of Bill Brown

Anon

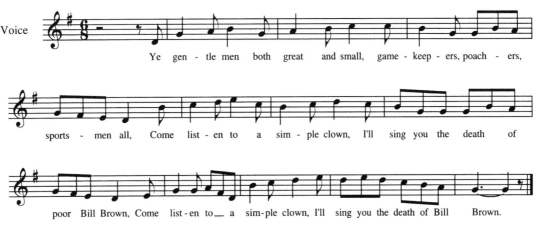

Fig. 8.24

Ye gentlemen both great and small, gamekeepers, poachers, sportsmen all,
Come listen to a simple clown, I'll sing you the death of poor Bill Brown,
Come listen to a simple clown, I'll sing you the death of Bill Brown.

One stormy night, as you shall hear, it was in the season of the year,
We went to the woods to catch a fat buck, but, ah! that night we had bad luck—
Ah! that night we had bad luck—Bill Brown was shot and his dog was stuck.

When we got to the woods our sport begun, I saw the gamekeeper present his gun,
I call'd on Bill to climb the gate to fetch the fat buck, but it was too late,
Fetch the fat buck, but it was too late, for there he met his untimely fate.

Then dying he lay upon the ground, and in that state poor Bill I found,
And when he saw me he did cry, "Revenge my death!" "I will," said I,
"Revenge my death!" "I will," said I, "For many a hare have we caught hard by."

I know the man that shot Bill Brown, I know him well and could tell the clown;
And to describe it in my song—black jacket he had, and red waistcoat on:
Black jacket he had, and red waistcoat on, I know him well, and they call him Tom.

I dressed myself up next night in time, I got to the wood, and the clock struck nine;
The reason was, and I'll tell you why, to find the gamekeeper I'll go try,
To find the gamekeeper I'll go try, who shot my friend, and he should die.

I ranged the wood all over, and then I looked at my watch and it was just ten;
I heard a footstep on the green, I laid myself down for fear of being seen,
Laid myself down for fear being seen, for I plainly saw that it was Tom Green.

Then I took my piece fast in my hand, resolved to fire if Tom did stand;
Tom heard the noise and turned him round, I fired and brought him to the ground,
I fired and brought him to the ground—my hand gave him his deep death wound.

Now revenge, you see, my hopes have crowned, I've shot the man that shot Bill Brown;

Poor Bill no more these eyes will see—Farewell, dear friend, farewell to ye,
Farewell, dear friend, farewell to ye, I've crowned his hopes and his memory.[69]

Other aspects of rural life were reflected in humorous ditties such as "The Grey Mare," "Robin Tamson's Smiddy," and "An Auld Man He Courted Me." Two other highlights of the collection not already mentioned were a lament about the hardships of married life, "When I Was a Maid" (noted from Allan Wardill) and a ballad of female inconstancy, "Green Bushes" (collected from Mrs. Holt of Alderhill). Drinking songs included "The Jolly Shilling" and "The Card Song." Religious and other moralistic songs were rare, but two that Kidson admired were "The Stolen Child" and "Time to Remember the Poor." About the latter he commented that it was "a great deal in advance of the usual street ballad, and the air is an excellent one."[70]

Time to Remember the Poor

Anon

Fig. 8.25

Cold winter is come with its cold chilling breath,
And the leaves are all gone from the trees,
And all seems touch'd by the finger of death,
And the streams are beginning to freeze;
When the young wanton lads o'er the river slide,
When Flora attends us no more;
When in plenty you're sitting by a warm fireside,
That's the time to remember the poor.

The cold feather'd snow will in plenty descend,
And whiten the prospect around;
The keen, cutting wind from the north will attend,
And cover it over the ground;

When the hill and the dales are all candied with white,
And the rivers are froze on the shore;
When the bright, twinkling stars they proclaim the cold night,
That's the time to remember the poor.

The poor, timid hare through the woods may be traced,
With her footsteps indented in snow,
When our lips and our fingers are dangling with cold,
And the marksman a shooting doth go,
When the poor robin redbreast approaches your cot,
And the icicles hang at the door,
And when your bowl smokes reviving and hot,
That's the time to remember the poor.

The thaw shall ensue, and the waters increase,
And the rivers vehemently grow,
The fish from oblivion obtains release,
And in danger the travellers go;
When your minds are annoyed by the wide swelling flood,
And your bridges are useful no more,
When in plenty you enjoy everything that is good,
Do you grumble to think on the poor?

The time will come when our Saviour on earth,
All the world shall agree with one voice,
All nations unite to salute the blest morn,
And the whole of the world shall rejoice;
When grim death is deprived of his killing sting,
And the grave rules triumphant no more,
Saints, angels, and men Hallelujah shall sing,
Then the rich must remember the poor.[71]

Many Yorkshire villages were scenes of industrial activity, either mining or textile production. Weaving was mechanized and moved to factories much later than spinning, and the late eighteenth and early nineteenth centuries had witnessed a great expansion of handloom weaving as a cottage industry. Only one song in *Traditional Tunes* directly reflected this industrial side of village life, "The Roving Heckler Lad," which was about an itinerant worker in the flax trade. "The Brewer Laddie" was another occupational song, but the principal aspect of commercial and industrial Britain reflected in Kidson's collection was the maritime life of the nation. Yorkshire and Northumberland had sea coasts, many fishing villages, and several large ports, including Hull and Newcastle, so it was hardly surprising that there were some songs about the sea and sailors. Charles Lolley collected several ballads about seamen's encounters with the fair sex ("Just As the Tide Was Flowing" and "The Indian Lass"), and just one shanty, which had also been noted by Laura Smith. This is Lolley's version of "Outward Bound":

To Liverpool docks we bid adieu,
To Suke and Sal, and Kitty too;
The anchor's weigh'd, the sails unfurled,
We're bound to cross the watery world.
Chorus: For we are outward bound,
          Hurrah! We're outward bound.

The wind blows from east-nor-east,
Our ship will sail ten knots at least;
The purser will our wants supply,
So while we live we'll ne'er say die.
For huzza! We're outward bound, etc.

And should we touch at Malabar,
Or any other port as far,
Our purser he will tip the chink,

And just like fishes we will drink.
For huzza! We're outward bound, etc.

And now we're haul'd into the docks,
When the pretty girls they come in flocks;
And one unto the other will say,
"Here comes Jack with his three years' pay."
For huzza! We're homeward bound.

And now we're off to the "Dog and Bell,"
Where good liquors they always sell;
In comes the landlord with a smile,
Saying, "Drink, lads, drink, it's worth your while,
For don't you see you're homeward bound," etc.

But when our money is gone and spent,

There's none to be borrowed, nor any to be
                                              lent;
In comes the landlord with a frown,

Saying, "Get up, Jack, let John sit down,
For don't you see he's homeward bound," etc.[72]

Outward Bound

Anon

To Liv-er-pool docks we__ bid a - dieu, To Su-ke and Sal and

Kit - ty__ too; The an - chor's weigh'd, the sails un - furled, We're bound to cross the__

wat - ery world, For we are out - ward bound ... ... Hur - ah! We're out-ward bound!

Fig. 8.26

Most of the other songs about the sea and ships reported specific incidents, such as shipwrecks, naval battles, or fights with pirates. They included "The *Nightingale*," "As We Were A-Sailing," "The Bold Privateer," "On Board a Man-of-War," and "Captain Death."

The wider world of national and international affairs only occasionally found its way into the folksongs collected by Kidson and his associates. When it did the songs were usually broadside ballads, such as "The Plains of Waterloo," celebrating major military or naval victories. Directly political songs were uncommon, but Kidson did include a tune (with just one verse and chorus) for "With Henry Hunt We'll Go," a song about the Peterloo massacre. He had not collected this himself but had obtained it from a fellow enthusiast on the other side of the Pennines, James B. Shaw of Cornbrook, Manchester, who had also supplied him with a Lancashire Morris dance tune. These are the only words Kidson had for the song:

> 'Twas on the sixteenth day of August,
> Eighteen hundred and nineteen,
> A meeting held in Peter Street
> Was glorious to be seen;
> Joe Nadin and his big bull-dogs,
> Which you might plainly see,
> And on the other side
> Stood the bloody cavalry.
>
> *Chorus:*
> With Henry Hunt we'll go, my boys,
> With Henry Hunt we'll go;
> We'll mount the cap of liberty
> In spite of Nadin Joe.[73]

And here is Shaw's melody for "Henry Hunt," which also sounds like a dance tune:

With Henry Hunt We'll Go

Anon

Voice

With Hen-ry Hunt we'll go, my boys, With Hen-ry Hunt we'll go;   We'll

mount the cap of lib-er-ty, In   spite of Nad-in Joe.

Fig. 8.27

As we have seen, a substantial proportion of the material in *Traditional Tunes* was not collected personally by Kidson but had been recalled or noted by one of several friends and helpers. Although a few of Kidson's tunes and texts were Scottish, the vast majority derived from Yorkshire. *Traditional Tunes* was therefore essentially a collaborative effort and primarily a regional collection. It was particularly important for its emphasis on tunes, since previous Victorian collections of Yorkshire songs had concentrated almost exclusively on texts.

Kidson as Editor

It remains to assess Kidson's approach to editing in his first two, groundbreaking, publications. At this early point in his career as a collector and scholar, Kidson believed that genuine folksongs antedated any variants of the song that were printed as broadsides or "ballad sheets." Printed versions rarely provided tunes and in any case few rural purchasers of broadsides from itinerant pedlars could read music. The wonderful tunes that he was discovering in the villages, towns, and ports of Yorkshire had either been passed on from generation to generation or created by the singers themselves out of a store of communal melody. Broadsides, he recognized, tended to stabilize the words, but they also corrupted them. He remarked that "the corruptions that have crept in by reason of the blunders of the reciter or the illiterateness of the printer have frequently turned a ballad, originally good, into an absurdity; it must also be conceded that the rustic muse produced better melody than poetry or even rhyme."[74] His antiquarian reverence for the tunes thus did not extend to the words of the songs in his collection, a fact that was evident as soon as one perused the first few items in *Traditional Tunes*. The first, "The Three Ravens," had an incomplete text; the second, "Chevy Chace," included only two verses of the ballad with the offhand assertion that it was "much too long and too well known for insertion here"; and the third, "The Knight and the Shepherd's Daughter" was given with a fragmentary text that appeared to have been censored.[75]

In editing his song texts Kidson was faced with two problems. One was that many of the texts collected from his source singers were incomplete: the informants simply had been unable to remember all the words. The other was that some of the words they had remembered were, in his opinion, indecent or otherwise unfit to print. His solution to both problems was to publish incomplete texts, omitting entire verses or sets of verse, or merely substituting a row of dots for a censored or forgotten line. To his credit Kidson did not attempt to rewrite song texts. But he was less than candid in indicating when he had used his editorial red pencil. It is often difficult to tell for sure whether a given text was incomplete as collected or had been rendered incomplete by censorship. To judge from the subject matter of the songs, however, it appears probable that of the eighty-three songs in *Traditional Tunes* some fourteen were censored, mostly on grounds of indecency but occasionally merely because Kidson considered the words to be "poor doggerel."

Let us briefly examine the songs that Kidson likely censored because they describe sexual encounters. "The Banks of Sweet Dundee," obtained from Benjamin Holgate, had two verses omitted. Holgate may not have been able to supply a full text, but Kidson had a copy of a Catnach broadsheet with the complete ballad, so he evidently took a deliberate decision to leave out the offending verses. A second offering from Holgate, "Three Maidens A-Milking Did Go" fared even worse. Kidson deigned to print only one verse, commenting that "it could be wished that the succeeding verses to the first…were equally meritorious and more suitable for this work."[76] Evidently casual sex in the countryside was not deemed by Kidson suitable content for his book. "Brocklesby Fair" received the same treatment, with only one verse printed, presumably because the lifestyle of the protagonist, young 'Ramble Away,' was judged too immoral to be seen or heard. As his justification for printing only one verse of Lolley's "My Valentine," Kidson invoked aesthetic rather than ethical criteria: "the whole song," he maintained, "is poor doggerel."[77] However, since his line of dots was inserted just at the point where the "pretty, pretty maid came to my bedside" one suspects that his motives were, at the very least, mixed. From "The Sprig of Thyme" just one verse was omitted, and since Kidson had taken his text from Johnson's *Museum* this cut too was evidently a conscious choice. One of Washington Teasdale's contributions, "The Brewer Laddie," which he had collected at Brough in Westmoreland, had at least one verse trimmed, with the result that the rambling lass's sorry fate remained untold, presumably because it was unsuitable for delicate ears to hear. Only one verse of Allan Wardill's "An Auld Man He Courted Me," which dealt, albeit humorously, with impotence and infidelity, was seen fit for print, and even the second half of the chorus, which detailed the elderly bridegroom's deficiency, was censored. Sailors' songs, such as Lolley's "Just As the Tide Was Flowing" and "Outward Bound" were given incomplete, and the same was true for "The Indian Lass," which Kidson noted on the North Yorkshire coast, despite the fact that he possessed the full text on a broadside. Similarly, "Down By the Derwent Side" and "The Bonny Irish Boy" were truncated, with only two verses printed from the former ballad and three from the latter. Again, from the well-known broadside ballad "Polly Oliver's Ramble" Kidson excerpted only four verses. This may not have been censorship, however, but merely an unwillingness to reprint a text that Kidson considered was already very well known.

Kidson had plenty of other incomplete texts in *Traditional Tunes,* but in most cases it would appear that the omissions simply reflected his informants' poor memories. Where he provided more than one variant of a ballad, as in the case of "Henry Martin" or "Barbara Allen," he did his best to include a full text, as well as additional fragments from other informants. By and large that was also true for songs such as "My True Love Once He Courted Me," "Forty Miles" and "The Farmer's Boy," for which he obtained several different variants. Nonetheless, one still receives the impression that Kidson cared less about the words of folksongs than about their melodies. Had he made more of a concerted effort to track down the missing lines, he might have obtained more complete songs and less in the way of fragments. As for his elimination of any overt sex from the texts he printed, this was understandable in the context of the moral climate of the Late Victorian era, but it was not forced upon him by a publisher. Since *Traditional Tunes* was self-published in a limited edition, Kidson had ultimate control over its content. A few Victorian editors before him, most notably Frederick Furnivall, had stood out against bowdlerization, and printing texts fully and accurately was the official policy of the Ballad Society. Kidson, too, was in principle in favor of a scientific approach to editing, and he could have joined the ranks of the minority willing to brave Victorian public opinion for the sake of accuracy and authenticity. He chose not to.

Despite these irritating problems with incomplete or censored texts, *Traditional Tunes* was an exceptionally impressive and useful collection. In terms of both presentation of tunes and provision of information about informants and other sources, it set a standard that no previous folksong collection had achieved and that, regrettably, many subsequent ones would also fail to match. In a note at the end of the book Kidson announced his intention to publish a "supplementary volume" of more traditional tunes, and he appealed to his readers to send him items that they had collected. In the event, this second volume never appeared. The reason may have been financial, but it seems more likely that Kidson simply decided to devote his time to his numerous other projects. If so, it was a regrettable decision. Kidson's personal vernacular song collection may have been less than a third of Baring-Gould's in size, but it was, in the main, of high quality. It was a pity that many years would elapse before more of it was made available in printed form.

Notes

1. Lucy Broadwood, "Obituary: Frank Kidson, M.A. Born November 15th, 1855. Died November 7th, 1926," *Journal of the Folk-Song Society* 8, no. 31 (1927): 48-49.

2. Frank Kidson, ed., *Traditional Tunes: A Collection of Ballad Airs* (Oxford: Taphouse, 1891).

3. For a biographical sketch of Kidson's life, focusing on his early career as a landscape painter, see: John Francmanis, "The Roving Artist: Frank Kidson, Pioneer Song Collector," *Folk Music Journal* 8, no. 1 (2001): 41-66.

4. Francis Kidson, *Hebrew, Moslem, and Moorish Melodies* (Leeds: Charles Goodall, 1869).

5. Frank Kidson to Lucy Broadwood, 24 November 1893 [Vaughan Williams Memorial Library, Lucy Broadwood Collection, LEB/4/159].

6. Joseph and Frank Kidson, *Historical Notices of the Leeds Old Pottery* (Wakefield, U.K.: SR Publishers, 1970 [reprint of the 1892 edition]).

7. Francmanis, "Roving Artist," 46-47.

8. Francmanis, "Roving Artist," 50.

9. Frank Kidson, "Yorkshire Folk Song," Mitchell Library, M. 18052. Lecture delivered to the National Convention of Choirmasters at Sheffield, 15 September 1906, and summarized in the *Musical Herald,* October 1906.

10. Kidson, *Traditional Tunes,* 84.

11. Kidson, *Traditional Tunes,* 85-86.

12. Frank Kidson, ed., *Old English Country Dances* (London: William Reeves, 1890. Reprinted, Louth: Celtic Music, 1983).

13. Roy Palmer, "Kidson's Collecting," *Folk Music Journal* 5, no. 2 (1986): 150-75.

14. Roy Palmer, *Checklist of Manuscript Songs and Tunes collected from Oral Tradition by Frank Kidson* (Glasgow & London: Mitchell Library & EFDSS, 1986).

15. Frank Kidson, "Notes on Old Tunes," thirty-two articles, *Leeds Mercury Weekly Supplement,* 6 November 1886–25 June 1887.

16. Frank Kidson, "Notes on Old Tunes: Dr. Greene's Setting of 'The Fly,'" *Leeds Mercury Weekly Supplement,* 6 Nov 1886.

17. Kidson, "Fly."

18. Frank Kidson, "Notes on Old Tunes: Early Collections," *Leeds Mercury Weekly Supplement,* 11 December 1886.

19. Kidson, "Early Collections."

20. Frank Kidson, "Notes on Old Tunes: 'The Beggar's Opera,'" *Leeds Mercury Weekly Supplement,* 12 February 1887.

21. Frank Kidson, "Notes on Old Tunes: Ballad Operas," *Leeds Mercury Weekly Supplement,* 19 February 1887.

22. Frank Kidson, "Notes on Old Tunes: A Wassail Song, &c.," *Leeds Mercury Weekly Supplement,* 25 December 1886.

23. Kidson, "Wassail Song."

24. Frank Kidson, "Notes on Old Tunes: 'Johnnie Faa', or 'The Gypsy Laddie,'" *Leeds Mercury Weekly Supplement,* 13 November 1886.

25. Frank Kidson, "Notes on Old Tunes: 'Lochaber No More,'" *Leeds Mercury Weekly Supplement,* 29 January 1887.

26. Frank Kidson, "Notes on Old Tunes: 'The Keel Row,'" *Leeds Mercury Weekly Supplement,* 26 March 1887.

27. Frank Kidson, "Notes on Old Tunes: 'Bow, Wow, Wow,'" *Leeds Mercury Weekly Supplement,* 23 April 1887.

28. Kidson, "Bow Wow Wow."

29. Kidson, *Old English Country Dances,* iii.

30. Kidson, *Old English Country Dances,* 1.

31. Kidson, *Old English Country Dances,* 19.

32. Kidson, *Old English Country Dances,* 8.

33. Kidson, *Old English Country Dances,* 32.

34. Kidson, *Old English Country Dances,* 32.

35. Kidson, *Old English Country Dances,* 6.

36. Kidson, *Old English Country Dances,* 31.

37. Frank Kidson, "New Lights upon Old Tunes, No. V: Airs in the Early Ballad Operas," *The Musical Times* (1 June 1896): 378-79.

38. Frank Kidson and Alfred Moffat, eds., *The Minstrelsy of England: a collection of 200 English songs with their melodies, popular from the 16th century to the middle of the 18th century* (London: Bailey and Ferguson, 1901), 284.

39. Kidson, *Traditional Tunes,* 114-15.

40. Kidson, *Traditional Tunes,* 153-54. James Henry Dixon, ed., *Ancient Poems, Ballads and Songs of the Peasantry of England* (London: Percy Society, 1846), 230-32.

41. Kidson, *Traditional Tunes,* 19.

42. Kidson, *Traditional Tunes,* 25-26.

43. Kidson, *Traditional Tunes,* 54-55.

44. Kidson, *Traditional Tunes,* 63-64.

45. Kidson, *Traditional Tunes,* 112-13.

46. Kidson, *Traditional Tunes,* 38-40.

47. Kidson, *Traditional Tunes,* 102-3.

48. Kidson, *Traditional Tunes,* 108-9.

49. Kidson, *Traditional Tunes,* 104.

50. Kidson to Lucy Broadwood, 24 September 1907, as quoted by Francmanis, "Roving Artist," 50, from Vaughan Williams Memorial Library, "Lucy Broadwood Collection," Box 1.

51. Kidson, *Traditional Tunes,* 21-22.

52. Kidson, *Traditional Tunes,* 22-23.

53. Broadwood, "Obituary: Frank Kidson, M.A.," 48.

54. Kidson, *Traditional Tunes,* xi-xii.

55. Kidson, *Traditional Tunes,* xii-xiii.

56. Kidson, *Traditional Tunes,* xiii.

57. Kidson, *Traditional Tunes,* xii-xiv.

58. Kidson, *Traditional Tunes,* xvi.

59. Kidson, *Traditional Tunes,* v-vi.

60. Kidson, *Traditional Tunes,* xv. One wonders whether this claim was based entirely on Kidson's personal experience as a song collector in the field. Evidence is lacking that he himself noted any songs in Berkshire and Oxfordshire, but it is difficult to see to what printed collection he might have been referring, since he made this statement before the publication of *English County Songs.*

61. Kidson, *Traditional Tunes,* xv.

62. Kidson, *Traditional Tunes,* 31-32.

63. Kidson, *Traditional Tunes,* 51-53.

64. Kidson, *Traditional Tunes,* 155-56.

65. Kidson, *Traditional Tunes,* 77-78.

66. Kidson, *Traditional Tunes,* 69.

67. Kidson, *Traditional Tunes,* 67-68.

68. Kidson, *Traditional Tunes,* 138-39.

69. Kidson, *Traditional Tunes,* 131-32.

70. Kidson, *Traditional Tunes,* 170.

71. Kidson, *Traditional Tunes,* 170-71.

72. Kidson, *Traditional Tunes,* 107-8.

73. Kidson, *Traditional Tunes,* 163.

74. Kidson, *Traditional Tunes,* xvi.

75. Kidson, *Traditional Tunes,* 17-21.

76. Kidson, *Traditional Tunes,* 72.

77. Kidson, *Traditional Tunes,* 60.

Part 3

The Growth of a Movement, 1890-1903

9

Interlude: England in the 1890s

In chapter 3, before beginning our exploration of the birth of the Late Victorian folksong revival, we surveyed the state of the country in the 1880s in order to gauge the kind of society and culture within which the new movement would find a place. It is now time to follow briefly the new developments that were occurring in the England of the 1890s at the same time as folksong collecting gathered momentum and the isolated efforts of individuals gradually cohered into a cultural movement. As in chapter 3, we will survey the main trends in the economic and political life of the nation and outline the most significant contributions made to thought, literature, and the fine arts before tracing briefly the new developments in English musical life. Finally we will again examine briefly the specialized intellectual activity of ballad editing because of its particular relevance to the business of folksong collecting. Our focus there will be on the work of two key individuals: Francis James Child and Joseph Ebsworth.

Population and Economy

The late Victorian era witnessed a steady rise in population. During the decade of the 1880s the number of people living in the United Kingdom had grown by nearly eight percent, reaching 37.7 million in 1891. It would continue to climb at a similar rate during the next decade, reaching 41.5 million by the end of Queen Victoria's reign. While England shared in this general demographic picture the trend was exacerbated there by a flow of people from Scotland and Ireland to urban areas, resulting in an even higher rate of expansion. The result was that from twenty-six million in 1881 the English population grew to twenty-nine million in 1891 and to 32.5 million in 1901. This over-crowded land, which was already unable to feed itself, was thus becoming ever more dependent on imports of food paid for by wealth earned from the export of industrial goods.[1]

Although its rate of growth had slowed considerably since the boom years of the Industrial Revolution, the British economy was still expanding, sustained by large export markets in Europe, the British Empire, and South America. Despite heavier competition from Western Europe and North America, the value of British exports rose by ten million to £233 million between 1880 and 1899, and this occurred during a period in which prices on average fell, although that trend saw the beginnings of a reversal in the last three years of the century. It was an age of coal and steel. Coal was the principal fuel for long-distance transportation (rail and shipping), for the steam-powered factories and for domestic heating. Steel had replaced iron as the building material of choice for most large-scale uses, and the remarkable growth in steel production, which had easily outstripped the expansion of most other industries, continued, albeit at a lesser pace, rising from 3,637 thousand tons in 1890 to 4,901 thousand in 1900.[2] This was also increasingly an age of electricity, with electric street and domestic lighting becoming much more widespread, and electric trams making their appearance or expanding their networks of lines in most of the larger cities. The automobile was not yet a significant factor in transportation—the internal combustion engine had only just been invented, the number of horseless vehicles on the roads was still very small, and they were possessed only by the rich or by enthusiasts of what was regarded as a new sport—but England possessed an extensive rail network. Trains were pulled by steam engines that provided fast mainline services and also operated on a myriad of branch lines that have since disappeared. They permitted convenient access to many country towns and villages, and, when used in combination with a bicycle, made folksong collecting in the field much easier than before. British engineering skill was renowned world-wide, and this was a time when ships (luxury liners and freighters both) grew in size, some of the fastest ever steam-powered railway locomotives were built, and imaginative projects such as the very long Firth of Forth bridge and the huge Manchester Ship Canal were conceived and brought to fruition.

As in the previous decade, the poor cousin of the British economy was agriculture. Between 1890 and 1900 the acreage devoted to corn crops continued to fall significantly, from approximately 9,500 to approximately 8,700, a trend which was compensated for only partially by a seven percent growth in cattle production. This progressive abandonment of more marginal lands reflected the difficulty of making anything but the most efficient arable farming turn a profit at a time when wheat prices continued to fall, from approximately thirty-two shillings per quarter in 1890 to twenty-seven shillings in 1900.[3] For the consumer, on the other hand, this was good news, with the price of bread declining from about six pence for a four lb. loaf in 1890 to around five pence in 1900. Most other basic commodities, including tea, sugar, meat, and the imported raw material, cotton, on which the English textile industry depended so heavily, saw some price fluctuations in these years, but there were no serious long-term increases, so the overall cost of living remained relatively stable. This meant that the 1890s were fairly good times for the middle classes and for working class families whose breadwinner remained permanently employed.

Continuous employment, however, was not a given for a significant percentage of the workforce. Still an unbridled *laissez-faire* system, the British economy continued to undergo that bane of industrial capitalism, a cycle of boom and bust that resulted in severe bouts of unemployment for several years at a time. 1889 had seen the crest of an economic wave, and as the new decade began exports and other economic activity began to decline. By 1893-94 the economy had slumped into a trough almost as severe as the terrible year of 1886, with unemployment hitting nearly eight percent. At a time when unemployment insurance was unknown in Britain and the only social security net was the dreaded workhouse, that meant at least one in twelve working class families had joined the underclass of the permanently unemployed. From mid-decade, however, the economy improved again, and the remainder of the century brought prosperity, with the boom cresting in 1899 and unemployment at a low of two percent. Of course, the good times would not last and another, albeit milder, slump was in the offing before the Edwardian era had seen more than a few years.[4]

The successful London Dock Strike of 1889 had provided an impetus for the trade-union movement, and the 1890s are usually seen as the time when a "new unionism" emerged. The term perhaps overemphasizes the change, but there was during the decade a more concerted attempt to organize industrial unions on a national scale, superseding in part the older craft unions and also unions with merely regional or even local bases. The new formations included the Miners' Federation and the Amalgamated Society of Engineers, both of which were involved in major strike actions during the 1890s. Neither were particularly successful in this decade. The miners' strike of 1893, for example, was actually a lockout, precipitated by the colliery owners' unilaterally imposing a 10 percent roll-back in wages, and, because it took place during a downturn in the economy when demand for coal was weaker than normal, was defeated, although not before the workers' families had suffered tremendous hardship and government troops had fired on strikers picketing Featherstone Colliery, killing two of them. That had been a defensive strike, its only goal the protection of the miners' standard of living. The Amalgamated Society of Engineers' strike in 1897-98, on the other hand, took the offensive, with an eight-hour day its central demand. Its failure reinforced the conviction already held by some union leaders, and led others to recognize, that since the state and the employers normally worked hand in glove and together constituted formidable adversaries, some form of political action was needed to complement industrial action.[5]

This conviction led to the formation of the Independent Labour Party in 1893, and to the election of Keir Hardie to the House of Commons. Yet Hardie lost his seat in 1895, and the new unionism, even when effective, could only help an elite of workers employed in the biggest industries.[6] In terms of living standards, that was not where the need was sorest. Quite apart from the ranks of the permanently unemployed, there was still a large stratum of Victorian society that lived a hand to mouth existence, barely keeping body and soul together. Friedrich Engels, of course, had already demonstrated this problem in the 1840s (using government statistics), but it took the work of pioneer urban sociologist Charles Booth to reinforce the message. He concluded in the first volume of *Life and Labour of the People of London* that over 30 percent of the inhabitants of London lived in poverty.[7] Overcrowded housing and a dearth of sanitation and running water contributed to the problem, not only in London but in numerous cities and industrial towns from the South Wales coalfields to Liverpool, Leeds, Newcastle, and Glasgow. Moreover, the situation was in many cases getting worse, because the rise in population was outstripping the provision of tenements.

Late Victorian England was thus a society in crisis, but the crisis only affected the disempowered, so it was possible for most politicians at the national level to ignore it, and ignore it they did. At the municipal level, on the other hand, not only were socialists or labor representatives beginning to secure seats on local councils but a significant number of idealistic and scientifically trained professionals, most of whom supported the Liberal Party nationally, were determined to bring clean water, sewers, parks, and trams to their cities. This was the movement called, somewhat misleadingly, municipal socialism, and it dovetailed with parallel concerns about the lack of care for orphans and for the provision of elementary education for the children of the poor. The men and women with social consciences who saw the need for drastic action on these issues hardly expected the national government, especially when it was in Conservative hands, to act decisively to solve them. But they did call for legislation to provide an enabling framework for local action, and for a greater devolution of authority to the municipal government level. National politics thus had a significant bearing on real-life issues in urban England, as well as continuing to be the leading spectator sport for the middle classes.[8]

Political Life

Apart from a period of Liberal rule under Gladstone and Rosebery between August 1892 and June 1895, the United Kingdom was governed by the Conservative party, in alliance with the Liberal Unionists led by Joseph Chamberlain, for the remainder of the Victorian era.[9] The decade of the 1890s began with a Conservative government, led by Salisbury, still in power, but it was defeated in the general election of July 1892. The Liberals, led by the octogenarian Gladstone, ran on the celebrated "Newcastle Programme," which promised Irish Home Rule, the disestablishment of the Anglican Church in Wales and Scotland, further electoral reform, the creation of district and parish councils, a local veto on the sale of intoxicating liquor, limits on working hours, workmen's compensation (for industrial accidents), and other reforms. Not surprisingly, this reformist platform appealed to a diverse coalition of nonconformists, lower-class and Celtic voters, but alienated the middle ground of public opinion in England. The result of the 1892 election was a House of Commons in which Liberals and Conservatives were almost evenly balanced, but the Irish Home Rulers outnumbered the Liberal Unionists. Gladstone, recognizing that this would be his last chance, determined to solve the Irish question once and for all. His fourth (and final) term in office was dominated by his attempt to pass his second Home Rule Bill through the House of Commons. After interminable debate and eighty-five sittings he succeeded, only to see the measure rejected by the Conservative majority in the House of Lords. Gladstone was eager to fight another election on the issue, in order to obtain a mandate to curb the powers of the second chamber, but his cabinet colleagues, recognizing the Home Rule Bill's unpopularity in England, had no stomach for another campaign.

Gladstone then resigned as Prime Minister, and Queen Victoria chose Lord Rosebery as his successor.[10] A Liberal government therefore continued in office for another sixteen months, and tried periodically to enact various pieces of legislation stemming from the Newcastle Programme. Most of these bills were either rejected or drastically emended by the House of Lords. For example, a Workmen's Compensation Act was gutted by allowing employers to opt out of its provisions, which rendered it impotent. An attempt to permit the local prohibition of alcohol was killed. Two important reforms survived substantially intact, however: the introduction of death duties (as a way of paying for the modernization and expansion of the navy, which the Conservatives supported), and the Local Government Act of 1894, which set up parish and district councils, giving them fairly sweeping powers but only a very limited capacity to raise revenue for municipal improvements through local property taxes.

In the general election of 1895 the Conservatives, again in coalition with the Liberal Unionists, won a decisive majority against a Liberal party whose policies of Home Rule and (partial) prohibition were unpopular among many English voters. Gladstone had had little taste for multiplying colonies in Africa, fearing (wisely) that they would end up costing more than they were worth as sources of raw materials or as potential export markets. The Conservatives, on the other hand, had readily embraced an ideology of imperialism that was increasingly popular in the country at large.[11] For better or for worse, Salisbury and Chamberlain were more in tune with the mood of the country than were Rosebery's Liberals, and they believed they had been given a mandate to employ force against Irish reformers, strikers, and anyone who stood in the way of an expanding British Empire. The Salisbury administration that took over government in 1895 would endure until 1902, and even then it would be replaced by another Conservative cabinet led by Salisbury's nephew, A. J. Balfour.[12]

The Liberal Unionist leader Joseph Chamberlain played a leading role as Colonial Secretary in a government that was determined not to grant Home Rule for Ireland and was, on the whole, indifferent to demands for reform at home, but was an enthusiastic champion of imperial expansion.[13] Chamberlain was particularly active in promoting British commercial interests in West Africa and the West Indies, but he also faced the issue of how to handle developments in South Africa. Gladstone and the Liberals had followed policies designed to avoid expensive military involvement in colonial conflicts, but Chamberlain, albeit reluctantly, was willing to resort to force if necessary. His more aggressive approach to solving African issues resulted in the Boer War, the event that dominated British political life in the last years of the Victorian era. A gold rush in the Transvaal had transformed this Boer republic (led by Paul Kruger) into a wealthy state, but one which was almost hemmed around by British protectorates. Cecil Rhodes, the premier of the Cape Colony, was determined to retain a land corridor (and to build a railway) linking the Cape with Rhodesia to the north, while Kruger hoped to annex the territory between Transvaal and the eastern coast of Africa. The unsuccessful Jamieson Raid on Johannesburg in January 1896 was the work of Rhodes but was perceived by the Boers as British policy, and resulted in Transvaal receiving diplomatic and even some military support from Germany. Chamberlain had not authorized the raid, and was eventually exonerated from the charge of fomenting the uprising, but the incident underlined the potential conflict between Boer and British ambitions in East Africa, and it left the unsatisfactory situation of the British Uitlanders in the Transvaal unresolved.

The problem flared up again in 1898 when the Uitlanders petitioned the British government to do something to stop the systematic discrimination that Kruger was practicing against them. Chamberlain, using Sir Alfred Milner as his envoy, attempted to negotiate a solution, but Kruger refused to give in to British pressure. Believing that the Orange Free State and the Transvaal's combined forces could defeat any British military expedition launched to help the Uitlanders, he judged the time was right to create a Dutch federal state that would be completely independent of Britain. Neither side was prepared to back down, and the result was the Boer War (1899-1902), which began when the Boers invaded British territory. English public opinion was divided, but the majority supported war, and early British defeats merely resulted in the sending of more troops. The relief of Ladysmith and Mafeking permitted the British forces to take the offensive, and a successful invasion of the Transvaal resulted in its formal annexation, as well as that of the Orange Free State. The war was not yet over, however, since the Boers resorted to effective guerrilla tactics, but eventually they were defeated, although at great cost in terms of money (£222 million) and lives (those of twenty-two thousand troops). Meanwhile, in North Africa, Britain had, during the Fashoda incident of 1899, successfully faced down French expansion in the Sudan, while in West Africa Chamberlain resisted similar attempts by French forces to take over the coastal territories where Britain had imposed her hegemony. Another significant development at the end of the decade was the creation of a federation of the six Australian colonies: parliament passed the Commonwealth of Australia Act in 1900.[14]

The Salisbury government, at Chamberlain's urging, used the British military victory in South Africa as a way of extending its term in office by holding the so-called Khaki election of October 1900 at a time of public euphoria. The Liberals were at the time an ineffective opposition because they were split over the war; Rosebery supported it, but the more radical wing of the party, which included John Morley and David Lloyd George, opposed it, as did the Independent Labour Party, which that year was effectively replaced by the Labour Representation Committee, the forerunner of the Labour Party.[15] During this period of Conservative ascendancy and imperialist xenophobia, reformers of all stripes had difficulty in getting a hearing or making any progress for their causes. Nonetheless, they were getting better organized. For example, the National Union of Women's Suffrage Societies was founded in 1897: it was committed to moral suasion and would oppose, often quite bitterly, the tactics of more militant suffragettes in the Women's Social and Political Union who caught the attention of the press in the Edwardian era. By remaining respectable, it was able to gain support among women whose politics were in other respects conservative (including, for example, Lucy Broadwood), and its membership grew rapidly. Its first success was the increasing involvement of women in local government, as voters in elections to district councils, as elected officials, and as employees of local boards.

Thought and Literature

Early feminism was but one of several intellectual movements that flourished in Late Victorian England. Imperialism, for example, was not only a mixture of trade, missionary activity, and Conservative foreign policy, it was also an ideology with its theorists and popularizers. C. H. Pearson's *National Life and Character* was perhaps the most influential attempt to provide an intellectual justification for the racist version of colonialism, and it played a role in the deliberate adoption of a 'White Australia' policy in that country.[16] Kipling, who coined the phrase "the white man's burden," was not the aggressive imperialist that he is usually portrayed as; he had a detailed knowledge of and respect, even love, for Indian religion and culture, as is evident from his novel *Kim*.[17] Nonetheless, unlike Annie Besant, he accepted without question the benefits and obligations of colonialism, and through his poems and short stories, in particular, played a considerable role in justifying and promoting it. His more important publications during the 1890s included his first novel, *The Light That Failed* (1891), a very popular collection of vernacular poetry called *Barrack-Room Ballads* (1892), a book of short stories, *Many Inventions* (1893), his brilliant children's tales, *The Jungle Book* and *The Second Jungle Book* (1894-95), and his sea yarn set in Newfoundland, *Captain Courageous* (1897). His most famous apology for imperialism, which actually emphasized the responsibilities and duties of Western administrators in the colonies, was published on the eve of the Boer War in 1899, while his best Indian novel, *Kim*, appeared during the war in 1901 and the popular *Just So Stories* (for children) a year later.[18]

Christianity, although in overall terms its appeal (and active support) was gradually declining, was still a major force in late Victorian society and intellectual life. Evangelicalism, with its literal interpretation of the bible, was under attack, and in the 1890s found no new champion with arguments to refute either Darwinism, the comparative anthropology of Sir James Frazer's *The Golden Bough* (1890-1915),[19] or the textual criticism of liberal theologians. The Oxford movement, too, had largely run its course, although a significant minority of Anglican clergy were now high churchmen and they persisted—against somewhat half-hearted opposition from their bishops—in reintroducing quasi-Catholic theological formulations and rituals into their churches.

In nonconformist circles, particularly among Methodists, the social gospel had considerable appeal, and Christian Socialism often seemed a suitable way of retaining's one faith while professing solidarity with the poor and the working class.[20] William Booth, however, offered a powerful alternative. Initially the Salvation Army had been created as a missionary body on revivalist lines, but working among the poorest, most disadvantaged, and most neglected members of the underclass had opened his and his wife's eyes to an extent of urban misery that shocked them and changed their focus. In 1890 Booth published *In Darkest England, and the Way Out*,[21] and throughout the decade of the 1890s and thereafter built a network of agencies aimed at not only feeding and clothing the poor while saving their souls but also at job training and facilitating emigration to the colonies. Urban sociologist Charles Booth—(who, incidentally, was not related to the Salvation Army's founder)—reinforced the message by continuing to publish the fruits of the research he had begun in 1886 into the conditions of life among the lower classes. *Life and Labour of the People of London*, which, as we have seen, proved an unpleasant revelation to many when the first volume was published in 1889, was gradually completed during the 1890s, with a nine volume edition issued between 1892 and 1897, and a revised fourteen volume version, divided into three series (*Poverty, Industry,* and *Religious Influences*) published in 1902.[22] Although the Salisbury government was indifferent to "the social problem," it was clear to many Christians and non-believers alike that something had to be done, and quickly. The question was what, and how. It was perhaps not surprising that composer Hubert Parry would be moved to set to music William Blake's poem "The New Jerusalem," but while the anthem stirred the soul it provided no blueprint for action.

Not everyone was convinced that Christianity was part of the solution rather than part of the problem. Although Charles Bradlaugh died in 1891, the free-thought movement, which championed not only agnosticism and Darwinism but also birth control, continued unabated its highly vocal critique of all forms of orthodox Christianity.[23] One of its star speakers, Annie Besant, who had been converted to socialism in the mid-1880s and had organized a strike of match-girls in 1888, now became a convert to theosophy.[24] Helena Blavatsky, the movement's founder and leading personality, died in 1891, but theosophy continued to flourish in England during the 1890s, despite Besant's move to India in 1893.[25] It combined an ecumenical form of belief in a World Spirit, which it saw as finding expression in a variety of different regional religions, with a putatively scientific investigation of the paranormal and supernatural. George R. S. Mead, formerly Blavatsky's private secretary, took up her torch, from 1894 onwards editing (jointly with Besant) the Theosophical Society's periodical *Lucifer* and its successor *The Theosophical Review,* and quickly emerging as the movement's authority on Gnosticism and comparative religion.[26] He would become a close friend and influence on Lucy Broadwood. An alternative to theosophy, for those who wanted an intellectual framework that supplanted Christian dogma but rejected materialism and retained a spiritual universe, was provided by the Idealist school of philosophy, led by such figures as T. H. Green, Edward Caird, F. H. Bradley, and Bernard Bosanquet; their most famous and influential work was Bradley's *Appearance and Reality*.[27]

Although each was brilliant in his or her own way, individuals such as Besant, Mead, and even Bradley were seen as mavericks by most Victorians. That was still true, too, for any writer who espoused a form of socialism, even one as gifted as William Morris or as ebullient as George Bernard Shaw. Late Victorian socialism was by no means homogenous as an ideology: there were, among others, pragmatists such as Keir Hardie, Christian socialists, Marxists, followers of William Morris, and Fabians. The first set of *Fabian Essays* had been published in December 1889, but more were to come and the 1890s was the decade in which the Fabian Society flourished not only as a debating chamber but as a fecund source of practical ideas for much needed social reforms.[28] Among its leading lights were Sidney Webb and Beatrice Potter (they married in 1892),[29] whose pioneering *History of Trade Unionism* appeared in 1894[30] and whose principal contribution to socialist theory, *Industrial Democracy*, was published in 1897.[31] George Bernard Shaw, who had contributed to the first *Fabian Essays* and who served on the Society's executive committee, earned his living as a music critic and, from 1895, as drama critic for *The Saturday Review*. His early career as a novelist had been unsuccessful commercially, but in the 1890s he emerged as a major playwright. A great admirer of Ibsen, he chose social issues as the subjects of most of his plays, but treated them with such wit and humor that even conservative critics were won over.[32] His first play, *Widowers' Houses*, was not a success, but from *Arms and the Man* (1894) onwards Shaw began creating the works for which he is most famous, including *The Devil's Disciple* (1897), *Mrs. Warren's Profession* (1898), which ran afoul of the censor, *You Never Can Tell* (1899), and *Caesar and Cleopatra* (1900). His first published collection, *Plays Pleasant and Unpleasant*, appeared in 1898.[33] Despite Shaw's attempt to promulgate his concerns and reformist ideas through the theatre, Fabianism never attracted the mass audience reached by such imaginative American books as Laurence Gronlund's *Co-operative Commonwealth* (1884)[34] and Edward Bellamy's *Looking Backwards* (1887).[35] Yet these were in any case supplemented—and to some degree supplanted—in the 1890s by home-grown utopian literature: William Morris's *News from Nowhere* (1891)[36] and, above all, *Merrie England* (1894) by Robert Blatchford, whose lively periodical, *The Clarion*, was a significant advocate not only for socialism but also for the back-to-the-land movement, vegetarianism, feminism, arts-and-crafts, music, and literature.[37]

George Gissing was the novelist who most systematically set out to portray the grim realities of lower-class life. His best-known work, *New Grub Street*, was published in 1891, and his other most popular novel, *Born in Exile*, followed it the next year. Other of Gissing's books printed in the 1890s included five more novels, *The Odd Women* (1893), *Sleeping Fires* (1895), *The Whirlpool* (1897), *The Town Traveller* (1898), and *The Crown of Life* (1899), and a critical work on Charles Dickens.[38] Gissing's friend, H. G. Wells, a disciple of T. H. Huxley and a future member of the Fabian Society, would emerge in the Edwardian era as a gifted satirist who, like Shaw and Gissing, took important social issues for the subject matter of his novels. In the 1890s he was more important as a pioneer of science fiction, his popular scientific romances including *The Time Machine* (1895), *The Island of Dr. Moreau* (1896), *The Invisible Man* (1897), *The War of the Worlds* (1898), and *When the Sleeper Wakes* (1899).[39] Although his fiction drew attention to the potential dangers of scientific invention, Wells nonetheless believed firmly in science and in progress through the increasing application of scientific method to human problems. Scientific method, as applied to the solving of crimes, was the *leitmotif* of Arthur Conan Doyle's fiction, especially his celebrated tales featuring Sherlock Holmes, which were serialized in *Strand Magazine* and collected in *The Adventures of Sherlock Holmes* (1892), *The Memoirs of Sherlock Holmes* (1894), and *The Hound of the Baskervilles* (1902).[40]

Gissing, Wells, and Doyle were all predominantly urban in orientation, whereas Thomas Hardy continued to examine the plight of human beings in an indifferent and meaningless world through a lens aimed at rural and small town Dorset (Wessex in his novels). Although Hardy was by now widely recognized as a major literary figure, his masterpieces *Tess of the D'Urbervilles* (1891) and *Jude the Obscure* (1895) were met with hostile reviews that deplored his pessimism and his allegedly immoral vision. Apart from publishing a collection of short stories as *Life's Little Ironies* in 1894, Hardy was content to see these two magnificent if controversial novels as his final testament as a prose writer, and from the mid-1890s he concentrated on writing poetry. His first collection of shorter poems, *Wessex Poems*, appeared in 1898, but it would be 1904 before the first volume of his epic poem in blank verse, *The Dynasts*, was published. Hardy never achieved the critical and commercial success as a poet that he had as a novelist, but his work stood out from the profusion of other Late Victorian poetry published during the last decade of the century.[41] Another writer whose distinctive cycle of poems captured the mood of that minority of Late Victorians who were disenchanted with industrialization, urbanization, imperialism, and the xenophobic hysteria that accompanied the Boer War was A. E. Housman.[42] Initially published in 1896 (it would be subsequently revised and expanded), *A Shropshire Lad* would gradually find an audience in the Edwardian era, helped, no doubt, by composer Arthur Somervell's setting of some of the poems in 1903.

Other Late Victorian poets with highly distinctive styles were Algernon Charles Swinburne and William Morris, but Swinburne's *Poems and Ballads: Third Series* (1889) was one of his last important publications, while Morris, apart from his artistic work with the Arts and Crafts movement, had turned to socialism (as already noted, his influential *News from Nowhere* was published in 1891) and to such historical romances as *The Roots of the Mountains*, *The Story of the Glittering Plain* (both 1890), and *The Wood Beyond the World* (1894), which Shaw denounced as "a startling relapse into literary Pre-Raphaelitism." They were published, in beautiful editions, by Kelmscott Press, which Morris had founded in Hammersmith in 1890 and for which he designed the type fonts, ornamental borders, and cover designs. The Press also published reprints of English classics, including the Kelmscott *Chaucer* and Caxton's *The Golden Legend*.[43]

Other important novelists of the 1890s included Mrs. Humphry Ward, George Moore, Henry James, and Joseph Conrad. Mary Augusta Ward, of whose work Gladstone was a great admirer, had a gift for capturing accurately the mode of life—habits, speech, preoccupations, opinions, and amusements—of the social and political elite who governed the country. She was also particularly interested in the Victorian crisis of faith and in the clash between traditional beliefs and the views espoused by scientists and freethinkers. Her novels along these lines included *The History of David Grieve* (1892), *Marcella* (1894), and *Helbeck of Bannisdale* (1898).[44] George Moore, who incidentally played a role in spreading knowledge about the French Impressionists through his 1893 work *Modern Painting*, was moving away from his earlier Zola-influenced naturalism, and in 1894 published what is usually regarded as one of his finest novels, *Esther Waters*. But a somewhat fallow period followed, while Moore sought for a new, more psychological approach, that focused more on the intellectual, aesthetic, and emotional inner lives of his characters. It found expression in a collection of short stories, *Celibates* (1895) and a pair of related novels, *Evelyn Innes* (1898) and *Sister Teresa* (1901), with which Moore later expressed his dissatisfaction. By then, horrified by the Boer War and revelations about Kitchener's concentration camps, he had returned to Ireland and thrown himself into the Irish Literary Renaissance associated with Yeats, Synge, and Lady Gregory (among others).[45]

Henry James, an American living in England, had already established himself as a major force in Late Victorian literature. In 1890 he published *The Tragic Muse,* which championed the cause of the artist against society, but he then abandoned the novel for a while, focusing on short stories and on drama. By 1897 he had evolved his later, more dense and convoluted style, with which he sought to penetrate beneath the surface of the human psyche and to capture the nuances of appearance and reality. This first found expression in *The Spoils of Poynton* and *What Maisie Knew* (both 1897), but these fairly slight works were merely a prolegomena to one of his masterpieces, *The Wings of the Dove* (1902).[46] The geographical subjects of Joseph Conrad's novels—set in Malaya, the Congo, and the East China Sea—suggested a kinship with Kipling, but the complexity of his narrative techniques and his preoccupation with ambiguities of character and motive place him closer artistically to Henry James. His first full-length novel, *Almayer's Folly,* was published in 1895, followed the next year by *An Outcast of the Islands.* More autobiographical was the first of his critically-acclaimed works, *The Nigger of the 'Narcissus'* (1897), which would be followed by one of his most successful experiments with indirect narration techniques, *Lord Jim* (1900).[47] Both Conrad and James would continue to produce important novels and novellas in the Edwardian era, but each had laid the groundwork for their later work by means of their stylistic experiments in the 1890s.

The 1890s are often characterized as an era of aestheticism and/or 'decadence' in literature and the fine arts. In fact, as we have seen in chapter three, the leading theorist and practitioner of literary aestheticism, Walter Pater, published most of his important works in the 1870s and 1880s, including his masterpiece, *Marius the Epicurean.* However, there was still *Plato and Platonism* to come in 1893 and the unfinished *Gaston de Latour,* which was printed posthumously in 1896, along with three collections of essays that brought together a mix of previously published and unpublished material.[48] Pater was certainly influential, not the least on Oscar Wilde, as evidenced by the latter's early *The Critic as Artist,* which elaborated his theory of the divorce between the artistic impulse, on the one hand, and ethics and subject matter, on the other. *The Soul of Man under Socialism* (1891), however, suggested that Wilde was by no means indifferent to social issues or lacking in sympathy with the poor. Wilde's masterpiece as a novelist, *The Picture of Dorian Gray,* which could be seen as ushering in the transition from aestheticism to 'decadence,' was published the same year, and the appropriateness of the label was perhaps underlined by his later play, *Salomé,* which was banned in Britain but produced in Paris by Sarah Bernhardt in 1894. The script would subsequently be employed by Richard Strauss as the libretto for an equally controversial opera. By the time *Salomé* was staged, Wilde had written two of the four witty and commercially successful comedies that were the talk of the town in the years 1892-95: *Lady Windermere's Fan, A Woman of No Importance, The Ideal Husband,* and *The Importance of Being Ernest.* Wilde's imprisonment after the scandal over his homosexual relationship with Alfred Douglas resulted in a return to more serious subjects: *De Profundis* (written in jail in 1897) was published only posthumously in 1905 and even then in a censored version, but the *Ballad of Reading Gaol* (1898) was (and is) a profoundly moving poem that belongs with *Dorian Gray* and *Salomé* as examples of his greatest work.[49]

Wilde had in fact little to do with the other literary figures and artists whose style and interests have caused the 1890s to be called the 'mauve decade.' The real leader of the so-called 'decadence' movement was the artist Aubrey Beardsley (about whom more later), who during 1894 and 1895 was the art editor for John Lane's quarterly publication, *The Yellow Book.*[50] This was a vehicle not only for Beardsley's striking and distinctive drawings but also for the poetry and short stories written by (among others) members of the Rhymers' Club, the most notable of whom was Frederick William Rolfe, who went by the name Baron Corvo. Corvo published *Stories Toto Told To Me* in 1898, followed by *Chronicles of the House of Borgia* in 1901, although it would be 1904 before his masterpiece, *Hadrian the Seventh,* appeared.[51] Meanwhile in 1896, Beardsley, having been effectively fired from *The Yellow Book,* founded *The Savoy,* with poet Arthur Symons as editor, and successfully solicited contributions from, among others, George Bernard Shaw and poets Ernest Dowson and William Butler Yeats. Symons was undoubtedly influenced by the French poets Verlaine and Mallarmé, but he found his own voice as a poet, and also contributed an important manifesto for the group of writers to whom he belonged, *The Symbolist Movement in Literature* (1899).[52]

Fine Arts

The Yellow Book and the subsequent Beardsley/Symons collaboration, along with the work of William Morris, underlined the connections between the fine arts, literature, and music that were evident in the 1890s. Perhaps the most significant occurrence in the world of Late Victorian art was an extraordinary multiplication of art galleries. Between 1887 and 1900 the following public galleries were opened in London: an extension to the National Gallery (1887), the City of London Corporation Gallery (1890), the National Portrait Gallery (1896), the National Gallery of British Art (1897), the Victoria and Albert Museum (1899), and the Wallace Collection (1900), while important municipal galleries were opened (or expanded) in Birmingham, Manchester, Liverpool, and Dublin.[53] Clearly there was plenty of public interest in art, and viewing paintings in galleries had become a significant form of middle-class recreation, especially on wet weekends. In these galleries the public found a mix of old masters and more recent works by contemporary artists. Victorian painting continued to be divided between a conservative orthodoxy that centered on representational portraiture and landscapes and alternative schools based on different theories of art or using different techniques.

English painting in the 1890s is usually regarded as something of a backwater, largely cut off from the important innovations happening on the continent of Europe. It is true that English art critics and the gallery-going public had been slow to appreciate French Impressionism in the 1880s, and the initial impact of that movement was already over in France, the last collective Impressionist exhibition having been held in Paris in 1886, the same year as a parallel exhibition took place in New York. Elements of what would be labeled Post-Impressionism was already emerging in the work of Gauguin, Van Gogh, and Cézanne; Van Gogh, for example, painted *Starry Night* in 1889, the year before his suicide, Gauguin returned to Tahiti in 1895, and that same year an influential exhibition by Cézanne was held in Paris. Meanwhile, back across the Channel, The New English Art Club, which was open to the radical new ideas and styles being developed in Europe, had been founded in 1886, but it was not until 1889 that a major exhibition of French Impressionist works was held in London. That year also a group of artists from the Club exhibited in London under the collective title of "The London Impressionists," so that by the 1890s Impressionism was established as a controversial minority current within the world of English art. [54] This belated recognition of the school and its methods indirectly benefitted Whistler, and a significant retrospective exhibition of his work was held in London in 1892.

These, however, were minority currents. The English art establishment remained oriented to a more traditional form of representational art, although it was not entirely immune to the new influences.[55] Important figures from the previous decade continued to paint. They included Frederic Leighton, Lawrence Alma-Tadema, and John Singer Sargent. Leighton, who had taken over as president of the Royal Academy of Arts in 1878, represented the establishment in Victorian art. He died in 1896, but his last paintings included the luminous *Flaming June* (1895), which showed that he was not uninfluenced by younger artists.[56] Alma-Tadema continued in his previous vein, concentrating on subjects taken from the ancient world, but his compositional technique, already highly accomplished, became more adventurous. This new freedom found expression in his dramatic classical scenes (which now sometimes included nudes) and above all in his masterpiece of perspective, *Coign of Vantage* (1895).[57] Yet if one artist might be said to have been a dominant figure among the more conventional painters of the decade, that individual would probably be John Singer Sargent. His works were a leading attraction in exhibitions at the Royal Academy in the last years of the decade, and among his most celebrated portraits were *Asher Wertheimer* (1898) and *Lady Elcho and her Two Sisters* (1900). By this time, however, Sargent, although essentially an establishment figure, had been influenced by Impressionism, so his later more fluid and colorful paintings helped win acceptance of a style that had been widely scorned and rejected in the previous decade.[58] Another distinctive, if stylistically orthodox, painter of the epoch was Helen Allingham, whose accurate and charming reproductions of village scenes, and particularly old cottages, documented a rural world that still existed but was beginning to disappear as the railway integrated the countryside more fully into the now predominantly urban society and culture. Examples of her work from the early 1890s include *Hook Hill Farm* and *At Pound Green*, both painted at Freshwater on the Isle of Wight, as well as a series of paintings that portrayed Aldworth House and its surrounding estate, the property of the Poet Laureate, Alfred, Lord Tennyson, with whom the Allinghams were close friends. In addition to painting many brilliantly colorful garden and landscape scenes, Allingham continued to search for (and find) exceptional examples of medieval and Tudor-era timbered buildings, such as *The Six Bells* (an ale house at Bearsted in Kent) and a cottage at *Ide Hill* (also in Kent, in the Westerham Valley).[59]

The 1890s also witnessed the swansong of the Pre-Raphaelite school. Of the principal founders of the Brotherhood, John Everett Millais had long abandoned its original ideals, joined the Royal Academy establishment, and focused his talents on portraiture. He died in 1896. Edward Burne-Jones died two years later, but there was a last flourishing of his art in such paintings as *The Vampire* (1897), *The Quest of Perseus* and *The Last Sleep of Arthur* (both 1898). Holman Hunt remained faithful to the original Pre-Raphaelite vision, as is evident in his late 1890s paintings, such as *The Miracle of the Holy Fire* (1899) and a canvas that took thirteen years to complete, *The Lady of Shalott* (1889-1902).[60] Of the younger painters influenced by the movement, John William Waterhouse was perhaps the individual who most authentically embraced its ideals, style, and characteristic subject matter. This can be seen in a set of three pictures illustrating Homer's *Odyssey*: *Ulysses and the Sirens*, *Circe Offering the Cup to Odysseus* (both 1891), and *Circe Invidiosa*

(1892). These were followed by *La Belle Dame Sans Merci* (1895) and *The Lady of Shalott Looking at Lancelot* (1894), while other notable works included *St. Cecilia* (1895), *Juliet* (1898) and *Mermaid* (1900).[61]

Perhaps the most original of all Late Victorian artists was Aubrey Beardsley. He died young, in 1898 (the same year as Burne-Jones), but the few years before he became seriously ill saw him creating much of his most distinctive and famous work. In 1894-95, for example, he created the prospectus, cover designs, and many illustrations for the *Yellow Book* (1894-95). Exceptional too in invention and execution were his controversial illustrations for Wilde's *Salomé* and Malory's *Morte d'Arthur*, both done in 1894, while his last, even more daring, creations included designs for Aristophanes's *Lysistrata* and Pope's *The Rape of the Lock* (both 1896).[62] Beardsley's work was a major influence on the Art Nouveau movement, which sought to beautify by embellishment all kinds of objects in daily use from chairs and wallpaper to entire buildings. Art Nouveau had had its beginnings in England, and one can see the influence on it of both Pre-Raphaelite painting and the Arts and Crafts Movement. Burne-Jones, Morris, and Sumner remained associated with it in the 1890s, along with Beardsley's and Morris's disciples Walter Crane and C. R. Ashbee. The other British wing of the movement was located in Scotland at the Glasgow School of Art, under the direction of Francis Newbery. The movement rapidly spread to the continent of Europe, with strong wings emerging in Belgium, France, Italy, Germany, and elsewhere. The Belgian group, Les Vingt, for example, organized an exhibition in Brussels in 1892 which included not only paintings but illustrated books, posters, embroidery, silver, ceramics, stained glass, wallpapers, fabrics, and a completely furnished studio interior. Morris, Ashbee, and Beardsley were among the artists/craftsmen represented. In Liège in 1896 a follow-up exhibition featured the work of the Glasgow School as well as works by Ashbee, Burne-Jones, Crane, Morris, and architect C. Harrison Townsend, the designer of London's Whitechapel Art Gallery, a good example of English Art Nouveau applied to architecture, although his 1902 building, the Horniman Museum in South London, is even more characteristic.[63]

In the realm of English architecture, however, Art Nouveau was a minority current.[64] Victorian Gothic was still going strong, for example in the cathedrals designed by J. L. Pearson and Giles Gilbert Scott, but the most characteristic style associated with the period was 'Old English,' the joint invention of Arts and Crafts architect Philip Webb and the man who has been called "the most brilliant of all later Victorian architects," Richard Norman Shaw.[65] The rather rambling 'Old English' style suited country houses better than urban dwellings, however, so Shaw and his colleague William Eden Nesfield had developed the so-called 'Queen Anne' style for town houses. This was quickly taken up by a host of younger architects, including Edward Godwin, who was an admirer of Beardsley's designs and alive to the ideals of the Art Nouveau movement. Shaw's own urban style evolved further, and by the 1890s he had adopted a form of neo-Georgianism, of which celebrated examples are No. 170 Queen's Gate, London, and the huge Bryanston House in Dorset (the seat of Viscount Portman). One other significant, but unusual, architectural development in this decade was the decision to employ for the new Roman Catholic cathedral in Westminster an 'Italo-Byzantine' style featuring three domes and a striped red and white exterior, an appearance which certainly distinguished it from Westminster Abbey and all the Gothic and neo-Gothic Anglican cathedrals and churches scattered around the United Kingdom.[66]

Music

Just as important new movements—Impressionism and Symbolism—were belatedly having an impact on English painting and literature respectively, so in the world of English classical music it was a matter of finding a balance between important foreign influences and the desire on the part of several leading composers to recreate a distinctly English art music that would draw on earlier English music, particularly that of the Tudor and Stuart periods, as well as folksong. The foreign influences came mainly from Germany/Austria and France, although Russia and Italy require mention too. The death of Wagner in 1883 left Johannes Brahms as the contemporary German composer whose works were most often played in England, but he too died in 1897 and none of his greatest compositions date from the last years of his life, although he did write several chamber works featuring the clarinet, as well as eleven choral preludes for organ and "Four Serious Songs" in memory of Clara Schumann. Brahms's Viennese rival, Anton Bruckner, died in 1896, leaving behind him three movements of his unfinished Symphony No. 9 in D minor, perhaps his greatest work. Brahms's and Bruckner's principal successors on the Vienna music scene were Gustav Mahler and Richard Strauss, who were both friends and rivals. Mahler worked as a journeyman conductor for much of the decade, but in 1897 he became director of the Vienna Opera. He composed his symphonies during his summer vacations, completing his second in 1894, his third in 1896, and his fourth in 1900. The symphonic poems of Richard Strauss became known in England more quickly, thanks to their being championed by the influential conductor Hans Richter: the chief ones from the 1890s were *Till Eulenspiegel's Merry Pranks* (1895), *Thus Spake Zarathustra* (1896), *Don Quixote* (1897), and *A Hero's Life* (1898).

The most influential French composers were Gabriel Fauré, who blended modal melodies within a tonal framework and set the work of Symbolist poets such as Verlaine, and Claude Debussy. Debussy also knew several of the Symbolist writers, and in 1894 he completed *Prélude à l'après-midi d'un faune*, an impressionist invocation of Mallarmé's poem. His opera, *Pelléas et Mélisande*, which he worked on from 1893 to 1902, consolidated his impressionist style, and he would create many of his best-known orchestral works (including *La Mer*) in its wake. Debussy's technique of orchestration was derived, in part, from the Russian composer Nikolai Rimsky-Korsakov. Known in England mainly for three orchestral works written in the late 1880s (*Cappriccio espagnole, Scheherazade,* and *Russian Festival Overture*), he was the leading creator of Russian opera in this era, producing a revised version of *The Snow Maiden* in 1895 and his popular *Sadko* the next year. Tchaikovsky was probably the Russian composer best known in the West, and before he died in 1893 he added to his earlier works the opera *The Queen of Spades* (1890), his much-loved music for *The Nutcracker* ballet, and his most popular symphony, No. 6 (*Pathétique*). As for Italy, Giuseppe Verdi composed his last great opera, *Falstaff,* in 1893, the same year as his successor, Giacomo Puccini, created *Manon Lescaut*, with *La Bohème* following in 1896 and *Tosca* in 1900. The most popular Italian opera of the decade, however, was *Cavalleria Rusticana,* the work of Pietro Mascagni in 1890, although it was rivaled by Ruggiero Leoncavallo's *Pagliacci,* which appeared two years later.[67]

Of the leading English composers from the previous decade, Arthur Sullivan was eager to leave comic operetta behind and create the major works that he believed his lucrative alliance with Gilbert had crowded out. He did produce his sole grand opera, *Ivanhoe* in 1891, but after that he turned back to operetta, composing *Haddon Hall, Utopia Limited, The Chieftain, The Grand Duke, The Rose of Persia,* and *The Emerald Isle* between 1892 and 1901. None was as successful as his very popular collaborations with Gilbert in the 1880s. Sullivan also wrote incidental music for several theatre productions, including *The Foresters* (1892), *King Arthur* (1895), and *The Beauty Stone* (1898), as well as for the ballet *Victoria and Merrie England* (1897). Apart from settings of poems by Tennyson, Kipling, and others, his last important work was his *Te Deum* (1900).[68]

While teaching at both Cambridge University and the Royal College of Music, Charles Villiers Stanford continued to compose the occasional opera, a considerable number of choral works (both sacred and secular), a variety of orchestral, chamber, and instrumental music, and many songs. His most successful opera was *Shamus O'Brien* (1896), which was performed in both London and New York, while his adaptation of the Shakespearean comedy *Much Ado About Nothing* (1900) similarly pleased the audiences who flocked to see it. Of his many large-scale choral works performed in the 1890s, notice should be made of his oratorio *Eden* to a text by Robert Bridges (1891), the *Mass* in G (1893), the *Requiem* (1897), and the *Te Deum* in B-flat composed for the Leeds Music Festival in 1898. Stanford's most important orchestral music from this decade included a symphony inspired by Milton, No. 5, "L'Allegro ed il Penseroso" (1894), and his violin concerto of 1899, but it was not until the early years of the twentieth century that he would begin creating the series of orchestral works, such as *An Irish Idyll* (1901) and *Irish Rhapsody No. 1* (1902), that attempted to capture in music the spirit of his native Ireland. However, one can detect the beginnings of this impulse in his chamber music, in particular with *Legend* (1893) and *Irish Fantasies* (1893). Stanford composed other chamber music, including three string quartets and a cello sonata (1893), as well as a large number of pieces designed for individual performers on the piano or organ. He was also an amazingly prolific composer of part-songs and songs for solo voice. The former included three sets of *Elizabethan Pastorales,* a nine-song cycle on Tennyson's *The Princess* (1897), and, at the end of the decade, *Choral Songs in Honour of Queen Victoria,* while the latter included many settings of poems by Tennyson, Robert Bridges, Robert Louis Stevenson, and Arthur Quiller-Couch, although perhaps the most popular of all was his version of A. P. Graves's "The Rose of Killarney" (1896).[69]

Stanford's colleague, Charles Hubert Parry, the director of the Royal College of Music, was regarded by many as the leading English composer of his era. While not as prolific as Stanford, he still maintained a substantial output of compositions during this decade. His stage works included incidental music for Aristophanes's comedy *The Frogs* (1892), which was produced in both Oxford and Leipzig, for two London productions, *Hypatia* (1893) and *A Repentance* (1899), and for a Cambridge production of Aeschylus's *Agamemnon* in 1900. His oratorios *Job* (1892) and *King Saul* (1894) were major works, and his religious music also included a *Magnificat* (1897) and a *Thanksgiving Te Deum,* both of which were performed in Hereford. Parry was well-known for his love of choral works with orchestra, and he added significantly to this repertoire during his lifetime. He had already contributed one of his most popular pieces, *Blest Pair of Sirens,* in 1887, but during the next decade he added a cantata based on Milton's *L'Allegro ed Il Penseroso* (1890), a setting of Tennyson's *The Lotus-Eaters* (1892), and several odes, including *Eton* (text by Swinburne), *Invocation to Music* and *A Song of Darkness and Light* (both by Robert Bridges). Like Stanford, he set much poetry as either part-songs (including *Six Lyrics from an Elizabethan Song Book, Six Modern Lyrics,* and *Eight Four-Part Songs*) or songs for solo voice. In 1889 Parry had composed his third and fourth symphonies; the fifth would not appear before the twentieth century, but orchestral works of significance composed during the 1890s included *Overture to an Unwritten Tragedy* (1893), the *Lady Radnor Suite* (1894), his moving *Elegy for Brahms* (on the latter's death), and *Symphonic Variations* (1897). He also wrote various chamber works, such as *Twelve Short Pieces* and *Romance,* and instrumental pieces. Parry, moreover, believed strongly in the importance of educating the public in music history and in the discipline of musicology. He put his convictions into practice in two important books: *Summary of the History and Development of Mediaeval and Modern European Music* (1893) and *The Art of Music* (1893), which he revised and enlarged as *The Evolution of the Art of Music* (1896). He also wrote over a hundred and twenty articles for Sir George Grove's *Dictionary of Music and Musicians,* the first (four volume) edition of which was completed in 1890 but which was continuously revised thereafter.[70]

Of the next generation of English composers, four names stand out: Granville Bantock, Edward Elgar, Frederick Delius, and Arthur Somervell. Bantock, initially an enthusiastic disciple of Wagner and Richard Strauss, received his training at the Royal Academy of Music. His earliest compositions included a cantata, *The Fire Worshippers* (1892), and two one-act operas, *Caedmar* (1892) and *The Pearl of Iran* (1893), while in 1894 he wrote incidental music for a London production of Sophocles's play *Electra.* Bantock next made his living as the editor of the *New Quarterly Music Review* and as a conductor, touring England with Stanford's comic opera *Shamus O'Brien,* but he returned to composing in the second half of the 1890s, producing the overture *Saul* in 1897 and following it with such works as the *Helena Variations, Russian Scenes,* and the tone poem *Thalaba the Destroyer* (all 1899).[71] Elgar's significant early orchestral compositions included the *Froissart Overture* (1890) and *Serenade for String Orchestra* (1892), but the work that marked his breakthrough to public recognition was his very popular *Enigma Variations* of 1899, which he followed the same year with the attractive song-cycle *Sea Pictures.* A major choral work, the oratorio *The Dream of Gerontius,* was premiered in 1900.[72]

Frederick Delius chose not to live in England, but his early music evoked the countryside in such tone poems as *Summer Evening* and *Spring Morning* (1890) and the overture *Over the Hills and Far Away* (1897). Another notable orchestral composition was the *Appalachia: American Rhapsody* (1896), while his Piano Concerto in C minor appeared the next year. Delius set five songs from Tennyson's *Maud* in 1891, but his most popular composition during the early 1890s was the "Prelude" from his first opera *Irmelin* (1892). Other lyric dramas followed later in the decade: *The Magic Fountain* (1895), *Koanga* (1897), and *A Village Romeo and Juliet,* often regarded as the greatest of his large-scale works, which was begun in 1899 but completed only in 1901.[73] A miniaturist and part-time composer, Arthur Somervell specialized during his early career in setting poetry, often in the form of song cycles. His Blake settings, *Songs of Innocence,* had made his mark in 1889 but a decade later he published one of his most successful song cycles, a setting of Tennyson's *Maud* that became more popular than that by Delius. Early in the new century Somervell would follow this with the first setting of poems chosen from A. E. Housman's *A Shropshire Lad.*[74]

The Edwardian era would witness a flourishing of English music at the hands of not only Parry, Stanford, Elgar, Delius, Bantock, and Somervell but also by a plethora of younger composers, many of whom were, to some degree, students or disciples of Parry and/or Stanford. Of this group, which included Arnold Bax, Rutland Boughton, Frank Bridge, George Butterworth, George Dyson, Ivor Gurney, and Gustav Holst, Ralph Vaughan Williams would eventually emerge as the leading champion of the movement to build on the work of earlier composers and create a large body of distinctively English orchestral and choral music. Along the way Vaughan Williams would set several Housman texts, but that was in the future. His most successful earliest song settings, among his earliest works composed in the 1890s, were of songs from Shakespeare's plays, and it was only in 1901 that he published the song, "Linden Lea," that first brought his name to the attention of the sheet-music buying public.[75] Two years later he would begin collecting folksongs, and bring his 'finds' to Lucy Broadwood for evaluation.[76]

Ballad Editing

Before we return to the story of folksong collecting during the 1890s it is necessary to canvass briefly developments in the realm of ballad editing. Although the ballad scholars of the era were concerned almost exclusively with texts, their work nonetheless had a resonance within folk music circles, especially as the leading collectors came to appreciate better the systematic and methodologically advanced nature of Francis James Child's great project, and also the degree to which English oral tradition was derived from and interlinked with the corpus of broadside balladry. In the sphere of ballad editing the beginning of the 1890s found two major projects well underway but still far from completion. Francis James Child had now published three of five projected volumes of *The English and Scottish Popular Ballads,*[77] while

Joseph W. Ebsworth had seen the sixth volume of *The Roxburghe Ballads* through the press but still had at least two more volumes to go.[78]

Public interest in old ballads seemed to be increasing, and as neither of these two mammoth projects was geared to a mass audience, there was room in the field for smaller works by editors who could draw upon the accomplishments of Victorian scholarship and create selected editions aimed at a wider readership. For example, we have already seen that John Ashton published his third broadside collection, *Real Sailor Songs*, in 1891. John Roberts and Rosamund Watson were among the others who had contributed to this task of publicizing the ballad in the 1880s, and in the next decade they were joined by Brimley Johnson and Francis Gummere. Nonetheless, it was Child and Ebsworth who really carried the torch for ballad editing, and so our focus should be on their work in the 1890s. We will complete the story of Child's endeavors and also continue that of the Ballad Society's edition of *The Roxburghe Ballads*.

Francis James Child and *The English and Scottish Popular Ballads*

By 1890 *The English and Scottish Popular Ballads* was well on its way to becoming the definitive published collection of traditional ballad texts. Child had published the first three volumes between 1882 and 1889. Volume 4 followed immediately at the beginning of the new decade, and the first part of Volume 5, the last segment that he saw personally through the press, in 1894.

Continuing the pattern established by earlier volumes, Volume 4 of *The English and Scottish Popular Ballads* was published in two halves, the first, which appeared as Part VII (covering ballad clusters nos. 189-225) in 1890 and the second, Part VIII (covering ballad clusters nos. 226-265), two years later, in 1892.[79] Scottish material again predominated in both parts. Child had English versions for only eleven of the thirty-seven ballads in Part VII, the other twenty-six apparently being entirely Scottish in provenance. Three of these English texts were border ballads, the most notable being "The Death of Parcy Reed." More significant items with English versions included the Jacobite ballad "Lord Derwentwater," the very popular "Gypsy Laddie," and two other ballads that had been collected in multiple versions, "Geordie" ("Georgie" in the English variants) and "The Braes of Yarrow." Other ballads in this section included "Sir James the Rose," "The Broom of the Cowdenknowes," "The Gardener," and "The Bonny Lass of Anglesey."

Of the forty ballads in Part VIII, Child had recovered only five English variants. For example, one of the most powerful of tragic love ballads, "Lord Saltoun and Auchanachie," lacked any English version, as did the equally tragic "Andrew Lammie." There were, however, a few important ballads in this group that were well known on both sides of the border, including "James Harris (The Daemon Lover)," "The Grey Cock," and the pirate ballad "Henry Martin."

As mentioned, Part IX, the first half of Volume 5, was published in 1894.[80] This fascicule set forth the final group of source materials (ballad clusters nos. 266 to 305) to be included in Child's *magnum opus*. He was now getting near the bottom of the barrel, and this part represented something of a mopping-up operation. It consisted of a miscellaneous bunch of comic songs and broadsides, together with a number of items that had missed their places in earlier volumes, including some narrative ballads that Child apparently dated back to the Tudor period. The highlights of the set were "John of Hazelgreen," "The Trooper and the Maid," and "The Brown Girl." Various broadside ballads that Child thought might have traditional sources were included, such as "The Suffolk Miracle," "The Crafty Farmer," "John Dory," and "The Mermaid." There were several ballads about incidents at sea, for example "The *George Aloe* and the *Sweepstake*," "The *Sweet Trinity*" (aka "The *Golden Vanity*"), and "Captain Ward and the *Rainbow*," and a goodly number of comic ballads, including "Our Goodman," "Get Up and Bar the Door," "The Farmer's Curst Wife," and "The Friar in the Well."

Despite his attempt to be systematic and comprehensive, Child was not always able to include every known variant of a ballad in the appropriate section of *The English and Scottish Popular Ballads*. He therefore added to each part an "Additions and Corrections" section which he used to add variants that he had missed earlier. As we have seen, the late Victorian folksong revival was now gathering steam in England, and although the majority of songs recovered from oral tradition during these years did not fit Child's stringent criteria for popular balladry, nonetheless a number of variants of traditional ballads did surface, as well as other narrative songs that he might well have included in his canon had he been so inclined. The question therefore arises of the extent to which Child succeeded in obtaining and printing versions of the ballads that had been noted in England since 1876. In his final volumes he used the "Additions and Corrections" sections as places to temporarily locate such items when it was too late to place them within the ballad clusters to which they belonged—provided, of course, that he decided that they warranted admission at all. He certainly did not include everything that he might have done. Baring-Gould was the English collector who provided him with the most extra material, and Child's reaction to it was cautious. As we shall see in chapter 12, various of the Devon cleric's submissions were rejected on one ground or another, although quite a few were accepted with thanks.

By this time Child had largely decided what British ballads he regarded as "popular" (read "traditional") and admissible, and he was very reluctant to add to their number. But, in the main, if it was merely a question of adding another variant to an existing member of the canon he was prepared to do so, although sometimes rather grudgingly. For example, in the "Additions and Corrections" section at the end of Volume 4, Child noted that Frank Kidson had printed in *Traditional Tunes* a variant of "Scarborough Fair" that had been sung in the streets of Whitby some "twenty or thirty years ago."[81] He also included a new version of "The Braes of Yarrow," the one that Kidson had noted from Mrs. Calvert of Gilnockie, Eskdale. But at this point he was still in the process of catching up with the most recent folksong and ballad collections published during the 1880s and early 1890s, with the result that most of the significant material that he derived from the English revival was to be found in the "Additions and Corrections" section of Volume 5. For example, for his very first ballad cluster, "Riddles Wisely Expounded," Child belatedly printed Mason's text in *Nursery Rhymes and Country Songs,* "There Was a Lady in the West." Similarly, for "The Elfin Knight" (no. 2) he now incorporated the variant titled "Scarborough Fair" that H. M. Bower had noted from Whitby fisherman William Moat, and that Broadwood and Fuller Maitland had included in *English County Songs.* Similarly, from the same source he added Heywood Sumner's "The Prickly Bush" to ballad cluster no. 95, "The Maid Freed from the Gallows." For "Sir Hugh, or, The Jew's Daughter" (no. 155) Child now included Harriet Mason's version, "Little Sir William," while with regard to "The Sweet Trinity" (no. 286) he acknowledged that Lucy Broadwood and Alec Fuller Maitland had printed a variant in *English County Songs,* although his dismissive comment that this was merely a "retouched copy" of a broadside seemingly underestimated the significance of the ballad being noted from oral tradition in several different regions of England and Scotland.[82]

With the appearance of installment IX in 1894 the canon of Child ballads was, for better or for worse, complete: the extant corpus of British traditional balladry in the English language thus comprised, in Child's opinion, just 305 ballad clusters, no more, no less. Implementing the great project had been a lengthy and formidable struggle, which had taken its toll on the mental and physical reserves of the mastermind behind it. Child was now elderly and ailing, but he planned, and in part assembled, a final fascicule that would consist of a final set of "Additions and Corrections" and various kinds of scholarly apparatus. Significantly, he at long last recognized that traditional ballads are not merely texts but narrative *songs,* in which words and tune fuse together to make an integral whole. The melodies were therefore very important, and Child included an appendix in which he set out the tunes found in the various manuscript sources (mainly Scottish) that he had mined for authentic ballad texts, as well as a few other items that he had received from correspondents. He did not, however, include any of the ballad tunes that had been noted in England by Mason, Burne, Baring-Gould, Kidson, and others during the previous two decades. Child died in 1896, before he could complete Part X and see it through the press, but his disciple George Kittredge completed the job, and the last segment of *The English and Scottish Popular Ballads* finally appeared in print in 1898.[83]

Joseph Ebsworth and *The Roxburghe Ballads*

Joseph W. Ebsworth was now in sole charge of the Ballad Society's major project, the ongoing serial publication of *The Roxburghe Ballads.* As the new decade opened, this still had a very long way to go, despite the fact that six volumes had already been mailed to subscribers. Ebsworth was worried that because the Ballad Society's membership was in decline the available funds would prove insufficient to complete the massive project. In an "Important Notice" printed at the end of Volume 6,[84] and intended to encourage the remaining subscribers to ante up enough cash to pay for the paper and printing of the next installment, he lamented the "heavy loss" resulting from the deaths of elderly subscribers and the "dropping away" of payments by the "lukewarmness, fickleness, or abatement of interest, in heedless members."[85] Death was indeed on his mind; he revealed that he had lost several personal friends during the last few years, and he had become more conscious of his own mortality. The great project undoubtedly would be left incomplete, he warned, if he should die before the remaining volumes had all been printed, since there was no alternative editor available who had the enthusiasm, knowledge, and experience to do the job:

> The few subscribers who remain might well take the warnings…and avoid the risk of the *Roxburghe Ballads* being left incomplete, in case the health or life of the Editor should be prematurely ended. Death must come to him as to the others. To no one could he willingly or hopefully transfer his duties; for now that J. P. Collier, William Chappell, and J. O. Halliwell-Phillipps, have passed away…there is absolutely no man known to him in England, and certainly not in America, possessing the qualifications to adequately carry on the work, in case death deprived the Members of the willingly-rendered services of their ill-supported friend.[86]

The "certainly not in America" may have been a gratuitous—and unfair—swipe at Francis James Child's competency as a ballad editor, but Child's dislike of broadsides was by now well known, and in any case he was elderly and in too poor health to be a realistic choice of successor. Frank Kidson, a younger man with a small private income, might have taken over effectively, but he considered the Roxburghe project an unrealistically huge undertaking, and, moreover, he had publicly doubted whether it would ever be completed. Ebsworth was therefore very conscious of the weight of responsibility on his own shoulders. He was still eager to finish the project, and he now claimed that this could be done in one final volume.[87] It is doubtful that Ebsworth actually believed this; more likely it was a ploy to convince subscribers that there was light at the end of the tunnel.

In the event, the money for printing was somehow found, and Volume 7 appeared in three parts between 1890 and 1893.[88] Most of the contents dated from the late seventeenth century, from either the Restoration era or the reign of William and Mary, but Ebsworth was able to include a few black-letter items from the Jacobean era that had been missed earlier, and also a smattering of Civil War ballads. As usual, he faced the editorial task of how to organize the voluminous material at his disposal. His method in Volume 7 was to arrange ballads by subject matter and to include 'answer' ballads and texts from other collections that he judged closely related to the main Roxburghe entries. Wherever possible he provided citations to, and sometimes exemplars from, the other major broadside ballad collections known to him, especially the Pepys, Douce, Wood, Rawlinson, Jersey, Huth, Euing, and Trowbesh collections.[89] This was a good idea, and it significantly enhanced the value of the collection.

The first major group of material in Part 1 of this volume (also known as Part XX of the entire collection) Ebsworth called ballads of "tradesmen and sportsmen." Most of these were linked in some way with occupations, the male tradesmen being weavers, shoemakers, tinkers, tapsters, pedlars, butchers, and ploughmen, although other ballads celebrated the lives of milkmaids, pudding-sellers, clerks, and even robbers and other criminals. His next category was a group of ballads about male/female sexual encounters that he titled a "Group of Cupid Ballads." Several of these were written by one of Ebsworth's favorite ballad-mongers, Laurence Price, but, on the whole, they were not a very distinguished bunch. The delights and drawbacks of the status so ardently desired by slighted maids was the subject of the next, and very large, batch of broadsides, which Ebsworth called a "group of matrimonial ballads." Not all these songs were pro-matrimony, however; for example "A Young Man Put to His Shifts; or, Ranting Resolution" was a flagrant defense of a "love 'em and leave 'em" strategy designed to leave the rake free from children and other cares, while "Rock the Cradle, John" was Laurence Price's warning against foolishly choosing a loose or lazy woman as a mate. And many were the ballads, written by men of course, on the subject of the scold. In the main, despite a number of mildly humorous ballads describing joyous scenes, the pitfalls of matrimony were more thoroughly explored than the rewards. In addition, Ebsworth was reluctantly reconciled to the fact that Volume 7 had perforce to include certain items, such as "The Wanton Wife of Bath," "A Young Man Put to His Shifts," and "The New Way of Marriage," that endorsed, or at least condoned, a cavalier attitude to sexual morality which he, and presumably the majority of his readers, abhorred. As an antidote, he made sure to include also a few ballads in which the would-be seducer was outwitted and received his just deserts.

More ballads on the same or similar themes were to be found in Part 2 of Volume 7 (aka Part XXI). For example, Ebsworth had found a seventeenth-century broadside version of "The False Knight Outwitted," a ballad often known in oral tradition as "The Outlandish Knight" and which, as we have seen, Child had admitted to his canon as "Lady Isabel and the Elf Knight" (Child no. 4).[90] Ebsworth divided the very large number of ballads available to him on the subject of male/female relationships into four categories: a "Group of Merry Adventures" (comic ballads), "Some Willow-green Ballads" (tragic ballads of unhappy love), "Ballads of Love's Mischances" (mainly laments or tales of the tragic parting of lovers), and a "Tom the Taylor Group" (stories of cuckoldry, often involving tailors). The massive Volume 7 was rounded out with batches of ballads on several other miscellaneous themes: sailors and their loves, cross-dressing, religion, the Civil War and the Commonwealth era, plus a group of twenty Christmas carols. Taken as a whole, it was an impressive achievement, and Ebsworth could feel with some justification that he had put the Ballad Society's project back on track. The problem now was how to finish it.

Ebsworth claimed in 1893 that just one more part would suffice to print the remaining ninety ballads of the Roxburghe collection.[91] That was very far from the truth. In fact there was still a great deal of material to be covered, and although the rest of the Ballad Society edition of *The Roxburghe Ballads* would be counted as Volume 8, that huge final volume was actually divided into five parts and was, as Ebsworth admitted, not only Volume 8 but effectively also Volume 9.[92] By 1895 the Ballad Society was in dire financial straits. It had used up all its initial capital—a good part of it frittered away, in Ebsworth's opinion, in hiring overpaid copyists on the accuracy of whose work he could not rely—and it was in arrears with its publisher for printing costs. From now on, each issue had to be paid for in advance, so that the money required for printing would be available up front. This new approach did work but it caused frustrating delays for the editor. Ebsworth apparently had the first three parts of Volume 8 prepared by 1895, and the remaining two parts ready by 1897, yet he was still seeing the last of these through the press when the new century dawned. The publication dates indicated on the various fascicules of Volume 8 are therefore misleading; the first three parts actually appeared between 1895 and 1897 and the remaining two only in 1899 and 1901.

Part 1 of Volume 8 (fascicule XXIII) was divided into four uneven sections, titled respectively "Group of Romantic and Religious Ballads," "Group on Unhallowed Marriages," "Group of Historical Ballads: Reign of Queen Anne," and "Group of Historical Ballads: Troubles under the Three Georges." There were also two fairly long lists: one of garlands in the Roxburghe collection, and the other of "Slip-Songs" in collection. The second of these sections involved some material that Ebsworth regarded as morally troubling: "The Young Woman's Complaint; or, A Caveat to All Maids to Have a Care How They Be Married to Old Men" was a lament by an energetic maid of fifteen married to a man of seventy-two. "The Old Man's Complaint" showed the other side of the picture, the lack of self-esteem felt by the elderly man unable to satisfy his young wife's sexual needs and his fear that she will be unfaithful to him. In "The Jealous Old Dotard; or, The Discovery of Cuckoldry" this fear proved only too real, the man was pronounced "Horn-mad," and the woman was denounced as a "slut."[93] It was an item that Ebsworth declined to print in full, providing the first and last verses and a summary of the story. Other ballads in this group were about courting: in "The Mother and Daughter" a young woman admitted that she had given herself to her chosen lover, and, when chastised, reminded her mother of her own affairs with a weaver, a tinker, and a tailor. The wholehearted enjoyment of sex depicted in this ballad was echoed in another, "The Young Farmer's Answer to his Sweetheart Nanny," in which the young couple's urgent desire to go to bed together was solved by the expedient of a hastily arranged marriage. Ebsworth, a down-to-earth clergyman who was irritated by coyness and sanctimoniousness but who nonetheless disapproved of extramarital sex, no doubt approved heartily of this particular example of the ballad-monger's art.

As a historian, Ebsworth tended to view broadsides more as primary sources than as literature. He cared little that they were written in doggerel if they were useful historical documents. He was most interested in sets of broadsides that, when taken together, reflected the attitudes, values, and customs of a particular era, as well as illuminating the political struggles of the time. For the reign of Queen Anne (1702-1714) he had such a set, but it was fairly small since there were less than a dozen items in Roxburghe and he felt compelled to add a few Jacobite songs from other sources to round it out. The Roxburghe collection also provided a record, albeit a sparser one, of political life in Georgian England. There were political broadsides from the reigns of each of the first three Hanoverian monarchs, although they took the story only as far as 1780. Unlike previous reigns, however, they were insufficiently numerous to provide the continuous view from the streets of contemporary politics that so fascinated Ebsworth.

Part 2 of Volume 8 (fascicule XXIV of the entire publication), was apparently issued in 1896. It contained four main groups of ballads, titled "Group of Semphill Ballads," "Final Group of Anglo-Scotch Ballads," "Final Group of Robin Hood Ballads," and "Group of Merry Ballads and Humorous Tales," the latter split in two parts but mainly inserted between the Semphill and Anglo-Scotch sets. Ebsworth placed at the front of the fascicule a lighthearted and mildly salacious broadside that had evidently caught his fancy, "The Female Highway Hector." The Semphill ballads, the group with which Part 2 really opened, were unique. They were the oldest ballads in the entire Roxburghe collection, and were Scottish in provenance, covering a series of events in the dramatic life of Mary Queen of Scots. Also particularly valuable were the Roxburghe collection's group of seventeen interrelated Robin Hood ballads. Interesting, too, was the batch of ballads, all of which related to the county of Kent, with which Ebsworth concluded Part 2.

The next year, 1897, saw the appearance in print of Part 3 of Volume 8 (fascicule XXV). It began with a continuation of a group of "Merry Ballads and Humorous Tales" that had featured prominently in the previous fascicule. One of the themes in this group was the dealings of men, often but not always portrayed as merchants or sailors, with "beggar wenches" and prostitutes in London and other ports such as Bristol, Plymouth, Liverpool, and Hull. Such encounters were portrayed as a kind of guerrilla warfare, in which sometimes one side won and sometimes the other. By abandoning the roughly alphabetical order in which the originals had been grouped by the successive owners of the collection, Ebsworth had been at liberty to defer printing ballads on topics that were liable to offend polite society. But if he was to come even close to editing a complete edition of the Roxburghe material he had eventually to decide how to handle such 'problem' ballads. In the course of editing successive volumes he seems to have become more tolerant and broadminded. He was no longer shocked by even the coarsest material in the broadsides about sexual encounters, and he had come to realize that it was very difficult to draw the line between what was immoral and reprehensible and what was merely broad but humorous. He appears to have actually enjoyed some of the comic ballads dealing with extramarital sex, and was no longer afraid to say so. This was evident in the second section of Part 3, titled "Group on the Rogueries of Millers," in which he printed uncensored "The Lusty Miller's Recreation," a ballad detailing the sexual exploits of a randy miller in which various women were depicted as eagerly seeking and enjoying what the miller had to offer.[94]

Ebsworth had already printed quite a few broadsides about prostitutes, female thieves, and other free-living women, but there were many more such items in Roxburghe, including some that he had deferred from previous sections. He now figured out a solution. It was to dump a large number of these 'iffy' ballads into a category that he called "Group of Female Ramblers," and to warn his readers explicitly about the nature of its contents. Such songs, he claimed, illuminated a recurrent phenomenon found in every country and every period of history: "unchanging in vice although diverse in costume and language." They were hardly titillating; rather they could and should function as a warning to any "silly moths" who might be dazzled by their "baleful light."[95] This "Female Ramblers" group comprised approximately three dozen items, and most of the ballads portrayed women whose conduct or philosophy of life contravened the moral standards supposedly upheld by polite society in the Victorian era. An example is "The Wanton Wenches of Wiltshire." The overt discussion of feminine sexual needs found in this ballad is hardly shocking nowadays, but at the time the sentiments expressed were too brazen for polite ears. The ballad-monger employed the usual code words ("brisk," "kiss," "laughter") but it was easy to infer that this was a tale of masturbation, lesbian sex, and voyeurism that ended in an orgy.[96] As Ebsworth recognized, this group of male-authored ballads hardly painted a flattering picture of the female sex. Women were usually portrayed as cheats, scolds, or shrews, as spendthrifts, or simply as lascivious and wanton, all too ready to make cuckolds of their husbands, especially if the latter were older than they. There were limits to Ebsworth's tolerance, and such ballads of loose living brought out the stern moral judge in the clergyman editor. He evidently felt it necessary to make clear to Ballad Society subscribers—(who included Queen Victoria)—that he condoned neither drunkenness nor libidinousness, at least in females. His emphatic condemnation of "The Wanton Wenches of Wiltshire" was in sharp contrast to his defense of "The Lusty Miller's Recreation," and one senses a double standard at work here. On the other hand, he did metaphorically shed a tear for a few of his "Female Ramblers," those who (like Mary Jones, executed in 1771 for stealing a single item of clothing) had been driven to break the law through hunger and poverty. As a social historian Ebsworth knew about the cynical mores of the London streets and he was well aware of the harsh conditions under which many poor women had lived. One can sense in his comments a tension between the sympathy he felt and the condemnation he felt obliged to pronounce.

In the preface that he appended to Part 3 of Volume 8 Ebsworth declared the Ballad Society's edition of *The Roxburghe Ballads* to be complete.[97] Yet in fact two more parts had yet to appear. Formally they were counted as additional fascicules of Volume 8, although they could easily and quite reasonably have been counted as Volume 9. Part 4 (aka Part XXVI), dated 1897 but actually issued in 1899, ostensibly contained only editorial matter, although in fact Ebsworth inserted a considerable number of additional ballads. There were three main sections. The first was an extended essay titled "Introduction to the Final Volume." The second reproduced an extremely useful document for anyone interested in the history of English balladry, the broadside publisher William Thackeray's complete list of ballads in stock in 1685. The third section, an extensive set of "Additional Notes" to each of the preceding volumes, was where most of the extra ballads were to be found.[98]

Ebsworth was still not done. There was still Volume 8, Part 5 (aka Part XXVII) to come.[99] This was the last fascicule of *The Roxburghe Ballads*, and it marked Ebsworth's swansong as a ballad editor. In it he tried to fill out as completely as possible the corpus of political balladry from the time period for which the Roxburghe collection was particularly rich: that of the early Restoration era, especially the years 1660-1661. This he did by adding relevant broadsides from other collections, especially the Euing (which had been compiled by his friend James Orchard Halliwell) and the British Museum's. He also included as many as he could of the items that he had been saving for a separate publication on the balladry of the English Civil War and the Commonwealth. And, as a parting gift, he slipped in a few other interesting non-Roxburghe ballads that he had come across during his research and especially wanted to share with his readers. In this way Ebsworth created two last sections of ballad texts, titled "Final Group of Restoration Ballads" and "Fifty-four Political and Miscellaneous Ballads, 1654 *et seq.*," together with a small group of seven miscellaneous ballads placed between them. Perhaps the most interesting last-minute addition was a partial text for "The Loving Ballad of Lord Bateman and the Fair Sophia," which he had found on a stall copy in the Manchester Reference Library, although it was the work of a London broadside printer, W. Gilbertson.[100] He noted that it was not included in Thackeray's list of broadsides extant in 1685, and he had hunted for, but failed to find, a black-letter copy of it. Child had similarly failed to find an old English broadside of the ballad, and had resorted to reprinting an 1839 stall copy as part of his ballad cluster no. 52, "Young Beichan."[101] Ebsworth was nonetheless convinced that the ballad dated back to at least the seventeenth century, and he claimed that a version titled "Young Bicham" was known in the north of England around 1760. "Although indisputably modernized," he commented, "the story is less distorted in the English stall-copies than it is in the absurdly elongated Scottish 'traditional' versions cited by Jamieson, Motherwell, Kinloch, and Peter Buchan."[102] Ebsworth's version was in fact virtually identical to a broadside in Frank Kidson's collection and to the oral text collected by Kidson from an anonymous Shropshire informant.[103]

The remainder of Part 5 was editorial matter: a contents list, new frontispieces for the first three volumes (sporting woodcuts that Ebsworth had specially made), a ballad index for the massive Volume 8, a list of known ballad-mongers responsible for texts in the volume,[104] and a list of subscribers to the project in 1897. They included Queen Victoria, Julia de Vaynes, and Frederick Furnivall but, perhaps surprisingly, not such names as Sabine Baring-Gould, Frank Kidson, Lucy Broadwood, Charlotte Burne, or Francis James Child. However, the inclusion of such institutional subscribers as Leeds Public Library and Harvard College Library meant that the great work was easily available to Kidson and that Child had seen much of it before he died in 1896. In the British Isles other copies could be found in libraries in Birmingham, Bristol, Dublin, Durham, Glasgow, Liverpool, London, Manchester, Newcastle, and Preston; the USA numbered a dozen subscribers, Canada was represented by the University of Toronto, and Australia by Melbourne Public Library.[105] And even if Baring-Gould felt unable to purchase his own copy, he was nonetheless listed among the many supporters that Ebsworth thanked for providing information and encouragement.

And that, at long last, was it. The Ballad Society's grand project ground to a halt at the turn of the century, with the last segment actually reaching subscribers only in 1901, although it was dated 1899. It had taken over thirty years and had consumed a large amount of funds and goodwill, not to mention an enormous expenditure of time and energy on the part of editors Chappell and Ebsworth. Effectively *The Roxburghe Ballads* had run the Ballad Society into the ground. It would attempt no more publishing projects. Ebsworth acknowledged ruefully that there was "no longer any reasonable hope of the thirty-years old Ballad Society, with its insufficient funds, printing quickly the series of 'Civil War and Commonwealth Ballads'" that he had already prepared for publication.[106]

According to Ebsworth's arithmetic, *The Roxburghe Ballads* reprinted a total of 1,468 ballads from Roxburghe and other collections, including all the black-letter broadsides in the original collection as owned by Roxburghe.[107] Moreover, it provided a significant window into the Pepys collection at Magdalen College, Cambridge, reproducing nearly five hundred black-letter broadsides found in that collection (either because they were duplicated in Roxburghe or because Ebsworth inserted them as related extras, of which he included some three hundred in total). Although it was in fact still not quite complete (that is, in the sense of a total reproduction of the entire Roxburghe collection in the British Museum), *The Roxburghe Ballads* was considerably broader in scope than its title suggested, and it offered its purchasers a comprehensive and representative illustration of the world of the seventeenth-century broadside ballad, including almost all the Roxburghe collection, a good selection from the Pepys collection, and a variety of examples from most of the other extant broadside collections. Notwithstanding its faults, it was a tremendous achievement.

Notes

1. Census data from www.visionofbritain.org.uk/census/index.jsp.

2. On the economic history of Late Victorian England, in addition to the standard works on the British Industrial Revolution, see especially the following: N. F. R. Crafts, S. J. Leybourne, and T. C. Mills, *The Climacteric in Late Victorian Britain: A Reappraisal of the Evidence* (Leeds: University of Leeds School of Economic Studies, 1987); François Crouzet, *The Victorian Economy* (New York: Routledge, 1982); Maurice Flamant and Jeanne Singer-Kérel, *Modern Economic Crises and Recessions* (New York: Harper & Row, 1970); James Foreman-Peck, *New Perspectives on the Late Victorian Economy: Essays in Quantitative Economic History, 1860-1914* (New York: Cambridge University Press, 2003); Eric J. Hobsbawm, *Industry and Empire*, vol. 3 of *The Pelican Economic History of Britain* (Harmondsworth: Penguin, 1969); Eric J. Hobsbawm, *The Age of Empire, 1875-1914* (London: Weidenfeld & Nicolson, 1987); Deirdre N. McCloskey, *Enterprise and Trade in Victorian Britain* (London: Routledge, 1981); R. S. Sayers, *A History of Economic Change in England, 1880-1939* (London: Oxford University Press, 1967).

3. On rural England, see David J. Eveleigh, *The Victorian Farmer* (Princes Risborough, England: Shire, 1991); David Souden, *The Victorian Village* (London: Collins and Brown, 1991); Sadie B. Ward, *Seasons of Change: Rural Life in Victorian and Edwardian England* (London: Allen & Unwin, 1982); for a snapshot of one county, see John Lowerson, *Victorian Sussex* (London: BBC, 1972).

4. Crafts, Leybourne and Mills, *The Climacteric in Late Victorian Britain*; Flamant and Singer-Kérel, *Modern Economic Crises and Recessions*.

5. David Kynaston, *King Labour: The British Working Class, 1850-1914* (Totowa, N.J.: Rowman & Littlefield, 1976); Harvey Mitchell and Peter N. Stearns, *The European Labor Movement, the Working Classes and the Origins of Social Democracy, 1890-1914* (Itasca, Ill.: Peacock, 1971).

6. Henry Pelling, *The Origins of the Labour Party, 1880-1900* (2nd edition, Oxford: Clarendon Press, 1965).

7. Charles Booth, *Life and Labour of the People of London, Volume 1: East London* (London and Edinburgh: Williams and Norgate, 1889).

8. There appears to be no systematic social history of Victorian Britain that covers these decades comprehensively and in detail, but aspects of the subject are treated in the following: Eugene C. Black, *Victorian Culture and Society* (New York: Harper & Row, 1973); Simon Gunn and Rachel Bell, *Middle Classes: Their Rise and Sprawl* (London: Cassell, 2002); Elizabeth T. Hurren, *Protesting About Pauperism: Poverty, Politics and Poor Relief in Late Victorian England, 1870-1900* (Woodbridge, England: Boydell Press, 2007); Gareth Stedman Jones, *Outcast London: A Study in the Relationship Between Classes in Victorian Society* (Oxford: Clarendon Press, 1971); Helen M. Lynd, *England in the Eighteen-Eighties: Toward a Social Basis for Freedom* (New Brunswick, N.J.: Transaction Books, 1984); John M. Mackenzie, ed., *The Victorian Vision: Inventing New Britain* (London: V&A Publications, 2001); Hugh McLeod, *Class and Religion in the Late Victorian City* (London: Croom Helm, 1974); Henry Pelling, *Popular Politics and Society in Late Victorian Britain: Essays* (London: Macmillan, 1968); Clarence Swisher, ed., *Victorian England* (San Diego, Calif.: Greenhaven Press, 2000); Donna Thomas, *The Problem of the Aged Poor: Social Reform in Late Victorian England* (Edmonton, Canada: University of Alberta Press, 1969).

9. Standard works on the general history of Late Victorian England include R. C. K. Ensor, *England, 1870-1914* (Oxford: Clarendon Press, 1960) and J. F. C. Harrison, *Late Victorian Britain, 1875-1901* (London: Routledge, 1991).

10. John Morley, *The Life of William Ewart Gladstone* (London: Macmillan, 1903); Philip Magnus, *Gladstone: A Biography* (New York: Dutton, 1954); Peter Stansky, *Gladstone: A Progress in Politics* (Boston: Little, Brown, 1979); Roy Jenkins, *Gladstone: A Biography* (New York: Random House, 1997); Richard Shannon, *Gladstone*, 2 vols. (Chapell Hill: University of North Carolina Press, 1984 & 1999).

11. There is a large secondary literature on British Imperialism. One of the most useful books is a documentary collection edited by George Bennett, *The Concept of Empire: Burke to Attlee, 1714-1947* (London: Black, 1962). A systematic overview of the subject is provided in Woodruff D. Smith, *European Imperialism in the 19th & 20th Centuries* (Chicago: Nelson Hall, 1982), while an extensive sampling of different perspectives can be found in Harrison M. Wright, ed. *The "New Imperialism": Analysis of Late Nineteenth-Century Expansion* (Lexington, Mass.: Heath, 1976). James Morris, *Pax Britannica*, 3 vols. (London: Faber and Faber, 1973-78) provides a systematic and colorful narrative account of the British experience. Particularly valuable for its blend of description and incisive analysis is Eric J. Hobsbawm, *The Age of Empire, 1875-1914* (London: Weidenfeld & Nicolson, 1987). More recent treatments include Andrew S. Thompson, *Imperial Britain: The Empire in British Politics, c. 1880-1932* (Harlow, England: Pearson Longman, 2000), Anthony Webster, *The Debate on the Rise of the British Empire* (Manchester, England: Manchester University Press, 2006); E. Spencer Wellhofer, *Democracy, Capitalism and Empire in Late Victorian Britain, 1885-1900* (London: Palgrave Macmillan, 1996).

12. Michael Blake, *Lord Salisbury's World: Conservative Environments in Later Victorian Britain* (Cambridge, England: Cambridge University Press, 2001); Robert Blake and Hugh Cecil, *Salisbury: The Man and His Policies* (New York: St. Martin's Press, 1987); Peter Marsh, *The Discipline of Popular Government: Lord Salisbury's Domestic Statecraft, 1881-1902* (Hassocks, England: Harvester Press, 1978); E. D. Steele, *Lord Salisbury: A Political Biography* (London: UCL Press, 1999); Robert G. Taylor, *Lord Salisbury* (New York: St. Martin's Press, 1975).

13. Thompson, *Imperial Britain*. For other secondary literature on British Imperialism, see note 11.

14. R. C. K. Ensor, *England, 1870-1914* (Oxford: Clarendon Press, 1960); J. F. C. Harrison, *Late Victorian Britain, 1875-1901* (London: Routledge, 1991); James Morris, *Pax Britannica*, 3 vols. (London: Faber and Faber, 1973-78); E. Spencer Wellhofer, *Democracy, Capitalism and Empire in Late Victorian Britain, 1885-1900* (London: Palgrave Macmillan, 1996).

15. Henry Pelling, *The Origins of the Labour Party, 1880-1900* (2nd edition, Oxford: Clarendon Press, 1965).

16. Charles Henry Pearson, *National Life and Character: A Forecast* (London: Macmillan, 1893).

17. Rudyard Kipling, *Kim* (London: Macmillan, 1901).

18. John Adams, *Kipling* (London: Haus Books, 2005); Charles Allen, *Kipling Sahib: India and the Making of Rudyard Kipling* (London: Little, Brown, 2007); Andrew Lyall, *Rudyard Kipling* (London: Weidenfeld & Nicolson, 1999); Phillip Mallett, *Rudyard Kipling: A Literary Life* (New York: Palgrave Macmillan, 2003); Harry Ricketts, *Rudyard Kipling: A Life* (New York: Carroll & Graf, 2006); Martin Seymour-Smith, *Rudyard Kipling* (London: Papermac, 1990).

19. Sir James Frazer, *The Golden Bough*, vol. 1 (London: Macmillan, 1890).

20. Peter d'Alroy Jones, *The Christian Socialist Revival, 1877-1914: Religion, Class, and Social Conscience in Late Victorian England* (Princeton, N.J.: Princeton University Press, 1968).

21. William Booth, *In Darkest England, and the Way Out* (London: International Headquarters of the Salvation Army, 1890).

22. Charles Booth, *Life and Labour of the People of London*, 9 vols. (London: Macmillan, 1892-97; revised edition in three series: *Poverty; Industry;* and *Religious Influences*, 14 vols., 1902).

23. J. M. Robertson, *Charles Bradlaugh* (London: Watts, 1920); James P. Gilmour, *Champion of Liberty: Charles Bradlaugh* (London: Watts, 1933); Walter L. Arnstein, *The Bradlaugh Case: A Study in Late Victorian Opinion and Politics* (Oxford: Clarendon Press, 1965).

24. Roger Manvell, *The Trial of Annie Besant and Charles Bradlaugh* (London: Elek, Pemberton, 1976); Annie Wood Besant, *Annie Besant: An Autobiography* (Madras, India: Theosophical Publishing House, 1939); Rosemary Dinnage, *Annie Besant* (Harmondsworth: Penguin, 1986); Arthur H. Nethecot, *The First Five Lives of Annie Besant* (Chicago: Chicago University Press, 1960); Arthur H. Nethecot, *The Last Four Lives of Annie Besant* (Chicago: Chicago University Press, 1963); Anne Taylor, *Annie Besant: A Biography* (Oxford: Oxford University Press, 1992).

25. S. L. Cranston, *HPB: The Extraordinary Life and Influence of Helena Blavatsky, Founder of the Modern Theosophical Movement* (New York: Putnam, 1993); Bruce F. Campbell, *Ancient Wisdom Revived: A History of the Theosophical Movement* (Berkeley: University of California Press, 1980); [Theosophical Society], *The Theosophical Movement, 1875-1925: A History and Survey* (New York: Dutton, 1925).

26. Clare Goodrick-Clarke and Nicholas Goodrick-Clarke, eds., *G. R. S. Mead and the Gnostic Quest* (Berkeley, Calif.: North Atlantic Books, 2005).

27. F. H. Bradley, *Appearance and Reality: A Metaphysical Essay* (London: Swan Sonnerschein, 1893).

28. Norman I. MacKenzie and Jeanne MacKenzie, *The Fabians* (New York: Simon and Schuster, 1977); Edward R. Pease, *The History of the Fabian Society* (London: Cass, 1963); A. M. McBriar, *Fabian Socialism and English Politics, 1884-1918* (Cambridge, England: Cambridge University Press, 1962); Margaret Cole, *The Story of Fabian Socialism* (Stanford, Calif.: Stanford University Press, 1961).

29. Lisanne Radice, *Beatrice and Sidney Webb: Fabian Socialists* (London: Macmillan, 1984); Jeanne MacKenzie, *A Victorian Courtship: The Story of Beatrice Potter and Sidney Webb* (New York: Oxford University Press, 1979); Margaret Cole, *Beatrice and Sidney Webb* (London: Fabian Society, 1955); Margaret Cole, *The Webbs and Their Work* (London: Muller, 1949); Royden Harrison, *The Life and Times of Sidney and Beatrice Webb: 1858-1905, the Formative Years* (Basingstoke, England: Palgrave, 2000).

30. Sidney and Beatrice Webb, *The History of Trade Unionism* (London: Longmans, Green & Co., 1894).

31. Sidney and Beatrice Webb, *Industrial Democracy* (London: Longmans, Green & Co., 1897).

32. Harold Bloom, *George Bernard Shaw* (New York: Chelsea House, 1987); Eldon C. Hill, *George Bernard Shaw* (Boston: Twayne, 1978); George Eric Brown, *George Bernard Shaw* (New York: Arco, 1971); Homer E. Woodbridge, *George Bernard Shaw, Creative Artist* (Carbondale, Ill.: Southern Illinois University Press, 1963); Maurice J. Valency, *The Cart and the Trumpet: The Plays of George Bernard Shaw* (New York: Oxford University Press, 1973); C. D. Innes, ed., *The Cambridge Companion to George Bernard Shaw* (Cambridge, England: Cambridge University Press, 1998).

33. George Bernard Shaw, *Plays Pleasant and Unpleasant* (London: Grant Richards, 1898).

34. Lawrence Gronlund, *The Cooperative Commonwealth: An Exposition of Modern Socialism* (London: Swan Sonnerschein, 1891).

35. Edward Bellamy, *Looking Backwards (2000-1887)* (London: William Reeves, 1887).

36. William Morris, *News From Nowhere, or An Epoch of Rest* (London: Reeves and Turner, 1891).

37. Robert Blatchford, *Merrie England* (London: Clarion Press, 1894).

38. Jacob Korg, *George Gissing: A Critical Biography* (London: Methuen, 1965).

39. John Batchelor, *H. G. Wells* (New York: Cambridge University Press, 1985); Harold Bloom, *H. G. Wells* (Philadelphia, Pa.: Chelsea House, 2004); Richard H. Costa, *H. G. Wells* (New York: Twayne, 1967); Norman I. MacKenzie and Jeanne MacKenzie, *H. G. Wells: A Biography* (New York: Simon and Schuster, 1973); Frank McConnell, *The Science Fiction of H. G. Wells* (New York: Oxford University Press, 1981); David C. Smith, *H. G. Wells: Desperately Mortal: A Biography* (New Haven, Conn.: Yale University Press, 1986); Darko Suvin and Robert M. Philmus, *H. G. Wells and Modern Science Fiction* (Lesisburg, Penn.: Bucknell University Press, 1977); W. Warren Wager, *H. G. Wells: Traversing Time* (Middleton, Conn.: Wesleyan University Press, 2004); Anthony West, *H. G. Wells: Aspects of a Life* (New York: Random House, 1987).

40. Martin Booth, *The Doctor, the Detective and Arthur Conan Doyle: A Biography of Arthur Conan Doyle* (London: Hodder and Stoughton, 1997); Ivor J. C. Brown, *Conan Doyle: A Biography of the Creator of Sherlock Holmes* (London: Hamilton, 1972); Owen D. Edwards, *The Quest for Sherlock Holmes: A Biographical Study of Arthur Conan Doyle* (Edinburgh, U.K.: Mainstream, 1983); Pierre Nordon, *Conan Doyle: A Biography* (New York: Holt, Rinehart and Winston, 1967); Andrew Lycett, *The Man Who Created Sherlock Holmes: The Life and Times of Sir Arthur Conan Doyle* (New York; Free Press, 2007); Daniel Stashower, *Teller of Tales: The Life of Arthur Conan Doyle* (New York: Holt, 1999).

41. James Gibson, *Thomas Hardy: A Literary Life* (New York: St. Martin's Press, 1996); Molly Lefebvre, *Thomas Hardy's World: The Life, Times and Works of the Great Novelist and Poet* (London: Carlton Books, 1997); Norman Page, *The Oxford Reader's Companion to Hardy* (New York: Oxford University Press, 2000); Norman Page, *Thomas Hardy* (London: Routledge & Kegan Paul, 1981); F. B. Pinion, *Thomas Hardy: His Life and Friends* (New York: St. Martin's Press, 1992); Ralph Pite, *Thomas Hardy: The Guarded Life* (New Haven, Conn.: Yale University Press, 2006); Claire Tomain, *Thomas Hardy* (New York: Penguin, 2007); Paul Turner, *The Life of Thomas Hardy: A Critical Biography* (Oxford: Blackwell, 1998); Carl T. Weber, *Hardy of Wessex: His Life and Literary Career* (New York: Columbia University Press, 1965); Sarah B. Wright, ed., *Thomas Hardy A to Z: The Essential Reference to His Life and Work* (New York: Facts on File, 2002).

42. Jeremy Bourne, *The Westerly Wanderer: A Brief Portrait of A. E. Housman, Author of 'A Shropshire Lad,' 1896-1996* (Bromsgrove, England: Housman Society, 1996); Richard P. Graves, *A. E. Housman: The Scholar Poet* (New York: Scribner, 1980); Norman Marlow, *A. E. Housman: Scholar and Poet* (Minneapolis: University of Minnesota Press, 1958); P. G. Naiditch, *Problems in the Life and Writings of A. E. Housman* (Beverley Hills, Calif.: Krown and Spellman, 1995); Norman Page, *A. E. Housman, A Critical Biography* (New York: Schocken, 1983).

43. E. P. Thompson, *William Morris: Romantic to Revolutionary* (London: Lawrence and Wishart, 1955); Florence S. Boos and Carole G. Silver, eds., *Socialism and the Literary Artistry of William Morris* (Columbia: University of Missouri Press, 1990); Paul Meier, *William Morris, the Marxist Dreamer* (Sussex, England: Harvester Press, 1978); Paul Richard Thompson, *The Work of William Morris* (New York: Oxford University Press, 1991); Linda Parry, *William Morris* (New York: Abrams, 1996); Diane Waggoner,

"The Beauty of Life": William Morris and the Art of Design (New York: Thames and Hudson, 2003); Elizabeth Wilhide, *William Morris: Décor and Design* (New York: Abrams, 1991); Rosalind P. Blakesley, *The Arts and Crafts Movement* (London: Phaidon, 2006); Peter Stansky, *Redesigning the World: William Morris, the 1880s, and the Arts and Crafts Movement* (Princeton, N.J.: Princeton University Press, 1985).

44. Stephen L. Gwynn, *Mrs. Humphry Ward* (London: Nisbet, 1917); Enid H. Jones, *Mrs. Humphry Ward* (New York: St. Martin's Press, 1973); John Sutherland, *Mrs. Humphry Ward: Eminent Victorian, Pre-eminent Edwardian* (New York: Oxford University Press, 1990).

45. Adrian W. Frazier, *George Moore, 1852-1932* (New Haven, Conn.: Yale University Press, 2000); Tony Gray, *A Peculiar Man: A Life of George Moore* (London: Sinclair-Stevenson, 1996); Elizabeth Grubgeld, *George Moore and the Autogenous Self: The Autobiography and Fiction* (Syracuse, N.Y.: Syracuse University Press, 1994).

46. George Bishop, *Henry James: Life, Work and Criticism* (Fredericton, N.B.: York Press, 1991); Leon Edel, *Henry James: A Life* (London: Flamingo, 1996); Kenneth Graham, *Henry James: A Literary Life* (New York: St. Martin's Press, 1995); Philip Horne, ed., *Henry James: A Life in Letters* (New York: Penguin, 1999); Fred Kaplan, *Henry James: The Imagination of a Genius: A Biography* (Baltimore, Md.: Johns Hopkins University Press, 1999); Harry T. Moore, *Henry James* (London: Thames & Hudson, 1974); Miranda Seymour, *A Ring of Conspirators: Henry James and His Literary Circle* (London: Scribner, 1988).

47. Harold Bloom, *Joseph Conrad* (Philadelphia, Pa.: Chelsea House, 2003); Albert Guérard, *Conrad the Novelist* (Cambridge, Mass.: Harvard University Press, 1958); Paul Kirschner, *Conrad: The Psychologist As Artist* (Edinburgh, U.K.: Oliver and Boyd, 1968); Owen Knowles and Gene M. Moore, eds., *The Oxford Reader's Companion to Conrad* (New York: Oxford University Press, 2000); Bernard C. Meyer, *Joseph Conrad: A Psychoanalytic Biography* (Princeton, N.J.: Princeton University Press, 1967); Leonard Orr and Theodore Billy, *A Joseph Conrad Companion* (Westport, Conn.: Greenwood Press, 1999); Norman Sherry, *Conrad's Eastern World* (London: Cambridge University Press, 1966).

48. William E. Buckler, *Walter Pater: The Critic As Artist of Ideas* (New York: Cambridge University Press, 1982); Hilary Fraser, *Beauty and Belief: Aesthetics and Religion in Victorian Literature* (New York: Cambridge University Press, 1986); Wolfgang Iser, *Walter Pater: The Aesthetic Moment* (New York: Cambridge University Press, 1987); Elizabeth Prettejohn, *Art for Art's Sake: Aestheticism in Victorian Painting* (New Haven, Conn.: Yale University Press, 2007); Margaret D. Stetz and Mark Samuels Lasner, *England in the 1880s: Old Guard and Avant-garde* (Charlottesville, Va.: University Press of Virginia, 1989).

49. J. Edward Chamberlin, *Ripe Was the Drowsy Hour: The Age of Oscar Wilde* (New York: Seabury Press, 1977); Richard Ellmann, *Oscar Wilde* (New York: Knopf, 1988); Peter Raby, *The Cambridge Companion to Oscar Wilde* (New York: Cambridge University Press, 1997).

50. Miriam J. Benkovitz, *Aubrey Beardsley: An Account of His Life* (New York: Putnam, 1981); Stephen Calloway, *Aubrey Beardsley* (London: V&A, 1998); David Colvin, *Aubrey Beardsley: A Slave to Beauty* (London: Orion, 1998); Aileen Reid, *Beardsley* (London: Bison Group, 1991); Matthew Sturgis, *Aubrey Beardsley: A Biography* (Woodstock, N.Y.: Overlook Press, 1999); Stanley Weintraub, *Beardsley: A Biography* (New York: Braziller, 1967).

51. Miriam J. Benkovitz, *Frederick Rolfe, Baron Corvo: A Biography* (New York: Putnam, 1977); Arthur J. A. Symons, *The Quest for Corvo: An Experiment in Biography* (Harmondsworth, U.K.: Penguin, 1950); Donald Weeks, *Corvo: Saint or Madman?* (New York: McGraw-Hill, 1972).

52. Arthur Symons, *The Symbolist Movement in Literature* (London: Heinemann, 1899).

53. Ensor, *England, 1870-1914,* 326.

54. François Mathey, *The World of the Impressionists* (London: Thames & Hudson, 1961).

55. Russell Ash, *Victorian Masters and their Art* (London: Pavillion, 1989); Hugh Brigstocke, ed., *The Oxford Companion to Western Art* (New York: Oxford University Press, 2001); Françoise Cachin, ed., *Arts of the Nineteenth Century: Volume Two, 1850 to 1905* (New York: Abrams, 1999); Peter Corbett and Lara Perry, *English Art, 1860-1914: Modern Artists and Identity* (New Brunswick, N.J.: Rutgers University Press, 2001); Paula Gillett, *The Victorian Painter's World* (Gloucester, England: Sutton, 1990); Luke Hermann, *Nineteenth Century British Painting* (London: Giles de la Mare, 2000); Lionel Lambourne, *Victorian Painting* (London: Phaidon, 1999).

56. T. J. Barringer, ed., *Frederic Leighton: Antiquity, Renaissance, Modernity* (New Haven, Conn.: Yale University Press, 1999); Wyke Bayliss, *Five Great Painters of the Victorian Era: Leighton, Millais, Burne-Jones, Watts, Holman Hunt* (London: Low, Marston, 1904).

57. Russell Ash, *Sir Lawrence Alma-Tadema* (New York: Abrams, 1990); R. J. Barrow, *Lawrence Alma-Tadema* (New York: Phaidon, 2001); Edwin Becker and Elizabeth Prettejohn, *Sir Lawrence Alma-Tadema* (New York: Rizzoli, 1972); Jennifer G. Lovett, *Empire Restored, Elysium Revisited: The Art of Sir Lawrence Alma-Tadema* (Williamstown, Mass.: Sterling and Francine Clark Art Institute, 1991).

58. Elizabeth Prettejohn, *Interpreting Sargent* (New York: Stewart, Tabon & Chang, 1998).

59. J. Marsden, ed., *The Victorian World of Helen Allingham* (London: Brockhampton Press, 1999).

60. Timothy Hilton, *The Pre-Raphaelites* (New York: Abrams, 1971); Elizabeth Prettejohn, *The Art of the Pre-Raphaelites* (Princeton, N.J.: Princeton University Press, 2000); Edmund Swinglehurst, *The Art of the Pre-Raphaelites* (New York: Shooting Star Press, 1994); Tate Gallery, *The Pre-Raphaelites* (London: Penguin, 1984); Jon Whiteley, *Oxford and the Pre-Raphaelites* (Oxford: Ashmolean Museum, 1989); Christopher Wood, *The Pre-Raphaelites* (New York: Viking, 1981).

61. Carol L. Gerton, "John William Waterhouse," CGFA website, http://cgfa.sunsite.dk//waterhou/index.html.

62. See note 50.

63. S. Tschud Madsen, *Art Nouveau* (London: Weidenfeld and Nicolson, 1967); Nikolaus Pevsner, *Pioneers of Modern Design* (Harmondsworth: Penguin, 1960).

64. Hugh Braun, *A Short History of English Architecture* (London: Faber, 1978); David Watkin, *English Architecture: A Concise History* (London: Thames and Hudson, 1979).

65. Watkin, *English Architecture*, 172.

66. Watkin, *English Architecture*, 170-79.

67. Standard histories of European classical music include Donald Jay Grout, *A History of Western Music* (3rd edition, New York: Norton, 1980), and K. Marie Stolba, *The Development of Western Music* (2nd edition, Dubuque, Iowa: Brown & Benchmark, 1994); see also articles in *Grove Music Online*.

68. Arthur Jones, *Arthur Sullivan: A Victorian Musician* (New York: Oxford University Press, 1984). There is a fairly extensive literature on Gilbert and Sullivan, including: Michael Ainger, *Gilbert and Sullivan: A Dual Biography* (New York: Oxford University Press, 2002); Leslie Baily, *Gilbert and Sullivan: Their Lives and Times* (Harmondsworth: Penguin, 1974); David Eden, *Gilbert and Sullivan: A Creative Conflict* (Rutherford, N.J.: Fairleigh Dickinson University Press, 1986); Alan James, *Gilbert and Sullivan* (New York: Omnibus Press, 1989).

69. J. A. Fuller Maitland, *The Music of Parry and Stanford: An Essay in Comparative Criticism* (Cambridge: Heffer, 1934); John F. Porte, *Sir Charles V. Stanford* (New York: Da Capo, 1976); Paul Rodmell, *Charles Villiers Stanford* (Burlington, Vt.: Ashgate, 2002); Nicholas Temperley, ed., *The Athlone History of Music in Britain, Volume 5: The Romantic Age, 1800-1914* (London: Athlone Press, 1981); Nicholas Temperley, ed., *Music in Victorian Society and Culture: A Special Issue of Victorian Studies* (Bloomington: Indiana University Press, 1986).

70. Michael Allis, *Parry's Creative Process* (Burlington, Vt.: Ashgate, 2003); Jeremy Dibble, *C. Hubert Parry: His Life and Music* (New York: Oxford University Press, 1992); J. A. Fuller Maitland, *The Music of Parry and Stanford: An Essay in Comparative Criticism* (Cambridge: Heffer, 1934); Nicholas Temperley, ed., *The Athlone History of Music in Britain, Volume 5: The Romantic Age, 1800-1914* (London: Athlone Press, 1981); Nicholas Temperley, ed., *Music in Victorian Society and Culture: A Special Issue of Victorian Studies* (Bloomington, Ind.: Indiana University Press, 1986); Donald F. Tovey, *Some English Symphonists* (New York: Oxford University Press, 1941).

71. Pieter J. Pirie and David Brock, "Bantock, Sir Granville," *Grove Music Online*; H. O. Anderton, *Granville Bantock* (London: John Lane, 1915); Myrrha Bantock, *Granville Bantock: A Personal Portrait* (London: Dent, 1972).

72. Robert Anderson, *Elgar* (New York: Schirmer, 1993); Michael Kennedy, *The Life of Elgar* (Cambridge, England: Cambridge University Press, 2004); Michael Kennedy, *Portrait of Elgar* (New York: Oxford University Press, 1982); Diana M. McVeagh, *Edward Elgar: His Life and Music* (Westport, Conn.: Hyperia, 1979); Jerrold N. Moore, *Edward Elgar: A Creative Life* (New York: Oxford University Press, 1984); Christopher Redwood, ed., *An Elgar Companion* (Ashbourne, England: Sequoia Press, 1982); Percy M. Young, *Elgar, O.M.: A Study of a Musician* (Westport, Conn.: Greenwood, 1980).

73. Thomas Beecham, *Frederick Delius* (London: Hutchinson, 1959; revised edition, 1975); Lionel Carley, *Delius: The Paris Years* (London: Triad Press, 1975); Lionel Carley, ed., *Frederick Delius: Music, Art and Literature* (Aldershot, England: Ashgate, 1998); Eric Fenby, *Delius As I Knew Him* (New York: Cambridge University Press, 1981); Eric Fenby, *Delius* (London: Faber and Faber, 1971); Arthur Hutchings, *Delius* (London: Macmillan,1948); Eric Fenby and Christopher Redwood, eds., *A Delius Companion* (London: Calder, 1976); Alan Jefferson, *Delius* (London: Dent, 1972); Gloria Jahoda, *The Road to Samarkand: Frederick Delius and His Music* (New York: Scribner's Sons, 1969); Christopher Palmer, *Delius: Portrait of a Cosmopolitan* (London: Duckworth, 1976); Robert Threlfall, *Delius' Musical Apprenticehip* (London: Delius Trust, 1994); Peter Warlock [Philip Heseltine], *Frederick Delius* (London: The Bodley Head, 1952).

74. Gordon Cox, ed., *Sir Arthur Somervell on Music Education: His Writings, Speeches and Letters* (Woodbridge, England: Boydell Press, 2003); Frank Howes, *The English Musical Renaissance* (London: Secker and Warburg, 1966); Michael Hurd, "Somervell, Sir Arthur," *Grove Music Online*; Michael Pilkington, *Delius, Bridge and Somervell* (London: Thames, 1993); Nicholas Temperley: *The Lost Chord: Essays on Victorian Music* (Bloomington: Indiana University Press, 1989).

75. James Day, *Vaughan Williams* (New York: Oxford University Press, 1998); Simon Heffer, *Vaughan Williams* (London: Weidenfeld and Nicolson, 2000); Paul Homes, *Vaughan Williams: His Life and Times* (New York: Omnibus Press, 1997); Michael Kennedy, *The Works of Ralph Vaughan Williams* (New York: Oxford University Press, 1964); Wilfrid Mellers, *Vaughan Williams and the Vision of Albion* (London: Barrie and Jenkins, 1989); Ursula Vaughan Williams, *R. V. W.: A Biography of Ralph Vaughan Williams* (Oxford, England: Oxford University Press, 1964).

76. Lucy Broadwood, diary entry for 15 June 1903. Broadwood Collection, LEB no. 6782. Surrey History Centre, Woking, England.

77. Francis James Child, ed., *The English and Scottish Popular Ballads,* 10 parts in 5 vols. (Boston: Houghton, Mifflin & Co., 1882-98; reprinted, New York: Dover, 1965). Subsequent references are to the Dover edition, vols. 1-5.

78. William Chappell and Joseph W. Ebsworth, eds., *The Roxburghe Ballads*, 8 vols. (Hertford, U.K.: The Ballad Society, 1869-99 [actually 1901]. [There was confusion over the numbering of the last volume, which, while in fact volume 9, was labeled as if it was an extra part of volume 8].

79. Francis James Child, ed., *The English and Scottish Popular Ballads,* vol. 4 (Parts VII and VIII) (Boston: Houghton, Mifflin & Co., 1890-92).

80. Francis James Child, ed., *The English and Scottish Popular Ballads,* vol. 5 (Part IX) (Boston: Houghton, Mifflin & Co., 1894).

81. Child, *The English and Scottish Popular Ballads,* vol. 4 (Part VIII), 440 and 522-23.

82. Child, *The English and Scottish Popular Ballads,* vol. 5 (Part IX), 204, 206, 233-34, 241, and 135-36.

83. Francis James Child, ed., *The English and Scottish Popular Ballads,* Vol. 5 (Part X) (Boston: Houghton, Mifflin & Co., 1898).

84. Joseph W. Ebsworth, ed. *The Roxburghe Ballads,* vol. 6, Parts 3-4 (Hertford, England: The Ballad Society, 1888-89).

85. Ebsworth, *The Roxburghe Ballads,* vol. 6, 855.

86. Ebsworth, *Roxburghe Ballads,* vol. 6, 855.

87. Ebsworth, *Roxburghe Ballads,* vol. 6, 855.

88. Joseph W. Ebsworth, *The Roxburghe Ballads,* vol. 7, Parts 1-3 (Hertford, England: The Ballad Society, 1890-93).

89. The last of these was actually Ebsworth's own collection. He sometimes wrote poetry under the pen-name of Trowbesh von Nirgends.

90. Child, *The English and Scottish Popular Ballads,* vol. 1, 22-62.

91. Ebsworth, *Roxburghe Ballads,* vol. 7, Part 3, viii.

92. Joseph W. Ebsworth, *The Roxburghe Ballads,* vol. 8, Parts 1-5 (Hertford, England: The Ballad Society, 1895-1901). See, for example, Ebsworth's "Prefatory Note to Second Division of Vol. VIII, Roxburghe Ballads. Virtually Vol. IX," *Roxburghe Ballads,* vol. 8, Part 5, ix.

93. Ebsworth, *Roxburghe Ballads,* vol. 8, Part 1, 198.

94. Ebsworth, *Roxburghe Ballads,* vol. 8, Part 3, 618-20 (Hertford, England: The Ballad Society, 1897).

95. Ebsworth, *Roxburghe Ballads,* vol. 8, Part 3, x.

96. Ebsworth, *Roxburghe Ballads,* vol. 8, Part 3, 651-52.

97. Ebsworth, *Roxburghe Ballads,* vol. 8, Part 3, vii.

98. Ebsworth, *Roxburghe Ballads,* vol. 8, Part 4 (Hertford, England: The Ballad Society, 1897 [actually 1899]).

99. Ebsworth, *Roxburghe Ballads,* vol. 8, Part 5 (Hertford, England: The Ballad Society, 1899 [actually 1901]).

100. Ebsworth, *Roxburghe Ballads,* vol. 8, Part 4, 843-44.

101. Child, *The English and Scottish Popular Ballads,* Vol. 1, 476-77.

102. Ebsworth, *Roxburghe Ballads,* vol. 8, Part 4, 844.

103. Frank Kidson, "Traditional Tunes Collected by Frank Kidson," manuscript tune-book M.19057, Frank Kidson Collection, Mitchell Library, Glasgow.

104. Ebsworth, *Roxburghe Ballads,* vol. 8, Part 5, 881.

105. Ebsworth, *Roxburghe Ballads,* vol. 8, Part 5, 932-33.

106. Ebsworth, *Roxburghe Ballads,* vol. 8, Part 5, ix.

107. Ebsworth, *Roxburghe Ballads,* vol. 8, Part 4, 739.

10

Birth of a Movement, 1890-92

The early 1890s were particularly fecund years in the domain of folksong collecting and publishing, and the fruits of this half-decade demonstrate beyond a shadow of doubt that a revival of English folksong was underway. From this time onwards we can legitimately talk of a folksong *movement*, in which many of the participants corresponded and collaborated with each other, sometimes even meeting in person. A handful of particularly important publications jointly provided the foundations upon which the movement was built. We've already examined several of these keystones: Bruce and Stokoe's *Northumbrian Minstrelsy*, Burne's *Shropshire Folk-Lore*, Baring-Gould's *Songs and Ballads of the West*, and Kidson's *Traditional Tunes*. The first years of the decade saw the appearance of another important songbook: William Alexander Barrett's groundbreaking *English Folk-Songs*.[1] This was the first major Victorian printed folksong collection to be genuinely national in scope since Robert Bell's revised (1857) edition of James Henry Dixon's pioneering *Ancient Poems, Ballads and Songs of the Peasantry of England*.[2] It was published in 1891, the same year as *Traditional Tunes* and two years before Broadwood and Fuller Maitland's equally significant *English County Songs*.[3] The first two years of the 1890s also witnessed the publication of several other contributions to the growing corpus of collected and printed English vernacular song. These included works by Thomas Allan, Charles Forshaw, and John Stokoe, as well as by the individual who would later assume a pivotal role in the new movement, Lucy Broadwood. In this chapter we survey first the more minor publications, then examine William Barrett's substantial contribution to the corpus of English song, and finally explore Lucy Broadwood's early involvement with folksong. However, in chapter 8 with Frank Kidson and *Traditional Tunes* we were based in Yorkshire, and to begin with we return to that large county.

Holroyd's Collection of Yorkshire Ballads

The mid-Victorian period had seen two collections of Yorkshire vernacular songs and poetry: James Halliwell's *The Yorkshire Anthology* (1851)[4] and Davison Ingledew's *The Ballads and Songs of Yorkshire* (1860),[5] and, as we have seen, *Traditional Tunes* was also based primarily, although not exclusively, on Yorkshire sources.[6] These three works were joined in 1892 by a fourth collection, Charles Forshaw's *Holroyd's Collection of Yorkshire Ballads*.[7] As the title indicates, this compilation had actually been made by Abraham Holroyd, a Yorkshire antiquarian who had died four years earlier, so the material in it had been collected earlier than most of that in Kidson's book. Some of it may even have antedated Ingledew's collection, since it included texts that Holroyd had obtained from James Henry Dixon.[8] Forshaw, the editor, was a lawyer, and evidently a friend of Holroyd's and admirer of his work who had agreed to see the collection into print when it became unlikely that Holroyd would be unable to do so himself. It is not clear whether the mode of organization employed in the book was due to Forshaw or Holroyd, but one suspects the latter.

Holroyd's Collection of Yorkshire Ballads was a substantial work, running to over three hundred pages. It reprinted the texts of 117 songs and ballads, but contained no tunes. Although there was considerable overlap between its contents and the two earlier Yorkshire collections, it nonetheless contained much additional material, most (although not all) of it regional in nature. The first third of the book was devoted to what Forshaw called "Place Ballads," by which he meant songs and poems reflecting particular cities, towns, villages, or other localities in the county of Yorkshire. A few examples of the songs are "Sheffield Is a Wonderful Town," "Mother Shipton," "The Craven Churn-Supper Song," "Scarboro' Sands," "The Dallogill Hunt," "The Fisher Lad of Whitby," and "The Wensleydale Lad." This overtly regional material was followed by six Robin Hood ballads that Holroyd believed to be connected in some way with Yorkshire:

"The Bishop of Hereford's Entertainment by Robin Hood and Little John in Merry Barnsdale,"
"The Jolly Pindar of Wakefield,"
"The Bold Pedlar and Robin Hood,"
"Robin Hood and the Curtall Friar,"
"The Noble Fisherman; or, Robin Hood's Preferment," and
"Robin Hood's Death and Burial."

The remainder of *Holroyd's Collection* was divided into five categories: patriotic ballads, tragic ballads, humorous ballads, love ballads, and miscellaneous ballads. As in Part 1, the word ballad was used loosely: by no means all these songs had narrative form or content. Humorous songs formed the largest category in Part 2, and they included various comic ditties ("Unfortunate Miss Bailey," "Harry the Tailor," "Old Wicket and his Wife"), as well as some dialect material, including (among others) "Dolly Dugging," "The Yorkshire Tyke," and "The Goodmanham Mule." Most of the eleven patriotic pieces were poems but "The Sword-Dancers Song" was clearly vernacular in nature, and there were several broadsides, including "Colonel Thompson's Volunteers" and "Paul Jones, the Cumberland Militia, and Scarborough Volunteers." Such broadside ballads as "The Yorkshireman in London," "The Crafty Plough Boy," and "King James First and the Tinker" formed the heart of the collection. Picking just one of them for illustrative purposes is arbitrary, but "The Merchant's Son and the Beggar Wench of Hull" is as good as any: it is a humorous broadside about the war of the sexes and also about one of the many skirmishes between the respectable members of society and the underclass. In this version it also has a Yorkshire connection, although it was actually the product of a London broadsheet printer:

You gallants all, I pray draw near,
And you a pleasant jest shall hear,
How a beggar wench of Hull
A merchant's son of York did gull,
Fal, la, &c.

One morning on a certain day,
He clothed himself in rich array,
And took with him, as it is told,
The sum of sixty pounds in gold.

So mounting on a prancing steed,
He towards Hull did ride with speed,
Where, in his way, he chanc'd to see
A beggar wench of mean degree.

She askèd him for some relief,
And said with tears of seeming grief,
That she had neither house nor home,
But for her living was forced to roam.

He seemed to lament her case,
And said, thou hast a pretty face:
If thou wilt lodge with me, he cry'd,
With gold thou shalt be satisfy'd.

Her silence seemed to give consent,
So to a little house they went;
The landlord laughed to see them kiss
The beggar wench, a ragged miss.

He needs must have a dinner drest,
And call'd for liquor of the best,
And there they toss'd off bumpers free,
The jolly beggar wench, and he.

A dose she gave him, as 'tis thought,
Which by the landlady was brought;
For all the night he lay in bed
Secure as if he had been dead.

Then she put on all his cloaths,
His coat, his breeches, and his hose;
His hat, his periwig likewise,
And seis'd upon the golden prize.

Her greasy petticoat and gown,
In which she rambled up and down,
She left the merchant's son in lieu,
Her bag of bread and bottle too.

Down stairs like any spark she goes,
Five guineas to the host she throws,
And smiling then she went her way,
And ne'er was heard of to this day.

When he had took his long repose,
He look'd about and mist his cloaths,
And saw her rags lie in the room,
How he did storm, nay fret and fume.

Yet wanting cloaths and friends in town,
Her greasy petticoat and gown
He did put on, and mounted strait,
Bemoaning his unhappy fate.

You would have laugh'd to see the dress
Which he was in, yet ne'ertheless
He homewards rode, and often swore,
He'd never kiss a beggar more.[9]

Almost all the tragic ballads in the collection derived from broadsides, and many of them were grisly accounts of murders, usually purporting to be eve-of-hanging confessions by the criminal concerned. Examples are "The Leeds Tragedy, or The Bloody Brother," "The Bowes Tragedy," "The Cropton Murders," and "The Hartlepool Tragedy." The same section also included an outlaw ballad in the Robin Hood tradition, "Bold Nevison, the Highwayman," and this ballad about the death of a poacher and the failure of the justice system to condemn his murderer, "Bill Brown, the Poacher":

In seventeen hundred and sixty-nine
As plainly doth appear then,
A bloody scene was felt most keen
Till death it did draw near then;
Of poor Bill Brown, of Brightside Town,
A lad of well-known fame then,
Who took delight, both day and night,
To trace the timid hare then.

With wires strong they marched along,
Unto brave Thriberg town then,
With nut-brown ale that ne'er did fail,
And many a health went round then;
Bright Luna bright did shine that night,
To the woods they did repair then,
True as the sun their dogs did run,
To trace the lofty hare then.

A lofty breeze amongst the trees,
With shining he came on them,
Like Cain he stood seeking for blood,
With his bayonet and his gun then;
Then he did charge with shot quite large,
George Miller did him spy then;
This rogue's intent was fully bent,
One of us poor lads should die then.

His cruel hand he did command
That instant for to fire then,
And so with strife took poor Brown's life,
Which once he thought entire then.
His blood aloud for vengeance cried,
The keeper he came on then,
Like cruel Cain up to him came,
And so renewed his wounds then.

Now this dear soul ne'er did controul
Nor think that man no ill then;
But to Dalton Brook his mind was struck,
While his clear blood did spill then;
For help he cried but was denied,
No one there nigh him stood then,
And there he lay till break of day,
Dogs licking his dear blood then.

Farewell dear heart, now we must part,
From wife and children dear then;
Pity my doom, it was too soon,
That ever I came here then.
Farewell unto the brave dear lads
Whoever range the fields then,
This cruel man's murdering hand,
Has caused me for to yield then.

In grief and pain till death it came,
To embrace his dear soul then,
Who took its flight to heaven straight,
Where no man can controul them.
The country round heard of the sound,
Of poor Brown's blood being spilt then,
'Twas put in vogue to find the rogue
That justice might be done then.

With irons strong they marched along
Unto York Castle fair then;
In a dark cell was doomed to dwell,
Till the judge he did appear then;
George Miller, as I've been told,
Deny it here who can then,
He ne'er was loath to take his oath,
Brown was a murdered man then.

There was a man who there did stand,
Whose heart did shake amain then;
But gold did fly they can't deny,
Or at Tyburn he'd been hung then.
They'd ne'er been bold to hear it told,
To hear of Shirtly's doom then;
The judge put it off to God on high
Or else they might have judged him soon then.

There was brave Ned Greaves never did fail,
To crown poor Bill's name then;
George Miller brave defies each knave
That travels o'er the plain then.
With sword and gun now we will run,
Though the law it doth maintain them,
Yet poor Brown's blood lost in the wood
For vengeance cries amain then.[10]

This version of "The Death of Bill Brown" appears to have been intended to be sung to the old ballad tune of "John Dory." Its author was evidently not the most skillful of wordsmiths, but despite the doggerel and the ambling rhythm a passionate sincerity (and hatred) shines through. The text reveals much about the depth of class conflict in the eighteenth-century or perhaps the early nineteenth-century English countryside. Its author would have had no difficulty in supporting the activities of Captain Swing.[11]

Holroyd's Collection was short on love songs, but did include "The Bonnet o' Blue" and rather surprisingly re-printed a ballad that celebrated adultery in an engagingly forthright manner, "The Wanton Wife of Castle-Gate; or, The Boatman's Delight." Forshaw's editorial licence had its limits, however, and he felt obliged to "make an alteration" to the last verse of "Harry's Courtship," in which the suitor abandoned his wooing to return to the arms of a more accom-modating lover. The "love ballads" section also included this dialect song of teenage rebellion, "Jenny! Tak' Care o' Thysen":

> When I was a wee little totering bairn, an' had nobbud just gitten short frocks,
> When to gang I at first war beginnin' to larn, on my brow I got monie hard knocs.
> For se waik, an' se silly, an' helpless was I, I was always a tubling down then,
> While mi mother wad twattle me gently an' cry, "Honey, Jenny! tak care o' thysen."
>
> When I grew biggar, an' gat to be strang, 'at I cannily ran all about,
> By mysen whor I liked, then I always mud gang, bithout bein' telled about ought.
> When, however, I com' to be sixteen year auld, an' rattled an ramp'd amang men,
> My mother wad call o' me in, an' would scauld, and cry—"Hussy, tak' care o' thysen!"
>
> I've a sweetheart come now up o' Setterday nights, an' he swears 'at he'll mak' me his wife;
> My mam grows stingy, she scaulds and she flytes, an' she twitters me out of my life.
> But she may lewk sour and consait hersen wise, an' preach again likin' young men;
> Sen I's grown a woman her clack I'll despise, an' I'se marry! tak' care o' mysen.[12]

The miscellaneous category in the collection included two items collected by James Dixon: "Begone Dull Care" and the border ballad "Jack and Tom" (an allegorical account of a journey made by Prince Charles in 1623). Other interesting items were a fox-hunting song, a "Mummer's Song" (aka "Poor Old Horse"), "The Wassail Hymn" (aka "Here We Come a-Wassailing"), and a fragment of a "Hagmena Song" (sung on New Year's Eve at Richmond).

All in all, *Holroyd's Collection of Yorkshire Ballads* was a varied and interesting compilation that included a consi-derable number of vernacular songs as well as many broadsides of a regional nature and a multitude of verses by local poets. Forshaw's approach as an editor was minimalist, with the result that the *Collection* appeared to be a jumble of ill-sorted material, but since his editing was only rarely intrusive he allowed some items to appear in print that most other Victorian editors would have excised or amended. Holroyd appears to have been quite catholic in the material that he collected. Yet in methodological terms the book was a throwback to the mid-Victorian era rather than a contribution to the new movement begun by *Nursery Rhymes and Country Songs*[13] and *Northumbrian Minstrelsy*.[14] Neither Holroyd nor Forshaw were interested in noting tunes for the vernacular songs in the collection, which meant that an opportunity had been missed to expand the body of Yorkshire folksong for which both melodies and words had been recovered beyond that recorded in Kidson's *Traditional Tunes*. Nonetheless, Kidson's and Forshaw's books, taken together, put Yorkshire on the map as far as the Late Victorian folksong revival was concerned. Thomas Allan and John Stokoe jointly did the same for Northumberland and Durham.

Allan's Illustrated Edition of Tyneside Songs and Readings

Starting in 1862, Newcastle-upon-Tyne publisher Thomas Allan had printed several small booklets of songs and poems by Northumbrian writers. Although no tunes were provided, the booklets found sufficient local sales to warrant reprint-ing in a single volume, and an expanded version appeared in 1872. This was still aimed at a local market, with a small print run, and is now a very rare item. It was not until 1891, when the book had metamorphosed into a large (580-page) compendium of folksongs, other vernacular songs, poems, and prose items, that it attracted a national audience. It was now titled *Allan's Illustrated Edition of Tyneside Songs and Readings*.[15] Much, but by no means all, of the material was in Geordie dialect. The collection, which was in fact not limited strictly to material from Newcastle-upon-Tyne, provided no tunes, but it was the most thoroughgoing attempt made so far to bring together in one volume the vernacular poetry of urban Northumberland and Durham.

The opening section of *Tyneside Songs* consisted mainly of traditional lyrics, most of which were in dialect. Exam-ples are "Weel May the Keel Row!" "The Waggoner," "Bobby Shaftoe," "The Bonny Pit Laddie," "Bonny Keel Lad-die," "Ride Through Sandgate," "My Eppie," "The Northumbrian's Sigh for His Native Country," and the poignant la-ment, "Sair Fyel'd, Hinney." In compiling this segment of the book Allan drew heavily on a limited number of previous publications, especially Joseph Ritson's *Northern Garlands*, John Bell's *Rhymes of Northern Bards*, and Cuthbert Sharp's *The Bishoprick Garland*. He also borrowed material from early nineteenth-century garlands and chapbooks, such as the *Newcastle Garland* (c. 1805), the *Northern Minstrel* (1807), from regional newspapers, and from two rare local collections published by John Marshall, *Marshall's Chapbook* (1823) and *Marshall's Collection* (1827). Allan inserted more anonymous traditional songs in an apparently random fashion throughout much of the book. In addition to a number of well-known non-dialect items, such as "Elsie Marley," "Andrew Carr," and the simple but beautiful "The Water of Tyne," the reader encounters (among others) such familiar dialect lyrics as "The Collier's Rant," "The Keel Row," "The Little P. D.," "Dol Li A," and "Ma' Canny Hinny." Here, as an example of this kind of traditional dialect material, is "A You A, Hinny Burd," which Allan had borrowed from John Bell's 1812 collection, *Rhymes of Northern Bards*:

It's O but I ken well,
A you, hinny burd;
The bonny lass of Benwell,
A you a.

She's lang-legg'd and mother-like,
A you, hinny burd;
See she's raking up the dyke,
A you a.

The Quayside for sailors,
A you, hinny burd;
The Castle Garth for tailors,
A you a.

The Gateshead Hills for millers,
A you, hinny burd;
The North Shore for keelers,
A you a.

There's Sandgate for aud rags,
A you, hinny burd;

And Gallowgate for trolly-bags,
A you a.

There's Denton and Kenton,
A you, hinny burd;
And canny Lang Benton,
A you a.

There's Tynemouth and Cullercoats,
A you, hinny burd;
And Shields for the sculler-boats,
A you a.

There's Horton and Holywell,
A you, hinny burd;
And bonny Seaton Delaval,
A you a.

Hartley Pans for sailors,
A you, hinny burd;
And Bedlington for nailers,
A you a.[16]

Although *Tyneside Songs* provided a useful service in conveniently gathering together a considerable number of traditional folksong texts from the northeast of England, Allan added little that was not already available in print. Moreover, the book's usefulness in this regard was reduced by its omission of tunes. Ultimately, then, it was another aspect of Allan's collection that made it a remarkably original and uniquely valuable undertaking. *Tyneside Songs* was, in effect, a history of the region's popular verse, and it contained many hundreds of poems and song lyrics by several dozen local poets and musicians. Not all of these were truly *vernacular* songs, even when their authors wrote them in local dialect and intended them to be sung to well-known melodies, since Allan often printed them from manuscripts and there is no evidence that they were actually sung on the streets of Newcastle. Yet many of these regional pieces evidently did catch on with the local populace. One such was the signature tune of a celebrated local actor-musician, Blind Willie Purvis, who took a traditional folksong and reworked it as "Buy Broom Busoms." This piece, which dated from the late eighteenth century, was one of the oldest songs in the collection to which Allan could ascribe an author. As we saw in chapter 4, it had been printed (with a tune) as "Buy Broom Buzzems" in *Northumbrian Minstrelsy*. Other early Newcastle area songwriters included Thomas Whittle, the composer of "Sawney Ogilvy's Duel with His Wife" and "Little Moody, Razor-Setter," John Cunningham, the author of "Holiday Gown," and George Pickering, the composer of "Donocht Head."

Allan attempted to provide commentaries on the lives and works of these and most of the other songwriters commemorated in his book. Some of his notes were very brief, but others extended to several pages. More than two dozen local poet/lyricists were featured in *Tyneside Songs;* they included such figures as John Shield, John Selkirk, William Stephenson (father and son), William Mitford, Robert Gilchrist, Joe Wilson, Robert Emery, Joseph Robson, Bobby Nunn, and Edward Corven. Of the hundreds of song texts penned by these and other writers, a few of the many that struck chords with the local audience were Tommy Thompson's "Canny Newcastle," Shield's "My Lord Size," Selkirk's "Bob Cranky's Size Sunday," Mitford's "Cappy; or, The Pitman's Dog," Robson's "The Collier's Pay Week," John Leonard's "Winlaton Hopping," Bobby Nunn's "Drucken Bella Roy, O!" and Joe Wilson's "Aw Wish Yor Muther Wad Cum." These became regional vernacular songs, and they often gave rise to parodies, a few of which, such as "Aw Wish Pay Friday Wad Cum" (by a Northumbrian miner named Anderson), rivaled the originals in popularity. New versions of traditional songs were also created by these regional songsmiths, and Allan printed a handful of them, including Tommy Thompson's "The New Keel Row," William Watson's "Dance to Thy Daddy" and the anonymous "Weel May the Keel Row That Gets the Bairns Their Breed." Apart from "The Keel Row" and "The Collier's Rant," however, few of these songs seem to have had great appeal outside the northeast of England. The dialect speech in which many of them were written was no doubt a significant barrier.

The one Tyneside songwriter who had some success in reaching a larger audience was George Ridley from Gateshead. His regional successes included "The Sheels Lass for Me," "The Bobby Cure," and "Johnny Luik-Up!" but it was in 1862, when he wrote new words to an old melody ("Brighton"), that he broke through to a national audience. "Blaydon Races" owed its popularity as much to its rollicking tune as for its devil-may-care lyrics, but they were a perfect match. The song has been belted out on bus trips, in pubs, and at soccer matches from that day to this:

> Aw went to Blaydon Races, 'twas on the ninth of Joon,
> Eighteen hundred an' sixty-two, on a summer's efternoon;
> Aw tyuk the bus frae Balbra's, and she wis heavy laden,
> Away we went alang Collingwood Street, that's on the way to Blaydon.
>
> [chorus, after each verse]
> O lads, ye shud only seen us gannin,'
> We pass'd the foaks upon the road just as they wor stannin';
> Thor wes lots o' lads an' lasses there, all wi' smiling faces,
> Gawn alang the Scotswood Road, to see the Blaydon Races.
>
> We flew past Airmstrang's factory, and up to the "Robin Adair,"
> Just gannin doon te the railway bridge, the bus wheel flew off there.
> The lasses lost their crinolines off, an' the veils that hide their faces,
> An' aw got two black eyes an' a broken nose in gan te Blaydon Races.
>
> When we gat the wheel put on away we went agyen,
> But them that had their noses broke, they cam back ower hyem;
> Sum went to the dispensary, an' uthers to Doctor Gibbs,
> An' sum sought out the Infirmary to mend their broken ribs.
>
> Noo when we gat to Paradise thor wes bonny gam begun;
> Thor wes fower-and-twenty on the bus, man, hoo they danced an' sung;
> They called on me to sing a sang, aw sung them "Paddy Fagan,"
> Aw danced a jig an' swung my twig that day we went to Blaydon.
>
> We flew across the Chain Bridge reet into Blaydon toon,
> The bellman he was callin' there—they call him Jackey Brown;
> Aw saw him talkin' to sum cheps, an' them he was pursuadin'
> To gan an' see Geordy Ridley's concert in the Mechanics Hall at Blaydon.
>
> The rain it poor'd aw the day, an' myed the groons quite muddy,
> Coffy Johnny had a white hat on—they war shootin' "Whe stole the cuddy."
> There was spice stalls an' munkey shows, an' aud wives selling ciders,
> An' a chep wiv a happeny roondabout shootin' "Now, me boys, for riders."[17]

Ridley's career as a popular songwriter and music-hall entertainer was short. He had his first success with a humorous song about a local jockey, "Joey Jones," in the late 1850s, and he died at the age of thirty in 1864, before "Blaydon Races" had become more than a local favorite. Ned Corven, the acknowledged disciple of and successor to Blind Willie Purvis and author of such local hits as "He Wad Be a Noodle," "O, What a Price for Sma' Coals," "Asstrilly; or the Pitman's Fareweel," and "The Fire on the Kee," was perhaps Ridley's greatest rival, but he died a year later in 1865. Their mantle was assumed by Joe Wilson and by a host of lesser names that Allan featured in the last section of *Tyneside Songs*, which he titled "Living Writers." They included Thomas Kerr, who composed "When the Gud Times Cum Agyen" and "Aw's Glad the Strike's Duin" during the 1870s, Richard Heslop, who published such songs as "Newcastle Toon Nee Mair," "A Tow for Nowt," "The Singin' Hinney," and "The Tyneside Chorus" on broadsheets and in *The Newcastle Chronicle* in the early 1880s, and song-collector Joseph Crawhall, whose own compositions included "The Hot-Trod" and "The Wife's Remonstrance."

As was the case with *Holroyd's Collection of Yorkshire Ballads,* Allan's *Tyneside Songs* was a poorly organized and rather undiscriminating compendium of song texts and related items, but it, too, contained a wealth of fascinating material which it helped preserve for posterity. It demonstrated that vernacular song in the northeast of England was beyond doubt a living tradition, and that the boundaries between music-hall, vernacular poetry, and folksong were difficult to draw with clarity. But it lacked tunes, and so another publication was required to underscore the fact that Northumberland was one of the principal wellsprings of English traditional melody. The folksong texts of northern England needed reuniting with their tunes, and the man who led the way in doing this was John Stokoe.

Songs and Ballads of Northern England

John Stokoe and Samuel Reay's *Songs and Ballads of Northern England* was published in 1892, the same year as *Holroyd's Collection* and a year after the omnibus edition of *Tyneside Songs.*[18] Like Allan, Stokoe was a resident of Newcastle-upon-Tyne, and this was reflected in his research into the vernacular songs sung locally. As we have seen, he had been a longtime member of the Newcastle Antiquarian Society, and he had collaborated with Collingwood Bruce on *Northumbrian Minstrelsy* and with Joseph Crawhall on *A Beuk o' Newcassel Sangs.*[19] However, his new work, like Laura Smith's, ranged in compass beyond Tyneside, and it was aimed at a national market among music teachers and amateur singers and musicians.

Heavily dependent on Stokoe's earlier collaborations, *Songs and Ballads of Northern England* shared many of the virtues and faults of *Northumbrian Minstrelsy.* Indeed, no pretence could be made that this new songbook provided a fully representative selection of the music of the laboring classes of the northeast. The songs of miners, textile workers, and most other urban dwellers were largely ignored. Not entirely, admittedly: there were a few Newcastle songs ("Canny Newcastle," "The Fiery Clock Fyece," and "Newcastle Is My Native Place"), there was a handful of songs about miners ("The Collier's Rant," "Success Unto the Coal Trade," "'Cappy', or the Pitman's Dog," "The Pitman's Courtship," and a couple about local celebrity Bob Cranky), and there were also some dialect songs (including, among others, "Bob Cranky's Adieu," "Up the Raw," "Sair Fyel'd, Hinny," "Maw Canny Hinny," and "A, U, Hinny Burd." As a short example of this kind of local Newcastle song, partly in Geordie dialect, here is "Dol-li-a":

Dol-li-a

Anon

Fresh aw cum frae Sand-gate Street,   Dol - li, Dol - li,   Maw best fri-ends here to meet,

Dol - i - a,   Dol - li the dil-len dol,   Dol - li   Dol - li,   Dol - li the dil-len dol,   Dol - li - a.

Fig. 10.1

Fresh aw cum frae Sandgate Street,
Dol-li, dol-li,
Maw best friends here to meet,
Dol-li-a, Dol-li the dillen dol,
Dol-li, dol-li,
Dol-li the dillen dol,
Dol-li-a.

The Black Cuffs is gawn away,
Dol-li, dol-li,
An that'll be a crying day,

Doli-li-a, etc.

Dolly Coxon's pawned her shirt,
Dol-li, dol-li,
To ride upon the baggage-cart,
Dol-li-a, etc.

The Green Cuffs is cummin' in,
Dol-li, dol-li,
An' that'll make the lasses sing,
Dol-li-a, etc.[20]

Stokoe did not print as many of these traditional dialect songs as had Allan in *Tyneside Songs,* but his book had the great virtue of including tunes for those that he did reproduce. So, for example, where Allan gave only the words of "A You A, Hinny Burd," Stokoe's version, titled "A, U, Hinny Burd," came equipped with melody as well as lyric, and it even included an extra verse that Allan had omitted. Here is the tune, with the additional verse:

A, U, Hinny Burd

Anon

Fig. 10.2

It's O, but aw ken well,
A, U, hinny burd;
The bonny lass o' Benwell,
A, U, A.

She's lang legg'd and mother-like,
A, U, hinny burd;
See, she's raking up the dyke,
A, U, A.

There's Tynemouth and Cullercoats,
A, U, hinny burd;
And North Shields for sculler boats,
A, U, A.

There's Westoe lies in a neu,
A, U, hinny burd;
And South Shields the place for seut,
A, U, A.[21]

Notwithstanding these regional items, an entire tradition of industrial song, especially protest song, was almost completely absent from *Songs and Ballads of Northern England.* From the material selected for *Songs and Ballads* one would hardly have guessed that this collection represented one of the geographical heartlands of the British Industrial Revolution. For example, there was not a single ballad about a mining disaster, and not a single song about the plight of the handloom weavers. Of course, Stokoe never intended his book to fully represent each and every type of local vernacular song. Rather, his principal aim was merely to republish the most accessible material from *Northumbrian Minstrelsy* and *A Beuk o' Newcassel Sangs* in a format more conducive to use by trained-voice singers performing in drawing rooms and concert halls. This time around, the tunes were harmonized for piano accompaniment.

One of the virtues of *Northumbrian Minstrelsy* had been the quite thorough and extensive notes provided to each song. In this respect *Songs and Ballads of Northern England* regressed. No information whatsoever was provided for forty-one of the ninety-two songs in the book. Only five songs were stated to have been collected from oral tradition, and only three informants were identified by name: Kitty Hall, Mrs. Andrews, and Blind Willie Purvis. In only three cases were broadsides cited as the source of the words of a ballad, although on twelve other occasions printed sources (such as Playford's *Dancing Master,* D'Urfey's *Pills,* Bell's *Rhymes of the Northern Bards,* Topliff's *Melodies of the Tyne and Wear,* and three Garlands) were referenced.

No attempt was made to distinguish between traditional folksongs and the compositions of a dozen or more local poets, except that the latter were usually given credit for their lyrics. It would have been possible to separate out these two types of material into different sections of the book, but this was not done. Indeed there was no evident principle of organization whatsoever; just a jumble of songs in no apparent order, and no alphabetical index. In short, Stokoe seems to have largely abrogated his editorial responsibilities. Unlike *Traditional Tunes* or even *Northumbrian Minstrelsy*, *Songs and Ballads of Northern England* was not intended as a scholarly work designed to preserve traditional song that was in danger of being lost. It would appear that Stokoe saw the publication as merely a money-making spin-off from his earlier work, nothing more than a songbook intended for the use of amateur (and perhaps also professional) musicians. That, after all, was why he brought in Samuel Reay to harmonize the tunes.

All that said, we must recognize that Stokoe's collection did make accessible a wealth of fine traditional songs. How authentic were the versions given is very difficult to judge. One cannot have confidence that they were not tampered with, given the motives of the editors and their heavy reliance on the imperfect *Northumbrian Minstrelsy*. Notwithstanding this qualification, *Songs and Ballads of Northern England* included a goodly number of folksongs of various types. The traditional narrative ballads (not yet referred to by Stokoe as Child ballads) included English versions of such border ballads as "Chevy Chace," "Jock o' the Side," and "Derwentwater." One of the shorter of these was "Hughie the Graeme," which Child would include in *The English and Scottish Popular Ballads* as no. 191:

Hughie the Graeme

Anon

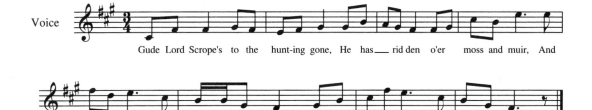

Voice

Gude Lord Scrope's to the hunt-ing gone, He has___ rid den o'er moss and muir, And

he has grip - it Hughie the the Graeme, For___ steal ing o' the Bish - op's mear

Fig. 10.3

Gude Lord Scrope's to the hunting gone,
He has ridden o'er moss and muir,
And he has grippit Hughie the Graeme
For stealing o' the Bishop's mear.

"Now, good Lord Scrope, this may not be!
Here hangs a broadsword by my side;
And if that thou canst conquer me,
The matter it may soon be tryed."

"I ne'er was afraid of a traitor thief,
Although thy name be Hughie the Graeme;
I'll make thee repent thee of thy deeds,
If God but grant me life and time."

"Then do your worst now, good Lord Scrope,
And deal your blows as hard as you can;
It shall be tried within an hour
Which of us two is the better man."

But as they were dealing their blows so free,
And both so bloody at the time,
Over the moss came ten yeoman so tall,
All for to take brave Hughie the Graeme.

Then they hae grippit Hughie the Graeme
And brought him up through Carlisle town,
The lasses and lads stood on the walls
Crying, "Hughie the Graeme, thou'se ne'er gae down."

Then hae they chosen a jury of men,
The best that were in Carlisle town,
And twelve of them cried out at once,
"Hughie the Graeme, thou must gae down."

Then up bespak' him gude Lord Hume
As he sat by the judge's knee—
"Twenty white owsen, my good lord,
If you'll grant Hughie the Graeme to me."

"O no, O no, my gude Lord Hume,
Forsooth and sae it mauna be,
For were there but three Graemes o' the name,
They sud be hangit a' for me."

'Twas up and spak the gude Lady Hume
As she sat by the judge's knee—
"A peck o' white pennies, my gude Lord Judge,
If you'll grant Hughie the Graeme to me."

"O no, O no, my gude Lady Hume,
Forsooth, and so it mustna be;
Were he but the one Graeme of the name
He sud be hangit high for me."

"If I be guilty," said Hughie the Graeme,
"Of me my friends shall have small talk;"
And he has louped fifteen feet and three,
Tho' his hands were tied behind his back.

He looked over his left shouther
And for to see what he might see;
There was he aware of his auld faither,
Cam tearing his hair most piteously.

"O hald your tongue, my faither," says he,
"And see that ye dinna weep for me;
For they may ravish me o' my life,
But they canna banish me frae heaven hie."

"Fare ye weel, fair Maggie, my wife,
The last time we came frae the toon,
'Twas thou bereft me of my life
And wi' the Bishop thou played the loon."

"Here, Johnie Armstrong, take thou my sword
That is made o' the metal sae fine;
And when thou cames to the English side,
Remember the death of Hughie Graeme."[22]

There were also two tragic ballads: "The Brave Earl Brand" and "Binnorie; or, The Cruel Sister," while other narrative songs included "The Fair Flower of Northumberland," "Lay the Bent to the Bonny Broom," "The Outlandish Knight," the dubiously authentic "Laidley Worm," the humorous "Keach i' the Creel," and this version of the ballad usually known as "The Baffled Knight" but here titled "Blow the Winds, I-Ho!":

Blow the Winds, I-Ho!

Anon

Fig.10.4

There was a shepherd's son,
He kept sheep on yonder hill;
He laid his pipe and his crook aside,
And there he slept his fill.

CHORUS: And blow the winds, I-ho!
Sing, blow the winds, I-ho!
Clear away the morning dew,
And blow the winds, I-ho!

He lookèd east, he lookèd west,
He took another look,
And there he spied a lady gay
Was dipping in a brook.

She said, "Sir, don't touch my mantle,
Come, let my clothes alone;
I will give you as much white money
As you can carry home."

"I will not touch your mantle,
I'll let your clothes alone,
I'll take you out of the water clear,
My dear, to be my own."

He did not touch her mantle,
He let her clothes alone,
But he took her from the clear water,
And all to be his own.

He set her on a milk-white steed,
Himself upon another,
And there they rode along the road,
Like sister and like brother.

And as they rode along the road,
He spied some cocks of hay;
"Yonder," he says, "is a lovely place
For men and maids to play."

And when they came to her father's gate,
She pulled at a ring,
And ready was the proud porter
For to let the lady in.

And when the gates were opened,
This lady jumped in;

She says, "You are a fool without,
And I'm a maid within.

"Good morrow to you, modest boy,
I thank you for your care;
If you had been what you should have been,
I would not have left you there.

"There is a horse in my father's stable,
He stands behind the thorn,
He shakes his head above the trough,
But dares not prie the corn.

"There is a bird in my father's flock,
A double comb he bears,
He claps his wing and crows full loud,
But a capon's crest he bears.

"There is a flower in my father's garden,
They call it marigold;
The fool that will not when he may,
He shall not when he wold."

Said the shepherd's son, as he doft his shoon,
"My feet they shall run bare,
But if ever I meet another maid,
I rede that maid beware."[23]

Shorter lyrics included in *Songs and Ballads of Northern England* that would become well known in later decades included "The Oak, the Ash and the Bonny Ivy Tree," "Bonny at Morn," "The Willow Tree, or Rue and Thyme," "Bobby Shaftoe," "D'ye Ken John Peel?" and the beautiful "Blaw the Wind Southerly." Stokoe had taken the tune and the traditional words from Cuthbert Sharp's *Bishoprick Garland*, but he added a set of three new verses written by John Stobbs that he had found on a nineteenth-century broadside. Here is the traditional chorus, followed by the new words and the tune:

CHORUS:
Blaw the wind southerly, southerly, southerly,
Blaw the wind southerly, south or south-west.
My lad's at the bar, at the bar, at the bar;
My lad's at the bar, whom I love best.
Then blaw the wind southerly, southerly, southerly;
Blaw the wind southerly, south or south-west.

NEW VERSES:
Blow the wind southerly, southerly, southerly,
Blow the wind south o'er the bonny blue sea;
Blow the wind southerly, southerly, southerly,
Blow, bonny breeze, my lover to me.

They told me last night there were ships in the offing,
And I hurried down to the deep rolling sea;
But my eye could not see it, wherever might be it–
The bark that is bearing my lover to me.

Blow the wind southerly, southerly, southerly,
Blow the wind south that my lover may come;
Blow the wind southerly, southerly, southerly,
Blow bonny breeze, and bring him safe home.

I stood by the lighthouse the last time we parted,
Till darkness came down o'er the deep rolling sea;
And no longer I saw the bright bark of my lover,
Blow, bonny breeze, and bring him to me.

Blow the wind southerly, southerly, southerly,
Blow, bonny breeze, o'er the bonny blue sea;
Blow the wind southerly, southerly, southerly,
Blow bonny breeze, and bring him to me.

Is it not sweet to hear the breeze singing,
As lightly it comes o'er the deep rolling sea?
But sweeter and dearer by far when 'tis bringing
The bark of my true love in safely to me.[24]

Blaw the Wind Southerly

Anon

Blaw the wind south - er - ly,   south-er-ly, south-er-ly,   blaw the wind south - er - ly,

south or south west.   My   lad's at the bar,   at the bar, at the bar,   My   lad's at the bar,

whom I love best. Then blaw the wind south er-ly,   south er-ly, south-er-ly, Blaw the wind south-er-ly,

south or south west.

Fig.10.5

Less well known, but also endowed with a haunting tune, was a night-visiting song in which the course of true love did not run smooth, "I Drew My Ship into the Harbour." The lyric included some pithy and poetic observations about the fragile nature of human relationships:

I Drew My Ship Into the Harbour

Anon

I   drew my ship in - to the har bour, I drew her up where my   true love lay; I

drew her close   by   up   to the wind - ow, To   list - en what   my dear   girl did say.

Fig. 10.6

I drew my ship into the harbour,
I drew her up where my true love lay;
I drew her close by up to the window,
To listen what my dear girl did say.

"Who's there that raps so loud at my window—
That raps so loud and fain would be in?"

"It is your true love that loves you dearly,
So rise, dear girl, and let him in."

Then slowly, slowly, got she up,
And slowly, slowly, came she down;
But before she got the door unlocked,
Her true love had both come and gone.

"Come back, come back, my only true love,
Come back, my ain one, and ease my pain;
Your voice I knew not, your face I saw not,
Oh, John! My heart will break in twain."

The ripest apple is soonest rotten,
The hottest love is soonest cold;

Seldom seen is soon forgotten,
True love is timid, so be not bold.

He's brisk and braw, lads, he's far awa', lads,
He's far beyond yon raging main,
When fishers dancing, and dark eyes glancing,
Have made him quite forget his ain.[25]

The collection also included a substantial number of regional folksongs, including "Elsie Marley," "The Sandgate Lass's Lament," "The Water of Tyne," "The Hexhamshire Lass," "The Shoemakker," "Captain Bover," and "Here's the Tender Coming." Stokoe's version of "The Keel Row" included two sets of lyrics. The first was traditional, the second set was written by Thomas Thompson in the local dialect and titled "The New Keel Row." Here is the traditional lyric, followed by the tune and the new words:

As I cam' thro' Sandgate, thro' Sandgate, thro' Sandgate,
As I cam' thro' Sandgate, I heard a lassie sing:
"Weel may the keel row, the keel row, the keel row,
Weel may the keel row that my laddie's in.
And weel may the keel row, the keel row, the keel row,
Weel may the keel row that my laddie's in."

"He wears a blue bonnet, blue bonnet, blue bonnet,
He wears a blue bonnet, a dimple in his chin.
Weel may the keel row, the keel row, the keel row,
Weel may the keel row that my laddie's in.
And weel may the keel row, the keel row, the keel row,
Weel may the keel row that my laddie's in."[26]

The Keel Row

Anon

Fig. 10.7

Whe's like my Johnny, sae leish, sae blithe, sae bonny,
He's foremost 'mang the mony keel lads o' coaly Tyne.

He'll set or row so tightly, or in the dance so sprightly,
He'll cut or shuffle sightly, 'tis true—were he not mine.
And weel may the keel row, the keel row, the keel row,
Weel may the keel row that my laddie's in.

He's ne mair learning than tells his weekly earning,
Yet reet frae wrang discerning, tho' brave, ne bruiser he;
Tho' he no worth a plack is, his awn coat on his back is,
And nane can say that black is the white o' Johnny's e'e.
And weel may the keel row, etc.

Each pay-day nearly, he takes his quairt right dearly,
Then talks O latin O cherly, or mavies jaws away;
How caring not a feather, Nelson and he together,
The springy French did lether, and gar'd them shab away.
And weel may the keel row, etc.

Were a' kings comparely in each I'd spy a fairly,
An' aye wad Johnny barly: we hae sic bonny bairns;
Go bon, the queen, or misses, but wad for Johnny's kisses,
Luik upon as blisses, scrimp meals, caff beds, and dairns.
And weel may the keel row, etc.

Wour lads, like their deddy, to fight the French are ready,
But gie's a peace that's steady, and breed cheap as lang syne;
May a' the press-gangs perish, each lass her laddy cherish,
Lang may the coal trade flourish upon the dingy Tyne.
And weel may the keel row, etc.

Bright Star o' Heaton, your aye wour darling sweet'en,
May heaven's blessings leet on your leddy, bairns, and ye;
God bless the king and nation, each bravely fill his station,
Our canny Corporation, lang may they sing wi' me.
And weel may the keel row, etc.

There were also northern versions of folksongs found in other regions of England, such as "Whittingham Fair" (aka "Scarborough Fair"), "The Nobleman and the Thrasher," "The Poor Old Horse," "The Miller and His Sons," and "Down in Cupid's Garden."

Finally one should not ignore some of the compositions by local musicians and poets, whether or not these are counted as folksongs; for example Robert Surtees's ballad to a Jacobite air, "Derwentwater's Farewell," John Selkirk's "Swalwell Hopping," William Mitford's "The Pitman's Courtship," Richard Heslop's "The Folks o' Shields," and the several songs about Bob Cranky. Here, as an example of such vernacular songs by known composers, is Thomas Doubleday's arrogant but evocative lyric to a beautiful tune that he collected from a Newcastle street singer *circa* 1820, "The Snow It Melts the Soonest":

Oh, the snow it melts the soonest when the winds begin to sing,
And the corn it ripens fastest when the frosts are settling in;
And when a woman tells me that my face she'll soon forget,
Before we part, I wad a croon, she's fain to follow't yet.

Oh, the snow it melts the soonest when the winds begin to sing,
And the swallow skims without a thought as long as it is Spring;
But when Spring goes and Winter blows, my lass, an' you'll be fain,
For all your pride, to follow me, were't across the stormy main.

Oh, the snow it melts the soonest when the winds begin to sing,
The bee that flew when Summer shone in Winter cannot sting;
I've seen a woman's anger melt between the night and morn,
And it's surely not a harder thing to tame a woman's scorn.

Oh, never say me farewell here—no farewell I'll receive,
For you shall set me to the stile, and kiss, and take your leave;
But I'll stay here till the woodcock comes and the martlet takes his wing,
Since the snow it melts the soonest when the winds begin to sing.[27]

The Snow It Melts the Soonest

Anon/Thomas Doubleday

Oh, the snow it melts the soon-est when the winds be-gin to sing, And the corn it ri-pens fast-est when the frosts are set-tling in'; And when a wom-an tells me that my face she'll soon for get, Be - fore we part, I wad a croon, she's fain__ to foll-ow't yet.

Fig. 10.8

"The Snow It Melts the Soonest" was but one of many attractive songs in *Songs and Ballads of Northern England*. The book's faults, if judged as a work of scholarship, were obvious, but it was an interesting and useful publication, a convenient source for a great deal of valuable material. Lucy Broadwood came to believe that many of the tunes had in fact been taken from James Telfer's manuscript music book in the library of the Newcastle-upon-Tyne Society of Antiquaries, but Samuel Reay, in a paper on "Northumberland Ballad Music," read before the National Society of Professional Musicians in January 1892, emphasized John Stokoe's efforts as a field-collector, citing "The Water of Tyne" as an example, taken down by Stokoe from the singing of an old man at Hexham. It would appear, therefore, that Stokoe's sources were varied, and it is indeed regrettable that he was not more explicit about them. Nonetheless, along with Stokoe's earlier publications and Allan's *Tyneside Songs,* the collection reinforced the importance of the northeast in England's treasury of folksong. In short, by publishing an accessible digest of much of the best material from *Northumberland Minstrelsy* and *A Beuk o' Newcassel Sangs,* Stokoe did folksong enthusiasts a useful service, although the book actually added few new items to the existing stock of northern English folksong.

English Folk-Songs

William Alexander Barrett (1834-1891) was a well known figure in London music circles, and *English Folk-Songs* was his swansong, published less than a year before his death.[28] Although for much of his life he earned his living as a journalist, as music critic for the *Morning Post* and as editor of *Monthly Musical Record, The Orchestra,* and *Musical Times,* he was a church musician with a longstanding involvement with the choir of St. Paul's Cathedral. For twenty years he also served as assistant Inspector of Music in the London school system, working under the composer John Stainer. A musicologist and music historian with a Bachelor of Music degree from Oxford University, Barrett jointly edited with Stainer a *Dictionary of Musical Terms* (1876), and he also published several books on English madrigals and church composers. He had collected folksong texts and melodies for nearly two decades and he was also interested in broadside balladry.

The basic goal of Barrett's research into vernacular song was to try to reunite broadside and other printed texts with the tunes to which they had originally been sung. In this respect his work paralleled that of Frank Kidson. He focused his efforts on fifty-four songs "gathered from various sources during many years," the majority of which he claimed had been "noted down from the lips of the singers in London streets, roadside inns, harvest homes, festivals on the occasion of sheep shearing, at Christmas time, at ploughing matches, rural entertainments of several kinds, and at the 'unbending' after choir suppers in country districts."[29] In all cases, he stated, the melodies (which he presented in fairly simple piano arrangements) were "derived" from his source singers, and in some cases the words were too, but he had tried, wherever possible, to "collate" all the known broadside versions "in order to avoid obvious corruptions of the text."[30] His aim, in short, was to create the best possible composite texts to accompany the tunes he had collected in the field.

Barrett commented in his preface to *English Folk-Songs* that in his experience folksongs did not "belong to any particular county" and hence finding a song in a given place did not necessarily prove that it had originated there; rather, variants were to be found in many locales with "each district where the same song is found embellishing it with local peculiarities of dialect."[31] This was a plausible anticipatory criticism of the method of organization Lucy Broadwood would employ in *English County Songs*, but Barrett had great difficulty coming up with any alternative plan. Eschewing Chappell's historical, Broadwood's geographical, and Grundtvig's metrical approaches, he might at least have plumped for an alphabetical one, but that he apparently rejected as too prosaic. The net result was an apparently random jumble of songs, and unfortunately no alphabetical index was provided to help the reader locate individual items. Moreover Barrett's notes to the songs were often perfunctory, although he did sometimes indicate the county or town in which he had noted an item. He rarely provided details about the source singers themselves.

Although this is not immediately evident to the reader (or user) of *English Folk-Songs,* Barrett does seem to have employed three principles in selecting material for his book. Notwithstanding his skepticism about a county-by-county approach to folksong collecting, he did endeavor to include songs from all the major regions of England: the north, the West Midlands, the East Midlands, the home counties, London, and the south. He also tried to provide examples of songs from five historical periods: the Tudor era, the seventeenth century, the eighteenth century, the period of the French Revolution and Napoleonic wars, and the Early Victorian era. Furthermore, he chose songs that illustrated certain major topics or fitted into certain categories, including agriculture, hunting, the sea, true love, patriotism, and merrymaking. We can therefore view the contents of his book from these three different angles to see what material he found in each instance.

From the rather scanty information he provides in *English Folk-Songs* one can infer that Barrett traveled quite extensively around England and picked up traditional songs in a variety of locales between Yorkshire in the northeast and Somerset in the southwest. His relatively few north-country songs, which were collected mainly in Yorkshire and Lancashire, included "The Painful Plough" and two May songs. His material from the West Midlands was more extensive. For example, while in Cheshire he obtained a pace-egging song, a ballad titled "William and Mary," and "The Lost Lady Found." Further south, in Gloucestershire, he collected "Good Morning, Pretty Maid," which he chose to open the collection, and a sheep-shearing song. The East Midlands were also represented by five items. In Nottinghamshire and Northamptonshire he found several fox-hunting songs, collected one of three versions of "The New-Mown Hay" in Lincolnshire, and noted "The Old Farmer" in two different places in East Anglia.

However, by far the majority of Barrett's collection derived from southern England. Since he lived in London he found it most convenient to collect songs either in the city itself or, more often, in the surrounding countryside. In Berkshire, for example, he found a harvest home song, and in Bedfordshire two variants of songs obtained elsewhere ("William and Mary" and "The New-Mown Hay"). Yet he also found the streets, pubs, wharves, and factories of East London a fertile source of songs. Those collected in London included a boatman's song, "The Jolly Waterman," a factory girls' song, "Saucy Sailor Boy," a broadside ballad, "The Gallant Hussar," a fishing song, "The Barbel," and "The Buffalo," an eighteenth-century emigrants' song about the delights of the New World. Barrett also collected songs from navvies engaged in railway construction, obtaining from this source "Ye Sons of Albion" and "Drink Little England Dry," both patriotic songs from the period of the Napoleonic wars. Although he failed to identify his informants, Barrett may have noted several of the drinking songs in his collection in London taverns. They included this popular but unusual lyric that cheerfully and philosophically looks death in the face, "Old Rosin the Beau":

> I've travelled the wide world all over, and now to another I'll go,
> I know that good quarters are waiting to welcome old Rosin the beau.
> To welcome old Rosin the beau, to welcome old Rosin the beau,
> I know that good quarters are waiting to welcome old Rosin the beau.
>
> When I'm dead and laid out on the counter, a voice you will hear from below,
> Singing out for some whiskey and water, to drink to old Rosin the beau.
> To welcome old Rosin the beau, &c.

And when I'm laid out then I reckon my friends will be anxious, I know,
Just to lift off the lid of the coffin, to peep at old Rosin the beau.
To welcome old Rosin the beau, &c.

You must get just a dozen good fellows, and stand them all up in a row,
And drink out of half-gallon bottles, to the memory of Rosin the beau.
To welcome old Rosin the beau, &c.

Get four or five jovial young fellows, and let them all staggering go,
And dig a deep hole in the meadow, and in it toss Rosin the beau.
To welcome old Rosin the beau, &c.

Then get you a couple of tombstones, place them at my head and my toe,
And mind do not fail to scratch on the name of old Rosin the beau.
To welcome old Rosin the beau, &c.

I feel the grim tyrant approaching, that cruel, implacable foe,
Who spares neither age nor condition, not even old Rosin the beau.
So welcome old Rosin the beau, &c.[32]

Old Rosin the Beau

Anon

Fig. 10.9

Like Lucy Broadwood, Barrett found Sussex and Surrey good counties for collecting: for example, at Shoreham (Sussex) he noted "The Country Lass," "The Seasons," and a sheep-shearing song, while at Cranleigh (Surrey) he collected "The Birds in the Spring." While visiting Melksham in Wiltshire he picked up a drinking song, "A Jug of This." On the other hand, he seems not to have bothered much with the West Country, since none of the items in the collection are identified as deriving from Dorset, Devon, or Cornwall. However, he did spend some time collecting in Somerset, and in that county he noted "Somerset Hunting Song," "Richard of Taunton Dean," and the tragic sea ballad titled "The *Nightingale.*" The latter, which told the sad tale of a young farm laborer, the victim of a press-gang, who ended his days in a storm at sea, was very popular with the female operatives of a glove-making factory in Yeovil.

The Nightingale

Anon

My love he was a farm-er's son, When first my tend-er heart he won; His

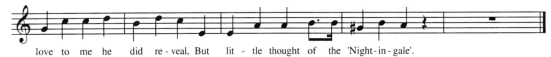

love to me he did re-veal, But lit-tle thought of the 'Night-in-gale'.

Fig. 10.10

My love he was a farmer's son,
When first my tender heart he won;
His love to me he did reveal,
But little thought of the *Nightingale*.

My cruel dad contrived it so,
That this young lad to sea should go,
He told the press-gang not to fail
To press my love for the *Nightingale*.

On the fourteenth of November last,
The wind it blew a bitter blast,
My love was in the dreadful gale,
And went to the bottom in the *Nightingale*.

The very night my love was lost,
Appeared to me his deadly ghost,

In sailor's dress and visage pale,
And told his fate in the *Nightingale*.

"O lovely Nancy, cease surprise,
In Biscay's Bay my body lies,
With all my mates, who once set sail
On board the hapless *Nightingale*."

I raised my head from my pillow high,
His pallid ghost from me did fly,
I little thought when he set sail
He'd end his days in the *Nightingale*.

My father's dwelling I'll forsake,
And far away my way I'll take,
By lonesome wood or distant vale,
I'll mourn his fate in the *Nightingale*.[33]

As mentioned, Barrett made an effort to include songs from all the main periods of English history from the reign of Elizabeth onwards. He had two songs that he could date confidently to the Tudor era, "Go No More a Rushing" and "Go from My Window." About the latter he commented,

> The words of this song are quoted by Beaumont and Fletcher and other poets of the reign of Queen Elizabeth. The melody, in a major key, is in Queen Elizabeth's Virginal Book, and is printed in "A New Booke of Tablature," 1596, and in other books of the same period. The version here given is traditional, and is similar to one of the airs usually sung by Ophelia in "Hamlet."[34]

This is Barrett's traditional version:

Go from my window, my love, my love,
Go from my window, my dear.
The wind is blowing high and the ship is lying by,
So you cannot get a harb'ring here.

Go from my window, my love, my love,
Go from my window, my dear.
The wind's in the west, and the cockle's in his nest,
So ye cannot get a harb'ring here.

Go from my window, my love, my love,
Go from my window, my dear.
The wind and the rain have brought you back again,
But you cannot get a harb'ring here.

Go from my window, my love, my love,
Go from my window, my dear.
The devil's in the man that he will not understan'
That he cannot get a harb'ring here.[35]

Go From My Window

Anon

Go from my win-dow, my love, my love, Go from my win-dow my dear, The

wind is blow-ing high, and the ship is ly-ing by, So you can-not get a har-b'ring here.

Fig. 10.11

The only song that Barrett explicitly dated to the seventeenth century was a "May Song" that he had encountered in both Lancashire and Yorkshire, and even in this instance his attribution was approximate and tentative.[36] But he also collected broadsides, and *English Folk-Songs* included quite a large number of items where the words were clearly taken from popular ballad sheets. A few of these probably dated from the Jacobean period or the Restoration era, the oldest likely being "Ward the Pirate" (aka "Captain Ward and the *Rainbow*"). Some of these ballads were obviously rural in nature, such as "The Honest Ploughman" and "The Old Farmer," whereas others dealt with highway robbery ("Flash Lad"), international politics ("Grand Conversation with Napoleon"), warfare ("Britons Strike Home" and "Paul Jones"), and the domestic consequences of warfare ("Bonny Light Horseman" and "The Soldier's Farewell"). Only a few of the broadsides were datable. "Marboro,'" for example, was likely written to commemorate the death of John, Duke of Marlborough, in 1716, and "Polka Mad" was evidently a late broadside, composed *circa* 1843. Other assorted broadside ballads included "The Gallant Hussar," "The Lost Lady Found," "The Masonic Hymn," and "Advice to Bachelors." One of the most powerful was a transportation ballad, "Botany Bay," which warned of the fate awaiting convicted poachers and thieves.

Come all you young men of learning,
And a warning take by me,
I would have you quit night walking
And shun bad company;
I would have you quit night walking,
Or else you'll rue the day;
You'll rue your transportation, lads,
When you're bound for Botany Bay.

I was brought up in London town
At a place I know full well;
Brought up by honest parents,
For the truth to you I'll tell.
Brought up by honest parents,
And rear'd most tenderly,
Till I became a roving blade,
Which proved my destiny.

My character soon was taken,
And I was sent to jail;
My friends they tried to clear me,
But nothing could prevail.
At the Old Bailey Sessions
The judge to me did say —
"The jury's found you guilty, lad,
So you must go to Botany Bay."

To see my aged father dear,
As he stood near the bar,
Likewise my tender mother,
Her old grey hairs to tear.
In tearing of her old grey locks,
These words to me did say—
"O son! O son! What have you done,
That you're going to Botany Bay?"

It was on the twenty-eighth of May
From England we did steer,
And all things being safe on board
We sailed down the river clear.
And every ship that we passed by,
We heard the sailors say—
"There goes a ship of clever hands,
And they're bound for Botany Bay."

There is a girl in Manchester,
A girl I know full well;
And if ever I get my liberty,
Along with her I'll dwell.
O, then I mean to marry her,
And no more to go astray;
I'll shun all evil company,
Bid adieu to Botany Bay.[37]

Botany Bay

Anon

Come all you young men of learn - ing, And a warn - ing take by me, I would have you quit night - walk - ing and shun bad com - pan - y; I would have you quit night walk - ing or— else you'll rue the day, You'll rue your trans por - ta - tion, lads, When you're bound for— Bot - a - ny Bay.

Fig. 10.12

Much of this broadside literature was eighteenth century in origin, and Barrett had some other items that he could with confidence ascribe to the Georgian era. They included "William and Mary" (from a broadsheet published in 1794), "Cupid, the Pretty Ploughboy" (one of the songs most frequently printed by Catnach, Pitts, and others at Seven Dials), "Good Morning, Pretty Maid," the emigrant song "The Buffalo," and "The Churchwarden's Song," the words for which Barrett had found in a garland published *circa* 1780 titled *The Charms of Cheerfulness*. The fairly short period of England's conflict with the revolutionary French Republic and with its successor, the Napoleonic Empire, was also well represented in *English Folk-Songs*. Examples of broadsides from the early nineteenth century include "Drink Little England Dry," "Grand Conversation of Napoleon" (which was unusually sympathetic to the French emperor), and this stirring patriotic ditty, "Ye Sons of Albion," which was sung to the tune of "To Be a Farmer's Boy:"

Ye sons of Albion, rise to arms and meet the haughty band,
They threaten us with war's alarms and ruin to our land.
But let no rebel Frenchman sans-culottes,
Nor the dupes of tyranny boast
To conquer the English, the Irish, and the Scots,
Or to land upon our coast.

There's hopeless Holland wears their yoke, and so doth faithless Spain,
But we will give them hearts of oak and drive them from the main.
So let no rebel Frenchman, etc.

The rulers of the universe they proudly wish to be,
But they shall meet with due reverse, for England shall be free.
So let no rebel Frenchman, etc.[38]

Ye Sons of Albion

Anon

Voice

Ye sons of Al-bion, rise to arms, And meet the haugh-ty band; They

threat - en us with war's al-arms, And ru - in to our land; But let no reb-el Frenchman

sans - cul ottes, nor the dupes of tyr - an-y boast ...._ To_ con-quer the Eng-lish, the

Ir ish and the Scots, Or to land up-on our coast ...._ or to land up-on our coast.

Fig. 10.13

Barrett was primarily interested in old songs, so it is hardly surprising that his collection included only a few items that seemingly dated from the Victorian era. Those that did were from the early years of Victoria's reign, such as "A Jug of This," a drinking song that had been included in a garland titled *Little Warblers* printed *circa* 1838, and "Polka Mad," which reflected the craze for polka dancing in the 1840s. "A Jug of This" was a rare instance in which Barrett provided fairly detailed information on both words and tune, ascribing the text to broadside publisher Ryle of Seven Dials and the melody to a farm laborer at Melksham, Wiltshire, whose singing he had listened to in 1857.

It seems clear that Barrett took pains to ensure that his book had plenty of variety in types of songs and in the subject matter that they dealt with. Because most of his collecting was done in the countryside, there were naturally many items dealing in one way or another with agriculture and other aspects of rural life. Some of these country songs were joyous evocations of farming as a vocation and celebrations of the working life of the agricultural laborer. Examples include "The New Mown Hay," "The Seasons," "The Country Lass," "Sheep Shearing," and "Harvest Home Song." Almost as often, however, they were quasi-political compositions with a message. Songs such as "The Painful Plough," "The Old Farmer," and "Good Morning, Pretty Maid" stressed the value of agriculture to the nation and reminded listeners of the hardships of farming and of the farm laborer's life of unremitting toil. The sentiment that rural England had changed for the worse since the mid-eighteenth century, and that neither the aged nor the lowly husbandman received the respect that they deserved was expressed trenchantly in "The Honest Ploughman" (aka "Ninety Years Ago"):

Come all you jolly husbandmen and listen to my song,
I'll relate the life of a ploughman, and not detain you long;
My father was a farmer, who banished grief and woe,
My mother was a dairy maid—that's ninety years ago.

My father had a little farm, a harrow and a plough,
My mother had some pigs and fowls, a pony and a cow;
They didn't hire a servant, but both their work did do,
As I have heard my parents say, just ninety years ago.

The Honest Ploughman

Anon

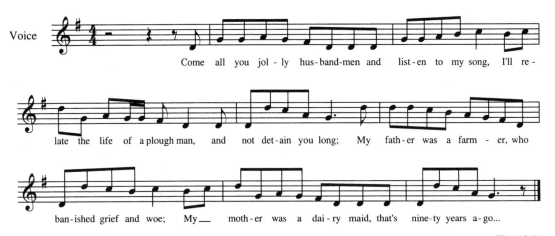

Voice

Come all you jol - ly hus-band-men and list-en to my song, I'll re -

late the life of a plough man, and not det-ain you long; My fath-er was a farm - er, who

ban-ished grief and woe; My__ moth-er was a dai-ry maid, that's nine-ty years a-go...

Fig. 10.14

The rent that time was not so high, but far as I will pen,
For now one family's nearly twice as big as then was ten;
When I was born my father used to harrow, plough and sow,
I think I've heard my mother say, 'twas ninety years ago.

To drive the plough my father did a boy engage
Until that I had just arrived to seven years of age;
So then he did no servant want, my mother milked the cow,
And with the lark I rose each morn to go and drive the plough.

The farmers' wives in every part themselves the cows did milk,
They did not wear the dandy veils and gowns made out of silk,
They did not ride blood horses, like the farmers' wives do now,
The daughters went a-milking, and the sons went out to plough.

When I was fifteen years of age, I used to thrash and sow,
I harrowed, ploughed, and harvest time I used to reap and mow;
When I was twenty years of age, I could manage well the farm,
I could hedge and ditch, and plough and sow, or thrash within the barn.

At length when I was twenty-five, I took myself a wife,
Compelled to leave my father's house, as I have changed my life,
The younger children in my place, my father's work would do,
Then daily as an husbandman to labour I did go.

My wife and me, tho' very poor, could keep a pig and cow,
She could sit and knit, and spin, and I the land could plough;
There nothing was upon a farm at all but I could do,
I find things very different now—that's many years ago.

We lived along contented, and banished pain and grief,
We had not occasion then to ask parish relief;
But now my hairs are grown quite grey, I cannot well engage
To work as I had used to do—I'm ninety years of age.

But now that I'm ninety years of age, and poverty do feel,
If for relief I go, they shove me in a Whig Bastille,

Where I may hang my hoary head, and pine in grief and woe,
My father did not see the like, just ninety years ago.

When a man has laboured all his life, to do his country good,
He's respected just as much when old as a donkey in a wood,
His days are gone and past, and he may weep in grief and woe,
The times are very different now, to ninety years ago.[39]

Hunting songs were common enough, Barrett found; they included "Tally Ho! Hark Away" and a "Somerset Hunting Song" that Barrett remarked was popular in other counties too. He had collected one fishing song, "The Barbel," and one transportation ballad intended as a warning against poaching. Two other common types of rural song were songs of occasion and drinking songs. The former were mainly associated with either harvest time or the return of fertility to the earth in spring; they included two May songs and a "Peace-Egger's Song" from Cheshire that was sung at Easter. The latter included "Sheep Shearing Day," "John Barleycorn," and the previously mentioned "Harvest Home Song." Other drinking songs, such as "The Punch Ladle," "A Jug of This," "Drink Little England Dry," and "Churchwarden's Song," were of a more general provenance, and Barrett apparently noted some of them in urban locations, such as the taverns of London's docklands.

As might be expected, *English Folk-Songs* included several patriotic songs, such as "Britons, Strike Home" as well as "Ye Sons of Albion." There were quite a few sea songs: the oldest were "Go from My Window" and "Ward the Pirate." "Paul Jones" and "The *Nightingale*" were maritime ballads, while "Saucy Sailor Boy," which was sung by factory girls in East London, was a song about a carefree sailor lover. It is not clear whether Barrett actually noted any of these songs from mariners, but he confidently stated that "The Cuckoo," although a woman's lament, was very popular among sailors in the early decades of the nineteenth century.

The Cuckoo

Anon

Fig. 10.15

Come all you pretty fair maids, wherever you be,
And never fix your mind on a sailor so free;
For the leaves they will wither and the root will decay,
O, I am forsaken, ah! woe, well-a-day.

The cuckoo is a fine bird, and she sings as she flies,
She brings us good tidings, she tells us no lies;
She sucks little birds' eggs to make her voice clear,
And never sings cuckoo till the summer draws near.

O, meeting is a pleasure, and parting is a grief,

An inconstant lover is worse than a thief—
A thief can but rob you, and take all you have,
An inconstant lover will bring you to the grave.

O the hours that I've passed in the arms of my dear
Can never be thought of without shedding a tear;
All hardships for him I would cheerfully bear,
And at night on my pillow forget all my care.[40]

"The Cuckoo" was one of relatively few love laments to be found in *English Folk-Songs,* although others included "The *Nightingale*" and "Bonny Light Horseman" (about a soldier lover who met his death on foreign soil). Most of the love songs in the collection were ballads. Some, such as "Lost Lady Found" and "William and Mary," related tales that ended with the reunion of lovers after years of separation. In "The Gallant Hussar" a young woman overcomes opposition from her parents and her soldier lover's commitment to a military career to obtain her goal of matrimony, while in "Undaunted Mary" (aka "The Banks of Dundee") the heroine murders a wealthy suitor and her uncle to avoid rape and to vindicate her right to marry a ploughboy. "Cupid, The Pretty Ploughboy" similarly celebrates the triumph of love in overcoming the class barrier between lady and agricultural laborer. Not all these broadsides about lovers had happy endings. In "The Soldier's Farewell" (aka "The White Cockade") the young woman is left bewailing the loss of her lover to the military, while, as we have seen earlier, "Mary of the Moor" is a tragic ballad in which an unmarried woman with a young baby attempts to return to her father but dies from exposure on his doorstep. The collection also included several songs that might be characterized as anti-matrimonial in spirit, such as "Advice to Bachelors" (stay single), "Good Morning, Pretty Maid" (the girl refuses to become a farmer's wife), and the comic ballad "Richard of Taunton Dean," which describes a failed attempt at courtship.

Barrett's documentation of his sources, never elaborate, was sometimes non-existent. He slipped into his book a number of items, some of them particularly attractive traditional songs, about which he provided no information. For example, one is left in the dark as to where he found texts and tunes for "John Barleycorn," "Derry Down Dale," "Mary of the Moor," and even the beautiful "The Banks of Sweet Primroses":

The Banks of Sweet Primroses

Anon

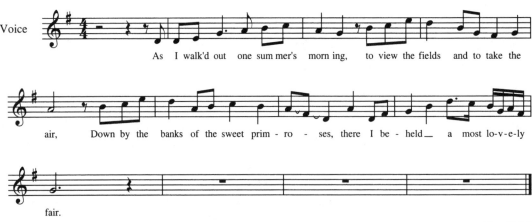

Fig. 10.16

As I walk'd out one summer's morning to view the fields and to take the air,
Down by the banks of the sweet primroses, there I beheld a most lovely fair.

I said, "Fair maid, where are you going, what is the reason for all your grief?"
For she was crying and deeply sighing—"Tell me your sorrows, I may give relief."

"Stand off! Stand off! you're quite deceitful, 'tis you have caused all my grief and pain;
Without your knowledge I have loved you dearly, and now your comforting is all in vain."

"I'll go down to some lonesome valley, where none on earth shall my troubles find,
Where the pretty birds shall sing songs of sweetness, and bring true comfort to my wearied mind."

"Dear maid, believe me, I will ne'er deceive thee; give your consent, we will married be;
Your days of sadness I'll change to gladness, and love shall change all your thoughts to me."

Come, all you maidens, that go a courting, pray give attention to what I say;
For there's many a dark and cloudy morning turns out to be a sunshiny day.[41]

As is evident from the song titles mentioned above, Barrett's collection included a wealth of interesting material and more than a handful of beautiful, expressive, and powerful songs, both narrative ballads and folk lyrics. It provided a handy compendium for the use of singers, but it was frustratingly inadequate as a work of scholarship since Barrett was far from systematic in his provision of information about when, where and from whom he had collected his material and neither did he include much in the way of discussion of the songs. However, like Baring-Gould's, Kidson's, and Stokoe's publications, *English Folk-Songs* served as a stimulus to further collecting. This, it seemed, was merely the tip of the iceberg, and it appeared likely that there were many, many more folksongs to be discovered in the counties and towns of England. What was now needed was an attempt to investigate each of the regions of England in more depth. Clearly the counties of Sussex and Surrey in the south of England were going to repay further attention, but regions further away from London also looked very promising, especially the northeast.

The Making of a Folksong Collector

Of all the contributors to the Late Victorian folksong revival Lucy Etheldred Broadwood (1858-1929) developed the broadest vision of what should be attempted, although she came to this perspective only gradually, over the course of a decade.[42] Many individuals were involved in the wave of vernacular song collecting that we call the Late Victorian folksong revival, but, as we have seen, the most substantial contributions during the 1880s were made by Burne, Stokoe, Baring-Gould, and Kidson.[43] Broadwood's name must be added to this list of key collectors although her publications date from 1890 onwards. Of this group of pioneer collectors she was the only one who lived and noted songs in the home counties.[44] Her proximity to (and later residence in) London meant that unlike the others she was able to combine her interest in traditional song with ongoing participation in the capital city's music scene. This, together with the leisure afforded by a private income, allowed her to play a leading role in the Folk-Song Society when it was established in the late 1890s. But why was Broadwood eager to play such a role? How had she developed a burning interest in folksong, and why in 1898 would she be regarded as already a figure of some stature in the movement? This and subsequent chapters will attempt to answer these questions. Broadwood's first significant publication appeared in 1890, and so it is to her work that we now turn.

Born in 1858, Lucy Broadwood was the youngest daughter of Henry Fowler Broadwood, a successful businessman whose firm had a long history of building high quality Broadwood pianos.[45] Although their money came from trade, the Broadwoods had been accepted into the local country gentry, and they were acquainted socially with several aristocrats. Unmarried, Lucy was thus an upper-middle-class spinster, and she had a private income, initially in the form of an allowance from her parents, later derived from investments in the family firm and in other stocks. The family had a London residence as well as a large manor house at Lyne, near Rusper, on the Surrey-Sussex border, and after her father's death in 1893 Lucy made London rather than Lyne her principal residence, eventually obtaining her own apartment, which she shared with her niece Barbara Cra'ster.

Lucy Broadwood might be said to have inherited her interest in folk music from her uncle, the Reverend John Broadwood, an important early Victorian collector and the editor of the 1847 publication *Old English Songs*.[46] She stated on one occasion that she had been "fired" by her uncle's collection when she first became aware of it, around 1870.[47] But Uncle John was not the only source of folksongs in the Broadwood house. Her father had also collected a number of old songs locally during the 1830s and 1840s, and he occasionally sang them at home.[48] Lucy's first encounter with folksong was probably in the mid-1860s: she recalled that when she was a child of six a small group of old laborers in smock frocks came around at Christmas time to sing ballads, apparently a rare event even then. She also remembered an old man with two sons coming to Lyne and singing "The Green Mossy Banks of the Lea" outside the front door. The last verse ended with the lines "Go home to your father and mother, and thus you may tell them from me; There's many a poor maiden far fairer than them as has great propertee." When the singers were invited into the house and asked to repeat the song, the old man violently nudged his boys and tried to prevent them from singing what might wound the feelings of the family.[49] Moreover, throughout much of her early childhood Lucy had a Scottish nurse who taught her nursery rhymes and sang ballads to her. She learned to play the piano and had singing lessons as part of her education as a young lady, and a handful of folksongs seem to have been part of her repertoire from quite an early age.

In studying Lucy Broadwood's life and her role in the folksong revival we can draw upon a primary source that is not available for any other figure of similar stature: a set of personal diaries.[50] These diaries offer a unique record of her increasing involvement with the folksong revival, revealing her own circumstances and something of her relationships with her friends and her informants. They permit us to date with more accuracy some of her collecting, and make possible a more intimate account of her contribution than that of any other participant in the movement.[51] The diaries—at least, those that are still extant in the Surrey History Centre—begin in October 1882 when Broadwood was aged 24 and living at the family country house at Lyne. The entries for 1883 make it evident that in her mid-twenties she was already an accomplished amateur musician who sang and played piano frequently at public as well as private 'entertainments.' She was already looking for repertoire other than "the usual drawing room ballads" (her phrase).[52] That year she supplemented "Home, Sweet Home" with "Croodlin' Doo," "Jock o' Hazeldean," and "How Could Ye Gang, Lassie?"

The early diaries also make it possible for us to picture the lifestyle of this Victorian young lady. Her health was always delicate and she suffered rather frequently from feverish colds that affected her throat and periodically prevented her singing. Although she sometimes had family responsibilities, such as helping to look after sick or aging relatives, Lucy evidently had plenty of time to devote to her chosen pursuits. The main ones were religion, art, reading, and music. There were several clergymen in the Broadwood family, and Lucy was a practicing Church of England Christian, who played the organ in church and trained the local choirboys. She read books on theology and on the history of Christianity, and she sometimes praised or criticized sermons in her diary entries. Without seriously questioning basic dogma she inclined to a rather liberal and rationalist version of the faith, and she was unsympathetic to fundamentalism or evangelicalism. Lucy's father owned a collection of valuable paintings, and she had a strong interest in art history. She sketched and painted (mainly landscapes), and she often visited art galleries. She read a lot of novels, including some of Baring-Gould's, and she also regularly scanned literary periodicals in French and German as well as English, a particular favorite being the *Revue des Deux Mondes*. She enjoyed biography, especially biographies of musicians and composers. Which brings us to her first love: classical music.

To a large degree Lucy's life centered around music: concert-going (several times a week when she was in London for a 'season'), piano practice (she was a talented pianist, capable of accompanying professional singers), singing lessons (her principal singing teacher was named Wallace Shakespeare), choirs (including membership in the prestigious Bach Choir), musical 'at-homes' and dinner parties, fund-raising 'entertainments' and charity concerts, collaborations with other musicians, either as pianist or singer, composing piano arrangements, and editing music manuscripts. There is an evident evolution in her musical tastes over the years: she began as a Wagnerite, came to prefer Beethoven and Brahms, and then discovered the works of Johann Sebastian Bach. Bach quickly became her favorite composer, although in the late 1880s she fell in love with the music of Edvard Grieg. She also explored the work of such contemporary British composers as Frederic Cowen,[53] George Alexander Macfarren,[54] Alexander Mackenzie,[55] Charles Hubert Parry, Charles Villiers Stanford, Arthur Sullivan, and Arthur Somervell.[56] Art songs by one or more of these composers were usually included in her concert programs. Mackenzie, Parry, Somervell, and Stanford she came to know personally, through her close friendship with another musician and family friend, J. A. "Alec" Fuller Maitland. Fuller Maitland introduced her to Elizabethan madrigals and lute music, and to the compositions of William Lawes and Henry Purcell. Lucy joined the Purcell Society, and in the mid-1890s undertook to edit the scores of two unpublished Purcell operas, *Amphitreyon* and *The Gordian Knot Untied*. Lucy's own composing was limited to a handful of songs, such as "Annie's Tryst" and "Nae Mair," and a fairly large number of piano arrangements of vernacular songs. Some of the latter were published as sheet music by Boosey, the most successful in terms of sales being "Jess Macpharlane." These royalties seem to have been Lucy's only form of earned income apart from the royalties she received from her published folksong collections.[57]

That, however, is to jump ahead. It was in 1884, when she was in her mid-twenties, that her brother James's engagement to her friend Evelyn Fuller Maitland resulted in Lucy getting to know Alec Fuller Maitland better, and he appears to have immediately encouraged her interest in folksong as well as Renaissance and Baroque music. By November of that year Lucy had obtained a British Museum reader's ticket and begun making good use of it.[58] She discovered the publications of the Percy Society, including Dixon's *Ancient Poems, Ballads and Songs of the Peasantry of England,*[59] as well as the carol collections of Davies Gilbert[60] and William Sandys.[61] The next summer a chance encounter at the

British Museum with musicologist Ellis Wooldridge,[62] who would subsequently edit a truncated edition of Chappell's *Popular Music of the Olden Time*,[63] stimulated her interest in the Victorian song collectors and in the modal character of folksong tunes.[64] Then in November she also met antiquarian F. E. Sawyer. At the time Sawyer was doing the research for a paper titled "Sussex Songs and Music" that he would read at a meeting of the British Archaeological Association and also publish as a pamphlet in 1886.[65] Sawyer emphasized to Lucy the importance of her uncle John's *Old English Songs,* and gave her copies of a few folksongs he had himself collected in Sussex.[66] She then apparently discovered that her father possessed the words (but no tunes) of some other folksongs that he and/or his brother John had noted in Sussex in the late 1830s or early 1840s.[67] She also inquired whether any more were to be found locally, and received one (the title is unfortunately not recorded) on 1 December from a Mr. J. Cobb.[68] This seems to have been her first attempt at song-collecting.

February of the next year (1886) found Lucy vacationing in South Wales. At the village of Dinas Powys she attended a local 'entertainment' and was delighted to hear a Mr. O. Fisher sing "Sally in Our Alley" and "Bold Robin Hood."[69] The latter sent her researching Robin Hood ballads in the Roxburghe and other broadside collections, while later that year, when her cousin Aubrey Birch Reynardson sang "Jockey to the Fair" at a charity concert in Stepney, she discovered that he and his brother Herbert shared her interest in folksong.[70] Although it is just possible that this combination of events stimulated Lucy to conceive the idea of a new edition of *Old English Songs,* there is nothing else in the diaries to indicate that she was thinking along those lines in 1886. The genesis of Lucy's first publication therefore seems to have taken place during the years 1887-88.

Sussex Songs

Lucy's friendship with Herbert Birch Reynardson blossomed during the winter of 1887-88. She greatly admired the music that Herbert composed for *A Masque of Flowers,* a production at the Prince of Wales Theatre in London; her diary records that she was "enchanted with it."[71] By now she had thought of the idea of editing a new edition of *Old English Songs,* and Herbert agreed that Geoffrey Dusart's piano arrangements needed to be replaced. She sent him a copy of one of the songs, "Rosebuds in June," and he obliged by re-harmonizing it.[72] By February 1888 Lucy was visiting her cousin in his London apartment and playing his new composition, a piece for two pianos, with him.[73] This was the year that she discovered the music of Edvard Grieg, and also Stanford's "Irish Symphony," which she loved. Reading between the lines, one can sense that Lucy and Herbert had jointly come to realize that there could be a renaissance of English national art music if it were re-rooted in folksong, an aesthetic vision that Vaughan Williams was later to champion so successfully.[74] Their first way of exploring this idea was for Herbert to write some new piano arrangements of folksongs, and what better ones to choose than those collected by Uncle John?

That summer Lucy began looking for additional material to complement that in *Old English Songs.* Her initial strategy was to write to people she knew who she thought might possess or might be able to locate suitable songs.[75] She also solicited help from the family's friends and acquaintances in the area, and followed up some of their suggestions. In this way she obtained material from local huntsmen, mummers, and participants in village 'harvest homes.' She also sought her father's help, but bouts of sickness apparently prevented her collecting anything from him until the spring of 1889 when she noted "Troy Town" from his singing.[76] He appears to have given her about twenty songs in total, although several of these were the same as those noted by his brother John.[77] By that time Lucy's editorial project was well under way, and it was already the stuff of gossip in London music circles. William Barrett, who had begun putting together *English Folk-Songs* (which, as we have seen, would be published in 1891),[78] contacted her, "begging for Sussex tunes to include in his book" (as Lucy put it), but she declined to contribute on the grounds that "HFBR [Herbert] has them already in hand."[79] The Reverend Sabine Baring-Gould, who had just published the first volume of *Songs and Ballads of the West,* also heard about the project and wrote to her about Devon and Cornish traditional song, a letter that marked the effective beginning of their spasmodic collaboration.[80]

Sussex Songs (Popular Songs of Sussex) was published in April 1890, although the publication date is usually given as 1889.[81] The cover carried Herbert's name, not Lucy's, but she nonetheless proudly dispatched a complimentary copy to Baring-Gould.[82] The book contained twenty-six songs, of which ten were additions made by Lucy, the remainder reprinted from her uncle's *Old English Songs* of 1847. So although they were mixed together in the book, the items in *Sussex Songs* really fell into two categories: those reissued from John Broadwood's collection, and the new offerings. As Ellis Wooldridge and F. E. Sawyer had pointed out, the old material was still interesting and valuable, in part because Broadwood had made a real effort to capture the modal tunes accurately. According to Lucy, her uncle had had considerable trouble in making sure that his collaborator Geoffrey F. Dusart, a music teacher and organist, did not alter the tunes. She related that "Dusart made great outcries over intervals which shocked his musical standards. A flat seventh never WAS and never COULD be! It is recorded that Mr. Broadwood, confirming his vocal intervals by vehement blasts on his flute, replied: 'Musically it may be wrong, but I will have it exactly as my singers sang it.'"[83] Such an articulate commitment to absolute authenticity in tune collection was unusual at the time, and marked an important step forward. On the other hand, John Broadwood had been more interested in saving tunes than words, and in several instances he neglected to obtain more than one verse of a song. But, at its best, the 1847 publication had united traditional melodies and full texts, and both had been collected in the field. That complete reliance on oral tradition had been a methodological breakthrough of sorts, although isolated instances of the same approach had occurred before in the work of earlier collectors. Nonetheless, the small book had its weaknesses, notably the absence of complete texts for many of the songs, weaknesses that Lucy had an opportunity to remedy, if she so chose.

Although a systematic replacement of the old piano arrangements with new ones meant that *Sussex Songs* would be much more than a new edition of *Old English Songs* even without the addition of extra songs, Lucy declined to alter her uncle's work much in other respects. She did partially rename one of the songs: "The Damsel in the West" became, although only in the table of contents, "The Maiden in the West." On the other hand, "Gipsy Song," which was really "The Lost Lady Found," retained its original title, as did "The Poacher's Song" which is better known as "In Thorny Woods." It is possible that the melody of the latter was actually collected by Lucy's father, Henry Broadwood, since a manuscript copy appears to be in Henry's hand rather than John's.

In Thorny Woods

Anon

Fig. 10.17

In Thorny Woods in Buckinghamshire, right fol lol lo de li de O,
Three keepers' houses stood three square, fol de rol lol de ri da,
Three keepers' houses stood three square, about a mile from each other they were,
In order to look after the deer, fol de rol lol de rol li do.

I and my dogs went out one night, right fol lol lo de li de O,
The moon and stars they shone so bright, fol de rol lol de ri da,
O'er hedges, ditches, gates and stiles, with my two dogs close at my heels,
To look for a buck in Parkmoor fields, fol de rol lol de rol li do.

The very first night I had bad luck, right fol lol lo, &c.,

For my very best dog in the breast got stuck, fol de rol, &c.,
He came to me so limping lame, he was not able to follow the game,
How sorry was I to see the same! Fol de rol, &c.

I searched his wounds and found them slight, right fol lol lo, &c.,
'Twas done by the keeper out of spite, fol de rol, &c.,
I took my pikestaff in my hand, and ranged the woods to find out the man,
To see whether I his hide could tan, fol de rol, &c.

When I had ranged all that night, right fol lol lo, &c.,
Until the next morning it was daylight, fol de rol, &c.,
When I had ranged all that night, until the next morning it was daylight,
I thought it high time to take my flight, fol de rol, &c.

Then I went home and went to bed, right fol lol lo, &c.,
And limping Jack went in my stead, fol de rol, &c.,
In Parkmoor fields, oh! there he found a brave fat buck running over the ground,
And my two dogs soon pulled him down, fol de rol, &c.

I listened a while to hear their note, right fol lol lo, &c.,
Jack drew a quivy, and cut his throat, fol de rol, &c.,
How you'd have laughed to see limping Jack come hopping along with a buck at his back,
And hide it under the miller's haystack, fol de rol, &c.

We sent for a butcher to dress up our game, right fol lol lo, &c.,
And likewise another to sell the same, fol de rol, &c.,
A very fine haunch we offered for sale, 'twas to an old woman that sold bad ale,
And, hang her! she brought us all to jail, fol de rol, &c.

Now sessions are over, assizes are near, right fol lol lo, &c.,
Now Jack and I we must appear, fol de rol, &c.,
Your bucks and does may range so free, but hares and rabbits they are for me,
A poacher's life is the life for me, fol de rol, &c.[84]

The subject matter of several of the other items from *Old English Songs* was daily work or everyday life in the English countryside, as in "The Woodcutter," "The Ploughboy," and "The Serving-man and the Husbandman." Although John Broadwood had collected his texts or text fragments (as well as tunes) from rural informants, several appear to be derived indirectly from broadsheets. That was true, for example, of two sea ballads ("The Privateer" and "The Fourteenth of July"), of "The Noble Lord," and of "The Lost Lady Found." It may also be true for "The Maiden in the West" and "In Lancashire," but he had obtained the words for only one verse of each of these songs, so it is more difficult to tell. Lucy declined the option of searching out and adding the missing verses, even when the song was obviously a broadside ballad and the full text was available in the British Museum.

Sussex Songs did not inherit many traditional ballads from *Old English Songs.* John Broadwood had noted tunes for just two: "The Bailiff's Daughter of Islington" and "Lord Bateman." He had also written down his unnamed informant's text of "The Bailiff's Daughter." Lucy therefore gave both, commenting that the tune differed from "the traditional one to which the ballad is commonly sung" as well as from that printed by Chappell in *Popular Music of the Olden Time.* Her comment revealed that she had previously heard the ballad sung, presumably by a local singer, and that she was already familiar with one of the greatest accomplishments of the Victorian vernacular song revival, Chappell's *magnum opus.* This is the version collected by John Broadwood, as reprinted in *Sussex Songs.*

There was a youth, and a well bred youth,
And he was a squire's son,
And he fell in love with the bailiff's daughter dear,
That liv'd in fair Islington.

The Bailiff's Daughter of Islington

Anon

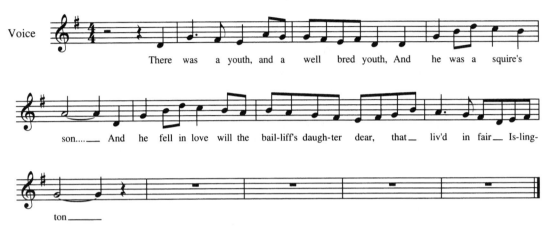

There was a youth, and a well bred youth, And he was a squire's son..... And he fell in love will the bail-liff's daugh-ter dear, that liv'd in fair Is-ling-ton

Fig.10.18

As soon as his father came for to know
His fond and foolish mind,
He sent him away up to fair London town
As apprentice there to bind.

And when he had served his seven long years,
His true love he ne'er had seen;
Whilst he had shed many a tear for her,
She had little thought of him.

As he was riding out one day,
The weather being fine and dry,
He thought he saw his own true love,
As he was riding by.

She stepped up to his horse's head,
Took hold of his bridle rein;
And she said, "Kind sir, will you let me ride a
mile
Just to ease my weary, weary pain?"

He said, "Fair maid, where came you from?
Oh, where were you bred and born?"

"In fair Islington, kind sir," said she,
"Where I have had many a scorn."

"Pray did you know the bailiff's daughter dear
That lived in fair Islington?"
"Yes, kind sir, I knew her very well,
But she hath been dead so long agone."

"Then I'll saddle up my milk white steed,
And take my arrow and bow;
And I'll go down to some foreign country
Where no one doth me know!"

"Oh no! kind sir, do not do so!
For she is by your side!
And here she doth stand at your fair horse's head
All ready to be your bride!"

"Oh farewell to father, farewell to mother!
Farewell to friend and foe!
For now I'll enjoy my own true love,
Who I thought was dead so long ago!"[85]

John Broadwood had noted only a fragment of a text for "Lord Bateman," but the words he printed were sufficient to indicate that his informant had probably learned the words from a broadside. We have seen in chapter 5 that Charlotte Burne had collected a somewhat similar version of the ballad and that she published both tune and text in *Shropshire Folk-Lore*. Lucy thus had the option of providing a full set of verses derived either from an old printed source or from oral tradition. It would have been quite easy to include the broadside text but she decided not to do so. In her view the tune—and, of course, Herbert's arrangement—was what mattered. This is the melody that John Broadwood had collected:[86]

Lord Bateman

Anon

Lord Bate-man he had a mind to trav-el in - to some for - eign coun -
try, Where he was tak-en and put in pris - on, till of his life__ he was quite wear - y.

Fig.10.19

The new material in *Sussex Songs* appears to have been collected by Lucy in the villages near Lyne. It reflected different aspects of rural life in the south of England. "The Nobleman and the Thresherman" was a broadside ballad that had evidently been taken into local oral tradition because it reflected the hardships and aspirations of landless agricultural laborers living in the area. It captures the pride and self-reliance of the rural worker but at the same time his sense of grievance about his landless condition and low wages.

> A nobleman there lived in the village of late;
> There was a poor thresherman, his family was great;
> He had got seven children and most of them were small;
> He'd nothing but hard labour for to maintain them all.
>
> This nobleman he met with this poor man one day,
> And unto this poor thresherman these very words did say:
> "You are a poor thresherman, I know it to be true,
> And how do you get your living so well as you now do?"
>
> "Sometimes I do reap, and sometimes I do sow,
> And sometimes I a-hedging, and a-ditching too, do go;
> There's nothing goes amiss with me, my harrow or my plough:
> And so I get my living by the sweat of my brow."
>
> "When my day's work is done I go home late at night;
> All in my wife and family I take a great delight;
> My children they come round me with their prattle and their toys;
> And that is all the pleasure, that a poor man enjoys."
>
> "My wife she is willing to join me in the yoke;
> We live like unto turtle-doves, and ne'er a one provoke,
> These times are very bad, and we are very poor,
> But still we get our living, and we keep cold from the door."
>
> "You are an honest fellow, you speak well of your wife;
> And you shall both live happy all the last part of your life:
> Here's forty acres of good land I'll freely give to thee
> For to maintain your wife and self, and your sweet family!"
>
> God bless all the farmers that take pity on poor men,
> I wish of them with all my heart their souls in heav'n may stand;
> And may those that are left behind, a better pattern take,
> That they may follow after as quick as they can.[87]

The Nobleman and the Thresherman

Anon

Voice

A nob - le-man there liv - ed in the vill - age of late,____ There
was a poor____ thresh - er man, his fam - i - ly was great;____ He had got sev - en
____ chid ren and most of them were small.... He'd no - thing but hard lab - our for
to main tain them all....____

Fig. 10.20

Lucy had picked up two carols sung locally, one of them ("A Glorious Angel") from a mummers' play titled *St. George, the Turk and the Seven Champions of Christendom.* Her text was a composite which combined lyrics that she had obtained from two of the actors in the play, neither of whom was able to write out a complete version from memory. The other religious song, "The Moon Shines Bright," which Lucy, perhaps erroneously, believed to be a traditional folk-carol, was evidently intended to be sung on Christmas morning.

The moon shines bright and the stars give a light,
In a little time it will be day;
The Lord our God, He calls upon us all,
And bids us awake and pray.
The Lord our God, He calls upon us all,
And bids us awake and pray.

Awake, awake, good people all!
Awake and you shall hear
How Christ was born all upon this morn,
For the Lord loved us so dear,
How Christ was born, etc.

So dear, so dear Christ loved us,
And for our sins was slain
So pray leave off your wickedness,
And turn to the Lord again.
So pray leave off, etc.

The fields so green, so wondrous green,
As green as any leaf;
The Lord our God, He watered them

With His heavenly dew so sweet.
The Lord our God, etc.

The life of man, it is but a span,
His beauty is like any flower;
Today he is strong, and to-morrow he is gone,
For he fadeth in less than an hour.
Today he is strong, etc.

Repent, repent, good people all,
Repent, while yet you may,
For it is too late for to repent
When dead and turned to clay.
For it is too late, etc.

Now my song it is done, and I must be gone,
No longer can I tarry here;—
So God bless you all, both great and small,
And send you a happy new year.
So God bless you all, etc.[88]

The Moon Shines Bright

Anon

Voice

The moon shines bright and the stars give a light, In a lit - tle time it will be day.... The Lord our__ God, He calls up-on us all, And__ bids us a - wake and pray._____ The Lord our__ God, He calls up-on us all, And bids us a - wake and pray...._____

Fig. 10.21

From local village festivities she had collected a harvest supper song ("Bango") and three drinking songs ("Fathom the Bowl," "I've Been to France, I've Been to Dover," and "Drink Old England Dry"). There were also three new hunting songs: "Bold Reynard the Fox," "Last Valentine's Day," and a pretty lyric titled, "The Sweet Rosy Morning."

> The sweet rosy morning smiles over the hills,
> With blushes adorning the meadows and rills;
> The sweet rosy morning smiles over the hills,
> With blushes adorning the meadows and rills.
> And the merry, merry, merry horn cries "Come, come away!"
> And the merry, merry, merry horn cries "Come, come away!"
> Awake from your slumbers and hail the new day,
> Awake from your slumbers and hail the new day.
>
> The fox runs before us, he seems for to fly,
> And pants to the chorus of the hounds in full cry;
> The fox runs before us, he seems for to fly,
> And pants to the chorus of the hounds in full cry.
> And the merry, merry, merry horn &c.
>
> When our days work is ended we home do retire,
> And we pull off our boots by the light of the fire;
> When our days work is ended we home do retire,
> And we pull off our boots by the light of the fire.
> And the merry, merry, merry horn &c.[89]

The Sweet Rosy Morning

Anon/Richard Leveridge

Fig. 10.22

Lucy clearly regarded "The Sweet Rosy Morning" as a folksong, but it raises the tricky issue of the relationship between folksongs and other vernacular songs. It was an eighteenth-century song, probably composed sometime during the early decades of the century and printed in several songbooks published during the reign of George II. This printed version, called "The Sweet Rosy Morn," had a fine tune composed by Richard Leveridge, the author of quite a number of vernacular songs that lived on in popular memory for several centuries, and the text was slightly different from Broadwood's.[90] Leveridge's "Sweet Rosy Morn" had apparently entered oral tradition in the county of Sussex about a century-and-a-half prior to its collection as a folksong, and during that interval of time it had metamorphosed to some degree. The tune had altered more than the words, with the result that it had turned into a somewhat different song from that composed by Leveridge. Yet it was still a very close relative. So had it become a folksong or was it still a vernacular song with a known author? The classification is arbitrary, and in a sense matters little, but "The Sweet Rosy Morning" provides a good example of the sometimes close relationship between urban popular song and rural tradition.

Sussex Songs was essentially a family affair, something that Lucy did primarily for her father and her cousin, but it had stimulated in her a fascination with folksong that she would never lose. During the next three years her involvement took four main forms: incorporating a few folksongs into her singing repertoire, research in the British Museum and other libraries designed to make sure that she was familiar with all existing printed collections of old songs, collaboration with Alec Fuller Maitland on a ground-breaking printed collection of 'county songs,' and collecting vernacular songs herself whenever and wherever she had an opportunity.

Contacts, Research, and Collecting, 1891-92

In the fall of 1890 Lucy began collecting again. Somehow—the diaries do not make it clear exactly how and when they initially met—she had found a valuable informant in the village of Cuckfield, Sussex. This was Samuel Willett, the village baker, who supplemented his income by performing at local events.[91] Sometime in September 1890 Lucy apparently contacted him by mail, enclosing a copy of *Sussex Songs*. Willett replied to her inquiries on 1 October in the following terms:

> Respected madam, I desire to acknowledge the receipt of letter and Book of Songs with many thanks. I cannot see any way clear to be of service to you unless I spend a convenient day at your residence and give a general recital of songs and music. I am sometimes requested to furnish a song (words and music) for which my usual charge is half a crown. As, however, you would like a considerable variety, say 40 or 50, the task would occupy some days and then, perhaps, the whole would hardly be acceptable for circulation. My late father was a man of many songs of which I have retained to memory about 60 and to indite these with piano arrangements would involve much time and consequently, a monetary consideration. If it is your wish I will willingly come to Lyne and assist you in compiling some of the best of my stock, and also I will leave the question of remuneration to your generosity.[92]

Before arranging such a session as Willett proposed, Lucy wanted to find out more about his repertoire, and he obliged by sending her several song lists. One such list contained thirty-five items, of which Lucy seemingly identified twenty of interest, and she apparently noted several of the tunes from his singing. For some twenty other songs Willett wrote out the tunes (with partial words) from memory in a small music manuscript book, which he mailed to her.[93] By July Lucy had selected twenty-seven items that she was willing to purchase, for which she paid twenty-seven shillings, a considerable reduction from Willett's normal asking price.[94] The songs included "John Appleby" (a hop-pickers' song from Kent), "Maying," "The Curly Headed Boy," "The Farmer's Boy," and a drinking song about a blacksmith that would subsequently turn up again in the Copper Family's repertoire, "Twankydillo":[95]

Twankydillo

Anon

Voice

Here's a health to the jol-ly black-smith, the best of all fel-lows. who

works at his an-vil while the boy blows the bel-lows; Which makes my bright ham mer to

rise and to fall, Here's to old Cole, and to young Cole, and to old Cole of all, Twan-ky

dill-lo, twan ky dil-lo, dil lo, dil lo, dil-lo, dil-lo, dil-lo; A roar-ing pair of bag-pipes made

of the green wil-low

Fig. 10.23

> Here's a health to the jolly blacksmith, the best of all fellows,
> Who works at his anvil while the boy blows the bellows,
> Which makes my bright hammer to rise and to fall;
> Here's to old Cole, and to young Cole, and to old Cole of all,
> Twankydillo, twankydillo, twankydillo, dillo, dillo, dillo,
> A roaring pair of bagpipes made of the green willow.
>
> If a gentleman calls his horse for to shoe,
> He makes no denial of one pot or two,
> For it makes my bright hammer to rise and to fall;
> Here's to old Cole, and to young Cole, and to old Cole of all,
> Twankydillo, twankydillo, twankydillo, dillo, dillo, dillo,
> And he that loves strong beer is a hearty good fellow.
>
> Here's a health to King Charlie and likewise his queen,
> And all the royal little ones where'er they are seen,
> Which makes my bright hammer to rise and to fall;
> Here's to old Cole, and to young Cole, and to old Cole of all,
> Twankydillo, twankydillo, twankydillo, dillo, dillo, dillo,
> A roaring pair of bagpipes made of the green willow.[96]

Willett subsequently also supplied Lucy with several harvest home songs, wassails, and carols. In total she appears to have collected about forty songs from him, although they included several items that were not traditional (for example, "Black-eyed Susan"), and even a song ("Hush Hush") composed by Willett himself.[97]

Lucy was now eager to meet other collectors, and in February 1891 she was delighted to encounter artist and song-collector Heywood Sumner at a musical party at which she was singing Elizabethan madrigals with Alec Fuller Maitland.[98] Sumner's *The Besom Maker* had been published in 1888, and the two authors spent hours together enthusiastically discussing the tunes they had collected. This chance encounter marked the beginning of an enduring friendship. Sumner was undoubtedly an important influence on Lucy because he encouraged her to keep on collecting. The Reverend Sabine Baring-Gould was another influence. Lucy treasured her copy of *Songs and Ballads of the West,* purchasing the fourth part of the first edition of this collection of Devon and Cornish folksongs in May 1891.[99] She was not uncritical of Baring-Gould's editorial methods, however: she regretted that he had chosen in some instances to set his own verses to traditional tunes rather than reproducing the original texts. Nor did she like the piano arrangements by H. Fleetwood Sheppard. Nonetheless, Lucy was soon in correspondence with the clerical author, swapping songs and sending him "many notes" about the items they were discussing.[100] Then in June 1891 she obtained a copy of Frank Kidson's *Traditional Tunes,* and confided to her diary that it was "very interesting."[101] It would be six months before she plucked up the courage to write to Kidson, but in January 1892 she did so and his prompt reply, enclosing a copy of his book, was the beginning of another close friendship.[102] She had now begun collaborative relationships with the three men—Kidson, Baring-Gould, and Fuller Maitland—with whom she would work most closely within the folksong movement during the Late Victorian era, although in the 1900s Ralph Vaughan Williams would also come to play a similar role.

In March 1891 Lucy paid two long visits to her musical mentor, Alec Fuller Maitland, and the next day she went to do research in the British Museum.[103] Her diary does not record what she and Alec discussed or what she read in the museum, but it does include a list of material that she intended to consult there. Periodic entries during the next twelve months indicate that she fairly frequently went back to the Museum to "make researches."[104] Among the books that she studied were Ritson's *Ancient Songs,*[105] Evans' *Old Ballads,*[106] Sandys's *Christmas Carols,*[107] the many publications of the Percy Society, Robert Bell's version of *Ancient Poems, Ballads and Songs* in addition to Dixon's,[108] and Christie's *Scottish Traditional Ballad Airs,*[109] as well as the periodical *Notes & Queries.*[110] Not all of these books were new to her, but Lucy had evidently now decided, with her characteristic thoroughness, to make herself familiar with all the important extant collections of ballads and other old songs. She continued doing so for the rest of her life. It seems likely that Sabine Baring-Gould, Heywood Sumner, Alec Fuller Maitland, and subsequently Frank Kidson, were her initial guides in the endeavour.

Next May (1892) Lucy attended a demonstration Morris Dance and met for the first time Charlotte Burne, the author of *Shropshire Folk-Lore;*[111] the two women got on well together and would subsequently meet whenever Charlotte traveled up to London to attend meetings of the Folklore Society.[112] She introduced Lucy to several leading folklorists, including Laurence and Alice Gomme. Lucy's friendship with the Somervells blossomed during 1891,[113] and Arthur

Somervell was a significant influence; full of praise for her arrangement of "Jess Macpharlane" and for her own composition "Nae Mair," he encouraged her to keep on with her own songwriting and arranging.[114] Lucy, moreover, was now feeling more confident about her singing, thanks to unexpected praise from her singing teacher Wallace Shakespeare and from another new friend, the professional singer Plunkett Greene, whom she much admired, so she had begun looking again for new and unusual material to use in her concert performances.

The Broadwoods had an extended network of relatives and friends, and Lucy's new project was common knowledge in such circles. In consequence it was often other people who located source singers for Lucy, although she then went to visit them herself if they appeared to have promising material. For example, on 18 November 1891 her cousin Herbert took her to the village of Kings Langley in Hertfordshire, where she noted several songs from Clara Wilson, the wife of a local gardener, and a week later she collected a Hertfordshire "May Day Song" from a Mr. Marshall in the same village.[115] She also noted a variant of "The Moon Shines Bright" from Mrs. Marshall.

Clara Wilson proved to be one of Lucy's most valuable informants. She had grown up in Northamptonshire, and her songs included two carols ("In Bethlehem City" and "As I Sat on a Sunny Bank"), the folk lyric "The Sprig of Thyme," the Child ballad "Lord Bateman," and this decidedly feminist broadside ballad, "The Undaunted Female":

The Undaunted Female

Anon

Fig. 10.24

'Tis of a fair damsel in London did dwell,
A-waiting in her beauty, which none there could excel,
Her master and her mistress she servéd seven year,
And what follows after you soon shall quickly hear.

She packed up her box with her red cloak and gown,
She packed up her box all to leave London town,
Her red cloak and gown, and the rest of her clothes,
And with her box upon her head from service she goes.

She put her box upon her head, and carried it along,
The first that she met was an able man and strong,
He said, "My pretty fair maid, pray will you come with me,
And I'll put you in a nearer way across this country?"

He took her by the hand, and he led to a lane,
He said, "My pretty fair maid, I'll tell you plump and plain,
Deliver up your money without fear or strife,
Or else this very moment I'll take away your life."

The tears from her eyes like two fountains did flow,
Saying, "Where shall I wander, or where shall I go?"
And while this young fellow was feeling for his knife,
This beautiful damsel she took away his life.

She put her box upon her head, and with it trudged along,
The next that she met was a noble gentleman,
He said, "My pretty fair maid, where are you going so late,
Or what was that noise I heard at yonder gate?"

"That box upon your head to yourself does not belong,
To your master or your mistress you have done something wrong,
To your master or your mistress you have done something ill,
For one moment from trembling you cannot keep still."

"This box upon my head to myself it does belong,
To my master and my mistress I have done nothing wrong;
To my master and my mistress I have done nothing ill,
But I fear in my heart that a young man I did kill."

"He demanded my money, and I soon let him know,
For while he was fumbling I proved his overthrow."
She took him by the hand and led him to the place
Where this able young fellow lay bleeding on his face.

This gentleman got off his horse to see what he had got;
He had three loaded pistols, some powder, and some shot,
Beside three loaded pistols, some powder, and some ball,
A knife, and a whistle, some robbers for to call.

He put the whistle to his mouth, and he blew it loud and shrill,
Then four stout and able fellows came tripping o'er the hill;
This gentleman shot one of them, and that most speedily,
And this beautiful damsel she shot the other three.

When this noble gentleman saw all the robbers dead,
He took the damsel by the hand, and thus to her he said,
"I'll take you for my own bride, for the deed that you have done,
In taking of your own part, and firing off your gun."[116]

In December of the same year Lucy's sister-in-law Ada brought her back some songs from the hamlet of Anstie, near Holmwood, Surrey, where she had obtained them from an elderly carter named George Grantham.[117] On 6 January 1892 Lucy followed up this lead, traveling to Anstie and noting several items from Grantham's repertoire, including "The Sweet Nightingale," "Venus and Adonis," "Sheepcrook and Black Dog," and "The Painful Plough."[118]

Come, all you jolly ploughmen, of courage stout and bold,
That labour all the winter, in the stormy winds and cold;
To clothe your fields with plenty, your farmyards to renew,
For to crown them with contentment behold the painful plough.

Says the gardener to the ploughman, "Don't count your trade with ours,
Walk down in those fair gardens, and view these pretty flowers;
Also those curious borders, and pleasant walks to view,
There's no such peace nor pleasure performèd by the plough."

Says the ploughman to the gardener, "My calling don't despise,
For each man for his living upon his trade relies;
Were it not for the ploughman both rich and poor would rue,
For we are all dependent upon the painful plough."

Adam in the garden was sent to keep it right,
The length of time he stayed there I believe it was one night;
Yet of his own labour I call it not his due,
Soon he left his garden, and went to hold the plough.

For Adam was a ploughman when ploughing first begun,
The next that did succeed him was Cain, his eldest son;
Some of the generation this calling now pursue;
That bread may not be wanting, remains the painful plough.

Samson was the strongest man, and Solomon was wise,
Alexander, for to conquer was all his daily pride,
King David he was valiant, and many thousands slew,
There's none of your brave heroes can live without the plough.

Behold the worthy merchant that sails on foreign seas,
That brings home gold and silver for those who live at ease;
With fine silks and spices, and fruits also, too
They were all brought from the Indies by virtue of the plough.

Them that brings them over will find what I say true,
You cannot sail the ocean without the painful plough,
For they must have bread, biscuits, rice pudding, flour, and peas,
To feed the jolly sailors as they sails upon the seas.

I hope there's none offended with me for singing this,
For it was not intended for anything amiss;
If you consider rightly you'll own what I say's true,
There's no trade you can mention as can live without the plough.[119]

The Painful Plough

Anon

Fig. 10.25

Another of Lucy's informants was John Burberry,[120] a retired gamekeeper, from whom she noted "The Mistress's Health," "The Carter's Health," and "The Seasons of the Year" in September 1892.[121] The latter song bore only slight resemblance to the one with the same name collected by Baring-Gould in Devon. This is the Sussex version:

The Seasons of the Year

Anon

Fig. 10.26

The sun it goes down, the sky it looks red,
Down on yonder pillow I lay down my head,
I lift up my eyes to see the stars shine,
But still this young damsel she runs in my mind.

When the sap it goes up the tree it will flaw,
We'll first branch him round, boys, and put in the saw;
But when we have sawed him, and tumbled him down,
Then we do flaw him, all on the cold ground.

When flawing is over, haying draws near,
With our scythes and our pitchforks some grass for to clear;
But when we have mowed it and carried it away,
We first called it green grass, we now call it hay.

When haying is over, then harvest draws near,
We'll send for the brewer, to brew us strong beer;
To brew us strong beer for the hard working man,
For they work late and early till harvest does end.

When the sap it goes down then the leaves they do fall,
The farmer to his hedging and ditching to call,
But when it's hard weather there's no working there,
Then into the barn, boys, some corn for to clear.

When Spring it comes on, the maid to her cow,
The boy to his whip, and the man to his plough,
And so we bring all things so cheerfully round,
Success to the ploughman that ploughs up the ground![122]

That same autumn Lucy went to stay with Herbert Reynardson at his father's mansion, Adwell House, in Tetsworth, Oxfordshire, where she noted "many rustic songs" (her phrase) from the gardener's wife, Mrs. Patience Vaisey, who was rewarded with a present of six handkerchiefs in a box.[123] In all, Patience Vaisey provided Lucy with fifteen songs that she had learned while growing up in the county of Hampshire, where she was born.[124] They included "My Bonnie, Bonnie Boy," "Banks of the Sweet Primroses," "The Banks of Sweet Dundee," "The Oyster Girl," and "Barbara Allen."[125] Of these, Lucy was particularly enchanted by "My Bonnie, Bonnie Boy" and incorporated it in her own repertoire:

My Bonnie, Bonnie Boy

Anon

Fig. 10.27

I once lov'd a boy, a bonnie, bonnie boy,
I lov'd him, I'll vow and protest;
I lov'd him so well, and so very, very well,
That I built him a berth on my breast,
That I built him a berth on my breast.

'Twas up the green valley and down the green
                                                grove
Like one that was troubled in mind,
She whooped and she halloed and she played
                                          upon her pipe,
But no bonnie boy could she find,
But no bonnie boy could she find.

She lookèd up high, and she lookèd down low,
The sun did shine wonderful warm;
Whom should she spy there but her bonnie,
                                             bonnie boy,
So close in another girl's arm,

So close in another girl's arm.

I passèd him by, on him ne'er cast an eye,
Though he stretched forth his lily-white hand,
For I thought he'd been bound to love but one,
So I would not obey his command,
So I would not obey his command.

The girl that was loved of my little bonnie boy,
I am sure she is greatly to blame,
For many's the night he has robbed me of rest,
But he never shall do it again,
But he never shall do it again.

My bonnie, bonnie boy is gone over the sea,
I fear I shan't see him again;
But were I to have him, or were I to not,
I will think of him once now and then,
I will think of him once now and then.[126]

By the spring of 1892 Lucy had thus collected several dozen folksongs in four counties: Oxfordshire, Hertfordshire, Surrey, and Sussex. The material she had in hand was already sufficient in both quality and quantity to warrant publication, and, fortuitously, an opportunity had already arisen for her to contribute to a printed collection. In the next chapter we will examine her collaboration with Alec Fuller Maitland on *English County Songs,* which was the last of the several important developments that occurred, approximately simultaneously, during the early 1890s.

It may seem hyperbolic to claim that the years 1890-92 witnessed the birth of a *movement* to recover and publicize English folksong. Perhaps one should extend the time period back to 1889, when the first segment of Baring-Gould's *Songs and Ballads of the West* appeared, and forward to 1893, to include *English County Songs,* the main subject of the next chapter. But if we take these five years as a whole, it is evident that a breakthrough did occur during this short period of time. These critical years were a time of consolidation: the publications of Allan and Stokoe jointly built on earlier work done in Northumberland and Durham, while Kidson's and Forshaw's books consolidated earlier work in the county of Yorkshire. They were also a time of expansion, with new counties, especially Devon and Sussex, coming into prominence, and William Barrett providing the first attempt at a major, England-wide, folksong collection since Bell's edition of *Ancient Poems, Ballads and Songs of the Peasantry of England.*[127] Not only did the early 1890s see the publication of major works by Baring-Gould, Barrett, Broadwood, Kidson and Stokoe, this was also the time when English folksong enthusiasts, many of whom knew each other personally, began to develop an informal network. We can see this occurring through the window of Lucy Broadwood's diaries. Lucy, although she was as yet a neophyte, had by the end of 1892 developed contacts with such figures as Baring-Gould, Barrett, Burne, Fuller Maitland, Kidson, Sawyer, Somervell, Stanford, Sumner, and Wooldridge, not to mention an even larger number of sympathetic friends and relatives upon whose help she would soon draw. One of the early fruits of this networking was the book that she edited jointly with Alec Fuller Maitland in 1892-93, *English County Songs.* It is to this work, and to Broadwood's subsequent collecting in the mid-1890s, that we now turn.

Notes

1. William Alexander Barrett, ed., *English Folk-Songs* (London & New York: Novello, Ewer & Co., 1891).

2. James Henry Dixon, ed., *Ancient Poems, Ballads and Songs of the Peasantry of England* (London: Percy Society, 1846); Robert Bell, ed., *Ancient Poems, Ballads and Songs of the Peasantry of England* (London: John Parker & Sons, 1857; a revised and expanded edition of Dixon's 1846 publication).

3. Lucy E. Broadwood and J. A. Fuller Maitland, eds., *English County Songs: Words and Music* (London: The Leadenhall Press, 1893; reprinted London: Cramer, 1915). This work is discussed extensively in the next chapter.

4. James Orchard Halliwell, ed., *The Yorkshire Anthology* (London: Halliwell, 1851).

5. C. J. Davison Ingledew, ed., *The Ballads and Songs of Yorkshire* (London: Bell & Daldy, 1860).

6. Frank Kidson, ed., *Traditional Tunes: A Collection of Ballad Airs* (Oxford: Taphouse, 1891).

7. Charles F. Forshaw, ed., *Holroyd's Collection of Yorkshire Ballads* (London: Bell & Sons, 1892).

8. Dixon, *Ancient Poems, Ballads and Songs.*

9. Forshaw, *Holroyd's Collection,* 217-19.

10. Forshaw, *Holroyd's Collection,* 185-87.

11. Widespread rioting took place in the English countryside during the fall and winter of 1830, in what has been called "the last labourers' revolt." Although the immediate cause of the revolt was the introduction of threshing machines at a time of exceptional distress in the rural economy, the protesters' grievances were more wide-ranging, extending to their treatment at the hands of the local clergy and magistrates as well as discontent with the national government. A manifesto circulated over the signature of 'Captain Swing' declared: "We will destroy the corn stacks and the threshing machines this year, next year we will have a turn with the parsons, and the third year we will make war upon the statesmen." Quoted by A. L. Morton in *A People's History of England* (London: Gollancz, 1938), 363.

12. Forshaw, *Holroyd's Collection,* 267-68.

13. M[arianne] H[arriet] Mason, ed., *Nursery Rhymes and Country Songs: Both Tunes and Words from Tradition* (London: Metzler, 1878).

14. J. Collingwood Bruce and John Stokoe, eds., *Northumbrian Minstrelsy: A Collection of the Ballads, Melodies, and Small-Pipe Tunes of Northumbria* (Newcastle-upon-Tyne, U.K.: Society of Antiquaries of Newcastle-upon-Tyne, 1882. Reprinted, with a foreword by A. L. Lloyd, Hatboro, Pa.: Folklore Associates, 1965).

15. Thomas Allan, ed., *Allan's Illustrated Edition of Tyneside Songs and Readings* (Revised edition, Newcastle-upon-Tyne: Thomas & George Allan, 1891. Reprinted, with an introduction by Dave Harker, Newcastle-upon-Tyne: Frank Graham, 1972).

16. Allan, *Tyneside Songs,* 29-30.

17. Allan, *Tyneside Songs,* 451-52.

18. John Stokoe and Samuel Reay, eds., *Songs and Ballads of Northern England* (London: Walter Scott, 1892).

19. Joseph Crawhall, ed., *A Beuk o' Newcassel Sangs* (Newcastle-upon-Tyne: Mawson, Swan, & Morgan, 1888. Reprinted: Newcastle-upon-Tyne: Harold Hill, 1965).

20. Stokoe and Reay, *Songs and Ballads,* 86-87.

21. Stokoe and Reay, *Songs and Ballads,* 160-61. The punctuation of the first part of this title seems to vary. This is how Stokoe gives it.

22. Stokoe and Reay, *Songs and Ballads,* 98-99.

23. Stokoe and Reay, *Songs and Ballads,* 112-13.

24. Stokoe and Reay, *Songs and Ballads,* 18-19.

25. Stokoe and Reay, *Songs and Ballads,* 35-36.

26. Stokoe and Reay, *Songs and Ballads,* 41-42.

27. Stokoe and Reay, *Songs and Ballads,* 120-21.

28. William Alexander Barrett, ed., *English Folk-Songs* (London: Novello, Ewer & Co., [1891]; reprinted, 1973).

29. Barrett, *English Folk-Songs,* preface (unpaginated).

30. Barrett, *English Folk-Songs,* preface (unpaginated).

31. Barrett, *English Folk-Songs,* preface (unpaginated).

32. Barrett, *English Folk-Songs,* 92-93.

33. Barrett, *English Folk-Songs,* 47. Unfortunately I was unable to put *Nightingale* in italics in the song title.

34. Barrett, *English Folk-Songs,* 46.

35. Barrett, *English Folk-Songs,* 46.

36. Barrett, *English Folk-Songs,* 28.

37. Barrett, *English Folk-Songs,* 90-91.

38. Barrett, *English Folk-Songs,* 22-23.

39. Barrett, *English Folk-Songs,* 32-33.

40. Barrett, *English Folk-Songs,* 81.

41. Barrett, *English Folk-Songs,* 80.

42. For alternative perspectives on Lucy Broadwood, see Christopher Bearman, "The Lucy Broadwood Collection: An Interim Report," *Folk Music Journal* 7, no. 3 (1997): 357-65; Dorothy De Val, "The Transformed Village : Lucy Broadwood and Folksong," in *Music and British Culture, 1785-1914: Essays in Honour of Cyril Ehrlich,* ed. Christina Bashford and Leanne Langley (Oxford: Oxford University Press, 2000), 341-66; Walter Ford, "Lucy Etheldred Broadwood," *Journal of the Folk Song Society* 8, no. 3 (1929): 168-69; Vic Gammon, "Folk Song Collecting in Sussex and Surrey, 1843-1914," *History Workshop Journal* 10 (1980): 61-89; Lewis Jones, "Lucy Etheldred Broadwood: Poet and Song Writer," *English Dance and Song* 57, no. 4 (December 1995): 2-3; Lewis Jones, "Lucy Broadwood's Diaries: The Early Years," *English Dance and Song* 62, no. 3 (Autumn 2000): 2-3; Lewis Jones, "Lucy Etheldred Broadwood: Her Scholarship and Ours," in *Folk Song: Tradition, Revival, and Re-Creation,* ed. Ian Russell and David Atkinson (Aberdeen: The Elphinstone Institute, University of Aberdeen, 2004), 241-52; Ralph Vaughan Williams, "Lucy Broadwood: An Appreciation," *Journal of the Folk Song Society* 8, no. 1 (1927): 44-45; Ralph Vaughan Williams, "Lucy Broadwood, 1858-1929," *Journal of the English Folk Dance and Song Society* 5, no. 3 (December 1948): 136-38; Mary Venables, "Lucy Etheldred Broadwood" (unpublished, February 1930), Surrey History Centre, Accession no. 2297/6.

43. Mention should also be made of (among others) William Barrett, Alec Fuller Maitland, Harriet Mason, Laura Smith, and Heywood Sumner.

44. I should like to thank Keith Chandler, Martin Graebe, Irene Shettle, and Maureen Shettle for their generous and invaluable help in tracking down biographical information on a number of Lucy's source singers. Despite their laborious searches through census data, however, I regret that I still do not know the first names of several of her informants. In most instances Lucy refers to source singers in her diaries and her field notes only as Mr. or Mrs., the conventional usage of the time.

45. The best Broadwood pianos were of exceptional quality, and a number of prominent musicians owned them. Famous composers with Broadwoods included Franz Josef Haydn, Wolfgang Amadeus Mozart, Ludwig van Beethoven, Frédéric Chopin, Franz Liszt, and Edward Elgar. On the Broadwood firm, see David Wainwright, *Broadwood by Appointment* (London, Quiller Press, 1982).

46. [John Broadwood] and Geoffrey F. Dusart, eds., *Old English Songs, as now sung by the Peasantry of the Weald of Surrey and Sussex* (London: Betts & Co., [1847, not 1843, as is often given; galley proofs of *Old English Songs* at the Surrey History Centre, Woking, are stamped 1847 (Accession no. 2185) and the book was catalogued by the British Museum (now British Library) that same year]).

47. Lucy Broadwood, "Re Collecting," manuscript notes, n.d. [c. 1893]. Woking, Surrey, U.K., Surrey History Centre. Broadwood papers, Accession no. 2185/LEB/1/446.

48. London, Vaughan Williams Memorial Library, Lucy Broadwood Collection, LEB/1/1.

49. Broadwood, "Re Collecting."

50. Lucy Broadwood diaries. Broadwood Collection, Accession no. 6782, Surrey History Centre, Woking, Surrey, England, U.K. The most convenient way of identifying individual entries is by date (day, month, and year). Subsequent citations from the diaries are given in this fashion. In all cases the accession number at the Surrey History Centre is the same, namely 6782.

51. For an alternative account of the early diaries, see Lewis Jones, "Lucy Broadwood's Diaries: The Early Years," *English Dance and Song* 62, no. 3 (Autumn 2000): 2-3.

52. Lucy Broadwood, diary entry for 12 April 1883.

53. Frederic Hymen Cowen (1852-1935) had a successful career as a pianist and conductor. His compositions included six symphonies, of which his Symphony No. 3 in C minor "Scandinavian," first performed in London in 1880, was the most popular and established his reputation as a significant figure in Late Victorian art music. See chapter 3.

54. George A. Macfarren (1813-87) was a leading British composer during the mid-Victorian era. For several decades a professor at the Royal Academy of Music, he became its Principal in 1876. His compositions included operas, oratorios, and a considerable body of orchestral music including eight symphonies. His Symphony No. 7 in C-sharp minor is regarded as one of his finest achievements. Macfarren was a personal friend of Victorian vernacular song collector and editor William Chappell. One of the results of their collaboration was William Chappell, G. A. Macfarren, Natalia Macfarren, and J. Oxenford, eds., *Old English Ditties, selected from W. Chappell's "Popular Music of the Olden Time," with a New Introduction*, 2 vols. (London: Chappell & Co., n.d.) See chapter 3 for more details on Macfarren's composing.

55. Sir Alexander Campbell Mackenzie (1847-1935) was a Scottish composer who spent much of his early career in Italy but in 1888 took over as Principal of the Royal Academy of Music in London. His most famous compositions included the oratorio *The Rose of Sharon*, his *Scotch Rhapsodies*, his incidental music for the Shakespeare plays *Twelfth Night* and *Coriolanus*, and various works for violin, including a violin concerto and *Six Pieces for Violin*. More details about Mackenzie's compositions are given in chapter 3.

56. Sir Arthur Somervell (1863-1937) played a significant role during the Edwardian phase of the English folksong revival. As Inspector for Music he had a tremendous influence on the kind of music employed by school teachers in their classrooms, and he strongly encouraged the teaching of English 'national' songs to primary school children. Attacked by Cecil Sharp for not including enough 'genuine' folksongs (i.e., those collected by Sharp and others from oral tradition), Somervell initially defended vigorously his more eclectic concept of folksong, but he later compromised with Sharp and facilitated the introduction of many more of the folksongs collected by Baring-Gould, Broadwood, and Sharp (among others). As a composer Somervell is best remembered for two song-cycles: his setting of Tennyson's *Maud* and his very influential setting of A. E. Housman's *A Shropshire Lad* (the first of very many such settings). I am assuming that Sir Charles Hubert Parry, Sir Charles Villiers Stanford, and Sir Arthur Sullivan, the three pillars of Late Victorian art music in England, are too well-known to need further introduction here. Their work as composers is discussed, along with Somervell's, in chapter 9. Incidentally, although most of these Victorian composers received knighthoods they had not necessarily been so honored when Lucy first discovered their music. That was true of Sir Edward Elgar too, but I have seen no evidence that Lucy was familiar with any of his compositions before the late 1890s.

57. This paragraph is based on multiple diary entries during the years 1884-89.

58. Diary entries for 15-26 November 1884.

59. Dixon, *Ancient Poems, Ballads and Songs*.

60. Davies Gilbert, ed., *Some Ancient Christmas Carols with the Tunes to which they were formerly sung in the West of England, together with Two Ancient Ballads, A Dialogue, etc.* (2nd edition: London: John Nichols, 1823). The first, much smaller, edition was published the previous year.

61. William Sandys, ed., *Christmas Carols, Ancient and Modern, including the most popular in the West of England, and the airs to which they are sung. Also specimens of French Provincial Carols* (London: Richard Beckley, 1833).

62. Wooldridge was an expert on medieval and early Renaissance polyphonic church music. See H. Ellis Wooldridge, *The Polyphonic Period, Part I: Method of Musical Art, 330–1400* (New York; Cooper Square, 1973).

63. H. Ellis Wooldridge, ed., *Old English Popular Music*, 2 vols. (London: Novello & Ewer, 1893 [a revised and truncated version of Chappell's *Popular Music of the Olden Time*]).

64. Diary entry for 2 June 1885.

65. F. E. Sawyer, *Sussex Songs and Music*. Paper read to The British Archaeological Association, 21 August 1886, and published as a pamphlet (reprinted from the Association's *Proceedings*) by the author [copy at Surrey History Centre, Accession no. 6192/2/42].

66. Diary entries for 25 and 29 November 1885.

67. London, Vaughan Williams Memorial Library, Lucy Broadwood Collection, LEB/1/1.

68. Diary entry for 1 December 1885.

69. Diary entry for 18 February 1886.

70. Diary entry for 2 November 1886.

71. Diary entry for 16 July 1887.

72. Diary entry for 13 July 1887.

73. Diary entry for 9 February 1888.

74. In my view the project, initiated by Macfarren and Parry but continued by Vaughan Williams and many others, of creating a new 'national' school of classical music with its roots in English folk music, was hugely successful. Meirion Hughes and Robert Stradling provide a surprisingly negative reading of this movement in *The English Musical Renaissance 1860-1940: Construction and Destruction* (London: Routledge, 1993; revised as *The English Musical Renaissance 1840-1940: Constructing a National Music.* Manchester: Manchester University Press, 2001).

75. Diary entries for 27 July 1888 and 16 January 1889.

76. Diary entry for 23 May 1889.

77. London, Vaughan Williams Memorial Library, Lucy Broadwood Collection, LEB/1/1.

78. Barrett, *English Folk-Songs*.

79. Diary entry for 15 April 1889.

80. Diary entry for 17 December 1889.

81. [Lucy E. Broadwood] and Herbert Birch Reynardson, eds., *Sussex Songs (Popular Songs of Sussex)* (London: Lucas & Weber, 1889 [actually 1890]).

82. Diary entries for 16 and 25 April 1890.

83. Lucy Broadwood, as quoted in Stanley Godman, "John Broadwood, the Earliest English Folksong Collector," *West Sussex Gazette*, 30 January 1964, pagination missing from photocopy of newspaper cutting in my possession.

84. [Broadwood] and Reynardson, *Sussex Songs*, 12-13.

85. [Broadwood] and Reynardson, *Sussex Songs*, 10-11.

86. [Broadwood] and Reynardson, *Sussex Songs*, 43.

87. [Broadwood] and Reynardson, *Sussex Songs*, 28-29.

88. [Broadwood] and Reynardson, *Sussex Songs*, 4-5.

89. [Broadwood] and Reynardson, *Sussex Songs*, 38-39.

90. Frank Kidson and Alfred Moffat, eds., *The Minstrelsy of England* (London: Bailey & Ferguson, 1901), 256.

91. Although born in Fulking, near Brighton, Samuel Willett had lived in Cuckfield for at least twenty years. He was aged 59 or 60, and his wife Sarah hailed from Shoreham. They had three sons and four daughters.

92. London, Vaughan Williams Memorial Library, Lucy Broadwood Collection, LEB/2/71. Samuel Willett, letter to Lucy Broadwood, 1 October 1890. Willett's price per song of "half a crown" was two shillings and six pence in the currency of the time.

93. London, Vaughan Williams Memorial Library, Lucy Broadwood Collection, LEB/2/72. Undated, but probably April or May 1891.

94. Diary entries for 2 and 3 July 1891.

95. Diary entries for 1 and 6 May 1891.

96. Broadwood and Fuller Maitland, *English County Songs*, 138-39.

97. London, Vaughan Williams Memorial Library, Lucy Broadwood Collection, LEB/2/69-92. The following is an attempt to list all the songs that Lucy probably obtained from Willett, one way or another; however, this may list some songs twice (where Lucy's and Willett's titles for the same song differ), and it includes several songs that were not traditional: "Adam and Eve," "Arthur o' Bradley," "The Battle of the Mill," "The Beggar Girl," "Black-eyed Susan," "Brave sportsmen pause," "Christians Awake," "Country Lass," "The Curly-headed Boy," "The Echoing Horn," "The Farmer's Boy," "Fayther and I," "Five and Twenty," "The Grey Mare," "Hark, Hark What News the Angels Sing," "Hare Hunting Song," "Harvest Home," "Hush, Hush," "John Appleby," "King James and the Tinker," "Lads Push the Bowl About," "Lashed to the Helm," "Master's Health," "May and December," "Maying," "Mistress's Health" (No. 1), "Mistress's Health" (No. 2), "Mr. and Mrs. Simkins," "Mr. Tompkins," "Now Christmas Is Come," "One Midsummer's Morning," "Poor Jack," "Remember, Love, Remember," "Richard Short," "Sary Sykes," "There Was an Old Woman," "Twankydillo," "Vernal Fields," "William and Mary," and "Young Roger the Miller."

98. Diary entry for 15 February 1891. Heywood Sumner was an accomplished artist and a member of the Arts and Crafts movement associated with William Morris. The small illustrated book of folksongs that he published, *The Besom Maker*, was a work of art. See Heywood Sumner, ed., *The Besom Maker and Other Country Folk Songs* (London: Longmans Green, 1888).

99. Diary entries for 11 and 16 May 1891.

100. Diary entries for 1, 6, 10, 11, 22, and 24 May 1891.

101. Diary entry for 30 June 1891. It was lent, or perhaps given, to her by A. J. Hipkins.

102. Diary entries for 16 and 18 January 1892.

103. Diary entries for 24, 25, and 26 March 1891.

104. Diary entries for 26 March, 23 June, 27 November, and 7 December 1891.

105. Joseph Ritson, ed., *Ancient Songs from the Time of King Henry the Third to the Revolution* (London: J. Johnson, 1790; revised and expanded edition: *Ancient Songs and Ballads from the Reign of King Henry the Second to the Revolution*, 2 vols. London: Payne & Foss, 1829).

106. Thomas Evans, ed., *Old Ballads, Historical and Narrative, with some of Modern Date, Collected from Rare Copies and Mss.*, 2 vols. (London: Evans, 1777. 2nd edition, 4 vols.: London: Evans, 1784. Revised edition, ed. R. H. Evans, *Old Ballads, Historical and Narrative*, 4 vols. London: Evans, 1810).

107. William Sandys, ed., *Christmas Carols, Ancient and Modern* (London: Beckley, 1833).

108. Bell, *Ancient Poems, Ballads and Songs*. See note 2.

109. William Christie, ed. *Traditional Ballad Airs*, 2 vols. (Edinburgh: Edmonston & Douglas, 1876 and 1881).

110. List at end of Diary no. 8, which begins 26 March 1891. The item by Christie is given as *Scottish Tunes* but this appears to be an uncharacteristic error.

111. Charlotte Sophia Burne, ed., *Shropshire Folk-Lore: A Sheaf of Gleanings from the Collections of Georgina F. Jackson* (London: Trubner & Co., 1883-86).

112. Charlotte Burne would become the first female President of the Folklore Society. See Gordon Ashman and Gillian Bennett, "Charlotte Sophia Burne: Shropshire Folklorist, First Woman President of the Folklore Society, and First Woman Editor of *Folklore*. Part 1: A Life and Appreciation," *Folklore* 111, no. 1 (2000): 1-22. Also Gillian Bennett, "Charlotte Sophia Burne: Shropshire Folklorist, First Woman President of the Folklore Society, and First Woman Editor of *Folklore*. Part 2: Update and Preliminary Bibliography," *Folklore* 112, no. 1 (2001): 95-96.

113. Diary entries for 30 March and 12 April 1891.

114. Diary entries for 30 and 31 March and 7 and 12 April 1891.

115. Diary entries for 18, 20, and 24 November 1891.

116. Broadwood and Fuller Maitland, *English County Songs*, 60-61.

117. My thanks to Irene Shettle for tracking down a census entry for George Grantham. He lived in Holmwood.

118. Diary entries for 16 December 1891 and 6 January 1892.

119. Broadwood and Fuller Maitland, *English County Songs,* 126-27.

120. John Burberry, who was aged 68, had been the gamekeeper at Lyne. He was born in the nearby village of Newdigate, Surrey, and now lived at Ridgebrook Cottage in Warnham, Sussex. His son Mark, who had taken over as Lyne gamekeeper, probably suggested to Lucy that his father might prove a valuable informant.

121. London, Vaughan Williams Memorial Library, Lucy Broadwood Collection, LEB/2/2.

122. Broadwood and Fuller Maitland, *English County Songs,* 143.

123. Diary entries for 16, 18, 20, and 21 September 1892.

124. Patience Vaisey (née Cooper) was aged 42 in 1892. Her husband, whom she had married in 1880, was Richard Walter Vaisey. The couple had two children, a boy and a girl, and they had moved to Oxfordshire within the last five years, since their children had been born in Barnet, Hertfordshire.

125. London, Vaughan Williams Memorial Library, Lucy Broadwood Collection, LEB/2/66-68. The other ten were "Sailor Boy, or Fair Phoebe," "Jenny of the Moor," "Ploughing Song," "I Courted a Bonny Lass," "How Sweet in the Woodlands," "When the Morn Stands on Tiptoe," "Oh Why Was I Born," "Nothing Else to Do," "The Beautiful Damsel, or In Rochester City," and "The Garland of Love." However, in many cases Lucy noted only the melody, or the tune with just a few of the words. "I Courted a Bonny Lass" was apparently noted twice, perhaps on different occasions.

126. Broadwood and Fuller Maitland, *English County Songs*, 146-47.

127. Bell, *Ancient Poems, Ballads and Songs*. See note 2.

11

Lucy Broadwood and *English County Songs*

During the 1890s Lucy Broadwood became a lynchpin of the Late Victorian folksong revival. Her activities within the movement were multifaceted: she collected folksongs, edited them for publication, sang them at concerts, encouraged professional singers to perform them, and kept up an active correspondence with other collectors and enthusiasts, meeting them when they came to London and even traveling to different parts of England to visit them. In short, she became the hub of a folk music network that would eventually develop into the Folk-Song Society. Most of this was still in the future in the summer of 1891, but Broadwood's enthusiastic resumption of collecting and her growing knowledge of the literature on English vernacular song had not been lost on her friend and mentor, Alec Fuller Maitland, a busy musician/journalist with multiple obligations, who was looking for help with a book project that he had recently conceived. On 11 August 1891, at Fuller Maitland's prompting, Lucy was asked by his publisher, Andrew Tuer, of Leadenhall Press, to co-edit a collection of English folksongs, to be called *English County Songs*.[1] The idea was to print both tune and words of at least one folksong from every county. Fuller Maitland would be the senior partner in the project, and, in effect, Broadwood would be his research assistant, although she would also share the work of writing piano arrangements. She agreed eagerly, in part because her friend had requested her help but mainly because the project seemed an excellent way of further developing her knowledge of folksong. Moreover, it offered a vehicle for publishing any more songs that she might collect.[2]

English County Songs

In the event, Lucy Broadwood did more than her anticipated share of the work on *English County Songs*, and she certainly earned her equal billing as co-editor. Her first tasks were to compose an accompaniment for "The Croodlin' Doo" and to write to a dozen acquaintances asking them to collect traditional songs in their regions. She would write many more begging letters during the ensuing months, and a handful of them produced results. The arrival by mail of some, but by no means all, of various "country songs" (Lucy's favorite way of describing them) is catalogued in her diary entries for the months of August to December 1891. For example, on 25 September the mail brought two tunes from Somerset correspondent A. H. Frere, one of which, "Young Herchard," found its way into the book. Similarly, on 20 October Lucy received from Robert C. Thompson the version of "The *Golden Vanity*" that she would slip into the final "Sea Songs" section.[3]

By April of the next year the two editors decided they had more than enough material for the book. After several intensive meetings they settled on the songs that would be included, reconciling themselves to the fact that there would be a few gaps in their attempted coverage of all the English counties, while a plethora of items for certain regions entailed that some good songs would have to be omitted.[4] After that it was mainly a matter of harmonizing the tunes for piano accompaniment, a task that Lucy worked at throughout the summer of 1892. The proofs were corrected by the end of the year, and the book eventually appeared in June 1893. Although a number of the songs included in it had been collected by Lucy herself and others were reprinted from such published sources as *The Besom Maker, Nursery Rhymes and Country Songs*, and *Shropshire Folk-Lore*, the bulk had been gathered by correspondents, most of whom were individuals whom either Broadwood or Fuller Maitland knew personally. In a sense, then, *English County Songs* was a collective enterprise, and as such it marks an important early stage in the emergence of a movement to collect and preserve English folksong before it disappeared in the face of urbanization and industrialization.

In the Preface to *English County Songs* the editors provided a list of forty-three correspondents or source singers whose contributions they wished to gratefully acknowledge. It was not exhaustive, but it read as follows:

Mr. Bennell	A. J. Hipkins, Esq.
Miss C. Bovill	Mrs. Lawson
Mr. J. Burberry	Miss Manisty
Mrs. H. J. T. Broadwood	Miss F. Medycott
Miss Collyer	Miss Peacock
Mrs. Pocklington Coltman	Mrs. Arthur Playne
Misses K. and B. Cra'ster	F. Scarlett Potter, Esq.
Miss J. Gordon Cumming	L. Powell, Esq.
The Hon. Mrs. Dickinson (the late)	A. H. Birch Reynardson, Esq.
Miss G. Dixon	Miss Margaret Royds
Miss J. Dixon	Rev. John Shearme
Quayle C. Farrant, Esq.	Miss Edith A. Slingsby
Mrs. G. L. Gomme	Mrs. Squarey
Rev. S. Baring-Gould	Rev. W. B. Stillman
Mr. Grantham	H. Strachey, Esq.
Lady Guise	Miss E. Thorold
Miss F. Hamond	Mrs. Vaisey
Miss Handley	Miss Wakefield
Mrs. Harley	Mr. Willett
R. L. Harrison, Esq.	Mrs. Wilson
Miss M. Curtis Hayward	&c., &c.[5]
Captain G. Heath, R.E.	

Some of these (Burberry, Grantham, Vaisey, Willett, and Wilson) were Lucy's source singers. Others (Broadwood, Craster, Reynardson, and Shearme) were members of Lucy's extended family. As might be expected, Sabine Baring-Gould was on the list, although, surprisingly, Harriet Mason's, Charlotte Burne's, and Frank Kidson's names are missing. Mason and Burne, however, were thanked for permitting songs to be reprinted from their publications. If the omission of Kidson was not merely an oversight, it is to be explained by the fact that, although Lucy had discovered him and *Traditional Tunes* by this time, the county of Yorkshire was Fuller Maitland's responsibility and the material included from there was contributed by his friend Herbert M. Bower of Ripon. Bower, however, was another surprising omission, an indication perhaps that Broadwood was more conscientious in listing her helpers than Fuller Maitland was in thanking his. Other omissions, whose names were included in footnotes, included Rev. W. Miles Barnes, Mrs. T. H. Farrer, G. K. Fortescue, A. H. Frere, J. F. Frye, Thomas Gray, Captain Hincks, Rev. M. P. Holme, Mr. Huttley, Mrs. Marshall, John Stokoe, Arthur Thompson, Robert C. Thompson, and Mark Wyatt. When all these contributors are added together, it becomes evident that approximately sixty people were involved in one way or another with Broadwood and Fuller Maitland's ambitious project.

If we examine the contents of *English County Songs* it becomes evident that some of the more prolific contributors among the correspondents (as opposed to the source singers) were:

Sabine Baring-Gould (Lew Trenchard, Devon)
R. Bennell (Oxfordshire)
Herbert M. Bower (Ripon, Yorkshire)
Margaret Harley (Bewdley, Worcestershire)
Alfred J. Hipkins (Westminster, London)
Margaret Royds (Heysham, Lancashire)
Frederick Scarlett Potter (Halford, Shipston-on-Stour, Worcestershire)[6]
Lavinia Squarey (Downton, Wiltshire)
Heywood Sumner (Hampshire and Somerset)
Mary Wakefield (Kendal, Lake District)
Clara Wilson (a correspondent as well as a singer; King's Langley, Hertfordshire).

Another dozen or so contributors supplied one song each, and there were many other correspondents whose offerings were, in the event, not included in the book due to lack of space.

Information on many of the threescore contributors is scarce or lacking altogether. On the other hand, some important ones can be identified. We are already familiar with Baring-Gould, Burne, Mason, Stokoe, and Sumner, and we know something about Broadwood's various source singers. Herbert M. Bower was an amateur musician who played in a string quartet while an undergraduate at Cambridge University; he knew several European languages and translated an Italian poetry collection and a German work on botany. A historian and folklorist, he had a keen interest in the Kirkby Malzeard Sword Dance, and he contributed articles on English, Italian, and French history and tradition for the Folk-Lore Society and other journals.[7] Mrs. G. L. Gomme was Lucy's future friend Lady Alice Gomme, the wife of prominent folklorist Laurence Gomme, and herself a folklorist and expert on traditional childrens' games and game songs.[8] Margaret Harley was a disciple of John Ruskin who, together with her husband Thomas, was an active member of Ruskin's Guild of St. George. In 1889 they had moved to the Wyre Forest, near Bewdley in Worcestershire, to develop a small-holding on a large estate owned by another Guild member, in an attempt to put into practice Ruskin's vision of a return to a lifestyle closer to nature.[9]

Alfred J. Hipkins was the principal technical designer of high quality instruments with the Broadwood piano manufacturing company, and a close friend of both Alec Fuller Maitland and the Broadwood family. As a musician, musicologist, and leading authority on keyboard instruments and their history, he played an important role in the English early music movement, championing the revival of the harpsichord and clavichord.[10] Frederick Scarlett Potter was a sculptor, historian, and prolific novelist, who would produce over fifty books (mainly fiction and children's books, but also local history and folklore) in his lifetime, one of the most successful being *Heroes of the North; or, Stories from Norwegian Chronicles* (1876).[11] Margaret Royds, the daughter of a Heysham clergyman, was well known locally as an accomplished amateur singer and musician; she was also a composer who saw several of her works published. She was an acquaintance of Fuller Maitland's.[12] Edith A. Slingsby was the sister of mountain climber William Cecil Slingsby, who specialized in conquering Norwegian peaks. A climber herself, Edith recorded her experiences of an expedition to Norway in 1875 in *An English Lady in Jotunheimen*.[13] Lavinia M. Squarey, who lived in a small village near Salisbury, was the sixty-year-old wife of local land agent Elias R. Squarey. The couple had two grown-up daughters and a son.[14]

Mary Wakefield, who lived at Sedgwick Hall, near Kendal, was also a friend and disciple of John Ruskin. A music student in London during the 1870s, she knew Parry and Stanford, and subsequently, as a singer, gave concert tours throughout England. She had the talent and training to become a professional musician but, blessed with a private income, she opted instead to play a major role in promoting wider public participation in music education and performance, starting the Competitive Music movement in 1885.[15] She was a friend of both Fuller Maitland and Broadwood. Mark Wyatt of Enborne, Berkshire, a gardener's son, came from a lower social background than any of these other correspondents; he worked for Robert Harris Valpy, the husband of Fuller Maitland's sister Jane, and should probably be counted as a source singer rather than a collector/correspondent.[16]

Despite the rather haphazard way in which its contents were assembled, *English County Songs* was one of the foundation stones of the first folksong revival. It has been called "a landmark in the history of English music, for it made the musical world aware of the treasures preserved in the memories of unlettered country people."[17] It was the first attempt since Chappell to go beyond a regional collection to a systematically national one, although its mode of organization was geographical rather than historical.[18] Indeed it was an ambitious attempt to survey, systematically, the traditional song of the whole of England, county by county. And its editors recognized that ideally such songs would be collected entirely from oral tradition, and they would be presented exactly as performed by the source singers. In her "Preface" to *English County Songs* Lucy emphasized that (with one exception, a late medieval song in which the spelling was modernized) her policy was to leave the lyrics "absolutely unaltered" and in no instance to "tamper with" the melodies.[19] In fact, because so many people had a hand in collecting material for *English County Songs*, it is very difficult to be sure that the tunes and lyrics printed in the book reflect with reasonable accuracy what the original informants actually sang. The diaries cast a little light on this problem, by helping one pick out the songs noted in the field by Lucy herself, but in the main they merely confirm that most of the others simply arrived in the mail. The truth is that most of the time Broadwood and Fuller Maitland had no choice but to assume that their collaborators had got down the words and tunes accurately.

In the event, the two editors were unable to carry out their plan to the letter. They failed to obtain any songs from three counties, Bedfordshire, Huntingdonshire, and Monmouthshire. Moreover, in some other instances they were reduced to ascribing songs to counties other than those in which they were actually collected, although they always found some more or less plausible excuse for doing so. For example, Cambridgeshire was represented by a single song, "Ground for the Floor," obtained from Edith Slingsby of Skipton, Yorkshire. The item was reassigned from Yorkshire to

Cambridgeshire on the basis of rather shaky hearsay evidence: the Reverend J. B. Healy of Ripon, Yorkshire, had mentioned to Alec's friend Herbert M. Bower that he remembered a fragment of the song as having been "formerly very popular among fens shooters from Cambridge."[20] Similarly the seven songs supplied by a former resident of Northamptonshire, Mrs. Clara Wilson of King's Langley, Hertfordshire, who happened to employ a servant girl from Leicestershire, were distributed rather cavalierly, according to need, among Leicestershire, Hertfordshire and Northamptonshire. Representation by county in *English County Songs* was thus patchy and uneven, with certain counties (Yorkshire, Northamptonshire, Middlesex, Surrey, Sussex, Somerset, and Devon) receiving more than their fair share of space. In any case, as Broadwood admitted in her "Preface," few if any traditional songs were "the exclusive property of a particular county," nor was it possible "from internal evidence to assign any tune to any one county"[21]. Yet the approach, although difficult to implement, had an evident benefit: by the very fact of focusing attention at the county level it induced collectors to try to fill in the most evident gaps. As Broadwood remarked:

> The arrangement here adopted, by which an attempt has been made to represent each county of England by at least one song, may seem an arbitrary one, since the county boundaries cannot be expected to confine the music of each shire to itself; it has, however, been indirectly of great service, since it has stimulated effort in places that at first seemed altogether unpromising, and these have sometimes proved to contain more than the average amount of good material. "We are such an unmusical neighbourhood, you will certainly not find anything in this county," is a remark which has often preceded some of the most interesting discoveries; for, strange as it may appear, the districts in which music is largely cultivated among the poorer classes are not those in which the old tunes are most carefully preserved and handed down. [22]

The format of *English County Songs* was thus rather arbitrary, and the editors might have been well advised to stick with the simpler division into six regions (North, Northwest, Midlands, East, Home Counties, and South Coast) that they used to structure their work. Broadwood had most editorial control over the material that she had collected herself, and, as we have seen, she noted personally at least ten of the songs, in Surrey and Sussex. But for the bulk of the collection she and her co-editor had to rely on the work of those sixty or so correspondents, friends and co-enthusiasts living in localities that spanned the length and breadth of England, from Yorkshire and the Lake District in the north to Devon and Cornwall in the southwest.

English County Songs opened with nine songs from the very north of England, which, it had been agreed, was primarily Fuller Maitland's remit. This northern region comprised the counties of Northumberland, Cumberland, Westmorland, Durham, and Yorkshire, thereby stretching much further south on the eastern side of the Pennines than on the western side. First came three songs from Northumberland, a county particularly rich in folksong, and already represented in print by such important publications as Harriet Mason's *Nursery Rhymes and Country Songs* and Bruce and Stokoe's *Northumbrian Minstrelsy*.[23] Each of these collections provided one song: the beautiful "The Water of Tyne" from *Northumbrian Minstrelsy* and "There Was a Lady in the West," a variant of Child no. 1, "Riddles Wisely Expounded," from *Nursery Rhymes and Country Songs*. The third putatively Northumbrian item, "Robbie Tamson's Smiddie," had actually been collected in Canada by Mrs. T. H. Farrer from one Richard Turner, presumably a former resident of Northumberland. The song's provenance was normally the Scottish lowlands, although it had been included in Kidson's *Traditional Tunes,* which was mainly a Yorkshire collection (Kidson, however, had failed to specify where his version had been noted).

Moving west along Hadrian's Wall, the next county, Cumberland, was represented by just one song, "Sally Gray," collected by Mary Wakefield from an old man in the northern part of the Lake District.[24] It was a dialect song with a known author, R. Anderson, and dated from 1802, so Lucy may have had some doubt about whether it should be counted as a folksong at all; however, there seem to have been no other candidates from Cumberland so any scruples about its suitability had to be put aside. Wakefield, who, as we have seen, lived in Kendal, had picked up elsewhere in the Lake District another song, "A North Country Maid," which could be ascribed to Westmorland, the county that bordered Cumberland to the south. The melody in local oral tradition was not in Lucy's eyes as beautiful as that most commonly associated with the lament, but it was good enough to be worth printing, and the Westmorland variant's words differed considerably from those found in *Northumbrian Minstrelsy*. This is the Westmorland version:

> A north-country maid up to London had stray'd,
> Although with her nature it did not agree;
> She wept, and she sighed, and she bitterly cried,
> "I wish once again in the north I could be.
> Oh, the oak and the ash and the bonny ivy tree,
> They flourish at home in my own country."

"While sadly I roam, I regret my dear home,
Where lads and young lasses are making the hay;
The merry bells ring, and the birds sweetly sing,
And maidens and meadows are pleasant and gay.
Oh, the oak and the ash, etc."

"No doubt, did I please, I could marry with ease,
Where maidens are fair, many lovers will come;
But he whom I wed must be north-country bred,
And carry me back to my north-country home.
Oh, the oak and the ash, etc."[25]

A North Country Maid

Anon

Fig. 11.1

Little information was given about Mary Wakefield's sources, and Fuller Maitland (who was in charge of this section and wrote the piano arrangements) had a similar problem with regard to Durham county. Lacking any items noted from oral tradition, he was forced to rely on "The Collier's Rant" from Cuthbert Sharp's 1834 publication *A Bishoprick Garland,* the sub-title of which was *A Collection of Legends, Songs, Ballads, etc., belonging to the county of Durham.* The song, associated with the pits of the Northumberland and Durham coalfield, was a strong choice, but no editorial information was provided to indicate its provenance or to help the reader make sense of the dialect phrases that it incorporated.[26]

For Yorkshire, on the other hand, there was an abundance of usable material, and not all of it could be included. The county was covered by the local collector mentioned earlier, Herbert M. Bower, who lived in Ripon but evidently spent time (perhaps his vacations) on the coast north of Scarborough.[27] Bower supplied an interesting version of "Scarborough Fair," noted from William Moat, a fisherman from Whitby in the North Riding. This variant lacked the usual refrain of "parsley, sage, rosemary and thyme," but it was evidently derived from Child no. 2, "The Elfin Knight," having retained elements of the riddling dialogue in that ballad of the supernatural:

Is any of you going to Scarborough Fair?
Remember me to a lad as lives there,
Remember me to a lad as lives there;

For once he was a true lover of mine.
Tell him to bring me an acre of land,
Betwixt the wild ocean and yonder sea strand,

Betwixt the wild ocean and yonder sea strand;
And then he shall be a true lover of mine.

Tell him to plough it with one ram's horn,
And sow it all over with one peppercorn,
And sow it all over with one peppercorn;
And then he shall be a true lover of mine.

Tell him to reap it with a sickle of leather,
And bind it together with one peacock feather,
And bind it together with one peacock feather;
And then he shall be a true lover of mine.

And now I have answered your questions three,
I hope you'll answer as many for me,
I hope you'll answer as many for me;
And then thou shalt be a true lover of mine.

Is any of you going to Scarborough Fair?
Remember me to a lass as lives there,
Remember me to a lass as lives there;

For once she was a true lover of mine.

Tell her to make me a cambric shirt,
Without any needles or thread or owt through't,
Without any needles or thread or owt through't;
And then she shall be a true lover of mine.

Tell her to wash it by yonder wall,
Where water ne'er sprung, nor a drop o' rain fall,
Where water ne'er sprung, nor a drop o' rain fall;
And then she shall be a true lover of mine.

Tell her to dry it on yonder thorn,
Where blossom ne'er grew sin' Adam was born,
Where blossom ne'er grew sin' Adam was born;
And then she shall be a true lover of mine.

And now I have answered your questions three,
And I hope you'll answer as many for me,
And I hope you'll answer as many for me;
And then thou shalt be a true lover of mine.[28]

Scarborough Fair

Anon

Fig. 11.2

Bower, an amateur folklorist, was very interested in local customs, a fact that was reflected in two other items he offered to Lucy and Alec, the lyrics and music for the Kirkby Malzeard sword dance (which he had taken down from Thomas Wood),[29] and the text and tune of a local wassail, collected in Galphay (near Ripon), and also heard at Anston, in South Yorkshire. Here is "The Wassail Bough":

Here we come a-wassailing, among the leaves of green,
Here we come a-wandering, so fairly to be seen.
Our jolly wassail, our jolly wassail,

Love and joy come to you, and to our wassail bough;
Pray God bless you, and send you a happy New Year,
A New Year, A New Year,
Pray God bless you and send you a happy New Year.

We are not daily beggars, that beg from door to door;
We are the neighbours' children, whom you have seen before.
Our jolly wassail, etc.

I have a little purse, it is made of leather skin;
I want a little sixpence, to line it well within.
Our jolly wassail, etc.

Bring us out the table, and spread it with the cloth;
Bring us out the bread and cheese, and a bit of your Christmas loaf.
Our jolly wassail, etc.

God bless the master of the house, and the mistress too;
Also the little children, which round the table grew.
Our jolly wassail, etc.[30]

The Wassail Bough

Anon

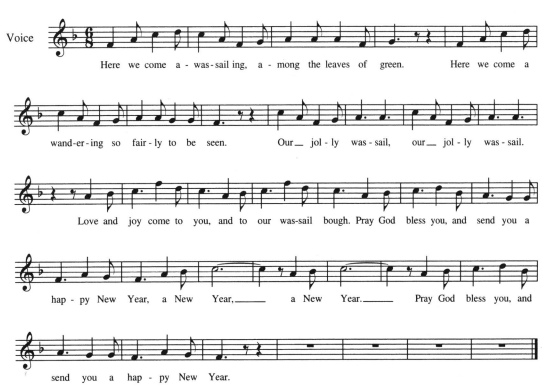

Fig. 11.3

Wassails were extant in other parts of England, and we have seen (in chapter 5) that Charlotte Burne collected a "Wassail Cup Carol" in Shropshire, while Heywood Sumner included "The Wassail Song" in *The Besom Maker*. "The Wassail Bough" also makes an interesting comparison with the following item, collected on the other side of the Pennines by Margaret Royds of Heysham, Lancashire. It was one of two 'peace-egging' songs noted by Royds. Peace (or pace) egging songs were the Easter equivalent of wassails. The name 'peace' or 'pace' appears to be a corruption of paschal, and the songs were associated with a mumming play or Morris Dancers' play in which St. George and a doctor who revived the dead had central roles. The play was usually performed on Easter Monday but the songs might be performed at other times during Easter Week, as a means of raising the wherewithal for continuing the celebrations. Like wassails, they legitimized and licensed begging.

Peace-Egging Song

Anon

Fig. 11.4

Here's two or three jolly lads all in one mind,
We are comed a peace-egging, and I hope you'll prove kind;
And I hope you'll prove kind, with your eggs and strong beer,
For we'll come no more nigh you until the next year.
Fol-de-rol-de-ray, fol-de-ray, fol-de-riddle, addle-i-o.

O the next that comes in is Lord Nelson, you'll see,
With a bunch of blue ribbons tied down to his knee;
And a star on his breast like silver doth shine—
And I hope you'll remember it's peace-egging time.
Fol-de-rol-de-ray, &c.

O the next that comes in is a jolly Jack Tar,
He sailed with Lord Nelson a-during last war;
He's arrived from the sea old England to view,
And he's comed a-peace-egging with our jovial crew.
Fol-de-rol-de-ray, &c.

O the next that comes in is Lord Collingwood,
He fought with Lord Nelson till he shed his blood;
He fought with Lord Nelson through sorrow and woe—
And I hope you'll reward us before we do go.
Fol-de-rol-de-ray, &c.

O the next that comes in is old Tosspot you see,
He's a valiant old man in every degree;
He's a valiant old man, and he wears a pig-tail,
But all his delight is in drinking mulled ale.
Fol-de-rol-de-ray, &c.

Then in comes old miser, with all her brown bags,
For fear of her money she wears her old rags;
So mind what you're doing and see that all's right;
If you give nought, we'll take nought, farewell and good night.
Fol-de-rol-de-ray, &c.

Come ladies and gentlemen that sits by the fire,
Put your hands in your pockets and give us our desire,
Put your hands in your pockets and pull out your purse,
And give us a trifle, you'll not be much worse.
Fol-de-rol-de-ray, &c.[31]

The two peace-egging songs were part of the second main section of *English County Songs*. This dealt with a region that Broadwood and Fuller Maitland characterized as the Northwest. It consisted of the counties of Lancashire, Cheshire, Shropshire, and the Isle of Man. Lancashire dominated this section, providing five items out of eleven. Two of the Lancashire items, "Green Gravel" and "There Was a Pig Went Out to Dig," both children's songs, actually appeared to be associated with other counties: the former, submitted by Mrs. Margaret Harley of Bewdley, appeared to have been collected in Worcestershire (with variants from Derbyshire and Shropshire), while the latter, taken from Mason's *Nursery Rhymes and Country Songs,* was seemingly from Northumberland. No explanation was provided for their allocation to Lancashire, so one was left to assume that, notwithstanding appearances, they had in fact been collected in the County Palatine. The fifth Lancashire item was a comic ballad, "King Arthur," collected by R. L. Harrison and similar to "King Arthur's Servants," as printed by Mason in *Nursery Rhymes and Country Songs.* Regrettably little detailed information was provided about the sources of these Lancastrian songs, not even the names of the informants nor (except in one instance) the exact locations where the songs were collected.[32]

Cheshire, the other part of the County Palatine, was represented by three items. There was a "Souling Song," the Hallowe'en equivalent of a wassail or peace-egging song, collected by the Reverend M. P. Holme from a girl at Tattenhall school in October, 1891. It was similar to one of those collected by Charlotte Burne in the neighboring county of Shropshire and printed in *Shropshire Folk-Lore.* Lucy noted that a detailed account of 'souling' had been given by Burne in her book, and that the custom was still practiced in Cheshire and Shropshire on All-Souls' Day.[33] The other Cheshire contributions were "The Cheshire Man" taken from Edward Jones's *Popular Cheshire Melodies,* and "I Will Give You the Keys of Heaven" collected by the Reverend F. Partridge. As we have seen in chapter 7, Baring-Gould had printed in *Songs and Ballads of the West* a version of the same song, collected from John Woodrich, under the title "Blue Muslin." He had also obtained a copy of Partridge's "Keys of Heaven" and had forwarded it to Lucy. This was an incomplete fragment of the ballad but the tune and first two stanzas had indeed come originally from Cheshire. The rest of the text, as Lucy admitted, had been "restored from an East country version." She also possessed a variant from Masham, Yorkshire, and she was aware that Harriet Mason had included a Northumbrian version in *Nursery Rhymes and Country Songs.* In some versions the courted lady is portrayed as extremely avaricious, eventually giving in when her cupidity is assuaged by an especially magnificent offer, only to be spurned in turn by her suitor. In this variant, however, she is interested not in material things but in genuine emotion and fidelity. The song (in its more idealistic version) particularly appealed to Broadwood, and she would make it part of her active repertoire as a concert singer. The version in *English County Songs* was thus her composite, although based on Partridge's Cheshire variant.

I will give you the keys of heaven,
I will give you the keys of heaven,
Madam, will you walk? Madam, will you talk?
Madam, will you walk and talk with me?

Though you give me the keys of heaven,
Though you give me the keys of heaven,
Yet I will not walk; no, I will not talk,
No, I will not walk or talk with thee.

I will give you a blue silk gown,
To make you fine when you go to town;
Madam, will you walk, etc.

Though you give me a blue silk gown,
To make me fine when I go to town,
Yet I will not walk, etc.

I will give you a coach and six,

Six black horses as black as pitch,
Madam, will you walk, etc.

Though you give me a coach and six,
Six black horses as black as pitch,
Yet I will not walk, etc.

I will give you the keys of my heart,

And we will be married till death us do part,
Madam, will you walk, etc.

Thou shalt give me the keys of thy heart,
And we'll be married till death us do part;
I will walk, I will talk,
I will walk and talk with thee.[34]

I Will Give You the Keys of Heaven

Anon

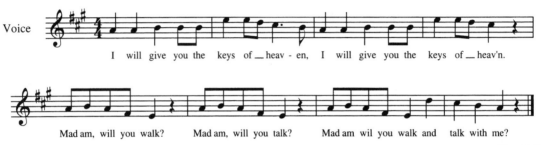

I will give you the keys of — heav - en, I will give you the keys of — heav'n.

Mad am, will you walk? Mad am, will you talk? Mad am wil you walk and talk with me?

Fig. 11.5

Both Manx songs in this section were in Gaelic, although translations were provided, and in one instance, "Ny Kirree Fo-Sniaghtey," not only the informant's full name (Quayle C. Farrant) was volunteered, but also his location (Greeba Towers, St. John's, Isle of Man). Shropshire—potentially a very fruitful hunting ground—was represented by one song only, "Cold Blows the Wind" (aka Child no. 78, "The Unquiet Grave"), from Charlotte Burne's *Shropshire Folk-Lore.*[35] Evidently neither Burne nor anyone else had seen fit to supply more songs from the county, although Burne had given permission to use material from her book.

The third main section of *English County Songs* covered the Midlands, from the Welsh marches in the west to Sherwood Forest in the east. The list of counties in this region comprised thirteen, two of which (Huntingdonshire and Monmouthshire) had no songs at all, and others of which were represented by one song only. Such was the case for Staffordshire, and the ballad, "Lord Thomas and Fair Eleanor" (Child no. 73), although collected in Eccleshall, was taken from *Shropshire Folk-Lore.*[36] Moving eastwards to the county of Derbyshire, the editors drew once again on the collecting of Harriet Mason, reprinting "The Spider" from *Nursery Rhymes and Country Songs.* "The Derby Ram" was a predictable choice, and Lucy gave three versions, one collected in Northumberland and another in Yorkshire. This is the Derbyshire version, in the form collected by Mason:

As I was going to Derby, sir, 'twas on a summer's day,
I met the finest ram, sir, that ever was fed on hay;
And indeed, sir, 'tis true; sir, I never was giv'n to lie,
And if you'd been to Derby, sir, you'd have seen him as well as I.

It had four feet to walk on, sir, it had four feet to stand,
And every foot it had, sir, did cover an acre of land;
And indeed, sir, etc.

The horns that were on its head, sir, held a regiment of men,
And the tongue that was in its head, sir, would feed them every one.
And indeed, sir, etc.

The wool that was on its back, sir, made fifty packs of cloth,
And for to tell a lie, sir, I'm sure I'm very loth.
And indeed, sir, etc.

The wool that was on its sides, sir, made fifty more complete,
And it was sent to Russia to clothe the Emperor's fleet.
And indeed, sir, etc.

The tail was fifty yards, sir, as near as I can tell,
And it was sent to Rome, sir, to ring Saint Peter's Bell.
And indeed, sir, etc.[37]

The Derby Ram

Anon

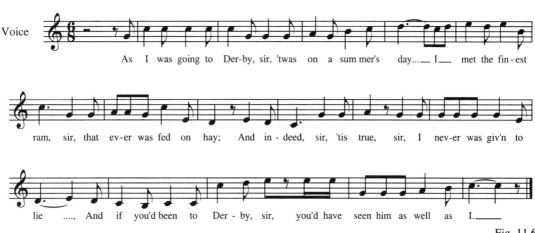

Fig. 11.6

Lacking a contributor from Nottinghamshire, Broadwood and Fuller Maitland represented this county by "The Poacher's Song" (aka "In Thorny Woods") from *Sussex Songs*[38] but re-titled it "The Nottinghamshire Poacher" for the occasion. As collected by the Reverend John Broadwood on the Sussex/Surrey border, the first line of the song clearly described the activities of a Buckinghamshire poacher, but, as Lucy remarked, in Robert Bell's edition of *Ancient Poems, Ballads and Songs of the Peasantry of England* the location had been identified as Nottinghamshire. So Lucy took the liberty of replacing the word "Buckinghamshire" with "Nottinghamshire" in the text of the song but in other respects reproduced her uncle's version.

Rutland also presented a difficulty, since neither editor had any contacts in that tiny county or knew of any folksongs that demonstrably originated there. The best they could do was a modernized version of a medieval canon, "Now Robin, Lend to Me Thy Bow," which was linked to Rutland only by a reference in the words to the town of Uppingham. Leicestershire also posed a problem, but a different solution was found: one of the songs that Lucy had noted from Hertfordshire informant Mrs. Clara Wilson had in turn been learned by her from a maidservant who conveniently hailed from Leicestershire. "I'll Tell You of a Fellow" thus became the lone item that represented Leicestershire. Mrs. Wilson herself, although she now lived near King's Langley, Hertfordshire, came originally from Northamptonshire, so that county was allocated four songs that she knew from her childhood: the broadside ballad given earlier, "The Undaunted Female" (aka "The Beautiful Damsel"), "In Bethlehem City," "Lord Bateman," and "The Sprig of Thyme." Lucy renamed the latter "The Seeds of Love" and appended two other versions, one from the Sussex/Surrey border that she had presumably noted herself near Lyne, and one, probably collected by Baring-Gould, from the West Country. She added a comment encouraging her readers to search out other English variants of "The Seeds of Love" in Bell's *Ancient Poems, Ballads and Songs,* Baring-Gould's *Songs and Ballads of the West,* and Kidson's *Traditional Tunes.* About "Lord Bateman" (aka Child no. 53, "Young Beichan") she remarked that variants could be found in a variety of collections, including Allingham's *Ballad Book,* Bruce and Stokoe's *Northumbrian Minstrelsy,* Burne's *Shropshire Folk-Lore,* Christie's *Traditional Ballad Airs,* Kidson's *Traditional Tunes,* and her own *Sussex Songs,* while Child had provided "full information" about it under the heading of "Young Beichan" in *The English and Scottish Popular Ballads.*[39]

There were four songs from Oxfordshire, all supplied by Mr. R. Bennell (about whom no information was given): "Turmut-hoeing," "'Twas Early One Morning," "The Thresher and the Squire," and a drinking song, "The Good Old Leathern Bottle." Lucy had been forced to do some compositing here. While the tune of "'Twas Early One Morning" was Bennell's, his lyric had been fragmentary, and Lucy had obtained a full set of words from a gardener's boy in Berkshire. For "Leathern Bottle" Bennell had similarly supplied the tune and the first two verses, but the remainder had to be taken from Sumner's *The Besom Maker*.

Coverage of the West Midlands (the counties of Warwickshire, Worcestershire, Herefordshire, Gloucestershire, and Monmouthshire) was uneven. Frederick Scarlett Potter, of Halford, near Shipston-on-Stour, was the source of the two Warwickshire songs, "Bedlam City" and "The Garden Gate." Lucy concluded that the former was a fragment of a longer broadside ballad, while the latter was a variant of a song printed in Bell's edition of *Ancient Poems, Ballads and Songs*. Mrs. Lawson of Upton-on-Severn provided two of the three Worcestershire items, "Poor Mary" and "The Three Dukes," both of which were children's game songs. The other, a lament, came from Mrs. Margaret Harley of Bewdley, and was titled "Sweet William." Lucy repeated Mrs. Harley's comment that "this song is a great favourite with the boys of Bewdley, who can give no account of it, except that 'there was an old man as used to sing it.' The best singer when he has ended the song always turns to the audience, remarking emphatically 'Till apples grows on an orange-tree,' probably the usual custom of the old ballad-singers."[40]

Sweet William

Anon

Fig. 11.7

O father, father, come build me a boat,
 That on this wild ocean I may float,
And ev'ry ship that I chance to meet,
I will enquire for my William sweet.

I had not sailed more than half an hour
Before I met with a man on board,
"Kind captain, captain, come tell me true,
Is my sweet William on board with you?"

"Oh no, fine lady, he is not here,
That he is drownèd most breaks my fear,

For the other night when the wind blew high,
That's when you lost your sweet sailor boy."

I'll set me down, and I'll write a song,
I'll write it neat, and I'll write it long,
And at every word I will drop a tear,
And in every line I'll set my Willie dear.

I wish, I wish, but it's all in vain,
I wish I was a sweet maid again.
For a maid, a maid I never shall be
Till apples grow on an orange tree.[41]

Two items, "Feast Song" and "The Shepherd's Song," were allocated to Gloucestershire, although the latter came from Warwickshire correspondent Frederick Scarlett Potter. It had been noted mainly from a shepherd named Thomas Coldicote, who lived in the Gloucestershire village of Ebrington. The editors were reduced to scraping the bottom of the barrel for Herefordshire: it was rather questionably represented by a carol, "A Virgin Unspotted," the tune of which was taken from Chappell's *Popular Music of the Olden Time.* Monmouthshire, along with most of the English-speaking counties of the Welsh marches, remained unrepresented.

Broadwood and Fuller Maitland separated Lincolnshire from the rest of the Midlands and included it instead in their fourth region, the Eastern Counties, by which they meant East Anglia and the Fenlands. This section was rather thin, comprising only eight items in total. Lincolnshire was represented by a children's game song called "Oats and Beans" and by a traditional ballad, "Little Sir William," a variant of Child no. 155 "Sir Hugh, or the Jew's Daughter." This was borrowed from Mason's *Nursery Rhymes and Country Songs,*[42] and elicited the editorial comment that the ballad was obviously a version of the legend of Saint Hugh of Lincoln, as told by the Prioress in Chaucer's *Canterbury Tales,* and that "Sir" was a corruption of "Saint."[43] From Norfolk came "Twenty, Eighteen," a curious mix of lyrics taken from the folksong commonly known as "Oh, No, John" and a children's backwards counting song. Words and tune had been collected in Besthorpe, near Attleborough, and Fuller Maitland had found it serendipitously in the September 1891 issue of the *Musical Herald.*[44] The other Norfolk song had been contributed by Miss F. Hamond of Swaffham and was a variant from oral tradition of the popular broadside ballad "Green Broom." Lucy pointed out that the broadside was included in *The Jolly Brown Man Garland,* a copy of which could be found in the British Museum, and that the song had been collected from singers in both the north and the southwest of England, having appeared in each of *Northumbrian Minstrelsy, Traditional Tunes* and *Songs and Ballads of the West.* This is the Norfolk version:

Green Broom

Anon

Fig. 11.8

Ah! there was an old man, and he lived in the East,
And his trade it was cutting o' broom, green broom,
And he had a son, a lazy boy John,
Who would lie a-bed till 'twas noon, 'twas noon,
Who would lie a-bed till 'twas noon, 'twas noon.

His father came up to his bedroom one day,
And swore he would fire the room, the room,
If Jack did not rise, and sharpen the knives,
And go to the wood to cut broom, green broom,
And go to the wood to cut broom, green broom.

Master Jack being sly, he git up by and bye,

And go into the town to cry broom, green broom;
So loud did he call, and so loudly did bawl,
"Pretty maids, do you want any broom, green broom?
Pretty maids do you want any broom, green broom?"

A lady looked out of her lattice so high,
And spied Jack a-crying o' broom, green broom;
Says she, "You young blade, won't you give up your trade,
And marry a maid in full bloom, full bloom?
And marry a maid in full bloom, full bloom?"

So they sent for the parson, without more delay,
And married they was in the room, the room;

There was eating and drink, and a kiss when you please;   Says Jack, "This is better than cutting o' broom."[45]
Says Jack, "This is better than cutting o' broom,"

Suffolk, the county located in East Anglia south of Norfolk, provided "Robin-a-Thrush," a comic song about a lazy wife whose cheese takes on a life of its own. This, according to its contributor, A. H. Frere, had been sung by a nurse at the end of the eighteenth century; Lucy noted that other variants of the song were to be found in *Nursery Rhymes and Country Songs* and *The Besom Maker*.[46] The other item ascribed to the same county, a chorus song called "Oliver Cromwell," had been learned by Lucy herself from a boy who presumably came from Suffolk, but she provided no details of when and where she had encountered the piece.[47] Essex, the southernmost county in East Anglia, was represented by only one song, a "May Day Carol" from J. F. Frye of Saffron Walden. Mr. Frye had apparently noted the song from children in Debden in 1857 and subsequently printed the tune and text, which he had forwarded to Fuller Maitland. It was an instance when pre-editing of otherwise valuable and interesting source material had evidently occurred, but Broadwood and Fuller Maitland, having nothing else available for that particular county, were, perhaps reluctantly, willing to trust the probity of the original editor turned contributor.[48] As mentioned earlier, "Ground for the Floor," a piece actually collected in Yorkshire, was linked unconvincingly by hearsay evidence to Cambridgeshire.[49] Neither Huntingdonshire nor Bedfordshire was represented at all. All in all, this Eastern segment was disappointingly meager, one of the least adequate sections of *English County Songs*.

The south of England, on the other hand, was Lucy Broadwood's home turf, and the quality of the collection improved once one reached London and the surrounding counties. The fifth section of the book was subtitled "Songs of the Home Counties," and it comprised sixteen items from the counties of Middlesex, Hertfordshire, Buckinghamshire, Berkshire, and Surrey. Only Bedfordshire was unrepresented. From Middlesex (read London) came four items, one of which was "Tripping Up the Green Grass," a children's game song noted by Margaret Collyer from the singing of an old family servant.[50] The other three were contributed by Alfred (A. J.) Hipkins, a Westminster organist, piano-tuner, and musicologist who (as we have seen) was a close friend of the Broadwood family and an employee of the Broadwood firm. "Farewell My Joy and Heart" was a short love lament that appeared to be a fragment of a ballad, "The Pair of Turtle-Doves," which Lucy located in the British Museum's Roxburghe collection. "Lavender Cries" was a set of four London street cries by sellers of lavender bunches, as heard in the streets of Kensington about a decade before.

Hipkins's most impressive contribution was "Lazarus," an organ tune that Lucy judged a particularly fine one, fitting the atmosphere and cadence of the ballad perfectly. But Hipkins knew of no words associated with his melody, and so a speculative leap was required to link it with the similarly titled religious ballad (Child no. 56 "Dives and Lazarus"). Fuller Maitland undertook some musical detective work in the tradition of William Chappell. Under the title "Worcestershire Carol" the words to "Diverus and Lazarus" had been printed in *Notes and Queries,* and, with Hipkins's help, in December 1892 he tracked down an old woman in Westminster who recognized the tune as belonging to the carol. He therefore included the *Notes and Queries* text in *English County Songs,* albeit with the disclaimer that "it is not claimed that these words belong to the beautiful tune here given, but they suit it so well that there is a great probability of their having at one time been associated together."[51] Fuller Maitland noted that another variant of the ballad could be found in Henry Husk's *Songs of the Nativity,* and there was strong evidence that it dated from at least the early seventeenth century, since it was alluded to in two Jacobean dramas, Fletcher's *Monsieur Thomas* and Beaumont and Fletcher's *Nice Valour.* Francis James Child had reprinted both Husk's variant and that from *Notes and Queries* in the second volume of *The English and Scottish Popular Ballads,* but without any tune. The bringing together of text and tune was thus a significant accomplishment. Here are the verses that Fuller Maitland took from *Notes and Queries,* followed by the beautiful "Lazarus" melody.

As it fell out upon one day,
Rich Diverus he made a feast,
And he invited all his friends,
And gentry of the best.

And it fell out upon one day,
Poor Lazarus he was so poor,
He came and laid him down and down,
Ev'n down at Diverus' door.

Then Lazarus laid him down and down,
Even at Diverus' gate:

"Some meat, some drink, brother Diverus,
For Jesus Christ his sake."

"Thou art none of mine, brother Lazarus,
Lying begging at my gate;
No meat, no drink will I give thee,
For Jesus Christ his sake."

And it fell out upon one day,
Rich Diverus he sickened and died;
There came two serpents out of hell,
His soul thereto to guide.

"Rise up, rise up, brother Diverus,
And come along with me;

There is a place prepared in hell,
For to sit upon a serpent's knee."[52]

Lazarus

Anon

As it fell out up - on one day, Rich Di-ver-us he made a

feast, And he in-vit-ed__ all his friends, and gent-ry of__ the best. And

it fel out up - on one day, Poor La-za-rus he was so poor, He came and laid him

down and down, Ev'n down at Di ver us' door. And it fell out up - on one day, Poor

La-za-rus he was so poor, He came and laid him down and down, Ev'n

down at Di-ver-us' door

Fig. 11.9

The county of Hertfordshire presented no problems. It was the new home of one of Lucy's favorite informants, Clara Wilson of King's Langley, and she offered "As I Sat on a Sunny Bank" (a variant of "I Saw Three Ships"):

As I sat on a sunny bank, a sunny bank, a sunny bank,
As I sat on a sunny bank, on Christmas Day in the morning.

I saw three ships come sailing in, come sailing in, come sailing in,
I saw three ships come sailing in, on Christmas Day in the morning.

I askèd them what they had in, what they had in, etc.

They said they had the Saviour in, etc.

I askèd them where they found Him, etc.

They said they found Him in Bethlehem, etc.

Now all the bells on earth shall ring, etc.

And all the angels in Heaven shall sing, etc.[53]

As I Sat on a Sunny Bank (I Saw Three Ships)

Anon

Fig. 11.10

Another King's Langley resident, Mrs. Marshall, was the source for a version of the May-Day carol, "The Moon Shines Bright," which Broadwood had already included in *Sussex Songs*.[54] A third local Hertfordshire singer, another of her informants, Thomas Gray of Weston, near Hitchin, also sang "The Moon Shines Bright," albeit to a different tune, and he contributed a courting ballad usually known as "The Fisherman" that he titled "As I Walked Out."[55]

Broadwood and Fuller Maitland lacked a contributor in neighboring Buckinghamshire, but they included "A Dashing Young Lad from Buckingham," supplied by Worcestershire correspondent Frederick Scarlett Potter.[56] In *Notes and Queries* they had also found the words of "The Prickly Bush," a version of Child no. 95 "The Maid Freed from the Gallows," contributed by Edmund Venables, a clergyman from Lincoln, who had learned them from a nurse who hailed from Buckinghamshire. As it happened, a variant of the same ballad had been submitted by Heywood Sumner, although he had actually collected it in Somerset. Sumner's version came equipped with a tune, so it was preferable to Venables's, but, by a sleight of hand, the item was still ascribed to Buckinghamshire. It hardly mattered, since the ballad would prove to be quite common throughout the southern counties of England, although Lucy did not yet know this. Here is Sumner's version of "The Prickly Bush":

"O hangman, hold thy hand," he cried, "O hold thy hand awhile,
For I can see my own dear father, coming over yonder stile."

"O father, have you brought me gold? Or will you set me free?
Or be you come to see me hung, all on this high gallows tree?"

"No, I have not brought thee gold, and I will not set thee free,
But I am come to see thee hung, all on this high gallows tree."

Oh, the prickly bush, the prickly bush, it pricked my heart full sore,

If I ever get out of the prickly bush, I'll never get in any more.

The Prickly Bush

Anon

Voice

"O hang man hold thy hand," he cried, "O hold thy hand a - while, for

I can see my own dear father com ing ov-er yon - der stile." Oh, the pri-ck - ly bush

..., the pr-ck-ly — bush, It pricked — my heart full — sore, If ev-er I get out of the

pri-ck-ly — bush, — I'll never get in — an-y more. —

Fig. 11.11

"O hangman, hold thy hand," he cried, "O hold thy hand awhile,
For I can see my own dear mother, coming over yonder stile."

"O mother, have you brought me gold? Or will you set me free?
Or be you come to see me hung, all on this high gallows tree?"

"No, I have not brought thee gold, and I will not set thee free,
But I am come to see thee hung, all on this high gallows tree."

Oh, the prickly bush, the prickly bush, it pricked my heart full sore,
If I ever get out of the prickly bush, I'll never get in any more.

"O hangman, hold thy hand," he cried, "O hold thy hand awhile,
For I can see my own dear brother, coming over yonder stile."

"O brother, have you brought me gold? Or will you set me free?
Or be you come to see me hung, all on this high gallows tree?"

"No, I have not brought thee gold, and I will not set thee free,
But I am come to see thee hung, all on this high gallows tree."

Oh, the prickly bush, the prickly bush, it pricked my heart full sore,
If I ever get out of the prickly bush, I'll never get in any more.

"O hangman, hold thy hand," he cried, "O hold thy hand awhile,
For I can see my own dear sister, coming over yonder stile."

"O sister, have you brought me gold? Or will you set me free?
Or be you come to see me hung, all on this high gallows tree?"

"No, I have not brought thee gold, and I will not set thee free,
But I am come to see thee hung, all on this high gallows tree."

Oh, the prickly bush, the prickly bush, it pricked my heart full sore,
If I ever get out of the prickly bush, I'll never get in any more.

"O hangman, hold thy hand," he cried, "O hold thy hand awhile,
For I can see my own dear sweetheart, coming over yonder stile."

"O sweetheart, have you brought me gold? Or will you set me free?
Or be you come to see me hung, all on this high gallows tree?"

"Yes, I have brought thee gold," she cried, "And I will set thee free,
And I am come, but not to see thee hung, all on this high gallows tree."

Oh, the prickly bush, the prickly bush, it pricked my heart full sore,
If I ever get out of the prickly bush, I'll never get in any more.[57]

For Berkshire, Broadwood and Fuller Maitland had two songs from Mark Wyatt of Enborne. "The Farmer's Daughter" was a variant of the feminist broadside usually called "The Banks of Sweet Dundee" or "The Undaunted Female," and the text of Wyatt's version was similar to that printed by William Barrett in *English Folk-Songs*, although in Lucy's opinion Wyatt's tune was clearly superior. She noted that Kidson had also included the broadside text and two tunes for the ballad in *Traditional Tunes*.[58] Wyatt's other offering was a version of "The Farmer's Boy," again similar to that collected by Kidson. A correspondent named G. K. Fortescue supplied the tune of a third item, "The Barkshire Tragedy." Confusingly, this was not a version of the broadside murder ballad often found under that title but also known as "The Oxford (or Wexford) Girl." It was instead an interesting variant of "The Two Sisters" or "Binnorie" (Child no. 10), in which the victim survived until reaching the mill pond and was then murdered by the miller:[59]

The Barkshire Tragedy

Anon

Fig. 11.12

Fuller Maitland was reduced to taking the words of this broadside ballad from a book by Thomas Hughes, *The Scouring of the White Horse*.[60] A footnote observed:

> This is one of very many variants of the ballad usually known as "Binnorie," which appears in different forms in many countries. The peculiarities of the English ballad are the presence of a third sister, not required by the story; the fact that the maiden was alive when she reached the mill; the brutal cruelty of the miller; the Crowner; the fate of the miller, and the horrible ending of the elder sister. In *The Scouring of the White Horse* there is

another ballad, which takes up the story at the point where the harper discovers the body and strings his harp with the maiden's hair. In this instance the instrument is a "fiddoll," and the process of stringing is described most realistically.[61]

It is not clear which of the two editors wrote that accompanying note, but it revealed that they knew the Lancastrian version of the text printed by John Harland in *Ballads and Songs of Lancashire*, and also of the existence of another broadside variant titled "The King and the Miller's Daughter," which was dated to 1656 and said to be the work of Dr. James Smith (1604-1667). They were also aware that Francis James Child had compiled multiple variant texts of the ballad, but since the footnote only cited vaguely "Child's *Ballads*" it is not clear whether this was the first volume of *The English and Scottish Popular Ballads* or Child's earlier published collection, *English and Scottish Ballads*. Here is Hughes's text, but to save space I have omitted the repeat of the first line and the two chorus lines except in the first verse (they should be included in each stanza when the ballad is sung):

A varmer he lived in the West Countree,
With a hey down, bow down;
A varmer he lived in the West Countree,
And he had daughters, one, two, and three,
And I'll be true to my love, if my love'll be true to me.

As they were walking by the river's brim,
The eldest pushed the youngest in.

"O sister, O sister, pray gee me thy hand,
And I'll gee thee both house and land."

"I'll neither gee thee hand nor glove,
Unless thou'lt gee me thine own true love."

So down she sank, and away she swam,
Until she came to the miller's dam.

"O vather, O vather, here swims a swan,
Very much like a drownded gentlewoman."

The miller he got his pole and hook,
And he fished the fair maid out of the brook.

"O miller, I'll gee thee guineas ten,
If thou'lt fetch me back to my vather again."

The miller he took her guineas ten,
And he pushed the fair maid in again.

But the Crowner he came, and the Justice too,
With a hue and a cry and a hullabaloo.

They hanged the miller beside his own gate,
For drowning the varmer's daughter Kate.

The sister she fled beyond the seas,
And died an old maid among black savages.

So I've ended my tale of the West Countree,
And they calls it the Barkshire Tragedee.[62]

That left Surrey, an easy county since Lucy had done some collecting of her own there from George Grantham, the carter discovered by her sister-in-law Ada at Anstie, near Holmwood. Four of his songs were included: "Venus and Adonis," "The Sweet Nightingale," "Sheepcrook and Black Dog," and the song quoted in the previous chapter, "The Painful Plough."[63] "The Sweet Nightingale" was a pretty duet song which Grantham had learned from two farmers named Upfold and Stanford at Cranleigh in Surrey. Lucy pointed out in a note that William Barrett had included a different version in *English Folk-Songs*. This is how she had noted it from her own source, the carter:

One morning in May by chance I did rove,
I sat myself down by the side of a grove,
And there did I hear the sweet nightingale sing,
I never heard so sweet, I never heard so sweet,
I never heard so sweet as the birds in the Spring.

All on the green grass I sat myself down,
Where the voice of the nightingale echoed around,
"Don't you hear how she quivers the notes?" I declare
No music, no songster, no music, no songster,
No music, no songster with her can compare.

Come all you young men, I'll have you draw near,
I pray you now heed me these words for to hear,
That when you're grown old you may have it to sing,
That you never heard so sweet, that you never heard so sweet,
That you never heard so sweet as the birds in the Spring.[64]

The Sweet Nightingale

Anon

One morn-ing in May by chance I did rove, I sat my-self down by the side of a grove, And there did I hear the sweet night-in-gale sing, I nev-er heard so sweet, I nev-er heard so sweet, I nev-er heard so sweet as the birds in the Spring.

Fig. 11.13

Broadwood and Fuller Maitland's last region, the South Coast, was a large one, and might well have been divided into southeast and southwest. There was a wealth of material available for this section, which comprised the counties of Kent, Sussex, Hampshire, Wiltshire, Dorset, Somerset, Devon, and Cornwall. Twenty-two items were selected for inclusion in the book. Sussex was easy, except for the problem of what to leave out. Lucy's own collecting provided almost all the items, although one exception was "Faithful Emma," which might have been more appropriately titled "Faithless Mary." It had been noted by Heywood Sumner from a man in his local church choir. The tune was a favorite of Lucy's but she regarded the text as an imperfect fragment, the result, she suggested, of the first three verses of one ballad tacked on to the ending of another. As she justly remarked, "the connection between Emma's faith and Mary's fickleness is not apparent," but she nonetheless printed the text as the informant had sung it to Sumner:

The lambs they skip with pleasure,
And the meadows are so green,
One of the finest mountains
That ever eyes have seen.
There's fine hunting, fine fishing,
And fine fowling also,
On top of yonder mountain
Where the finest flowers grow.

On the top of yonder mountain
There my true love's castle stands,
It is decked up with ivy
From the top down to the strands.
There's fine arches, fine porches,
And there's diamond stones so bright,
It's a pilot for the sailors
On a dark and stormy night.

At the bottom of the mountain
There's a river runs so clear,
And a ship from the West Indies
Once lay at anchor there;
With a red flag a-flying
And the beating of a drum,
Sweet instruments of music,
And the firing of a gun.

If little Mary had proved faithful
She might have been my bride,
But her mind it was more fickle
Than the rain upon the tide,
Like a ship upon the ocean
That is tossed to and fro,
May the angels now direct her
Wherever she may go![65]

Faithful Emma

Anon

The lambs they skip with pleas ure, and the mead ows are so green, One___
of the fin - est moun - tains That ev - er eyes have seen. There's fine hunt - ing, fine
fish ing, And fine fowl - ing al - so, On the top of yond-er moun tain Where the fin - est flow-ers
grow.

Fig. 11.14

Lucy's own informant, the gamekeeper John Burberry, provided three other jolly items credited to Sussex, "The Mistress's Health," "The Carter's Health," and a song reproduced in the previous chapter, "The Seasons of the Year."[66] Her first discovery, Samuel Willett of Cuckfield, contributed "The Farmer's Boy" and the blacksmithing song given earlier, "Twankydillo."[67] He also did the honors for Kent, having learned "John Appleby," a hop-picker's song, while working in the hop fields of that county.[68]

Hampshire was a little more of a problem, as neither Lucy nor any of her correspondents except Heywood Sumner had done any collecting from oral tradition in that county. However, Davies Gilbert's *Some Ancient Christmas Carols* was raided for "The Servingman and the Husbandman," while "The Reaphook and the Sickle" was borrowed from Sumner's *The Besom Maker*. Moreover, Lucy's informant Mrs. Patience Vaisey, the gardener's wife at Adwell House (the Reynardsons' country estate in Oxfordshire), had grown up in Hampshire, and so her rendition of "My Bonnie, Bonnie Boy" (reproduced in the previous chapter) was counted as a Hampshire item. Lucy commented that this song was similar to a ballad in Chappell's *Popular Music of the Olden Time* called "My Bonnie Bird, or Cupid's Trepan," which dated from the reign of Charles II, and that the same words as sung by Mrs. Vaisey had been printed in an eighteenth-century songbook, *The New Cabinet of Love, songs sung at Vauxhall*. The tune, she remarked, showed the influence of the Dorian mode, which suggested that the song had either begun its life as a folksong or had been modified in oral tradition.[69] For the county of Wiltshire Lucy could rely on three contributions noted locally by Mrs. Lavinia Squarey, a correspondent from the village of Downton, near Salisbury. They were a "Sheep-shearing Song," a "Harvest Song," and "The Jolly Ploughboy," although the latter was only a fragment and had to be completed from a Hampshire version supplied by Heywood Sumner.[70]

Moving on to the southwest, we find Dorset represented by two items: "I'm a Man That's Done Wrong to My Parents" (collected by H. Strachey from a collier at Bishop Sutton and also from a whistling laborer at Shillingham), and an interesting cumulative song, "The Twelve Apostles." Lucy was fascinated with the symbolism in this song and its multiple variants, and she would subsequently devote much time and energy to collecting them and trying to determine their meaning (if any), which she came to suspect had some connection with Freemasonry. The Dorset version, which had been collected by the Reverend W. Miles Barnes, had a very simple tune and some rather puzzling words:

The Twelve Apostles

Anon

Come, I will sing to you. What will you sing to me? I will sing you one oh! What may your one oh be? One and one is all a-lone and ev-er more shall be___ so. Two of them are li-ly white babes, cloth-ed all in green___ oh! Three of them are thri-vers. Four are the Gosp-el preach-ers.

Fig. 11.15

Come, I will sing to you.
What will you sing to me?
I will sing you one oh!
What may your one oh be?
One and one is all alone,
And evermore shall be so.

Come, I will sing to you.
What will you sing to me?
I will sing you two oh!
What may your two oh be?
Two of them are lilywhite babes,
Clothèd all in green oh!
One and one is all alone,
And evermore shall be so.

Three of them are thrivers.

Four are the Gospel preachers.

Five are the flamboys all in a row.

Six are the six bold waiters.

Seven are the seven stars in the sky.

Eight are the Gabriel angels.

Nine and nine of the brightest shine.

Ten are the ten commandments.

Eleven and eleven went to heaven.

Twelve are the twelve apostles.[71]

Lucy also printed a variant titled "Green Grow the Rushes, Oh!" which she had found in an Eton College songbook, in which some of the words seemed, at first glance, to make a little more sense, for example "three, three for the rivals" and "five for the symbol at your door." In an extensive two-page commentary she appended a detailed discussion of some of the other alternative lines submitted by readers to *Notes and Queries*. For example, alternatives to "thrivers" for number three included not only "the rivals" but also "drivers," "divers," "rhymers," "wisers," "arrows," "rare O's," and "strangers," but it was difficult to see how any of these were corruptions of a term for the three Persons of the Trinity, the usual suggestion for the underlying meaning of the line. A more plausible alternative, suggested by "wisers" and "strangers" was that the number actually referred to the three Wise Men from the East. As for number six, she suggested that "bold waiters" was a corruption of "bowls of water," a reference to the six water-pots employed in the miracle of Cana in Galilee.[72]

Lucy also knew of a Somerset version of "The Twelve Apostles" but she declined to print it, on the grounds that the words were complete nonsense, made so for the sake of rhyming. She had, in any case, plenty of material available to represent that county. "Bristol City," a broadside ballad credited to the singing of a Mr. Huttley "at the Convivial Societies of Bath and Bristol," was not, she admitted, a traditional song and so was "strictly speaking, outside the scope of the collection," but she included it because of its pretty tune.[73] Somersetshire also produced a hunting song, "The Cheerful Arn" (collected by Arthur Thompson in the pub of an unidentified village), and a humorous courting song in local dialect, "Young Herchard" (aka "Richard of Taunton Dene"), supplied by A. H. Frere. Heywood Sumner had also noted in the county a version of Child no. 4 ("Lady Isabel and the Elf Knight") titled "The Outlandish Knight," which Lucy described as a "fine ballad…known all over the north of Europe." She pointed out that an alternative version could be found in Burne's *Shropshire Folk-Lore,* and she referred her readers to Kidson's *Traditional Tunes* for a discussion of different melodies to which the ballad was sung in the north of England.[74]

Cornwall was under-represented, with only "Adam and Eve," collected, presumably from a parishioner, by Lucy's relative, the Reverend J. Shearme,[75] but there were three songs from Devon. Two of them, "The Green Bushes" and "The Loyal Lover" came courtesy of the Reverend Sabine Baring-Gould,[76] while the other, a cumulative song, "The Tree in the Valley," was taken from Harriet Mason's *Nursery Rhymes and Country Songs.* Lucy confirmed that it had in fact been collected in Devon, and that Baring-Gould had noted another version of it in the same county.[77] Although both of Baring-Gould's items had been included in *Songs and Ballads of the West* the versions printed by Lucy were not duplicates. In both cases the tunes were different. "The Green Bushes," for example, appears to have been James Parsons's variant, rather than the one sung by Robert Hard, which Baring-Gould had preferred to use in *Songs and Ballads.*

The Green Bushes

Anon

Fig. 11.16

As I was a-walking one morning in May,
To hear the birds whistle, see lambkins at play,
I spied a fair damsel, Oh sweetly sang she:
"Down by the green bushes he thinks to meet me."

"Oh, where are you going, my sweet pretty maid?"
"My lover I'm seeking, kind Sir," she said,
"Shall I be your lover, and will you agree
To forsake the old love, and foregather with me?"

"I'll buy you fine beavers, a gay silken gown,
With furbelowed petticoats flounced to the ground,
If you'll leave your old love, and following me,

Forsake the green bushes, where he waits for thee."

"Quick, let us be moving from under the trees,
Quick, let us be moving, kind Sir, if you please;
For yonder my true love is coming, I see,
Down by the green bushes he thinks to meet me."

The old love arrived, the maiden was gone,
He sighed very deeply, he sighed all alone,
"She is on with another, before off with me,
So adieu ye green bushes, for ever," said he.

"I'll be as a schoolboy, I'll frolic and play,
No false-hearted maiden shall trouble my day,

Untroubled at night I will slumber and snore,   So adieu, ye green bushes, I'll fool it no more!"[78]

   English County Songs was rounded out with four sea songs that the editors were unable or unwilling to link with any particular county, although "All on Spurn Point," collected by Herbert M. Bower from a Whitby fisherman (probably William Moat), was clearly from the northeast of England and could have been included with other Yorkshire songs. As we shall see later, Frank Kidson had also collected this disaster ballad from a sailor (Charley Dickenson) on the North Yorkshire coast, and he had picked up a copy of the full broadside text. It is reproduced, along with Dickenson's tune, in chapter 14. Another broadside ballad—a comic one this time—had been noted from an elderly workman at Buckland Newton, Dorset, in 1891. It was a seafarer's equivalent to "The Derby Ram," titled "The Crocodile."[79] Of a more generic nature were "My Johnny Was a Shoemaker," taken from Sumner's *The Besom Maker,* and a version of Child ballad no. 286, "The *Golden Vanity*." In her notes to the song Lucy referenced other variants in several Victorian publications, including W. H. Logan's *A Pedlar's Pack of Ballads,* Laura Smith's *Music of the Waters,* Baring-Gould's *Songs and Ballads of the West,* and the ubiquitous *Notes & Queries.*[80] The version she printed, however, had been obtained by her cousin Herbert Birch Reynardson from Robert C. Thomson:

The Golden Vanity

Anon

There was a ship came from the___north coun-try,   And the name of the ship was the Gold-en Va-ni-ty,   And they feared she might be tak-en by the Turk-ish en-e-my,   That sails up-on the Low-land, Low-land, that sails up on the Low-land sea.

Fig. 11.17

There was a ship came from the north country,
And the name of the ship was the *Golden Vanity*,
And they feared she might be taken by the Turkish
                                           enemy,
That sails upon the Lowland, Lowland,
That sails upon the Lowland sea.

There up there came a little cabin-boy,
And he said to the skipper, "What will you give to me,
If I swim alongside of the Turkish enemy,
And sink her in the Lowland, Lowland,
And sink her in the Lowland sea?"

"O I will give you silver and I will give you gold,

And my only daughter your bride to be,
If you'll swim alongside of the Turkish enemy,
And sink her in the Lowland," etc.

Then the boy made him ready, and overboard sprang he,
And he swam alongside of the Turkish enemy,
And with his auger sharp in her side he bored holes three,
And he sank her in the Lowland, etc.

Then the boy turned round, and back swam he,
And he cried out to the skipper of the Golden Vanity,
But the skipper did not heed, for his promise he would need;
And he left him in the Lowland, etc.

Then the boy swam round, and came to the port side,
And he looked up at his messmates, and bitterly he cried,
"O messmates, take me up, for I'm drifting with the tide,
And I'm sinking in the Lowland, etc."

His messmates took him up, but on the deck he died,
They sewed him in his hammock that was so large and wide,
And they lowered him overboard, but he drifted with the tide,
And he sank beneath the Lowland, etc.[81]

Broadwood and Fuller Maitland's readers had now traveled in song from the Scottish border to Land's End and even out to sea. *English County Songs* included ninety-two songs in all, and, taken as a whole, it was an impressive achievement. Yet the collection clearly had its limitations and problems. As we have seen, Lucy and her co-editor had to rely for the bulk of the collection on submissions from correspondents, friends, and co-enthusiasts, and there was no guarantee that songs mailed in by these contributors had been taken down accurately or submitted exactly as collected. Some texts were incomplete and had to be completed from broadsides, usually from those in the Roxburghe collection in the British Museum. Moreover, as we have seen, other songs were taken from earlier publications: Marianne Harriet Mason's *Nursery Rhymes and Country Songs,* Heywood Sumner's *The Besom Maker,* Davies Gilbert's *Some Ancient Christmas Carols,* Sabine Baring-Gould's *Songs and Ballads of the West,* and two other regional compilations, Edward Jones's *Popular Cheshire Melodies,*[82] and Charlotte Burne's *Shropshire Folk-Lore.* Twenty-two items were taken, in whole or in part, from these printed sources. Here it was a question of trusting the probity of the respective editors, and again Broadwood and Fuller Maitland had little choice in the matter since they needed to fill the geographical gaps left by their other collaborators' submissions. Despite this, coverage of England was still uneven, with some remaining gaps and other thin areas.

Another defect was that the editors often did not know, or chose not to reveal, source singers' names and places of residence. This editorial practice was contrary to that adopted by Sabine Baring-Gould in *Songs and Ballads of the West.*[83] The format in which the songs were presented was also controversial: forty-seven were harmonized for piano by Lucy and most of the rest by Fuller Maitland. This practice, although standard for the time, was in noticeable contrast to that adopted by Frank Kidson in *Traditional Tunes,* which eschewed piano arrangements.[84] The editors apparently did have some reservations about including piano arrangements, which effectively presented folksongs as if they were art songs, but they were quick to defend their practice in the preface:

> While to give the tunes without accompaniment is doubtless the most scientific method of preserving the songs, it has the disadvantage of rendering them practically useless to educated singers. The accompaniments have been kept as simple as possible, and in all cases the editors have endeavoured to preserve the character of the period to which they suppose the tune to belong.[85]

In other words, Lucy *was* sensitive to an editorial conflict between the most scholarly way of presenting the collection and Fuller Maitland's (and her own) desire that it be used as a songbook by 'educated' (read middle-class, often trained-voice) singers. Her (and Fuller Maitland's) choice was the pragmatic option.

Despite its faults, *English County Songs* was a significant achievement. The editors claimed, apparently correctly, that nearly two-thirds of the songs in the collection had never been published before. The book certainly demonstrated that traditional song was alive and available to be noted in most corners of England (including the streets of London), and it provided a basis upon which subsequent regional collections could build. Moreover, it proclaimed the aim of collecting folksongs from oral tradition rather than from library manuscripts and broadsides. It also stated the principle that a collector should publish a song exactly as it was sung to him or her: neither the tune nor the words should be modified.[86] This "antiquarian" policy was highly controversial at the time, and in Broadwood and Fuller Maitland's embracing of it we can see at work the influence of Joseph Ritson (the first collector to champion the approach), Frederick Furnivall and the Ballad Society, and, even more recently, that of Francis Child, with whose editorial approach in *The English and Scottish Popular Ballads* Lucy had recently become acquainted.

In practice, *English County Songs* did not fully implement these principles, but it was nonetheless a pioneering work that marked an important first step. The book suggested a methodological framework within which regional collecting could be pursued with increased vigor, albeit along lines already demonstrated by John Stokoe, Frank Kidson, and Sabine Baring-Gould. Only William Barrett had previously published a nation-wide survey of English folksong in which authentic traditional texts and tunes were both provided, and his smaller collection had not attempted to cover the various regions of England in the same comprehensive manner.[87] However, the full significance of what Broadwood and Fuller Maitland had attempted does not seem to have been fully appreciated at the time. Reviews were mixed, and Lucy must have become very tired of being told that a given song was not the exclusive property of the county to which it was assigned in the book, a complaint she had anticipated and tried to disarm in the preface. Nonetheless, the collection sold quite well, affording Lucy a small but fairly steady income for two decades.[88]

Collecting, Singing, and Networking, 1893-96

Harmonizing songs for *English County Songs* and correcting the proofs of the book took up most of Lucy's time during the summer and fall of 1892, although, as we have seen, she continued to do some collecting, Patience Vaisey of Tetsworth, Oxfordshire, being one of her most valuable informants. Early in the new year Lucy dispatched the last set of proofs to the publisher and thereafter her diaries show a renewed focus on her own singing, with folksong playing a larger role in her repertoire. She had been asked to provide the musical illustrations for a lecture by Mr. W. Frere to the Society for Plain Song Music on the subject of "Tonality of Popular Songs," and on 24 January 1893 she did so, singing "My Bonny Boy," "Adieu Lovely Mary," and "Cupid, the Pretty Ploughboy."[89] After the talk she chatted with the Reverend H. Fleetwood Sheppard, who had helped Baring-Gould with noting the tunes in *Songs and Ballads of the West*. As mentioned previously, Lucy was not a fan of Fleetwood Sheppard's piano arrangements but she was eager to resume her friendship with Baring-Gould, with whom she had corresponded several times during 1891 but temporarily lost touch the next year. They resumed their correspondence that February.[90] Frank Kidson was by now another regular correspondent,[91] and on 22 February Lucy was delighted to receive a present of an autographed and annotated copy of *Traditional Tunes* that Kidson had personally bound in leather.[92] April 1893 saw her traveling to Leeds where she performed in a concert, met Kidson for the first time, and was shown his extensive collection of old songbooks and broadsheets.[93] *English County Songs* was finally in the bookstores at the beginning of July, just in time for Lucy to show a copy to her father, who was very ill and in fact died on 8 July.[94]

If her father's passing was the low point of 1893 for Lucy, the high point was her discovery of Henry Burstow. The diaries do not reveal exactly how and when this occurred, but we know that on 2 May Lucy noted a batch of songs from him, apparently for the first time.[95] Burstow was a 68-year-old shoemaker, who had lived all his life in Horsham, Sussex, so it is likely that she traveled to Horsham to interview him. A music-lover whose hobby was bell-ringing, he was a willing informant and delighted in singing items from his extensive repertoire. He eventually penned an autobiographical account of Horsham and his life there.[96] Lucy later wrote the following brief account of her informant:

> As a boy he was apprenticed to the shoemaking trade, but [he] is best known as a bell-ringer. It has lately been written of him that his reputation "stands unrivalled in England, and there is hardly a belfry in the land where his name and fame are not known and respected." And this, although during eighty-three years he has slept only six nights away from his native town. Mr. Burstow has from childhood made bell-ringing and song-singing his hobbies. He has a list of more than four hundred songs, old and new, which he knows by heart. Amongst them [are] about fifty or sixty of the traditional ballad type, and these have been noted and preserved. Mr. Burstow learned some of his songs from his parents, and many "old songs and ballets off shoemakers singing at their work." Others he learned from labourers, many of whom could not read. His excellent ear and sense of rhythm have probably been developed by constant bell-ringing, in which he still joins…with energy and skill.[97]

During the three occasions that Lucy collected songs from Burstow during 1893 and 1894, he sang her (and she noted down) at least forty-three items, although this was only one tenth of his repertoire which was approximately 420 in total.[98] In alphabetical order those songs that Lucy definitely collected from Burstow (and copies of which are extant) are:

"The Ages of Man"
"Americans That Stole My True Love"
"As I Was A-Walking"
"Banstead Downs" (aka "Georgie")
"Belfast Mountains"
"Bitter and Cold Was the Night,"
"Bold Collins"
"The Bold Pedlar and Robin Hood"
"Boney's Lamentation" (or "Boney's Abdication")
"Bristol Town"
"The Cobbler"
"Come All You Lads and Lasses Gay"
"Come Forth Noble Masters…" (untitled),
"Death and the Lady"
"The Duke of Marlborough"
"Female Sailor, a true song"
"Female Smuggler, or Highwayman"
"Four and Nine"

"The Gallant Poachers" (aka "Van Diemen's Land")
"Gibson, Wilson and Johnson" (aka "The Three Butchers")
"Gilderoy"
"Green Bushes"
"Hay Makers"
"I Must Live All Alone"
"King Pharim"
"Madame, Do You Know My Trade Is War"
"The Merchant's Daughter" (aka "The Constant Farmer's Son")
"Months of the Year"
"The Moon Shines Bright"
"My Friend and Pitcher"
"Plough Bob"
"Poor Fisherman's Boy"
"Rosetta and her Gay Ploughboy"
"The Rover"
"Salt Seas" (aka "Henry Martin")
"The Scarlet Flower"

Burstow lent Lucy his song-list, but he refused to sing some of the items on it to her, on the grounds that the words were not fit for a lady's ears. These unfortunately included quite a few which, by their titles, promised to be among the very oldest ballads, and since he could not detach the tunes from the words, Lucy was unable to note even the melodies. One of the songs that he did sing, and which enchanted her at that first meeting on 2 May, was "Belfast Mountains," a simple lament with a haunting tune. Although the song depicted a scene in Northern Ireland, the text was on a broadside published initially in Manchester, although likely reprinted in London, since Burstow had learned it in the south of England.

Belfast Mountains

Anon

Fig. 11.18

All on the Belfast mountains I heard a maid complain,
Making forth her lamentations down by some purling stream,
Saying, "I am confined all in the bands of love,
All by a false pretender who doth inconstant prove."

"Oh, Johnny! My dear jewel, don't treat me with disdain!
Nor leave me here behind you in sorrow to complain!"
With her arms she clasps around him, like violets round the vine,
Saying, "My bonny Cheshire lad, you've stole this heart of mine."

"My dear, I'm sorry for you, that you for me should grieve,
I am engaged already; 'tis you I can't relieve."
"Since it is so, my Johnny, for ever I'm undone,
All by this shame and scandal I shall distracted run."

"If I'd but all those diamonds on yonder rock that grow,
I would give them to my Cheshire lad, if his love to me he'd show."
Wringing her hands and crying, "My Johnny dear, farewell!

Unto those Belfast mountains my sorrow I will tell."

"It's not those Belfast mountains can give to me relief,
Nor is it in their power to ease me of my grief;
If they'd but a tongue to prattle, to tell my love a tale,
Unto my bonny Cheshire lad my mind they would reveal."[100]

Lucy was so impressed by Burstow's extensive repertoire, reliable memory, and the quality of his singing that she arranged for him to travel to Lyne on 20 May to perform for two house-guests, Alec Fuller Maitland and A. J. Hipkins.[101] Her diaries do not reveal which songs Burstow sang on this occasion, but it is likely that "The Bold Pedlar and Robin Hood" (Child no. 132) was one of them. It was one thing to find Robin Hood texts on old broadsheets, but quite another to locate one with a tune, in oral tradition. Finding a vernacular version of "The Bold Pedlar and Robin Hood" was therefore something of a *coup,* and it is likely that Lucy wished to show off this 'find' to her fellow enthusiasts. Burstow's text was derived from a Such broadside, and was similar to that reprinted by Robert Bell in his edition of *Ancient Poems, Ballads and Songs of the Peasantry of England.* The ballad related essentially the same story as that in "Robin Hood Newly Revived" (aka "Robin Hood and the Stranger"), in which the protagonist is called Gamwell, a common seventeenth-century broadside found in the Pepys, Wood, and Douce collections and reprinted in *Robin Hood's Garland.*

The Bold Pedlar and Robin Hood

Anon

Fig. 11.19

There chanced to be a pedlar bold,
A pedlar bold there chanced to be;
He put his pack all on his back,
And so merrily trudgèd o'er the lea.

By chance he met two troublesome men,
Two troublesome men they chanced to be,
The one of them was bold Robin Hood,
And the other was Little John so free.

"O, pedlar, pedlar, what is in thy pack?
Come speedily and tell to me."
"I've several suits of the gay green silks,
And silken bowstrings by two or three."

"If you have several suits of the gay green silk,

And silken bowstrings two or three,
Then, by my body," cries Little John,
"One half of your pack shall belong to me."

"O, nay, O nay," said the pedlar bold,
"O nay, O nay, that never can be,
For there's never a man from fair Nottingham,
Can take one half of my pack from me."

Then the pedlar he pulled off his pack,
And he put it a little below his knee,
Saying, "If you do move me one perch from this,
My pack and all shall gang with thee."

Then Little John he drew his sword,
The pedlar by his pack did stand,
They fought until they both did sweat,

Till he cried, "Pedlar, pray hold your hand."

Then Robin Hood he was standing by,
And he did laugh most heartily,
Saying, "I could find a man of smaller scale,
Could thrash the pedlar and also thee."

"Go you try, master," says Little John,
"Go you try, master, most speedily,
For by my body," says Little John,
"I am sure this night you will know me."

Then Robin Hood he drew his sword,
And the pedlar by his pack did stand;
They fought till the blood in streams did flow,
Till he cried, "Pedlar, pray hold your hand."

"O pedlar, pedlar, what is thy name?
Come speedily and tell to me."
"Come, my name I ne'er will tell,
Till both your names you have told to me."

"The one of us is bold Robin Hood,
And the other Little John so free."
"Now," says the pedlar, "it lays to my good will,
Whether my name I choose to tell to thee."

"I am Gamble Gold of the gay green woods,
And travelled far beyond the sea,
For killing a man in my father's land,
And from my country was forced to flee."

"If you are Gamble Gold of the gay green woods,
And travelled far beyond the sea,
You are my mother's own sister's son,
What nearer cousins can we be?"

They sheathed their swords, with friendly words,
So merrily they did agree,
They went to a tavern and there they dined,
And cracked bottles most merrily.[102]

Lucy's third session with Burstow took place at Lyne on 1 January 1894, at which time she noted the melodies of twelve of his songs: "Americans That Stole My True Love," "The Female Smuggler" (a tune Burstow also used for "The Female Highwayman"), "Green Bushes," "Henry Martin" (which Burstow knew as "Salt Seas"), "King Pharim," "The Moon Shines Bright," "Poor Fisherman's Boy," "The Rover," "Stinson the Deserter," "The Three Butchers" (which Burstow called "Gibson, Wilson and Johnson"), and "Yarmouth Is a Pretty Town."[103] Of these items Lucy was particularly taken with the last two and with the traditional pirate ballad "Henry Martin" (Child no. 250). Burstow's version of the latter was quite similar to that printed by Kidson in *Traditional Tunes,* but it was not the only Child ballad that he sang. In addition to "Henry Martin" and "The Bold Pedlar and Robin Hood," he also knew a version of "Geordie" (Child no. 209), although his title for it was "Banstead Downs." As we have seen in chapter 8, Frank Kidson's collaborator Charles Lolley knew a Yorkshire version of the ballad, the tune of which had appeared in *Traditional Tunes* with a set of Scottish words borrowed from Johnson's *Museum.* Burstow's variant, of course, was English, and it probably derived from a broadside titled "The Life and Death of George of Oxford." It differed markedly in both tune and text from that printed by Kidson.

As I rode over Banstead Downs,
One mid-May morning early,
There I espied a pretty fair maid,
Lamenting for her Georgie.

Saying, "Georgie never stood on the King's
                                highway,
He never robbèd money,
But he stole fifteen of the King's fat deer,
And sent them to Lord Navey."

"Oh, come and saddle my milk-white steed,
And bridle it all ready,
That I may go to my good Lord Judge
And ask for the life of my Georgie."

And when she came to the good Lord Judge,
She fell down upon her knees already,

Saying, "My good Lord Judge, come pity me,
Grant me the life of my Georgie."

The judge he looked over his left shoulder,
He seemed as he was very sorry:
"My pretty fair maid, you are come too late,
For he is condemned already."

He will be hung in a silken cord
Where there has not been many,
For he came of royal blood
And courted a virtuous lady."

"I wish I was on yonder hill,
Where times I have been many!
With a sword and a buckler by my side
I would fight for the life of my Georgie."[104]

Banstead Downs (Georgie)

Anon

Voice

As I rode ov - er Ban - stead Downs, One mid - May morn - ing

ea - r - ly, There I esp - ied a pret - ty fair maid, La - ment - ing for her

Georg - ie. Say - ing, "Georg - ie nev - er stood on the King's high - way, He __ nev - er rob - bed

mon - ey, __ But he stole fif - teen of the King's fat deer, And sent them to Lord

Nav - cy.

Fig. 11.20

Henry Burstow was the most prolific informant that Lucy ever found, and when she eventually (in 1908) published a book-length selection from her collecting, his songs featured heavily in it. *English Traditional Songs and Carols* would include eighteen items noted from Burstow, more than half the book's contents. All eighteen had been collected in 1893-94, most of them were narrative ballads of one kind or another, and most of the ballads were based on broadside texts. Several of these dealt with the triumph over adversity by a pair of lovers upon whom fate had not initially looked kindly, for example "Rosetta and her Gay Ploughboy," "Through Moorfields," "Bristol Town," and "The Wealthy Farmer's Son." Others, such as "Belfast Mountains," "Yarmouth Is a Pretty Town," and the well-known broadside, "The Merchant's Daughter, or the Constant Farmer's Son," told love stories with sadder outcomes. The last-named had the same theme as Child no. 69 "Clerk Saunders," telling of the murder of a young woman's lover by her brothers who oppose the match.[105]

It's of a merchant's daughter in London town did dwell,
So modest, fair and handsome, her parents loved her well.
She was admired by lord and squire, but all their thoughts were vain,
For only one, a farmer's son, young Mary's heart did gain.

Long time young William courted her, and fixed their wedding day,
Their parents all consented, but her brothers both did say
"There lives a lord who pledged his word, and him she shall not shun;
We will betray, and then we'll slay, her constant farmer's son."

The Merchant's Daughter

Anon

Voice

It's of a mer-chant's daugh-ter in Lon-don town did dwell, So

mod-est, fair and hand-some, her par-ents loved her well. She was ad-mired by

lord and squire, but all their thoughts were vain, For on-ly one, a farm-er's son, young

Mar-y's heart did gain.

Fig. 11.21

A fair was held not far from town, these brothers went straightway,
And asked young William's company with them to pass the day;
But mark—returning home again, they swore his race was run,
Then, with a stake, the life did take of her constant farmer's son.

These villains then returning home, "O sister," they did say,
"Pray think no more of your false love, but let him go his way,
For it's truth we tell, in love he fell, and with some other one;
Therefore we come to tell the same of the constant farmer's son."

As on her pillow Mary lay, she had a dreadful dream,
She dreamt she saw his body lay down by a crystal stream,
Then she arose, put on her clothes, to seek her love did run,
When dead, and cold, she did behold her constant farmer's son.

The salt tear stood upon his cheeks, all mingled with his gore,
She shrieked in vain, to ease her pain, and kiss'd him ten times o'er;
She gathered green leaves from the trees, to keep him from the sun,
One night and day she passed away with the constant farmer's son.

But hunger it came creeping on; poor girl she shrieked with woe;
To try to find his murderer she straightway home did go,
Saying, "Parents dear, you soon shall hear, a dreadful deed is done,
In yonder vale lies, dead and pale, my constant farmer's son."

Up came her eldest brother and said, "It is not me,"
The same replied the younger one, and swore most bitterly,
But young Mary said, "Don't turn so red, nor try the laws to shun,
You've done the deed, and you shall bleed for my constant farmer's son!"

These villains soon they owned their guilt, and for the same did die;
Young Mary fair, in deep despair, she never ceased to cry;
The parents they did fade away, the glass of life was run,
And Mary cried, in sorrow died, for her constant farmer's son."[106]

Of course, not all Burstow's broadside ballads were on the subject of true love frustrated or vindicated. "The Three Butchers" was a dramatic tale of deception, robbery, and murder, while "Boney's Lamentation" and "The Duke of Marlborough" were historical broadsides dealing with war and international politics. "The Gallant Poachers" was a powerful ballad about poaching and transportation that is normally titled "Van Diemen's Land." John Ashton had reprinted a broadside version of this song in *Modern Street Ballads*, but Burstow had his own variant text and he could also provide the tune to which it was sung.[107]

Van Diemen's Land

Anon

Fig. 11.22

Come, all you gallant poachers, that ramble free from care,
That walk out of a moonlight night, with your dog, your gun, and snare;
Where the lofty hare and pheasant you have at your command,
Not thinking that your last career is on Van Diemen's Land.

There was poor Tom Brown from Nottingham, Jack Williams, and poor Joe,
Were three as daring poachers as the country well does know;
At night they were trapannèd by the keepers hid in sand,
And for fourteen years transported were unto Van Diemen's Land.

Oh! when we sailed from England we landed at the bay,
We had rotten straw for bedding, we dared not to say nay.
Our cots were fenced with fire, we slumber when we can,
To drive away the wolves and tigers upon Van Diemen's Land.

Oh! when that we were landed upon that fatal shore,
The planters they came flocking round, full twenty score or more;

They ranked us up like horses, and sold us out of hand,
They yoked us to the plough, my boys, to plough Van Diemen's Land.

There was one girl from England, Susan Summers was her name,
For fourteen years transported was, we all well knew the same;
Our planter bought her freedom, and he married her out of hand,
Good usage then she gave to us, upon Van Diemen's Land.

Oh! oft when I am slumbering, I have a pleasant dream:
With my sweet girl I am sitting, down by some purling stream,
Through England I am roaming, with her at my command,
Then waken, brokenhearted, upon Van Diemen's Land.

God bless our wives and families, likewise that happy shore,
The isle of sweet contentment which we shall see no more;
As for our wretched females, see them we seldom can,
There are twenty to one woman upon Van Diemen's Land.

Come all you gallant poachers, give ear unto my song,
It is a bit of good advice, although it is not long;
Let be your dog and snare; to you I do speak plain,
If you knew the hardships we endure, you ne'er would poach again.[108]

Not all of Lucy's favorite Burstow songs were ballads. His other offerings included a rambling song, "Travel the Country Round," plus two items with more literary texts that betrayed the hand of an educated author, "The Ages of Man" and "Death and the Lady." In contrast, there were also simple folk lyrics, laments with pretty melodies that appealed to Lucy. An example is "I Must Live All Alone," which Lucy also included in *English Traditional Songs and Carols*, although she felt the need to consolidate the text, making four verses out of the original five. It was not standard broadside material, but Lucy did find, in Baring-Gould's personal collection of broadsides, a similar text, so it is likely that a broadsheet had been Burstow's original source for the song.[109]

I Must Live All Alone

Anon

Fig. 11.23

As I was a-walking one morning by chance,   "When I was eleven, sweethearts I had seven,
I heard a maid making her moan;   And then I would look upon none;
I asked why she sighed, and she sadly replied,   But now all in vain I must sigh and complain,
"Alas! I must live all alone, alone,   For my true love has left me alone, alone,
Alas! I must live all alone."   For my true love has left me alone."

I said, "My fair maid, pray whence have you strayed?   "Oh! come back from the sea, dear Johnny, to me,
And are you some distance from home?"   And make me a bride of your own!
"My home," she replied, "is a burden to me,   Or else for your sake, my poor heart it will break,
For there I must live all alone, alone,   And here I shall die all alone, alone,
For there I must live all alone."   And here I shall die all alone."[110]

Although seeing *English County Songs* in print and discovering Henry Burstow were the most important folksong-related happenings in Lucy's life during 1893, there were some other exciting events too. In addition to visiting Frank Kidson in Leeds, she met the Reverend Sabine Baring-Gould for the first time. On 4 September she made a complicated train journey to Coryton in Devon, in order to stay for two weeks with the Baring-Gould family in the rectory at Lew Trenchard.[111] Her diary records that the next day she "looked through many vols of Mr. Baring-Gould's traditional songs, broadsides, etc., and had long talks with him." That evening they attended a "folk song concert" in Launceston, organized by the daughter of Baring-Gould's collaborator, F. W. Bussell. Lucy's opinion of it was mixed; she commented that "Mr. Ferguson (good baritone) and two indifferent professional ladies sang, in costumes (poor). Tunes very brisk. Mr. Ferguson especially exulted in 'Ormond the Brave.'"[112] The next day included another long session discussing folk music with Baring-Gould and exploring his collection and library.

The highlight of the trip came on 7 September when the two enthusiasts went song-hunting together. In the morning they walked over to Down House, a farm on Baring-Gould's estate, and Lucy noted two tunes, "Green Gravel" and "The Summer Is Over—Nothing Else to Do," from Louisa and/or Elizabeth Hamley.[113] In the afternoon they drove in a carriage to the village of Milton Abbott for tea with Alice Cann, the local rector's wife. In the nearby hamlet of Dunterton they found another informant, Jane Jeffrey. Although elderly and frail (she had only partly recovered from a debilitating stroke), Jane sang them several verses of Child no. 78, "The Unquiet Grave." Like the version collected in Shropshire by Charlotte Burne, which Lucy had included in *English County Songs,* this was titled "Cold Blows the Wind" and the lyric was similar, except for Jane Jeffrey's two concluding stanzas, which delighted Lucy. The tune was somewhat different from the Shropshire variant, although obviously related. Lucy apparently only wrote down three stanzas, the first and the last two.[114]

Cold Blows the Wind

Anon

Fig. 11.24

Cold blows the wind o'er my true love,   Tomorrow or to-day,
Cold blow the drops of rain,   Sweet Christ in heaven will have my soul,
I never had but one true love,   And take my life away.
In the greenwood he was slain.

My time be long, my time be short,   Don't grieve, don't grieve for me, true love,
                                                No mourning do I crave;

I must leave you and all the world,   And sink down in my grave.[115]

This was not the end of Lucy's collecting in Devon. On 21 September, the day before she left the county to visit relatives on the Isle of Wight, she and Baring-Gould drove to the village of Lifton, near Launceston, where Lucy noted three songs from a farmer's wife named Mary Fletcher: "Damon and Phyllis," "Why, What's the Matter Now?" and "The Outlandish Knight."[116]

Back in London for the pre-Christmas concert season, Lucy divided her musical activities between singing, writing songs, concert-going, and networking with other folksong enthusiasts and folklorists. She had written some more songs of her own ("Tammy" and "The Woodlark"), and her performances usually included a mixture of her own compositions, German *lieder* (she was particularly fond of Mendelssohn's "Der Frühling"), and folksongs from *English County Songs.* For example, at a concert in Poplar on 11 November she performed "A North Country Maid" and "The Loyal Lover."[117] Now interested in the non-musical aspects of folklore as well as in folk music, Lucy had begun attending meetings of the Folklore Society, and she was happy to pursue her friendship with Charlotte Burne, whom she met at a meeting of the Society on 15 November and then entertained at home a week later.[118] Baring-Gould was also in London, and he was invited to lunch on 6 December. Together they attended a "Ballad Concert" at which Lucy's favorite professional male singer of *lieder,* Harry Plunket Greene, performed two items from *English County Songs,* "Twankydillo" and "The Golden Vanity."[119]

Lucy also gave Baring-Gould copies of two carols that she had recently noted from three male travelers (as was normal at the time, she called them "gypsies") from a family named Goby, who often camped in the Surrey/Sussex border country near Lyne.[120] She had encountered them on nearby farmland at Pleystowe, Surrey. "The Moon Shines Bright" was a traditional Christmas carol that Lucy had previously found to be sung frequently in local villages, but "King Pharim" was more unusual. She concluded that it was related to two Child ballads, no. 22, "St. Stephen and Herod" (a late medieval poem in the Sloane collection in the British Museum, printed in 1856 by Thomas Wright in his collection, *Songs and Carols from a Manuscript in the British Museum of the Fifteenth Century*)[121] and no. 55, "The Carnal and the Crane," which had been collected by William Sandys in the West Country and by William Henry Husk in Worcestershire.[122] Both ballads included the miracle of a roasted cock crowing three times in affirmation of the birth of Christ; "King Pharim" (which Lucy believed to be a corruption of "King Pharaoh") also shared some text with "The Carnal and the Crane."

King Pharim

Anon

Fig. 11.25

King Pharim sat a-musing,
A-musing all alone;
There came the blessed Saviour,
And all to him unknown.

"Say, where did you come from, good man.
Oh, where did you then pass?"
"It is out of the land of Egypt,
Between an ox and an ass."

"Oh, if you come out of Egypt, man,
One thing I fain I known,
Whether a blessed Virgin Mary
Sprung from an Holy Ghost?"

"For if this is true, is true, good man,
That you've been telling to me,
That the roasted cock do crow three times
In the place where they did stand."

Oh, it's straight away the cock did fetch,
And feathered to your own hand,
Three times a roasted cock did crow,
On the place where they did stand.

Joseph, Jesus and Mary
Were travelling for the west,
When Mary grew a-tired
She might sit down and rest.

They travelled further and further,
The weather being so warm,

Till they came unto some husbandman
A-sowing of his corn.

"Come husbandman!" cried Jesus,
"From over speed and pride,
And carry home your ripened corn
That you've been sowing this day."

"For to keep your wife and family
From sorrow, grief and pain,
And keep Christ in your remembrance
Till the time comes round again."[123]

Around this time, too, Lucy was contacted by Cambridge writer Brimley Johnson, with a request to help him choose and edit material for a projected four-volume edition of traditional ballads. She alerted him to the work of Francis James Child, and for the other assistance that she provided Johnson was sufficiently grateful to reward her with a copy of the set, when *Popular British Ballads, Ancient and Modern* was published the next year.[124] This was another example of Lucy's networking, an activity which she continued over the next two years, 1894 and 1895. Her musical friends, with whom she played and sang at informal gatherings, included, in addition to composers Alexander Mackenzie, Charles Villiers Stanford and Arthur Somervell, such instrumentalists as Fanny Davies,[125] Alec Fuller Maitland, Arnold Dolmetsch,[126] and Josef Joachim,[127] and singers Kate Lee,[128] Harry Plunket Greene,[129] and James Campbell McInnes.[130] She maintained her correspondence with Frank Kidson and Sabine Baring-Gould, and on 11 May 1894 attended a lecture by the latter on "Traditional Song" at the Royal Institution. This, she considered, was spoiled by "bad singing" and by Fleetwood Sheppard's irritating piano arrangements.[131] Her most exciting trip of that year was undoubtedly a visit to Bayreuth, during which she attended performances of *Lohengrin, Tannhäuser*, and *Parsifal*. As mentioned previously, Lucy had been an enthusiastic Wagnerite when she was younger, but her taste in classical music now inclined more to the Baroque period, in particular the works of Bach and Purcell, and she was less receptive to German Romantic music than she had been a decade earlier. *Tannhäuser*, she confessed, now left her "cold and unmoved," but she still found *Parsifal* "altogether most impressive and touching."[132]

Although she was still an amateur, Lucy's singing was by now recognized in London musical circles as professional in standard, and she was asked to sing the role of Elvira in a successful production of Mozart's *Don Giovanni* and that of Dorabella in a follow-up production of *Così fan tutti*.[133] This was a major undertaking and may be reckoned the highlight of her brief career as an opera singer. She also continued to perform shorter recitals at numerous charity concerts, on occasion mixing such folksongs as "The Loyal Lover" and "A North Country Lass" with art songs by Somervell, Stanford, and Brahms.[134] Her involvement with the Early Music movement included singing Elizabethan lute songs, songs by William Lawes, Henry Lawes, and Jean-Jacques Rousseau, and vocal works by Johann Sebastian Bach and George Frideric Handel.[135]

All this musical activity took Lucy away from collecting and from her scholarly research on folksong, but she did not neglect the latter entirely. She acted as Baring-Gould's researcher in the British Museum, and she helped composer and Principal of the Royal Academy of Music Alexander Mackenzie prepare a series of lectures on "English County Songs."[136] A throat and ear infection, which temporarily rendered her deaf and left her with a sore throat for several months, prevented her from acting as Mackenzie's singer for those lectures, but on other occasions she performed similar services (research and singing musical examples) for Somervell and Fuller Maitland.[137] Fuller Maitland's lecture series covered the history of English music, and his eloquence reinvigorated Lucy's love for medieval song (she incorporated "Summer Is Icumen In" and a piece by Dunstable into her repertoire), for Elizabethan madrigals, and for the music of the English Baroque era, especially that of Henry Lawes, John Blow, and Henry Purcell.[138]

By the fall of 1895 Broadwood was again in fine voice, and her reputation as an interpreter of Purcell had grown to the point where (in November) she was offered a professional engagement at a concert of Purcell's music.[139] This was the closest she came to a professional singing career, and, although she declined, she must have hesitated before doing so because she took her singing very seriously, and she was usually on the lookout for ways to supplement her income. But the family would have disapproved, and in any case Lucy was only too aware of the problems she had earlier experienced with her throat, so she probably decided that a singing career would overtax her strength. For the folksong movement it was a fortunate decision.

In September 1895 Lucy began collecting folksongs again. While staying with a friend at Swannington House, near Coalville in Leicestershire, she noted songs from two local colliery workers, William Wardle[140] and Hoseah Heywood,[141] although she concluded that "none [of their offerings] were really very old."[142] William Wardle sang for her "Phoebe Dearest" and a coal-mining version of "Come, Let's Sit Down and Merry, Merry Be." Hoseah Heywood contributed "The Father's Welcome, or All Day Long in the Cornfields So Weary."[143] Later that month, while staying with relatives at Craster, near Alnwick in Northumberland, she noted several songs and singing games from children in the village of Embleton.[144] These included "Bingo," "Hullabaloo," "Round and Round the Village," and "Newcastle Races." Lucy was familiar with Alice Gomme's published collections of nursery rhymes and children's games, and she recognized "Dinah, or Jenny Jones" and "When I Was a Lady" as items that Gomme had previously collected. Some of the melodies were already known to her; for instance, "Amongst the Bush of Tansy" employed the tune of "Nancy Dawson," while "Oh What Is Mary Weeping For?" had the same tune as "Poor Mary," a Worcestershire game-song that Lucy had included in *English County Songs*.[145]

On her way back to London Lucy stopped off in Leeds for the annual music festival, visiting Frank Kidson and introducing him to Alec Fuller Maitland.[146] Her friendship with Fuller Maitland and with British Museum musicologist W. Barclay Squire now led to closer involvement with the work of the Purcell Society. Her major scholarly project in 1896 was to edit for publication the scores of two recently rediscovered Purcell operas, *Amphitreyon* and *The Gordian Knot Untied,* for which she also constructed piano arrangements. This time-consuming scholarly work again took her away from collecting, but she was still including folksongs in her recitals, which might include such traditional ballads as "Edinbro'" (a version of "The Cruel Sister") and "The Three Ravens" as well as her standbys "A North Country Lass" and "The Loyal Lover." One of Lucy's proudest achievements this year, apart from her editions of the Purcell operas, was learning to bicycle, a skill she learned in part in the hope of becoming less dependent on others when noting songs in the countryside around Lyne.

After a break of nearly a year, Lucy once more resumed collecting in the fall of 1896, following up a tip from a friend named Mrs. Carr,[147] who was singer Kate Lee's sister.[148] On this occasion the results were more substantial. Lucy recorded her visit to the Surrey village of Dunsfold in her diary as follows:

> [W]ent to a small old cottage done up by Mr. & Mrs. Carr. Mrs. Carr received me...Walked with her to see some cottagers about old songs. In afternoon ditto. In evening 10 or 12 old men, labourers, none able to read, came to supper and to sing to us. They sang sitting with eyes shut. Amongst others they knew and sang "Banks of Sweet Dundee," "The Lady and the Box," "Bailiff's Daughter of Islington," "Cold Blows the Wind," "The Trees They Are So High," "Young Lamkin," "Abroad As I Was Walking," "A Ship Lies in the Harbour," etc., etc., etc. Interesting evening. I noted 14 old tunes.[149]

While none of the Dunsfold informants was in the same league as Henry Burstow, this group of singing villagers, who apparently knew each other well and had shared songs together before, was nonetheless a notable discovery. It is by no means certain that they all lived in Dunsfold; although some were residents of the village, others may have walked in from nearby farms or hamlets, or from neighboring villages. In the main they were not as elderly as Lucy perceived them to be, since most of them were in their forties or fifties. The singers from whom she noted items included George Baker,[150] James Bronham,[151] Edward Cooper,[152] George Ede,[153] Richard Lough,[154] George and Mary Ann Rugman,[155] Mr. Sparks,[156] and Thomas Whittington.[157] The lone female, Mary Ann Rugman, sang "How Cold the Winds Do Blow," a variant of "Cold Blows the Wind."[158] Her husband George contributed "The Sheffield Apprentice" (about an innocent man hanged)[159] and a well known broadside ballad of requited love, "The Blind Beggar of Bethlem Green," a ballad which Richard Lough also sang, to a slightly different tune.[160] James Bronham offered a different variant of "Cold Blows the Wind," as well as "The New Irish Girl,"[161] while Edward Cooper provided "The Pleasant Month of May," another ballad of requited love.[162]

Lucy was aware that Baring-Gould had collected the traditional ballad "The Trees They Do Grow High" in Devon (see chapter 7) and had included an edited version of it in *Songs and Ballads of the West.* She also knew of a broadside text (printed by Such) titled "My Bonny Lad Is Young, but He's Growing." The version sung in Dunsfold by George Ede had a different tune and some variation in the words from that noted in Devon. For example, the age of the young lovers was even younger, namely twelve and thirteen respectively. Lucy first heard it sung when Ede was trimming hedges, and she reported that the fierce snap of his shears at the words "so there was an end to his growing" came with "a startling dramatic effect."[163] She would publish Ede's text, without censoring it, in 1902, in the *Journal of the Folk-Song Society,*[164] but in *English Traditional Songs and Carols* she transposed or altered words "where rhyme and metre absolutely necessitated it" and she omitted the penultimate stanza.[165] This is the version that George Ede sang (with his variant of the title):

The Trees Are Getting High

Anon

Voice

Oh! the trees are get-ting high, and the leaves are get-ting green, The

time is past and gone, my love, you and I have seen, 'Twas on a win-ter's ev-en-ing, as

I sat all a-lone, There I spied a bon-ny boy, young, but grow-ing.

Fig. 11.26

Oh! the trees are getting high, and the leaves are getting green,
The time is past and gone, my love, you and I have seen.
'Twas on a winter's evening, as I sat all alone,
There I spied a bonny boy, young, but growing.

"Oh mother! Dear mother! You've done to me much wrong!
You've married me to a bonny boy, his age it is so young!
His age is only twelve, and myself scarcely thirteen!"
Saying, "My bonny boy is young, but a-growing."

When it's "Daughter, dear daughter, I have done to you no wrong,
I've married you to a bonny boy, he is some rich lord's son,
And a lady he will make you, that's if you will be made,"
Saying, "Your bonny boy is young, but a-growing."

Saying, "Mother, dear mother, I am but a child,
I will go back to my old college for a year or two more;
I will cut off my yellow hair, put my box upon my head,
And I'll gang along with it to the college."

And 'twas on one summer's morning by the dawning of the day,
And they went into some cornfields to have some sport and play,
And what they did there she never will declare,
But she never more complained of his growing.

And at the age of thirteen then he was a married man;
And at the age of fourteen he was father of a son;
And at the age of fifteen then his grave was growing green:
So there was an end to his growing.[166]

If demonstrating that "The Trees They Do Grow High" was in English oral tradition elsewhere than the West Country was significant, so too was finding a southern English version of Child no. 93, "Lamkin." The Dunsfold singer who contributed it was Thomas Whittington and he called his version "Bold Lankon."[167]

Bold Lankon

Anon

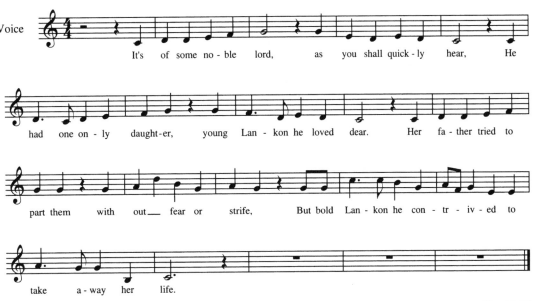

Voice

It's of some no-ble lord, as you shall quick-ly hear, He had one on-ly daught-er, young Lan-kon he loved dear. Her fa-ther tried to part them with out__ fear or strife, But bold Lan-kon he con-tr-iv-ed to take a-way her life.

Fig. 11.27

It's of some noble lord as you shall quickly hear,
He had one only daughter, young Lankon he loved dear.
Her father tried to part them without fear or strife,
But bold Lankon he contrived to take away her life.

It was contrived between young Lankon and the nurse
To murder the lady and baby at her breast.
Said the lord unto the lady, "I am a-going out,
Beware of Bold Lankon while I am about."

"Beware of Bold Lankon, not of any man,
For all my doors are all bolted, and my windows are all pinned."
Bold Lankon he came in, in the dead of the night,
He pinched the tender boy, which made it for to cry.
While the nurse sat singing "Hush a lullaby!"

"Oho! Nurse, oho! Nurse, how soundly you do sleep!
Can't you hear my tender baby, so bitterly does weep?"
"I cannot keep it quiet with sop nor with pap,
So come down, my dearest lady, and take it in your lap."

"How can I come down in the dead of the night,
Where no fire is shining, nor candle alight?"
This lady she came down, oho! Not thinking of any harm,
Bold Lankon he stood ready, and caught her in his arm.

"Oho! Spare my life, Bold Lankon! Oho! Spare my life so sweet,
I'll give you as much gold as stones lie in the street."
"Before I have as much gold as stones lie in the street
I'd rather see your heart's blood run down to your feet!"

"Oho! Spare my life, Bold Lankon! Oho! Spare it for one hour,
There is my eldest daughter, she is the branch flower."
"That for your oldest daughter! She [may] do me some good,
She might hold the silver basin to catch her mother's blood."

There's blood in the kitchen, there's blood in the hall,
There's blood in the parlour where this lady did fall.
The lord he came home, the same he came for to know,
His eyes like two fountains with water did o'erflow.

The nurse shall be hangèd on the gallows high,
Bold Lankon shall be burnt in the fire close by,
The bells shall be muzzlèd to make a dismal sound
Where this lady and the baby lay dead on the ground.[168]

The importance of this version of "Lamkin" lay more in the fact of its existence in oral tradition in the south of England than in its somewhat doggerel text or rather pedestrian tune. Some of the other ballads sung in Dunsfold, although likely more recent creations by eighteenth-century ballad-mongers, came with more attractive melodies. Whittington, for example, also sang a version of "The Bailiff's Daughter of Islington," and while Lucy did not bother to write down the well-known words she did note his tune.[169] The same was true for "The Seeds of Love," which Lucy had previously collected from Henry Burstow, and for which she now obtained different tunes from George Ede and from Mr. Sparks.[170] This is Ede's tune, with the "well-known version of the words" (Lucy's phrase), to which he sang it.

The Seeds of Love

Anon

Fig. 11.28

I sowed the seed[s] of love,
And it blossomed all in the Spring,
In April, or May, or else in June,
When the small birds they do sing.

A young gardener was standing by,
I asked him to choose for me,
He chose for me the lily, the violet, and pink,
But I really did refuse them all three.

The lily I did not like
Because of its fading so soon,
The violet and the pink I did fairly overlook,
So I vowed I would tarry till June.

In June there is a red, rosy bud,
A red, rosy bud for me!
Oft times I have aimed at that red, rosy bud,
But I gained the green willow-tree.[171]

Mr. Sparks also contributed "The Labouring Man," a song about the hard times experienced by rural workers.[172] He had learned the words from a ballad sheet, but had made up the tune himself.

One of the songs mentioned in Lucy's diary entry, "A (or Our) Ship She Lies in Harbour," had a tune that particularly appealed to her, and her field notes credit it to Edward Cooper. Her manuscript is a little indistinct, but I believe this is an accurate rendition of the tune that she noted for the ballad from Cooper. A comment underneath the melody emphasizes that the singer definitely sang the F in the second bar as a natural rather than the sharp that would be normal in the key of G.

A Ship She Lies in Harbour

Anon

Fig. 11.29

"Our Ship She Lies in Harbour" was also sung by Mr. Sparks, and it was his tune that Lucy would subsequently choose for publication in *English Traditional Songs and Carols*. It was an unusually concise broadside ballad in which a patient young woman outmaneuvers her parents' opposition to her marriage with a sailor. One verse was omitted by the singer, but was included in a broadside text printed by Such, which Lucy was able to track down with the help of Frank Kidson.[173]

Our Ship She Lies in Harbour

Anon

Fig. 11.30

"Our ship she lies in harbour,
Just ready to set sail,
May heaven be your guardian, love,
Till I return from sea."

Said the father to the daughter,
"What makes you so lament?
Is there no man in all the world
Could give your heart content?"

Said the daughter to the father,
"I'll tell the reason why:

You have sent away the sailor lad
That could me satisfy."

"If that's your inclination,"
The father did reply,
"I wish he may continue there,
And on the seas may die!"

She, like an angel, weeping,
On the rocks sighed every day,
Awaiting for her own true love
Returning home from sea.

[When nine long years were over,
And ten long tedious days,
She saw the ship coming sailing in
With her true love from the seas.]

"Oh, yonder sits my angel!
She's waiting there for me,
To-morrow to the church we'll go,
And married we will be."

When they had been to church, and were
Returning back again,

She espied her honoured father
And several gentlemen.

Said the father to the daughter,
"Five hundred pounds I'll give,
If you'll forsake that sailor lad
And come with me to live."

"It's not your gold that glittered,
Nor yet your silver that shined,
For I'm married to the man I love
And I'm happy in my mind!'[174]

Another striking ballad that Lucy collected at Dunsfold was one that, curiously, she did not mention in her diary. Sung by George Baker, who also contributed "The Pretty Sailor, or the Lowland Maid,"[175] this was a feminist broadside titled "The Valiant Lady."[176] It tells the unusual story of a young woman, apparently trained in medicine, who volunteers to go to sea as a surgeon to keep an eye on her lover, the victim of a press-gang. Her medical skill saves his life, and she then buys his release. Lucy discovered that this song was a variant of a longer black-letter broadside in the Roxburghe collection titled "The Valiant Virgin, or Philip and Mary," and in printing the ballad in *English Traditional Songs and Carols* she restored one verse and two other lines that Mr. Baker, her Dunsfold informant, had forgotten. The seventeenth-century broadside was intended to be sung to the tune of "When the Stormy Winds Do Blow," and Lucy argued that Baker's tune, which she regarded as a fine, vigorous air, was a more authentic version of "Stormy Winds" than that printed by Chappell in *Popular Music of the Olden Time,* which she dismissed as "weak and monotonous."[177] This, then, was one of the fairly rare instances in which a centuries-old ballad tune had been recovered from oral tradition along with much of the original text. Here is Broadwood's reconstruction of "The Valiant Lady":

It's of a brisk young lively lad
Came out of Gloucestershire;
And all his full intention was
To court a lady fair.

Her eyes they shone like morning dew,
Her hair was fair to see;
She was grace, in form and face,
And was fixed in modesty.

This couple was a-walking,
They loved each other well;
And someone heard them talking
And did her father tell.

And when her father came to know
And understand this thing,
Then said he, "From one like thee
I'll free my daughter in the spring!"

'Twas in the spring-time of the year
There was a press begun;
And all their full intention was
To press a farmer's son.

They pressèd him, and sent him out
Far o'er the raging sea,
"Where I'm sure he will no more
Keep my daughter company!"

[In man's apparel then she did
Resolve to try her fate;
And in the good ship where he rid

She went as surgeon's mate.

Says she, "My soldier shall not be
Destroyed for want of care;
I will dress, and I will bless,
Whatsoever I endure!"]

The twenty-first of August
There was a fight begun,
And foremost in the battle
They placed the farmer's son.

He there received a dreadful wound
That struck him in the thigh,
Every vein was filled with pain,
He got wounded dreadfully.

Into the surgeon's cabin
They did convey him straight,
Where, first of all the wounded men,
The pretty surgeon's mate

Most tenderly did dress his wound
Which bitterly did smart,
Then said he, "Oh! one like thee
Once was mistress of my heart!"

She went to the commander
And offered very fair,
"Forty or fifty guineas
Shall buy my love quite clear!

No money shall be wanted,

No longer tarry here!"   My own and lovely child!"
"Since 'tis so, come let's go!
To old England we will steer!"   Cried she, "Since I have found him
                                                                          And brought him safe to shore,
She went unto her father's gate   Our days we'll spend in old England,
And stood there for a while;   Never roam abroad no more!"[178]
Said he, "The heavens bless you!

The Valiant Lady

Anon

Fig. 11.31

Other vernacular songs heard by Lucy in Dunsfold included three contributions by Richard Lough, who sang two songs about requited love ("The Bonny Labouring Boy," "It's Of a Pleasant Month of May"), and one about unrequited love ("Some Rival Has Stolen My True Love Away"). The first of these was a fairly lengthy broadside ballad about parental opposition to their rich daughter's desire to marry a handsome ploughboy, and Lucy was more interested in the tune, which she ascribed to the mixolydian mode and which resembled that of "The Painful Plough" in *English County Songs*, than the words, which were to be found on a Such broadsheet.[179] Lough's May song also had a familiar tune; it was similar to "Down by a Riverside" in Baring-Gould's *Songs and Ballads of the West*.[180] "Some Rival" was another one of Lucy's favorites: a simple but eloquent folk lyric with an attractive tune that was reminiscent of "Love Will Find Out the Way."[181] It may serve as a final example of Broadwood's collecting during the years 1892 to 1896:

> Some rival has stolen my true love away,
> So I in old England no longer can stay.
> I will swim the wide ocean around my fair breast,
> To find out my true love whom I love the best.
>
> When I have found out my joy and delight,
> I'll welcome her kindly by day and by night,
> For the bells shall be a-ringing and the drum make a noise
> For to welcome my true love with ten thousand joys.

Here's a health to all lovers that are loyal and just,
Here's confusion to the rival that lives in distrust,
For it's I'll be as constant as a true turtle-dove,
For I never will at no time prove false to my love.[182]

Some Rival Has Stolen My True Love Away

Anon

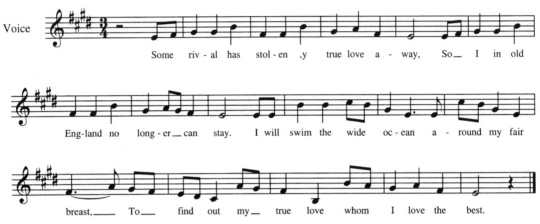

Fig. 11.32

Despite her enthusiasm for the cause, and for much of the material that she had collected, Lucy's involvement with folksong was only an occasional activity during the winter of 1896-1897. However, she was still including folksongs in her performances at amateur concerts. For example, at a 'Popular Ballad Concert' held at Toynbee Hall, Aldgate, in London, on 22 October 1896, she sang "A North Country Maid," "Edinbro', or the Cruel Sister," and "Young Colin," the latter her own arrangement of an eighteenth-century vernacular song by William Shield. After dinner that evening she sang the entire fifteen verses of "Edinbro'" into a phonograph owned by a Mr. Aves, her first experience with the new technology.[183] The next year (1897) saw Lucy continuing her work for the Purcell Society and occasionally attending meetings of the Folklore Society, where she made new contacts, including the new President, A. Nutt, who gave his inaugural lecture on fairies.[184] She continued to see the Stanfords, Somervells, Fuller Maitlands, and other musical friends socially, and made music with them at dinner parties, tea-parties, and 'at homes.' By now her standard folksong repertoire also included "I Will Give You the Keys to Heaven," an item that Sabine Baring-Gould had contributed to *English County Songs*.[185] Her most significant new friendship was with the young composer Ralph Vaughan Williams, whom she invited to dinner on 15 January and again to tea on 31 January.[186] He would be on her guest list for periodic musical 'at homes' and tea parties throughout the year, and by May he was arranging songs by Bach for the two of them to perform together.[187] Even more significant, at least in the short term, was an impromptu collaboration in December with singer Kate Lee at a party held at the house of Mr. and Mrs. Herbert Carr. Kate, a professional singer, had incorporated into her repertoire a number of songs from *English County Songs* and was an enthusiastic supporter of the burgeoning movement. It was time, they agreed, that it had a formal organization, similar to the Folklore Society. They met again on 15 January 1898 to plan the creation of a Folk-Song Society.[188]

Lucy Broadwood's early involvement with the birth of the Folk-Song Society is a topic that will be addressed in a subsequent chapter, but it may be useful at this point to summarize briefly her principal accomplishments in the realm of folk music from the time that she first began to take a serious interest in folksong in 1884 to her initial involvement in planning the Folk-Song Society in 1897.

Lucy had been exposed to folksong on various occasions during her childhood but it was her decision in the winter of 1887-88 to co-edit with her cousin Herbert Birch Reynardson a new edition of John Broadwood's *Old English Songs* that prompted her to begin her career as a folksong collector. Although this project was primarily a family affair, it resulted in her taking up vernacular song-collecting as a hobby. She began noting extra material in the summer of 1888, *Sussex Songs* was published in the spring of 1890, and during the next year she began building her network of contacts in the fields of folklore and folksong. Friendships with Heywood Sumner, Arthur Somervell, Charlotte Burne, Sabine Baring-Gould, and Frank Kidson developed during the next few years. She resumed collecting in 1890, and her most important informants during the next two years included Samuel Willett, Clara Wilson, Patience Vaisey, George Grantham, and John Burberry.

The invitation to work with Alec Fuller Maitland on *English County Songs* was the next major stimulus that kept Lucy engaged wholeheartedly with folksong. During 1891-93 this second project led her to delve systematically into the extant Georgian and Victorian literature on English folksong, and within a few years she made herself the most knowledgeable person on the subject in Late Victorian England. Collecting material for the book also necessitated developing a nation-wide network of friends and correspondents who were interested in the folklore and folk music of their local areas. Lucy helped publicize the book by singing her (and Fuller Maitland's) arrangements of folksongs from it at charity concerts, and by persuading professional singers, including Harry Plunket Greene, Kate Lee, and, later, James Campbell McInnes, to incorporate such folksongs in their repertoires.

While very few of the items contributed by Fuller Maitland, family members, or correspondents to *English County Songs* are extant in manuscript form, we are fortunate that some of Lucy Broadwood's field manuscripts have survived, although they are now inconveniently divided between two archives, the Vaughan Williams Memorial Library at Cecil Sharp House (London) and the Surrey History Centre (Woking). They are far from complete, and not always easy to read, but they provide us with some ability to confirm that what Broadwood published from her own collecting in *English County Songs,* in articles in the *Journal of the Folk-Song Society*, and (eventually) in *English Traditional Songs and Carols* accurately reflected what she had noted in the field. Essentially they do. One finds a few minor amendments (the name "Floral" changed to "Flora," for example) but the songs appear to be noted conscientiously and changes are trivial in nature compared to the kinds of modification one finds so often in Baring-Gould's publications. As a female, Broadwood was spared the problem of dealing with bawdy songs or other lyrics that might be deemed unsuitable for polite ears, because her source singers simply declined to furnish her with such material. She regretted this fact, but there was little she could do about it. Well aware of the problem that male collectors faced in this regard, she sympathized with Kidson's approach rather than Baring-Gould's: it was, she thought, better to leave out the offending stanzas rather than rewrite them. Like Kidson, too, she tended to take down in the field only the tunes of the songs that she had discovered, often prevailing upon her source singers to write out the lyrics for her, or simply relying—as Kidson so often did—on the relevant broadside text. Clearly she was more interested in tunes than texts, but she recognized that songs were unique combinations of both elements and, in her publications, she strove to provide both. In *English County Songs* and *English Traditional Songs and Carols*, both of which were intended as commercial publications aimed at the drawing room market, she willingly (although not without some scholarly misgivings) provided piano arrangements. These, however, she kept simple, having strongly negative opinions about the work of musicians such as Fleetwood Sheppard who composed more florid and obtrusive settings.

Broadwood continued collecting in the mid-1890s, after the *English County Songs* project was complete, but she did so only episodically, and her other musical interests tended to take prominence in her life. This was the time when her unpaid but demanding career as an opera and concert singer was at its height. Yet her continuing friendships with Frank Kidson and Sabine Baring-Gould kept her involved with folksong, and she was fortunate to discover such valuable new informants as Henry Burstow and the Dunsfold villagers. She also continued networking, bringing into her orbit leading folklorists and such big names in the world of Late Victorian art music as Sir Alexander Mackenzie, Sir Charles Hubert Parry, Sir Charles Villiers Stanford, and the young Ralph Vaughan Williams. It was, however, due to her friendship with singer Kate Lee that she became involved in the planning and eventual foundation of the Folk-Song Society.

It seems reasonable to conclude that during the decade 1887-1897 folksong was initially little more than a hobby for Lucy but that it gradually became an avocation. Yet, except for a few months here and there, it was not her primary occupation. She was at least as committed to her amateur career as a singer, and to her involvement with the Early Music movement. She undoubtedly viewed her contribution to the Purcell Society as of equal importance to her work with folksong. Indeed, looking back over the decade, Lucy Broadwood may well have been a little surprised at how much she had accomplished in the latter field, but her role in the development of the late Victorian folksong revival was indeed a major one.

Notes

1. Lucy E. Broadwood and J. A. Fuller Maitland, eds., *English County Songs: Words and Music* (London: The Leadenhall Press, 1893; reprinted London: Cramer, 1915).

2. Lucy Broadwood diaries, Broadwood Collection, Accession no. 6782, Surrey History Centre, Woking, Surrey, U.K.; diary entry for 11 August 1891.

3. Broadwood diary entries for 25 September and 20 October 1891.

4. Broadwood diary entry for 4 April 1892.

5. Broadwood and Fuller Maitland, *English County Songs,* vi.

6. I am grateful to Keith Chandler for pointing out that Shipston-on-Stour, although surrounded by Warwickshire, was at this date administratively in Worcestershire.

7. For this information I am indebted to John Francmanis, "Letter to the Editor of *Folk Music Journal,*" a copy of which was forwarded to me by David Atkinson.

8. Robert Gomme, "Gomme [née Merck], Alice Bertha, Lady Gomme (1853-1938), folklorist," *Oxford Dictionary of National Biography,* www.oxforddnb.com:80/view/article/38616.

9. Francmanis, "Letter."

10. Anne Pimlott Baker, "Hipkins, Alfred James (1826-1903), writer on musical instruments," *Oxford Dictionary of National Biography,* www.oxforddnb.com:80/view/article/33890.

11. Information from John Francmanis and from Google and World Cat searches. Surprisingly there is no entry for Potter in the *Oxford Dictionary of National Biography* or other standard reference works.

12. Francmanis, "Letter."

13. Francmanis, "Letter."

14. For this information I am grateful to Keith Chandler's research into census data.

15. Francmanis, "Letter."

16. Francmanis, "Letter."

17. Ursula Vaughan Williams, *R.V.W.: A Biography of Ralph Vaughan Williams* (Oxford: Oxford University Press, 1964), 62.

18. William Barrett's smaller compilation, *English Folk-Songs,* has marginally chronological priority as a national collection of folksongs with tunes, so the operative word here is "systematically." *English County Songs* deliberately set out to cover the whole country in a way to which Barrett had not aspired. It was conceived as a project well before the publication of *English Folk-Songs,* but Broadwood and Fuller Maitland were certainly familiar with Barrett's book before they completed their own publication.

19. Broadwood and Fuller Maitland, *English County Songs,* v.

20. Broadwood and Fuller Maitland, *English County Songs,* 97.

21. Broadwood and Fuller Maitland, *English County Songs,* iii.

22. Broadwood and Fuller Maitland, *English County Songs,* iv.

23. Broadwood and Fuller Maitland, *English County Songs,* 3-7.

24. Broadwood and Fuller Maitland, *English County Songs,* 8-9.

25. Broadwood and Fuller Maitland, *English County Songs,* 18.

26. Broadwood and Fuller Maitland, *English County Songs,* 10-11.

27. Broadwood and Fuller Maitland, *English County Songs,* 12-17.

28. Broadwood and Fuller Maitland, *English County Songs,* 12-13.

29. Broadwood and Fuller Maitland, *English County Songs,* 16-17. Kirkby Malzeard is a village near Ripon.

30. Broadwood and Fuller Maitland, *English County Songs,* 14-15.

31. Broadwood and Fuller Maitland, *English County Songs,* 22-23.

32. Broadwood and Fuller Maitland, *English County Songs,* 20-28.

33. Broadwood and Fuller Maitland, *English County Songs,* 31.

34. Broadwood and Fuller Maitland, *English County Songs,* 32-33.

35. Charlotte Sophia Burne, ed., *Shropshire Folk-Lore: A Sheaf of Gleanings from the Collections of Georgina F. Jackson* (London: Trubner & Co., 1883-86), 542-43 and 651. For Burne's collecting in Shropshire, see chapter 5.

36. Burne, *Shropshire Folk-Lore,* 545-546 and 651.

37. Broadwood and Fuller Maitland, *English County Songs,* 44-45

38. [Lucy E. Broadwood] and Herbert Birch Reynardson, eds., *Sussex Songs (Popular Songs of Sussex)* (London: Lucas & Weber, 1889 [actually 1890]), 12-13.

39. Lucy uncharacteristically mixed up Child's two collections, referring to his "English and Scotch Ballads" when she undoubtedly meant the first volume of *The English and Scottish Popular Ballads.*

40. Broadwood and Fuller Maitland, *English County Songs,* 75.

41. Broadwood and Fuller Maitland, *English County Songs,* 74-75.

42. M[arianne] H[arriet] Mason, ed., *Nursery Rhymes and Country Songs: Both Tunes and Words from Tradition* (London: Metzler, 1878), 46. See chapter 4 for an account of Mason's collecting.

43. Broadwood and Fuller Maitland, *English County Songs*, 86.
44. Broadwood and Fuller Maitland, *English County Songs*, 91.
45. Broadwood and Fuller Maitland, *English County Songs*, 88-89.
46. Broadwood and Fuller Maitland, *English County Songs*, 93.
47. Broadwood and Fuller Maitland, *English County Songs*, 94-95.
48. Broadwood and Fuller Maitland, *English County Songs*, 98-99.
49. Broadwood and Fuller Maitland, *English County Songs*, 96-97.
50. Broadwood and Fuller Maitland, *English County Songs*, 106-7.
51. Broadwood and Fuller Maitland, *English County Songs*, 103.
52. Broadwood and Fuller Maitland, *English County Songs*, 102-3.
53. Broadwood and Fuller Maitland, *English County Songs*, 111.
54. Broadwood and Fuller Maitland, *English County Songs*, 108-9.
55. Broadwood and Fuller Maitland, *English County Songs*, 110.
56. Broadwood and Fuller Maitland, *English County Songs*, 114-15.
57. Broadwood and Fuller Maitland, *English County Songs*, 112-13.
58. Broadwood and Fuller Maitland, *English County Songs*, 116-17. See chapter 7.
59. Broadwood and Fuller Maitland, *English County Songs*, 118-19.
60. [Thomas Hughes,] *The Scouring of the White Horse; or, The Long Vacation Ramble of a London Clerk* (London: Macmillan, 1859), 158-60.
61. Broadwood and Fuller Maitland, *English County Songs*, 119.
62. Broadwood and Fuller Maitland, *English County Songs*, 118-19.
63. Broadwood and Fuller Maitland, *English County Songs*, 125.
64. Broadwood and Fuller Maitland, *English County Songs*, 124-25.
65. Broadwood and Fuller Maitland, *English County Songs*, 136-37.
66. Broadwood and Fuller Maitland, *English County Songs*, 140-43.
67. Broadwood and Fuller Maitland, *English County Songs*, 134-35 and 138-39.
68. Broadwood and Fuller Maitland, *English County Songs*, 132-33.
69. Broadwood and Fuller Maitland, *English County Songs*, 147.
70. Broadwood and Fuller Maitland, *English County Songs*, 149-53.
71. Broadwood and Fuller Maitland, *English County Songs*, 154-55.
72. Broadwood and Fuller Maitland, *English County Songs*, 158-59.
73. Broadwood and Fuller Maitland, *English County Songs*, 162-63.
74. Broadwood and Fuller Maitland, *English County Songs*, 164-65.
75. Broadwood and Fuller Maitland, *English County Songs*, 176-77.
76. Broadwood and Fuller Maitland, *English County Songs*, 170-73.
77. Broadwood and Fuller Maitland, *English County Songs*, 174-75.
78. Broadwood and Fuller Maitland, *English County Songs*, 170-71.
79. Broadwood and Fuller Maitland, *English County Songs*, 184-85.
80. Broadwood and Fuller Maitland, *English County Songs*, 183.
81. Broadwood and Fuller Maitland, *English County Songs*, 182-83.
82. Edward Jones, ed., *Popular Cheshire Melodies* (London: Jones, 1798).
83. Sabine Baring-Gould and H. Fleetwood Sheppard, eds., *Songs and Ballads of the West, a Collection made from the Mouths of the People*, vols. 1-4 (London: Patey & Willis, [1889-92]. 2nd edition, London: Methuen and Patey & Willis, [1891-95], reprinted in one volume, 1895).
84. Frank Kidson, ed., *Traditional Tunes, a Collection of Ballad Airs, chiefly obtained in Yorkshire and the South of Scotland, together with their appropriate words from broadsides and from oral tradition* (Oxford: Charles Taphouse & Son, 1891; reprinted, East Ardsley, U.K.: S.R. Publishers, 1970).
85. Broadwood and Fuller Maitland, *English County Songs*, v.
86. Broadwood and Fuller Maitland, *English County Songs*, v.
87. William Alexander Barrett, ed., *English Folk-Songs* (London: Novello, Ewer & Co., [1891]. Reprinted, Darby, Pa.: Norwood Editions, 1973).
88. The Broadwood diaries periodically record the arrival in the mail of a small royalty cheque from The Leadenhall Press.
89. Broadwood diary entry for 24 January 1893. "My Bonny Boy" was almost certainly "My Bonnie, Bonnie Boy."
90. Broadwood diary entries for 10, 22, 24, 25 May and 5 June 1891, and 6, 8, and 21 February 1893.
91. Broadwood diary entries for 16 and 18 January, 27 February, 25 September, and 28 December 1892.
92. Broadwood diary entry for 22 February 1893.
93. Broadwood diary entry for 10 April 1893.
94. Broadwood diary entries for 1, 6, 7, and 8 July 1893.

95. London, Vaughan Williams Memorial Library, Lucy Broadwood Collection, LEB/2/3: mss. dated 2 May 1893: list of 43 items: "songs noted from singing of H. Burstow, bellringer, born and lived all his life (68) at Horsham." This seems to have been Lucy's master-list of songs that she collected from Burstow, or at least those noted during her earliest sessions with him.

96. Henry Burstow, *Reminiscences of Horsham: being Recollections of Henry Burstow the Celebrated Bellringer and Songsinger* (Horsham, Sussex: Free Christian Book Society, 1911. Reprinted, with a foreword by A. E. Green and Tony Wales: Norwood, Pa.: Norwood Editions, 1975). On Burstow, see Andrew R. Turner, "Burstow, Henry (1826–1916)," *Oxford Dictionary of National Biography*.

97. Lucy Broadwood, ed., *English Traditional Songs and Carols* (London: Boosey, 1908), xi.

98. For Burstow's entire repertoire, see the *Folkopedia* article on Burstow, http://folkopedia.efdss.org/Henry_Burstow.

99. Lucy Broadwood Collection, Vaughan Williams Memorial Library, Cecil Sharp House, London, LEB/2/3-23, except 2/6. This list of forty-three songs is not definitive. There may well have been more. In the Burstow section of the VWML Broadwood collection [LEB/2/3-23] there are several lists of Burstow's songs, usually written on (empty) envelopes, some of which contain other song titles, but these other items may have been songs that Burstow refused to sing, or that Lucy decided she did not want, or items that have somehow been lost, or duplicates under alternative titles.

100. Lucy E. Broadwood, "Folk Songs Collected in Sussex and Surrey," *Journal of the Folk-Song Society* 1, no. 4 (1902): 170-171.

101. Broadwood diary entry for 20 May 1893.

102. Broadwood, *English Traditional Songs and Carols*, 4-5.

103. Broadwood diary entry for 1 January 1894; also London, Vaughan Williams Memorial Library, Lucy Broadwood Collection, LEB/2/5.

104. Broadwood, *English Traditional Songs and Carols*, 32-33.

105. Broadwood, *English Traditional Songs and Carols*, 28-29.

106. Broadwood, *English Traditional Songs and Carols*, 28-29.

107. Broadwood, *English Traditional Songs and Carols*, 2-3.

108. Broadwood, *English Traditional Songs and Carols*, 2-3.

109. Broadwood, *English Traditional Songs and Carols*, 16-17.

110. Broadwood, *English Traditional Songs and Carols*, 16-17.

111. Broadwood diary entry for 4 September 1893.

112. Broadwood diary entry for 5 September 1893.

113. Broadwood diary entry for 7 September 1893; also London, Vaughan Williams Memorial Library, Lucy Broadwood Collection, LEB/2/25. I am very grateful to Martin Graebe for telling me about Lucy and Sabine's visit to Louisa and Elizabeth Hamley, who at the time were aged 20 and 18 respectively. These two informants are not named by Lucy in either her diary entry or her field notes, although the two tunes that she noted from them are in LEB/2/25. However, the two songs are included in the *Personal Copy*, volume 1, no. 422 ("Green Gravel") and volume 2, no. 224 ("Nothing Else to Do"), with the tunes in Lucy's handwriting. Baring-Gould's annotation indicates they were collected from "Miss Hamley." See the Baring-Gould microfiche collection (copies at VWML and Plymouth Central Public Library).

114. London, Vaughan Williams Memorial Library, Lucy Broadwood Collection, LEB/2/25. I would like to thank Martin Graebe for informing me that Jane Jeffrey lived in the hamlet of Dunterton, not in the neighboring village of Milton Abbott as is recorded, erroneously, in Lucy's diary.

115. Broadwood, *English Traditional Songs and Carols*, 54-55.

116. Broadwood diary entry for 21 September 1893; Also: London, Vaughan Williams Memorial Library, Lucy Broadwood Collection, LEB/2/24 and LEB/2/26. Mary Fletcher (née Uglow) had been born in Cornwall. She was now a widow aged 69 with four grown-up sons. She had fairly recently lost her husband John, and had then taken up residence with her brother Wymond Uglow and his family on a farm near the village.

117. Broadwood diary entry for 11 November 1893.

118. Broadwood diary entries for 15 and 22 November 1893.

119. Broadwood diary entries for 22 November and 6 December 1893.

120. London, Vaughan Williams Memorial Library, Lucy Broadwood Collection, LEB/2/6.

121. Thomas Wright, ed., *Songs and Carols from a Manuscript in the British Museum of the Fifteenth Century* (London: T. Richards for the Warton Club, 1856).

122. William Sandys, ed., *Christmas Carols, Ancient and Modern, including the most popular in the West of England, and the airs to which they are sung. Also specimens of French Provincial Carols* (London: Richard Beckley, 1833); William Henry Husk, ed., *Songs of the Nativity; Being Christmas Carols, Ancient and Modern* (London: John Camden Hotten, 1864; revised edition, 1868).

123. Broadwood, *English Traditional Songs and Carols*, 74-75; Lucy Broadwood Collection, VWML, LEB/2/6.

124. Broadwood diary entry for 7 December 1894. R. Brimley Johnson, ed., *Popular British Ballads, Ancient and Modern*, 4 vols. 1-4 (London: Dent, 1894).

125. Fanny Davies (1861-1934) was a student of Clara Schumann's who specialized in playing the piano music of Schumann, Beethoven, and Brahms. She also played English music for virginals and harpsichord. She and Lucy would become very close friends in the Edwardian era.

126. Arnold Dolmetsch (1858-1940) was a musical craftsman who specialized in building replicas of old instruments; as a musician he accompanied Lucy on the lute, but he also played other instruments and was a pioneer of the 'authentic' school of performing with period instruments.

127. Joseph Joachim (1831-1907) was one of the finest violinists of his generation. A protégé of Felix Mendelssohn, he was later a close friend of Johannes Brahms and did much to popularize Brahms's music in England, as a soloist, as the leader of a string quartet, and as a conductor.

128. Kate Lee was a professional singer, song collector (she discovered the Copper family), founder member of the Folk-Song Society, and its first Honorary Secretary. She and Lucy became friends and collaborators, although there was also some rivalry between them. On Kate Lee, see Christopher J. Bearman, "Kate Lee and the Foundation of the Folk-Song Society," *Folk Music Journal* 7, no. 5 (1999): 627-643.

129. Harry Plunket Greene (1865-1936) was a professional bass baritone. A pre-eminent interpreter of English art song, he popularized some of Lucy's compositions and also several of her arrangements of folksongs, thereby enhancing the visibility and sales of *English County Songs.*

130. James Campbell McInnes (1873 or 1874-1945) was a professional baritone who achieved considerable success and popularity during the 1900s. A protégé of Lucy's, he regularly practised with her as his accompanist, and the two became very close friends. Despite the disparity in their ages, they may also have been lovers. After a failed marriage to Angela Mackail, McInnes later emigrated to Canada to become a professor of English and Music at the University of Toronto. His archives are held at the Toronto Public Library.

131. Broadwood diary entry for 11 May 1894.

132. Broadwood diary entries for 2, 5, and 6 August 1894.

133. Broadwood diary entries for 31 October and 9 November 1894 and 1 and 9 January 1895.

134. Broadwood diary entry for 10 November 1894.

135. Broadwood diary entries for 4 December 1894 and 10 January and 20 April 1895.

136. Broadwood diary entries for 17, 24, 25, and 26 December 1894 and 20 January 1895.

137. Broadwood diary entry for 13 November 1895.

138. Broadwood diary entries for 21 and 28 May, 11 and 18 June, and 2 July 1895.

139. Broadwood diary entry for 30 November 1895.

140. William Wardle was aged 60 and worked as the driver of a stationary engine (presumably one that drove the pit machinery); he and his wife had five sons. One of these, Thomas, aged 24, was a coal miner, so it is just possible that he rather than William was Lucy's informant.

141. Hoseah Heywood was a coal miner from the nearby village of Worthington. He was aged 31 and lived with his wife Fanny and their young son and daughter. The Heywood and Wardle families lived next door to each other in Swannington, a village very close to Coalville.

142. Broadwood diary entry for 2 September 1895.

143. London, Vaughan Williams Memorial Library, Lucy Broadwood Collection, LEB/2/38-41.

144. Broadwood diary entry for 21 September 1895.

145. London, Vaughan Williams Memorial Library, Lucy Broadwood Collection, LEB/2/36-37.

146. Broadwood diary entry for 3 October 1895.

147. Mrs. Carr, whose Christian name(s) I have yet to discover, was the wife of Herbert Carr, and had a strong interest in local folklore. The Carrs, who were members of the Broadwood family's social circle in London, appear to have acquired their cottage in Dunsfold as a country retreat. The fact that Mrs. Carr, who evidently discovered the Dunsfold singers, asked Lucy rather than Kate Lee to come and note tunes from them suggests that Kate had not begun collecting at this time. If she had not, it was probably the combination of Lucy's example and her sister's interest in vernacular song that stimulated her to begin doing so in the late 1890s.

148. Broadwood diary entry for 4 September 1896.

149. Woking, Surrey, U.K., Surrey History Centre. Broadwood papers, Accession no. 2185/LEB/4/65-73.

150. George Baker, who was aged 55, had been born in Cranleigh, Surrey, a town about five miles northeast of Dunsfold. He had a wife named Anne, and was employed as a wheelwright.

151. Regrettably I have no biographical information on James Bronham.

152. Edward Cooper, who had been born in the West Sussex village of Kirdford, was married to a woman named Mary and had a young son called Philip. He was aged 28, and worked as an agricultural laborer and as a laborer in a brickyard. As he was clearly not an old man in 1896, it is possible that Lucy's informant was not him but rather his father. However, Edward appears to have been the only man named Cooper living in Dunsfold at the time, unless his father was missed in the 1891 census and had died before the 1901 census. It is possible, of course, that Edward's father lived in another nearby village.

153. George Ede, who was aged 49 or 50, worked as an agricultural laborer. He and his wife Jane had three sons and four daughters.

154. I have so far been unable to trace Richard Lough. He does not appear to have been living in Dunsfold in either 1891 or 1901. His name sounds Irish, which might suggest that he was not a permanent local resident, but this is mere speculation.

155. George Rugman was a brickyard laborer, aged 43. He had married Mary Ann Cobbitt, who was now aged 39, in 1878, and they had a son William and a daughter Edith. Although now living in Dunsfold, they both came from Bramley, Surrey, a village just south of Guildford.

156. Mr. Sparks has so far eluded me. He does not appear to have been living in Dunsfold in either 1891 or 1901. He was probably from a neighboring village.

157. Thomas Whittington was an agricultural laborer aged 49. He and his wife Jane both came from Kirdford, Sussex. They had two sons and two daughters, of whom only the youngest (aged 9) had been born in Dunsfold. The Whittingtons had previously lived in Alfold, Surrey, a village a few miles to the southeast of Dunsfold. Lucy, incidentally, consistently gives his name as Whitington, but the census records give Whittington and that seems to be the normal spelling.

158. Lucy E. Broadwood, "Folk Songs Collected in Sussex and Surrey," *Journal of the Folk-Song Society* 1, no. 4 (1902): 192. Broadwood, *English Traditional Songs and Carols*, 52-53.

159. *Journal of the Folk-Song Society* 1, no. 4 (1902): 200-201.

160. *Journal of the Folk-Song Society* 1, no. 4 (1902): 202-203.

161. *Journal of the Folk-Song Society* 1, no. 4 (1902): 190-193. Also Broadwood, *English Traditional Songs and Carols*, 50-51 and 60-65.

162. *Journal of the Folk-Song Society* 1, no. 4 (1902): 194-195.

163. Broadwood, *English Traditional Songs and Carols*, 120.

164. *Journal of the Folk-Song Society* 1, no. 4 (1902): 214-215.

165. Broadwood, *English Traditional Songs and Carols*, 120.

166. *Journal of the Folk-Song Society* 1, no. 4 (1902): 214-215.

167. *Journal of the Folk-Song Society* 1, no. 4 (1902): 212-213.

168. Broadwood, "Songs Noted Chiefly in Sussex and Surrey," 212-213.

169. *Journal of the Folk-Song Society* 1, no. 4 (1902): 209.

170. *Journal of the Folk-Song Society* 1, no. 4 (1902): 209.

171. Tune as recorded in Alec Fuller Maitland's annotated copy of *English County Songs* in the Lancashire County Archives, Lancaster, U. K. Given slightly differently in *Journal of the Folk-Song Society* 1, no. 4 (1902): 209-211.

172. *Journal of the Folk-Song Society* 1, no. 4 (1902): 198-199.

173. *Journal of the Folk-Song Society* 1, no. 4 (1902): 196-197. Also *English Traditional Songs and Carols*, 58-59.

174. Broadwood, *English Traditional Songs and Carols*, 58-59.

175. *Journal of the Folk-Song Society* 1, no. 4 (1902): 188-189.

176. Broadwood, *English Traditional Songs and Carols*, 72-73.

177. Broadwood, *English Traditional Songs and Carols*, 121.

178. Broadwood, *English Traditional Songs and Carols*, 72-73.

179. *Journal of the Folk-Song Society* 1, no. 4 (1902): 206-207.

180. *Journal of the Folk-Song Society* 1, no. 4 (1902): 204.

181. *Journal of the Folk-Song Society* 1, no. 4 (1902): 205. Also *English Traditional Songs and Carols*, 108 and 125.

182. *Journal of the Folk-Song Society* 1, no. 4 (1902): 205.

183. Broadwood diary entry for 22 October 1896.

184. Broadwood diary entry for 19 January 1897.

185. It had actually been collected in Cheshire by the Reverend F. Partridge. Broadwood and Fuller Maitland, *English County Songs*, 32-33.

186. Broadwood diary entries for 15, 19, and 31 January 1897.

187. Broadwood diary entries for 2 and 11 May 1897.

188. Broadwood diary entries for 8 December 1897 and 15 January 1898.

12

The Revival of National Song

There was another aspect to the movement that emerged during the first years of the 1890s. The revival embraced not only songs noted from oral tradition in the countryside but also a resurgence of interest in national song. The idea that there existed a corpus of English national songs—songs that were not necessarily overtly patriotic but that expressed or captured in a special way the spirit of the country—goes back at the very least to William Kitchiner's publications in the 1820s, *The Loyal and National Songs of England* and *The Sea Songs of England*.[1] In the 1850s William Chappell's groundbreaking *Popular Music of the Olden Time* was broader in scope, yet his huge compilation included many more examples of the kind of material that Kitchiner had championed, and there was no more patriotic music editor and publisher in Victorian England than he.[2] *Popular Music of the Olden Time*, however, was essentially a scholarly work that by its sheer size and the detailed, rather antiquarian, nature of its text, was daunting for the average mid-Victorian purchaser of songbooks. In an effort to tap a much larger, more popular, market, Chappell authorized the creation of *Old English Ditties,* a two-volume selection from his *magnum opus* made by Natalia Macfarren and John Oxenford.[3] This work, which featured piano arrangements by a leading Victorian art music composer, George Macfarren, gave the notion of national song much wider currency in the mid-Victorian era than Kitchiner's pioneering efforts had achieved earlier in the century.

By the late Victorian period national songs were a standard component of the country's musical life, and one might feel that there was scarcely any need in the 1890s to revive a genre that was perfectly alive and well. Nonetheless, in that decade we find a renewed interest in the concept and tradition of national songs—or, to put it another way, in quintessentially English songs of various kinds. Significantly, several of the late Victorian folksong collectors would take leading roles in this renaissance of national song, in particular Alexander Barrett, Sabine Baring-Gould, and Frank Kidson. Not that they were the only ones: other prominent late Victorian musicians and composers, most notably Arthur Somervell, also played a part in the movement, which had actually been initiated by John Hatton as early as 1873. During the decade of the 1890s this renewed interest came in two bursts, the first in 1890-92 and the second from 1895 onwards. In this chapter we explore the first wave, leaving the second part of the story until chapter 15.

Most 'national' songbooks included a substantial number of items that could not really be counted as vernacular songs: they were not folksongs, nor had they caught the popular imagination sufficiently to be whistled in the streets. Above all, they had not demonstrated that they possessed the 'vital melodies' or appealing lyrics that would enable them to survive from generation to generation. In the main they were drawing-room ballads that had known some success in their day but had been largely superseded by later commercial offerings. I shall ignore most of these items in my discussion of the revival—I say 'most' not 'all,' because a few of them, such as "Home, Sweet Home," did exhibit sufficient durability to be counted as vernacular songs—but it is necessary to recognize that such drawing-room ballads *were* included in their collections by most, although not all, late Victorian editors of national songs. Providing an example of the genre is perhaps the best way of indicating the kind of song that they so often championed but which I am excluding from this account. "Fly Away, Pretty Moth," composed by Thomas H. Bayly, seems to have found many performers and appreciative listeners in its hey-day. It had an attractive tune and an evident, although suitably allegorical, moral message that appealed to respectable middle-class Victorians, especially, perhaps, to women who had somewhat reluctantly acquiesced in a comfortable but conventional married life rather than fully exploring their interests and talents in the face of a disapproving society. The song appeared in several collections and, prima facie, was good enough to stand a reasonable chance of returning to the popular repertoire for a while, although, in the event, it seems to have been too characteristically Victorian to have had much appeal to twentieth-century audiences.

Fly Away, Pretty Moth

Thomas H. Bayly

Fig. 12.1

Fly away, pretty moth, to the shade
Of the leaf where you slumber'd all day.
Be content with the moon and the stars, pretty moth,
And make use of your wings while you may.
Though yon glittering light may have dazzled you quite,
Though the gold of yon lamp may be gay,

CHORUS: Many things in this world that look bright, pretty moth,
Only dazzle to lead us astray.
Many things in this world that look bright, pretty moth,
Only dazzle to lead us astray.

I have seen, pretty moth, in the world,
Some as wild as yourself, and as gay,
Who bewitch'd by the sweet fascination of eyes,
Flittered round them by night and by day.
But tho' dreams of delight may have dazzled them quite,
They at last found it dangerous play.[4]

As the last quarter of the century opened, the music publisher Boosey and Company made a determined move to corner the lucrative market on simple piano arrangements of national songs. John L. Hatton was commissioned to edit a user-friendly collection that would rival *Old English Ditties*. Hatton's work started off in 1873 as a single-volume collection, but by the end of the 1870s the commercial success of the initial venture had encouraged Boosey to bring out a second volume, and two decades later a third would be added, under the aegis of a new editor, Eaton Faning, since Hatton died in 1886. While *Old English Ditties* no doubt continued to garner respectable sales, it was the two-volume edition of Hatton's *The Songs of England* that had, by 1880, become the benchmark against which any future collections of national songs would be judged.

John L. Hatton's *The Songs of England* [first edition]

The full title of Hatton's expanded collection was *The Songs of England: A Collection of 200 English Melodies, including the most popular traditional ditties, and the principal songs and ballads of the last three centuries*, and the subtitle provided a fair indication of its contents.[5] The work, however, reflected the fact that it had begun life as a slimmer, single-volume, songbook, and that Hatton's initial task had been to choose the one hundred songs that best reflected the nation's musical spirit since Shakespeare's time. We will start, therefore, by examining Hatton's initial songbook, and his choice of the best one hundred national songs.

The structure of Hatton's first volume appears random in nature: the songs are not ordered alphabetically, but neither is there any attempt to arrange them in even approximate chronological order. On the other hand, if one examines the contents closely, it is evident that Hatton did have in mind a broad scheme as to how he would go about selecting the material for the book. Essentially he saw his river of national song as having three well-springs: (i) anonymous traditional or "old English" songs which probably dated from the sixteenth century or even earlier; (ii) the songs of Shakespeare and his contemporaries; and (iii) songs from the seventeenth century, many of which were also anonymous. To these early sources he then added what he considered the best of eighteenth-century song, beginning with material from *The Beggar's Opera* and other songs by John Gay but including representative samples of the work of a good variety of other eighteenth-century songwriters and musicians, such as (among others) Richard Leveridge, William Shield, Thomas Arne, Richard Stevens, and Charles Dibdin. Finally, in his fifth category he sought to show how the tradition of national song had continued to bear fruit in the first half of the nineteenth century, giving as examples songs by such composers as Michael Balfe, Henry Bishop, John Braham, and Charles Horn.

Of his one hundred songs, Hatton classified less than one tenth as "traditional" or "Old English," the two terms that he used to describe material that was both old and anonymous. He included eight items in this first category. He recognized that not all of them in fact dated from Elizabethan England (or earlier), but he had no way of verifying the exact time when ballads such as "The Bailiff's Daughter of Islington," "Barbara Allen," and "The Three Ravens" had been composed. The last-named was published in the first decade of the seventeenth century but probably dated from the Wars of the Roses, and it was already familiar to most Victorians interested in old songs and ballads. Arthur Bullen would reprint the text in his 1887 compilation *Lyrics from the Song-Books of the Elizabethan Age*, a collection that did much to re-popularize songs from the Tudor era.[6] The difference between Hatton and Bullen, however, was that Hatton provided his readers with a tune:

There were three ravens sat on a tree,
Down a down, hey down, hey down;
They were as black as they might be,
With a down.
And one of them said to his mate,
"Where shall we our breakfast take?"
With a down, derry, derry, derry down, down.

"Behold! alas, in yon green field,
Down a down, etc.
There lies a knight, slain under his shield,
With a down.
His hounds lie down beside his feet,
So well do they their master keep."
With a down, etc.

"His faithful hawks so near him fly,
Down a down, etc.
No bird of prey dare venture nigh,
With a down.
But see! there comes a fallow doe,
And to the knight she strait doth go."
With a down, etc.

She lifted up his ghastly head,
Down a down, etc.
And kiss'd his wounds that were so red,
With a down.
She buried him before the prime,
And died herself, ere even-song time,
With a down, etc.[7]

The Three Ravens

Anon

Fig. 12.2

Other songs that Hatton included in the same "traditional" category were "Early One Morning," "The Leathern Bottel" and "The Girl I Left Behind Me," although, confusingly, he suggested that the last-named, although anonymous, was probably an eighteenth-century composition. Other surprising inclusions in his first category were "There Was a Jolly Miller (*aka* "The Miller of Dee"), which he believed to have been in circulation before Isaac Bickerstaffe incorporated it into the ballad opera *Love in a Village* (Hatton counted it as seventeenth-century), and "The British Grenadiers," which he over-confidently ascribed to the sixteenth century. This, a good, if well-known, example of the overtly patriotic kind of national song, would find a place in virtually every subsequent compilation of compositions of this type.

The British Grenadiers

Anon

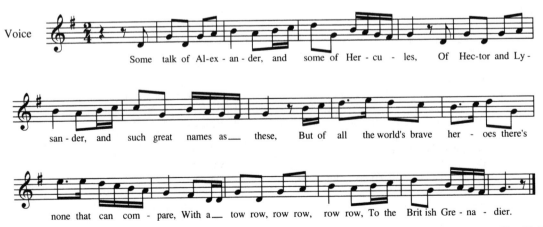

Fig. 12.3

Some talk of Alexander, and some of Hercules,
Of Hector and Lysander, and such great names as these;
But of all the world's brave heroes there's none that can compare
With a tow row, row row, row row, to the British Grenadier.

When e'er we are commanded to storm the palisades,
Our leaders march with fusees and we with hand grenades;
We throw them from the glacis about the enemies' ears,
Sing tow row, row row, row row, the British Grenadiers.

Then let us fill a bumper and drink a health to those
Who carry caps and pouches and wear the louped clothes;
May they and their commanders live happy all their years,
With a tow row, row row, row row, for the British Grenadiers.[8]

If Hatton's category of traditional songs turned out to include material spanning the centuries, the same, curiously enough, was also true of his second group: songs by Shakespeare and his contemporaries. The lyrics all dated from the late sixteenth or early seventeenth century, but the tunes were sometimes much later creations, since both Thomas Arne and Henry Bishop had specialized in setting Shakespearean texts to music. Of songs by Shakespeare's contemporaries, Ben Jonson's "Drink to Me Only" was accorded its traditional (and presumably Jacobean) melody. Hatton believed that "Down among the Dead Men" was the work of Elizabethan courtier-poet Sir Edward Dyer, best known for the poem-lyric "My Mind to Me a Kingdom Is," although he thought the tune a later creation, dating from the end of the seventeenth century. As for Shakespeare himself (whom Hatton insisted on calling Shakspeare), his lyric from *As You Like It*, "It Was a Lover and His Lass," employed a contemporary tune by Thomas Morley. The melody of "O, Willow, Willow" (sung by Desdemona in *Othello*), on the other hand, was designated "traditional," with both words and music ascribed vaguely to "Shakspeare's time":

O Willow, Willow

Anon/Shakespeare

Fig. 12.4

A poor soul sat sighing by a sycamore tree,
Sing willow, willow, willow,
With his hand in his bosom, and his head upon his knee,

> Oh! willow, willow, willow, willow,
> Oh! willow, willow, willow, willow,
> My garland shall be,
> Sing all a green willow, willow, willow, willow,
> Ah! me...the green willow my garland must be.
>
> He sighed in his sighing, and made a great moan,
> Sing willow, willow, willow,
> I am dead to all pleasure, my true love she is gone!
> Oh! willow, willow, willow, willow,
> Oh! willow, willow, willow, willow,
> My garland must be,
> Sing oh! the green willow, willow, willow, willow,
> Ah! me...the green willow my garland must be.[9]

Several of the other Shakespearean settings chosen by Hatton were by eighteenth-century composers. Thomas Arne, for example, provided "Blow, Blow, Thou Winter Wind" (also from *As You like It*), "Where the Bee Sucks" (from *The Tempest*), and "Under the Greenwood Tree," while R. J. S. Stevens was responsible for "Sigh No More, Ladies." Nineteenth-century composer Sir Henry Bishop contributed the tunes and arrangements for other poems attributed to Shakespeare: "Bid Me Discourse," "Lo! Here the Gentle Lark," and "Should He Upbraid."

It is not entirely clear why Hatton made a distinction between those seventeenth-century songs that he classified as "traditional" or "Old English" and those he simply regarded as anonymous compositions from the same century, although he may have considered the former as rural in provenance and the latter as products of the urban music industry, despite the loss of the names of their creators. Anonymous items in his third category included "Begone! Dull Care," "Come Lasses and Lads," "Jockey to the Fair," "Near Woodstock Town," "The Oak and the Ash" (aka "The North Country Maid"), and "The Vicar of Bray." Another anonymous seventeenth-century tune was "My Lodging It Is On the Cold Ground," although Hatton attributed the words to John Gay. For other songs from this century he could confidently indicate a composer of either the melody or the lyric (or both): John Dryden, for example, was the writer of "What Shall I Do to Show How Much I Love Her," while the music was the creation of Henry Purcell, who was also responsible for "I Attempt From Love's Sickness to Fly" and "Ye Twice Ten Hundred Deities." Hatton might have been hard pressed to make a convincing case that these two examples of Purcell's artistry were really vernacular songs, and the same was true of John Milton's "Now Phoebus Sinketh in the West," which had been set to a tune by Thomas Arne. However, he would have had no difficulty championing as national songs such other seventeenth-century items as Richard Sheridan's "Here's to the Maiden of Bashful Fifteen" and Robert Herrick's "Cherry Ripe," although he presented the latter in an arrangement by nineteenth-century composer Charles E. Horn.

Moving on to the eighteenth century, Hatton surprisingly ignored entirely the songwriting of Thomas D'Urfey, but John Gay and the phenomenon of the ballad opera clearly demanded representation. From *The Beggar's Opera* came "Cease Your Funning," and, as we have seen, Gay was also credited with the words of "My Lodging It Is On the Cold Ground," although Hatton recognized that in both cases the tune was traditional. On the other hand, the prolific Richard Leveridge was the acknowledged composer of the melody for Gay's most popular creation, "Black-eyed Susan":

> All in the Downs the fleet was moor'd,
> The streamers waving in the wind,
> When black-ey'd Susan came on board,
> "O where shall I my true love find?
> Tell me ye jovial sailors, tell me true,
> If my sweet William,
> If my sweet William sails among your crew?"
>
> William was high upon the yard,
> Rock'd by the billows to and fro,
> Soon as her wellknown voice he heard,
> He sigh'd and cast his eyes below;
> The cord slides swiftly thro' his glowing hands,
> And quick as lightning,
> And quick as lightning, on the deck he stands.

> "Believe not what the landsmen say,
> Who tempt with doubts thy constant mind,
> They'll tell thee sailors when away
> In ev'ry port a mistress find,
> Yet, yes, believe them when they tell thee so,
> For thou art present,
> For thou art present where-so-e'er I go."
>
> "Oh, Susan, Susan, lovely dear,
> My vows for ever true remain,
> Let me kiss off that falling tear,
> We only part to meet again;
> Change as ye list, ye winds, my heart shall be
> The faithful compass,
> The faithful compass that still points to thee."

The boatswain gave the dreadful word,
The sails their swelling bosoms spread;
No longer must she stay on board:
They kiss—she sigh'd—he hangs his head:

The less'ning boat unwilling rows to land,
"Adieu," she cries,
"Adieu," she cries, and waves her lily hand.[10]

Black-eyed Susan

John Gay & R. Leveridge/Hatton

Fig. 12.5

Hatton chose fewer examples of Leveridge's song writing than might have been expected, but he could not omit one of the classic national songs from the Georgian musician's pen, "The Roast Beef of Old England." Similarly *de rigueur* was the David Garrick/William Boyce collaboration, "Hearts of Oak" (Hatton gave the plural form of the title rather than the original singular). We have already seen that he included several of Thomas Arne's settings of Shakespeare and Milton, but he also slipped in "We All Love a Pretty Girl under the Rose" and "When Forced from Dear Hebe," the latter a setting of one of William Shenstone's poems. And, of course, there was no avoiding "Rule Britannia," which had originally appeared in Arne's masque *Alfred*, with words by the Scottish poet and librettist James Thomson. Other national songs from the early Georgian period that virtually chose themselves were Henry Fielding's "A Hunting We Will Go" (which Hatton dated to 1760), Henry Carey's "Sally in Our Alley," and Leonard McNally's "Lass of Richmond Hill."

William Shield was another eighteenth-century composer from whom Hatton liberally borrowed songs. He attributed the music for Prince Hoare's "The *Arethusa*" to Shield, as well as that for Pearce's "The Heaving of the Lead," H. B. Dudley's "The Streamlet that Flow'd Round," and two songs by John O'Keefe, "The Thorn" and "The Wolf." Shield himself was apparently responsible for the words as well as the music of "Tell Her I'll Love Her." As might have been expected, the other songwriter who dominated the material chosen by Hatton from the second half of the century was Charles Dibdin. Hatton included twelve of Dibdin's compositions, favoring those with marine connections, such as "The Anchorsmiths," "Blow High, Blow Low," "The Jolly Young Waterman," "The Sailor's Journal," "Then Farewell, My Trim-built Wherry," "The Token," and the inevitable "Tom Bowling," although, strangely enough, "Poor Jack" was missing. The others were mainly love songs, such as "Love Has Eyes," "Lovely Nan," and "While the Lads of the Village." Choosing just one Dibdin song for illustrative purposes is difficult, but one of his more contemplative yet still popular creations was an allegorical lament titled "I Lock'd Up All My Treasure":

I lock'd up all my treasure,
And journey'd many a mile,

And by my grief did measure,
The passing time the while;

I lock'd up all my treasure,   Like an expecting lover
And journey'd many a mile,   To view it once again,
And by my grief did measure,   But this delight was stifled
The passing time the while,   As it began to dawn,
And by my grief did measure   I found my casket rifled
The passing time the while.   And all my treasure gone,
                                                 I found my casket rifled,
My business done and over,   And all my treasure gone.[11]
I hasten'd back amain,

I Lock'd Up All My Treasure

Charles Dibdin

Fig. 12.6

When he reached the nineteenth century, Hatton privileged the compositions of Henry Bishop beyond any other pre-Victorian musician, although he did also insert a few songs with tunes written by Charles Horn, Michael Balfe, and Thomas Bayly. The most notable inclusion by Balfe was his setting of Longfellow's "The Arrow and the Song," while Bayly contributed "Gaily the Troubadour" and "We Met—'Twas in a Crowd." Horn provided the music not only for Herrick's "Cherry Ripe" but also for Mrs. George Sharpe's "The Deep, Deep Sea" and George Soane's "I've Been Roaming." Apart from "Cherry Ripe" none of these were sure-fire candidates for vernacular status, but there were a couple of obviously national songs among the eleven items for which Bishop had composed the music. We have already noticed his popular Shakespeare settings, and he was also responsible for the tune of one of Dibdin's best-loved songs, "Love Has Eyes." Hatton also admired his collaborations with Bayly ("Oh, No, We Never Mention Her") and with T. Morton ("Pretty Mocking Bird," and "Tell Me, My Heart"), but it will be for the melodies that he composed for General Burgoyne's "The Dashing White Sergeant" and J. Howard Payne's "Home, Sweet Home" that he will be best remembered.

Mid pleasures and palaces, though we may roam,
Be it ever so humble, there's no place like home!
A charm from the skies seems to hallow us there,
Which seek thro' the world, is ne'er met with elsewhere.
Home! Home! Sweet, sweet home!
There's no place like home, there's no place like home.

An exile from home splendour dazzles in vain,

Oh! give me my lowly thatch'd cottage again!
The birds singing gaily that came at my call,
Give me them with the peace of mind dearer than all.
Home! Home! Sweet, sweet home!
There's no place like home! There's no place like home.[12]

Home, Sweet Home

Henry Bishop & J. Howard Payne

Fig. 12.7

The Songs of England, Volume 2

When, in the late 1870s, John Hatton came to compile the second volume of *The Songs of England*, he included a brief preface in which he remarked that he had not thought initially that it would be possible to find a second hundred old songs of equal quality to those chosen for volume one. Only the fact that the first book had been "so universally popular" had induced him to do the necessary research. He claimed, however, that the result had exceeded his expectations, and the plethora of available good songs had meant that, in his estimate, the "second selection [was] hardly less interesting and valuable than the first."[13] While this might have been a piece of self-puffery designed to help sell the book, the contents of volume two suggest that Hatton was both sincere and correct. To be sure, this was in part because some idiosyncratic omissions from the first hundred were still available, but second time around Hatton made no mistake over such well-loved and popular items as Arne's "My Dog and Gun," Shield's "Old Towler," Dibdin's "Poor Jack," and W. T. Parke's "The Garden Gate": all four were included. Another reason seems to have been that Hatton was somewhat more willing than before to include anonymous material from the sixteenth and seventeenth centuries. As we have seen, he had done so to a limited degree in volume one, but this time the number of items (fourteen) falling into his category of "traditional/old English" was nearly double, while he still included nine other seventeenth-century songs. His coverage of the eighteenth century still leaned heavily on the output of Thomas Arne, William Shield, and Charles Dibdin, but if anything his selections from their works were stronger than those in the first volume. And if, as before, he filled the book out with numerous compositions by Bayly, Bishop, and Horn, on this occasion he made better use of compositions by John Davy and John Braham.

It is doubtful whether many of Hatton's group of anonymous old English songs—the ones that he apparently regarded as folksongs—dated back to the Tudor era. He was unable to ascribe even an approximate date to them, but they did include a few that he might legitimately have assigned to the seventeenth century, if not the sixteenth. Probably the oldest, and perhaps the best candidate for the label "traditional," was the drinking song "How Stands the Glass Around?" There were two well-known songs about relations between the sexes, one ("Phillada Flouts Me") negative and the other ("Cupid's Garden") positive. Hatton borrowed the latter, which he was content to characterize merely as an "old song," from Chappell's *Popular Music of the Olden Time*. He provided only a truncated version of the lyric, which made the story in the song even less intelligible than the fuller, if still confused, version that John Ashton printed in *Real Sailor Songs*.[14] This was the item that Frank Kidson regarded as one of the most over-rated of English vernacular love songs, but it was undeniably popular, with a pretty tune that no doubt saved the undistinguished text from oblivion. It was a modest but useful service to make the melody once again available for drawing-room use:

Cupid's Garden

Anon

Fig. 12.8

'Twas down in Cupid's garden for pleasure I did go,
To see the fairest flowers that in that garden grow;
The first it was the jessamine, the lily, pink and rose,
And surely they're the fairest flowers that in that garden grows,
That in that garden grows.

I'd not walk'd in that garden the past of half an hour,
When there I saw two pretty maids sitting under a shady bow'r;
The first was lovely Nancy, so beautiful and fair,
The other was a charming maid who did the laurel wear,
That did the laurel wear.

I boldly stepp'd up to her and unto her did say—
"Are you engag'd to any young man? Do tell to me I pray!"
"I'm not engag'd to any young man—I solemnly do swear;
I mean to live a single life and still the laurel wear,
And still the laurel wear."

Then hand in hand together this lovely couple went,
Resolved was the sailor boy to know her full intent;
To know if he would slighted be, when to her the truth he told:
"Oh no! oh no! oh no!" she cried, "I love a sailor bold!"[15]

Hatton's group of "old English songs" also included a hunting song, "A Southerly Wind and a Cloudy Sky," a smoking song ("Tobacco Is an Indian Weed"), and a poaching song "The Poacher" (this was, in fact, a Somerset version of the song better known as "The Lincolnshire Poacher"). And there was one that he described as an "old English ballad" but which was actually a sailors' tavern song, "You Gentlemen of England" (*aka* "When the Stormy Winds Do Blow"):

You Gentlemen of England

Anon

Fig. 12.9

You gentlemen of England, who live at home at ease,
How little do you think upon the dangers of the seas;
Give ear unto the mariners, and they will plainly show,
All the cares, and the fears, when the stormy winds do blow,
All the cares, and the fears, when the stormy winds do blow.

All you that will be seamen must bear a valiant heart,
For when you come upon the seas you must not think to start,
Nor once to be faint-hearted in rain, hail, blow or snow,
Nor to think for to shrink, when the stormy winds do blow,
Nor to think for to shrink, when the stormy winds do blow.

The lawyer and the usurer that sit in gowns of fur,
In closets warm can take no harm, abroad they need not stir;
When winter fierce with cold doth pierce, and beats with hail and snow,
We are sure to endure, when the stormy winds do blow,
We are sure to endure, when the stormy winds do blow.

Then courage, all brave mariners, and never be dismay'd,

Whilst we have bold adventurers we ne'er shall want a trade;
Our merchants will employ us to fetch them wealth, I know,
Then behold, work for gold, when the stormy winds do blow,
Then behold, work for gold, when the stormy winds do blow.

When tempests are blown over and greatest fears are past,
In weather fair, and temperate air, we straight lie down to rest;
But when the billows tumble and waves do furious grow,
Then we rouse, up we rouse, when the stormy winds do blow,
Then we rouse, up we rouse, when the stormy winds do blow.

When we return in safety, with wages for our pains,
The tapster and the vintner will help to share our gains;
We'll call for liquor roundly, and pay before we go,
Then we'll roar on the shore, when the stormy winds do blow,
Then we'll roar on the shore, when the stormy winds do blow.[16]

The oldest material in volume two was, as Hatton put it, "from the time of Shakspeare." This second category included two anonymous items, "The Milking Pail" and "To the Maypole Haste Away," one text by Ben Jonson ("From Oberon in Fairyland"), and three songs connected with Shakespeare. Only one of the Shakespearean lyrics had a sixteenth-century melody, namely "When That I Was a Little Tiny Boy," from *Twelfth Night*:

When That I Was a Little Tiny Boy

William Shakespeare

Fig. 12.10

When that I was a little tiny boy,
With a heigh! ho! the wind and the rain,
A foolish thing was but a toy,
For the rain it raineth every day,
With a heigh! ho! the wind and the rain,
For the rain it raineth every day.

But when I came to man's estate,
With a heigh! ho! the wind and the rain,
'Gainst thieves and knaves men shut their gate,
For the rain it raineth every day,
With a heigh! ho! the wind and the rain,
For the rain it raineth every day.

But when I came, alas! to wive,
With a heigh! ho! the wind and the rain,
By swaggering never could I thrive,
For the rain it raineth every day,
With a heigh! ho! the wind and the rain,
For the rain it raineth every day.

A great while ago the world began,
With a heigh! ho! the wind and the rain,
But that's all one, our play is done,
And we'll strive to please you every day,
With a heigh! ho! the wind and the rain,
For the rain it raineth every day.[17]

Other settings of poems and songs attributed to Shakespeare were the work of nineteenth-century composers Sir Henry Bishop ("Come Live With Me and Be My Love") and Charles Horn ("Crabbed Age and Youth" and "Titania's Song").

Moreover, there was at least one other anonymous song that Hatton also assigned to the Tudor era, "The Hunt Is Up!" (which mentions "Harry, our king" in the lyric), while he dated "Come You Not from Newcastle?" to the year 1600.

The group of material that Hatton assigned to his third category, the seventeenth century, included two songs derived from John Milton's poetry, "By Dimpled Brook" and "By the Gaily Circling Glass," although they both appeared in later settings by Thomas Arne. George Herbert's poem "Sweet Day, So Cool," on the other hand, had a seventeenth-century melody, and the same was true for various anonymous compositions that Hatton believed were entirely Stuart-era creations, text and tune both. These included "Love Me Little, Love Me Long," "Love Will Find Out the Way," "Dulce Domum," "We Be Three Poor Mariners" (which he dated to 1609), and two lyrics associated with ceremonies welcoming the advent of spring, "The Queen of the May" and "To the Maypole Away."

Moving on to the eighteenth century, Hatton ascribed to this time period the anonymous "Haste to the Wedding." He had nothing from either Thomas D'Urfey or John Gay, but to Thomas Arne's Milton settings he added three other Arne compositions, "Fresh and Strong the Breeze is Blowing," "My Dog and Gun" and that quintessential national song, the composer's tribute to Shakespeare's birthplace, "Thou Soft-flowing Avon":

Thou Soft-flowing Avon

Thomas Arne

Fig. 12.11

Thou soft-flowing Avon, by thy silver stream,
Of things more than mortal thy Shakespeare would dream,
Would dream, would dream, thy Shakespeare would dream.
The fairies by moonlight dance round the green bed,
For hallow'd the turf is which pillow'd his head;
The fairies by moonlight dance round the green bed,
For hallow'd the turf is which pillow'd his head.

The love stricken maiden, the soft-sighing swain,
Here rove without danger, and sigh without pain;
The sweet bud of beauty no blight shall here dread,

For hallow'd the turf is which pillow'd his head;
The sweet bud of beauty no blight shall here dread,
For hallow'd the turf is which pillow'd his head.

Here youth shall be fam'd for their love and their truth,
And cheerful old age feel the spirit of youth;
For the raptures of fancy here poets shall tread,
For hallow'd the turf is that pillow'd his head;
For the raptures of fancy here poets shall tread,
For hallow'd the turf is that pillow'd his head.

Flow on, silver Avon, in song ever flow!   And the turf ever hallow'd which pillow'd his head;
Be the swans on thy borders still whiter than snow!   Ever full be thy stream, like his fame may it spread,
Ever full be thy stream, like his fame may it spread,   And the turf ever hallow'd which pillow'd his head![18]

In this section Hatton also included six songs for which William Shield had supplied the music and, in most cases, probably the words too: "Ere Round the Huge Oak," "Let Fame Sound the Trumpet," "My Friend and Pitcher," "My Heart with Love Is Beating," "Old Towler," and "The Storm." The other major eighteenth-century songwriter to figure in a substantial way in this volume was Charles Dibdin. Hatton reprinted nine of his songs, and one, "The Bee Proffers Honey but Bears a Sting," from his son, Charles Dibdin Jr. The elder, more famous, Dibdin's compositions included a drinking song ("The Flowing Bowl"), a hunting song ("The High-mettled Racer"), an ironically humorous survey of the uses to which felled trees are put ("The Woodman"), and "True Courage, " a philosophical meditation on the theme of the parable of the Good Samaritan. The others were on the military or maritime themes for which he was best known: "The Soldier's Adieu," "All's One to Jack" (about death in a naval battle), "Jack Rattlin" (on a sailor's love for his girl ashore), and "Poor Jack," a fatalistic but much-loved reflection on the dangers of life at sea. "The Lass That Loves a Sailor," one of the most popular of his many drinking songs, was also included:

The Lass that Loves a Sailor

Charles Dibdin

Fig. 12.12

The moon on the ocean was dimm'd by a ripple,
Affording a chequered delight;
The gay jolly tars pass'd the word for the tipple,
And the toast, for 'twas Saturday night.
Some sweetheart or wife, he loved as his life,
Each drank and wished he could hail her;
But the standing toast, that pleas'd the most,

Was "The wind that blows, the ship that goes,
And the lass that loves a sailor."

Some drank "The Queen" and some her brave ships,
And some "The Constitution,"
Some "May our foes, and all such rips,
Yield to English resolution."

That fate might bless some Poll or Bess,
And that they soon might hail her;
But the standing toast, that pleased the most,
Was "The wind that blows, the ship that goes,
And the lass that loves a sailor."

Some drank "The Prince," and some "Our Land,"
This glorious land of freedom;

Some "That our tars may never want
Heroes brave to lead them."
"That she who's in distress may find
Such friends as ne'er will fail her."
But the standing toast, that pleased the most,
Was "The wind that blows, the ship that goes,
And the lass that loves a sailor."[19]

Most of the other material in volume two was the work of later musicians and songwriters, with John Davy, John Braham, Thomas Bayly, Charles Horn, and, of course, Henry Bishop the most prominent names. There was some interesting material here, including Bayly's "Fly Away, Pretty Moth" and "Isle of Beauty." Others included Horn's Shakespeare settings and Bishop's settings of Scott ("County Guy") and Byron ("My Boat Is on the Shore"), but most of this material had yet to prove its staying power in the collective consciousness of the nation. Songs such as Braham's "The Beautiful Maid" or Bishop's "The Bloom Is on the Rye" and "The Sun is o'er the Mountain" may have been potentially national songs but they were not yet vernacular songs. In contrast, such composed items as W. T. Parke's "The Garden Gate" and Shield's "Old Towler," let alone such anonymous ditties as "Cupid's Garden" and "The Poacher," were commonly to be found in oral tradition and were definitely songs that the public had taken to heart and made part of the English national musical heritage.

Eaton Faning's *The Songs of England*, Volume 3

A decade passed before a new edition of *The Songs of England* appeared; this now had 272 songs in three volumes, and was edited by Eaton Faning.[20] Faning left the first two volumes much as before, but he was entirely responsible for the third, which comprised seventy-two extra "English melodies and ballads" that were billed as "popular during the last fifty years."[21] It opened with Michael Balfe's setting of Tennyson's "Come into the Garden, Maud," and many of Faning's proposed additions to the national song canon were nineteenth-century compositions by such familiar names as Balfe, Bayly, Bishop, and Horn, often setting lyrics by Longfellow, Edward Fitzball, and the prolific Alfred Bunn. Former editor John L. Hatton was another of the nineteenth-century composers whose work was included, and such eminent figures as W. Sterndale Bennett and Arthur Sullivan were also represented. Sullivan's contributions, for example, were "Golden Days" and "Once Again," both of which were collaborations with lyric writer Lionel H. Lewin. None of this had anything to do with folk music, and few of these drawing-room poems and ballads were even on their way to becoming vernacular songs, let alone tunes that were already being whistled in the streets.

On the other hand, Faning had slipped in one patriotic drinking song from the Napoleonic era that was a fairly typical representative of the national song genre, and it was certainly a vernacular song, since Frank Kidson had collected a version of it from oral tradition in Yorkshire. This was "He Swore He'd Drink Old England Dry":

Drink round, brave boys, and never give o'er,
Drink round, brave boys, as I have said before;
Old Boney he has sent to us a fresh reply,
And swears that he will come and drink old England dry.

CHORUS: Dry, dry, dry, boys, dry!
         He swears he'll come and drink old England dry, dry, dry.

Often times, often times old Boney he has said,
If England would receive him no taxes need be paid;
We'd rather not believe him for fear that he should lie,
Should play the knave and come and drink old England dry.

'Twas Collingwood, of gallant renown,
Swore he'd fight for his king, his country and the crown;
For his crown, king and country, he would fight until he die,
Before that they should come and drink old England dry.

If we meet his ships all on the high seas,
Ten thousand to one that we shall not agree;

Our cannons they shall rattle, and bullets swiftly fly,
Before that he shall come and drink old England dry.[22]

He Swore He'd Drink Old England Dry

Anon

Fig. 12.13

Faning had also delved into the past to find a dozen or so old songs that he believed had survived the ravages of time. There were more lyrics by "Shakspeare" (Faning, like Hatton, preferred the older spelling), including "When Daisies Pied" from *As You Like It* in Thomas Arne's arrangement, although other texts attributed to the Bard ("By the Simplicity of Venus' Doves," "Over Hill, Over Dale," and "Take, Oh! Take Those Lips Away") were accorded more modern settings by Bishop or T. Cooke. The seventeenth century received rather nominal coverage: Henry Purcell was represented by "Arise, Ye Subterranean Winds" and "Let the Dreadful Engines," Edmund Waller's "The Self-Banished" appeared in a setting by John Blow, and George Wither's poem "Woman" was set to music by H. Phillips. The eighteenth century did not fare a lot better, although three more songs by Charles Dibdin were added to those in the previous two volumes: "Tom Tough," "The True English Sailor," and "The Tight Little Island." There was, however, one other anonymous song that it was surprising Hatton had omitted from the earlier volumes, and it probably dates from the eighteenth century. Although it was a regional song—the lyric unequivocally identifies it with the Lake District—there is no question that this popular celebration of fox hunting belongs in the corpus of national songs: "D' Ye Ken John Peel?":

D' ye ken John Peel with his coat so gay?
D' ye ken John Peel at the break o' the day?
D' ye ken John Peel when he's far, far away,
With his hounds and his horn in the morning?

CHORUS:
For the sound of his horn brought me from my bed,
And the cry of his hounds which he oft-times led,
Peel's "view hal-loo" would awaken the dead,
Or the fox from his lair in the morning.

Yes, I ken John Peel, and Ruby too,
Ranter and Ringwood, Bellman and True;

From a find to a check, from a check to a view,
From a view to a death in the morning.

Then here's to John Peel, from my heart and soul,
Let's drink to his health, let's finish the bowl;
We'll follow John Peel through fair and through foul,
If we want a good hunt in the morning.

D' ye ken John Peel with his coat so gay?
He lived at Troutbeck once on a day;
Now he has gone far, far away,
We shall ne'er hear his voice in the morning.[23]

D' Ye Ken John Peel?

Anon

Voice

D' ye ken John Peel with his coat so gay? D' ye ken John Peel at the

break o' the day? D' ye ken John Peel when he's far, far a way, With his hounds and his horn in the

morn - ing? For the sound of his horn brought me from my bed, And the cry of his hounds, which he

oft-times led, Peel's "view haloo" would a - wak - en the dead, Or the fox from his lair in the

morn - ing.

Fig. 12.14

Faning's expanded version of Hatton's collection would undergo further modification in 1900, with the addition of another nine songs, but it was the first three-volume edition (1890) that seems to have been the one most frequently employed by such late Victorian song-collectors as Lucy Broadwood and Frank Kidson. They were also very familiar with a rival collection that appeared the same year, edited by a fellow collector, William Barrett.

William Alexander Barrett's *Standard English Songs*

In the preface to the second volume of *The Songs of England* Hatton had used, instead of the term "national songs," the phrase "our Standard Songs and Ballads" (his capitals).[24] The scholar selected by the publisher Augener to edit a rival collection of national songs picked up on this terminology and decided—or the publisher decided—to call his book *Standard English Songs*.[25] William Alexander Barrett was a musician, journalist, and academic, whose work was mainly in the field of art music. In 1886 he had authored *English Glees and Part-Songs: An Inquiry into their Historical Development*,[26] but, as we have seen in chapter 10, he had also collected folksongs in the south of England and would publish them as *English Folk-Songs* in 1891.[27] Although no date is given at the front of *Standard English Songs* it was apparently issued in 1890, and it rapidly became the normal one-volume alternative to *The Songs of England*. Its contents therefore contributed to defining the corpus of national song for the late Victorian generation.

Barrett's underlying approach was quite similar to Hatton's, and a considerable number of his choices were identical. Like Hatton initially, he was restricted to one hundred songs, and, within this limit, he aimed to provide a fairly comprehensive coverage of the history of national song, beginning with a few traditional ballads and lyrics and moving through the seventeenth and eighteenth centuries to the early Victorian era. Unlike Hatton, he largely ignored the songs of the Elizabethan theatre, even those of Shakespeare. His oldest songs that can be dated securely were probably three from the Jacobean era, two by court lutenist and composer Robert Jones ("Love in Jealousy" and "Tell Me, Dearest, What Is Love") and Ben Jonson's "Drink to Me Only With Thine Eyes." Hatton had included the latter in his collection, but he had been unable to identify the composer of the tune; Barrett confidently attributed it to Colonel R. Mellish:

Drink To Me Only

Ben Jonson

Fig. 12.15

Drink to me only with thine eyes,
And I will pledge with mine,
Or leave a kiss within the cup,
And I'll not ask for wine.

The thirst that from the soul doth rise,
Doth ask a drink divine,
But might I of Love's nectar sip,
I would not change for wine.

I sent thee late a rosy wreath,
Not so much hon'ring thee,
As giving it a hope that there
It could not wither'd be.

But thou thereon didst only breathe,
And sent'st it back to me,
Since when it grows, and smells, I swear,
Not of itself but thee.[28]

Barrett selected more anonymous traditional material that may also have dated from the early seventeenth century, such as the broadside ballad "The Bailiff's Daughter of Islington" and another old lyric chosen by Hatton, "Near Woodstock Town." And, again like Hatton, he opted to include "Come Lasses and Lads," a song that he felt sure was a seventeenth-century production:

Come lasses and lads, get leave of your dads,
And away to the maypole hie.
For every he has got a she,
And the fiddler's standing by.
For Willie shall dance with Jane,
And Johnny has got his Joan,
To trip it, trip it, trip it, trip it,
Trip it up and down,
To trip it, trip it, trip it, trip it,
Trip it up and down.

"You're out" says Dick, "Not I" says Nick,
"'Twas the fiddler played it wrong,"
"'Tis true," says Hugh, and so says Sue,
And so says ev'ry one.
The fiddler then began
To play the tune again,
And ev'ry girl did trip it, trip it,
Trip it up and down,
And ev'ry girl did trip it, trip it,
Trip it up and down.

Then after an hour they went to a bow'r,
And played for ale and cakes,
And kisses too, till they were due,
The lasses held the stakes.
The girls did then begin
To quarrel with the men,
And bade them take their kisses back,
And give them their own again,
And bade them take their kisses back,
And give them their own again.

And there they sat until it was late,
And tired the fiddler quite,
With singing and playing, without any paying,
From morning until night.
They told the fiddler then,

They'd pay him for his play,
And each gave twopence, twopence, twopence,
Twopence, and went away,
And each gave twopence, twopence, twopence,
Twopence, and went away.

Goodnight, says Harry, goodnight, says Mary,
Goodnight, says Dolly to John,
Goodnight, says Sue, goodnight says Hugh,
Goodnight, says ev'ry one.
Some walk'd and some did run,
Some loiter'd on the way,
And bound themselves by kisses twelve,
To meet next holiday,
And bound themselves by kisses twelve,
To meet next holiday.[29]

Come Lasses and Lads

Anon

Voice

Come lass es and lads, get leave of your dads, And a - way to the may pole hie,___ For

ev-ery he___has got a she, And the fid - dler's stand - ing by.___ For Wil - lie shall dance with

Jane,___ And John-ny has got his Joan,___ To trip it, trip it, trip___it, trip it, trip___it up and

down,___ To trip it, trip it, trip___it, trip it, trip___it up and down.___

Fig. 12.16

Barrett clearly felt that this celebration of May Day merrymaking, like Ben Jonson's poetic love lyric, was one of the foundation stones of the national song tradition. Another essential item was "The British Grenadiers," although he rejected Hatton's claim that it was a sixteenth-century effusion and more cautiously dated it to *circa* 1700. He also decided that two of the important seventeenth-century art music composers, Henry Purcell and John Blow, should be represented in the collection, so he allotted them a song each, "Nymphs and Shepherds" in the case of Purcell and "To Phyllis" for Blow. He also slipped in "Woman," a collaboration between poet George Wither and musician H. Phillips. Moreover, he believed that Isaac Bickerstaffe's "The Jolly Miller" employed a seventeenth-century tune, although the well-known words were added later, as part of the libretto of the ballad opera *Love in a Village*.

Mention of Bickerstaffe brings us to the eighteenth century, a period with which Barrett seemed more comfortable. He identified three anonymous compositions as worthy to be counted as "standards" in the national song repertoire, namely "A Country Life Is Sweet," "The Invitation," and, more plausibly, the popular vernacular lyric "The Girl I Left Behind Me." Not surprisingly, he agreed with Hatton that it was essential to include Richard Leveridge's "Roast Beef of

Old England," Henry Carey's "Sally in Our Alley," and also "My Lodging It Is On the Cold Ground," although he ascribed the words of the latter song to William Davenant rather than John Gay, and took the melody from the 1775 edition of *Vocal Musick*. He included one other song by Carey, "Flocks Are Sporting," and one other by Leveridge, "The Cure of Care." William Shield was allocated three compositions, "Tell Her I'll Love Her" and two of his collaborations with John O'Keefe, "Ere Around the Huge Oak" and "The Thorn." Thomas Linley, the composer who set to music Richard Sheridan's "Here's to the Maiden of Bashful Fifteen," was also represented by "Young Lubin."

Charles Dibdin's songs were far less numerous in Barrett's collection than in Hatton's, but to the unavoidable "Tom Bowling" was added "Bright Gems" and "The Last Shilling," two items that Hatton had omitted, despite his penchant for Dibdin's work. James Hook, a composer somewhat slighted by Hatton, was represented by "The Voice of Love," "My Friend Is a Man I Would Copy," and, predictably, his popular collaboration with wordsmith Leonard McNally, "The Lass of Richmond Hill":

The Lass of Richmond Hill

James Hook and Leonard McNally

Fig. 12.17

On Richmond Hill there lives a lass,
More bright than May-day morn,
Whose charms all other maids surpass,
A rose without a thorn.

CHORUS:
This lass so neat, with smiles so sweet,
Has won my right good will,
I'd crowns resign to call her mine,
Sweet lass of Richmond Hill,
Sweet lass of Richmond Hill,
Sweet lass of Richmond Hill,

I'd crowns resign to call her mine,
Sweet lass of Richmond Hill.

Ye zephyrs gay that fan the air,
And wanton thro' the grove,
O whisper to my charming fair,
"I die for you, my love."

How happy will the shepherd be,
Who calls this maid his own,
O may her choice be fix'd on me,
Mine rests on her alone.[30]

As for Thomas Arne, "Rule Britannia" was there, as was Arne's setting of Milton's "Now Phoebus Sinketh in the West," both choices with which Hatton concurred, but Barrett also opted for Arne's well-loved collaboration with Bickerstaffe, "My Dog and My Gun":

My Dog and My Gun

Thomas Arne and Jack Bickerstaffe

Fig. 12.18

Let gay ones and great make the most of their gate,
From pleasure to pleasure they run,
From pleasure to pleasure they run,
Well, who cares a jot, I envy them not,
While I have my dog and my gun,
While I have my dog and my gun.

For exercise, air, to the fields I repair,
With spirits unclouded and light,
With spirits unclouded and light,
No blisses I find, no sting leaves behind,
But health and diversion unite,
But health and diversion unite.[31]

There was one other eighteenth-century song that clearly could not be omitted, and Barrett gave it pride of place as the opening item in his collection. "Heart of Oak" (Barrett correctly retained the original singular spelling of the first word of the title) had been written in 1759 to a melody composed by William Boyce, and it was a quintessential national song, one of a dozen or so that really defined the genre:

Come cheer up my lads, 'tis to glory we steer,
To add something new to this wonderful year,
To honour we call you, not press you like slaves,
For who are so free as the sons of the waves?

CHORUS:
Heart of oak are our ships, jolly tars are our men,
We always are ready, steady boys steady,
We'll fight and will conquer again and again.

We ne'er see our foes but we wish them to stay,
They never see us but they wish us away,
If they run, why, we follow and run them ashore,
And if they won't fight us, we cannot do more.

They swear they'll invade us these terrible foes,
They frighten our women, our children, our beaux,
But should their flat bottoms in darkness get o'er,
Still Britons they'll find to receive them on shore.[32]

Heart of Oak

William Boyce and David Garrick

Voice

Come cheer up my lads, 'tis to gl - ry we steer, To add some thing new to this

won-der ful year. To— hon-our we call you, not press you like slaves, For who are so free as the

sons of the waves. Heart of oak are our ships, jol-ly tars are our men, We al ways are read-y

Stead y boys, stead-y, We'll fight and will con-quer a - gain and a-gain.

Fig. 12.19

Moving on to the nineteenth century, Barrett, like Hatton, was hard pressed to find genuinely vernacular items that had entered the consciousness of previous generations and already become part of the national heritage. In the main, it was simply too early for the work of his favorite composers, who clearly included Thomas Bayly, Michael Balfe, and G. H. Rodwell, to have attained the same status as the classic national songs from the previous two centuries. There were a few candidates, however. Barrett was not as enthusiastic about the music of Henry Bishop as was Hatton, but he could agree that both "Home, Sweet Home" and "The Dashing White Sergeant" were part of the standard repertoire, and for good measure he added "The Pilgrim of Love." He concurred with Hatton that Charles Horn's setting of Herrick's "Cherry Ripe" had to be on the list of standard national songs, and he slipped in four more of Horn's compositions, "I've Been Roaming," "Through the Wood," and two collaborations with Thomas H. Bayly, "He Loves and Rides Away" and "After Many Roving Years." Bayly was also represented by "Welcome Me Home," "I'd Be a Butterfly" and two songs that Hatton had also picked, "Isle of Beauty" (a collaboration with composer C. S. Whitmore) and, of course, "Fly Away, Pretty Moth."

Barrett was a committed champion of the songs of Michael W. Balfe, about whom he also wrote a book. On this occasion he selected five of Balfe's compositions, "When I Beheld the Anchor Weighed," a setting of Thomas Moore's "They Told Me Thou'rt the Favoured Guest," two collaborations with Alfred Bunn ("Then You'll Remember Me" and "I Dreamed I Dwelt in Marble Halls"), and "The Peace of the Valley." The latter had lyrics by Edward Fitzball, who also collaborated with composer G. H. Rodwell on "Return, O My Love" and "The Banks of the Blue Moselle." Barrett also included three other Rodwell compositions: "The Wind and the Beam" (words by Edward Bulwer Lytton), "Violets" and "The Beautiful Maid of My Soul." Yet, although all these songs were undoubted favorites in Victorian drawing-rooms, none of them became true vernacular items, and it is doubtful if any really belonged in the corpus of national songs.

Boulton and Somervell's *Songs of the Four Nations*

Two years later, in 1892, another competitor joined the market for piano arrangements of national songs. *Songs of the Four Nations*[33] was the work of Harold Boulton and art music composer Arthur Somervell, a friend of Lucy Broadwood who was already making a name for himself in London music circles for his song settings and other compositions. Somervell had yet to compose the three song cycles for which he would become famous, his settings of Tennyson's

Maud, Browning's *James Lee's Wife*, and, above all, Housman's *A Shropshire Lad*. But he was already interested in the idea of creating a new kind of English art music that would be rooted in the nation's cultural heritage, and he counted national songs (as well as folksong) as an important part of that heritage. In his art songs Somervell strove for a musical purity and simplicity that he believed was too often lacking in Victorian music—he disliked the element of bombast so evident in many Victorian concert overtures (including some of Sullivan's, and, later, Elgar's, compositions)—and he found that simplicity in the best examples of the national song tradition. In the preface to *Songs of the Four Nations* he wrote:

> The first thing to be remembered is the extreme simplicity of the national tune. It takes in music the same place as the simplest lyric takes in poetry [and] answers absolutely to Mr. F. T. Palgrave's definition of a lyric, that it "shall turn on some simple thought, feeling, or situation." So with National Songs; the tunes are of the simplest possible construction, and are repeated again and again, quite regardless of the varying character of the words…Such songs as these, have, for the larger part, sprung anonymously from the people, and, handed down by them, have sufficed to express their narrow (not necessarily shallow) range of feeling on the subjects of love, war, and other primary emotions of mankind.[34]

For Somervell, then, there was little difference between national songs and folksongs, and he was clearly prepared to include a goodly number of the latter within the standard canon of national music. Boulton concurred, and noted in the preface to the book that in order to "fully represent the individuality and beauty of the national music hailing from all parts of our country" they had had to look for material beyond that already reprinted in such collections as Hatton's and Barrett's.[35]

Yet because *Songs of the Four Nations* was limited to fifty items and the intention of its editors was to include also Cornish, Manx, Welsh, Scottish, and Irish material, only ten examples of the best of English national song were to be found in the book. Several of these—"The Three Ravens," "My Lodging It Is On the Cold Ground," "Old Towler," and "Cupid's Garden"—we have already seen printed by Hatton or Barrett or both. Most of the others were also anonymous, including "Floodes of Tears," "Pretty Polly Oliver," and "The Happy Farmer," although "When the King Enjoys His Own Again" was known to be the work of Stuart-era ballad-monger Martin Parker. "Ye Mariners of England" was attributed to Thomas Campbell and Dr. Calcott. Unfortunately Boulton had taken it upon himself to rewrite the lyrics of three songs, "When the King," "The Happy Farmer," and "Polly Oliver." Apart from "The Three Ravens," the first printed version of which was found in Thomas Ravenscroft's *Melismata* (1611), the oldest English item in *Songs of the Four Nations* was "Thou Wilt Not Go and Leave Me Here," which Boulton and Somervell had found in the Advocates Library in Edinburgh. Dating from 1639, the text was evidently an example of early Stuart metaphysical poetry while the tune possessed the kind of melodic simplicity that appealed to Somervell. Boulton retained seventeenth-century spelling and much of the original Scottish flavor of the song in his reproduction of the lyrics.

Thou wilt not goe and leave me heir,
Oh do not so my deirest deir,
The sune's depairting clouds the sky,
But thy depairting maks me die.

Thow can'st not goe, my deirest heart,
Bot I must quyt my choisest pairt;
For with two hearts thou must be gone,
And I shall stay at home with none.

Meanwhill, my pairt sall be to murne,
Telling the houres whill thow returne;
My eyes sall be but eyes to weip,
But nether eyese to sie nor sleipe.

Prevent the hazard of this ill,
Goe not at all, stay with me still;
I'll bath thy lips with kisses then,
And look for mor ease back againe.

Since thou will needs goe, weill away!
Leave, leave one hart with me to stay;
Take mine, lett thine in pane remaine,
That quicklie thow may come againe.

Fairweill, deir hearte, since it must be,
That thow wilt not remain with me;
My greatest greife it still sall be,
I love a love that loves not me.[36]

Thou Wilt Not Go and Leave Me Here

Anon

Thow wilt not goe and leave me heir, O do not so my deir-est deir, The

sune's de-pairt ing clouds the sky, Bot they de-pairt-ing maks me die. Thow canst not

goe my deir-est heart, Bot I must quyt my chois-est part, For with two hearts thow

must be gone, And I shall stay at home with none.

Fig. 12.20

Boulton and Somervell declined to enter the scholarly argument about who had written the words of "My Lodging It Is On the Cold Ground," simply calling it an anonymous "old English song" with an "old English air," although by so doing they implicitly rejected both Hatton's ascription of the text to John Gay and Barrett's to Sir William Davenant. Boulton admitted to editing the text slightly. This is the version printed in *Songs of the Four Nations*:

> My lodging it is on the cold ground,
> And hard, very hard is my fare,
> But that which troubles me most,
> Is the coldness of my dear.
> Yet still I cry, "Oh, turn my love,
> And prithee love turn to me,
> For thou art the one that I long for,
> And alack, what remedy?"
>
> I'll crown thee with a garland of straw, love,
> I'll marry thee with a rush ring;
> My frozen hopes they will thaw then,
> And merrily will we sing.
> Yet still I cry, "Oh, turn my love,
> And prithee love turn to me,
> For thou art the one that I long for,
> And alack, what remedy?"[37]

My Lodging It Is On the Cold Ground

Anon

Voice

My lodg ing it is on the cold ground, And hard, ver y hard is my fare,___ But

that which trou-bles me most, Is___ the cold - ness of my dear. Yet still___ I cry, "Oh,

turn love, And pri-thee love turn to me,___ For thou art the one that I long for, And a-

lack,___ what re - me - dy?"

Fig. 12.21

The remainder of the book consisted of material from other regions of the British Isles, including, as might be expected, Scottish songs by Robert Burns and Lady Nairne, such Welsh songs as "The Ash Grove" and "All Through the Night," and over a dozen Irish favorites including "Kitty Magee," "Shule Agra," and "Kathleen ni Hoolihan." The lone Cornish item in the book came courtesy of Sabine Baring-Gould, and was titled "Where Be Going?" ("Kan Kerniw" in Cornish), although this was actually the song known elsewhere in England as "Dabbling in the Dew." Somervell reproduced the old Cornish air faithfully enough but Boulton made a composite English-language version of the lyric, although he did also print the original Cornish text. This is the tune, together with the text in both languages:

"Pa le ere w why moaz moz vean sheg,
Gen alaz they hagaz bleu melyn?"
"Mi a moaz a ha leath ba firra wheg,
A delkiow sevi gura muzi teg!"

"Ka ve moaz gan a why, moz vean wheg,
Gen alaz they hagaz bleu melyn?"
"Gel loll and collan sirra wheg,
A delkiow sevi gura muzi teg!"

"Pa le'r ew an Bew, moz vean wheg,
Gen alaz they hagaz bleu melyn?"
"En park an mow, ba firra wheg,
A delkiow sevi gura muzi teg!"

"Where be going to, dear little maiden,
With your red rosy cheeks and your black curly hair?"
"I be going a milking, kind little man," she said,
"'Tis dabbling in the dew makes the milkmaids fair."

"Shall I go with you, dear little maiden,
With your red rosy cheeks and your black curly hair?"
"With all my heart, my kind little man, she said,
"'Tis dabbling in the dew makes the milkmaids fair."

"Say, shall I wed you, dear little maiden,
With your red rosy cheek and your black curly hair?"
"With that I agree, my kind little man," she said,
"'Tis dabbling in the dew makes the milkmaids fair."[38]

Where Be Going? (Kan Kerniw)

Anon

Voice

"Where __ be __ go - ing to, dear lit - tle maid - en, With your red ro - sy cheeks and your

black cur - ly hair?" "I be go - ing a - milk - ing, kind lit - tle man," she said, "Tis

dab - bling in the dew makes the milk maids __ fair."

Fig. 12.22

As mentioned earlier, one of the interesting aspects of *Songs of the Four Nations* was that Boulton and Somervell saw their publication as one that not only reprinted some "established favourites" but also revived songs that had "dropped out of common cognizance even where they were once wellknown."[39] To that end they deliberately included folksongs as well as items from old printed sources, and while neither of its editors had done folksong collecting in the field (although they had done library research on old songs) they saw fit to consult, and to draw upon the work of, various people who had. In his preface Boulton thanked not only Baring-Gould and Alec Fuller Maitland but also W. H. Hadow (of Oxford) and Mary Wakefield, two of Lucy Broadwood's correspondents who provided material for *English County Songs*.

The three publications discussed in this chapter—Hatton and Faning's three-volume edition of *The Songs of England*, Barrett's *Standard English Songs*, and Boulton and Somervell's *Songs of the Four Nations*—together defined the Late Victorian notion of national song. But they would not have the field to themselves for very long. Two of the leading folksong collectors of the period, Sabine Baring-Gould and Frank Kidson, also came to believe there might be a sizeable market for old songs of this type. We will see in chapter 15 how they each approached the task of assembling and editing their own collections of national songs. Before then, however, we must explore their ongoing activities as folksong collectors during the 1890s, beginning in the West Country with Baring-Gould and his second major song collection, *A Garland of Country Song*.

Notes

1. William Kitchiner, ed., *The Loyal and National Songs of England, for one, two, and three voices, selected from original manuscripts and early printed copies in the Library of W. Kitchiner* (London: Hurst, Robinson & Co., 1823); William Kitchiner, ed., *The Sea Songs of England, selected from original manuscripts and early printed copies in the Library of W. Kitchiner* (London: Hurst, Robinson & Co., 1823).

2. William Chappell, *Popular Music of the Olden Time, a collection of Ancient Songs, Ballads and Dance Tunes, illustrative of the National Music of England*, 2 vols. (London: Cramer, Beale & Chappell, 1858-59; reprinted, New York: Dover, 1965).

3. William Chappell, G. A. Macfarren, Natalia Macfarren, and J. Oxenford, eds., *Old English Ditties, selected from W. Chappell's "Popular Music of the Olden Time," with a New Introduction*, 2 vols. (London: Chappell & Co., n.d.)

4. William Alexander Barrett, ed., *Standard English Songs* (London: Augener, [1890]), song no. 92 [unpaginated].

5. John Liptrott Hatton, ed., *The Songs of England: A Collection of 200 English Melodies, including the most popular traditional ditties, and the principal songs and ballads of the last three centuries*, 2 vols. (London: Boosey & Co., 1873 & 1879).

6. Arthur Bullen, ed., *Lyrics from the Song-Books of the Elizabethan Age* (London: John C. Nimmo, 1887).

7. Hatton, *Songs of England,* vol. 1, 105.

8. Hatton, *Songs of England,* vol. 1, 26.

9. Hatton, *Songs of England,* vol. 1, 20-21.

10. Hatton, *Songs of England,* vol. 1, 163-65. Melody reproduced for first verse only; Hatton also gives Shield's minor variations of the tune to fit the other verses.

11. Hatton, *Songs of England,* vol. 1, 168.

12. Hatton, *Songs of England,* vol. 1, 213-15.

13. Hatton, *Songs of England,* vol. 2, preface [unpaginated].

14. John Ashton, ed., *Real Sailor Songs* (London: Leadenhall Press, 1891; reissued, New York: Benjamin Blom, 1972), 199. See chapter 6.

15. Hatton, *Songs of England,* vol. 2, 128-29.

16. Hatton, *Songs of England,* vol. 2, 168-69.

17. Hatton, *Songs of England,* vol. 2, 127.

18. Hatton, *Songs of England,* vol. 2, 146-47.

19. Hatton, *Songs of England,* vol. 2, 20-21.

20. John L. Hatton and Eaton Faning, eds., *The Songs of England: A Collection of 272 English Melodies, including the most popular Traditional Ditties, and the Principal Songs and Ballads of the Last Three Centuries,* 3 vols. (London: Boosey & Co., [1890]).

21. Eaton Faning, ed., *The Songs of England, Vol. III: A Further Collection of 72 English Melodies and Ballads Popular During the Last Fifty Years* (London: Boosey & Co., 1890). The third volume of the previous item.

22. Faning, *Songs of England,* vol. 3, 225.

23. Faning, *Songs of England,* vol. 3, 186-87.

24. Hatton, *Songs of England,* vol. 2, preface [unpaginated].

25. William Alexander Barrett, ed., *Standard English Songs* (London: Augener, [1890]).

26. William Alexander Barrett, *English Glees and Part-Songs: An Inquiry into their Historical Development* (London: Longmans, 1886).

27. William Alexander Barrett, ed., *English Folk-Songs* (London: Novello, Ewer & Co., [1891]).

28. Barrett, *Standard English Songs,* song no. 49 [unpaginated].

29. Barrett, *Standard English Songs,* song no. 47.

30. Barrett, *Standard English Songs,* song no. 10.

31. Barrett, *Standard English Songs,* song no. 67.

32. Barrett, *Standard English Songs,* song no. 1.

33. Harold Boulton and Arthur Somervell, eds., *Songs of the Four Nations: A Collection of Old Songs of the People of England, Scotland, Ireland and Wales* (London: Cramer, 1892).

34. Arthur Somervell, "On the Singing of National Songs," unpaginated preface, in Boulton and Somervell, *Songs of the Four Nations.*

35. Boulton, "Preface" to *Songs of the Four Nations,* vi.

36. Boulton and Somervell, *Songs of the Four Nations,* 8-12. Boulton modernized the spelling of the word "heir" in the title but not in the text of the song.

37. Boulton and Somervell, *Songs of the Four Nations,* 24-28.

38. Boulton and Somervell, *Songs of the Four Nations,* 58-60.

39. Boulton, "Preface" to *Songs of the Four Nations,* vi.

13

Sabine Baring-Gould in the 1890s

The Reverends Sabine Baring-Gould and H. Fleetwood Sheppard continued to collaborate during the early 1890s, and in 1895 they followed *Songs and Ballads of the West* with another, somewhat more general, collection of songs, titled *A Garland of Country Song*. This publication comprised fifty more items, proclaimed in the subtitle of the book to be "English folk songs with their traditional melodies," which had been noted mainly, although not entirely, in Devon and Cornwall. In his introduction to the new work Baring-Gould attempted to distinguish between the two collections by arguing that the tunes in *Songs and Ballads of the West* were unique to Devon and Cornwall and were of Celtic derivation whereas the melodies in *A Garland of Country Song* were to be found in many other counties of England as well as the southwest. This Celtic/non-Celtic distinction was not very convincing, and the second songbook may be regarded as primarily another installment of the fruits of the two clergymen's collecting trips in the West Country. There was actually a higher proportion of Cornish material in *A Garland* than in *Songs and Ballads* because Baring-Gould had discovered some new informants in the Duchy.

As we have seen in chapter 7, it is often necessary to make a careful distinction between what Baring-Gould collected and what he published, because he adopted a very activist approach as an editor, frequently truncating, modifying, or even completely rewriting lyrics that he deemed not publishable in their original state. For his later collecting there is no equivalent to "The Plymouth Manuscript," nor do the "Rough Copy" notebooks provide much useful information, so one has to rely mainly on "The Personal Copy" [microfiche collection, 2.2].[1] While the entries in the three volumes of this document are fair copies of what Baring-Gould noted in the field or received in manuscript form from his collaborators, one sometimes finds that a degree of censorship has already affected the material. Verses deemed indelicate or "coarse" (one of his favorite pejorative epithets) are occasionally omitted or modified, although he seems to have been fairly conscientious about indicating whenever this has been done.

Before discussing Baring-Gould's publications in the 1890s it is therefore necessary to try to reconstruct his field collecting, to the extent that "The Personal Copy" reveals information about this, although one has to bear in mind that our principal source is already a step removed from the field. Most of Baring-Gould's collecting during the new decade took place in Devon, as before, but he also noted some songs—and dealt with some correspondents—in Cornwall, and indeed a higher proportion of his material came from that county than had been the case in the 1880s. The Cornish market town of Launceston, just across the county boundary, was only about twelve miles from Lew Trenchard. Yet, apart from a fairly small region near the border with south Devon, most of Cornwall, although not so very far away, was accessible to Baring-Gould only during special trips, such as vacations. The same was true of north Devon, whereas he could work into his routine as an Anglican minister visits to nearby villages and, occasionally, more extended forays across Dartmoor.

We will therefore begin by examining briefly his collecting in Devon during the decade of the 1890s. This was done mainly, although not entirely, with H. Fleetwood Sheppard who, as before, noted the tunes while Baring-Gould wrote down the words and did further research on the songs. As before, Frederick W. Bussell was his other principal co-collector. On other occasions, however, the vicar of Lew Trenchard worked on his own and tried to capture both words and tunes. He played the piano and had a good ear, but, as we have seen, he nonetheless experienced some difficulty in noting melodies from informants in the field, and so one must be a little cautious with regard to the accuracy of his own transcriptions.

Collecting in Devon

By the end of the 1880s Baring-Gould had built up a network of informants in the villages around his parish of Lew Trenchard, on and around Dartmoor, and, to a lesser extent, in north Devon. In chapter seven we saw that there were more than a dozen individuals who contributed at least a handful of songs each, and a core group of singers whose repertoires were extensive. They were mainly elderly men, and a few of them died or became too infirm to contribute additional songs, but others kept singing to the visiting clergymen. Although by no means all the entries in "The Personal Copy" are dated, sufficient of them are to allow us to trace to some extent the pattern of Baring-Gould's collecting in the 1890s. We can identify those of his regular informants from whom he obtained new material, and we can also see which new singers he discovered and the songs that they gave him.

Sally Satterley (aka Mary Satcherley) of Huccaby Bridge was the only female member of Baring-Gould's initial core group. He continued to visit her in the early 1890s, and, among other items, she sang "The False Lover" and "The Scornful Dame." The latter was one of her favorites and Baring-Gould noted it on several occasions before he was satisfied that he had the correct tune and a full set of words. Among his informants women were still in a minority, but there were a few more of them and Baring-Gould was also now more effective in persuading them to sing to him. Three individuals seem to have been the most prolific, or to have contributed the most valuable items. Anne Roberts of Scobitor, near Widdecombe, contributed "The Loyal Lover," "Souls on the Wind," and "Tobacco." Then in January 1893 Baring-Gould discovered two new women singers: Mary Knapman of Kingswear and Mary Langworthy of Stoke Flemming. The latter's fairly large repertoire included "Old Times and New," "Too Many Lovers Will Puzzle a Man," "The Old Couple," "The Old Maid's Song," and "Come All You Jolly Sailors." Several of these songs had been learned from her mother, Anne Quarm, and in obtaining their tunes Baring-Gould had help from Miss B. Bidder, the daughter of a musician-friend, George Bidder, who lived in the same village.[2] Mary Knapman contributed "The Quaker Song," "Country Courtship," "Limbo," and "One Michaelmass Morn."

Baring-Gould's male informants in the early 1890s were more numerous, indeed too numerous to list in full. The more important—in terms of number and quality of songs—included William Aggett of Chagford, Matthew Baker of Lew Down, Sam Fone of Mary Tavy, Edmund Fry of Lydford, Richard Gregory of Two Bridges, William Nankivell of Merrivale Bridge, and William Nichols of Whitchurch. In fact most of the clerical songhunter's old contingent continued to provide him with additional material, but a few, including John Helmore and John Masters, had already died or become too infirm to sing. The most prolific of his regulars from the previous decade were Robert Hard, James Parsons, and John Woodrich. Hard, too, died in the early 1890s, but the continuity between Baring-Gould's earlier collecting and the later Devonian material included in *A Garland of Country Song* may be illustrated by examples of songs noted from these three stalwarts.

Robert Hard, from whom Baring-Gould collected some forty songs in total, contributed during the three years before his death in 1892 such items (found in Volume 2 of "The Personal Copy") as "Adieu to Old England," "The Gallant Poacher," "Do You See My Billy Coming?" "The Flailman," "What Did Your Sailor Leave You?" "A Frigate Well Mann'd," "Molly O!" "The Cuckoo," "A Week's Work," and "Fan Left on Shore." He also came up with a version of "The Greenland Whale Fishery." He was not the only singer from whom Baring-Gould heard this ballad—others included Matthew Ford, Richard Gregory, Mary Langworthy, and Sam Fone—but Hard's tune was the one that would be selected for *A Garland of Country Song*. It was reproduced in that book with just a slight variation from Baring-Gould's own noting in the field. About this whaling ballad, of which he printed only ten of the "thirteen or fourteen" verses commonly found on broadsides, Baring-Gould commented:

> The melody is not very original, but pleasant; and it is known throughout England, especially on the sea-coast, and wherever seamen are who are engaged on the Greenland fishery. The air is always the same. We have taken down half-a-dozen variants, but the variations are very slight. It is singular that this well-known song should not have found a place in Mr. Kidson's collection from Yorkshire, nor in Mr. Stokoe's from Northumberland, as "The Greenland Fishery" is certainly well known in the ports of Hull and Newcastle.[3]

The text Baring-Gould obtained from Hard was fragmentary but Richard Gregory had provided a more complete version when singing the ballad in January 1890. Here is Robert Hard's tune[4] with one verse of his version of the ballad, followed by the text (Gregory's) which Baring-Gould gave in the Plymouth Fair Copy Manuscript.[5] Baring-Gould also reproduced in that manuscript the longer broadside version printed by Catnach. Gregory's first verse was equivalent to the third verse in the broadside. The broadsheet version was evidently a nineteenth-century one, and this may have been an instance when a late broadside was derived from oral tradition, since there were obvious corruptions, perhaps resulting from the ballad-monger mishearing the singer. On the other hand, Hard, Gregory, Ford, Langworthy, and Fone may each have made their own inadvertent alterations to the broadside text.

The Greenland Fishery

Anon

In seven-teen hund-red and nine-ty four, On March the twen-ti-eth day, We hoist our col-ours to the mast, and for Green-land bore a-way, brave boys, and for Green-land bore a-way.

Fig. 13.1

We may no longer stay on shore,
Since deep we are in debt,
So off to Greenland let us steer,
Some money, boys, for to get—brave boys,
So to Greenland bear away.

In eighteen hundred and twenty four,
On March the twenty third,
We hoist' our colours to th' mast head,
And for Greenland bore away—brave boys,
And for Greenland bore away.

John Sargeant was our Captain's name,
Our ship the *Lion* bold,
We weighed our anchor at the bow
To face the storms and cold—brave boys,
And to Greenland bore away.

We were twenty gallant men on board,
And to the North did steer,
Old England left we in our wake,
We sailors knew not fear—brave boys,
And to Greenland bore away.

Our boatswain to the mast head went,
With a spy-glass in his hand,
He cries, "A whale! A whale fish blows,
She blows on every span"—brave boys,
And to Greenland bear away.

Our captain on the quarter deck,
A violent man was he,
He swore the devil should take us all
If that fish were lost to we—brave boys,
And to Greenland bear away.

Our boat being launch'd, and all hands in,
The whale was full in view,
Resolved was every sea-man bold
To steer where the whale fish blew—brave boys,
And to Greenland bear away.

The whale was struck, the line paid out,
She gave a flash with her tail,
The boat capsized, we lost five men,
And never caught the whale—brave boys,
And to Greenland bore away.

Bad news we to our Captain brought,
We'd lost five 'prentice boys,
Then down her colours he did haul
On hearing the sad news—brave boys,
And from Greenland bore away.

"The losing of this whale," said he,
"Doth grieve my heart full sore,
But the losing of my five brave men,
Doth grieve me ten times more"—brave boys,
And from Greenland bore away.

"The winter star doth now appear,   For Greenland is a barren place,
So boys the anchor weigh,   A land where grows no green,
'Tis time to leave this cold country,   But ice and snow where the whale fish blow,
And for England bear away—brave boys,   And the daylight's seldom seen—brave boys
And from Greenland bear away.   So for England bear away.[6]

During the early 1890s Baring-Gould continued to collect extensively from James Parsons, one of his favorite local informants, bringing the total number of items noted from this singer to over fifty. A few of these that were identified in "The Personal Copy" as having been collected in 1891 or later are "Rosemary Lane," "The Dilly Song," "As Polly Walked Out," "The Fox," "The Green Gown," "Hunting the Hare," "Ramble Away," "O, No, My Love, Not I," and "Billy, My Billy." Other undated items sung by Parsons that found their way into the second volume of "The Personal Copy" included "The Ragged Beggar Man," "Richard Malvin," "The Cuckold's Song," "The Jolly Wagoner," "On the Dew So Pearly," and "Where Are You Going, My Pretty Maid?." The third volume of "The Personal Copy" included Parsons's versions of "Cupid's Garden," "The Leicester Chambermaid," "Botany Bay," and "Catch Me If You Can." Baring-Gould described the latter as "a very saucy song," and this was not the only item in Parsons's repertoire he deemed unsuitable for publication. Some songs, such as "The Ragged Beggar Man," were merely bowdlerized by the omission of indelicate verses. Others were rewritten entirely, or rejected as inappropriate. An example of one that the clergyman sanitized is "The Mower," noted initially in 1888 but collected for a second time in 1891. The text is to be found in the "Killerton Notebook" [microfiche 1.3] and both tune and text were included in "The Personal Copy" [microfiche 2.2]:

The Mower

Anon

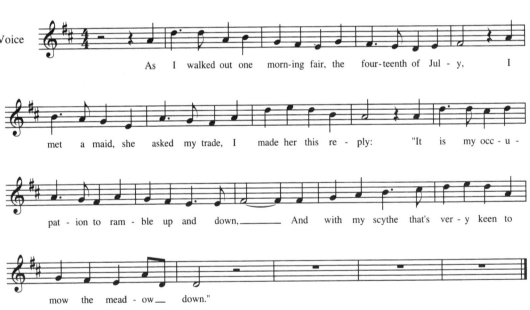

Fig. 13.2

As I walked out one morning fair, the fourteenth of July,
I met a maid, she asked my trade, I made her this reply:
"It is my occupation, love, to ramble up and down,
And with my scythe that's very keen to mow the meadow down."

She said, "My pretty young man, a mower if you be,
I'll find you some employment, if you'll go along with me;
My mother hath a meadow that's kept for you in store,

It's on this day, I tell thee true, t'was never mowed before.

All in my little meadow, you'll find no hills nor rocks,
I pray you do not leave me till my hay is all in pokes,
O mower man you promised me, you promised me that day
You would not bear your scythe elsewhere till you had cut my hay."

I answered, "Dearest maiden, I can no longer bide,
For I must go across the hills, far, far away and wide,
But if the grass be all cut down in the country where I go,
Then I'll return to you again, your meadow for to mow."

Now summer being over past and harvest being o'er,
The mower gone, I'm left alone, my folly to deplore.
And where he's gone, I cannot tell, 'tis far beyond the hill,
And I must yield and quit the field when the grass is growing still.[7]

Baring-Gould deemed these lyrics, and other versions of the song that he had found on broadsides, thoroughly objection-able. He was not very keen on the melody either, which he dismissed as "without much character."[8] But he recognized that the song was "a very favourite one throughout England" and decided for that reason to include it in *A Garland of Country Song*, but with a completely rewritten lyric, one of his own meditations on the loss of loved ones, longing for death, and the joys of an anticipated afterlife:

A mower in the month of June
With tarring scythe am I.
To left, to right, I sweep and smite,
Before the dew is dry.
The daisy and the buttercup,
Before me bow the head,
What bloomed fair in summer air,
Lies withered, cold, and dead.

There's one doth mow, full well I know,
That passeth through the land,
With scythe more keen, he mows the green,
And letteth little stand.

Me unforgot, he sought my plot
Where bloomed babies three,
And pretty wife, there with his scythe
He shore them all for me.

At fall of e'en, when skies are green,
Above the sun's decline,
I there behold blow flowers of gold,
And think those flowers are mine.
On scythe I stoop, in humble hope,
That mower'll ease my pain,
In Eden sweet, I then shall greet
My pretty flowers again.[9]

John Woodrich,[10] whom Baring-Gould often called by his nickname "Ginger Jack," also contributed a large number of songs that were under consideration for inclusion in *A Garland of Country Song*. Woodrich has already been intro-duced in chapter 7, but because he became one of Baring-Gould's mainstays in the 1890s it is worth recalling who he was and how he obtained his large repertoire of songs. This is how the cleric described the itinerant singer in his pen portrait of rural Devon and Cornwall, *Old Country Life*, and in his autobiography, *Further Reminiscences*:

Another minstrel is a little blacksmith; he is a younger man than the others, but he is, to me, a valuable man. He was one of fourteen children, and so his mother sent him, when he was four years old, to his grandmother, and he remained with his grandmother till he was ten. From his grandmother he acquired a considerable number of old dames' songs and ballads. His father was a singer; he had inherited both the hereditary faculty and the stock-in-trade. Thus my little blacksmith learned a whole series which were different from those acquired from the grand-mother....His story [is] peculiar. When aged fourteen he ran away from home and rambled about the country pick-ing up work and wages, and did not return to his parents during their lives. As he was not a strong man, and the vein of roving was in him, he could not remain in any situation for a length of time. He was really not fit for more at the forge than to blow the bellows, and that was work which he found monotonous. Finally he became a stone-breaker on the roads. He had married a pretty young woman and she had given him children; but this did not chain him down. He deserted them and went to Wales. For this, and for throwing his family on the rates, he was sent to prison. His wife died of cancer; his children scattered, and finally he died, nursed by one child. By wandering about he was able to collect a good many songs, and, having a good pipe, was a favourite in the taverns, where he got his drink for nothing out of his pocket.[11]

Woodrich's repertoire also ran to over forty songs. Those noted from him in the 1890s included (among many others) "Cupid the Ploughboy," "The Everlasting Circle," "Pretty Barbara Allen," "Rock the Cradle, John," "I Had Two Ships," and "Jacky My Son." Others for which Baring-Gould gave no collecting date in "The Personal Copy" included "The Bailiff's Daughter of Islington," "Go from My Window," "Mother and Daughter," "I Can Let It Alone," "The Banks of Sweet Primroses," "The British Young Miner," and "Let Bucks A-Hunting Go." One of Woodrich's sea songs was a well known broadside, "The Mermaid," which Baring-Gould had also noted from James Parsons and Robert Hard. All three men sang words that were virtually identical with the broadside version. In this instance Baring-Gould noted the tune himself, apparently from Hard. The following illustration reproduces his transcription in "The Personal Copy" [microfiche 2.2], although it seems likely that in fact Hard's first note was E-flat rather than D, and also that he sang it in the key of E-flat rather than B-flat (i.e., that whenever the note A comes in the tune below it should be flattened). The standard broadside text is reprinted from John Ashton's *Real Sailor Songs*:[12]

The Mermaid

Anon

Fig. 13.3

On Friday morning we set sail,
It was not far from land,
O, there I spy'd a fair pretty maid,
With a comb and a glass in her hand.

The stormy winds did blow,
And the raging seas did roar,
While we poor Sailors went to the top,
And the land lubbers laid below.

Then up and spoke a boy of our gallant ship,
And a well speaking boy was he,
I've a father and mother in Portsmouth town,
And this night they weep for me.
The stormy winds did blow, etc.

Then up spoke a man of our gallant ship,
And a well speaking man was he,

I've married a wife in fair London town,
And this night she a widow will be.
The stormy winds did blow, etc.

Then up spoke the Captain of our gallant ship,
And a valiant man was he,
For want of a boat we shall be drown'd,
For she sunk to the bottom of the sea.
The stormy winds did blow, etc.

The moon shone bright, and the stars gave light,
And my mother was looking for me,
She might look and weep with watery eyes,
She might look to the bottom of the sea.
The stormy winds did blow, etc.

Three times round went our gallant ship,
And three times round went she,

Three times round went our gallant ship,   The stormy winds did blow, etc.[13]
Then she sank to the bottom of the sea.

It is difficult to tell when Baring-Gould paid his last visit to Woodrich, who usually lived in the tiny and remote hamlet of Thrushelton, but the evidence of the first two volumes of "The Personal Copy" indicates that it was no earlier than 1896 and probably as late as 1905. There are at least eight items ascribed to Woodrich in the third volume, and most of these likely date from the middle of the 1890s, although since "The Personal Copy" is not always in chronological order it is difficult to say this with complete certainty.[14] Among the more than forty credited to Woodrich in "The Personal Copy" is this version of the Child ballad "Geordie," in its anglicized form of "Georgie." As we've seen in chapters 8 and 11, both Frank Kidson (in Yorkshire) and Lucy Broadwood (in Sussex) had also collected variants of the ballad, from Charles Lolley and Henry Burstow respectively. John Woodrich's version was different from either, although closer to Burstow's than to Kidson's Yorkshire/Scottish composite.

Georgie

Anon

Fig. 13.4

As I rode over London Bridge, it was one morning early,
I spied there a maiden fair, all in the dew so pearly.

"O Georgie never stole ox nor cow, of calves he ne'er stole any,
But six King's deer he stole I know and sold them in Broad Hembury."

"Come saddle me my milk white steed, come saddle it so easy,
To my good lord judge I'll ride with speed to beg the life of Georgie."

And when she came into the hall, there were lords and ladies many,
And she did fall on knee and call, "Spare me the life of Georgie!"

The judge looked over his left shoulder, "Lady, I pray, be easy,
He has confessed, he shall not be pressed, but the Lord ha' mercy on Georgie."

"He shall be hanged in a chain of gold, such as you ne'er saw other,
For it shall be told, he was a gentleman bold, and was loved by a virtuous lady."

"Now I for him shall weep and pray, and I for him will sorrow,
And may God speed on my dying day, my Georgie and me good morrow."

"Were I at the top of Prockter's Hill, where times I have been many,
With pistol cocked or good stout bill I'd fight for the life of Georgie."[15]

The Devon singer whose material would be utilized the most in *A Garland of Country Song* was one of Baring-Gould's more recent finds. Samuel Fone's name is largely (although not completely) absent from the first volume of "The Personal Copy,"[16] and Baring-Gould probably first discovered him only in 1891, noting "The Buffalo" from him at that time.[17] His collecting from Fone became extensive in 1892 and continued throughout most of the decade. Fone was an itinerant mason but by then he was based in Mary Tavy, on the western flank of Dartmoor, where Baring-Gould found him again and began noting his songs more systematically, first in October and again just before Christmas. Of the seventeen items collected from him that year, "Holland Smock" is as representative as any, with its simple tale of seduction and its unusual melody. It is evident that Baring-Gould had some difficulty capturing the tune, because Fone decorated the basic melody with numerous grace notes, but this is the simplified version found in "The Personal Copy":

The Holland Smock

Anon

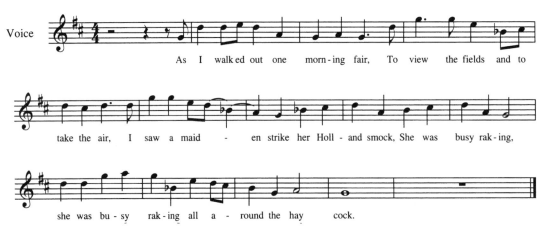

Fig. 13.5

As I walked out one morning fair
To view the fields and to take the air,
I saw a maiden strike her Holland smock,
She was busy raking, she was busy raking,
[All] around the hay cock.

I said, "Fair maid, lay by your rake,
And go with me to yonder wake."
"To go with you I leave my master's hay,
He'll pay no wages, he'll pay no wages,
And turn me down away."

With sweet enticement and kind compliment
I laboured till I gained this maid's consent,
She downed her press and laid aside her rake,
And went a fair day, and went a fair day
With me to the wake.

And after as we got to yonder wake,
I treated her with wine and cake,
I treated her with ribbons, rings and gloves,
And so I gained this, and so I gained this
Pretty maiden's love.

When fourteen weeks was gone and past,
Her rosy cheeks waxed pale at last,
She cursed the hour, she cursed the very day,
That she went with me, that she went with me,
And left her master's hay.

Then here's adieu to Holland smock,
Red rosy cheeks and curly locks,
And here's a health to saucy merry maid
Will kiss a sailor boy, will kiss a sailor boy
And never be afraid.[18]

Sam Fone turned out to be Baring-Gould's single most prolific informant, and he had a prodigious memory for tunes and texts. The cleric believed that this was due, at least in part, to the circumstances of Fone's childhood and adolescence. On one occasion he recalled the singer explaining how he had acquired his repertoire:

Now, when a little urchin, Sam was wont to carry milk every day for an aged widow, and as she was too poor to pay him with coin, she rewarded him with an old ballad that she taught him; these he has never forgotten, and lo! now after nearly seventy years, he gets repaid in shillings for every can of milk he carried and every ballad he then acquired. At one time Fone worked with an old mason who was a great singer. This man fell from a ladder and broke his neck, but Fone has all his store of songs by heart. I believe this man knows well nigh a hundred and fifty or two hundred songs, ballads, words, and melodies. The other day, a concert of old west country songs was given at Tavistock by professionals in costume. Fone was present, at the back of the hall, and would sing out every song with which he was familiar, along with the performer, somewhat to the disconcertion [*sic*] of the artist, but to the amusement of the audience.[19]

In total approximately ninety songs noted from Sam Fone are reproduced in "The Personal Copy," although, of course, many of these are also attributed to other singers as well. About a third of them were collected during 1893, with Baring-Gould visiting the singer at Mary Tavy on a number of occasions in late February, March, July, and October. Just a few of the songs and ballads noted were "I Would that the Wars Were Over," "The Gipsy Countess" (a variant of "The Gipsy Laddie"), "Gilderoy," "High Germany," "Ramble Away," "Jordan," "Poverty No Sin," and "The Setting of the Sun" (a variant of "Polly Vaughan"). Baring-Gould continued collecting from Fone until at least 1897, and possibly later (more than a dozen items attributed to Fone towards the end of Volume 3 of "The Personal Copy" have no date), but the harvest was never again quite as abundant. Of the ten or more songs noted in 1894 mention may be made in particular of "The Pack of Cards," "If I Had a Thousand a Year," and "Hard Times in England," while the eight songs noted in 1895 included "My Mother Did So Before Me," "Ground for the Floor," and "The Springtime of the Year." Among the undated songs may be found "Brennan on the Moor," "The Lost Lady Found," "Richard of Taunton Dean," "Cupid's Garden," "Flora, the Lily of the West," and "The Death of Queen Jane." In short, Sam Fone's repertoire was very large and varied, and he was one of the most important of all song-carriers to be discovered during the late Victorian folksong revival. A summary account cannot do him justice, but here as a token gesture is a second example of the material that Baring-Gould collected from him. "The Setting of the Sun," a variant of the ballad also known as "Polly Vaughan" or "The Shooting of His Dear," was collected from Fone on 12 July 1893, the tune by F.W. Bussell and the words by Baring-Gould:

The Setting of the Sun

Anon

Fig. 13.6

Come all you young fellows that carry a gun
Beware of late shooting when daylight is done,
For its little you reckon what hazards you run,

I shot my own true love at the setting of the sun.

CHORUS: In a shower of rain as my darling did run

All under the bushes a shower for to shun,
Her apron about her neck I took her for a swan
I shot the only maid I loved, at the setting of the sun.

I'll fly from my county, I nowhere find rest,
I shot my own true love as a bird in her nest
[two lines missing]
CHORUS: In a shower of rain....

O it's son! dearest son! don't you run away

Don't leave your own country till the trial day,
Don't leave your own country till the trial is done
For shooting of your true love at the setting of the sun.
CHORUS: In a shower of rain....

In a night to her uncle the fair maid appeared
Saying, Uncle! dear uncle of me be not afraid
As my apron about my neck in the rain I did run
He shot me as a swan, at the setting of the sun.
CHORUS: In a shower of rain....[20]

There were many other Devon informants from whom Baring-Gould collected just one or two songs each. Thanks to "The Personal Copy" we know many of their names and usually the village in which they resided. Brief mention may therefore be made of William Andrews of Sheepstor, Charles Arscott of South Zeal, John Dingle of Coryton, George Doige, Joseph Dyer of Golant, Lucky Fewins, J. Gerrard of Cully Hole (near Chagford), James Glanville of South Zeal, W. Horne of Plympton, William Houghton of St. Austell, Adam Laundry of Northill, Thomas Morris of Fowey, John Richards of Lamerton, and Harry Westaway of Belstone. This list is not complete, but about most of the other informants we know only their surname and the first letter of a Christian name. Moreover, a few of the singers have remained anonymous, such as the navvy from whom Baring-Gould noted this plaintive folk lyric on a train journey from Tavistock to Yelverton, "The Queen of Hearts"[21]:

The Queen of Hearts

Anon

Fig. 13.7

To the queen of hearts he's the ace of sorrow,
He is here today, he is gone tomorrow.
Young men are plenty but sweethearts few,
If my love leaves me, what shall I do?

When my love comes in, I gaze not around,
When my love goes out, I fall in a swound,
To meet is pleasure, to part is sorrow,
He is here today, he is gone tomorrow.

Had I the store in yonder mountains
Where gold and silver is had for counting,
I could not count for the thoughts of thee,
My eyes so full that I could not see.

I love my father, I love my mother,
I love my sister, I love my brother,
I love my friends, my relations too,
But I'd leave all for the love of you.

My father left me both house and land
And servants many at my command,
At my command they ne'er shall be,
I'll forsake them all for to follow thee.

An ace of sorrow to the queen of hearts!
O how my bosom bleeds and smarts
Young men are plenty but sweethearts few,
If my love leaves me, what shall I do?[22]

A considerable amount of Baring-Gould's collecting in Devon remained hidden in the pages of "The Personal Copy" rather than finding public exposure in *Songs and Ballads of the West* and *A Country Garland.* In some instances this was by design, since numerous were the song texts that Baring-Gould considered unfit for publication in the form in which he had collected them. Yet much of the time it was because space limitations forced difficult choices among the available material. This difficulty was compounded by the fact that the clerical songhunter's trips to Cornwall, although neither very numerous nor very extensive, nonetheless provided him with much good material, some of which was of very high quality.

Collecting in Cornwall

Songs and Ballads of the West had included a few items that Baring-Gould had collected in Cornwall, including "Hal-an-Tow" from the Furry Day ceremonies at Helston and several songs noted from a resident of Launceston, James Olver, whom we met in chapter 7. As mentioned, Launceston was only just over the border from the western part of south Devon where Baring-Gould did most of his collecting, and he continued to note songs from Olver during the early 1890s. Most of the items attributed to Olver in Volume 2 of "The Personal Copy" are undated, but the evidence suggests that Baring-Gould visited him in 1891 and perhaps again later. Among the songs noted in the early 1890s may probably be numbered "The Poor Man's Lament," "Jolly Fellows That Follow the Plough," "Where Are You Going, My Pretty Maid?" "The Buffalo," and "A Bachelor's Easy Life." Olver will go down in history as the informant from whom Baring-Gould first noted "The Streams of Nancy" and he also seems to have been the only West Country source for "The Baffled Knight." Another of his notable items was a version of a ballad that Francis James Child included in *The English and Scottish Popular Ballads* as no. 110, "The Knight and the Shepherd's Daughter," although Olver left the guilty male out of the title. It was the story of a rape and of the resourcefulness of the victim in obtaining retribution.

The Shepherd's Daughter

Anon

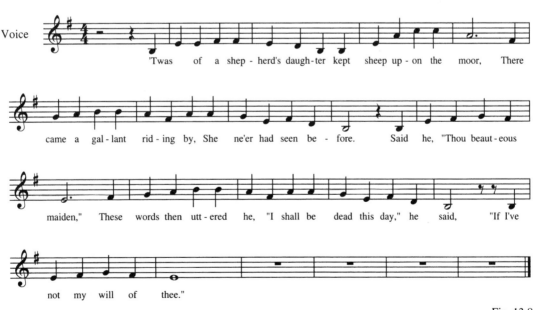

Fig. 13.8

'Twas of a shepherd's daughter,
Kept sheep upon the moor,
There came a gallant riding by,
She ne'er had seen before.

Said he, "Thou beauteous maiden,"
These words then uttered he,
"I shall be dead this day," he said,
"If I've not my will of thee."

"Now if I trust thee, what's thy name,
Thy name straightway declare,
For promises are empty words
And falsest words sound fair."

"O some do call me Jack," he said,
And some do call me James,
But when I'm in the King's high court,
Then William is my name."

He took his horse all by the head
And straight away did ride,
She gathered up her skirts and ran
Hard by his stirrup side.

And when she to a river came
She set her breast and swam,
And when she was on the green grass
Then swift afoot she ran.

He never was a courteous knight
To have her mount and ride,
And she was such a simple maid,
She bade him not abide.

"Now stay, the night is falling dark
And weary thou must be."
"I will not stay by night or day,
But run along side of thee."

And when they came to London town,
He from his horse did fling;
She headed to the King's palace
And there did knock and ring.

There was no servant in the hall,
Nor noble heard the din,
And so there came the king himself
And let the fair maid in.

"What would'st thou have of me?" he said,
"O what do'st seek?" said he,
"Thou hast a knight in thy fair court
That has a-robbèd me."

"What hath he robbed thee of, fair maid,
Of purple or of pall?
Or hath he took the red gold ring
From off thy finger small?"

"He hath not robbed me, gentle sir,
Of purple or of pall,

But he hath ta'en my maidenhead
That grieves me most of all."

"How dost thou know this robber knight,
What dost thou know him by?"
"By his locks that are as yellow wheat
And by his bright blue eye."

"Oh, if he is a married man
I'll hang him on a tree,
But if he be a bachelor
His body I'll give to thee."

The King he callèd down his men,
By one, by two, by three.
Sir William once was first of all,
But now as last came he.

Then out he held full fifty pounds
All wrappèd in a glove.
"Fair maid, I'll give the same to thee,
Go seek another love."

"Oh, I want nothing of thy gold,
Nor nothing of thy fee,
But I will have thy body whole
Which the King hath granted me."

"Would I had drunk the water clear,
When I did drink the wine,
Rather than any shepherd's maid
Should be a lady of mine.

Would I had drunk this puddle foul
When I did drink the ale,
Rather than any shepherd's maid
Should be telling me this tale."

"A shepherd's maiden though I was,
You might have let me be;
I never had come to London town,
To ask of aught from thee."

He sat her on a milk white steed,
Himself upon a grey,
And forth he rode with his shepherd maid
From London town away.

The very first town they came upon
He bought her a golden ring,
The very next town they came upon
He made her a gay wedding.[23]

Baring-Gould had first collected this ballad from James Parsons in 1888, but he obtained Olver's version in 1891. The two singers had different, if related, tunes, and apparently virtually identical texts. Neither of them included the chorus that was part of the broadside version, titled "The Beautifull Shepherdesse of Arcadia," in the Roxburghe collection, and they omitted the final verses in which the woman reveals her aristocratic lineage.

Baring-Gould made a number of trips to Cornwall during 1891-93, and there are certain other locales (in addition to Launceston) that we can identify as proving fruitful venues for song collecting. Some twelve miles south of Launceston is the town of Liskeard, and nearby is the village of Menheniot. In both places—as indeed elsewhere in Cornwall—

Baring-Gould found good singers with traditional songs and ballads in their repertoires. Some of them were undoubtedly 'characters.' In *Old Country Life* Baring-Gould, who was something of a 'character' himself, recalled one of them, whose identity he chose to keep secret.

> There is a Cornishman whose name I will give as Elias Keate—a pseudonym—a thatcher, a very fine, big-built man, with big, sturdy sons. This man goes round to all sheep-shearings, harvest homes, fairs, etc., and sings. He has a round, rich voice, a splendid pair of bellows; but he has an infirmity, he is liable to become the worse for the liquor he freely imbibes, and to be quarrelsome over his cups. He belongs to a family of hereditary singers and drinkers. In his possession is a pewter spirit-bottle—a pint bottle—that belonged to his great-grandfather in the latter part of the last century. That old fellow used to drink his pint of raw spirit every day; so did the grandfather of Elias; so did the father of Elias; so would Elias—if he had it; but so do not his sons, for they are teetotalers.[24]

According to Martin Graebe, Elias Keate was Edmund Fry, a champion sheep-shearer who died as the result of a fall from a roof he was thatching.[25] This was a Cornishman who had moved to Devon; when Baring-Gould knew him he lived at Lydford, on the western edge of Dartmoor, just a few miles east of Lew Trenchard. However, we can canvass Baring-Gould's other Cornish informants and indicate the contribution they each made to his collection of West Country song.

Baring-Gould's Launceston singers included John Richards, who sang "The Fox Hunt" and "The Painful Plough," Otho B. Peter, who provided "The Three Poor Baronets," and T. Bennet who offered "Three Oxford Scholars." His Liskeard informants included fiddler Peter Isaacs and N. Wilkey, who contributed "The Alterman Volunteer."[26] More prolific was J. Peake, who worked as a tanner. From him the songhunting cleric noted several songs with military themes: "The Black and the Grey," "The Siege of St. Malo," "The Drum Major," "True Blue," and "Brave, Brave, Old England's Forces." Peake also contributed an interesting political and historical ballad titled "Ormond the Brave" and a well-known broadside ballad, "Bold General Wolfe," about the British conquest of New France. Julia de Vaynes had found a fairly similar version on a broadside in Kent.

> Bold General Wolfe to his men did say,
> "Come, lads, and follow without delay,
> To yonder mountain that is so high.
> Don't be down-hearted, don't be down-hearted,
> But gain the victory."
>
> "There stand the French on the summit high,
> While we poor lads in the valley lie;
> I see them falling, like motes in the sun,
> Through smoke and fire, through smoke and fire,
> All from the British gun."
>
> The first of volleys to us they gave,
> In his left breast wounded Wolfe so brave.
> Yonder he lies, for he cannot stand,
> Yet fight on boldly, yet fight on boldly,
> But he can still command.
>
> "Here's all my treasure that you behold,
> A thousand guineas in shining gold;
> Share it among you," brave Wolfe did say,
> "You're welcome to it, you're welcome to it,
> Since you have gained the day."
>
> "When to old England you do return,
> Tell all my friends I am dead and gone;
> And bid my mother, so kind and dear,
> No tears to shed for me, no tears to shed for me,
> A hero's grave awaits me here."[27]

Bold General Wolfe

Anon

Voice

Bold Gen-eral Wolfe to his men did say, "Come, lads and fol-low with-out de-

lay, To yond er mount ain that is so high, Don't be down - heart - ed, Don't be down - heart - ed, But

Last verse

gain.... .....___ the vic-to-ry." "When to old Eng land you do re - turn, Tell all my friends I am dead and

gone. And bid my mo - ther, so kind and dear, No tears to shed for me, No tears to

shed for me, A he - ro's grave a - waits me here."

Fig. 13.9

A few miles away, the village of Menheniot was a nest of singing birds. Here Baring-Gould discovered shoemaker Matthew Ford, whose repertoire included "The Streams of Nancy," "The Greenland Whale Fishery," "Toby," "Roger the Ploughboy," and "The Oxen Ploughing." Neighbor J. Benney sang "The Haymakers" and "The Buffalo." Another Menheniot singer, William Nichols, who actually hailed from Whitchurch, near Tavistock, contributed "In Bodmin Town," "The Rout of the Blues," and "The False Swain." Women and children added to Baring-Gould's haul in this location: Mary Treise provided "Put Down Your Stick" and "The Stranger from America," and local schoolchildren demonstrated three play songs, "The Three Dukes," "The Ring," and "The Robber, or London Bridge." On the southern Cornish coast the most productive villages turned out to be Fowey and Golant. Thomas Morris of Fowey sang "William Combe" and an untitled May Day song, while at nearby Golant the village's leading singer was Joseph Dyer, who contributed "The Oxen Ploughing," "The Turkey and the Bear," "When Pensive I Thought," and "In Southampton City."

Baring-Gould was an archeologist and folklorist, fascinated by anything to do with West Country history and customs. As we have seen, he was very interested in the May Day ceremonies at Helston, and he was equally eager to view the parallel customs at Padstow, on the north Cornish coast. He apparently went to Padstow on 1 May 1890, and seemingly made extensive notes about the ceremonies. He also may have taken down the words and tune of the Padstow May Day songs from the actors and dancers themselves. In *A Garland of Country Song* he set out his interpretation of the tradition and also tried to reconstruct the musical side of the ceremony.[28] This is his version of the Padstow May Song:

Chorus: Unite and unite, now let us unite,
For summer is a-come in today;
And whither we are going we will all go in white,
In the merry morning of May.

And for to fetch the summer home,
The summer and the May, O,
For summer is a come in,
And winter is away, O!

Go to the green wood, youths every one,
The summer and the May, O,
To fetch the May-bush home,
And winter is away, O.
Unite and unite, etc.

Where are the young men that should dance?
The summer and the May, O;
Some are away in France,
And winter is away, O.
Unite and unite, etc.

Where are the maidens that should sing?
The summer and the May, O;
They're all gone flower gathering,

And winter is away, O.
Unite and unite, etc.

Young men of Padstow, ye could,
The summer and the May, O;
Gild you a ship of gold,
And winter is away, O.
Unite and unite, etc.

You maids of Padstow, ye might,
The summer and the May, O,
Weave you a garland of white,
And winter is away, O.
Unite and unite, etc.[29]

The Padstow May Song (Unite and Unite)

Anon

Fig. 13.10

The above is actually a composite of verses sung at different times during the Padstow ceremony, comprising material that Baring-Gould (or someone else) had initially taken down as two separate items. However, a convincing case can be made that they belong together, in part because the melody and rhythm fit the lyrics well.

Further down the northern Cornish coast, just north of Newquay, Baring-Gould had discovered the village of Mawgan-in-Pyder, in the Vale of Lanherne, where he enjoyed staying at a local hostelry, the Falcon Inn. It turned out that the elderly landlord there had been a fine singer in his younger days, and that he had other singers in his family. Sam Gilbert's repertoire was no doubt derived, at least in part, from that of the regulars in his public bar. It does not seem to have been very extensive, but it included some gems. This was one of the first songs that Baring-Gould noted from him:

The lark in the morn as she rises from her nest
Mounts through the white air, with the dew on her breast,
'Long with the pretty ploughboy, she'll whistle and she'll sing,
And returns to her nest in the cool evening,
And returns to her nest in the cool evening.

One morning she mounted so cheerily on high,
She look'd round about her and at the dark sky,
And loudly she was singing and twittering her lay,
There's no life like the ploughboy's in the sweet month of May,
There's no life like the ploughboy's in the sweet month of May.

When day's work is ended and over, he'll go
To fair or to market to buy him a bow,
And whistle as he walks, O, and shrilly too will sing,
There's no life like the ploughboy's all in merry spring,
There's no life like the ploughboy's all in merry spring.

Good luck to the ploughboy wherever he may be,
A fair pretty maiden he'll take on his knee,
He'll drink the nut-brown ale, and this song the lad will sing,
Oh! the ploughboy is happier than noble or king,
Oh! the ploughboy is happier than noble or king.[30]

The Lark in the Morn

Anon

Fig. 13.11

One of the most extrovert singers that Baring-Gould found in the Falcon Inn at Mawgan was Peter Sandry, a possible alternative model for the fictional Elias Keate. He regaled Baring-Gould and Fleetwood Sheppard with "The Foggy Dew," "The Maid and Lantern," "Paddy's Blunder," "My Old Friend John," and even a traditional drinking song adapted to the present, "Here's a Health to Victoria." Most interesting of all was the fact that Sandry sang a version of "The Merry Doe" (aka "The Keeper"), although he apparently sometimes omitted the familiar chorus. Unfortunately Baring-Gould decided that most of this song was "gross" (his word), and he failed to write down a full set of lyrics. "The Personal Copy" contains fragments of two versions, apparently noted on different occasions. It is not entirely clear that both were obtained from Sandry, although he is the only informant credited in "The Personal Copy"; nor is there an obvious fit between tune and words. The first two stanzas were definitely Sandry's, and the fifth (in square brackets in the manuscript, as here) was composed by Baring-Gould. Reading between the lines, it appears that Peter Sandry was a powerful singer with a fairly large and interesting repertoire, but that much of it offended clerical taste. As a result only a portion of what he had to offer was noted down, and even that was sometimes censored. In this case Baring-Gould did his best to turn an allegorical song about sexual encounters in the forest into one that softened the image and ended with an image of cosy domesticity.

The Merry Doe (The Keeper)

Anon

Voice

Fig. 13.12

One morn in autumn at dawn of day
My bed in order I went my way,
All through the woods so fresh and gay,
Among the leaves so green.

In search of game I first did fare
And through the woods my way did steer
And there I spied a bonny May hare,
Among the leaves so green.

There was a keeper a shooting did go
And under his arm he bore a bow
And all for to shoot the merry doe,
Among the leaves so green.
CHORUS; Jack my Master, sing you well

Very well with my derry down
With my down, down, down.

The first doe he shot at he miss'd
The second doe went where no one wist
The third doe he did catch & kiss'd
Among the leaves so green,
Jack my Master, sing you well, etc.

[My pretty doe, said he, wherefore roam?
O with me you henceforth shall come,
And you shall tarry all in my home
Among the leaves so green,
Jack my Master, sing you well, etc.][31]

Another singer that Baring-Gould found at Mawgan-in-Pyder was Mary Gilbert, who was probably the publican's wife, daughter or grand-daughter, since her repertoire overlapped considerably with his. Among the songs she sang were "O That I Had a Heart," "The Flowers in the Valley," "While Pensive I Thought," and, most likely, an exceptionally pretty song that dated back at least to the seventeenth century, although Baring-Gould actually noted "Lemonday" from Sam Gilbert.

As I was a-walking one midsummer morning,
The fields and the flowers were green and were gay;
The birds and the blossoms the summer adorning,
So early in the morning, at breaking of day.
The world was awaking, all drowsiness scorning,
I thought and I warbled of sweet Lemonday.

O hark and O hark to the nightingale's singing,
The lark she is taking her flight in the air,
The turtle-doves now through the green wood are winging,
The sun is just glimm'ring—arise up, my fair!
O Lemonday! Lemonday! Through my heart ringing,
The name is as bells, between hope and despair.

O Lemonday! Lemonday! Thou art the flower,
The sweetest of flowers adorning the May;
I'll play on my pipes in the green summer bower,
So early in the morning at the breaking of day.
I'll stand at thy window and watch by the hour,
As the daffodil waiteth the sun's early ray.

Arise, love, arise, I have pluck'd thee fair posies,
The choicest of flowers that grow in the grove;
I've gathered them all for thee, lilies and roses,
And pinks, for my Lemonday; maiden, approve!
The sun's on the roof where my fair love reposes,
Then Lemonday waken! My own pretty love![32]

Lemonday

Anon

As I was a-walk-ing one mid - sum-mer morn - ing, The fields and the flow - ers were green and were gay; The birds and the bloss - oms the sum - mer a-dorn - ing, So ear-ly in the morn - ing, at break - ing of day. The world was a-wak ing, all drows - i-ness scorn - ing, I thought and I war - bled of sweet____ Le - mon - day.

Fig. 13.13

Other songs collected from the Gilberts included "Do You See My Billy Coming?" "A Merry Little Soldier," and "Ground for the Floor." Evidently Mawgan rivaled Menheniot as *the* place in Cornwall to find traditional songs.

Ballads for Francis James Child

During the period 1890 to 1893 there was an exchange of letters between Baring-Gould in Lew Trenchard and Francis James Child at Harvard College in Cambridge, Massachusetts. Unless, by a miracle, Child's side of the correspondence turns up in an as yet unsorted box at the Devon Records Office, only Baring-Gould's half of the exchange is extant. It is part of the Francis James Child Collection at the Houghton Library, Harvard University,[33] and it has been included in the Baring-Gould microfiche collection in the form of a single document, edited by George Kittredge in 1913, titled "The Harvard Manuscript." This is part of Kittredge's description of the material:

> This manuscript, which is in the handwriting of the Rev. S. Baring-Gould, was for the most part sent to Professor Child by him in 1890. But it was not all sent at once, and there was no pagination. I have tried to arrange the sheets in a reasonable order, and have added page-numbers...On June 6, 1890, Baring-Gould wrote to Child, expressing his intention to send him what ballads he had collected, and on July 14, 1890, he wrote: "I send you a budget of copies." In October, 1890, Child remarked (in the Advertisement to Part VII): "The Rev. S. Baring-Gould has done me the great favor of furnishing me with copies of traditional ballads and songs taken down by him in the West of England." On p. 62 of the same part (Vol IX) Child acknowledges the receipt of two versions of "The Gipsy Countess" from Baring-Gould, and these are contained in that part of the ms. now under consideration (pp. 1-34), on pp. 1-5. In a letter of August 14, 1890, Baring-Gould included a version of "The Trees [they are] so High"—that is, obviously, a version in addition to that included in this same part of the ms. (on pp. 13-15).

It is therefore practically certain that the "budget of copies" sent by Baring-Gould on July 14, 1890, consisted of at least pp. 1-34 of the ms. (as now paged)...The appearance of the ms. when I examined it (folds of paper, etc.) makes me quite sure that pp. 35-42 (which belong together), were also part of the "budget." Other portions of the ms. which belong together in groups are pp. 43-66, pp. 67-86, and pp. 87-90. All or most of these were undoubtedly sent soon after the "budget"...Pp. 91-92 were enclosed in a letter of October 18, 1890; pp. 93-94 in a letter of Jan 9, 1891; and pp. 95-98 in a letter of Feb. 26, 1892. To the ms. itself I have appended various letters from Baring-Gould to Child, some of which contain additional texts.[34]

In short, Kittredge combined into one large document two kinds of (related) material: Baring-Gould's letters to Child and several batches of manuscript copies of songs that he had collected in Devon and Cornwall. We know that Baring-Gould also sent Child a copy of the first edition of *Songs and Ballads of the West*, and that he saw it as his task to make sure that Child was apprised of other late Victorian published collections that included ballads. This probably accounts for the quite comprehensive listing of such material in the bibliography included in the last fascicule of *The English and Scottish Ballads*.

Kittredge's account of "The Harvard Manuscript" is misleading on one count, since his first sentence could be taken to suggest that this interaction between Baring-Gould and Child took place almost entirely in the year 1890. In fact it occurred over a four-year period, 1890-93 (the last item, a postcard, is dated 23 November 1893), and some of the later material that Child received was a product of Baring-Gould's collecting in the 1890s (especially from Sam Fone), although the initial "budget" mentioned by Kittredge reflected his earlier collecting in the late 1880s. Child and Baring-Gould had been briefly in contact with each other a decade earlier, but in relation to folksong the first important letter from Baring-Gould, which renewed their correspondence after a ten-year gap, was dated 6 June 1890. Baring-Gould wrote that while working in the British Museum he had just come across the first volumes of *The English and Scottish Popular Ballads*, which he judged to be an "admirable" new edition of Child's earlier *English and Scottish Ballads*. The discovery, he continued, had revealed to him a solution for a problem that had been nagging at him since he had begun editing *Songs and Ballads of the West*. This is how he characterized problem and solution:

> I have been engaged mainly in collecting the old melodies in Devon & Cornwall, but in so doing have collected the old ballads and songs as well. In publishing for the general public it has not been possible to give <u>all</u> the ballads, nor all such as we do give in quite their original form, as some have a looseness in morals that will not suit the pianoforte. Now I have been rather puzzled what to do with the originals, but now I have seen your book my difficulty ceases. I will send them to you.[35]

To convince Child of the value of what he was offering—manuscript texts of the narrative items in *Songs and Ballads of the West* plus other material that he had collected but deemed unpublishable because of its sexual explicitness or promiscuous sentiments—Baring-Gould added a little context and a possible explanation of why the West Country was a special region for English folksong collecting:

> I have come to the conclusion that a vast mass of ballad poetry existed in the British Isles common to England & Scotland & English-speaking Ireland, but in Scotland only hitherto have the ballads been taken down from the mouths of the people, whereas the English collectors have gone to the old black letter broadsides and Garlands. I do not think that printers cared to print the older traditional ballads, as they were so well known, & printed instead the newly produced compositions. I find that in Devon and Cornwall our old fellows sing ballads and songs that were found in Scotland also, not only so, and they sing portions of the ballads not heard in the Scottish, and on the other hand the Scottish have verses not found in ours...Our old West Country songmen are absolutely illiterate, they inherit the ballad and songs usually—in nine cases out of ten—from their fathers, and in some cases I have been able to satisfy myself that the grand-fathers were also song-men. I think in most cases these old men are the last members existing of a class of hereditary singers. Hardly ever will their sons sing the same old songs and ballads, nor do they like the old minor melodies...[W]hat is peculiar with us is that our melodies are not the same as those to which the same songs and ballads are sung elsewhere in England in the vast majority of cases. The songs are, naturally, more numerous than the ballads! It is really too late to recover the ballads, and the men are less inclined to remember the ballads than are the women, and I have not tried to get results from old women so far.[36]

He also tried to give Child some sense of the corpus of balladry to which he was referring and the extent to which he had felt compelled to censor some of the items that he had included in *Songs and Ballads of the West*. Material that he could send to Child included "Henry Martyn," "The Jolly Sportsman," "The Maid and the Box," "Pretty Polly Oliver," "The Miraculous Hen, or the Cuckold's Cap," "The Wooer's Tasks," "The Baffled Knight," "Young Riley," "Richard Malvine," "The Squire of Tamworth," "The Beggar-Man and the Maid," "The Silly Doe," "The Fiend Knight," and

"The Outlandish Knight." Moreover, Child could have the full versions of ballads that he had published in truncated form, such as "The Trees They Are So High," "Cold Blows the Wind," "Brixham Town," "Widdecombe Fair," "The Silly Old Man," "The Squire and the Fair Maid," "The Gipsy Countess," "The Spotted Cow," "The Painful Plough," and "Strawberry Fair." He also had available an even larger number of shorter folk lyrics, but he supposed (correctly) that Child did not want non-narrative songs.[37]

Child evidently wrote back and encouraged Baring-Gould to send him manuscript copies of West Country ballads, although he may have expressed reservations about some of the material on offer, such as "The Miraculous Hen," "The Spotted Cow," and "Widdecombe Fair." The result, in any case, was that on 14 July Baring-Gould wrote again, enclosing with his letter "a budget of copies."[38] His letter revealed something of his changing view of the relationship between oral tradition and broadsides. When he started collecting, he observed, he had assumed that the words to most ballads sung by his informants derived from broadsides, and that the texts were hardly worth noting down in most instances (a view to which Frank Kidson firmly subscribed). After a while, however, he had begun to doubt that this was always the case. Sometimes, at least, the ballad seemed to have been in oral circulation well before the first broadside version. In other cases the old singers started with the broadside text but adapted, altered, and modified it as they saw fit. One of his illiterate West Country singers, for example, composed verses of his own when the text that he had learned seemed to be missing a stanza or two. In short, Baring-Gould had come to realize that the texts were as worth collecting as the tunes, and he now believed that later broadside texts were often corrupt derivations from folk ballads.[39]

He also commented on the similarity between many of the Devonian and Cornish texts that he had come across and the Scottish versions that James Johnson had included in his *Scots Musical Museum.* But, he added, although the texts were similar the melodies were never the same, and, moreover, the words were "sufficiently different to show that they are independent versions of the same story." Since the likelihood of direct transmission from Scotland to Cornwall or vice versa was very low, he could only conclude that "a vast number of the Scottish songs and ballads are actually English, and that they have been imported into Scotland, as they have been imported into Cornwall, where Cornish was the prevailing tongue in Queen Elizabeth's days." It was all very odd, he remarked, but he could account for this empirical evidence "no other way."[40] He may not have realized it, but in putting forward this diffusion theory of the spread of English folksong throughout the British Isles he was echoing the views of William Chappell.

As for the "budget of copies," it is difficult to know for certain which of the West Country texts in "The Harvard Manuscript" came in this first batch, but given the list of titles that Baring-Gould had offered a month before, it seems very likely that they included "Brixham Town," "The Squire and the Fair Maid," "Strawberry Fair," "Richard Malvine," "The Maid and the Box," "The Wooer's Tasks," "Cold Blows the Wind," "The Gipsy Countess," "The Ragged Beggar-Man," and "Henry Martyn." It was a mixed bunch of broadside ballads and traditional ballads that would give Child some challenges in sorting out what he would deem genuinely "popular" and what he would reject as mere derivatives of late broadsides. At this point in his editorial process the elderly American scholar, who in any case was in ill-health, was apparently reluctant to add new ballad clusters to the canon of 305 on which he had already decided, but he still welcomed additional variants from oral tradition of items that he had already approved as traditional. So while Child was far from enamored of everything that Baring-Gould sent, there was sufficient good material in the "budget" for him to express his thanks in the Advertisement to Part VII of *The English and Scottish Popular Ballads* and to encourage the cleric to send more.[41]

Baring-Gould's next letter was undated, but it was probably written soon after. He had mentioned "The Trees They Are So High" in his letter of 14 July, suggesting that the melody dated from as early as the reign of Henry VII, but he had apparently neglected to include it in the "budget." Child had inquired about it, and so Baring-Gould forwarded a copy of the text that he had obtained from oral tradition. He remarked that the ballad had been "taken down from the same old hedger at Lew Down" [i.e., James Parsons]; "also from an old cripple at the same place" [i.e., Matthew Baker]; and "also from a moor-man at Widdecombe" [i.e., Roger Hannaford]. He continued, "the refrain three lines and a half are necessary for the very early and peculiar melody. The lines get shifted about somewhat. The stall copy cannot be sung to the melody used in Devon and Cornwall as the metre is different. At first we obtained only a fragment from our man. Later he was able to repeat some more verses, and a music peddler version was obtained still later." He added that the broadside version, issued by both Catnach and Disley, comprised seven verses, the last one of which was not sung in Devon, and that there was also a Scottish version in James Maidment's *A North Country Garland.*[42] Not long afterwards, Baring-Gould sent Child another, Irish, version of "The Trees They Are So High," which he had obtained from a correspondent named Mary O'Bryan who lived in Tipperary.[43] Just over a week later, on 23 August 1890, he wrote again, stating Fleetwood Sheppard had confirmed his opinion that the melody of the Tipperary version was almost identical to Roger Hannaford's tune, but quite distinct from that sung by James Parsons.[44]

This was one of the longest and most interesting of Baring-Gould's letters to Child. Child had evidently asked if he could purchase or borrow Baring-Gould's manuscript books, but the cleric demurred: he could not spare the notebooks because they were in constant use as he obtained more songs and more versions of songs he already had. He did promise to make copies for Child of everything new that he obtained, and gradually to provide on a selective basis copies of anything else Child wanted from the source material for *Songs and Ballads of the West*. Child had also asked him whether it was still possible to purchase Catnach broadsides in London. He replied that Catnach's editions and other old printings were now very hard to find, but that there were three broadside printers who were still active in London, namely Fortey of Seven Dials, Such of Borough, and Taylor of Spitalfields. The best collection of broadsides that he knew of was that owned by William Alexander Barrett, but he himself possessed about 1,700 broadsheets and he had also gone through all those in the British Museum (which included the Roxburghe and Bagford collections, as well as some smaller ones). Child was welcome to all the duplicates in his collection, but he cautioned the American scholar not to overestimate their value:

> I am quite satisfied that the broadside ballads are bad representations of the original. Catnach, Pitts, Fortey, etc. employed fellows to pick up ballads for them, or to rhyme murders. They paid them 1/- [1 shilling] for each they purchased. To earn their money they patched together scraps of various ballads, they rewrote old songs, and when they got hold of a genuine ballad they got hold of a base form of it, as they picked up their ballads in <u>town</u> and not in the country where the purest forms were preserved. Then the printed ballads seemed to corrupt the springs in the country. That is what I find. The younger singers nearly always follow a broadside, whereas the old and ignorant men follow the traditional version.[45]

This opinion no doubt served to further reinforce Child's ingrained prejudice against broadside texts. Nor was Baring-Gould's account of the way some singers readily modified tradition calculated to make him more receptive to variants recently obtained from oral sources. The cleric contrasted James Parsons, one of his favorite source singers, with other singers he had encountered in pubs, harvest homes, and sporting events. Parsons, he explained, was "a most valuable man [because] his family have been from time immemorial song men [and because] he is absolutely illiterate and devoid of imagination." Consequently one could be sure that any songs and ballads noted from him were entirely traditional, being neither derived from modern broadside texts nor modified by the singer himself. Other West Country singers, on the other hand, were not so reliable purveyors of tradition, although one had to admire their creativity, especially their ability to improvise at the drop of a hat:

> Now some of our minstrels are in their own way poets and can extemporize on the spur of the moment, for instance there was a fellow now dead, Dicky Down, who at a wrestling match would sing through the whole match swaying from one foot to the other, and narrating in rhyme to a tune the terms of the game [indistinct] in reference to all those present. Another man I know does much the same at a harvest. The old fellow, when I asked him if he had a song about cider, a day or two after sung us one. I questioned him about it, and he told me he had composed it, words and air, to suit me. The air no doubt he adapted from some previous song he had learned, and he certainly worked into the words passages I recognized as belonging to other ballads. and, indeed, the singers do not always sing their ballads as fully one time as another. One evening on Dartmoor in a tavern kitchen a moor man was singing a ballad, when a maid came in. He sang on, and I did not quite follow his story, and he told me after "it was a bit rough" and because the girl was in the room he altered it.[46]

Child had evidently been puzzled by the copy of "The Gipsy Countess" that he had received as part of the "budget." In *Songs and Ballads of the West*, he pointed out, Baring-Gould had printed it in two parts, as if there were two different songs, but in the manuscript copy it was a single ballad credited entirely to James Parsons. Which was correct? Baring-Gould's answer was unequivocal: his informants never sang the ballad in two parts, and the division into two was entirely his work as an editor. He had done so simply in order to make use of the two different but equally good melodies that he and Bussell (who was helping him at the time) had noted down from Parsons and John Woodrich. This was Parsons's text of "The Gipsy Countess" as sent by Baring-Gould to Child:

"There came an Earl a riding by
A gipsy maid espied he,
"O nut-brown maid," to her he said,
"I prithie come away with me."

"I'll take you up, I'll carry you home,
I'll put a safeguard over you,

Your shoes shall be of the Spanish leather
And silken stockings all of blue."

"My brothers then no more I'll see
If that I went along with you,
I'd rather be torn by thistle or thorn
With my bare feet all in the dew."

"I'll lock you up in a castle tall,
I'll bar you up in a room so high,
Thou gipsy maid from green wood glade,
That ne'er a gipsy shall come nigh."

"Thou shall no more be set in the stocks
And trudge about from town to town,
But thou shalt ride in pomp and pride,
In velvet red and broidered gown."

"I'll pawn my hat, I'll pawn my gown,
I'll pawn my silken stockings too
I'll pawn my petticoat next my shift
To follow along with the gypsies O."

"All night you lie 'neath the starry sky,
In rain and snow you walk all day,
But now thy head shall have feather-bed,
And in the arms of a husband lay."

"I love to lie 'neath the starry sky,
I do not heed no rain and snow,
And I will away, come night, come day,
To follow along with the gypsies, O."

"I will thee wed, sweet maid, he said,
I will thee wed with a golden ring,
Then thou shalt dance, and merry, merry be,
I'll make for thee a gay wedding."

"I will not wed, kind Sir," she said,
I will not wed with a golden ring,
For fickle as wind I fear I'll find
The man that would make my wedding."

[verses 11 & 12 missing]

Three gypsies stood at the castle gate,
They sang so high, they sang so low,
The lady sat in her chambers late,
Her heart it melted away as snow.

They sang so sweet, they sang so shrill,
That fast her tears began to flow,
And she laid down her silken gown,
Her golden rings and all her show.

O she put off her gilded shoes
That were of the Spanish leather, O,
All forth to go, in the rain or snow,
All forth in the stormy weather, O.

O she put off her gilded shoes
That were of the Spanish leather, O,
And down the stairs went the lady fair
To go away with the gypsies, O.

At past midnight he did come home,
And where his lady was would know,
The servants replied on every side,
"She's gone away with the gypsies, O."

"Come saddle my horse, come saddle my mare,
And hang my sword from my saddle hard,
That I may ride for to seek my bride
That is gone away with the gypsies, O"

They saddle his horse, they saddle his mare,
They hung his sword from his saddle hard,
That he might ride to seek his bride,
That was gone away with the gypsies, O.

Then he rode high and he rode low,
He rode through hills and valleys O,
He rode till he spied his own fair bride,
Following along with the gypsies, O.

"What makes you leave both house and lands,
What makes you leave your money, O?
What takes you abroad from your wedded lord,
To follow along with the gypsies, O?"

"O I want none of your house and lands,
And I want none of you money,
Neither care I for my wedded lord,
I will follow along with the gypsies, O."

"Last night you slept in a feather-bed,
Rolled in the arms of your husband O,
And now you must lie down on the cold, cold ground
And walk along in the rain and snow."

"I care not to sleep in a feather-bed,
Rolled in the arms of a husband, O,
I'd rather lie down on the cold, cold ground,
And walk along in the rain and snow."

"That never shall be, I vow," said he,
He drew his sword from his saddle bow,
And [?] he smote on her lily white throat
And then the red blood down did flow.[47]

[B-G: "Almost certainly another verse missing."]

These are the notes that Baring-Gould provided to Child *à propos* the ballad:

Taken down from an old and illiterate hedger [Parsons], son of a more famous singer. Neither able to read or write. The father died some years ago—is said to have known 200 ballads and songs. The son knows about 60. Tune in *S. of W.*, part II, p. 54. Another version, beginning at 2.13 from a blacksmith [Woodrich], but his follows the stall copy. He can read. His tune is in *S. of W.*, part II, p. 56: it bears a resemblance to a Scottish Jacobite melody, though different from any such it has the character. Another version, very fragmentary, from an old shoemaker at Tiverton. The principal divergences are as follows. He began at verse 13 and sang verses 15, 17-21, remainder forgotten…Stall copy: Catnach, 2 Monmouth Court, Seven Dials. Another broadside, "Gipsy Laddy, O" by Such, 177 Union St., Borough.[48]

In the event, despite all this documentation, Child refused to print Baring-Gould's oral texts of the ballad as variants of "The Gipsy Laddie" (no. 200), although he did make a passing reference to them in Volume IV of *The English and Scottish Popular Ballads*.[49]

Baring-Gould's final letter to Child in 1890 was dated 18 October, and it is interesting for the snapshot it gives of his fieldwork as a collector. He had recently spent a week with Fleetwood Sheppard collecting songs in the villages in and around Dartmoor, and they had obtained what he judged to be "a most successful harvest." He claimed to have noted fifty-six different melodies, although many items were variants of previously collected songs and others were, in his opinion, inferior in quality. The "haul" (his word) included a nearly complete version of "Lord Bateman" [from J. Bennett of Chagford], another "Trees They Are So High" to a different tune [from William Aggett of Chagford], a "curious form" of "Barbara Allen" from "a mostly illiterate old fellow who has lived all his life on the moor" [William Nankivell of Merrivale Bridge], another variant of "Cold Blows the Wind" from an elderly woman [Anne Roberts of Scobitor], and, best of all, "Midsummer Carol," sung to "a splendid, rugged old melody" by "a paralyzed old moor-man" [William Aggett]. With this letter Baring-Gould enclosed the texts of "Barbara Allen" and "Midsummer Carol" as well as newly collected fragments of "The Trees They Are So High" and "The Gipsy Countess."[50]

In his letter acknowledging the receipt of these items Child expressed particular interest in the various versions Baring-Gould had obtained of "Cold Blows the Wind" (aka Child no. 78, "The Unquiet Grave"). Writing again in January of the next year, the Devon cleric promised to provide Child with all his variants of this ballad. He recognized that Child was puzzled as to why he had previously sent only a composite text, and he provided an honest explanation which revealed much about his initial approach to collecting:

> I could not [do so] at first, as it was one of the first ballads I got; and at a time when I was more keen on the melodies than the words, to the latter I attributed no importance, believing them to be all taken from broadsides: so I mixed my verses, but I have found Mrs. Gibbons' ms. and seen Woodrich since, and also got a third version from an old woman on Dartmoor.[51]

In fact, the combined evidence of "The Personal Copy" and the material sent to Child indicates that Baring-Gould obtained this ballad from Devon oral tradition on at least six occasions: first, in 1888 from Harry Westaway of Belstone; second, from John Woodrich (to whom he returned for a second hearing in 1890); third, from Anne Roberts (the "old woman on Dartmoor"—this was the variant to which he referred in the previous letter); fourth, from another female informant who lived on Dartmoor, Sally Satterley (aka Mary Satcherley) of Huccaby Bridge; fifth, from Elizabeth Doidge of Brentor (this was actually recalled for him by a lady named Miss Gibbons, whose nurse Elizabeth Doidge had been in the 1820s); and sixth, from Jane Jeffrey of Dunterton (he would send this variant to Child in a letter dated 1 September 1892). Of these, Child received four versions (those sung by Woodrich, Roberts, Doidge, and Jeffrey), and he printed three of them (Woodrich, Roberts, and Doidge) in *The English and Scottish Popular Ballads*.

Baring-Gould sent Child two more communications in February 1891, the second of which was a letter enclosed with some additional texts.[52] These were probably versions of "The Jolly Beggar" (Child no. 279) and "The Carpenter's Wife" (aka Child no. 243, "James Harris, or The Daemon Lover"). The former was credited by Baring-Gould to "a Dartmoor labourer"; he had in fact noted it from William Setter, a Dartmoor moorman, and from J. Gerrard, a workman who lived at Cullyhole, near Chagford, as well as from James Parsons. Child failed to print this oral text in *The English and Scottish Ballads*, although he did make reference to it, dismissing it as a derivation from a broadside titled "The Jovial Beggerman" in *The Forsaken Lover's Garland*, which he called a "*rifacimento*, and a very inferior piece."[53] He was no more appreciative of "The Carpenter's Wife," which Baring-Gould had noted from Joseph Paddon of Holcombe Burnell in 1889, even though he reprinted two English broadside texts ("A Warning for Married Women" from the Pepysian collection and "The Distressed Ship-Carpenter" from *The Rambler's Garland*). Presumably he also dismissed "The Carpenter's Wife" as an inferior *rifacimento*. Child's opinion notwithstanding, here is Joseph Paddon's account of the ballad, as mailed to Harvard by Baring-Gould (there are some minor differences from the text ascribed to Paddon in "The Personal Copy"):

Well met, well met my own true love,   I might have had a king's daughter,
Long time have I been seeking of thee,   She gladly would have married me,
I am lately come from off the salt sea,   But I naught did hold for her crown of gold,
And all for the sake, sweet love, of thee.   And all for the sake, sweet love, of thee.

If you might have had a king's daughter
I think you were much to blame,
I would not 'twas found for a hundred pound
That my husband should know the same.

For my husband he is a ship's carpenter,
A carpenter so good is he,
By him I have gotten a little son,
Or else I would go—sweet love—with thee.

But if I should leave my husband dear,
And my fair sweet baby also,
O what have you got far, far away,
That with thee—sweet love—I should go?

I have seven ships that sail on the seas,
It was one of them brought me to land,
I have mariners many to wait on thee,
To be sweet-love at thy command.

A pair of slippers thou shalt wear,
They are made of beaten gold,
They are lined within with a coney's skin
To keep thy feet, sweet love, from cold.

A gilded boat thou shalt also have,
The oars they'll be gilded also,
And the mariners they shall pipe and sing
As thro' the waves, sweet love, they row.

They had not rowed a bowshot off,
A bowshot off from the land,
But over her shoulder she looked back,
And said, "Set me once more on the land."

"For I have a child in my little chamber,
And I think I hear him loudly cry,
And I would not, I would not my babe should wake
And his mother should not be standing by."

The captain he smiled and he stroked his arms,
And he said "This may not, lady, be,

Behind is the shore and the sea before,
And thou must go, sweet love, with me."

They had not been long time on the sea,
They had not been long time on the deep
Before that she was a wringing her hands
And loudly did she wail and weep.

"O why do you wail and why do you weep,
And why do you wring your hands?" said he,
"Do you weep for my gold that is in the hold,
Or do you weep for my octoes (?) fee?"

"I do not weep for your gold," she said,
"Nor yet do I weep for your silver fee,
But by the masthead stands my baby dead,
And I weep, I weep, for my dead baby."

She had not been upon the seas
The days they were but three or four,
When never a word she spoke or she stirred
And she looked over towards the shore.

She had not been upon the seas,
Upon the seas six days of the week
Before that she lay as cold as the clay
And never a word she more could speak.

They had not sailed upon the seas
Of weeks they were but three or four
But down to the bottom the ship did go,
And never the ship was heard of more.

And when the tidings to England came
That the carpenter's wife was drowned,
The carpenter rent his hair and wept
And then as dead he fell and swoun'd.

A curse be on all sea captains
That do lead such a godless life,
They will ruin a good ship carpenter
And his little son and his dear loved wife.[54]

The Devon cleric included one other interesting text with this letter, a fragment titled "Flowers in the Valley," which he believed to be an incomplete version of either "The Cruel Brother" (Child no. 11) or "Riddles Wisely Expounded" (Child no. 1). He had noted it at Mawgan-in-Pyder in 1891, and would print it himself in *A Garland of Country Song* (see below). Child surprisingly rejected this also, making no mention of it in *The English and Scottish Popular Ballads*.

Baring-Gould presumably did not realize how little impressed Child was with the first set of oral ballad texts that had arrived in the mail from Lew Trenchard. So he kept on sending new material throughout 1892 and 1893. On 5 June 1892, for example, he sent "The Golden Ball," and on 1 September Jane Jeffrey's version of "Cold Blows the Wind." Child then apparently heard nothing from him for nine months, but on 15 June 1893 the cleric sent a long letter accompanied by at least seven interesting new texts. They included three ballads noted from Sam Fone, ("The Death of Queen Jane" (Child no. 170), "A Maiden Sweet in May," and "Ward the Pirate" (aka Child no. 287, "Captain Ward and the *Rainbow*"). There was also the striking "Dead Maid's Land" from Joseph Paddon and the folk-lyric "The Sprig of Thyme" from Joseph Dyer, and Baring-Gould alerted Child to two related broadsides, "The Gardener" and "The Sprig of Thyme," copies of which he supplied. In his letter he also mentioned "The Merry Doe" (aka "The Keeper"), which he had collected in Mawgan-in-Pyder, and quoted the first verse. His other news was that he was now working with Fleetwood Sheppard on a new project, a publication based on their more recent collecting, to be titled *A Garland of Country Song*.[55]

With his next letter, dated 29 July 1893, Baring-Gould enclosed his last contribution to *The English and Scottish Popular Ballads*. This was a variant of "The Elfin Knight" (Child no. 2), which he called "The [Lover's] Tasks." He had found an Irish version of the ballad in a publication titled *Ulster Ballads* that he had come across in the British Museum, and this discovery reminded him that he had intended to send his Devonian and Cornish versions to Child.[56] There were three of them: the first he had obtained in 1888 from a friend named Philip Symons who had taken it down from an informant near Camelford; the second, titled "Whittingham Fair," he and F. W. Bussell had collected on Dartmoor from John Hext of Two Bridges in 1890; and the third had been noted from Joseph Dyer at Mawgan-in-Pyder in 1891. Baring-Gould would subsequently obtain two more variants, both collected later that same year (1893) from Mrs. Knapman of Kingswear and from S. Lobb, while "The Personal Copy" also includes a version of "Scarborough Fair" noted in Whitby, Yorkshire, by Frank Kidson. None of these additional texts ever reached Child, however, and he printed only the Camelford version in its entirety, although he did subsequently include some variant stanzas from Dartmoor (Hext) and Mawgan (Dyer).[57]

Baring-Gould's note revealed that he was concerned that Child might not be keeping abreast of the important work that was being done in England by other folksong collectors. He had previously mentioned Harriet Mason's *Nursery Rhymes and Country Songs* and Francis Hindes Groome's *In Gipsy Tents*, and now he drew Child's attention to the recent publication of Lucy Broadwood and Alec Fuller Maitland's *English County Songs*. He remarked that the latter book was "very interesting," although he had reservations about the attribution of certain songs to specific counties. He also criticized the inclusion of "printed songs" (by which he meant published compositions by known authors) such as "The Farmer's Boy" and "The Garden Gate."[58] Baring-Gould's final communication with Child was a postcard that he sent from France on 23 November 1893, responding positively to Child's request to borrow a copy of *Nursery Rhymes and Country Songs*. His suggestion that Child should check out these various recent English publications did bear fruit: Child would include items from Mason's, Groome's, and Broadwood's collecting in the last volume of *The English and Scottish Popular Ballads*. He would also include some of the material that Baring-Gould had sent him, though not nearly as much as the Devon cleric hoped and expected.

So which of Baring-Gould's texts did win admittance into the canon of Child balladry? He had sent versions of twelve (or possibly thirteen, if one includes "Flowers in the Valley") of the putatively traditional ballads that would receive Child numbers. As we have just seen, three of Baring-Gould's texts for "The Elfin Knight" (Child no. 2) were printed in whole or in part by Child. "Flowers in the Valley" was rejected. Child printed three oral texts of "The Undutiful Daughter" (Child no. 24, "Bonnie Annie"): one noted from an old man at Bradstone, one from an old man at Holne, and one from a younger man on Dartmoor (these informants were probably Richard Gregory, Harry Small, and Sam Fone, the three singers named in "The Personal Copy"). With regard to "The Unquiet Grave" (Child no. 78) three of Baring-Gould's four texts were accepted (those by informants Elizabeth Doidge, John Woodrich, and Anne Roberts). On the other hand, Child rejected William Nankivell's version of "Barbara Allen" (Child no. 84), but he did print Sam Fone's "The Death of Queen Jane" (Child no. 170). As for Child no. 200, Baring-Gould offered not only James Parsons's lengthy, two-part "Gipsy Countess" but also shorter variants of "The Gipsy Laddie" by John Woodrich of Thrushelton and Peter Cheriton of Tiverton. None was printed by Child, although he did mention the existence of Parsons's and Cheriton's variants. In contrast, Joseph Paddon's "Dead Maid's Land" was accepted as a variant of "The Gardener" (Child no. 219), although the same singer's version of Child no. 243 ("James Harris, or The Daemon Lover") was rejected. The Devon variants of "Henry Martyn" (Child no. 250) fared better: both Matthew Baker's and Roger Luxton's were printed by Child. He rejected, although he made reference to, Baring-Gould's oral texts for "The Jolly Beggar" (Child no. 279) and "Captain Ward and the *Rainbow*" (Child no. 287). Finally he accepted and printed John Woodrich's version of "The Brown Girl" (Child no. 295).[59]

With regard to ballads that Child recognized as "popular," Baring-Gould's track record in getting his variants accepted was thus rather mixed: he succeeded in seven instances and failed in six, although for a few of the latter he received honorable mentions. This, however, was far from the whole of the story. The other half of the tale concerned ballads that were excluded from the canon. Baring-Gould submitted at least sixteen other items that he thought warranted inclusion, but not once did he succeed in convincing Child to expand the canon. It seems surprising that Child was so adamant in refusing "The Trees They Are So High," despite several attempts by Baring-Gould to convince him that it was a traditional ballad of high quality. "Death and the Lady" (Roger Hannaford's account, noted in May 1890) would seem a good candidate also, not to mention James Parsons's "The Dilly Song" (noted in 1891). Other contenders offered by Baring-Gould were clearly broadside ballads, although they were not obviously inferior to other broadsides that Child did include in the canon, such as "The Crafty Farmer" or "The Trooper and the Maid." Here, for example, is "The Squire and the Fair Maid," which Baring-Gould had noted from James Parsons in 1888, from John Masters of Bradstone, and from a taverner's son, H. Smith of Two Bridges, on Dartmoor in 1890. He gave Child all three versions, but this was the best one, Masters's text:

As I walked out one May morning
Down by a river's side,
I heard a fair maid singing sweet,
It filled my heart with pride.
"May heaven blessings on thee rain,
Sing me another song,
Then I'll make thee my bride, fair maid."
"Kind sir, I am too young."

"The younger you are, the better you are,
The better you are for me,
I vow and swear and do declare
I'll marry none save thee.
I'll make of thee my sweet lady,
My sweet lady," he said,
"And all the world shall see and know
My wife she is a maid."

He took her by the lily-white hand,
Together forth they went,
And all the bushes sweet with flowers
They passed through, and bent,
He led her to a pleasant room,
She kissed his ruddy cheek,
She stroked his furry (?), flaxen hair,
No word the squire might speak.

In the beginning of the night
They both did jest and play,
And the remainder of the night
Close to his breast she lay.
The night being gone, the day come on
The morning shined clear,
The youth arose, drew on his clothes
And said – "Farewell, my dear."

"Is this the promise that you made,
Down by the riverside?
You promised me you'd marry me,
And make of me your bride."
"If I to you a promise made,
That's more than I can do,
Man loveth none so easy won,
So unafraid as you."

"Go get you where are gardens fair
There sit and cry your fill,
And when you think on what you've done,
Then blame your forward will.
There is a herb in your garden,
I think they call it rue,
When fishes fly as swallows high,
Then young men will prove true."

She went all down to her garden,
She sat her down to cry,
"Was ever found on God's good ground
One crossed in love as I?
A maid again I ne'er shall be
A maid without a stain,
On orange trees when apples grow
My love will come again."

"Was e'er a maid in field or town
So used as I have been?
Was e'er a maid so used as I
For wearing gown of green?
Whilst others roam, I stay at home,
The cradle rock and cry:-
"Alack a day! At home to stay
And sing lul-lul-aby![60]

All that remains to be done in providing an account of the intriguing epistolary encounter between these two major figures is to note the other songs that were sent by Baring-Gould and rejected by Child, together with various others that Baring-Gould offered (or mentioned in his letters) but Child was not sufficiently interested to request. To provide a more useful picture of the kind of English material that Child decided, for whatever reason, was insufficiently "popular" (i.e., not really traditional) to be included in *The English and Scottish Popular Ballads*, I will include the variants of Child ballads that he deemed not worth printing as well as the broadside ballads and other songs that he refused outright. I have omitted a few Irish variants, as their geographical origin obviously ruled them out. This is the list of rejects, in alphabetical order, using Baring-Gould's titles. Asterisks indicate material in "The Harvard Manuscript":

"A Brisk Young Man Courted Me"
"All in the May Morning"*
"As I Went Out"
"As Johnny Walked Out"*
"The Baffled Knight"
"Barbara Allen"*
"Brixham Town"*
"By Chance It Was"*
"The Carpenter's Wife"*
"Death and the Lady"*
"The Dilly Song"*

"Fair Rosamund"
"The Farmer's Son"*
"The Fiend Knight"
"Flowers in the Valley"*
"The Fly and the Bee"
"The Golden Ball"*
"The Gipsy Countess"*
"The Jolly Sportsman"*
"Lowlands of Holland"
"The Maid and the Box"*
"A Maiden Sweet in May"

"The Merry Doe"
"Midsummer Carol"*
"The Miraculous Hen; or, the Cuckold's Cap"
"The Mower"*
"Our Good Man"
"The Outlandish Knight"
"Peggy Bawn"
"Pretty Polly Oliver"
"The Ragged Beggar-Man"*
"Richard Malvine"*

"The Silly Doe" [probably the same song as "The Merry Doe"]
"The Sprig of Thyme"
"The Squire and the Fair Maid"*
"The Squire of Tamworth"
"Strawberry Fair"*
"Three Pretty Maidens"
"The Trees They Are So High"*
"Ward the Pirate"*
"Young Riley"

A few of these items were perhaps better classified as folk lyrics or carols than ballads and others were undoubtedly broadside ballads. All the same, it seems a pity that Child was not more flexible with regard to the West Country oral texts that he received (or could have received), and more open to Baring-Gould's suggestions. Evidently the two men had quite different notions of what ballads were worth collecting, studying, and promoting. Despite his conviction that many recent broadsides were corrupt derivatives of better versions in oral tradition, Baring-Gould already had a strong, even passionate, interest in the history and provenance of broadside balladry. This fascination was reflected in the material that he included in his later publications, including *A Garland of Country Song*, which he worked on from 1893 onwards and which appeared in print in 1895.[61]

A Garland of Country Song

The wealth of song that Baring-Gould encountered in the Falcon Inn at Mawgan-in-Pyder, Cornwall, was displayed prominently in *A Garland of Country Song*. The book opened with Devon versions of "The Cuckoo" and "High Germany," but the third song was "Flowers in the Valley," which Baring-Gould had collected from both Sam and Mary Gilbert in 1891. "Lemonday" was the twelfth song in the book, and "The Lark in the Morn" was number 27. In his notes to "Flowers in the Valley" Baring-Gould commented that the song had an "exquisite melody" and that Sam had learned it from a nonagenarian called Thomas Williams, who had died in 1881. Unfortunately neither Sam nor Mary could remember all the words, and Baring-Gould had been forced to do some reconstruction work on the lyric. The fragments that they could recall (the chorus and the enumeration of musical instruments), together with the distinctive tune, suggested that "Flowers" was derived from an old song that had evolved in Scotland into "Fine Flowers o' the Valley," which had first been collected by David Herd. Similarly, that song had probably been the source of the ballad known as "Three Knights," which Davies Gilbert had collected in Cornwall in the 1820s. Baring-Gould speculated that the original version of the song had been sung "all over England and Scotland, from Land's End to John o' Groat's house," but that it had subsequently been modified in different ways in different regions. Drawing on these related texts, Baring-Gould came up with a composite lyric for the Cornish version of "Flowers in the Valley." It was one of his better efforts. The result may not have been an authentic folksong, but it was a laudable achievement that helped preserve a beautiful tune and probably also the spirit of the original song.

O there was a woman, and she was a widow,
Fair are the flowers in the valley,
With a daughter as fair as a fresh sunny meadow,
The red, the green, and the yellow.
The harp, the lute, the pipe, the flute, the cymbal,
Sweet goes the treble violin.
The maid so rare and the flowers so fair,
Together they grew in the valley.

There came a knight all clothed in red,
Fair are the flowers in the valley,
"I would thou wert my bride," he said,
The red, the green, and the yellow.
The harp, the lute, the pipe, the flute, the cymbal,
Sweet goes the treble violin.
"I would," she sighed, "ne'er wins a bride!"
Fair are the flowers in the valley.

There came a knight all clothed in green,
Fair are the flowers in the valley,
"This maid so sweet might be my queen,"
The red, the green, and the yellow.
The harp, the lute, the pipe, the flute, the cymbal,
Sweet goes the treble violin.
"Might be," sighed she, "will ne'er win me!"
Fair are the flowers in the valley.

There came a knight, in yellow was he,
Fair are the flowers in the valley,
"My bride, my queen, thou must with me!"
The red, the green, and the yellow.
The harp, the lute, the pipe, the flute, the cymbal,
Sweet goes the treble violin.
With blushes red, "I come," she said,
"Farewell to the flowers in the valley."[62]

Flowers in the Valley

Anon

O there was a wom-an and she was a wid-ow, Fair are the flowers in the

val - ley, With a daugh-ter as fair as a fresh sun-ny mead-ow, The red, the _ green, and the

yel - low. The harp, the lute, the pipe, the flute, the cym-bal, Sweet goes the tre-ble vi-o-

lin. The maid so _ rare and the flowers so fair, To-geth-er they grew in the val - ley.

Fig. 13.14

Baring-Gould included "Bold General Wolfe," "The Padstow May Song," "The Lark in the Morn," "Lemonday," and "Flowers in the Valley" in *A Garland of Country Song* but omitted "The Shepherd's Daughter," presumably because he thought its subject matter (rape) was unsuitable. Other Cornish material printed in the book included "The Jolly Wagoner" (noted from both James Olver and James Parsons), "The Greenland Fishery" (collected from Matthew Ford of Menheniot), "The Virgin's Wreath" (a rewritten version of Peter Sandry's "The Virgin's Garland"), "The Carrion Crow" (ascribed to an unidentified Cornishman), and "Bodmin Town" and "The Rout It is Come for the Blues" (both from William Nichols of Menheniot).

A few locations in Devon also stand out as sources of the material in *A Garland*. For example, the village of Stoke Flemming, a coastal community south of Dartmouth, was where both Mary Langworthy and Elizabeth Burgoyne lived and where Baring-Gould's collaborator Miss B. Bidder did her collecting. The two women singers contributed "Lovely Nancy" (aka "Lonely Nancy, Sad Lamenting") and "Some at Eighteen" (aka "The Old Maid's Song"). Lew Down was well represented because that was where one of Baring-Gould's regulars, James Parsons, lived, and he was associated with such songs as "The Jolly Wagoner," "Cupid's Garden," "The Beggar-Man," "The Gipsy Countess" (aka "The Gipsy Laddie"), "Across the Fields the Other Morn," and "The Mower." Thrushelton, the home base of itinerant blacksmith John Woodrich, was a geographical source for "The Gipsy Countess," "Let Bucks A-Hunting Go," and "Where Hast Thou Been Today?" The village that contributed the most songs to *A Garland*, however, was undoubtedly Mary Tavy, because Baring-Gould drew heavily upon Sam Fone's repertoire, which included (among others) "High Germany," "I Would That the Wars Were Over," "Jordan," "Kitty Alone," "One Night at Ten O'Clock," "A Farmer's Son So Sweet," "The Drummer Boy," "Leave Me Alone," "Hark! Hark! The Wars" (aka "Harmless Molly"), and the controversial "Gipsy Countess."

Although most items in *A Garland* had been noted in the West Country, Baring-Gould went out of his way in his introduction to the book to underline that he and Fleetwood Sheppard had sometimes drawn on material collected elsewhere in England. Although almost all the songs came from the countryside, there were a few items with urban sources, London in particular. For example, one of Sheppard's contributions was "All Around My Hat," a song that he regarded as a London street song since that was where, a half-century previously, he had first heard it. Its survival demonstrated that it was a vernacular song, but whether it was really a folksong was questionable. Sheppard knew he was stretching the envelope by including it, but he clearly loved the song.

All Around My Hat

Anon

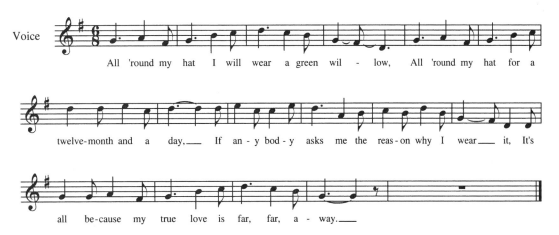

All 'round my hat I will wear a green wil - low, All 'round my hat for a twelve-month and a day,___ If an - y bod - y asks me the reas - on why I wear___ it, It's all be-cause my true love is far, far, a - way.___

Fig. 13.15

All 'round my hat I will wear a green willow,
All 'round my hat for a twelvemonth and a day;
And if anybody asks me the reason why I wear it,
It's all because my true love is far, far away.

My love she was fair, and my love she was kind, too,
And many were the happy hours between my love and me;
I never could refuse her whatever she'd a mind to,
But now she's far away, far across the stormy sea.

O will my love be true, and will my love be faithful,
Or will she find another swain to court her where she's gone?
The men will all run after her, so pretty and so graceful,
And perhaps she may forget me, lamenting all alone.

So all round my hat I will wear a green willow,
All round my hat for a twelvemonth and a day;
And if anybody asks me the reason why I wear it,
It's all because my true love is far, far away.[63]

Another example of a song in *A Garland* that was not collected in Devon or Cornwall was "The Somerset Wassail," which had been noted at Baring-Gould's request by a collaborator named Mr. C. L. Eastlake from Christmas wassailers at Langport in Somerset. Sheppard believed that the words of this wassail had been borrowed from another one in Gloucestershire, but he had no doubt that the tune was a good West Country one. It was, he observed, a "specimen of the best class of folk songs."

Wassail! Wassail! All 'round the town,
For the cup is white and the ale is brown,
For 'tis our wassail! And 'tis your wassail!
And 'tis joy come to our jolly wassail!

The cup is made of the ashen tree,
And the ale is made of the best barley.
For 'tis our wassail, etc.

The great dog of Langport burnt his tail,
The night that we went singing wassail.
For 'tis our wassail, etc.

O maid, fair maid, in holland smock,
Come ope the door, and turn the lock.
For 'tis our wassail, etc.

O maid, fair maid, with golden tag,

Come ope the door and show a pretty leg.
For 'tis our wassail, etc.

O master, mistress, that sit by the fire,
Consider us poor travellers all in the mire.

For 'tis our wassail, etc.

Pour out the ale, and the raw milk cheese,
And then you shall see how happy we be's.
For 'tis our wassail, etc.[64]

Somerset Wassail

Anon

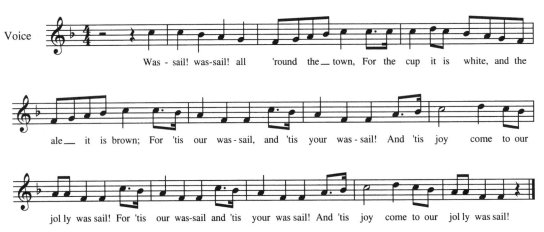

Fig. 13.16

Sheppard's emphasis that the "Somerset Wassail" was a genuine old folksong echoed a theme upon which Baring-Gould elaborated in his introduction to *A Garland of Country Song*. As the following quotation indicates, he explicitly and categorically distinguished between the 'Old English' songs printed by Chappell in *Popular Music of the Olden Time* and the real folksongs collected by himself and Sheppard:

> It is singular how little notice has been accorded to English folk music. Mr. Chappell, in his *Popular Music of the Olden Time* has given us a most learned and precious treatise on the airs of Old England, but has hardly touched on folk music. He probably did not suspect that so much was to be found of real ancient melody, still living in our midst, and not printed and laid by on the shelves of the British Museum...When by chance a genuine folk song did come to the surface—as when Chappell produced "The Mermaid"—at once more than half-a-dozen composers laid hold of it and arranged it. It did not occur to them to inquire whether there were others quite as good to be heard in country taverns, or in the milking-shed. It is one thing to go into the reading room of the British Museum, and in a few days pick out sufficient old-fashioned airs to form a volume of English songs; it is quite another thing altogether to hunt after old singers—few and far between, only to be heard of after diligent search, and, when found, to win their confidence, overcome their reserve, and get them to disclose the treasures buried in the inmost recesses of their memories. Not only is this difficult and a matter of much time and tact, but it is expensive work, requiring long journeys and lodging at inns, entertainment of the singers, and also much disappointment.[65]

This manifesto on behalf of field collecting as opposed to antiquarian research in libraries and archives would find a sympathetic echo in the hearts and minds of such Edwardian song-collectors as Cecil Sharp and Ralph Vaughan Williams. Unfortunately it set a fashion for undervaluing the work of Dixon, Rimbault, Chappell, and other mid-Victorian collectors. Baring-Gould's curious denial of the large folksong component in *Popular Music of the Olden Time* seems to stem from a desire to emphasize the importance and value of his own field collecting. It is obvious that he poured a great deal of time, energy, and money into his field trips, and successful collecting did not always come easy. He made an interesting observation about the difficulties he found in collecting outside Devon and Cornwall in places where he had no common ground with his potential informants:

> I venture to think that such a work as the collection of folk airs from the old singers would be impossible, or nearly so, to a man who had not lived the greater portion of his time in the country, and who did

not know the ins and outs of the countryman's mind. I find myself that, though I can rapidly unlock the hearts of our Devon and Cornish singers, I find more difficulty elsewhere—I do not understand the peasant in other parts so thoroughly as I do in the West, for there we have a score of subjects in common; we know about each other and each other's friends and companions, about places associated with each other's old recollections—we are on common ground very soon.[66]

Given Baring-Gould's heartfelt appreciation of both the obstacles facing the collector and the unique nature and value of the material he had collected, it seems surprising and unfortunate that he did not present the fruits of his labors as collected. In fact, as before, those fruits were subjected to heavy editing. Eleven songs in *A Garland* were provided with completely new words, while another seventeen were cut or modified in significant ways. Baring-Gould was less conscientious than before about giving details of his sources, but he was more ready to include in his notes some of the stanzas omitted from his chosen text. On occasion, as in the case of "When Joan's Ale Was New," he even gave two sets of words: his own "up to date" text and the original one as collected. There were many fine folksongs in *A Garland,* which made it all the more regrettable that their texts were so often served up censored and/or truncated. For example, only four of the eight stanzas of "High Germany" were printed, with the opinionated comment: "this song, in hopelessly bad metre and of no poetic merit, is given with only some slight modifications to suit *les convenances*." As Baring-Gould also noted, the ballad had a "particularly fine" melody:

High Germany

Anon

Fig. 13.17

As I was a-walking, a-walking along,
I heard two lovers talking and singing of a song.
Said the young one to the fair one, "Dearest, this way!
For the King he has commanded us, and his orders we must obey."
O it's "Do not me forsake, but pity on me take, for great is my woe!

And thro' France, Scotland, and Ireland, with thee, my love, I'll go."

"O, love you are too venturesome to risk your precious life;
You cannot go along with me, although you are my wife.
The rough roads and the rugged rocks your tender feet would wound,
And foes they would molest you and beset you all around.
And O t'would never yield to lie in th'open field all the night lang,
And your friends then would be angry if with me that you should gang."

"O, my friends I do not value, and my foes I do not fear,
But along with my valiant soldier I'll travel far and near;
That no one may molest me, I'll wear a soldier's suit,
And march with my dear husband in a regiment of foot.
With William at my side, all hardships I'll deride, and always be gay;
And with songs and merry stories beguile the weary way."

"Yes, you shall march and beat a drum, and when the trumpet sounds
In battle to your side I'll come, and shelter you from wounds.
All dangers we will share, my love, as hand in hand we go;
And that you are so fair, my love, no man shall ever know.
So, dearest, dry your tears, and banish all your fears, sure as man and wife we be,
You shall hear the drums and trumpets sound in the wars of High Germany."[67]

"The Drummer Boy" received similar treatment: four of ten stanzas were printed with the excuse that "the original words of this song are hardly acceptable. We have for good reason re-written this ballad." Other bowdlerized songs were "All Around My Hat," "Jordan," "The Beggar Man," "The Lark in the Morn," "The Frigate," and "Down to the Ground," while "The Mower" and "The Gipsy" were among those completely rewritten. Baring-Gould claimed that the problem with the original version of "Jordan" was that "some of the stock verses are coarse," and that it was "obviously impossible" to use the original words of "Down to the Ground." About "The Mower" he commented that although the song existed in several versions they were all objectionable, so he had been compelled to rewrite it entirely. Curiously, he let the original words of "Green Besoms" stand, perhaps because he was oblivious to the implicit sexual allegory (which is evident only if the singer is female). Cuts were not always made on moral grounds. Baring-Gould pronounced lengthy ballads to be unsingable and he ruthlessly cut them down to half-a-dozen verses at most, regardless of the harm done to the ballad's storyline or dénouement. Examples of such truncations are "The Three Sisters," "Outward Bound," "The Witty Shepherd," and "The Sad Recruit."

The editorial liberties taken by Baring-Gould and Fleetwood Sheppard significantly reduced the value to the scholar of what could have been a very important collection. Nonetheless, it still contained approximately two dozen folksongs that seem to have been presented as collected or only slightly modified. These included such fine songs as "The Cuckoo," "Bold General Wolfe," "Lovely Nancy," "Lemonday," "The Jolly Waggoner," "Bodmin Town," "Somersetshire Wassail," and "The Padstow May Song." Other highlights of the collection were the Child ballads "The Three Sisters" and "Where Hast Thou Been Today?" the latter a version of "Lord Randall." Since, with the exception of a two-verse fragment from Suffolk, all the many variants of this ballad assembled by Francis Child had been Scottish, Irish, or American, this was quite a find. According to Baring-Gould's notes, it had first been collected fifty years previously by Miss F. J. Adams, who noted it from her old nurse, near Kingsbridge (Devon), but more recently he had also found the ballad (or fragments of it) in the repertoires of "several old singers." Regrettably he left these informants unnamed, but they certainly included John Woodrich. This is the Devon version of the ballad, as reproduced in *A Garland:*

> Where has thou been today, Jacky, my son?
> Where has thou been today, my honey man?
> I have been a-courting, mother, O make my bed soon;
> For that I'm sick to heart, mother, fain would lie down.
>
> Where shall I make it to, Jacky, my son?
> Where shall I make it to, my honey man?
> Lowly in the churchyard, mother, O make my bed soon;
> For that I'm sick to heart, mother, fain would lie down.
>
> What didst thou eat this day, Jacky, my son?

What did thou eat this day, Jacky, my son?
Nothing but a little fish, O make my bed soon;
For that I'm sick to heart, mother, fain would lie down.

Who gave the fish to thee, Jacky, my son?
Who gave the fish to thee, Jacky, my son?
'Twas my pretty sweetheart, mother, O make my bed soon;
For that I'm sick to heart, mother, fain would lie down.

What wilt thou leave thy mother, Jacky, my son?
What wilt thou leave thy mother, Jacky, my son?
All my money I leave thee, mother, O make my bed soon;
For that I'm sick to heart, mother, fain would lie down.

What wilt thou leave thy father, Jacky, my son?
What wilt thou leave thy father, Jacky, my son?
All my land I leave him, mother, O make my bed soon;
For that I'm sick to heart, mother, fain would lie down.

What wilt thou leave thy sweetheart, Jacky, my son?
What wilt thou leave thy sweetheart, Jacky, my son?
Hempen rope to hang her, mother, O make my bed soon;
For that I'm sick to heart, mother, fain would lie down.[68]

Where Hast Thou Been Today?

Anon

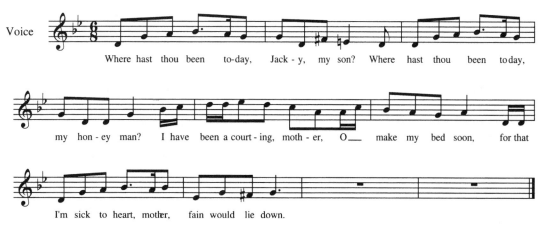

Where hast thou been to-day, Jack-y, my son? Where hast thou been to day, my hon-ey man? I have been a court-ing, moth-er, O__ make my bed soon, for that I'm sick to heart, mother, fain would lie down.

Fig. 13.18

A Garland of Country Song was the last major selection of songs from "The Personal Copy" that Baring-Gould published, although there would be a new edition of *Songs and Ballads of the West* (with an abbreviated title, some change of contents, and simplified piano arrangements by Cecil Sharp) in 1905. A few more of the songs that he had collected in the West Country would find their way into his next major music-publishing project, which occupied him for most of the second half of the decade. This was an eight-volume compendium titled *English Minstrelsie* and it will be discussed in chapter 15.[69] The last time that Baring-Gould collected folksongs on a large scale appears to have been 1894, a year in which he noted some forty songs. It is probable that in no year during the decade from 1895 to 1905 would he add more than a dozen items to Volume 3 of "The Personal Copy," although it is difficult to be certain because of the large number of undated items in the volume, especially at the end of it. He did continue to add a few dated items most years. For example he noted a version of "Tarry Sailor" in 1896, "The Queen of Hearts" in 1897, and "Flora, the Lily of the West" in 1899, and it appears that John Woodrich was still singing "The Rout Is Out" and "Jacky, My Son" (aka "Where Hast

Thou Been Today?") to him as late as 1905, perhaps because the work involved in preparing *Songs of the West* for publication had re-stimulated his interest in the old songs and the West Country men and women who sang them. The truth of the matter, though, is that from 1895 onwards Baring-Gould became primarily an armchair songhunter, turning more to archives than informants for additional old songs with which to expand his already very large collection.

Evaluating Baring-Gould: The Pluses and Minuses

Like *Songs and Ballads of the West,* Baring-Gould's *A Garland of Country Song* was a valuable but flawed work. As an editor the Reverend Sabine had three virtues: an obvious enthusiasm for his material and his sources, an extensive knowledge of his subject (including the broadside literature), and candidness about his methodology that wins him a certain, albeit grudging, respect. Despite the class difference between himself and his informants, Baring-Gould apparently succeeded in creating a rapport of trust and friendship with them. He communicated his genuine love of their "old songs" and they responded with a willingness to share them with him. According to Martin Graebe's count, Baring-Gould obtained songs from more than 150 informants. It is not possible to give an exact figure because it is sometimes difficult to decide whether a given item was noted by Baring-Gould personally or sent to him by someone else; moreover, there are inconsistencies in the spelling of informants' names which may disguise the fact that two apparently different singers were in fact the same person. We have met an instance of this in the case of Sally Satterley/Mary Satcherley. Nonetheless, it is clear that Baring-Gould's songhunting was on a larger scale than that of either Frank Kidson or Lucy Broadwood. Furthermore, in the main he appears to have established a remarkable rapport with most of his informants. He came to respect them as individuals, and made some efforts to help a few of them financially by giving them the profits from local concerts given by himself and his musician friends. In the introduction to *A Garland of Country Song*, Baring-Gould wrote:

> I cannot pass to another portion of my subject without a word on the great happiness it has been to me to make the acquaintance—I venture to believe the friendship – of so many of our old singing men, of getting to know them intimately, and of hearing the simple and often touching stories of their lives, and of cheering them in their old age with the assurance that English people are beginning to value what they themselves valued some forty or fifty years ago, but which it has been the fashion among the new generation to despise and laugh down.[70]

This was sincere, and there seems little question that the informants that Baring-Gould knew best, including Robert Hard, Richard Helmore, James Parsons, John Woodrich, and Sam Fone, regarded him as a good friend as well as a clergyman and song collector. Moreover, there is no question that Baring-Gould appreciated the melodic beauty of Devon and Cornish folksongs. He saw it as his personal mission to save them from oblivion and to publicize them to a wider audience. He also perceived the folk music of his region as an expression of a vanishing rural culture, and he had a social historian's interest in that traditional way of life, with its values, customs, and songs. This is reflected in some of his other publications, in particular *Old Country Life* and *A Book of Folk-lore.*[71] In his books he not only attempted to preserve the songs, he also wrote about the people from whom he collected them and the lives they lived. One of his other enthusiasms was archeology, and in his approach to folksong one can see at work the mind of an anthropologist and folklorist as well as that of an Anglican minister who happened to be an amateur musician and a successful novelist.

Neither Baring-Gould nor his collaborators H. Fleetwood Sheppard and Frederick W. Bussell were fraudulent in their dealings with the folksongs they had collected. Fundamentally they were honest in their approach to their material, however unfashionable that approach may now be. They did not attempt to pass off their own compositions as traditional lyrics. If they replaced the words of a folksong with their own, they said that they had done so, and they gave the reason why. Their compositions were thus not 'fakesongs,' but merely composed songs that utilized traditional melodies. Moreover, Baring-Gould did not censor texts secretively, as, for example, Kidson sometimes did. On the contrary, he was quite open about his bowdlerizing, cutting, and rewriting of lyrics that he regarded as indelicate or doggerel. When he edited texts, he sought to produce good, singable versions in the spirit of the original. "Singable" is the key word here. In compiling and editing *Songs and Ballads of the West, A Garland of Country Song,* and (later) *English Minstrelsie,* Baring-Gould's basic aim was to put folksongs (and, in the case of *English Minstrelsie,* some other good old national songs too) into the hands of middle-class singers who would perform them in the drawing rooms and concert halls of the nation. He believed it essential to do whatever was necessary to achieve that goal.

As a result, while Baring-Gould's work apparently presented accurately the tunes of the folksongs he chose to publish, this was far from the case with regard to the words. The lyrics in *Songs and Ballads of the West* and *A Garland of Country Song* fall into five categories: (i) those composed entirely by one or other of the editors; (ii) those substantially re-worked by Baring-Gould although based on an original folksong and containing elements of that song; (iii) those editorially emended or abridged but still consisting mainly of the original words; (iv) those composed entirely of verses noted down from a number of source singers; and (v) those printed exactly as collected from an individual informant. In some instances, where Baring-Gould had only one source for a song and he deemed the singer's words acceptable, one does apparently find the song exactly as collected. But such instances appear to be quite rare. The majority of folksongs in his published collections fell into categories (iii) and (iv), that is, folksongs that were essentially genuine but which had been polished and tidied up for use by potential singers.

The problem with Baring-Gould's published collections was (and is) thus quite simple: they contained a rather haphazard mixture of several quite different kinds of items. There was a fairly small number of imitation folksongs (i.e, songs with completely new lyrics written by Baring-Gould to traditional tunes), but these lyrics can easily be discounted and at least the device was a vehicle for preserving some beautiful tunes. There were larger numbers of heavily emended and/or truncated songs that bore a resemblance to the original but had nonetheless been tampered with quite extensively. There were also many other traditional songs that appeared to be quite genuine, but Baring-Gould had the habit of making minor editorial changes to these too, sometimes without informing his reader. The net result is that one can never be quite sure that a folksong published by Baring-Gould is *exactly* the same as he collected it. Unfortunately even "The Personal Copy" is not totally reliable, although Baring-Gould often used square brackets to indicate his additions or 'improvements.' Ultimately editing involves a question of trust, and, regrettably, one has to make the harsh judgment that Baring-Gould's approach to folksong editing, however well-meaning, forfeited that trust. By modern standards, and despite his good intentions, his collections were insufficiently scholarly. He did have a good excuse: he *was* dealing with many songs that exhibited a "looseness in morals unsuitable for the pianoforte" and he wanted to preserve and publicize beautiful melodies that he believed would otherwise be lost for ever. One therefore has to recognize that his method, if in the last analysis unsatisfactory, was understandable, pragmatic, and legitimate within its own terms. It was, in fact, what one might expect of a Victorian clergyman who loved the songs but had an accurate sense of what polite society would not tolerate.

Notes

1. Baring-Gould microfiche collection, 2.2, "The Personal Copy." For an account of the Baring-Gould microfiche collection and a discussion of "The Personal Copy," see chapter 7.

2. Baring-Gould apparently portrayed Bidder as "The Calculating Boy" in *Devonshire Characters and Strange Events* (London: John Lane, 1908). For this information I am indebted to Martin Graebe.

3. "The Personal Copy," no. 158. Sabine Baring-Gould and H. Fleetwood Sheppard, eds., *A Garland of Country Song: English Folk Songs with their Traditional Melodies* (London: Methuen, 1895), 56-57.

4. Baring-Gould, "The Personal Copy," no. 158.

5. In "The Personal Copy" Baring-Gould also reproduces the Catnach broadside, which includes three verses that Richard Gregory omitted. The Catnach version was reprinted by other broadsheet publishers, including Fortey and Such, and it was also reproduced by John Ashton in his edited collection *Real Sailor Songs* (London: Benjamin Blom, 1891; reissued 1972). I have so far been unable to track down the broadsheet in Baring-Gould's own broadside collection, which has been scattered among several archives and is incomplete on microfiche, but there are several copies in Frank Kidson's broadside collection which Baring-Gould on occasion consulted. He and Kidson sometimes swopped duplicates of broadsheets.

6. "Plymouth Fair Copy Manuscript," 373-76. The Such broadsheet version is in Kidson's *Folio Collection of Broadsheets.* A broadsheet version is also printed by Ashton in *Real Sailor Songs,* 242-43.

7. "The Personal Copy," no. 102.

8. Baring-Gould and Sheppard, *Garland of Country Song,* 85.

9. Baring-Gould and Sheppard, *Garland of Country Song,* 85.

10. Woodrich's correct surname may have been Woodridge, since that is the way it was recorded by a Census taker. However, it is also possible that the latter misheard the name, and in any case Baring-Gould consistently wrote Woodrich.

11. Sabine Baring-Gould, *Old Country Life* (London: Methuen, 1890), 277-78; Sabine Baring-Gould, *Further Reminiscences* (London: John Lane, 1925), 199. In *Old Country Life,* written at the time that Baring-Gould knew Woodrich well, the young man is said to have left home at the age of sixteen rather than fourteen.

12. "The Personal Copy," no. 293.

13. Ashton, *Real Sailor Songs,* 119.

14. The last song with a collecting date attributed to Woodrich in "The Personal Copy" appears to be "Where Hast Thou Been Today?" (aka "Jacky My Son," which is found in volume 2 as number 328a. There are two dates given, namely 1 September 1896 and

12 September 1905. Although this second date seems very late, one other song attributed to "Ginger Jack" (Woodrich's nickname), "The Rout Is Out," also has a collecting date of 1905, although it is included in volume 1 of "The Personal Copy." This evidence seems to suggest, therefore, that Baring-Gould's last collecting session with Woodrich in the 1890s took place in September 1896 but that he did eventually return to visit the singer nine years later.

15. "The Personal Copy," no. 514.

16. Five songs are credited to him but these are usually additional versions of items noted previously from other singers.

17. "The Personal Copy," no. 201. Baring-Gould's annotation indicates that he collected "The Buffalo" from Sam Fone at Micheldean in 1891, but Martin Graebe suspects that this is an error and that the village was actually Mary Tavy.

18. "The Personal Copy," no. 333.

19. Sabine Baring-Gould, ed., *English Minstrelsie: A National Monument of English Song,* 8 vols. (Edinburgh: Jack & Jack, 1895-1898). Quotation from volume 7, vi.

20. "The Personal Copy," no. 409.

21. Baring-Gould's handwriting is difficult to read, and it is possible that his informant was a nurse rather than a navvy.

22. "The Personal Copy," no. 458.

23. "The Personal Copy," no. 117.

24. Baring-Gould, *Old Country Life,* 276-77.

25. Martin Graebe, "Sabine Baring-Gould and his old singing-men," in *Folk Song: Tradition, Revival, and Re-Creation,* ed. Ian Russell and David Atkinson (Aberdeen, U.K.: The Elphinstone Institute, University of Aberdeen, 2004), 181-82.

26. Although Baring-Gould collected from him in Liskeard, Isaacs was not Cornish and in fact spent much of his time wandering around Dartmoor and the South Hams region in the southern part of the county of Devon.

27. "The Personal Copy," no. 232, as "General Wolfe"; *Garland of Country Song,* 14-15, as "Bold General Wolfe."

28. Baring-Gould and Sheppard, *Garland of Country Song,* 92-94. This lengthy account by Baring-Gould of the Padstow ceremonies certainly sounds as though it is based on personal observation. However, Martin Graebe informs me that he has some doubt as to whether Baring-Gould actually went to Padstow.

29. Baring-Gould and Sheppard, *Garland of Country Song,* 90-91.

30. "The Personal Copy," no. 255.

31. "The Personal Copy," no. 402.

32. "The Personal Copy," unnumbered at end of volume 1 [where no. 113 would be].

33. Francis James Child Collection, Houghton Library, Harvard University, shelf-marks fMS Eng 863 and r.f. 25241.45*.

34. George Kittredge, "The Harvard Manuscript", Baring-Gould microfiche collection 1.4.

35. Sabine Baring-Gould, letter to Francis J. Child, 6 June 1890 in "The Harvard Manuscript."

36. Baring-Gould to Child, 6 June 1890.

37. Baring-Gould to Child, 6 June 1890.

38. Sabine Baring-Gould, letter to Francis J. Child, 14 July 1890 in "The Harvard Manuscript."

39. Baring-Gould to Child, 14 July 1890.

40. Baring-Gould to Child, 14 July 1890.

41. Francis James Child, ed., *The English and Scottish Popular Ballads,* 5 vols. (Boston, Mass.; Houghton, Mifflin & Co., 1882-1898), vol. 4, "Advertisement to Part VII," unpaginated.

42. Sabine Baring-Gould, letter to Francis J. Child, undated but evidently late July or early August 1890; "The Harvard Manuscript."

43. Sabine Baring-Gould, letter to Francis J. Child, 14 August 1890 in "The Harvard Manuscript."

44. Sabine Baring-Gould, letter to Francis J. Child, 23 August 1890 in "The Harvard Manuscript."

45. Baring-Gould to Child, 23 August 1890.

46. Baring-Gould to Child, 23 August 1890.

47. Baring-Gould to Child, 23 August 1890.

48. Baring-Gould to Child, 23 August 1890.

49. Child, *English and Scottish Popular Ballads,* vol. 4, 62.

50. Sabine Baring-Gould, letter to Francis J. Child, 18 October 1890 in "The Harvard Manuscript."

51. Sabine Baring-Gould, letter to Francis J. Child, 9 January 1891 in "The Harvard Manuscript."

52. Sabine Baring-Gould, letter to Francis J. Child, 26 February 1892 in "The Harvard Manuscript."

53. Child, *English and Scottish Popular Ballads,* vol. 5, 109.

54. Baring-Gould to Child, 26 February 1892.

55. Sabine Baring-Gould, letter to Francis J. Child, 15 June 1893 in "The Harvard Manuscript."

56. Sabine Baring-Gould, letter to Francis J. Child, 29 July 1893 in "The Harvard Manuscript."

57. Child, *English and Scottish Popular Ballads,* vol. 4, 439-40, and vol. 5, 206.

58. Sabine Baring-Gould, letter to Francis J. Child, 29 July 1893 in "The Harvard Manuscript."

59. For an alternative account of the variants of ballads sent by Baring-Gould to Child and their reception, see David Atkinson, "Sabine Baring-Gould's Contribution to *The English and Scottish Popular Ballads*" in *Ballads into Books: The Legacies of Francis James Child,* ed. Tom Cheeseman and Sigrid Rieuwerts (Bern: Peter Lang, 1997), 41-52.

60. Baring-Gould, "Harvard Manuscript," 35; also "The Personal Copy," no. 23.

61. Sabine Baring-Gould and H. Fleetwood Sheppard, eds., *A Garland of Country Song: English Folk Songs with their Traditional Melodies* (London: Methuen, 1895).

62. Baring-Gould and Sheppard, *Garland of Country Song*, 8-9; cf. "The Personal Copy" [microfiche collection 2.2], no. 213.

63. Baring-Gould and Sheppard, *Garland of Country Song*, 26-27.

64. Baring-Gould and Sheppard, *Garland of Country Song*, 44-45.

65. Baring-Gould and Sheppard, *Garland of Country Song*, vi.

66. Baring-Gould and Sheppard, *Garland of Country Song*, vi.

67. Baring-Gould and Sheppard, *Garland of Country Song*, 6-7; cf. "The Personal Copy" [microfiche collection 2.2], no. 146.

68. Baring-Gould and Sheppard, *Garland of Country Song*, 82-83; cf. "The Personal Copy" [microfiche collection 2.2], no. 328, as "Jacky, My Son."

69. Sabine Baring-Gould, ed. *English Minstrelsie: A National Monument of English Song,* 8 vols. (Edinburgh: Jack & Jack, 1895-98).

70. Baring-Gould and Sheppard, *Garland of Country Song*, viii.

71. Sabine Baring-Gould, *A Book of Folk-lore* (London: Collins, 1900).

14

Frank Kidson in the 1890s

In the Late Victorian era Frank Kidson was the leading, although not the only, collector of folksongs in the county of Yorkshire. As we have seen in chapter 8, his major publication *Traditional Tunes*, although it did not appear in print until 1891, reflected the fruits of his collecting in the 1880s. By the early 1890s he had in his possession additional material noted from oral tradition that had not found a place in the book, either because he had decided to omit it (for example, he deliberately avoided overlap with the items in Baring-Gould's *Songs and Ballads of the West*) or because he had collected it more recently. He was already thinking in terms of editing a companion volume, but he was not a rich man, and self-financing the first volume had put a strain on his resources. Moreover he was becoming increasingly fascinated with the history of popular song publishing, a topic upon which he rapidly became an acknowledged expert. We have already seen that between November 1886 and June 1887 he contributed a series of thirty-two articles to the *Leeds Mercury Weekly Supplement* under the general title "Notes on Old Tunes."[1] This he now followed with a second thirty-two part series titled "Old Songs and Airs: Melodies Once Popular in Yorkshire," which appeared in the same newspaper's *Weekly Supplement* between January 1890 and June 1891.[2]

"Old Songs and Airs: Melodies Once Popular in Yorkshire"

The first article in the "Old Songs and Airs" series set the tone for the rest. It discussed the former popularity of country dancing in the county, demonstrating Kidson's familiarity with both Playford's *English Dancing Master* and various regional collections of dance tunes. He argued that the history of country dancing was not only interesting in itself but could cast considerable light on the origins of folksongs and other vernacular songs. "The old country dance music," he wrote, "besides having a value in itself as being frequently good and pure melody, is interesting from the light it throws upon the evolution of popular airs." As an example he cited "The Keel Row," the tune of which he had found associated with an early dance called "The Yorkshire Lad," which could be dated back to 1748.[3]

That phrase "the evolution of popular airs" provides the key to Kidson's interests and expertise. The search for musical origins clearly fascinated him, and many of the next thirty-one articles would attempt to explore the history of tunes that he believed to be familiar to his readers in a present-day disguise but which had actually had more than one previous incarnation under a different name. One of many examples provided the substance of his third article, on "The Crafty Ploughboy" (aka "The Crafty Farmer," Child no. 283). He reprinted the tune and sixteen verses of this ballad, which was also known as "The Highwayman Outwitted" or "The Yorkshire Bite," from an early broadside in his possession, and then pointed out that the tune was the same as that commonly used for an early broadside, "The King and the Abbot of Canterbury," which could be found in Thomas D'Urfey's *Pills to Purge Melancholy*, Volume IV (1719).[4] "The Crafty Ploughboy" was an example of a humorous ballad well known in Yorkshire but by no means exclusive to the county, having been collected as far away as the West Country and the north of Scotland. Kidson was critical of collectors and enthusiasts who focused on the song culture of their own region to the exclusion of all else, and who saw in their local songs the fount of the entire country's musical culture. But he was also a Yorkshireman, with a strong affection for and pride in his native county. He therefore strove in his articles to preserve a balance between the regional and the national in terms of the material that he discussed. His second, fourth, and eighth articles emphasized local productions, in particular the comic ballad "The Yorkshire Horse Dealers," the song "The Honest Yorkshireman," and a plaintive lyric titled "The Lass of Humberside." The latter was a lament about the loss of a fisherman-lover on a whaling trip to Greenland, beginning with the words "In a lonely cot on Humberside, I sit and mourn my hours away, For constant Will was Peggy's pride, But now he sleeps in Iceland Bay." Kidson reminded his readers that Hull and Whitby were the principal Yorkshire ports from which whaling vessels sailed, and he speculated that the whaling industry must have given rise to a large number of songs, only a few of which had survived.[5]

In his sixth article Kidson tackled a Robin Hood ballad that appeared to have a Yorkshire connection, "The Noble Fisherman, or Robin Hood's Preferment." He argued that Robin and his band had ranged as far north as the North York Moors, a fact that was reflected in place names in the Scarborough area, in particular Robin Hood's Bay. His commentary left no doubt that he was thoroughly familiar with the broadside literature about Robin, and also that he had a strong admiration for Joseph Ritson and the work he had done in assembling and collating the extant ballad texts about the outlaw and his deeds:

> Joseph Ritson, at the end of the last century, made special research into Robin Hood lore, and his wide and extensive inquiry seems to have left no fresh materials for future historians. There is little doubt that such a person existed as an outlaw, and had great power in the wild and extensive forests in Yorkshire and Nottingham...With regard to the history of the various ballads on Robin Hood, it is this—the earliest we have is a small quarto volume in black letter, printed by Wynkin de Worde (circa end of the fifteenth century). It is preserved at Cambridge. There is also another...book, a little later in date, printed by William Copland, in the British Museum...there is also in the Cambridge library a manuscript poem [from the reign of Henry VII] called "Robyn Hode." Later than this date are found as many as thirty more different ballads having him as a hero...Most of these are in blackletter, and several of the original ballads are in the Roxburghe gathering and in the Cambridge collections, which appear particularly rich in Robin Hood lore. Bishop Percy published one or two Robin Hood ballads from MS., but by far the greatest number (twenty-eight) were first reprinted from broadsides in Evans' *Collection of Old Ballads*, Vol 1 (1784), the "Noble Fisherman" being one of these. Some few are included in a collection of old ballads, in three volumes, dated 1723. In 1795 Joseph Ritson issued his invaluable book in two volumes...The airs to the ballads are much less frequently met with. A great many songs were sung to the same air. Some of these tunes are found in early MS. collections; others are printed alongside the ballads on broadsides; [but the tune for the "Noble Fisherman" is found in] the old ballad opera, *The Jovial Crew*, acted and published in 1731. It is there titled "Arthur a Bland" and is the tune to which "Robin Hood and Arthur a Bland" (or the Tanner) was chanted. It is also more than probable that other Robin Hood ballads...were sung to it.[6]

This is a good example of Kidson's historical, even antiquarian, approach to folksong and balladry, and it reveals his extensive knowledge of the work of previous folklorists, collectors, and ballad editors. An admirer of William Chappell and, methodologically speaking, his disciple, Kidson shared Chappell's catholic interest in any and all kinds of old songs and tunes, from street cries and hornpipes to folksongs, carols, traditional ballads, broadsides, songs from the London pleasure gardens, and ballad operas.

Later articles in the series dealt with such broadside ballads as "The King and the Countryman," "The Yorkshire Farmer," "The Old Maid," "The Saucy Sailor Boy," and "Old Christmas Returned" as well as the folk carol "The Twelve Days of Christmas," but the majority were devoted to vernacular songs with known authors, most of which would usually be classified as national songs rather than folksongs. They included "The Roast Beef of Old England" (by Richard Leveridge), "Ye Banks and Braes" (words by Robert Burns to an old Scottish air titled "The Caledonian Hunt's Delight"), "The Jolly Miller" (aka "The Miller of Dee," text by Isaac Bickerstaffe, but to an earlier tune called "The Budgeon, It Is a Fine Trade" from the ballad opera, *The Fashionable Lady; or, Harlequin's Opera*, 1730), and "The Dusky Night" (words by Henry Fielding to a tune also found in *The Fashionable Lady* but probably older still). Kidson was not equally enthusiastic about all of this vernacular material. For example, although he devoted an article to "'Twas Down in Cupid's Garden," printing a Yorkshire version from oral tradition that differed slightly in tune and text from that included in Chappell's *Popular Music of the Olden Time*, he regarded it as a very inferior production. Rejecting Chappell's eminently sensible suggestion that Cupid's Garden was a corruption of Cuper's Garden, one of the pleasure gardens in eighteenth-century London that rivaled in popularity the more famous Vauxhall Gardens, he commented:

> The song has every mark of being of the banal kind of doggerel love ditty popular in the last century. It is astonishing to think what sentimental ditties amused our forefathers. "Cupid's Garden" would do credit to a professional valentine-writer, and perhaps we are indebted for its creation to one. During most of the last century, before Burns wrote his sterling love songs, amatory versification could get no further than the allegory which represented the lovers as shepherds and shepherdesses...The Chloes, the Damons, the Phillidas, and the Lucindas who sighed

for each other, and spoke of each others' charms in such far-fetched metaphors, had their run for more than a century. How in the world such vapid productions ever held public esteem for so long a period is a wonder, for from 1650 to the beginning of this century we find that they monopolized a great deal of space in the music and song books of that period. They, however, got into polite society, and being perfectly artificial and unnatural, were eminently suited for that sphere. Moreover, they were very easily manufactured…During all this time, though, the real shepherds and shepherdesses sang their loves in a very different fashion, and the Corydon and Phillis class of song scarcely ever reached them. This class of song, however, never got into print, except very occasionally as a broadside.[7]

So much for "Cupid's Garden," which Chappell had judged to be one of the most popular of all street songs in late Georgian England.

On the other hand, Kidson had a high regard for what he considered the best of eighteenth-century song writing, the work of Richard Leveridge, Henry Carey, William Shield, Charles Dibdin, and, of course, the incomparable Robert Burns. One song that he particularly liked was "Nancy Dawson," to which he devoted an entire article. The subject of the song, he had discovered, was a stage dancer who first appeared at Sadler's Wells Theatre in 1760 and shortly afterwards at Covent Garden. Her dancing made a great sensation, especially when she appeared between acts at a revival of *The Beggar's Opera*, a common practice at the time. The air "Nancy Dawson," which has been ascribed to George Alexander Stevens, was a hornpipe, composed especially for her to dance to, and Kidson had found it in several country dance tunebooks of the time under the title "Nancy Dawson's Hornpipe." The song "Nancy Dawson" was written to the dance tune and appeared during the time that she was performing; it was printed for the first time in 1768 in *The Universal Magazine*, from which source Kidson reproduced it. It was very different from the children's version that Harriet Mason had noted from oral tradition and printed in *Nursery Rhymes and Country Songs*, although some resemblance between the two tunes was evident. This is the original composition by Stevens:

Nancy Dawson

George Alexander Stevens

Fig. 14.1

Of all the girls in our town,
The black, the fair, the red, the brown,
That prance and dance it up and down,
There's none like Nancy Dawson.

Her easy mien, her shape so neat,
She foots, she trips, she looks so sweet,
Her ev'ry motion is complete,
I die for Nancy Dawson.

See how she comes to give surprise,
With joy and pleasure in her eyes,
To give delight she always tries,
So means my Nancy Dawson.

Was there no task to obstruct the way,
No Shuter bold nor house so gay,
A bet of fifty pounds I'd lay
That I gain'd Nancy Dawson.

See how the opera takes a run,
Exceeding Hamlet, Lear, and Lun,
Tho' in it there would be no fun
Was it not for Nancy Dawson.

Tho' Beard and Brent charm every night
And female Peachums jointly right,
And Filch and Lockyt please the sight,
'Tis kept up by Nancy Dawson.

See little Davy strut and puff,
Frown on the opera and such stuff,
"My house is never full enough,
A curse on Nancy Dawson."

Tho' Garrick he has had his day
And forced the town his laws t'obey,
Now Johnny Rich is come in play
With help of Nancy Dawson.[8]

If Kidson's *Traditional Tunes* had proclaimed his interest in and love for the melodies (and, to a lesser extent, the lyrics) of songs extant in Yorkshire oral tradition, "Old Songs and Airs: Melodies Once Popular in Yorkshire" thus demonstrated that he was equally interested in national songs, country dances, and broadside balladry. Indeed, he was convinced that there was a symbiotic relationship between the printed broadsheet and the old English and Scottish melodies that could still be found in oral tradition and often also proved to be the source of the "vital melodies" borrowed by eighteenth-century songwriters for their most popular compositions. The old (sixteenth- and seventeenth-century) balladmongers, he suspected, had written their song lyrics with contemporary tunes in mind, a practice followed by many of their eighteenth-century successors, whether the latter were aiming their songs at the country ballad market, the urban pleasure gardens, or the popular theatre. Later songwriters also frequently borrowed tunes from older songs, perhaps modifying them slightly in the process. Moreover, the ballad sellers were often inclined to chant their wares rather than faithfully reproduce the intended tunes, so country singers re-created the melodies or even used different ones that they already knew. Some even invented their own tunes. The result of these natural processes was a wealth of old English melody that had been created over the centuries in London, in provincial towns and in the countryside. If an old air was collected in the countryside from oral tradition it would conventionally be called a folksong, but if it had been created or employed by an urban songwriter whose lyric attained lasting popularity it would be called a national song. In Kidson's opinion both kinds of lyric—urban street song and rural folksong—owed their status as vernacular songs largely to the special quality of their melodies. If a song, whatever its origins, possessed what he called a "vital melody," it would survive in popular culture. Then it would be worth reprinting, and worth studying its evolution from its origins down to the present day. Research into the history of old songs and collecting from oral tradition thus went hand in hand for Kidson, as it had done for William Chappell before him. The beautiful old airs that he so loved could be found both in the memories of tradition carriers and in old printed and manuscript tune books. Both sources were important and their products were equally valuable.

Materials for a Second Volume

Kidson's love of traditional melody explains why, despite his fascination with the history of popular music and music publishing, he had not abandoned folksong collecting. In fact he continued to collect quite vigorously for at least another decade, and he was still noting down new items in the 1900s, although by then most of his collecting seems to have been done only at local music festivals at which he had been asked to adjudicate singing competitions.[9] As we have seen, he planned a second volume of *Traditional Tunes*, and he had no lack of material for it, although it would never appear in print, at least in the form that he initially envisaged. There are three main clues as to what this book would have contained. One is the material that Kidson offered to the *Journal of the Folk-Song Society* during its first years of publication.[10] Another is the body of previously unpublished songs from his collection printed in three books edited primarily by Alfred Moffat between 1926 and 1929: *A Garland of English Folksongs*,[11] *Folk Songs from the North Countrie, with their Traditional Airs*,[12] and *English Peasant Songs, with their Traditional Airs*.[13] The third is a set of six manuscript notebooks extant in the Kidson Collection in the Mitchell Library, Glasgow. Since much of the material in this chapter derives, directly or indirectly, from these manuscripts, it is worth describing them and their contents.

All six manuscript volumes contain tunes, although sometimes lyrics (often just one or two verses) are included too, or, alternatively, references to broadsheets in Kidson's extensive personal collection of broadsides (which he bound in ten large folio volumes). There is considerable overlap in contents between the manuscripts, and it appears that while one of them was a field notebook, the others were fair copy notebooks. At the Mitchell Library these documents are catalogued as M.18056, M.18057, M.18058, M.18060, M.18061, and M.18109. The last of these (M.18109) is a fiddler's tune book that belonged to Kidson's friend and informant Charles Lolley, and it is in Lolley's handwriting. The first (M.18056) comprises a collection of 37 tunes for children's games and nursery songs, some but perhaps not all of which were collected by Kidson. M.18061 is a large fair copy tune book titled "Traditional Airs" containing 396 items. It appears to have been the repository into which Kidson copied out tunes that he found in printed sources or in manuscripts lent to him by Sabine Baring-Gould, William Barrett, Lucy Broadwood, Alec Fuller Maitland, or other late Victorian collectors.

In contrast to these three notebooks, the other three volumes are manuscript tune books that directly reflect Kidson's personal collecting. M.18057 is a quarto-size bound volume; the paper is plain but Kidson inserted ruled lines for music notation at the top of each page and then wrote lyrics underneath; occasionally he pasted in the words of a song from a broadsheet or newspaper cutting. Before the first page with a song there is an almost blank page on which is written "Traditional Tunes Collected by Frank Kidson" and a date, 1903. This contains 88 items, the first of which is "The Swan Swims Bonny O," as noted from W. H. Lunt. M.18060 is a fairly small manuscript music book, wider than it is long; the entries look as if they are fair copies. The inside cover contains the words "Traditional Airs Collected by Frank Kidson Book II." It also has written "F. Kidson, 5 Hamilton Avenue, Chapeltown, Leeds" and a date, 1915. The first of 93 items is "Blow the Candle Out." It would appear that both of these are fair copy notebooks rather than field notebooks, and the dates (1903 and 1915, respectively) suggest that they represented two different drafts of the putative second volume of *Traditional Tunes*. The 1903 draft was clearly intended to include extensive lyrics, while the 1915 version focused primarily on melodies.

M.18058, on the other hand, although it is a bound folio-size music manuscript book, appears to be a field notebook. The contents, 221 items, are less neat, and the material is not arranged in any kind of order. The first page, after a pasted-in, typed, contents list, has a title: "Traditional Tunes, collected by Frank Kidson, Leeds." It begins with an untitled item from Mr. Carr, Bradford, dated 1890: "Then up starts an officer of credit and renown...," which is in fact "Drink Old England Dry." This manuscript, then, is the best source we have for the songs (especially the tunes) that Frank Kidson collected from his various informants during the 1890s. It clearly provides a record of material that he noted personally from 1890 onwards, and consequently most of the examples of Kidson's collecting given in this chapter are taken from this manuscript. The two fair copy notebooks, on the other hand, give us clues as to what he found most valuable in the material he collected, and the items that he had at various times under consideration for inclusion in volume two of *Traditional Tunes*.

At the very least, these extant documents demonstrate that during the 1890s Kidson continued to be an active collector of folksongs and other vernacular songs. He was an equally avid collector of broadside ballads, and he quickly amassed many hundreds of them, which he bound in ten folio volumes that he called his *Folio Collection of Broadsheets*.[14] Unfortunately it is often difficult to pinpoint exactly when and where he found the new material that he obtained in this decade. He was not consistent in his documentation of his field collecting, which is perhaps a little surprising for a man normally so meticulous in his habits. Many of the items in the field notebook are undated, although he did occasionally note when he obtained songs from certain of his informants, especially some of his more frequent sources. For example, we know that in 1891 he collected the first five of the twenty-five songs that he would note from Leeds charwoman, Kate Thompson. Certain of Kidson's earlier informants and collaborators, such as Charles Lolley and Allan Wardill, evidently continued to supply him with new material, and he occasionally noted the date (or at least the year) they did so. He apparently visited the seaside town of Scarborough quite frequently, and over the years he obtained a number of songs from an informant who lived there called T. C. Smith, while another of his regular informants was a family friend called Alf Mooney. Other, more casual, informants we find identified only by their names (Charley Dickenson, Mr. Anderson, Edward Kaye, Mrs. Hollings) or by the locality in which they had been found ("street whistler in Leeds," "Shropshire woman," "pipe & tabor player, Oxford"). On some occasions Kidson recorded the complete words and tune of a song, along with the full name of the informant, and the date and place when it was noted, but too often he failed to include one or more of these particulars.

Collecting, 1890-1892

Reconstructing a chronological and geographical picture of Kidson's collecting in the 1890s is therefore not easy, but to some extent it can be done, and so I will make an attempt in this chapter. To begin with, it is evident from the manuscript tune books that not everything that Kidson had noted in the 1880s found its way into *Traditional Tunes*. For example, his fruitful relationship with T. C. Smith began at least as early as 1888, when he noted "I'Anson's Racehorse" from the

Scarborough native. Between then and 1896 Kidson obtained another twelve songs from Smith; the undated ones included a version of the Child ballad "The *Golden Vanity*," a popular broadside ballad about the notorious highwayman Dick Turpin ("Turpin Hero"), a conversation ballad extolling the joys of a simple country life ("The Rich Man and His Labourer"), a folk carol ("God Rest You Merry Gentlemen"), and the well-known folk lyric "Seventeen Come Sunday." During the years 1889 and 1890 Kidson was mainly preoccupied with compiling and editing his first two publications in the field of folk music: *Old English Country Dances* and *Traditional Tunes*, both of which were discussed in an earlier chapter. He did, however, find time to do a small amount of collecting in 1890. On 12 August he noted "In Leinster There Dwelt a Young Damsel" from an anonymous Irish street singer whom he came across by chance in Leeds. This was also the year in which he obtained three items ("Drink Old England Dry," "The One Pound Note," and "The Cuckoo's Nest") from a Mr. Carr of Bradford. As mentioned, "Drink Old England Dry" is the first entry in Kidson's field notebook (M.18058), and so it was likely the first song that he noted when he began collecting seriously again after the publication of *Traditional Tunes*. His notes to the song indicate that Mr. Carr informed him he had learned the song around 1861, and his research into its provenance led him to believe that it probably related to one of Napoleon's threatened invasions during the 1800s. By this time he was familiar with Lucy Broadwood's edition of *Sussex Songs*, and he noted that she had included a variant of the song on page 46 of that work. Apparently Mr. Carr could only remember the following verse and chorus of the song:

> Then up starts an officer of credit and renown
> Who swore he would fight for his country and crown,
> The cannons they shall rattle and the bullets they shall fly
> Before that they shall drink old England dry.
>
> CHORUS: Dry, dry, dry, my boys, dry
> Before that they shall drink old England dry.[15]

This was the melody that Kidson noted from him. The last seven bars are the chorus.

Drink Old England Dry

Anon

Fig. 14.2

That same year Kidson also noted one song each from Robert Holliday ("The Foggy Dew") and from Mr. Clarke of Wortley, near Leeds ("The Pretty Ploughboy").[16] He identified the tune for the latter as "The Lark in the Morning" and he possessed a broadsheet with the words of the song, so he did not bother to note down Clarke's words since they were essentially the same as the printed ones. This is the broadside text:

It is of a pretty ploughboy was gazing o'er his plough,
His horses stood under the shade,

'Twas down in yonder grove he went whistling to his plough,

And he chanced to meet a pretty maid.

And this was the song as he walked along,
Sweet maid you are of high degree,
If I should fall in love and your parents should know,
The next thing they would send me to sea.

Oh when these loving parents came for to know,
The ploughboy was ploughing on the plain,
A press gang was sent and press'd her love away,
Then sent him in the wars to be slain.

She dressed herself in all her best,
Her pockets she well lined with gold,
To see her walk the streets with tears in her eyes
When in search of her jolly sailor bold.

The first that she met was a jolly sailor bold,
Have you seen my pretty ploughboy, she cried,
He has just crossed the deep in sailing for the fleet,
Then he said, my pretty maid, will you ride?

She rode till she came to the ship her love was in,
Then unto the captain did complain,
Says she I'm come to seek for my pretty plough boy,
That is sent to the wars to be slain.

A hundred bright guineas she quickly pulled out,
And gently she told them all o'er,
And when she got him in her arms,
She hugged him till she got on shore.

When she got her pretty ploughboy in her arms,
Where oft she had had him before,
She set the bells to ring, and sweetly she did sing,
Because she met with the lad she did adore.

So blessed be the day when all true lovers do meet,
Their sorrows are at an end;
The last cruel war called many lads away,
And their true lovers will never find them more.[17]

The Pretty Ploughboy

Anon

Fig. 14.3

Because he had already printed a version in *Traditional Tunes*, Kidson did not regard this ballad as a contender for his second volume. But he liked it a lot and judged it to be much older than the late eighteenth century, when it was collected for the first time in Scotland by Robert Burns. He had located a copy of the text in an old garland in the British Museum, titled *Four Excellent New Songs…The Ploughman's Glory* (Edinburgh, 1778), which antedated Burns by a few years. He was also aware that it was extant in oral tradition in Surrey, information that he obtained from either Lucy Broadwood or Kate Lee.

In the summer of 1891 Kidson discovered one of his most valuable and important source singers. Kate Thompson was a Leeds charwoman who had been brought up in Knaresborough where, as a child, she had learned most of the songs in her repertoire. The first of twenty-five songs that Kidson collected from her between 1891 and 1897 was the well-known traditional ballad "Barbara Allen." He noted this on 6 June, but it seems to have been November of the same year before he obtained three more items from her: "The Indian Lass," "The Manchester Angel," and "Young Reilly the Fisherman." Kate remembered the tunes of these three broadside ballads but had difficulty recalling all the words, although she knew enough of "The Manchester Angel" for Kidson to conclude that her source for the lyrics was the broadside version with which he was familiar. The same was true of "Young Reilly," a tune that Kidson particularly liked, and he marked it out as a candidate for inclusion in the putative second volume of *Traditional Tunes*. In his fair copy notebook he transcribed the tune and included the words of two very similar but not quite identical broadsides, one "Riley, the Fisherman" printed by H. P. Such, the other, anonymous and apparently somewhat older, titled "Young Riley the Fisherman." This is the melody, [18] followed by the latter text:

Young Reilly the Fisherman

Anon

Fig. 14.4

As I went out one evening clear, down by the sea,
I overheard a fair maid, the tears rolling down did glide;
This is a cold stormy night, these words I heard her say,
My love is on the ocean wide bound for America.

John Riley they do call him, reared near the town of Hull
He is a nice young man as ever my eyes did see;
My father he has riches, and Riley he is poor,
Because I loved a sailor they could not me endure.

My mother took me by the hand, and this to me did say
Your father says he'll have his life—so shun his company,
If you be fond of Riley, let him leave this country,
For your father says he'll have his life, so take advice from me.

Oh mother dear, don't be severe, where must I send my love,
My heart lies in my breast, as constant as a dove:
Oh daughter I'm not severe, here is a thousand pound
Send Riley to America to purchase there some ground.

Soon as she got the money to Riley she did run,
To take your life, this very night my father charged a gun;
Here is a thousand pounds in gold my mother sent to you
Sail you to America and I'll soon follow you.

As soon as he got the money, next day he sailed away
He hadn't got a foot on board, she these words to him did say-
Here is a token of my love, and we will break it in two
You have my heart and half my ring until I find you out.

In the course of three months after she was walking on the quay,
When Riley he came home again, and took his love away,
The ship was wrecked, all hands were lost, her father grieved full sore,
He found Riley in her arms, drownded on the shore.

And they found a letter in her breast, and it was wrote with blood,
Saying bad was my parent that thought to shoot my love,

That this may be a warning to all fair maidens gay,
Never let the boy you love sail to America.[19]

The next month, December 1891, Kidson collected additional material from Kate Thompson, including a traditional ballad, "Fair Margaret and Sweet William," that he concluded was definitely one of the oldest items in her repertoire, in terms of both tune and text. Kate told him that she had learned it at her mother's knee, when a child of six or seven years old, during the early 1850s, but she could remember only four verses of the ballad.

Fair Margaret and Sweet William

Anon

Fig. 14.5

There sat two lovers on yon hill
All on yon hill on high,
They sat together for a long summer's eve
And they never could tell their mind.

Miss Margaret sat in her bedroom
Combing out her long brown hair,
Who should she spy but her own true love
Riding by with a lady fair.

She had a penknife in her hand
And it was long and sharp,
She made no more of her use of it
But she rammed it to her heart.

The day being spent and the night coming on
When all was fast asleep,
Miss Margaret appeared at twelve o'clock
And stood at his bed feet.[20]

Kidson noted more songs from Mrs. Thompson on at least three occasions during the next year (1892). In January she sang to him "The Banks of Sweet Primroses," and this appears to have been another item that he placed on his shortlist for inclusion in the second volume of *Traditional Tunes*. It appears he did not bother to write down the words that Kate sang because he already had them on a broadsheet in his collection, and, as we have seen in chapter 10, William Barrett had recently printed a version of the same song in *English Folk-Songs*. This is Kidson's broadside text, which differs somewhat from Barrett's, followed by Kate's tune:[21]

As I walked out one mid-summer morning,
To view the fields and to take the air,
Down by the banks of the sweet primroses,
There I beheld a most lovely fair.

Three long steps I took up to her,
Not knowing her as she passed me by;
I stepp'd up to her, thinking to view her,
She appeared to me like some virtuous bride.

I said, fair maid, where are you going,
Or what is the occasion of all your grief;
I'll make you as happy as any lady,
If you will grant me some small relief.

Stand off, stand off, you are quite deceitful,
You've been a false deceitful man 'tis plain,
It's you that's caused my poor heart to wander,
To give me comfort it is all in vain.

I'll go down into some lonesome valley,
No man on earth shall e'er me find;
Where the pretty birds shall change their voices,
At every moment shall blow boisterous wind.

Come all you young maids that go courting,
Pray give attention to what I say,
For there's many a dark and cloudy morning
Turns out to be a sun-shining day.[22]

The Banks of Sweet Primroses

Anon

Voice

Fig. 14.6

By that September Mrs. Thompson was sufficiently comfortable with Kidson to sing him a ballad—"As I Was Walking in Rippleton Gardens"—which dealt with the subject of prostitution and venereal disease. He found the tune appealing and commented in his notebook that although probably Irish in origin it was one that traditional singers often used for other songs, such as "All Jolly Fellows That Follow the Plough" and "As Maggie Was Milking One Morning in May." He nonetheless concluded that the ballad was unsuitable for inclusion in his projected publication because the words were "objectionable." It was, he recognized, a variant of "The Unfortunate Rake," and he possessed a broadsheet version titled "The Unfortunate Lad." Here is Kate's tune,[23] followed by the broadside text:

The Unfortunate Rake

Anon

Voice

Fig. 14.7

As I was walking down by the Hospital,
As I was walking one morning of late,
Who did I spy but my own dear comrade,
Wrapped in flannel so hard is his fate.

CHORUS:
Had she but told me when she disorder'd me
Had she but told me of it in time,
I might have got salts & pills of white mercury,
But now I'm cut down in the height of my prime.

I boldly stepped up to him and kindly did ask him,
Why was he wrapp'd in a flannel so white?
My body is injured and sadly disorder'd,
All by a young woman my own hearts delight.

My father oft told me, and oftimes chided me,
And said my wicked way would never do,
But I never minded him, nor ever heeded him,
Always kept up in my wicked ways.

Get six jolly fellows to carry my coffin,
And six pretty maidens to bear up my pall,
And give to each of them bunches of roses,
That they may not smell me as they go along.

Over my coffin put handfuls of lavender,
Handfuls of lavender on every side,
Bunches of roses all over my coffin,
Saying there goes a young man cut down in his prime.

Muffle your drums, play your pipes merrily,   And fire your guns right over my coffin,
Play the dead march as you go along,   There goes an unfortunate lad to his home.[24]

Kate Thompson was not Kidson's only informant in 1892. It was a year in which he collected extensively, and his other informants included T. C. Smith, Charles Lolley, Sarah Jackson, Allan Wardill, and W. H. Lunt. Probably while on vacation on the Yorkshire coast, Kidson picked up more songs from T. C. Smith, including the somewhat ribald comic song, "An Auld Man He Courted Me," which Smith had learned from a singer hailing from Rillington in the Derwent valley between York and Scarborough. Then in November of the same year Kidson found another important new informant. Back in Leeds, he discovered Sarah Jackson, a young woman who had learned various ballads and traditional songs from her mother, who lived in Nottingham. His tune notebooks ascribe five songs to "Miss Jackson," and they may have all been noted in 1892, although this is not certain. But we know that on 12 November Sarah sang "The Sprig of Thyme," although Kidson noted only the tune and not the words. He was already familiar with the song, having printed Charles Lolley's version in *Traditional Tunes* (see chapter 8), and he possessed a broadsheet with the following text, which was presumably either identical or very similar to that sung by Sarah. This is Sarah Jackson's tune,[25] followed by the broadside text, which has one additional verse to those earlier noted from Yorkshire oral tradition.

The Sprig of Thyme

Anon

Fig. 14.8

Come all you fair pretty maids,   I've got no room for any new,
That's just in your prime,   For in that place where my old thyme grew
I would have you weed your gardens clear   It run to a running, running rue.
Let no one steal your thyme.
                                             But I'll put a stop to that running, running rue
I once had a sprig of thyme,   And plant a fair oak tree,
It prospered both night and day,   Stand up you fair oak tree,
By chance there came a false young man   And do not wither and die,
And he stole my thyme away.   For I'll prove true to the lad I love,
                                             As the stars prove true to the sky.
Thyme is the prettiest flower
That grows under the sun,   It's very well drinking ale,
It's time that brings all things to an end,   And it's very well drinking wine,
So now my time runs on.   But it's far better sitting on a young man's knee
                                             That's won this heart of mine.[26]
But now my old thyme is dead,

About this song Kidson commented in his notebook: "This is one of many sets of 'The Sprig of Thyme' or 'The Seeds of Love.' Another set appears in *Traditional Tunes*, and Miss Broadwood has collected some versions in North Lancashire and Sussex. See *Traditional Tunes*, p. 69." He would later reprint the tune and part of the text in *Journal of the Folk-Song Society*,[27] so he evidently valued it and it is likely that he placed it on his shortlist for inclusion in the second volume of *Traditional Tunes*. The other ballads that he noted from Sarah Jackson were all broadsides, although Francis Child would count "Lord Bateman" as traditional ("popular" in his terminology). The other three were "The Female Highwayman," "At Plymouth Town" (aka "Gosport Beach"), and "The Sailor from Dover." "At Plymouth Town" provided a good example of Kidson the musical Sherlock Holmes at work. Sarah Jackson remembered the tune and only one verse of the song, which went as follows:

At Plymouth Town (Gosport Beach)

Anon

Fig. 14.9

At Plymouth town we landed
That place of noted fame,
I called for a bottle of brandy
To treat my bold flash dame.[28]

This fragment, Kidson recognized, was a variant of a Such broadside in his collection, "Gosport Beach," the lyrics of which closely paralleled the stanza remembered by Sarah Jackson:

On Gosport beach I landed,
That place of noted fame,
When I called for a bottle of brandy,
To treat my flashy dame;
Her outside rigging was all silk,
Her spencer scarlet red,
We spent that day quite merrily,
And at night all sorrow fled.

It was early the next morning,
All by the break of day,
He says my handsome fair maid,
What brought you down this way?
I am a rich merchant's daughter,
From London I came down,
My parents turned me out of doors,
Which caused me for to roam.

He says, my handsome fair maid,
I am sorry for to say,
That you have strayed so far from home,
To throw yourself away;

But no reflections I will cast,
But ever I'll prove true,
And when from Chatham I return,
Sweet maid I'll marry you.

They both shook hands and parted,
Tears from her eyes did flow,
Then on ship-board with her own true love,
She saw she could not go;
But as a token of true love,
A gold ring she broke in two,
One half she gave to her own true love,
Saying, adieu! sweet lad, adieu!

But scarce six months were over,
From Chatham he came back,
Saying, now sweet girl I'll marry you,
I've shiners in my sack.
Then to the church they hastened,
The marriage knot to tie,
And now they both live happy
Until the day I die.[29]

He also remembered that in the notes to *Songs and Ballads of the West* Baring-Gould had acknowledged collecting a West Country version of "Gosport Beach" but, on grounds of propriety, had declined to reproduce the text, and had instead used the tune for one of his own compositions, "Furze and Bloom." Baring-Gould's tune, he pointed out, while it was not identical to Sarah Jackson's, did have a certain resemblance to it.

Another of the informants from whom Kidson collected extensively that year was W. H. Lunt of Liverpool. Lunt was probably a sailor or ex-sailor, and he clearly had a connection with Ireland, since his varied repertoire included such items as "Boyne Water" and "Paddy Haggerty's Leather Breeches." He was fond of drinking songs, giving Kidson versions of "When Joan's Ale Was New" and "There Is an Alehouse in Yon Town." He also sang two children's songs: "We Are Three Jews Come Out of Spain" and "Are You Ready for a Fight?" Yet quite a few of the seventeen songs that Kidson noted from Lunt either in 1892 or the next year were broadside ballads; they included "Banks of the Nile," "The Bold Trooper," "The Highwayman," and "Sam Hall." Among the items in his repertoire that most appealed to Kidson were "Blow the Candle Out" and "The Swan Swims So Bonny." The tune of the former, Kidson remarked, was practically the same as the version of "The Banks of Sweet Dundee" that he had published in *Traditional Tunes*, which ruled it out as a candidate for inclusion in volume two. "The Swan Swims So Bonny," on the other hand, was a distinctive variant of the traditional ballad known as "The Cruel Sister" or "The Two Sisters." Kidson only wrote down one verse of Mr. Lunt's text, but he preserved the tune as follows:

The Swan Swims Bonny O

Anon

Fig. 14.10

> The farmer's daughter being dressed in red,
> My oh my bonny O,
> She went for some water to make her bread
> Where the swan swims so bonny oh.[30]

The last of Kidson's many informants in 1892 was another old friend, Allan Wardill, the railway pointsman from Goathland, on the edge of the North York Moors. He had already included in *Traditional Tunes* eight songs noted from Wardill, and between 1892 and 1895 he collected six more. They were "Broom, Green Broom," "Horncastle Fair," "I Designed to Say No and Mistook and Said Yes," "Seventeen Come Sunday," "Spencer the Rover," and a "Sword Dancer's Song." Of these at least one, "Seventeen Come Sunday," was noted on 11 December 1892, and Kidson preferred Wardill's version to others that he had noted.[31] It included the lines "Stockings white and shoes so bright, and her buckles shone like silver, She had a dark and rolling eye, and her hair hung down her shoulder," which Kidson recognized as very similar to those in a broadsheet that he possessed. Here is the broadside version of the lyrics, followed by Wardill's tune:

> As I walked out one May morning,
> One May morning so early,
> I overtook a handsome maid,
> Just as the sun was rising,
> > With my ru rum ra.
>
> Her stockings white, her shoes so bright,
> Her buckles shone like silver,
> She had a black and rolling eye,
> And her hair hung o'er her shoulders.
> > With my ru rum ra.
>
> Where are you going my fair pretty maid,
> Where are you going my honey?
> She answered me right cheerfully,

> An errand for my mammy.
> > With my ru rum ra.
>
> How old are you, my pretty maid,
> How old are you my honey?
> She answered me right modestly,
> I'm seventeen come Sunday.
> > With my ru rum ra.
>
> Will you take a man my pretty maid,
> Will you take a man my honey,
> She answered me right cheerfully,
> I dare not for my mammy.
> > With my ru rum ra.

If you will come to my mammy's house,   Soldier will you marry me,
When the moon shines bright and clearly,   For now is the time or never,
I'll come down and let you in,   For if you do not marry me,
My mammy shall not hear you.   I am undone for ever.
            With my ru rum ra.   With my ru rum ra

I went to her mammy's house   Now I'm with my soldier lad,
When the moon so bright was shining,   Where the wars they are alarming,
She came down and let me in,   A drum and fife is my delight,
And I lay in her arms till morning.   And a pint of rum in the morning.
            With my ru rum ra.   With my ru rum ra.[32]

Seventeen Come Sunday

Anon

Fig. 14.11

1892 was not only a gala year in terms of Kidson's collecting, it was important for another reason. In January he received a letter from Lucy Broadwood, who had recently borrowed *Traditional Tunes* from her family friend Alfred Hipkins, enquiring if she could purchase a copy of the book. He responded by return post, sending her a complimentary copy, and this proved the beginning of a close and lasting friendship between the two collectors.[33] They corresponded frequently that year, while Lucy was hard at work obtaining and selecting material for *English County Songs*, and on several occasions Kidson sent her manuscript copies of songs that he had recently collected, offering them for possible inclusion in her and Fuller Maitland's book. He also prepared for her a special annotated copy of *Traditional Tunes*, which Lucy was delighted to receive early the next year, noting in her diary on 22 February: "Heard from Mr. Kidson with handsome bound edition of his *Traditional Tunes* annotated and interleaved, also books lent to me from him."[34] Lucy usually attended the annual Leeds Music Festival, which was noted for its high quality choral singing, and when she did so that April she took the opportunity to visit Kidson at his residence in the city. They got on well together, and Kidson wrote thanking her for the visit and praising her "exquisite singing." They had discussed another of Lucy's collector friends, the Reverend Sabine Baring-Gould, and Lucy had evidently expressed sufficient reservations about Baring-Gould's editorial methods in *Songs and Ballads of the West* to encourage Kidson to be frank about his opinion of the man and his published collection. He wrote:

> You asked me my opinion of Baring Gould's *Songs of the West*, but we had so little time that I think I failed to give you it. This is it:—He is among a perfect treasury of old traditional song but I am afraid his ear is not quick enough or his memory too defective to retain the subtle points in an air (in note and in time) that makes the air so beautiful and so removed from the commonplace, for unless great attention is paid to this it is terribly easy to snip the corners off an air. The airs that he thus gets imperfectly he sends to Mr. Sheppard who possibly seeing technical defects in the tune thus noted down again alters or corrects them, as they confess they do not give the different versions of the air as noted down but give what they imagine to be the correct form of it—compiled from all

the ones they have found. This accounts for the character of the <u>airs</u> in *Songs of the West*. Regarding the words, upon the plea of doggerel or coarseness they suppress even the <u>title</u> or first few lines of a song, & in place of it write songs totally out of keeping with the spirit of the original (compare Robert Burns' handling of the old Scotch songs he collected for Johnson's *Museum*). To me I cannot in the least believe that a single song is there placed as it was sung to Baring Gould, the general spirit of the book being opposed to unadulterated country song. Witness a couple of songs and airs composed by Shepherd [*sic*] and Gould being inserted in the body of the collection without comment until part IV was published.[35]

This was a harsh judgment, and not entirely fair to Baring-Gould, who in fact prided himself on reproducing as accurately as possible the tunes that he or Fleetwood Sheppard had noted. Kidson was, of course, correct that the first edition of *Songs and Ballads of the West* had included two of Sheppard's compositions (with words by Baring-Gould), but both were omitted from the second edition and replaced with folksongs. To a degree it was a case of the pot calling the kettle black, since Kidson, when editing *Traditional Tunes*, had faced the same problem of how to deal with lyrics that were, according to the conventions of the time, unfit for drawing room society, and his own solution had been to omit entirely the problematic verses. Whether this was a much better course of action than Baring-Gould's attempt to provide appropriate substitute verses was somewhat debatable. It is possible that Kidson, normally the most mild-mannered and charitable of men, was lashing back in anger at Baring-Gould's criticism of his own book, which evidently Lucy had passed on to him. He defended himself vehemently from the charge that his chief informants, and in particular Charles Lolley, were not members of "the people," i.e., the lower classes:

> From what you hinted he does not think much of my book because he has an impression that I have not gone among <u>the people</u> to collect my tunes. He is in this mistaken. I have not sat at home and secured tunes ready noted down by post. People to whose names I prefix the title "Mr" he would have spoken of as:—"Old John so & so, very illiterate." Mr. Lolley is a bricklayer whose father kept a country inn in the East Riding & Lolley being a good fiddler can play the tunes which he remembers hearing sung when he was a lad at the old country inn. He and I have noted the tunes down together, and with this exception all the rest I have myself noted down from the several singers & I have been <u>very</u> careful. I believe I have got them fairly right as far as musical notes will give the air as sung.[36]

Broadwood apparently agreed with Kidson on both counts, and they continued to correspond amicably and enthusiastically about old songs and their discoveries in the field, although Lucy also kept up her friendship with Baring-Gould and did her best to smooth ruffled feathers and reconcile the two men, both of whom she admired, if not uncritically. Kidson's subsequent visits to London were rare, but, just like Baring-Gould, whenever he did make the trip he tried to include a visit with Lucy, and he also became a close friend of Alec Fuller Maitland. In the meantime he kept on collecting, and frequently apprised Lucy by mail of his discoveries.

As for Charles Lolley, Kidson had no intention of abandoning his collaboration with the bricklayer turned construction foreman, and in August 1892 he had again got together with his old friend, informant and fellow collector. On this occasion Lolley sang him "The Coach and Six," although this was but one of twenty-two new songs that Lolley would contribute to Kidson's collection, in addition to the twenty-four that he had already provided for *Traditional Tunes*. Moreover, Mrs. Lolley also provided over a dozen ballads and folk lyrics, including "The Drowned Lover," "The Fighting Cock," "My Bonny Boy," "When the Stormy Winds Do Beat," and "Young Roger the Ploughboy."[37] Unfortunately most of this additional material is undated, although presumably "The Coach and Six" was not the only item that Charles Lolley gave Kidson in the summer of 1892. Here is an alphabetical list of the songs that are clearly identified with Lolley in Kidson's manuscript tune books:

"The Armada"
"As I Was A-Travelling the North Country"
"As Tim and Harry Went to Plough" (aka "Sir Lionel")
"The Basket of Oysters"
"The Blackbird"
"The Bonny Bunch of Roses O"
"The Coach and Six"
"The Deserter"
"Fair Margaret and Sweet William"
"Fair Phoebe and Her Dark Ey'd Sailor"
"Female Smuggler"
"Fragment of Air"

"I'll Be True to My Love" (aka "Barkshire Tragedy" or "The Two Sisters")
"Irish Air"
"Lady Franklin's Lament"
"The Mariner's Grave"
"The Outlandish Knight"
"Poor Old Horse"
"Sorry the Day I Was Married"
"The Wanderer" (aka "Cease Awhile Ye Winds To Blow")
"The Warbling Waggoner" (aka "The Jolly Waggoner")
"Young Banker"

As is evident from this list, Kidson noted from Lolley a goodly mixture of traditional ballads, broadside ballads, sea songs, and folk lyrics, although, as usual, he tended to focus on the tunes rather than the texts, relying on his broadside collection to provide the latter. There were two traditional songs that Francis Child would admit to his canon of 305 "popular" ballads, namely "Fair Margaret and Sweet William" and "The Outlandish Knight." We have seen that Kate Thompson also supplied Kidson with a version of the former, so here is Lolley's tune for the latter, which he had picked up in the East Yorkshire town of Driffield:[38]

The Outlandish Knight

Anon

Fig. 14.12

"The Outlandish Knight" seems to have been a popular song in various parts of England. We have seen that Bruce and Stokoe reproduced a northern version in *Northumbrian Minstrelsy* (see chapter 4) and Charlotte Burne noted a quite similar West Midlands variant in Shropshire (see chapter 5). Charles Lolley's was not the only version of this ballad that Kidson would collect; he noted another from Mrs. Corker in Knaresborough, and a third was sent to him by a Mr. Rathbone, who had obtained it in Westmorland.[39] Kidson apparently had the item in mind for inclusion in the second volume of *Traditional Tunes*, and he would eventually submit it for publication in the *Journal of the Folk-Song Society*.[40] Although none of his informants remembered a complete set of words they knew enough to convince him that they were all singing the version he had on a broadsheet.[41] His broadside text was in fact identical to that provided by Bruce and Stokoe, so it can be omitted here.[42]

As the list indicates, Charles Lolley's repertoire contained a substantial number of broadside ballads, including "The Basket of Oysters," "The Bonny Bunch of Roses," "The Deserter," and "The Female Smuggler," and it is difficult to choose just one example to represent such a wealth of material. In chapter 7 we saw that Baring-Gould collected from John Helmore and Robert Hard two versions of the broadside ballad known variously as "The Dark-Eyed Sailor" and "The Broken Token." This is Charles Lolley's Yorkshire version of the same ballad, which he knew as "Fair Phoebe and Her Dark Ey'd Sailor." The tune, although different, is clearly related melodically to Robert Hard's.

Fair Phoebe and her Dark Ey'd Sailor

Anon

Fig. 14.13

It's of a comely lady fair,
Was walking out to take the air,
She met a sailor by the way,
So I paid attention to hear what they did say.

Said William—lady, why roam alone?
The night is coming, and the day near gone,
She said, while tears from her eyes did fall,
It's a dark-ey'd Sailor, that's proved my downfall.

It's two long years since he left the land,
I took a gold ring from off my hand,
We broke the token—here's part with me,
And the other rolling at the bottom of the sea.

Said William: drive him all from your mind,
Some other sailor as good you'll find,
Love turns aside, and soon cold do grow,
Like a winter's morning when lands are clothed
                                        with snow.

These words did Phoebe's fond heart inflame,
She said on me you shall play no game,

She drew a dagger and then did cry,
For my dark-ey'd sailor a maid I'll live and die.

His coal-black eye and his curly hair,
And his pleasing tongue did my heart ensnare,
Genteel he was, but no rake like you,
To advise a maiden to slight the jacket blue.

But still said Phoebe I'll ne'er disdain
A tarry sailor, but treat the same,
So to drink his health—here's a piece of coin,
But my dark-ey'd sailor still claims this heart of mine.

Then half of the ring did young William show,
She seem'd distracted 'midst joy and woe,
Oh, welcome William, I've lands and gold,
For my dark ey'd sailor so manly, true, and bold.

Then in a village down by the sea,
They join'd in wedlock and do well agree,
So maids be true when your love's away,
For a cloudy morning oft brings a pleasant day.[43]

Lolley was not in fact the only informant whom Kidson heard sing this ballad; he also found it in oral tradition in Goathland on the North York Moors, perhaps in the repertoire of Allan Wardill, although he seems to have neglected to record that local singer's name. In both cases the words were apparently those found on a very common broadsheet, of which Kidson picked up several copies, one of which is to be found in his *Folio Collection of Broadsheets*.[44] One more example of the kind of material that Charles Lolley helped Kidson collect must suffice. There were various fishing villages and a few larger seaports—including, of course, Hull—on the East Yorkshire coast, so it is not surprising that Lolley's repertoire included a number of sea songs, including "The Armada" and "The Mariner's Grave" as well as "The Female Smuggler" and "The Dark Ey'd Sailor." One of the more striking and unusual was a song that Lolley called "You Seamen Bold" but which is also known as "Lady Franklin's Lament" or simply as "Seamen Bold." It was a broadside composed about the ill-fated Franklin expedition to seek the North-West Passage. Lolley knew the tune and an evidently corrupt fragment of the words, but could not remember the rest, although he was sure that they were about Sir John Franklin and his crew. This is what he gave Kidson:

You Seamen Bold (Lord Franklin)

Anon

Fig. 14.14

You seamen bold I [who?] have long withstood the storms of nature,
Bring flood [Attend?] to these few lines which I now name
[They?] Will put you in mind of a sailor's fame.[45]

Drawing on his extensive knowledge of broadside literature, Kidson identified Lolley's somewhat nonsensical fragment with a ballad printed by H. P. Such, titled "Lament on the Fate of Sir. J. Franklin and His Crews."[46] About Lolley's melody, which he thought a good match with his broadside text, he commented that it was a variant of a common but good tune usually known as "Charles Reilly" which had also appeared in print since 1808 as "The Rambling Boy." He also noted that the ballad had been collected from oral tradition in Scotland. Here is the Such broadside text:

You tender Christians I pray attend,
To these few lines that I have penn'd,
Of Sir John Franklin and his brave band,
Who've perished far from their native land.
CHORUS: So listen now while I tell to you,
The fate of Franklin and his brave crew.

It's now fifteen years since he set sail,
With joyous hearts and a pleasant gale,
In frozen regions to cruise about,
The north-west passage for to find out.

There was many a sad and an aching heart,
As from their friends these brave men did part,
To plough their way o'er the raging main,
For fear they should ne'er return again.

When six dreary years they had been away,
Some other vessels without delay,
Were sent to search for the missing crews,
But, alas! of them they could hear no news.

A gloomy mystery for nine long years,
Their wives and children has kept in tears,
In deepest anguish they did await
The ship sent out to learn their fate.

Poor Lady Franklin in great despair,
In anguish wild she tore her hair,
Saying "Ten thousand pounds I'll give for news
Of my loving Franklin and his brave crews."

The government in this present year
Did pensions give to their families dear,

But Lady Franklin refused the grant,
Crying "Give me my husband, I no money want."

At length sad tidings of this brave band,
Has reached the shores of their native land,
By which we hear they are all dead,
Tho' suffering much ere their souls had fled.

As through the frozen seas they pushed,
Their ships by blocks of ice was crushed,
And offering prayers for their babes and wives,
Many brave souls did lose their lives.

Forty poor creatures from a watery grave,
With one of their boats their lives did save,
And o'er the ice they now took their way,
To reach in safety famed Hudson Bay.

What horrid sufferings of pain and want,
These frozen regions no food did grant,
At length, oh horrid! for want of meat
Their dying comrades they had to eat.

How horrid was the sight when found,
Their limbs and bodies lay scattered round,
The flesh gnaw'd off from every bone,
O may their souls to heaven have gone.

Now for to finish and to make an end,
May God their families from want defend,
And while their loss we sadly deplore,
We hope such horrors to hear no more.[47]

Collecting, 1893-95

In 1893 Kidson added a new informant, Charley Dickenson (or Dickerson or Dickinson; all three spellings are found in Kidson's notebooks), to his roster. Dickenson was also a retired sailor, and his repertoire consisted almost entirely of shanties and songs about sea battles and shipwrecks. In March Kidson noted from him a version of "The *Bold Princess Royal*," and later that year, in August, he added the shanty "Poor Old Horse." It seems likely that another song, "Heave Ho, Blow the Man Down," was collected at the same time. This was another version of the shanty we saw in chapter 6 printed in different forms by Laura Smith (in *Music of the Waters*) and Davis and Tozer (in *Sailors Songs or "Chanties"*).

Heave ho, blow the man down,
Give him some time to blow the man down.[48]

Blow the Man Down

Charley Dickenson/Frank Kidson

Fig. 14.15

The above version is how Kidson noted it in his field notebook (the folio ms. tunebook M.18058); it is there followed by "Poor Old Horse" (August 1893), "The *Golden Vanity*" and "The *Bold Princess Royal*."[49] However, in his fair copy notebook (the quarto ms. M.18057), which was probably a draft of the intended second volume of *Traditional Tunes*, he modified his transcription of the melody as follows:

Heave Ho, Blow the Man Down

Anon

Fig. 14.16

In this notebook Kidson added the comment: "Sailors chantie from Charley Dickenson. A sailors' chanty used in lowering cargo. Possibly the words should be 'Heave ho, roll (low or low'r) the man down.' Another version is 'Roll the man down, Teddy, roll the man down, Give him some time to roll the man down.'"[50] To judge from the fair copy notebook, the other song noted from Dickenson that Kidson had under active consideration for inclusion in volume two was the shipwreck ballad "All on Spurn Point." He had written down not only the tune but all the words sung by his informant, and the ballad provides an interesting case of the relationship between oral tradition and broadside balladry. Here, to begin with, is the tune, followed by Dickenson's text:

All On Spurn Point

Anon

Fig. 14.17

Good people all pray listen well,
A dreadful story to you I'll tell.
A vessel called the *Industry*
Was lost upon the raging sea.

About seven o'clock on Sunday night
She struck ground all on Spurn Point,
The swelling waves ran mountains high,
In a dismal state the ship did lay (lie).

We hail'd her captain who stood at the stern,
We have come to save you and your men,

We want no saving he then did cry
We shall get off at high water he reply'd.[51]

Kidson's comment in his notebook reads: "There is a fragment of the above taken down from a Whitby fisherman in *English County Songs* and set to the tune "Charley Reilly." I have the whole ballad on a ballad sheet, V 128." And sure enough, the broadside can be found in Kidson's *Folio Collection of Broadsides*, titled "*Industry* off Spurn Point":

Good people all pray listen well,
A dreadful story to you I'll tell,
A vessel called the *Industry*,
Who was lost upon the raging sea.

About seven o'clock on Sunday night,
She struck the ground all on Spurn point,
The swelling waves ran mountains high,
In a dismal state the ship did lay.

But when on shore we came to know,
To their assistance we did go,
We manned the lifeboat stout and brave,
Expecting every man to save.

We hail'd the captain who stood at stern,
We have come to save you & your men,
We want no relief he then did cry,
I'd thank you to move off immediately.

In the space of half an hour or more,
The lifeboat's crew reached the shore;
We watched her till eleven at night,
Then in distress they hoisted a light.

Into the lifeboat once more we got,
And hastn'd to the fatal spot,
Before we reached the fatal crew,
The light disappeared from our view.

O then we heard one poor man cry,
For God's sake help me or I shall die,
My shipmates are gone and so must I,
And down he went immediately.

The captain was so obstinate,
Into our lifeboat he would not get,
Or else all hands we might have saved,
And kept them from a watery grave.[52]

Kidson's collecting in 1894 appears to have been less extensive than in the previous two years. Nonetheless, he found at least one new informant, a Leeds ballad seller named Mr. Anderson, from whom he noted "Joe Muggins" and "James Waller (or Walker) the Poacher." He was not impressed with the quality of Anderson's singing, but he commented that his tune for the poaching broadside was typical of those employed by ballad hawkers. He identified the melody as a variant of "The Highwayman" or "Charles Reilly," and jotted down the following comment about it in his notebook: "From Mr. Anderson, 20th December 1894. James Walker was a poacher, executed at York circa 1860-65. The above is excellent as a specimen of a ballad singer's chant. It is curious to compare this version with the original of Charles Reilly." This was how he noted it down:

James Walker the Poacher

Anon

Fig. 14.18

Come all ye poachers pray lend an ear and listen to my sad career,
My poaching habits have caused strife and now I'm charged with taking life.[53]

Apart from Anderson, the one informant that we know Kidson definitely collected from in 1894 was T. C. Smith of Scarborough, whom he visited just before Christmas. It was a time for merry-making, and the song with which Smith regaled Kidson was appropriate to the season, the humorous drinking song "When Joan's Ale Was New," although Smith knew it as "Chandler's Ale":

> There was a jovial tinker who was a good ale drinker,
> He was no small beer drinker and merry his jovial crew.
> He came from the Weald of Kent
> And all his money was gone and spent
> Which made him look like a Jack a lent,
> When Joan's ale was new.[54]

When Joan's Ale Was New

Anon

Voice

Fig. 14.19

As usual Kidson supplemented the words that he had collected from Smith with a fuller set that he had found on a broadsheet:

There were six jovial tradesmen,
And they all sat down to drinking,
For they were a jovial crew;
They sat themselves down to be merry,
And they called for a bottle of sherry,
You're welcome as the hills, says Nelly,
While Joan's ale is new, brave boys,
While Joan's ale is new.

The first that came in was a soldier,
With his firelock over his shoulder,
Sure no one could be bolder,
And a long broadsword he drew.
He swore he'd fight for England's ground
Before the nation should be run down,
He boldly drank their healths all round,
While Joan's ale was new.

The next that came in was a hatter,
Sure no one could be blacker,
And he began to chatter,

Among the jovial crew.
He threw his hat upon the ground,
And swore every man should spend his crown,
And boldly drank their health all around,
While Joan's ale was new.

The next that came in was a dyer,
And he sat himself down by the fire,
For it was his heart's desire,
To drink with the jovial crew.
He told the landlord to his face,
The chimney corner should be his place,
And there he'd sit and dye his face,
While Joan's ale was new.

The next that came in was a tinker,
And he was no small beer drinker,
And he was no small beer drinker,
Among the jovial crew.
For his brass nails were made of metal,
And he swore he'd go and mend a kettle,

Good heart, how his hammer and nails
                   did rattle
While Joan's ale was new.

The next that came in was a tailor,
With his bodkin, shears, and thimble,
He swore he would be nimble,
Among the jovial crew.
They sat and they called for ale and stout,
Till the poor tailor was almost broke,

And was forced to go and pawn his coat,
While Joan's ale was new.

The next that came in was a ragman,
With his ragbag over his shoulder,
Among the jovial crew.
They sat and call'd for pots and glasses,
Till they were all as drunk as asses,
And burnt the old ragman's bag to ashes,
When Joan's ale was new.[55]

Kidson was back in Scarborough for Easter of the next year, and on 6 April he again visited T. C. Smith and collected songs from him. They included "The Golden Glove," "The Knight's Dream, or The Labouring Man's Daughter," and a fine anti-war ballad titled "Banks of the Nile." This was Smith's tune for the last-named song:[56]

The Banks of the Nile

Anon

Fig. 14.20

Kidson apparently did not bother to write down any of the words that Smith sang because he recognized them as the same as a broadside ballad in his collection that he had picked up from a local Leeds broadsheet publisher, H. Andrews:

Hark I hear the Drums beating, no longer can I stay,
I hear the trumpet sounding, my love, I must away,
We are ordered from Portsmouth many a long mile,
For to join the British soldiers [on] the banks of the Nile.

Willie, dearest Willie, don't leave me here to mourn,
You'll make me curse and rue the day that ever I was born,
For the parting of my own true love is parting of my life,
So stay at home, dear Willie, and I will be your wife.

I will cut off my yellow locks and go along with you,
I will dress myself in velveteens, and see Egypt too,
I will fight or bear your banner, while kind fortune
                   seems to smile,
And we'll comfort one another on the Banks of the Nile.

Nancy, dearest Nancy, with me you cannot come,
Our Colonel he gives orders no woman there shall go,
We must forget our own sweethearts besides our native soil,

And go and fight the Blacks and Heathens on the Banks of the
                   Nile.

Your waist it is too slender, love, your waist it is too small,
I'd be afraid you would not answer me when on you I would
                   call,
Your delicate constitution would not bear the unwholesome
                   clime,
Nor the cold sandy deserts on the Banks of the Nile.

My curse attends the war, and the day it first begun,
It has robbed old Ireland of many a clever man,
It took from us our own true loves, the protectors of our soil,
To fight the Blacks and Negro[e]s on the Banks of the Nile.

So now the war is over, and homeward we'll return,
Unto our wives and sweethearts we left behind to mourn,
We'll embrace them in our arms until the end of time,
And we'll go no more to battle on the Banks of the Nile.[57]

In 1895 Kidson also spent some time further along the North Yorkshire coast at Whitby, and there he found an informant named Mrs. Agar. The maritime connection was very strong: Mrs. Agar was not only the daughter of a sailor, she was also married to one, and the songs she sang all had something to do with the sea and ships. Kidson noted from her three broadside ballads: "The Dockyard Gate," "William Taylor and Sally Brown," and another version of "The *Bold Princess Royal*." The second of these three songs Kidson also noted from another informant, Anne Noble of Bradford, who sang it to the same tune and with the same set of words. This is the tune, with the fragment of a lyric that Kidson included in his tune notebook when he noted the melody from Mrs. Agar:

William Taylor and Sally Brown

Anon

Fig. 14.21

I'll sing you a song of two young lovers,
Two young lovers of this town;
The young man's name was William Taylor,
The fair maid's name was Sally Brown.[58]

As usual Kidson was familiar with the broadside text of the song, which he commented was essentially that sung by both informants. It was one of the first broadsides he had ever purchased, and the only substantial difference was in the name of the vengeful female:

I'll sing you a song about two lovers,
Who from Lichfield town did come;
The young man's name was William Taylor,
The maiden's name was Sarah Dunn.

Now for a sailor William enlisted,
Now for a sailor William's gone;
He's gone and left his charming Sally [*sic*],
All alone to make me mourn.

She dress'd herself in man's apparel,
Man's apparel she put on,
And for to seek her own true lover,
For to find him she is gone.

One day as she was exercising,
Exercising among the rest;
A silver locket flew from her jacket,
And exposed her milk-white breast.

O then the captain stepped up to her,
And asked her what brought her there;
All for to seek my own true lover,
For he has proved to me severe.

If you are come to find your lover,
You must tell to me his name.

His name is bold William Taylor
And from Lichfield town he came.

If your lover's name is William Taylor,
He has proved to you severe;
He is married to a rich lady,
He was married the other year.

If you will rise early in the morning,
In the morning by the break of day;
There you will see bold William Taylor,
Walking with his lady gay.

Then she called for a brace of pistols,
A brace of pistols I command;
Then she shot bold William Taylor,
With his bride at his right hand.

O then the captain was well pleased,
Well pleased with what she'd done.
And soon she became a bold commander,
On board the ship with all the men.

Then the captain loved her dearly,
Loved her dearly as his life;
Then it was three days after,
Sarah became the captain's wife.[59]

As was often the case, Kidson was more interested in the tune than the text. It was, he remarked, one that was often employed for execution ballads, for example the broadside of "Elsie Sykes" which he had noted from Kate Thompson (Sykes had murdered Hannah Brooke and committed suicide in Armley Gaol in 1865 after being condemned to die).[60]

"New Lights upon Old Tunes"

Following Kidson's collecting to the middle of the decade has caused us to skip over an important development that occurred in 1894. In October of that year Kidson resumed his earlier career as a musical journalist by contributing an article on the ballad "Sir Hugh of Lincoln" to the "Local Notes and Queries" section of the *Leeds Mercury Weekly Supplement*.[61] Calling it "one of the most curious and earliest of our old ballads" with an "endless and perplexing" variety of English and Scottish variants and even one in Norman French, he argued that it was evidently based on an incident related by Matthew Paris that took place in 1255, although the alleged ritual slaying may have been a pure invention that revealed more about contemporary hatred of the Jewish community than the facts of the case. Although the ballad bore a considerable resemblance to Chaucer's "Prioress's Tale," it apparently first appeared in print in England only in 1765, in Percy's *Reliques*, and that was actually a Scottish version, similar to one in David Herd's *Scottish Songs* (1776), although Herd also printed another, different, version. Kidson noted that the first time an air had been given for the ballad was in Johnson's *Scots Musical Museum* (1803), while Robert Jamieson had collected it from Mrs. Brown of Falkland and published her version in *Popular Ballads and Songs* (1806). William Motherwell subsequently also found text and tune in oral tradition in southern Scotland. Kidson pointed out that several French versions of the ballad had been collected together in a book published in Paris in 1834, *Huges de Lincoln: Receuil de ballades, Anglo-Normande et Ecossoises relatives au meurtre de cet Enfant Commis par des Juifs en MCCLV*. Moreover, it was still extant in oral tradition in England, having been collected recently in Lincolnshire by the Reverend George Hall and also, from travelers, by Francis Hindes Groome, who had included their version in *In Gipsy Tents* (1881).

Kidson himself had heard another traditional version sung by schoolgirls in Liverpool to "a peculiar chant-like melody, one portion resembling "Yankee Doodle," and he quoted the words that they sang:

Two little children were playing ball,
One went up and the other went down,
One fell into the Jew's garden,
[line missing].

The Jew came out as white as a sheet
And stabbed him like a sheep.
He took him into the barber's [or butcher's] shop
And laid him on a table.

Lay the bible at my head,
The Testament at my feet;
An[d] if my mammy calls for me,
Tell her I am asleep.

My coffin shall be black,
Six angels at my back—
Two to sing, and two to pray,
And two to carry my soul away.[62]

About this "terribly corrupt version," Kidson remarked wryly that its only value was in showing how ballads and other traditional lyrics were mangled by being repeated by children and "other uninformed persons." Oral tradition was by no means always an evolutionary process by which a somewhat doggerel broadside text was honed into a work of folk art.[63]

Two years later we find Kidson again contributing to the *Leeds Mercury Weekly Supplement*, and this article, about Charles Dibdin's celebrated "Tom Bowling,"[64] demonstrated that he was just as interested in eighteenth-century national songs as in traditional ballads with medieval roots. He clearly loved the song, stating that "for real honest feeling and pathos, as opposed to many clever songs where the writer has not had his heart in his subject, it not only stands above most of Dibdin's other work, but equals any lyric in the English language." It was, he continued, "one of the score or so by which Dibdin can hold a foremost place among song writers," citing "Poor Jack," "The Token," "Blow High, Blow Low," and "Ben Backstay" as other examples of Dibdin at his most creative, although he admitted that Dibdin had also been responsible for his fair share of "atrocities," including some pseudo-Yorkshire items and some racist "Jew Songs." Kidson clearly felt some affection as well as admiration for Dibdin, and he gave the following pen-picture of the man and artist:

> There were few harder worked men than Charles Dibdin; he wrote novels, he drew and etched in aquatint a series of illustrations for a picturesque tour in two volumes quarto, a rare work...He wrote his *Life*, his *Musical Tour*, he managed a theatre, and built another for himself. He established a music publisher's business, and was at different

times in his life a harpsichord tuner, an actor and singer, a composer and writer of many successful operas, and author of over two thousand songs, to most of which he composed the airs. Amid all this work, much poor stuff is to be expected, but though now-a-days poor Dibdin is often sneered at, yet, to sweep away all his rubbish, there is sufficient good matter left to rank among the best of its time. The song "Tom Bowling" was written on the death of the author's eldest brother, Thomas Dibdin, who was captain of a merchant vessel, and was drowned at sea. Dibdin first introduced it to the public in 1789, in an entertainment called *The Oddities*, the second of many monologues he appeared before the public in. This form of entertainment, wherein one person is singer, actor, and lecturer, all in one, was first instituted by George Alexander Stevens, and carried forward by Dibdin and the elder Charles Mathews…Companions to "Tom Bowling" in *The Oddities* were several ditties which attained a vastly increased popularity over it. The "Greenwich Pensioner," which commences "'Twas in the good ship *Rover*," was the chief favourite, and of this song, from first to last, he sold 10,750 copies. "The Lamplighter" was another which held the people's ear. The three songs named, he tells us in his *Life*, cleared him more money in four months than he had ever [before] made by music in his life.[65]

A similar focus on songs by known composers was evident in a series of eight articles that Kidson wrote for *The Musical Times* between October 1894 and August 1897 under the general title "New Lights upon Old Tunes."[66] They were similar in length and scope to his *Leeds Mercury Weekly Supplement* pieces, except that there was no need for a Yorkshire angle and he deliberately chose songs and other subjects that were national in scope and importance. The fairly short pieces usually presented the results of Kidson's musical detective work into the pre-history of well-known popular songs. For example, he argued in the first article that the melody of the naval song "The *Arethusa*" had not been composed by William Shield (as commonly thought) but was based on an air titled "The *Princess Royal*" that first appeared in print in Walsh's *Compleat Country Dancing Master* in 1730. The words (not given) were by Prince Hoare, but this is the tune:[67]

The Arethusa

Prince Hoare

Fig. 14.22

The following excerpts from this article indicate Kidson's evidence for his claim, and they also provide a good sense of his wide-ranging knowledge and method as a song-detective:

It is certainly to be expected that a great nation like England, which has done so much of her fighting on the high seas, should have a goodly store of sea songs. This, indeed, we have. Ships have changed from wood to iron, and every detail of the Service has been altered; yet, in default of better, the songs of Charles Dibdin and other scattered naval and patriotic lyrics of the last century will touch the same chord as they did when originally written, and will find as quick a response...Dibdin did not, however, monopolise the best naval song-writing of his time; there are many other songs of this period which will rank alongside the best of Dibdin's—from David Garrick's "Hearts of Oak" down to Allan Cunningham's "A Wet Sheet and a Flowing Sea," and among this number the vigorous song "The *Arethusa*" holds a prominent place.

    "The *Arethusa*" appeared originally in a small opera, or musical entertainment, entitled *The Lock and Key*, which was acted in 1796. The libretto was by Prince Hoare, author of the popular opera *No Song, No Supper*, and a water-colour painter of ability. He died in 1834. Prince Hoare was, presumably, author of the words of the song, but the fine and spirited air is in all modern collections put down as the composition of William Shield. This error I wish in the following paper to dispel. First, however, as to the song itself. It exactly chronicles an engagement which took place in the English Channel on the evening of June 17, 1778. The *Arethusa* was commanded by Captain Marshall...The song, from the time of its production in *The Lock and Key* down to our own day, never waned in its popularity. Charles Incledon's singing of it gave it great impetus in its first day. William Shield wrote and arranged the musical portion of *The Lock and Key*, and this is the reason why Shield's name has ever been associated with the air...Dr. Kitchiner, in his *Sea Songs*, 1823, prints Shield's name to the air, but his work contains other inaccuracies. As a matter of fact, the air is really a dance tune named "The Princess Royal"; and this again has been, I believe wrongly, attributed to an Irish origin as the composition of Carolan, the Irish bard...I have found the tune in three collections of this period, the first being a volume of Walsh's *Compleat Country Dancing Master*, c. 1730, [where it is titled "Princess Royal, The New Way"]. A comparison of the air will at once show that Shield had the good sense to refrain from tampering with so fine a melody when he used it for "The *Arethusa*." Another copy of the tune is found a little later in Wright's *Complete Collection of Celebrated Country Dances both old and new*, Vol. 1, oblong 8vo. Here it is entitled "New Princess Royal," and is identical with Walsh's...In several song books, issued about 1808 to 1810, in which "The Arethusa" is printed, florid additions are given to the air, but the [above], from an early music sheet, appears to be the original form.[68]

Similarly, in a subsequent article Kidson traced the melody of "The Campbells Are Coming" back to "Hob or Nob," a tune found in Walsh's *Caledonian Country Dances* of 1740.[69] He also argued that the tunes of certain well-known political songs and folksongs also derived from eighteenth-century printed sources; for instance, "With Henry Hunt We'll Go," "The Jolly Ploughman," and "The Nut Girl" were all, in his view, variations on a melody associated with a broadside popular during the American War of Independence, titled "The Brags of Washington."[70]

    "New Lights upon Old Tunes" revealed Kidson's fascination with such early eighteenth-century song collections as Thomas D'Urfey's *Pills to Purge Melancholy* and John Watts's *Musical Miscellany* (1729-31), and with the vogue for ballad operas that began with John Gay's *The Beggar's Opera*. From D'Urfey's *Pills*, for example, he reprinted tune and text (three verses this time) of "The Dame of Honour." He obviously felt an affinity with the songs of the early Georgian era, which he regarded as a golden age of English song writing, and he made the ballad operas of the 1720s and 1730s an object of special study. Significantly, he was just as interested in the 'composed' songs of the sixteenth, seventeenth and early eighteenth centuries as he was in the anonymous folksongs that happened to have been preserved in *Pills to Purge Melancholy*, in Watts's *Musical Miscellany*, and in the various ballad operas. Watts, he pointed out, was the only music publisher of the day to print the scores of these works, and in the thirty or so that he published were to be found in total over one thousand "old and named airs." Among them could be discovered the melodic originals of such vernacular songs as "Do You Ken John Peel?" (a dance tune titled "Red House"), and "The Miller of the Dee" (the tune was borrowed from "The Budgeon It Is a Fine Trade," a song in the 1730 ballad opera *Fashionable Lady*).[71]

    Kidson's fifth article in *The Musical Times* was devoted to "Airs in the Early Ballad Operas," and his basic thesis was that the scores of these early eighteenth-century productions were a treasure mine for a songhunter seeking traditional English melodies. This is an excerpt from his account of the phenomenon:

When, in 1727 (as Handel complained), *The Beggar's Opera* pelted the Italian opera off the stage with "Lumps of Pudding" its great success gave immediate birth to dozens of ballad operas founded upon its model. The principal point (musically) about the *Beggar's* and the other ballad operas was the employment of traditional or of other popular melodies for the songs, instead of, as in other periods, airs composed especially for the piece. The musical arranger had but to compose an overture, to add simple basses to the melodies, and his work was finished. The musical success of an opera treated thus was ensured, for the tunes were all familiar and each had passed safely the ordeal of public taste. From an antiquarian point of view this was a fortunate arrangement, inasmuch as many old and beautiful specimens of folk-melody are preserved to us which would otherwise have inevitably been lost. The *Beggar's Opera* is generally credited with having been the first constructed on these lines, but John Gay merely followed Allan Ramsay's lead in writing the songs to the old airs. Ramsay had already written and published his Scotch pastoral *The Gentle Shepherd* (the songs in which were set to old Scotch tunes), when (the year after), in 1726, Gay visited him in Edinburgh. There is a probability that Gay was guided by Ramsay's example or suggestion in this matter, and the credit of the invention of the ballad opera thus belongs to Scotland.

In the two or three years following, the stage was swamped with more or less weak imitations of Gay's work. Most of them are as dull and insipid as the original is bright and sparkling. If we may except the half-dozen or so by Fielding, the best written of these early ballad operas were by Charles Coffey, his most favourite one, having at the time a popularity almost as great as *The Beggar's [Opera]*, being *The Devil to Pay, or Wives Metamorphosed,* acted in 1731. This was an adaptation of a much earlier play, and had also many a hand in its ultimate concoction. The songs in this opera were retained in the public ear long after the piece itself had gone into the limbo of forgotten productions. Mrs. Clive as *Nell,* the cobbler's wife, in this opera, made her first step on the road to success. Charles Coffey wrote other ballad operas, but absolutely the first in imitation of *The Beggar's[Opera]* was *The Quaker's Opera* written by Thomas Walker, the original actor of Captain Macheath, and acted in 1728 at Lee and Harper's booth in Bartholomew Fair. Then followed *Momus Turned Fabulist, The Village Opera, The Beggar's Wedding, The Cobbler's Opera, Love in a Riddle,* all in 1729. The next three years brought forth many more. *Polly,* Gay's sequel to *The Beggar's Opera,* had been printed but not acted, and *Achilles* in 1733 was acted after his death. The collapse of the ballad opera came as suddenly as its rise, and after the last date we hear no more of it till 1762, when Isaac Bickerstaffe revived it in all its force with *Love in a Village,* and the ballad opera, in a modified form, lasted from then till our fathers' days.[72]

Having sketched the history of the ballad opera, Kidson argued that these musical dramas had preserved the traditional melodies for many old ballads, citing as examples "Death and the Lady," "The Bailiff's Daughter of Islington" and "The Oxfordshire Tragedy." He concluded that the operas had saved for posterity a "store of seventeenth and eighteenth century airs" that would otherwise have been lost, and therefore that possessing "a collection of these operas is essential to the student of national song."[73]

Like other examples of his journalism, Kidson's article on ballad operas was thus a manifesto for the kind of musical detective work at which he excelled and which his mentors, Joseph Ritson and William Chappell, had pioneered before him. It also implicitly challenged any attempt to draw a hard-and-fast line between folksongs and other vernacular songs by arguing that the "vital melodies" used for many seventeenth and eighteenth-century national songs had their roots in older, more traditional, tunes, often those associated with early English country dances. All vernacular songs with distinctive melodies were of interest to Kidson, and he believed that the interactions between the different strands within the broad corpus of English vernacular song were complex and often elusive. The relationships between oral tradition, broadside balladry, ballad operas, and commercial popular song, he believed, could only be elucidated by painstaking historical research, and it was highly probable that such research would reveal a complicated net of causal interplay. Folksong, for Kidson, was only part—although a very important part—of a much bigger musical picture.

Collecting, 1896-99

Perhaps because of his renewed focus on national songs and ballad operas, 1896 appears to have been a year in which Kidson did little collecting, but 14 January of that year was one occasion on which he got together with Alf Mooney of Liverpool and his wife Ethel. Mooney was a singer who had obtained some of his repertoire from the Irish community in the port city; he tended to favor Irish songs, comic songs, and shanties, and Kidson noted one of each genre from him: respectively, "Shule Agra," "The Peeler and the Goat" and "Poor Old Horse." But he also knew some English ballads and folk-lyrics, such as "The *Golden Vanity*," "I Will Tell You of a Fellow," and "The Banks of the Roses," while Ethel sang "Queen Mary" and "Down by a Riverside." "The Banks of the Roses" was one of the songs that Mooney had learned from an old Irishman in the streets of Liverpool, and it appears to have been one of the few ballads for which Kidson could not readily identify a broadside text, although he really liked the tune. These are the only words he had for the song:

On the banks of the roses
My love and I sat down,
He pulled out his German flute
And played a charming tune.

In the middle of his tune
Sure I sobbed and sighed and said
Darling Johnny, darling Johnny,
Do not leave me.[74]

The Banks of the Roses

Anon

Fig. 14.23

Kidson was always ready to spend time listening to Irish street singers, and on 30 July 1897 he came across one in the streets of Leeds. In October he also found an Irish street whistler. From both performers he noted tunes that the musicians called "The Shamrock Shore," and when writing to Lucy Broadwood the next January he gave her an account of these two collecting incidents. They provide an insight into his method of obtaining material:

> I have been wanting to send you an air I have picked up from an Irish street singer. I recognized it was old and fine although screamed at the top of his voice and I got him home after giving him a good dinner. I noted his tune down. The words were of the usual Irish street ballad type, and the tune he said he had learned from his father in Ireland many years ago. I think it is old and very beautiful being quite Irish in character. It is different to Dr. Joyce's "Shamrock Shore" though it bears the same title, also different to a sheet ballad I have. I got hold of another street performer some little time ago who whistled on a brass whistle exquisitely. He was whistling an old hornpipe which I knew. So I got him home and from him what I think is as pretty a set of "The Banks of Sweet Dundee" as I have heard. It is quite an Irish set of it, and I am confirmed in my original opinion that it is Irish. He called it, I fancy at haphazard, "The Shamrock Shore," perhaps because I had mentioned that air to him.[75]

Kidson not only enjoyed his encounters with street singers in Leeds and Liverpool, he also loved to find ballad sellers touting their wares, a phenomenon that was becoming much rarer than it had been in the past, although it still existed in late Victorian England. He was, of course, fascinated by the phenomenon of the broadside ballad, and, as we have seen, amassed a huge quantity of them in his personal collection. In 1896 he wrote for the *Leeds Express* a short piece on the subject of the street ballad. His perspective was interesting, and portions of the article bear quoting as a further illustration of his approach to vernacular song. He began by providing a general description of the genre and the colorful characters who scratched a living from selling broadsheets:

> The street ballad has disappeared, and the street balladist, of the type once common, is almost, if not quite, extinct. The reader need not be middle-aged to remember when an inevitable feature at feast and fair was a long stretch of canvas, on which hundreds of sheets of ballads were pinned, or hung over lines of string. And a brisk business used to be done in the sale of these at a half-penny each, or three sheets a penny. The head of some of the verses was adorned by a "cut," which, though it had but the remotest relevancy to the letterpress, seemed to stimulate the sale. These ballads were of all kinds—sentimental, amatory, humorous, pathetic, and comic, in striving for which latter quality decency was not infrequently sacrificed. Itinerant vendors of these productions used to do a good business by rambling through the poorer districts of towns, and chanting, in unmelodious tones, specimens of their wares. Especially brisk was the trade accomplished when a murder had been committed, or an execution had occurred, the "horful tragedy" minutely described in halting lines, or the "last dyin' speech an' confession" rendered into rhyme (often before they had been made) meeting with a rapid sale at increased prices. Sometimes these descendants of the troubadours would be represented by two or three melancholy-looking cripples in dilapidated sailor costume. If the wooden legs and white 'ducks' failed to carry conviction as to the genuineness of the 'tars,' the jack-knife slung across the hip, and the stiff, black, shiny hats (similar to the 'tomtits' now becoming popular with the ladies), put every doubt to flight, and one was almost compelled to believe that they had taken part in the naval battles of which they dolorously sang.[76]

He then discussed a handful of ballads that he regarded as typical of the genre but also of particular interest because of their subject matter or attitudes to life:

> There is a certain amount of curious interest in many of these forgotten ballads, and it will not be amiss to reproduce a few examples from a rare collection to which I have access. Some are so quaint and indecorous that quotation is out of the question, but others are not open to this objection. Such a one is the ballad of "Fair Phoebe and Her Dark-eye'd Sailor"... The Crafty Ploughboy" contains a tribute to Yorkshire acuteness. The composers of these effusions were great admirers of constancy of affection. Then they had an overpowering fondness for finishing off each verse with a repetition of a line which also furnishes the title. This is illustrated in "The Bonny Blue Handkerchief," amongst others—sometimes with grotesque effect...The dangers of bad company and poaching were urged in some of these ballads by metrical moralisings on the miseries of the convict settlements. "Botany Bay" has its key-note in the lines "I'll have you quit night-walking, or else you'll rue the day, When you are transported and going to Botany Bay." Then "Young Henry the Poacher" exposes "The fate of us poor transports as you shall understand, The hardships which we undergo upon Van Dieman's Land."...Quite in a different vein is "A Week's Matrimony," which relates, with more breadth than might be acceptable here, how the hero courted on Sunday, married on Monday, was jealous on Tuesday, fought with his wife on Wednesday, found her out on Thursday, was released by her suicide on Friday, got drunk for joy on the Saturday, the next day "saw her in the grave all right, And made love to another on Sunday night!" Even less capable of transcription is the artless candour of "The Bunch of Rushes, oh," of the whimsical freedom of such songs as "The Cunning Cobbler," "The Female Cabin Boy," and "The Indian Lass." But many quaint, entertaining, and not unpicturesque examples remain....[77]

Writing this piece re-stimulated Kidson's desire to collect as many broadside ballad tunes as he could before the opportunity to do so had completely disappeared. Early in 1897 he had arranged another collecting session with Kate Thompson, and it was on 8 January that he noted the racehorse song "Creeping Jane" from her. As mentioned earlier, Kidson had been noting songs episodically from the Knaresborough charwoman since the summer of 1891, and he obtained twenty-five songs in all. Indeed, apart from Charles Lolley, Kate was his most prolific source singer, and we have seen that she sang him several fine ballads, broadside and traditional, in 1892. That he greatly valued her as an informant is evident from a letter to Lucy Broadwood that he wrote on 19 January, in which he inquired whether Lucy knew "Creeping Jane," which he was convinced was a traditional air, although he already had the text on a broadsheet.

> Do you know a traditional song called "Creeping Jane," it is a description of a race in which the horse Creeping Jane wins at last. I have it on a ballad sheet, it is fairly old & I got the tune for the first time ever from our invaluable charwoman. The introduction of her grave tol de dol in a cadenza like manner is quite funny. I have the words on a ballad sheet.[78]

Unfortunately Kidson did not always note the details of his sessions with Kate, so some of her most interesting material is undated. Nor was he always able to obtain all the verses of a song, even when he wanted to. Two of her shorter folklyrics are a case in point. Kidson had no broadside texts for these songs so he was limited to noting down the fragments of the lyrics that Kate could remember. Here, for example, is "The Orange and the Blue," about which he remarked only "What this fragment means I don't know" and, unusually, had nothing to say about variants and other usages of the tune. It was one of those occasions when oral tradition produced something unexpected and somewhat mysterious.

> Green grows the laurel and so does the rue,
> Sorry was I when I parted from you,
> By our next meeting our sorrows will be o'er,
> And we will change the green willow
> From the orange and the blue.
>
> Often I have wondered why maids they love men,
> Oft have I wondered why men do love them,
> Tell him that you love him and set his mind at ease
> And we'll change the green willow
> From the orange and the blue.[79]

The Orange and the Blue

Anon

Voice

Fig. 14.24

Kidson, of course, valued the tune of "The Orange and the Blue," and much the same was true of another fragment that he picked up from Kate Thompson, titled "One Moonlight Night." This, too, had a pretty tune and a fragmentary lyric that might have derived from a broadside ballad, but Kidson was unsure which. He was fairly sure that both tune and text were old, and indeed he rather speculatively linked the song to a story by a medieval chronicler, commenting "I don't know whether there are any more of these verses but the story is that an appointment having been made by a lover with his sweetheart whom he had betrayed, she seeing two persons (one of whom was her sweetheart) digging a grave became suspicious and climbed a tree to watch. The story is said to be told by Matthew Paris."[80] The sexual metaphor in the one verse that Kate Thompson sang made it the kind of song that Kidson would in any case not have printed in full in the putative second volume of *Traditional Tunes*, but on this occasion no censorship seems to have been involved, unless on the part of Kate herself. This is the melody that Kidson noted from Kate Thompson's singing, followed by the lone extant verse:

One Moonlight Night

Anon

Voice

Fig. 14.25

One moonlight night as I sat high
I looked for one but two passed by
The boughs did bend & the leaves did shake
To see the hole the fox did make.[81]

When Kidson published *Traditional Tunes* he was already aware of the early work of Sabine Baring-Gould and possessed a copy of the first edition of *Songs and Ballads of the West*. It influenced his choice of material for the book because he decided, as far as possible, to avoid duplication of songs, especially where the melodies were similar. For example, he omitted "The Trees They Do Grow High" although he had apparently already collected Yorkshire versions from both Charley Dickenson and Kate Thompson. He also had a broadside text for it. He apparently only wrote down one verse of the ballad as Kate sang it but he did note her tune:

Oh father dear father I'm afraid you have done wrong,
You've married me to a college boy,
His age it is too young,
For his age is [but sixteen] twenty four
And the fairest of it is
That my bonny lad is young
But he's growing.
Oh! my bonny lad is young
But he's growing.[82]

My Bonny Lad Is Young But He's Growing

Anon

Fig. 14.26

Kidson knew that the same ballad was extant in Scottish oral tradition, and that it had been included in both Johnson's *Scots Musical Museum* and Maidment's *North Countrie Garland* of 1824. He jotted down in his notebook that "Baring-Gould has a copy of the song taken from a Devonshire singer. His air, though in 6/8 time, bears a very slight resemblance to the Yorkshire air. The song in various forms seems to have been much printed on ballad sheets all over the country." This was clearly a strong candidate for inclusion in the second volume of *Traditional Tunes*, and Kidson included in his fair copy notebook a broadside version printed by H. Such. A very similar, but slightly different and apparently somewhat older, broadside version, titled "My Bonny Boy Is Young But He's Growing," can also be found in his *Folio Collection of Broadsides*, but he may have obtained that later.[83] This is the Such version that he apparently intended to reprint with Kate Thompson's tune:

O the trees that do grow high, and the leaves that do grow green,
The days are gone and past, my love, that you and I have seen,
On a cold winter's night when you and I alone have been,
My bonny lad he's young but he's growing.

O father, dear father, you to me much harm have done,
You married me to a boy, you know he is too young,
O daughter dear, if you will wait you'll quickly have a son,
And a lady you'll be while he's growing.

I will send him to the college for one year or two,
And perhaps in that time, my love, he then may do for you,
We'll buy him some nice ribbons to tie round his bonny
                                                                waist too,

And let the ladies know he is married.

She went to the college and looked over the wall,
Saw four-and-twenty gentlemen playing there at ball,
They would not let her go through, for her true love
                                                                she did call,
Because he was a young man growing.

At the age of sixteen, oh, he was a married man,
At the age of seventeen she brought him forth a son,
At the age of eighteen the grass did grow over his
                                                                gravestone,
Cruel death put an end to his growing.

I will make my love a shroud of the fine Holland brown,
And all the time I'm making it the tears they shall run down,
Saying, once I had a sweetheart but now I have got none,
Farewell to thee my bonny lad for evermore.

O now my love is dead and in his grave doth lie,
The green grass grows over him so very high,
There I can sit and mourn until the day I die,
But I'll watch o'er his child while he's growing.[84]

Kidson's session with Kate Thompson in 1897 appear to have been the last time he collected from her, and by this time too he appears to have ceased his active collaboration with Charles Lolley. At some point, perhaps when he quit playing his fiddle, Lolley gave Kidson his personal tunebook, which added over a hundred items to the latter's collection. Most, but not all, were instrumental pieces, but Lolley was obviously fond of playing certain airs associated with songs, such as "The Bold Dragoon," "Gee Ho Dobbin," "Green Grow the Rushes O," "My Lodging It Is On the Cold Ground," and "Ye Banks and Braes." One of his favorites was "The Cuckoo."[85]

The Cuckoo

Anon

Fig. 14.27

Although the tune is not exactly the same, this is identifiably the same song as that printed by William Barrett in *English Folk-Songs* (see chapter 10). Kidson's field notebook contains another version of the same song.

The cuckoo is a bonny bird,
He sings as he flies,

He brings us good tidings
And tells us no lies. [86]

The Cuckoo

Anon

Fig. 14.28

He had noted this melody and fragment of the lyric from a young Leeds informant named Miss Mary Riley, who also sang him a children's game song ("Sally Walker") and a sea song titled "Jolly Sailor Boys."

There is no datable collecting in Kidson's tunebooks that can be pinned to 1898, although we know that in May 1899 he noted an "Irish Air" with Gaelic words from an Irish informant named Frank Kelly, and that he also obtained at least two of the items in Alf Mooney's repertoire that year, namely "Poor Old Horse" and "I Will Tell You of a Fellow." The item that may have pleased him most was a version of the traditional ballad "Lord Bateman." We have seen in chapters 5 and 10 that the ballad was extant in oral tradition in Shropshire (as collected by Charlotte Burne and reproduced in *Shropshire Folk-Lore*) and, at least earlier in the century, in Sussex (as noted by John Broadwood and reprinted by Lucy Broadwood in *Sussex Songs*). Kidson's variant was noted from an unnamed Shropshire woman on 5 January (she had learned it as a child in Shrewsbury). The tune is closely related to Burne's melody, although not identical. The texts are in the main very similar, except that this version, derived no doubt from a broadside, has six more verses:

Lord Bateman

Anon

Fig. 14.29

Lord Bateman was a noble Lord,
A noble Lord of high degree,
He shipped himself on board a ship,
Some foreign Country he would go see.

He sailed east and he sailed west,
Until he came to fair Turkey,
Where he was taken and put in prison,
Until his life was quite weary.

And in this prison there grew a tree,

It grew so stout and it grew so strong,
Where he was chained by his middle,
Until his life was almost gone.

The Turk he had an only daughter,
The fairest creature ever my eyes did see,
She stole the keys of her father's prison,
And swore Lord Bateman she would set free!

Have you got houses, have you got lands,
Or does Northumberland belong to thee?

What would you give to the fair young lady
That out of prison would set you free?"

"I have got houses, I have got lands,
And half Northumberland belongs to me,
I'll give it all to the fair young lady,
That out of prison would set me free.

O then she took him to her father's palace,
And gave to him the best of wine,
And every health she drank unto him,
I wish Lord Bateman that you were mine.

Now for seven long years I'll make a vow,
For seven long years and keep it strong,
If you will wed no other woman,
That I will wed no other man.

O then she took me to her father's harbour,
And gave to me a ship of fame,
Farewell, farewell, my dear Lord Bateman,
I'm afraid I shall never see you again.

Now seven long years were gone and past,
And fourteen long days well known to me,
She packed up her gay clothing,
And Lord Bateman she would go see.

And when she came to Lord Bateman's castle,
So boldly now she rang the bell,
Who's there?" cried the young porter,
Who's there?—now come unto me tell.

O is this Lord Bateman's castle,
Or is his Lordship here within,
O yes, O yes, cried the proud young porter,
He's just taking his young bride in.

Oh then tell him to send me a slice of bread
And a bottle of the best wine,
And not forgetting the fair young lady,
That did release him when close confined.

Away away went that proud young porter,
Away away and away went he,
Until he came to Lord Bateman's door,
Down on his bended knees fell he.

What news, what news, my young porter,
What news have you brought unto me?
There is the fairest of all young ladies,
That ever my two eyes did see.

She has got rings on every finger,
And round one of them she has got three,
And such gay gold hanging round her middle
As would buy Northumberland for thee.

She tells you to send her a slice of bread,
And a bottle of the best wine,
And not forgetting the fair young lady,
That did release you when close confined.

Lord Bateman then in a passion flew,
And broke his sword in splinters three,
Saying, I will give all my father's riches,
If that Sophia has crossed the sea.

Then up spoke this young bride's mother,
Who never was heard to speak so free,
You'll not forget my only daughter,
If Sophia has crossed the sea.

I own I made a bride of your daughter,
She's neither the better nor worse for me,
She came to me with her horse and saddle,
She may go home in her coach and three.

Lord Bateman prepared another marriage,
With both their hearts so full of glee,
I'll range no more in foreign countries,
Now since Sophia has cross'd the sea.[87]

About this Kidson commented in his notebook: "Words practically the same as ordinary ballad sheet, except 'proud Turkey' for 'fair Turkey' in second verse, as Miss Jackson also sings it." This was a reference to the version of the same ballad that he had previously noted from Sarah Jackson, but Kidson had not been very satisfied with Sarah's rendition, commenting that it was "a particularly poor sung Lord Bateman." He remarked that he had recently come across another fine version of the song in a printed source: "In addition to the versions of airs set to this ballad and named in *Traditional Tunes* may be added a very good tune in the late Mr. Crawhall's book *Olde Tayles Newly Related.* The tune there given is doubtless a traditional Northumbrian setting of an air but it is written down (musically speaking) in an impossible manner."[88]

Kidson did continue to do a small amount of collecting in the 1900s, but by then he was one of the stalwarts of the recently formed *Folk-Song Society*, and this last episode in the history of the late Victorian revival will be treated in chapter 16. In the same letter to Lucy Broadwood in which he mentioned collecting "Creeping Jane" from Kate Thompson he also mentioned the major project that increasingly consumed his time and energy in the last years of the 1890s. "I have been working," he explained, "on a list of old London musical publishers from about Playford's time downwards to about 1825. Giving the various dates and changes of addresses already I have found what I have got together a great service in fixing the dates of sheets and books of music. I have been limited mostly to my own library and odd memoranda which I have from time to time made. It is now pretty well arranged & if it would interest you or perhaps would like to look it over I would send it...”[89] Whether he did in fact send Lucy the draft version of this reference book is uncertain, but the results of his research were published in 1900 as *British Music Publishers, Printers, and Engravers: London, Provincial, Scottish and Irish: From Queen Elizabeth's Reign to George the Fourth's*.[90] And, as we shall see in chapter 15, he had also been compiling, with his musician friend Alfred Moffat, a large collection of national songs titled *The Minstrelsy of England*.[91] In his fascination with vernacular songs that had their origins in the commercial popular music industry of the sixteenth, seventeenth, and eighteenth centuries Kidson was by the late 1890s less of a maverick. He would soon take part in a revival of English national song—composed songs as well as folksongs—that he had helped to stimulate. In the next chapter we shall see how such 'national songs' again caught the attention of the music publishing industry and English art music circles of the time. They would continue to play a significant, if controversial, role in the first folksong revival.

Notes

1. Frank Kidson, "Notes on Old Tunes," thirty-two articles published in the *Leeds Mercury Weekly Supplement* between 6 November 1886 and 25 June 1887.

2. Frank Kidson, "Old Songs and Airs: Melodies Once Popular in Yorkshire," thirty-two articles published in the *Leeds Mercury Weekly Supplement* between 4 January 1890 and May or June 1891 [the exact date of the last article is not indicated on the clipping held in the Lucy Broadwood collection at the Surrey History Centre, Woking].

3. Frank Kidson, "Old Songs and Airs: Melodies Once Popular in Yorkshire, I," *Leeds Mercury Weekly Supplement*, 4 January 1890.

4. Frank Kidson, "Old Songs and Airs: Melodies Once Popular in Yorkshire, III: 'The Crafty Ploughboy,'" *Leeds Mercury Weekly Supplement*, 25 January 1890.

5. Frank Kidson, "Old Songs and Airs: Melodies Once Popular in Yorkshire, II: 'The Lass of Humberside,'" *Leeds Mercury Weekly Supplement*, 11 January 1890.

6. Frank Kidson, "Old Songs and Airs: Melodies Once Popular in Yorkshire, VI: 'The Noble Fisherman, or Robin Hood's Preferment,'" *Leeds Mercury Weekly Supplement*, 1 March 1890.

7. Frank Kidson, "Old Songs and Airs: Melodies Once Popular in Yorkshire, XXV: 'Twas Down in Cupid's Garden,'" *Leeds Mercury Weekly Supplement*, 18 October 1890.

8. Frank Kidson, "Old Songs and Airs: Melodies Once Popular in Yorkshire, XV: 'Nancy Dawson,'" *Leeds Mercury Weekly Supplement*, 7 June 1890.

9. On Frank Kidson's later collecting, see Roy Palmer, "Kidson's Collecting," *Folk Music Journal* 5, no. 2 (1986):150-75; Roy Palmer, ed., *Checklist of Manuscript Songs and Tunes collected from Oral Tradition by Frank Kidson* (Glasgow & London: Mitchell Library & EFDSS, 1986); Ray Cowell, "Kidson's Informants," *Folk Music Journal* 5, no. 4 (1988): 482-88.

10. See especially "Songs from the Collection of Mr. Frank Kidson," *Journal of the Folk-Song Society* 1, no. 5 (1904): 228-57.

11. Frank Kidson and Alfred Moffat, eds., *A Garland of English Folksongs* (London: Ascherberg, Hopwood & Crew, [1926)].

12. Frank Kidson and Alfred Moffat, eds., *Folk Songs from the North Countrie, with their Traditional Airs* (London: Ascherberg, Hopwood & Crew, 1927).

13. Frank Kidson, Ethel Kidson, and Alfred Moffat, eds., *English Peasant Songs, with their Traditional Airs* (London: Ascherberg, Hopwood & Crew, 1929).

14. Frank Kidson, *Folio Collection of Broadsheets*, Vols. 1-10. Unpublished bound volumes in Frank Kidson Collection, Mitchell Library, Glasgow.

15. Frank Kidson, "Traditional Tunes, collected by Frank Kidson, Leeds," manuscript tune book (M.18058), 1, in Frank Kidson Collection, Mitchell Library, Glasgow.

16. Kidson, manuscript tune book (M.18058), 12-13.

17. Frank Kidson *Folio Collection of Broadsheets*, 2: 42. No broadside publisher indicated.

18. Kidson, manuscript tune book (M.18058), 22; also Frank Kidson, "Traditional Tunes, c. 1903," fair copy manuscript tune book (M. 18057), 6a.

19. Kidson, *Folio Collection of Broadsheets*, 5: 84. No broadside publisher indicated. Kidson also collected two broadside versions of a related ballad, "Young Riley," *Folio Collection of Broadsides*, 7: 119 & 7: 181. These were published by H. Such and J. Catnach (London) respectively.

20. Kidson, manuscript tune book (M.18058), 21.

21. Kidson, manuscript tune book (M.18058), 20.

22. Kidson possessed four broadsheets of "The Banks of Sweet Primroses," *Folio Collection of Broadsides*, 5: 66; 6: 105; 7: 150; and 9: 248. They were printed respectively by W. S. Fortey (London), Taylor (n.l.), H. P. Such (London), and J. Cadman (Manchester).

23. Kidson, manuscript tune book (M.18058), 28.

24. Kidson, *Folio Collection of Broadsheets*, 2: 73. No broadside publisher indicated.

25. Kidson, manuscript tune book (M.18058), 17.

26. Kidson, *Folio Collection of Broadsheets*, 4:32. No broadside publisher indicated on the broadsheet, but a penciled note by Kidson states "bought at Bolton, Lancashire."

27. "Songs Collected by Frank Kidson," *Journal of the Folk-Song Society* 2, no. 9 (1906): 288-89.

28. Kidson, manuscript tune book (M.18058), 17.

29. Kidson, *Folio Collection of Broadsheets*, 6: 36. Broadsheet published by H. P. Such (London).

30. Kidson, manuscript tune book (M.18058), 16; fair copy manuscript tune book (M.18057), 1.

31. Kidson, manuscript tune book (M.18058), 2, 35, and 39.

32. Kidson, *Folio Collection of Broadsheets*, 3: 33. Broadsheet published by John O. Bebbington of Manchester. Also *Folio Collection of Broadsheets*, 6: 87. Broadsheet published by H. P. Such (London), with a different text for the last verse.

33. Lucy Broadwood, diary entries for 16 and 18 January 1892. Broadwood Collection, Surrey History Centre, Woking, U.K.: LEB 6782.

34. Lucy Broadwood, diary entry for 22 February 1893. Broadwood Collection, Surrey History Centre, Woking, U.K.: LEB 6782.

35. Frank Kidson to Lucy Broadwood, 14 May 1893, Lucy Broadwood Collection, Vaughan Williams Memorial Library, Cecil Sharp House, Camden Town, London, U.K.: LEB/4/100.

36. Frank Kidson to Lucy Broadwood, 14 May 1893, Lucy Broadwood Collection, Vaughan Williams Memorial Library, Cecil Sharp House, Camden Town, London, U.K.: LEB/4/100.

37. There is no indication in the manuscript whether this Mrs. Lolley was Charles Lolley's wife or his mother but on other occasions Lolley did obtain material from his mother.

38. Kidson, manuscript tune book (M.18058), 37.

39. Kidson, manuscript tune book (M.18058), 3 and 7.

40. "Songs Collected by Frank Kidson," *Journal of the Folk-Song Society* 2, no. 9 (1906): 282.

41. Kidson, *Folio Collection of Broadsheets*, 7: 95. No broadside publisher indicated on the broadsheet.

42. J. Collingwood Bruce and John Stokoe, eds., *Northumbrian Minstrelsy: A Collection of the Ballads, Melodies, and Small-Pipe Tunes of Northumbria* (Newcastle-upon-Tyne: Society of Antiquaries of Newcastle-upon-Tyne, 1882. Reprinted, with a foreword by A. L. Lloyd: Hatboro, Pennsylvania: Folklore Associates, 1965), 48-50. See chapter 4, where it is reprinted.

43. Kidson, manuscript tune book (M.18058), 26.

44. Kidson, *Folio Collection of Broadsheets*, 3: 97. Published by R. Barr (Leeds). The broadside title was "Fair Phoebe and The Dark-eye'd Sailor."

45. Kidson, manuscript tune book (M.18058), 18.

46. Kidson, *Folio Collection of Broadsheets*, 5: 129.

47. Kidson, *Folio Collection of Broadsheets*, 5: 129. Published by H. P. Such (London).

48. Kidson, manuscript tune book (M.18058), 40.

49. Kidson, manuscript tune book (M.18058), 40.

50. Kidson, fair copy manuscript tune book (M.18057), 66.

51. Kidson, fair copy manuscript tune book (M.18057), 67.

52. Kidson, *Folio Collection of Broadsheets*, 5: 128. Broadsheet published by W. Forth (Hull).

53. Kidson, manuscript tune book (M.18058), 45.

54. Kidson, manuscript tune book (M.18058), 44.

55. Kidson, *Folio Collection of Broadsheets*, 9: 322. No publisher indicated.

56. Kidson, manuscript tune book (M.18058), 49.

57. Kidson, *Folio Collection of Broadsheets*, 10: 175. Broadsheet published by H. Andrews (Leeds).

58. Kidson, manuscript tune book (M.18058), 51.

59. Kidson, *Folio Collection of Broadsheets*, 1: 6. Broadsheet published by W. Fortey (London).

60. Kidson, manuscript tune book (M.18058), 22.

61. Frank Kidson, "Sir Hugh of Lincoln," in "Local Notes and Queries," *Leeds Mercury Weekly Supplement*, 20 October 1894.

62. Kidson, "Sir Hugh."

63. Kidson, "Sir Hugh." Not surprisingly, Kidson would have his reservations about the truth of Cecil Sharp's Darwinian theory of the evolution of folksong as elaborated in the latter's *English Folk Song: Some Conclusions* (Taunton, U.K.: Barnicott and Pearce, 1907).

64. Frank Kidson, "Tom Bowling," *Leeds Mercury Weekly Supplement,* 26 September 1896.

65. Kidson, "Tom Bowling."

66. Frank Kidson, "New Lights upon Old Tunes," eight articles, *Musical Times,* 1 October 1894, 1 February 1895, 1 May 1895, 1 September 1895, 1 June 1896, 1 July or 1 August 1896, 1 September 1896, and 1 August 1897.

67. Frank Kidson, "New Lights upon Old Tunes—'The *Arethusa*,'" *Musical Times* (1 October 1894): 666-68.

68. Kidson, "New Lights—'The *Arethusa*.'"

69. Frank Kidson, "New Lights upon Old Tunes, No. VIII: 'The Campbells Are Coming,'" *Musical Times* (1 August 1897): 521-22.

70. Frank Kidson, "New Lights upon Old Tunes, No. III: The Evolution of a Tune: 'The Low-backed Car,'" *Musical Times* (1 May 1895): 301-3.

71. Frank Kidson, "New Lights upon Old Tunes, No. V: Airs in the Early Ballad Operas," *Musical Times* (1 June 1896): 378-79.

72. Frank Kidson, "New Lights, No. V," 378-79.

73. Frank Kidson, "New Lights, No. V," 378-79.

74. Kidson, field notebook (M.18058), 51.

75. Frank Kidson to Lucy Broadwood, 9 January 1898. Lucy Broadwood Collection, Vaughan Williams Memorial Library, Cecil Sharp House, Camden Town, London, U.K.: LEB/4/95.

76. Frank Kidson, "Street Ballads," *Leeds Express,* 16 January 1896.

77. Kidson, "Street Ballads."

78. Frank Kidson to Lucy Broadwood, 19 January 1897. Lucy Broadwood Collection, Vaughan Williams Memorial Library, Cecil Sharp House, Camden Town, London, U.K.: LEB/4/111.

79. Kidson, manuscript tune book (M.18058), 19.

80. Kidson, fair copy manuscript tune book (M.18057), 5.

81. Kidson, manuscript tune book (M.18058), 21.

82. Kidson, manuscript tune book (M.18058), 47; fair copy manuscript tune book (M.18057), 37 and 40.

83. Kidson, *Folio Collection of Broadsheets,* 1: 7. No publisher indicated.

84. Kidson, fair copy manuscript tune book (M.18057), 37 and 40.

85. Charles Lolley, manuscript tune book (M.18109), 51.

86. Kidson, manuscript tune book (M.18058), 45.

87. Kidson, manuscript tune book (M.18058), 60.

88. Kidson, fair copy manuscript tune book (M.18057), 58-59. Kidson's first comment is on p. 58 and the second is on p. 59. The broadside text of the ballad is interleaved between these two pages.

89. Frank Kidson to Lucy Broadwood, 19 January 1897. Lucy Broadwood Collection, Vaughan Williams Memorial Library, Cecil Sharp House, Camden Town, London, U.K.: LEB/4/111.

90. Frank Kidson, *British Music Publishers, Printers, and Engravers: London, Provincial, Scottish and Irish: From Queen Elizabeth's Reign to George the Fourth's* (London: W. E. Hill, 1900).

91. Frank Kidson and Alfred Moffat, eds., *The Minstrelsy of England: a collection of 200 English songs with their melodies, popular from the 16th century to the middle of the 18th century* (London: Bailey & Ferguson, 1901).

15

National Song as Minstrelsy

There was a brief lull after the burst of renewed interest in national song in the early 1890s, but the burgeoning folksong movement took up the subject again at mid-decade. Boulton and Somervell's view of national song as vernacular song (including folksong) was one that sat easily with several of the leading late Victorian folksong collectors, including Lucy Broadwood, Fuller Maitland, Kidson, and Baring-Gould. The last-named had begun by asserting the value and distinctiveness of West Country folksong when compared with the productions of both ballad-mongers and commercial songsmiths, but by the middle of the 1890s he had come to modify his views significantly. Although he still championed the superiority of the folk airs that he had noted down from his Devonian and Cornish informants, he had lost his disdain for other kinds of vernacular song. He now had much more time for broadside ballads (he was amassing his own large collection of them), and he was exploring the large corpus of "old English songs" (his term) that could be found in old printed (and manuscript) sources. In short, like Frank Kidson, he was now treading in the footsteps of William Chappell. This partial change of heart would be evident in his next major undertaking, which was designed to bring together both currents in the river of national song.

Baring-Gould's *English Minstrelsie*

The increasing vogue for old 'composed' songs, together with the commercial success of *Songs and Ballads of the West* and *A Garland of Country Song*, encouraged Baring-Gould to attempt a third, even more ambitious, project. This was *English Minstrelsie: A National Monument of English Song*, an eight-volume work that appeared between 1895 and 1898.[1] *English Minstrelsie* was not primarily a folksong collection, although it included many folksongs. Rather it was an attempt to supplement (or perhaps supplant) Chappell's *Popular Music of the Olden Time*, which had been republished in a new edition, revised by H. Ellis Wooldridge, under the title *Old English Popular Music*.[2] Wooldridge had truncated Chappell's sprawling *opus*, omitting most of the traditional songs, an editorial decision that infuriated Baring-Gould, who admired Chappell's work, notwithstanding his belief that it contained relatively few genuine folksongs. In this opinion he was at one with Frank Kidson who regarded Wooldridge's edition as a travesty of the original. Baring-Gould commented:

> The highest honour is due to the late Mr. William Chappell for his labours in the field of old English Music, of which "The Popular Music of Olden Time," 1855, is a *monumentum aere perennius*. But this work took little account of the living traditional song of the people, and the Editor of the new edition (1894) has excluded from the work all the traditional airs not found in print. Consequently this work is a monument erected over the corpses of dead melodies, which indeed it enshrines and preserves. It in no way represents the living music of the English people...As a National Monument of English Song, it seems only just that the music of all classes should be included in this work [i.e., in *English Minstrelsie*], that it should not confine itself to such songs as have been written for the harpsichord and the piano, by skilled musicians, but should include also the lark and thrush and blackbird song of the ploughman, the thrasher, and the milkmaid; that it should give songs as dear to their hearts as are "Cherry Ripe," "The Wolf," and "Love's Ritornella" to the gentlemen and ladies in the drawing-room...The English labourer is now an important factor in politics; that he has been a factor in

461

English music has not been recognised as it ought. Of the freshness and sweetness of our English folk-airs one cannot speak too highly, and the time has now come when the music of the ploughboy demands to be recognised as an integral portion of our "English Minstrelsy," just as his opinion demands a hearing in all that concerns our commonwealth.[3]

Baring-Gould evidently appreciated the significance of Joseph Chamberlain's successful campaign to extend manhood suffrage to the English countryside, a campaign that had contributed to the passing of the Reform Act of 1884. He was also much readier to recognize William Chappell's achievements than he had been when he wrote the introduction to *A Garland of Country Song*. This may seem a sudden *volte face*, but in fact Baring-Gould was still drawing a sharp distinction between two kinds of English vernacular songs: on the one hand, anonymous traditional ballads and folk lyrics that he believed to have been created by the unlettered rural dwellers of past centuries, and, on the other, the most enduring products of educated songsmiths from the upper and middle classes, many of whom were professional writers, musicians, or both. He recognized that the lyrics of some of the former sometimes turned up on broadsheets, and that the authors of the latter were not always known by name, but he firmly believed that there were basically two kinds of English vernacular songs, namely folksongs and national songs, in addition to art songs and the more ephemeral products of the pleasure gardens and music halls. *English Minstrelsie* was intended to draw upon both musical streams, but throughout the work he tried conscientiously to distinguish between them, labeling certain songs "folk songs" and for the others providing information on the lyric writer and the composer of the tune. Where a national song was anonymous he labeled it as an "old English Song" or an "old air," as opposed to a "folk song" or "folk air."

Given Baring-Gould's eloquent plea for greater democracy in music as well as politics, one might have expected *English Minstrelsie* to give equal representation to rural workers' songs. In fact, of the 347 songs in the work, less than seventy were folksongs. Baring-Gould's conservative count was 25; mine is 63, but any figure is arbitrary, depending on which way one classifies various marginal items. I am more inclined to count as folksongs most anonymous vernacular songs that have been found in oral tradition, irrespective of their origins. For example, "The Vicar of Bray," "Oh Dear, What Can the Matter Be?" and "The Garden Gate" are just three examples of composed songs that nonetheless became part of oral tradition. They are—or were—undoubtedly vernacular songs, but perhaps not folksongs. Baring-Gould did not reckon them as such. Furthermore it is arguable whether the thirteen traditional tunes for which Baring-Gould or Sheppard wrote completely new words should still count as folksongs, even if the original songs obviously were folksongs and their tunes classified as "folk airs." Incidentally, ten other traditional songs were significantly modified or truncated by Baring-Gould, leaving a total of only forty folksongs or other vernacular and anonymous "old English" songs that appear to have been printed unaltered in *English Minstrelsie*. So, however one classifies the songs, the reality was less impressive than the claim made in Baring-Gould's introductory essay. Folksongs were a long way from receiving parity with composed songs.

All the same, *English Minstrelsie* did print several more of the folksongs that Baring-Gould and his collaborators had collected in Devon and Cornwall. And there were a few other songs, borrowed from earlier printed works, that were also deemed to be folksongs. Yet only four items in Volume 1 were classified by the editors as folksongs: "When Once I Was a Shepherd Boy," "As Dolly Sat Milking Her Cow," "Lubin's Rural Cot," and "The Farmer's Boy." In his notes to the last-named song Baring-Gould commented:

> One of the most popular and widely-known folk-songs in England. It would be hard to find an old labourer who has not heard it...Mr Kidson gives four versions as acquired in Yorkshire. The words were printed by Bell in his "Songs of the English Peasantry...." An interesting circumstance may be mentioned in connection with this song. Not then knowing the traditional air, Mr. Sheppard set it to one of his own, and very delightful it was. Some twelve years ago, I sang this at a village concert, when an old labourer stood up, and saying to those near him, "He's got the words right, but the tune be all wrong—I b'ain't going to listen to old songs spoiled wi' new-fangled moosic," he left the room. This was what first drew my attention to the fact that there was extant, among our peasantry, a body of folk-melody that had never been collected.[4]

Baring-Gould's version of "The Farmer's Boy" is quite similar to that given earlier from Kidson's *Traditional Tunes*, so there is no need to reprint it here. Two other folksongs, "Marigold Lane" and "A Damsel Possessed of Great Beauty," were thoroughly rewritten by the editors but retained the original tunes of the folksongs on which they were loosely based.

Other vernacular songs that might be counted as folksongs included "Come Lasses and Lads," and a very truncated version of "The Bailiff's Daughter of Islington." The anonymous old English songs included "Charming Phyllis," "Take a Bumper and Try," "Sweet Nellie, My Heart's Delight," and the very popular "The Vicar of Bray." Although it had obviously been composed by a witty and sophisticated songsmith, the ballad was anonymous.

The Vicar of Bray

Anon

Fig. 15.1

In good King Charles's golden days, when loyalty no harm meant,
A zealous High Church man I was, and so I got preferment;
To teach my flock I never miss'd, kings were by God appointed,
And damned are those that do resist, or touch the Lord's Anointed.
And this is law I will maintain until my dying day, sir.
That whatsoever king may reign, still I'll be the vicar of Bray, sir.

When Royal James obtain'd the crown, and popery came in fashion,
The penal laws I hooted down, and read the Declaration:
The church of Rome I found would fit full well my constitution;
And had become a Jesuit, but for the Revolution.
And this is law I will maintain, &c.

When William was our King declar'd, to ease the nation's grievance;
With this new wind about I steer'd, and swore to him allegiance;
Old principles I did revoke, set conscience at a distance;
Passive obedience was a joke, a jest was non-resistance.
And this is law I will maintain, &c.

When gracious Anne became our queen, the Church of England's glory,

Another face of things was seen, and I became a Tory:
Occasional conformists base, I damn'd their moderation;
And thought the Church in danger was, by such prevarication.
And this is law I will maintain, &c.

When George in pudding-time came o'er, and moderate men look'd big, sir,
I turn'd a cat-in-pan once more, and so became a Whig, sir,
And thus preferment I procur'd from our new faith's defender;
And almost ev'ry day abjur'd the Pope and the Pretender.
And this is law I will maintain, &c.

Th' illustrious house of Hanover, and Protestant succession;
To these I do allegiance swear—while they can keep possession:
For in my faith and loyalty, I never more will falter,
And George my lawful king shall be—until the times do alter.
And this is law I will maintain, &c.[5]

Other national songs included in this volume were by known songwriters. "Down among the Dead Men" is an example of a vernacular song dating from the mid-seventeenth century. It was a Cavalier drinking song written by John Dyer, and it maintained its popularity into the Victorian era, when the gender of the monarch referenced in the lyric had to be changed. Baring-Gould made the appropriate modification, but here is the original:

Down Among the Dead Men

John Dyer

Fig. 15.2

Here's a health to the King and a lasting peace,
To faction an end, to wealth increase,

Come let us drink it while we have breath,
For there's no drinking after death.
And he that will this health deny,
Down among the dead men, down among the dead men,
Down among the dead men, down, down, down, down,
Down among the dead men let him lie.

Let charming beauty's health go round,
In whom celestial joys are found;
And may confusion still pursue
The senseless woman-hating crew;
And they that will this health deny,
Down among the dead men, etc.
Down among the dead men let them lie.

May love and wine their rites maintain,
And their united pleasures reign!
While Bacchus' treasure crowns the board,
We'll sing the joys that both afford!
And they that won't with us comply,
Down among the dead men, etc.
Down among the dead men let them lie.[6]

Vernacular songs with disputed authors included "Pastime With Good Company," which was confidently attributed by Baring-Gould to King Henry VIII, and "The Northern Lass," ascribed to William Fisher of Hereford. The national anthem "God Save the Queen" was another difficult case, but Baring-Gould provided a detailed explanation of why he attributed the tune to John Bull and the words to Henry Carey. National songs with firmly identified authors included (among others) "Amo Amas" (John O'Keefe and Samuel Arnold), "Come, If You Dare" (John Dryden and Henry Purcell), "Here's to the Maiden of Bashful Fifteen," (Richard Sheridan), "Where the Bee Sucks" (Thomas Arne's setting of Ariel's song in *The Tempest*), "Cherry Ripe" (words by Robert Herrick and music by Charles E. Horn), "I Went to the Fair" (John Whitaker), "I Am a Friar of Orders Grey" (John O'Keefe and William Reeve), "Listen to the Voice of Love" (James Hook), "The Wolf" (John O'Keefe and William Shield), "Poor Jack" (Charles Dibdin), "The Bay of Biscay" (Andrew Cherry and John Davy), and "The Garden Gate" (W. Upton and W.T. Parke). About the last of these Baring-Gould commented:

Bell included this song in his "Songs and Ballads of the English Peasantry," not knowing its origin. He says of it: "One of the most pleasing ditties. The air is very beautiful. We first heard it sung in Malham dale, Yorkshire, by Willy Bolton, an old Dales' minstrel, who accompanied himself on the union-pipes." The song was published in 1809. Mr. Bell heard it sung in Yorkshire, somewhere about 1856-60; so that the song took half a century to be, so to speak, naturalized among the Yorkshire peasantry. I myself have heard it sung by a little blacksmith who goes by the nickname of "Ginger Jack," and from whom I have taken down a great many songs, new and old. Mr. Sheppard also noted it down from a crippled stone-breaker, whose memory was richly furnished with old songs. Alas! the dear old man, for whom I had a particular regard, is dead. He was found stiff in a ditch one bitter winter night. That the song became popular is shown by its having descended to the condition of broadside. As such it was issued by Catnach, Pitts, Fortey, Such, etc. Moreover, an "Answer to his Garden Gate," that is to say, a sequel, was published by the broadside ballad printers.[7]

The blacksmith was John Woodrich, and the crippled stone-breaker Robert Hard. As for the song, the tune was better than the lyrics, and Baring-Gould was perhaps correct to reject Robert Bell's classification of it as a folksong, although it certainly seems to have become a vernacular song, given its longevity and provenance.

The day was clos'd, the moon shone bright,
The village clock struck eight,
When Lucy hastened with delight
To ope the garden gate;
But sure as if to drive her mad,
The gate was there but not the lad,
Which made poor Lucy grieving cry,
"Was ever maid so us'd as I?"

She pac'd the garden here and there,
The village clock struck nine;
When Lucy cried in wild despair,
"He sha'n't, he sha'n't be mine!
Last night he vowed the garden gate
Should find him there this eve at eight;
But this I'll let the creature see,
He ne'er shall make a fool of me."

She ceas'd—a voice her ear alarms,   He shewed the ring, to wed next day,
The village clock struck ten,   He'd been to buy, a long, long way;
When William caught her in his arms,   How then could Lucy cruel prove
And ne'er to part again.   To one that did so fondly love?[8]

The Garden Gate

W. Upton and W. T. Parke

Fig. 15.3

The material that Baring-Gould selected for volume 2 of the *Minstrelsie* followed the same pattern of mixing a handful of folksongs with older vernacular songs and a smattering of popular national songs by well-known composers. The latter included "Black-eyed Susan" by John Gay and Richard Leveridge, "The Bonny Gray-eyed Morn" by Jeremiah Clark, "Fairest Isle" by Henry Purcell, "Home, Sweet Home" by Howard Payne and Henry Bishop, "Poor Tom" by Charles Dibdin, and "Rule Britannia!" by Thomas Arne. "Come, Come, Sweet Molly," a lyric written by Captain William Hicks, was set to "a folk air…sung by country folk in the West of England."[9] There were numerous lyrics by anonymous wordsmiths which employed "old English airs" but were nonetheless not counted by Baring-Gould as folksongs, presumably because he had never come across them in oral tradition. Some of them were overtly patriotic national songs, such as "The British Grenadiers," but most were simply old songs whose authors' identities had been lost over the years. They included "Cupid's Courtesy," "The Dumb Wife," "The Fine Old English Gentleman," "Gathering Peascods," "In Limbo," "Last Night the Dogs Did Bark," "The Leather Bottel," "Phillida Flouts Me," "Sir Thomas, I Cannot," "Twang Lango Dillo Day," and "You Gentlemen of England." Only four songs were classified by the editors as unequivocally folksongs, namely "Spring and Winter" (aka "The Four Seasons"), "All of a Row," "The Oxen Ploughing," and "Early One Morning."

Early one morning, just as the sun was rising,   How could you use a poor maiden so?"
I heard a maid sing in the valley below:
"O don't deceive me, O do not leave me!   "O! gay is the garland, and fresh are the roses,
How could you use a poor maiden so?"   I've culled from the garden to bind on thy brow;
                                                         O don't deceive me, O do not leave me!
"Remember the vows that you made to your Mary,   How could you use a poor maiden so?"
Remember the bow'r where you vowed to be true;
O don't deceive me, O do not leave me!   Thus sang the poor maiden, her sorrows bewailing,

Thus sang the poor maid in the valley below: How could you use a poor maiden so?"[10]
O don't deceive me, O do not leave me!

Early One Morning

Anon

Fig. 15.4

About "Early One Morning" Baring-Gould remarked that Chappell had named it as one of the three most popular songs among the servant-girls of his generation—the others were "Cupid's Garden" and "The Seeds of Love"—and that the tune was an excellent example of the beauty that could be drawn from "that bubbling spring of pure melody," English folksong. Concerning "Oxen Ploughing," he remarked that the song was "full of freshness and life. And there is in the last verse that spirit of self-confidence and self-consequence, so marked a feature in the English ploughman. The 'ploughboy' songs of the country form a class of their own; they are all delightful, breathe a contented spirit, joyous as that of the lark."[11] Baring-Gould's interpretation of this song may be overly romantic, but it illustrates his infectious enthusiasm for the material he had collected and for the source singers from whom he had obtained it. Moreover, his notes to "Oxen Ploughing" provide a good indication of the way he went about collecting in the field and also his method of editing the results of that collecting:

> For several years I had come upon snatches of it, old men remembered portions—the chorus almost always, and a fragment of the song itself, here and there, none perfect. At last I received information that there was an old fellow near Liskeard in Cornwall who sang it. Mr. Sheppard and I went thither, arrived at his door to hear that he had been speechless for three days, and his death was hourly expected. One day I was engaged in excavating a prehistoric village on the Bodmin moors near Trewortha Marsh, when a workman told me that there was in the parish of Northill an old man, a bit of a white witch, who could sing. I made three excursions after him, driving a distance of eighteen miles, and the same distance back. On two occasions he was not to be found, on the third I caught him cutting fern on a bank. A fine old man with snowy hair and beard, dark eyes, and a nose like the beak of a hawk. I at once asked him if he knew the song of "Oxen Ploughing." He struck up at once. I sat on a heap of fern he had cut as bedding for cattle, and sang with him, till I had learned the song by heart, then I drove home the eighteen miles, singing it the whole way so as to make sure of the tune. The following year I was in the Vale of Lanherne in Cornwall, where the old innkeeper, over ninety, was once a great singer. I asked him about this song. He told me there was a bell-ringer in the place, who sang it every year at the ringers' supper, and it was his "one song." I sent for this man. Mr. Bussell was with me, and we got it down from him, words and music. It was now easy out of these two complete copies, differing somewhat from one another, and the eight or nine fragments, to arrive at the original form of the song.[12]

The white-haired farm laborer from Northill was Adam Laundry, and the elderly publican at Mawgan in the Vale of Lanherne was Sam Gilbert, but the bell-ringer's identity is not evident, since no informant from that village is listed in "The Personal Copy." It appears that the earlier fragments, including three versions of the tune, had been noted from

Joseph Dyer, Matthew Ford, and Harry Westaway. What all this indicates is that the "Oxen Ploughing" printed in *English Minstrelsie* was a composite, Baring-Gould's best guess at what the text and tune 'should' have been. Rather than print one or more of the variants actually collected, he saw it as his duty as editor to try to put together an 'original' version, which may in fact never have existed. He clearly saw nothing wrong in doing this; rather he saw himself as an advocate on behalf of something he loved, and he was trying to provide the best version possible for his readers. This is the song of country life that so delighted the rural cleric, in the version that he reconstructed and printed:

The Oxen Ploughing

Anon

Fig. 15.5

Prithee, lend your jocund voices, for to listen we've agreed,
Come sing of songs the choicest, of the life we ploughboys lead.
There are none that live so merry as the ploughboy does in spring,
When he hears the sweet birds whistle and the nightingales to sing.
   Chorus: "With my Hump along! Jump along! Here drives my lad along!
   Pretty, Sparkle, Berry! Good luck, Speedwell, Cherry!
   We are the lads that can follow the plough,
   Oh, we are the lads that can follow the plough!"

For it's, O my little ploughboy, come awaken in the morn,
When the cock upon the dung-hill is a-blowing of his horn,
Soon the sun above Brown Willy with his golden face will show,
Wherefore hasten to the linney, yoke the oxen to the plough.

Chorus: With my Hump along! Jump along! &c.

In the heat of the daytime it's but little we can do,
We lie beside our oxen for an hour or for two.
On the banks of sweet violets I'll take my noon-tide rest,
And it's I can kiss a pretty girl as hearty as the best.
  Chorus: With my Hump along! Jump along! &c.

When the sun at eve is setting and the shadows fill the vale,
Then our throttles we'll be wetting with the farmer's humming ale;
And the oxen home returning we will send into the stall;
When the logs and peat are burning we'll be merry ploughboys all.
  Chorus: With my Hump along! Jump along! &c.

O the farmer must have seed, sirs, or I swear he cannot sow,
And the miller with his mill-wheel is an idle man also.
And the huntsman gives up hunting, and the tradesman stands aside,
And the poor man's bread is wanting, so 'tis we for all provide.
  Chorus: With my Hump along! Jump along! &c.[13]

Baring-Gould probably did much the same kind of intrusive editing on many of the other vernacular songs to be found in the other volumes of *English Minstrelsie.* The items he classified in Volume 3 as folksongs were "Farewell and Adieu, Ye Spanish Ladies," "Midsummer Carol," and a variant of "The Lincolnshire Poacher" that he titled "The Gallant Poacher":

The Gallant Poacher

Anon

Fig. 15.6

When I was bound apprentice in famous Lincolnshire,
Full well I serv'd my master for more than seven years,
Till I took up to poaching, as you shall quickly hear;
Oh, 'tis my delight on a shining night, in the season of the year.

As me and my companions were setting of a snare,
'Twas then we spied the gamekeeper, for him we did not care,
For we can wrestle and fight, my boys, and jump o'er anywhere;
Oh, 'tis my delight on a shining night, in the season of the year.

As me and my companions were setting for a drive,
And taking on 'em up again, we caught a hare alive;
We took the hare alive, my boys, and thro' the woods did steer;
Oh, 'tis my delight on a shining night, in the season of the year.

I threw him on my shoulder, and then we trudged home,
We took him to a neighbour's house and sold him for a crown,
We sold him for a crown, my boys, it surely wasn't dear;
Oh, 'tis my delight on a shining night, in the season of the year.

Success to ev'ry gentleman that lives in Lincolnshire,
Success to ev'ry poacher that wants to sell a hare,
Bad luck to ev'ry gamekeeper that will not sell his deer,
Oh, 'tis my delight on a shining night, in the season of the year.[14]

Another folksong that might have been included was "The Sailor's Return," but instead of the original text Baring-Gould substituted an entirely new set of words by Fleetwood Sheppard titled "Within a Garden." It was one of the more annoying instances of his unnecessary editorial tampering. Other anonymous vernacular songs with old English airs that might have been counted as folksongs (but were not) were "Ragged, Torn and True," "My Lodging It Is On the Cold Ground," and "With Jockey to the Fair." Baring-Gould even remarked about the latter that he had "heard the song sung by old labouring men in the West of England," but he was convinced that it had been composed for use in the Vauxhall or Ranelagh pleasure gardens *circa* 1750 and was therefore a product of the commercial music industry. He had found it in the 1772 edition of *Vocal Music; or, The Songster's Companion*.[15] Volume 3 also included various national songs, of which a few of the most notable were "The Lass of Richmond Hill" by James Hook, Henry Purcell's "If Love's a Sweet Passion" and "I'll Sail Upon the Dog-Star," and "The *Arethusa*" by Prince Hoare and William Shield.

Neither volume 4 nor volume 5 of *English Minstrelsie* had much in the way of traditional material, and more recent vernacular songs were only slightly more plentiful. The national songs in volume 4 included Thomas Arne's Shakespeare setting "When Daisies Pied," John Dowland's "Now, O Now I Needs Must Part" and "Awake Sweet Love," Charles Dibdin's "Tom Bowling," "Heart of Oak" by art music composer William Boyce and Shakespearean actor David Garrick, Joseph Wade's "Meet Me in the Moonlight Alone," and Richard Leveridge's "The Roast Beef of Old England." "Cease Your Funning," from *The Beggar's Opera* by John Gay and Christopher Pepusch, which was first performed in 1728, probably adapted an old tune by an unknown composer. Other anonymous items with old English airs were "The Girl I Left Behind Me," "The Gallant Sailor," and "Love Lies A-Bleeding." As for folksongs, they were not numerous. "Dear Love, Regard My Grief" and "Old Adam" were described by the editors as "folk airs." About "Old Adam" Baring-Gould wrote the following note, which again provides some insight into his collecting methods and, at least on this occasion, goes some way to excuse his interventionist editing:

This curious air was taken down from William Andres, a fiddler at Sheepstor, on the edge of Dartmoor. I made two visits to the old man, one in 1890 with Mr. Sheppard, when we failed to extract much from him. I went again in 1892 with Mr. Bussell, and then his shyness was broken down, and we spent two hours with him, noting down his old airs. We might have got more, but the Rector most kindly came in and insisted on our going to tea with him. We could not refuse, and then had to hasten to catch our train to return, and as we passed, more than an hour after having left the old man, we heard him still fiddling. His memory was stored with old airs. As he told me, in ancient days when there were dances in the farm-houses, all the young folk sang as they danced, and the "burden" or refrain served to mark the turns in the dance. Unhappily he could not recall much of the words of the ballads thus sung. As he told me, he "minded his viddle more than them zingers;" consequently we could obtain the words [only] in a fragmentary condition—rarely more than the first verse. The poor old fellow died last autumn, and there is an end to his music on earth. "Old Adam" was one of the songs of which he could recall but a scrap of words, and I have therefore been compelled to write new verses, following as far as I could the idea of the ancient song. The air is peculiar in character, and the metre unusual. One would like to know what was the dance performed to it.[16]

The only other folksongs in this volume were a poaching song, "Hares in the Old Plantation," and a bell-ringing song, "The Ringers of Torrington Town." The former was a Yorkshire ditty, taken from Kidson's *Traditional Tunes* but modified by Baring-Gould, who deleted several verses but added a chorus and a conclusion. By Baring-Gould's own testimony, "Torrington Ringers," obtained from an elderly ringer at Exbourne, near Hatherleigh, was just one of many songs about bell-ringing that he had noted on his field trips around Devon and Cornwall.

Volume 5 of *English Minstrelsie* opened with an informative, if rather discursive, essay by Baring-Gould on eighteenth-century concert halls and pleasure gardens and the professional singers who performed in them. The remaining contents, however, were, in the main, less interesting. The most notable national songs by known composers and lyricists were "Behold I Am a Village Lass" by Prince Hoare and Stephen Storace, "The Cabin Boy" by Thomas Dibdin (from the highly successful pantomime, *Harlequin and Mother Goose*, first performed at Christmas, 1806), and "Harvest Home" by one of George III's court musicians, Luffman Atterbury. "Drink to Me Only with Thine Eyes" was an example of a song for which the lyricist was known—in this case Ben Jonson—but the composer of the tune was anonymous. Similarly, "When Daffodils Begin to Peer," taken from Shakespeare's *The Winter's Tale*, used a melody by an unknown Tudor tunesmith. Other songs with old English airs and anonymous lyric-writers included "Dearest Kitty," the broadside ballad "I Once Loved a Maiden Fair" (Baring-Gould found the text in the Roxburghe collection and the tune in Playford's *The English Dancing Master*), "The Ploughman's Ditty," and "Joan's Placket Is Torn." In some instances Baring-Gould took it upon himself to modernize, supplement, or replace the traditional songtexts. For instance, instead of giving the text of the broadside ballad "The Plot Rent and Torn" in the Roxburghe collection, which was written to the tune "Joan's Placket Is Torn," he composed new words of his own, although he included one stanza from the broadside in his note about the song. The only item in volume 5 that he designated as a folksong was "Down among the Banks of Roses," and this was actually a commercial song composed for use in the Vauxhall gardens and published in 1780.

For the reader interested in folksongs, volume 6 was much more promising. In addition to the five items that Baring-Gould classified as folksongs, a number of other compositions could reasonably be counted as vernacular songs that had appealed to successive generations of street singers and indeed continued to do so. National songs of note included "Gather Ye Rose-buds" (by Robert Herrick and William Lawes), "Here's a Health unto His Majesty" (by Jeremiah Saville), Henry Purcell's "A Jewel Is My Lady Fair," and the beautiful "The Banks of Allan Water" (words by M. G. Lewis, set to a melody by an anonymous tunesmith). Songs described as "old English" included "Well-a-Day!" (although Baring-Gould had partly rewritten the words), "I Am a Poor Shepherd Undone," "Begone! Dull Care," "Love Will Find Out the Way," "The Miller of Dee," "Shepherd, Have You Seen My Pastora?" "Here's a Health to the Lass" (a traditional drinking song that Baring-Gould saw fit to bowdlerize), "My Dog and I" (from the Roxburghe collection of broadside ballads), and "Phillis On the New-Mown Hay" (another Roxburghe broadside, with a tune from Playford's *English Dancing Master*).

The designated folksongs were "The Stammering Lovers" (a humorous ditty, taken down from an old mason on Dartmoor), "The Cheshire Cheese," "The Mermaid" (Baring-Gould truncated the song, but provided a full set of verses in his notes), "George Ridler's Oven" (for which Baring-Gould rejected any allegorical interpretation), and "Adieu to Old England." The latter had been noted from Robert Hard in 1890, and also collected from William Friend of Lydford. Baring-Gould counted it as a folksong since he had twice found it in oral tradition, although he recognized that the ballad, which he claimed to have "come upon repeatedly, for the last ten years…in the West of England," had the same theme and a certain textual and melodic resemblance to a song of the same title printed in a collection published *circa* 1778, *Vocal Music, or, The Songster's Companion*. The folksong version, he concluded, was aesthetically superior, and, moreover, was probably older than the commercial song inspired by it. The version given in *English Minstrelsie*, however, seems to have been a composite derived from both the published song and the fruits of Baring-Gould's field collecting. It was the cleric's practice to draw upon all available sources to create the best version that he could construct:

> My father in leather was clad, my mother in sheep's russet gray,
> They work'd in fine weather and bad that I might go gallant and gay,
> My rapier, hat, feathers and knot, a heart, too, as light as a cork,
> What frugality raked and got, I spread all abroad with a fork.
> CHORUS: So adieu to old England, adieu,
>   And adieu to some thousands of pounds,
>   If the world had been done, e'er my life had begun,
>   My sorrows would then have had bounds.
>
> My fortune is pretty well spent, my lands and my cattle and corn,
> I must put on a face of content when as naked as when I was born.

No more I'll be troubled with wealth, my pockets are drainèd full dry,
I walk where I please for my health, And never fear robbing, not I.
   So adieu to old England, etc.
O, once I would eat of the best, the finest of bread that was white,
Now glad if a crust may be had and thankful to have it to bite.
And once I would drink of the best, the best of ale, humming and brown,
Now fain some clean water to gain that runneth from mountain or down.
   So adieu to old England, etc.

O, once I could lie on the best, the best of good beds made of down,
If sure of a flock of dry straw I am glad to keep off the cold ground.
Some say, that old care kill'd the cat, and starv'd her for fear she should die;
Henceforth I'll be wiser than that, to my cares bid for ever goodbye.
   So adieu to old England, etc.[17]

Adieu to Old England

Anon

My fath-er in leath-er was clad, My moth-er in sheep's russ-et gray, They

work'd in fine weath-er and bad,___ That I might go gall-ant and gay. My

rap-ier, hat, feath ers and knot,___ A heart, too, as light as a cork, What fru-gal-it-y rak ed and

got,___ I spread all a-broad with a fork. So ad-ieu to old Eng land, ad-ieu,___ And ad

ieu to some thous ands of pounds,___ If the world had been done, e'er my life had be-gun, My

sor-rows would then have had bounds.

Fig. 15.7

The trend towards including a greater proportion of genuinely vernacular songs continued with the final two volumes of *English Minstrelsie*. Volume 7 opened with a fascinating "Introductory Essay on English Folk-Music," a series of reminiscences by Baring-Gould about his experiences collecting and the men and women from whom he obtained the songs. It revealed some of the experienced songhunter's considered conclusions about the singers, the songs, the difficulties involved in collecting, and the importance of the enterprise:

> Tunes and words must be taken down when the opportunity offers, these opportunities must be seized without the least delay…Unhappily, collectors have spent money and pains on gathering the printed broadsides, and have supposed that these constituted the ballad poetry of the people. This was a mistake. They ought to have gone to the peasantry, and from them they would have reaped as rich a store of good early ballads as have been collected in Scotland. Most of our English ballads were re-written in the Stuart period in very villainous taste, and were then printed. But the people continued to sing the older ballads, and never took kindly to those which were re-shaped, because the metre was unsuited to the airs with which they were familiar. Now it is too late. All that we can recover are fragments, but the melodies are not wholly lost, and a fragment of an early ballad is precious when united to an ancient air. The freaks of tradition are extraordinary….As a matter of fact, the peasant singer knows no time; he sings as suits the sense of his words and according to the character of his ballad. This makes it a difficult matter to note down his melodies correctly; and indeed it is not possible to do them justice apart from the words…It must be admitted that a very large percentage of the ballads and songs have a breadth and frankness in them in dealing with certain topics, which render it impossible to give them verbatim. It is not that the songs are licentious, far from it; they are moral in their aim, but they enter into particulars with undesirable minuteness, and treat of matters to which we prefer to shut our eyes….It is easy for a critic to sneer at such work, because he is himself wholly unacquainted with our English peasant class; but if this rapidly perishing music is to be saved, it must be done at once, and it must be done by some one with enthusiastic love for the old music, and who is familiar with the twists and turns of the mind of the agricultural labourer. Much might be done by ladies; I have by no means worked among old women singers as much as I have among men. But women love old songs even more than do men.[18]

Items in volume 7 reckoned to be folksongs by Baring-Gould numbered only two: "Richard of Taunton Dean" and "Polly Oliver." In his notes to the latter, a bowdlerized version rewritten by Fleetwood Sheppard, Baring-Gould, perhaps in a fit of conscience, printed nine verses from the original as collected but admitted to excluding other verses as "not very delicate" and having "no poetic merit." But if designated folksongs were few and sometimes tampered with, this volume did include a large number of anonymous songs with "old English" tunes. Some of these, for example "Came You Not from Newcastle?" "Under the Greenwood Tree," "The Spanish Lady" (actually a truncated version of Thomas Deloney's broadside ballad), "O Good Ale, Thou Art My Darling," "To Drive the Cold Winter Away," and "There Was an Old Woman Liv'd Under a Hill," were well-known vernacular songs that might well have been included in the folksong category. Others, less popular in the countryside, included "Ay Me! What Shall I Do?" (extensively rewritten by the editors), "Be Lordly, Willy, Be Lordly," "Britons, Where?" "Can You Now Leave Me?" "From Thee to Me She Turns Her Eyes," "Maidens, Beware Ye," "Songs of Shepherds," "Sparabella's Complaint," "When Fanny, Blooming Fair," and "Where, Dear Maid?" There were the usual hybrids and problem cases. For instance, Baring-Gould ascribed the words of "The Dame of Honour," "All On a Misty Morning," and "Lady, Thee I Love" to Thomas D'Urfey, but argued that all three tunes were old and anonymous. National songs included "It Was a Lover and His Lass" (from Shakespeare's *As You Like It*, the tune credited to Thomas Morley), "The Heaving of the Lead" by W. Pearce and William Shield, and "Brave Men of Kent" by Thomas D'Urfey and Richard Leveridge.

The last volume of *English Minstrelsie* included, according to Baring-Gould's judgment, just two more folksongs. They were the celebrated "Widdecombe Fair" (which Baring-Gould had already published in *Songs and Ballads of the West* and *A Garland of Country Song*) and "I'm a Man That's Done Wrong to My Parents," one of the last songs noted by Baring-Gould from Sam Fone, in 1897. The beautiful "I Live Not Where I Love," on the other hand, was classified as a broadside text written to an "old English" melody:

> Loyal lovers that are distant from your sweethearts many a mile,
> Come and help me at this instant, mirthfully to spend the while;
> Singing sweetly and completely commendations of my love,
> Swearing ever to part never, though I live not where I love.
>
> Though our bodies they be parted and asunder many a mile,
> Yet I vow to be true hearted, to be faithful all the while.
> With mine eye I cannot spy distance great, my dearest love,
> Still I'm with her altogether, though I live not where I love.
>
> When I sleep I do dream on her, when I wake I take no rest,
> Ev'ry moment think upon her, she's so fixèd in my breast.

So my tears, my groans and fears, wat'ry eyes my passion prove,
I will never love dissever, though I live not where I love.

Birds may leave their airy region, fishes in the air may fly,
All the world be one religion, living things may cease to die,
All things change to shapes most strange, ere that I disloyal prove,
Any way my faith decay, though I live not where I love.[19]

I Live Not Where I Love

Peter Lowberry

Fig. 15.8

Baring-Gould had reworked this songtext to avoid any suggestion of adultery, although his excuse on this occasion was that the original broadside ballad by Peter Lowberry simply had too many stanzas and that he had merely consolidated them. It was a good example of a vernacular song with a vital melody (to use Frank Kidson's term), and it was perhaps surprising that he had never found it in oral tradition since it had undoubtedly been very popular in the past. Chappell had included it in *Popular Music of the Olden Time* but with a new, nineteenth-century, lyric. Baring-Gould's version was therefore closer to the original, although regrettably truncated.

Volume 8 had a large number of other anonymous songs with "old English" tunes, some of which, such as the vernacular drinking songs "He That Will Not Merry Merry Be" and "How Stands the Glass Around?" might easily have been counted as folksongs. The same was true of "Nancy Dawson" and the carol "The Morning Break." Songs written to traditional melodies composed by anonymous tunesmiths included Collins's "The Golden Days of Good Queen Bess," "Oh! The Oak and the Ash" (aka "A North Country Maid," a broadside ballad that Baring-Gould credited to Martin Parker), "What Though I Be a Country Lass" (another broadside by Martin Parker, using the dance tune "Oil of Barley"), and Thomas D'Urfey's "The Lass of Lynn." Other songs with airs judged to be "old English" were "A Health to All Honest Men," "Come Sweet Lass," "Spring Is Coming," "The Hop-Planter's Song," "In Praise of a Dairy," "Marriage; or, The Mousetrap," "Roger and Cicely," "My Dear and Only Love," "O Jenny, Jenny, Where Hast Thou Been?" and "A Valentine."

National songs that had achieved lasting popularity included "Nottingham Ale" (the tune of which had been composed by Henry Purcell), William Elderton's broadside "York! York for My Money" (which used the tune of "Greensleeves"), Robert Herrick's "To Anthea," Henry Carey's "Sally in Our Alley," and "Blow, Blow, Thou Winter Wind" (Thomas Arne's setting of a song from Shakespeare's *As You Like It*). This volume thus included plenty of vernacular songs, but it was vitiated by a spate of editorial rewriting. "Northern Nancy" and "Bonny Nell," for example, were imitation folksongs composed by Baring-Gould and Sheppard respectively. "The Maid of Doncaster" was a cleaned-up version of "The Northern Lass," while the quite innocuous words of "Hal-an-Tow" were replaced by a lyric composed by the poet Southey titled "The Well of St. Keyne." Baring-Gould also felt constrained to rewrite "The Lass of Lynn" because he found the original lyric "eminently objectionable." By this time the reader could hardly have been surprised at such interventionist editing.

As we have seen, the editorial method employed in *English Minstrelsie* was firmly in the tradition of Sir Walter Scott and William Allingham and certainly would not have pleased either Frederick Furnivall or Francis James Child. The collection depended heavily on composite texts, it had its *longueurs*, and, at eight volumes, seemed somewhat overblown. Yet, on the whole, it was an impressive work. It stands as a systematic and fairly successful attempt to place folksongs and other older vernacular songs within the broader compass of English national song.

Kidson and Moffat's *The Minstrelsy of England*

In writing the song notes for *English Minstrelsie* Baring-Gould had not hesitated to ask for Lucy Broadwood's help when he needed information that could be found most readily in the British Museum. Similarly he drew on Frank Kidson's advice and extensive antiquarian knowledge of old songs and their composers. Kidson was now William Chappell's most able disciple, and although, as we have seen, he continued folksong collecting in the 1890s, his avocation as a music historian increasingly took more and more of his time and energy. Consequently his major publications during the first decade of the new century were mainly outside the field of folk music. They included a ground-breaking dictionary of *British Music Publishers, Printers and Engravers,* [20] and two collaborative works with Alfred Moffat: *The Minstrelsy of England* [21] and *English Songs of the Georgian Period.* [22]

The first of these two collections in particular was an important publication because it brought a body of valuable but largely neglected song back into the public eye. The *Minstrelsy* did include a number of folksongs but by far the majority of the reprinted songs were compositions by such musicians and lyricists as (among others) Henry Lawes, Henry Purcell, Richard Leveridge, Thomas Arne, Charles Dibdin, James Hook, William Reeve, and William Shield. In commercial terms the book was obviously intended to compete with Hatton's *Songs of England* and Barrett's *Standard English Songs* rather than Baring-Gould's *English Minstrelsie*, since Kidson and Moffat had only one, albeit large, volume at their disposal. In approach, however, it was closer to Baring-Gould than to his predecessors. Despite some minor errors, Baring-Gould had set a high editorial standard, researching composers and lyric-writers and providing informative notes in a way that was noticeably lacking in the collections by Hatton, Barrett, and Boulton and Somervell. Kidson, of course, was an expert in this field, and although he could be something of a maverick, his decisions over song attributions were likely to be even more accurate than Baring-Gould's and much more reliable than Hatton's or Barrett's.

Unfortunately Kidson and Moffat's volume, scholarly though it was in most respects, was vitiated by a major flaw. Space restrictions led them to make a draconian editorial decision: to curtail the length of songtexts. Their rule of thumb was that if a song had more than four verses some of them would be omitted, in order to avoid using up another page of the book on mere text. This approach was disastrous in the case of most narrative ballads, rendering them nonsensical. It also would seem to have been counterproductive, since *The Minstrelsy of England* was intended, first and foremost, to be a useful songbook, and any singer finding the Kidson and Moffat version of a chosen song to be annoyingly incomplete would perforce have recourse to a rival publication. The texts of very many of the items in *The Minstrelsy of England* were thus truncated, and its main value lay in the tunes that Kidson had unearthed for songs previously printed as texts only. In this sense, the book carried on the good work of Rimbault's *Musical Illustrations of Bishop Percy's Reliques* and Chappell's *Popular Music of the Olden Time.*

The contents of *The Minstrelsy of England* fell roughly into one of three categories. There were anonymous traditional ballads, broadside ballads and folk lyrics. There were compositions by prominent authors and musicians that had already become part of the better-known heritage of English national vernacular song. Thirdly, there were many old songs that had been popular in their day but had since been forgotten: interesting or charming compositions that might well have become vernacular songs but, in the event, had failed to become part of oral tradition, even in the streets of London and other cities. Kidson and Moffat believed that these obscure but charming old songs deserved a second chance, and about half *The Minstrelsy of England* comprised old 'pop' songs by known (if largely forgotten) authors in which they were hoping to revive public interest. It is not clear if they regarded all these songs as national songs. Most likely they simply included a number of items that they thought had been unjustly neglected and ought to be part of the national song corpus, although as yet they were not really vernacular songs.

Other items were beyond doubt national songs, and Kidson and Moffat referred to them as such. There was no problem with these but most had already found their way into earlier national song collections. So Kidson and Moffat naturally wanted to add some extra material to the category. A few examples will suffice to illustrate the sort of lesser-known songs they had in mind. The early eighteenth-century singer and musician Richard Leveridge, the author of three tunes that had become, in Kidson's phrase, "typical National Melodies" ("The Roast Beef of Old England," "Black-eyed Susan," and "The Sweet Rosy Morn"), had set to music a poem by John Donne, "Send Home My Long-stray'd Eyes to Me," and the result was, in Kidson's opinion, far too good to be left in oblivion. Other Leveridge compositions deserving a new lease of life were "Sweet Are the Charms of Her I Love" and "To All You Ladies Now at Land." In Kidson's opinion the same was true of Henry Lawes's setting of Robert Herrick's lyric "Love's Votary." Lawes was one of his favourite composers, and he included several of his other tunes, including "Amidst the Myrtles as I Walk," "The Angler's Song," and "I Prithee, Send Me Back My Heart," the latter a setting of a lyric by Jacobean poet Sir John Suckling. Again, Kidson thought that one of Thomas D'Urfey's songs, "We All to Conqu'ring Beauty Bow," equipped with a new tune by John Blow, deserved to endure, and he had a similar brief for "Come, Come My Lovers," a pretty ditty by seventeenth-century musican Walter Porter whose music had often been included in Playford's publications. One could easily multiply such examples, but enough have been given to demonstrate the main thrust of *The Minstrelsy of England,* namely the revival of songs that in the editors' opinion should never have died.

This large songbook naturally contained many national songs that had captured the hearts and minds of ordinary English men and women during successive centuries. Many examples could be given of vernacular songs (usually by known composers) selected by Kidson and Moffat for inclusion in the volume. One type, the patriotic song, was well represented. The book opened with "God Save the King" and others included "Rule Britannia," "The British Grenadiers," "Heart of Oak," and "Here's a Health to His Majesty." Another political item was that most famous of all Cavalier songs, Martin Parker's "When the King Enjoys His Own Again." To illustrate this kind of material here is a patriotic song that at the same time makes a political point, "The Roast Beef of Old England":

The Roast Beef of Old England

Henry Fielding and Richard Leveridge

Fig. 15.9

When mighty roast beef was the Englishman's food,
It ennobled our hearts and enriched our blood,
Our soldiers were brave, and our courtiers were good,
O! the roast beef of old England!
And O! for old England's roast beef!

Our fathers of old were robust, stout and strong,
And kept open house with good cheer all day long,
Which made their plump tenants rejoice in this song.

O! the roast beef of old England!
And O! for old England's roast beef!

When good Queen Elizabeth sat on the throne,
Ere coffee or tea or such slip-slops were known,
The world was in terror if e're she did frown.
 O! the roast beef of old England!
And O! for old England's roast beef![23]

Of course, not all the national songs chosen by Kidson and Moffat were political or overtly patriotic. Some reflected characteristically English attitudes and values, such as "The Vicar of Bray," "The Miller of Dee," and "The Hunt Is Up." Most were love songs of one kind or another that had simply become part of the common heritage of singing English men and women. Examples are Shakespeare's "O Mistress Mine" and "It Was a Lover and His Lass," Christopher Marlowe's "Come Live with Me and Be My Love," Ben Jonson's "Drink to Me Only with Thine Eyes," Robert Herrick's "Gather Ye Rosebuds," Jeremiah Clark's "The Bonny Grey-Ey'd Morn," and Henry Carey's "Sally in Our Alley."

Certain early eighteenth-century musicians, such as Richard Leveridge, had been gifted with a flair for inventing what Kidson named "vital tunes," melodies that made almost immortal the songs of which they were a part; as we've seen, Leveridge's included "The Sweet Rosy Morn," "Black-eyed Susan," and "The Roast Beef of Old England." Such "vital tunes," whatever their source, were what Kidson most wanted to fill the pages of *The Minstrelsy of England*. A number of these vernacular songs with haunting melodies had been written initially for the musical theatre but had subsequently taken on an independent existence. Examples were "Golden Slumbers" (from Dekker and Chettle's *The Pleasant Comedy of Patient Grisel* (1603), "Cease Your Funning" (from Gay's *The Beggars' Opera*), and "There Was a Maid Went to the Mill" (from the 1731 ballad opera *The Jovial Crew*), all of which found a home in the collection. Kidson also slipped in a few drinking songs; early ones that he liked ("Come All You Jolly Watermen") and better known ones such as "Down among the Dead Men" and "He That Will Not Merry, Merry Be." Most of these vernacular songs had previously been included in Chappell's *Popular Music of the Olden Time*, and the concordance between Chappell's taste and Kidson's is striking.

The line between folksongs and other vernacular songs is not always easy to draw, and *The Minstrelsy of England* contained a number of marginal songs that might be classified in either category. Those drinking songs are good examples, and others included several songs that Kidson had rescued from D'Urfey's *Pills to Purge Melancholy*, including "The Dumb Wife Cured" and "Love Will Find Out the Way." Another was "As Down in the Meadows I Chanced to Pass," resurrected by Kidson from Walsh's *Merry Musician, or Cure for the Spleen* (1728) but essentially the same as the folk lyric "Down in a Meadow" (aka "Susan's Complaint"). "Jockey to the Fair" is similarly difficult to classify; Kidson reproduced it from J. Bew's edition of *Vocal Music* (1781), remarking that it was "a popular favourite, probably first sung at Vauxhall or some similar public garden, ...[and] in great vogue about 1779-80...In its original form the air is of more extended compass and not so vocal as the present traditional set which has been its recognised form for half a century."[24] "Jockey" thus appears to be a good example of a professionally composed ditty that was not only commercially successful when first introduced but also became so popular that it lived on as a perennial favourite in the streets and taverns of London, subsequently migrating to the countryside and entering rural oral tradition as well.

The Minstrelsy of England also contained quite a few old, anonymous songs that were still current in oral tradition in rural England, a good number of them reprinted from Kidson's *Traditional Tunes*. These may be grouped into four main categories: traditional ballads, broadside ballads, lyrics about male-female relationships, and other folksongs. Although he printed only truncated texts, Kidson slipped nine English versions of Child ballads into the book. "The Three Ravens" was reprinted from *Melismata* (1611), the later version of "Chevy Chace" was set to an Elizabethan tune ("In Pescod Time") and "Robin Hood and the Bishop of Hereford" was taken from Ritson's collection of *Robin Hood Ballads*. For his material Kidson relied quite heavily on the combination of Percy's *Reliques* and Rimbault's *Musical Illustrations:* from this dual source came "Barbara Allen's Cruelty" and "The Bailiff's Daughter of Islington," while for "Queen Eleanor's Confession" he took the text from Percy but used the tune given in the appendix to Motherwell's *Minstrelsy*. Broadside texts for "The Mermaid" and "The *Golden Vanity*" were supplemented with tunes taken from Chappell and Baring-Gould respectively. To illustrate the traditional ballad component of *The Minstrelsy of England*, here is Kidson and Moffat's version of "The Knight and the Shepherd's Daughter," with the addition of missing verses from the broadside in the Roxburghe collection that Kidson cited as the source for the five stanzas that he did print. It may be compared with the West country variant titled "The Shepherd's Daughter" that Baring-Gould noted from James Olver in 1891 (see chapter 13). On this occasion Kidson did not print a tune from oral tradition because he had found a seventeenth-century melody for the ballad in Playford's *Dancing Master:*

The Knight and the Shepherd's Daughter

Anon

There was a shep - herd's daugh - ter came trip - ping on — the

way.   And   there   by chance a — knight she met, which caus - ed — her   to   stay.

Fig. 15.10

There was a shepherd's daughter came tripping on the way,
And there by chance a knight she met, which caused her to stay.

"Good morrow to you, beauteous maid," these words pronounced he,
"O I shall dye this day," he said, "If I have not my will of thee."

"The Lord forbid," the maid reply'd, "that such a thing should be,
That ever such a courteous young knight should dye for love of me."

He took her by the middle so small and laid her down on the plain,
And after he had had his will, he took her up again.

"Now you have had your will, good sir, and put my body thus to shame,
Even as you arc a courteous knight, tell me what is your name."

"Some men do call me Jack, sweet heart, and some do call me John,
But when I come to the king's [fair] court, they call me Sweet William."

He set his foot in the stirrop, and away then did he ride;
She tuckt her kirtle about her middle, and run close by his side.

But when she came to the broad water, she set her brest and swom,
And when she was got out again, she took her heels and run.

He never was the courteous knight to say, "Fair maid, will you ride?"
Nor she never was so loving a maid to say, "Sir Knight, abide."

But when she came to the king's fair court, she knocked at the ring;
So ready was the king himself to let this fair maid in.

"O Christ you save, my gracious liege, your body Christ save and see!
You have got a knight within your court this day hath robbed me."

"What hath he robbed thee of, fair maid? Of purple or of pall?
Or hath he took thy gay gold ring from off thy finger small?"

"He hath not robbed me, my liege, of purple nor of pall;
But he hath got my maidenhead, which grieves me worst of all."

"Now if he be a batchelor, his body I'le give to thee;
But if he be a married man, high hanged shall he be."

He called down his merry men all, by one, by two, and by three;
Sweet William was us'd to be the first, but now the last comes he.

He brought her down full forty pound, ty'd up within a glove:
"Fair maid, I give the same to thee, and seek another love."

"O, I'le have none of your gold," she said, "nor I'le have none of your fee;
But I must have your fair body, the king hath given me."

Sweet William ran and fetched her then five hundred pound in gold,
Saying, "Fair maid, take this unto thee, thy fault will never be told."

"Tis not your gold that shall me tempt," these words then answered she,
"But I must have your own body, so the king hath granted me."

"Would I had drank the fair water when I did drink the wine,
That any shepherd's daughter should be a fair lady of mine!

Would I had drunk the puddle-water when I did drink the ale,
That ever any shepherd's daughter should have told me such a tale!"

"A shepherd's daughter as I was, you might have let me be;
I'd never come to the king's fair court to have craved any love of thee."

He set her on a milk-white steed, and himself upon a gray;
He hung a bugle about his neck, and so they rode away.

But when they came unto the place where marriage rites were done,
She proved herself a duke's daughter, and he but a squire's son.

"Now you have married me, sir knight, your pleasures may be free;
If you make me lady of one good town, I'le make you lord of three."

"Accursed be the gold," he said, "If thou hadst not bin true,
That should have parted thee from me, to have chang'd thee for a new."

Their hearts being then so linked fast, and joyning hand in hand,
He hath both purse and person too, and all at his command.[25]

A dozen or so ballads of the type regarded as non-traditional by Child and usually found on broadsides also found their way into *The Minstrelsy of England.* Examples included "Admiral Benbow," "Richard of Taunton Dean," "Sir Eglamore," "There Were Three Travellers" (aka "The Jovial Companions, or The Merry Travellers Who Paid Without a Stiver of Money"), and "Near Woodstock Town" (aka "The Oxfordshire Tragedy"). For tunes to match these texts Kidson had raided D'Urfey's *Pills,* Fielding's *Vocal Enchantress* (1783), and Chappell's *Popular Music of the Olden Time.* In *Pills to Purge Melancholy* he also found a tune for "Broom, Green Broom" that he preferred to the one he had collected in Yorkshire, although he remarked in a note that "this song, set to several different airs, has been picked up traditionally in Devonshire, Yorkshire, Northumberland, and Norfolk; these traditional versions are to be seen in the several recently published collections of folk melodies [and] copies of the words are also to be found on old ballad sheets and in song garlands."[26] Nonetheless he censored D'Urfey's lyrics, expunging the subtext of sexual attraction across the class barrier. Similarly Kidson took another ballad relating an amorous encounter, "The Northumberland Bagpiper," from *Pills,* and although he retained D'Urfey's tune he again felt constrained to modify the words for the sake of propriety.[27]

Playford's *Dancing Master* (1650, and numerous later editions) was another of Kidson's favorite collections of old music, and he used it as a plentiful source for the tunes to which broadside ballads had been written. On this occasion Playford provided melodies for "The Oak and the Ash" and "Once I Loved a Maiden Fair" (both texts came from the Roxburghe collection). Thomas Deloney's "The Spanish Lady's Love" was credited to Percy's *Reliques* rather than to Deloney's own *Garland of Good-Will,* while "The Lost Lady Found," a common broadside which Kidson, perhaps surprisingly, described as "a folk ballad," was taken from John Broadwood's *Old English Songs* and given Broadwood's erroneous title, "Gipsy Song." "Just As the Tide Was Flowing" was reprinted from *Traditional Tunes,* and Kidson remarked that while the words were from a broadside "the tune was taken down in the East Riding of Yorkshire from traditional singing and has been heard to the same words in the North Riding."[28]

Another broadside ballad preserved in *The Minstrelsy of England* was "Turpin Hero" (aka "O Rare Turpin"). The story of this ballad had considerable popular appeal because it combined sympathy for that thorn in the side of the state, the highwayman, with a joke at the expense of lawyers, who were often regarded as grasping and untrustworthy parasites. Kidson borrowed the tune, which he called a "traditional ballad air," from Chappell's *Popular Music of the Olden Time.* It had been noted by Chappell from the singing of Charles Sloman in 1840. The words were from a broadsheet but Kidson admitted that he had reproduced "merely a selection from the lengthy ballad." They were, however, enough to indicate the main thrust of the tale:

Turpin Hero

Anon

Fig. 15.11

On Hounslow Heath as I rode o'er, I spied a lawyer riding before,
"Kind sir," said I, "Aren't you afraid of Turpin, that mischievous blade?"
O rare Turpin hero, O rare Turpin, O!

Says Turpin, "He'd ne're find me out, I've hid my money in my boot."
The lawyer says, "There's none can find, my gold is stich'd in my cape behind."
O rare Turpin hero, O rare Turpin, O!

As they rode by the powder mill, Turpin commands him to stand still;
Said he, "Your cape I must cut off, my mare she wants a saddle cloth."
O rare Turpin hero, O rare Turpin, O!

This caused the lawyer much to fret, to think he was so fairly hit,
And Turpin robbed him of his store, because he knew he'd lie for more.
O rare Turpin hero, O rare Turpin, O![29]

As usual, many of the folksongs in the collection took as their subject matter relations between the sexes. These included "Come You Not from Newcastle" (tune from Playford's *Dancing Master,* text from Percy's folio manuscript), "Cupid's Trick" (aka "Once I Had a Sweetheart"), and "Cupid's Garden," which Kidson described as "a quaint old-fashioned love song which, even so late as the forties and fifties, was a great favourite traditionally in most country places...the present tune has not appeared in print much more than forty or fifty years, but it is certainly an early air."[30] "As I Walked Forth One Summer's Day" (aka "A Forsaken Lover's Complaint") was taken from Robert Johnson's *The Treasury of Musick* (1669), although Kidson had no doubt that it was "a folk ballad." The text of "It Was a Maid of My Countrie" was an Elizabethan poem found by Ritson in a manuscript at the Cotton library, to which had been fitted a traditional tune, noted by Edward Jones and printed in *Musical and Poetical Relics of the Welsh Bards* (1784). As for "Go from My Window, Go," this was a sixteenth-century folk ballad, the tune of which was in *Queen Elizabeth's Virginal Book*. The original text was to be found in Beaumont and Fletcher's comedy *The Knight of the Burning Pestle*, but Kidson and Moffat had found it too rude to reproduce; on this occasion Kidson sounded just like Baring-Gould, commenting that "for sufficient reasons we have decided to reject all old copies of the words, and for the purpose of popularizing the exquisite old melody, have adopted the above verses."[31]

Fortunately not all the folksongs about love and sex reproduced in *The Minstrelsy of England* had been censored or rewritten. Kidson never altered tunes, although Moffat's piano arrangements were a mixed blessing. One of the more beautiful melodies in the collection was "Early One Morning," which Kidson described as a "traditional English melody" that had been noted from oral tradition by Chappell and printed in his *National English Airs* (1838). "The Pretty Ploughboy," on the other hand, had been collected by Kidson himself from a North Yorkshire ploughman and was reprinted from *Traditional Tunes*. *Traditional Tunes* was also the source for this genial piece of male fantasy, "The Spotted Cow," a version of which we saw (in chapter 7) had also been collected in Devon by Sabine Baring-Gould from John Helmore.

The Spotted Cow

Anon

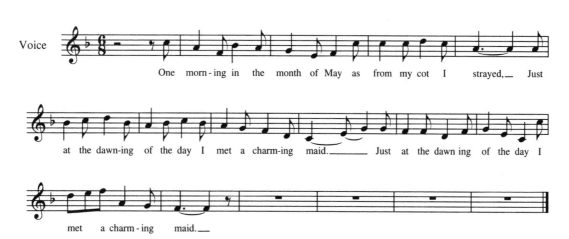

Fig. 15.12

One morning in the month of May, as from my cot I strayed,
Just at the dawning of the day, I met a charming maid;
Just at the dawning of the day, I met a charming maid;
"Good morning, fair maid, whither go so early? Tell me now."
The maid replied, "Kind sir," she said, "I've lost my spotted cow."
The maid replied, "Kind sir," she said, "I've lost my spotted cow."

"No more complain, no longer mourn, your cow's not lost, my dear.
I saw her down in yonder bourne; come, love, I'll show you where.
I saw her down in yonder bourne; come, love, I'll show you where."
"I must confess you're very kind; I thank you, sir," said she;
"You will be sure her there to find, come sweetheart, go with me;
You will be sure her there to find, come sweetheart, go with me."

And in the grove we spent the day, and thought it pass'd too soon,
At night we homeward bent our way, when brightly shone the moon;
At night we homeward bent our way, when brightly shone the moon.
If I should cross the flow'ry vale, or go to view the plough,

> She comes and calls, "Ye gentle swains, I've lost my spotted cow!"
> She comes and calls, "Ye gentle swains, I've lost my spotted cow!"[32]

As mentioned earlier, several of the folksongs reprinted in *The Minstrelsy of England* were drawn from the Reverend John Broadwood's *Old English Songs, as now Sung by the Peasantry of the Weald of Surrey and Sussex,* a rare copy of which Kidson had been loaned by Lucy Broadwood, although he also had a copy of her *Sussex Songs.* He described *Old English Songs* as "practically the first collection of peasant song and folk melodies published as such, and for the avowed purpose of rescuing traditional English songs in their primitive state," and he seems to have been especially attracted to those songs in the collection that reflected everyday life in rural England.[33] For inclusion in *The Minstrelsy* he selected "The Rosebuds in June," "The Woodcutter," "The Poacher's Song" (aka "In Thorny Woods"), and "The Ploughboy." About the latter he commented that it was "one of the numerous songs in praise of a ploughman's life over any other worldly occupation ...It is to be noticed that while in the south country the folk song is frequently one having for its theme the pleasures of rural life, yet as we advance northward this kind of ditty is gradually left behind, and probably the more barren land and the greater hardness of winning crops make the farmer and his labourer less inclined to sing of the joys of farming."[34] Other songs of rural life in *The Minstrelsy* included another poaching song, "When I Was Bound Apprentice" (aka "The Lincolnshire Poacher"), the text for which came from James Henry Dixon's *Ancient Poems, Ballads and Songs of the Peasantry* and the tune from Chappell's *A Collection of National English Airs.* There was a fox-hunting song, "Bucks A-Hunting Go," reprinted from Kidson's *Traditional Tunes,* about which Kidson remarked that "the tune was commonly sung on the borders of Staffordshire, Cheshire and Shropshire, between 1820 and 1840, and the words are in early song garlands printed by T. Evans and by J. Pitts."[35]

Humorous songs in *The Minstrelsy* included "Good Morrow, Gossip Joan" and "The Jovial Beggar" (aka "A-Begging We Will Go"), both of which could be found in D'Urfey's *Pills to Purge Melancholy.* The collection also reproduced a goodly number of drinking songs, not all of which were folksongs. Those that were included "In Praise of Ale" (from Ritson's *A Select Collection of English Songs*) and "The Leather Bottel," about which Kidson remarked that it was a favorite song of his grandfather's in the last decade of George III's reign. His version was taken from a seventeenth-century broadside in the Roxburghe collection (set to a traditional air collected by Chappell), but a variant was to be found in D'Urfey's *Pills,* and other traditional songs in praise of the leather bottle were printed in Dixon's *Ancient Poems, Ballads and Songs of the Peasantry of England* and Broadwood and Fuller Maitland's *English County Songs.*[36] James Dixon had also printed two versions of the words of the very popular West Country drinking song called "The Barley Mow," and Chappell had provided a melody in *Popular Music of the Olden Time.* The song had a distinctive tune and was normally sung with cumulative lyrics (as indicated by the square brackets added to Kidson's text):

> Here's a health to the barley mow, my boys, a health to the barley mow.
> We'll drink it out of the nut-brown bowl, a health to the barley mow.
> The nipperkin, pipperkin, and the brown bowl,
> A health to the barley mow, my boys, a health to the barley mow!
>
> Here's a health to the barley mow, my boys, a health to the barley mow.
> We'll drink it out of the pint [pot], my boys, a health to the barley mow.
> The [pint pot, the] nipperkin, pipperkin, and the brown bowl,
> A health to the barley mow, my boys, a health to the barley mow.
>
> Here's a health to the barley mow, my boys, a health to the barley mow.
> We'll drink it out of the gallon, my boys, a health to the barley mow.
> The [gallon, the pint pot, the] nipperkin, pipperkin, and the brown bowl,
> A health to the barley mow, my boys, a health to the barley mow.
>
> Here's a health to the barley mow, my boys, a health to the barley mow.
> We'll drink it out of the river, my boys, a health to the barley mow.
> The [river, the gallon, the pint pot, the] nipperkin, pipperkin, and the brown bowl,
> A health to the barley mow, my boys, a health to the barley mow.
>
> Here's a health to the barley mow, my boys, a health to the barley mow.
> We'll drink it out of the ocean, my boys, a health to the barley mow.
> The [ocean, the river, the gallon, the pint pot, the] nipperkin, pipperkin, and the brown
> bowl,
> A health to the barley mow, my boys, a health to the barley mow.[37]

The Barley Mow

Anon

Voice

Here's a health to the bar-ley mow, my boys, a health to the bar-ley

mow!__ We'll drink it out of the nut__brown bowl, a health to the bar-ley mow.__ The

nip-per kin, pip-per kin, and the brown bowl, a health to the bar-ley mow, my boys, a

health to the bar-ley mow!__

Fig. 15.13

More surprising, but indicative of Kidson's interest in local customs and folklore, was the insertion of such items as "The Cheshire Man" (a song in praise of Cheshire cheese, from Edward Jones's small 1798 collection *Popular Cheshire Melodies*), "The May Pole" (the words of which had been written by seventeenth-century lyricist Robert Cox to a traditional dance tune, "Staines Morris," printed in Playford's *Dancing Master*), and "Robin Hood and Little John." This latter song was not a Robin Hood ballad but rather a version of "Hal-an-Tow," a song associated with May Day ceremonies at Helston in Cornwall. Kidson commented that

> The Helston Furry Dance is one of the most singular customs still retained in England. The dance is a survival of a "morris" and is performed to the tune given above, every old May Day (i.e., 8th May), at Helston, in Cornwall. Parties of ladies and gentlemen dressed in bright attire with a profusion of flowers trip in couples, to the number of thirty or forty, through the streets and even through the houses of the little town. While a band plays the historical old tune given above, the couples sing the verses here given under the music. The festival is supposed to be a survival of a very ancient rite dating from an early British period. The air is distinctly an old "morris" dance tune.[38]

Other folksongs in the *Minstrelsy* included "We Be Three Poor Mariners" and "Come and Listen to My Ditty" (aka "The Sailor's Complaint"), both reflections on the hardships of life at sea. There was only one industrial song, "The Collier's Rant," which Kidson described as "purely a Northumbrian pitman's ditty [that had] evolved from the pit itself"; he had taken the words from Ritson's *Northumberland Garland, or Newcastle Nightingale* and the tune from Topliff's *Selection of the Most Popular Melodies of the Tyne and Wear.*[39]

Despite his regrettable decision to truncate lyrics, Kidson's scholarship as a music historian was far superior to that of all previous editors of national songs except William Chappell and, to a lesser degree, Sabine Baring-Gould. If he did nothing else, he almost put editing national songs on the same scientific footing as had Francis J. Child for ballad editing. He also reinforced the notion—which by now was becoming fairly widely accepted—that folksongs were an important part of the national music heritage. Although he was increasingly preoccupied with the urban popular songs of previous centuries (and with the history of their publication and re-publication), Kidson did not abandon folksong after the appearance of *The Minstrelsy of England.* As we shall see in the next chapter, he was a founder-member of the Folk-

Song Society, he would be a prominent contributor to its *Journal*, and, although his involvement with the movement was more episodic, to the Edwardian folksong revival in general.

It is perhaps surprising that *The Minstrelsy of England* was such a late contribution to the vogue for national song that was so evident in the late Victorian period. Kidson, after all, was (with Chappell and Hatton) one of the pioneers of the national song revival. When he was writing his first series of articles in the *Leeds Mercury Weekly Supplement* in the late 1880s he must have felt that his was a lonely voice championing a genre that most people were happy to ignore. Moreover, his perspective—that folksongs, broadside ballads, and the best commercial "pop" songs were complementary elements within the same, vibrant tradition of English song—had initially very little support, although Arthur Somervell clearly looked at things in much the same way by 1892. Lucy Broadwood, Alec Fuller Maitland, and, surprisingly, Sabine Baring-Gould were converts to the same vision by the middle of the decade, and, for a while it became the dominant outlook among the circle of people who would later form the nucleus of the Folk-Song Society. Small wonder, then, that when Cecil Sharp championed an alternative, more doctrinaire vision in the Edwardian era he met stubborn, if polite, resistance from Kidson, Broadwood, and their supporters. But that is to anticipate the future. Before Sharp could attempt his takeover of the Folk-Song Society it had first to exist. The story of how it came into being, and the nature of its early work, is the last major episode in the history of the Late Victorian phase of the first folksong revival.

Notes

1. Sabine Baring-Gould, ed., *English Minstrelsie: A National Monument of English Song,* 8 vols. (Edinburgh: Jack & Jack, 1895-98).

2. H. Ellis Wooldridge, ed., *Old English Popular Music,* 2 vols. (London: Novello & Ewer, 1893) [a revised and truncated version of Chappell's *Popular Music of the Olden Time*].

3. Baring-Gould, *English Minstrelsie,* vol. 1, xxii-xxiii.

4. Baring-Gould, *English Minstrelsie,* vol. 1, xxx.

5. Baring-Gould, *English Minstrelsie,* vol. 1, 14-17.

6. Baring-Gould, *English Minstrelsie,* vol. 1, 46-47.

7. Baring-Gould, *English Minstrelsie,* vol. 1, xxxi-xxxii.

8. Baring-Gould, *English Minstrelsie,* vol. 1, 84-85.

9. Baring-Gould, *English Minstrelsie,* vol. 2, xv.

10. Baring-Gould, *English Minstrelsie,* vol. 2, 126-28.

11. Baring-Gould, *English Minstrelsie,* vol. 2, xii.

12. Baring-Gould, *English Minstrelsie,* vol. 2, 97-99.

13. Baring-Gould, *English Minstrelsie,* vol. 2, 97-99.

14. Baring-Gould, *English Minstrelsie,* vol. 3, 28-29.

15. Baring-Gould, *English Minstrelsie,* vol. 3, x.

16. Baring-Gould, *English Minstrelsie,* vol. 4, v.

17. Baring-Gould, *English Minstrelsie,* vol. 6, 108-9.

18. Baring-Gould, *English Minstrelsie,* vol. 7, ix-xiii.

19. Baring-Gould, *English Minstrelsie,* vol. 8, 36-37.

20. Frank Kidson, *British Music Publishers, Printers, and Engravers: London, Provincial, Scottish and Irish: From Queen Elizabeth's Reign to George the Fourth's* (London: W. E. Hill, 1900).

21. Frank Kidson and Alfred Moffat, eds., *The Minstrelsy of England: a collection of 200 English songs with their melodies, popular from the 16th century to the middle of the 18th century* (London: Bailey & Ferguson, 1901).

22. Frank Kidson and Alfred Moffat, eds., *English Songs of the Georgian Period* (London: Bailey & Ferguson, 1907).

23. Kidson and Moffat, *Minstrelsy of England,* 233.

24. Kidson and Moffat, *Minstrelsy of England,* 206-7.

25. Kidson and Moffat, *Minstrelsy of England,* 161. Text from Francis J. Child, ed., *The English and Scottish Popular Ballads,* 5 vols. (Boston: Houghton Mifflin, 1882-1898), vol. 2, 459-60.

26. Kidson and Moffat, *Minstrelsy of England,* 234.

27. Kidson and Moffat, *Minstrelsy of England,* 292.

28. Kidson and Moffat, *Minstrelsy of England,* 288.

29. Kidson and Moffat, *Minstrelsy of England,* 160.

30. Kidson and Moffat, *Minstrelsy of England,* 302.

31. Kidson and Moffat, *Minstrelsy of England,* 24.

32. Kidson and Moffat, *Minstrelsy of England,* 124-25.

33. Kidson and Moffat, *Minstrelsy of England*, 94.
34. Kidson and Moffat, *Minstrelsy of England*, 304.
35. Kidson and Moffat, *Minstrelsy of England*, 200.
36. Kidson and Moffat, *Minstrelsy of England*, 148.
37. Kidson and Moffat, *Minstrelsy of England*, 236.
38. Kidson and Moffat, *Minstrelsy of England*, 311.
39. Kidson and Moffat, *Minstrelsy of England*, 172.

16

Birth of the Folk-Song Society

The creation of the Folk-Song Society in 1898 marks the culmination of the Late Victorian phase of the first folksong revival in England. This event had a long genesis, going back to 1892. The foundation for the Society's successful formation lay in the network of correspondents that Lucy Broadwood and Alec Fuller Maitland had developed while accumulating suitable materials for *English County Songs*. But the organization needed not only sufficient dues-paying rank-and-file members to provide an audience for its publications and to sustain it financially, it also needed enthusiasts who were prepared to sit on its executive committee and do the routine administrative chores because they shared a vision of the society's *raison d'être*, its potential, and its goals. And above all it required active and sustained participation by a core group of folksong collectors and scholars. Before the Folk-Song Society became a real possibility, rather than a mere aspiration, that nucleus of activists had had to come together. The core group coalesced during a five-year period (1892-97) and the catalyst was Lucy Broadwood. It was mainly she who brought together in the cause such diverse personalities as Sabine Baring-Gould, Charlotte Burne, W. Frere, Alec Fuller Maitland, Frank Kidson, Kate Lee, Arthur Somervell, W. Barclay Squire, and Mary Wakefield, among many others. Broadwood's diaries allow us to see, to some degree, the emergence of what might be called a 'folksong social circle,' although it overlapped with her larger circle of musical friends, many of whom were involved in one way or another with the early music revival and, in particular, the rediscovery of the work of Henry Purcell.

The Growth of an Informal Network

Even before she became heavily involved with collecting and editing folksongs, Lucy Broadwood's circle of musical friends included such figures as Alec Fuller Maitland, W. Barclay Squire, and Alfred J. Hipkins. Through them—and through her own performances as a soprano at charity concerts and musical at-homes—she came to meet such eminent late Victorian composers as Sir Alexander Mackenzie, Sir Hubert Parry, Charles Villiers Stanford, Sir John Stainer, and Arthur Somervell. Later, in 1897, she would add the singers Plunket Greene and Kate Lee as well as the young Ralph Vaughan Williams to her social list. All these musicians would be involved—although some of them only marginally—with the genesis and early activities of the Folk-Song Society. Three of them (Fuller Maitland, Lee, and Squire) would be members of the initial core group. To be effective, that founding nucleus also needed participation from some of the other important folksong collectors in late Victorian England. Charlotte Burne, Sabine Baring-Gould, and Frank Kidson were among those willing to make the required commitment of time and energy. Since all three lived away from London, Broadwood's contacts with them are documented, albeit incompletely, in her extant diaries and correspondence. Those documents allow us to trace her ongoing relationships with the three collectors, and, to a lesser extent, with other members of the growing folksong circle that embraced London, the Home Counties, and the Midlands. They reveal the gradual building of a network of personal ties that would later provide the backbone of the Folk-Song Society.

When they first became interested in folksong, Lucy Broadwood, Kidson, and Baring-Gould did not know each other personally. They seem to have become aware of each other's work in the field of folk music only through the publication of *Songs and Ballads of the West* and *Traditional Tunes*. Lucy already knew of Baring-Gould as a novelist (she read his *Richard Cable* in early July 1888), but it was not until she had perused the first volume of *Songs and Ballads of the*

West in 1889 that she wrote to him at Lew Trenchard. They then corresponded for several years, and during 1891-92 Baring-Gould sent her a fairly large number of Devon folksong tunes and texts for possible use in *English County Songs*. After the publication of that book, he continued to send her copies of West Country variants of songs that she had published in it, and she reciprocated, keeping him informed of her own collecting efforts. They also discussed frankly the merits and defects of various published collections of folksongs, including Barrett's *English Folk Songs* and Kidson's *Traditional Tunes*. As we saw in chapter 11, Lucy eventually took a vacation in Devon in September 1893 and visited Baring-Gould at Lew Trenchard. During her stay she looked through his song manuscripts and broadside collections, and the two collectors had long discussions about their fieldwork and editing issues. She also accompanied him on several collecting expeditions, noting songs from the Hamley sisters, Jane Jeffrey, and Mary Fletcher.[1]

This initially warm relationship subsequently cooled just a little as Lucy grew increasingly critical of what she came to regard as Baring-Gould's rather cavalier methods of collecting and editing folksongs.[2] However, she was tactful and polite, and he was thick-skinned, so their disagreements hardly affected their ongoing friendship. Baring-Gould continued to write to her, telling her about his discoveries in the field, complaining about his collaborators Sheppard and Bussell, and outlining his plans for future publications. Lucy not only answered his letters promptly, she readily helped him by doing odd bits of research for him in the British Museum.[3] The two collectors continued to regularly exchange songs that they had noted, and the Broadwood archives contain a substantial number of items that Baring-Gould collected in Devon and Cornwall, as well as his discussions of various singers and songs.[4] For example, early in 1894 Lucy received a letter that included a transcription of a ballad that Baring-Gould had recently noted from John Woodrich. The cleric wrote: "I have just taken this down from my little blacksmith J. Woodrich. It is your 'Sweet William.' The air is old and good. I do not believe your last verse belongs to 'Sweet William' but is pieced on from another song. The first verse of Woodrich's is no gain…[But] this seems to me more correct than yours. There certainly needs a revision in verses 1 & 2…the verse about the moon came out of another I have." Baring-Gould's version may be compared with the quite different one printed by Broadwood and Fuller Maitland in *English County Songs*, which had been collected in Bewdley, Worcestershire, by Margaret Harley (see chapter 11, p. 318). Despite the obvious differences, elements of both tune and text are sufficiently similar to indicate that the Devon cleric was correct to identify Woodrich's song as a variant of the same ballad.

Sweet William

Anon

Fig. 16.1

"So early, early in the Spring
I went abroad to serve the King
I left my pretty love behind
She often said her heart was mine.

O father, father, build me a boat,
And on the ocean blue I'll float,
And every King's ship passing by
I'll hail it for my sailor boy.

She had not sailed far on the deep
Before a King's ship she chanced to meet;

O Brother Sailor pray tell me true,
Is my sweet William among your crew?

O no fair lady he is not here,
Drowned is sweet William I greatly fear,
One stormy night the winds blew high,
We heard a loud and a bitter cry.

The moon shone out upon the sea,
Sweet William drowning discussed we.
                    [two lines missing]

She wrung her hands, she tore her hair,	I'll set me down, and I'll write a song,
All like a lady lost in despair,	I'll write it fair, I'll write it long,
Then her little boat on the rocks did run,	And at every word I will drop a tear,
She said with William I am undone.	And in every verse set my William dear."[5]

Whenever Baring-Gould planned a trip to London he always inquired whether there was any chance of meeting Lucy, and occasionally such meetings took place. He was usually invited for lunch or dinner, but sometimes the two met at the British Museum or at a concert or musical evening in London. Their relationship was never less than cordial, and it lasted for many years. Lucy also became acquainted with Fleetwood Sheppard through their mutual interest in the Society for Plain Song Music, which met periodically in the Chapter House at St. Paul's Cathedral.

Charlotte Burne was another out-of-town friend whom Broadwood normally entertained whenever she came up to London. The first time they met was probably in May 1892 when Lucy, together with the eminent folklorists Laurence and Alice Gomme, attended a fancy dress party at which the Burne family demonstrated Oxfordshire Morris dances. Lucy had already read *Shropshire Folk-Lore* and at the time she was looking for material for *English County Songs*, so the two women had plenty in common and much to talk about. Charlotte gave permission for Lucy to reprint any songs she wanted to from *Shropshire Folk-Lore* and from November 1893 onwards became a regular, if fairly infrequent, guest at Lucy's table.

With Frank Kidson, Lucy struck up a warm friendship that would endure until Kidson's death. As we have seen, she first came across his *Traditional Tunes* in June 1891, and she wrote to him early the next year, beginning a correspondence that would continue for more than thirty years. They were soon lending each other books, but it was not until April 1893 that Lucy first visited Kidson in Leeds. The next month she sent him copies of nineteen songs she had collected from Henry Burstow in Sussex, and from then on they collaborated closely.[6] Kidson encouraged Lucy to look in second-hand bookstores for a copy of the original edition of William Chappell's *Popular Music of the Olden Time*, and he usually sprang to Chappell's defense when the latter's work was criticized. Chappell, he acknowledged, had his blind spots—his hostility to all things Scottish being the worst one—but in the main his work was remarkably solid and informative: "Chappell's book," he wrote, "is on the whole a <u>marvel of accurate research</u> but one or two times he let his prejudices so run away with him that in certain matters he is <u>very inaccurate</u>."[7] Lucy and Kidson continued to correspond, exchanging songs and information about songs, and they met once or twice a year. In October 1895 Lucy took Alec Fuller Maitland to visit Kidson in Leeds, while they were attending Leeds Music Festival, and this was the beginning of a friendship between the two men, who would attend concerts together whenever Kidson made the trip down to London.[8]

Kidson soon got to know Baring-Gould better, and his opinion of the Devon cleric improved, although he still had some sharp criticisms of *Songs and Ballads of the West* and *A Garland of Country Song*. About the latter he wrote the following to Lucy: "It is unfortunate that Mr. B. Gould has such reckless musical collaborators who don't seem to care two pins about the <u>spirit</u> of the airs they harmonize, and make no bones at any alterations they think fit."[9] Baring-Gould, he recognized, was not entirely happy with the work of Fleetwood Sheppard and Bussell, but he was dependent on their services and had little control over them. Kidson had some criticisms of *English Minstrelsie* too, but on the whole he thought it a valuable work that had been given an unfairly rough ride by the music press: "I think the critics are a bit too much 'down' on Baring Gould… The book (to me) is interesting for the discovery from a garland of the original song 'The Mermaid' which was first published by Chappell from traditional singing and is not found elsewhere except from Chappell's source."[10] Although Kidson's and Baring-Gould's relationship had got off to a rocky start, Lucy successfully poured oil on troubled waters and acted as a mediator between them, defending each man against the other's criticisms. In any case, their interests had moved closer together, as Baring-Gould was bitten by the broadsheet-collecting bug and became less dismissive of national songs with known authors. He even asked Kidson's advice and help with the editorial matter for *English Minstrelsie*, so that by the late 1890s the two men had changed from being uncharitable rivals to well-disposed, if still not uncritical, colleagues.

Yet if an informal network of English folksong enthusiasts existed by the mid-1890s, it still required determination and energy—and, of course, a broad consensus that it was a good idea—to build this network into a formal organization. The conditions for the next step appeared ripe towards the end of 1897. A number of music events took place in London between late October of that year and the end of the pre-Christmas season, including several "popular ballad concerts" by the People's Concert Society at which Lucy performed such folksongs as "Edinbro', or the Cruel Sister" and "I Will Give You the Keys of Heaven." Then on 8 December she played piano accompaniment for Kate Lee, a professional concert singer who routinely included folksongs in her repertoire, and who had been asked to sing a number of items from *English County Songs* at a party thrown by Mrs. Herbert Carr.[11] It was at events like these that a consensus emerged that it was now time for action, and that an attempt should be made to test the waters, to see if there was indeed enough support for a folksong society to make it a viable proposition.

Kate Lee apparently took the initiative to get the ball rolling just after Christmas. On 9 January 1898 we find Kidson again writing to Lucy, reporting that he had received a circular letter broaching the idea. He commented, "I have received today (probably at your suggestion) a circular about a proposed Folk Song Society. Such a Society, worked on proper lines, would be a capital idea but its success and its usefulness would really depend on the managing committee and their earnestness. I trust that you will be on this committee as your absolute knowledge of the subject would stand in such good stead. I shall be glad to belong to the Society if the subscription is not excessive."[12] Naturally he was in favor of the project, provided only that the enterprise was well organized and managed by people who knew what they were doing. Broadwood's participation on the executive committee would be his litmus test of whether the ship was sound and the voyage looked promising.

Birth of the Folk-Song Society

Kidson, of course, was right in suspecting that Lucy was one of the moving spirits behind the drive to form a folksong society. Personal contacts between the pioneer collectors were invaluable, but she had gradually come to recognize that a more formal organizational framework was needed to help coordinate their work. She was not the only one to think this way. The idea seems to have been also the brainchild of Irish folklorist Alfred (A. P.) Graves (the Secretary of the Irish Literary Society) and of Kate Lee. Sir Ernest Clarke, E. F. Jacques, and Alec Fuller Maitland were also among those involved at the very beginning of the project. The first practical initiative was taken in early January 1898 when the circular letter that Kidson received was mailed by Lee to various interested parties, including Alfred Nutt, President of the Folk-Lore Society.[13] Lee and Broadwood met to discuss the response on 15 January, and they both attended an inaugural meeting on 27 January, at which a planning committee was elected and exploratory discussions were held with officers of the Irish Literary Society and the Folk-Lore Society. The original idea seems to have been to create a new section of the Folk-Lore Society, but negotiations with Nutt proved abortive, and Kidson (among others) championed the need for an independent organization with a lower membership fee. This alternative strategy was decided upon at a meeting of the steering committee held on 23 March, attended by Lucy, Kate, Graves, Jacques, and Fuller Maitland.[14] After one more planning meeting on May 4 it was duly implemented, and the Folk-Song Society formally came into existence on 16 May 1898.[15]

In creating an independent Society the founding committee had five main aims. One was to create a formal body that could serve as a means of communication between the several hundred people scattered across England who were interested in collecting, studying, and/or performing folksongs. A second aim was to recruit as members various wealthy sympathizers and eminent musicians who might be persuaded collectively to fund the Society and to lend prestige to its activities. The third goal was to hold regular—preferably twice-yearly—meetings or conferences at which reports on new collecting would be given and examples of newly collected folksongs would be performed. A fourth aim was to publish a scholarly journal. This was intended as the means by which the fruits of members' collecting would be preserved for posterity, but it was also seen as an opportunity for academic scholarship. And, last but not least, the new Society was seen as a vehicle for promoting folksong through lectures and performances. Significantly, Kate Lee, a professional contralto whose hobby was collecting and singing traditional songs, was chosen as Secretary of the new Society. Its achievements during its first few years owed much to her efforts.

The first thing Kate Lee and her colleagues did was to undertake a membership drive. They signed up Lord Herschell to be the Society's first president, and then, when he died suddenly, they found a replacement in Lord Cobham. Equipped with a suitably prestigious aristocrat as its titular president, the Society also needed support from the musical establishment. This was achieved by making three of the leading English composers of the time, Sir Alexander Mackenzie, Sir Hubert Parry, and Charles Villiers Stanford, vice-presidents. Drawing on Lucy Broadwood's existing network of correspondents, a body of rank-and-file members was also recruited, and they were asked to submit to the executive committee the fruits of their own local collecting for communication to other members at an inaugural general meeting to be held in London early the next year.

Lucy had not done much collecting for the last year or two, but she now threw herself back into folk music, not only regularly attending committee meetings and singing folksongs at concerts but also resuming field work. On 17 and 18 September 1898 she went back to Dunsfold to revisit some of the singers from whom she had previously collected old songs, and again she "noted down numerous fine airs."[16] Then on 20 September, after traveling to St. Albans, she collected several songs from a young shepherd named Frederick Page and his thirteen-year-old cousin, J. Page, and on the evening of the twenty-second she obtained more items from the two teenagers.[17] In early October Lucy was off to Leeds for the annual music festival, and naturally she had tea with Frank Kidson while she was there. Back in London, she dined with Edward Elgar and his wife on the twelfth but was unable to persuade the composer to become an honorary vice-president of the Society, although he did promise to buy a membership. More committee meetings followed, on 15 and 30 December 1898 and 4 January 1899, and at the last of these Lucy was asked to prepare a paper on "Collecting Folk Songs" for delivery at the inaugural Annual General Meeting. She duly set to work on it the next day, although in the event she decided that she was not ready to give it at the AGM or even at the next general meeting held on 23 November of that year.[18] She did, however, make some rough notes for herself, and the following extracts suggest a few of the anecdotes that she might have included in the talk, had she given it. LEB, of course, refers to herself, the bell-ringer is Henry Burstow, the carter is George Grantham, and the gypsies are members of the Goby family:

> Great disappointments await collectors. LEB was told by an old and intelligent woman that she had a book of old songs her son had left in her charge—it proved to be a programme of the Christy Minstrels! On the other hand, one may stumble on a mine unexpectedly. LEB was talking about songs to a labourer at her old home and he said he was not musical but that he knew a bell-ringer who kept a written list of all the songs he knew and made old songs his hobby. The book was kindly lent, and proved to be of the greatest value, giving the titles of more than 300 songs old and modern which the bell-ringer had by heart, and which contained from 90 to 100 of real value, and from 70 to 80 of undoubted archaeological interest. The only difficulty in getting at these valuable songs was that the singer despised the narrative ballads and the simple or archaic words and tunes, and insisted on singing Eliza Cook's "The Haymakers," "Robin Adair" and "Let Me Kiss Him for His Mother" in preference. Fortunately his pride in the fact that he can remember more songs than anyone else incites him to collect from everyone and everywhere. His best so-called traditional songs he collected from unlettered labourers and shoemakers of more than half a century ago.
> One excellent singer—a carter in Surrey—told me that he had learnt most of his songs from older carters and labourers in Sussex, which was his birthplace. This old man could not read or write. He said to LEB, "I'm not much of a musician, but I dersay if we puts our heads together we may make something out." He was intensely interested when LEB went to the piano and reproduced what he sang, and said "Well, I never knew how it was done afore! That do seem wonderful!" From this carter LEB got "Sheepcrook and Blackdog" and many excellent songs.
> A short time ago two gipsies near to LEB's old home sang an Xmas carol beginning "King Pharim (meaning 'Pharaoh') sat a-musing." This carol turned on the legendary infancy of Christ. 'King Pharim' says to the infant Christ: "If it be true, true, good man, All that you say to me, Make that a roasted cock do crow, In the place where we do stand." Naturally one supposed the 'roasted cock' to be a corruption of 'roosting cock'. But in the British Museum LEB found early legends, one in a ms. of Henry VI's time, of Christ, and saints also, causing a roasted fowl to come to life and crow in its dish. This shows the importance of re-printing the words in the exact form in which they have been given to one. Words become much corrupted, for in another Xmas carol the word 'sepulchre' was sung and written as 'music-port.'
> In Sussex a good singer is called by his admiring friends "an outway songster." He clears his throat lustily before beginning and then begins with a sort of scoop up from the dominant to the tonic or tonic to the dominant, and this defect in attacking the first note is I believe the origin of the very characteristic feature in English song. The rustic singer delights in triplets by way of ornament, and continually uses them where the cultivated musician would use two equal notes, or two short and one long...At the end of the song the old fashion still obtains of speaking the last line, or at all events the last few words.[19]

Perhaps the most significant line of all in this document is Lucy's reflection on the lesson that she learned over the roasted cock. She had become a firm adherent of the scientific school of editing and now believed that the collector's first duty was to record faithfully and exactly what an informant sang. Precision and fidelity came first, interpretation second, and revision for performance or publication later, if at all.

The first Annual General Meeting of the Folk-Song Society, duly held on 2 February 1899, took the form of a mini-conference, chaired by Mackenzie. Parry gave the opening address. This excerpt from his remarks captures the ideological context in which the Folk-Song Society had been founded:

> Ladies and Gentlemen—I think I may premise that this Society is engaged upon a wholesome and seasonable enterprise. For, in these days of high pressure and commercialism...there is a tendency with some of us to become cynical; and the best remedy available is to revive a belief in, and love of our fellow-creatures. And this love and well-thinking of our fellow-creatures must come to those who study folk-music; for...in true folk-songs there is no sham, no got-up glitter, and no vulgarity...and the pity of it is that these treasures of humanity are getting rare...Moreover, there is an enemy at the doors of folk-music which is driving it out, namely the common popular songs of the day; and this enemy is one of the most repulsive and most insidious...it is made with a commercial intention out of snippets of musical slang. And this product it is will drive out folk-music if we do not save it. For

even in country districts where folk-songs linger, the people think themselves behindhand if they do not know the songs of the seething towns; and as soon as the little urchins of distant villages catch the sound of a music-hall tune, away goes the hope of their troubling their heads with the old fashioned folk-songs. But the old folk-music is among the purest products of the human mind. It grew in the hearts of the people before they devoted themselves so assiduously to the making of quick returns; and it grew there because it pleased them to make it, and because what they made pleased them; and that is the only way good music is ever made...Folk-song...outlasts the greatest works of art, and becomes a heritage to generations. And in that heritage may lie the ultimate solution of the problem of characteristic national art.[20]

Parry thus made it quite clear that he saw in collecting "the old folk-music" a moral crusade to save a national treasure that was being destroyed by industrialization, urbanization, and the popular trash purveyed by the music hall. Other active members of the Folk-Song Society were perhaps motivated more by a simple love of the unusual, often modal, tunes found in oral tradition, and a desire to note, preserve, and publish them. There was general agreement, however, that other European countries and even Scotland and Ireland were well ahead of England in collecting and publishing their folksongs, but that England possessed just as fine a body of traditional music. It was high time to collect, publish, and publicize this, and thereby disprove the oft-repeated slur that England had no national music. The recovery of English traditional music was seen as a valuable aim in its own right, but Parry and others who agreed with him had a second agenda too: a renaissance of English art music fueled by the heritage of English folksong. As he remarked, "in that heritage may lie the ultimate solution of the problem of characteristic national art."[21]

Parry also had some controversial things to say about folksong collecting. He stressed the difficulty of noting down tunes accurately, claiming that "in reality, the collection of folk-songs requires the most extraordinary facility of accurate attention, of accurate retention, of self-criticism and practice as well, to distinguish what is genuine from what is emasculated. The attention required makes it almost impossible to take down folk-songs with certainty. To my mind the only way to do it with absolute accuracy would be to make use of the phonograph..."[22] In 1899 Parry found few supporters of this position. Kate Lee, Lucy Broadwood, J. A. Fuller Maitland, and other pioneer practitioners of song-collecting in the field were well aware of the practical difficulties that they had encountered, but they did not think that noting tunes was "almost impossible." Tricky, yes. Impossible, by no means. Nor did they believe that at the time of collecting one needed to distinguish the genuine from the corrupted; it was better to take down as accurately as possible whatever the source singers had to offer, and then sort out later the authenticity of the material so obtained. It was easy to assume, erroneously, that a song was a recent composition of a ballad-monger when in fact the broadside from which the informant had learned the words was actually based on a centuries-old traditional song. As for using a phonograph, that was a newfangled idea that never appealed to the first generation of pioneer collectors. Parry himself apparently failed to act on his own advice, and neither did Baring-Gould, Barrett, Burne, Kidson, Lee, or Stokoe. It would be left mainly to a second generation of collectors to experiment with mechanical recording devices, with Percy Grainger and Ralph Vaughan Williams the most enthusiastic converts to the technology. Broadwood would eventually be won over to recording informants on wax cylinders but she employed a phonograph principally when collecting Gaelic songs in the Edwardian era.

The Society's first AGM also saw the delivery of papers by Kate Lee and E. F. Jacques. Lee's was entitled "Some Experiences of a Folk-Song Collector" and described her field work in Norfolk, East London, and Sussex.[23] She had begun collecting traditional songs when on vacation at the seaside town of Wells in Norfolk in 1897, and she recalled noting at that time a Welsh song, "Llandaff," from a gardener and ex-soldier called Mr. Edge. She also mentioned two songs, "The Bonny Irish Boy" and "The Cottage by the Wood," that she had collected in East London from an old lady called Mrs. Mainwaring Bodell, who had learned them as a child in the hamlet of Prees Green, Shropshire. Lee's most successful collecting trip was to Rottingdean in Sussex where she discovered James Copper, the landlord of the Plough Inn and his brother William, a foreman on a local farm. Of the "half a hundred" songs the Copper brothers said they knew, Lee collected six in November 1898: "Claudy Banks," "The Banks of Sweet Primroses," "Wedding Song," "The Week Before Easter," "Adieu, Sweet Lovely Nancy," and "As I Walked Out" (aka "The Irish Girl").[24] Here is one of them, "The Claudy Banks":

'Twas on one summer's morning, all in the month of May,
Down by our flow'ry garden where Betsy did stray.
I overheard a damsel in sorrow to complain,
All for her absent lover that ploughs the raging main.

I stepped up to this fair maid and put her in surprise,
She owned she did not know me, I being in disguise.

I said, "My charming creature, my joy and heart's delight,
How far have you to travel on this dark and rainy night?"

"The way, kind Sir, to the Claudy Banks, if you will please to show;
Pity a poor girl distracted, for there I have to go.
I am in search of a young man, and Johnnie is his name,
And on the Banks of Claudy I'm told he does remain."

"Young Johnnie, if he was here this night, he'll keep me from all harm.
He's in the field of battle, and in his uniform.
He's in the field of battle, his foes he will destroy,
Like some roaming king of honour, who fought in the wars of Troy."

"It was six weeks or better since my true love left the shore.
He's a-cruising the wide ocean where the foaming billows roar,
He's a-cruising the wild ocean for honour or for gain."
"I was told the ship got wrecked all on the coast of Spain!"

When Betsy heard this dreadful news she fell into despair,
In wringing of her hands, and in tearing of her hair.
"Since Johnnie has gone and left me, no man on earth I'll take,
But in some lonesome valley, I'll wander for his sake."

Young Johnnie hearing her say so, he could no longer stand,
He fell into her arms, saying, "Betsy, I'm the man!
I am the faithless young man, and whom you thought was slain,
And since we met on Claudy Banks, we'll never part again."[25]

The Claudy Banks

Anon

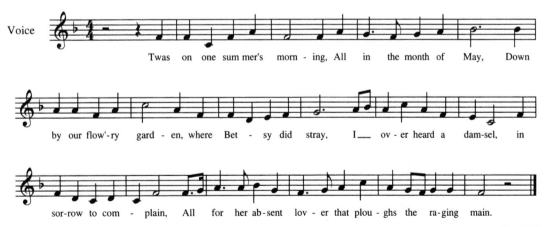

Fig. 16.2

Lee illustrated her paper by singing a few of the songs she had mentioned, including "Claudy Banks," "Llandaff," "As I Walked Out" and "The Wedding Song." She also had Gregory Hast sing "The Week Before Easter" and her friend Mrs. Helen Trust sing "The Cottage by the Wood" and "The Banks of Sweet Primroses." From its very beginning, then, the Folk-Song Society was more than a collectors' club and an academic forum. It was also a vehicle for the performance of folksongs by its members, many of whom were amateur (or even professional) musicians and some of whom had voices trained to deliver operatic arias and art songs.

The other paper, delivered by E. F. Jacques, was a collaborative effort with Alec Fuller Maitland on the subject of "Modal Survivals in Folk-Song." Claiming that no one interested in folksong could afford to be without an accurate and comprehensive knowledge of the Ecclesiastical Modes, Jacques argued that the Dorian, Mixolydian, and Aeolian modes were often to be found in folk music. The modes, he suggested, were not "eccentric deviations" from modern major and minor keys but rather were the normal scales used by musicians in the Mediterranean and India in the time of the ancient Greeks and in Western Europe during the Middle Ages. Older folksongs, too, used modal melodies, which is why they sometimes "sound[ed] wrong" to ears accustomed to modern tonality. Modern ears, claimed Jacques, were simply not adequately prepared for the "modal peculiarities" of traditional song, which was why there was a very regrettable propensity for "those called upon either to play, sing, or edit [traditional] music...to spoil it, by altering or 'correcting' what they suppose to be wrong."[26] To illustrate the use of the Mixolydian mode in folksong, Jacques had Hammet Drake sing "Napoleon's Farewell to Paris," a song collected by Lucy Broadwood and Alec Fuller Maitland from a gamekeeper at Lyne, Sussex, in 1893.[27] "Napoleon's Farewell to Paris" illustrated two things that were to become characteristic of the next (Edwardian) phase of the folksong revival: the song had been thought interesting enough to collect and analyse primarily because of its modal melody, and the words (noted only in fragmentary form from the singer) had been "completed" from a broadside ballad-sheet. Here is "Napoleon's Farewell":

Napoleon's Farewell to Paris

Anon

Fig. 16.3

Farewell, ye splendid citadel, Metropolis, called Paris,
Where Phoebus every morning shoots forth refulgent beams,
Where Flora's bright Aurora advancing from the Orient,
With radiant light adorning the pure shining streams.

At eve, when Centaur does retire, while the Ocean gilds like fire,
And the universe admires our merchandise and store,
Commanding Flora's fragrance the fertile fields to decorate,
To illuminate the royal Corsican again on the French shore.

My name's Napoleon Bonaparte, the conqueror of nations,
I've banished German legions, and drove kings from their throne,
I've trampled dukes and earls, and splendid congregations,

Though they have now transported me to St. Helena's shore.

Like Hannibal I've crossed the Alps, the burning sands and rocky cliffs,
O'er Russian hills, through frost and snow, I still the laurel wore;
I'm on a desert island where the rats the devil would affright,
Yet I hope to shine in armour bright through Europe once more.

Some say the cause of my downfall was parting from my consort,
To wed the German's daughter who wounded my heart sore;
I stole Malta's golden gates, I did the works of God disgrace,
But if He gives me time and place, to Him back I will restore.

My golden eagles were pulled down by Wellington's allied army,
My troops all in disorder could no longer stand the field,
I was sold that afternoon, on the eighteenth day of June,
My reinforcements proved traitors which caused me to yield.

I am an allied oak, with fire and sword I made them smoke,
I have conquered Dutch and Danes, and surprised the grand signor;
I have defeated Austrians and Russians, both Portuguese and Prussians,
Like Joshua, Alexander, or Caesar of yore.

And to the south of Africa, and the Atlantic ocean,
To view the wild emotions and flowings of the tide;
Banished from the royal crown of Imperial promotion,
From the French of glory to see those billows glide.

Three days I stood the plain, liberty's cause for to maintain,
Thousands I left slain and covered in their gore;
I never fled without revenge, nor to the allied army cringed,
But now my sword is sheathed, and Paris is no more.[28]

The inaugural General Meeting of the Society was counted by most who attended as a great success. Broadwood did not play a prominent role in it because she was at the time preoccupied with moving house, a major upheaval that saw her at last obtaining what she had long desired, a permanent London residence of her own. Nonetheless, her involvement with the planning committee had been a significant development in her life, and she was easily persuaded by Fuller Maitland and Kidson to stand for election to the new executive committee. She was duly elected, and her diary for 1899 provides a record of her continued involvement with the Society as well as her other folksong-related activities. The first day of February 1899 saw her moving into her new apartment, and two days after the AGM she was traveling up to Yorkshire, where, on the seventh, she sang various madrigals and folksongs as illustrations for a lecture in Hull by Arthur Ferguson on folklore and customs.

Back in London in March, Broadwood entertained Frank Kidson on the ninth, and the next day the two of them attended a Folk-Song Society committee meeting. More committee meetings took place on the twenty-first and the twenty-fourth of the same month. April saw her collaborating again with Kate Lee, and also with a new singer who would in future play an important role in her personal and musical life, James Campbell McInnes. A summer of music making was followed in August by a trip to Northumberland, which included a visit to Newcastle-upon-Tyne. There she visited the Society of Antiquarians Library at the castle and scrutinized James Telfer's manuscript collection of Northumbrian tunes. Returning to London in the autumn, she again sang musical illustrations for another of Arthur Ferguson's lectures and resumed attending Folk-Song Society committee meetings. These were now focused on preparing the agenda of the second general meeting of the Society, to be held in November, and making sure that the first issue of the *Journal of the Folk-Song Society* would be available for distribution at that meeting.

Journal of the Folk-Song Society, 1899-1900

The Society's *Journal* was intended primarily as a place to print the fruits of members' collecting expeditions, and secondarily as a vehicle for scholarly commentary upon those songs. Together, the founding of the Society and the subsequent creation of the *Journal* represented an attempt to formalize, institutionalize, and thereby consolidate and make more permanent, the efforts of various individuals who had previously been working in isolation. The very first issue of the *Journal of the Folk-Song Society* was published later that same year, 1899. It provided a record of the Society's first AGM. In addition to Parry's "Inaugural Address" it contained printed texts of Jacques's and Lee's papers, plus transcriptions of "Napoleon's Farewell to Paris" and nine of the songs Lee had noted down in Norfolk, East London, and Sussex.[29]

The second issue of the *Journal* was devoted to reporting the Society's second General Meeting, held on 22 and 23 November 1899. The proceedings included a paper by the Reverend Francis L. Cohen on "Folk-Song Survivals in Jewish Worship Music" and one by Frank Kidson on "Sailors' Songs." Broadwood, Lee, and Fuller Maitland all contributed musical illustrations to one or both of the presentations. The three of them were also re-elected to the Society's executive committee.

Kidson's paper was less specialized in nature than Cohen's and therefore of more interest to the general membership.[30] He distinguished between shanties and songs sung by sailors for their own amusement. He concentrated on the latter, discussing hornpipes and ballads of various types. For illustrative purposes Louis Hillier played a couple of hornpipes, although on what instrument is unclear. However, the ballads were what interested Kidson most. He divided them into a number of different categories: (i) old ballads based on historical incidents such as "The *Golden Vanity*," "Captain Ward and the *Rainbow*," and "The Death of Admiral Benbow," (ii) pirate ballads such as "Henry Martin" and "The *Bold Princess Royal*," (iii) "long dismal ballads" of wrecks, fires, and murders at sea, such as "The Gosport Tragedy, or the Cruel Ship's Carpenter," (iv) press-gang songs, such as "The Brisk Young Lively Lad," and (v) songs of the sailor's return, either triumphantly (as in "In Fair Plymouth City") or as a drowned corpse (as in the Yorkshire song "Stowbrow").

Kidson had arranged for a number of singers to sing some of the examples that he mentioned, and Kate Lee performed "Just As the Tide Was Flowing." As we saw in chapter 8, Kidson had found a complete set of words on a broadside, his collaborator Charles Lolley had noted the tune in the North Riding of Yorkshire and the ballad was included in *Traditional Tunes*.[31] Charles Phillips performed "Henry Martin" and "Outward Bound," both of which had also been printed in *Traditional Tunes*, while Kathleen Fell sang "The *Nightingale*," a version of which had been collected by William Barrett and published in his *English Folk-Songs*.[32] Because most of the songs Kidson mentioned were already available elsewhere only one of his collection of sea songs was printed for illustrative purposes in the *Journal*. This was "The *Bold Princess Royal*." He had noted down two different versions of the ballad, one from retired sailor Charley Dickenson and the other from Mrs. Agar of Whitby, a sailor's daughter who had learned the song from her father. With one minor modification (to better fit the rhythm of the words) he printed the tune as Mrs. Agar had sung it, adding a set of words based on broadsides in his collection:

Bold Princess Royal

Anon

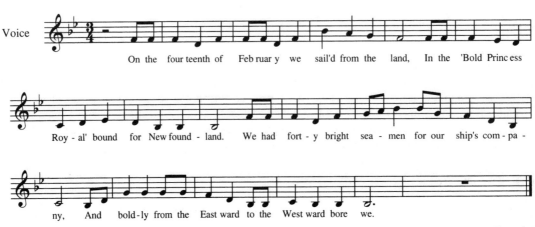

On the four teen of Feb ruar y we sail'd from the land, In the 'Bold Princ ess Roy-al' bound for Newfound-land. We had fort-y bright sea-men for our ship's com-pa-ny, And bold-ly from the East ward to the West ward bore we.

Fig. 16.4

On the fourteenth of February we sail'd from the land
In the *Bold Princess Royal* bound for Newfoundland.
We had forty bright seamen for our ship's company,
And boldly from the Eastward to the Westward bore we.

We had not been sailing past two days or three,
When a man from our masthead a sail he did see;
She bore down upon us, our ship for to view,
While under her mizzen black colours she flew.

"Good Lord!" says our captain, "what shall we do now?
Here comes a bold pirate, to rob us I know."
"Oh, no!" cries our chief mate, "that ne'er shall be so,
We'll shake out a reef, boys, and from her we'll go."

Now when this bold pirate she hove alongside,
With a long speaking trumpet "Whence you come?" they cried;
Our captain being aft, boys, he answered them to,
"We came from fair London: we're bound for Cairo."

"Come, haul up your courses and heave your ship to,
For I have a letter I'll send home by you."
"I will haul up my courses and heave my ship to,
But it shall be in harbour, and not alongside you."

They fired shots after us but could not prevail,
For the *Bold Princess Royal* soon showed them her tail;
She chased us to windward but could not make way,
So she hail'd up her mainsail and then bore away.[33]

Apart from the two papers, the main business of the meeting was the presentation, by Alec Fuller Maitland, of some thirty or so songs collected by members of the Society since its inauguration. Of these, the largest number had been submitted by Kate Lee. Lee had continued her field-work in Norfolk, East London, and Sussex, and she was present to sing some of the eleven tunes she had collected. Four came from Norfolk: two hornpipes, and two songs noted from Mr. Cater, an eighty-year-old shepherd from Baconsthorpe: "In Plymouth Fair City" and "Eggs in Her Basket." As sung (and as subsequently printed in the *Journal*) the lyrics of the latter were truncated, the reason for which Fuller Maitland explained as follows: "the rustic situation of which 'Eggs in Her Basket' treats is of a nature which would tax the powers of Mr. Thomas Hardy to describe without giving offence, and only part of the story is presentable in performance."[34] There was apparently no such problem with "In Fair Plymouth City," despite the *double entendre* in verses 7 and 8:

In the city fair of Plymouth
A fair damsel did dwell,
Her modest, fair and handsome,
Her father loved her well.

When gazing round the mainmast,
And there she chanced to spy,
Oh! a jolly young sailor
Who was there standing by.

She called for her maid Betsy
And unto her did say,
"Come take this here letter
And carry it straight away."

"Come take this here letter,
And carry it to my dear,
And go to him and tell him from me,
A lady wants him here."

Now the sailor being come,
He was in the other room,
Hearing of this fair lady
A-making of her moan.

She turned her head aside,
Saying, "Sailor, are you come?"
Another answer that he made,
"Yes, madam, that I am."

"Oh! do you well remember,
It was on the other day,
On board of my father's ship
The hammock it did sway?"

"'Twas then I lost my jewel,
More precious far than gold,
And you are the man that found [it]
As I have been told."

And he picked up his hat
And she gave him a kiss,
And she said, "Dear jolly sailor,
Don't take this amiss."

Now this couple got married,
As you shall quickly hear,
Her father died and left her
A thousand a year.

Beside five hundred guineas
He left all his gold,

Because she'd got married
To a jolly sailor bold.

So you ladies of honour,
Wherever that you be,
Do not despise a sailor
Of any degree.

For they are lads of honour
And they'll spend their money free,
And they'll venture their lives
For Queen and counterie.[35]

In Fair Plymouth City

Anon

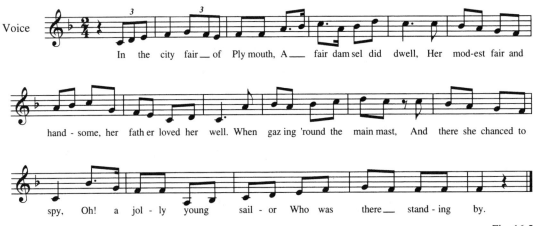

Voice

In the city fair ___ of Ply mouth, A ___ fair dam sel did dwell, Her mod-est fair and

hand - some, her fath er loved her well. When gaz ing 'round the main mast, And there she chanced to

spy, Oh! a jol - ly young sail - or Who was there ___ stand - ing by.

Fig. 16.5

Since the last annual meeting of the Folk-Song Society Kate Lee had also been back to Rottingdean in Sussex, revisiting the Coppers and noting more of their repertoire. Her new songs from this source included "Seaman Bold," "Sweep Chimbly Sweep," "Spencer the Rover," "The Jolly Ploughman," and "The Sun Is Down."[36] She had also tried collecting in the streets of London. From William Walker, of Poplar, East London, she had collected two songs that he had learned as a boy, while he lived in Cheshire: "The Moon Is Up" and "The Plains of Waterloo." Lee particularly liked the tune of "The Plains of Waterloo" and it was one of the songs that she performed for the assembled gathering. It appears that she had obtained only two verses from her informant; at least, they were all that were performed on this occasion:

Come all ye loyal lovers, and pray you lend an ear,
And listen unto these few lines which I have written here.
And while these lines I do indite, the tears my cheek bedew,
Lamenting for my darling boy that was slain at Waterloo.

My hands they are so feeble, with pain they scarce can move,
I'm troubled in my mind and my blood is running cold.
I mourn like a turtle dove, what more can I do?
Lamenting for my own true love that was slain at Waterloo.[37]

The Plains of Waterloo

Anon

Voice

Come all ye loy - al lov - ers and pray you lend an ear, And
list - en un - to these few lines which I have writ - ten here. And while these lines I
do in - dite, the tears my cheeks be - dew, la - ment - ing for my darl - ing boy that was
slain at Wat - er - loo.

Fig. 16.6

Other Society members who had contributed songs included Mrs. C. Milligan Fox (seven tunes) and Mr. J. T. N. Lee (two items), both of whom Fuller Maitland criticized for providing insufficient information about their sources. He remarked pointedly that "it is always worthwhile to give every detail as to the sources from which the contributions have come, exactly how they were heard, and from whom."[38] This was a counsel of perfection to which he and Broadwood had failed to adhere when editing *English County Songs,* but it was an admirable sentiment nonetheless. Unfortunately, many of the leading Edwardian collectors would choose to do as Fuller Maitland did rather than as he said.

The executive committee of the Folk-Song Society had received a wealth of material from a variety of sources. Clearly there was widespread enthusiasm for the cause, and the movement was picking up a considerable number of active rank-and-file members. For example, William Welch of Cranleigh, Surrey submitted "The Echoing Horn," a Dr. Bland had noted "'Tis Better to Marry than Die an Old Maid," Lieutenant-Colonel Wilkingson of Dolgelly had collected a Somerset wassail song, and the Reverend W. Marcon of Edgefield, Norfolk, had sent in "John Hodge." More prolific was Mr. E. T. Wedmore of Bristol: the fruits of his collecting in Somerset and Devon included "In Cupid's Garden," "Come All You Jolly Seamen Bold," "Rise Up, Young William Raleigh," "Captain Dicky Fleming," "Barnstable Fair" (a variant of "Widdecombe Fair"), and, most interesting of all, "Come, Mother," a ballad noted from Joseph Spillers of North Petherton, near Bridgwater, that seemed to combine elements from several different Child ballads, including "Lord Randal," "Matty Groves," and "Lord Thomas and Fair Eleanor." All this was very promising, and it was evident that, notwithstanding his criticisms, Fuller Maitland was very pleased with the amount of collecting activity stimulated by the establishment of the Society.

To conclude his review Fuller Maitland selected "The Green Bed," a ballad submitted by Isabel Hearne; the words, he remarked, were "not very edifying" but the tune was an "interesting old one":

> It was a jolly sailor boy, who ploughed the radiant main,
> Who had lately had a pleasant voyage, but now he's on the shore;
> He called at an alehouse, where he used to resort,
> In his ragged apparel, like one who is poor.
>
> He told them his money was growing short,
> He asked them to trust him, but the answer was nay.

He asked them to trust him, but the answer was nay:
"Friend, if you've no money, you must call another day."

Now John being worried, he hung down his head,
And called for a candle to light him to bed,
"Our beds are all full, John, and has been for this week,
So now for fresh lodging you must go and seek."

"Oh, what is your reckoning, since you've been so bold;
Oh, what is your reckoning, since you've been so bold?"
"It's five and forty shillings, John, you've owed me from old."
And with that he pulled out two handfuls o' gold.

The sight of the money made the old landlady rue,
The sight of the money made the old landlady to grue:
"My daughter is not busy, John, she can come down to you,
Or either I will trust you with a pot or two."

Down came her daughter, she was dressed in her best;
"Oh, what has been said, John, was only in jest!"
She kissed him and she cuddled him, and called him her dear,
"The Green Bed is empty, John, you can lie there."

"Before I would lie there, I would lie in the street,
And now for fresh lodging I will surely go and seek;
For if I'd had no money, out o' door I'd be turned,
So you and your mother do deserve to be burned."

Come, all you jolly sailor boys, that plough the radiant main,
That do get your living through the cold wind and rain;
Now if you have any money, I pray you lay it in store.
'Twill be a noble companion when you get turned out o' door."[39]

The Green Bed

Anon

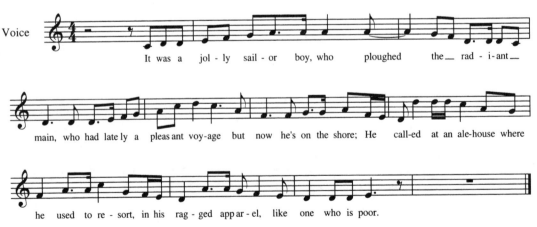

Fig. 16.7

The audience at the meeting was spared five of these supposedly unedifying verses (Mr. Phillips sang three only), but
readers of the *Journal* would be able to read the entire ballad, as sung by farm laborer John Butler of Shottery, near

Stratford-on-Avon. Fuller Maitland, however, was much more interested in the melody which, he commented, was "obviously modal" but seemed to fluctuate between Dorian and Phrygian.[40]

That second issue of the *Journal*, which actually did not appear in print until the end of 1900, was taken up almost entirely with printing Fuller Maitland's report and the two papers by Kidson and Cohen. Space was found at the end, however, for one song collected by Lucy Broadwood in Surrey ("The Brisk Young Lad") and the one by Frank Kidson quoted earlier ("The *Bold Princess Royal*"). However, this conception of the *Journal* as a report of the proceedings of the Folk-Song Society's meetings would not endure. From 1901 on the *Journal* would rarely report on the Society's AGMs, which were subsequently devoted mainly to matters of routine administrative business. Successive editors would concentrate instead on using precious space (there were only one or two issues per year) to print traditional songs and tunes collected by members.

In the meantime the musical life of the Folk-Song Society and its London members went on without pause. The new millennium had opened with more committee meetings, more music-making, and more networking. Broadwood was now also elected to the Council of the Folk-Lore Society, she occasionally entertained Ralph Vaughan Williams and Sabine Baring-Gould, and she regularly played piano and/or sang with Alec Fuller Maitland and James Campbell McInnes.[41] At the beginning of February she traveled to Oxford to perform in a concert put on by the Oxford Ladies Musical Society. This consisted of spinet solos (tunes of songs and dances by William Byrd, Thomas Morley, John Munday, Giles Farnaby, John Bull, Peter Philips, and Orlando Gibbons) taken from the *Fitzwilliam Virginal Book,* edited by W.B. Squire and J. A. (Alec) Fuller Maitland; and folksongs sung by Lucy. The latter included eight songs from *English County Songs*: "In Bethlehem City" (Northamptonshire), "The Wassail Bough" (Yorkshire), "Little Sir William" (Lincolnshire), "The Reaphook and the Sickle" (Hampshire), "Cold Blows the Wind" (Shropshire), "The Thresher and the Squire" (Oxfordshire), "Of All the Horses in Merry Greenwood" (Surrey), and "The Sweet Nightingale" (Surrey); four songs from Lucy's own collecting: "As I Went Forth" (Sussex: new words), "Some Rival Has Stolen My True Love Away" (Surrey), "Belfast Mountains" (Sussex), and "Bristol Town" (Sussex); and three others: "The Ripest Apples" (arranged J. A. Fuller Maitland), "Henry Martin" (Yorkshire, from *Traditional Tunes,* arranged by Frank Kidson), and "The Rosebuds in June" (from *Sussex Songs,* arranged by Herbert Birch Reynardson). Lucy's comment in her diary read, "In evening satisfactory concert by Alec Maitland and self, both much appreciated."[42] Later that same month she was again singing folksongs in a concert setting, this time "A North Country Maid," "The Loyal Lover," "Little Sir William," and "The Sweet Nightingale" (all from *English County Songs*) at Essex Shire Hall, Chelmsford, in aid of the St. Alban's Diocesan Institution for Trained Nurses.[43]

Broadwood continued dutifully to attend Folk-Song Society committee meetings throughout 1900 and 1901, although of the elected committee only Kate Lee was showing the same commitment to the cause as in the initial burst of enthusiasm for the project. At one meeting, on 13 March, only Kate, Lucy, and Alec showed up, and only one other meeting was held during the summer of 1900.[44] The Folk-Lore Society was now taking up some of Lucy's time, as was the Purcell Society and her close friendship with James Campbell McInnes. But Kate Lee revived the Folk-Song Society committee at the beginning of 1901, and Lucy also renewed her friendships with Charlotte Burne and Frank Kidson, entertaining them on 29 January and 15 February respectively. Another engagement in Harrow, singing illustrations for Arthur Ferguson's lecture on "Sea Songs," followed in March, and in June she got together again with Sabine Baring-Gould. It was a while since Broadwood had done any collecting, but in early October she traveled to the village of Bury in West Sussex where her friends Mr. and Mrs. Carr now had a cottage, and that evening Mrs. Carr invited to supper four local singers, John, Walter and Ed. Searle (all quarrymen) and Mr. Hoare (a laborer). Lucy "noted down numerous tunes" and, observing that Bury was only about four miles away from Wiggenholt, where her Uncle John Broadwood had collected some of his songs, she also remarked that "these men sang 'The Bailiff's Daughter' to precisely his same tune."[45] The final Folk-Song Society committee meeting of the year, on 13 November, approved the printing of the third issue of the Society's *Journal.*

Percy Merrick: Collecting in Sussex

Getting issue No. 3 (1901) of the *Journal* published appears to have been a collective effort, the joint work of secretary Lee and the nominal editor Mr. Kalisch (who was unfortunately hampered by health problems), with assistance from Broadwood and Kidson. It was devoted entirely to fifty-two songs collected by W. Percy Merrick from Henry Hills, a farmer at Lodsworth, near Petworth, Sussex.[46] Merrick, who lived in Sussex, was sight-impaired and had been assisted by his friend Albert Burnell. The songs were presented with melody lines but no harmonization, with full texts as collected (with two exceptions), and with brief commentaries by Broadwood and Kidson, usually pointing out other versions of tunes or texts to be found in broadsides or printed collections. These commentaries demonstrated their authors' thorough familiarity with such Victorian collections as Chappell's *Popular Music of the Olden Time* and Dixon's and Bell's *Ancient Poems, Ballads and Songs of the Peasantry of England,* as well as their own more recent publications and those of Baring-Gould, Barrett, Christie, Stokoe, and Sumner. They also revealed that Broadwood and Kidson had not yet fully assimilated the work of Francis Child, since they made no reference to Child's *English and Scottish Popular Ballads* when discussing such ballads as "Barbara Allen," "The Unquiet Grave," and "The Elfin Knight."

Merrick's collection from Henry Hills was fascinating in its variety and scope. He arranged the fifty-two songs according to a number of loose categories, although he left to the end various incomplete songs and fragments. In the main, Merrick presented exactly what he had collected, but there were two unfortunate exceptions where censorship reared its ugly head. The songs in question were "The Nut Girl" and "The Foggy Dew," from which verses depicting sexual encounters, although sung by Mr. Hills, were omitted. This was unfortunate; whatever the validity of arguments about the impossibility of including indelicate texts in songbooks intended for use in the drawing rooms of polite society, there was no excuse for employing the same intrusive editorial method in an academic journal intended for a small, specialist audience. Apart from this error of judgment, Merrick's presentation of his material was scholarly, indicating the month and year (late 1899 or early 1900) when he had obtained the songs. He also relayed any information that Hills had vouchsafed to him about the songs' geographical location (usually but not always Lodsworth) and social function, or about the singer(s) from whom he had learned them.

Quite a number of Hills's songs were 'healths' or 'catches' sung at harvest-home or rabbit-hunt suppers at Lodsworth "upwards of thirty years ago," whereas others, including but not exclusively carols, were sung at Christmas by parties of singers who went from house to house. The former included "The Mistress's Health," "Poor Tom," "I've Been to France," and "Poor Old Horse," and the latter "Come Pretty Maids" and "Come, All You Worthy Christians." Some songs, such as "John Barleycorn," Hills had learned from his parents, but others he had picked up from local laborers, artisans, and carters whose jobs brought them to the village. Agricultural songs were fewer in number than might have been expected, but Hills did sing "The Farmer's Glory," "The Thresherman and the Squire" and "John Barleycorn":

John Barleycorn

Anon

Fig. 16.8

There were three men came out of the West, they sold their wheat for rye;
They made an oath and a solemn oath, John Barleycorn should die,
Oh! and John Barleycorn should die.

They ploughed him into islands deep, the clods fell over his head,
They made an oath, a solemn oath, John Barleycorn was dead,
Oh! and John Barleycorn was dead.

And there he lay for three long weeks, some rain from heaven did fall,

John Barleycorn sprung up again, and he did surprise them all,
Oh! he did surprise them all.

And there he stood till Midsummer, he looked both pale and wan;
John Barleycorn he grew a beard, and soon became a man,
Oh! he soon became a man.

They hired two men, with their sharp scythes, to cut him off at knee,
And then they served him worse than that—they served him barbarously,
Oh! they served him barbarously.

They hired two men with their pitchforks to pitch him to the heart,
And then they served him worse than that—they bound him to the cart,
Oh! they bound him to the cart.

They wheeled him round and round the field until they came to a barn,
They mowed him in the mow so close because he shouldn't take any harm,
Oh! because he shouldn't take harm.

They hired two men with their clap-sticks to whip him skin from bone;
The miller he served him worse than that—he ground him betwixt two stones,
Oh! he ground him betwixt two stones.

And in the mash-tub he was put, and they scalded him stark blind;
And then they served him worse than that—they cast him to the swine,
Oh! they cast him to the swine.

We'll make the huntsman follow the hounds without a whip or horn,
We'll lay the tinker on the ground, says little John Barleycorn,
Oh! says little John Barleycorn.

We'll tip white wine into a glass, and scarlet into a can;
John Barleycorn and his brown bowl shall prove the stronger man,
Oh! shall prove the stronger man.[47]

Hills also sang three other songs which reflected the seasonal rhythms of country life: two fragmentary May songs and a complete version of "The Four Seasons of the Year." There was only one poaching song, "The Northamptonshire Poacher," but two highwayman songs ("Captain Grant" and "In Newry Town") and four songs of transportation and/or exile: "Here's Adieu to All Judges and Juries," "The Isle of France," "The Irish Stranger," and "Erin's Lovely Home."

The impact of the military and of the sea on rural Sussex was very evident in Merrick's collection. Songs of soldiering and warfare included "Bold General Wolfe," "The Blues," "It's of a Young Soldier," and "Come, All You Maids of Honour." "Six Joyful Welchman [sic]" expressed Welsh opposition to political rule from England, and reflected the Tudors' conflict with the Yorkists in the late Middle Ages. Songs about ships, the sea and the life of a sailor comprised the largest category of Hills's songs, although within this broad grouping there was considerable diversity. Commercial fishing was portrayed in "The Greenland Whale Fishery" and life in the Royal Navy by "The *Bold Princess Royal*" and "Our General Bold Captain." Class distinctions at sea were reflected in "The *Golden Vanity*" and the activities of the press-gang in "The Lowlands of Holland" and "It's of a Pretty Ploughboy," while the sadness of the wife or lover left behind on shore was expressed in "Farewell, My Dear Nancy" and "Our Captain Cried." In some of Hills's songs the missing lover returned safely to marry his waiting lover, but more often he was drowned, as in "Young Edwin in the Lowlands Low" and "A Sailor's Life." The latter ballad might even be counted as a variant of "Sweet William," the song that Baring-Gould had noted from John Woodrich and sent to Lucy Broadwood in 1894:

A sailor's life is a merry life, they rob young girls of their heart's delight,
Leaving them behind to sigh and mourn, they never know when they will return.

Here's four-and-twenty all in a row, my sweetheart cuts the brightest show;
He's proper, tall, genteel withall, if I don't have him, I'll have none at all.

O, father, fetch me a little boat that I might on the ocean float,

And every Queen's ship that we pass by, we'll make enquire for my sailor boy.

We had na' sailed long upon the deep, before a Queen's ship we chanced to meet;
"You sailors all, come tell me true, does my sweet William sail among your crew?"

"O, no, fair lady, he is not here, for he is drowned, we greatly fear;
On yon green island as we passed by, there we lost sight of your sailor boy."

She wrung her hands, and she tore her hair, much like a woman in great despair;
Her little boat 'gainst a rock did run: "How can I live, now my William's gone?"

She wrung her hands, and she tore her hair, much like a woman in great despair;
She threw her body into the deep, in William's arms to lay fast asleep.[48]

A Sailor's Life

Anon

Fig. 16.9

Only one of these tragic ballads evoked the supernatural: "How Cold the Wind Do Blow," a variant of "The Unquiet Grave." Another song was the nursery rhyme "Sing Ivy," derived from "Scarborough Fair," itself a fragment of the Child ballad usually titled "The Elfin Knight," but in Hills's version of the song the supernatural element was disguised, although still implicit. Similarly his "Turkish Lady" was actually a detached fragment of a much longer Child ballad, "Lord Bateman."

In addition to these songs and ballads about the loss of a lover at sea or his return from abroad, more than a dozen of Hills's songs dealt with relationships between the sexes. Ballads about inconstant lovers or unrequited love included "The Seeds of Love," "Barbara Allen," "Young Collins," "Sheepcrook and Black Dog" (aka "Faithless Floro"), "My True Love I've Lost," and "Come All You Little Streamers." Requited love leading to marriage was celebrated in "Green Broom," "The Fisherman," and "The Bailiff's Daughter of Islington." Sexual encounters of a more casual nature were depicted in "The Foggy Dew," "The Nut Girl," and "Seventeen Come Sunday." As we have seen, Merrick censored two of these songs but it was to his (and Kate Lee's) credit that the last verse of "Seventeen Come Sunday," which revealed the subtext of this pretty song to be teenage sexuality, was printed as sung. From the standpoint of scientific editing this was a step forward, despite the two steps backward noted above. This is the version of "Seventeen Come Sunday" collected by Merrick from Henry Hills in November 1899:

As I walked out one May morning, one May morning so early,
I overtook a handsome maid, just as the sun was rising,
To my right, tol-loo-ro loo-ro lo, to my right tol-loo-ro lee ro.

"Where are you going, my pretty maid, where are you going, my honey?"

She answered me right cheerfully, "I'm on an errand for my mammy."
To my right, &c.

"How old are you, my sweet pretty maid, how old are you, my honey?"
She answered me right cheerfully, "I'm seventeen come Sunday."
To my right, &c.

Her shoes were black, her stockings white, her buckles shone like silver,
And she had a dark and a rolling eye, and her hair hung down on her shoulder.
To my right, &c.

"Will you take a man, my sweet pretty maid, will you take a man, my honey?"
She answered me right cheerfully, "I dare not for my mammy."
To my right, &c.

"Will you come to my mammy's house when the moon shines bright and clearly?
And I'll come down and let you in, and my mammy shall not hear me."
To my right, &c.[49]

Seventeen Come Sunday

Anon

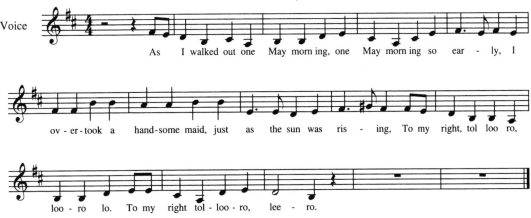

Fig. 16.10

Five additional songs collected by Percy Merrick from Henry Hills would be published in issue No. 5 of the *Journal* (1904). They included a night-visiting song ("O, Who Is That that Raps at My Window?"), a fine variant of "Reynardine" called "One Night Upon My Rambles," a variant of "My Bonny Boy" called "Many a Night's Rest," and a bittersweet love song for a departed lover, "Farewell Lads." The fifth song, "One Noble Knight," was inserted as a fragment only, with the terse editorial comment "words objectionable."[50] Once again the censor's red pencil had struck to protect the morals of *Journal* subscribers.

Eight years later, fifteen of Henry Hills's songs appeared, dressed up with piano accompaniments by Ralph Vaughan Williams, in *Folk Songs from Sussex*.[51] This was one volume in a series of songbooks issued by Novello under the general title *Folk Songs of England*. Edited by Cecil Sharp, the series was designed to present selections from the best folksongs collected in various English counties, and would eventually be reissued as a single volume under the title *English County Folk Songs*.[52] The collection opened with "Bold General Wolfe," followed by "Low Down in the Broom," "The Thresherman and the Squire," "The Pretty Ploughboy," and "O Who Is That that Raps at My Window?" They were followed by Hills's version of "The Unquiet Grave," supplied with additional words taken from variants of the same ballad collected by Baring-Gould, Sharp, and H. E. D. Hammond. Next came "Captain Grant," "Farewell Lads," and a religious song, "Come All You Worthy Christians," followed by the truncated version of "Lord Bateman" called "The

Turkish Lady." A fine version of "The Seeds of Love" was one of the highlights of the collection, which also included "The Maid of Islington," "Here's Adieu to All Judges and Juries," and a version of "The Baffled Knight" called "Lovely Joan." The final song, the only one arranged by Albert Robins instead of Vaughan Williams, was the transportation ballad "The Isle of France."

Broadwood and Kidson's practice of adding scholarly notes to the folksongs published in the *Journal* would be continued in the next year's issue. One important difference in their approach was evident. Broadwood had now discovered *The English and Scottish Popular Ballads,* and on every appropriate occasion she referred the *Journal's* readers to Child's extensive commentary on the ballad in question.

Lucy Broadwood: Collecting in Surrey and Sussex

Although the third issue of the *Journal* was excellent in terms of content, it was evident that organizing an annual mini-conference and publishing the *Journal* had become the *raison d'être* of the Folk-Song Society since nothing much, except committee meetings, happened during the rest of the year. One member of the executive group, W. Barclay Squire, decided that, in the circumstances, he had little to contribute and resigned from the committee, effective the end of 1901. Lucy contemplated doing the same herself, decided not to, but wrote a humorous poem about the situation which expressed her frustration with the way the Society was going:

> Horrid Mr. Barclay Squire! How, oh how could you retire!
> Leaving me on this committee? Had you not a grain of pity?
> Don't you know how ill it makes L.E.B. to sit near Jacques?
> How she hates Sir Ernest Clarke's vapid, wandering remarks?
> How she quivers as she braves monologues from A.P. Graves?
> Mr. Kalisch (often ill,) seldom comes; and Mr. Gill
> Dreads Mrs. Lee, and won't confront her, neither will the wise Todhunter.
> Words of sense drop often from worthy Mrs. Laurence Gomme,
> But the Folk Lore Council claims her—for her absence no one blames her.
> Mr. Maitland, good and great, often comes, but often late.
> Hilda Wilson, great and good, seldom comes ('tis understood
> Mr. Jacques she can't endure him.) Now you've left, and lo! Miss Joachim!
> Mr. Squire's voice is dumb; Eugenie instead has come!
> Joachim, and Clarke, and Jacques—shall I linger for their sakes?
> Shall I, squirming, drink my tea with all these, and Mrs. Lee?
> Base deserter! Tell me true: What, oh what am I to do?
> Shall I quit my golden throne, leaving Alec all alone?
> Or urge my kind collaborator to quit with me, a little later?[53]

One reason why Lucy could not resign at this time was that the 1902 issue (No. 4) of the *Journal* was devoted almost exclusively to her own collecting in the counties of Sussex and Surrey.[54] She had agreed to this just before Christmas, and it meant that she was the *de facto* editor for the issue. She consequently spent much of January and February 1902 going through her traditional song manuscripts, sorting them out, deciding which to use, and then making fair copies for the nominal *Journal* editor, Arthur Kalisch. By 26 February she was ready to send them off to him. She had chosen forty-seven songs in all, of which twenty-one were noted from Henry Burstow of Horsham (Sussex), four were collected at Amberley in Sussex, and fifteen were obtained from nine inhabitants (mainly farm laborers and their wives) of the village of Dunsfold, Surrey. There were also included a few miscellaneous but interesting items, including a "Christmas Mummers' Carol" from Kingsclere, Hampshire, May Day songs from Fowlmere in Cambridgeshire and Hinwick, Bedfordshire, and two carols "The Moon Shines Bright" and "King Pharim" (the latter a variant of the Child ballad "The Carnal and the Crane") collected from the Goby family of gypsies at Capel in Surrey. All in all, it was another impressive collection, although many of the song texts were clearly derived from broadsheets, even when noted down "in the field" from local singers. This was the case, for example, with Henry Burstow's songs; wherever he had obtained his tunes (something that Broadwood failed to establish), he had evidently learned their words from the versions printed by commercial 'ballad-mongers.'

As we have seen, Broadwood had visited Henry Burstow in 1893, when he was sixty-eight years old. He had a varied repertoire, less oriented to agriculture and the sea than that of Henry Hills, a reflection, perhaps, of the different geographical locations of Horsham and Lodsworth within the county of Sussex. About half of Burstow's songs dealt with relations between the sexes. Two ballads about amorous encounters ("Salisbury Plain" and "As I Was A-Walking") he deemed unfit for Lucy Broadwood's ladylike ears, with the result that she was able to note only the tunes. Of the others, three were tales of lovers triumphing over the opposition of cruel or unsympathetic parents: "Through Moorfields" (in which the girl was rescued from a madhouse), "Bristol Town" (in which the hired assassin allowed his victim to escape), and "Rosetta and Her Gay Ploughboy" (in which the heroine endured imprisonment until the timely death of her oppressive father). Another of Burstow's songs was a 'broken token' ballad of separation in which the faithful lovers were eventually reunited, "The Wealthy Farmer's Song." Three others were ballads of unrequited love and yearning for a lost lover: "Belfast Mountains," "The Americas that Stole My True Love Away," and "The Seeds of Love."

Burstow's songbag included three Child ballads. Two were outlaw ballads: "Banstead Downs, or Georgie," (a version of Child # 209) and "The Bold Pedlar and Robin Hood" (Child # 132); the other was about the pirate "Henry Martin" (Child # 250). He sang one carol ("The Moon Shines Bright"), one set-piece about the different stages of human life, "The Ages of Man," a poaching song ("The Gallant Poachers"), and one fragment about the Grim Reaper, "Death and the Lady." Finally there were three ballads of warfare and soldiering ("The Duke of Marlborough," "Boney's Lamentation" and "Stinson the Deserter"), and three murder ballads: "The Three Butchers," "The Merchant's Daughter, or, Constant Farmer's Son" and "The Cruel Ship Carpenter." Both "The Merchant's Daughter" and "The Cruel Ship Carpenter" included supernatural elements; in one of these the daughter dreamed (correctly) that her lover had been murdered by her brothers, while in the second a ghost tracked down her murderous lover aboard a ship at sea. Lucy Broadwood was impressed neither by the melodramatic text nor by the commonplace tune of "The Cruel Ship Carpenter," which she dismissed as "of the 'Villikins and his Dinah' type, so often met with in country songs."[55] Yet, as Frank Kidson remarked, this ballad, which was also known as "Polly's Love" or "The Gosport Tragedy," was one of the commonest of all broadsides, and had still been until recently for sale on a ballad-sheet published by Such. Whether one agreed or disagreed with the masses' taste, there was no question that this murder ballad with a vindictive ghost had been a hugely popular vernacular song:

The Cruel Ship Carpenter

Anon

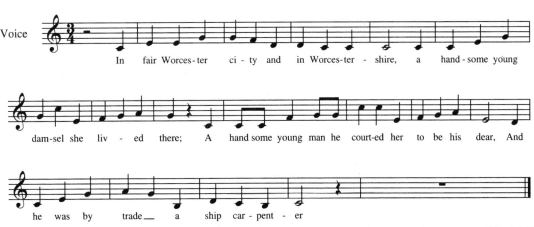

Fig. 16.11

In fair Worcester city and in Worcestershire, a handsome young damsel she lived there,
A handsome young man he courted her to be his dear, and he was by trade a ship carpenter.

Now the king wanted seamen to go on the sea, that caused this young damsel to sigh and to say:
"O William, O William, don't you go to sea, remember the vows that you made to me."

It was early next morning before it was day, he went to his Polly, these words did he say:
"O Polly, O Polly, you must go with me, before we are married, my friends for to see."

He led her through groves and valleys so deep, and caused this young damsel to sigh and to weep:
"O William, O William, you have led me astray, on purpose my innocent life to betray."

"It's true, it's true," these words he did say, "for all the long night I've been digging your grave."
The grave being open, the spade standing by, which caused this young damsel to sigh and to cry.

"O William, O William, O pardon my life, I never will covet to be your wife,
I will travel the world over to set you quite free—O pardon, O pardon, my baby and me."

"No pardon I'll give, there's no time for to stand," So with that he had a knife in his hand,
He stabb'd her heart till the blood it did flow, then into the grave her fair body did throw.

He covered her up so safe and secure, thinking no one would find her he was sure,
Then he went on board to sail the world round, before that the murder could ever be found.

It was early one morning before it was day, the captain came up, these words he did say:
"There's a murderer on board, and he it lately has done; our ship is in mourning and cannot sail on."

Then up stepp'd one: "Indeed it's not me." Then up stepp'd another, the same he did say.
Then up starts young William to stamp and to swear: "Indeed it's not me, sir, I vow and declare."

As he was turning from the captain with speed, he met his Polly, which made his heart bleed;
She stript him and tore him, she tore him in three, because he had murdered her baby and she.[56]

More recently, in 1901, Broadwood had collected five songs in the villages of Houghton and Amberley, Sussex. From Mr. Hoare at Houghton she obtained "The Bob-tailed Mare," and from Walter Searle of Amberley two more ballads about cruel parents attempting to thwart the union of young lovers ("The Young Servant-Man" and "The Rich Merchant and his Daughter"). The latter was a murder ballad, and Walter's relative John Searle provided another, "Poor Mary in the Silvery Tide," in which the victim was a young woman who refused to marry as directed. His other offering was much pleasanter, a paean to the joys of the simple life unencumbered by riches, "The Cobbler and the Miser." The remainder of Broadwood's collection was noted at different places in Surrey. As we saw earlier, in 1892 she had found a Sussex native, the carter named George Grantham, in retirement near Holmwood, Surrey. Yet of the many songs she noted from him, only two found their way into the pages of the *Journal*: "The Rich Nobleman and His Daughter" and another version of "The Merchant's Daughter" (aka "The Constant Farmer's Son").

Much more extensive were Broadwood's records of her fruitful collecting trip in 1896 to Dunsfold, near Chiddingfold. Here she also noted two murder ballads, "The Pretty Sailor, or the Lowland Maid" and a version of the grim Child ballad "Lamkin," here titled "Bold Lankon." Other 'finds' were "How Cold the Winds Do Blow," a full version of the Child ballad "The Unquiet Grave," a good broadside about the hanging of an innocent man, "The Sheffield Apprentice," and one traditional ballad that had escaped Francis Child, "The Trees They Are So High." There was another ballad about lovers faced with opposition from cruel parents ("The Bonny Labouring Boy"), and several songs about parted lovers at last reunited ("The Pleasant Month of May," "Our Ship She Lies in the Harbour," and "The Blind Beggar of Bethlem Green"). There were also two songs of unrequited love, "The New Irish Girl" and "Some Rival Has Stolen My True Love Away," and Broadwood obtained variant tunes for "The Seeds of Love" and "The Bailiff's Daughter of Islington." Finally she collected from Mr. Sparks of Dunsfold a very interesting ballad of social protest, "The Labouring Man," which glorified the patriotism and reliability of the ordinary working man while bemoaning the hard times that he was now forced to endure in the English countryside:

You Englishmen of each degree, one moment listen unto me,
From day to day you all may see the poor are frowned on by degrees.
To please you all I do intend, so listen to the lines I've penned,
By them, you know who never can do without the labouring man.
Old England's often led the van, but not without the labouring man.

In former days you all must know, the poor man cheerfully used to go
Quite neat and clean, upon my life, with his children and his darling wife;
And for his wages it is said, a fair day's wages he was paid,
But now to live he hardly can—May God protect the labouring man.
Old England's often led the van, but not without the labouring man.

There is one thing we must confess if England finds they're in a mess,

And has to face the daring foe, unto the labouring man they go,
To fight their battles, understand, either on sea or on the land;
Deny the truth we never can, they call upon the labouring man.
Old England's often led the van, but not without the labouring man.

Some for soldiers they will go, and jolly sailors too we know,
To guard Old England day and night, and for their country boldly fight,
But when they do return again, they are looked upon with great disdain;
Now in distress throughout the land, you may behold the labouring man.
Old England's often led the van, but not without the labouring man.

When Bonaparte, and Nelson too, and Wellington at Waterloo,
Were fighting both by land and sea, the poor man gained these victories!
Their hearts are cast in honour's mould, the sailors and the soldiers bold;
And every battle, understand, was conquered by the labouring man.
Old England's often led the van, but not without the labouring man.

The labouring man will plough the deep, till the ground and sow the wheat,
Fight the battles when afar, fear no dangers or a scar,
But still they're looked upon like thieves by them they keep at home at ease,
And every day throughout the land they try to starve the labouring man.
Old England's often led the van, but not without the labouring man.

Now if the wars should rise again and England be in want of men,
They'll have to search the country round for the lads that plough the ground.
Then to some foreign land they'll go to fight and drub the daring foe;
Do what they will, do what they can, they can't do without the labouring man.
Old England's often led the van, but not without the labouring man.[57]

The Labouring Man

Anon

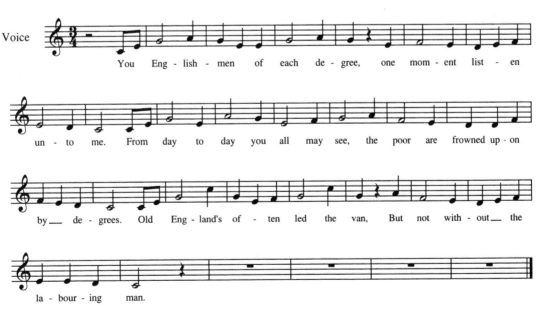

Fig. 16.12

Broadwood would eventually publish more of her early collecting in *English Traditional Songs and Carols* (1908), and, as editor of the *Journal of the Folk-Song Society,* she would play a very important role in the Edwardian phase of the folksong revival. But for now she was simply glad to find that her small collection had found a handful of admirers who wrote to her expressing their gratitude to her for preserving the songs. Her fans that autumn included the Reverend Atherton, Dr. Ernest Walker, Walter Ford, and Mary Venables.[58] On 23 October 1902 she got together again with Ralph Vaughan Williams and agreed to sing ten illustrations at a lecture on "Folk Song" that he was soon to give in Boscombe, a suburb of Bournemouth. That took place on 17 November, with an audience of 112 people at the Bournemouth Hall of Fine Arts, and Lucy, who was presented with an enormous bouquet of chrysanthemums, concluded that at the very least it was good publicity for *English County Songs*, the source from which she and Vaughan Williams had chosen most of the illustrations.[59]

Frank Kidson: Collecting In Yorkshire

All four early issues of the *Journal of the Folk-Song Society* were valuable and successful in their different ways, and the body of material that had been collected and published was already impressive. Broadwood and Kidson, who provided most of the annotations to the songs printed, were rapidly making names for themselves as highly knowledgeable folksong scholars. The outlook for the Society appeared to be set fair. It was disappointing, therefore, when no issue of the *Journal* appeared in 1903 and no collectors' meeting was held either. The reason was the protracted illness and incapacity of one of the Society's mainstays, Kate Lee. Lucy, who may have been a little jealous of Kate's strong voice and poise as a professional artist, was annoyed by her apparent dilatoriness, and disinclined to believe that her illness was as serious as Kate had confided it was. The lack of committee meetings that year did not bother Lucy too much, however, as she had ceased to regard them as particularly valuable or effective. Instead she went back to cultivating—and extending—her own network of musicians who were also folksong collectors. This was the year that she got to know Percy Merrick, who on two occasions (1 May and 15 June) sent her more folksongs that he had collected, including some French ones. They subsequently corresponded, comparing notes about their collecting in Sussex and elsewhere.[60]

Broadwood's friendship with Ralph Vaughan Williams also bloomed this year. He called on her on 11 January with a request that she and James McInnes premier a new composition of his, "Willowwood." They agreed, and several rehearsals took place during the next two months before the performance took place on 12 March. Then in April Vaughan Williams asked Lucy to sing illustrations at another of his lectures on "English Folk Song," and this took place in Kidderminster on 10 June. In his talk he mentioned songs that he had himself recently collected in Essex, and Lucy naturally expressed an interest in seeing them; five days later he provided her with copies of his Essex collecting. Then on 10 July she received from him two songs that he had composed, one of which he had dedicated to her. It was not until November that Lucy heard from him again, but on 11 November she received a letter from him asking about her Sussex collecting, to which she replied immediately. They kept in touch by mail, and on 20 December Lucy entertained him and his wife at a dinner party in her London apartment. Vaughan Williams played the company a folksong setting that he had recently composed.[61] He was now part of the Broadwood social circle as well as a member of the Folk-Song Society and of Lucy's informal folk music network.

Lucy's third new folk music acquaintance in 1903 was also a figure of some note. She had heard through the grapevine, perhaps from Vaughan Williams, that Cecil Sharp, the Principal of Hampstead Conservatoire, was interested in folksongs and was giving lectures on the subject. On 28 November she wrote to him inquiring about his lectures, and received a prompt reply on the thirtieth, and then another letter from Sharp on 4 December. Sharp, it appeared, not only gave talks about folksongs, but had been collecting them in Somerset. Intrigued, Lucy immediately invited him to lunch, and on 6 December she recorded in her diary that "Mr. Cecil Sharp, Principal of Hampstead Conservatoire, came to luncheon and showed me 40 folk songs collected by himself in Somersetshire."[62] It was the beginning of a productive, if often stormy, relationship. Lucy would rarely agree with Sharp's ideas, which she saw as too doctrinaire, and she found his personality rather pushy and authoritarian, but she always respected his achievements as a collector. She immediately encouraged him to become an active member of the Folk-Song Society and to contribute to its *Journal*.

The *Journal of the Folk-Song Society* was one of Lucy's biggest worries at this time. A 1903 issue of the *Journal* had been planned under Kate Lee's aegis but her illness had prevented her doing the necessary editorial work. Lucy eventually took it over, and it finally appeared as Volume 1, No. 5, in 1904. The issue was devoted mainly to twenty-five Yorkshire songs from Frank Kidson, but it also included some other items. There were three songs performed in local singing competitions at Frome and Kendal, and the five additional Sussex songs collected by Percy Merrick from Henry Hills that have already been mentioned.[63] Also included were three versions of the Child ballad "Barbara Allen," all collected by Lucy Broadwood: a Kentish one from Mrs. Grahame of St. Leonard's-on-Sea, a Yorkshire one from Mr. Thomas (a gardener at Wakefield), and a Hampshire one from Patience Vaisey, the wife of a gardener at Adwell, Oxford-shire.

Highlights of Kidson's collection were three Child ballads: "Robin Hood and the Keeper" (noted from the singing of a farmer near Huddersfield), "Lord Bateman" (two versions, one from Shropshire and one from Nottingham), and "The Outlandish Knight." There were some interesting broadsides too: a ballad of unfaithfulness and revenge ("William Taylor and Sally Brown"), an execution ballad ("Eli Sykes"), a story of unsuccessful robbery ("The Highwayman Out-witted"), and this ballad expressing discontent with military life, "The Deserter":

The Deserter

Anon

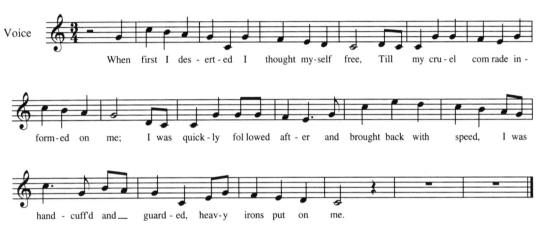

Fig. 16.13

When first I deserted I thought myself free,
Till my cruel comrade informed on me,
I was quickly followed after and brought back with speed,
I was handcuffed and guarded, heavy irons put on me.

As I wanderd down Ratcliffe Highway,
The recruiting party came beating that way;
They enlisted me and treated me, till I did not know;
Then to the Queen's barracks they forced me to go.

When next I deserted I thought myself free,
When my cruel comrade informed against me;
I was quickly followed after, and brought back with speed,
I was handcuffed and guarded, heavy irons put on me.

Court martial, court martial they held upon me,
And the sentence they passed on me was three hundred and three.
May the Lord have mercy on their souls for their sad cruelty,
For now the Queen's duty lies heavy on me.

Then again I deserted and thought I was free,
When my cruel sweetheart informed against me,
I was quickly followed after and brought back with speed,
I was handcuffed and guarded, heavy irons put on me.

Court martial, court martial was very soon got,
And the sentence they passed was that I should be shot.
May the Lord have mercy on their souls for their cruelty,

For now the Queen's duty lies heavy on me.

Then up rode Prince Albert in his coach and six:
"Bring to me that young man whose death it is fixed.
Release him from his irons and let him go free,
For he'll make a clever soldier for his Queen and country."[64]

Several other songs, collected on or near the coast of northeast England or southern Scotland, reflected the importance of the sea in the lives of Kidson's informants: "All on Spurn Point" (about a shipwreck), "Jack the Sailor," and "The Fisherrow Guidwife." A few items were about animals: "Creeping Jane" (about a racing horse) and "A Farmer's Dog," a drinking song better known as "Bingo." Others were courting songs, or songs of unrequited love (including "There Is an Alehouse in Yonder Town" and "Sorry the Day I Was Married"). Kidson also included a few instrumental tunes, of which the most interesting was a sword-dancing air, played at a 'pleugh-stotting' ceremony (a traditional custom akin to Morris dancing) at Goathland on the North Yorkshire Moors.

Unfortunately Kidson often failed to provide complete texts to accompany the tunes that he had noted. This was the case for several of the ballads. He omitted the words of "Lord Bateman" on the specious grounds that it was "too long and too well known to be repeated here," while his excuse for not providing a text for "The Outlandish Knight" was that it had been included in his *Traditional Tunes.* Similarly, "The Banks of Sweet Dundee," a song that he considered to be "one of the best known among our rustic ditties," was included with only the first verse of the text, presumably because he assumed that all the *Journal*'s readers already knew the lyric. Kidson's readiness to suppress texts was even more evident in his treatment of "The Unfortunate Lad." His informant, Kate Thompson of Knaresborough, had been unable to remember all the words but it was clear that she was singing the broadside ballad often titled "The Unfortunate Rake." Kidson, aware that the subject of this song was the death of a soldier from venereal disease, provided the first verse only, remarking that the ballad would "scarcely bear reprinting in its entirety."[65] Despite these regrettable editorial decisions, this small collection nonetheless provided a valuable supplement to *Traditional Tunes,* although it also served as a reminder that the promised second volume of that pioneering work had never appeared. As a final illustration of Frank Kidson's important contribution to the late Victorian folksong revival, here is one more example of the material that he collected in Yorkshire, in this case from an unnamed farmer near Huddersfield. "Robin Hood and the Keeper" was a typical broadside, overly prolix and prone to degenerate into doggerel, but Robin Hood ballads were rare and so it was quite an achievement to find it in oral tradition. The farmer's oral text was similar, although not identical, to "Robin Hood and the Ranger" (Child no. 131), an eighteenth-century broadside probably written by William Stukely in 1741 and printed by the London broadsheet publisher C. Dicey. It was subsequently included in the Yorkshire version of *Robin Hood's Garland.*[66]

When Phoebus had melted the ic'les of ice
And dissolved all the mountains of snow,
Bold Robin Hood in a frolicsome mood
Went wand'ring about with his bow.
He had left all his merry men waiting behind,
And travelled the woods far and near,
When by the woodside the gamekeeper he spied,
Who questioned him how he came there, how he came there,
When by the woodside the gamekeeper he spied,
Who questioned him how he came there.

"I'm coming," said Robin, "to shoot a fat buck
For me and my men in the wood,
And besides, e'er I go, I must have a young doe,
For I think they are tender and good."
"You had best have a care," said the keeper in wrath,
"For these are his majesty's deer,
Before you do shoot, your right I dispute, your right I dispute,
For I am chief forester here."
[repeat last two lines, as before; also in subsequent verses]

"These thirteen long summers," bold Robin replied,
"I've thus let my arrows all fly;

So freely I've ranged and to me it seems strange
That you should have more right than I!
These woods and these valleys I count as my own,
And so does the nimble deer too,
I therefore declare, and I solemnly swear, I solemnly swear,
That I'll not be commanded by you.

The keeper had got a large staff in his hand,
Likewise a broadsword by his side,
Without more ado his scabbard he drew,
And swore that the truth should be tried.
Bold Robin likewise had a sword of the best,
He swore he would suffer no wrong;
His courage was flush, and he long'd for a brush, long'd for a brush,
For to prove if that it was strong.

The keeper struck first and he gave such a bang
That he made his broad weapon cry 'twang';
He struck Robin's head, and he fell down for dead,
For he'd never received such a bang.
But soon he recovered and jumped on his feet,
And quickly maintained his own ground.
The very next stroke, both weapons were broke, weapons were broke
 Without either giving a wound.

Their large oaken cudgels they next took in hand
Because they would have a new bout,
Bold Robin Hood in jeopardy stood,
Unwilling to yield or give out.
At length the bold keeper became quite in a rage,
He cudgeled poor Robin so sore
Till he scarcely could stand, so shaking his hand, shaking his hand,
Cries Robin, "Let's fairly give o'er!"

"For thou art a good fellow, bold, skilful, and brave,
I never knew any so good.
A very fit man to be one of my clan
And dwell in yon merry greenwood.
I'll give thee a ring as a token of love,
If thou to my wish art inclined,
For a man that can fight I behold with delight, behold with delight,
For I love them with heart and with mind."

Robin then took his horn to assemble his men
And loudly he made it to blow,
His archers soon heard and in order appeared
And each of them had his long bow.
Little John was their leader, he marched at their head,
And wore a rich mantle of blue;
The rest were all seen, dressed in garments of green, in garments of green,
A beautiful prospect to view.

"These are my bowmen," bold Robin he cried,
"And thou shalt be one of my train,
A quiver and bow and a dress I'll bestow
On those whom I thus entertain."
The keeper survey'd them with pleasant surprise,
They made such an excellent show;
At length in his mind he became quite inclined, became quite inclined
Along with bold Robin to go.

Robin Hood and the Keeper

Anon

Voice

When Phoe bus had melt-ed the ic'-les of ice, And dis - solved all the moun tains of

snow,__ Bold Rob-in Hood in a frol ic some mood Went wand' ring a-bout with his bow. He had

left all his mer - ry men wait-ing be-hind, And trav - elled the woods far and near, When

by the wood-side the game - keep-er he spied, Who quest ioned him how he came there,__

how____ he__ came there, When by the wood - side the game - keep - er he spied, Who

quest ioned him how he came there.__

Fig. 16.14

What singing and dancing there was in the wood
For the joy of another new mate!
With mirth and delight they employed the whole night
And they lived at a plentiful rate.
Next day Robin gave him a mantle of green,
A quiver and a curious long bow,
And when he was dressed quite as gay as the rest, gay as the rest,

Robin ranged all his men in a row.

"So all my brave comrades be true to your trust,
And then we have nothing to fear,
We'll range the wood wide with our arms by our side,
And live without sorrow or care."
They all with a shout made the elements ring,
And swore they would ever be true;
So he marched them away, looking gallant and gay, looking gallant and gay,
Their pastimes and sports to renew.[67]

The year 1904 had opened with a flurry of activity by London members of the Folk-Song Society. Alec Fuller Maitland had been invited by the Royal Institution of Great Britain to give a series of three lectures on British folksong. These, titled "Celtic Elements in British Folk Song," "Modal Influences in British Folk Song" and "Folk-Songs in the Modern Scales," were duly delivered on 16, 23, and 30 January, and Lucy was naturally a member of the audience.[68] She had agreed to help out Vaughan Williams with another of his folksong lectures, so on 21 January they got together to rehearse seven items that he intended to include as illustrations, and on 2 February they traveled to Hertford to deliver the talk. Meanwhile Lucy was back in contact with Percy Merrick about his folksong collecting, and she was also writing a long letter to the *Morning Post* newspaper on the subject of folksong. It duly appeared on 1 February, along with another by Cecil Sharp.[69] Sharp, Lucy concluded, was undoubtedly energetic and enthusiastic, and the Folk-Song Society could certainly use a few more activists with those qualities since several of the founding members had proven to be less than reliable.

During January Lucy also received several letters from Kate Lee about Folk-Song Society matters. Kate, who was dying of cancer, had decided that Lucy was the person to take over the secretarial and editing work that she had been doing for the Society and its *Journal*. Lucy was not convinced that this transfer was really necessary, and on 1 February she went to see Kate to discuss the situation. Although Kate revealed that her illness was terminal, Lucy somewhat callously confided to her diary that night that she "suspected more than ever not fatal illness but nervous, etc." Unfortunately her diagnosis proved to be erroneous. Lucy was, however, now convinced that left to Kate and other members of the old guard, the Folk-Song Society would gradually sink into oblivion. Sharp had expressed to her personally, and now in print in the *Morning Post*, his dissatisfaction with the Society's track record and his aspirations for what might be achieved in the future. He was obviously the new broom that was needed to sweep the executive clean. On 6 February Lucy, Cecil Sharp, and Ralph Vaughan Williams met to discuss what should be done. Lucy recorded in her diary that the three of them had conducted an inquest on "the Folk Song Society and [had] made a scheme for reviving its dying embers."[70]

This conversation, together with Kate Lee's death in July 1904, marked a turning-point in the history of the first phase of the English folksong revival. The "scheme" was in effect a strategy for a palace revolution. After a brief pause to mourn, new hands would take over the administration and leadership of the Society. Lucy Broadwood, with the help of her northern collaborator Frank Kidson, had already been shouldering part of the burden. She would now resume leadership of the revival, becoming the new editor of the *Journal*. Broadwood recognized that above all the cause needed new energy and enthusiasm, so she welcomed new recruits to the movement. She may have got more than she bargained for, since her authority would soon be challenged by several of the new participants. Initially, however, the old guard and the new guard worked well together, constituting a 'gang of five' that comprised Broadwood, Fuller Maitland, Kidson, Sharp, and Vaughan Williams. But that—the beginning of the Edwardian phase of the folksong revival—is another story.

Notes

1. Lucy Broadwood, diary entries for September, 1893. Surrey History Centre. Broadwood's diaries for the period 24 October 1882 to 22 September 1893 have been summarized by Lewis Jones in "Lucy Broadwood's Diaries: The Early Years," *English Dance and Song* 62, no. 3 (Autumn 2000): 2-3.

2. Lewis Jones, "Lucy Broadwood's Diaries," 2.

3. Broadwood, diary entries for 6 December 1893, 11 May 1894, 1 June 1894, 1 and 25 January 1895, and 15 March 1895, Broadwood Collection, LEB 6782, Surrey History Centre, Woking, U.K.

4. Lucy Broadwood Collection, Vaughan Williams Memorial Library, Cecil Sharp House, Camden Town, London, U.K., LEB 3 and LEB 4.

5. Sabine Baring-Gould to Lucy Broadwood, undated letter, Lucy Broadwood Collection, Vaughan Williams Memorial Library, Cecil Sharp House, Camden Town, London, U.K., LEB 4.

6. Broadwood, diary entries for 16 and 18 January 1892, 27 February 1892, 25 September 1892, 28 December 1892, 22 February 1893, 10 April 1893, and 18 April 1894.

7. Frank Kidson to Lucy Broadwood, letter dated 15 December 1893; Broadwood Collection, Vaughan Williams Memorial Library, LEB/4/108.

8. Broadwood, diary entry, 3 October 1895.

9. Frank Kidson to Lucy Broadwood, letter dated 26 September 1896; Broadwood Collection, Vaughan Williams Memorial Library, LEB/4/86.

10. Frank Kidson to Lucy Broadwood, letter dated 19 January 1897: Broadwood Collection, Vaughan Williams Memorial Library, LEB/4/111.

11. Broadwood, diary entries for 21 October, 27 November, and 7 and 8 December 1897.

12. Frank Kidson to Lucy Broadwood, letter dated 9 January 1898: Broadwood Collection, Vaughan Williams Memorial Library, LEB/4/95.

13. I have been unable to find a copy of the circular letter. It may have gone out under Alfred Graves's name, although Kate Lee probably wrote it and took charge of the mailing.

14. Broadwood, diary entries for 27 January, 8 February, and 23 March 1898.

15. For more details, see Christopher J. Bearman, "Kate Lee and the Foundation of the Folk-Song Society," *Folk Music Journal* 7, no. 5 (1999): 627-43. See also Michael Kennedy, *The Works of Ralph Vaughan Williams* (London: Oxford University Press, 1964), 24. Kennedy gives 16 June 1898 as the Society's date of birth.

16. Broadwood, diary entries for 17 and 18 September 1898.

17. Broadwood, diary entries for 20 and 22 September 1898.

18. Broadwood, diary entries for 6 and 12 October 1898, 15 and 30 December 1898, and 5 January 1899.

19. Lucy Broadwood, "Re Collecting," manuscript, 2185/LEB/1/446, Broadwood Collection, Surrey History Centre, Woking, U.K.

20. Sir Hubert Parry, "Inaugural Address to the General Meeting of the Folk-Song Society, 2 February 1899," *Journal of the Folk-Song Society* 1, no. 1 (1899): 1-2.

21. Parry, "Inaugural Address," 3.

22. Parry, "Inaugural Address," 2.

23. Kate Lee, "Some Experiences of a Folk-Song Collector," *Journal of the Folk-Song Society* 1, no. 1 (1899): 7-25. The main article on pp. 7-13 was followed by an appendix of eleven songs, nine of which had been collected by Lee, on pp. 14-25.

24. The Copper family would keep their local singing tradition alive throughout the interwar period, and would play a significant role in the post-war revival. Members of the family are still performing and recording today.

25. Lee, "Some Experiences of a Folk-Song Collector," 19-20.

26. E. F. Jacques, "Modal Survivals in Folk-Song," *Journal of the Folk-Song Society* 1, no. 1 (1899): 4-6.

27. Jacques, "Modal Survivals," 4-6.

28. "Napoleon's Farewell," *Journal of the Folk-Song Society* 1, no. 1 (1899): 14. Two modal Gaelic tunes are on p. 15.

29. Lee, "Some Experiences of a Folk-Song Collector," 14-25.

30. Frank Kidson, "Sailors' Songs," *Journal of the Folk-Song Society* 1, no. 2 (1900): 39-42.

31. Frank Kidson, ed., *Traditional Tunes* (Oxford: Charles Taphouse & Son, 1891), 108-9.

32. See chapters 8 (for Kidson's *Traditional Tunes*) and 10 (for Barrett's *English Folk-Songs*).

33. "The *Bold Princess Royal*," *Journal of the Folk-Song Society* 1, no. 2 (1900): 62.

34. J. A. Fuller Maitland, "Report to the Second Meeting of the Folk-song Society," *Journal of the Folk-Song Society* 1, no. 2 (1900): 27-31.

35. Of the songs collected by Kate Lee and mentioned by Fuller Maitland, the following were included (tunes and text, or tune only in the case of the hornpipe) in the *Journal*, 46-51: "Eggs in Her Basket," "The High Road to Lynn" (hornpipe), "The Plains of Waterloo," and "In Fair Plymouth City." "In Fair Plymouth City" is on pp. 50-51.

36. Fuller Maitland, "Report to the Second Meeting," 28-29.

37. "The Plains of Waterloo," *Journal* 1, no. 2 (1900): 49.

38. Fuller Maitland, "Report to the Second Meeting," 29.

39. "The Green Bed," *Journal* 1, no. 2 (1900): 48.

40. Fuller Maitland, "Report to the Second Meeting," 30-31.

41. Broadwood, diary entries for 15, 20, 24, and 26 January 1900.

42. Broadwood, diary entries for 1 and 2 February 1900.

43. Broadwood, diary entry for 20 February 1900.

44. Broadwood, diary entries for 13 March and 15 June 1900.

45. Broadwood, diary entries for 29 and 31 January, 15 February, 6 March, 23 May, 30 June, and 3 October 1901.

46. W. Percy Merrick, "Sussex Songs collected from Mr. Hills," *Journal of the Folk-Song Society* 1, no. 3 (1901): 64-105.

47. Merrick, "Mr. Hills," 81.

48. Merrick, "Mr. Hills," 99.

49. Merrick, "Mr. Hills," 92-93.

50. W. Percy Merrick, "Sussex Songs," *Journal of the Folk-Song Society* 1, no. 5 (1904): 268-74. The quotation is on p. 270.

51. W. Percy Merrick, ed., *Folk Songs from Sussex* (London: Novello, 1912). Fourteen of the piano accompaniments were by Vaughan Williams but one was by Albert Robins.

52. Cecil J. Sharp (series editor), *Folk Songs of England,* 5 vols. (London: Novello, 1908-1912). Reprinted in a one volume edition as *English County Folk Songs* (London: Novello, 1961).

53. Broadwood, diary entry for 1 January 1902.

54. Lucy E. Broadwood, "Folk Songs Collected in Sussex and Surrey," *Journal of the Folk-Song Society* 1, no. 4 (1902): 139-223.

55. Broadwood, "Folk Songs Collected in Sussex and Surrey," 173.

56. Broadwood, "Folk Songs Collected in Sussex and Surrey," 172-73.

57. Broadwood, "Folk Songs Collected in Sussex and Surrey," 198-99.

58. Broadwood, diary entries: 29 September, and 6 and 16 October 1902.

59. Broadwood, diary entry for 17 November 1902.

60. Broadwood, diary entries for 1 May, 15 June, 5 and 7 October 1903.

61. Broadwood, diary entries for 11 January, 17 and 24 February, 12 March, 22 April, 10 and 15 June, 10 July, 11 November, and 5 and 20 December 1903.

62. Broadwood, diary entries for 28 and 30 November, and 4 and 6 December 1903.

63. *Journal of the Folk-Song Society* 1, no. 5 (1904): 227-74.

64. Frank Kidson, "Songs from the Collection of Frank Kidson," *Journal of the Folk-Song Society* 1, no. 5 (1904): 234-35.

65. Kidson, "Songs from the Collection," 228-55. The quotations are from pp. 232, 240, 246, and 254.

66. Kidson noted that the broadside had been included by Joseph Ritson in *Robin Hood: A Collection of All the Poems, Songs and Ballads now extant relative to that celebrated English Outlaw,* 2 vols. (London: Johnson, 1795). He commented "the farmer told me he had never heard of its being in print."

67. Kidson, "Songs from the Collection," 247-49.

68. Broadwood, diary entries for 16, 23, and 30 January 1904.

69. Broadwood, diary entries for 21, 22, and 30 January and 2 February 1904.

70. Broadwood, diary entry for 6 February 1904.

17

Epilogue and Conclusions

Queen Victoria died in 1901, so, technically speaking, the Late Victorian phase of the revival also came to an end with the very beginning of the new century. The real time of transition, however, was the three-year period 1903-1905, the years that saw the advent of a second generation of folksong collectors that included Cecil Sharp and Ralph Vaughan Williams. Sharp's conversion to the cause while visiting Rev. Charles Marson at his Hambridge vicarage in August 1903, his extraordinary field work in Somerset during the next few years, and his decision to become involved in a serious way with the activities and publications of the Folk-Song Society together constituted a landmark in the evolution of the first English folksong revival. Vaughan Williams also began song collecting in the field in 1903 although his friendship with Lucy Broadwood and his interest in English folksong dated from several years earlier. For better or for worse, things would never be the same again after 1904. The palace revolution that occurred behind the scenes in the Folk-Song Society that year was reflected, albeit with a lag, in the issues of its *Journal:* the 1904 issue may be counted as the last Late Victorian one, devoted in part to Kidson's collecting in Yorkshire during the last decade of the nineteenth century; the 1905 and 1906 issues featured more recent collecting by Sharp and Vaughan Williams respectively and signal the advent of a new Edwardian phase of the folksong revival. Although the change was significant, even dramatic, there was also a strong element of continuity. Lucy Broadwood and Frank Kidson, and to a much lesser extent Alec Fuller Maitland and Sabine Baring-Gould, would remain mainstays of the Society, while Charlotte Burne would go on to play a major role in the Folklore Society. But they would no longer dominate the movement and other names would come to the fore, not only Sharp and Vaughan Williams but also George Butterworth, George Gardiner, Annie Gilchrist, Percy Grainger, Ella Leather, Percy Merrick, and the Hammond brothers, among others.

The story of the Edwardian phase of the revival requires another book, but we cannot leave our principal characters without providing a brief indication of what happened to them in the years after 1903. Some, such as Collingwood Bruce, William Barrett, Joseph Crawhall, John Harland, and Kate Lee, had already died, or would soon do so. Others, such as Laura Smith, disappeared from public view as song collectors and subsequently lived unrecorded private lives. Some found their vocation in another field. Harriet Mason, for example, enjoyed a productive career as a Local Government Board inspector of the condition of children placed in foster care under Poor Law legislation. Heywood Sumner concentrated on his career as an artist and craftsman, playing an important role in the Arts and Crafts movement. Alec Fuller Maitland and Arthur Somervell remained prominent figures in the musical life of the nation, but, in the main, focused their energies elsewhere than folksong collecting and editing.

Charlotte Burne had a distinguished career in the related field of folklore. She joined the Folk-Lore Society in 1883 and in recognition of the value of *Shropshire Folk-Lore* was elected to its Council in 1887. An admirer of George Laurence Gomme, one of the dominant personalities in Folk-Lore Society circles, she soon became a close friend of his wife, Alice Bertha Gomme. Together they played an active part in organizing the 1891 International Folklore Congress. For a while during the 1890s Burne dropped out of active involvement with the Council, but in 1900 she moved to London and took over as editor of *Folk-Lore*. The next year she was elected vice-president of the Society. In 1908 she resigned as editor, but agreed instead to edit a new edition of the Society's *Handbook of Folk-Lore*. In 1910 she took over as president, a role she filled for two years, the first woman to do so. Finally in 1914 she brought the project of re-editing the *Handbook of Folk-Lore* to a successful conclusion, and also published her last update to the material in *Shropshire Folk-Lore,* in the form of an article titled "Souling, Clementing and Catterning: Three November Customs of the Western Midlands." Although she continued to be interested in the Society's activities and occasionally reviewed books for *Folk-Lore,* ill-health precluded her undertaking any new projects during the last decade of her life. She suffered a stroke in 1922, and died the next year.[1] *Shropshire Folk-Lore* remains her most enduring legacy.

John Stokoe continued to play a significant role, as both performer and folklorist, in traditional music circles in Newcastle-upon-Tyne and elsewhere in the northeast of England. Sabine Baring-Gould also continued to lead an active life, and never lost his interest in West Country folksong and in broadside balladry, but his collecting days were largely, although not quite completely, over. During the Edwardian era he kept on writing and publishing, albeit at a slower pace than during the 1880s and 1890s. As we have seen, his omnibus edition of West Country folksongs, with revised piano accompaniments by Cecil Sharp, was published in 1905 as *Songs of the West: Folk Songs of Devon and Cornwall, Collected from the Mouths of the People.* His other collaboration with Sharp, *English Folk Songs for Schools,* was published a year later. After that he focused his efforts mainly on folklore and local history, continuing to research and describe in print the people and folklore of the county he loved; later books included *Devonshire Characters and Strange Events* (1908), *A Book of Folk-lore* (1913), and *Further Reminiscences* (1925). He died in January 1924.

The two Late Victorian figures who had the most to contribute to the next phase of the revival were Lucy Broadwood and Frank Kidson. For the sake of completeness, the following sketches briefly some of the highlights of their later endeavors in the field.

Frank Kidson after 1904

Kidson's involvement with folk music after 1904 was more episodic than his friend Lucy Broadwood's, but he still had some important contributions to make to the promotion of English vernacular song. For example, in 1915 he would collaborate with Mary Neal to create a much-needed popular introduction to the folk music revival titled *English Folk-Song and Dance.*[2] Many more of the songs that he and his helpers collected during the years 1890-1908 would eventually be published, although unfortunately only decades later. Their belated appearance during the mid-late 1920s was a lot better than nothing, yet by failing to publish the songs in a timely manner Kidson forwent the opportunity to make a second outstanding contribution to the Late Victorian or even the Edwardian phase of the folksong revival. It was a classic case of a folksong collector discovering valuable and important material in the field and then neglecting to make all the fruits of his labors available to the public.

Although his continued presence in the movement would be evident during the war years and the 1920s, Kidson's involvement with the Folk-Song Society was more muted throughout much of the Edwardian era. Temperamentally averse to public controversy, and living somewhat out of the mainstream of English cultural and intellectual life, he preferred to make his opinions known privately to his friends, or, when he expressed them in print, he did so in an oblique and muted manner. Like Lucy Broadwood, he felt that the movement should not wash its dirty linen in public, and that it was important to put on a public face of unity, notwithstanding disagreements on details. In consequence, when he came in 1908 to review *English Folk-Song: Some Conclusions* for the *Musical Times* he was broadly supportive of Sharp's controversial endeavours to publicize the wealth of neglected tunes already recovered from oral tradition, although he also twice remarked that Sharp's conclusions would not be everybody's.[3] Carefully read, his short article, "English Folk-Song," revealed that he had strong reservations about the gospel according to Sharp, but he adroitly disguised just how fundamental those reservations were. He pronounced that Sharp's book was one that "no folk-song student can afford to be without" and generously described it as "a well-considered scientific treatise" and "a vigorous book full of thoughtful reasoning which cannot lightly be set aside." On the other hand, he withheld his support on a series of key points. For example, he criticized Sharp's definition of folksong as too vague and lengthy, and concluded that "a compact definition of 'folk-song' is still needed." He questioned the adequacy of Sharp's account of the winnowing process of oral tradition, contenting himself with the observation that "there remain many puzzling things about folk-song—or rather folk-melody—which are not solved by such obvious reasoning." He indicated his unease with Sharp's central argument that folksong was communal in nature while art song was individual, commenting that many folksongs had been "individually and personally created" but had later become communal by winning the "affections of the people."[4] Further, he took exception to Sharp's attack on early eighteenth-century ballad operas, and suggested that Sharp had been "unduly severe" on their authors. In Kidson's opinion the printed versions of such tunes as "The Miller of the Dee" and "Constant Billy" were accurate and, moreover, they compared favorably with "the versions known among folk-singers today," so that it was wrong to charge eighteenth-century musicians with corrupting them. In short, he was not at all convinced by Sharp's hard-and-fast distinction between genuine folksongs collected from oral tradition and other "old English songs" found in early printed music books (which Sharp excluded from the canon). The latter, Kidson believed, were often as worth preservation and revival as the former, and in any case it was often difficult to distinguish one from the other.[5]

Although he glossed over most of these differences in his review article, burying them in a generally positive account of Sharp's insights, Kidson detailed some of them in a letter to Sharp.[6] As this revealed, the "details" on which Kidson disagreed with Sharp were actually quite fundamental. The truth of the matter was that Kidson simply did not accept Sharp's central arguments. He was flatly opposed to Sharp's core theories and to his strategy for the revival. Sharp, he suggested, was making a "cult" out of folksong by adulating its supposed communal and national character.[7] From Kidson's point of view the supposed communal origin of English folksong was an unproven hypothesis, and an unlikely one at that. In fact, he thought it much more likely that the individual origin theory of folksong was correct, and that the original composer of an old song might often be found through diligent scholarly research among manuscript and early printed sources.

Kidson was therefore unable to embrace the Sharpean faith in folk music as fundamentally different from both art music and commercial popular music, and he felt considerable unease with Sharp's and Vaughan Williams's claim that folksong was the key to recreating a national music. Although he loved folksongs he had no strong belief in their racial or ethical worth. Indeed, he considered some of them immoral, and thought that they should be kept out of the hands of those who might be corrupted by them. Writing to Sharp in December 1910, he remarked that "it isn't every folksong that is suitable for a child. They very often deal with man's & woman's passion & it is hard to turn this into meat for children."[8] Indeed, he was firmly opposed to Sharp's strategy of popularizing folksongs through their employment in the school curriculum. He had seen school children performing folksongs and he cringed at the way the songs he loved were massacred. He stated this bluntly to Sharp:

> My chief objection to folk song in schools is that folk songs are too good for school singing, that it is like putting a very delicate & fragile thing into the hands of a child who cannot understand its full beauty & really destroys it; because it is a fact that public singers will not sing what bears the ban of a school song. When Miss Kay sings "The Seeds of Love" or similar song she understands it, & pulls the full meaning out of it, & her audience also understands its passionate pathos; but to the child it is Greek, or ought to be. Also such songs are only suitable for individual singing, not for chorus singing...No, school, in my idea is not the place for folk songs.[9]

On this matter Kidson and Sharp agreed to disagree and there appears to have been no acrimony in this private debate between the two men. Kidson consented to appear on the platform with Sharp when the latter gave a public lecture in Leeds. Despite his quarrel with Marson, Sharp usually avoided fights with friends who quietly but firmly indicated their reservations about his opinions—he kept on good terms with both Grainger and Vaughan Williams, for example—and he seems to have held Kidson in respect as a pioneer and as a highly knowledgeable scholar. Kidson was independent-minded and stubborn, but he was a genial personality who was generous with praise for the achievements of others. He saw Sharp's faults, but he also admired his tenacity and accomplishments. As J. L. Lightwood commented in his obituary of Kidson:

> His kindly nature ever prevented him from criticising in public the 'discoveries' of certain modern folk-song enthusiasts who have turned the art into a commercial undertaking. No, Kidson could have told them a thing or two that would have surprised them, but he was content to let them go their own way.[10]

Kidson continued to assist Lucy Broadwood with editorial work on the *Journal* during the half-decade before World War I, but he did not take as high a profile in the Folk-Song Society as he had in its early years. He now saw himself more as a music historian and journalist rather than as a folksong collector, and much of the time he kept to his book-lined study in Leeds. His visits to London were rare, and he attempted no further systematic collecting of folksongs in Yorkshire, Northumbria, or the Scottish border country. Yet if he was doing little new collecting, he still had a lot of unpublished material that he had assembled during the 1890s. In the mid-1900s he hoped that the folk-music boom would create sufficient demand for a new edition of his *Traditional Tunes,* which in 1891 had been published in only a limited edition of two hundred copies. He also hoped for an opportunity to put together a follow-up volume of the songs he had collected since 1891. In both cases he was disappointed and neither plan came to fruition before World War I.

Kidson did publish two more specialized collections: *Eighty Singing Games*[11] and *Seventy-Five British Nursery Rhymes*[12] came out during the Edwardian era. These were both collaborations with arranger Alfred Moffat, who seems to have initiated the projects and found publishers for them. Essentially they were songbooks in which simple tunes were decked out in piano arrangements. They seem to have been aimed at the elementary school market. Judged by the number of items they printed both were quite substantial collections, but in neither publication was Kidson given much space to discuss the significance of the material or to relate it to the main body of English folksong. Nor was any systematic attempt made to inform the reader how and where the various chants, rhymes, and songs had been obtained, although it appeared that occasional Yorkshire items were the result of Kidson's own collecting. What was most significant about these two works was their preoccupation with areas of folklore that Sharp, Vaughan Williams, Grainger, and others had neglected. By their very publication *Eighty Singing Games* and *Seventy-Five British Nursery Rhymes* proclaimed Kidson's conviction that the mainstream of the revival was too narrow in its focus, and that singing games and nursery rhymes were as worth collecting and studying as ballads and folk lyrics.

Although Kidson spent little time outside Leeds in these years and only on rare occasions noted new songs from singers he met on trips to the North York Moors or the Yorkshire coast in the region of Scarborough and Whitby, he kept busy working in his library at home. At one point a new edition of *The Minstrelsy of England* looked possible but this project also failed to see the light of day. On the other hand, Kidson contributed historical notes to Moffat's *English Songs of the Georgian Period,* a compilation of tunes and lyrics from printed sources that Sharp would have dismissed as a collection of Old English songs rather than a folksong collection.[13] Kidson's extensive research for this book gave him new insight into the history of popular tunes, and he summarized his findings in a paper delivered to a learned society, the Musical Association, on 17 March 1908. It was subsequently published as "The Vitality of Melody."[14] The article reveals Kidson's firm conviction that England was a "tune-loving nation" that possessed a "wealth of fine melody" and that it scarcely mattered whether individual items were classified as "folk melodies" or as "art tunes."

> Our national English tunes are the outcome of spontaneous musical feeling and the growth from English, or at any rate British minds. It would be...unreasonable to expect the musician to hark back to a primitive treatment of harmony...but in regard to melody it seems to be that we cannot go farther back and fare worse, and many of our earliest tunes [from Chaucer's time onwards] would appeal today equally as they did several hundred years ago. Types of melody may occur in certain definite periods, but these types are generally the known works of recognised musicians whose education and feeling are entirely of the age in which they composed. Such tunes are those by Shield, Hook, Dibdin, Bishop, etc., prior to which may be named as of a different cycle melodies by Arne, Worgan, Boyce and Greene. While these tunes have been popular in their own, and sometimes in a later day, yet there are others which appear to belong to no assignable period, and seem to be for all time. Such I call *vital melodies.* Some of these go to sleep for fifty or sixty years, or even a century, but they, like musical Rip Van Winkles or Sleeping Beauties, are roused from slumber and take their place in the rank of modern music. Strange as it may appear, the man in the street accepts them quite readily and never notices that there is anything different from the rest of their fellows.[15]

In other words, the real distinction between art music and music of the common people should be drawn not between folksong and composed song (as Sharp would have it) but between period songs and timeless songs. The latter were just as "communal" as songs collected from oral tradition since they possessed "vital melodies" to which ordinary people would be attracted time and time again.

As the oldest example of a "vital melody" Kidson gave the thirteenth-century tune "Sumer Is I Cumen In," but he remarked that in the seventeenth century some of the most effective political songs had made use of timeless tunes of this kind. For example, the Jacobite cause had employed "The King Shall Enjoy His Own Again," "Johnny Cope," "Charlie Is My Darling," and "The White Cockade," while on the other side of the political fence the Orangemen made parallel use of "Lilliburlero" and "Boyne Water." Kidson gave many more examples of "vital melodies," including "Joan's Placket Is Torn" (aka "The Cock o' the North"), "Blowzabella," "The Weaver's March," and "Yorkshire Lasses." He even traced one such tune (which began in 1760 as "To Rodney We Will Go") through a series of metamorphoses as, in turn, "The Brags of Washington," "With Wellington We'll Go," "Moll Roone," "With Henry Hunt We'll Go," "Jack the Jolly Ploughboy," "The Nut Girl," and, most recently, "The Low-Back'd Car." Kidson concluded that "a good tune never dies" and that such vital melodies have been used time and time again precisely because of their melodic value. Whether they turned up in the guise of folksongs, political songs, or art songs, the important point was that the tunes were timeless and popular: "people like familiar friends, and we all laugh loudest at old jokes."[16] Kidson did not draw the obvious conclusion in his paper, but it was implicit for all to infer: anyone who rejected or ignored such old friends on the grounds that, strictly speaking, they were not folksongs was throwing the baby out with the bathwater. He had effectively put his weight behind the eclectic Stanford/Somerville position that so appalled Sharp in 1906 and led to the public controversy that preceded the writing of *English Folk-Song: Some Conclusions.*

Kidson's major project after his collaboration with Moffat was a second and greatly expanded edition of *British Music Publishers, Printers, and Engravers.* This work seems to have been completed in manuscript, but the new edition was never printed. He was unable to find a publisher who saw in printing the bulky manuscript a viable commercial proposition, and his attempt to find sufficient subscribers to finance a private publication was also unsuccessful. Between 1908 and 1911 he kept a low public profile, but in 1912 he came out of the closet, writing two interesting articles for *The Choir* magazine, one titled "Folk-Song" and the other "Folk-Song and the Popular Song."[17] It was evident that he was still wrestling with the question of just how different folksong was from 'Old English' songs of the type that Sharp spurned. Traditional folksong, he now suspected, was no more than *archaic* popular song, and it was therefore a mistake to place it on a pedestal as a fundamentally different kind of communal or national music.[18] This, of course, amounted to a public repudiation of Sharp's central doctrines in *English Folk-Song: Some Conclusions*. Kidson, however, was still tentative in his analysis and he was not yet willing to follow his line of thought to its logical conclusion. An article that finally spelled out bluntly his disagreements with Sharpean orthodoxy appeared in *The Musical Herald* in August 1913.[19] It was not written by Kidson but was based on a lengthy interview with him. The anonymous piece, which was titled simply "Mr. Frank Kidson," provided a portrait of the man, his background, his beliefs, and a brief history of his publications. Some of the opinions ascribed to him were placed in quotation marks, but others were interpretations of his ideas based on his recent articles in *The Choir* and on his answers to questions posed by the interviewer. This, for example, was the journalist's account of Kidson's current views on the issue of the communal origin of folksongs:

> Are folk-songs heaven born, or of communal origin—or were they not born at all—like Topsy? Mr. Kidson knocks on the head a good deal of nonsense which has been heard on this score. Conjectures are not conclusions, for such must stand the scrutiny of men who want proofs. And there is no particular sanctity in the form in which an old air is sung by an old man or woman before whom a reverent collector sits with a phonograph. It is merely the version which the singer personally remembers or gives forth. So much the worse for the singer if his incapacity for time and tune leads him to change every measure and every phrase out of the recognition of those who possess printed originals. As we sit in Mr. Kidson's study he shows us such original songs, free from modal eccentricities and innocent of 5/4 time. He loves the old songs and seeks to secure their preservation in their purity. If he can trace the name of the composer, or poet, he gives them due credit. The mystery of so-called communal origin can often be solved by research among early printed matter.[20]

"Conjectures are not conclusions, for such must stand the scrutiny of men who want proofs." That criticism was obviously aimed at Sharp. Kidson, polite as ever, did not name names, but the remark was in character. He concluded that "on the whole" oral tradition had proved to be "wonderfully accurate" in transmitting songs over several generations, but he argued that many, perhaps most, of the songs that Edwardian collectors were noting in the field were derived ultimately from broadsides or other early printed sources. In his opinion that fact in no way disqualified such songs as folksongs; the ballad-mongers, he emphasized, had been poorly educated members of the lower classes, as were the singers who purchased their creations. The entire question of "authenticity," he concluded, was a very tricky one, and it was inadvisable to rush to judgment:

> Ballads were often written by people who were little better educated than the singers. Sometimes, and especially in Irish songs, one comes across classical references which can hardly have been familiar to the genuine peasant, and are evidently the production of some hedge schoolmaster. It is difficult to dismiss this subject in a word or two.[21]

Kidson was thus not prepared to dismiss as "inauthentic" or "inaccurate" songs that were not "peasant" in origin, and he argued for a broader understanding of popular song than that espoused by Sharp in *English Folk-Song: Some Conclusions*. There was an intricate relationship, he believed, between folk tradition and composed song, and in the area of overlap between folk music and art song were often to be found those "vital melodies" that he so admired. Careful research was therefore required to sort out and to comprehend the complicated history of popular song, and doctrinaire romantic theories would hinder, not help, the painstaking scientific work.

Kidson's methodology was eclectic, based not on theory but on a catholic love of old songs of various types and an unwillingness to discriminate in favor of one kind rather than another. It reflected the empirical, even antiquarian, side of his approach to traditional song. As *British Music Publishers, Printers, and Engravers* had demonstrated, he was a music historian first and foremost, and he pursued with tenacity the challenge of tracing tunes and words to their source. This "musical Sherlock Holmes" (as the interviewer called him) cared little for speculative theories about folksong but he loved collecting broadside ballads, garlands, and first editions of songbooks. His intellectual heroes were still Joseph Ritson and William Chappell, antiquarian editors whose instinct had been to try to check the text and tune of any song collected from oral tradition against early manuscript and print sources. Insistence on this comparative method was Kidson's most important contribution to the Edwardian revival, and he believed that it was the surest way of shedding light on the accuracy and authenticity of received versions of songs. How far in practice he was from embracing Sharp's and Vaughan Williams's concept of folksong was evident in 1913 when he published, jointly with Martin Shaw, a new book titled *Songs of Britain: A Collection of One Hundred English, Welsh, Scottish and Irish National Songs.*[22] While this included many English folksongs (in piano arrangements, to which Kidson had now become reconciled), it was essentially a collection in the tradition of Sharp's 1902 publication, *A Book of British Song for Home and School,*[23] and Stanford's *National Song Book* of 1905.[24] No clearer repudiation of *English Folk-Song: Some Conclusions* was possible than a work that, in effect, ignored everything that Sharp had said, written, or done in the previous decade.

Kidson's long-time collaborator Alfred Moffat eventually persuaded him that it was high time to remedy the regrettable fact that the planned second volume of *Traditional Tunes* had never appeared. Moffat offered his services as an arranger of the best folksongs that Kidson had collected well before World War I, suggesting a new edition of *Traditional Tunes* (with piano accompaniments) and at least one companion volume of additional material. Kidson had previously declared his belief that folksong tunes should not be harmonized but should be printed only as simple melody lines. He now reluctantly abandoned this purist stance, and accepted Moffat's offer. His tardy decision—made, apparently, sometime in 1925—to publish material that he had collected more than thirty years previously, came too late. His health was failing, he had less than two years to live, and he died in November 1926. In the event, he was able to see only a single volume, *A Garland of English Folk Songs*, through the press.[25] His niece and collaborator, Ethel Kidson, aided by arranger Alfred Moffat, was responsible for editing the second and third publications in what amounted to a mini-series that purported to make public the best of Kidson's legendary collection of Yorkshire folksongs. The titles of the other two songbooks were *Folk Songs from the North Countrie, with their Traditional Airs*[26] and *English Peasant Songs, with their Traditional Airs.*[27]

Kidson presumably still had some control over the editing of the first volume of the trilogy. *A Garland of English Folk Songs* reveals something of how, as an elderly music historian, he now viewed the songs that he had collected with such enthusiasm during the last decades of the nineteenth century.[28] His views had changed somewhat over the years, and he now subscribed to the pessimistic school that believed English folk music had become moribund and was doomed to disappear in the face of industrialization and urbanization. Yet the best folksong tunes were still for Kidson something extraordinary and very special. And it had become very obvious to him over the years that a given folksong might be found with more than one tune that was worth preserving. Each district of the United Kingdom had its own tunes, he concluded, and asserted bluntly that "the same ballad or song is found united to many different airs, and no two singers give it the same melody." As an example he cited "Lord Bateman," a ballad which he claimed had been collected "probably thirty or forty times" and in no instance was one tune like another.[29] This fact was his primary justification for issuing yet another collection of English folksongs.

All the songs in *A Garland* were variants collected in the northeast of England, mainly in Yorkshire, and they stood comparison with the same or similar songs noted in the south and the Midlands. Their traditional tunes were their glory, and in Kidson's opinion that was the principal reason they deserved to be preserved and appreciated. He remarked:

> Strange it is that folk-song and folk-melody ran, until recent years, as an obscure stream ignored by the musician, who is now quick to recognise its merits and value. The beautiful melodies which have come down to us from the memories of old men and women have in them the essentials of pure English melody, purer than any other music we possess; a melody unaffected by fashion or the influence of the music of any other nation. In the course of our musical history we have accepted the Italian, the French and the German standards, but our folk-melody has remained pure and unbiassed by any but its own formula. It has, therefore, for many reasons, great claims upon our consideration.[30]

It was thus, in Kidson's view, still the melodies that really mattered, and he was now quite willing to make the editorial compromises necessary to see those tunes preserved in printed form. For someone who had spent a lifetime involved with the folk music movement, he was surprisingly diffident about the quality of even the best songs that he had selected for the volume. He was also much readier than he had been in 1891 to wield the editorial knife and to compose new text where words, lines, or stanzas were missing. When he had published *Traditional Tunes* Kidson had been ahead of his time in his approach to editing folksongs. Now he seemed a reactionary. His defence of editorial license was reminiscent of Baring-Gould's or even Percy's:

> The folk-song has its limitations, and confined itself solely to events and sentiments which were within the scope of the singer's thought and experience. Frequently, the verse was so rude and unpolished as to be faulty in metre and rhyme. In these cases I have ventured to carefully amend glaring instances, and here and there to shorten ballads which, now-a-days, are too long for singing. In addition to these revisions I have completed a few imperfect songs, imperfect through the faulty memory of the singer, but this has been done carefully and in full sympathy with the original.[31]

Kidson's reader was thus warned not to rely on the authenticity of the texts in *A Garland of English Folksongs,* especially as its editor rarely bothered to indicate when he had been constrained to amend or recompose the songs. Nor did he provide any information about the informants from whom the songs had been noted or the dates and places of collecting. Clearly he and Moffat intended the work as a songbook, not as a precise record of what Charles Lolley, T. C. Smith, and Kidson himself had actually heard in the field.

Most of the songs in the book would have been known already to readers familiar with the various English folksong collections published before World War I. There was the usual handful of Child ballads, in this instance "Lord Bateman," "Fair Margaret and Sweet William," "The Cruel Sister," "Barbara Allen," and "The *Golden Vanity*." More numerous were broadside ballads about love found or lovers reunited. They included "The Golden Glove," "Green Broom," "Fair Phoebe and Her Dark-eyed Sailor," "The Dover Sailor," and "The Wealthy Farmer's Son." Less common were ballads in which the departed lover was drowned or the outcome in some other way tragic, but two examples were "'Twas Early, Early All in the Spring" and "Young Riley the Fisherman." Other broadsides dealt with recurrent problems of rural life or with unusual incidents that had caught the popular imagination. "As I Was A-Travelling the North Countrie" was a song about gambling, "Creeping Jane" the story of a horse race, "The Peelers and the Pig" a comic tale about an encounter between a hog and a police patrol, and "Jack Hall" the confession of a defiant criminal about to be hanged. "The Female Highwayman" and "Turpin Hero" were broadsides sympathetic to robbers, but "The Highwayman Outwitted" and "The Yorkshire Farmer" saw matters from the intended victims' point of view and celebrated their success in turning the tables on the highwayman. Some ballads or songs, such as "High Germany," "The Gallant Hussar," "John o' Greenfields Ramble," and "The Deserter" reflected the impact of the military on rural life, while broadsides about ships, sailors, life at sea or emigration included "Captain Glen" (aka "The Cruel Captain"), "The *Bold Princess Royal*," "Jack the Sailor," "On Board a Ninety-Eight," and "The Shamrock Shore."

Approximately half of the sixty items were folk lyrics rather than ballads. Unlike most collections of English folksongs there were relatively few laments about false or departed lovers. The few that Kidson did select included such beautiful songs as "Sprig of Thyme," "A Brisk Young Sailor Courted Me," "Three Pretty Maids," and "My Bonny, Bonny Boy." Love lyrics were rather more numerous, and the songbook offered versions of such well-known items as "The Banks of Sweet Primroses" and "Seventeen Come Sunday" as well as "Cupid's Garden" and "My Johnny Was a Shoemaker." Songs of courtship included "Colin and Phoebe," "The Knight's Dream," "The Queen of the May" and "I Designed to Say 'No' But Mistook and Said 'Yes.'" Kidson slipped into the collection a couple of pub songs ("When Joan's Ale Was New" and "Tobacco"), and he seems to have retained his fondness for songs celebrating the joys of rural life. There were a lot of these, some expressing general contentment with country living, such as "Cottage Well Thatched With Straw" and "Ground for the Floor," others championing the life of the carter ("The Warbling Waggoner"), the ploughman ("The Pretty Ploughboy," "Saucy Ploughboy," and "We Are Jolly Fellows That Follow the Plough") or the small farmer ("The Farmer's Boy"). Because of the number of these old songs of country life, and because Kidson's introduction stressed the changes that had afflicted the English countryside since they had been collected, *A Garland of English Folk Songs* projected an air of nostalgia for a lost rural past not unlike Alfred Williams's *Folk-Songs of the Upper Thames.*[32]

In addition to issuing *A Garland of English Folk Songs,* Moffat had planned a new edition, with piano arrangements, of *Traditional Tunes.* Kidson never lived to see the project come to fruition, but in 1927 Ethel Kidson and Moffat collaborated on *Folk-Songs of the North-Countrie,* which comprised another sixty songs from Kidson's files.[33] They persuaded Lucy Broadwood to write a foreword for the new volume. Broadwood welcomed it as "a modern edition of Frank Kidson's *Traditional Tunes* arranged for medium voice with piano accompaniment" and lamented that Kidson himself had been unable to see this new version of his pioneering work in print.[34] The truth was that *Folk-Songs of the North-Countrie,* although based on *Traditional Tunes,* was hardly a new edition of that book. The original had contained eighty-three songs, the new work contained only sixty. Three of the sixty ("The Dawn of the Day," "The Gentleman Gay," and "The Golden Ring") had not been in *Traditional Tunes* for the simple reason that they were new songs composed by Ethel Kidson. That meant that twenty-six songs were missing from the supposed "new edition." To be sure, a few had already appeared in *A Garland of English Songs.* That was true of "Lord Bateman," "Barbara Allen," "The Golden Glove," "Colin and Phoebe," "The Farmer's Boy," and "The Sprig of Thyme." But that still left twenty omitted, and they included many interesting items. Some of the missing songs were such well-known Child ballads as "Lord Thomas and Fair Eleanor," "The Outlandish Knight," "The Dowie Dens of Yarrow," and "Chevy Chace," while others were Scottish pieces such as "Braes of Strathblane," "Robin Tamson's Smiddy," and "Glowerowerum." The others that were omitted included "The Bold Privateer," "The Gown of Green," "The Goose and the Gander," "The Plains of Waterloo," "Saddle to Rags," "Spencer the Rover," "The Stolen Child," and "With Henry Hunt We'll Go."

The difference in content and the addition of piano arrangements were not the only things that had changed in the evolution of *Traditional Tunes* into *Folk-Songs of the North-Countrie*. The original book had often included more than one variant of a song, sometimes providing an alternative tune and sometimes alternative words. The new edition presented a single composite version in each case. In some instances the new versions had been cut down and quite ruthlessly rewritten, as for example in the transformation of "The Death of Bill Brown" into "Bill Brown." Similarly "The Jolly Shilling" had metamorphosed into "The Jolly Sixpence" and been shortened in the interests of brevity. On the other hand, some fragments had been expanded into full songs, and indelicate lines rewritten. Such was the case with "My Valentine" (the new version of which was twice as long but left out any suggestion of the young lady jumping into bed) and "The *Nightingale*" (which expanded from eight lines to twenty-four). Clearly if the reader wanted to see what Kidson had actually collected he had no choice but to seek out the scarce original edition of *Traditional Tunes*. Not that the original publication had been completely faithful to its sources, but it represented an earlier stage in the evolution of traditional songs into manicured products aimed at an established middle-class market. This was a process that Frank Kidson had long resisted, and one can only speculate about how he might have reacted to some of his niece's editorial decisions. It is likely that had he lived to edit *Folk-Songs of the North-Countrie* himself it would have been a genuine second edition of *Traditional Tunes* and there would have been no missing items.

Ethel Kidson still had an opportunity to include the lost songs in the third songbook, *English Peasant Songs*,[35] but apart from "The Goose and the Gander" she neglected to do so. She apparently disliked the book's inappropriate title although she failed to fight hard enough to prevent its adoption. She was, however, mainly responsible for the contents and for the way it was edited. Her uncle, more interested in folksong tunes than texts, had often neglected (or been unable) to obtain full sets of words for the songs he had collected. Ethel understandably wanted to provide full texts for the songs, and therefore had to resort to broadsides, to other published versions of the same songs, and, if necessary, to her own creative imagination. Two of the songs in the collection ("The Maiden's Garden" and the shanty, "Whiskey Johnny") were not from her uncle's collection but from her own memory of how she had heard them sung as a child in Liverpool. The remaining fifty-eight items were apparently derived from Kidson's manuscripts, and presumably the tunes, at least, were much as he had obtained them from his informants, apart from the added piano arrangements. However, those informants were never identified in *English Peasant Songs*, nor were any dates and places of collection provided.

Despite the misleading title there was a strong non-rural element to the collection. Songs of country life were relatively few. Examples of those that were included are "May Dew," "Come All Ye Pretty Maids!" "Come All Ye Bold Young Countrymen," and "Yorkshire Too!" to which may be added such humorous courting songs as "Joe Muggins" and "I Once Went A-Courting" and the one wassail, "Here We Come A-Wassailing." There were also three hunting songs ("The Morning Looks Charming," "The White Hare," and "Holmbank Hunting Song") but these, although rural in nature, reflected the activities of a higher social class than the so-called peasantry. Sailors' songs were almost as well represented as those of agricultural workers. They included "The Dockland Gate," "The Town of Liverpool" (aka "The Jolly Roving Tar"), "The Armada," and "In a British Man-of-War," not to mention an emigration ballad ("Patrick's Farewell") and three shanties: "All For My Grog and Tobacco," "Whitechapel Road," and "Whiskey Johnny."

There were no Child ballads but about two dozen broadside ballads were included. Some of the finest were tragic or horrific in nature, such as "My Bonny Lad Is Young" (aka "The Trees They Do Grow High"), "The Manchester Angel" (about lovers parting), "William Taylor" (a tale of revenge for unfaithfulness), "Spurn Point" (about a shipwreck), and "The Cruel Ship's Captain" (a story of supernatural reckoning for murder). Many were on the theme of parted lovers eventually reunited, for example "Rosetta and Her Gay Ploughboy," "Gosport Beach," and "Pretty Rosaline." A large number told of male/female encounters that resulted, sooner or later, in courtship and/or marriage; these included, among others, "Caroline of Gosport," "Horncastle Fair," "The Young Cobbler," "The Carrier's Cart," "Canada I O," and "Naught Else to Do." In a few of these broadsides ("The Oyster Girl" and "The Coach and Six") the women were more interested in the man's wallet than in marriage and left him poorer and wiser. Others, on the other hand, portrayed unexpected kindness and altruism, as in "The Poor Fisher Boy" and the transportation ballad "The Isle of France."

About one third of the collection consisted of love lyrics and laments by deserted lovers. Some examples of the love songs are "Come, Come, Bonny Lass," "Pretty Jennee," "A Case of Needles," "The Country Garden," "The Orange and the Blue," "My Heart Is Light As a Feather" and "Green Broom Besoms." As usual, many of the love laments had particularly beautiful tunes, for instance "With Fife and Drum He Marched Away" (aka "Shule Agra"), "The Bonny Lighthorseman," "Irish Molly O," and "Let Him Go!" Other laments included "Sorry the Day I Got Married," "The Maid Lamenting," "The Yorkshire Weaver," "The Maiden's Garden," "Young Willie Brown," and "The Banks of the Roses." There was thus a variety of singable material in this third collection, but, as with the first two books in the series, *English Peasant Songs* was marred by a lack of information about the songs, their singers, and how and when Kidson had collected them. It was difficult to be sure what was traditional song and what had been contributed by the creative mind of Ethel Kidson.

Although quite different in approach and in editorial standards, Kidson's collections, like those of John Stokoe's, demonstrated beyond question that the north of England, especially the counties of Yorkshire and Northumberland, was still a most fertile source of English folksong. Narrative ballads (with traditional melodies) could still be found in oral tradition, although only a fraction of those in Child's *English and Scottish Popular Ballads* had so far turned up. Local versions of folksongs found elsewhere in England (and, for that matter, Scotland) were fairly common, and there was apparently a considerable body of folksong special to the region. There was also clearly a regional tradition of sung poetry, some but not all of it in dialect, which supplemented the local oral traditions. Whether or not this material should be counted as "folksong" was a difficult question. The answer depended on how one conceived and defined a folksong. Intuitively a song such as "Buy Broom Buzzems" was obviously a folksong, and it certainly circulated by word of mouth in Tyneside, yet there was a known author, in this case Blind Willie Purvis. Similarly "D'ye Ken John Peel?" was composed by John Graves, albeit to a traditional Border air. Again, "Bob Cranky's 'Size Sunday'" was the work of John Selkirk of Gateshead, while "Bob Cranky's Adieu" was composed by John Shield of Broomhaugh, near Hexham.

Kidson's work confirmed that a broader rather than narrower definition of folk music would be appropriate to reflect fully the diversity of lower class song and tune-making in a region that was urban as well as rural, as much industrial as agricultural. Folksong evidently remained an ambiguous concept, and exactly how the term should be applied was still unclear. Perhaps for that reason Kidson avoided the word in the titles of the collections published during his lifetime. His legacy was essentially two-fold: a wealth of folksong tunes collected mainly, but not exclusively, in Yorkshire, and a perspective on the history of British vernacular music that integrated oral tradition into a broader river of popular song including broadside balladry, ballad operas, and national songs.

It is a shame that Kidson's collecting from the 1890s and early 1900s was bequeathed to posterity in a rather unsatisfactory form, so that his best effort as a folksong collector and editor remained his groundbreaking work, *Traditional Tunes,* published back in 1891. When one adds to the approximately two hundred songs in these four books the other items that he published in the *Journal of the Folk-Song Society* and the contents of the manuscripts in the Mitchell Library, it is evident that a significant proportion of his collecting remains difficult of access and largely neglected by modern scholarship.[36] One would eventually like to see a multi-volume scholarly edition of his entire *oeuvre* as a folksong collector and editor, including, of course, those songs and tunes actually noted by his various collaborators, especially Charles Lolley. In the meantime, however, a reconstruction of the never published second volume of *Traditional Tunes* as Kidson himself envisaged it would be an eminently worthwhile scholarly project.

Lucy Broadwood in the 1900s

If Frank Kidson withdrew somewhat from Folk-Song Society circles after 1904, Lucy Broadwood would remain at the heart of the English folksong revival for several more decades. During its Edwardian phase she was one of its most powerful and influential figures. When Kate Lee became no longer able to carry on as the Honorary Secretary of the Folk-Song Society she took over its administrative reins for the best part of a decade. She was formally elected to the post of Secretary in March 1904, but she had in fact already been doing most of the duties for more than a year. She formally held the position until her resignation in 1908 but in practice she continued to function thereafter as the Society's administrative lynch-pin until well after World War I. This was in part due to her role as the principal editor of the *Journal of the Folk-Song Society.* She performed this essential (and very demanding) task from 1904 until 1911, although she was formally named Honorary Editor only in 1908. She resumed the editorship during the First World War, and continued to be a key member of the editorial board until her resignation in 1927. Although she was not always the titular editor during this lengthy period, in effect she largely controlled the contents and methodology of the *Journal* for over twenty years.

Broadwood's secretarial and editorial duties left her less time for her own collecting, but she was perceived by the educated public as a leading collector and an authority on the subject. On 14 March 1905 she gave an illustrated paper to a meeting of the Royal Music Association that was subsequently printed in the Association's *Proceedings.* Titled "On the Collecting of English Folk-Song" it summarized her perspective on the nature of English traditional music.[37] She walked a careful line between, on the one hand, the ideas and opinions that Baring-Gould had expressed to her, and on the other the insights and knowledge that she had derived from Kidson. After distinguishing firmly between traditional ballads and "the genteel 'Phoebe and Colin' song of the eighteenth century," which she did not count as folk music, Broadwood nonetheless emphasized the central role played by the broadside industry in preserving ballads and folk lyrics. In the early years of the nineteenth century, she remarked, Catnach and other broadsheet publishers had "saved many a genuine ballad of the people"; moreover, earlier black-letter broadsides often have texts virtually identical to the words of folksongs collected from oral tradition. Adopting Baring-Gould's theory concerning the minstrel origins of traditional song, she speculated that even the earliest printed versions of ballads derived from oral transmission that had roots at least as far back as the folklore of the Middle Ages. As regards folksong tunes, Broadwood admitted that their origins were usually unknown but argued that they often exhibited certain melodic characteristics that made them instantly identifiable and suggested that they were related historically to the music of the medieval Church. She commented:

> The pure English folk-tune is exceedingly simple in construction; often it is but eight bars long. Its subjects are repeated with artless economy. Yet it has the most beautiful, original, and varied cadences to be found in music, and the melody frequently moves in superb curves...Our true folk-tune is purely diatonic, and it is often purely modal. Mr. Cecil Sharp finds that amongst 500 songs collected by him in Somerset, 125 are modal. Nor is this proportion unusual, judging from other collections, my own included. Indeed, the most characteristic English folk-tune is more closely allied to the plainsong of the Office Book or Gradual than to any other form of music.[38]

In short, folksong collectors should pay attention to both oral and print traditions since they were closely interrelated, but it was only in the field that they were likely to come across those modal melodies that made folksong so special. Some of those tunes, Broadwood recognized, came attached to song texts that were, in the words of Surrey carter George Grantham, "outway rude," a fact that made it particularly difficult for women collectors to obtain a source singer's full repertoire.[39] However, she believed that the main problem facing the Folk-Song Society lay not with the lack of songs but with the lack of active collectors. Anticipating a vision that would be embraced eagerly by Cecil Sharp, Ralph Vaughan Williams, George Butterworth, Percy Grainger, and many others, she also appealed for a renaissance of English art music that would be based on folksong and would appeal not only to an educated elite but to the vast majority of the country's population. As she put it,

> [I]t is not our folk-music that has been lacking. It has been the *collector*. We are a century behind the Buntings, the Moores, the Burns's, yet I believe that England has still at this moment a rich harvest of pure, noble melody...a harvest which we may save if we choose, and which offers a natural basis for our National Musical Education. *And surely we must build upon the healthy artistic instincts of our people, should we hope for the coming of another Purcell*, and should we wish to train our growing generations to reject of themselves the enervating slow poison dished up so attractively for them by vulgar caterers in the art, literature, and popular amusements of today.[40]

The lecture was apparently very well received by those in attendance, and it was quite influential. Percy Grainger, for example, credited it with recruiting him to folksong collecting, and Ralph Vaughan Williams always remembered it as a significant event in the history of the movement.

Some indication of what Broadwood had recently been doing in the field was to be found in the *Journal of the Folk-Song Society* in 1907. The first issue of Volume 3 (No. 10) was devoted to the fruits of her collecting in Ireland, and to songs noted by a variety of members of the Society in Cumberland, Northumberland, and the southern counties of England: twenty-two items in all. Lucy herself had spent the previous August vacationing in County Waterford, and at Camphire, near Cappoquin, she had noted English-language songs from an elderly farm-laborer and his daughter, Michael and Bridget Geary. Both informants sang in a highly decorated style, varying "intervals and ornaments much more than any English or Scottish singer" Lucy had ever come across, and she found Michael's melodic lines particularly difficult to note down. She had encountered an Irish traditional singing style in all its intricate glory, and she marveled at it:

> Nothing but a series of phonographic-records could satisfactorily reproduce any one song as given by Michael Geary, for he varies both his intervals, graces, and rhythm endlessly. The flexibility of his voice is amazing, and is contrived by that very nasal manner of producing the voice (met with so much amongst Orientals), which makes it possible for the untaught singer to perform feats that a skilled violinist might envy. Michael Geary will often sing a rapid run of eight or more notes as a preliminary to the essential note of the tune...The rapidity of his arpeggios, and the power of dwelling on favourite notes, swelling them out to a *fortissimo,* and sustaining them, are extraordinary. His singing indeed sounds like a rhapsodical improvisation; in all its main characteristics it is startlingly like that of the peasants of Southern Europe, especially of South Italy and Spain, and also of many Eastern races. [41]

Broadwood thus raised, at least implicitly, two major issues that she and her colleagues in the first phase of the revival would never deal with satisfactorily. Could and should mechanical or electrical recording devices be employed in collecting to ensure complete accuracy and to capture informants' singing styles as well as the tune of the song itself?

And given the huge difference between traditional singing styles and those normally employed by trained-voice singers, was it appropriate to perform traditional songs as if they were *lieder* or arias? Nowadays to most folklorists the standard answers are "yes" and "no" respectively, but these were not obvious answers in the Edwardian era. They were, in fact, the views of a tiny minority of folksong enthusiasts. Broadwood herself backed away from answering either question, which meant that in practice she endorsed the status quo: noting songs by ear, and singing them art-music style.

The detailed story of Lucy Broadwood's ongoing activities as the Folk-Song Society's Secretary and principal *Journal* editor must wait for another occasion, but it is important to recognize that she still had something to contribute as a song collector/editor during the Edwardian era. Fifteen years elapsed between the publication of *English County Songs* in 1893 and that of her next book-length collection, *English Traditional Songs and Carols*, in 1908.[42] Viewed superficially, this publication belongs to the Edwardian phase of the folksong revival. Yet when one examines Broadwood's sources one finds that most, although not quite all, of the songs contained in the new book had actually been collected during the 1890s. A brief discussion of it will therefore round off our investigation of her work as a Late Victorian song collector and editor.

Broadwood's preface to the tunes and texts in *English Traditional Songs and Carols* was brief, just over three pages in length, but it revealed much about her own views on folksong. Like most of the other late Victorian and Edwardian collectors she loved traditional modal tunes, and she agreed with Vaughan Williams that the preoccupation of traditional singers with melody rather than harmony was folksong's greatest strength. She candidly admitted that folksong had its weaknesses, remarking that "the country ballad" often exhibited "doggerel narrative, faulty rhyme, and irregular metre." On the other hand, folk poetry had its strengths too: an emotional directness and sincerity that sometimes found expression in penetrating insights and hauntingly beautiful verses. As examples she quoted the line "Oh, love it is a killing thing! Did you ever feel the pain?" and the following verse from the "Bedfordshire May-Day Carol":

> When I am dead, and in my grave, and covered with cold clay,
> The nightingale will sit and sing, and pass the time away.[43]

To explain the uneven quality of folksong texts, Broadwood pointed out that many "country ballads" were derived, directly or indirectly, from broadsides, and she devoted about a third of her introduction to discussing the relationship between traditional song and the printed broadside. Broadsides, she argued, provided a unique record of the popular culture of England in the early modern era, and they preserved, among many other things, both "orally-traditional" ballads and those "newly-made" by strolling minstrels and tavern-bards:

> Before the days of cheap literature, the broadside, indeed, took the place of the newspaper, political pamphlet, history, novel, poetry-book, and hymnal of our times; and upon the ballad-sheets - largely circulated by pedlars, themselves often singers—the country folk relied for fresh information, amusement, and moral instruction, the more easily assimilated when in homely verse...Many ballads were common to most broadside printers, but the versions of these, as given by different publishers, are rarely identical. Indeed, the kaleidoscopic shifting of lines, or whole verses, the additions, curtailments, borrowings, diversity of metre, and the strange corruptions in these printed versions (ancient or modern), go to prove that, however much the country singer or local bard may be beholden—directly or indirectly—to the broadside, the broadside is equally indebted to the ballad-singer and hedge-poet.[44]

Broadwood specifically mentioned James Catnach as "an astute Northumbrian printer" who had settled in London and "paid men to collect ballads from singers in country taverns" which he then published as broadsides.[45] Her tolerant, even sympathetic, perspective on broadside texts as valuable historical documents and as sources of otherwise lost folksong texts was quite different to the attitude exhibited by Francis Child, Cecil Sharp, or Ralph Vaughan Williams, each of whom had recourse to broadsides only reluctantly, when there appeared to be no alternative. It no doubt reflected the influence of Kidson, who not only was keenly interested in the history of music publishing but had researched the activities of such broadside entrepreneurs as Catnach.

Broadwood's new collection, then, was more than a bunch of traditional melodies. She paid equal attention to texts as to tunes, and she started with the premise that just as a folksong editor had an obligation to print the tunes faithfully so he or she should attempt as far as possible to do the same for the lyrics. She described her own practice in *English Traditional Songs and Carols* as follows:

> Every tune in the book is faithful to the version noted from the singer at the time named. The original words of the singers remain also unaltered, save in trifling instances where a false rhyme, forgotten line, nonsensical corruption, or the like, has made it absolutely necessary to correct them...In two cases a verse has been omitted, and the wording of a line slightly

changed. One song has been partly re-written...The unaltered words may in many cases be found in the *Journal of the Folk-Song Society...*"[46]

This represented a slight retreat from the uncompromising stance she had adopted earlier in 1893, but it still indicated her opposition to the heavier kind of editing that so many late Victorian and Edwardian collectors, from Baring-Gould to Butterworth, believed to be acceptable or even desirable.

Another innovative and scholarly aspect of Broadwood's book was her clear and up-front acknowledgement of her source singers, whom she listed in the preface. They were fourteen individuals plus a gypsy family by the name of Goby, and most of them lived in either Sussex or Surrey. Not surprisingly, the single most important informant—in terms of the number and quality of the songs he provided—was Henry Burstow, the Horsham shoemaker and bellringer.[47] Of Burstow's four hundred songs, Broadwood chose eighteen for reproduction in *English Traditional Songs and Carols*, which meant that he had supplied more than half of the book's contents. All eighteen had been collected in 1893, and most of them were ballads of one kind or another. To start with there were his three Child ballads: "Banstead Downs" (aka "Georgie"), "Henry Martin," and "The Bold Pedlar and Robin Hood." Of his other narrative songs, several dealt with the triumph over adversity of a pair of lovers upon whom fate had not initially looked kindly, for example "Rosetta and Her Gay Ploughboy," "Through Moorfields," "Bristol Town," and "The Wealthy Farmer's Son." Others, such as "The Merchant's Daughter, or the Constant Farmer's Son," "Belfast Mountains," and "Oh, Yarmouth is a Pretty Town" told love stories with sadder outcomes. "Van Diemen's Land" was a powerful ballad of poaching and transportation, "The Three Butchers" was a dramatic tale of deception, robbery and murder, while "Boney's Lamentation" and "The Duke of Marlborough" were historical broadsides dealing with war and international politics. Burstow's remaining songs included a lyrical lament, "I Must Live All Alone" and a rambling song, "Travel the Country Round," plus two more literary items that betrayed the hand of an educated author, "The Ages of Man" and "Death and the Lady."

Another Sussex singer to whom Broadwood was indebted was Walter Searle, whom she described as a young quarryman from Amberley. He had sung "The Young Servant Man" (or "The Two Affectionate Lovers") to her in 1901, and, like Henry Burstow, he would subsequently contribute songs to the notebooks of other collectors to whom Broadwood gave his name and address. Another younger singer—at least, relatively so when Broadwood visited him in 1897—was Mr. Foster, a farm laborer at Milford in Surrey who sang "The Poor Murdered Woman," while at Holmwood (also in Surrey) she had noted "The Rich Nobleman and His Daughter" from George Grantham.

As we have seen, the locality in Surrey where Lucy had found the most and the best songs was the village of Dunsfold and the surrounding neighborhood. Here in 1896 she had discovered many fine singers, including five farm laborers and the wife of another farmhand. To *English Traditional Songs and Carols* Mary Ann Rugman contributed a Child ballad, "How Cold the Winds Do Blow" (aka "The Unquiet Grave"), and James Bromham offered a variant of the same ballad plus another song, "The Irish Girl." Another fine ballad, "The Trees Are Getting High" had been noted by Lucy from George Ede, while George Baker had sung two items that she still treasured more than a decade later: "The Little Lowland Maid" and "The Valiant Lady" (aka "The Brisk Young Lively Lad"). She had also collected from Richard Lough "Some Rival Has Stolen My True Love Away," and from Mr. Sparks "Our Ship She Lies in Harbour." All these found a place in the book.

One category of material featured in *English Traditional Songs and Carols* and alluded to in its slightly misleading title was that of the folk-carol. In fact there was only a handful of such carols in the collection, although the specimens included were excellent examples of the genre. Like Ella Leather, Lucy Broadwood loved folk-carols, and she was very interested in the folklore surrounding them, especially their relationship to mumming plays. When collecting material for *Sussex Songs* in 1880-81 she had noted from a group of mummers at Horsham a "Sussex Mummer's Christmas Carol," and in 1904 she had obtained from five Sussex villagers other variants, with additional verses; the version printed seems to have combined the original tune with a text based mainly on one of these later variants. For comparative purposes Broadwood inserted a similar "Hampshire Mummers' Christmas Carol" collected by Godfrey Arkwright from the Kingsclere Mummers. She also included a May carol collected by Sir Ernest Clarke at Hinwick in Bedfordshire, commenting that its words obviously alluded to pagan May Day ceremonies but also reflected the Christian gloss placed upon them by "gloomy" Puritan preachers.[48] Two other folk-carols that Broadwood had collected in 1893 from the Goby family of gypsies camped between Horsham and Dorking on the Sussex/Surrey border rounded out this small group of religious folksongs. They were "The Moon Shines Bright" and "King Pharim," a variant of the Child ballads "St. Stephen and Herod" and "The Carnal and the Crane." Broadwood's extensive and erudite notes revealed her familiarity with the history of carol collecting in England and the various previously published collections of English carols, including those by Sandys and Rimbault, as well as her acquaintance with *The English and Scottish Popular Ballads* and the scholarly work of Francis Child.

Yet if *English Traditional Songs and Carols* was intended primarily to showcase Broadwood's collecting in Sussex from Henry Burstow and in Surrey from the villagers of Dunsfold, she also took the opportunity to include various miscellaneous items that she regarded as of particular value. For example, she wanted to see in print some of the very first folksongs that she had noted, and for which she felt special affection. In 1893 she had learned from her old family nurse, Mrs. Hills (who hailed from Stamford in Lincolnshire), a version of "The Lost Lady Found," while the same year (while visiting Baring-Gould) she had noted from Jane Jeffrey, an elderly cottager in Devon, a beautiful version of "How Cold the Winds Do Blow" (aka "The Unquiet Grave"). These ballads duly appeared in the book, as did a variant of "Lord Randal" titled "King Henry, My Son" that one of her friends, Miss M. B. Lattimer of Carlisle, had learned from a maidservant called Margaret Scott from Wigton in Cumberland as long ago as the 1860s.

Broadwood also included a small sample from her collecting in the Edwardian era. In 1906 she had noted "Died of Love" (or "A Brisk Young Lad He Courted Me") from Joseph Taylor, the singing estate bailiff from Saxby-All-Saints, Lincolnshire. Taylor, from whom "Brigg Fair" had been collected, had subsequently become one of Percy Grainger's main informants. Lucy included "Died of Love" in her collection, with the following notes about Mr. Taylor and the song:

> He has been a choirman in his village for forty-two years, but familiarity with modern major and minor scales has not destroyed his power of singing purely modal tunes. His voice is a flexible true tenor, and his genius for delicately ornamenting his melodies, whilst exquisitely preserving the rhythm, is one which many a skilled musician might envy...[He] remembered only two verses of words. Of these the first verse, though beautiful, is too painfully tragic for general use. It has therefore been omitted here, and two stanzas from a variant of a similar ballad, noted by Mr. H. E. D. Hammond in Dorsetshire, have by his kindness been used for verses 1 and 2. The words of this song belong to a type of ballad which is extraordinarily popular amongst country singers both in England and Scotland. The subject (of a forsaken and broken-hearted girl, who directs how her grave shall be made), is the same in all versions, which however vary astonishingly in detail, whilst having certain lines or stanzas always in common...For copious references, and various tunes, see Kidson's *Traditional Tunes*, "My true love once he courted me"; and *Journal of the Folk Song Society* under the titles of "Died for Love," "A Bold Young Farmer" (or "Sailor"), "In Jessie's City," "There is an Alehouse (or Tavern) in Yonder Town," etc. Usually the tunes sung to these ballads are especially beautiful, and most often modal...The fine Dorian tune here given has striking points of likeness to the ancient "Song of Agincourt," thought to be a folk-tune (see Chappell's *Popular Music*).[49]

These notes give an indication of the depth of Lucy's knowledge of the body of material assembled by the Victorian and Edwardian folksong collectors, but they also reveal that she was now willing to censor her sources for the sake of providing what she regarded as a more singable text. Deleting Taylor's first verse, however "painfully tragic" the words may have been, was hardly adherence to that policy of leaving songs "absolutely unaltered" that she had once proclaimed in *English County Songs*.

"Died of Love" was one of the very few items in *English Traditional Songs and Carols* that reflected Broadwood's collecting since the Folk-Song Society had been revived by the enthusiasm of Sharp, Vaughan Williams, Grainger, and other members of the second generation of collectors. The truth was that after taking over the editorial reins of the *Journal of the Folk-Song Society* Lucy now did relatively little field-work herself, although she acted as the central coordinator of the collecting effort. For example, she encouraged Percy Merrick, and she was instrumental in persuading Henry Hammond that Dorset should be the primary focus of his and his brother's collecting efforts. She collaborated with Sharp and Vaughan Williams, making sure that substantial samples of their field work would appear in the *Journal*. But she no longer actively sought out additional folksongs, although she was still happy to note them when they came her way. That was the main reason why *English Traditional Songs and Carols* documented an earlier phase of her contribution to the movement. Another was her desire to provide substantial scholarly notes, for which she drew upon her past contributions as editor of the *Journal*; as she put it, in making her selection for publication she had "preferred such songs as had already undergone my more leisurely examination and annotation."[50]

During the Edwardian years and the post-war decade Broadwood continued to study (and sing) folksongs, and her well-researched articles on the subject set high standards. She also became very interested in the subject of Gaelic song, as well as such non-folksong topics as Freemasonry, theosophy, and the paranormal. And she maintained her close involvement with the classic music scene in London. She did still have in manuscript form some additional unpublished songs from her earlier collecting, but *English Traditional Songs and Carols* would be her last major publication. From 1908 onwards Lucy Broadwood was essentially a scholar, editor, and administrator, who left to others the ongoing work of English-language folksong collection. She remained actively involved with the Folk-Song Society and its *Journal* until 1927, briefly serving as the Society's President before her death in 1929. Her close involvement with English folksong thus extended from the mid-1880s until the end of the 1920s, a period of over forty years. During the Late

Victorian and Edwardian eras she was a key figure in the movement. A full-length study of her song-collecting, her method as an editor, and her administrative role within the Folk-Song Society is obviously needed.

Some Conclusions

The history of the first folksong revival in England divides naturally into three phases: the Late Victorian era, the Edwardian decade, and a final period from World War I until the mid-1930s, when the Folk-Song Society merged with the English Folk Dance Society. The Edwardian years undoubtedly saw the movement at its peak: they were a time of intense energy during which a large body of vernacular songs was collected by quite a number of figures, including, but certainly not limited to, such big names as Cecil Sharp, Ralph Vaughan Williams, and Percy Grainger. The Late Victorian phase, however, laid the groundwork for these achievements. In comparison with the Edwardian phase it has been unjustly neglected by scholars, or, when discussed at all, its history has been distorted.[51] If during its Edwardian phase the first folksong revival burned with a brilliant flame like a meteor in the night, the earlier Late Victorian phase was no less important. It lasted longer—a quarter century—and it produced an equally impressive body of collected folksongs. Looking back on the period between 1878 and 1903 we can, with the benefit of hindsight, see its achievements, its failings, and some of its unique characteristics. What, then, were the principal achievements of the Late Victorian revival, and in what way did this phase of the movement differ from the later phases?

The Emergence of a Cultural Movement

My decision to treat the Late Victorian phase of the revival in two chronological stages, focusing first on the 1880s and subsequently on the 1890s, was not made lightly. A topical mode of organization was an alternative, and in the case of key individuals and special topics such as sea songs and national songs it is an approach that I have tried to integrate within a broadly developmental perspective. Because of the fundamental division of the book between the two decades and the fact that crucial contributions were made by Baring-Gould and Kidson in each of them, I was compelled to split my discussion of these figures into more than one chapter each, with Baring-Gould appearing mainly in chapters 7, 13, and 15, and Kidson in chapters 8, 14, 15, 16, and 17. Similarly, Broadwood's story can be found in chapters 10, 11, 16, and 17. From one perspective such splits are regrettable, and as a result the reader may initially lose a sense of these individuals' work as a whole, although that can be remedied fairly easily by going back and reading the appropriate sections consecutively. Nonetheless, the great advantage of a mainly chronological approach is that it underlines the fundamental change that took place during these two decades: the recovery of English folksong evolved from a number of scattered individual initiatives into a partially organized movement with an institutional base, the Folk-Song Society.

The first half of the book deals essentially with pioneering individual initiatives, while the second half examines the genesis and emergence of the movement. Chapter 10, "Birth of a Movement, 1890-92," is pivotal, providing a bridge between the two halves of the book. It encapsulates my thesis that the Late Victorian era witnessed the consolidation of individual collecting efforts into a whole that was more than the sum of the parts, namely a cultural movement aimed at a renaissance of English music founded on the sturdy base of a revival of English folksong. This overarching goal was not a conscious motive for the pioneer collectors in the 1880s but from *English County Songs* onwards it became increasingly recognized as not only desirable but also feasible. One suspects that it helped motivate many of the movement's participants. The idea was certainly embraced by Lucy Broadwood and her circle, which included Fuller Maitland, Somervell, Stanford, Parry, and, significantly, the young Ralph Vaughan Williams, and it found early expression in *Sussex Songs*, Lucy's collaboration during 1888-89 with her cousin Herbert Birch Reynardson.

All the work of song-collecting, collating, and editing done by the many individuals discussed in this book certainly had some cumulative results. One major effect was a refocusing of Victorian songhunting away from the library into the field. Another was a renewed emphasis on tunes, sometimes, unfortunately, at the expense of texts. At its best, however, the Late Victorian movement recognized that traditional songs are organic entities in which words and melody combine to create a whole that is more than the sum of its parts. It also recognized that oral and print sources were—and are—symbiotic, and that the collector-scholar needs to pay careful attention to both and to the complicated relationship between them. And, as we have seen, folksong was understood to be part of a wider body of vernacular song, which in turn was part of a wider stream of popular music, but could also provide the basis for a renaissance of English art music.

But what of the songs themselves? What overall picture of English folksong emerged from the collecting done in these two-and-a-half decades?

The Ballad

To begin with it was evident that the traditional ballad—what Child called the "popular" ballad—still flourished in most regions of the country. They were not yet referred to as Child ballads, but versions of more than forty of those that Child accepted into his canon surfaced in English oral tradition. For example, to take the fifty-three ballad clusters in Child's first volume, we find the Late Victorian collectors turning up variants of the following fourteen:

> "Riddles Wisely Expounded" (Child no. 1)
> "The Elfin Knight" (Child no. 2)
> "Lady Isabel and the Elf-Knight" (Child no. 4)
> "Earl Brand" (Child no. 7)
> "The Fair Flower of Northumberland" (Child no. 9)
> "The Twa Sisters" (Child no. 10)
> "Lord Randal" (Child no. 12)
> "Babylon" (Child no. 14)
> "The Cruel Mother" (Child no. 20)
> "St. Stephen and Herod" (Child no. 22)
> "Bonnie Annie" (Child no. 24)
> "The Three Ravens" (Child no. 26)
> "Clerk Colville" (Child no. 42)
> "Young Beichan" (Child no. 53)

Versions of other well-known Child ballads collected in this period included the following:

> "Lord Thomas and Fair Annet" (Child no. 73)
> "The Unquiet Grave" (Child no. 78)
> "The Wife of Usher's Well" (Child no. 79)
> "Bonny Barbara Allan" (Child no. 84)
> "Lamkin" (Child no. 93)
> "The Maid Freed from the Gallows" (Child no. 95)
> "The Bailiff's Daughter of Islington" (Child no. 105)
> "The Knight and the Shepherd's Daughter" (Child no. 110)
> "The Baffled Knight" (Child no. 112)
> "Robin Hood and the Ranger" (Child no. 131)
> "The Bold Pedlar and Robin Hood (Child no. 132)
> "Sir Hugh, or The Jew's Daughter" (Child no. 155)
> "The Hunting of the Cheviot" (Child no. 162)
> "The Death of Queen Jane" (Child no. 170)
> "Hughie Grame" (Child no. 191)
> "The Gypsy Laddie" (Child no. 200)
> "Lord Derwentwater" (Child no. 208)
> "Geordie" (Child no. 209)
> "The Braes of Yarrow" (Child no. 214)
> "The Gardener" (Child no. 219)
> "James Harris (The Daemon Lover)" (Child no. 243)
> "Henry Martyn" (Child no. 250)
> "Our Goodman" (Child no. 274)
> "The Jolly Beggar" (Child no. 279)
> "The Crafty Farmer" (Child no. 283)
> "The *Sweet Trinity* (The *Golden Vanity*)" (Child no. 286)
> "Captain Ward and the *Rainbow*" (Child no. 287)
> "The Mermaid" (Child no. 289)
> "The Brown Girl" (Child no. 295)

Ballads that were apparently traditional which Child disregarded or was not aware of included "The Broken Token," "Just As the Tide Was Flowing," "The Trees They Are So High," and "The Setting of the Sun" (aka "The Shooting of

His Dear"). Added to these were at least an equal number of splendid broadside ballads that Child rejected as merely the work of seventeenth- and eighteenth-century ballad-mongers but which clearly found favor among source singers. Another list even longer than the second of the two above would be tedious, but to illustrate the point let me at least mention ten of them: "The Banks of Dundee," "Bold General Wolfe," "The Bonny Bunch of Roses," "The Death of Bill Brown," "The Deserter," "Napoleon's Farewell to Paris," "Spencer the Rover," "Turpin Hero," "The Unfortunate Rake," and "Van Diemen's Land." In short, the broadside ballad was alive and well in the Late Victorian era. Not only were broadsheets still being printed and sold, large numbers of the genre had taken root in oral tradition and become vernacular songs.

The Songs

If the vernacular ballad—traditional and broadside—comprised a significant component of the body of song that the Late Victorian collectors found in the English countryside, what of other kinds of folk lyric and popular song? They were certainly varied in nature. Folk lyrics there were in abundance, and again a few examples will have to serve as a substitute for a list that could be much longer. Many of the folksongs that Sharp and others would also collect and champion in the Edwardian phase of the revival had in fact been already discovered or rediscovered by Baring-Gould, Kidson, Broadwood, et al. They included such gems as "All Around My Hat," "The Cuckoo," "Early One Morning," "The Keys of Heaven," "Lemonday," "The Merry Doe (The Keeper)," "Scarborough Fair," "Seventeen Come Sunday," "Sweet Nightingale," and even "The Seeds of Love" (the song that so delighted Sharp when he heard it at Hambridge in 1903). Added to these were many vernacular lyrics such as "Black-eyed Susan," "Cupid's Garden," "The Garden Gate," "John Peel," "Old Rosin the Beau," "The Queen of Hearts," and "The Lass of Richmond Hill" that might or might not be counted as folksongs (depending on one's definition of the term) but were seemingly just as popular among singers.

Occupational songs fell mainly into two groups: those associated with rural life, especially agriculture, and sea-shanties. The former included "The Bell Ringing," "The Cottage Thatched with Straw," "The Farmer's Boy," "The Nobleman and the Thresherman," "The Reaphook and the Sickle," "The Seasons," and "Twankydillo," but also hunting songs ("The Sweet Rosy Morning") and such poaching ballads as "In Thorny Woods" and "Bill Brown the Poacher." As we saw in chapter 6, shanties were abundant, but sea-songs were by no means limited to shanties. They included broadside ballads such as "All on Spurn Point," "The *Bold Princess Royal*," and "The Greenland Fishery" as well as lyrics like "A-Roving," "Blaw the Wind Southerly," and "The Lass That Loves a Sailor." Songs about sailors as lovers, whether lost at sea (as in "The Drowned Sailor"), too long away ("I Drew My Ship into the Harbour"), or returning at last after years away ("The Dark-eyed Sailor"), were particularly prevalent.

There was much else. Comic ditties were often favored by source singers, and they ranged from "Aw Wish Thy Muther Wad Cum" to "The Derby Ram," "John Dory," and "The Loppington Bear." Drinking songs included "The Barley Mow," "Down among the Dead Men," "Drink Old England Dry," "The Drunken Maidens," and "When Joan's Ale Was New." Wassails were not so numerous but some were located, as were such related songs of ceremony and occasion as "Hal-an-Tow," a "Peace-Egging Song," and two Souling songs. Children's play-songs, such as "Green Gravel," "King Arthur's Servants," "The Frog's Wooing," and "Johnny Todd," deserve mention too. And there were many songs that were regional in provenance, often incorporating local dialect words but often joined to fine melodies. Examples include "Bonny at Morn," "The Bonnie Pit Laddie," "The Collier's Rant," "Elsie Marley," "The Keel Row," "Sair Fyel'd, Hinny," "The Sandgate Lass's Lament," "Up the Raw," and "Widdecombe Fair."

One other category of song deserves special attention. The Late Victorian era saw a resurgence of the 'national' song and at least a partial breakdown of the rather artificial division between folksongs collected from rural source singers and other vernacular songs that were often sung by the same informants. These national songs included a number of flagrantly patriotic ditties—"The British Grenadiers," "Heart of Oak," and "He Swore He'd Drink Old England Dry" come immediately to mind—but the majority of them were not chauvinistic. Rather they were popular songs that a varied group of editors from Hatton to Baring-Gould and Kidson regarded as in some sense expressing a spirit of Englishness. They were a mixed bag, some anonymous and others by 'name' songsmiths from Shakespeare to Dibdin, but all possessed 'vital melodies' that had helped them live on from generation to generation. A few were satirical and quasi-political: "The Vicar of Bray" is a good example. Some, such as "The Oxen Ploughing," "My Dog and Gun," "D'Ye Ken John Peel?" and even "The Gallant Poacher," celebrated rural life, or, as in "The Roast Beef of Old England" and "Adieu to Old England," expressed regret for the passing of a simpler, pre-industrial mode of existence. Drinking songs like "Down among the Dead Men" and "The Barley Mow" are to be found among them, and celebrations of the mariner's vocation are common, as in "You Gentlemen of England" and "The Lass That Loves a Sailor." Yet other national songs were simply examples of English song-making at its best. They included many love songs, some rather sentimental ("The Garden Gate" and "Cupid's Garden"), some mildly suggestive ("The Spotted Cow"), and some sad or wistful ("Early One Morning" and "I Live Not Where I Love"). Even such traditional ballads as "The Three Ravens" and "The Knight and the Shepherd's Daughter" were included in this category, as well as some of the most popular broadside ballads such as "Bold Wolfe" and "Turpin Hero." National song was a mixed bag, to be sure, but the quality was usually high and many of these ditties were destined to become the standard fare of twentieth-century community songbooks. They expressed ideas and sentiments with which their listeners could identify, and they were, above all, catchy and singable.

It is evident, therefore, that, whatever their faults and idiosyncrasies, the Late Victorian collectors demonstrated conclusively that there existed an extraordinary wealth and variety of vernacular song in the small towns and counties of England. Earlier Victorian songhunters had suggested that this was the case, but it was the work of the Late Victorians that proved it beyond a doubt. They built upon the efforts of their predecessors, but they supplanted them in one crucial regard: their focus on recovering tunes from oral tradition. In a word, Baring-Gould, Barrett, Broadwood, Burne, Kidson, Stokoe, and the others demonstrated the persistence of melody in the English countryside. And they recovered those melodies for the entire nation to sing and enjoy. Others would follow in their footsteps, most notably Sharp and Vaughan Williams, but they had laid the foundations for both the first and second English folksong revivals.

The Concept of Folksong

There emerged during the Late Victorian era a vision of folksong that was more ecumenical and tolerant than that which later came to be associated with Cecil Sharp, Maud Karpeles, and the English Folk Dance and Song Society. It was, in part, a reaction to the great variety of song—including national and occupational songs—that had been recovered. It was also the result of the emergence of a new body of popular music scholarship that had been inaugurated by William Chappell in the mid-Victorian era but which was developed further in the 1880s and 1890s. Frank Kidson, in particular, recognized that English folksong was an integral part of, and inextricably connected with, a larger body of British vernacular music that had also found expression through broadside balladry, dance music, ballad opera, and the best of commercial popular song.

For Kidson as a historian of popular culture, the crucial question was whether a song possessed a 'vital melody.' If it did, it would become a vernacular song, and quite frequently several different sets of lyrics would become associated with it. Conversely, if a certain ballad text or song lyric had enduring appeal but initially lacked a distinctive melody, it would soon pick up a good and appropriate tune; in fact, different, although usually somewhat related, melodies might be found linked with it in different regions of the British Isles. The name of the tune composer and/or the name of the author of the song text might be known or the item might be anonymous, but for Kidson this did not matter very much. What really mattered was whether the song had survived and become part of vernacular culture. This was a view that neither Sharp nor, initially, Vaughan Williams would embrace. Sharp, in particular, never understood—or, at least, never accepted—Kidson's perspective on the role of folksong and folk dance within the broader history of British popular music, and he fought long and hard, if unsuccessfully, to persuade the Folk-Song Society to adopt his own Darwinian interpretation of the genesis and evolution of folksong as a unique species.[52] My own studies in the history of folksong and popular music have led me to conclude that Kidson was essentially correct and that Sharp was mistaken.

This said, it has to be acknowledged that not even Kidson, and certainly neither Lucy Broadwood nor Sabine Baring-Gould, systematically conflated the notion of folksong with that of vernacular song. They still sometimes —although not always—made a distinction between songs noted aurally from rural tradition bearers, items they readily labeled folksongs, and other vernacular songs, in which they were still interested but which they tended to call old songs, country songs, county songs, or national songs. While they insisted that the broadsides were a highly important source for ballad and folksong texts they usually argued that the best tunes were to be found in oral tradition, irrespective of their known or unknown origin. Searching for a broader term to encompass the wider field of vernacular song, Baring-Gould latched on to the word 'minstrelsy,' which had the advantage of suggesting a musical tradition that went back to the Middle Ages but yet could embrace later, even much more recent, exponents of the popular art of song-making. Kidson followed his example. The term had been used early on by Bruce and Stokoe but it was not one that achieved widespread adoption; 'folksong,' for all its ambiguity, won the day. However, that should not disguise the fact that the Late Victorian era witnessed not only a fairly systematic attempt to recover vernacular melodies from rural tradition bearers but also a renewed interest in broadside balladry, occupational songs—especially sea songs—and national songs.

The Role of Women

One of the most striking features of this Late Victorian cultural movement was the central part in it played by women. Harriet Mason must be given credit for starting the ball rolling in the late 1870s with *Nursery Rhymes and Country Songs*. She demonstrated that old ballads were still extant in oral tradition and that children (and their grandparents and nurses) might be valuable tradition bearers. Yet this fairly slight publication could easily have remained an isolated phenomenon and soon been forgotten had not others seen its worth and taken up the cause. Charlotte Burne was the young folklorist who first perceived the importance of music in rural culture. She also recognized that melody was an integral component of traditional song and that anyone attempting to preserve local musical customs and present them in a scholarly manner to a wider audience needed to capture tunes as well as texts. Doing so was not easy for her but, like Baring-Gould in Devon, she took the trouble to find musician-helpers who could note the melodies more accurately than she felt able to do on her own. Burne was catholic in her approach to song-collecting: she not only preserved the traditional and broadside balladry of her native Shropshire, she noted folk lyrics, carols, wassails, souling-songs, and recently composed comic songs about local events. As might be expected, she searched for songs among the elderly female residents of villages near her home, but she also saw that the itinerant travelers of the region possessed a wealth of unique folklore, including song. Like Harriet Mason, Burne recognized too that children—in this case gypsy children—could prove a fecund source of songs that their parents might be more reluctant to perform to outsiders. All in all, *Shropshire Folk-Lore*, although it contained much more than local music, was a pioneering work for the folksong revival in several ways. It set folksong within the broader social context of village life, it demonstrated that traditional ballad was alive and well in rural England, and it showed how valuable the traveler community was as a carrier of English as well as Romany song traditions.

It was Burne's collecting from Shropshire gypsies that seems to have inspired Laura Smith to do the same in the Scottish border country and in London and the Home Counties. Smith's *Through Romany Songland* promised more than it delivered, but together with Francis Hindes Groome's *In Gipsy Tents* it demonstrated the variety and abundance of song to be found among English and Scottish travelers. Nor was it Laura Smith's only contribution to the Late Victorian folksong revival. Her major work, *The Music of the Waters*, was the only publication that attempted to document and present a panorama of English sea song. While her main focus was on the occupational songs of English mariners—she made a brave attempt at sorting out and categorizing various different kinds of shanty—her collection included some broadside ballads and other songs sung by sailors when at leisure. As such it was less specialized than either Davis and Tozer's shanty collection or John Ashton's broadside collection, both of which works served to flesh out further Smith's pioneering work in the field.

Important though the published collections by Mason, Burne, and Smith were, they pale in comparison with the work of Lucy Broadwood. Broadwood's initial publication, *Sussex Songs*, was a modest contribution to the revival, although it served the double function of reminding its readers of the Reverend John Broadwood's pioneering work and also printing some of the first folksongs ever noted by his niece. *English County Songs*, on the other hand, was a major achievement, and Broadwood certainly played her full part in its creation, as both collector and editor. The network of folk music enthusiasts that she and Alec Fuller Maitland developed while researching the book helped provide a core membership for the Folk-Song Society when it was eventually formed in 1898, and the publication itself certainly stimulated song-collecting in various regions of England. As the first real attempt at a systematic survey of folksong in the length and breadth of the country it provided a roadmap for the burgeoning movement, and, while it had its imperfections, it was clearly one of the most important products of the Late Victorian phase of the revival, a milestone of sorts. Broadwood's subsequent collecting—from Henry Burstow and from the Dunsfold villagers, in particular—found an outlet in the *Journal of the Folk-Song Society* and in her belatedly published *English Traditional Songs and Carols*, a book which, despite its publication date of 1908, really belongs in the Late Victorian phase of the revival. But, of course, Lucy Broadwood played a central role in the movement not merely as a collector but as the secretary of the Folk-Song Society and, above all, as its long-serving *Journal* editor. Essentially she was the one who held everything together, keeping in regular communication with not only Fuller Maitland but also Baring-Gould, Burne, Kidson, Somervell, Kate Lee, and, later, Sharp and Vaughan Williams. It is no exaggeration to say that Broadwood was the administrative heart of the folksong movement from the early 1890s until the mid-1920s.

Other Key Figures

If Lucy Broadwood was one of the pillars of the first folk music revival, the two other key figures during its Late Victorian phase were Sabine Baring-Gould and Frank Kidson. Of the two, Baring-Gould has received the more attention from scholars but this has been mainly negative in character. I have discussed at some length the criticisms that have been made of his published work, criticisms that were anticipated by Kidson's private comments to Broadwood about *Songs and Ballads of the West*, and I have attempted to indicate the limited extent to which they were, and are, justified. None of the several biographies of the man do justice to the importance of his work as a folksong collector, nor is there yet any book that studies this in detail. Baring-Gould is clearly due for rehabilitation, and we look to Martin Graebe for a thorough and balanced study of his collecting that will tell us as much as can be rediscovered about the songs as originally noted and the source singers who performed them. One would also love to see a new edition of *Songs of the West* which could dispense with the unnecessary piano arrangements but which would include all the items in *Songs and Ballads of the West* and *A Garland of Country Song* in the versions preserved in the Killerton and Plymouth notebooks or, where this is not possible, in the form given in the Personal Copy manuscripts.

Frank Kidson has not been totally neglected by scholars, since there are valuable articles by Roy Palmer and John Francmanis, but there is to date no biography and no systematic full-length study of his work as a song collector or as a historian of popular music. He was obviously a major figure in both regards: apart from Joseph Ebsworth he was the only important disciple of William Chappell, and the only Yorkshire collector of the period to note and print tunes as well as texts. His influence on the Late Victorian phase of the revival was covert rather than overt, filtered mainly through Lucy Broadwood, but it was huge: he forced upon other collectors, including Baring-Gould and John Stokoe, the recognition that print and oral traditions were inextricably interwoven and that the song collector needed to pay extensive attention to the products of the broadside press, although he was less successful in extending this interest to the scores of ballad operas. He has been criticized on the grounds that many of the folksongs he published in *Traditional Tunes*, in articles in the *Journal of the Folk-Song Society*, and in the books that appeared just before and after his death were actually noted by others, in particular by his close friend and collaborator Charles Lolley. That criticism has some truth to it, although he did in fact also do a considerable amount of collecting on his own, but it ultimately misses the mark, since it was clearly Kidson who provided the enthusiasm behind the Leeds collecting cooperative and who edited the results. As an editor he was guilty of some silent bowdlerization of texts and a too-ready reliance on broadsides, but his focus on tunes was a valuable corrective to the work of earlier Yorkshire collectors. His failure to publish in the 1890s the second volume of *Traditional Tunes* amounts to a minor tragedy, and it should be belatedly rectified by a scholarly reconstruction of the book that errs on the side of inclusiveness. We have enough source materials and clues to its intended contents to do the job. A major study of the man and his work is obviously also required.

Two other, more minor yet nonetheless important, figures also badly require scholarly attention: John Stokoe and William Barrett. We know that Stokoe was responsible for the music in the *Northumbrian Minstrelsy* and it seems likely that he was the real engine behind bringing a much-delayed project to fruition. The book itself was a compilation from a variety of sources: collecting done nearly half a century earlier, manuscript sources, broadsides, other publications, and the work of local musicians. Despite its faults, for which it has been roundly criticized, it was a pioneering work: the first attempt to unite tunes and texts in a fairly comprehensive survey of a region's vernacular music. Stokoe's other significant contribution to the movement, *Songs and Ballads of Northern England*, was derivative from his earlier work but it came at an opportune time and thereby helped to reinforce the sense of a burgeoning revival of folk music that was occurring simultaneously in the north (especially Lancashire, Yorkshire and Northumbria) as well as the West Midlands and southern counties of England. Stokoe lacks a biographer and even a substantial scholarly article, and so he is a figure to whom we must hope attention will soon be paid by a historian or ethnomusicologist located in or near Newcastle-upon-Tyne.

William Barrett is a better-known figure because of his work as a music journalist and church musician, his collaboration with composer John Stainer, and his various publications on madrigals and religious music. His contributions to the folksong revival were made just before his death, and, although he corresponded briefly with Lucy Broadwood, he remained on the fringes of the nascent movement. Nonetheless, his published collection of *English Folk-Songs* was an important contribution to it, coming (like Stokoe's second book) at an opportune time and complementing *English County Songs*. Barrett also played a significant part in the revival of national song with his *Standard English Songs*, although primary credit for pioneering this aspect of the revival must be accorded to the successive editions of John Hatton's *The Songs of England* and, as we have seen, mention should also be made of Boulton and Somervell's popular *Songs of the Four Nations*. It was a relatively neglected area of popular music that both Baring-Gould and Kidson quickly recognized as an important cousin to rural oral tradition and sought to integrate into the revival.

The Source Singers

Important though the collectors were, the first folksong revival would also have been impossible without the source singers. We do not yet know enough about them, and it is to be hoped that future research will uncover many of the missing names, as well as much more information about those informants whose names and occupations we do already know. During the Late Victorian era collectors and editors varied considerably in their conscientiousness about noting down (and subsequently including in their books) data on the sources of the songs they published.

We have seen that the renewed search for ballad and folksong melodies began, approximately simultaneously, in the northeast of England, the West Midlands and the counties of Devon and Cornwall in the southwest. Let us take the northeast first. Our knowledge of the source of the items in *Nursery Rhymes and Country Songs* is clearly inadequate, although more than half of them were obtained by Harriet Mason from the Mitford family and many of those can be attributed to her grandmother. We would like biographical information about not only Mrs. Mitford but also the unidentified Derbyshire agricultural laborer who sang "Spencer the Rover" and the anonymous Welsh nurse who taught her charges "The Cutty Wren." The situation is only a little better with regard to the seminal *Northumbrian Minstrelsy*, although we are aware that local pipers William Vickers and Robert Bewick provided many of the Northumbrian pipe tunes. We also know that Stokoe obtained much of the regional and dialect material in the book from such Tyneside musicians as Blind Willie Purvis. A concerted investigation into the field collecting of James Henry Dixon and Robert White might better illuminate some of the sources of the ballads and other folk lyrics, and two of the informants on whom White drew, his sister, Mrs. Andrews and Liddesdale shepherd James Telfer, are clearly good candidates for further research. Joseph Crawhall conscientiously identified the authors of the composed items in *A Book o'Newcassel Sangs* but about the identity of the pub and street singers who provided the vernacular songs we unfortunately have few if any clues.

Moving to the West Midlands, we can rejoice that Charlotte Burne at least recorded the names of several of her group of Edgmond singers, but we would wish for much more information about the lives of Jane Butler, Harriet Dowley, Sally Withington, and their friends. Other of Burne's informants, such as the old nurse at Ross, the elderly fisherman at Bridgnorth, or Mrs. Dudley of Much Wenlock, are more shadowy figures, and it will be a challenge indeed to find out more about travelers Eliza Wharton and her brothers. Much the same is true of Laura Smith's gypsy musicians Jim and Job Lee. Francis Hindes Groome had a much better opportunity to get to know his Romany informants than did Charlotte Burne or Laura Smith and he created pen-portraits of several of them. Consequently, although factual data is lacking, we have mental images of Anselo, Pyramus, Sinfi, Amy North, and three members of the Lovell family: Lementina, Starlina, and Lucretia. Unfortunately even that cannot be said for the anonymous Hampshire informants who provided most of the substance of Heywood Sumner's *The Besom Maker*. William Barrett's collecting ranged widely over the regions of England but although he often noted the locality (or at least the county) in which he found a particular song, he rarely provided much detail about his informants' occupations and almost never their names. It would be left to Lucy Broadwood and, later, Percy Merrick to record for posterity the names and sometimes the occupations of their Sussex and Surrey singers.

Among the pioneer Late Victorian collectors Sabine Baring-Gould stands out as a folklorist with a respect and warm affection for many of his informants. This shines through his informative notes in *Songs and Ballads of the West* and *A Garland of Country Song* and his descriptions and anecdotes in *Old Country Life* and *Further Reminiscences*. He found more good source singers than any other collector before Cecil Sharp, and we know something, although not always very much, about almost all of them. More than fifty are referenced in the notes to *Songs and Ballads of the West* and more appear in *A Garland of Country Song*. It is evident that Baring-Gould had a core group of informants from whom he obtained much of his best material. We have line-drawings of three of them (Robert Hard, John Helmore, and James Olver) in *Old Country Life* and there are pen-portraits of others (James Parsons, Roger Luxton, Jonas Croaker, and Edmund Fry). Other important Devon singers were Matthew Baker, William Kerswell, Harry Westaway, and Joseph Paddon, while the Cornishmen included J. Peake, Matthew Ford, Joseph Dyer, and Peter Sandry. Even more prolific were his two stalwarts: John Woodrich (aka "Ginger Jack") and Sam Fone, the man who gave Baring-Gould more songs than anyone else. The clergyman was not so adept at collecting from women, but he did have a few female informants, of whom Sally Satterley, Mary Gilbert, Jane Jeffrey, and Ann Roberts were perhaps the most important.

Baring-Gould's songhunting in Devon and Cornwall was paralleled by that of Frank Kidson in Yorkshire but Kidson was less systematic in recording the names and occupations of his source singers. All too often a song is credited to "a fisherman at Whitby," "an Irish street singer" or some other tantalizingly imprecise attribution. Moreover, a significant proportion of Kidson's collection was obtained by his helpers, in particular Charles Lolley, and they seem to have been unconcerned to document their sources. Lolley, about whom we do know quite a lot, was a major informant as well as a collector. Songs were also contributed by such members of Kidson's circle of friends in Leeds as Benjamin Holgate, Washington Teasdale, and William Cheetham. Kidson's other early source singers included Allan Wardill of Goathland, T.C. Smith of Scarborough, Robert Holliday of Newtondale, and Mr. Carr of Bradford, but none of these possessed a repertoire rivaling in size and quality that of Kate Thompson whom he discovered in Leeds in 1891. Sarah Jackson was another important female singer from whom Kidson noted tunes during the 1890s, while among his male informants W. H. Lunt of Liverpool and Charley Dickenson were valuable additions. In the main, however, his later stalwarts were singers whom he had discovered earlier, especially Wardill, Smith, Thompson, and, of course, Charles Lolley.

We do not know the names of the local singers who contributed new material to *Sussex Songs*, but from 1890 onwards Lucy Broadwood left a fairly comprehensive record of her singers and their repertoires. Samuel Willett was the first of her important Sussex informants, from whom she obtained about forty items. Willett's offerings were supplemented by those from carter George Grantham of Anstie and local gamekeeper John Burberry. Even more valuable source singers were two women, Clara Wilson of Kings Langley in Hertfordshire and Patience Vaisey of Tetsworth, Oxfordshire. Broadwood included some of the best of her early informants' material in *English County Songs* but, in the main, we know little about most of the singers who provided the contents of that work. Again the problem seems to have been that Broadwood and Fuller Maitland's helpers were less conscientious than Broadwood herself about supplying detailed information on their informants. There are a few other exceptions, such as Whitby fisherman William Moat and Kidson's informant, ex-sailor Charley Dickenson, but we usually know only the names of the collectors although occasionally, as in the case of Mark Wyatt of Enborne, Berkshire, they were apparently also the source singers. When Broadwood began collecting again after the publication of *English County Songs* she was fortunate to discover Henry Burstow, the Horsham shoemaker and bell-ringer with a repertoire of four hundred songs. Although he was reluctant to share some of those items because of their indelicate content, Burstow nonetheless proved Broadwood's most prolific informant, and he yielded more of his store to later collectors such as Ralph Vaughan Williams. Other notable singers located by Broadwood included the Goby family of travelers and the Dunsfold villagers, who included George Baker, James Bronham, Edward Cooper, George Ede, Richard Lough, Mr. Sparks, Thomas Whittington, and George and Mary Ann Rugman.

The renewed burst of collecting that accompanied the birth of the Folk-Song Society meant that a number of new source singers were located by Kate Lee and others at the end of the 1890s. Lee's informants included Mrs. Mainwaring Bodell, two Norfolk singers, Mr. Edge of Wells and Mr. Cater of Baconsthorpe, and her most important discovery, James and William, the Copper brothers of Rottingdean, Sussex. Another female collector, Isabel Hearne, recorded the name, occupation, and place of residence of one of her informants, John Butler, a farm laborer who lived near Stratford-on-Avon. The most prolific new source singer to contribute material to the pages of the *Journal of the Folk-Song Society* at the close of the Later Victorian era was Sussex farmer Henry Hills. His repertoire of fifty-two songs was noted by Percy Merrick.

There were many other source singers from whom songs were noted during the 1880s and 1890s whose names and occupations we do not know, although, in the main, they tend to have contributed just one or two items to the growing body of recovered ballad and folksong tunes and texts. Only too often when we have a record of a singer's name and location, at present that is all we know. Census and parish records offer the possibility of tracking down more information about these vitally important informants, but the search process can be difficult and longwinded. For the Late Victorian era we unfortunately have very few visual records of the singers, although luckily in the Edwardian period some collectors, including, notably, Cecil Sharp, began taking photographs of their informants. Much work still remains to be done before we will have a comprehensive picture of the tradition bearers whose memories and love of song made possible the Late Victorian folksong revival.

Censorship and Authenticity

The question of the accuracy and authenticity of the ballads and folk lyrics published during the Late Victorian period is one that I raised at the beginning of the book. The previous scholarly literature, such as it was, vigorously denied the authenticity of many of the songs published by the Late Victorian collectors. When I began my research it was perhaps the most major issue I expected to have to come to terms with. Was it true that I would be dealing primarily with 'fakesongs' created by bourgeois 'mediators' who were either unprincipled exploiters of the workers' music or, at best, misguided neo-Romantics with a rose-colored vision of a mythical 'folk' living in an 'imagined village'? The short answer turned out to be 'no.' However the critique, although misdirected, was not totally groundless. It quickly became clear to me that not everything collected was deemed publishable at the time. There was the problem of what was acceptable to publishers, and one also had to keep in mind the social conventions of middle-class society.

It will be evident from the various chapters that no single answer of a general nature is possible. The amount of *de facto* censorship varied considerably from source singer to source singer and from collector to collector. Different songhunters had different ways of dealing with the problem of song lyrics that they deemed unacceptable to polite ears. Clearly there was fairly systematic censorship of bawdy material, the simplest solution being to leave out offending verses or entire songs. Evidence that this was the case can be found in the discrepancies between broadside texts and published versions, in shortened and clearly incomplete texts, and in the candid admissions of certain collectors, including Baring-Gould, Laura Smith, and Lucy Broadwood. And it seems to have been fairly often the case that source singers were too shy to sing the 'outway rude' portions of their repertoires to ladies or even clerics. So in these late nineteenth-century collections we are missing one dimension of English vernacular song, and an important one at that. However, to judge from the proportion of bawdy material in the big broadside collections, it probably did not amount to more than, at most, ten per cent of the total. And it is a distortion that we can easily recognize and compensate for, given the fairly abundant body of this kind of song that was printed before the Victorian age and also collected from oral tradition after it.

In other respects there is little reason to suspect either incompetence or a desire to mislead on the part of the Late Victorian collectors. Baring-Gould, the collector-editor who has come most under attack, was in fact open and informative about his collecting methods and editorial decisions. One may not always agree with his decisions, but I have come to respect his honesty and candor. Kidson, although not a cleric, had similar views on what could and could not be printed, but since he was keen to identify the broadsides with which he believed his singers were familiar it is usually possible to supplement the partial texts he published. Broadwood, like Joseph Ebsworth, proclaimed her commitment to printing songs exactly as noted, and, although she believed that some editorial discretion was required in songbooks, her contributions to the *Journal of the Folk-Song Society* are almost certainly reliable. As regards the tunes, all the collectors believed that it was highly important to record them accurately. They did their level best to do so. A few of them—Sabine Baring-Gould, Charlotte Burne, and Laura Smith—had some difficulty noting tunes themselves, so they may have made some inadvertent mistakes, but in any case they usually sought from more experienced musicians help with capturing melodies. Occasionally one suspects a given note, rhythm or time-signature may not be quite right, but in the vast majority of cases there seems no reason to doubt the accuracy of the tunes. In short, the men and women whose work I have surveyed in these pages collectively demonstrated beyond a shadow of doubt that a wealth of English melody had survived in oral tradition. They proved that English vernacular song—balladry as well as non-narrative lyrics of all kinds—was not only alive and healthy but also very varied in character.

This book represents no more than a first attempt to provide a reasonably systematic and fairly detailed overview of the first phase of the English folksong revival. Obviously much more research has to be done before we have a really comprehensive and in-depth understanding of this cultural movement. More detailed studies of the most important individual collectors, especially Sabine Baring-Gould, William Barrett, Lucy Broadwood, Frank Kidson, and John Stokoe, need to be undertaken. At present we know very little about the dozens of more minor but still important collectors and enthusiasts who also contributed to the movement in various ways during these decades. And the source singers themselves deserve much more attention than they have received so far. It will not be easy to research the backgrounds and activities of the more obscure informants and minor collectors, but the effort must be made. There is much to be done, but at least a beginning has been made. With any luck it will stimulate further exploration of this treasury of song, of the tradition bearers who kept it alive, and of the work of the men and women who first recognized its value and preserved it. To both groups jointly we owe the persistence of English melody.

Notes

1. For additional biographical information, see Gordon Ashman and Gillian Bennett, "Charlotte Sophia Burne: Shropshire Folklorist, First Woman President of the Folklore Society, and First Woman Editor of *Folklore*. Part 1: A Life and Appreciation," *Folklore* 111, no. 1 (2000): 1-22; Gillian Bennett, "Charlotte Sophia Burne: Shropshire Folklorist, First Woman President of the Folklore Society, and First Woman Editor of *Folklore*. Part 2: Update and Preliminary Bibliography," *Folklore* 112, no. 1 (2001): 95-98.

2. Frank Kidson and Mary Neal, *English Folk-Song and Dance* (Cambridge: Cambridge University Press, 1915; reprint, E.P. Publishing, 1972).

3. Frank Kidson, "English Folk-Song," *Musical Times* (1 January 1908): 23-24.

4. Kidson, "English Folk-Song," 23.

5. Kidson, "English Folk-Song," 24.

6. Frank Kidson, letter to Cecil Sharp, 31 January 1908. Sharp Mss., Correspondence, Vaughan Williams Memorial Library, Cecil Sharp House, London.

7. Frank Kidson, "English Folk-Song: What Collectors are Doing," *Leeds Mercury,* 21 February 1907.

8. Frank Kidson, letter to Cecil Sharp, 26 December 1910. Sharp Mss., Correspondence, Vaughan Williams Memorial Library, Cecil Sharp House, London.

9. Frank Kidson, letter to Cecil Sharp, 29 December 1910. Sharp Mss., Correspondence, Vaughan Williams Memorial Library, Cecil Sharp House, London.

10. L [J. T. Lightwood], "Frank Kidson," *The Choir,* no. 205 (January 1927): 7-8. For the identification of the author of this obituary I am indebted to John Francmanis.

11. Frank Kidson, ed., *Eighty Singing Games* (London: Bayley & Ferguson, 1907).

12. Frank Kidson, ed., *Seventy-Five British Nursery Rhymes* (London: Augener, n.d.)

13. Alfred Moffat, ed., with historical notes by Frank Kidson, *English Songs of the Georgian Period* (London: Bayley & Ferguson, 1907).

14. Frank Kidson, "The Vitality of Melody," *Proceedings of the Musical Association* 34 (1907-08): 81-95.

15. Kidson, "Vitality," 82.

16. Kidson, "Vitality," 95.

17. Frank Kidson, "Folk-Song," *The Choir* (February 1912): 30-31; Frank Kidson, "Folk-Song and the Popular Song," *The Choir,* no. 32 (August 1912): 149-151.

18. Frank Kidson, "Folk-Song and the Popular Song," 149-51.

19. "Mr. Frank Kidson," *Musical Herald* (1 August 1913): 227-30.

20. "Mr. Frank Kidson," 228.

21. "Mr. Frank Kidson," 229.

22. Frank Kidson and Martin Shaw, eds., *Songs of Britain: A Collection of One Hundred English, Welsh, Scottish and Irish National Songs* (London: Boosey, 1913).

23. Cecil J. Sharp, ed., *A Book of British Song for Home and School* (London: John Murray, 1902).

24. Sir Charles Villiers Stanford, ed., *The National Song Book: A Complete Collection of the Folk-Songs, Carols, and Rounds suggested by the Board of Education* (London: Boosey, 1905).

25. Frank Kidson and Alfred Moffat, eds., *A Garland of English Folksongs* (London: Ascherberg, Hopwood & Crew, [1926]).

26. Frank Kidson and Alfred Moffat, eds., *Folk Songs of the North Countrie, with their Traditional Airs* (London: Ascherberg, Hopwood & Crew, 1927).

27. Frank Kidson, Ethel Kidson, and Alfred Moffat, eds., *English Peasant Songs, with their Traditional Airs* (London: Ascherberg, Hopwood & Crew, 1929).

28. Frank Kidson, "Preface" and "Foreword," in Kidson and Moffat, *Garland,* iii-v.

29. Kidson, "Foreword," in Kidson and Moffat, *Garland,* v.

30. Kidson, "Foreword," in Kidson and Moffat, *Garland,* iv.

31. Kidson, "Preface," in Kidson and Moffat, *Garland,* iii.

32. Alfred Williams, ed., *Folk Songs of the Upper Thames* (London: Duckworth, 1923; reprint, Wakefield, U.K.: E.P. Publishing, 1972).

33. Kidson and Moffat, *Folk Songs of the North Countrie.* See note 26 above.

34. Lucy Broadwood, "Foreword," in Kidson and Moffat, *Folk Songs of the North Countrie,* iii.

35. Frank Kidson, Ethel Kidson, and Alfred Moffat, eds., *English Peasant Songs, with their Traditional Airs* (London: Ascherberg, Hopwood & Crew, 1929), preface [unpaginated].

36. Roy Palmer lists 223 items in his *Checklist of Manuscript Songs and Tunes collected from Oral Tradition by Frank Kidson* (London: EFDSS, 1986). However, the manuscripts upon which this list is based do not include all the items in Kidson's published folksong collections. Some of his notebooks must have been destroyed or lost, and the total number of songs that he collected was evidently considerably more than 223.

37. Lucy E. Broadwood, "On the Collecting of English Folk-Song," *Proceedings of the Royal Music Association* 31 (1905): 89-109.

38. Broadwood, "On the Collecting of English Folk Song," 91.

39. Broadwood, "On the Collecting of English Folk Song," 101.

40. Broadwood, "On the Collecting of English Folk Song," 97.

41. Lucy E. Broadwood, "Songs from County Waterford, Ireland," *Journal of the Folk-Song Society* 3, no. 10 (1907): 4.

42. Lucy E. Broadwood, ed., *English Traditional Songs and Carols* (London: Boosey, 1908).

43. Broadwood, *English Traditional Songs and Carols,* ix.

44. Broadwood, *English Traditional Songs and Carols,* ix-x.

45. Broadwood, *English Traditional Songs and Carols,* x.

46. Broadwood, *English Traditional Songs and Carols,* x.

47. Broadwood's collecting from Burstow was discussed in chapter 11. For a portrait of the man and his musical abilities, see *English Traditional Songs and Carols,* xi.

48. Broadwood, *English Traditional Songs and Carols,* 123.

49. Broadwood, *English Traditional Songs and Carols,* xi and 123-24.

50. Broadwood, *English Traditional Songs and Carols,* x.

51. In particular the perspectives advanced by Dave Harker in *Fakesong:The Manufacture of British 'Folksong' 1700 to the Present Day* (Milton Keynes, U.K.: Open University Press, 1985) and by Georgina Boyes in *The Imagined Village: Culture, Ideology and the English Folk Revival* (Manchester: Manchester University Press, 1993).

52. A decade after Sharp's death the English Folk Dance and Song Society, as well as the International Folk Music Council, would eventually adopt a Sharpean definition of folksong, albeit at a time when developments in North America were again demonstrating that it was too narrow.

Appendix

Alphabetical Song List

This list includes only songs for which text or tune (or both) are provided as illustrations. It is primarily an alphabetical arrangement of the musical figures but it also includes songs for which only texts or partial texts are given. Songs for which only text is provided have no Fig. numbers. The source of each illustration is indicated; full bibliographical details will be found in the Bibliography and/or Notes.

Bibliography

Primary sources (unpublished)

Baring-Gould, Sabine. *Baring-Gould Microfiche Collection.* This collection reproduces archival materials at Plymouth Central Library and West Devon County Records Office, Plymouth, Devon, U.K., at East Devon County Records Office, Exeter, Devon, U.K., at the British Library, London, U.K, and at Harvard University Library, Cambridge, Mass. Copies of the microfiche are held at Plymouth Central Library and at Vaughan Williams Memorial Library, London.

Broadwood, Lucy. *Broadwood Collection.* Surrey History Centre, Woking, Surrey, U.K. The Lucy Broadwood holdings are part of a larger Broadwood family collection.

Broadwood, Lucy. *Lucy Broadwood Collection.* Vaughan Williams Memorial Library, London, U.K.

Fuller Maitland, John A. *J. A. Fuller Maitland Collection.* Lancaster Public Library, Lancaster, Lancashire, U.K.

Kidson, Frank. *Frank Kidson Collection.* Mitchell Library, Glasgow, Scotland, U.K.

Kidson, Frank and Ethel Kidson. *Kidson Collection.* Leeds Central Library, Leeds, Yorkshire, U.K.

Primary sources (printed)

Allan, Thomas, ed. *Allan's Illustrated Edition of Tyneside Songs and Readings.* Rev. ed., Newcastle-upon-Tyne, U.K.: Thomas and George Allan, 1891. Reprint, with an introduction by Dave Harker, Newcastle-upon-Tyne, U.K.: Frank Graham, 1972 [first ed. published in 1872].

Allingham, William, ed. *The Ballad Book: A Selection of the Choicest British Ballads.* London: Macmillan, 1864.

Ashton, John, ed. *A Century of Ballads.* London: Elliot Stock, 1887.

———, ed. *Modern Street Ballads.* London: Chatto and Windus, 1888.

———, ed. *Real Sailor Songs.* London: Leadenhall Press, 1891. Reissued, New York: Benjamin Blom, 1972.

Axon, William E. A. *Folk Song and Folk-Speech of Lancashire.* Manchester, U.K.: Tubbs and Brook, n.d. [1871, reissued 1887].

Baring-Gould, Sabine. "Among the Western Song Men." *English Illustrated Magazine* 102 (1892): 468-477.

———. *A Book of Folk-lore.* London: Collins, 1900. Reprint of 1913 ed., N.l.: Forgotten Books, 2007.

———. *The Book of Were-Wolves.* London: Smith, Elder, 1865.

———. *Curious Myths of the Middle Ages.* London: Rivingtons, 1866.

———. *Devonshire Characters and Strange Events.* London: John Lane, 1908.

———. *Further Reminiscences.* London: John Lane, The Bodley Head, 1925.

———. *Lives of the Saints,* 15 Vols. London: Hodges, 1872-88.

———. *Mehalah.* London: Smith, Elder, 1880.

———. *Old Country Life.* London: Methuen, 1890.

———. *The Origin and Development of Religious Belief.* London: Rivingtons, 1870.

———. *Through Flood and Flame.* London: Smith, Elder, 1868.

————. *The Vicar of Morwenstowe: A Life of Robert Stephen Hawker.* London: King, 1876.

————, ed. *English Minstrelsie: A National Monument of English Song,* Vols. 1-8. Edinburgh: Jack and Jack, 1895-98.

Baring-Gould, Sabine, and Cecil J. Sharp, eds. *English Folk Songs for Schools.* London: Curwen, 1906.

Baring-Gould, Sabine, and H. Fleetwood Sheppard, eds. *A Garland of Country Song: English Folk Songs with their Traditional Melodies.* London: Methuen, 1895.

————, eds. *Songs and Ballads of the West, a Collection made from the Mouths of the People,* Vols. 1-4. London: Patey and Willis, [1889-92]. 2nd ed., London: Methuen and Patey and Willis, Vols. 1-4 [1891-95]. Reprint in one volume, 1895.

Baring-Gould, Sabine, H. Fleetwood Sheppard, F. W. Bussell and Cecil J. Sharp, eds. *Songs of the West: Folk Songs of Devon and Cornwall, Collected from the Mouths of the People.* London: Methuen, 1905.

Barrett, William Alexander. *English Glees and Part-Songs: An Inquiry into their Historical Development.* London: Longmans, 1886.

————, ed. *English Folk-Songs.* London: Novello, Ewer and Co., [1891]. Reprint, Darby, Pa.: Norwood Editions, 1973.

————, ed. *Standard English Songs.* London: Augener, [1890].

Bell, John, ed. *Rhymes of Northern Bards.* Newcastle-upon-Tyne, U.K.: Bell and Angus, 1812. Reprint, Newcastle-upon-Tyne, U.K.: Frank Graham, 1971.

Bell, Robert, ed. *Ancient Poems, Ballads and Songs of the Peasantry of England.* London: John Parker and Sons, 1857. [A revised edition of Dixon's 1846 publication of the same title.]

Bell, Robert, ed. *Early Ballads Illustrative of History, Traditions and Customs.* London: John Parker and Sons, 1856.

————, ed. *Songs from the Dramatists.* London: John Parker and Sons, 1854.

Bellamy, Edward. *Looking Backwards (2000-1887).* London: William Reeves, 1887.

Blatchford, Robert. *Merrie England.* London: Clarion Press, 1894.

Borrow, George. *The Romany Rye.* London: John Murray, 1857.

————, ed. *Romano Lavo Lil: World Book of the Romany; or, English Gypsy Language.* London: John Murray, 1874.

Boulton, Sir Harold, and Arthur Somervell, eds. *Songs of the Four Nations: A Collection of Old Songs of the People of England, Scotland, Ireland and Wales.* London: Cramer, 1892.

The British Minstrel, 3 Vols. Glasgow, U.K.: William Hamilton, S. J. Machen and Simkin, Marshall and Co., 1844-45.

[Broadwood, John,] and Geoffrey F. Dusart, eds. *Old English Songs, as now sung by the Peasantry of the Weald of Surrey and Sussex.* London: Betts and Co., [1847] [the publication date is often given erroneously as 1843].

Broadwood, Lucy E., ed. *English Traditional Songs and Carols.* London: Boosey, 1908.

————. "Folk Songs Collected in Sussex and Surrey." *Journal of the Folk-Song Society* 1, no. 4 (1902): 139-223.

————. "On the Collecting of English Folk-Song." *Proceedings of the Royal Music Association* 31 (1905): 89-109.

————. "Re Collecting." Ms. notes, n.d. [c. 1893]. Broadwood papers, Accession # 2185/LEB/1/446, Surrey History Centre, Woking, Surrey, England, U.K.

————. "Songs from County Waterford, Ireland." *Journal of the Folk-Song Society* 3, no. 10 (1907): 4.

[Broadwood, Lucy E.,] and Herbert Birch Reynardson, eds. *Sussex Songs (Popular Songs of Sussex).* London: Lucas and Weber, 1889 [actually 1890].

Broadwood, Lucy E., and J. A. Fuller Maitland, eds. *English County Songs: Words and Music.* London: The Leadenhall Press, 1893; Reprint London: Cramer, 1915.

Bronson, Bertrand H., ed. *The Traditional Tunes of the Child Ballads,* 4 Vols. Princeton, N.J.: Princeton University Press, 1959, 1962, 1966, and 1973.

Bruce, J. Collingwood, and John Stokoe, eds. *Northumbrian Minstrelsy: A Collection of the Ballads, Melodies, and Small-Pipe Tunes of Northumbria.* Newcastle-upon-Tyne, U.K.: Society of Antiquaries of Newcastle-upon-Tyne, 1882. Reprint, with a foreword by A. L. Lloyd, Hatboro, Pa.: Folklore Associates, 1965.

Buchan, Peter, ed. *Ancient Ballads and Songs of the North of Scotland,* 2 Vols. Edinburgh: Laing and Stevenson, 1828.

————, ed. *Gleanings of Scarce Old Ballads.* Peterhead, U.K.: Buchan, 1825.

Bullen, A. H., ed. *Lyrics from the Dramatists of the Elizabethan Age.* London: John C. Nimmo, 1889.

————, ed. *Lyrics from the Song-Books of the Elizabethan Age.* London: John C. Nimmo, 1887.

————, ed. *More Lyrics from the Song-Books of the Elizabethan Age.* London: John C. Nimmo, 1888.

Burne, Charlotte Sophia, ed. *Shropshire Folk-Lore: A Sheaf of Gleanings from the Collections of Georgina F. Jackson.* London: Trubner and Co., 1883-86.

Burstow, Henry. *Reminiscences of Horsham: being Recollections of Henry Burstow the Celebrated Bellringer and Songsinger.* Horsham, Sussex: Free Christian Book Society, 1911. Reprint, with a foreword by A. E. Green and Tony Wales, Norwood, Pa.: Norwood Editions, 1975.

Campbell, Donald. *A Treatise on the Language, Poetry and Music of the Highland Clans.* Edinburgh: Collie, 1862.

Chappell, William, ed. *A Collection of National English Airs consisting of Ancient Song, Ballad and Dance Tunes,* 2 Vols. London: Chappell, Simkin, Marshall and Co., 1838.

————, ed. *The Crown Garland of Golden Roses, consisting of Ballads and Songs by Richard Johnson, from the Edition of 1612.* London: Percy Society, 1842.

————, ed. *The Crown Garland of Golden Roses, Part II, from the Edition of 1659.* London: Percy Society, 1845.

————, ed. *Popular Music of the Olden Time, a collection of Ancient Songs, Ballads and Dance Tunes, illustrative of the National Music of England,* 2 Vols. London: Cramer, Beale and Chappell, 1858-9. Reprint, New York: Dover, 1965.

Chappell, William, and J. W. Ebsworth, eds. *The Roxburghe Ballads,* 8 Vols. Hertford, U.K.: The Ballad Society, 1869-99 [actually 1901]. [There was confusion over the numbering of the last volume, which, while effectively Volume 9, was labeled as if it was an extra part of Volume 8].

Chappell, William, G. A. Macfarren, Natalia Macfarren, and J. Oxenford, eds. *Old English Ditties, selected from W. Chappell's "Popular Music of the Olden Time," with a New Introduction,* 2 Vols. London: Chappell and Co., n.d.

[Child, Francis James]. "Ballad Books." *The Nation* 7 (September 3, 1968): 192-93.

Child, F[rancis] J[ames]. "Ballad Poetry." 464-68 in *Johnson's Universal Cyclopedia,* ed. Rossiter Johnson. New York: Johnson, 1874. Reprint as 365-67 in *Universal Cyclopedia and Atlas,* ed. Rossiter Johnson. New York: Johnson, 1884.

[Child, Francis James], "Bishop Percy's Folio Manuscript." *The Nation* 5 (August 29, 1867): 166-67.

Child, Francis James. Letter to Professor Svend Grundtvig, August 25, 1872. Reprint in Appendix A of Sigurd B. Hustvedt, *Ballad Books and Ballad Men: Raids and Rescues in Britain, America, and the Scandinavian North since 1800.* Cambridge, Mass: Harvard University Press, 1930.

Child, Francis James, ed. *English and Scottish Ballads,* 8 Vols. Boston, Mass.: Little, Brown and Co., 1857-59. 2nd ed., 1860. 3rd ed., 1866.

————, ed. *The English and Scottish Popular Ballads,* 10 Parts in 5 Volumes. Boston, Mass.: Houghton, Mifflin and Co., 1882-98. Reprint, New York: Dover, 1965.

Christie, William, ed. *Traditional Ballad Airs,* 2 Vols. Edinburgh: Edmonston and Douglas, 1876 and 1881.

Clare, John. *Poems Descriptive of Rural Life and Scenery.* London: Taylor, Hessey and Drury, 1820.

————. *The Rural Muse.* London: Whittaker, 1835.

————. *The Shepherd's Calendar, with Village Stories and Other Poems.* London: Taylor, 1827.

————. *The Village Minstrel and Other Poems,* 2 Vols. London: Taylor, Hessey and Drury, 1821.

A Collection of Old Ballads, Corrected from the best and most Ancient Copies Extant, with Introductions Historical, Critical or Humorous, 3 Vols. London: J. Roberts, 1723-25.

Collier, John Payne, ed. *Old Ballads from Early Printed Copies.* London: Percy Society, 1840.

Cowell, Sam, ed. *Sam Cowell's New Universal Illustrated Pocket Songster,* 4 Vols. London: W. Barker, 1856.

Cox, Gordon, ed. *Sir Arthur Somervell on Music Education: His Writings, Speeches and Letters.* Woodbridge, England: Boydell Press, 2003.

Crawhall, Joseph, ed. *A Beuk o' Newcassel Sangs.* Newcastle-upon-Tyne, U.K.: Mawson, Swan, and Morgan, 1888. Reprint, Newcastle-upon-Tyne. U.K.: Harold Hill, 1965.

Davidson, G. H., ed. *Davidson's Universal Melodist,* 2 Vols. London: Davidson, 1848.

Davis, Frederick, and Ferris Tozer, eds. *Sailors' Songs or "Chanties."* London: n.d. [1886 or 1887]. 3rd ed., London: Boosey and Co., [1907].

Deacon, George. *John Clare and the Folk Tradition.* London: Sinclair Browne, 1983.

Deloney, Thomas. *The Garland of Good Will.* London: publisher unknown, c. 1595. Republished, ed. J. H. Dixon, as part of Vol. 30 of *Early English Poetry, Ballads, and Popular Literature of the Middle Ages.* London: C. Richards for the Percy Society, 1851.

————, *The Pleasant History of John Winchcomb, In his younger years called Jacke of Newberie, the famous and worthy Clothier of England.* London: Young and Wright, 1633 [originally published 1597].

————. *Strange Histories, or, Songes and Sonets, of Kings, Princes, Dukes, Lordes, Ladyes, Knights, and Gentlemen.* London: W. Barley, 1607. Reprint as *Strange Histories, consisting of Ballads and other Poems.* London: Percy Society, 1841.

————, [attrib. ed.] *Wit Restor'd.* London: n.p., 1658. Reprint in *Facetiae: Musarum Deliciae, Wit Restor'd and Wits Recreations,* 2 Vols. London: n.p., 1817.

De Vaynes, Julia H. L., ed. *The Kentish Garland,* 2 Vols. Hertford, U.K.: Austin and Sons, 1881-82.

Dixon, James Henry, ed. *Ancient Poems, Ballads and Songs of the Peasantry of England.* London: Percy Society, 1846.

————, ed. *Chronicles and Stories of the Craven Dales.* London: Simpkin, Marshall and Co., 1881.

————, ed. *The Garland of Good-Will of Thomas Deloney.* London: Percy Society, 1851.

————, ed. *Scottish Traditional Versions of Ancient Ballads.* London: Percy Society, 1846.

D'Urfey, Thomas, ed. *Wit and Mirth: or Pills to Purge Melancholy,* 6 Vols. London: D'Urfey, 1719-20. Reprint, New York: Folklore Library Publishers, 1959.

Dusart, Geoffrey [and John Broadwood], eds. *Old English Songs, as now sung by the Peasantry of the Weald of Surrey and Sussex.* London: Betts and Co., 1843.

Ebsworth, Joseph Woodfall, ed. *The Amanda Group of Bagford Poems.* Hertford, U.K.: The Ballad Society, 1880.

————, ed. *The Bagford Ballads,* 2 Vols. Hertford, U.K.: The Ballad Society, 1876-78.

————, ed. *Choyce Drollery: Songs and Sonnets, being a Collection of Divers Excellent Pieces of Poetry. Of Several Eminent Authors, to which are added the extra songs of Merry Drollery, 1661, and an Antidote Against Melancholy, 1661.* Boston, U.K.: Robert Roberts, 1876.

————, ed. *Merry Drollery Compleat, being Jovial Poems, Merry Songs, both parts, 1661, 1670, 1691.* Boston, U.K.: Robert Roberts, 1875.

————, ed. *Westminster Drolleries, both parts, of 1671, 1672, being a Choice Collection of Songs and Poems sung at Court and Theatres.* Boston, U.K.: Robert Roberts, 1875.

Ebsworth, Joseph Woodfall, and William Chappell, eds. *The Roxburghe Ballads,* 8 Vols. Hertford, U.K.: The Ballad Society, 1869-99 [actually 1901].

Engel, Carl. *An Introduction to the Study of National Music.* London: Longmans, Green, Reader and Dyer, 1866.

————. *The Literature of National Music.* London: Novello, Ewer and Co., 1879.

Evans, R. H., ed. *Old Ballads, Historical and Narrative,* 4 Vols. London: Evans, 1810. Rev. ed. of *Old Ballads, Historical and Narrative,* ed. Thomas Evans.

Evans, Thomas, ed. *Old Ballads, Historical and Narrative, with some of Modern Date, Collected from Rare Copies and Mss.,* 2 Vols. London: Evans, 1777; 2nd ed., 4 Vols.: London: Evans, 1784.

Fairholt, Frederick W., ed. *The Civic Garland: A Collection of Songs from London Pageants.* London: Percy Society, 1845.

————, ed. *Poems and Songs relating to George Villiers, Duke of Buckingham, and his assassination by John Felton, August 23, 1628.* London: Percy Society, 1850.

————, ed. *Satirical Songs and Poems on Costume: From the 13th to the 19th Century.* London: Percy Society, 1849.

Faning, Eaton, ed. *The Songs of England, Vol. III: A Further Collection of 72 English Melodies and Ballads Popular During the Last Fifty Years.* London: Boosey and Co., 1890.

Finlay, John, ed. *Scottish Historical and Romantic Ballads, Chiefly Ancient.* Edinburgh: J. Ballantyne for J. Smith and Son, 1808.

Forshaw, Charles F., ed. *Holroyd's Collection of Yorkshire Ballads.* London: Bell and Sons, 1892.

Fuller Maitland, J. A. *A Door-Keeper of Music.* London: John Murray, 1929.

————. *English Music in the Nineteenth Century.* London: Richards, 1902.

————. "Report to the Second Meeting of the Folk-Song Society." *Journal of the Folk-Song Society* 1, no. 2 (1900): 27-31.

Furnivall, Frederick J., *The Ballad Society. First Report (by Mr. Furnivall), January, 1869.* London: The Ballad Society, 1869.

————. *The Ballad Society: Fourth Report by Mr. Furnivall, October 1873.* Hertford, U.K.: The Ballad Society, 1873.

————, ed. *Ballads from Manuscripts,* 2 Vols. London: The Ballad Society and Taylor and Co., 1868-73.

————, ed. *Captain Cox, His Ballads and Books; or, Robert Laneham's Letter to Humfrey Martin.* Hertford, U.K.: The Ballad Society, 1871.

————, ed. *Jyl of Brentfords Testament, The Wyll of the Deuyll and his Last Testament, A Talk of Ten Wives on their Husbands' Ware, A Balade or Two by Chaucer, and Other Short Pieces.* London: Furnivall, 1871.

Gammer Gurton's Garland, or, The Nursery Parnassus. London: n.p., 1810.

Gilbert, Davies, ed. *Some Ancient Christmas Carols with the Tunes to which they were formerly sung in the West of England, together with Two Ancient Ballads.* 2nd ed.: London: John Nichols, 1823.

Groome, Francis Hindes. *In Gipsy Tents.* Edinburgh: Nimmo, 1881.

————. "The Influence of the Gypsies on the Superstitions of the English Folk." *International Folk-Lore Congress: Papers and Transactions, 1891*: 292-308. London: n.p., 1892.

————. *Kriegspiel.* New York: Ward, Lock and Bowden, 1896.

————, ed. *Gypsy Folk-Tales.* London: Hurst and Blackett, 1899.

Grundtvig, Svend, Axel Olrik, et al., eds. *Danmarks gamle Folkviser,* 12 Vols. Kjöberhavn: Samfundet til den danske literaturs fremme, 1853-1976.

Gummere, Francis B., ed. *Old English Ballads.* Boston, Mass.: Ginn and Co., 1894.

Gutch, John Mathew, ed. *The Robin Hood Garlands and Ballads, with the Tale of 'The Lytell Geste': A Collection of Poems, Songs and Ballads relating to this Celebrated Yeoman,* 2 Vols. London: J. R. Smith, 1850.

Hales, John W., and Frederick J. Furnivall, eds. *Bishop Percy's Folio Manuscript.* 3 Vols. and Supplement of "Loose and Humorous Songs." London: Trubner, 1867-68.

Halliwell, James Orchard, coll. *The Euing Collection of English Broadside Ballads,* ed. David Murray, Macneile Dixon, W.R. Cunningham and Douglas Jackson, with introduction by John Holloway. Glasgow, U.K.: University of Glasgow Press, 1971.

———, ed. *Ballads and Poems respecting Hugh of Lincoln.* Brixton Hill, U.K.: [Halliwell,] 1849.

———, ed. *The Early Naval Ballads of England.* London: Percy Society, 1841.

———, ed. *The Loyal Garland: A Collection of Songs of the seventeenth Century.* London: Percy Society, 1850.

———, ed. *The Norfolk Anthology: A Collection of Poems, Ballads, and Rare Tracts Relating to the County of Norfolk.* Brixton Hill, U.K.: Halliwell, 1852.

———, ed. *The Nursery Rhymes of England, collected principally from oral tradition.* London: Percy Society, 1842.

———, ed. *The Palatine Anthology: A Collection of Ancient Poems and Ballads Relating to Lancashire and Cheshire.* London: Halliwell, 1850.

———, ed. *Palatine Garland, being a Selection of Ballads and Fragments Supplementary to the Palatine Anthology.* London: Halliwell, 1850.

———, ed. *Popular Rhymes and Nursery Tales, a sequel to the Nursery Rhymes of England.* London: John Russell Smith, 1849.

———, ed. *The Yorkshire Anthology.* London: Halliwell, 1851.

Harland, John, ed. *Ballads and Songs of Lancashire, chiefly older than the 19th Century.* London: Whittaker, 1865. 2nd ed., 1875.

———, ed. *Lancashire Lyrics: Modern Songs and Ballads of the County Palatine.* London: Whittaker, 1866.

Harland, John, and T. T. Wilkinson, eds. *Ballads and Songs of Lancashire.* Rev. ed., London and Manchester: Heywood, 1882 [incorporates *Lancashire Lyrics*].

Hatton, John Liptrott, ed. *The Songs of England: A Collection of 200 English Melodies, including the most popular Traditional Ditties, and the Principal Songs and Ballads of the Last Three Centuries,* 2 Vols. London: Boosey and Co., 1873 and 1879.

Hatton, John Liptrott, and Eaton Faning, eds. *The Songs of England: A Collection of 272 English Melodies, including the most popular traditional ditties, and the principal songs and ballads of the last three centuries,* 3 Vols. London: Boosey, 1890.

Henderson, George, ed. *The Popular Rhymes, Sayings and Proverbs of the County of Berwick.* Newcastle-upon-Tyne: W. S. Crow, 1856.

Henderson, W., ed. *Victorian Street Ballads.* London: Country Life, 1937.

Hindley, Charles. *The History of the Catnach Press, at Berwick-upon-Tweed, Alnwick and Newcastle-upon-Tyne, in Northumberland, and Seven Dials, London.* London: Charles Hindley, 1887. Reprint, Detroit: Singing Tree Press, 1969.

———. *The Life and Times of James Catnach (Late of Seven Dials), Ballad Monger.* London: Reeves and Turner, 1878; Reprint, Detroit: Singing Tree Press, 1968.

[Hughes, Thomas]. *The Scouring of the White Horse; or, The Long Vacation Ramble of a London Clerk.* Cambridge and London: Macmillan, 1859.

Husk, William Henry, ed. *Songs of the Nativity; Being Christmas Carols, Ancient and Modern.* London: John Camden Hotten, 1864. Rev. ed., 1868.

Ingledew, C. J. Davison, ed. *The Ballads and Songs of Yorkshire.* London: Bell and Daldy, 1860.

Jacques, E. F. "Modal Survivals in Folk-Song." *Journal of the Folk-Song Society* 1, no. 1 (1899): 4-6.

Jewitt, Llewelynn F. W., ed. *Ballads and Songs of Derbyshire.* London: Bemrose and Lothian, 1867.

———. *Notes on the Folk-lore of Fungi.* London, n.p., 1860.

Johnson, Brimley R., ed. *Popular British Ballads: Ancient and Modern,* 4 Vols. London: Dent, 1894.

Jones, Edward, ed. *Popular Cheshire Melodies.* London: Jones, 1798.

Kidson, Francis. *Hebrew, Moslem, and Moorish Melodies.* Leeds: Charles Goodall, 1869.

Kidson, Frank. *British Music Publishers, Printers, and Engravers: London, Provincial, Scottish and Irish: From Queen Elizabeth's Reign to George the Fourth's*. London: W. E. Hill, 1900.

———. "English Folk-Song: What Collectors Are Doing." *Leeds Mercury,* February 21, 1907.

———. "English Folk-Song." *Musical Times,* January 1, 1908: 23-24.

———. "Folk-Song." *The Choir,* February, 1912: 30-31.

———. "Folk-Song and the Popular Song." *The Choir,* August, 1912: 149-51.

———. "John Playford and Seventeenth Century Music Publishing." *The Musical Quarterly* 4 (1918): 516-34.

———. "New Lights upon Old Tunes." *Musical Times*, October 1, 1894; February 1, 1895; May 1, 1895; September 1, 1895; June 1, 1896; September 1, 1896; and August 1, 1897.

———. "Notes on Old Tunes." Thirty-two articles published in the *Leeds Mercury Weekly Supplement* between November 6, 1886 and June 25, 1887.

———. "Old Songs and Airs: Melodies Once Popular in Yorkshire." Thirty-two articles published in the *Leeds Mercury Weekly Supplement* between January 4, 1890 and May or June 1891 [the exact date of the last article is not indicated on the clipping held in the Lucy Broadwood collection at the Surrey History Centre, Woking].

———. "Sailors' Songs." *Journal of the Folk-Song Society* 1, no. 2 (1900): 39-42.

———. "Sir Hugh of Lincoln." in "Local Notes and Queries." *Leeds Mercury Weekly Supplement,* October 20, 1894.

———. "Songs Collected by Frank Kidson." *Journal of the Folk-Song Society* 2, no. 9 (1906): 250-94.

———. "Songs from the Collection of Frank Kidson." *Journal of the Folk-Song Society* 1, no. 5 (1904): 228-55.

———. "Street Ballads." *The Leeds Express,* January 16, 1896.

———. "Tom Bowling." *Leeds Mercury Weekly Supplement,* September 26, 1896.

———. "Traditional Tunes Collected by Frank Kidson." Manuscript tune-book M.19057, Frank Kidson Collection, Mitchell Library, Glasgow, U.K.

———. "Traditional Tunes, Collected by Frank Kidson, Leeds." Field notebook M.19058, Frank Kidson Collection, Mitchell Library, Glasgow, U.K.

———. "The Vitality of Melody." *Proceedings of the Musical Association* 34 (1907-1908): 81-95.

———. "Yorkshire Folk Song." Mitchell Library, M. 18052. Lecture delivered to the National Convention of Choirmasters at Sheffield, September 15, 1906, and summarized in the *Musical Herald,* October 1906.

———. ed. *Eighty Singing Games*. London: Bayley and Ferguson, 1907.

———. ed. *Folio Collection of Broadsides*, 10 Vols. Unpublished bound volumes, Mitchell Library, Glasgow.

———, ed. *Old English Country Dances*. London: William Reeves, 1890. Reprint, Louth: Celtic Music, 1983.

———, ed. *Seventy-Five British Nursery Rhymes*. London: Augener, n.d.

———, ed. *Traditional Tunes, a Collection of Ballad Airs, chiefly obtained in Yorkshire and the South of Scotland, together with their appropriate words from broadsides and from oral tradition*. Oxford: Charles Taphouse and Son, 1891. Reprint, East Ardsley, U.K.: S.R. Publishers, 1970.

Kidson, Frank, and Alfred Moffat, eds. *English Songs of the Georgian Period*. London: Bayley and Ferguson, 1907.

———, eds. *Folk Songs from the North Countrie, with their Traditional Airs*. London: Ascherberg, Hopwood and Crew, 1927.

———, eds. *A Garland of English Folksongs*. London: Ascherberg, Hopwood and Crew, [1926].

———, eds. *The Minstrelsy of England: a collection of 200 English songs with their melodies, popular from the 16th century to the middle of the 18th century*. London: Bailey and Ferguson, 1901.

Kidson, Frank, and Martin Shaw, eds. *Songs of Britain: A Collection of One Hundred English, Welsh, Scottish and Irish National Songs*. London: Boosey, 1913.

Kidson, Frank, and Mary Neal. *English Folk-Song and Dance*. Cambridge: Cambridge University Press, 1915. Reprint, E.P. Publishing, 1972.

Kidson, Frank, Ethel Kidson, and Alfred Moffat, eds. *English Peasant Songs, with their Traditional Airs*. London: Ascherberg, Hopwood and Crew, 1929.

Kidson, Joseph, and Frank Kidson. *Historical Notices of the Leeds Old Pottery*. Wakefield, U.K.: SR Publishers, 1970 [a reprint of the 1892 ed.].

Kitchiner, William, ed. *The Loyal and National Songs of England, for one, two, and three voices, selected from original manuscripts and early printed copies in the Library of W. Kitchiner*. London: Hurst, Robinson and Co., 1823.

———, ed. *The Sea Songs of Charles Dibdin, with a Memoir of his Life and Writings*. London: G. and W. B. Whittaker and Clementi and Co., 1823.

———, ed. *The Sea Songs of England, selected from original manuscripts and early printed copies in the Library of W. Kitchiner*. London: Hurst, Robinson and Co., 1823. [a continuation of *The Loyal and National Songs of England*].

Lee, Kate. "Some Experiences of a Folk-Song Collector." *Journal of the Folk-Song Society* 1, no. 1 (1899): 7-12.

Leeds Mercury Weekly Supplement, 1886-87, 1890-91, and 1894.

Leland, Charles Godfrey. *The Gypsies*. Boston: Houghton Mifflin, 1882.

Lilly, Joseph, et al, eds. *A Collection of 79 Black Letter Ballads and Broadsides printed in the Reign of Queen Elizabeth*. London: Lilly, 1867.

Logan, W. H., ed. *A Pedlar's Pack of Ballads and Songs, with Illustrative Notes*. Edinburgh: William Paterson, 1869. Reprint, Detroit, Mich.: Singing Tree Press, 1968.

Lytton, Bulwer. *The Disowned*. London: H. Colburn, 1829.

Mackay, Charles, ed. *The Book of English Songs, from the Sixteenth to the Nineteenth Century*. London: Office of the National Illustrated Library, 1851.

———, ed. *The Cavalier Songs and Ballads of England from 1642 to 1684*. London: G. Bohn and Co., 1863. Reprint as *The Songs and Ballads of the Cavaliers*. London: C. Griffin and Co., 1864.

———, ed. *A Collection of Songs and Ballads relative to the London Prentices and Trades, and to the Affairs of London Generally*. London: Percy Society, 1841.

———, ed. *The Illustrated Book of Scottish Songs, from the Sixteenth to the Nineteenth Century*. London: Illustrated London Library, 1852.

———, ed. *The Jacobite Songs and Ballads of Scotland from 1688 to 1747, with an appendix of modern Jacobite songs*. London: R. Griffin, 1861.

———, ed. *The Legendary and Romantic Ballads of Scotland*. London: Griffin, Bohn, 1861.

Mann, Francis Oscar, ed. *The Works of Thomas Deloney*. Oxford: Clarendon Press, 1912.

Mason, M[arianne] H[arriet], ed. *Nursery Rhymes and Country Songs: Both Tunes and Words from Tradition*. London: Metzler, 1878.

Merrick, W. Percy, ed. *Folk Songs from Sussex*. London: Novello, 1912.

———. "Sussex Songs." *Journal of the Folk-Song Society* 1, no. 5 (1904): 268-74.

———. "Sussex Songs collected from Mr. Hills." *Journal of the Folk-Song Society* 1, no. 3 (1901): 64-105.

Morris, William. *News From Nowhere, or An Epoch of Rest*. London: Reeves and Turner, 1891.

Motherwell, William, ed. *Minstrelsy Ancient and Modern*. Glasgow: John Wylie, 1827.

"Mr. Frank Kidson." *The Musical Herald*, August 1, 1913: 227-30.

Musical Herald, October 1906.

Musical Times, 1894-97.

The Musical Times and Singing Class Circular 30, no. 557, July 1, 1889, 393-94.

Palmer, John Williams, ed. *Folk Song*. New York: Scribner, 1865.

Parry, Sir Hubert. "Inaugural Address to the General Meeting of the Folk-Song Society, 2nd February 1899." *Journal of the Folk-Song Society* 1, no. 1 (1899): 1-2.

Percy, Thomas, ed. *Reliques of Ancient English Poetry, consisting of old heroic ballads, songs, and other pieces of our earlier poets (chiefly of the lyric kind)*, 3 Vols. London: Dodsley, 1765. 5th ed., London: Rivington and Longman, 1812.

Playford, Henry, ed. *Wit and Mirth: or Pills to Purge Melancholy*, 4 Vols. London: Playford, 1698-1706. A fifth volume was issued in 1714.

Playford, John, ed. *The English Dancing Master*. London: Playford, 1651.

Ramondon, Lewis, ed. *The Merry Musician, or, A Cure for the Spleen*, 3 Vols. 2nd ed., London: J. Walsh, 1730.

Ramsay, Allan, ed. *The Tea-Table Miscellany, or A Collection of Choice Songs, Scots and English*, 4 Vols. Edinburgh: Ramsay, 1724-1732. Rev. ed., 1740.

Ravenscroft, Thomas, ed. *Deuteromelia*. London: n.p., 1609.

———, [attrib. ed.] *Melismata: Musicall Phansies, Fitting the Court, Cittie, and Countrey Humours*. London: n.p., 1611.

Reeves, James, ed. *The Everlasting Circle: English Traditional Verse from the Manuscripts of S. Baring-Gould, H. E. D. Hammond and George Gardiner*. London: Heinemann, 1960.

———, ed. *The Idiom of the People*. London: Heinemann, 1958.

"Review of *Shropshire Folk-Lore*." *Folk-Lore Journal* 4 (1886): 365.

Reynardson, Herbert Birch, and [Lucy E. Broadwood,] eds. *Sussex Songs (Popular Songs of Sussex)*. London: Lucas and Weber, 1889 [actually 1890].

Rimbault, Edward F., ed. *Christmas Carols*. London: Chappell and Co., n.d.

————, ed. *A Little Book of Christmas Carols, with the Ancient Melodies to which they are Sung*. London: Cramer, Beale and Co., 1847.

————, ed. *A Little Book of Songs and Ballads*. London: Smith, 1851.

————, ed. *Musical Illustrations of Bishop Percy's Reliques of Ancient English Poetry*. London: Cramer, Beale and Co., 1850.

————, ed. *Musical Illustrations of the Robin Hood Ballads*. London: Smith and Lilly, 1850.

————, ed. *Nursery Rhymes*. London: Cramer, Beale and Co, 1849.

————, ed. *Old Ballads illustrating the Great Frost of 1683-84 and the Fair on the River Thames*. London: Percy Society, 1844.

Ritson, Joseph, ed. *Ancient Songs from the Time of King Henry the Third to the Revolution*. London: J. Johnson, 1790. Expanded ed. as *Ancient Songs and Ballads from the Reign of King Henry the Second to the Revolution*, 2 Vols. London: Payne and Foss, 1829.

————, ed. *Northern Garlands*. London: Triphook, 1810. A reprint, in one volume, of four small collections made by Ritson and published separately between 1784 and 1802: *The Bishopric Garland, or Durham Minstrel* (1784, Rev. ed. 1792), *The Yorkshire Garland* (1788), *The Northumberland Garland* (1793), and *The North-Country Chorister* (1802).

————, ed. *Robin Hood: A Collection of All the Ancient Poems, Songs and Ballads now extant relative to that celebrated English Outlaw*, 2 Vols. London: J. Johnson, 1795. 2nd ed.: London: William Pickering, 1832.

————, ed. *A Select Collection of English Songs in Three Volumes*, 3 Vols. London: J. Johnson, 1783.

Roberts, John S., ed. *The Legendary Ballads of England and Scotland*. London: Frederick Warne, 1887.

Sandys, William, ed. *Christmas Carols, Ancient and Modern, including the most popular in the West of England, and the airs to which they are sung. Also specimens of French Provincial Carols*. London: Richard Beckley, 1833.

————. *Christmastide, its History, Festivities and Carols*. London: John Russell Smith, 1852.

————, ed. *Festive Songs, principally of the Sixteenth and Seventeenth Centuries*. London: Percy Society and T. Richards, 1848.

————, ed. *Specimens of Cornish Provincial Dialect...[and] a Selection of Songs and other pieces connected with Cornwall*. London: J. R. Smith, 1846.

Sargent, Helen G., and George L. Kittredge, eds. *English and Scottish Popular Ballads*. Boston: Houghton Mifflin, 1904.

Sawyer, F. E. *Sussex Songs and Music*. Paper read to The British Archaeological Association, 21 August 1886, and published as a pamphlet (a reprint from the Association's *Proceedings*) by the author. Copy at Surrey History Centre, Accession # 6192/2/42.

Scott, Sir Walter, ed. *Minstrelsy of the Scottish Border, consisting of historical and romantic ballads, collected in the southern counties of Scotland, with a few of modern date, founded on local tradition*, 2 Vols. Kelson, U.K.: J. Ballantyne, 1802. 2nd ed., 3 Vols. Edinburgh: Ballantyne, 1803. 5th ed., 1812. New edition, ed. T. F. Henderson, 3 Vols. Edinburgh: William Blackwood and Sons, 1902.

Sharp, Cecil J. *English Folk Song: Some Conclusions*. Taunton: Barnicott and Pearce, 1907.

————, ed. *A Book of British Song for Home and School*. London: John Murray, 1902.

————, ed. *English Folk-Chanteys*. London: Schott, 1914.

————, ed. *Folk Songs of England*, Vols. 1-5. London: Novello, 1908-1912. Reprint in a one volume ed. as *English County Folk Songs*. London: Novello, 1961.

————. "Some Characteristics of English Folk-Music." *Folk-Lore* 19 (1908): 132-46.

Sharp, Cecil J., and Charles L. Marson, eds. *Folk Songs from Somerset*, 5 Vols. Taunton: The Wessex Press, 1904-9. Reprint, London: Simpkin, Marshall, Hamilton, Kent and Co., 1904-11.

Sharp, Cecil J., and Sabine Baring-Gould, eds. *English Folk Songs for Schools*. London: Curwen, 1906.

Sharp, Sir Cuthbert, ed. *The Bishoprick Garland, or a collection of Legends, Songs, Ballads, etc., belonging to the county of Durham*. London: Nichols and Baldwin and Cradock, 1834.

Sheldon, Frederick, ed. *The Minstrelsy of the English Border, being a collection of Ballads, ancient, remodelled, and original, founded on well known Border legends*. London: Longman, Brown, Green and Longmans, 1847.

Smith, Laura Alexandrine, ed. *The Music of the Waters: A Collection of the Sailors' Chanties, or Working Songs of the Sea, of All Maritime Nations. Boatmen's, Fishermen's, and Rowing Songs, and Water Legends*. London: Kegan Paul, Trench and Co, 1888.

————, ed. *Through Romany Songland*. London: David Stott, 1889.

Somervell, Arthur. "On the Singing of National Songs." Unpaginated preface, in Sir Harold Boulton and Arthur Somervell, eds. *Songs of the Four Nations.* London: Cramer, 1892.

Somervell, Arthur, and Sir Harold Boulton, eds. *Songs of the Four Nations: A Collection of Old Songs of the People of England, Scotland, Ireland and Wales.* London: Cramer, 1892.

Stanford, Sir Charles Villiers, ed. *The National Song Book: A Complete Collection of the Folk-Songs, Carols, and Rounds suggested by the Board of Education.* London: Boosey, 1905.

Sternberg, Thomas. *The Dialect and Folk-lore of Northamptonshire.* London: J. R. Smith, 1851.

Stokoe, John, and J. Collingwood Bruce, eds. *Northumbrian Minstrelsy: A Collection of the Ballads, Melodies, and Small-Pipe Tunes of Northumbria.* Newcastle-upon-Tyne, U.K.: Society of Antiquaries of Newcastle-upon-Tyne, 1882. Reprint, with a foreword by A. L. Lloyd, Hatboro, Pa.: Folklore Associates, 1965.

Stokoe, John, and Samuel Reay, eds. *Songs and Ballads of Northern England.* London: Walter Scott, 1892.

Struthers, John, ed. *The British Minstrel, a Selection of Ballads, ancient and modern, etc.,* 2 Vols. London: n.p., 1822.

Sumner, Heywood, ed. *The Besom Maker and Other Country Folk Songs.* London: Longmans Green, 1888.

Thoms, William J. *The Folk-lore of Shakespeare.* London: J.R. Smith, 1847.

Tomson, Graham R. [pseud. for Rosamund Watson], ed. *Border Ballads.* London: Walter Scott, 1888.

———, ed. *Ballads of the North Countrie.* London: Walter Scott, 1888.

Topliffe, Robert, ed. *Selection of the Most Popular Melodies of the Tyne and Wear, consisting of 24 original airs peculiar to the counties of Durham and Northumberland.* London: R. Topliffe, 1820.

Totnes Times and Devon News, December 3, 1892.

Turner, Andrew R. "Burstow, Henry (1826–1916)." *Oxford Dictionary of National Biography.* London: Oxford University Press, 2004. www.oxforddnb.com/view/article/57089.

The Universal Songster, or, Museum of Mirth, forming the most complete, extensive, and valuable collection of Ancient and Modern Songs in the English Language, 3 Vols. London: Jones, 1825-27. Rev. ed., 1834.

[Utterson, Edward V., ed.] *A Little Book of Ballads.* Newport, U.K.: Yelf and Co., for the Roxburghe Club, 1836.

Wilkins, W. Walker, ed. *Political Ballads of the Seventeenth and Eighteenth Centuries,* 2 Vols. London: Longman, Green, Longman and Roberts, 1860.

Williams, Alfred, ed. *Folk Songs of the Upper Thames.* London: Duckworth, 1923. Reprint, Wakefield, U.K.: E.P. Publishing, 1972.

Williams, Maria Jane, and Daniel Huws, eds. *Ancient National Airs of Gwent and Morganwg.* Llandovery, Wales: W. Rees, 1844.

Wooldridge, H. Ellis, ed. *Old English Popular Music,* 2 Vols. London: Novello and Ewer, 1893. [a revised and truncated version of Chappell's *Popular Music of the Olden Time*].

———, *The Polyphonic Period, Part I: Method of Musical Art, 330–1400.* New York: Cooper Square, 1973.

Wright, Thomas, ed. *Political Ballads Published in England during the Commonwealth.* London: Percy Society, 1841.

———, ed. *Political Poems and Songs relating to English History from Edward III to Richard III,* 2 Vols. London: Longman, Green, Longman and Roberts, 1859-61.

———, ed. *The Political Songs of England, from the Reign of John to that of Edward II.* London: Camden Society, 1839.

———, ed. *Songs and Ballads, chiefly from the Reign of Philip and Mary.* London: J.B. Nichols and Sons, 1860.

———, ed. *Songs and Carols from a Manuscript in the British Museum of the Fifteenth Century.* London: T. Richards for the Warton Club, 1856.

———, ed. *Songs and Carols now first printed from a Manuscript of the Fifteenth Century.* London: Percy Society, 1847.

———, ed. *Specimens of Old Christmas Carols selected from Manuscripts and Printed Books.* London: Percy Society, 1841.

Wright, Thomas, and James Orchard Halliwell, eds. *Reliquiae Antiquae: Scraps from Ancient Manuscripts*, 2 Vols. London: n.p., 1845.

Secondary Sources

[Note: *Grove Music Online* is now included in the *Oxford Music Online* suite of databases.]

Ainger, Michael. *Gilbert and Sullivan: A Dual Biography.* New York: Oxford University Press, 2002.

Allis, Michael. *Parry's Creative Process.* Burlington, Vt.: Ashgate, 2003.

Anderson, Robert. *Elgar.* New York: Schirmer, 1993.

Anderton, H.O. *Granville Bantock.* London: John Lane, 1915.

Ashman, Gordon, and Gillian Bennett. "Charlotte Sophia Burne: Shropshire Folklorist, First Woman President of the Folklore Society, and First Woman Editor of *Folklore.* Part 1: A Life and Appreciation." *Folklore* 111, no. 1 (2000): 1-22.

Atkinson, David. "Sabine Baring-Gould's Contribution to *The English and Scottish Popular Ballads.*" 41-52 in *Ballads into Books: The Legacies of Francis James Child,* ed. Tom Cheeseman and Sigrid Rieuwerts. Bern, Switzerland: Peter Lang, 1997.

Atkinson, David, with Tom Cheeseman. "A Child Ballad Study Guide with Select Bibliography and Discography." 259-80 in *Ballads into Books: The Legacies of Francis James Child,* ed. Tom Cheeseman and Sigrid Rieuwerts. Bern, Switzerland: Peter Lang, 1997.

Baily, Leslie. *Gilbert and Sullivan: Their Lives and Times.* Harmondsworth: Penguin, 1974.

Baker, Anne Pimlott. "Hipkins, Alfred James (1826-1903), writer on musical instruments." *Oxford Dictionary of National Biography.* www.oxforddnb.com/view/article/33890.

Bantock, Myrrha. *Granville Bantock: A Personal Portrait.* London: Dent, 1972.

Barbour, Jane. "Sumner, (George) Heywood Maunoir (1853-1940), Artist and Archaeologist." *Oxford Dictionary of National Biography.* London: Oxford University Press, 2004. www.oxforddnb.com/view/article/38033.

Bashford, Christina, and Leanne Langley, eds. *Music and British Culture, 1785-1914: Essays in Honour of Cyril Ehrlich.* Oxford: Oxford University Press, 2000.

Bearman, Christopher J. "The English Folk Music Movement 1898-1914." Ph.D. thesis, University of Hull, 2001.

———. "Kate Lee and the Foundation of the Folk-Song Society." *Folk Music Journal* 7, no. 5 (1999): 627-43.

———. "The Lucy Broadwood Collection: An Interim Report." *Folk Music Journal* 7, no. 3 (1997): 357-65.

Beecham, Thomas. *Frederick Delius.* London: Hutchinson, 1959. Rev. ed., 1975.

Bell, Michael J. "'No Borders to the Ballad Maker's Art': Francis J. Child and the Politics of the People." *Western Folklore* 47 (1988): 285-307.

———. "'To Realize the Imagined Community': Francis Barton Gummere and the Politics of Democracy." 53-68 in *Ballads into Books: The Legacies of Francis James Child,* ed. Tom Cheeseman and Sigrid Rieuwerts. Bern, Switzerland: Peter Lang, 1997.

Bennett, Gillian. "Charlotte Sophia Burne: Shropshire Folklorist, First Woman President of the Folklore Society, and First Woman Editor of *Folklore.* Part 2: Update and Preliminary Bibliography." *Folklore* 112, no. 1 (2001): 95-98.

Blakesley, Rosalind P. *The Arts and Crafts Movement.* London: Phaidon, 2006.

Blom, Eric, ed. *Grove's Dictionary of Music and Musicians,* 10 Vols. 5th ed., New York: St. Martin's Press, 1954-61.

Boyes, Georgina. *The Imagined Village: Culture, Ideology and the English Folk Revival.* Manchester: Manchester University Press, 1993.

Boyes [Smith], Georgina. "Literary Sources and Folklore Studies in the Nineteenth Century: A Re-assessment of Armchair Scholarship." *Lore and Language* 2, no. 9 (1978): 26-39.

Broadwood, Lucy. "Obituary: Frank Kidson, M.A. Born November 15th, 1855. Died November 7th, 1926." *Journal of the Folk-Song Society* 8, no. 31 (1927): 48-49.

Caldwell, John. *The Oxford History of English Music,* Vol. 2: *From c. 1715 to the Present Day.* Oxford: Oxford University Press, 1999.

Carley, Lionel. *Delius: The Paris Years.* London: Triad Press, 1975.

———, ed. *Frederick Delius: Music, Art and Literature.* Aldershot, England: Ashgate, 1998.

Cheeseman, Tom and Sigrid Rieuwerts, eds. *Ballads into Books: The Legacies of Francis James Child.* Bern, Switzerland: Peter Lang, 1997.

Colloms, Brenda. "Gould, Sabine Baring- (1834-1924)." *Oxford Dictionary of National Biography.* ww.oxforddnb.com/articles/30/30587-article.html.

Cowell, Ray. "Kidson's Informants." *Folk Music Journal* 5, no. 4 (1988): 482-88.

Cox, Gordon, ed. *Sir Arthur Somervell on Music Education: His Writings, Speeches and Letters.* Woodbridge, England: Boydell Press, 2003.

Day, James. *Vaughan Williams.* New York: Oxford University Press, 1998.

De Val, Dorothy. "The Transformed Village: Lucy Broadwood and Folksong." 341-66 in *Music and British Culture, 1785-1914: Essays in Honour of Cyril Ehrlich,* ed. Christina Bashford and Leanne Langley. Oxford: Oxford University Press, 2000.

Dibble, Jeremy. *C. Hubert Parry: His Life and Music.* New York: Oxford University Press, 1992.

Dickinson, Bickford. *Sabine Baring-Gould: Squarson, Writer and Folklorist, 1834-1924.* Newton Abbot, U.K.: David and Charles, 1970.

Disher, Maurice Willson. *Victorian Song: From Diva to Drawing Room.* London: Phoenix House, 1955.

Dorson, Richard M. *The British Folklorists: A History.* London: Routledge and Kegan Paul, 1968.

Eden, David. *Gilbert and Sullivan: A Creative Conflict.* Rutherford, N.J.: Fairleigh Dickinson University Press, 1986.

Ensor, R. C. K. *England, 1870-1914.* Oxford: Clarendon Press, 1960.

Fenby, Eric. *Delius.* London: Faber and Faber, 1971.

Fenby, Eric, and Christopher Redwood, eds. *A Delius Companion.* London: Calder, 1976.

Field, Katherine. "Mason, (Marianne) Harriet." *Oxford Dictionary of National Biography.* London: Oxford University Press, 2004. www.oxforddnb.com/articles/48/48847-article.html.

Ford, Walter. "Lucy Etheldred Broadwood." *Journal of the Folk Song Society* 8, no. 3 (1929): 168-69.

Francmanis, John. "The 'Folk-Song' Competition: An Aspect of the Search for an English National Music." *Rural History* 11, no. 2 (2000): 181-205.

———. "The Musical Sherlock Holmes: Frank Kidson and the English Folk Music Revival, c. 1890-1926." Ph.D. thesis, Leeds Metropolitan University, 1997.

———. "National music to national redeemer: the consolidation of a 'folk-song' construct in Edwardian England." *Popular Music* 21, no. 1 (2002): 1-25.

———. "The Roving Artist: Frank Kidson, Pioneer Song Collector." *Folk Music Journal* 8, no. 1 (2001): 41-66.

Fuller Maitland, J. A. *The Music of Parry and Stanford: An Essay in Comparative Criticism.* Cambridge: Heffer, 1934.

Gammon, Vic. "Folk Song Collecting in Sussex and Surrey, 1843-1914." *History Workshop Journal* 10 (1980): 61-89.

Gardham, Steve. "'The Brown Girl' (Child 295B): a Baring-Gould concoction?" 363-76 in *Folk Song: Tradition, Revival, and Re-Creation,* ed. Ian Russell and David Atkinson. Aberdeen, U.K.: Elphinstone Institute, University of Aberdeen, 2004.

Godman, Stanley. "John Broadwood, the Earliest English Folksong Collector." *West Sussex Gazette,* 30 January 1964.

Gomme, Robert. "Gomme [née Merck], Alice Bertha, Lady Gomme (1853-1938), folklorist." *Oxford Dictionary of National Biography.* www.oxforddnb.com:80/view/article/38616.

Goodrick-Clarke, Clare, and Nicholas Goodrick-Clarke, eds. *G.R.S. Mead and the Gnostic Quest.* Berkeley, Calif.: North Atlantic Books, 2005.

Graebe, Martin. "Sabine Baring-Gould and his old singing-men." 175-85 in *Folk Song: Tradition, Revival, and Re-Creation,* ed. Ian Russell and David Atkinson. Aberdeen, U.K.: Elphinstone Institute, University of Aberdeen, 2004.

Gregory, E. David. "Before the Folk-Song Society: Lucy Broadwood and English Folk Song, 1884-97." *Folk Music Journal* 9, no. 3 (2008): 372-414.

———. "The Emergence of a Concept in Victorian England: From 'Old Ballads' and 'Songs of the Peasantry' to 'Folk-Song.'" in *Vom Wunderhorn zum Internet: Perspektiven des Volkslied-Begriffs und der wissenschaftlichen Edition populärer Lieder,* ed. David Atkinson and Ekhard John. Freiburg, Germany: Kommission für Volksdichtung, forthcoming.

———. "Frank Kidson: The Formative Years, 1886-1890." 64-71 in *Folk Music, Traditional Music, Ethnomusicology: Canadian Perspectives, Past and Present,* ed. Gordon Smith and Anna Hoefnagels. Newcastle-upon-Tyne, U.K.: Cambridge Scholars Press, 2008.

———. *Victorian Songhunters: The Recovery and Editing of English Vernacular Ballads and Folk Lyrics, 1820-1883.* Lanham, Md.: Scarecrow Press, 2006.

Gregory, Rosaleen, and David Gregory. "Jewels Left in the Dunghills: Broadside and other Vernacular Ballads Rejected by Francis Child." *Canadian Journal for Traditional Music* 29 (2002): 69-80.

Grout, Donald Jay. *A History of Western Music.* 3rd ed., New York: Norton, 1980.

Harker, Dave. *Fakesong: The Manufacture of British 'Folksong' 1700 to the Present Day.* Milton Keynes, U.K.: Open University Press, 1985.

———. "Francis James Child and the 'Ballad Consensus.'" *Folk Music Journal* (1981): 146-64.

———. "The Making of the Tyneside Concert Hall." *Popular Music* 1 (1981): 27-56.

———. "Thomas Allan and 'Tyneside Song.'" vii-xxviii in *Allan's Illustrated Edition of Tyneside Songs,* ed. Dave Harker. Newcastle-upon-Tyne, U.K.: Frank Graham, 1972.

Heffer, Simon. *Vaughan Williams.* London: Weidenfeld and Nicolson, 2000.

"Henry Burstow." *Folkopedia.* http://folkopedia.efdss.org/Henry_Burstow.

Homes, Paul. *Vaughan Williams: His Life and Times.* New York: Omnibus Press, 1997.

Howes, Frank. *The English Musical Renaissance.* London: Secker and Warburg, 1966.

Hughes, Meirion, and Robert Stradling. *The English Musical Renaissance 1840-1940: Constructing a National Music.* Manchester: Manchester University Press, 2001. [2nd ed. of Robert Stradling and Meirion Hughes, *The English Musical Renaissance 1860-1940: Construction and Deconstruction.* London: Routledge, 1993.]

Hurd, Michael. "Somervell, Sir Arthur." *Grove Music Online.*

Hustvedt, Sigurd B. *Ballad Books and Ballad Men: Raids and Rescues in Britain, America, and the Scandinavian North since 1800.* Cambridge, Mass.: Harvard University Press, 1930.

Hutchings, Arthur. *Delius.* London: Macmillan, 1948.

Jahoda, Gloria. *The Road to Samarkand: Frederick Delius and His Music.* New York: Scribner's Songs, 1969.

James, Alan. *Gilbert and Sullivan.* New York: Omnibus Press, 1989.

Jefferson, Alan. *Delius.* London: Dent, 1972.

Jones, Arthur. *Arthur Sullivan: A Victorian Musician.* New York: Oxford University Press, 1984.

Jones, Lewis. "Lucy Broadwood's Diaries: The Early Years." *English Dance and Song* 62, no. 3 (Autumn 2000): 2-3.

———. "Lucy Etheldred Broadwood: Her Scholarship and Ours." 241-52 in *Folk Song: Tradition, Revival, and Re-Creation,* ed. Ian Russell and David Atkinson. Aberdeen, U.K.: Elphinstone Institute, University of Aberdeen, 2004.

———. "Lucy Etheldred Broadwood: Poet and Song Writer." *English Dance and Song* 57, no. 4 (December 1995): 2-3.

Jones, Michael Owen. "Francis Hindes Groome: 'Scholar Gypsy and Gypsy Scholar.'" *Journal of American Folklore* 80 (1967): 71-80.

Kennedy, Michael. *The Life of Elgar.* Cambridge, England: Cambridge University Press, 2004.

———. *Portrait of Elgar.* New York: Oxford University Press, 1982.

———. *The Works of Ralph Vaughan Williams.* London: Oxford University Press, 1964.

Kirk-Smith, Harold. *'Now the Day Is Over': The Life and Times of Sabine Baring-Gould, 1834-1924.* Boston, U.K.: Richard Kay, 1997.

Laws, G. Malcolm, Jr. *American Balladry from British Broadsides: A Guide for Students and Collectors of Traditional Song.* Philadelphia, Pa.: American Folklore Society, 1957.

L. [Lightwood, J. T.] "Frank Kidson." *The Choir* 205 (January, 1927): 7-8.

Lloyd, A. L. *Folk Song in England.* London: Lawrence and Wishart, 1967.

Marsden, J., ed. *The Victorian World of Helen Allingham.* London: Brockhampton Press, 1999.

Marsh, Jan. *Back to the Land: the Pastoral Impulse in England, from 1880 to 1914.* London: Quartet Books, 1982.

McVeagh, Diana M. *Edward Elgar: His Life and Music.* Westport, Conn.: Hyperia, 1979.

Mellers, Wilfrid. *Vaughan Williams and the Vision of Albion.* London: Barrie and Jenkins, 1989.

Moore, Jerrold N. *Edward Elgar: A Creative Life.* New York: Oxford University Press, 1984.

Morton, A. L. *A People's History of England.* London: Gollancz, 1938.

Palmer, Christopher. *Delius: Portrait of a Cosmopolitan.* London: Duckworth, 1976.

Palmer, Roy, ed. *A Ballad History of England from 1588 to the Present Day.* London: Batsford, 1979.

———. *Checklist of Manuscript Songs and Tunes collected from Oral Tradition by Frank Kidson.* Glasgow and London: Mitchell Library and EFDSS, 1986.

———. "Kidson's Collecting." *Folk Music Journal* 5, no. 2 (1986): 150-75.

———. *The Sound of History: Songs and Social Comment.* Oxford: Oxford University Press, 1988.

———. "'Veritable Dunghills': Professor Child and the Broadside." *Folk Music Journal* 7, no. 2 (1996): 155-66.

Patrick, David. "Groome, Francis Hindes (1851-1902): Scholar of Gypsy Life and Writer." *Oxford Dictionary of National Biography.* www.oxforddnb.com/view/article/33588.

Pearsall, Ronald. *Edwardian Popular Music.* Newton Abbot, U.K.: David and Charles, 1975.

———. *Victorian Popular Music.* Newton Abbot, U.K.: David and Charles, 1973.

Pegg, Dave. *Folk: A Portrait of English Traditional Music, Musicians and Customs.* London: Wildwood House, 1976.

Pevsner, Nikolaus. *Pioneers of Modern Design.* Harmondsworth: Penguin, 1960.

Pilkington, Michael. *Delius, Bridge and Somervell.* London: Thames, 1993.

Pirie, Pieter J., and David Brock. "Bantock, Sir Granville." *Grove Music Online.*

Porte, John F. *Sir Charles V. Stanford.* New York: Da Capo, 1976.

Purcell, William E. *Onward Christian Soldier: A Life of Sabine Baring-Gould.* London: Longman, Green, 1957.

Redwood, Christopher, ed. *An Elgar Companion.* Ashbourne, England: Sequoia Press, 1982.

Reeves, James, ed. *The Everlasting Circle: English Traditional Verse from the Manuscripts of S. Baring-Gould, H.E.D. Hammond, and George B. Gardiner.* London: Heinemann, 1960.

———. *The Idiom of the People: English Traditional Verse from the Mss. Of Cecil James Sharp.* London: Heinemann, 1958.

Reppert, James Donald. "F. J. Child and the Ballad." Harvard, Mass.: Ph.D. thesis, Harvard University, 1953.

———. "F. J. Child and the Ballad." 197-212 in *The Learned and the Lewd: Studies in Chaucer and Medieval Literature,* ed. Larry D. Benson. Harvard English Studies 5. Cambridge, Mass.: Harvard University Press, 1974.

Rieuwerts, Sigrid. "The Ballad Society: a forgotten chapter in the history of English ballad studies." 28-40 in *Folk Song: Tradition, Revival, and Re-Creation,* ed. Ian Russell and David Atkinson. Aberdeen, U.K.: The Elphinstone Institute, University of Aberdeen, 2004.

———. "The Folk-Ballad: The Illegitimate Child of the Popular Ballad." *Journal of Folklore Research* 33 (1996): 221-26.

———. "From Percy to Child: The 'Popular Ballad' as 'a distinct and very important species of poetry.'" 13-20 in *Ballads and Boundaries: Narrative Singing in an Intercultural Context,* ed. James Porter. Los Angeles: Department of Ethnomusicology and Systematic Musicology, University of California at Los Angeles, 1995.

———. "'The Genuine Ballads of the People': F. J. Child and the Ballad Cause." *Journal of Folklore Research* 31, nos. 1-3 (1994): 1-34.

———. "In Memoriam: Francis James Child (1825-1896)." 19-25 in *Ballads into Books: The Legacies of Francis James Child,* ed. Tom Cheeseman and Sigrid Rieuwerts. Bern, Switzerland: Peter Lang, 1997.

Roberts, David. "His 'Magpie Mind' Made Baring-Gould a Rare Bird Indeed." *Smithsonian* 24, no. 4 (1993): 74-83.

Rodmell, Paul. *Charles Villiers Stanford.* Burlington, Vt.: Ashgate, 2002.

Rouse, Andrew C. *The Remunerated Vernacular Singer: From Medieval England to the Post-War Revival.* Frankfurt am Main: Peter Lang, 2005.

Russell, Dave. *Popular Music in England, 1840-1914: A Social History.* Manchester, U.K.: Manchester University Press, 1987. 2nd ed., 1997.

Russell, Ian, and David Atkinson, eds. *Folk Song: Tradition, Revival, and Re-Creation.* Aberdeen, U.K.: The Elphinstone Institute, University of Aberdeen, 2004.

Sadie, Stanley, ed. *The New Grove Dictionary of Music and Musicians,* 20 Vols. London: Macmillan, 1980.

Simpson, Claude M. *The British Broadside and Its Music.* New Brunswick, N.J.: Rutgers University Press, 1966.

———. "Ebsworth and the Roxburghe Ballads." *Journal of American Folklore* 61, no. 242 (October-December 1948): 337-44.

Stansky, Peter. *Redesigning the World: William Morris, the 1880s, and the Arts and Crafts Movement.* Princeton, N.J.: Princeton University Press, 1985.

Steeves, Harrison Ross. *Learned Societies and English Literary Scholarship in Great Britain and the United States.* New York: Columbia University, 1913. Reprint, New York: AMS Press, 1970.

Stolba, K. Marie. *The Development of Western Music.* 2nd ed., Dubuque, Iowa: Brown and Benchmark, 1994.

Sykes, Richard. "The Evolution of Englishness in the English Folksong Revival, 1890-1914." *Folk Music Journal* 6, no. 4 (1993): 446-90.

Temperley, Nicholas. *The Lost Chord: Essays on Victorian Music.* Bloomington: Indiana University Press, 1989.

———, ed. *The Athlone History of Music in Britain, Vol. 5: The Romantic Age, 1800-1914.* London: Athlone Press, 1981.

———, ed. *Music in Victorian Society and Culture: A Special Issue of Victorian Studies.* Bloomington: Indiana University Press, 1986.

Threlfall, Robert. *Delius' Musical Apprenticeship.* London: Delius Trust, 1994.

Tovey, Donald F. *Some English Symphonists.* New York: Oxford University Press, 1941.

Vaughan Williams, Ralph. "Lucy Broadwood: An Appreciation." *Journal of the Folk Song Society* 8, no. 1 (1927): 44-45.

——— "Lucy Broadwood, 1858-1929." *Journal of the English Folk Dance and Song Society* 5, no. 3 (December 1948): 136-38.

Vaughan Williams, Ursula. *R.V.W.: A Biography of Ralph Vaughan Williams.* Oxford: Oxford University Press, 1964.

Venables, Mary. "Lucy Etheldred Broadwood." Unpublished manuscript, February 1930. Surrey History Centre, Woking, U.K. Accession # 2297/6.

Vicinus, Martha. *The Industrial Muse: A Study of Nineteenth Century British Working-Class Literature.* London: Croom Helm, 1974.

Wainwright, David. *Broadwood by Appointment.* London, Quiller Press, 1982.

Warlock, Peter [Philip Heseltine]. *Frederick Delius.* London: The Bodley Head, 1952.

Willeby, Charles. *Masters of English Music.* London: Osgood, McIvaine and Co., 1893.

Wittgenstein, Ludwig. *Philosophical Investigations*, tr. G. E. M. Anscombe. 2nd ed., Oxford: Basil Blackwell, 1967.

Young, Percy M. *Elgar, O.M.: A Study of a Musician.* Westport, Conn.: Greenwood, 1980.

Index

About the Author

Dr. E. David Gregory was born in Hitchin, Hertfordshire, U.K., and grew up in southern England. As a child he lived in a variety of English towns and villages, including Paignton (Devon), Abinger Hammer (Surrey), Lane End, and Denham (both Buckinghamshire). He spent most of his teenage years in Cambridge, where he attended the Perse School. He then studied history and literature at the University of Keele and was awarded a B.A. with first class honours in 1967. He subsequently received an M.A. in the History of Ideas from the University of Sussex (1968) and a post-graduate Certificate in Education from the University of London (1969).

In the autumn of 1969 he and his wife, Rosaleen, emigrated to Kingston, Ontario, Canada, where they lived for ten years and started a family; they now have three grown-up daughters, Fiona, Karina, and Rhiannon. David obtained his Ph.D. in Modern History from Queen's University (Kingston) in 1978, having also taught for several years in Queen's department of history. In 1979 he moved to Alberta and joined Athabasca University, the Canadian Open University, where he is currently employed as Professor of History and Humanities, teaching mainly European history and music history. During his career at Athabasca University he has also served as Dean of Arts and twice as Chair of the Centre for Global and Social Analysis. He and Rosaleen, who is a fine singer of traditional and contemporary folk music with a repertoire of over three hundred ballads and songs, currently live in the town of Athabasca, in northern Alberta. They enjoy hiking and canoeing in summer and snow-shoeing and Nordic skiing in winter.

Dr. Gregory is a former president of the Folklore Studies Association of Canada and is currently a director of the Canadian Society for Traditional Music. He co-edits the quarterly periodical *Canadian Folk Music/Musique folklorique canadienne*. He has made several radio series on the history of popular music for the Alberta radio network CKUA. Those currently broadcast are titled *The Long Weekend* (covering 1900 to 1940), *From Bop to Rock* (on the 1940s and 1950s), and *The Rocky Road* (on the 1960s and 1970s). His book-length publications include *The Athabasca Ryga* (1990), *Athabasca Landing: An Illustrated History* (2nd edition, 1998), and *Victorian Songhunters: The Recovery and Editing of English Vernacular Ballads and Folk Lyrics, 1820-1883* (2006). He has also published numerous articles in such academic journals as *Folk Music Journal, The Canadian Journal for Traditional Music, Canadian Folk Music, B.C. Folklore, Newfoundland Studies, History of Intellectual Culture*, and *Historical Reflections*. He is currently editing a volume in a multi-volume edition of *Songbooks of the Romantic Period*, and is doing further research on the life and work of English folksong collector Lucy Broadwood. He also hopes to write a history of the Edwardian phase of the English folksong movement. This would continue the story narrated in *The Late Victorian Folksong Revival: The Persistence of English Melody, 1878-1903* and complete a trilogy of books on the origins and development of the first English folksong revival begun with *Victorian Songhunters*, which is also published by Scarecrow Press.